Contemporary
Literary Criticism

Guide to Gale Literary Criticism Series

When you need to review criticism of literary works, these are the Gale series to use:

If the author's death date is:	You should turn to:
After Dec. 31, 1959 (or author is still living)	***CONTEMPORARY LITERARY CRITICISM*** for example: Jorge Luis Borges, Anthony Burgess, William Faulkner, Mary Gordon, Ernest Hemingway, Iris Murdoch
1900 through 1959	***TWENTIETH-CENTURY LITERARY CRITICISM*** for example: Willa Cather, F. Scott Fitzgerald, Henry James, Mark Twain, Virginia Woolf
1800 through 1899	***NINETEENTH-CENTURY LITERATURE CRITICISM*** for example: Fedor Dostoevski, Nathaniel Hawthorne, George Sand, William Wordsworth
1400 through 1799	***LITERATURE CRITICISM FROM 1400 TO 1800*** *(excluding Shakespeare)* for example: Anne Bradstreet, Daniel Defoe, Alexander Pope, François Rabelais, Jonathan Swift, Phillis Wheatley ***SHAKESPEAREAN CRITICISM*** Shakespeare's plays and poetry
Antiquity through 1399	***CLASSICAL AND MEDIEVAL LITERATURE CRITICISM*** for example: Dante, Homer, Plato, Sophocles, Vergil, the Beowulf Poet

---

Gale also publishes related criticism series:

CHILDREN'S LITERATURE REVIEW

This ongoing series presents criticism on authors of all eras who write for the preschool through high school audience.

SHORT STORY CRITICISM

This series covers the major short fiction writers of all nationalities and periods of literary history.

ISSN 0091-3421

Volume 49

Contemporary Literary Criticism

Excerpts from Criticism of the
Works of Today's Novelists, Poets,
Playwrights, Short Story Writers, Scriptwriters,
and Other Creative Writers

**Daniel G. Marowski
Roger Matuz**
EDITORS

**Sean R. Pollock
Robyn V. Young**
ASSOCIATE EDITORS

 *Gale Research Inc.*
Book Tower
Detroit, Michigan 48226

STAFF

Daniel G. Marowski, Roger Matuz, *Editors*

Sean R. Pollock, Robyn V. Young, *Associate Editors*

Jane C. Thacker, Thomas J. Votteler, Bruce Walker, *Senior Assistant Editors*

Cathy Beranek, Kent Graham, Michele R. O'Connell, David Segal, *Assistant Editors*

Melissa Reiff Hug, Debra A. Wells, *Contributing Assistant Editors*

Jeanne A. Gough, *Production & Permissions Manager*
Lizbeth A. Purdy, *Production Supervisor*
Kathleen M. Cook, *Production Coordinator*
Suzanne Powers, Kristine E. Tipton, Lee Ann Welsh, *Editorial Assistants*
Linda M. Pugliese, *Manuscript Coordinator*
Maureen A. Puhl, *Senior Manuscript Assistant*
Donna Craft, Jennifer E. Gale, Rosetta Irene Simms, *Manuscript Assistants*

Victoria B. Cariappa, *Research Supervisor*
Maureen R. Richards, *Research Coordinator*
Mary D. Wise, *Senior Research Assistant*
Joyce E. Doyle, Kevin B. Hillstrom, Karen D. Kaus, Eric Priehs,
Filomena Sgambati, Laura B. Standley, *Research Assistants*

Janice M. Mach, *Text Permissions Supervisor*
Kathy Grell, *Text Permissions Coordinator*
Mabel E. Gurney, *Research Permissions Coordinator*
Josephine M. Keene, *Senior Permissions Assistant*
Eileen H. Baehr, H. Diane Cooper, Anita Lorraine Ransom,
Kimberly F. Smilay, *Permissions Assistants*
Melissa A. Kamuyu, Martha A. Mulder, Lisa M. Wimmer, *Permissions Clerks*

Patricia A. Seefelt, *Picture Permissions Supervisor*
Margaret A. Chamberlain, *Picture Permissions Coordinator*
Pamela A. Hayes, Lillian Tyus, *Permissions Clerks*

Copyright © 1988 by Gale Research Inc.

Library of Congress Catalog Card Number 76-38938
ISBN 0-8103-4423-8
ISSN 0091-3421

Printed in the United States of America

Contents

Preface

Literary criticism is, by definition, "the art of evaluating or analyzing with knowledge and propriety works of literature." The complexity and variety of the themes and forms of contemporary literature make the function of the critic especially important to today's reader. It is the critic who assists the reader in identifying significant new writers, recognizing trends in critical methods, mastering new terminology, and monitoring scholarly and popular sources of critical opinion.

Until the publication of the first volume of *Contemporary Literary Criticism (CLC)* in 1973, there existed no ongoing digest of current literary opinion. *CLC,* therefore, has fulfilled an essential need.

Scope of the Work

CLC presents significant passages from published criticism of works by today's creative writers. Each volume of *CLC* includes excerpted criticism on about forty authors who are now living or who died after December 31, 1959. Nearly 2,000 authors have been included since the series began publication. The majority of authors covered by *CLC* are living writers who continue to publish; therefore, criticism on an author frequently appears in more than one volume. There is, of course, no duplication of reprinted criticism.

Authors are selected for inclusion for a variety of reasons, among them the publication of a critically acclaimed new work, the reception of a major literary award, or the dramatization of a literary work as a film or television screenplay. For example, the present volume includes Gwendolyn Brooks, who in 1950 became the first black author to win a Pulitzer Prize, which she received for her poetry collection *Annie Allen;* Günter Grass, whose acclaimed novel *The Tin Drum* was recently adapted for film; and George C. Wolfe, whose play *The Colored Museum* prompted diverse reactions and critical controversy upon its debut in 1986. Perhaps most importantly, authors who appear frequently on the syllabuses of high school and college literature classes are heavily represented in *CLC;* John Hawkes and Randall Jarrell are examples of writers of this stature in the present volume. Attention is also given to several other groups of writers—authors of considerable public interest—about whose work criticism is often difficult to locate. These are the contributors to the well-loved but nonscholarly genres of mystery and science fiction, as well as literary and social critics whose insights are considered valuable and informative. Foreign writers and authors who represent particular ethnic groups in the United States are also featured in each volume.

Format of the Book

Altogether there are about 600 individual excerpts in each volume—with approximately fifteen excerpts per author—taken from hundreds of literary reviews, general magazines, scholarly journals, and monographs. Contemporary criticism is loosely defined as that which is relevant to the evaluation of the author under discussion; this includes criticism written at the beginning of an author's career as well as current commentary. Emphasis has been placed on expanding the sources for criticism by including an increasing number of scholarly and specialized periodicals. Students, teachers, librarians, and researchers frequently find that the generous excerpts and supplementary material provided by the editors supply them with vital information needed to write a term paper, analyze a poem, or lead a book discussion group. However, complete bibliographical citations facilitate the location of the original source and provide all of the information necessary for a term paper footnote or bibliography.

A *CLC* author entry consists of the following elements:

• The **author heading** cites the author's full name, followed by birth date, and death date when applicable. The portion of the name outside parentheses denotes the form under which the author has most commonly published. If an author has written consistently under a pseudonym, the pseudonym will be listed in the author heading and the real name given on the first line of the biographical and critical introduction. Also located at the beginning of the introduction to the author entry are any important name variations under which an author has written. Uncertainty as to a birth or death date is indicated by question marks.

- A **portrait** of the author is included when available.

- A brief **biographical and critical introduction** to the author and his or her work precedes the excerpted criticism. However, *CLC* is not intended to be a definitive biographical source. Therefore, *cross-references* have been included to direct the reader to these useful sources published by Gale Research: *Contemporary Authors,* which includes detailed biographical and bibliographical sketches on more than 90,000 authors; *Children's Literature Review,* which presents excerpted criticism on the works of authors of children's books; *Something about the Author,* which contains heavily illustrated biographical sketches of writers and illustrators who create books for children and young adults; *Dictionary of Literary Biography,* which provides original evaluations and detailed biographies of authors important to literary history; *Contemporary Authors Autobiography Series,* which offers autobiographical essays by prominent writers; and *Something about the Author Autobiography Series,* which presents autobiographical essays by authors of interest to young readers. Previous volumes of *CLC* in which the author has been featured are also listed in the introduction.

- The **excerpted criticism** represents various kinds of critical writing—a particular essay may be descriptive, interpretive, textual, appreciative, comparative, or generic. It may range in form from the brief review to the scholarly monograph. Essays are selected by the editors to reflect the spectrum of opinion about a specific work or about an author's literary career in general. The excerpts are presented chronologically, adding a useful perspective to the entry. All titles by the author featured in the entry are printed in boldface type, which enables the reader to easily identify the works being discussed. Publication information (such as publisher names and book prices) and parenthetical numerical references (such as footnotes or page and line references to specific editions of a work) have been deleted at the editor's discretion to provide smoother reading of the text.

- A complete **bibliographical citation** designed to help the user find the original essay or book follows each excerpt.

Other Features

A list of **Authors Forthcoming in *CLC*** previews the authors to be researched for future volumes.

- An **Appendix** lists the sources from which material in the volume has been reprinted. It does not, however, list every book or periodical consulted during the preparation of the volume.

- A **Cumulative Author Index** lists all the authors who have appeared in *CLC, Twentieth-Century Literary Criticism, Nineteenth-Century Literature Criticism, Literature Criticism from 1400 to 1800,* and *Classical and Medieval Literature Criticism,* with cross-references to these Gale series: *Short Story Criticism, Children's Literature Review, Authors in the News, Contemporary Authors, Contemporary Authors Autobiography Series, Contemporary Authors Bibliographical Series, Dictionary of Literary Biography, Something about the Author, Something about the Author Autobiography Series,* and *Yesterday's Authors of Books for Children.* Readers will welcome this cumulated author index as a useful tool for locating an author within the various series. The index, which lists birth and death dates when available, will be particularly valuable for those authors who are identified with a certain period but whose death date causes them to be placed in another, or for those authors whose careers span two periods. For example, Ernest Hemingway is found in *CLC,* yet a writer often associated with him, F. Scott Fitzgerald, is found in *Twentieth-Century Literary Criticism.*

- A **Cumulative Nationality Index** alphabetically lists all authors featured in *CLC* by nationality, followed by numbers corresponding to the volumes in which they appear.

- A **Title Index** alphabetically lists all titles reviewed in the current volume of *CLC.* Titles are followed by the corresponding page numbers where they may be located. In cases where the same title is used by different authors, the authors' surnames are given in parentheses after the title, e.g., *Collected Poems* (Berryman), *Collected Poems* (Eliot). For foreign titles, a cross-reference is given to the translated English title. Titles of novels, novellas, dramas, films, record albums, and poetry, short story, and essay collections are printed in italics, while all individual poems, short stories, essays, and songs are printed in roman type within quotation marks; when published separately (e.g., T.S. Eliot's poem *The Waste Land*), the title will also be printed in italics.

• In response to numerous suggestions from librarians, Gale has also produced a **special paperbound edition** of the *CLC* title index. This annual cumulation, which alphabetically lists all titles reviewed in the series, is available to all customers and will be published with the first volume of *CLC* issued in each calendar year. Additional copies of the index are available upon request. Librarians and patrons will welcome this separate index: it saves shelf space, is easily disposable upon receipt of the following year's cumulation, and is more portable and thus easier to use than was previously possible.

Acknowledgments

No work of this scope can be accomplished without the cooperation of many people. The editors especially wish to thank the copyright holders of the excerpted essays included in this volume, the permissions managers of many book and magazine publishing companies for assisting us in securing reprint rights, and the photographers and other individuals who provided portraits of the authors. We are grateful to the staffs of the Detroit Public Library, the Library of Congress, the University of Detroit Library, the University of Michigan Library, and the Wayne State University Library for making their resources available to us. We also wish to thank Anthony Bogucki for his assistance with copyright research.

Suggestions Are Welcome

The editors welcome the comments and suggestions of readers to expand the coverage and enhance the usefulness of the series.

Authors Forthcoming in *CLC*

Contemporary Literary Criticism, Volume 50, will be a yearbook devoted to an examination of the outstanding achievements and trends in literature during 1987. Volumes 51 and 52 will feature criticism on a number of authors not previously covered in this series as well as excerpted reviews of newer works by authors included in earlier volumes.

To Be Included in Volume 51

Chinua Achebe (Nigerian novelist, short story writer, poet, and essayist)—One of Africa's most important contemporary writers, Achebe chronicles the cultural and psychological effects of European colonization on the Ibo, a native Nigerian tribe. His entry will include reviews of his recent novel, *Anthills of the Savannah.*

Anita Brookner (English novelist, nonfiction writer, and critic)—Best known as the author of *Hotel du Lac,* for which she received the Booker McConnell Prize for fiction, Brookner writes novels that focus upon well-educated, affluent women whose lives are often disrupted by unfaithful husbands and lovers. Recent works to be covered in her entry include *Family and Friends* and *The Misalliance.*

Noël Coward (English dramatist, lyricist, novelist, short story writer, scriptwriter, and autobiographer)—A prolific and versatile playwright, Coward is best remembered for whimsical social comedies that display his talent for creating imaginative plots and witty, acerbic dialogue. Recent revivals of such popular Coward plays as *Private Lives, Blithe Spirit,* and *Design for Living* have renewed interest in his work.

Kenneth Fearing (American poet, novelist, and editor)— Best known for the thriller novel *The Big Clock,* from which the recent film *No Way Out* was adapted, Fearing also distinguished himself during the Depression era as a poet whose verse attacked the dehumanizing effects of a capitalistic industrialized society.

Nadine Gordimer (South African novelist, short story writer, critic, and editor)—Gordimer is respected for examining the effects of the South African apartheid system on both ruling whites and oppressed blacks. Criticism in Gordimer's entry will focus upon her recent novel, *A Sport of Nature.*

Katherine Govier (Canadian novelist, short story writer, and journalist)—In her fiction, Govier often depicts female characters who must confront elements of their past in order to live contentedly in the present. Govier's interest in history is reflected in her recent novel, *Between Man,* which intertwines the stories of a contemporary history professor and an Indian woman who died mysteriously in the 1880s.

Patrick Hamilton (English dramatist, novelist, and scriptwriter)—Best known for his psychological plays *Rope* and *Angel Street,* Hamilton also wrote several novels during the 1930s and 1940s set in and around English pubs that portray the disordered lives of criminals, outcasts, and misfits.

Lisel Mueller (German-born American poet and critic)—Using such traditional techniques as metaphor, simile, and personification, Mueller concentrates on discovering the extraordinary aspects of ordinary objects and events. Collections of verse to be covered in her entry include *The Private Life* and *Second Language.*

Tom Wolfe (American essayist, journalist, editor, critic, and novelist)—Regarded as one of the most original stylists in contemporary literature, Wolfe figured prominently in the development of New Journalism, a form of expository writing that blends reporting with such techniques of fiction as stream of consciousness, extended dialogue, shifting points of view, and detailed scenarios. This entry will focus upon Wolfe's recent first novel, *The Bonfire of the Vanities.*

Yevgeny Yevtushenko (Russian poet and novelist)—Among the most outspoken and controversial poets to emerge in the Soviet Union since the death of Stalin, Yevtushenko has written two recent novels, *Wild Berries,* and *Ardabiola,* in which he expands on the personal themes of his poetry.

Peter Ackroyd (English novelist, biographer, and critic)—An acclaimed biographer of such esteemed writers as T.S. Eliot and Ezra Pound, Ackroyd has also elicited significant praise for his novels focusing upon prominent literary figures. Among the works to be covered in his entry are *The Last Testament of Oscar Wilde, Hawksmoor,* and *Chatterton.*

Conrad Aiken (American poet, novelist, short story writer, critic, dramatist, memoirist, and autobiographer)—A major figure in twentieth-century American literature who was awarded the Pulitzer Prize in Poetry in 1930, Aiken employed formal stylistic techniques and an often somber tone in his verse to examine themes related to such topics as spirituality, philosophy, psychology, and science.

Woody Allen (American dramatist, short story writer, scriptwriter, and director)—Best known for his work as a comedian, actor, and filmmaker, Allen is also a noted author of fiction and drama. Criticism in his entry will focus upon the short story collections *Getting Even, Without Feathers,* and *Side Effects* and such plays as *Don't Drink the Water* and *Play It Again, Sam.*

Gregory Benford (American novelist and short story writer)—Benford has written several works of speculative science fiction in which he contrasts the negative and positive aspects of such phenomena as alien contact and technological advancement.

Maryse Conde (Guadeloupean-born French novelist, short story writer, and dramatist)—Conde's novels often portray the lives of contemporary Caribbean and African women. Included in her entry will be criticism of *Moi, Tituba, sorcière, Noire de Salem,* a fictionalized biography of Tituba, a Barbadian slave who was tried for witchcraft in colonial Massachusetts.

William Faulkner (American novelist, short story writer, poet, and scriptwriter)—A seminal figure in modern literature, Faulkner was best known for novels and short stories set in his fictional locale of Yoknapatawpha County. Criticism in this volume will focus upon *Absalom, Absalom!,* one of Faulkner's most frequently analyzed works.

Christopher Hope (South African novelist, poet, short story writer, and dramatist)—In his novels *A Separate Development* and *Kruger's Alp,* Hope employs black humor, surrealism, allegory, and satire to explore the implications of racial discrimination in South Africa under the apartheid system.

Louis MacNeice (Irish-born English poet, critic, translator, dramatist, scriptwriter, and novelist)—A member of the "Oxford Group" of poets of the 1930s that included W.H. Auden, C. Day Lewis, and Stephen Spender, MacNeice is best known for verse in which he examines social concerns and the vagaries of the human condition.

Gloria Naylor (American novelist and short story writer)—Recognized as the author of *The Women of Brewster Place,* for which she received the American Book Award for best first novel, Naylor often examines the experiences of black American women in her fiction. Criticism in Naylor's entry will focus upon her novels *Linden Hills* and *Mama Day.*

Erika Ritter (Canadian dramatist, essayist, and short story writer)—Ritter's plays follow the plight of intelligent contemporary women who attempt to balance love and careers in the wake of the feminist movement. Ritter's entry will also include criticism of her collection of satirical essays, *Urban Scrawls.*

Richard Aldington

1892-1962

English poet, novelist, autobiographer, editor, translator, critic, biographer, essayist, short story writer, and dramatist.

Remembered primarily as a leading proponent of the Imagist movement, Aldington achieved critical recognition for his works as a poet, novelist, and nonfiction writer. Throughout his career, he documented his search for beauty in a world he depicted as increasingly unresponsive to art. Attributing humanity's lack of cultural awareness to its break with tradition, Aldington dedicated much of his writing to reestablishing Greek and Renaissance principles, an ideal he eventually abandoned as irreconcilable with contemporary civilization. In his verse, Aldington rejected regular metrical constructions, creating instead a heavily cadenced, sometimes prosaic poetry that Roy Campbell characterized as ''a stricter and more difficult form which can hardly be called free verse because of the masterful control which regulates and balances every detail with the minutest precision: and which enables him to perpetuate moments of illumination in forms as hard and clear as gems.'' The sensual content and aesthetic concerns of Aldington's poetry have prompted comparisons to the work of such nineteenth-century Pre-Raphaelites as Algernon Charles Swinburne and William Morris.

Aldington's verse was first published in *Poetry* magazine in 1912, along with several poems by his future wife, Hilda Doolittle, and Ezra Pound's first Imagist manifesto. Pound later included works by Aldington and Doolittle in the anthology *Des Imagistes*, and pieces by Aldington also appear in subsequent Imagist anthologies edited by Amy Lowell. Aldington's first collection, *Images (1910-1915)* (1915), features free verse that derives more from the choruses of Greek tragedies than from the French Symbolists emulated by the majority of Imagist poets. While Pound insisted on poetry that required associative leaps by the reader, Aldington relied on such conventional devices as simile and metaphor. *The Love Poems of Myrrhine and Konallis* (1917), Aldington's next major volume, is a rendering of a lesbian love affair in ancient Greece that exemplifies the aesthetic intentions of his verse. He explained: ''I wanted something sterile and passionate and lovely and melancholy.''

Despite his affinities to Imagism, Aldington evidenced his growing impatience with the movement's restrictions in his succeeding volumes. *Images of War* (1919) and *Images of Desire* (1919), while chronicling his experiences as a soldier during World War I, display similarities in style to the verse of Walt Whitman. In *Images of War*, Aldington vividly evokes horrifying aspects of battle and suggests that personal solace may be found in nature. *Images of Desire* contains pieces that imitate and parody the styles of such diverse authors of love poems as Catullus, Dante, and Swinburne. In these works, Aldington again proposes that life may be affirmed by a closeness to nature as well as through art and romantic love. Aldington's concise diction and subject matter in the sequence ''Words for Music,'' from *Exile and Other Poems* (1923), recalls the works of such seventeenth-century poets as Robert Herrick and Andrew Marvell. Other poems in *Exile* explore

John E. Read
HOLLYWOOD

The Granger Collection

personal effects of World War I and Aldington's perception of British cultural stagnation.

Following the publication of *Exile*, Aldington began writing extended poems that develop romantic and sexual themes and examine the modern world in light of historical achievements. In *A Fool i' the Forest: A Phantasmagoria* (1925), considered by many critics his finest verse accomplishment, Aldington explores the relationship between reason and imagination by creating three protagonists, each of whom represents different aspects of an individual personality. *A Fool i' the Forest* is often compared to T.S. Eliot's *Waste Land* for its employment of extensive literary allusions and passages in different languages. Both *The Eaten Heart* (1929) and *A Dream in the Luxembourg* (1930: published in the United States as *Love and the Luxembourg*) present lengthy discourses on love. The title of *The Eaten Heart*, a reference to the Provençal story about a woman who is served her lover's heart by the husband whom she has made a cuckold, metaphorically represents Aldington's views of Platonic and sexual love. *A Dream in the Luxembourg* focuses on a relationship that parallels Aldington's romance with Brigit Patmore, to whom the volume is dedicated. *Life Quest* (1935) recounts a spiritual odyssey rendered in the Modernist fashion of *A Fool i' the Forest*. In *The Crystal World* (1937), Aldington assembles verse units of varied lengths to create ''a world which has no battlefield, / No factions and no bitter strife for power, / And scarcely touches yours.'' The resolution of *The Crystal World* has been perceived by critics as implying that Aldington no longer regarded poetry as either a viable alternative to the real world or an accurate representation of life. Pieces from various periods in Aldington's career are collected in *The Poems of Richard Aldington* (1934) and *The Complete Poems of Richard Aldington* (1948).

Aldington also garnered substantial critical attention for his prose works. His novels, which include the acclaimed *Death of a Hero* (1929), *The Colonel's Daughter* (1931), *All Men Are Enemies* (1933), *Women Must Work* (1934), *Very Heaven* (1937), *Seven against Reeves* (1938), and *Rejected Guest* (1939), were compared to the works of Aldous Huxley and Evelyn Waugh for their satirical attacks on British society. His short story collection, *Soft Answers* (1932), lampoons the English post-World War I literary community. *The Duke: Being an Account of the Life and Achievements of Arthur Wellesley, First Duke of Wellington* (1946) was awarded the James Tait Black Memorial Prize in biography. Aldington also authored biographies of D.H. Lawrence and T.E. Lawrence as well as his autobiography, *Life for Life's Sake: A Book of Reminiscences* (1941).

(See also *Contemporary Authors*, Vols. 85-88 and *Dictionary of Literary Biography*, Vols. 20, 36.)

JOHN GOULD FLETCHER

One of the highest pleasures that the intelligent and discriminating reader of poetry can have, is to discover some poet who employs throughout his work a clean and sure technique. There have been few such poets in English, but in France, Italy, and wherever the classic spirit has shown itself strongly, we can discover many examples to prove the crudity of our usual slap-dash Anglo-Saxon methods. Recently there have been in England signs of a return to that simplicity and restraint which are the qualities of highest art, and it is to be hoped that the war will have the effect of still further clarifying the English spirit, over-muddied with floods of Victorian sentiment and rhetoric. Of this admirable tendency Mr. Aldington is the precursor and the most shining example.

The impression one gains from the reading of the thirty-five pieces which he has now gathered together and given to the public [in *Images Old and New,* published in Great Britain as *Images (1910-1915)*], is one of uniform technical excellence. Here is a style like a sword-blade, bright, keen, nervous, and never exuberant. Nowhere does the poet say too much, nowhere does he permit his image to become clouded with long accumulations of detail, vague sentiments or indefinite moralizings. In fact, it may be that he sometimes says too little for those who seek to read as they run, or for those who are too readily inclined to look for that heroic strumming and smashing which is vulgarly considered to be the chief characteristic of ''major'' poetry. But it is necessary to point out that this common view of poetry is not that of the great artists, whether they be Greeks, Chinese, Japanese, or Johann Wolfgang von Goethe. ''In restraint the master first displays himself.'' By such standards Mr. Aldington must be judged, and he is neither ''major'' nor ''minor,'' but simply a poet.

These *Images Old and New* as he calls them, divide themselves roughly into two classes, the first dealing with Greek antiquity, the second with modern life. In either case, whatever be the subject, the unity is preserved, and it is a unity of style, of attitude. Mr. Aldington is a poet who speaks the truth. He is never vaguely romantic, or sentimental, or writing to satisfy anything but his own artistic conscience. There is scarcely a page in this small volume in which we cannot find something that will satisfy us at the first reading, and yet more fully with successive readings; but there are some pages which will begin by shocking us and end by convincing us. Here is a force which attracts us the more completely for its apparent simplicity: and it is the force not of realism but of reality. (pp. 49-50)

Mr. Aldington is a poet, as Simonides and Turgenev were poets.

We in America, at least, have much to learn from him. The inchoate vastness of our material and of its intertangled racial currents, the haphazardness of our methods and institutions, all tend to drive us towards a poetry which is ephemeral in that it is hectic, disorganized, lacking in reflective judgment. Europe has already taught us to distinguish the vital elements in the work of such men as Whitman and Poe from the unvital: Europe can teach us more. There are at least a dozen poets in this country who could not do better than to keep a copy of *Images Old and New* on their shelves, for constant reference and comparison. (p. 51)

John Gould Fletcher, ''Mr. Aldington's Images,'' in
Poetry, *Vol. VIII, No. 1, April, 1916, pp. 49-51.*

MAY SINCLAIR

It is more than six years since the first poems of Richard Aldington appeared in the first *Imagiste* anthology. They were followed by seven other poems in *Some Imagist Poets* in 1915; by *Reverie* and *Myrrhine and Konallis* in 1917; and in 1919 by *Images of War, Images of Desire* and *Images*.

In these six years other poets have become well known who were not known at all when Mr. Aldington, a very young man, was writing his **''Choricos''** and **''To a Greek Marble,''** but he still waits for that intelligent comprehension which might have been his if he had been more conspicuously the child of his own nation and his own age; or even if, keeping his Greek soul, he had been more ductile and placable, if he had bent his mind to compromise and conciliation—if he had been the sort of person and the sort of poet that he is not. He might have found his inspiration in Anyte of Tegea, in Theocritus, in Meleager or where he pleased, he might have written about the

> lithe, pale girls
> Daughters of Oceanus,

about Argyria,

> Swayer of reeds, whisperer
> Among the flowering rushes.
>   .   .   .
> Swallow-fleet,
> Sea-child cold from waves,

about Isis,

> Straight and slim. . .
> As a marble phallus,

as much as he liked, and comprehension, more or less intelligent, would have followed, if only he had written in familiar verse forms that by an irresistible association of ideas, and the stirring of a thousand literary reminiscences suggest to the hypnotised reader and reviewer, "This is poetry." As it is, he puts them off by writing about unfamiliar things in unfamiliar forms of *vers libre,* and in an unfamiliar manner. His austerity puts them off; they mistake it for coldness; they are apt to think he is both perverse and insincere because, being a subject of the British Empire, born in a Christian age and a Christian country, he celebrates the loves of Myrrhine and Konallis as a Greek would have celebrated them, without a suggestion of ugliness and without shame.

And yet it is his achievement of this manner, this complete trinity of form, spirit and substance that prove his sincerity and his naturalness and the reality of his inspiration. Richard Aldington is possessed by the sense of beauty, the desire of beauty, the absolute emotion, as no English poet since Shelley has been yet possessed, with the solitary exception of H.D. The pre-war Richard Aldington refuses to recognise the reality of anything else but beauty on this earth. He gets beauty, "Elysian beauty, melancholy grace," out of grief and death. His **"Choricos"** recalls the grave music of the Greek tragic chorus. (pp. 397-98)

[**"Choricos"** and **"To a Greek Marble"** were the first poems] that Mr. Aldington published. They were written before he was twenty. Already they show a certainty, a fine finish. Already he has the command of a form, and of a rhythm absolutely right for his purposes. His rhythm, at its best, is distinguished, more decided, more stressed than Mr. Flint's, less subtle than H.D.'s or Ezra Pound's. In technique he has not done better than these first poems; or the later **"Stele."** . . . (p. 399)

So far there is no mistaking his affinity. The error is in his date. He should have been born some centuries B.C.; he should have been young when Sappho or Anyte of Tegea were young. Then his spirit could have maintained itself without conflict and without misgiving, in that "harmonious adjustment of internal to external relations" which is happy life. To be born at the end of the nineteenth century and to be young in the youth of the twentieth must be counted as misfortune to a poet like Richard Aldington. For there is no mistaking his modernity. One half of him is not Greek, and it brings into his poetry an element which is not Greek, a pain, a dissatisfaction, a sadness that the purely Greek soul did not know. Whatever it may have been for other people, life for the ancient Greek poet of any age before the decadence seems to have been harmonious and beautiful beyond our conception. His aesthetic sensibilities were not outraged at every turn; there was no intense conflict between his soul and its surroundings; he was not harassed and handicapped by exacting moralities. Beyond an occasional sense of satiety and the prevision of death, nothing came between him and the joy of life. He knew little of the Roman poets' *Taedium vitae.* His complaint was not against life but against death that puts an end to the happy sequence of sensations. His sadness was mainly elegiac.

The modern poet is not greatly worried about death. Death to him is only one more disagreeable incident closing a series of disagreeable incidents. He even finds it acceptable because of its finality. His quarrel is with life itself because so much of life is ugly and discordant. And so Richard Aldington brings his sad modernity into the heart of his Greek world. His joy in beauty which was pure joy to the ancient Greek who had to do with beauty unadulterated and unstained, his joy has in it a deep, incurable dissatisfaction. Beauty hurts him as it did

not and could not hurt the Greek; because he sees that its position in the modern world is dangerous and impermanent.

And for a time the modern world gets the better of him, and the poems that succeed **"Choricos"** and the rest are mainly records of this defeat. He has waked up from his pagan dream to find himself a modern. He is convinced unwillingly that a modern poet must *be* modern; he must assimilate the world as it is now, or die to his time, perhaps to all time. He realises that there is beauty—capricious, bizarre, discordant, yet piercing and overwhelming beauty—in the modern world. But he is divorced from it. He cannot yet seize it, and make it his own. He can see nothing but ugliness. Hence the impression of conflict, of profound incompleteness conveyed by these poems of his transition. (pp. 400-01)

[While] other war-poets were trying with feverish pertinacity to make songs of the infinite brutality and filth and squalor of the trenches, Richard Aldington turned back to his beautiful Greek world, and wrote his *Myrrhine and Konallis,* a sequence of the most exquisite love poems in the language, poems that, if he had never written another line, ought to be enough to secure for him a high and permanent place in literature.

To be sure, the love is Lesbian, but Mr. Aldington has kept for us its pagan innocence and candour, its mortal pathos, and left us no image that is not beautiful. The figures, exquisite and fragile, pass shining as in some processional frieze of marble overlaid by gold, washed clean by the light of a world too remote, too long dead to excite our repulsion or our blame: a world not quite real. (p. 403)

It is because I cannot separate the post-war from the pre-war Richard Aldington, the poet of *Myrrhine and Konallis* from the poet of **"Choricos"** that I find myself disconcerted by some of his war poems (*Images of War*). They belong to that incomplete modern half of him so imperfectly fused with the other finished half. They seem not so much to have sprung spontaneously from himself as to have been torn from him by a cruel external compulsion, a compulsion that does violence to his genius. They are sincere, they are direct, they are faithful transcripts of experience. . . . They have lines, passages of great beauty:

> Night after night comes the moon
> Haughty and perfect;

they have one or two perfect poems, but, for the rest, somthing vital and necessary has been extinguished in them between their conception and their birth. They are too calm. It is as if the superhuman restraint that makes possible the endurance of great danger, of great horror, had checked the first passionate impulse of their being. They have not that quality which, in spite of its hysterical violence, makes a war-poem of D.H. Lawrence an intolerable, a shattering thing. (p. 405)

However admirable Mr. Aldington's work as a translator his *Myrrhine and Konallis* will remain as his highest tribute to the genius of Greek love, of Greek poetry. (p. 408)

If we are to find his sources and affinities it is clear that Richard Aldington owes an immense debt to Walter Savage Landor. There is no other writer of "prose poetry" with whom he can be more fitly compared. True, he has not in the last three years written anything comparable with his own best, with the exception of the **"Epilogue"** to *Images of Desire.* Yet it is impossible to think of arrested development in his case. It may happen at twenty, but not at five-and-twenty. It was the Greek Richard Aldington who ripened to a precocious mastery; the modern poet that is no less surely in him has not even approached maturity. He is perhaps not yet fully aware of himself. Incredible that the spirit that lived unbeaten and unabated through five years of war should not survive the Peace, that so fine and essentially sound a talent should not develop and endure. His style has no vices of fantasy, of eccentricity or obscurity, but always the clearness and directness of sincere speech. No perverse turns of phrase, no artificial inversions. At his worst, here and there, an exhausted rhythm, a cadence unsustained or undeveloped, a flat-footed line here and there. If he has nothing like H. D.'s range of subtle and complex emotions, his language is clearer and simpler than hers, his rhythm, at its best, not less musical. He has got more sheer music into his unrhymed cadence than any other contemporary writer of *vers libre*.

It has happened that this poet who so detested war, was so detached from modern time, from the state of Europe and destiny of empires, it has so happened that he cannot be considered apart from the European War; its influence has been too profound, his reactions too decided. It is a very great thing, a very wonderful thing that through all he has kept his clearness and his sanity, his hold on beauty and his technical excellence undiminished, that the danger, the horror he lived with never wrung from him one ignominious cry nor one phrase beneath the dignity of heroism. He never stoops to find abuse for the murderous stupidity of generals, but carries his complaint to a higher court in the magnificent protest of his **"Disdain."**

> Have the gods then left us in our need
> Like base and common men?
> Were even the sweet grey eyes
> Of Artemis a lie,
> The speech of Hermes but a trick
> The glory of Apollonian hair deceit?
> Desolate we move across a desolate land,
> The high gates closed,
> No answer to our prayer;
> Naught left save our integrity,
> No murmur against Fate
> Save that we are juster than the unjust gods,
> More pitiful than they.

If you ask me what he "stands" for I should say he stands for just that: indomitable endurance and defiance—that and an incorruptible faithfulness to reality, to beauty. These are moral qualities, but they have their aesthetic counterparts.

I don't want to talk about a poet as though he were a parliamentary candidate, otherwise I should say that, technically, he stands for freedom, freedom of subject, freedom of form and treatment, freedom from cramping tradition and convention. He might not now subscribe to the manifesto of "Imagism" except so far as to defend the concrete image against the abstract word, but he would, I think, agree with Mr. Flint's axiom: "The test of poetry is sincerity, the test of sincerity is style, and the test of style is personality."

The statement admits of the criticism that the term "personality" itself calls for some definition which will have to include poetic quality, and this brings us into a vicious circle; but the truth remains that *without* personality there can be no style, and without style no poetry.

Personality. Judged by this test, Richard Aldington's work will surely stand, whether you take his earliest poems, **"Choricos,"** or **"Bromios,"** or one of his latest—**"Epilogue."** . . . (pp. 408-10)

May Sinclair, "The Poems of Richard Aldington," in The English Review, *Vol. XXXII, May, 1921, pp. 397-410.*

PAUL ROSENFELD

The title [of this essay, "The Importance of Richard Aldington"], must appeal ironically to all who have been irritated by the gentleman's leannesses. They're not to be overlooked; Aldington is wooden, of the second strings. In spite of the international literary adventure in which he's participated, he remains a kind of Englishman of letters. There is even something of the masculine old maid about him; vivid currents, moments and imports turning so gingerly at his touch. You cannot with the best of wills place him on a level with Eliot, Pound, H. D. and the rest of the epoch-making poets of war and post-war London, whose companion he was and whose innovations he appreciated. He is as far behind them in sensuous responsiveness as they as a group are behind D. H. Lawrence in fire. Nonetheless, it is not possible to read his excessively *soignée* poetry, so dainty in its form and fine in its expression, and not receive an impulse and feel a personality. It embodies an idea, thin as its play may be found to be; an idea of aloofness, of detachment in stuff and handling.

Aldington has had what in his best Greek manner he calls "an intuition of the unalterable gods." Of course, the Greek manner, "Phoibus Apollon," "the Kuprian's breasts," "Kimmerian dusk" and the rest, are a trifle insipid; summoning to mind an Oxford student in a tunic being corybantic according to the books. But the poetry does lie in line of things; is "objective" and lapidary. Aldington's verse is imagistic, metaphoric; composed of crisp figures in several sensuous fields, chiefly in the visual; the the workmanship is as precise as the material. Laxness of line remains nobly foreign to it. Rhythms and verbal combinations echo

> The brief shrill clang of glass on ice
> The note of fragile metal sharply struck.

There is a keen tactility, our finger tips continually running on rims acute as

> the line of near hills
> Cut out in thin blue steel
> Against red haze.

A world has been caught in action. The movement is unfailingly serene and impersonal, subtle with hesitation and pause, and controlled by the will to "gather something of repose—some Attic gesture." The war's very introduction of harsh notes, pain and sensuality, does not break the detachment; and the hardness of matter and exactness of workmanship, the slender sound and firm handling, compensate for absent *brio* and authority.

Which immediately suggests the importance of Richard Aldington. An Oxford student in a tunic, he has none the less naturalized "pure" American poetry in England. He was the first of his countrymen to recognize the value of the experiments of what has since been discerned to be the most important contemporary movement in poetry; the first to refresh his art with the new vision. That vision, of course, was of a pure, a self-contained poetry which, "free of loose relative reference, using symbols without association outside the literary range of the poem itself, and effective through a great technical rigidity," would lean on nothing for its meaning, and be thinglike, lapidary, objective. The experiments made in sympathy with it moved in a direct line toward those uncompromisingly ''absolute'' minor masterpieces, *The Waste Land*, ''The Comedian as the Letter C'' of Wallace Stevens, and the Sordello-like *Cantos* of Ezra Pound. Perhaps because of its references, the adjective ''symbolistic'' ought to be adopted in place of ''absolute.'' . . . So, if in this note on Richard Aldington's conciliatory rôle, we persist in calling the group he naturalized in England poetic absolutists, it is merely for the purpose of insisting a little longer on their vision of independent poems: forms, creations, things complete in themselves.

Aldington's fullest embodiment of their principles is to be found in his phantasmagoria *A Fool i' the Forest*. Previous to the time of its composition, and since his commencements as a pallid, post-Swinburnian atticist, invocation of the Greek divinities and all, he had developed into a full-fledged imagist. The direction was Pound's. We would like to think Aldington more the collaborator than the disciple, since so little in his adaptations is slavish. He is always personal; beneath his constant stylizations, one invariably meets the mind of the English gentleman struggling to face what the day has brought his world, and preserve a manly sweetness amid the crass decay. No question but Aldington learned for himself from his patterns, as he has learned from Landor, the Athenian choruses, and the Restoration lyrists. But *A Fool i' the Forest* scarcely bids us call him free at forty; no more than his earlier poems; even the vignettes of the war. If the little work's reliance on rhythm, phrase and image as the chief agents of meaning, is of the time; as rightfully Aldington's method as it is Pound's or Gertrude Stein's, Joyce's or Hart Crane's, the use to which he has put it, the significations he has bodied forth with it, are scarcely original. *A Fool i' the Forest* is another Poem of Doubt, an absolutistic work in the spirit of the famous *Cantos* and *The Waste Land*. Undoubtedly, what made Pound and Eliot write their minor masterpieces was likewise at work in Aldington. It must have been the Englishman's own disconnection that originally drew him into a group whose common characteristic was unconnectedness. Pound, Eliot, Stevens and Company are not mere minor poets. They are major poets out of whack, twisted and balked by unwill. Almost oriental in their sensitivity to their material, concerned for daintiness of shape and fineness of expression, leaders in the exquisite advance of poetry, they front life neither robustly nor steadily; most constrainedly in comparison to D. H. Lawrence, their major contrast. . . . While their poetry has epigrammatic succinctness and delicacy of rhythm and expression, it quite lacks fire, warmth and gusto. It is cast in cool, oblique, ironic forms, and much of the sarcasm seeks out the authors' egos. Fragmentariness mars some of the liveliest of their attacks: Pound almost never rounds out an idea, and Eliot, more successful in his shorter pieces, fails of giving *The Waste Land* the unity necessary to its prosperity as a work of art.

In any case there is nothing vicious in the circumstance that like several of his group, Aldington should have applied his most ambitious and sustained efforts to the production of a Poem of Doubt. The Poem of Doubt remains an ultimate expression of his group, much as the poem of passion and weariness of passion (Cynara, The Sphinx) remains the ultimate expression of that of the orchidean nineties. Unwill, conflict, defensiveness commonly takes the form of painful suspension between the equally positive poles of affirmation and negation, and attachment to passive suffering. Objective reality, so seductive to the passions, appears simultaneously insignificant and treacherous to unwill's weak, uncertain lights; unsteady, unpleasurable, offering only the cheerless choice of shipwreck

on the ocean of adjustments and starvation and insanity in the waterless waste-land of unrelation. Of course, the war and the peace were prolific in justifications of tragic stinginess. Hence, the smoky funeral pall lying on the ''London'' of Eliot's great poem of doubt, the feeling of falling worlds, . . . the brutal miscarriages of lyricism; despair assuming the parodistic jerks of jazz; and the ignoble couplings half amusing, half torturing the poet's mind. Hence, too, the rôle played by the war in *A Fool i' the Forest*; the despairing conclusion in the picture of adjustment to the world purchased through betrayal of the inner man.

But while expression through a poem of doubt may have been natural to Aldington, his is no improvement on Eliot's which preceded it; nor on Pound's, brilliant and meaty for all its emptiness, important for all its asininity, which preceded that. (pp. 236-44)

Now, *A Fool i' the Forest* is anything but a poor poem: the ''gemlike cutting of the Greek'' invariably delights in Aldington. The little work's outline is clearer, the material more unified, than that of *The Waste Land*. An amount of this unity may be due the circumstance that Aldington is telling a story, recounting the adventures of an ''I'' and several symbolic characters from the Commedia del Arte, and may therefore be superficial. But an equal amount is due consistency of purpose. And where Aldington writes directly, permits himself simplicity and gravity, his phantasmagoria is really moving. There are portions of it as poignant, sharp and delicate as the best of his earlier pieces and **''The Lover''** in the *Images of War;* and the motives displayed in *Exile,* his immediately preceding volume are developed in it. The rising of the moon on the Acropolis, the Landor-like lament for youth, the midnight patrol (one of the succinctest evocations of the war) and the funereal vision of sleeping London, with its ''million breathing corpses,'' belong among the achievements of the recent literature of precision. Not, alas, the irony, the romantic parody, the sardonic realism, distinctly derived from Eliot, and wanting Eliot's verve and fine diablerie. To be sure, Aldington is exquisitely appreciative, a cultivated intelligence in a eclectic age; a respectable workman. But irony is distinctly not his vein. Eliot's handling of his second-rate material, the depressed and mocking voices of psychic conflict, was first rate, happy and inventive; while Aldington's dislocated moods, acrid turns of language and rhythm, despairing parodies of Campbell, Byron, the liturgy and American advertising, are wooden in comparison, and make one feel the Englishman of letters.

Which one again brings us to the ostensible subject of this harangue, the importance of this secondary author. Is it not precisely in his secondariness that Aldington's consequence lies? In mediating, attempting to integrate the experiments of the verbal relativists with the tradition, has he not put his minor gift to uses momentous for both American and English letters? On the one hand, there was a number of rebels; on the other, an old tradition. The rebels were disconnected, psychic exiles, strangers in more than a strange land, and the tradition was decadent, dying with Hardy, deteriorating with Bridges. Doubtless under some personal necessity, Aldington stood between the two, unconsciously interpreting them to each other, making what was racial in himself understand the new feelings, and harmonizing them with his ancestors' religion. In thus combining them, in vivifying the old English feeling and belief with the new American daring, he was not only furthering his own heritage. He was corroborating a band of experimentalists in their own direction, and assuring them of a wide influence.

Pound and the rest must be deeply indebted to the welcome and understanding given them by this gentleman in whose blood the culture of old Europe ran. Not alone Pound; was it so long ago that word went about New York Richard Aldington had said, "the best English prose is being written by Americans today"? And do not the Sitwells and the other English experimenters who have learned so much from the Americans, stand in a direct line behind this English officer of liaison? (pp. 245-48)

> Paul Rosenfeld, "The Importance of Richard Aldington," in his By Way of Art: Criticisms of Music, Literature, Painting, Sculpture, and the Dance, Coward-McCann, Inc., 1928, pp. 236-49.

PAULL F. BAUM

When a living author permits his *Collected Poems* to be issued, we may begin to judge him with such security as one contemporary can judge another. Already he sits to posterity for his portrait, and posterity, though unprepared, must do what it can. Moreover, Mr. Aldington's verse is to be taken seriously, partly because some of it is altogether admirable, and partly also because some of its weaknesses are characteristic and illustrative of much in modern verse that is frequently admired.

Mr. Aldington appeared first on the poetic scene as an Imagist. Imagism, however, was but a phase and has almost disappeared unless it survives in his own work and that of "H. D." (Mrs. Aldington). It has developed into something else, and that something appears also in Mr. Aldington; and the trend of development is highly interesting. It began as perhaps a species of polite advertisement, a banner. Then came the war (which changed other things besides verse), and the *japanoiserie* movement (a very small eddy), and the natural growth of the young poets themselves. The Imagists, moreover, when they wrote *poetry* proved to be not much different from other poets—and when they did not write poetry it matters little what they were. Descriptive poetry lives by its imagery, which is sometimes clear and sharp, as the Imagists would have it, and sometimes vague and suffused, as with the romanticists. In intellectual poetry the image tends toward the Marinistic conceit, which is not always bad in itself, but needs to be buoyed and balanced by smething more. The Imagists seem to have sought a combination, rendering description by means of the bold, recherché trope, that is, imagery born of the intellect, though addressed to the imagination; whereas the older imagery sprang apparently full-formed from the imagination alone. (This terminology, one may note, is out of date and will be repudiated by recent psychological critics and poets; but its meaning is plain enough, and it is after all quite as clear as the more complicated technical language of today.) Then when the combination proved to be insoluble, the intellectual tendency came to predominate; which is a perhaps natural development reinforced by the external circumstances of contemporary life. This, with the added note of his late Greek interests, seems to have been Mr. Aldington's story.

The *Collected Poems* opens with this grecizing note. Mr. Aldington is saturated with the Anthology and the Sicilian idylists. His imagination is filled with "Maenads dancing to a Faun's pipe." He is haunted by fauns and dryads and "naked wanton hamadryads"; they keep returning, even in his war poetry. (pp. 201-02)

The simplest and purest expression of this nostalgia, which is of course a form of decadence, is in the first five poems of the volume: **"Choricos"** (as fine as anything of the kind can

be, and echoed in the later poem **"The Lover"**), **"To a Greek Marble,"** **"Argyria,"** **"At Mitylene,"** and **"Stele."** . . . Here are the sense of music become silence, of human loveliness become marble, of ultimate beauty ended in a sadness which is warm only with remotest memories. Think of Pater's Mona Lisa done from a late Greek model, and you have the feeling of these first poems: clarity, chastened sensuousness, a cold fire, a beauty of lips that smile and eyes that stare like a statue's; that which is at once cruel and exquisite, life under "the very grey sky of Persephone," with a burden of "Love me, for I must depart." Then comes the sixth poem, **"Lesbia,"** which reveals the weakness of the whole manner and reveals it in a final line of stabbing sarcasm.

> And through it all I see your pale Greek face;
> Tenderness
> Makes me as eager as a little child to love you,
> You morsel left half-cold on Caesar's plate.

From this it is but a step to the modernistic, sub-poetic style which mars the verse of Mr. Aldington and a large group who today pass for poets. . . . These poets are infected with what Théophile Gautier called *le triste amour du laid*. Ugliness is a passion, an obsession with them. Not content with a sub-poetic, often they pass to a sub-prosaic level. They pretend to be careless and offhand about things. They mumble and speak in an undertone. They choose a commonplace subject, deprecate any real interest in it, write of it casually, and ask us to be moved by it. Reacting perhaps from the elaborately self-conscious art of the decadents, they fly to the opposite extreme. But poetry remains an art and will not be treated contemptuously. The imagination will not be sprung by such light fingering. It is one thing to cultivate simplicity, as Wordsworth did, sometimes with success; but quite another to cultivate barrenness, dulness, and incoherence. And it is one of the interesting and surprising contrasts of Mr. Aldington that he represents both schools, that he even tries to combine them. To illustrate this adequately would require abundant quotation; but by reference one may cite **"Childhood"** as an example of the worst and the **"Meditation"** as an example of the best;—the former being unrelieved dulness, the latter a sort of prose lifted by the dignity of its thought and warmed by an inner repressed glow.

The next step of a decadent intellectualism is to recognize the discrepancy of the two modes and deliberately exploit the discord. The result is a conscious grotesquerie. We know that the thing is bad and ugly; we know we are beaten; and we seize our nettle with a loud laugh at the hurt. (pp. 202-04)

[The] prime illustration of this débâcle of intellectual poetry is the longish work (fifty-odd pages) at the end of the volume called *A Fool i' the Forest*, with the subtitle "A Phantasmagoria" and a note explaining the allegory. Here three characters, "I", the typical man "struggling to attain a harmony between himself and the exterior world"; Mezzetin, a figure from the Commedia dell' arte, symbolizing the imaginative faculties, including "irresponsible gaiety"; and the Conjuror, a malicious fellow, symbolizing the intellectual faculties, that is, "age, science, righteous cant, solemnity, authority"; these three, being "one person split into three," take ship to Athens, get drunk on the Acropolis, sing and declaim and argue; presently wander into the catacombs (apparently), and on down to the Italian Renaissance, and still on to the World War in France, and still on to post-war London. Mezzetin dies; the Conjuror pesters "I" with well-meant advice until he is pushed off London Bridge, and "I" becomes a respectable commonplace

Englishman. All this comprises much raving in English, French, and Italian; in various meters and no-meters; with beauty (including the "echoing calls of fauns and dryads Happy in flower-sweet recesses") and ribaldry; with nonsense and serious reflections on the "miserable condition of humanity";—a precious mixture which out-herods "The Barren Land"; a phantasmagoria indeed. There is no point in passing judgment on this work; it is a document, a summary. It is a verbal counterpart of so much contemporary painting which is the perversion of art, and contemporary music which is technical proficiency gone mad. It also reveals a mental history.

Without assuming or implying necessarily that it is the personal story of Mr. Aldington, one traces a certain similar change and conflict through the succession of *Collected Poems.* One imagines a youth among none too lovely surroundings becoming enamoured of the vanished idyllic beauty of the Greek world, the idealized Arcadia of Theocritus and parts of the Anthology. Here was a frank sensuousness, a clear bright sweetness, a simple-hearted cheerfulness, and withal a golden richness, which offered the perfect escape from the drab day-by-day of Modern England. Into this pagan retreat the youth withdraws deeper and deeper. As he grows up to take his place in the actual world the contrast possesses him more powerfully. Youthful disillusion gives way to a mature disillusion, and the result is as ashes in the mouth. The War comes, exaggerating still further this contrast and feeling of misfit. He hopes, however, to be purified by experience, to be strengthened by trial, to be exalted by sacrifice. And the miracle is slow of fulfillment. He passes through stages of **"Terror," "Defeat," "Doubt," "Resentment," "Disdain."**

> You beat against me,
> Immense waves, filthy with refuse. . . .
> I shudder at the contact;
> Yet I pierce through you
> And stand up torn, dripping, shaken,
> But noble and fierce.

And this he calls **"Doubt."** In the **"Epilogue"** of *Images of War* he clings to love as the solvent. Then follow the *Images of Desire* with their "quick flower-flames that sear into the soul Sharp wounds of pleasure"; and though there is a brave Epilogue, it is the bravery of despair. **"Eumenides,"** in the section called "Exile," raises the old questions, and ends: "Tell me, what answer shall I give my murdered self?" Finally, in solitude, "innocent peace," and silence he has recovered the old raptures and "Almost that vanished purity"; in the humble Berkshire meadows the "wounds of war" have been cleansed. Yet one wonders if the cleansing is more than momentary. One feels that it is scarcely a permanent recovery. The ashes and bitterness predominate still.

This is the story, perhaps an imaginary one. He who would have lived happily in a pastoral of Theocritus finds himself at bay among the complexities of civilization and the brutalities of war. He whose gods are Silenus, the fauns, and white-armed Aphrodite can hardly be at home among

> All the wheels of the traffic,
> All the cold indifferent faces,
> All the fronts of the houses,
> All the stones of the street.

This is the story; yet one's faith in its veracity, even in its artistic sincerity, is undermined by the sense of strain throughout. Is it more than partly true? The war poems are genuine enough, though they are not always successful as poems. But in the love poems the note is forced to a shrillness, sometimes,

which begets doubt. The "fleshliness" of some of these (**"Daybreak"** for example) would have made Buchanan stare and gasp. (The "Songs for Puritans," perfect as they are in the late seventeenth century manner, are too much obviously exercises to be reckoned in this charge.) There is too much of breasts, weary eyes, cruel lips, burning pain—the sensual language of decadence—so that we feel it all to be shallow, artificial, deliberately stimulated. The sensual is a part, to be sure, of all passion, but never rightly for its own sake; but rather as a means of kindling the black earth till it achieve the gemlike flame. There must be flame; not, however, as a consuming force, but for its light and shadow, its warming and transmuting power. And here it is that Mr. Aldington's verse tends to betray its insincerity. He is always fanning his fire with strange images—

> Her mouth is a crushed flower
> That unpetals marvelously
> Beneath my lips.

And "the perfume of the flesh" is acrid; "She is so shudderingly beautiful." He may call upon Dante and those *che son contenti nel fuoco*, but he has not, in his *Collected Poems*, found the other love, that of Beatrice and the Paradiso.

A final word must be added on Mr. Aldington's prosody; it deserves fuller treatment. Most of the poems are in free-verse, part of which is plain prose of assorted lengths, that is, of discontinuous rhythms, and part in very delicately modulated patterns. Often the lines will scan readily, though the rhythm may seem to shift from line to line. Often there is a close approach to blank verse. Always in the best poems there is a true melody, not formal, but the more subtle for being continually varied. If for no other reason, Mr. Aldington's poetry would be important for its metrical mastery. And if we find it too frequently in substance a harsh wine (in Bacon's phrase) that tastes of the grape-stone, if (in his own phrase)

> We have beauty that is diseased and wanton,
> Art that plays with ugliness and fantasy,

still it is beauty and art sufficiently to warrant his place in our attention. To call it decadent and Alexandrian is fair enough, provided one remember that decadence and Alexandrianism are not altogether bad; and there is enough of the *vrai beau*, along with the *faux bon*, to make one hope that Mr. Aldington will complete the story with a satisfying resolution of his Arcadian-modernistic discord. (pp. 204-08)

Paull F. Baum, "Mr. Richard Aldington," in South Atlantic Quarterly, *Vol. XXVIII, No. 2, April, 1929, pp. 201-08.*

THE TIMES LITERARY SUPPLEMENT

It is chiefly of the contrast between the actual and the ideal, to put it very roughly, that Mr. Aldington writes: of the horrible comic song and the voices of children singing in the cupola. Sometimes the contrast seems to imply some kind of connexion, more often the opposites are simply confronted. For Mr. Aldington scorns obvious reconciliations, and refuses to infer a smiling face simply from the evidence of a frowning Providence. [Mr. Aldington's *Collected Poems*] begins with several conjurations of an exquisite ideal, the delicate images of antiquity. . . . Mr. Aldington makes us feel the remote cleanliness of epicurean simplicity, the integrity of these classical delights.

But we turn over one or two pages and are confronted with the loss which the world has suffered since the Greeks:—

> Millions of human vermin
> Swarm sweating
> Along the night-arched cavernous roads.
> (Happily rapid chemical processes
> Will disintegrate them all.)

And in the poems here collected from *Images of War* the contrast increases between the integrity and cleanliness of the Greeks, the unimpeachable sentiment of Nature, and the dingy muddle of the present. . . .

While the contrast is still a naked confrontation of opposites, though the ideal often gains in beauty by comparison with the actual, Mr. Aldington is most a poet when he writes of such beautiful subjects as naturally charm the poet. If such subjects are the common stock of poetry, Mr. Aldington succeeds in stripping them of all the luxury which poets have added to them so that they are still fresh and clean. He is an ascetic in the associations which he allows his poetic images to evoke. But he is not always able to walk easily amongst what is distasteful, relishing its horror and turning it into fine phrases as the born satirist will. His descriptions of the tedious and the horrible are both adequate and very sincere, so that they fall into their place in the contrast and do not overcome the beautiful, but as poetry, at any rate in the earlier poems, they take a second place and are not always appreciable for their own sake.

If in the earlier poems there is the blunt contrast of impotent clamour or tedious horror with temperate beauty, the contrast becomes in the later poems more involved, and the battle is more spiritual and subjective. Mr. Aldington turns from the external world, which contains both the mess that human beings have made and its own natural beauties assisted by the modest artifice of the ancients, to a contrast within himself. . . .

There is a complete break in the sequence of the poems when we come to some few essays in the manner of Restoration lyrics, admirable in artifice and wit; but the volume ends with Mr. Aldington's most elaborately metaphysical poem *A Fool i' the Forest,* where the actual and the ideal have now turned into personifications of the different aspects of the poet's mind. The "I" of the poem is, as Mr. Aldington explains, shown at a moment of turmoil "as he struggles to attain a harmony between himself and the exterior world." Here Mr. Aldington is at his most complicated; and since he has to express so many varieties of mood, his metre and verse are often apparently formless, though actually sincerity, and perhaps sincerity alone, seems to make form out of formlessness. The poem has a despairing conclusion, but it is a subtle statement of a problem which possibly does not admit of a solution, and in any case it is the statement, and not the solution, that matters to the reader, if not to the poet.

In *The Eaten Heart* Mr. Aldington has an even more difficult if not so large a problem, since his poem treats of love. The legend of the eaten heart tells of a Provençal knight who was killed by his mistress's husband. This husband then gave her lover's heart to his wife to eat, and when the lady discovered what she had done she killed herself. So in the past men died for love, but, Mr. Aldington asks—

> But who would die for sex?
> Would you die for an appetite,
> Die for food or drink?

So, the argument of the poem continues, do the moderns think of love. Yet they are right to be so hard—

> . . . to question and to destroy,
> Pitching out gods and fools, lumber and riches,
> Clearning away the falsities and pretensions.

Even so Mr. Aldington wonders whether we have been too hard, "mistaken the problem, overlooked the tragedy," and are incapable of reaching the tragic and beautiful intensity of the lovers in the tale of the eaten heart. For, if intense, it must be a tragedy. This is a conclusion in the sense that no more can be said about the problem, but it is not a solution; and of this nature appears to be the inevitable and sincere end of all Mr. Aldington's poems. But in this poem the doubt and difficulty begin again at the end, as if another poem were beginning. The knight is dead and inquires about the lady:—

> Well, but has she played her part?
> She ought to fall from the lip of the tower,
> And there she is prettily eating fruit.

The dead man is then reproved for not lying still, and thus this last poem has the same form as that of the *Fool i' the Forest,* where the two conflicting forces of the soul being removed, the "I" of the poem settles down to respectability. But we may suppose that he only settles down until he shall, with impassioned sincerity, again point the contrast between the actual and the ideal in another poem.

> *"Mr. Aldington's Poems," in* The Times Literary Supplement, *No. 1436, August 8, 1929, p. 620.*

HAROLD MONRO

The new practice of publishing collected poems during the life, even during the comparative youth, of their author, is not only misleading; in some cases it may be damaging. Recently the 'Collected Works' of a young poet and his latest new volume were published on the same day, in the former, chronological order being entirely discarded, the poems being rearranged under six new headings according to their subjects. It may be thought seemly for an elderly and altered Wordsworth, with his eyes on posterity, and his muse having one foot in the grave, to deal in such manner with the bulky product of the greater part of a lifetime. But, generally speaking, during his own life, a poet's admirers prefer to have and keep his works in their different successive volumes, unrevised, and each representing its period of development. To collect or collate is rather the work of a posthumous editor. The living poet is misrepresenting himself and misleading his public in suggesting that works to which he will constantly be adding can as yet be termed *collected*. Finally such meticulous craftsmen as Robert Bridges or W. B. Yeats have been known to damage some of their best poems by revising the impulses of youth in terms of a critical consciousness of some thirty years later.

Mr. Richard Aldington has a far larger following in America than in England, and, as his [*Collected Poems*] carries the imprint of a U.S.A. printer, or, if only because the pages never need be cut at the *fore-edge*, or, perhaps chiefly, on account of its large and imposing format, it may be assumed that the volume was produced mainly to meet the requirements of an American demand.

Moreover, the above general remarks about Collected Poems only in part apply to the present volume. First, it does not appear that many, or indeed any, revisions have taken place. Secondly, the volume as a whole conveys an impression of finality. Mr. Aldington appears before us as a writer who has turned aside from poetry, which impression is strengthened by the appearance simultaneously of his novel *Death of a Hero,* an important book which appears to mark a turning-point in his literary life.

It is not for me, however, to lay down these dicta for him. I am only suggesting what outside appearances denote. Yet on the clearest internal evidence, any new beginning will now be necessarily, as it were, a superstructure to the present volume. Mr. Aldington will have to be reborn as a poet. The *Collected Poems* constitutes a career in itself, divided into three periods.

The first period is chiefly pre-war. It belongs to the days of *The Egoist: a Weekly Individualist Review,* and of the young poets who first met in 1909 to discuss theories of poetry, and subsequently grouped themselves together under the term *Imagist.* (pp. 518-19)

Like many similar French movements, 'Imagism' (I prefer it without the final *e*) did not long survive but I think it has been stronger as an influence than it ever was as a movement.

Mr. Aldington retained the word for many years in its application to his own poetry, and we had from him between 1910 and 1919 several thin volumes such as *Images, Images of War, Images of Desire,* the last of which is undoubtedly the most powerful. (p. 520)

His style and method remain simple—chiefly description and comment, with hot outbursts of indignation. The verse flows in natural, rather conversational rhythms, with hardly ever a formal stanza, or a rhyme. In fact some poems are what one must call ingenuous, and there may be those people who find it nearly impossible to imagine why Mr. Aldington should have included in such a volume as this certain pieces that would appear to be early note-book versions, rough sketches, rather than the finished poem which ought certainly to have been resultant. (p. 521)

The poems in *Images of Desire* are passionate and sincere, the most *real* poetry in the book. Those under the heading **"Exile"** are less ardent and natural, and in the **"Words for Music"** Mr. Aldington has reined himself in (where he should have trusted his passion and instinct), and has turned neat and unnatural little stanzas in the manner of Prior.

Lastly, he emerges as a man with a confession to make, and a complaint and we have *The Fool i' the Forest (A Phantasmagoria)* more formless than anything he has yet written, entirely undisciplined and not a little obscure. It is a strange development, altogether an extraordinary evolution.

The Fool i' the Forest fails to be generally disturbing: it is too personal a complaint. There are certain other poems to-day of the same kind, which seem, however, as works of literature, to have more intellectual vitality, or concentrated force of discontent. Perhaps the plot of *The Fool* is ill-planned, or the structure too loose; but I think chiefly that it is too conversational. Language so wantonly *ordinary* can seldom be impressive. However this may be, it is impossible not to think that Mr. Aldington wrote it too quickly and fluently—gave perhaps one or two years to it where he should have given five.

It is not easy to figure what position Richard Aldington will ultimately hold on the strength of this volume. It is easy to be more struck by the remarkable personality of their author than by the face value of the poems as works of literature. He troubles us most when he seems least willing to take himself

seriously. The book is so graphic in its processes of development that it is too difficult to believe it can represent only a phase in a life wholly and faithfully devoted to literature; yet whatever new development or fresh beginning can now take place remains, for the moment, as already suggested, one of those enigmas that literary history delights to provide. (p. 522)

Harold Monro, in a review of "Collected Poems: Richard Aldington," in The Criterion, *Vol. IX, No. XXXVI, April, 1930, pp. 518-22.*

GLENN HUGHES

The essence of Aldington's character, the key to his poetry, is rebellion. He cannot tolerate the status quo. That is why he admires Pound and Lawrence and Wyndham Lewis, and why his god is Voltaire. The youngest of the imagists, he proved one of the staunchest defenders of the faith, a warrior eager for battle, and armed with much learning, tremendous mental energy, and a mocking, biting wit. His headstrong enthusiasms result sometimes in inconsistency and exaggeration, but generally he is a sound and penetrating thinker. He has been a professional critic almost as long as he has been a poet, and his reputation is as considerable in the field of prose as it is in that of verse. (pp. 86-7)

His early poems, written between 1910 and 1915, were published under the title, *Images.* Some of them had appeared first, of course, in the 1914 and 1915 imagist anthologies, and in periodicals. They are nearly all in unrimed free verse, beautifully cadenced.

The book opens with **"Choricos,"** a poem of studied and perhaps affected gravity, but one of Aldington's most effective efforts to recapture the Hellenic mood. (p. 88)

There are other lyrics in the collection which echo [the] classic mood, this coolness and dignity as of an Attic temple. But ere we have turned many pages we find ourselves in a more familiar world, with a poetry less archaic:

> The chimneys, rank on rank,
> Cut the clear sky;
> The moon
> With a rag of gauze about her loins
> Poses among them, an awkward Venus—
> And here am I looking wantonly at her
> Over the kitchen sink.

And presently we leave the kitchen sink for the streets of London, the underground trains, the cinemas, the iron and smoke of Whitechapel, a procession of cripples in Kensington. The flowery ways and glamorous gods of ancient Greece are almost forgotten; the poet glimpses them only now and then as welcome visions in a world of ugliness and pain. Since he cannot escape the life about him, he reviles it. Not only does he find the London of his young manhood awful; he comes to realize with terrible clarity that his childhood was spent in an atmosphere even worse. The horror of Dover in retrospect is too much for him. He does all that he can do now by way of getting even: he writes a rebellious poem [**"Childhood"**] in which the dreariness of an English town is etched in poison. (pp. 89-90)

What would have happened to Aldington as a poet had it not been for the War is a vain but inevitable query. It is safe to assume that he would have changed, for it is in him to change, but how no one can say. It is possible that without the experience of war he would have become as bitter and as cynical as he did with the experience. At any rate, his two and a half years of service, with fifteen months spent at the actual front, left him a quite different poet. Yet the change was not immediate. His poems written during the War period are a recognizable continuation of his early work, even though their tone is sterner and their details are more vivid. *Images of War* contains certainly some of the truest and most beautiful poems written by any soldier in modern times. In the opinion of Harold Monro, "Except Siegfried Sassoon, no 'war-poet' has represented the torments of military life with such candor and so entirely without bombastic rhetoric." (p. 93)

[In *Images of War,* we] see and feel the cataclysm of bombardment, the loneliness of ruined fields and villages; we lean against a trench in the frosty night, making wisps of poems to the moon; we march wearily through the night and to the dawn; again and again we hear the whispers of death, the imminent lover. Almost never in these poems does the author allow self-pity to master him, and never does he indulge in heroics. He is consistently honest, and consistently an artist.

To the same period as *Images of War* belong the love poems called *Images of Desire.* This small collection contains a surprising variety of manners. Indeed, it is as though the author had sought deliberately to celebrate his love in various ways—to weave a garland of diverse flowers, thus making the tribute as rich as possible. There are many short pieces, true images, of the Oriental type. . . . There are others in which passion awakens echoes of Swinburne. . . . In these and other modes appear the inevitable affirmations of love: the ecstasy of possession, the dread of loss, the agony of separation. Apart from their emotional content these poems are interesting to us because they indicate Aldington's transition from pure imagism to a less prescribed technique. They illustrate his rebellion against a method which at one time had satisfied him but which he now employs only on occasion.

To the same general period belongs *Myrrhine and Konallis,* a series of poems celebrating the love of two Greek maidens. The first of these were written between 1913 and 1915, the remainder in 1919. In style they are akin to Mr. Aldington's translations from Anyte of Tegea, Anacreon, and Meleager. They are rhetorical, archaic, and richly colored. The cadences are long and voluptuous; the imagery weighted with ornament. . . . (pp. 94-6)

I have spoken of the bitterness which the War brought to this poet. For its first violent expression we must turn to *Exile and Other Poems.* This book, though small, contains three sections. The first is composed of poems chiefly in free verse and blank verse, all of them voicing the disillusionment and despair which besieged the poet in the post-war days, when memories of horror were still fresh, and when it seemed impossible to make a readjustment of life along the lines of peace. He cannot sleep for the nightmare of the past, and in his spiritual pain he questions fate. . . . (p. 97)

The second section of [*Exile*] is composed of fourteen songs, titled explicitly **"Words for Music."** Ten of them are dedicated to Puritans and four to sensualists. As might be expected, the Puritans are invited to participate in the joys of the flesh, and the sensualists are treated to the purity of star and blossom. All these poems are exquisitely modeled upon seventeenth-century patterns, and one hears in them the scarcely disguised accents of Herrick and Carew. They contain little originality, but they testify to the virtuosity of their author.

The third section, called **"Metrical Exercises,"** consists of only two poems: **"The Berkshire Kennet"** and **"A Winter Night."** Both are written in rimed couplets, in rather an eighteenth-century manner, and both are in praise of country life. Apart from their intrinsic beauty they are interesting because of their biographical and psychological significance. After the War Mr. Aldington settled down to live in a little cottage in the heart of Berkshire, at Padworth, a parish not far from Reading. There among the marvelously green fields, through which winds the river Kennet, he found the quiet, the solitude, which his heart required. There he escaped the turmoil of modern life, and there he found the healing balm for bitter memories of hate and death. . . . (pp. 98-9)

The pastoral mood was authentic, but it was not permanent. How could it be, when it was only a phase of convalescence? The poet was still young and still rebellious. His spirit here waxed strong within him and produced *A Fool i' the Forest,* a long, phantasmagoric poem, an autobiographical harlequinade, in which three characters (who symbolize three aspects of the author's personality) dance their way madly through the spinning world of consciousness and memory, until two of them are dead and the other is ignominiously submerged in conventional society. (pp. 99-100)

Although Aldington is not the first man in the world to suffer such an inner conflict and to face such a crisis, he is, I should think, one of the best modern examples of the type. And certainly he is one of the most articulate. Another excellent example is T. S. Eliot. In fact, it has already been remarked by critics that *A Fool i' the Forest* owes much to *The Waste Land.* Humbert Wolfe's comment is that "Aldington . . . could only see life darkly in T. S. Eliot's looking-glass." But he adds that "that half-glimpse was worth the whole of the Imagist philanderings with verse which was only free in the sense that a bolting horse is free." His point is that in this work the poet has allowed life itself to dictate form, whereas in the early imagist poems an attempt was made to impose order upon a living organism. I cannot agree entirely with this generalization, but I do agree that *A Fool i' the Forest* is Aldington's finest poetic achievement.

The whole poem has extraordinary pace, and a great variety of rhythms. The narrative passages are in unrimed verse, irregular, but hovering about the norm of a four-beat line. Interpolated are many snatches of song, some of them rimed and metrical—some of them satirically doggerel—others in unrimed cadence. Moods alternate swiftly, thought flashes and disappears, scenes shift as in a dream—a method of presentation now common in fiction and drama as well as in poetry. The settings are Venice, Athens, the battlefields of France, and London. The time is the simultaneous past and present, for consciousness and memory are blended. Aldington the man is dragged from place to place by Aldington the poet and Aldington the scholar. The soul of the man is fought for by the poet and the scholar. First one gains it, then the other. They picnic in the shadow of the Parthenon. They all get drunk, and argue about life and art and science. (pp. 100-01)

[The ending of *A Fool i' The Forest*] holds the bitterest mockery of the whole poem. It represents the sort of thing which Aldington most despises; the hell which he has spent his life escaping. In that sense it is an autobiographical conclusion, but in that sense only, for actually the poet and the scholar both survived, and are still contending for the soul of man.

Something of this triangular struggle is reflected in Aldington's more recent poem, *The Eaten Heart,* a single piece of some three hundred lines of free verse, with a theme drawn from the medieval legend of the beautiful lady who is tricked by her husband into eating the heart of her slain troubadour lover. The contemplation of this romantic story, with its tragic end, leads the modern poet to an analysis of love, to a contrast between old and new ideals, and thence to a semi-autobiographical rhapsody in which the recurrent motif is the struggle of a romantic nature to adapt itself to the hardness and disillusionment of a deflowered age, a post-war, machine-governed world. The conclusion, reached by a tortuous and sometimes prosaic road, is that the soul of the poet survives. It hardens itself and tunes itself to the machines. The tragic suffering attendant upon the metamorphosis is but another poetic experience in a life which is always and inevitably tragic. One kind of beauty is lost, but another is gained. Sweetness goes, but with it goes falsehood; and bitterness brings honesty, a virtue compatible with our age. (pp. 105-06)

Artistically, I should say, [*A Dream in the Luxembourg*] is lacking in the merit belonging to *The Eaten Heart* and "**Passages toward a Long Poem.**" Here and there a line flashes fire, but many passages are dull prose, and the intensity of emotion which evidently inspired the poem is by no means communicated to the reader. At best it exhales the perfume of a long-pressed flower. (p. 108)

> Glenn Hughes, "Richard Aldington: 'The Rebel'," *in his* Imagism & the Imagists: A Study in Modern Poetry, *1931. Reprint by The Humanities Press, 1960, pp. 85-108.*

R. P. BLACKMUR

Mr. Aldington is a type of the poet—in intention, in attitude toward life and toward past literature, in vocabulary, in the tone of his thinking, and in his wilful assertion of personal inspiration. But he is, on the whole, not an example: his work is not poetry of a high order. The best evidence for this statement is that his poetry loses rather than gains when read all at one time, as [*The Poems of Richard Aldington*] invites us to read it. There is no single poem in the volume which persuades us to remember it complete, though there are many lines, especially beginning lines, which stick in the mind because of the boldness of statement or the lift of the rhythm. That is to say, while he presents us with a fund of substance and a talent for feeling, Mr. Aldington lacks either the genius or the arduous will for persistent execution; he lacks those elements of composition and of style which persuade us finally of a poem's existence.

This failure may be fundamental, the result of a radical defect of talent, or it may have an origin at least partly historical. Mr. Aldington began publishing with the imagist group of 1912, and that—as it has turned out for everyone in the group—was a heavy weight to bear. The excitement of a fresh, superficial view coupled with an easy, not to say laxative, method of writing produced or encouraged a good many rather fluid talents to whom the finished, the solid, the mature seemed stale. Success was accidental and fragmentary, and no poet can expect a lifetime of accidents unless the life is short. (p. 625)

Eliot and Pound deliberately obstruct by obscurity of reference the reader's view of the contents of their more important poems and accomplish their perversity with great clarity and beauty of language. Mr. Aldington, on the contrary, has not advanced that far in the attempt to make verse either difficult or private. You do not need, in reading him, either a specially designed encyclopedia or a faculty for telepathy. His subject matter is conventionally presented, his allusions may be found in a small classical dictionary, and he uses words in their normal connotations. His poems, however, appear with what Henry James called "the terribly fluidity" of self-revelation. Thus, like Eliot and Pound on one side, he sees neither the necessity nor the convenience of sustained tone and the dramatic presentation of material, and like Cummings on the other side, he uses words as he finds them without much effort to particularize them in the poems. Hence his rhythms break down as soon as they are established, his arrangements lack inevitability, and his language tends to be slovenly and therefore while intelligible cannot certify its meaning.

Perhaps nothing more orderly, especially in the realm of poetry and feeling—nothing less fragmentary, nothing less heretical—could have been expected of a generation whose young manhood was interrupted by the war and demolished by the peace, and whose imagination was thus driven by the need of exile or escape from the dreadful order that was laid everywhere upon it. We have Mr. Aldington's war poems and particularly his poem called "Exile" positively to suggest as much, and we have the later poems of the Eaten Heart Group and the new poems at the end of the book to demonstrate it negatively. The two longish poems, *A Fool i' the Forest* and *A Dream in the Luxembourg,* are so to speak interludes between the positive and negative poles, but rather resemble in their diffuseness and excessive romantic bitterness *The Death of a Hero* and *The Colonel's Daughter* than the poems. It was the war perhaps and what came after it that made Mr. Aldington in every case let himself go from a summit of emotion, of recognition, or of disillusionment. But when you let yourself go you do not often make great poetry, because without a form to mold you and a discipline to direct you, you cannot possibly know where to stop, know what has been presented specifically and what has been merely stated, what has come out good and what bad; you can, in fact, only push on to the corollary and let yourself run down.

That is what Mr. Aldington does. Experience catches him by the throat or beats him in the face, and he answers back as vigorously as he can. His subjects are war and love and hypocrisy. His weapons are sharp statement, bold image, snatches of masculine rhythm, and the catch-as-catch-can of tumultuous feeling. His retreat is into Greek poetry or the English land. He has a stubborn but crotchety honesty without ever the persuasion of tact, and he has an intense personal bitterness that never bothers with the only secure foundation for bitterness, which is irony. His poems make powerful personal documents of a life, but they do not often do the necessary work to make them powerful poetry. The success of many fragments only adumbrates the size of his failure. Reading him we may fortify the more honorable of our prejudices, but nothing is brought to the objective strength of that which can be contemplated all round.

> R. P. Blackmur, "Richard Aldington," *in* The Nation, *New York, Vol. CXXXVIII, No. 3595, May 30, 1934, p. 625.*

CONRAD AIKEN

To review Imagist poetry, after a lapse of twenty years, is a bewildering experience; for if one opens the pages of [*The Poems of Richard Aldington*], and if then one returns to the celebrated Imagist anthologies of 1915 and 1916, it is to marvel that there should ever have been such excitement about the thing. It is exactly a generation since, under the leadership of Ezra Pound, this little band of Balearic slingers advanced so truculently upon us and put us to rout. Their slogans we still remember—freedom in choice of subject, new rhythms, the language of common speech, the presentation of an ''image,'' concentration, and the production of poetry that was ''hard and clear, never blurred or indefinite.'' Sound enough notions— so sound, indeed, as to be the usual characteristics of *any* poet worth his salt! and just why we should have thought the program revolutionary, or should have imagined that we saw anything very new or subversive in the poetry itself, is now hard to conceive. Most of the poetry in the Imagist anthologies, if now revisited, looks quite mild and, on the whole, unimportant; perhaps the free verse with its look of novelty bemused us; at any rate, one many question whether H. D. was not the only genuine dyed-in-the-wool Imagist in the whole lot. Beside her, the others all lack ''concentration,'' and even her imitators (among whom was Mr. Aldington) never approached her skill in achieving a pure singleness of image or picture. (p. 272)

It was presumably the accident of his association with H. D. that brought Mr. Aldington into the group, for that she influenced him a great deal is obvious from his collected poems. But the influence was on the surface, chiefly. The essential character beneath was very different indeed, and successfully resisted the imposition: now that one reads him *en masse* one sees that he was really rather an old-fashioned if not definitely *fin-de-siècle* fellow, pretty lush and Swinburnian, very much given to nostalgic and erotic pallors and pinks, quite sentimental, and on the whole with little real distinction of style or idea. The verse has for the most part a confected appearance, and if it seldom achieves perfection of form or statement, it just as seldom compensates for that lack by any genuine approach to reality. There are exceptions—**''Bones''** is a good poem, and it is instructive to note that in this, and in one or two other of the more successful things, Mr. Aldington was for the moment abandoning free verse for strict octosyllabic couplets.

In his later work, Mr. Aldington has moved away from the decorative neo-Hellenic style to something plainer and prosier—one sees the influence of Eliot and the Sitwells, particularly in a noticeable increase in the use of irony. *A Dream in the Luxembourg* is the best thing in the book, a straightforward story told in a relaxed free verse, colloquial and vivid—but it is too like Mr. Ford's (or as he then was, Mr. Hueffer's) ''On Heaven'' even if it is as good; and moreover, one cannot help wondering if it could not better have been done frankly in prose as a short story. At all events, in this and in the other poems, one looks in vain for any singular sharpness of image or concentration, or for much hardness and clearness. A good deal of the diction is from the poetic ''stock,'' the rhythms are neither very various nor very new, and there is a noticeable paucity of ideas. It is often charming work, but one feels in the end that Mr. Aldington lacks the final energy for the essential that marks the true poet. His prose is far better. (pp. 272-73)

Conrad Aiken, ''Death of an Imagist,'' in The New Republic, *Vol. LXXIX, No. 1024, July 18, 1934, pp. 272-73.*

RICHMOND CROOM BEATTY

[Richard Aldington] is a writer who for twenty-two years has been doing the kind of verses which suited the hour, who gave us imagistic poems when imagism was fashionable, who gave us bitterly denunciatory war poems when war was fashionable, who was properly disillusioned when disillusionment was in order, and who, modern of moderns through two decades, has cried out savagely for the Truth—that bright star so long eclipsed by the miasmal mists of Victorianism. Perhaps one may attribute to Aldington the virtue of expressing his age. But one cannot avoid the suspicion that his point of view is predicated upon something rather shoddily journalistic in character. He emerges in [*The Poems of Richard Aldington*] an intellectual drifter, one who writes hurriedly, and with no significant style, about anything new or apt to be in demand.

In spite of his prolixity, his ideas are thin and unsatisfying: War is a tyranny fomented by bloated capitalists, the English hate life, the physical rapture of first love is man's supreme ecstasy. It is this last theme which Aldington belabors most tediously. In one work only, *The Eaten Heart*—a prose essay set down arbitrarily as verse—does he go beyond it, to declare that a spiritualized love may obliterate, in part, the loneliness of his generation. In the others, his is simply a pedestrian approach to a subject which Marvell, Marlowe, Herrick, Keats, Byron, and a host of others have treated exquisitely before him.

Of course these are generalizations, to which certain minor poems offer an occasional exception. It is only fair to add that at times Aldington's extensive knowledge of Greek literature invests his usually commonplace lines with wisdom and felicity. He is one of the few of many poets of a generation ago inclined to imagism who have found in Greek culture something more impressive than cameos and figurines. He may yet find something further, even stability, and his poetry may reflect it, when the date for a collected edition shall in honesty have arrived. (pp. 195-96)

Richmond Croom Beatty, ''Poets, English and American,'' in The Yale Review, *Vol. XXIV, No. 1, September, 1934, pp. 194-97.*

DOUGLAS BUSH

In intention and technique [Mr. Richard Aldington's] early Hellenic-Imagist poems were much the same as H. D.'s, but with a more diffuse softness, a more openly Victorian weariness and nostalgia. Greece was a symbol of the beauty of nature and art, of freedom and amorous nymphs. **''Choricos,''** which was too revolutionary for an English journal and consequently appeared in Miss Monroe's *Poetry* in 1912, was ''The Garden of Proserpine'' over again, without the Swinburnian music but with all the Swinburnian materials, melancholy regret, satiety, death and eternal sleep. *Images* (1915) was not wholly Greek; pictures of London streets and tubes and cinemas were realistic and angry. Then to the ugliness of peace was added a greater ugliness, and, as the poet had contrasted the statue of Eros and Psyche with the grime of Camden Town, so his images of war were mingled with visions of ''beauty and the women of Hellas,'' the sea and olive gardens, fauns and ''naked wanton hamadryads.'' But the mold of Mr. Aldington's Imagism was, along with other things, broken by the war. It was too delicate a vial for a wrath which one cannot condemn, though one may think an emotional indignation against all things established an inadequate creed for a serious writer. At any rate Mr. Aldington turned from Imagism to verse of the Pound-Eliot kind, and then to the novel, and has made a career of disillusioned bitterness.

The phantasmagoric poem, *A Fool i' the Forest* (1925), contains one person split into three: the narrator, a modern man of artistic temperament who is struggling "to attain a harmony between himself and the exterior world"; the Conjuror, who represents "the intellectual faculties—age, science, righteous cant, solemnity, authority"; and Mezzetin, "the imaginative faculties—art, youth, satire, irresponsible gaiety, liberty." The trio visit Athens and discourse upon Greek culture. For a time the Greeks did possess that perfect harmony of mind and senses which yielded "Science and beauty reconciled with health." They accepted life; even their sensual excesses were disciplined by a sense of beauty. Our minds and senses, our science and art, are unbalanced, diseased, mechanized. Finally, Mezzetin is killed in the war, through the Conjurer's blundering; back in London, the narrator throws the Conjurer into the Thames; and, left to himself, the lover of truth and beauty settles down as the complete suburbanite. Mr. Aldington's conception of Greece is here more realistic than it was, but it is still mainly emotional and sentimental. The evening star brings home the *Evening News* and the business man, "Sappho and Shelley you no longer bring"; such a line might have been written by Wilde.

Mr. Aldington has clung to a faith in life, which nowadays means love. His erotic philosophy is that of Lawrence enveloped in a mist of glamorous romantic idealism and classical allusion. In the neo-pagan idyll called *A Dream in the Luxembourg* (1930), the woman is a veritable wood-nymph "Because she is brave and frank and honest and herself" (as Shelley said, "frank, beautiful, and kind"), because (here the note is Swinburnian) such fair, uninhibited creatures fight against "The Jewish gloom and the gloomy Christ." Finally, there is *The Eaten Heart* (1933), a meditation on love, on an individual's escape from solitude to that complete union with another which yields complete satisfaction and enrichment. It is hard to discern any very felicitous aptness in the reinterpretation of Philoctetes as the symbol of "the dreadful inevitable loneliness of the human soul"; there is an unbridgeable gulf between the heroic masculine sufferer on the Lemnian isle and the modern lover's "weak squabble with despair." Altogether, Mr. Aldington is a sensitive romantic rebel who has found in Greek poetry, as any selective reader can find, support for his own temperament. He is superior to many such rebels in being aware of disharmony and confusion in himself. But he has always been, rather too self-consciously, a captive faun. (pp. 468-70)

> *Douglas Bush, "From the Nineties to the Present, II," in his* Mythology and the Romantic Tradition in English Poetry, *1937. Reprint by W. W. Norton & Company, Inc., 1963, pp. 457-80.*

A. E. [GEORGE WILLIAM RUSSELL]

When one likes a poet it is easy to write about him, to become eloquent in his praise. We try to convey to others the enchantment he has cast upon ourselves. But how are we to be truly critical? We cannot apply to poetry any tests such as we can apply to the formulas of the chemist. They can be proved to be true or false in a laboratory. There is no accepted technique of criticism, no proof of beauty. We have little else but the expression of opinion. I have tried to formulate to myself some philosophical principles of criticism, but am uncertain about these. I ask myself about a poet whether his poetry is opaque or transparent; that is, does he rest on the surface of things, or does he see through things, and, lastly, I ask myself out of how deep a life does he speak. I formulated these principles of criticism after reading the *Banquet* of Plato, where Socrates

suggests a hierarchy of beauty. First he says we are in love with a single person or form; then, as the soul becomes wiser, it realises that the beauty in one form is akin to the beauty in all other forms. We are released from this mean idea of beauty in one person or form only. Our search goes into the depths, and in this second stage of initiation into beauty we pass from the beauty of form into perception of the beauty of ideas, and at last are led to see beauty in its very essence. But he does not tell us by what criterion we are to esteem ideas. That is left to our intuition, and I could only think of this, that some ideas are opaque as some forms are, and stay us beside them, and that other ideas are transparent and we see through them as one looking through a glass at immense vistas. We are imprisoned—pleasurably, it may be—by the first order, and are liberated by the second order. I was started on this meditation by Richard Aldington's poems. This poetry, esteeming it as Socrates might, I class as largely opaque. It is imagist, resting on the surface or appearance of things, beauty of colour or form, and, indeed, the very titles of four of the volumes of verse from which [*The Poems of Richard Aldington*] was made suggest the poet's preoccupation with images. Here is a poem which has for substance little else than a charming imagination for the eyes:

> We will come down to you,
> O very deep sea,
> And drift upon your pale green waves
> Like scattered petals.
> We will come down to you from the hills,
> From the scented lemon-groves,
> From the hot sun.
> We will come down,
> O Thalassa,
> And drift upon
> Your pale green waves
> Like petals.

That is a poetry made of what the eye rests upon, and there is no attempt at transfiguration. The image is delicately selected, but there is nothing more in it than the image which has a charm. I think Socrates would say of many of these poems that the poet had not passed beyond the first conception of beauty as existing only in the forms of things. I can understand this fanatic passion for things lovely to look on, for in one of his poems he suggests childhood in an unlovely city. After a childhood like that we can forgive the poet dreaming of white marble forms, blue waters, Sicilian skies, old gardens, lutes and lyres, fauns and maenads, and other images of ancient beauty. Almost always it is by pain we are driven from a contented resting on the senses, and the war seems to have broken up that mould of mind in Richard Aldington from which came that early opaque imagist poetry. But the ideas are still opaque. There is in him rage and lamentation as he broods bitterly in the trenches, but as yet he can see no meaning in the carnage, perhaps nobody could. Now and then he is stirred to an elemental meditation, but it reveals nothing. There is only the tortured nerves, puddles of blood and flesh, rotting bodies; phantom images of that lost beauty of Sicilian sea, white forms, love, all remote and fading. But there is an increased intensity even if nothing is transfigured, even if he has not found some divine justice in the anguish he endures. But he is launched on that inner sea, and will never be able again to write contentedly of white marble beauties. Nature, when we pass from one phase to another, closes the door behind us, and we can never return to what we were, once we have passed away from ourselves. I could find no verses suggesting that he had come to the region of the psyche where images and ideas are transparent or liberating. Nothing like

> Thy friends are exultations, agonies.

That was written by one who saw that for which all the long labours of the soul were undertaken, who could press the thorns into the soul, knowing that they would take root there, that they would break out into immortal flowers.

In the later poetry we find him wandering about in that new internal world into which his anguish has pushed him, not all unhappy, able to laugh, be cynical or serious, but never quite coming to that transparency where a light shines through idea or emotion, two worlds meet in us, and in every breathing there are martyrdoms or exaltations of sense or soul. Anyhow, he has begun to think. He even develops an ironical humour which has its appeal. He may find his way to the third circle of poetry, where ideas and emotions are transparent. But at present he is making himself at home in the second circle, salving his wounds with humour. He is the first victim to whom my Platonic formulae have been applied. I hope that genuine sense of humour the poet has developed will enable him to endure without rage my attempts to probe into his psyche with the lantern Diotima gave to Socrates. (pp. 104-07)

> A. E. [*George William Russell*], "*A Platonic Criticism*," in his The Living Torch, *edited by Monk Gibbon, The Macmillan Company, 1938, pp. 104-07.*

C. P. SNOW

[*The essay excerpted below was originally published in the 1938 pamphlet "Richard Aldington: An Appreciation."*]

Anyone in touch with twentieth-century literature knows Richard Aldington to be a writer of great gifts. You cannot pin him down as simply a "novelist" or "poet" or "critic"; he has already produced a large volume of work in each genre, much of it high and secure beyond controversy and depreciation. His achievement exists. He has followed his own course, and won his special place. His books are translated in over a dozen countries and are read all over the world.

You can read scarcely any of his work and remain indifferent. It produces that immediate *impact* which is a mark of the most intense writers. To get the most out of him, however, as with any writer, one needs to appreciate something beneath the first impact.

Let me begin with a commonplace. His writing is full of life. No one can read him for ten minutes without feeling a glow of power and vitality: a gusto both of the senses and of the mind: a natural, fluid ease with words: an impression of someone seeing things ten times more vividly, and being both hurt and delighted ten times more intensely, than most of us can ever manage.

"Full of life"—read **All Men Are Enemies** or the **Collected Poems** or **A Dream in the Luxembourg.** You will feel that the phrase is *literally* true. The writing makes you share an experience of life which has been unusually complete; it glows with an appetite for living without which the experience would have been dead. That warmth and appetite for living shine through all his work: it is the essence of his gift and vitalises everything he has to say.

Few writers have possessed such a zest for the variety of experience in one man's life. I do not mean the observant second-

hand zest of Balzac—that is part of many writers' equipment—but the actual passionate sense of one's own pleasure and suffering as one goes alone through the world. It is that sense which Aldington communicates with such astonishing directness; he brings us nearer to another passionately felt experience than we thought we could ever come.

This experience, as I have said, is wide as well as deep. It is the life of "the here and now," as he calls it, the life of the senses as well as of the emotions and the mind. They all come home to us with the same absolute conviction and the certainty that we learn them at first hand. They are expressed with the greatest power and *authority*. The latter seems a curious word to use about a writer's communication of his joy in immediate life; yet there is no other which is quite so true. One never doubts the genuineness nor the intensity of the experience. For this man, one knows, it meant just that. A good many writers have rhapsodised about the life of the senses. There is something forced and bogus about many of them. They are, so to speak, yodelling through their pince-nez. But no one could conceivably read Aldington and entertain such a doubt. His passions, his delights and his suffering, come to us as deeply and honestly as they did to himself. He is a man with an unusual capacity for them all. That is why he can enrich us with moments unlike those of anyone alive. That is why he can give us an intimation of experience so deep and yet immediate that we shall not see the world with quite the same eyes again.

Some people have, however, also felt a "bitterness" and a "harshness" which they allow to dominate their other responses to his writing. Of course, as soon as a critical slogan is put forward, it is the easiest thing in the world for it to spread. We are all more suggestible than we like to think. Fashions in criticisms are accordingly too easy to start, and dangerous when they are on the move. With the catchword "bitter" in the back of one's mind, one can read a book and find the bitterness in every line—and spare oneself the trouble of looking for anything else.

Something like that has often seemed to happen with Aldington's work. It is a pity. The bitterness is there all right. But it only predominates in one or two books, and in them is accompanied by much else. In everything he has written we ought to find many qualities far different and far more important. In order to get all we can from him, we need to understand the "bitterness," put it in its place, and see beneath it the particular conception of life, the particular kind of passion and sensitivity, of which it is only one result.

Most of his work is "personal" in the best sense. It is a passionately felt experience. To begin to understand it properly, I think we must understand some parts of his own personality; it is not by accident that often in his books, particularly in the prefaces, he has given some careful and deliberate self-revelations.

A certain kind of indrawn sensitivity, acting within a powerful and passionate nature, runs through much of his work. His books are full of people more than ordinarily sensitive and proud, more deeply humiliated, more easily subject to shame: proud individuals, aware of their own loneliness, desperately sensitive even to a hostile glance. But when these people of his can feel assured that they are liked, the barriers come down in an instant. Just as their pride was great, so is their happiness and surrender in love and friendship.

That acute inner sensitiveness lies behind a great deal of his writings, particularly in the novels. We understand them better,

I think, as soon as we realise it; particularly if we also realise that it is coupled with force, authority and strength. That is, there is nothing passive about his sensitivity; if he feels suspicious of a hostile world, his impulse is to attack before he is himself attacked.

Often, then, he sees the world of human beings as remote, hostile and wounding. At other times, in friendship and essentially in love, he feels an ecstasy greater than the other enmity. It is from this other side, the happy side of his sensitivity, that he draws his hopes. He has called himself a ''romantic idealist''—and that is absolutely true. He knows that he expects more of life than the mixture and contradictions of living can give. He believes in ''integrity and comradeship,'' in his generation that ''hoped much, strove honestly and suffered deeply'': and most of all in his own romantic ideal of love, ''the finer fuller life.'' ''It is not only life with a woman he really loves, but the energy and beauty of existence which he wants to contribute to their joint possession. It is the life of the here and now, the life of the senses, the life of the deep instinctive forces.'' (pp. 134-38)

[*The Crystal World*] convinced many of what they had gradually been suspecting for some time: that Aldington has written some of the best love-poetry in English. Most of us are not over-willing to commit ourselves to a literary judgment on a contemporary; but that statement I would make myself without feeling that I was risking anything at all. (p. 140)

> *C. P. Snow, in a review in* Richard Aldington: An Intimate Portrait, *edited by Alister Kershaw and Frédéric-Jacques Temple, Southern Illinois University Press, 1965, pp. 134-40.*

ROY CAMPBELL

[*The essay excerpted below originally appeared as ''The Happy Pagan'' in* The Poetry Review, *April-May, 1949.*]

In literature the poet (that is the minority-man who is still performing the function of literature) depends for his contemporary fame and perhaps his livelihood, largely on whether his work can be used to illustrate the pet theories of the uncreative majority of politico-critical pedants who really for the time being call the tune. As Richard Aldington points out in his brief and masterly introduction to his [*Collected Poems*], commentators on verse are more interested in discussing what they call ''tendencies'' than on studying the work of the poet. One crossword-conscious pedant has the effrontery to tell us that he likes his poetry ''difficult,'' as ''something to be wrestled with,'' and for every clear-headed poet, like Aldington, there are at least three hundred crossword-conscious professors demanding, like this one does, to be *puzzled* by poetry which is more difficult to read than to write; poetry in which they can joyfully hunt the thimble of meaning through haystacks of self-bamboozlement; poetry which is vague and formless but offers (like Leonardo's mildewed wall) a million suggestions of half-meanings and glimmerings of sense. Whenever the reader, the listener, or the spectator wants, as in this case, to join in the show and ''be clever too'' he crashes a great donkey's hoof through the whole function of art and reduces it to collective barbarism and imbecility. Aldington does not cater for this collective craving. There is not enough hesitancy or obscurity in Aldington's work to nourish a single one of these parasitic interpreters, or employ even a part-time hack-translator of verse into literary officialese, the function of the modern critic. He is his own commentator; his verse, even though concerned with

great profundities of thought and feeling, is always explicit and clear. It is for his earlier rôle as a daring innovator that he has received more recognition than for his subsequent achievements as a poet, which entirely eclipses his earlier, better-known, anthologised work. It is only on reading this magnificent collection of work written during the last thirty-five years, that one realises how shamefully one of the best of living poets has been neglected: and also that in Aldington's case (as in the rare cases of Hardy and Lawrence) a first-rate novelist has been equalled if not excelled by his own achievement as a poet.

In his introduction he tells us that, in his experience, poetry was not the result of selfconscious effort but seemed to occur quite spontaneously and mysteriously. ''That is the moment of poetic ecstasy,'' he tells us, ''which almost invariably occurs in a mood of what Wordsworth called 'wise passivity'—all the rest is hard work.'' At a very early age Aldington was already endowed with such lapidary skill as a chiseller of poetical medallions, that he was able to discard the traditional aids to poetic form from the outset. By dint of sheer ''hard work'' that skill has become a second nature: so that under the stress of passions which tend to make most other poets long-winded by discursive love, anger, or hate it enables him to find the fullest expression in the fewest possible words. Brevity, with him, is not only the soul of wit, but of passion. Though he has written long poems of perfect construction, like *The Dream in the Luxembourg, A Fool i' the Forest* and *The Crystal World,* they are formed, like crystals, of smaller crystals, each of which is a separate whole, brief and crisp as an epigram.

Aldington was one of the first English poets of this century to discard the conventions of rhyme and metre, which were unnecessary to him. The vast majority of English poets have since discarded these conventions for looser and freer forms which are easier to write, but which often prove that the discarded conventions were of as great a necessity to them as a bellyband to a fat man. Aldington discarded them for a stricter and more difficult form which can hardly be called free verse because of the masterful control which regulates and balances every detail with the minutest precision: and which enables him to perpetuate moments of illumination in forms as hard and clear as gems, which, nevertheless, retain the warmth, fragrance, and freshness of the first impulse to write. If we compare his verse with much other rhymeless and metreless verse, we begin to see what rhyme and metre were originally intended for. The rhymes were intended as hurdles, ditches, and hedges, to tire out long-winded poets so that they would soon lose their breath and shut up. The metre was apparently intended to serve to the average poets' thoughts as a corral serves to a herd of jungle-happy nanny-goats to keep them from rambling, and straying, and getting lost. Together rhyme and metre acted as a sort of corset to Muses who suffered from Elephantiasis of the Soul (as they usually do when they have little to say).

Though Aldington was one of the few who originated the whole movement of what we call modern verse, he took no part in any of the commercially collectivised *''movements''* or *''tendencies''* during the nomadic inter-war period when almost every article was headed ''towards a new synthesis,'' ''towards'' a new this, ''towards'' a new that, and ''towards'' a new the other. . . . (pp. 5-8)

[It] is a delightful experience, which makes me revise some of my views, to meet in Aldington the one example I know of a happy pagan writer who enjoys life although (no, rather *because*) he had seen and felt a rougher side to it than our modern moaners, as one can see from his war poetry: who wears his vast erudition and scholarship lightly and gracefully, without pedantry; whose mature experience is not sour or vinegary but has the tartness of the real ripe apple of knowledge from the garden of Eden. He has written some of the finest love poetry of our time. He has none of the collective disillusionment which for so many years sold both itself and the public so successfully. One reads him not only for the poetry but for the companionship and comradeship of the man whom we feel to be so brave, sincere, generous, and full of charm. Robert Frost is the only other poet who gives me the feeling that I know him personally, as Aldington does, though I've never met either of them. His poetry has been obscured for us by the fake-screen of "movements" and "tendencies" for the last generation. But now it has come to us all together, and for good! (pp. 10-11)

> *Roy Campbell, in a review in* Richard Aldington: An Intimate Portrait, *edited by Alister Kershaw and Frédéric-Jacques Temple, Southern Illinois University Press, 1965, pp. 4-11.*

STANLEY K. COFFMAN, JR.

Like Pound, [Aldington] placed considerable emphasis upon the kind of poetic language for which Imagism stood. The Imagists, he said use as few adjectives as possible. Though stated as a separate principle, this related to another, perhaps more important:

> The exact word. We make quite a heavy stress on that. . . . All great poetry is exact. All the dreariness of nineteenth century poets comes from their not quite knowing what they wanted to say and filling up the gaps with portentous adjectives and idiotic similes.

Elsewhere, Aldington added a further note to his concept of the diction appropriate to modern poetry. He described its aim as "speakable English" and recommended that the poet observe this simple rule: syntax or vocabulary unsuitable to prose has no place in poetry. For another *Egoist* article he illustrated both good and bad diction by quoting a passage from the verse of H. D. In three lines otherwise stylistically perfect he objected to one word, *meads,* on the ground that it is a stock "poetic" word which would not be used in prose statement.

Aldington also shared Pound's admiration for the quality of "hardness" in poetry; the second of the principles he listed in **"Modern Poetry and the Imagists"** demanded of a poem a "hardness, as of cut stone. No slop, no sentimentality." His poems show a feeling for the beauty of natural objects, the human body, or physical passions, which he found best expressed through the art and mythology of classical Greece. For example, in **"To a Greek Marble"** he recreates the intense reaction to physical beauty which must have moved the sculptor of this piece; in **"Choricos"** he personifies death as a cold, chaste woman who brings rest and forgetfulness.

He did not confine his attention entirely to classical subjects, but when he turned to contemporary scenes he could not always adequately objectify his attitude toward them. Neither **"Childhood,"** which describes the dull, grimy town in which he was reared, nor **"Eros and Psyche,"** which argues the incongruity of these figures in a modern industrial city, is successful poetic statement because the poet never transcends his personal distaste for his material. Nor were other attempts to draw material from the scenes around him completely satisfactory. **"Au Vieux Jardin,"** a poem in the manner of H. D., offers the poet's

reaction to the rose and white colors of smooth flagstones and the pale, yellow grasses growing between them. The spectacle of a man so affected by the appearance of a blade of grass provoked rather unsympathetic comments from some critics, as Aldington fully realized: "I shall not be unwilling to counteract the somewhat 'precious' effect of the poems I have published in *Poetry* and that infernal Glebe anthology."

Aldington's interpretation of Imagism did not ignore matters more specifically Imagistic. At the head of his list of principles was "Direct treatment of the subject. . . . We convey an emotion by presenting the object and circumstances of that emotion without comment." Instead of using "twenty-five" adjectives to describe a woman, the Imagist presents her in an image. Thus Aldington, too, understood direct treatment as dependent upon the image; and he stated his conviction that the title of the movement appropriately reflected its basic doctrine. (pp. 164-66)

His use of the image does not permit dogmatic conclusions about what it meant to him. All one can safely say is that his theory and practice were similar to those of Pound: Imagism centered upon the image, but the image was not limited by Hulme's definition of it. **"To A Greek Marble"** presents a succession of images which make not only pictorial, but aural and tactile appeals: fragile pipes, cicada song, brown fingers moving over slim shoulders, the "sun upon thy breasts." The poem does not rely upon metaphor but bases its appeal upon the cumulative effect of a succession of separate images. Aldington, however, also employed imagery in another manner recommended by Pound: by sudden and apt comparison to communicate "an intellectual and emotional complex in an instant of time." (pp. 166-67)

> *Stanley K. Coffman, Jr., "Amygism," in his* Imagism: A Chapter for the History of Modern Poetry, *University of Oklahoma Press, 1951, pp. 163-86.*

NORMAN T. GATES

It is at once apparent that Richard Aldington had at his command an extremely lucid poetic style. Of the more than one hundred and fifty short poems and the five long poems in *The Complete Poems,* there are scarcely any that present syntactical or verbal problems. This clarity of style traces back to his early Imagist poetry. As the years passed, Aldington made it known that he did not like the direction in which some of his contemporaries were going, and that he knew exactly the kind of poetry that he wanted to write. In 1925 he wrote to [Sir Herbert Read]:

> I am rebelling against a poetry which I think too self-conscious, too intellectual, too elliptic and alembique. This poetry is (selon moi) distinguished by over-elaboration of thought and expression and by a costiveness of production.

The poetry he was particularly thinking of was, naturally, that of Eliot and Pound, and, despite what appear to be occasional desertions to the enemy camp, like *A Fool i' the Forest,* Aldington remained consistent in his position. (p. 122)

It should not be necessary to "excuse" Aldington's lucid poetic style; however, it does help to put it into a living tradition for those of us who have become accustomed to dealing with the ambivalent and ambiguous poetics of the more representative twentieth-century poets. Certainly the clarity of his poetic approach should not prevent our hearing what he has to say.

It is curious that the second primary attribute of Aldington's poetry, which does not today strike us as being particularly unusual, was the very thing that caused all of the hue and cry in the halcyon days of Imagism. The simplicity of his diction and style was accepted by his early readers as their due, but his prosody (and that of his fellow Imagist poets) aroused their ire. Aldington's use of free verse originated in the same period as his lucid style. . . . (pp. 123-24)

[Aldington's] free verse is finely cadenced and in perfect harmony with his clean, classic style. In the longer poems particularly, his individualistic rhythm plays a large part in conveying the emotion of the poem. He also wrote just enough poetry in traditional meter and rhyme to confound those critics who were anxious to convict all users of free verse of a subterfuge designed to conceal their inability to deal with the traditional prosody.

The two attributes of Aldington's poetry so far considered, lucidity of style and *vers libre,* are functions of form. The final and most important characteristic is concerned rather with content, although it is related to the use of free verse, as the poet himself points out. Writing in 1914 of the poetry of Amy Lowell and John Rodker, Aldington, again discussing cadence, says: "cadence, which is primarily the expression of individual emotion, may be ruined by inadequate technique as well as by insufficient emotion." (p. 125)

Mikhail Urnov, the Russian critic, reports on a discussion that took place just days before the death of the British poet. "In one of his conversations, Aldington defined the underlying idea of his creative work in the short and, at first sight, somewhat mysterious statement, 'To live here and now.'" C. P. Snow, writing of Aldington's early days, says, "It was also natural that he should begin as an 'imagist'—for in that way he could express the 'immediate life' which he has always instinctively felt to be his major task as an artist" [see excerpt above]. Emotion, passion, sensuousness, life—these were the keystones of Richard Aldington's poetic art.

In a broad view of Aldington's poetical work, such as we have been taking, we cannot overlook his importance as a unique spokesman for his times. The most important single event in the affairs of humanity during the first third of the present century was World War I. For all of Europe, certainly for all English-speaking peoples, it is a line of demarcation between two eras. For better or worse, the old world was lost in the battlefields of France along with thousands of its young men, and a new world came into being. No poet-novelist reflected this cataclysm in his work more completely than Richard Aldington. . . .

In Aldington's poetry, which covers the quarter-century from 1912 to 1937, we can trace the effect of the Great War on a sensitive writer who is able to speak for the thousands of his generation who also endured this holocaust and survived. We see the idealism of youth smashed on the battlefields of France, the long and bitter period of healing for a wound whose scar will never be entirely erased, and finally the way in which one man came to terms with a world that included this horror. (p. 126)

During the period when he wrote many of the poems that make up his first volume, *Images (1910-1915),* Aldington was in Italy. At age twenty in Italy in the springtime, it would be very difficult for any young man to remain in love only with an ideal of the cold, chaste past, being surrounded with so much warm beauty of a real present. In poems like **"Amalfi,"**

"**June Rain,**" and "**Images**" the youthful poet writes of the loveliness of this time and place.

Aldington, however, would have considered finally that he was evading life if his poetry failed to deal with the real world in terms of both its beauty and its ugliness. . . . In many of the poems of his first volume Aldington tries to come to terms with the real world's darker face. There is some question, however, whether he has been able "to accept," because in many of these poems he seems only to be making a contrast between the ideal world of his imagination and the misery and ugliness he finds surrounding him.

Even the most casual reading of the *Images of War* poems will quickly reveal the sharp impact of the reality of trench warfare on the still-young poet who had not yet completely resolved the conflict between his Grecian ideal and the world of his own time. In the hell of the trenches of France, Aldington hammered out the shape of his "life quest"; the remaining body of his poetry is an extension of this first accommodation to reality. He began to substitute nature for his unattainable Grecian ideal, and by taking comfort in the beauty that nature offered even during war, as well as by keeping alive the memory of love, he saved his creative self from complete destruction (although not from a scar it was to carry for the rest of his life). In *Images of Desire,* the volume of love poems written in the same years as the war poems, similar adjustments to reality occur, but here the power of passionate human love becomes the primary salvation.

Although Richard Aldington survived the war physically (which a great many of his fellow artists did not), and appeared in his poetry to have made an accommodation to it, he was in fact quite a number of years "healing" from its effects. The whole of his *Exile and Other Poems* reveals a period of convalescence during which he is striving to regain his psychological and also his poetic balance. In an article for *Poetry* magazine in 1921 he asks: "How can poetry, which is essentially order, affirmation, achievement, be created in an age, a *milieu,* of profound doubt and discouragement?" All of the poems of the **"Words for Music"** part of *Exile* are, as the poet quite frankly tells us, an effort to steep himself again in poetic tradition—to rehabilitate his craft while he is restoring his spirit.

In *A Fool i' the Forest* Aldington returns once more to a consideration of the schism between the world as it is and the world as it might be. In a "Note" to the poem he identifies the dichotomy as that between an artistic and a scientific civilization. The poem is inconclusive, however, since the poet leads us into the wasteland without Eliot's promise of regenerative fire and water. It is in the four long poems of the last ten years of his poetic work that Aldington gives final shape to the "conception of life" that he first glimpsed on the battlefields of France.

Life Quest expands the concept of the godhead in nature that Aldington first wrote of in his war poems; it urges man to "revere the real holy ones / Sun Sea and Earth." . . . [The] glorification of nature is one facet of Aldington's vision of life which was built up through the early poems like those in *Images of War,* and culminated in *Life Quest.* Besides being a part of his resolution of the conflict between ideal and real that troubled him even before the war, it is a bringing together of the classical vision and the beauty of his own world so that he never quite needs to relinquish the dream of his youth.

The other and more important facet of the poet's "conception of life," the power of love, is expressed in the three long love poems. *The Eaten Heart* marks the close of the ten years of "exile" during which the poet was trying to make himself whole again. The poem is first an assertion of the essential human condition: "The dreadful inevitable loneliness of the human soul." For this loneliness the poet, like D. H. Lawrence, prescribes quite simply the love of man for woman. . . . In the other two long love poems, *A Dream in the Luxembourg* and *The Crystal World*, the poet provides exempla for his text— he tries to prove on our senses the point he has argued reasonably in *The Eaten Heart*.

What Richard Aldington has to say to us in the body of his poetry is not new; his "conception of life" is not unique. It was said before by the classical Greek writers in the age he admired so much; it was said in part by Remy de Gourmont, the Frenchman whose works he edited and translated; and it is central to the message left by his friend and contemporary, D. H. Lawrence. Of Aldington's novels, *All Men Are Enemies* comes the closest to his poetry in the expression of his lifeview. It is written in the sensuous style which is his best, and is for this reason his finest novel. But it is to his poetry that we should turn for the clearest statement of his creed—to the "**Epilogue**" of *Images of Desire*, for instance, a poem that was probably written in 1917-1918 and to whose theme Aldington returned again and again in his poetry of the next twenty years. (pp. 127-29)

Richard Aldington was a better poet than his present reputation indicates. One of the things that has damaged his permanent reputation was the tendency, early in his career, to associate him with poets such as Eliot and Lawrence whose work is of a different order. Equally detrimental was his position as a leading Imagist poet which gave him, while still young, a station he could not maintain. There is also the question of the effect of his wartime service on his poetic art. While it made him a more representative poet of his period, it may also have hurt his poetry. It is possible that as a novelist Aldington used as a spring the traumatic shock of a wartime experience that proved injurious to him as a poet. (p. 129)

> *Norman T. Gates, in his* The Poetry of Richard Aldington: A Critical Evaluation and an Anthology of Uncollected Poems, *The Pennsylvania State University Press, 1975, 362 p.*

RICHARD EUGENE SMITH

Aldington was only twenty when he published the poems which launched the imagist movement in 1912. From the start, his verse is characterized by an adoration of natural beauty; and, in his early poems, the myriad deities of nature from the art and myths of ancient Greece provide him with the means by which he can express his sentiments. His paganism is genuine; for, as a general rule, he effectively communicates to the reader his feelings of awe or delight or reverence about his gods, dead gods, about whom he can do little more than lament their passing. He does manage to make them live again in a few poems in which he recaptures the color and animation of scenes from ancient art or from contemporary England.

On the whole, however, Aldington is unable to revivify Greek myth in modern terms, as Yeats, for example, has done. Aside from his use of free verse, he shows little technical and imaginative originality in many of the poems, for the imagery often resembles that of Swinburne and other late nineteenth-century poets, while other pieces appear to be less skillful imitations of the "perfect images" of his wife, H. D. Taken as a group,

Aldington's early poems (and even different stanzas of particular poems) indicate that he was unable to produce consistently good images. One has the impression that the imagist credo led him to believe that almost any image would do, as long as it was an image.

The same observation is applicable to Aldington's other early poems, including his imitation of Japanese *haiku, haikai,* and *tanka.* Here and there, one notes effective or striking images, but they are comparatively few in number. Aldington continues to pursue the vanishing shades of his Greek dream as he faces the terrible realities of the trenches and battlefields; but while he never ceases to take delight in the beauty of nature, his best war poems are those in which he forgets his dream and gives an objective account of the horrors of modern warfare. By the time one gets to his love poems, Aldington's dream has undergone a significant transformation: the poet is no longer trying to revive the Greek deities of nature in the world about him; he is seeking divine inspiration in his passion for beautiful women, describing their lips, breasts, and bodies as flowers, and endowing his ladies with goddesslike qualities. The poems are characterized by strong passions, and they contain many lovely images. Though some of Aldington's images resemble those of his wife, H. D., they are often equal—and sometimes superior—to hers in vividness and evocative power. Despite the high quality of certain pieces, however, the imagery continues to reflect the influence of poets of the past century, such as Swinburne. Aldington's poems of "exile" offer an account of his recovery from the horrors of the war. At first the poet feels only anguish and despair, but he gradually regains his peace of mind as he recalls his Greek dream of prewar years, while in other poems, he more or less ignores the dream as he appeals to modern attitudes regarding life and death; and these pieces also demonstrate his ability to create striking, original images.

As in the case of Aldington's earlier verse, his long poems are not consistent in their quality; they range from poems of high quality which present many evocative and original images to poems of doubtful merit which present prosaic narratives that are no more "poetic" than the average short story. Aldington's spiritual progress may also be noted in his long poems. Disillusioned with the postwar world, he begins with a farewell to his Greek dream; and he also rejects Christianity—just as he has in his earlier poems—but he is now unable to find anything to take its place. He fears that the poetic spirit within him has been destroyed and that he cannot escape a life of dull mediocrity in a materialistic world. He fails to overcome his loneliness and unhappiness by having a passionate affair with the woman he loves, for she is unable to love him as deeply as he loves her; then he seeks the "perfect" woman—one who can share his feelings to the extent of being unable to live without him—but realizes that such a hope is futile.

Up to this point, Aldington has been unsuccessful in his search for spiritual fulfillment. He has abandoned his Greek dream, rejected Christianity and other organized religions, and relinquished hope of finding the solution in love for other human beings. He sets forth again, as lonely and unhappy as before. As he wanders across Europe, he finds no comfort in contemplating the glories of the past or the present; for the works of men are subject to destruction, and he sees only death, decay, and desolation in the world about him. His quest seems hopeless until he finds inspiration in the more enduring beauty of nature. Aldington has returned to the adoration of natural beauty which is characteristic of his early poems, but he does so with a difference: he no longer relies upon the art and the myths of a dead civilization for the expression of his feelings; he worships nature itself as the life-giving source.

Aldington's quest for life, however, has not come to an end, for he makes an earnest request that his search may continue until he dies. To enjoy his discovery of new life fully, he also needs someone who can share it with him. He does not expect the perfect lovers to be willing to die for each other—it is far better if they can live for each other. Together, the poet and his lady create their own world—a world of beauty inhabited by them alone, since it exists only in the feelings which they share. Though others may smash their secret world, the lovers will recreate it; for, having once known happiness there, they will not be content to accept life in the ordinary world. (pp. 175-77)

> *Richard Eugene Smith, in his* Richard Aldington,
> *Twayne Publishers, 1977, 204 p.*

Gwendolyn Brooks

1917-

American poet, novelist, editor, autobiographer, and author of children's books.

A major contemporary poet and the first black American writer to win a Pulitzer Prize, Brooks is best known for her sensitive portraits of ordinary urban blacks who encounter racism and poverty in their daily lives. Her verse is characterized by objectivity, succinctness, and a fusion of Afro-American colloquialisms with the formal structures and language of traditional verse. In her early work, Brooks avoided overt statements about social injustice, prompting critics to find universal import in her poetry. During the late 1960s, however, her writing underwent a radical change in style and subject matter. Inspired by the black power movement and the militancy of such poets as LeRoi Jones and Don L. Lee, Brooks began to explore the marginality of black life through vivid imagery and forceful language and to recognize rage and despair among black people as her own.

Brooks's first volume of poetry, *A Street in Bronzeville* (1945), chronicles the aspirations and disappointments of citizens living in Bronzeville, a black district in her native Chicago that serves as the setting for many of her poems. The first part of *A Street in Bronzeville* provides a realistic picture of the neighborhood; the second section, a sequence of twelve sonnets entitled "Gay Chaps at the Bar," explores the unequal treatment of blacks in the Armed Forces during World War II. In this book, as in much of her early verse, Brooks employs such varied poetic forms as the ballad, the quatrain, blank verse, and free verse. This work also introduces her major thematic concerns of the next two decades: family life, war, the quest for contentment and honor, and the hardships caused by racism and poverty. Brooks's second collection, *Annie Allen* (1949), is an experimental volume for which she received the Pulitzer Prize in poetry. Similar in structure to a prose narrative, the poems in *Annie Allen* focus on the growth of the title character from childhood to adulthood in an environment replete with indigence and discrimination. Critics generally praised Brooks for her subtle humor and irony, her skillful handling of conventional stanzaic forms, and her invention of the sonnet-ballad, a verse structure integrating colloquial speech and formal language. Brooks's next major collection, *The Bean Eaters* (1960), details the attempts of ghetto inhabitants to escape from feelings of hopelessness. New pieces included in *Selected Poems* (1963) evidence Brooks's growing interest in social issues and the influence of the early years of the civil rights movement.

Brooks experienced a change in political consciousness and artistic direction after witnessing the combative spirit of several young black authors at the Second Black Writers' Conference at Fisk University in 1967. She later commented: "If it hadn't been for these young people, these young writers who influenced me, I wouldn't know what I know about this society. By associating with them I know who I am." With *In the Mecca* (1968), which most critics regard as her transitional volume, Brooks abandons traditional poetic forms in favor of free verse and increases her use of vernacular to make her works more accessible to black readers. This collection features naturalistic portraits of several residents of a dilapidated ghetto

apartment house who battle anguish and despair. In *Riot* (1969) and *Family Pictures* (1970), Brooks evokes the revolutionary legacy of such slain black activists as Medgar Evers, Malcolm X, and Martin Luther King, Jr. and examines the social upheavals of the late 1960s with a mixture of objectivity and compassion. While her concern for the black nationalist movement and racial solidarity continued to dominate her verse in the early 1970s, the energy and optimism of *Riot* and *Family Pictures* were replaced with disenchantment resulting from the divisiveness of the civil rights and black power movements. In *Beckonings* (1975) and *To Disembark* (1981), Brooks urges blacks to break free from the repression of white American society and advocates violence and anarchy if necessary. Critics are divided in their judgments of Brooks's work following her artistic and ideological transformation. Some believe that she has sacrificed formal complexity and subtlety for political polemic. According to D. H. Melhem, however, "[Brooks] enriches both black and white cultures by revealing essential life, its universal identities, and the challenge it poses to a society beset with corruption and decay."

In addition to poetry, Brooks has written an autobiography, *Report from Part One* (1972); several books of verse for children, including *Bronzeville Boys and Girls* (1956) and *Aloneness* (1971); and *Maud Martha* (1953), a novel that relates a young black woman's struggle to maintain dignity amid racism from both blacks and whites. Brooks has also edited numerous poetry anthologies featuring the works of black writers.

(See also *CLC*, Vols. 1, 2, 4, 5, 15; *Contemporary Authors,* Vols. 1-4, rev. ed.; *Contemporary Authors New Revision Series,* Vol. 1; *Something about the Author,* Vol. 6; *Dictionary of Literary Biography,* Vol. 5; and *Concise Dictionary of American Literary Biography, 1941-1968.*)

GARY SMITH

The critical reception of *A Street in Bronzeville* contained, in embryo, many of the central issues in the scholarly debate that continues to engage Brooks's poetry. As in the following quotation from *The New York Times Book Review,* most reviewers were able to recognize Brooks's versatility and craft as a poet:

> If the idiom is colloquial, the language is universal. Brooks commands both the colloquial and more austere rhythms. She can vary manner and tone. In form, she demonstrates a wide range: quatrains, free verse, ballads, and sonnets—all appropriately controlled. The longer line suits her better than the short, but she is not verbose. In some of the sonnets, she uses an abruptness of address that is highly individual.

Yet, while noting her stylistic successes, not many critics fully understood her achievement in her first book. This difficulty was not only characteristic of critics who examined the formal aspects of prosody in her work, but also of critics who addressed themselves to the social realism in her poetry. Moreover, what Brooks gained at the hands of critics who focused on her technique, she lost to critics who chose to emphasize the exotic, Negro features of the book. . . .

The poems in *A Street in Bronzeville* actually served notice that Brooks had learned her craft well enough to combine successfully themes and styles from both the Harlem Renaissance and Modernist poetry. She even achieves some of her more interesting effects in the book by parodying the two traditions. She juggles the pessimism of Modernist poetry with the general optimism of the Harlem Renaissance. (p. 35)

Because of the affinities *A Street in Bronzeville* shares with Modernist poetry and the Harlem Renaissance, Brooks was initiated not only into the vanguard of American literature, but also into what had been the inner circle of Harlem writers. Two of the Renaissance's leading poets, Claude McKay and Countee Cullen, addressed letters to her to mark the publication of *A Street in Bronzeville.* McKay welcomed her into a dubious but potentially rewarding career:

> I want to congratulate you again on the publication of *A Street in Bronzeville* and welcome you among the band of hard working poets who do have something to say. It is a pretty rough road we have to travel, but I suppose much compensation is derived from the joy of being able to sing. Yours sincerely, Claude McKay. (October 10, 1945.)

Cullen pinpointed her dual place in American literature:

> I have just finished reading *A Street in Bronzeville* and want you to know that I enjoyed it thoroughly. There can be no doubt that you are a poet, a good one, with every indication of becoming a better. I am glad to be able to say 'welcome' to you to that

> too small group of Negro poets, and to the larger group of American ones. No one can deny you your place there. (August 24, 1945.)

The immediate interest in these letters is how both poets touch upon the nerve ends of the critical debate that surrounded *A Street in Bronzeville.* For McKay, while Brooks has "something to say," she can also "sing"; and for Cullen, she belongs not only to the minority of Negro poets, but also to the majority of American ones. Nonetheless, the critical question for both poets might well have been Brooks's relationship to the Harlem Renaissance. What had she absorbed of the important tenets of the Black aesthetic as expressed during the New Negro Movement? And how had she addressed herself, as a poet, to the literary movement's assertion of the folk and African culture, and its promotion of the arts as the agent to define racial integrity and to fuse racial harmony?

Aside from its historical importance, the Harlem Renaissance—as a literary movement—is rather difficult to define. . . . Likewise, the general description of the movement as a Harlem Renaissance is often questioned, since most of the major writers, with the notable exceptions of Hughes and Cullen, actually did not live and work in Harlem. Finally, many of the themes and literary conventions defy definition in terms of what was and what was not a New Negro poet. Nonetheless, there was a common ground of purpose and meaning in the works of the individual writers that permits a broad definition of the spirit and intent of the Harlem Renaissance. Indeed, the New Negro poets expressed a deep pride in being Black; they found reasons for this pride in ethnic identity and heritage; and they shared a common faith in the fine arts as a means of defining and reinforcing racial pride. But in the literal expression of these artistic impulses, the poets were either romantics or realists and, quite often within a single poem, both. The realistic impulse, as defined best in the poems of McKay's *Harlem Shadows,* was a sober reflection upon Blacks as second class citizens, segregated from the mainstream of American socio-economic life, and largely unable to realize the wealth and opportunity that America promised. The romantic impulse, on the other hand, as defined in the poems of Sterling Browns's *Southern Road* (1932), often found these unrealized dreams in the collective strength and will of the folk masses. In comparing the poems in *A Street in Bronzeville* with various poems from the Renaissance, it becomes apparent that Brooks agrees, for the most part, with their prescriptions for the New Negro. Yet the unique contributions she brings to bear upon this tradition are extensive: 1) the biting ironies of intraracial discrimination, 2) the devaluation of love in heterosexual relationships between Blacks, and 3) the primacy of suffering in the lives of poor Black women.

The first clue that *A Street in Bronzeville* was, at the time of its publication, unlike any other book of poems by a Black American is its insistent emphasis on demystifying romantic love between Black men and women. The **"old marrieds"**, the first couple encountered on the walking tour of Bronzeville, are nothing like the youthful archetype that the Renaissance poets often portrayed:

> But in the crowding darkness not a word did they say.
> Though the pretty-coated birds had piped so lightly all the day.
> And he had seen the lovers in the little side-streets.
> And she had heard the morning stories clogged with sweets.
> It was quite a time for loving. It was midnight. It was May.
> But in the crowding darkness not a word did they say.

In this short, introductory poem, Brooks, in a manner reminiscent of Eliot's alienated *Waste Land* characters, looks not toward a glorified African past or limitless future, but rather at a stifled present. Her old lovers ponder not an image of their racial past or some symbolized possibility of self-renewal, but rather the overwhelming question of what to do in the here-and-now. Moreover, their world, circumscribed by the incantatory line that opens and closes the poem, "But in the crowding darkness not a word did they say," is one that is distinctly at odds with their lives. They move timidly through the crowded darkness of their neighborhood largely ignorant of the season, "May," the lateness of the hour, "midnight," and a particular *raison d'etre,* "a time for loving." Their attention, we infer, centers upon the implicit need to escape any peril that might consume what remains of their lives. The tempered optimism in the poem, as the title indicates, is the fact that they are "old-marrieds": a social designation that suggests the longevity of their lives and the solidity of their marital bond in what is, otherwise, an ephemeral world of change. Indeed, as the prefatory poem in *A Street in Bronzeville,* the "old marrieds," on the whole, debunks one of the prevalent motifs of Harlem Renaissance poetry: its general optimism about the future.

As much as the Harlem Renaissance was noted for its optimism, an important corollary motif was that of ethnic or racial pride. This pride—often thought a reaction to the minstrel stereotypes in the Dunbar tradition—usually focused with romantic idealization upon the Black woman. (pp. 36-8)

In *A Street in Bronzeville,* this romantic impulse for idealizing the Black woman runs headlong into the biting ironies of intraracial discrimination. In poem after poem in *A Street in Bronzeville,* within the well-observed caste lines of skin color, the consequences of dark pigmentation are revealed in drastic terms. One of the more popular of these poems, **"The Ballad of Chocolate Mabbie,"** explores the tragic ordeal of Mabbie, the Black female heroine, who is victimized by her dark skin and her "saucily bold" lover, Willie Boone. . . . Mabbie's life, of course, is one of unrelieved monotony; her social contacts are limited to those who, like her, are dark skinned, rather than "lemon-hued" or light skinned. But as Brooks makes clear, the larger tragedy of Mabbie's life is the human potential that is squandered:

> Oh, warm is the waiting for joys, my dears!
> And it cannot be too long.
> O, pity the little poor chocolate lips
> That carry the bubble of song!

But if Mabbie is Brooks's parodic victim of romantic love, her counterpart in **"Ballad of Pearl May Lee"** realizes a measure of sweet revenge. In outline, Brooks's poem is reminiscent of Cullen's *The Ballad of the Brown Girl* (1927). There are, however, several important differences. The first is the poem's narrative structure: Pearl May Lee is betrayed in her love for a Black man who "couldn't abide dark meat," who subsequently makes love to a white girl and is lynched for his crime of passion, whereas Cullen's "Brown Girl" is betrayed in her love for a white man, Lord Thomas, who violated explicit social taboo by marrying her rather than Fair London, a white girl. Moreover, Cullen's poem, "a ballad retold," is traditional in its approach to the ballad form. . . . Brooks's ballad, on the other hand, dispenses with the rhetorical invocation of the traditional ballad and begins *in medias res:*

> Then off they took you, off to the jail,
> A hundred hooting after.
> And you should have heard me at my house.
> I cut my lungs with my laughter,
>   Laughter.
>   Laughter.
> I cut my lungs with my laughter.

This mocking tone is sustained throughout the poem, even as Sammy, Pearl May Lee's lover, is lynched:

> You paid for your dinner, Sammy boy,
> And you didn't pay with money.
> You paid with your hide and my heart, Sammy boy,
> For your taste of pink and white honey,
>   Honey,
>   Honey,
> For your taste of pink and white honey.

Here, one possible motif in the poem is the price that Pearl May Lee pays for her measure of sweet revenge: the diminution of her own capacity to express love and compassion for another—however ill-fated—human being. But the element of realism that Brooks injects into her ballad by showing Pearl May Lee's mocking detachment from her lover's fate is a conscious effort to devalue the romantic idealization of Black love. Furthermore, Pearl May Lee's macabre humor undermines the racial pride and harmony that was an important tenet in the Renaissance prescription for the New Negro. And, lastly, Pearl May Lee's predicament belies the social myth of the Black woman as *objective correlative* of the Renaissance's romanticism. (pp. 39-41)

For Brooks, unlike the Renaissance poets, the victimization of poor Black women becomes not simply a minor chord but a predominant theme of *A Street in Bronzeville*. Few, if any, of her female characters are able to free themselves from the web of poverty and racism that threatens to strangle their lives. The Black heroine in **"obituary for a living lady"** was "decently wild / As a child," but as a victim of society's hypocritical, puritan standards, she "fell in love with a man who didn't know / That even if she wouldn't let him touch her breasts she / was still worth his hours." In another example of the complex life-choices confronting Brooks's women, the two sisters of **"Sadie and Maude"** must choose between death-in-life and life-in-death. Maude, who went to college, becomes a "thin brown mouse," presumably resigned to spinsterhood, "living all alone / In this old house," while Sadie who "scraped life / With a fine-tooth comb" bears two illegitimate children and dies, leaving as a heritage for her children her "fine-tooth comb." What is noticeable in the lives of these Black women is a mutual identity that is inextricably linked with race and poverty. (pp. 43-4)

Brooks's relationship with the Harlem Renaissance poets, as *A Street in Bronzeville* ably demonstrates, was hardly imitative. As one of the important links with the Black poetic tradition of the 1920s and 1930s, she enlarged the element of realism that was an important part of the Renaissance world-view. Although her poetry is often conditioned by the optimism that was also a legacy of the period, Brooks rejects outright their romantic prescriptions for the lives of Black women. And in this regard, she serves as a vital link with the Black Arts Movement of the 1960s that, while it witnessed the flowering of Black women as poets and social activists as well as the rise of Black feminist aesthetics in the 1970s, brought about a curious revival of romanticism in the Renaissance mode.

However, since the publication of *A Street in Bronzeville,* Brooks has not eschewed the traditional roles and values of Black women in American society; on the contrary, in her subsequent works, *Annie Allen* (1949), *The Bean Eaters* (1960), and *The Mecca* (1968), she has been remarkably consistent in identifying the root cause of intraracial problems within the Black community as white racism and its pervasive socio-economic effects. Furthermore, as one of the chief voices of the Black

Arts Movement, she has developed a social vision, in such works as *Riot* (1969), *Family Pictures* (1970), and *Beckonings* (1975), that describes Black women and men as equally integral parts of the struggle for social and economic justice. (p. 45)

> *Gary Smith, "Gwendolyn Brooks's 'A Street in Bronzeville', the Harlem Renaissance and the Mythologies of Black Women," in* MELUS, *Vol. 10, No. 3, Fall, 1983, pp. 33-46.*

HERBERT W. MARTIN

It has been twenty years since Gwendolyn Brooks' *Selected Poems* appeared and almost twelve years since a major commercial publisher issued *The World of Gwendolyn Brooks*. In those intervening years she has produced some remarkable work.... [*To Disembark*] proves that [Brooks] is a sure and durable poetic treasure. It is as if Miss Brooks, in this collection, has taken off on a new journey. It may be said that Gwendolyn Brooks gained a new sense of vitality when the angry sixties erupted in our consciousnesses, and whether she joined that movement, gave substance to it, or took sustenance from it, she was strong and gifted enough to survive the "hangers on." Miss Brooks has within her scope an ever-evolving vision.

One instance of that vision is her speech (**"To The Diaspora"**) to those who have fallen, who are falling and who will fall. The purpose is clear and steadfast. Courage, belief and endurance are the watchwords. This poem addresses itself to the age-old question of how to distinguish country from countryman. She writes:

> Because
> you did not know you were Afrika.
> You did not know the Black continent,
> that had to be reached
> was you.

There is something precious in the life-giving sun and in the reward that comes from self-recognition:

> I could not have told you then that some sun
> would come
> somewhere over the road,
> would come evoking the diamonds
> of you, the Black continent
> somewhere over the road.

There is an understandable awareness that emanates from a resistance that dies too soon. The persona has not believed in his or her time and, perhaps, even worse, has no investments to make in the future. It takes disaster to bring about sound belief. (p. 109)

The hardness that we as a people have acquired is apparent in **"The Boy Died In My Alley."** It is a summing up of all those experiences/incidents where we as a people have closed our eyes. However, there is a certain knowledgeable pain and perceptiveness presented in this poem. It is both the awareness and familiarity of those deaths which occur in black neighborhoods, and how such tragic ends have taken on the attitude of custom. The persona here, like individuals all over America, has learned to block out such pain, such awareness....

I do not wish to suggest that all is despair in Miss Brooks' latest volume. She is as inventive as she ever was, her metaphors are tightly turned, and despite the fact that she writes in an open rather than closed form, her poetry is still alive, vital, and strikes dead center. There are moments of joy in this book,

and the author comes to them when she is praising those individuals she admires in the public and creative life, those who are known and unknown. There are such personages as: Steve Biko, W. Bradford, Paul Robeson, K. Kgositsile, J. O. Killens, H. R. Madhubti, and Laini Nzinga. (p. 111)

This book is filled with gems; one need only turn from page to page. Consider Miss Brooks' poem **"The Life of Lincoln West."**

> Ugliest little boy
> that everyone ever saw.

No radical surgery is performed to give this little boy a new face, but through irony we are shown how he gains a new sense of self. This poem succeeds in the end because of the perceptive awareness Lincoln West arrives at on his own. It is a subtle twist of fate that allows him to perceive a searing insult with an unthought of and certainly an unintended meaning. Lincoln West (think of the implications of such a name) reflects about,

> When he was hurt, too much
> stared at—
> too much
> left alone—he
> thought about that He told himself
> "After all I'm
> the real thing."
> It comforted him.

And we can take comfort in the fact that Gwendolyn Brooks has continued to write first rate poems that are the envy of many of her contemporaries as well as many younger poets. She is a poet who continues to burn at first magnitude. (p. 112)

> *Herbert W. Martin, in a review of "To Disembark,"*
> *in* Great Lakes Review, *Vols. 9 & 10, Nos. 1 & 2,*
> *Fall, 1983 & Spring, 1984, pp. 109-12.*

PATRICIA H. LATTIN AND VERNON E. LATTIN

Since its publication in 1953, Gwendolyn Brooks's *Maud Martha* has been a novel in search of a critic. Major studies of the black American novel have either completely ignored it or have included only brief, general remarks.... The only full-length critical article on *Maud Martha*, Annette Oliver Shands's "Gwendolyn Brooks as Novelist" [see *CLC*, Vol. 4], is not perceptive. Shands treats the novel only as opportunity to quote parallels from Brooks's poetry. The comparisons are obvious and fail to provide the reader with any insights into *Maud Martha* as a work of fiction.

We are therefore left with a critical void. One reason is that critics have in general not written as much on black women writers as on their male counterparts. Also, Gwendolyn Brooks's going on to win a Pulitzer Prize as a poet and not as a novelist has encouraged critical studies of her poetry, not her novel. Had she written and won the prize for a later novel, certainly her first novel would have garnered more critical attention. (pp. 180-81)

Discussion of *Maud Martha* must begin with a recognition of what the novel is not. In 1940, Richard Wright told the story of Bigger Thomas growing up in black Chicago not far from where Maud Martha was to grow up. In 1953, the year *Maud Martha* was published, Ralph Ellison added the story of his protagonist harassed from the south to New York City. Judged by the standards of these two complex, powerful urban novels, *Maud Martha* could easily be dismissed. Maud does not experience the same intense search for identity that Bigger and Ellison's protagonist experience. Nor does the novel have comparable violent struggles between the black and white worlds, broad philosophical discussions of black nationalism, or tragic conflicts between characters. Maud Martha's stage is not the newspapers or courtrooms of Bigger's stage or the packed auditorium and street battles where Ellison's unnamed protagonist plays his role. Maud's stage is the home in which she grew up, the schools she attended, the kitchenette where she lives after marriage, and most often her own mind and heart as she struggles to be creative and to be an individual in a gray, oppressive world.

A reader cannot, therefore, approach *Maud Martha* expecting the epic or tragic dimensions of *Native Son* or *Invisible Man*. *Maud Martha* must be judged by its own standards. It is a unique work. With a very loose organization consisting of a series of short vignettes, and with lyrical language never far from poetry, this short novel has a deceptively light and simple exterior which belies the complexity of the interior. Although on the surface a comedy of the commonplace, *Maud Martha* is also a novel that looks directly at racial discrimination and its effects on Blacks, and anger often simmers underneath its calm surface. The protagonist, however, possesses a dual vision that allows her to see simultaneously beauty in ugliness, life in death, and a positive way of living by which one can maintain one's self-respect and creativity in the face of overwhelmingly negative forces.

Brooks's *Maud Martha* is first of all a comedy of the commonplace. Underlying the author's story is the constant recognition that the world is not populated with tragic or epic heroes. People generally exist in everyday settings, seldom reaching even the height of melodrama. (p. 181)

Maud has intuitively appreciated the common everyday world since she was a child. For example, she has always had a special feeling for dandelions, the flower she sees most often in her back yard. She would have liked to have "a lotus, or China asters or the Japanese iris, or Meadow lilies," but she nevertheless loves the common, ordinary dandelion, which she thinks of as "Yellow jewels for everyday, studding the patched green dress of her back yard." In contrasting herself with her sister Helen, who has "heart-catching beauty," Maud identifies with the dandelion: in its everydayness "she thought she saw a picture of herself, and it was comforting to find that what was common could also be a flower." Maud's subtle consciousness of beauty in the everyday leads her as a child to like "painted music," which she thinks of as "deep blue, or delicate silver," and to have a special sensitivity for the colors of the evening sky and the light it radiates. (pp. 181-82)

Maud's struggle to grow up, black and female, in the white-dominated Chicago of the thirties and forties is a day-to-day struggle made up of small events. These small events, however, generally reflected on silently and internally, create an awareness of racial segregation and its effects that is as great as that of Bigger as he is surrounded by whiteness or of Ellison's protagonist as he realizes his recurring nightmare with its engraved letter that reads "Keep This Nigger-Boy Running." As a child, Maud is aware of the color line when she goes with her mother for an evening walk "East of Cottage Grove" and sees so many white faces. Nothing happens on the walk, and the reader's interest in the event lies with Maud's later reaction to the walk. Asleep, she dreams of an escaped gorilla, and awake, lying in her bed, she instinctively associates the white world with her fear of the night, which she sees as "always

hunched and ready to close in on you."... Years later, when Maud and her husband attend a movie at the World Playhouse, with its all-white staff and audience, very little happens. No confrontation occurs. In fact, except for Paul's buying a ticket, there is no communication between the couple and the whites. However, the reader feels with Maud as she is nervous, uncertain, and afraid, yet also defiant and assertive. She hates Paul a little when he remarks that they are "the only colored people here," and she is angry that Paul is afraid to ask the "lovely and blonde and cold-eyed" woman about tickets. In the darkness of the movie house, she is happy with the idea of being there, of feeling that she is an equal with all the others. However, when the lights go on, the spell is broken. Although she wants to communicate with the whites around her, sharing perceptions of the film, she and Paul speak to no one, and no one speaks to them. (p. 182)

The reader feels with Maud as she experiences fear, anxiety, and doubt not unlike that felt by Wright's Bigger Thomas when he goes out to eat with Jan and Mary. The difference between Bigger and Maud is not their emotions but rather their understanding of the emotions and their ability to control them. Blinded by his anger and fear, Bigger wants to blot out the world he cannot change or even understand. On the other hand, Maud's awareness of the racism and injustice which threaten her ability to exist in a creative fashion challenges her to control her anger and frustration so that she can continue to develop and grow as a "good," loving human being. For example, Maud knows that her husband Paul has accepted the "white is better" philosophy and that he can never fully love her because she is darker than he. She knows that for Paul, as for many black men of the period, "Pretty would be a little cream-colored thing with curly hair," and when, at the Foxy Cats Club dance, Paul leaves her to dance with "someone red-haired and curved, and white as a white," Maud knows Paul is rejecting her on the basis of her blackness.... She does not, however, reject Paul because of his weakness; she lives with him in full understanding of why he is as he is. Haunted by the "white mountain" similar to the wall Maud sees Paul trying to jump, Bigger Thomas wants to "strike something with his fist," like Ahab attacking the white whale, and his overpowering frustration and rage are spent only after he has killed and been apprehended. Maud has thoughts of scratching, spitting at, and screaming at Paul's light-skinned dance partner but does not give in. Maud seems to realize that she will never have the opportunity to defy the gods and mountains responsible for her oppression, so she, like Paul, will simply keep jumping at the wall.

In this connection, it is important for a reader to recognize that Maud is not naive. The early Brooks has often been accused of failing to see racial oppression, and a superficial reader could use Maud Martha to support such a view of Brooks. In fact, Maud is clearly aware of ugliness and oppression, but she chooses to defy with grace, to live as best she can. She also recognizes and regrets that she and others often fall short even of the goal of defiance. (p. 183)

The complexity of Maud Martha's reaction to racism is perhaps best illustrated in the Christmas incident in which the white Santa Claus ignores her daughter Paulette, causing the child to ask, "Why didn't Santa Claus like me?" Maud resists the urge to take her scissors from her purse and "jab jab jab" Santa Claus' eyes. However, she realizes that she cannot resolve the incident in her mind, as her sister Helen would have been able to do, "Because it really would not have made much difference to Helen.'' Nor can she forget it or dismiss it from her mind, ''put off studious perusal indefinitely,'' as she knows her husband Paul would have done after his initial twitching and cursing, ''the first tough cough-up of rage.''. . . She hopes that tonight will not be the time the child will start asking questions. She hopes to allow Paulette to live a little longer in the world of ''fairies, with witches always killed at the end, and Santa every winter's lord, kind, sheer being who never perspires, who never does or says a foolish or ineffective thing, who never looks grotesque, who never has occasion to pull the chain and flush the toilet.'' The struggle within Maud is powerful and significant. She is learning to live without giving up her imagination, her quest for beauty and love. At one point Maud thinks that ''everything can be done with a little grace. I'm sure of it.'' As with most real people, Maud's rites of passage are not heralded by trumpets and fanfare, but they are nevertheless real and meaningful.

When Maud does carry out an act of resistance against racism, she exhibits insight premature for her times: even before the 1954 Supreme Court decision and before the civil rights movement, she understands that one can resist evil and discrimination by refusing to be part of the system. Her husband laid off from work, Maud goes to work as a cook for a white woman. After being reminded to use the back door next time, and after being treated all day ''As though she were a child, a ridiculous one, and one that ought to be given a little shaking,'' Maud knows that she cannot go back the next day, even though the wages are good. Although she cannot singlehandedly change the system, she can turn away and say ''No, in thunder!'' She can make a conscious decision not to be further dehumanized by these particular people at this particular place. She compares her act to that of one who ''walked out from that almost perfect wall, spitting at the firing squad. What difference did it make whether the firing squad understood or did not understand the manner of one's retaliation or why one had to retaliate?''

Maud's attitude toward this act of passive resistance underscores what should be clear by this point: alongside her recognition of racism and human weakness, Maud has developed an awareness of both the significance and insignificance of an individual's existence. She has managed to combine a subtle cynicism with a genuine acceptance of the human condition. Refusing to go back to her job is like spitting at a firing squad not only because it has positive significance for one's inner being but also because in many respects it is totally meaningless. Our acts are absolutely significant for ourselves, and yet they are also common and meaningless in the long march of history. With this dual vision, Maud is able to make her individual acts significant, maintaining her humanity, grace, and dignity in the face of the absurdity and violence of the world, to which she is never for one moment blind. . . . Both the richness and the absurdity of life seem to sustain Maud's existence. She has learned to see both sides without either being drowned in maudlin tears or consumed by anger.

It is not an overstatement to say that in *Maud Martha* Brooks suggests a positive way of life that can help one maintain one's self respect and creativity in the face of the racism and death which surround one. One can create in spite of the deadening realities of life. The novel is full of images of traps, walls, being cornered, and lying in a coffin-like bed. In the middle chapter of the novel, Maud's marriage and life in her kitchenette have become a trap. As the reader focuses on Maud in her dingy apartment, the camera shifts, and we see Maud capturing a mouse that has been eluding her for days. Having

captured the mouse, however, she begins to empathize with the creature, thinking that it may have a family and that it is regretting all the pleasure it will miss. She lets the mouse go. One can profitably contrast this scene with the opening scene of *Native Son*, where Bigger Thomas violently kills a fighting, frightened, cornered rat and then sadistically torments his sister with its dead body. In his limited, poverty-stricken, oppressed life, Bigger is as trapped as the rat. In contrast, Maud, at this midpoint in the novel, experiences an epiphany and ''sees'' that she has power ''to preserve or destroy.'' She ''sees'' that she need not blindly succumb to circumstances but that she can in her own fashion create value and meaning. Through her ''simple restraint'' she has created. ''She had created a piece of life.'' By letting the creature go, she has been not only an artist/creator but also a moral ''good.'' Uniting art and morality, she sees herself as having ''a godlike loving-kindness.'' Clearly for Brooks everyday existence can be invested with meaning and beauty.

Essential to the positive way of life Brooks suggests are the elements of love and the sense of place. Brooks seems to imply that these elements are not only necessary for the development of our ''precious private identities'' but also for the survival of Blacks as a people. Whereas Bigger Thomas grows up with little sense of ''family,'' Maud grows up surrounded by love reinforced by an almost mythical understanding of her place in time and space. (pp. 184-86)

In *Maud Martha,* Brooks has created a female character unique for the time period. Within the comedy of the commonplace, she allows us to see the effects of racism, the occasional absurdity of human behavior, and the quest of one individual for beauty, love, and meaning. *Maud Martha* remains a fresh novel even today because it balances the individual's struggles and hopes with an understanding of human mutability and limited existence. Although the novel ends on a positive note, as Maud awaits the birth of her second child and as the weather bids her ''bon voyage,'' this is tempered by the dual vision created within the novel, and the reader realizes that the seasons will change. We recognize that Maud has won human dignity for herself in the daily struggle against inertia, grayness, and hate. Suggesting that such is possible is a significant contribution for any novel to make. (p. 187)

Patricia H. Lattin and Vernon E. Lattin, ''Dual Vision in Gwendolyn Brooks's 'Maud Martha','' in Critique: Studies in Modern Fiction, *Vol. XXV, No. 4, Summer, 1984, pp. 180-88.*

GEORGE KENT

The consciousness producing *A Street in Bronzeville* (1945) was one making its first compassionate outreach to the broad range of humanity. On the one hand, it represented the mastered past: [Brooks'] old neighborhood and youth. On the other hand, it represented an intense getting acquainted with the present which was pressurized by the raw currents of Chicago's racial practices, and by World War II. Optimism prevailed, however, since the war situation had produced both threatening violence and some evidence that a broadened democracy would be born from it. In the poet's early work, one result is a deceptively simple surface. Syntax is most often either in close correlation with the usual subject plus verb plus object or complement pattern of a familiar prose sentence or within calling distance. Wielding this syntax is a friendly observer giving one a tour of the neighborhood or quick views of situations. Thus abrupt beginnings sound pretty much the way they do in our communications with friends with whom we share clarifying reference points. The observer [in **"The Old-Marrieds"**] begins: "But in the crowding darkness not a word did they say." Joining the group in "kitchenette building," the observer-narrator pitches at us a long question but one so well ordered that it is painless: "But could a dream send up through onion fumes / Its white and violet, fight with fried potatoes / And yesterday's garbage ripening in the hall, / Flutter, or sing an aria down these rooms . . . ?" At the end of three more lines we complete the question, and are then given quick relief through a series of short declarative statements whose brevity drives home the drama and the pathos of the situation.

There are poems with much simpler syntax within this group and one sonnet with a far more complex syntax. The simplest derive from closeness to conversational patterns, from reproduction of speech tones, and from the already mentioned patterning upon simple prose statements. A form such as the ballad also has conventions which allow for great simplicity of syntactical structure. The more complex structure which probably puzzles on a first reading actually derives . . . from exploitation of one of the more complex rhetorical but conventional structures—the periodic sentence. (pp. 89-90)

In terms of the relationship to conversational language and actual speech tones one will find in the style a range running from "folk" speech (the Hattie Scott poems) to that which is more self-consciously literate and affected by formal traditions (**"The Sundays of Satin Legs Smith"** and the sonnets, for example). Brooks is also alert to the richness provided by bringing contrasting traditions into strategic conjunctions or, by movement, into a very formal eloquence; again, examples of both may be seen in **"Satin Legs Smith."** And finally there is the colloquial and hip level provided by such a poem as **"Patent Leather"**: "That cool chick down on Calumet / Has got herself a brand new cat. . . ."

For the most part imagery goes beyond the simple functions of representing an object or pictorializing, activities characteristic of the most simple poems, and manages to do so quietly. "Pretty patent leather hair" obviously has its total effect in the literal picture it creates and the comment it makes upon the judgment of the cool chick. But Brooks expanded the range and function of the realistic image in several ways: attaching to it a striking descriptive term ("crowding darkness"), combining it with a figurative gesture ("could a dream send up through onion fumes / Its white and violet"), contrasting realistic and symbolic functions (crooked and straight in **"Hunchback Girl . . ."**), presenting expressionistic description of a condition ("Mabbie on Mabbie with hush in the heart"), and emphasizing the figurative role of a basically realistic or pictorial expression ("wear the brave stockings of night-black lace," and "temperate holiness arranged / Ably on asking faces").

Perhaps the foregoing elements may be allowed to stand for other devices making up the total struggle with language meant by the word *style.* I have tried to suggest that the central trait of most of the language devices is that they convey the impression of actual simplicity and thus offer the appearance of easygoing accessibility. It is certainly not a total accessibility, in several cases. On one level people and their life stories appear in sharply outlined plots presenting easily recognized issues from the daily round of existence, and move to definite decisive conclusions. However, recognizing certain devices or reading at the tempo required not only by the story but by imagery and

language changes will, at times, take us to another level. "Southeast corner," for example, seems interested in the artistry, as well as the vanity, of the deceased madam of the school of beauty, an interpretation suggested by the vivid image of shot silk shining over her tan "impassivity." **"Satin Legs"** has meanings which reveal themselves in the imagery, language shifts, and mixture of narrative attitudes, which go beyond the basic story, and so on.

But there is no question that in *A Street in Bronzeville* (and in individual poems over the body of her work) there is a general simplicity which seems easily to contain specific complexities. The fact makes Brooks a poet speaking still, not merely to critics and other poets, but to people.

It is probable that nearly all the stylistic developments of Brooks' subsequent works are embryonically present in *A Street in Bronzeville,* since, with its publication, she was emerging from a very long and earnest apprenticeship. Some clear foreshadowing of more complex stylistic developments is in the sonnets, and in **"The Sundays of Satin Legs Smith."** Whereas, for example, the full capacity of the narrator of the Hattie Scott poems may be shaded in the background, the sophistication and perception of the narrator of the sonnets and the life of Smith are clearly those of the narrator of *Annie Allen.* Yet it is understandable that people found the stylistic developments in this second work startling and complex.

If the opening poem of *A Street* makes things seem easy by providing a friendly narrator using language in seemingly customary ways, the opening poem of *Annie Allen,* **"the birth in a narrow room,"** makes the reader feel that the narrator's assumption is that he is to the poetic manner born. The poem demands the reader's absolute commitment, an acceptance of the role of a tougher elliptical syntax, and a comprehension of imagery which functions both realistically and mythically. Actually, the syntax is difficult largely because for several lines the infant remains the *unnamed* subject of the poem. The sources for imagery are the fairy and timeless world and the "real" objects of the "real" world, both of which function to sustain temporarily complete freedom for the young child in an Edenic world. Thus the first poem warns the reader to expect to participate in complex struggles with language.

The style of *Annie Allen* emerges not only from the fact that the poet of the highly promising first book naturally expects to present greater mastery of craft in the second but also from a changed focus in consciousness. In her first book Brooks' emphasis had been upon community consciousness. In [*Annie Allen*] her emphasis is upon self-consciousness—an attempt to give artistic structure to tensions arising from the artist's experience in moving from the Edenic environment of her parents' home into the fallen world of Chicago tenement life in the roles of young wife, mother, and artist. Her efforts, however, were not an attempt to be confessional but an attempt to take advantage of the poetic form to move experiences immediately into symbols broader than the person serving as subject. A thoroughgoing search of the territory and the aspiration for still greater mastery of craft called for a struggle with language, a fact which would require the reader to make also a creative struggle.

One device is to play conventional and unconventional structures against each other, and, sometimes, to work apparently conventional structures for very special effects. In **"the parents: people like our marriage, Maxie and Andrew,"** the reader abruptly confronts the synecdochial opening lines: "Clogged and soft and sloppy eyes / Have list the light that bites or terrifies.'' Afterward the poem gradually settles into the more conventional approach, though it demands that the reader absorb its realities from simple symbols instead of editorial statements. In such poems the reader's creative participation is sustained by other devices: unusual conjunctions of words, shifts in pace and rhythm, reproductions of speech tones at the point of the colloquial and at varying distances from it, figurative language, challenging twists in the diction, and others. (pp. 90-2)

The long poem on young womanhood entitled **"The Anniad"** has the task of taking Annie into maturity by carrying her from the epic dreams of maidenhood into the prosaic and disillusioning realities provided by the married life. More concretely, having inherited the romance and love lore of Euro-Americans and disabilities imposed upon Black identity, she is, at once, the would-be heroine of song and story and the Black woman whom ''the higher gods'' forgot and the lower ones berate. The combination of the realistic and romantic portrays the flesh and blood person and the dreamer. (p. 94)

To express the climax of accumulated problems, storms, and confusions of Annie's young life, Brooks turns completely to expressionistic imagery:

> In the indignant dark there ride
> Roughnesses and spiny things
> On infallible hundred heels.
> And a bodiless bee stings.
> Cyclone concentration reels.
> Harried sods dilate, divide,
> Suck her sorrowfully inside.

The last stanzas return to the language of the realistic scale, although the language itself is not simply mimetic or pictorial. Annie is described as salvaging something of the more usual day-to-day fruits from her experiences: ''Stroking swallows from the sweat. / Fingering faint violet. / Hugging gold and Sunday sun. / Kissing in her kitchenette / The minuets of memory.'' (p. 95)

On the level of telling the Annie Allen story, Brooks was thus able to experiment extensively with stylistic devices and license herself to move beyond realistic imagery. She did so by retaining realism as the base of conception and the norm for the behavior patterns the personalities must ultimately adopt. Thus the form includes devices for humor and pathos which register, in the world of the possible, Annie's excess of idealism, dreaminess, or self-absorption: intense pictures of imbalance, rhythms suggesting frenetic behavior, and a vocabulary suggesting the occupation of worlds which must prove incompatible. In short, the kindly satiric pat appears to halt unrealism, though the unrealism if it could be transformed into ''reality'' might make a richer world.

Annie Allen represents Brooks' most energetic reach for simply a great command of the devices of poetic style. Having developed this command, she could now wield the devices at will and make them relate more efficiently to form and intention. With this mastery of numerous devices came also the power to achieve originality by making variations in the contexts in which they were used and in the relationships one device makes with another. Then, too, a device which in the earlier stages of the artist's career could be completely summed up in the term *conventional* or *traditional* could, at times, now be put into innovative roles. In such a poem as **"Beverly Hills, Chicago,"** for example, the very precision of a syntax based upon the simple declarative sentence drives home the tension

of the rest of the structures: ''It is only natural, however, that it should occur to us / How much more fortunate they [the rich] are than we are.'' (pp. 95-6)

In *The Bean Eaters* (1960) and certain of the new poems of *Selected Poems* (1963), developments in style, for the most part, are responses to experimentations with loosened forms and the milage one can gain from very simple statements. In *Annie Allen* Brooks had loosened up the form of the sonnet in **"The Rites for Cousin Vit,"** with the use of elliptical syntax, the pressures of colloquial speech, and the cumulative capacity of all the poetic devices to create the impact of hyperbole. Cousin Vit was simply too vital to have died; thus Brooks interjects into the language of the sonnet the idiomatic swing and sensuality of the street: that Vit continued to do ''the snake-hips with a hiss. . . .'' In *The Bean Eaters* she again loosened up sonnet form in **"A Lovely Love"** by adapting the Petrarchan rhyme scheme to the situation of the tenement lovers, intermingling short and long complete statements with elliptical ones, and managing a nervous rhythm which imposes the illusion of being a one-to-one imitation of the behavior of the lovers. The diction of the poem is a mixture of the romantic (''hyacinth darkness''), the realistic (''Let it be stairways, and a splintery box''), and the mythically religious (''birthright of our lovely love / In swaddling clothes. Not like that Other one''). Although the elliptical structures are more numerous and informal in **"Cousin Vit,"** the rhythm of **"A Lovely Love"** seems to make that poem the more complex achievement.

Another technical development is the poet's bolder movement into a free verse appropriate to the situation which she sometimes dots with rhyme. The technique will be more noticeable and surer in its achievement in the next volume, *In the Mecca*. But the poem **"A Bronzeville Mother Loiters in Mississippi. Meanwhile, A Mississippi Mother Burns Bacon"** gives the technique full rein, except for the rhyming. The lines frequently move in the rhythms of easygoing conversation or in the loose patterns of stream of consciousness, as the poet portrays the movement from romantic notions to reality in the consciousness of the young white woman over whom a young Black boy (reminiscent of the slain Emmett Till), has been lynched by her husband and his friend. The dramatic situation determines the length of lines, and the statements vary in form; short declarative sentences, simple sentences, phrase units understandable from their ties to preceding sentences, and long, complex structures. Additional sources of rhythm are repetition, parallel structures, and alliteration.

One of the more interesting techniques of the poem is that of playing romantic diction against the realistic. Thus a stanza containing such terms as ''milk-white maid,'' ''Dark Villain,'' ''Fine Prince,'' and ''Happiness-Ever-After'' precedes one containing the following lines:

> Her bacon burned. She
> Hastened to hide it in the step-on can, and
> Drew more strips from the meat case. The eggs and sour-
>   milk biscuits
> Did well.

Two new poems in *Selected Poems*, **"To Be in Love"** and **"Big Bessie Throws Her Son into the Street,"** have lines and a use of rhyme closer to the method of the poems in *In the Mecca* in their tautness. **"To Be in Love,"** a portrait of that state of being, leans as close as possible to direct statement. ''To be in love / Is to touch things with a lighter hand.'' The next one-line stanza: ''In yourself you stretch, you are well.'' Rhymes then dot several areas of the poem and, near the end, combine with more complex diction to provide the emotional climax. "**Big Bessie**," a portrait of a mother encouraging her son to seize his independence, has similar strategies, although it is less realistic and moves toward the impressionistic. (pp. 96-7)

In the Mecca is comprised of the poem "**In the Mecca**" and several under the heading "**After Mecca**." The long poem "**In the Mecca**" has for setting a famous Chicago apartment building, half a block long, located between State and Dearborn streets, one block north of Thirty-fourth Street. The title poem in the company of the others marks Brooks' turn from Christianity and the hope of integration to that of nationalism. Obviously the situation means that motives different from those of the preceding works will place at the foreground the necessity for new stylistic developments. The language must emphasize Blacks developing common bonds with each other instead of the traditional "people are people" bonding. For a poet who has so intensively devoted herself to language, the situation means a turn to ways of touching deeply an audience not greatly initiated into the complexity of modern poetry and yet retaining a highly disciplined use of language. The challenge would seem all the greater since to acquire such brilliant command over so wide a range of poetic devices as Brooks had done over the years was also to build a set of reflexes in consciousness which, one would think, would weight the balance toward complex rendering. (pp. 97-8)

[*In the Mecca*] represents, on the one hand, the poet at the very height of her command and utilization of complex renderings. On the other, it represents change of concern and expansion of the use of free verse. Actually, the poem "**In the Mecca**" required complex resources and rendering. Its unifying story line is simple. Mrs. Sallie, a domestic worker, returns from work to find that she has lost her courageous battle to support and rear nine "fatherless" children. Her missing child Pepita, who seemed, at first, astray in the slum-blasted building, turns out to have been murdered and hidden under the bed of the mentally twisted murderer. However, the total story is complex: the rendering of the Mecca universe and what is happening to the holiness of the souls of nearly thirty people, if one counts only those characterized either by extended treatment or by the single incisive line or phrase. Obviously, all the resources the poet had accumulated over the years were needed.

The older stylistic resources seem, at times, to have received further growth. Mrs. Sallie leaves the repressive environment of her employer: "Infirm booms / and suns that have not spoken die behind this / low-brown butterball." The imagery, strategic repetitions, ritualized and moralizing lines—some of which are rhymed for special emphasis—give further revelation of Mrs. Sallie's strength, complex responses, and dogged determination. Imagery and unusual conjunctions of words make each child memorable and his or her situation haunting. Yvonne of "bald innocence and gentle fright," the "undaunted," once "pushed her thumbs into the eyes of a thief." Though given a touch of irony, her love story has something of the direct style of the poem "**To Be in Love**." (pp. 98-9)

The language usage extends from the realistic to the expressionistic, from actual speech tones to formal eloquence. It is a language which must extend itself to engage the balked struggle and melancholy defeat of Mrs. Sallie; the embattled but tough innocence of the children; the vanities, frustrations, insanity, futility, and ruthlessness of certain characters—and the pathos of others; and, finally, the desperation, philosophies, and intellectual reaches of the young hero intellectuals seeking

a way out. It also is a language which unites the disinherited of the Mecca Building with the disinherited across the universe. (p. 99)

[The] wide range of achievement in free verse is further tested by the varied functions it was required to serve in the remaining poems of the book. The function of "**In the Mecca**" was to continue deep definition, to lay bare, and to foreshadow. Though it contains rage, its central emotion is compassion, and Mrs. Sallie is bound within a traditional mode of responding and does not undergo a change of consciousness. Except for "**To a Winter Squirrel**," the succeeding poems are largely about new consciousness and the raw materials of the Black community. "**The Chicago Picasso**" is technically outside such a conclusion judged in its own right, but it is also present to highlight the communal celebration represented by "**The Wall**," since it represents individualism and conventional universalism.

The two sermons on the warpland represent the high point in the poet's struggle to move to the center of the Black struggle, with the first urging the building of solid bases for unity and communion and the second urging Blacks to bear up under the pains of the struggle and to "Live! / and have your blooming in the noise of the whirlwind." Parts I, III, and IV seem the more effective, since their style better combines the abstract and the concrete and their language moves more easily between the areas of formal eloquence and the colloquial. Effective poems addressing the communal concerns of Blacks are also in the pamphlet *Riot* (1969). . . . [The directness of "**Riot**"] and, above all, its satire regarding the privileged John Cabot are effective when read to a Black audience. The satiric approach was both an older device of Brooks' and a feature of the new movement. The last poem, "**An Aspect of Love, Alive in the Ice and Fire**," reproduces the directness and simplicity of the earlier "**To Be in Love**."

Gwendolyn Brooks' subsequent poetry has seen the observer of the poems evidence more easily and casually membership in the group. As part of her mission to help inspire the bonding of Blacks to each other, she wished to write poetry which could be appreciated by the person in the tavern who ordinarily did not read poetry. This ambition required some additional emphasis upon simplicity. She had already had the experience of writing prose of poetic intensity in her novel *Maud Martha* (1953) and in the short story "**The Life of Lincoln West**." . . . Making minor revisions she was able to rearrange "**The Life of Lincoln West**" in verse lines, and it became the lead-off poem in *Family Pictures* (1970), whose title signified the intimate relationship between the observer-writer and the community. It is the story of a little boy who is disliked because of his pronounced African features and who becomes reconciled to his situation when he learns that he "is the real thing." In style it creates an imagery, a syntax, and a diction which do not press greatly for meanings beyond the requirements of its narrative line and development. It moves close to what the poet would shortly be calling verse journalism in referring to her piece "**In Montgomery**," in which she evoked the current situation and mood of the survivors and descendants of the Montgomery Bus Boycott. (pp. 100-01)

In the long poem "**In Montgomery**," . . . [Brooks employs] realism but also ranges, extending from direct, prosy statement to a heightening produced by some of the older but simple approaches to diction in poetry. . . . The poet also clearly evidences the fact that she is visiting Montgomery as a concerned relative, a definite part of the family. In the opening passages she continuously announces her presence.

> My work: to cite in semi-song the
> meaning of Confederacy's Cradle.
> Well, it means to be rocking gently, rocking gently!
> In Montgomery is no Race Problem.
> There is the white decision, the white and pleasant
>   vow
> that the white foot shall not release the black neck.

In phrases which serve as structuring devices in parallel form, she continues to present the evidence of her presence, kinship, and role in the historical continuum.... (pp. 101-02)

Such poems as those devoted to Lincoln West and to Montgomery display many qualities of post-*In the Mecca* style, and they should be added to from other poems in *Family Pictures, Beckonings,* and *Primer for Blacks* and from new poems as they arrive. Some stylistic qualities can be listed: use of various types of repetition, alliteration, neologisms (crit, creeple, makiteer), abstract terms gaining depth of meaning from reference to the group's shared experiences, epithets ("whip-stopper," "Treeplanting Man"), variations in expressional patterns usually associated with the simple ballad, ritualistic echoing of childhood-game rhythms and rhyme, gestural words, and simple words forced to yield new meanings from dramatic context. To these one might add the creation of sharp contrasts, and become inclusive by stating that the repertoire involves all the traditional resources provided for simplicity by free verse.

But such a list does not say as much as it seems to, since many of the above devices were already used in the more complex style, and the true distinguishing point is the new combination made of many of them in the later poetry. Under the caption Young Heroes in *Family Pictures* is a poem devoted to a young African poet, **"To Keorapetse Kgositsile (Willie),"** which illustrates the new simplicity and some carry-over of older devices in a somewhat simpler pattern.... The poem is an introduction to Kgositsile's book *My Name Is Afrika!,* and concludes simply, "'MY NAME IS AFRIKA / Well, every fella's a Foreign Country. / This Foreign Country speaks to You.'" Certainly, the use of capitals and lower-case expressions, unusual word conjunctions ("pellmelling loneliness," "lenient dignity"), and repetition can be found in the more complex style, but here, for the most part, the usage adapts to the creative capacity of an audience not drilled in poetic conventions.

In the same work, **"To Don at Salaam"** retains simplicity throughout and creates a warm portrait suggestive of disciplined intensity. The first stanza creates a symbolic picture of a person who poises himself easily amid forces that are usually overwhelming, and is notable for depending almost entirely upon monosyllabic words.... The third stanza notes his affectionateness, the fourth registers his definiteness in an indefinite world, the fifth brief stanza points to his harmoniousness and capable action, and the sixth, a one-line stanza, ends simply but dramatically: "I like to see you living in the world." Part of the style is the structuring of stanzas according to function and place in the dramatic whole.

Poems dealing with persons or fraternal situations within the family of Blacks tend to be the more successful, especially those dealing with specific persons. But the sermons and lectures contain effective passages and, frequently, longer and more complex movements. In *Beckonings,* **"Boys, Black"** admonishes the boys to develop health, proper Blackness, and sanity, in their approach to existence, and urges heroic struggle.

The dramatic opening gives a sense of the positive direction suggested by the poem, and is noteworthy for drawing images and figures made simple by having been first validated by traditional usage.... The poem also gives an example of a distinctive use of repetition in the first line, and, in the first and second lines, the creative use of alliteration. As it proceeds, it accumulates an in-group set of references. Aside from such expressions as the opening one and the second address ("boys, young brothers, young brothers"), there is the stanza offering caution:

> Beware
> the easy griefs.
> It is too easy to cry "ATTICA"
> and shock thy street,
> and purse thy mouth,
> and go home to "Gunsmoke." Boys,
> black boys,
> beware the easy griefs
> that fool and fuel nothing.

The ending is one of love and faith and admonition: "Make of my Faith an engine / Make of my Faith / a Black Star. I am Beckoning." Much revised and addressed to Blacks in general, **"Boys, Black"** appears in a new collection of poems entitled *To Disembark*.... (pp. 101-04)

With the publishing of *To Disembark* it is apparent that Gwendolyn Brooks' change in outlook and consciousness has crystallized in an altered and distinctive style that offers the virtues of its own personality without denying its kinship with an earlier one. Most dramatic are the speaker's position in the center of her kinship group and the warmth and urgency of her speech. As indicated, the tendency of the language is toward a new simplicity. It can be seen in poems which, on the surface, remain very close to a traditional style of poetic realism but always evidence the fact that they proceed from an artist who is choosing from a wide range of resources. It can be seen in poems which will still, in particular passages, place language under great strain. Such patterns create also a recognizably new voice in the poetry. Thus the always-journeying poet sets the example of doing what she asks of others in the new poem **"To the Diaspora."**

> Here is some sun. Some.
> Now off into the places rough to reach.
> Though dry, though drowsy, all unwillingly a-wobble,
> into the dissonant and dangerous crescendo.
> Your work, that was done, to be done to be done to be
> done.

(pp. 104-05)

George Kent, "Gwendolyn Brooks' Poetic Realism: A Developmental Survey," in Black Women Writers (1950-1980): A Critical Evaluation, *edited by Mari Evans, Anchor Books, 1984, pp. 88-105.*

FREDERICK C. STERN

At least since her famous 1967 "conversion" Gwendolyn Brooks's politics have been primarily the politics of Blackness. That can hardly be doubted. (p. 111)

No one would suggest that Brooks's subsequent output was entirely different from her earlier work after this experience. Although she was to make a number of dramatic changes, including the well-known shift from Harper & Row as her major publisher to Dudley Randall's Black-owned and edited Broadside Press in Detroit as her most-favored outlet, she had always been a poet of Blackness. . . . Others, and Black critics in particular, are much more competent than I am to assess and evaluate this change in Brooks's poetry, and many have done so. I wish . . . to examine another, if related, aspect of Brooks's politics. I want to ask if we can place Brooks's political views somewhere within the spectrum of a more generalized American political ideology. Can we say of Brooks that her poetry indicates a view of society which will reflect a political ideology that includes her relatively recently expanded views about Blackness, but which also speaks to the general polity of the nation-state in which she makes her home?

The example of another Black writer whose views in this regard, at least at one point in his career, are quite clear can elucidate my question in regard to Brooks. Amiri Baraka leaves us in little doubt as to his general political views. Especially relevant in this regard is his 1976 play *S-1*. The play takes its title from a bill before the Congress which proposed a radical revision of the United States criminal code. The play can readily be identified as Maoist in approach. Its premise is essentially that the bill has passed. Many civil libertarians saw in Senate Bill S-1 a serious threat to the provisions of the first, fourth and fourteenth amendments to the Constitution of the United States, and in fact see such threats in the various attempts since then to change the criminal code, which have come to be known as "sons of S-1." Thus, Baraka's premise is that with the passage of the bill something akin to fascism has become the law of the land. The play's major opposing forces are, on the one hand, a group of Black leaders of working people, and, on the other rather stereotypic police officials, business leaders and politicians. The play's script provides a glossary of terms which reflect its Maoist ideology, and a set of notes, partly entitled "S-1, the FBI, Capitalism in Crisis, Fascism in the USA!," which clearly echo the then prevailing views of the Chinese Communist Party under the Leadership of Mao and those of his successors, now fallen from power, who have been called "the Gang of Four."

I do not mean to imply that Brooks's view is like Baraka's in 1975, nor do I mean to assert that Baraka holds the same views today, nine years after the play's original production as he did then. Rather, I use this example as an instance of the kind of political philosophy I wish to examine in Brooks's poetry. Is there, in Brooks's work, a politics analogous in function to, though surely different in perspective, than that which we find in this work of Baraka's?

The answer to the question is in no way as clear or as easily ascertained as in Baraka's case. Brooks has not offered the kind of explicit political statement that Baraka makes in *S-1*. Rather, we must extrapolate a political view from her poetry. I think it can be done, and I will call the view which I believe emerges "populist." What I mean by "populist" needs explaining, of course. I do not mean the often demagogic view we associate with such American political figures as Huey Long, the later William Jennings Bryan, or the racist populist Congressman Tom Watson. Rather, I use the term to identify a kind of belief in and caring about ordinary human beings, "the people," which one can most readily associate with Brooks's predecessor as Poet Laureate of Illinois, Carl Sandburg. In poem after poem, from his "Chicago," to the volume, *The People. Yes,* to such late poems as "Waiting for the Chariot," Sandburg asserts, from sources in his socialist and liberal convictions, a kind of faith in people, a belief in the possibilities and the beauty of "ordinary" men and women which, for lack of a better term, I am here calling populist.

I don't think Brooks's faith is as relatively simple as is Sandburg's. She is much more willing to articulate than is the older poet the possibility of evil in the individual which, whether socially caused or not, is terribly destructive of community. In this sense, her views are closer to those of another Chicago writer, Brooks's near contemporary, the novelist Nelson Algren. Algren's sympathies are all for the grifters, grafters, lowlifes and gamblers. . . . But Algren knows them to be dangerous. He also believes, however, that the source of their evil is not in themselves, but in the social conditions which determine their lives, and that the greatest evil lies in those who control the society—the "well-to-do" living in the suburbs mentioned in *The Man With The Golden Arm,* for instance. Brooks's social awareness, what I have called here her "populism," is much more like that of Algren then, than like the Maoism of Baraka in the 1970's, or than like Sandburg's less acerbic version of "populism."

A few instances of Brooks's verse which demonstrate this kind of populism may make the point clearer. **"The Blackstone Rangers,"** a three part poem in the volume *In the Mecca,* provides an interesting instance. The poem itself is startling, since it celebrates "the Rangers," usually thought of as a dangerous street gang. But Brooks sees in them precisely a form of proud, Black opposition to the powers that be, to "the downtown thing." The second part of the poem, sub-titled "The Leaders," reads, in part:

> Jeff. Gene. Geronimo. And Bop.
> They cancel, cure and curry.
> Hardly dupes of the downtown thing
> the cold bonbon,
> the rhinestone thing. And hardly
> in a hurry.
> Hardly Belafonte, King,
> Black Jesus, Stokely, Malcolm X or Rap.
> Bungled trophies.
> Their country is a Nation on no map.

The pride in the Black self sufficiency of the leadership of the Rangers is evident here. Their independence from downtown Chicago, that is, from the then-white power structure, is equally clear. They are, however, these self-possessed and powerful young men, quite different from other symbols of Black independence, like the activist-singer Harry Belafonte, or the Muslim leader Malcolm X, or the leaders of a new, anti-integration, renascent SNCC, Stokely Carmichael and Rap Brown, or the "Black Jesus," Dr. Martin Luther King, Jr. No Chicago street will be re-named after them. They are a "bungled trophy," not to be seen as evidence of the control of Black leadership potential which, no matter how militant, still somehow remains tied to the existing power structure. Their Nation, in a gang which was to call itself in time "The Black P Stone Nation," is on no map. They are so disconnected from the existing power structures of the United States that they are entirely separate. The populism here is quite powerful, an appreciation for those outside the system, which comes quite close to being revolutionary. (pp. 111-15)

Her earlier poetry reflects similar concerns, though not as steeped in the pride in Blackness which resulted from her "conversion," as such titles as *A Street in Bronzeville* and *The Bean Eaters* make clear. Later Brooks poetry, published since *In The Mecca,* is rather scant, but can be seen in the same populist light as the earlier volume. *Family Pictures* is a case in point. Perhaps the clearest instance of Brooks's populism in the volume can be found in the tributary poem **"Paul Robeson."** Robeson, long assigned by both blacks and whites to Coventry because of his radical political views, and, in 1970, already seized by the debilitating illness that was to keep him from public forums for the rest of his life, is here celebrated less as a spokesman for Blackness, than as one speaking for the concerns of all human beings for one another:

> That time
> we all heard it,
> cool and clear,
> cutting across the hot grit of the day.
> The major Voice.
> The adult Voice
> forgoing Rolling River,
> forgoing tearful tale of bale and barge
> and other symptoms of old despond.
> Warning, in music-words
> devout and large,
> that we are each other's
> harvest;
> we are each other's
> business:
> we are each other's
> magnitude and bond.

Notable here is the accent on all humanity—if one can, as would be true for Robeson, read the "we" of the last four lines this way. Furthermore, the poem seems to speak of the later Robeson, the one increasingly concerned with international peace and friendship, as the phrase "forgoing tearful tale of bale and barge," a reference to Robeson's famous rendition of "Old Man River," in which he changed the words "you get a little drunk / and you land in jail" to "you get a little spunk / and you land in jail," seem to suggest. (pp. 116-17)

Brooks's populism, though primarily directed at her own community, can well be applied to the entire polity in which she lives. The very forms of her poetry, and especially so in *In The Mecca,* relate her inevitably to the tradition in American letters which shows the whole of the community in action with both pity and caring. The form as well as the content of the poetry is, in that sense, populist. Like Baraka's Maoism in 1975, like Algren's left-influenced special awareness, like Sandburg's mildly Socialist-based concern, Brooks has a social philosophy which can be found in her poetry, and which, seen in connection with her emphasis on Blackness, by tradition and outlook can properly be called "populist." (p. 118)

> *Frederick C. Stern, "The 'Populist' Politics of Gwendolyn Brooks's Poetry," in* MidAmerica, *Vol. XII, 1985, pp. 111-19.*

WILLIAM H. HANSELL

In her first three major poetry anthologies, [*A Street in Bronzeville, Annie Allen,* and *The Bean Eaters*], Gwendolyn Brooks portrays "ghetto people" as being largely preoccupied with their personal experience. Busy with their own lives and practical matters, they have little time to reflect on their relationship to the larger society or even to their immediate community. This detachment is presented for the most part as a positive attribute.

In the early works, there are very few poems on the major themes of poems written since the mid-1960s: the nature of blackness and the role of the artist. However, analyses of some poems from the earliest volumes reveal Brooks' ideas about the appropriate subject matter of the artist, and her comments in interviews and elsewhere further substantiate what the analyses suggest.

That immediate and practical needs must take precedence over any "dreams" is the literal meaning of **"Kitchenette Building,"** a poem [included in *A Street in Bronzeville* which] Brooks described as typical of the bulk of her work. Somewhat reminiscent of Eliot's "Preludes," the world described in this poem is squalid, enclosed, almost a trap, and the people in it must devote themselves to the urgencies of their situation. The narrator's speculation on "dreams" gives them a very slim chance of surviving amidst "onion Fumes" and "yesterday's garbage ripening in the hall. . . ." The comic-pathetic overtones of the final description of the narrator rushing to use the bathroom now that "Number Five" is out give a more definite sense of what was implicit in the opening lines: "We are things of dry hours and the involuntary plan, / Grayed in, and gray."

Although **"Kitchenette Building"** portrays a way of life which ostensibly cannot afford the luxury of art, there are obvious ironies. The poem itself is a product of that environment. Although if circumstances seem to militate against art, *these* circumstances are the subject of this poem. Finally, **"Kitchenette Building"** illustrates Brooks' commitment to a concept of art which she has never surrendered: the artist must work with the materials most familiar to him, with his own milieu. Not until *Riot,* published in 1970, are ghetto people her primary audience. Before *Riot,* with few exceptions, white, middle-class buyers of books would seem to be the audience to which she directed her poems. Her subject matter, on the other hand, has always derived almost exclusively from an urban black milieu. In 1969, Brooks stated her attitude: "I think it is the task or job or responsibility or pleasure or pride of any writer to respond to her climate. You write about what is in the world." Brooks has also said that art should use familiar materials, because that will enhance its usefulness to the audience. More than the artist or sculptor, the poet should create things that "mean something, will *be* something that a reader may touch." (pp. 261-63)

The importance of imagination in the process of attaining to experiences and insights beyond the physical world is a theme in the four poems [collected in *Annie Allen*] to be discussed next. The characters in the poems are not artists as such; but Brooks surely would not argue that imagination in the individual can enrich life and transcend physical realities if she did not also believe it functioned similarly in the artist. **"The Birth in a Narrow Room,"** for example, accurately described by Stanley Kunitz as "in her most characteristic vein," argues explicitly that the imagination is not confined by seemingly restrictive circumstances. (p. 268)

Part Two of **"The Womanhood"** is a poem beginning "Life for your child is simple, and is good. . . ." Ostensibly on childhood, the poem also emphasizes the curiosity concerning the commonplace and the sense of adventurousness inborn in those who seek the truth. Trust in himself, aspiration, faith in "undeep and unabiding things," as seen in the child's discovery that he can spill or topple certain objects, are necessities of the spirit, even if sometimes he is injured. . . . The poem portrays the necessity for some individuals to give their curiosity free range, to trust in themselves, and to believe in the intrinsic value of the concrete world: "undeep and unabiding things." And even in the familiar, the immediate and concrete, there is always a risk, an adventure, and a challenge. Brooks' own curiosity and concern with "undeep and unabiding things" has, of course, been her primary source of poetic materials.

"Maxie Allen" is a poem depicting a generational conflict between a mother and her fanciful daughter, but the poem also stated the power of the imagination to enable an individual to escape the immediate environment. Nonetheless, the young girl in the poem is unable to persuade her mother (''Maxie'') that she desires more than material comfort, that vague dreams and aspirations are not satisfied by ''lots of jacks and strawberry jam.''. . . (p. 269)

''Memorial to Ed Bland'' is an elegy to a man ''killed in Germany, March 20, 1945; volunteered for special dangerous mission . . . wanted to see action. . . .'' The poem describes his intense curiosity, even from childhood, and emphasizes his wonderment at things others saw as quite ordinary. Because people saw what he saw but could not fathom what he thought, that is, could not really see into things as he did, they considered him very strange. . . . Explicitly stated here is the need ''people'' have to discover some kind of order and regularity in their world, a need that drives many of them to stifle natural curiosity and grow suspicious of the imagination. Because Brooks became increasingly more concerned with portraying in her poetry the relation of the artist to society, perhaps it is valid to say that an implication in this poem is that unless the artist (Bland, in this poem), with his curiosity and profounder vision, finds some way to convey his truth to people, they will be left only with a very crude and artificial sense of reality.

To sum up, several poems in *Annie Allen* illustrate Brooks' continuing desire to portray her belief that most people's lives would be improved if they allowed their imagination greater scope. They would thus enrich and deepen their awareness of reality.

In *The Bean Eaters* (1960), published eleven years after *Annie Allen*, Brooks continues to portray the immediate environment and ordinary people and events. Her manner and themes are almost identical to those in the two earlier books. But there are leanings or tendencies which will become definite paths in subsequent poems. To focus the better on these tendencies, I shall concentrate on some poems which reveal her concern with the nature and function of art and the artist. ''The Artists' and Models' Ball,'' for example, represents the commonplace as the truly ultimate mystery. The common object resists our perception by being too familiar and obvious and changeable; it refuses to be defined by conventional labels. Here is the entire poem:

> Wonders do not confuse. We call them that
> And close the matter there. But common things
> Surprise us. They accept the names we give
> With calm, and keep them. Easy-breathing them
> We brave our next small business. Well, behind
> Our backs they alter. How were we to know.

Artists can never exhaust the significance of the immediate and commonplace, and artists who ignore ''common things'' literally risk the loss of contact with reality.

In ''The Egg Boiler,'' Brooks ironically explores the false opposition between the practical and the imaginary. The contrast in the sonnet between the artist concerned with imaginative creations, things cut ''out of air,'' and the man preparing an egg seems intended to dramatize the idea that art must be rooted in the concrete world. The man cooking the egg is a poet of sorts—he cuts his ''poetry from wood''—in that he brings passion and love and skill to his task; but his is contemptuous of the ''gorgeous Nothingness,'' the imaginative creations of the artist. In the final line, the man eats his egg and laughs ''aloud'' at ''fools'' who have only poetry as the result of their work. But he is not really given the last laugh. The poem itself reveals that art is rooted in the physical world, can portray, in

fact, so simple a task as boiling an egg. The artist, therefore, when firmly tied to things, has both the physical world and the imaginative one, both reality and reality transformed into art.

Brooks' portrayal of the positive effects of art forms which respond directly to the needs of the people will begin in earnest in the ''New Poems'' section of *Selected Poems* (1963). In *The Bean Eaters*, though, she continues in a direction begun in *A Street in Bronzeville*; she continues, that is, to explore the harmful effects of art which is misunderstood and misleading. Reminiscent of ''The Sundays of Satin-Legs Smith,'' ''Strong Men Riding Horses: Lester after the Western'' portrays a young man's confusion and self-contempt as a result of having seen a film in which strong and courageous men seem such superior beings that Lester can only conclude that he, in contrast, is ''pitiful.'' . . . (pp. 270-72)

Perhaps none of Brooks' poems so explicitly portrays the human cost of actions motivated by hate as ''A Bronzeville Mother Loiters in Mississippi. Meanwhile a Mississippi Mother Burns Bacon,'' and no other more definitely links behavior and values to the arts and to the myths which shape the individual imagination. ''A Bronzeville Mother Loiters in Mississippi'' portrays the effects of a murder on the relationship between a husband and wife (the ''Mississippi Mother''), both of whom are white. The man has killed a black youth and has been acquitted. All the reader knows at the beginning of the poem, the day after the trial, is that the white woman is deep in fantasy. The recent events make her feel as if she is actually experiencing the action in ballads and fairy tales she read or heard as a child and schoolgirl, in which princesses are rescued from dark villains by adoring knights. We are also told she ''never quite / understood'' those ballads.

The first scene portrays the white mother fully involved in her own imaginative reconstruction of recent events while she prepares a meal for her family:

> . . . the milk-white maid, the ''maid mild''
> Of the ballad. Pursued
> By the Dark Villain. Rescued by the fine Prince.
> The Happiness-Ever-After.

She is abruptly brought out of her daydreaming by the smell of burnt bacon. Restored to the everyday world, she becomes literal and matter-of-fact in thinking of the events which triggered her fairy-tale imaginings. She begins to feel that the real-life ''villain'' was inadequate. . . . From this thought, she is led into a speculation on what the ''Dark Villain'' thought and felt when the men confronted him. She thinks of how a child would respond to suddenly brutal men, whom, she imagines, he was accustomed to regarding as standards of proper behavior. Thinking of the ''blackish child,'' especially of his defenselessness and his incomprehension of adult motivation, she reflects momentarily on the essential childishness of all men. Beneath a surface of strength and seeming knowledge and courage, all men are basically children, she thinks, no doubt subconsciously searching for an excuse for her husband's behavior. Further thought about the child, however, suddenly fills her with the ridiculousness of such ''combat.''

As she begins to remember her own part in the trial, especially the fact that she had helped her husband win acquittal, she is disturbed by the realization that she can no longer remember what the boy did to her. The curious and painful fact forces us to recall the opening line: ''From the first it had been like a / Ballad.'' That is, Brooks implies, the woman's fantasy of herself as the Princess assaulted by a black villain was probably more a factor in her accusation of the boy than anything he actually did. (pp. 273-74)

Her whole concern as she begins to reconsider the lynching with ''terrifying clarity'' becomes a frantic need to prove worthy of her husband's ferocity:

> It was necessary
> To be more beautiful than ever.
> The beautiful wife.
> For sometimes she fancied he looked at her as though
> Measuring her. As if he considered,
>   Had she been worth It?

She begins to imagine what her husband might think of her now and is tormented by the possibility that he may think she wasn't worth ''It.'' The fact that she can only refer to the murder as ''It'' and can no longer obscure the reality in fantasy, already confirms her repugnance for the actual deed.

She begins to imagine her husband's thoughts:

> Had she been worth the blood, the cramped cries,
>   the little stuttering bravado,
> The gradual dulling of those Negro eyes,
> The sudden, overwhelming *little-boyness* in that barn?

These thoughts and her determination never to seem unworthy are interrupted by her husband's appearance for dinner, the trial and publicity very much on his mind. Although he sneers at the Northern press, which had harshly criticized his deed, he appears nervous, self-conscious, especially attentive to his hands. It is clear, however, that his wife feels he is pretending, playing the role of a cold-hearted killer contemptuous of anyone else's opinion. . . . (pp. 274-75)

When the husband speaks, he is still rationalizing his deed. Ultimately, he says, all blacks should be killed; in the meanwhile smart-alecky blacks must be punished, and the North must be opposed. ''Mississippi'' must prevail: ''Nothing and nothing could stop Mississippi.'' His speech is interrupted by a squabble between two of his children:

> The Fine Prince leaned across the table and slapped
> The small and smiling criminal.

The wife is suddenly horror-struck and envisions the child covered with blood, blood that went everywhere, touched everything. Even after she has shaken away that sanguine fantasy, she must leave the table and try to conceal the new fear she feels—''The fear, Tying her as with iron.'' Her husband joins her. The touch of his hands on her shoulder again fills her with horror, and she realizes—or believes—she would be unable to protect herself or the children from him. He could murder them all. The vision of blood oozing everywhere, even ''over all of Earth and Mars,'' returns.

When he embraces her and turns her around to face him, she sees only the red of his lips. Sickness consumes her. Ugly and squalid images of the courtroom return. With a sharpening sense of guilt, she recalls the eyes of the child's mother, ''the Decapitated exclamation points in that Other Woman's eyes.'' Hatred for her husband floods over her as she understands that it was hate, not love, as she had imagined in her dream of knights and princesses, that impelled all his actions and talk. Her maternal sensibilities, aroused by violence against her own child, and her common sense have forced her to an awareness of the actual consequences of her fantasy and of her own share of the guilt. Hating her husband and his action, she must also hate herself. (pp. 275-76)

In portraying in ''**A Bronzeville Mother Loiters**'' the close relationship between literature and reality, in particular the fact that literature to some degree can influence behavior and shape reality, Brooks is in a sense developing further a theme in ''**The Sundays of Satin-Legs Smith.**'' In another sense, by explicitly relating this influence to racial conflicts in this country, Brooks is moving towards the concept of the black artist as political militant. (p. 277)

William H. Hansell, ''The Uncommon Commonplace in the Early Poems of Gwendolyn Brooks,'' in CLA Journal, *Vol. XXX, No. 3, March, 1987, pp. 261-77.*

D. H. MELHEM

In contemporary poetry, the world of the poem is often conceived as a beleaguered fortress against the real world; to enter one is to depart from the other. This limits the material of reality for the work and requires a choice between the two as means or end. Whether weighted toward solipsism or manipulation, the tendency results in an exclusive poetry, usually offered with matching poetics and criticism. The art of Gwendolyn Brooks makes no such dichotomy. It includes the world, its poetic emblems, and us. We are not merely to be ranked and shaped with the raw data of existence. We matter, in the vital properties of our thought, feeling, growth, and change, so that the poem becomes an interaction in a mutual process, socially resonant. (p. 236)

[Brooks's] work cries out against the subjugation of blacks, which may have inflicted more physical than spiritual damage, while it has hurt whites spiritually. Brooks embodies caritas, expressed in the poetic voice as it articulates a racial and communal vision. Hers is a unified sensibility, pragmatic and idealistic, shaped, in part, by the needs which it ventures to meet. This kind of artistic courage, risking ''the highest falls,'' is shown by a poet of the first rank, a major poet.

Brooks meets the criteria for major status on all four levels: craft and technique; scope or breadth; influence of the work in style, content, or productivity, upon others; and influence of the poet upon others. Technically, we have examined her mastery of form and cultivation of new and renewed forms. She has extended language itself, as Whitman did, by imaginative compounding, word-coinage, and use of black English vernacular. She belongs to that select category Pound called ''the inventors,'' the highest classification of poets who create and expand formal limits and, thereby, taste itself. Development toward a genre of contemporary heroic poetry, offering distinctive style and language, may be considered Brooks's outstanding achievement. Various types of heroic, exemplified by several other black poets, are examined elsewhere. Yet Brooks's heroic, direct though subtle, comprehensive in sensibility and range, whether ''grand'' or ''plain,'' socially responsive and evangelically fused, makes her work a paradigm of the genre. The unique authority with which she speaks to her people is based in mutual affection and esteem and a historically viable sense of kinship. Her call to Black pride, even when chiding or dismayed, has a familial intimacy. This kind of rapport hovered over the Fireside Poets who supported the Union during the Civil War. For the earlier tradition of literature in English, the configuration is Miltonic and Romantic, the poet as artist and activist. For the native tradition of the American and African American folk preacher, it is sermonic and communal.

A further complex of antecedence has been suggested: the Homeric bard, the Anglo-Saxon scop, the African griot, the balladeer. We have noted Black roots in African and African American culture: religion, religious and secular music (the latter emphasizing blues and jazz), language, and the legacy of oral tales and verbal artistry. Yet even here, we have chiefly studied formal intersection with content: visual, aural, semantic, and psycholinguistic elements that absorb and transcend boundaries of time and place. At what point or line do we separate blues from ballad? Where do we locate the ancestral balladeer: in Britain? New Orleans? Harlem? When does gut become "the slipping string" of a Stradivarius? And what of the sonnet—when it becomes a "sonnet-ballad"? Can we usefully ghettoize our cultural traditions? . . . Brooks is now. "Bees in the stomach, sweat across the brow. Now." She *is* our multiethnic, multiracial American artistic heritage. (pp. 237-38)

While examining Brooks's heroic style in terms of "contemporary fact," the background of African and African American culture, and the British and American poetic tradition(s), we should also bear in mind its relation to the American democratic impulse. Brooks's work, like that of the entire genre, shares idealistic strains of the culture, notable, for example, in the early Emerson and Whitman, and in Thoreau. Observe the continuity with Whitman, who wrote in 1888: "One main genesis-motive of the 'Leaves' was my conviction (just as strong to-day as ever) that the crowning growth of the United States is to be spiritual and heroic." The words call our subject, her art infused with the historic, communal quest for emancipation and leadership.

Brooks participates in the Black Rebellion, identified by [historian Lerone Bennett, Jr.] as "one of the longest and most varied upheavals by black people in the twentieth century." Her life and work illustrate his claim that "Blackness is the real repository of values Euro-Americans proclaimed and never lived," or—in the word rightly popular among blacks—repository of the American *soul*. Beyond Blackness, therefore, and the growing sense of a pan-African heritage, we arrive at spirituality, emphasized by Du Bois and more recently by Chancellor Williams. Speaking of Africa, the latter notes:

> our land, rather than any other land, was called the *spiritual* land, the land of the Gods by the non-African world. . . . So that we have been a very religious people, a very humble people. What reason for it overall is kind of difficult to understand because the same religion—which is an admirable quality, in our world—turned out to be that by which we were victimized.

Brooks's ambivalence toward Christianity stems partly from its very compatibility with the African tradition of humility and acceptance. One recalls Whitman's apt prediction: "There will be soon no more priests. Their work is done . . . the gangs of kosmos and prophets en masse shall take their place."

It is Brooks's fundamental humanism that prevents her from being trapped either in the Victorian conflict between religion and science or in the twentieth-century dilemma of reconciling spirit, idealism, and optimism with science, determinism, and pessimism. For Brooks, ideals are the given of existence, whether or not supernaturally endowed, and the task is to create a humane society in the benign image of an extended family. She is sophisticated enough to understand the vicissitudes of progress, and determined enough not to submit to a weary pessimism. Her gentle, amused mien accompanies a fervent seriousness. The prophetic role, once assumed, is not to be put

aside. In periods of confusion or disintegration, it orders vision. Since the prophet traditionally expects little or no honor in his or her own country, neither appreciation nor recognition are prerequisites for the task.

Perhaps Gwendolyn Brooks's most important contribution to the philosophy of literature is the challenge of her work to the cul-de-sac of the antiheroic ironic mode, as defined by Northrop Frye, retaining its intellectual virtues while moving toward reentry into the mythic/heroic. In this process, she also gathers historical strands of romantic and mimetic or realistic modes along with the ironic, into the heroic abode of epic genre. Frye's definition of epic is useful here. He writes, "The function of the epic, in its origin, seems to be primarily to teach the nation, or whatever we call the social unit which the poet is addressing, its own traditions." Madhubuti perceptively refers to *In the Mecca* as Brooks's "epic of black humanity." (pp. 239-40)

Brooks has not codified her transition to heroic as an "Adamic" celebration of the individual, to use the terminology of Roy Harvey Pearce. In his useful study, Pearce distinguishes an Adamic mode, embodied in Whitman and culminating in Stevens, and a mythic mode, also historically continuous, realized in Eliot. It would seem, however, that the political impulse of Whitman is distant from Stevens's detachment. Brooks is Whitmanic in a way she cannot be Stevensian. Faith in self, projected nationally, politicizes awareness. This diverges radically from poetic faith as a commitment to art, ultimately one's own. Nor can she be Eliotic, with a mythos based on stabilizing a society that she is bent upon altering. In her quest of heroic and its prosody, Brooks transforms the aristocratic concept of the hero or heroine from the conventional status of super-being—as Frye accepts the perspective for his heroic/mythic historical mode—toward redemption of that which is more compatible with the Judeo-Christian tradition of humble origins of beauty and power.

The creative by-product of Brooks's local and national efforts has been to encourage the making of poems. She has personally established a prodigious number of prizes and awards for poetry, funded student trips to Africa, anthologized, subsidized, and promoted student work. Her readings and workshops, undertaken on regular, cross-country travels, convey her to prisons and reformatories, as well as to schools, universities, and other environments. Whether journeying or at home in Chicago, she communicates the drama of current affairs with a concern that begins in the spirit. Her faithful representations of black experience define the nature of its white context. She enriches both black and white cultures by revealing essential life, its universal identities, and the challenge it poses to a society beset with corruption and decay.

Beyond critical analysis, we decide that we like a work, or we don't; we like a poet, or not. We care about the poetry of Gwendolyn Brooks in great measure because it cares about us and the existence we share. It does not lose us in a labyrinthine psyche, or make us claustrophobic to get out of life, or tax our patience with chronic self-pity. Its warmth is more immediate, for the most part, than that of Eliot, Pound, Williams, or Stevens. A social act, it hones an art of utility and beauty, at home in the world. . . . Its human terrain recalls John Dewey's observation that Williams found so compelling: "The local is the only universal, upon that all art builds." At the same time, Brooks's travels, her span of interests and enterprise, give her work a cosmopolitan breadth. She contributes a beauty of wholeness, of a fully articulated human being whose compassionate intelligence, wit and humor and anger transcend their tragic awareness.

It is especially just that Brooks's familial perspective on the Black Nation renders her animating quality. As we read her poems, we feel their indivisible affection, their cohering power. Acknowledging them, "an essential sanity, black and electric," we recognize a national resource, needed now. (pp. 240-42)

D. H. Melhem, in her *Gwendolyn Brooks: Poetry & the Heroic Voice, The University Press of Kentucky, 1987, 270 p.*

NORRIS B. CLARK

The evolution of the poetry of Gwendolyn Brooks from an egocentric orientation to an ethnocentric one is directly related to her advocacy of a black aesthetic and to the shifting aesthetic criteria in modern America. "For one thing, the whole concept of what 'good poetry' is is changing today, thank goodness . . . I'm just a black poet, and I write about what I see, what interests me, and I'm seeing new things."

Although she has always written poetry concerned with the black American experience, one that inheres the diversity and complexity of being black and especially being female, her poetics have primarily undergone thematic developments. Her emphasis has shifted from a private, internal, and exclusive assessment of the identity crises of twentieth-century persons to a communal, external, and inclusive assessment of the black communal experience. That change not only corresponds to the fluctuating social, political, and ideological positions of the national black American communities during the sixties and seventies, but it also correlates with the evolution of aesthetic humanism's fundamental concerns about the nature of reality, our relationship to it and its vast variety. (pp. 83-4)

Brooks's latest poetry, *Riot* (1969), *Family Pictures* (1970), *Aloneness* (1971), and *Beckonings* (1975), clearly incorporates a pronounced humanistic concern for a collective black America as well as accepting a black aesthetic ideology in terms of aesthetic relativism. Her transitional text *In the Mecca* (1968) clearly advocates and represents a turning point in her conception of art and of a black aesthetic, an artistic position in which she continues to use language as "our most faithful and indispensable picture of human experiences, of the world and its events, of thoughts and life. . . ." It is a position that remains attentive to the needs and the energetic struggle of the oppressed, as all writers of a black aesthetic persuasion maintain.

Gwendolyn Brooks's poetry, as black aestheticians have advocated, has always been committed to depicting the "simple" lives of black Americans in the medium of black language, black rituals, black experience; it has always been reflective of the multiple values inherent in the black community. Brooks's earliest poetry, for which she is most noted in academia, *A Street in Bronzevillle* (1945), *Annie Allen* (1949), *The Bean Eaters* (1960), and *Selected Poems* (1963), equally depicts, as does her latest poetry, the basic uncertainty of black people living amid the physical turbulence and psychic tensions of American society—the whirlwind of stasis within flux of twentieth-century America. One merely needs to look at Brooks's **"The Sundays of Satin-Legs Smith"** or **"Gay Chaps at the Bar"** to see her concern for the dilemma of the oppressed minorities' identity struggle. (pp. 84-5)

Critics suggest that Brooks's poetry, whether an extension of herself as an artist or as a black artist, can be divided into three groups: (1) *A Street in Bronzeville* and *Annie Allen,* primarily devoted to craft and exhibit an "objective and exquisite detachment" from the lives or emotions of individuals; (2) *The Bean Eaters, Selected Poems,* and *In the Mecca,* also devoted to craft but exhibit a strong awareness of black social concerns; and (3) *Riot, Family Pictures, Aloneness,* and *Beckonings,* less devoted to craft and more concerned about pronounced statements on a black mystique, the necessity of riots (violence), and black unity. Those categories can also be characterized in political language as traditional, prerevolutionary, and revolutionary; or in the language of sociologists as accommodationists, integrationists, and black nationalists; or in racial language as white, colored, and black. Regardless of how one chooses to classify Brooks's poetry, if one must, her corpus remains as an undeniable statement about the condition humane. More precisely, it is a statement about the myriad black American experiences as it communicates the feeling of brotherhood and love. In each phase, arbitrarily defined or not, Brooks has clearly been committed to, as black aesthetic advocates desire, black people.

Although the central theme of Gwendolyn Brooks's poems does not essentially change—to reveal the black person's presence and participation in the complexities of life—as her changing sensibility about the objectives of art evolves, the formal poetic techniques used to create art "to mean something, [that] will be something that a reader may touch" remain "technically proficient." A different emphasis between the thematic content of her earlier poems—self, motherhood, tenements, war heroes, racial ambivalence, joblessness, pretensions, poverty, religion—and her later "black" poems—a black aesthetic, black unity, black consciousness, contemporary black heroes, overt racism, riots—is noticeable. Yet, her poetry still continues to characterize not only the subtleties of racial tensions and to exhibit an intense and brilliant craftsmanship, a propriety of language in ordinary speech, but it also maintains the traditional reliance on rhetorical devices that elicit ambiguity, irony, paradox, tension and contrast. . . . It should constantly be remembered that "she knows the ways in which Shakespeare, Spenser, Milton, Donne, Keats, Wordsworth juxtaposed intense emotion . . . creating patterns of pull and push among its elements . . . the ways in which moderns like Pound, Eliot, Yeats and Frost break traditional poetic patterns." Brooks's varied use of the traditional formal elements of poetry: rhyme, meter, couplets, elocution—anaphora, assonance, dissonance, enumeration, gradation, isocola, prolepsis; combined with folk elements derived from the black community: jazz and blues rhythms, black speech patterns (only determined by idiom)—slurred rhymes, slant rhyme, sprung syntax, jarring locution—and black folk heroes give Brooks a distinction as a unique modern black poet. . . . Her formal concerns with poetry—to avoid clichés, to balance modern influences with intuitional phrasing, to unify rhythm with tonal effect, to discover and to create order, to avoid imitation, to use traditional forms as well as nontraditional forms, to use colloquial speech, rhyme, quick rhyme, to "blacken" English—give Gwendolyn Brooks a distinction among the ranks of contemporary modern American writers and among the ranks of most black American writers, especially advocates of a black aesthetic.

Clearly, Brooks's poetic sensibility, as a poet or as a black poet, is both modernist and traditionalist in style, form, language, and theme, rather than political. Not only does she combine in her poetic artifacts the formal, European, and American traditions, but she also infuses them with her point of view, that which any artist must do, and makes them uniquely

American, modern, and black. Unlike many of the poets of a black aesthetic ideology, Brooks displays a unique individualism in her work that is devoid of racial polemic or black rhetoric. Despite her present attentiveness to a black audience and her conscious linguistic strategies, as in **"My Name is Red Hot. Yo Name Ain Doodley Squat,"** she is neither a protest poet nor a practitioner of a popular cultural aesthetic. Whether her poems are of a dramatic nature or a narrative nature as in **"The Boy Died in My Alley"** or **"The Life of Lincoln West,"** respectively, or of song or elegy as in **"Steam Song"** or **"Elegy in a Rainbow,"** respectively, or not associated directly with "blackness" as in **"Horses Graze,"** Brooks remains a poet first, one who expresses her blackness through art. She does not, as Houston Baker suggests, have a white style and black content.

Brooks's continuous use of nontraditional technical elements, black English, or idioms of the street indicate that Brooks's poetic style is not white, rather it is black American—one which incorporates poetic techniques from a dual heritage. One should also keep in mind that some black Americans do not speak in the idiom or linguistic structure of black English. Indeed, W.E.B. Du Bois's assessment of a dual consciousness is what Brooks's poetry has always been about: "this longing to attain self-conscious [person]hood, to merge his double self into a better and truer self. In this merging he wishes neither of the older selves to be lost."

Although Brooks's poetry is modern, American, and black, some critics think her latest poetry has lost its "universality" because it deals with social themes or exhibits a conscious concern for the political, social, and economic circumstances that stultify the lives of black people. One critic, Daniel Jaffee, condescendingly objected to Brooks's definition of her art as black poetry rather than poetry: "The label 'black poetry' cheapens the achievement of Gwendolyn Brooks. It recommends that race matters more than artistic vocation or individual voice." Despite an opinion that Brooks's achievements are cheapened because of race, such critical sensibility points not to the dilemma of her changing concept of poetry, but to the inherent dilemma of artistic evaluations that do not view race as a significant aspect of aesthetic, social, and moral judgments. To uncritically assume that "black" cheapens art denies, a priori, unbiased aesthetic evaluation, artistic integrity to black art forms and the artist, consciously or subconsciously. Moreover, such views minimize the notion that literary style is the bridge that unifies the artistic sensibility, literature, and the cultural environment into a dynamic historical and social experience. It further stigmatizes and stereotypes that which is deliberately, and potentially beautifully, created in an historically accurate and representative manner. In addition, it denies validity to Brooks's black consciousness or poetic voice as well as her magnificent poetic sensibility that has always given credence to race as significant and thus important as thematic material. . . . (pp. 85-8)

As George Kent suggests, Gwendolyn Brooks's "dilemma" points to the dilemma of all black artists. On the one hand, critics want to acknowledge that artifacts transcend race, while on the other paradoxically emphasizing that an art construct tells or shows the reader what it has meant to be a black American. As Brooks has stated, emphasized from *In the Mecca* to *Beckonings,* her art is to be more committed not only to recreating artistically the lives of black people, but also to using technical devices that permit black people to see reflections of themselves and to feel the dynamics of those reflections in her

poetry. Brooks's recent artistic sensibility and criteria for art are akin to those to which many advocates of a black aesthetic adhere: to speak as a black, about blacks, to blacks. (p. 88)

Although Brooks's *The Bean Eaters* indicates a thematic change from general themes such as personal aspiration, motherhood, marriage, dreams, isolation, and birth, *In the Mecca* (1968) is Brooks's transitional text. *The Bean Eaters* illustrates that her increased social awareness began with **"A Bronzeville Mother Loiters in Mississippi. Meanwhile a Mississippi Mother Burns Bacon,"** **"The Last Quatrain of the Ballad of Emmett Till,"** and **"The Chicago *Defender* Sends a Man to Little Rock"** or the exquisite and subtle condemnation of racism in sonnet form, **"Gay Chaps at the Bar."** In contrast to those earlier poems, in *In the Mecca* Brooks makes explicit statements about how blacks think, the ideology of Negritude, a black aesthetic, and black power. In essence, those "political" statements evolve from her reawakened and redirected artistic consciousness and reflect the black cultural milieu of the 1960s and 1970s. Even though there is an emphasis on "blackness," Brooks, importantly, continues to explore the universal qualities—social and psychological—of blacks, as they *survive* in an interracial and intraracial society. *In the Mecca* isn't solely about black nationalism or a black aesthetic; rather, it is primarily a testimony to the undisputed fact that black persons are not curios, that they do have values, that there is dignity among the uncertainties of their lives. *In the Mecca* is actually a tribute to black existence, one that avoids castigating "Whitey" to emphasize liberation of those ordinary lives that blossom and wilt among "hock[s] of ham," "hopes as heresy," "roaches and gray rats." (p. 89)

In the Mecca also clearly indicates, via the character of Don Lee, who "wants a new nation . . . new art and anthem," Brooks's leanings toward a black aesthetic as suggested by Haki Madhubuti (Don L. Lee), whom Brooks regarded as a stimulus for a new renaissance. Yet the true significance of *In the Mecca* is not so much Brooks's advocacy of a black aesthetic or Alfred's ability to finally act (rebel) or Pepita's ignoble death—"a little woman lies in dust with roaches." The true aesthetic significance, thematically, is that the black lives, whether Way-out Morgan's, Alfred's, Darkara's, or Pepita's, are meaningful and reflect an "ultimate reality" in formal juxtaposition to expectations. It symbolically represents the existential dilemma of twentieth-century humankind—the province of art and especially the province of "black art." People living or dying in the Mecca exhibit the existential tensions confronting any people with human limitations and possibility. That epic poem reflects our madness, our helplessness, our pain and feelings of rejection. It represents the universal nature of oppression, self-imposed or externally imposed. Not to know and cherish the tragedy of our own lives is not to know the joy of being here.

Gwendolyn Brooks's later poetry after *In the Mecca* also does not only reflect a specific black aesthetic in which all black persons are "beauti-ful"; rather her art, from advocating militant resistance in **"Riders to the Blood-Red Wrath"** (1963) to wishing "jewels of black love" in **"A Black Wedding Song,"** thematically suggests a range of "ways"—"The Ways of the Mecca are in this Wise"—in which blacks can, should, and do respond to oppression. Although there is a stronger sense of a black nationalist perspective in **"Boys. Black.,"** it is one that extends the black nationalist perspective of action as suggested by Alfred's role in *In the Mecca* rather than scathe white America. Clearly, unlike the poetry of many young black writers of the sixties, especially those whom Arthur P. Davis regards as the poets of "black hate," Brooks's poetry is neither irrational nor propagandistic. She does not use devices such as incendiary polemics, militant slogans, four-letter expletives, fused words, slashed words, or phonetic spellings. Instead there is a clear use of language with some hip talk, some street talk and idiom to make her poetry less "obscurantis" to blacks in an attempt to advocate a sense of communal and individual responsibility for the spiritual and physical death of blacks. . . . (pp. 89-90)

In essence, Gwendolyn Brooks's thematic concerns, the tense and complex dimensions of living through the paths of petty destinies, have changed but have not eliminated an acceptance of those who choose to live and to love differently. Unlike the more radical black aesthetic poets, she does not condemn the "Intellectual Audience" as Nikki Giovanni has done, or equate Negroes with repulsive beasts as does Welton Smith in "The Nigga Section," or curse white people, as in Carolyn Rodgers's "The Last M. F." Brooks's later works, *Riot, Aloneness, Family Pictures,* and *Beckonings,* instead, emphasize a need for black unity by using "the exile rhythms of a Black people still seeking to establish at-homeness in America," but not to the exclusion of universal themes and subjects such as "brotherly love," literary critics, heroes, music, love between man and woman, false ideals, friendship, beautiful black blues. Nor like the more radical or political black poets of the sixties and early seventies such as Imamu Baraka, Sonia Sanchez, the "radical" phase of Nikki Giovanni, Welton Smith, or other black aesthetic advocates does Brooks create racist, propagandistic, and taciturn poems that advocate violence as therapeutic (Fanon's dictum), exhort whites to bring about equality, castigate or demean others. Instead, she depicts black realities without brutally frank language via her black voice, a voice that emanates a conscious humanistic concern for others. Similar to "great masters," Brooks's poetry does not tell us that there is evil, corruption, oppression, futility, or racism; rather, she shows us the tragedy and its relationship to individuals in hopes that we may learn a moral insight from the juxtaposition of beauty and horror, death in life as in **"The Life of Lincoln West."**

Brooks's unique voice in her latest poetry is one that not only ideologically varies from a narrowly defined black aesthetic, but also thematically deviates from its total reliance on obscure African references or Africa as a source of inspiration or upon a doctrine of how to live, as in Ron Karenga's Kawaida Doctrine, or a pro-Muslim religious orientation as some black aestheticians advocate:

> Blackness
> is a going to essences and to unifyings.
> "MY NAME IS AFRIKA!"
>   Well, every fella's a Foreign Country.
> This Foreign Country speaks to you.

Not surprisingly, Brooks's voice which contrasts the American ideals and practices—W.E.B. Du Bois's "Veil Metaphor"—especially the insensitivity and ignorance of whites toward blacks, as in *Riot,* is not filled with private symbolism or biting satire. Rather, self-identity in Brooks's poems leads to group-identity. She does not, as Baraka has done, only focus on a black nationalist, black Muslim, black power, or blacker-than-black perspective. Rather, her voice is one that recreates the feelings and thoughts of the unheard, as riots do, rather than merely languish in a black aesthetic of polemics devoid of lyricism. Even though Brooks's poetry calls for a black dignity and a black pride, erstwhile symbolized by Africa, she acknowledges

that blacks "know so little of that long leap languid land [Africa]" and suggests that enacting "our inward law"—unity (community, family) among black Americans—is more important than any external reliances upon a leader, a god or God(s) or the heat of "easy griefs that fool and fuel nothing." Her attempt to create black unity is not to establish a bond among third-world peoples but to establish a bond between those oppressed black Americans who "are defining their own Roof. . . ." (pp. 90-2)

Unlike the black writers of polemics and propaganda or the rhetoricians of hate and violence, Brooks doesn't attempt to impose her personal philosophy upon others; she does not demean or denigrate blacks whose psychological mechanism to survive leads them to be "Toms" or race traitors. (In fact, some critics have questioned her attitudes or personal voice as not being strong enough on issues such as abortion.) Brooks's poetry remains one of love and affirmation, one that accepts some hate and perhaps some violence as necessary without condemning or castigating those who have been pawns to interracial and intraracial forces. Adequately reflecting the hopes and aspirations of the black community, Brooks displays a love for her brothers and sisters regardless of psychosocial or socioeconomic position. In doing so, she clearly embraces "blackness" and the values of liberation, and thus the values of all humanity. That quality, despite an emphasis on embracing blacks first, is one that is universal in literature of self-affirmation and self-identity; the universal is revealed through the particular. As her sensitivity to the spirit of social revolution emanates from her sense of "love," Brooks advocates a sense of self-love and compassion while reflecting the tensions of her time period, a tension due to racial oppression: "On the street we smile. / We go / in different directions / down the imperturbable street."

Thematically and imagistically, Brooks's poetry after *In the Mecca* reflects a social sensibility that incorporates, as her earlier work has done, especially war poems, the expressive and mimetic aspects of a black experience rather than an arbitrary, political black aesthetic. An art form that has aesthetic qualities related to the black experience should, by definition, incorporate a sense of what it is like to face life's multitude of complexities as a person affected by racial values (Afrocentric and Eurocentric) pertaining to the black communities. Regardless of the ideological or social position the writer has, the genre should render that representation in a manner that is most particular, although not necessarily unique, to an existence as a person confronted with the issues of "blackness." This is not meant to imply that the central theme must be about blackness; rather it is to suggest that the world view that the art conveys, in theme as well as in image and structure, should provide a sense of what it is like to see historically, culturally, and psychologically through the eyes of a black person. The tensions of living as a black person—whether in blackness or whiteness—should be illustrated and discernible. To that end, Brooks's poetry extends. If one considers her multidimensional themes combined with her conscious attempt to fuse the traditional with the colloquial or common, it is evident that Brooks's later poetry is not thematically "more black" than her earlier poetry. Her poetry, despite her diminished reliance upon formal diction, continues to be an expression of her craftsmanship as well as an expression of her black voice as expressed in 1950. [In an article published in *Phylon,* Brooks stated:] "Every Negro poet has 'something to say.' Simply because he is a Negro he cannot escape having important things to say."

The technical proficiency with which Brooks creates those meaningful lives, whether heroic, mock heroic, or parody, is what poetry is about. It is to that specific end, exposing the truth of human existence in forms meaningful to the black community, that Brooks's poetry leads. Despite the extension of Gwendolyn Brooks's poetry to a new black consciousness of the late 1960s and 1970s, her formal devices remain as alive in her later poetry as they are in her earlier poetry. She does continue to pay attention to craft, to the neat turn of phrase: "Now the way of the Mecca was on this wise," "as her underfed haunches jerk jazz," or "In the precincts of a nightmare all contrary...." She "blackens English": "That Song it sing the sweetness / like a good Song can, . . .", "Unhalt hands," or uses extensive alliteration: "These merely peer and purr / and pass the passion over." She continues to infuse the traditional standard American English not only with her intuitional phrasing and coinage of words, but also with the "common folk phrasing" as exhibited in songs and folk sermons. In doing so, Brooks's poetry is more reflective of aesthetic relativism while maintaining some elements of traditional "white" culture as in "Que tu es grossier!" or "death in the afternoon." That relativism related to the black experience can be observed in her use of black folk heroes, or in **"The Wall,"** a poem in which art for art's sake is not a valid concept whereas the wall allows celebration and commitment (i.e., it is communal and functional as "Negritude" advocates). Specific references are made to black literary heroes as in **"Five Men Against the Theme,"** **"'My Name is Red Hot. Yo Name ain Doodley Squat,'"** or musical heroes as in **"Steam Song"** (Al Green) or **"The Young Men Run"** (Melvin Van Pebbles). Combined with the sounds and sense of sermons, jazz, blues, and double entendre, these references help to bring ghetto life alive and to enhance the significance of an idea and its "metaphysical function" as in **"Elegy in a Rainbow."** In addition, Brooks continues to exhibit irony, a complex sense of reality, a sensitivity to traditional line and beats, metered as well as in free verse. She juxtaposes lines that appear to move rapidly with those that tend to slow the reader down, as in **"The Boy Died in My Alley."** Furthermore, she uses sudden contrasts or repetition to make each word bear the full measure of weight and suggestion. (pp. 92-4)

Although the forms of Gwendolyn Brooks's poetry contribute to and enhance an understanding of the content—move it from the simple, mundane, and colloquial to a complex, eternal, and universal—her recent poetry does achieve aesthetic beauty and historical truth. It fails functionally in her terms only. Her latest objective: "I want to write poetry that will appeal to many, many blacks, not just to blacks who go to college but also those who have their customary habitat in taverns and the street. . . ." is not, as she acknowledges, achieved because it doesn't reach those "taverneers." Brooks acknowledges her failure of *Riot*—"It's too meditative"—and *Beckonings* has a dual impulse (a self-analytic commentary on the nature of her own poetry). She also states that only two love poems (songs), **"When you've forgotten Sunday"** and **"Steam Song,"** can be well received in tavern readings. Similar to some of the "Broadside poets," as well as other black writers who desire

to write for the black masses—as Walt Whitman and Ralph Waldo Emerson had also advocated—Gwendolyn Brooks falsely assumes that her task is to create art for those who don't appreciate formal art. As with most poetry, even that which infuses informal folk elements with formal literary elements, undereducated or subeducated persons—those to whom the fourth-to-sixth-grade reading level of newspapers appeals—cannot or choose not to be subjected to it. Rarely do they appreciate the subtlety and interrelationships of finely turned phrases or understand, reflectively or meditatively, the appeal of formal alliteration and repetition to a complex meaning or abstract idea. The unsophisticated generally expresses an emotional understanding or appreciation of rhythm or meter by nodding or tapping his or her foot; the sophisticated generally searches, from an objective distance, for rhetorical and metrical relationships or correlations to history, psychology, religion, or culture. Ironically, it is precisely because Brooks's poetry fails to appeal to the black masses that it appeals aesthetically to the "blacks who go to college" as well as those *littérateurs* who can and will reflect upon the "sound and sense" of a poetic artifact. (p. 95)

The aesthetic success of Gwendolyn Brooks's later poetry, and her sense of its failure, reflects the historical literary dilemma of cognitively and emotively appreciating the truth and beauty of a black experience and art per se. To create art reductively, only for one group, limits the art; to create art without letting it organically or ontologically exist limits the number of persons who have the faculties with which to appreciate it. Formal art can never be truly functional; folk art is always functional. To infuse, as Gwendolyn Brooks has, the informal with the formal, in a medium designed to be formal, subsumes the informal component, especially when it evolves from a self-conscious literary formalism. Thus attempting to reach those in taverns, the origins of some folk traditions, alters and negates the ontological component of art. It necessarily extends it beyond the folk to the formal by making it solely functional in a "literary" sense. What Brooks does with words, forms, and content—not consciously imitating anyone—is the essence of the aesthetic imagination unifying disparate elements into a coherent whole—structurally, semantically, and phonetically. As a spokesperson of the black masses, Brooks is literally different from those for whom she writes; consequently, she is the "seer and the sayer," the Emersonian poet, who articulates the needs, ideas, and aspirations of others. In doing so, she can only create, to make clear in terms she knows and understands, her perception of the raw material. Her quest, then, is to create works of an aesthetic nature and of a "black origin"—whether critics appreciate it or not. To do so, as she has, is not "to be content with offering raw materials. The Negro poet's most urgent duty, at present, is to polish his technique, his way of presenting his truths and beauties, that those may be more insinuating, and therefore, more overwhelming." (p. 96)

Norris B. Clark, "Gwendolyn Brooks and a Black Aesthetic," in A Life Distilled: Gwendolyn Brooks, Her Poetry and Fiction, *edited by Maria K. Mootry and Gary Smith, University of Illinois Press, 1987, pp. 81-99.*

Alejandro Casona

1903-1965

(Born Alejandro Rodríguez Álvarez) Spanish dramatist, poet, scriptwriter, and essayist.

One of Spain's foremost twentieth-century dramatists, Casona achieved international recognition for employing such elements as illusion, folklore, the supernatural, and imaginary settings to create plays rich in fantasy, symbolism, and moral meaning. While didactically conveying his belief that individuals must confront reality, Casona's plays maintain universal appeal through their infusion of humor, irony, idealism, and lyrical language. His dramas often depict the conflict between reality and illusion and the importance of balancing these integral components of humanity. In many of his works, Casona's protagonists escape the harshness of life by creating fantasies. This illusory existence is typically overcome when the characters adapt to the conditions of their lives. Kessel Schwartz noted: "Casona's characters, in their desire for flight from the world, exhibit essentially a negative attitude and only in their adaptation, complete or partial, do they convert to positive aspirations. Very often a return to a struggle for a positive end implies conversion, not only to reality, but to an ethical life, for the sense of duty and ethics is very strong in Casona, and very often ethical living and reality are synonymous for him."

Casona was born in a small village in the northern province of Asturias. Like both of his parents, he became an educator, and after teaching for several years, he was appointed superintendent of Madrid schools in 1931. Later that year, Casona was made director of the People's Theater, a traveling company established to bring cultural advances to Spain's rural population. His duties in this position included writing and producing plays for the troupe to perform. Casona established himself as a major dramatist in Spain with his first three plays, *La sirena varada* (1934), *Otra vez el diablo* (1935), and *Nuestra Natacha* (1935). The latter work, in which a group of idealistic young people attempt to improve the educational, social, and economic conditions of a Spanish community, was produced near the beginning of the Spanish Civil War and prompted Generalissimo Francisco Franco to ban Casona's works. After leaving Spain in 1937 and settling in Argentina, Casona garnered international acclaim with performances of his works throughout Latin America. Casona returned to his homeland in 1962.

In *La sirena varada,* which was awarded the Lope de Vega Prize, Casona underscores the importance of confronting reality by depicting a group of characters who have retreated from society and live in illusory worlds. Through the help of a doctor, these individuals eventually learn to cope with the unpleasant elements in their lives. *Otra vez el diablo* evidences Casona's interest in such literary forms as the fairy tale and the fable. Set in a fictitious kingdom, this play centers on a young student who overcomes his temptation to work with the Devil through moral fortitude and saves the princess he loves. Casona's unusual portrayal of a pitiable, semi-human Devil has been commented upon by several critics. *Nuestra Natacha,* which condemns inhumane teaching methods employed in Spanish reformatories, revolves around the efforts of a female student to improve educational programs for delinquent or-

phans. In addition to his main topic, Casona depicts the satisfaction and happiness attained by those who are devoted to their work.

Casona's first play written after his exile, *Prohibido suicidarse en primavera* (1937; *Suicide Prohibited in Springtime*), centers on a home established by a psychologist for suicidal individuals. Ostensibly providing the means for guests to kill themselves in idyllic settings, the home is eventually revealed to be a disguised rehabilitative institution. As case histories of the characters are presented during the course of the play, the psychologist helps his patients reconcile their unhappiness, and the beautiful surroundings prompt them to recognize positive elements of life. *La dama del alba* (1944; *The Lady of the Dawn*) is considered a haunting, poetic masterpiece by many critics. This play centers on the benevolent intervention of Death, which is personified as a beautiful and mysterious young woman called "the lady of the dawn." Poetic justice is served when Angelica, who has made a cuckold of her young husband, is spirited away by Death, and her husband finds true love with another woman. Casona's next play, *La barca sin pescador* (1945; *The Boat without a Fisherman*), again features the Devil as a central character. In this work, which is reminiscent of Christopher Marlowe's play *Doctor Faustus*, the Devil visits Ricardo, who is on the verge of financial ruin, and offers to restore his fortune if he will agree to break the only one of the Ten Commandments he has not already compromised—"Thou shalt not kill." After initially declining, Ricardo consents upon being informed that he merely has to sign a document for the deed to be accomplished. The remainder of the play details Ricardo's remorse and his struggle for redemption. As in *Otra vez el diablo,* the Devil in *The Boat without a Fisherman* is portrayed with sympathy and humor.

Casona's next major play, *Los árboles mueren de pie* (1949), is a comedy concerning an aged woman who finds happiness through a ruse concocted by her husband in which a delightful young couple is introduced as their grandson and his wife. The real grandson, a criminal and blackmailer, arrives on the scene, but the grandmother, preferring to continue the illusion, turns him away. *Siete gritos en el mar* (1952) revolves around seven people and a reporter aboard a passenger ship. While dining with the captain, the passengers are informed that the ship is serving as a decoy and will be attacked by enemy submarines. Facing impending death, the dinner guests reveal negative qualities about themselves. The audience gradually becomes aware, however, that the dinner conversation has occurred in the reporter's dream and has exposed personal truths that the real passengers had been concealing.

Two of Casona's final works are historical plays. *Corona de amor y muerte* (1955) blends legend and fact to detail the tragic love story of Pedro Fernandez de Castro, the crown prince of Portugal, and Ines de Castro, his illegitimate daughter. *El caballerro de las espuelas de oro* (1964) offers a portrait of satirist Francisco Gomez de Quevedo y Villegas, a renowned writer of the Spanish Golden Age who fought decadence and corruption through scathing social criticism. In addition to plays,

Casona wrote numerous film scripts and contributed journalistic pieces to several Latin American periodicals.

(See also *Contemporary Authors,* Vols. 93-96 [obituary].)

WILLIAM H. SHOEMAKER

[Until 1936, the] life and career of Alejandro Casona was framed within the many-sided civil struggle of his country—of a Spain seeking a new life of freedom against overwhelming odds. It was the life and career of a quiet, modest school teacher to whom education and culture were of vital significance and in whom the creative spark came to glow warm and bright as it embodied his ideals in stirring works for the Spanish stage. The next ten years were a decade of exile, of wandering and uncertainties, of devotion to dramatic art, of eventual establishment in Argentina, where . . . Casona at forty-three leads a life in theater and motion picture activities that is both busy and successful, but not untinged with nostalgic reminiscences and yearning. (p. xi)

The teacher and the dramatist in Casona received notable and perhaps unexpected development in the two years he spent in the Valle de Arán, whither the Primo de Rivera dictatorship sent him as elementary school superintendent in 1928. . . . [It] was in the Valle de Arán in 1929 that he wrote his play, *La Sirena varada,* his first to be performed—five years later and with spectacular success—in an established theater by a professional company.

With the birth of the Republic [of Spain] in April, 1931, a larger sphere of professional activity, both in the theater and in pedagogy, unfolded for Casona. . . . First, he took examinations in open competition and won the superintendency for Madrid. Second, D. Manuel Bartolomé Cossío, the spiritual father of modern teaching and teachers in Spain, selected Casona to organize and direct the *Teatro del Pueblo,* a part of an educational project of incalculable importance known as *Las misiones pedagógicas.*

In spite of the success and renown that began to come to him in 1934 and continued until the civil war violently altered Spanish life after July, 1936, Casona's life was most intimately and most actively bound up for five years (1931-1936) with the new mission which so happily united the two dominant tendencies in his nature—the teacher and the dramatist. One of the first acts of the Republic had been to establish the *Patronato de Misiones Pedagógicas* under the *Ministerio de Instrucción Pública y Bellas Artes.* . . . The work of the *misiones* furnishes one of the most inspiring stories in the annals of education for disinterested, nobly idealistic, and progressive yet sustained activity. Briefly stated, the *misiones* sought to perform a work of social justice by bridging the abyss between the cities and the rural districts and by removing through communication the isolation of the latter. . . . The school taught how to read, the *misión* awakened the love of reading. By opening the windows of the mind to new vistas of many sorts, the *misiones* were bringing hundreds of villages to life, reincorporating them into the Spanish nation.

Casona organized and directed the activities, wrote and arranged plays for the *Teatro del Pueblo,* and personally led eight of the twenty missions conducted in 1932, the first full year of activity. . . . Some fifty students formed the *Teatro del Pueblo,* mostly prospective teachers but with the other different professional schools represented. Their work was all voluntary and gratuitous and included over four hundred performances in villages of Castilla, La Mancha, Extremadura, León, Aragón, Asturias, and Galicia. For this group Casona wrote his three one-act plays: (1) *El entremés del mancebo que casó con mujer brava,* a dramatization with variations of the Taming-of-the-Shrew story found in Juan Manuel's fourteenth century *El Conde Lucanor;* (2) *Sancho Panza en la ínsula Barataria,* an arrangement for the stage of the corresponding chapters of *Don Quijote;* and (3) the *Balada de Atta Troll,* adapted from a literary satire of the German poet Heine and later incorporated in *Nuestra Natacha.* (pp. xv-xviii)

The remarkable success of *La Sirena varada,* first performed on March 17, 1934, at the Teatro Español in Madrid, opened up for Casona a new world, the world of the professional theater. (pp. xix-xx)

La Sirena varada is a highly original fantasy in which Casona deals with several facets of the problem of personal happiness—whether it is socially and morally free of responsibility and whether it can be found in the escape of sustained self-deception and in insanity, or must face life squarely and rest on truth and reality. (p. xx)

This play, with its weird psychological types may recall Unamuno and Pirandello (especially in *Henry IV*). But essentially it is an affirmative attack on the dehumanization of life so characteristic of much of the literature and drama throughout the Western World between the two world wars, the product of a civilization in crisis. It was widely recognized as a fresh and invigorating new note in the Spanish theater, all critics without exception finding something fine in this, the first work of an unknown author. Full of overtones and symbolical values, elements both intellectual and romantic, and composed with a sure and skillful technique, *La Sirena varada* reveals how close the modern theater may be to ancient allegory. (p. xxi)

Otra vez el diablo, written in 1927, was revised by Casona and performed . . . on April 26, 1935, just a year after their success with *La Sirena varada.* This second play, although not achieving the popular success of the first, greatly enhanced Casona's reputation among critics and has been played widely throughout the Americas in both professional and university theaters, published already in four different Spanish editions, with contracts drawn in the first year for translations into Danish and Italian.

Otra vez el diablo is a wholly unrealistic fantasy of a timeless morality: He, She, and the Devil. The *Infantina,* believed to be bewitched by the *Diablo,* is cured and saved by her lover, the *Estudiante*—captain of the bandits. The Devil, his identity unknown, has become the girl's tutor and has aided in preparing her fall in amorous conquest to her lover. But the latter at the crucial moment foregoes his opportunity, rejects and slays his Mephistophelian helper. He kills him in the only way evil can be killed, Casona tells us,—within himself. This assassination, being inner and moral, gives rise to much symbolism, lyricism, and originality of both thought and dramaturgy. Many stimulating and provocative allusions and the rejection or flaunting of many hoary traditions such as *donjuanismo* . . . reveal the teacher within the poetic dramatist. (pp. xxi-xxii)

Casona astounded the theatrical world of Spain and elsewhere with the unparalleled success of *Nuestra Natacha.* . . . From its first performance in Madrid . . . on February 6, 1936, this play achieved an unequaled run of over 500 consecutive performances—this in a country where the normal theater-going public is not large and runs are rare. No doubt the tensions of the day and even the military rebellion in July, while they made theatrical activities more difficult, enhanced the public's appreciation of the play. For *Nuestra Natacha* breathes the very spirit of young Spain—the sincerity of the generous, self-sacrificing zeal of its students, the humanly liberalizing régime with which their idolized leader Natacha seeks to reform the reform school, the courageous experiment of the community enterprise in which the group develops a profitable farm out of a run-down and abandoned property. The life and the serious, purposeful attitudes of the students, their theater, and even the *Balada de Atta Troll,* which they perform, derive directly from Casona's own experiences, especially with the *Teatro del Pueblo* of the *misiones pedagógicas*. (pp. xxii-xxiii)

The forces of habit and inertia, conservative and reactionary patronage, against which Natacha makes her unavailing struggle at the *Reformatorio de las Damas Azules* may recall such earlier works as, for example, Benavente's *Los malhechores del bien*. But Benavente's play was, like most of the work of the generation of '98, satiric, bitter, pessimistic, and negative. Natacha is obliged to abandon her position, and it may be assumed that the school will return to its old spiritless routine, spelling failure for her "reform." But this happens after the curtain falls. What Casona presents on the stage is a vigorous and inspiring affirmation of Natacha's ideas in action. Benavente and Casona created these plays from opposite standpoints, each writing with a focus, so to speak, on what the other implied but largely omitted. In *Nuestra Natacha* Marga's violation is charged to a class of Spanish society that never appears on the stage—the *señoritos,*—and these idle and irresponsible sons of wealth and position, these youths who had already flocked to Spain's Fascist party, the *Falange,* and were soon to raise their brutal malevolence with the rebellious army against the Republic, are bitterly criticized. But even here, Casona's attitude is mainly affirmative. The vicious attack on Marga is in the end the unintentional cause of her redemption through motherhood.

Some of the dramatic strength developed in the first two acts of *Nuestra Natacha* is lost in the third, probably because Casona presents a social-economic achievement near its moment of triumphant completion. There is no social or economic conflict on the stage, it is apparent largely in retrospect. To many it may not seem sufficient to justify Natacha's refusal to marry Lalo, whom she has come to love. But herein lies Casona's fundamental moral idea: duty and responsibility to the task set must not yield to personal pleasure and happiness.

For all its seriousness, *Nuestra Natacha* is pervaded by a gay humor: the enthusiasms of the students in the first act, of students and reform school youths in the third; the pathetic and intensely human delights of the *educandos* in the second. Casona does not contrive situations for their comic effect. The humor rises out of the nature of the characters: Lalo's optimism, which keeps him in the university through intentional failures in examinations because he doesn't know what direction to give his life until Natacha shows him; Mario's scientific absorption in the love life of insects to the utter unawareness of his own; Juan's superabundance of animal energy, which must expend itself on whatever it finds confronting it; the warden Francisco's need of his imposing uniform. Only the Marquesa of the school board and the old-line teacher Srta. Crespo lack a natural and sympathetic humanity; but this is intentional for Casona wishes to show them as having abandoned their humanity in falling into a rigid, static, dehumanized pattern of

thought and behavior. They contrast with Don Santiago, the University *rector* and foster uncle of Natacha, whose warm friendliness . . . differs so markedly from the traditional aloof formality of officialdom.

Nuestra Natacha is Casona's only *specifically* social drama and was the last one written and performed in Spain before the Franco rebellion succeeded in banning this and all his works from both press and stage. (pp. xxiii-xxv)

Throughout Casona's works runs a preoccupation with spiritual crises, often created by social problems, and revealing keen psychological understanding, tender human sympathy, and profound moral concern. An uncommon sensitiveness to these things has combined with a lyrical tendency and with the irresistible attraction of other-worldly Death and the Devil to make most of his plays non-realistic fantasies. *Nuestra Natacha,* by way of exception, is rooted in the soil and heart of Spain, less impressive perhaps for imaginative flights and universal timelessness but more powerful in the intense fervor and the sense of actuality of its theme and characters. (p. xxix)

William H. Shoemaker, "Life and Work of Alejandro Casona," in Nuestra Natacha *by Alejandro Casona, edited by William H. Shoemaker, D. Appleton-Century Company, Inc., 1947, pp. xi-xxix.*

VIRGIL A. WARREN

It may safely be predicted that the interest of the North American student will be aroused and retained in the study of [*Nuestra Natacha*] with its simple natural dialogue, and its humorous but natural varied student types, encountered on campuses in the United States as well as in Spain. He will feel sympathetically attracted to Lalo and the latter's intentional failures in examinations due to indecision concerning his life's career; to Mario, negligent of a personal love life in his concern over that of insects; to Francisco, ever in need of the security of his uniform; to Marga, seduced by the *señorito;* and to the attractive, intelligent Natacha, who will not permit personal pleasure and happiness to supersede duty and responsibility.

The thesis of the play is in perfect accord with present trends in welfare work. A humane, sympathetic treatment of the underprivileged in life is more effective in the creation of useful contented citizens than a rigid, static, dehumanized control of their thoughts and actions.

Virgil A. Warren, in a review of "Nuestra Natacha," in Hispania, *Vol. XXX, No. 3, August, 1947, p. 437.*

MELISSA A. CILLEY

[*Nuestra Natacha*] is based on the modern, progressive idea of youth: that in work and responsibility lies real happiness and that steadfast devotion to duty brings about a moral and spiritual self-reliance that is necessary for a satisfying life. It is a social drama depicting various types of young people, students mostly, their manner of thinking and their aspirations. As the curtain falls on the last act, we leave them working successfully and, in the main, unselfishly toward a better world in which every human being can achieve his own destiny.

The life of the university students, with their gaiety, their problems, their enthusiastic group spirit, their confidence that they or their leader Natacha can put to rights the world, or at least part of it, is representative of youth of all epochs and particularly of modern Spanish youth. These students give wholeheartedly a year of their lives to help Natacha work out a humanizing reform for the inmates of a reform school. But at the end of the year Natacha finds that the problems are not yet all solved; she cannot accept love when it first calls her, she must stay on at her post.

The contrasting element is seen in the rigid, old-fashioned ideas of the president of the school board of the reform school and in the first teacher, who shows little understanding of her pupils. On the other hand, don Santiago, head of the university and foster uncle of Natacha, shows how abreast of the times he is by his natural mingling and working with the students, his kindly attitude toward their pattern of thought and his sympathetic assistance in the new line of activities.

Faith in mankind permeates the entire play, and this means faith also in a new Spain that will emerge through sympathetic, keen understanding of social problems and the will to work out patiently spiritual and practical matters. (pp. 473-74)

> Melissa A. Cilley, in a review of "Nuestra Natacha," in The Modern Language Journal, *Vol. XXXI, No. 7, November, 1947, pp. 473-74.*

A. WALLACE WOOLSEY

From a certain point of view, life may be interpreted as a continuing attempt to escape on the part of man. The quest for food is escape from hunger; adventure is release from the boredom and the tedium of every day existence. Most men desire companionship to escape loneliness, but some seek solitude to escape the crowd. While this interpretation of life is possible, it is a negative approach: carried to the extreme, it gives a warped outlook on life. Alejandro Casona has made this desire for escape the main-spring of several of his plays; in others it is a most important element.

The plays in which the characters seeking escape are to be found are works of diverse and varied settings. *Otra vez el diablo* takes place in a fairy-tale land of the past, while *La dama del alba* presents customs and superstitions of Asturias in northern Spain. *Prohibido suicidarse en primavera* and *La sirena varada* unfold in a surrealist modern world, and *Nuestra Natacha* in the Madrid of 1936—very much in the world of reality. In *Los árboles mueren de pie* we find fantasy superimposed upon an extremely modern setting that might be any metropolitan center in the world. Among the characters are to be found the Devil himself, a royal princess, a university student, would-be suicides, the *segundón* overshadowed by the elder brother, a blind man and many others.

The psychological approach is not new to drama and literature in general, but Casona seems to have evolved something almost unique in his technique. He has drawn upon his knowledge of medieval folklore and witchcraft, modern psychology and his own knowledge of man gained from life and observation.

In *La sirena varada* a strange group of persons move and speak their parts. As is the case in most of Casona's plays, the setting and situation are unique and not likely to be duplicated. It is to a deserted house that these people have found their way. But every one in the group is drawn to this particular place by the consuming desire to escape from something. Ricardo, the owner, seeks, as he says, a republic of men where common sense does not exist. . . .

Another is Daniel who is humored in his whim of going about with his eyes bandaged; he says that he must flee from the monotony of the same colors day after day. When the bandage is removed, the awesome truth is revealed; he is blind. As long as he wears the bandage, he can pretend that he could see if he did not have it. . . . (p. 80)

But the most eerie, the most other-worldly, to join the assemblage is Sirena who has seemingly appeared out of the sea to make her way into Ricardo's arms and into his heart. Ricardo knows not who she is, nor whence she comes; nor does he care; she is the superb climax to this world of fancy in which he would live. . . . (pp. 80-1)

In truth Sirena has taken that last and almost final step into the world of illusion. She is insane.

Prohibido suicidarse en primavera has an even more unusual and unlikely setting than does *La sirena varada.* It is a sanatorium with its latch-string out to would-be suicides. The entire setting is conducive to thoughts on the morbid subject of taking one's own life. There are books and poems by famous people who have committed suicide; there are portraits of these people on the walls. Along the walks are provided all the classic devices for putting into effect the ultimate and absolute escape from life. Gathered in this refuge between life and death is a pathetic group of people, each of whom is fleeing from some problem of living.

For Alicia loneliness is the haunting specter, a loneliness known only to the soul alone among the crowds of a great city. The Imaginary Lover, enamoured of the opera star Cora Yako in the form of Brunhilde, Marguerite, Scherezade, Madame Butterfly, has stolen and would carry with him to the grave his illusion of love and escape the consequences of his act. . . .

Otra vez el diablo takes us back into a Cinderella-like royal kingdom of the past with a picaresque Spanish student, a starry eyed princess seeking adventure, and the Devil. The princess has rosy dreams of being abducted by dashing bandits of the mountains—a desire to escape the tedious security and decorum of the court. . . .

The student's struggle for escape is within his own soul. He strives to free himself from the power of his emotions and his baser self in order to be able to rise to a higher plane. It is a different sort of escape from that which we have seen previously.

Even the Devil himself wishes sometimes to escape from his diabolic existence and be something different for just one time in his eternal existence—"before he retires" as he puts it. The only way that the Devil can be non-Devil is to perform some good. That he wishes to do. . . .

Mauricio of *Los árboles mueren de pie* makes a business of weaving illusion into the lives of others, but when truth comes into conflict with his created world of fancy, he too wishes to escape. He would avoid the tragedy of seeing his illusory structure crumble before the light of unrelenting reality. . . .

The prime example of the desire to avoid the problems of life in the play *Nuestra Natacha* is the university student Lalo. He is a very real sort of fellow, the like of whom most of us have seen at one time or another. College life offers him a shelter from the vicissitudes of the world, and graduation would bring the necessity for leaving this place of refuge. All of this has caused Lalo to romanticize failure and to make of it his device for escape. (p. 81)

Others of *Nuestra Natacha* are also seeking escape. The Conserje must hide from his own lack of self-confidence behind the facade of his brilliant uniform. . . . Margo has always re-belled against the restrictions that life has placed upon her and finds release in walking endlessly, endlessly. (pp. 81-2)

La dama del alba records folkways and superstitions of the people of Asturias and their attempts to elude evil by certain custom-sanctioned actions. . . . In all of the examples that have been cited of the workings of the escape complex, imagination is naturally an important element. However, with some of the characters the realm of fancy is glorified above all else; the building up of illusion becomes an art wherein the imaginary situation is always thought to be better than any original from which it may have been copied.

Ricardo of *La sirena varada* exalts the imagination over reality. Although Pérez Galdós had asserted over fifty years earlier in *Doña Perfecta* in the words of Pepe Rey that ''la loca de la casa'' had become only the servant in the house, Ricardo would again lift up this mad woman into first place. He believes that he can build a community in which all the members can dwell in their world of illusion and ignore reality. . . .

In the play *Los árboles mueren de pie* Mauricio sees himself as an artist and one who creates illusion in the lives of others. For him the product of the imagination of the artist is always superior to matter of fact reality. The sympathetic tear, ecstatic delight, even the evidences of love, are always more convincing when they are produced by the imaginative artist than when they come forth spontaneously from real life situations.

Lalo of *Nuestra Natacha* in his desire for failure as a medical student is rebelling against a world of practicality and is seeking the realm of fancy. This he finds in his work as an entertainer and as a poet. Here the imagination has free play, and illusion becomes a man's stock in trade. Furthermore, this business of imagination on the part of the poet fits into the scheme of every day life. (p. 82)

Likewise the Imaginary Lover, whom we have seen earlier in *Prohibido suicidarse en primavera,* like Lalo also creates in real life a place for his own life of illusion in order to escape from a treadmill existence. In his imagination he is the hero and lover of the great operas; he has traveled to the glamorous points of the globe. These spots have their own romantic and imaginary existence for him which is his and his alone. The realities of the ugliness and discomfort of these places are unknown to him, and he refuses to allow them to cast a shadow over his fanciful musings. He too becomes an artist, a creator, a weaver of illusion. . . . (pp. 82-3)

But what is the final outcome of all this desire to escape? Can man create his own imaginary way of life and dwell therein? In almost every one of the cases cited the end result is that the romantic individual has to face the realities of life and adjust himself to them. Ricardo, the rebel against common sense, at last realizes that truth is relentless and inevitable. . . .

Sirena can no longer remain in her dream world of insanity. For the sake of her unborn child she must make the effort and return to the world of reason and reality. . . .

In *Prohibido suicidarse en primavera* Alicia finds that she can-not ignore the physical and consider her body as something immaterial when it is pointed out to her that to keep that body alive she has consumed many tons of meat and wagonloads of vegetables. Nor can she escape loneliness in death, for death is absolute loneliness. Such escape comes from service to oth-ers and through forgetfulness of self. The Imaginary Lover finds the reality of the places of his dreams and the girl of his

illusions far baser things than his imagination has pictured. For these would-be suicides then, not death but life is the solu-tion. . . .

Even more forcefully does *Otra vez el Diablo* set forth wherein true escape lies. We escape only by facing the issue squarely and conquering it within our own heart and soul. Throughout the play there are many references to a small jewelled dagger, supposed to be the only weapon capable of killing the Devil. When this dagger shall have blood upon it, it will be a sign that the Devil has been killed.

The Student, in order to restrain his own lustful intent towards the Princess, has Cascabel tie him to a chair and then go for the King. When the King arrives at dawn, the Student proves that the Devil is dead by showing the dagger dripping with blood. He has killed the Devil by his own superior will and self-denial; he has killed him in his own breast. . . .

In *Los árboles mueren de pie* Mauricio has fabricated the rosy illusion of the return of a prodigal grandson to the arms of a fond and loving grandmother. However, such an illusory cre-ation must inevitably give way before the brutal truth of the presence of the real person. Throughout the fantastic week he and Isabel have striven to weave into the Grandmother's ex-istence, Isabel has had misgivings. She has repeatedly indicated that the only real solution is the truth. When the curtain comes down upon their act, she feels that she must return to reality. She cannot leave this imaginary existence to enter another equally false. She has learned a great lesson. . . .

Natacha of *Nuestra Natacha* is throughout the play an avowed opponent of those who would escape into a world of romantic unreality. Repeatedly she states her firm conviction of the ne-cessity for facing the world squarely and realistically. . . . (p. 83)

She persuades Lalo to forego his romantic pose of martyr and to go forth and face the world instead of fleeing from it. Natacha opposes escape behind any sort of false front and finally causes the Conserje to abandon his pompous uniform. He must learn to accomplish his purpose through his own ability instead of hiding his ineffectiveness behind a false front.

Casona does not seem to rule out entirely the possibility at times of having the imagination serve the needs of life. Lalo does not have to abandon his world of illusion, but he does face the reality of its illusory nature and brings it to serve his fellow men. Other men realize the imaginative nature of Lalo's work and yet accept it, for it fills a need. Lalo has become a poet, a singer and an actor. Likewise, the Imaginary Lover puts his imaginative powers to work writing glowing descrip-tions of his dream travels with Cora Yako. It would appear that the author makes a place in the world of reality for the imaginative realm of poetry, drama, and fiction.

The most unusual and in a sense the most paradoxical of all situations is to be found in *Los árboles mueren de pie.* Truth has in reality destroyed the illusion of the penitent grandson so carefully created by Mauricio. However, Mauricio and Is-abel depart believing that their manufactured situation is reality for the Grandmother. She is a greater actor and a greater artist than they and allows them to go away still believing in the effectiveness of their artistic imagination. She shields them from the disillusionment which she herself has suffered. Age has lost its illusions, but youth can tarry yet a while longer in its world of fancy.

The foregoing cases and examples will serve to show the great importance of the escape motif in the works of Alejandro Casona. Man is confronted on every hand by the desire to escape from one thing or another—to substitute illusion for reality. But we can only reach the conclusion that the author feels that there is no escape other than to face reality. An illusory or imaginary way of life must fade away in the pitiless light of reality. (pp. 83-4)

A. Wallace Woolsey, "Illusion versus Reality in Some of the Plays of Alejandro Casona," in The Modern Language Journal, Vol. XXXVIII, No. 2, February, 1954, pp. 80-4.

KESSEL SCHWARTZ

A theme of conflict between reality and idealism or the interplay of the material and the visionary has been a characteristic of many Spanish authors, of whom Cervantes and Calderón are outstanding examples.

Alejandro Casona continues this tradition in his acceptance of the theme. He combines fantasy and reality in a special manner, insisting on the human quality of his fantastic creations in their relationships with worldly beings. His Devils in *Otra vez el Diablo* and in *La barca sin pescador* are more human than supernatural in their portrayal, as is the frustrated Peregrina in *La dama del alba.* Casona, however, adds further vigor to the tradition in keeping with twentieth-century psychological and philosophical concepts. His addition might be termed not so much acceptance of as adjustment to reality, as he insists that man's happiness lies in facing the truth instead of seeking to escape into a variety of fantasy worlds.

In schizophrenia, interest in adjusting to reality has become secondary to other interests. Casona has examined the lives of individuals whose experiences with other people have been painful or dangerous, so that avoiding them became a measure to preserve comfort or safety. His concern is with having these individuals adjust to reality, for his conclusion is that only in such adjustment, even when it entails giving up privileges, lies the enjoyment of a full and meaningful life.

Casona's characters, in their desire for flight from the world, exhibit essentially a negative attitude and only in their adaptation, complete or partial, do they convert to positive aspirations. Very often a return to a struggle for a positive end implies conversion, not only to reality, but to an ethical life, for the sense of duty and ethics is very strong in Casona, and very often ethical living and reality are synonymous for him.

Casona had to face difficulties in his own life in his partisanship of the Republican cause and in devoting himself, in his play *Nuestra Natacha,* to a truth he felt it was his duty to portray. (p. 57)

Casona's characters attempt to escape through illusion which will disguise the unhappiness or the sordidness they have known. In general, they make their temporary "escape" from reality through fantasy, evil, desertion or rejection of the world, and sacrifice.

The Infantina in *Otra vez el diablo,* Sirena and Don Joaquín in *La sirena varada* and the Amante in *Prohibido suicidarse en primavera* all weave their lives into a fantasy world to defend themselves from the cruelty of the real one. The Infantina thinks of life as a fairy tale and seeks her romantic ideal in the young and handsome bandit captain.... She is awakened from her dream world by the real advances of the Estudiante and realizes that life has many complications which she must accept in order to know true love. She stops seeking imaginary dangers and faces the real ones which confront her.

Sirena, in order to forget the sordidness of her circus life, creates for herself the fantasy that she is a mermaid. She tries to believe she had lived at the bottom of the sea and only recently has become a land prisoner. Through the help of Don Florín she forgets the false universe and adjusts to the real one. Her unborn child becomes the symbol of the future to her, and for its sake she will not return to the formerly attractive sea.... Though reality is not a perfect state, she recognizes it as the only way to a happy future. She rejects her beautiful fantasy and helps her husband reach a livable compromise.

The Amante Imaginario pretends to be the lover of a famous opera star.... When he finally meets her, he realizes that she is not the solution to his problems and that illusion cannot offer permanent escape.... He denies the fantasy that he has created and adapts to reality by becoming a travel writer.

Don Joaquín, the hired ghost, is not sure whether he has really died or not, but he finally realizes that he cannot be happy in his make-believe and decides to become a gardener....

Both Ricardo Jordan in *La barca sin pescador* and the Estudiante in *Otra vez el diablo* thought that they could rise above their reality through evil. Ricardo, betrayed by his friends, accepts the Devil's aid in order to escape the problems which face him. He wishes the death of an innocent man and rationalizes that since he doesn't know his victim, he will not be affected. He soon realizes that ["in the life of a man is the life of all men"]. Good triumphs over evil, reality over illusion, and through his love for the wife of the victim, he can begin to try to atone for the damage he has done. The final solution is not perfect, as Ricardo renounces the Devil and the evil Ricardo Jordan and makes an adjustment to a new life. In spite of the hardships involved, through his new found love he will find the way to happiness.

Ricardo in *La sirena varada* and Doctor Roda in *Prohibido suicidarse en primavera* remove themselves physically and spiritually from the everyday world. Ricardo has had material wealth but has missed much of childhood's pleasures, having been an unhappy and unloved child. He seeks to escape the sorrows of the world, which he finds boring and stupid, and establishes a refuge for others who seek escape.... He achieves temporary satisfaction in his love for Sirena but soon wants something more substantial in their relations than her mermaid story.... His new happiness is not without its bitterness and an occasional relapse.... But Sirena convinces him that even ugliness is better than illusion and Ricardo finally agrees, saved through love.

Doctor Roda rationalizes his *Hogar de Suicidas,* making much of the stages of readjustment of those seeking to flee their responsibilities, until he realizes that by giving the victims a refuge from the world with other unfortunates, he is not helping their recovery.... By withdrawing from society he failed to accomplish his noble purpose, and so he takes the advice to return to the real world and its problems.... His decision to close the *Hogar* is his first step in dealing with the problem of suicide in a realistic manner.

Some of Casona's characters refuse to accept reality. The Madre in *La dama del alba,* Daniel in *La sirena varada* and Hans in *Prohibido suicidarse en primavera* escape in this manner. The Madre grieves for the supposedly dead Angélica and refuses to live a normal life. She will not allow changes in her daughter's room. . . . She cannot agree with Abuelo's contention that what has happened has happened and that life must go on in positive rather than negative fashion. When Adela enters her life she begins to realize that life has meaning and she finds happiness again in reality. . . .

Daniel, the blind painter, is one of the few characters who never adjusts to reality and therefore can find no happiness. He is bitter about what he terms the "dirty world" and pretends he is trying to invent new colors. When Ricardo rips the blindfold from his eyes and accuses him of being a coward, Daniel demands his bandage back. He cannot allow himself to admit his blindness, even though Sirena encourages him to adjust. . . . (pp. 57-9)

Hans, too, is unable to face normal life. Ruined by the war, he has become obsessed with the thought of death and seeks pleasure only through the sufferings of others. He is doomed to a perpetual search for a contentment he will never find.

Martín of *La dama del alba* escapes by concealing the truth temporarily. He knew that Angélica was not the image of purity all thought her to be. By refusing to tell the truth he had been contributing to the world of fantasy, but when he fell in love with Adela he felt that real escape lay in building a life for himself elsewhere. He had been living one lie and wanted to escape now into a more involved one. He was spared the decision of a choice between the real and the unreal by finally telling the truth about Angélica, so his return to the real world is through truth. (p. 59)

Sacrifice and duty are key aspects of Casona's philosophy. Adela of *La dama del alba* sought escape in suicide, but later she found meaning in life in her love for Martín. [Though] she weakens momentarily when Martín reveals the truth to her, she resolves, with Peregrina's help, to continue to face life. Chloe, in *Prohibido suicidarse en primavera*, attempts to kill herself in order to bring two brothers together, and then tries to sacrifice her love by marrying Juan instead of Fernando, whom she really loves. She wants to create for Juan the illusion of being loved for once in his lonely life. . . . She discovers that her choice is false and one more illusory attempt at happiness. True happiness can come only from the real love she feels for Fernando and sacrificing that reality for an illusion would have brought unhappiness to all three. . . . Juan has attempted suicide to keep from murdering his brother. Full of guilt feelings, he maintains a paranoid obsession that his brother has robbed his life of love. He finally makes the adjustment in spite of his anguish and refuses Chloe's sacrifice, although he will need continuing help to maintain his adjustment. Alicia is another who sees temporary refuge in Roda's retreat. She is tired of struggling against solitude and hunger, but basically she is not a neurotic type and she is willing to help Dr. Roda adjust others to life and thus find happiness through service.

Isabel of *Los árboles mueren de pie*, like Adela, unhappy, friendless, and unable to recall any past happiness, seeks escape through suicide. When offered a chance for friendship and, more important, for service to fellow sufferers, she recovers her sense of belonging and becomes a useful member of society. Love saves her from a return to her cold room and dusty geraniums. Balboa in the same play, with noble motivation, has lied to his wife about her worthless grandson, seeking to create a false illusion to protect her, but when La Abuela learns the truth, she is willing to give up her fantasy. . . . Her sacrifice, like that of Natacha and others, is a positive one to further the happiness of those who have helped her.

In *Nuestra Natacha* the idea of adjustment to reality is not the central theme, but even here there prevails the idea that each person must find his own place in life and that moral responsibility must be met before personal happiness can be achieved. It is not only Natacha who sacrifices herself for the reform-school youths. Most of them go from rebellion and frustration to adjusted lives. Juan channels his animal energy into constructive channels for Marga. She ceases to rebel and seeks redemption, as did Sirena, through motherhood. Lalo, pictured in earlier scenes as an unmotivated, continual, intentional failure at the university, through his love for Natacha, becomes the man who works hard and faces honestly the problems of life. (pp. 59-60)

Most of Casona's characters forsake their worlds of fantasy and find happiness by adjusting to the world they wanted to leave. Some compromise with reality as the best solution possible. Very few continue to live in their world of illusion, as do Daniel and Hans, and their dissatisfaction and continuing unhappiness show how fruitless is the attempt to escape.

For Casona the idea of duty to society is all important. Don Florín, when asked whether he thinks he is doing good by returning reason to Sirena and opening her eyes again to the dirty world which surrounds her, can say only that it is his duty and that the truth, no matter how bitter, must be faced. Natacha is willing to work for others and give up her own rights, for as she tells Don Santiago, each person must seek his place in life. . . . Don Florín brings reason to Ricardo and shows him that his previous life was not good. The Abuelo in *La dama del alba* tries to convince the Madre that she should not live in the past but try to make a new life from the present. Cascabel, of *Otra vez el Diablo*, is the realistic gracioso opposed to the idealistic escapists.

Casona doesn't claim that all illusion is bad. The Abuela in *Los árboles mueren de pie* lets those who tried to help her believe they have succeeded, but, on the whole, Casona's conclusion is that the worlds of reality and happiness are synonymous. (p. 60)

Kessel Schwartz, "Reality in the Works of Alejandro Casona," in Hispania, Vol. XL, No. 1, March, 1957, pp. 57-61.

CHARLES H. LEIGHTON

Because of Alejandro Casona's concern with illusion it has become something of a critical commonplace to couple his name with that of Luigi Pirandello. These facile references, usually making use of *La sirena varada* as exemplar, do not really tell us too much. Granted that both are concerned with the question of illusion versus reality, the question remains of the precise extent to which one is justified in calling Casona a follower of Pirandello.

Pirandello's most productive and successful period was the troubled decade 1915-1924. During those years he wrote his best known works: *Cosi è (se vi pare)*; *Tutto per bene*; *Come prima, meglio di prima*; *La signora Morli, una e due*; *Sei personaggi in cerca d'autore*; *Enrico IV*; and *Ciascuno a suo modo*. An examination of these and later plays reveals that in them, Pirandello has activated artistically a number of philosophical commonplaces, all of which may be subsumed under the heading of rational solipsism. Literature has always provided a fertile field for the examination of this problem. Virtually every major writer in the Western tradition has been occupied with one or more of its facets. The most enticing of these has been the most general—the question of whether or not there is one objective truth or an infinite number of subjective truths. As Leo Spitzer has pointed out [in "Linguistic Perspectivism in the *Don Quijote*"], writers may be categorized with respect to their attitude toward this question. Some like Cervantes feel that there is one truth but that no finite creature ever apprehends all of it; others, like Pirandello, insist that whatever truth there is, like beauty, resides purely "in the eye of the beholder."

There is another side to the problem. As long as the writer or the philosopher concerns himself solely with the perception of inanimate objects, perspectivism is a relatively uncomplex matter. When, however, he turns to man, the complexities become manifest and manifold. (pp. 202-03)

A final aspect of the solipsistic problem is that of communication. If it is impossible or at least difficult to apprehend any truth, it is likewise impossible or difficult to communicate what we have apprehended to others. The resultant isolation of man from his fellows is one of the basic themes of Pirandello's theater and accounts for much of the tragedy found therein. . . .

The most apparently Pirandellist of Casona's plays is *Las tres perfectas casadas*. (p. 203)

The play raises several questions of the sort dear to Pirandello. There is first of all the contrast between appearance and reality. When confronted with the fact of his wife's infidelity, Javier thinks that, if the whole matter can be kept secret, he and the other two husbands can continue to play their accustomed roles despite their knowledge. The solution he proposes is thus quite similar to that of *Tutto per bene*.

Then there is the question of what love is. In their final meeting Gustavo and Ada hurl accusations at each other. Each accuses the other of pride and egotism and a possessiveness which passes for love but is a perversion of it. . . . (pp. 204-05)

Then the question of the nature of truth is raised in connection with the behavior of Ada. She insists again and again that she has never loved Gustavo. Yet in an access of emotion she seems to admit that she has indeed loved him all along. . . . Moreover, as the final curtain falls she is fervently kissing the dying man. Again, Casona never makes it quite clear as to what his version of the truth is. The audience must decide for itself.

Incidentally the question of Gustavo's motivation in writing the original letter is raised. The explanation he offers Ada for his despicable behavior are quite Pirandellist. . . . There is some evidence, however, that he does love Ada, for he has made a ritual of recreating the circumstances of their one stolen hour together. Each year on April 23 he reenacts in his imagination that delirious hour of love. But does he know what love really is any more than Ada?

Finally there is the question of the suicide. Did Gustavo fully intend to carry out the bargain? There is no doubt that it appealed to him. But there is throughout the whole last scene at least a suggestion of further deceit. It often seems that he has staged the whole thing just to facilitate another meeting with Ada under circumstances favorable to another seduction. But the strangest aspect of the whole play is that of the shooting itself. Neither Ada nor the audience can tell who did pull the trigger. And Gustavo's insistence that it was he may be a first and last bit of gallantry on the part of a defeated man. All of

these ambiguities of motivation are similar to those found in *Ciascuno a suo modo*.

Although he suggests to the audience the difficulties of ascertaining the truth about human beings, their acts, and motives, Casona by no means implies that the truth is nonexistent. His position seems to be similar to that of Cervantes. Behind Cervantes' perspectivism lies a unity, as Leo Spitzer has pointed out: the personality of the artist and in it a consciously presented analogue of the Mind of the Maker. Spitzer goes on to assert that "later thinkers and artists did not stop at proclaiming the inanity of the world: they went so far as to doubt the existence of any universal order and to deny a Creator. . . ." I would except Alejandro Casona from this group because, like Cervantes, he implies that he knows the truth with regard to his creatures, just as God knows that relative to His. Herein lies the greatest difference between Pirandello and Casona: the former is obviously an agnostic while the latter evidently believes in a personal God.

None of Casona's other plays comes close to *Las tres perfectas casadas* in utilization of situations or ideas that may be termed Pirandellist. Many of them do, however, contain a few such elements. *La sirena varada*, for example, has been compared to *Enrico IV* because of its "weird psychological types" [according to William H. Shoemaker, see excerpt above]. (p. 207)

It will be seen at once that the outcome of this play is exactly the opposite of that of *Enrico IV*. Reason triumphs here; Sirena refuses to go on with her role. Moreover, the Pirandellian theses are practically absent from the play. Indeed the thesis of this play is that reality is virtually inescapable except through suicide. Nevertheless, in some aspects the play does recall Pirandello. For instance, Casona admits that we may never know people fully. Yet, in opposition to Pirandello, he does insist that we can gradually apprehend a substantial amount of the truth concerning them. The process whereby this is accomplished is illustrated quite well by the play under discussion. During the first act we are presented characters who seem veritable symbols: Ricardo—the Rebel; Daniel—the Avant-garde Painter; etc. Yet as the action progresses we are surprised to find that behind these roles there are quite complex human beings.

The Ghost, one of the minor figures of *La sirena varada* finds himself in a situation similar to that of some of Pirandello's wretched creatures (e.g., Mattia Pascal, Enrico IV). He has tired of his assumed role, and, what is more, he is beginning to feel insecure about his true identity. . . . Yet once again Joaquín, unlike Pirandello's lost souls, does manage to reestablish his identity and to cultivate his garden.

Other plays make use of ideas that might be considered Pirandellian, but never with quite the same force that they have in the works of the Sicilian. The subtle changes that time effects in people and the irreversible nature of those changes is treated pessimistically in many of Pirandello's works (e.g., *Come tu mi vuoi; Come prima, meglio de prima*). His creatures are not only isolated from each other, but from themselves as they were at other times. Essentially the same theme is utilized by Casona in *La Dama del alba* and in *La barca sin pescador;* in both of these plays, however, the treatment of the theme is optimistic. In the first play Adela, the would-be suicide, has been accepted by Martín's in-laws to the point where she has replaced Angélica, his supposedly dead wife, in every way. In a delightful conversation with La Peregrina the change that the experience has wrought in her is made clear. . . . The idea that each hour has its own truth is again superficially Piran-dellian, yet the intent is obviously not the same. Rather it is once more a manifestation of that Cervantian perspectivism we have already detected in Casona's plays. The second play re-iterates the same notion. Ricardo Jordán, who has suffered a regeneration as a consequence of the love and warmth he has come to know in a tiny fishing village of Scandinavia, is able to tell the Devil that he will fulfill the pact he made by com-pleting the bloodless murder of his old self. . . . (pp. 208-09)

There is no doubt then that Casona is aware of the fact that no individual is monolithic, that he changes in keeping with the experiences which life brings. But far from looking upon this from a pessimistic point of view as does Pirandello, he is optimistic about it. For Pirandello, this multiplicity of possi-bilities inherent within an individual is tragic; it rules out the possibility of integration. The individual will never have the fixity and completeness of an artistic creation, and Pirandello is not willing to settle for less. Pirandello's solution to this problem is, as we have seen in the case of *Enrico IV*, to have his characters escape into illusions. . . . Here again we have a difference between the two playwrights. Although on occasion Casona has had one of his characters exalt art over life there is little doubt that he himself feels otherwise. He looks upon life as a duty and upon escapism of any sort as a dereliction of that duty.

Finally, it is worthy of note that Casona, unlike Pirandello, did not find concern with the precise mode of existence of his literary creatures either attractive or interesting. That he did not is even more significant when one considers that precedents were available in Spanish literature of his own day.

Preoccupation with the ontology of his literary creations derives ultimately from considerations on the part of the author anent that of his own person. The search of the characters for au-tonomy is but a reflection of the author's own search. Their confusion is his confusion; their revolt, his revolt. Thus in Unamuno's tragedy *El otro* one of the characters rebukes both him and the audience. . . . Now while the revolt of the char-acters is found in a sufficient number of modern play-wrights . . . Casona makes no use of it.

Certain conclusions seem to be justified on the basis of the foregoing discussion. First, while some critics have held that Casona belongs to the "New Theater" mainly because he evinces the influence of Luigi Pirandello, a close reading of his plays reveals that such influence is minimal. Second, it is obvious that while Casona has been immersed in the same emotional and intellectual currents as Pirandello, he has reacted quite differently to them. Third, the touchstone of any comparison between the two dramatists must be the problem of solipsism. Disillusioned with life, Pirandello accepted the three theses of Gorgias, and his only solution to the philosophical dilemma thus established is psychological. He resorts to illusion. Casona rejects both the Pirandellian theses and the Pirandellian solu-tion. He is indeed concerned with only one facet of the problem of solipsism and then only with its artistic exploitation. He is well aware of the difficulty of apprehending the truth about things and people, but he does assume the existence of such truth. He insists that, although it is impossible for humans to apprehend that truth in its entirety, they can nevertheless ap-proximate it. He is thus closer to Cervantes than to Pirandello. His "perspectivism" like that of Cervantes presupposes the existence of a personal God to whom alone is vouchsafed full vision and of whom the author is an analogue. Consequently, like Cervantes, he grants only a certain measure of autonomy

to his creatures; there are no anguished characters in search of an author in his plays. Again contrary to Pirandello's practice, Casona does not sanction illusion as an answer to the difficulties implicit in the pursuit of truth. He believes that life is a duty and regards all escapism as reprehensible.

Finally, there are differences of form. The spatial and kinetic patterns employed by the two playwrights are different. In the works of Pirandello the spatial pattern is "a center of suffering and a periphery of busybodies—the pattern of the Sicilian vil-lage." In those of Casona the usual pattern is a center of resistance to and a flight from reality (the bourgeois reality of materialism and scientism) and an opposing center of critical and subversive acceptance of that reality. The kinetic pattern utilized by Pirandello is "deception, outrage, and remedy by larger deceit." That employed by Casona is illusion, disillu-sion, and remedy by acceptance tempered by a modicum of subversive illusion. (pp. 210-12)

Charles H. Leighton, "Alejandro Casona's 'Piran-dellism'," in Symposium, *Vol. XVII, No. 3, Fall, 1963, pp. 202-14.*

CHARLES H. LEIGHTON

The Devil has always fascinated Casona. At least as early as 1926 he manifested great interest in Lucifer. That year as the topic for his thesis at the Escuela Superior del Magisterio he chose *El diablo en la literatura y en el arte*. Two years later he wrote *Otra vez el Diablo,* a play of diabolical intervention. Twice again he returned to the theme: in a play, *La barca sin pescador,* in 1945 and an article, **"Don Juan y el Diablo,"** in 1955. (p. 29)

The action of *Otra vez el Diablo* takes place in a fairy tale setting, an environment devoid of spatial or temporal precision. It is suggested vaguely that the country in question lies between Spain and Germany and that the time is the seventeenth century. The main figures are unmistakably symbolical: He [a student], She [a princess], and the Devil.

Casona's Devil is quite interesting yet quite orthodox. On the occasion of his first appearance he shocks the student by an assertion that like him he too is a Roman Catholic. In spite of the humor the statement is valid: it is a Roman Catholic Devil with which we have to do here—one which is theologically accurate. He is a rather pathetic creature trying to disprove the allegations of Catholic philosophers and theologians. . . . [At] another point he aggrandizes himself by insisting that all Chris-tians, even the saints, owe him a debt for without his efforts they would not have attained sainthood. . . .

It is arresting to note that Casona's Devil adduces in his own favor arguments almost exactly similar to those which Papini used to justify the Devil's existence in his extremely contro-versial *The Devil*. Casona, however, has had the wisdom to put such diabolical arguments where they belong—in the mouth of the Devil. (p. 31)

Satan in *Otra vez el Diablo* is a witty deceiver who blends truth and falsehood so cleverly that it is difficult to avoid being gulled by him. . . . The ending of the play suggests that the Devil is equivalent to Sin, and that he can be killed by a simple conscious effort on the part of each of us. This would seem to place Casona close to the position of the rationalists. Yet such an assumption does not appear to be justified by the treatment accorded the Devil in . . . *La barca sin pescador.*

In *La barca sin pescador* Ricardo Jordán, an unscrupulous young financier and apparently an American, finds himself on the verge of being ruined. The Devil appears at precisely the right moment and offers Ricardo the chance to recoup. All he need do is agree to will a death, that of a Scandinavian fisherman whom he does not even know. After some hesitation Ricardo agrees. The Devil permits him to hear the abrupt termination of his victim's joyful song as he plunges to his death from a cliff and the scream of a woman who has witnessed the event. Ricardo immediately begins to feel an unwonted emotion—remorse. For the first time in his life his blood begins to thaw. Despite the miraculous bouleversement on the stock market which restores his fortune he remains unhappy. Two years later and apparently after a prolonged search Ricardo finds Estela, the widow of his victim, Péter Ánderson. She is living with her aged grandmother trying to keep up the household all by herself. Ricardo spends two weeks with the two women and begins, quite literally, a new life. On the last day, just before his ship is to leave, Ricardo makes an effort to confess his crime but before he can do so Estela tells him that she saw the murder and recognized the murderer as her brother-in-law Cristián. Before Ricardo has a chance to say anything, Frida, Cristián's wife, bursts in with the news that her husband has been gravely wounded and wishes to see Estela. Estela leaves uneasily, feeling that she can never give Cristián the pardon he is apparently seeking. Once she is gone the Devil appears to Ricardo to remind him of his bargain. But Ricardo has realized that the Devil did not perform any miracle, that, indeed, all he did was to take advantage of events to provide the appearance of a miracle. When the Devil reminds him that in any case he has made a bargain, Ricardo argues that he has not succeeded in fulfilling his part; he has not willed the death of a man. Thereupon he confounds the Devil by stating that he will fulfill the contract by killing the old Ricardo Jordán, a process which he has already begun. The Deceiver, deceived, has no recourse but to concede defeat. Ricardo now is free to remain in the little village and pay court to Estela, whose love has made possible this regeneration.

Once again in this play Casona has created an intriguing, witty Devil. He appears dressed in a cutaway coat and carrying a briefcase looking every inch the successful denizen of Wall Street. Ricardo argues like a rationalist against the possibility of his appearance. . . . (pp. 32-3)

It will be seen at once that Casona again plays with some of the traditional ideas concerning the Devil. Satan here is well acquainted with the device so dear to Baroque dramatists of "engañar con la verdad." He admits jocosely that he has never been able to ruin souls without playing the role of night-hawk preacher. While this is quite true, it is a role forced upon him by those who would redeem him.

Once the pact is signed and the Devil departed, Ricardo tries to verify what he has witnessed. He calls his servant Juan and asks him to call back the visitor, but Juan has seen no one. Juan, looking for a rational explanation, assumes that his master has had an hallucination as a consequence of protracted insomnia and the effects of alcohol. But the relief is only momentary for Juan comes upon a black glove which the Devil has carelessly left behind. . . . Ricardo decides that the most prudent thing to do is to try to forget the whole matter, for any attempt to explain it to others will be met with misunderstanding and disbelief. . . . [The] Devil as a living figure does not exist for the majority of educated people. As an abstract idea of evil, yes; or as an illusion, perhaps; but certainly not in human form, and in a form so current. He is, as we have seen, accepted by "rational and free" minds as a myth, as a contrived figure used for literary purposes to express Evil, or as an unconscious projection of the evil inherent in each of us.

Why, then, does Casona present him in this fashion? Why does he have him leave the black glove as tangible evidence, a concrete artifact which cannot be explained away? Would it not have been to the author's advantage to leave the question of the mode of existence of the Devil open, in order to keep his audience pondering this ethical point? Certainly it would have given more philosophical depth to the drama. But no, Casona wants to leave no doubt in anyone's mind as to the reality of his Devil. The only conclusion to be drawn from this rejection of modern rational thought must be that, for Casona at least, the Devil is very much alive, and very much in evidence. Perhaps the author, ever the pedagogue, is trying to point out this fact to his audiences, to rouse them from their lethargic attitude toward evil. . . . Baudelaire believed that the Devil desires to have people believe he doesn't exist because it makes it easier for him to achieve his purposes. It may be that in his lifetime Casona has seen ample proof of the Devil's working thus in and through unbelieving people and that he wishes to convince such skeptics of the Devil's reality in this world by the only evidence they will accept—tangible evidence. In this play, then, Casona regards the Devil as really existing, as multiform, clever, and witty. He also regards him as pathetic. (p. 34)

Charles H. Leighton, "Alejandro Casona and the Devil," in Hispania, Vol. XLVIII, No. 1, March, 1965, pp. 29-36.

MICHAEL BENEDIKT

The work of Casona is shot through with a gentle, wistful feeling for the improbable and the imaginative; however, it is a feeling which is also characterized by a particularly calculated and deliberate relation to reality. *Suicide Prohibited in Springtime* was written in 1936-37, just before Casona's self-imposed exile in Argentina (where he lived until just before his death), yet it sets forth in no uncertain terms and with delightful wit and fancifulness the concerns which were to occupy him throughout his later life. (p. 240)

The play is the story of a Utopia of sorts, a home for suicides founded by a pupil of a certain mysterious Doctor Ariel, the figure who is also the absent patron saint of several other Casona plays. It is the apparent intention of Doctor Ariel's pupil that this establishment should encourage suicides by facilitating them. Every convenience for the pleasurable consummation of self-immolations is provided: a Gallery of Silence, Werther Gardens, perfumed gasses, poisoned flowers, and a whole series of places and devices apparently designed to make suicide irresistible. Actually, the purpose of all this is, by showing would-be victims the most alluring things they might think of, reconciliation with life. The Utopia is actually a kind of laboratory for the study of the relationship of the fantastic to reality. It is by learning to love something in life, even something odd, at the very end of life, that patients grow stronger, more willing to confront their difficulties. The outlandish and charming case histories presented during the play all seem to be on the road to survival at its close. Not all their lessons are based—as in the case of the Imaginary Lover who meets his great love in the flesh and is thereby cured—on the confrontation of reality; there is also a journalist, who understands that the factual side of life is only one side of it, and that fantasies, too, have their place. All these conversions relate not only to Surrealist championing of the real role of the imagination, and to Surrealism's official interest in the theories of Dr. Freud-Ariel, but also to the cultivation of connections between the ideal and the real which occurs throughout Spanish literature from its beginnings. Although Casona teaches a lesson of wisdom, the instruction is not grim, being as light and crystalline as that given in the tragicomedies of the seventeenth century. (pp. 240-41)

> *Michael Benedikt, in an introduction to "Suicide Prohibited in Springtime," in* Modern Spanish Theatre: An Anthology of Plays, *edited by Michael Benedikt and George E. Wellwarth, E. P. Dutton & Co., Inc., 1968, pp. 240-41.*

JOHN A. MOORE

It is my intention to consider how Casona, while using death as a theme, achieves great characterization and fine dramatic scenes, and exhibits a care in the management of the details of putting his stories on the stage. For a great characterization one should certainly turn to *La dama del alba*. Death seems to have entered the door of an Asturian family as Angélica, the oldest daughter, was apparently a suicide victim three days after her wedding. She is presumed to have drowned, but the river has not given up her body. Her mother tries to suspend her own life and that of her family, until the body can be found for burial. She is disturbed that the girl's grandfather and her widower, Martín, are involved in normal pursuits on the fourth anniversary of the young girl's disappearance. It is on this day that Martín rescues Adela, a girl about Angélica's age, who has tried to drown herself. She is taken into the family and gradually seems to take Angélica's place.

The great characterization is that of Peregrina, who is "la dama del alba.". . . Peregrina enters the home with the literal role of a tired pilgrim and the allegorical role of Death. She plays with the younger children and falls asleep. The Grandfather senses that she is Death and is worried about the children, but Peregrina's mission had been to take Martín, and her nap saved his life.

As Death personified and allegorized, Peregrina must instill awe in the audience but an awe that is dignified and ultimately soothing. She elicits sympathy from the audience. She is old and tired; she has emotions but she is not supposed to act according to her own whims, and perhaps most important, as Death, she cannot find relief by dying. None of this must take away any sense of her power. Casona accomplishes this, partly by having the Grandfather be the only one who recognizes her as Death. The rest is the task of the actress.

Peregrina's unobtrusive power is shown in a scene featuring Martín and Adela, who are unaware of her presence, although Martín feels a strange compulsion. He professes his love for Adela and confesses that he alone in the town knows that his wife Angélica is still alive. She had run off with another man. Peregrina has a dual role here. The audience realizes that she, more by woman's intuition than by Death's omniscience, perceives the state of Martín's soul and the situation that could have caused it. Secondly, Martín is being pushed into his confession by a kind of mental telepathy.

The crowning use of Peregrina's power and one of the subtlest touches of Casona comes when Peregrina persuades Angélica to kill herself. Angélica, having repented of her way of life, was returning home, unaware that she was considered dead and that her family thought that she was still pure and innocent. If she killed herself she could preserve that reputation and in some measure earn it. Casona's skill in this use of Peregrina's power will, for most spectators, completely overcome the effect of the terrible act. (pp. 51-2)

Excellent characterization and the dramatic effect of a fine ending are combined in *Los árboles mueren de pie*. Here again death plays a central role. The character in this case is the Grandmother. She is in the background throughout most of the play. The main characters in the first part are: "The Director" a man who makes a profession of providing illusions for those who need them for therapy; Marta, a girl whom he rescues from possible suicide; and the Grandfather, who has been providing illusions for the Grandmother concerning the rehabilitation of their delinquent grandson, Mauricio. Instead of achieving rehabilitation, Mauricio has descended from a delinquent to a hardened criminal.

The Grandfather persuades the Director to play the role of the grandson, with Marta to play that of his imagined wife, Isabel, to give Grandmother the illusion that her grandson is an attractive and socially acceptable person. When the real grandson, thought dead, appears, the Grandfather tries vainly to keep him away from Grandmother, thinking that this revelation will kill her.

Actually, it does, but it is a surprising, triumphant death and a great dramatic ploy. Just as dead trees remain standing, showing their enduring strength, Grandmother announces that she is still standing although this blow has killed her, and it has shown her where her real strength lies; she has overcome her need for illusion. The false Mauricio is the true friend. The reality of what he and Grandfather have done for her makes her see that her own life has been worthwhile and allows her to die as Casona wants everyone to die—standing firmly upon faith in the value of human life. The play's message comes through, loud and clear, but for the real dramatist, the special consideration is not the message but the impact of the action upon the audience. People with great ideas who can't achieve this impact should write novels.

Corona de amor y muerte likewise concentrates upon a dramatic ending in which death is the center of attention. Casona could not achieve here the originality of *Los árboles mueren de pie* since he was using a theme which many predecessors had used. The Inés de Castro tragedy comes from the conflict between the King of Portugal and his son Pedro, the Crown Prince. The King, for political reasons, wants Pedro to marry Constanza, Princess of Castile. Pedro has loved Inés de Castro and has had children by her. This love has transcended all parental and political opposition. In fact Casona has a strong suggestion that it is the very opposition which has welded a love which otherwise might not have been so constant. The King feels that he has no choice but to have Inés killed. In Casona's final scene, Inés appears to Pedro shortly after her death, presenting Casona's philosophical speculations about death in a memorable manner. Death guarantees that the love of Pedro and Inés will never be threatened by time, force, or the withdrawal of force. Living lovers are apt to quarrel and part; dead lovers are eternally joined.

Great characterizations and great scenes are certainly vital to a successful dramatist. One other claim can be made for Casona's superiority in dramatic construction—his loving care with detail, perhaps a legacy of his pedagogical background. In *Prohibido suicidarse en primavera* the idea of the play is to rehabilitate those who have contemplated suicide as an escape from their troubled or empty lives. Dr. Roda starts a *Sanatorio de almas,* inviting those who wish to commit suicide to do so where they can be taught the proper techniques and can perform the job in comfortable surroundings. His invitation is based upon two premises. The first is that those who are ready for suicide will do so without benefit of his counsel. Second, those who do come to him are people with unhappy life experiences, usually being unloved, but who lack the decisiveness to kill themselves.

These people come to him thinking that they are learning how to die, and indeed they are offered the various means: poisons, high places, weapons, but they are introduced to comfortable surroundings, beautiful landscapes, a lake, flowers, music. The heroism of the suicidal gesture is thus removed and they hesitate. . . . They are soon weeping. A meditation interval follows, next a desire for reading and for company. With this mental health therapy and a few fortunate circumstances, they end by being able to accept themselves as they are and to deal with their problems directly. Death is not the problem, only a symptom of it. Their goal is reconciliation with reality whether they know it or not. Learning that death is not unkind is a step on this path.

Casona's carefulness here is not simply with the staging; it is a detailed study of the psychological sequences in the suicide therapy. Starting with good clinical techniques, he can then concentrate upon his staging problems. One such problem is to simplify; his audience came to be entertained, not instructed. But Casona, as a good teacher, is always concerned about the twin problems of knowing the subject matter and knowing how to transmit it. In this instance he cannot strive for memorable characterizations. He must concentrate upon making sure that the audience is with him as the characters—all minor ones—advance from stage to stage in his therapeutic program. The audience wishes to feel that the cures are plausible and effective. Then, little features can be very meaningful. Hans, the Doctor's assistant, made German for naïveté, remarks early in the play that Dr. Roda is very unsuccessful in persuading the people to commit suicide. He serves mainly to reassure the audience that Dr. Roda does not really encourage suicide, but the characterization is interesting in itself.

Casona's stage effectiveness is not based upon clever tricks or even upon vivid imagination so much as it is upon his broad study of history and literature, his sympathetic understanding of human nature, and his careful attention to the relationship between the stories and ideas and their adaptation to the stage.

One final question is, why does Casona use death as a theme so often? He was preoccupied with death; so was Unamuno and the contrast is startling. Unamuno's great brain could not cope with the concept of death. He longed to understand immortality rationally. Casona approaches the subject so calmly that he leaves the impression that he has death on a leash and can exercise control over it since he has come to an understanding with it. As he presents the allegorical Peregrina, a philosophical acceptance of the invitable, the psychology of violent death, and the Christian sense of triumph over death,

he seems to have mastered death mentally and can persuade his audience that they can learn from him how to master it also. (pp. 53-5)

John A. Moore, "Death as a Theme in Casona's Plays," in South Atlantic Bulletin, Vol. XXXIX, No. 2, May, 1974, pp. 51-5.

EUGENE A. MAIO

No critic of Casona's drama fails to underscore the presence and function of *el trasmundo* (a meta-reality) that mingles with and becomes part of the world of sensible, experienced reality. Critics point out the dramatic interest created by the conflictive interaction between *el mundo* and *el trasmundo* [see, for example, essays by A. Wallace Woolsey and Kessel Schwartz excerpted above]. The narration of the history-fiction, precisely at the crisis in *La dama del alba,* is a strikingly creative attempt by Casona, through myth, to resolve the apparently irreconcilable experiences of fact and fiction, mortality and immortality, *mundo* and *trasmundo*.

The reality, *el mundo* of this drama, contains the episodes in the life of a peasant family in Asturias: the disappearance and apparent death four years before of a daughter, Angélica, the wife of Martín; the adoption of a stranger, Adela, who fills the void left by Angélica in the family and in the life of Martín; and the magico-religious festival of St. John the Baptist. The meta-reality, *el trasmundo,* contains the visit to the family of La Peregrina, Casona's original and paradoxical creation of death incarnate in the form of a beautiful young woman; the resultant intermingling at the narrative level of fantasy and fact, life and death; and finally the salvation of Angélica by La Peregrina who leads Angélica to a death that becomes a living legend of beauty and innocence.

What gives dramatic as well as mythic unity to an apparently chaotic action that takes place on different levels of reality, in disjointed time periods, in a narration that alternates between dream and reality, among characters that are historical and preternatural, is a cosmic agent, water, the archetype of purification, regeneration and return to origins that functions in this drama as the miraculous threshold that gives simultaneous entrance to the separate realities of reality and meta-reality, of life and death.

The narrative reveals that Angélica disappeared one night near the river and the people thought she had drowned. Actually she crossed the river in a boat and met her lover who was waiting on the opposite bank and the two of them fled away in the night. Angélica has been gone four years and returns to her home on the eve of St. John, repentant, remorseful and hopeful of regaining her husband, her family and her former happy life. (pp. 132-33)

According to the *historia-cuento* of La Peregrina, Angélica will return to her family and her absence will seem no longer than an instant. For La Peregrina will lead Angélica back to the water where she will be found by her family. La Peregrina does not call this experience death. La Peregrina simply offers to lead Angélica to the land of final pardon.

La Peregrina relates "la historia que parece cuento" in this abridged manner: Once upon a time near a small town ran a river at the bottom of which there lay a submerged village. One day a young girl disappeared in the river. She had gone to live in the submerged village. It was useless for the village to shout at her from above. She was asleep, in a misty dream.

Time passed, everyone forgot her. Only her mother kept on hoping. Finally a miracle. During an evening festival of bonfires and singing, the sleeping beauty of the river was found, her hair still lustrous, her hands warm, and on her lips a smile of peace, as if the years at the river depths had lasted only an instant.

This *historia-cuento* of La Peregrina is an example of mythopoesis, a technical term for imagination at work, the experience of creating fiction, or the myth-making process. As a mental process, mythopoesis stands midway between the strictly cognitive and the vaguely intuitive; and it is out of that limbo between rational intelligence and the unconscious that fictions are generated. La Peregrina's narration is at this point a *mythos* or *cuento,* for it is a vaguely intuitive account of what will eventually happen to Angélica. This same narration will transform itself into a *logos* or *historia* when Angélica at the climax of the drama is found at the river.

Mythopoesis is a form of insight, instruction, or understanding. It works its first effect upon La Peregrina herself. The articulation of this "historia que parece cuento" brings to La Peregrina an understanding of what her function is at this moment of the drama. The *historia-cuento* becomes the crisis within the play's structure. La Peregrina now knows that she has come to this house in the Asturian countryside to bring death to Angélica. (pp. 133-34)

For the children who listen to the *historia-cuento,* the narration assumes the form of a prophecy. Beneath dream, symbol and imagery the climax of the drama is detailed. Although the full meaning of the legend is lost on the children's ingenuous minds, the reader now shares the understanding of La Peregrina concerning the resolution of the dramatic conflict.

Water now will work its archetypal miracle and cleanse Angélica of her foolish infidelity, regenerate her and return her to her family physically dead but alive in a loving and cherished memory. Water assumes the most important symbolic and dramatic role because it makes clear an archetypal pattern of destruction and regeneration, periodic disappearance and reappearance, the myth of the eternal return. As part of our knowledge of archetypes we know that water symbolizes the whole of the potentiality, the source of all possible existence. Immersion symbolizes a return to the pre-formal, a total regeneration, a new birth, because immersion means a dissolution of forms, a reintegration into the formlessness of pre-existence.

The second disappearance of Angélica enters sacred time through mythical gestures and archetypes. Angélica's first trip to the river occurred in profane time, because it was irreversible and devoid of any religious significance. The second trip to the river is sacred and mythical. The essential difference lies in Angélica's ability to perceive a sacred or numinous power in natural events. (p. 135)

Regeneration necessarily occurs in sacred rather than profane time, because rebirth is bound up with a belief in another myth, the ability to attain to an absolute beginning. Angélica's death, looked at now not as *logos* but as *mythos,* is an archetypal ritual of water immersion that generates several levels of meaning and significance. The water-ritual is an initiation for it confers upon Angélica a new birth. . . . The water-ritual is also a healing process that expels from Angélica's life any taint of infidelity. . . . Finally the water-ritual is a passage through death to eternal life. (pp. 135-36)

Angélica's moment of salvation takes place in sacred time for still another reason—it repeats an indispensable part of the mythic return to the past. In mythical regeneration or return to primordial events, chaos must precede creation. A new creature can be built only upon the ruins of the old. The four years of Angélica's historical abandonment of her home and husband constitute to some extent an archetypal "chaos." (p. 136)

The "chaos-new creation" *mythos* of Angélica is represented in the drama by the ritual and symbolism that enliven the Asturian festival of St. John the Baptist. The people build enormous bonfires, an archetype that symbolizes the destruction of old forms, the purification necessary for the implantation of new forms under the numinous power of the Baptist. To religious people the creation of chaos marks the return to absolute beginnings. In the drama of Angélica, her four years of chaotic wandering . . . culminates in the final moment of chaos when she is immersed in the river. Immersion is the final, absolute abolition of the old self that gives way to the emersion of a new self—innocent, pure, primordial. To consider Angélica's ritual death as both sacred and mythical is to characterize it as a hierophany because it opens on to sacred time and becomes capable of revealing the absolute.

Angélica returns to absolute beginnings through the magical powers of water because the myth of the eternal return is intimately bound up with the cosmos. Human life is seen as moving synchronously with the cycles of the cosmos. The rhythm and cyclic patterns in the cosmos reveal to the religious person the presence of the numinous, a belief that goes back at least to the ancient Greek Eleusinian Mystery cult and its worship of the goddess Demeter.

Angélica's death and resurrection is a cosmogony: a transition from chaos to creation. Casona's drama repeats what is common to primitive mythologies, that death is never an irreversible destruction. Death is always the condition *sine qua non* of a transition to another mode of being. Immersion in water, symbolic of a return to the womb, has a cosmological significance. The universe itself symbolically returns with Angélica into cosmic darkness in order to be created anew. For both the cosmos and Angélica, it is necessary to abolish the work of Time, and to re-enter the instant prior to Creation. As a cosmogony, Angélica's death takes on a far wider significance. Death is not a cessation but a rite of passage, the supreme initiation, the beginning of a new spiritual existence.

The sequence of the four Acts in **La dama del alba** correspond to a cosmic rhythm. Acts I and II occur in the winter, a time of psychological withering and death for the characters. The mother grieves over the loss of Angélica; the grandfather sees the presence of La Peregrina as a threat to the family; Telva and the grandfather recall many local scenes of death over which La Peregrina has presided. Acts III and IV occur in summer, a time of love, rejuvenation, and salvation. The mother throws off her wintry isolation and rejoins the ongoing life of the village; Adela and Martín fall in love. The townspeople inundate the village with the sights and sounds of a religious festival; La Peregrina brings salvation to Angélica.

The most dramatic experience of the mythic continuity between the cosmos and human nature is the salvation of Angélica. Both in Act III by way of a prophecy to the children in the *historia-cuento,* and in Act IV at the climax of the play, Angélica finds salvation through an intimate union with the cosmos.

In terms of both the structure and the meaning of Casona's myth, La Peregrina is the indispensable point of convergence between *el mundo* and *el trasmundo*, reality and meta-reality. She herself is a form of *historia-cuento*. (pp. 136-37)

Human experience is at one sacred and profane, *historia* and *cuento*, reality and meta-reality. This is Casona's insight and while not entirely original it does allow him to construct through mythopoesis a drama like **La dama del alba** in which the par-adoxical experiences of reality and meta-reality constantly in-tersect. (p. 138)

Eugene A. Maio, ''Mythopoesis in Casona's 'La Dama del Alba','' in Romance Notes, *Vol. XXII, No. 2, Winter, 1981, pp. 132-38.*

Alfred Chester

1929?-1971

American novelist, short story writer, and essayist.

In his fiction, Chester celebrated the advantages of alternative lifestyles while denouncing values of conventional society. His writings, which are characterized by dark humor, eccentric characters, and surreal and fragmented narratives, typically focus on such thematic concerns as homosexuality, the power of emotion, the banality of reason, and the dominance of dream and fantasy over reality. Subversive and uninhibited, often containing explicit descriptions of sexual adventures, Chester's fiction has been compared to the works of Jean Genet and Louis-Ferdinand Céline but is distinguished by its combination of innocence and depravity which is central to his aesthetic sensibility. Theodore Solotaroff observed: "[Chester] is able to write about perversion from a fresh and complicated perspective that gives all proper and enthusiastic dues to the joys of the instinctual life, however a man chooses and needs to experience it, while at the same time remaining very precisely aware of the twists and turns and torments of its fantasies."

An expatriate writer who spent much time within the creative community of Tangier, Morocco, during the 1950s and 1960s, Chester contributed essays and fiction to the *New York Tribune,* the *New Yorker,* and the *American Review,* among other publications. His first book, *Jamie Is My Heart's Desire* (1957), is a seriocomic psychological novel focusing on the relationships that develop between the central characters and a human corpse that may or may not exist. Occurring within a bizarre, supernatural setting, this novel dramatizes humanity's inability to accept and confront life's complexities. The stories contained in Chester's second book, *Behold Goliath* (1964), explore such topics as the dynamics of sexual relationships, the struggle against authority and repression, and the horrors of social and sexual alienation. Although these pieces vary in subject matter, setting, tone, and style, Saul Maloff noted: "What gives Chester's collection such unity as it has is the motif, recurrent almost to the point of obsession, of homosexuality—the sodomist's frantic, unceasing quest through the great cities for the love that is . . . the hideous, loveless world's last hope for meaning and value."

Chester's final work, *The Exquisite Corpse* (1967), is a fragmented, symbolic novel featuring characters who freely change names and merge identities throughout a series of vignettes. Indebted to the surrealist parlor game in which players pass a folded piece of paper and create a composite picture or sentence without knowledge of the preceding players' contributions, this work has been interpreted as an exploration into the suffering of a single protagonist who is the embodiment of all the characters in the book. Michael Feingold stated: "*The Exquisite Corpse* is a game of 'let's pretend' played with genitalia and God, birth and death, blood and shit, parents and lovers as its stakes, a game that broadens and burgeons till it opens out in every direction, an imaginary toad with an infinity of real gardens in it."

(See also *Contemporary Authors,* Vols. 33-36, rev. ed. [obituary].)

MARY SHIRAS

In [*Jamie Is My Heart's Desire*], an undertaker named Harry Sutton who has been pretty much a spectator of both the living and the dead is suddenly knocked off his noncommittal balance when he is unable to see a corpse named Jamie that is really there. The visual failure shocks him into a psychical trial from which he emerges, chastened, dazed, and loving. In his most troubled moments he asserts, "I wanted to live my life in, to accept confusion if it meant that, to see Jamie, to love Tess." His counterpart, Mark the poet, shy, but vibrant with creative powers, feels the intensity of life through loving Jamie.

But just as Jamie empowers Harry to accept confusion and to love Tess, he also kills Mark's love, leaving him wretched and helpless. While Harry is resolving to live his life *in,* Mark says quietly and grimly, "I know what I'll do. I'll let it [life] live itself out." Emily, a social worker who moves somewhere between Mark and Harry is continually being distracted from life until Jamie makes her see that her work has been the one activity in her life that has brought out her strength and her love.

All three, Harry, Mark, and Emily, as they are portrayed until about halfway through, are quite credible; after their reappraisals they are disappointing. With Harry, for example, we are asked to believe that after a week of severe myopia and insomnia, this skeptical undertaker who regards all sentiment as human fabrication has transformed himself into a warm and sympathetic human being—an altogether charming and amiable person like ourselves. Furthermore, even granting the rejuvenated Harry, he is not nearly so interesting as his old plain and sarcastic self.

The difficulties in the novel result in part from a rather weak grasp of characterization: Mr. Chester hinders himself at the outset from producing full-bodied results by creating people who are too limited to see their own depths. What underlies this fault in characterization seems to be an awkward adjustment of serious and comic values. Comedy is Mr. Chester's real strength—the comedy of ironic, sidewise humor that thrives on understatement, wisecracks, and offbeat wit. Consider the absurdities and incongruities of some of the novel's themes: the hero is an undertaker; his antagonist, a corpse; the corpse throws everyone into a tailspin without batting an eyelash; the poet turns prosaic while the prosaic undertaker turns poet; the poet trembles with the conviction of a prophet and then crawls in humiliation to a pastry shop where he serves as a baker's boy—and collects his parents' life insurance to make ends meet; a gin-loving priest named Tulley has a dark passion for spiritualism and ouija boards; the social worker—like so many of course—is ill-at-ease in her closest friendships. Character is burlesqued for taking things seriously; yet in the conclusion of the novel we are meant to feel, as Harry does, that some things really matter, that to love someone, for example, is valuable and important. But Mr. Chester is not stalwart enough to follow through his own provocative ideas, so that the hero who comes out of his complacency into love, confusion, and other perils does not convince us that there ever was much of a heart's desire to begin with. (pp. 212-13)

Mary Shiras, "The Heart's Pain," in Commonweal, *Vol. LXVII, No. 8, November 22, 1957, pp. 212-13.*

MARTHA BACON

Jamie Is My Heart's Desire is a book which on its surface makes very little sense (or what we usually construe to be sense) but very good reading. Mr. Chester, an American writer who lives in Paris, seems well acquainted with the works of James Joyce and Samuel Beckett. Indeed, like *Waiting for Godot,* this book about Jamie defies attempts at summarization. However, we may go so far as to say that the novel opens in a funeral parlor in New York and Harry Sutton, who assists the manager of this establishment in his mournful duties, is the narrator. Harry has a great deal to narrate. He has a large circle of friends, among them Emily, a social worker who is good at her job and hates it; Wallace, a rather dim and semi-employed young man, intermittently beloved of Emily. There is Tess, who is simple and healthy and lovely and wonderful with men. There is Father Tulley, a priest of dubious emotional commitments. There is Kitty, an orange cat of the female sex, and there is Mark Akero, a young man. Depending on how you look at it, there is Jamie, but Jamie is dying and eventually dead—that is, if you can see him. Those who can see him say that he is beautiful. His very existence, even as a stinking near-corpse (he emits a very bad smell) seems to constellate Emily and Tulley, to make Wallace valid and Mark Akero, who claims to be Jamie's brother, something more than a wraith.

The beautiful corpse merely moves the dark-haired, loving Tess to pity and reverence, because Tess always feels emotions appropriate to the occasion. At this point there is a hitch in the proceedings of the story because Harry cannot see Jamie. Indeed, there seems to be some evidence that there is no corpse—no Jamie. Is there a solution to this problem? This is something which each reader must decide for himself. In my opinion, there is none. The author proposes an answer, but it is cryptic as the Mayan code. . . .

To take the spirit world for the subject and ambience of a novel is rushing in where angels fear to tread, and Mr. Chester arms himself with a wiry and saving humor which allows him to emerge at the end relatively unscathed by his dip into Acheron. For this book is funny, funny in the grain rather than in event or phrase. The anti-rhetorical contemporary idiom is wonderfully incongruous in its relationship to the burial ceremony and the séance, here referred to euphemistically as "a sitting."

And what of miserable humanity, priests, social workers and old neighbor women, mourning the death of a selfish and beautiful member of society—assuming the creature ever lived outside of their heads? Perhaps we are left with a conclusion arrived at a hundred-odd years ago; the one that made Lewis Carroll's Alice cry.

Martha Bacon, "What Goes On? The Answer's Up to You," in New York Herald Tribune Book Review, *December 22, 1957, p. 4.*

SAUL MALOFF

Alfred Chester's first collection of stories, **Behold Goliath,** follows the publication of his first novel, **Jamie Is My Heart's Desire,** by six years. It represents a garnering of nearly a decade, and it is most uneven, varying strikingly—sometimes dismayingly—from story to story both in quality of writing and in imaginative control.

What gives Chester's collection such unity as it has is the motif, recurrent almost to the point of obsession, of homosexuality—the sodomist's frantic, unceasing quest through the great cities for the love that is (for him, artistic and narcissistic as he is again and again portrayed to be) the hideous, loveless world's last hope for meaning and value. And there is a unity, also, of tone and style: a rhapsodic, ornate, excessive, cadenced prose placed at the service of (indeed, threatening to overpower) tales which are closer in conception to fable than to story as that latter term is usually understood—fables that transact freely with dream and nightmare, by intention putting at issue the world which is the common ground of fiction.

This opposition asserts itself so repeatedly as to become, in these stories, a world view: on the one hand, the square, frigid, 9-to-5 world; and on the other, the passionate, intensely deviate world of the queer bars and the *pissotières*. Indeed, one of the stories (**"In Praise of Vespasian"**) amounts virtually to a homosexual Baedeker of public conveniences, as the hero, a tireless martyr to love, cruises the "urinary stations of the cross" on at least two continents. The story is not unrepresentative; and it is, not always intentionally, hilarious.

On the whole, the author's prose is full of unrealized possibilities and faltering resolutions, lacking in that sufficiency of imaginative and dramatic power that alone could render a treacherously difficult theme. Some of the pieces are more fragments than stories; even some of the longer pieces are episodes failing of wholeness, whatever their length. Finally, one feels, they are blocked by their very means from achieving their ends—by a style that exerts a counterforce to the narrative movement, stopping it dead, holding it in a death grip while we are asked to admire the dazzling thing that is being dangled before us.

At its worst, the writing is compulsively self-indulgent, mannered, posturing, merely fancy; and even at its most effective, the narrative—the story, the fiction itself—cannot quite break loose and move to its destined end. Chester's resources, again and again, exceed his achievements.

Distressingly often, this collection seems a means for the display, certainly not of life, and not even of art and craft, but of personality—the author's. And that is not (it must be insisted again after all these years) what we seek in the art of narrative. We come to the short story as a literary form for what it is supremely fashioned to achieve—that elegant, bloodletting incision, saving or killing, which it can make in actual flesh.

Saul Maloff, "A Loveless World's Last Hope for Meaning," in The New York Times Book Review, *April 19, 1964, p. 38.*

THEODORE SOLOTAROFF

[*The essay from which this excerpt is taken was originally published in the* Sunday Herald Tribune Book Week, *June 7, 1964.*]

Behold Goliath is mainly about the skin and about those out-of-the-way and not very sanitary places and lives where the kingdom of its desires still reigns. **"Cradle Song"** tells of a girl who is so smitten by the skin of her lover that she murders their newborn infant in order not to lose it. **"As I Was Going Up the Stairs"** is a fantasy of a boy's struggle with social authority and repression to avoid being turned into another sensible middle-class ghost, and of the illumination he receives from a pregnant gypsy, a demented angel of the carnal underworld. [**"Behold Goliath"**] presents a series of vignettes on the alienations and resources of a female impersonator, while **"From the Phoenix to the Unnamable, Impossibly Beautiful Wild Bird," "In Praise of Vespasian,"** and **"Ismael"** are studies in the *Realpolitik* of sexual relationships and, in the latter two cases, fairly explicit accounts of the adventures of the skin that lurk in the doorways along Greenwich Avenue or in the *pissotières* of Paris.

What makes Chester an interesting writer in these matters is that he often has the radical honesty that both children and deviant adults may possess. He is himself a very curious combination of innocence and depravity—a sort of cross between the Baron de Charlus and Huckleberry Finn, however odd that may seem. Thus he is able to write about perversion from a fresh and complicated perspective that gives all proper and enthusiastic due to the joys of the instinctual life, however a man chooses and needs to experience it, while at the same time remaining very precisely aware of the twists and turns and torments of its fantasies. . . . (p. 162)

Yet Chester's stories, on the whole, are less daring than their subject matter and his attitude toward it would promise. His celebration of his own forms of ecstasy as well as his snide dismissal of the huffing and puffing routines of the straight world will seem grossly offensive to the mass of readers who have still moved up to only Grace Metalious. His more sophisticated readers, however, are likely to find that alongside of, say, Céline and Genet, Chester himself seems tame and rather vague and rhetorical in his imagination of deviancy and

in his revulsion from the ghostly squares. Indeed, in several of the other stories—of a dying girl who comes alive through sex, of a loveless marriage that has reached its moment of truth, of a fantastic but lovable Polish piano teacher—Chester seems to be writing with his coat and tie on, as if to show that he, too, can produce a presentable story.

The main problem of the other stories, I suspect, is that Chester has still not entirely liberated his perspective from the defensiveness that he feels in making use of it. The free flow of his sensibility circles around a certain inhibition of aim and requires a forcing of attitude to move it along. Thus, he tends to be a spokesman—indeed, at times an apologist—for the sexual underground he inhabits, so that there is an undue amount of explaining and arguing and position-taking, and too little inventing and representing. And though the world he describes and the levels of consciousness and tone at which he approaches it are richly imaginative, the point to which the reader is finally brought is usually the same. One feels that he is being told the same thing over and over again: that feeling—whatever pain and selfishness and perverseness it breeds—is all that matters in life, that conventional society—and its psychic surrogate, reason—deaden it and thereby turn us into phantoms.

I admire the courage of Chester's efforts to naturalize homosexuality, to give it its legitimate place in the sum of human nature's possibilities for joy and tenderness as well as morbidity and cruelty, particularly so after reading a book like *City of Night*, which is undermined by its author's hypocrisy about the nature of his feelings. Still, when Chester comes to write, say, of one of his "Unknown Soldiers" of love, so much of it is covered over with literary decorations and editorializing that one wishes he would be daring enough to do what he is always telling the world to do: let his characters be.

In **"From the Phoenix"** one does begin to see the possibilities of Chester's fiction when he liberates himself from his defensiveness and allows experience and imagination to make his point. The story involves a triangle, the apex of which is a young Greenwich Village roustabout and poet whose wife has just left him and who turns to his former lover for consolation. In the course of re-enacting both relationships—mainly through the dialogue of the two men—Chester takes entirely for granted their equally normal-abnormal character and discloses their common basis in the illusions of vanity and dependency. Male to his wife and female to his lover, Mario takes on genuine and moving significance as a walking, lusting, suffering example of sexual ambivalence.

All of this Chester understands very well: particularly the inexorable logic by which the passions are subverted by the fantasies they breed. Homosexual passion is, no doubt, the genuinely tragic ground of this logic, since it is apparently so unmitigated by the other sources of human connection. However, in order to explore this theme, Chester will have to be really audacious: he will have to give up the easy out of rebuking our problems of feeling and begin to accept and dramatize his own. (pp. 163-64)

Theodore Solotaroff, "Alfred Chester: Daring and Doing," in his The Red Hot Vacuum and Other Pieces on Writing in the Sixties, *Atheneum Publishers, 1970, pp. 161-64.*

JOHN SIMON

The stories in **Behold Goliath** fall chiefly into two categories: the weird, heterosexual, and unconvincing ones; and the sordid, homosexual, and convincing ones. There are two exceptions: **"As I Was Going Up the Stair,"** which is not homosexual but convincing and excellent; and **"In Praise of Vespasian,"** which is homosexual but unconvincing and dreadful.

In the first category, we find stories like **"Rapunzel, Rapunzel,"** in which a deranged, beautiful, dying young millionairess falls wildly in love with a repellent clairvoyant, who, however, is interested only in midnight window-shopping for sexual scenes to which he can masturbate. For her clairvoyeur's sake, she gives herself with clockwork regularity to a preposterous little Oriental whom she loathes, with the knowledge that her truelove is watching and the conviction that it is he who is possessing her. In **"Beds and Boards,"** a young couple about to separate for six months or, just possibly, forever, spend their last night—improbably—smashing and burning their furniture.

In the second category, there are stories like **"From the Phoenix to the Unnamable, Impossibly Beautiful Wild Bird"** or **"Ismael,"** which tell in different keys the same tale of mutual torture in homosexual ménages, and the illusory happiness to be snatched from a male pick-up, which, with the passage of time, proves equally bitter and impossible.

This is the theme of Mr. Chester's stories—what Jean Prévost made the subtitle of one of his novels—*l'impossibilité d'aimer*. "In this world it is dangerous to love," we read in one story. Another ends with, "perhaps love is only the moment before separation." Elsewhere: "in the equation of romance no plus can exist except by virtue of a minus"; and, again, we are "destined never to profoundly have whom we love nor to profoundly love whom we have." But the reason for this split is made hardly more clear than the reason for the split infinitives.

Probably this is where Chester's main difficulty lies: though he can evoke the How magisterially, he is not very good at the Why. One may be convinced by his style, but not by his motivation. At its best, the style produces images like "my pride . . . would not even allow me to admit that it has been wounded. My pride has pride." Or this, from a homosexual married to a narcissistic woman: "With her teeth in my throat and my teeth in hers, how could we avoid one flow of blood?" And there are passages of sustained horror, comic or cosmic, which give off a sinisterly dazzling light: not enough to illuminate, but enough to take one's breath away. There is the city which "offered its populace more than merely every-evening freedom; it offered a variety of slaveries to which the freedom might be put," the slaveries culminating in a vision of "the rectangular darkness of the national church with its two-dimensional gods in technicolor." Or, more transcendentally: "Then suddenly I felt something. I felt celestial disharmony. It's true we were chosen to act out murder. But it's God's will. God wills us to break God's laws. In the black night of hatred and demons and horror, in our violation of God's laws, all the saints and angels acquiesce. God too. He doesn't merely pardon us. He loves us."

This last, however, already verges on Chester's characteristic excesses. . . . (pp. 297-98)

Still, Mr. Chester is able to describe homosexual relationships with unflinching cogency, without edulcorating in the manner of Williams, or romanticizing in that of Genet. But then he will produce a story like **"In Praise of Vespasian,"** in which the pathetic progress of a catamite in search of love [sic] through Parisian *pissoirs*, London water closets, and the men's rooms

of New York is narrated in predominantly religious images and biblical language. The boy becomes a Christ figure, and when, in a posthumous apotheosis, he prepares for *fellatio,* he "opens his lips upon Life Everlasting." We are never allowed to be sure whether all this is to be taken as a joke—and if so, why?—or seriously—and if so, more than ever, why? One wonders whether Chester himself knows. (p. 298)

John Simon, "Where Love Has Gone," in Partisan Review, *Vol. XXXII, No. 2, Spring, 1965, pp. 294-99.*

MORDECAI RICHLER

Chester is an astonishingly good and original writer and *Behold Goliath,* his first book since *Jamie Is My Heart's Desire* nine years ago, is not the usual slight between novels offering—it's totally absorbing.

A really imaginative writer, Alfred Chester is somebody who cares deeply about language and uses it with enviable stylishness. The themes of some of his stories are, on the surface, unpromising—sensitive childhood; parched urban homosexuals on the prowl—but the treatment is so personal, so unusual, that it seldom matters. Childhood is charged with terror of the ordinary. In **"As I Was Going Up the Stairs,"** a child brought up on the usual run of harmless little lies, then put on display for his mother's guests in the parlour, comes to believe all people are ghosts ("There were no people anywhere").

Chester is never self-pitying about loneliness and homosexual love and his stories are enriched by a fine comic sense. In **"From the Phoenix to the Unnamable, Impossibly Beautiful Wild Bird,"** the narrator drinks the night through with Mario, once his lover, now just abandoned by the girl he left him for. Their duologue has the same nervy quality as the best of Albee in *Who's Afraid of Virginia Woolf?*. In **"Ismael,"** Chester is very bitchily funny about a Jewish homosexual's conversion to Catholicism, and about Madison Avenue queers in their Dacron suits ("cute as a button, most of them, this army of Tom Sawyers"). Only the obviously fantastic stories failed for me—Chester is much more rewarding when he heightens the ordinary so as to make *it* appear fantastic. Occasionally language runs away from him. It becomes self-inflated, as when he writes "the rectangular darkness of the national church with its two-dimensional gods in technicolor" when all he means is "the movies." But it's a small price to pay for a rare and enjoyable book.

Mordecai Richler, "Out of the Ordinary," in The Observer, *May 23, 1965, p. 27.*

EUGENE GOODHEART

[In the best stories in *Behold Goliath*], **"In Praise of Vespasian"** and **"Behold Goliath,"** Chester rises to, if he doesn't sustain, an heroic poetry that compels our admiration. His heroes are not only capable of choosing passion and disaster, they suffer their choice with an exuberant mixture of pain and joy that validates their self-heroizing, self-ironizing impulse, the pride of Joaquin, for instance, of **"In Praise of Vespasian"** that he is "still in one piece and still bearing his Catalan name, yet like the glorious soldier—Mutilated and Unknown." Joaquin, footloose and fancy free, lives only for his passion, lives for it against those who "fling slop at him" and "humiliate and wound the love in him," against those who "will ultimately bring him to a hospital in Barcelona where a further slit will be cut in his belly and where his arms will be sewn tight, more like judgment than treatment.''

This is the heroic homosexual: we know also of the bourgeois of the species who has learned the secret of accommodating his passions to the domestic pieties. But the heroic possibility, the old identity of love and death, exists for the likes of Joaquin. His passions are not attenuated by responsibilities: they keep the intensity of an obsession or a disease. What protects his heroes from psychoanalytic suspicion is Chester's concentration on action and the lyric effect, his lack of interest in motive or moral implication. Somewhere Mann speaks of homosexuality as '''free' love in the sense of infertility, hopelessness, lack of consequence and responsibility. Nothing comes of it, it does not found anything, it is *l' art pour l' art.*'' Chester never denies these qualities, he merely disengages them from Mann's (and our) moralistic understanding of them. The inconsequence and irresponsibility suddenly appears as a unique capacity for life, an ability to live in the present moment: to be careless of the risk, to find in the obscene embrace of a lover in a *pissotiere* ''a conversion and a revelation.'' We entertain no illusions about a character's ''capacity for love,'' the ''tenderized'' Christian giving of the hetersexual world. Chester's heroes focus narcissistically on their own feelings and passions, experience the *other* as an occasion for erotic solipsism. Chester's characters know—as do D. H. Lawrence's—that ecstasy is in the taking, not the giving, and what they take gives them power, makes them big and intense, Goliath-like.

If Chester's fiction ultimately disappoints, it is because it fails too often to fulfill its heroic ambitions. Too much license is given to the wayward fantasies of the characters, and the lyricism with its tendency toward confected beauty (''the crystal beauties of the ghosted night'') suppresses psychological complication. (Chester's fiction lacks the psychological and intellectual complexity of Genet, for instance, and it has only intermittently the demonism of Genet's vision.) The lyricism creates an insulation from the ordinary world, a reluctance to see the enemy as something other than unexplained vision or symbol: ''Medea with a murdered son limp across each arm,'' ''boys impaled upon the cold,'' ''children [bawling] like human brats,'' ''a cranky brood,'' ''a husband mad with worry,'' ''nature [flying] at the throat of the city,'' and the visions issue suddenly in execrations of ''this land and this life.'' The images and rhetoric (of **''Behold Goliath''**) may be powerful, but they do not coalesce into fully realized drama. The ordinary world is too shadowy, too passive in its resistance, and the heroic, defiant gesture dissolves all too easily into dream. Chester's refusal to dramatize the claims of the ordinary world, and his inclination to allow the dream to dominate reflects the myopia of affirmation. Chester seems unwilling to explore the other side: the expense of spirit in being deviant in a hostile world.

Despite its limitations, Chester's imaginative vitality is rare and moving. (pp. 82-4)

> *Eugene Goodheart, ''Behold Goliath to the Hanging Gardens,'' in* Critique: Studies in Modern Fiction, *Vol. VII, No. 3, Spring-Summer, 1965, pp. 82-5.*

JOSH GREENFIELD

The Exquisite Corpse is human ruin with a view—unremittingly homosexual—and that is its sole unity. The rest is fragments—some brilliant as diamonds, some sharp as cracked glass, some crude as costume-jewelry rhinestone, some dull as sidewalk cement. Every once in a while the diverse pieces seem to come together, almost as geometrically ordained as the pattern in a kaleidoscope—but then a slight shake, and the cohesion is gone again.

There is no story-line as such, and there are no consistent characters. There are images and shadows with names, and picturesque names at that: James Madison, John Anthony, Baby Poorpoor, Xavier, Ismael and TomTom Jim. And these names change, absorb and elide into each other like masturbatory fancies; have visions within visions, dreams within dreams, and change sex as matter-of-factly as Genet's prisoners.

Nor is there a singular event toward which the disparate actions of the book ascend—unless it is the violent death of one of the partners in a completely realized ''Zoo Story'' relationship. By and large, reality keeps bumping into fable, and then goes ricocheting (with English) into daydream: demi-worlds constantly colliding in a billiard game without rules.

But Chester is always capable of wild bursts of humor: He has a homosexual lover depict his plight—although not revealing his true sex—in a letter to Dr. Rose Franzblau of The New York *Post.* And often he achieves a perverse eloquence. For example, he has a ''master'' instruct his ''slave'' with a mock antiprayer:

> In your dream is my only awakening. In your fantasy is my only reality. In my hell is your only heaven. In your moment is my only eternity. In your devil is my only God. In my death is your only birth. In my destruction is your only creation. Come to me, murderer. Come to me, murderer.

Most of the scenes in *The Exquisite Corpse* are set within the geographic confines of New York City; others take place in some vague never-never land. One would require a key to unlock—or a magnet to draw together—all of its symbolism. But even if one does not fully understand or accept *The Exquisite Corpse,* one should not ignore it. Chester—like Henry Miller and William Burroughs, to cite but two other Americans working in the French tradition—is a born writer with a zestful imagination and a poet's gift for creating provocative and unforgettable images. Reason enough to forgive many of his proud multitude of sins. (p. 51)

> *Josh Greenfield, ''In the French Tradition,'' in* The New York Times Book Review, *March 5, 1967, pp. 5, 51.*

JOHN ASHBERY

Throwing the book—almost any book will do—at humanity for having made a mess of itself has become a kind of compulsory athletic credit for the budding novelist. . . . The journey to the end of night has been rerouted via the last exit to Brooklyn, where, as anyone who has never been there knows, human existence is ghastly beyond belief. And the implication is always that the reader is somehow to blame for this. ''*You* made the world this way, you faceless *hypocrite lecteur!* Do you think I enjoy writing like this? You make me do it and I hate you for it!'' So that it is increasingly difficult to approach a new work of fiction without feeling guilty about not feeling that collective guilt which is supposed to be as inherent in us as magnanimity was in the Noble Savage.

''Ah, the human estate, the human estate,'' sighs a character in *The Exquisite Corpse* who could be a spokesman for the author, and there are indeed signs that Alfred Chester was intending to sum up once more the prosecution's case against

John Doe (the name, alas, of another of the characters in this novel). He has assembled a large cast of freaks and ghouls to act in a Grand Guignol morality play intended to eclipse all other recent efforts in the genre. Fortunately the enthusiasm he brings to this task has carried him over into a world of make-believe that for all its horror is somehow companionable. At the very moment when he is piling the Pelion of perversion on the Ossa of scatology, Chester breaks into a schoolboy giggle and the whole edifice comes clattering down in multicolored fragments, some of them lovely. The novel is not an indictment nor a scream, but a lively macabre diversion, recommended to readers with strong stomachs—but is there still anybody who hasn't one?

The characters are introduced in a rapid series of vignettes. Xavier's curiosity about his dying father's body leads him to finger the exposed intestine, spraying the sickroom with liquid excrement. Mary Poorpoor has a lesbian "husband": the fairies steal her baby and leave a monstrous changeling in its place. Baby Poorpoor himself, a pudgy, unlovable fruit, metamorphoses into James Madison who in turn becomes the nymphomaniac Madame Madison. T. S. Ferguson, a happily married commuter, doubles as the sadistic John Doe, who keeps James Madison as a sex-slave in a city apartment. Tommy, whose handsome face turned hideous after an operation, is in love with a Puerto Rican named Ismael who writes letters signed "Isobel" to Dr. Rose Franzblau. The outlines of the characters merge freely. Is Tomtom Jim, the Negro "exterminating angel," a combination of Tommy and of James Madison? It is hard to say for sure, but the novel is so loosely constructed—like the Surrealist parlor game from which it takes its name—that this scarcely matters.

The looseness could have been exploited to better effect if Chester—as he sometimes seems about to do—had in the end drawn all the far-flung destinies of his characters into a Gordian knot, the way Dickens did in *Bleak House* for instance. Instead he has settled for an all-over, pointillist field that is otherwise effective. He has used the materials of a novel to make something like a poem—a hybrid thing, but a thing still very much worth doing, as the poisoned eloquence of his writing proves on almost every other page.

The endlessly varied theme of the novel, which in the end does associate the various limbs of the *cadavre exquis* into a kind of whole, is the familiar one of masks and identities. John Anthony, apparently yet another of Baby Poorpoor's alter egos, lives in a kind of Salvation Army warehouse of discarded costumes, where he fashions lifelike masks for himself and for disfigured Tommy. Mary Poorpoor's baby can be seen by others but not by herself (just as Chester's first novel dealt with a corpse who was visible to everyone but the narrator). Baby's name changes merely because he happens to be wearing a windbreaker marked "James Madison High School." And Ismael, disfigured himself at the end of the book, is delighted that terrified passersby think the new face is "really him."

These shifting Pirandellian transformations eventually take on tragic urgency through sheer repetition, and when a series of long-anticipated deaths finally arrives, it is as though a miniature world were crumbling. (The death of James Madison, which happens in a carnivorous forest connected by phone booth to the outside world, is one of the most haunting passages in the book.) Characters we have resisted believing in suddenly become larger than life as they appear for the curtain call.

In general *The Exquisite Corpse* is a far more satisfying book than *Jamie Is My Heart's Desire,* Chester's first novel. That work was highly praised, but in my opinion was aimless and carelessly written, its deliberate ugliness both gratuitous and half-hearted. Here, on the contrary, it is *meant;* and though rats scamper under the Brooklyn El and razor-wielding maniacs lurk under arc-lamps oftener in this novel than they do in real life, Chester can often rise to powerful evocations of metropolitan grandeur and misery and weave them into a disturbing metaphysical worldview. . . . (pp. 3, 13)

One is left feeling impatient with him for his occasionally slapdash handling of some marvelous raw materials; for loose ends; for his teenager's fascination with the gothic and grotesque and for things that look, smell, taste, and sound bad. And sometimes for his writing, which can pass from heights of incandescent evil to the homespun Thirties Surrealism of Saroyan's *The Man on the Flying Trapeze.* His next novel could be the major statement that has been awaited from him. Yet meanwhile, one still emerges from the acid-bath of this one feeling singularly toned up. (p. 13)

> John Ashbery, "Chester's Sweet Freaks," in Book Week—World Journal Tribune, *March 12, 1967, pp. 3, 13.*

CHARLES T. SAMUELS

Through a series of separate but interspersed narratives, [*The Exquisite Corpse*] constructs a crazy-house world of erotic anguish, a sort of queer *Grand Hotel.* In dizzying succession, we witness murder and ecstasy, high-comic satire of suburban motherhood (though these ladies tend children who don't exist), and pornographic descriptions of homosexual mechanics. Plotless, incisive, lyrical, repulsive, *The Exquisite Corpse* is a book for which the epithet "uneven" seems facetious.

In some bizarre subplots, Chester manages to find the right situation for his peculiar truth. . . .

In other parts of the novel, the action is so bizarre as to block any response except bemused curiosity. . . .

Yet when Chester controls the grotesqueness, he can be both insightful and liberatingly comic, as in the series of letters written to Dr. Franzblau by a girl who "sort of knew the facts of life but not too clearly," since she is probably a boy. At his best, Chester combines wicked humor with pathos. (p. 696)

The oddly named characters in Chester's *mélange* appear to merge and assume one another's identities, an obvious clue to the title's allusion. (*Cadavre Exquis* is a famous Surrealist parlor game in which the players draw physical parts on pleats of a page in order to learn what arbitrary organism they may ultimately create.) If a reader were ignorant of the parlor game, however, he would almost certainly fail to perceive, as Chester clearly intended, that the novel's subject is one twisted avatar of suffering composed of all the characters. But what is compositionally valid in visual terms need not be applicable to fiction.

The vivid details are sometimes revealingly focused, but too often they seem only to reflect a sort of private blue movie being run off in the author's mind. It is psychologically descriptive of John Anthony's character when Chester shows him worshiping a homosexual Christ (with its "high tough buttocks and one tiny crab among the pubic hair"); but what is being characterized by Chester's erotic descriptions of neutral objects like trains and ice-cream scoops, his homosexual puns concealed in passages of seemingly innocent narration, his leering plot details (most of the characters either become or search for a man named Dickie)?

After all the fun and games, the shocking events coming at us without intelligible order, the book begins to seem more and more unmistakably soft. Characters start exhaling about "how hard it is to live." The most important subplot (in which a man considerably masks his ruined face only to go unrecognized by his homosexual lover) would pass, under other circumstances, for "straight" O. Henry.

Though *The Exquisite Corpse* is ultimately unsuccessful, it remains interesting for what it exemplifies. In its pages, two contemporary developments coincide: fascination with forbidden subjects and impatience with the traditional art of fiction. The book's subject is still strange, having been rendered comprehensible to most readers neither by Rechy's coy evasions nor Burroughs' mad dreams; neither by Selby's mindless pseudo-naturalism nor Genet's metaphysical arabesques. The private pain in Chester's pages is authentic, but the technical dislocations make its source more marginal and the pain becomes more remote.

In our literary situation, going underground is the road to chic success. But true exploration requires a discovery which is not mere inversion of the natural. (p. 697)

> *Charles T. Samuels, "High Camp in the Underground," in* The Nation, *New York, Vol. 204, No. 22, May 29, 1967, pp. 696-97.*

LESLIE SCHAFFER

The Exquisite Corpse is, I would hazard, essentially a commentary on some of the varieties of obscenity, both in life and in literature, rather than the grotesquely obscene book that, ironically, it pretends to be. Its title is descriptive both of the form of Chester's satirical exercise and of his image of the form of those parodies of relation (including sex) that are the lot of the dispossessed population of the "drag" world from which his cast is drawn. André Breton has described the surrealist parlor game recalled by the title in this way:

> Game of folded paper played by several people, who compose a sentence or drawing without anyone seeing the preceding collaboration or collaborations. The now classic example, which gave the game its name, was drawn from the first sentence composed in this way: The - exquisite - corpse - will - drink - new - wine.

Chester has folded the paper so as to provide 49 scenes, each affording a brief glimpse of the apparent unfolding of the lives of the several members of the cast. The sketches are delightfully varied in style: some, for example, are cast in terms of fantastic allegory, others are elegantly contrived literary graffiti or pastiches of much that parades as realism in contemporary writing. I cannot tell exactly how many are included in the cast, but suspect that it matters not at all: the ambiguities of name, number and gender in this transvestite world serve as almost trivial reflections of other more nightmarish ambiguities.... The question arises then, not of how many constitute the cast, but whether there is, in any significantly human sense, any cast at all: each seems exclusively to be the fictitious invention of the other, and this other is no less a reductive fiction than his invention. This is quite spectacularly so in the occasional vignettes of the mothers, monstrously simple when they are not simply monstrous. The exquisite corpse, it will be recalled, was essentially a collaborative game.... Chester has suc-

ceeded admirably, even with a thoroughly ruthless precision, in portraying that absurdly reductive, almost hypochondriacal vision of the human condition that seems increasingly popular in our age. Nigel Dennis put it nicely when he wrote that "... we tend to believe nowadays that in studying an author's character we should look to the excrement if we are to find the fundament." Out of these manifold follies, Chester has made an appropriately unpleasant comedy which, like all good comedy, is never merely funny. (pp. 28, 30)

> *Leslie Schaffer, "The Hypochondriacal Vision," in* The New Republic, *Vol. 157, Nos. 8 & 9, August 19 & 26, 1967, pp. 26-8, 30.*

MICHAEL FEINGOLD

The opening chapter [of *The Exquisite Corpse*], a prologue of barely 20 lines, describes a man looking in a mirror and then shouting out, as he smashes it against his chin, "Why? Why must I suffer your destiny?" The rebellious questioner is John Anthony, sculptor and maskmaker, who has retreated from life to the attic of a church settlement house, where he lives among piles of donated clothes too old-fashioned for even the settlement's wino clientele to wear. Resenting his own destiny so much, in a later chapter he builds himself a new one. (p. 61)

As it turns out, John Anthony's new persona comes already equipped with a taste for boilermakers and a low social circle, including a panhandler who supplies it with a name (Veronica) and a history ("You always did look prettiest when you got a little mad"). Though certain scenes of *The Exquisite Corpse* are built to call up pictures of everyday reality, while others resemble the nightmare fantasies of artists from Fuseli to Frazetta, nothing can be taken for granted. When not circular, the primary movement of Chester's various worlds is a folding into one another, like a magician's silk scarves blossoming into flowers which then become doves.... Appropriately for its homosexual themes and sensibility, *The Exquisite Corpse* is in both senses of the word a series of tricks, a random matching of pairs of made-up selves in druggy nights of sexual combat.

Just as the costume of Veronica can conjure up, along with its own name, a panhandler boyfriend, every Papageno outfit in Chester's extensive wardrobe calls forth a compatible Papagena, with his or her own ability to transform from hostile witchlike garb into docilely matching fine feathers: John Anthony is in retreat from the unattainable international gigolo Dickie. Dickie himself, really just a hapless kid from banal Brooklyn, has adopted the name Xavier in his effort to escape his eternally dying Jewish-patriarch father. The rich, facially disfigured businessman Tommy is fatally entangled with the teenage Puerto Rican hustler Ismael. Penniless, pregnant Mary Poorpoor, in one narrative thread a figure of fable wandering through dreamscapes with her lover Tomtom Jim, in another is rescued from despair on the very real streets of New York by Emily, a hearty, old-fashioned-manly lesbian (who says, with memorable Chesterian topsy-turviness, "Your name can't be Mary. Mary is a boy's name.").

As the double-pronged stories of Dickie/Xavier and Mary Poorpoor suggest, even the most intensely bonded of these pairings is likely to snap apart, or twist into something else in the novel's destabilized structure: John Anthony, pining for Dickie, meets Xavier and fails to recognize him. Tommy's promiscuous but devoted Ismael pours out the chronicle of their infighting in hilarious letters to Dr. Rose Franzblau, under the name "Isobel." By the time his/her second letter is underway, Isobel's story has turned into something horrifically different. Arrogant, closeted T. S. Ferguson, a married man with children (who may be another version of Tommy), engages—as "John Doe"—in a brutal clandestine affair with a boy whom he names "James Madison," after the high-school logo on the boy's jacket, and whose mother duly turns up as "Mrs. Madison," though she is presumably not the "Madame Madison" who suffers for her propensity to cruise Tenth Avenue, naked except for her fur coat and pearls, picking up sailors.

"Madame Madison," of course, may just be another of John Anthony's costumes (if nakedness under fur can be called a costume), or another facet of "James," who has started out in any case as "Baby Poorpoor"—perhaps the child Mary Poorpoor is carrying, or the "poor poor baby" of the prologue, who is really only a bassinet in John Anthony's attic, with that significant mirror in it. In Mary's story, however, her *real* baby, if the word is applicable, dies hideously, while the imaginary child she and Emily have christened Emilio survives. So perhaps Baby Poorpoor is someone else altogether. His "John Doe" has a childhood friend named Dickie, who may or may not be either Dickie/Xavier or John Anthony's Dickie. The identities are as transferrable as Madame Madison's pearls, which, stolen from her, find their way to the unfortunate Isobel—whose lover, it develops, is also named Dickie, a name which, significantly, is both a false shirtfront and a childish euphemism for the male genital.

Rather than characters, Chester's inventions are vectors of force, nudging the story in this or that direction, clothing it in the tonality of different genres as each persona—each *impersonation*—summons up events appropriate to itself, much as the made-up alias James Madison makes a mother Madison inevitable. The story of Tommy and Ismael is jazzy New York naturalism; John Anthony brings on a Firbankian novel of manners and comic squalor; the shabby grotesquery Xavier wanders through is out of Céline, with an admixture of Saul Bellow; while Mary Poorpoor lives through what seems at first to be a primitive legend. But the gestures toward genre, like the personae, keep curving into their opposites, as if the genres themselves were having nightmares about their future in our categoryless world: Mary's jungle fable reaches its horrific nadir among the terraces of Gramercy Park; her jungle, it turns out, was only a movie set. Tommy and Ismael's tale, the nightmarishness of which has seemed an all too believable slice of life, comes to a purely Aesopian climax—an evil inversion of the sweetly moralistic ending to Max Beerbohm's *The Happy Hypocrite*—which is the definitive last word in Chester's dazzling play with the question of masks vs. faces.

The art of fiction has rarely seemed this fecund in its creativity, or this nakedly jerry-built in its impish lack of pretense. *The Exquisite Corpse* is a game of "let's pretend" played with genitalia and God, birth and death, blood and shit, parents and lovers as its stakes, a game that broadens and burgeons till it opens out in every direction, an imaginary toad with an infinity of real gardens in it. (pp. 61, 64)

Michael Feingold, "Tales from the Cryptic," in The Village Voice, *Vol. XXXI, No. 48, December 2, 1986, pp. 61, 64.*

Humberto Costantini

1924?-1987

Argentinian novelist, short story writer, dramatist, and poet.

In his novels, which are set in Argentina during the 1970s, Costantini employs humor and satire to convey his view of the arbitrariness of fate and the oppression wrought by military dictatorships. His works are widely admired for their depictions of innocent civilians unwittingly involved in political tumult. The plot of *De dioses, hombrecitos, y policías* (1979; *The Gods, the Little Guys, and the Police*), for example, revolves around twelve amateur poets who are wrongly suspected by military police of subversive activities. Costantini intensifies the absurdity of the situation by revealing that the poets are part of a scheme devised by the Greek god Hades to avenge the death of a sadistic general whom he admired. Aphrodite, Hermes, and Athena intervene and rescue the men, but twelve replacements for their execution are randomly selected by evil gods. *La larga noche de Francisco Sanctis* (1984; *The Long Night of Francisco Sanctis*) focuses on the decision the title character must make between remaining a passive citizen of a fascist regime or delivering information that could save the lives of two governmental enemies.

(See also *Contemporary Authors*, Vol. 122 [obituary].)

© *Jerry Bauer*

S. R. WILSON

[In *De dioses, hombrecitos y policías*], Humberto Costantini has created a narrative of assassination whose point of origin and departure is a dismemberment and reintegration of language usage. There is nothing resembling cubism in the novel. *De dioses, hombrecitos y policías* plainly and dramatically demonstrates the multiplicity of language as a form of violence. Costantini, an Argentine born in 1924, is a novelist and a poet. Two works, *Una vieja historia de caminantes* (*An Old Story about Travellers*, 1967) and *Háblenme de Funes* (*Talk to me about Funes*, 1970) received the *Premio municipal* of Buenos Aires. In 1977, his work as a short story writer was acknowledged in Mexico and he received special recognition from *Casa de la Cultura* in Puebla. *De dioses* was awarded first prize for narrative by *Casa de las Américas* in 1979.

In 1975, Buenos Aires was still under the control of Isabel Perón and her administrative advisor, José López Rega; repressive measures required a new terminology. Thus, language manipulation and political assassination formed a compliant if somewhat nepharious relationship. Poetry, mythology and police surveillance are inextricably merged in *De dioses* in Buenos Aires during November and December, 1975. "La agrupación polimnia" (The poetry circle of Polimnia), a small, innocuous, effusive gathering of rather whispy amateur poets, meets weekly in a modest, rented house in a tranquil area of Buenos Aires. Eleven, sometimes twelve people are present: a German teacher, a bank employee, the owner of a small restaurant, a textile worker, a primary school teacher in a Catholic school for girls—not exactly the type of candidates typical of subversive and

ominous anti-government activities. They recite opulent sonnets, poems that praise the rewards of bucolic existence, and modest attempts at elaborate love poetry that tentatively describes flowerings of romantic and nubile amorous relations:

> You would plant delicate flowers
> Never see the flower that is beside you
>
> Speak, oh wise gardener
> I will not fear light if God sends it

This is not the sort of writing normally associated with clandestine meetings and hidden arms *cache*. Nevertheless, suspicion is a primary nutritive element in the 1970's in Argentina. People who enter a house quietly, remain inside for a number of hours, then emerge and disperse with regularity immediately put on alert vigilant sectors of local police. Poetry and police are not the only confronting elements in Buenos Aires. A protective, observing body of gods and goddesses watch, with consternation, occurrences taking place in the city. Aphrodite, Hermes, and Athena watch the gathering of bucolic and romantic poets with tender curiosity. Another language emerges. From the solitude and heights of Olympus, the gods observe the timid and rather pathetic attempts at poetic expression. The language they use is filled with the opulence of mythological savoring and qualification. For Aphrodite, it is incomprehensible that these 12 inauspicious souls speak about love without experiencing it.

The vigilant police, who also observe the modest and gray house in Villa Devoto, have recourse to another and even more stylized language:

> As you must know, subversive crime, which has almost been wiped out in the rural sector, certainly will be found in more heavily populated areas.

The police, gods of love and sinister, death-like gods all view the circumstances with grave caution.

Perhaps the most unique interpretation of life in Buenos Aires that Costantini presents is the representation of death. Death comes from the capricious intervention of evil gods—gods who seek vengeance, gods who intransigently defend military and police operations. The destiny of the 12 bucolic poets, one of whom is blind, another paralyzed, depends exclusively on the scowling decision of a god from Hell. As Costantini indicates, politically organized death simply cannot be comprehended by any other means. The arbitrariness of trial by execution has no explanation. A decision or lack of decision by a mythological force grants the extension of life. The 12 poets are saved; 12 others, equally without reason or justification, are indifferently selected by evil gods as replacements.

Elements of language and inexplicable chance form the agglutinating feature of Argentine society. Language is a fascinating device in Argentina; in the early 1970's, large and admiring sectors of the population were equally enamored with the vocabulary of Perón, the Montoneros, and structuralism. Chance, only chance, offered survival as a possiblity. Life was a more precarious composition than language. For Costantini, presently in exile in Mexico, even the gods marvelled at the uniqueness of the human spirit that managed to persist despite the surveillance, the vigilance, the reprisals and the assassinations:

> It is also the destiny of splendid mortals to pass through life under the permanent threat of death. This gives a unique value to each of their actions, and creates an enormous respect in the Gods for the smallest and most insignificant of men.

(pp. 64-6)

S. R. Wilson, in a review of "De dioses, hombrecitos y policías," in Latin American Literary Review, *Vol. IX, No. 19, Fall-Winter, 1981, pp. 63-6.*

LYDIA HUNT

One of the concerns of Humberto Costantini's *Gods, the Little Guys and the Police* . . . [is] the question of accountability under a dictatorship.

The novel begins on a summer evening during the worst of Argentina's "dirty war," when the members of a group that calls itself "Polimnia" gather at a weekly meeting place to read their poetry. The poems were dreadful, but their endearing if somewhat silly authors are regarded fondly by Athena, Aphrodite and Hermes, for the poets are fragile beings "exposed to certain doom" on a fragile planet, "which endows each of their acts with singular value." The gods become alarmed when they notice the cloud of Hades hovering over the meetinghouse and learn that, based on evidence as irrelevant as it is contrived, a paramilitary death squad is preparing to kill 12 of the group's members to avenge the death of a general.

The distressed gods decide to make the mortals' last hours as happy as possible and permeate their meeting with what for the Polimnians is a rare spirituality, eroticism and harmony (and for the reader a rare hilarity). Suddenly it appears that the union of desire and intellect has made hatred and death impotent, and the Polimnians are saved. Their reprieve, however, is only temporary and conditional. Twelve other victims are chosen to replace them.

Several aspects of the question of accountability are addressed by this well-written, funny yet serious novel. One is the moral responsibility of individuals at lower levels of a repressive regime who claim they are only obeying orders from above. In the novel, the unacknowledged henchmen of officialdom clearly do not limit themselves to following orders. One calls torture "fun," and another becomes infuriated when a raid is called off. A second aspect has to do with the tendency to ignore official criminal behavior and underestimate its implications, an attitude that is reflected by the Polimnians in various ways. They remain oblivious to the plot against them, to what is occurring in their land.

But perhaps the most sinister and terrifying aspect of the accountability question—and the one Mr. Costantini stresses—is the role chance or randomness plays as an indiscriminate instrument of repression. Nothing succeeds in subduing an opposition movement more than a random terror that arbitrarily chooses its victims, while at the same time permitting the authorities to maintain the pretense of ignorance. The Polimnians are picked for extermination in part because their meetings bring together at least 12 people at a predictable time and place, making them efficiently manageable prey. And their substitutes are just as arbitrarily selected.

The Gods, the Little Guys and the Police contains some 40-odd short chapters written in diverse narrative styles. There is the precious prudery of one of the Polimnians, the imbecilic pedantry of bureaucratic communications, the dishonest detachment of news reports, the compassionate intrusions of a narrator, and several others. These chapters are interwoven to provide various perspectives, and great suspense is created, not only because the reader becomes privy to dreadful information unsuspected by the Polimnians, but also because the pace of the writing itself is often out of step with the furious action.

Lydia Hunt, "The Poets and the Death Squad," in The New York Times Book Review, *April 29, 1984, p. 34.*

KRISTIN HELMORE

[In *The Gods, the Little Guys, and the Police*, the] "Little Guys" are a strait-laced and ardent group of poetry buffs, calling themselves Polimnians, who meet on Wednesday evenings to read their own verses aloud. The exalted moments of a certain Wednesday's meeting are lovingly, though somewhat stuffily, recorded by one José María Pulicicchio, whose specialty is the sonnet. Tenderness, small personal details, and wry humor pervade his account, contrasting it strongly with the two other interweaving narrative strands.

For, unbeknownst to the Polimnians, a tough and trigger-happy right-wing death squad is bent upon engineering the poets' "disappearance," by means of abduction, torture, and murder, on the very Wednesday evening in question. Thus we are also treated to an inside view of the "Police," with their grandiose but tenuous hierarchy, their detailed files on each Polimnian's life history, and their Orwellian talent for turning the most innocent pursuits and connections into evidence of "subversive delinquency."

In his obvious despair at finding no sane explanation for the random violence that had prevailed so long in Argentina, Costantini ironically gives us the Greek gods, with their all too human rivalries and squabbles: as good, or as bad, an "explanation" as any. Athena, Aphrodite, and Hermes may be benign, and highly interested in preserving their mortal protégés, but Hades, in vengeance for the death of a fascist general, is bent on their destruction, and his schemes are not to be foiled.

While the Olympians waft down impulses of love and delight in an attempt to sweeten the Polimnians' last hours, Hades is issuing orders of Denunciation and Prompt Execution to the death-squad thugs. The tension builds, and doom seems inevitable. Even if there is a reprieve, it can be only temporary, for Costantini sees the forces of evil as an easy match for the forces of good as represented by the Olympians.

The book is absorbing, moving, and often sadly funny, but the Homeric accounts of the antics of the gods are a bit long-winded. Toby Talbot's adroit translation embodies the flowery Latin courtliness of the Little Guys and the offhand bureaucratic slang of the Police. It only falters when tackling the sweeping epic narrative relating the exploits of the gods, which was probably a bit tedious in the original, too.

To Costantini, the supreme irony seems to lie in the fact that the Little Guys are so wrapped up in their esoteric and emotional cocoon as to be totally oblivious to the violent death they so narrowly escape. Nor have they any idea that their salvation is only temporary, and that Hades will contrive soon again to destroy them. Toward the end of the book, the spokesman for Polimnia writes, "To summarize accounts, I can assert that in the wake of that memorable evening . . . happiness has entered our midst and there seems no reason for it ever to abandon us." (pp. 19-20)

> Kristin Helmore, *"Argentine's Haunting Satire of Military Repression,"* in The Christian Science Monitor, *May 23, 1984, pp. 19-20.*

MARGERY RESNICK

The Long Night of Francisco Sanctis is anchored in a single life amid the unimaginable terrors of Argentina in 1977. Mr. Costantini (who recently returned to Argentina after years of political exile in Mexico City), insists on literary artifice; his novel, with its chapter summaries anticipating action, has a Cervantine design and narrative voice. Yet he creates a powerful tension between the work as fiction and as a kind of documentary reflecting the world in which a prosaic accountant named Francisco Sanctis faces a major moral predicament on a fateful night in Buenos Aires.

Sanctis is a man at peace with his world. Despite his failures in a seminary and medical school, a disastrous marriage and a succession of lost jobs, he has at last attained an unremarkable security, and as head of the accounting department of a small wholesale firm, he is able to support his second wife and household. Sanctis has neither renounced his humanitarian ideals nor accommodated to the mediocrity of his colleagues. Oppressed by his banal existence, he immerses himself in music as a retreat from a crass society.

The novel centers on a dilemma Sanctis must face that will eventually determine the course of his life. A former university classmate, Elena, entrusts him with a mission, namely to warn two innocent citizens who are to be seized that night by Argentine Air Force Intelligence. Though Sanctis' youthful activism faded with the onset of middle age, he memorizes the names and addresses of the secret-police targets. The reader experiences the fluctuations of Sanctis' will in a 10-hour vigil during which he must decide whether to risk his personal gains on the mere chance he can save the lives of two strangers.

The originality of this taut, compassionate novel lies in its refusal to portray the protagonist's situation as a dark night of the soul. Sanctis is no superhero. But average as he is, he cannot be like those "guys who are mimics . . . who adapt with astonishing ease, who, like corks, always stay afloat no matter what happens. . . . Who in their loves and hates always identify with the loves and hates of those in the driver's seat." Mr. Costantini's novel shows the inevitability of personal moral choices even for those determined to remain uninvolved. Norman Thomas di Giovanni's translation admirably re-creates the wry humor with which the original Spanish conveys the hero's introspection.

> Margery Resnick, *"Those in the Driver's Seat,"* in The New York Times Book Review, *October 6, 1985, p. 38.*

DAVID T. HABERLY

The long Argentine night of dictatorship, torture, and thousands of disappearances—the long night to which the title of [*The Long Night of Francisco Sanctis*] obliquely refers—has inevitably come into sharp focus as a central topic of recent Argentine literature. As a literary subject, however, this experience presents problems, for the huge numbers of the disappeared and the grim details of the torture chambers are both overwhelming and emotionally deadening. It would seem that all of this suffering could only be understood and felt, through literature, at the level of the individual victim; but to emphasize individual experience might undermine the significance of the long night for Argentine society as a whole.

The Argentine experience differs, in fundamental ways, from two possible referents—the Holocaust and the Spanish Civil War. Thousands of Argentines were brutalized and slaughtered, but these atrocities were not perpetrated by a hostile external force; rather, the killers and torturers were almost always the ethnic, social, and cultural doubles of their victims. This identification would suggest that the Argentine experience could best be understood as a civil war, but a civil war that was almost invisible, particularly to those in Argentina and elsewhere who preferred not to look too closely. From a literary point of view, moreover, that war was not only invisible but the sum of thousands of recurring events—a knock on the door, a shot or a scream, a black sedan racing through deserted streets. However, such events, taken individually, seem utterly banal, trivialized by the commonplaces of popular culture—crime novels and gangster movies—which they reproduced.

Few Argentine authors have been as sensitive to these issues as Humberto Costantini. . . .

Costantini's 1979 novel *De dioses, hombrecitos y policías,* translated by Toby Talbot as *The Gods, The Little Guys and The Police,* is an original and intensely self-conscious attempt to deal with these issues through the creation of a mock-heroic prose epic, in which very human classical gods seek to protect ordinary Argentines from the bad guys. The novel is a technical tour de force, but Costantini's cleverness and his verbal brilliance . . . seem designed, in the end, to evade reality rather than to confront and comprehend it. (p. 63)

[*The Long Night of Francisco Sanctis*] is more traditional in form and less consciously clever than *De dioses,* and seems to me more successful. It appears, on the surface, to be no more than a straightforward account of ten hours in the life of a middle-class, middle-aged accountant in Buenos Aires. Costantini avoids the problem of describing horrors by ending his narratives before the horrors begin—but the suspense leading up to the novel's abrupt ending enables us to imagine those horrors when we reach the last page and find the name of Francisco Sanctis on one page of Amnesty International's list of the disappeared.

The inclusion of that list is one indication that Costantini's narrative is not quite as straightforward as it might appear. Francisco Sanctis's adventures begin with a mysterious telephone call from a woman he knew, years before, when they both worked for a student literary magazine. She tells him a quite implausible story to explain her call, and insists that she must see him. At their brief meeting, Elena—who in no way resembles the girl Sanctis used to know—reveals that the lives of two men he has never met depend upon him, and begs him to warn them that Air Force Intelligence is planning to pick them up that night. Thus Sanctis—in the tradition of Borges's Baltasar Espinosa and Denevi's Rosaura—becomes enmeshed in someone else's story; despite his better judgment, he decides to play along with Elena's tale, if only to find out where it leads—just as we find ourselves drawn into the fiction of the intrusive and gratingly patronizing narrator of *The Long Night.* Our dislike and distrust of the narrator very cleverly lead us to identify with Sanctis as he seeks to make sense of his ambiguous mission.

At the end of the novel, we come to realize that Elena's unfathomable fiction is simply part of Sanctis's predestined fate—the greater fiction of the godlike narrator. The context of that larger fiction, moreover, is essentially medieval—the exemplary account of a miracle that transcends the individual and the particular. The miracle here is that Francisco Sanctis, a product of the comfortable banality of bourgeois Argentine society, rises above that banality to sacrifice his life in an act of Christian charity and human solidarity worthy of his Borgesian double, Saint Francis. (p. 64)

> David T. Haberly, in a review of *"The Long Night of Francisco Sanctis,"* in Review: Latin American Literature and Arts, *Vol. 36, January-June, 1986, pp. 63-4.*

JOHN UPDIKE

Humberto Costantini, another Argentine recently returned from exile, has written *The Long Night of Francisco Sanctis* . . . , [which] describes a single nightmarish period of less than twenty-four hours. . . . Costantini's [style] is ruminative, chatty, with humorously elaborate chapter titles, such as "Chapter I. In which, so as to keep the reader from raising his hopes too high with regard to the entertainment value of this little book, it is here stated without further ado that its subject matter is of a more or less psychological nature—or, in other words, that the prospect ahead is fairly humdrum. Thus forewarned, the reader

can now be told something about a certain telephone call that came from out of the blue."

Francisco Sanctis, the forty-one-year-old head accountant for a small Buenos Aires grocery wholesaling firm, happily married and economically prospering, is phoned one day (Friday, November 11, 1977) at his desk by a ghost from his past—Elena Vaccaro, who seventeen years ago was an overweight fellow university student, like the youthful Sanctis active in literary and left-wing circles. Though their relationship was casual and unconsummated, she now asks him to meet her immediately, on the flimsy excuse that an old student poem of his is being reprinted in a Venezuelan magazine. He very grudgingly agrees to rendezvous on a street corner, and she, grown unexpectedly lean and glamorous, drives him around in her Renault while explaining that what she really wants is for Sanctis to notify two men that they are going to be abducted by the goons of Air Force Intelligence that night. He is naturally reluctant to become involved, contented bourgeois that he is, and yet enough of his old idealism lingers to let this abruptly assigned mission nag at him; he spends the rest of the novel, far into the night, indecisively wandering the streets of Buenos Aires.

The exposition is leisurely, confident, knowing. The gently erotic comedy of Sanctis's encounter with his old semi-flame (she admired him, in her plump radical days) is almost Cheeveresque, as he mentally takes her sociological temperature:

> Sanctis observes her closely and draws some hasty conclusions: solid economic background, a social life, a pitiless diet consisting of a small glass of grapefruit juice and such for breakfast, dance or body expression, swimming or tennis, beauty treatments and yoga, a very busy husband, independence, the odd light-hearted affair.

In his own apartment, where he briefly alights after ten o'clock, he notices that his wife, María Angélica, has put a bottle of wine in the refrigerator and that her remarks to him are accompanied "by a certain tone and a sleepy smile that Sanctis knows well and that have to do with bed, with a certain French perfume that only now he's aware he's been smelling without being conscious of it." Nevertheless, torn between domestic bliss and political conscience, he goes out into the streets again.

We have been here before, in Argentine novels, in this double invisible net where the secret police and the revolutionary underground intersect on a street corner—for example, Manuel Puig's *Kiss of the Spider Woman.* What struck me, following Sanctis's increasingly ominous perambulations, was how Borgesian this Buenos Aires is—the practically endless, undistinguished streets that gather to themselves a mysterious maziness wherein a specific address becomes charged with some unspeakable spiritual burden. (pp. 111-13)

> John Updike, *"The Great Paraguayan Novel and Other Hardships,"* in The New Yorker, *Vol. LXII, No. 31, September 22, 1986, pp. 104-16.*

MICHELENE WANDOR

You are male, in your forties; 20 years ago you were a student radical, active in cultural politics, with a couple of revolutionary poems to your published credit (under a pseudonym). . . . Your radical past is exactly that and you find consolation and escape from some of the more humdrum aspects of life in classical music. One day you get a phone call from a woman whom you remember as rather unimposing in your radical days. You meet her and she is now glamorous, assured. She asks you to memorise the names and addresses of two people and then tells you that the secret police are coming for them: will you warn them? It is early evening, and you only have a few hours. What do you do? . . .

For Francisco Sanctis it is the beginning of a night of agony in which, despite seeking help from an old friend and a wife, he is forced to return to the examination of his own conscience and the memories of his past. Like the names and addresses he's been given, these memories live on in his mind and reveal the limbo of isolation in which he has decided to live. He is forced to confront his past self and enter into dialogue with it. This he does during a night of wandering the city, encountering the silence and debris of fear, meeting young people on the run and finally facing the moral issue of whether he can really betray his own conscience and live with himself.

It may sound from this summary as if [*The Long Night of Francisco Sanctis*] is an exercise in doomy solemnity; but the author is chillingly clever in his chosen tone. . . . The chapter headings have the jaunty feel of a pre-20th-century novel, describing what's to follow in terms of trivial detail (a tie, French perfume) rather than of larger events, and jollying us along with a casual, cynical, self-deprecating elegance. This is the narrative voice, not that of the character, and the reader is teased and led into a world of an urban bewilderment which invokes echoes of Kafka, Joseph Heller and the young people in Stephen Poliakoff's early plays. The casualness of the narrator's tone conceals supreme power; while Sanctis is waiting to meet his telephone contact, the narrator nips in to give us a quick resumé of his past. But even the narrator cannot protect Sanctis from political persecution. The observer observes as the acts of violence continue. And this, of course, is Costantini's message. Whether you merely tell a story, or are one of the protagonists, you are still responsible. So what would you do?

Michelene Wandor, "No Hiding Place," in New Statesman, *Vol. 113, No. 2920, March 13, 1987, p. 27.*

MICHAEL DIBDIN

The Long Night of Francisco Sanctis describes a moral dilemma. Francisco Sanctis, an office worker, is telephoned by a woman he knew years before, when they were both at university. He is mildly intrigued at her interest, mildly irritated by the persistence with which she gets him to agree to a meeting that very evening—Francisco had been looking forward to listening to his new record of Corelli *concerti grossi*. The result is very different from anything he had imagined, for the woman gives him the names and addresses of two men who are to be abducted by Air Force Intelligence that very night. She advises Francisco not to act himself, but to pass the information on to some organisation unconnected with either of them: the leak may be a trap set for her husband, an Air Force officer. Ironically, it is the very fact that he is completely innocent of any connections with such organisations, that his only friends turn out to sympathise with the regime, which places Francisco in his terrible dilemma.

Costantini's stylistic strategy in this book is similar to Nabokov's in the work of the Berlin period: the brutal and tawdry ambience is played off against a manner of high-profile artifice, featuring elaborate chapter-headings and an insistently chatty authorial persona. Only in the final pages, where the Christian analogy is insisted on rather too stridently, does this tone falter. 'To keep the reader from raising his hops too high with regard to the entertainment value of this little book,' comments the heading to the first chapter, 'it is here stated without further ado that . . . the prospect ahead is fairly humdrum.' Nothing could be further from the truth: although the outcome is no more in doubt than that of a Classical tragedy—the final chapter is written not by Costantini but by Amnesty International—the skill and compassion with which Francisco Sanctis's lonely battle with himself is described, and the evocation of the late-night streets and bars of Buenos Aires, make this book as absorbing as any thriller. (p. 18)

Michael Dibdin, "How to Vanish," in London Review of Books, *Vol. 9, No. 8, April 23, 1987, pp. 18-19.*

Harry (Eugene) Crews

1935-

American novelist, essayist, autobiographer, and short story writer.

In his fiction, Crews focuses upon individuals whose attempts to discover self-esteem and meaning in their lives often result in emotional hardship and tragedy. Set in impoverished rural locales and materialistic urban environments of Georgia and Florida, Crews's novels feature protagonists whom Jack Moore described as "trying to make do, to cope, to love, desperately to blot out the nothingness of life and the everywhereness of death." Moore also noted that Crews's vivid evocation of place "provides a land upon which he can construct the odd blend of intense realism and uproarious, sick, dreamy fabulation that is the secret blend of his artistry." Several critics link Crews's work with the Southern Gothic literary style of Carson McCullers and Flannery O'Connor. Like these authors, Crews explores distinctive and universal qualities of Southern culture by depicting grotesque characters who represent extremes of human behavior.

Crews's first novel, *The Gospel Singer* (1968), examines the inability of the charismatic title character to find spiritual fulfillment. This work is set in the protagonist's hometown of Enigma, Georgia, where he returns each year to perform and preach. After learning that his best friend, a black man, has been lynched for allegedly raping and murdering a white woman, the singer confesses that he himself had seduced the same woman years before, and the townspeople respond by hanging him as well. In *Naked in Garden Hills* (1969), Crews parodies the biblical story of Creation. This novel takes place in Garden Hills, Florida, a town of prefabricated buildings and artificial parks developed by a mysterious unknown man who wants to mine phosphate in the region. When the phosphate resources are depleted, the inhabitants of Garden Hills lose their jobs and are left without hope for the future. Miss Dolly, a would-be savior and frustrated virgin, turns the town into a lewd, grotesque tourist resort, featuring a six-hundred-pound man as the main attraction. Jean Stafford described *Naked in Garden Hills* as "[macabre] and slapstick, howlingly funny and as sad as a zoo, ribald, admonitory, wry and deeply fond." Sex, death, religion, and old age are among the topics explored in Crews's next novel, *This Thing Don't Lead to Heaven* (1970). Set in a senior citizens' home, this novel evidences Crews's darkly humorous satire through an assortment of odd characters, including an enthusiastic salesman of cemetery plots, an atheistic minister who preaches that there is no death, a sexually frustrated proprietress named Pearl Lee Gates, and a midget who offers painful massages as a means for spiritual cleansing.

Karate Is a Thing of the Spirit (1971) is one of several novels in which Crews presents characters who seek satisfaction through physical power. Intense self-discipline and adherence to the rules of karate are the major motivations for the protagonist of this work. Through his protagonist's decision to leave the karate dojo for a life with the woman who is carrying his child, Crews suggests that love may serve to overcome the hopelessness of human existence. America's obsession with the automobile is at the center of Crews's next novel, *Car* (1972). When the idealistic Herman Mack, whose family owns a junk-

Photograph by Hank Rowland

yard, decides to eat a 1971 Ford Maverick, his stunt becomes a nationwide media event. As in *Karate Is a Thing of the Spirit*, love offers a potential escape from despair, as Herman abandons his absurd performance to care for a former prostitute. Allen Shepherd deemed *Car* "a fearful and bizarre story, precisely because it is continuously in contact with and grows out of a vision of life we know well and instantly recognize and is yet, simultaneously, a closed system." In *The Hawk Is Dying* (1973), disillusioned protagonist George Gattling must learn to discipline himself both emotionally and physically while training a captured hawk. Becoming increasingly isolated from humanity, George regards the hawk as nature's only redeeming element and his training of the bird as a way of ordering his existence. Frank W. Shelton asserted that *The Hawk Is Dying* reveals Crews's growing "despair at the ability of people to reach any real understanding of others." In *The Gypsy's Curse* (1974), Crews examines body-building as a method of self-control by depicting a legless deaf-mute whose upper-body strength allows him to perform acrobatic stunts. The man's well-ordered life collapses, however, when he murders the woman he loves after she undermines his relationships with other people.

A Feast of Snakes (1976) is generally considered Crews's finest novel and his bleakest portrayal of the human condition. Using the annual rattlesnake roundup in Mystic, Georgia, as his scenario, Crews reveals how love, sex, religion, and family fail to provide positive impetus for Joe Lon Mackey, an illiterate former high school football star. Unhappily married with two small children and no career prospects, Joe Lon attends the roundup and murders four people, thus gaining revenge against society and a measure of control over his fate. Crews's next novel, *All We Need of Hell* (1987), was published after a ten-year period during which he wrote several nonfiction works. Described by Christopher Lehmann-Haupt as "a fable about an overdriven man who is redeemed by the author's unusual vision of friendship and love," this book focuses on Duffy Deeter, a health and fitness fanatic who is rapidly losing contact with reality. After meeting Tump Walker, a professional football player, Duffy learns to care for others while maintaining and achieving his goals. Although containing such familiar elements of Crews's fiction as sex, violence, and the obsessive search for meaning in life, *All We Need of Hell* features an uncharacteristically optimistic conclusion.

Crews has also been praised for several nonfiction works. His autobiography, *A Childhood: The Biography of a Place* (1978), recounts the first six years of his life in Bacon County, Georgia. This book received widespread acclaim for Crews's evocation of his Southern upbringing and for its insights into the sources of his fiction. Michael Mewshaw observed: "Throughout *A Childhood* [Crews] maintains a precarious balance between sentiment and sensation, memory and madness, and manages to convince the reader of two mutually exclusive imperatives which have shaped his life—the desire to escape Bacon County and the constant ineluctable need to go back, if only in memory." Two other volumes, *Blood and Grits* (1979) and *Florida Frenzy* (1982), contain essays that originally appeared in *Esquire* and *Playboy* magazines. In these pieces, Crews explores such topics as sports, the modernization of the South, and media celebrities.

(See also *CLC*, Vols. 6, 23; *Contemporary Authors*, Vols. 25-28, rev. ed.; *Contemporary Authors New Revision Series*, Vol. 20; and *Dictionary of Literary Biography*, Vol. 6.)

JOHN SEELYE

On the surface, Crews' novels have many of the characteristics of the traditional Southern literary landscape, yet they make major revisions of the old agrarian map, eschewing the wilderness sanctuary for a chaotic territory of chromium and steel. Moreover, where for Faulkner the tenant farmer was an ambivalent symbol, half dirty clown (the inheritance of Southwestern humor), half redemptive man of the soil (the heritage of Jeffersonian agrarianism), for Harry Crews the generic term is "Grits," not the "true grit" of Western heroics but the soft mushy stuff that red-necks and white trash eat as a main staple of an otherwise pork-heavy diet. His "Grits" are an American version of Yahoo, ready to form a lynch mob at the drop of a coil of rope. If Harry Crews is an important writer, and I think he is, his works testify to the diminishing relevant force of William Faulkner and to the rising sun of Erskine Caldwell. We are moving geographically from the rich Mississippi Delta of plantation aristocracy to the red clay of Georgia farmland, a reduction of epic potential, perhaps, but with no consequent loss of violent traditions. (p. 616)

[It] was Caldwell's genius to popularize Faulkner's formulaics of rural violence and degeneracy (*pace* Richard Gilman) by instilling a dimension of social consciousness while adding also a quasi-pornographic element of explicit sex. There is sex in Faulkner's earliest novels, but it is not much enjoyed by anybody. . . . Caldwell's characters are often satyrs and nymphs thinly clad as hill-billies and -betties, introducing a bawdry that gained even wider national circulation after 1935 through the agency of Al Capp's libidinous *Dogpatch* [as depicted in his syndicated cartoon "Li'l Abner"]. (pp. 616-17)

This brings me back once again to Harry Crews, who not only shares a common Georgian nativity with Erskine Caldwell, but who continues to purvey a number of the characteristic Caldwell literary features, while managing also to transform Caldwell's country into a recognizably modern terrain: if *Tobacco Road* can be seen as a red-dirt track leading out of Yoknapatawpha County into *God's Little Acre*, Crews may be said to have picked it up on the other side of Dogpatch, where it becomes a six-lane superhighway that retains the blood-red clay as center-strip and shoulders. Not only are the familiar themes of sex and violence retained, but they become supercharged, and the same may be said of the obsessive manias that so often motivate Caldwell's country folk. Thus the brand new automobile whose gradual destruction is a central symbol of madness in *Tobacco Road* is reconstituted as the shiny red Ford Maverick that is eaten bit by bit in Crews' novel, *Car.* (p. 617)

[The] automobile in Southern writing is often associated with an element of perverse religiosity, a secular quest with an often vague even disparate goal which can also signal the falling apart and the death of families. *The Reivers* of course works to opposite ends, but it is one of Faulkner's least convincing if most optimistic works. For the most part, the automobile can be seen as a symbol of what is wrong with the South, of loss not gain, a direction epitomized by the self-destructive exodus undertaken by the Jeeter Lester family in what starts out a symbol of new found wealth.

In Crews' *Car,* this direction is carried to surrealistic extremes, the automobile as eaten object becoming a chromeplated eucharist, in which blood and bits of steel are intermixed. In most of Crews' novels we can detect a constant stress on religious quest, with a concomitant emphasis on the individual not the group: in *Car,* as in the best of Caldwell and in much of Faulkner, the focus is on a disintegrating, feuding family, but this is not typical of all his stories. Even when set in a family grouping, moreover, Crews' men and women are very much alone, even lonely, often depicted as living in the shadowy grip of long dead or distant parents. And the most of them are engaged in a religious search, whether figured as karate, or falconry, or eating a car, violent things of the spirit which for Crews always have as their coefficients the act of sexual congress. Where for Caldwell the act of sex is a Rabelaisian element, for Crews (as for Faulkner) it is if anything Swiftian in implication, presented in the ugliest possible light, as if to diminish in his readers the very appetites he is describing in his characters. Sex is, in a Crews novel, a metaphorical if not literal adjunct to anger, and sex coupled with anger is often called "rape." Faulkner in *Sanctuary* has been called a moralist with a corncob; Crews' characters might be called corncobs in search of a Temple, some sort of apocalyptic locus that will be the site of an apotheotic orgasm. (pp. 618-19)

One of the characteristics held in common by the people of Caldwell and Faulkner is their quality of silent outrage, a permanent psychic anger instilled by their impoverished, hopeless lives. Caldwell and Faulkner are not outraged, please note, they merely record the phenomenon. But Crews *is* outraged, and his novels seethe with anger, which takes the form of a relentless emphasis on the ugliest aspects of life. His characters are often literally freaks of nature, an element prefigured in the freak show that is a main feature of his first novel, *The Gospel Singer,* the hero of which is likewise a *lusus naturae,* being gifted with a marvelously charismatic voice. Still, despite this constant demonstration of the horror that is the human condition, Crews evinces what might be called a deeply spiritual drive, a version of Southern Baptist revivalism that constantly seeks some kind of transformation, some transfiguring apotheosis. The title and theme of his first novel provide a key to what becomes a covert motif in the books to follow: what is conventional and explicit in *The Gospel Singer* will take increasingly bizarre and [unlikely] forms.

The peculiar qualities of a Crews novel are best demonstrated by his third book, entitled *This Thing Don't Lead to Heaven,* set in a "home" for the aged and dying, the manager of which, a buxom blonde, is frustrated in her constant search for sexual fulfillment. It is in this novel also, with its stress on the most disgusting aspects of the aging process, that Crews makes clear his debt to the California tradition, most particularly to the novels of Nathanael West and Evelyn Waugh's *The Loved One.* I do not mean that Crews openly acknowledges any such debt, but his novel, set in Cumseh, Georgia, seems much closer to West's and Waugh's Hollywood than to any definable Southern literary terrain—call it Lost Atlantos if you will. It is here that the transmogrification of the South of Faulkner and Caldwell takes place, the recognizable rural and mining settings found in Crews' first two novels, *Gospel Singer* and *Naked in Garden Hills,* having been abandoned for a generalized modern urban landscape. The place names remain regional but through some creative wizardry the map takes on a definably Californian—which is to say insane—shape, a lay of the land which when called "Southern" brings to mind the surname "Terry."

The Gospel Singer ends with a lynch-mob scene, the depiction of which bears a detectable resemblance to the horrific climax of *Day of the Locust* but which remains nonetheless a traditional even ritualistic and quasi-religious Southern literary feature. In *Naked in Garden Hills,* the mob scene involves a beauty contest set against an abandoned phosphate mine, still recognizably Southern territory. But in *This Thing Don't Lead to Heaven,* the mob, if it can be called that, is a desperate group of superannuated senile people, set against that geriatric equivalent of a McDonald's hamburger stand, a place called "Axel's Senior Club," formerly known as "The Old Folks' Home." One of the major characters is a salesman of caskets and burial plots, an escapee clearly from Waugh's satire of Forest Lawn.

In the autobiographical note which accompanies *The Gospel Singer,* Crews seems at the start of his authorial career to have carefully cultivated a certain image of himself, commencing with his birth "at the end of a very long dirt road in Bacon County, Georgia," but stressing the fact that his college education was interrupted by what was in the 1950's and early 60's a typically modern American *wanderjahr. . . .* (pp. 619-21)

Crews has more recently, in his autobiography called *A Childhood,* expanded on the details of the years he spent growing up at the wrong end of the long, red-dirt road, presenting life in the rural South as a mixture of simple pleasures and stark horrors. I shall return presently to that book, but it is sufficient to state here that *A Childhood* reveals the very large extent to which his novels are autobiographical, in both literal and figurative—which is to say metaphorical—terms. *The Gospel Singer* begins with what has become a trope in Southern fiction, a description of a black man waiting in jail to be lynched for the rape and murder of a white woman. The name of the black man is Willalee Bookatee, which is the name also, Crews tells us in *A Childhood,* of a black boy with whom he grew up, much as the novel's Willalee is the childhood friend of the Gospel Singer, who is not only ineffective in his attempts to free the jailed man but who ends up hanging from the same tree. The Singer is clearly an autobiographical figure, his magical voice an equivalent to Crews' own creative gift.

Where in *A Childhood* Crews depicts his family, his mother in particular, in sympathetic even sentimental terms, evoking the images made familiar by sundry WPA publications, in *Gospel Singer* the family of the hero is presented as cracker caricatures, cousins germane to the Jeeter Lesters and Ty Ty Waltons of Erskine Caldwell. Since the novel is about the disastrous return home of the titular hero, who is lynched by his former neighbors and friends, it seems to have been intended by Crews as a ritual exorcism of his rural origins, an apotheotic farewell to his birthright acted out in the terms of a Caldwell novel but in the style and with the stress of Nathanael West's California stories. Thenceforth, as I have said, Crews' writing gradually abandoned the traditional landmarks of Southern literature, substituting instead equivalents of West's terrain, turning his back on the place where the Agrarian writers, including his own early writing master, Andrew Lytle, took their stand.

But in . . . *A Feast of Snakes,* which was published in 1976, the author, as in *A Childhood* (published two years later), seems to be undergoing a significant metamorphosis. For *A Feast of Snakes* is in many ways a revision of *The Gospel Singer,* signaling a return to the home place but with a number of significant changes. First of all, the central figure of the story is not a charismatic celebrity returning to his birthplace but an entrapped, desperate former high-school football star who cannot get away. Several years after graduation and with no hope of recovering his former lustre, Joe Lon Mackey lives in a trailer with his bedraggled wife and two screaming infants, making a meager income peddling illegal liquor from his father's tiny store. In short, Rabbit Redneckus. Where the characters in *Gospel Singer* were the wildly improbable Southern equivalents of Nathanael West types, Crews in *Feast of Snakes* is deeper than ever in Caldwell Country.

Joe Lon, with his sexual libido fueled by high octane anger, seems a compound of all the Walton boys [in *God's Little Acre*] . . .—frustrated, furious, a time bomb set with no certain moment to go off. His father, Big Joe, having driven his wife to suicide by his brutal treatment, spends his time breeding and training pit bulldogs, while Joe Lon's sister, Beeder, driven mad by her mother's death, sits alone in her filthy, darkened bedroom watching a television set turned up to deafening volume. There is also, among a number of ancillary grotesques, Sheriff Buddy Matlow, a one-legged Vietnam veteran who uses his police powers to coerce black women into granting sexual favors: Lottie Mae, one such girl, who in a fit of insane terror slashes off Matlow's penis with a razor; Berenice Sweet, the former high-school sweetheart of Joe Lon, and a champion baton twirler, who has returned home from college for the annual rattlesnake hunt—which gives Crews' book its title and finale—and her younger sister, Hard Candy, also a baton-twirler, whose football playing boyfriend, Willard, is Joe Lon's younger counterpart and drinking-and-violence companion. This list is certainly exotic enough, but it is one that seems much more generic to Caldwell's Country than to the California of Nathanael West.

The *Feast of Snakes* itself, with its open allusions to the snake-handling cults of the rural South, is an overwhelming regional event, albeit used as a backdrop to the beauty contest which Crews already employed in two of his earlier novels. But surrounding his regional cast of rednecks and good ol' boys is a mob of tourists who have invaded the town to take part in the rattlesnake hunt, providing the faceless, furious, howling human wall that is so essential to California apocalypses. Crews seems in his last novel, therefore, to be trying to achieve some kind of synthesis, to be recovering and exploiting his red-dirt roots while retaining the savagely satiric mood of Nathanael West's *Day of the Locust*. Where Enigma, Georgia, the setting of *Gospel Singer,* is Southern in locale, Mystic, Georgia, where the snake hunt and attendant mayhem takes place, is if anything much more tightly linked to Crews' native ground, yet the California coloration is likewise more intense.

Both place names share a common symbolism, obviously chosen with care, but where *The Gospel Singer,* like Crews' subsequent writing, deals openly with matters of the spirit, *Feast of Snakes* is entirely of the flesh, figured in the titular beast, with its ancient phallic connotation . . . , and the writhings of Joe Lon to escape himself through those characteristic Crews' channels, sex and violence—including violent sex. Spirit, save in the form of bootleg whiskey, is not much in evidence here, and aside from the rattlesnake hunt, the chief event around which the story is organized is a dogfight, in which the bloody struggles between the animals and occasional impromptu matches between the spectators are thoroughly (and purposefully) confused. Joe Lon, like the caged pit bulls, is a hopeless, doomed case, a trapped and savage satyr, whose final release comes when, in a fit of mad rage, he empties a shotgun into a crowd of snake hunters, who in turn fall on him in a howling vengeful mass of open mouths and bared teeth.

It is difficult to reconcile this horrific vision of Southern life with Crews' autobiographical version, in which the main stress evokes James Agee in its optimistic presentation of Southern tenant-farmer life, with its rural even Georgic rounds. Such a life, in Crews' account, is not without its grotesqueries and violence, and his childhood was one of crippling illnesses and accidents, of grinding poverty and memories of a drunken, abusive stepfather. (At times the book seems to be Mark Twain's *Autobiography* as written by a literate Huck Finn—which in a sense it was.) But the main figure in the field is Crews' mother, a strong-willed if dirty-mouthed farm-wife, who looms likewise in the background of a number of his novels, ruling over her fatherless children with a strong but loving hand. Once again, she most properly belongs to that "famous" breed of impoverished tenant farmers of which Agee once sang, not to the exotic South of Faulkner or Caldwell. Typically, in *Feast of Snakes* Crews transfers a number of his mother's qualities to Big Joe Mackey, the father figure, nor are there present many strong mother figures in his novels. Women in general are treated by Crews as sexual objects—as in *Feast of Snakes* a kind of life-size Barbie Doll with openings—or else are repugnant and asexual, like Joe Lon's sister, Beeder.

We can, that is to say, detect a characteristic disjunctiveness between the facts of Crews' rural boyhood and his use of those facts in his fiction, a version of the cultural schizophrenia that often takes place in the Southern novel, being a surrealistic

and satirical equivalent to the Gothicising of Mississippi in Faulkner's fictive world. That Crews would look to Nathanael West as a model, filling out Caldwell's world of sexually obsessed grotesques with an apocalytic mob is . . . part of what can be called the Hollywoodization of the South, a literary equivalent to the introduction of superhighways and fast-food restaurants in the Southern landscape. But it also serves to emphasize what amount to definitive differences between the apocalyptic visions of West and Crews: where California and Georgia may both serve as mystical, horrific terrain, there is notably no nativist element in West's landscape, for all his characters are aliens and exiles of a sort. To pervert an old saying, you can take the good ol' boy out of the country, but you can never remove the apostrophe. . . . Crews, while using a number of West's satiric and surreal formulas, while abandoning for a time his own rural backgrounds for a Southern version of Los Angeles, never quite succeeds in ridding himself of the soil on his motorcyclist's boots, and in *Feast of Snakes* we find him back home again—back, that is to say, in Erskine Caldwell's Georgia.

I have up until now purposefully avoided more than a scant mention of Flannery O'Connor, another Georgian whose early works were powerfully influenced by Nathanael West, nor do I want to engage in a lengthy comparison between her novels and stories and those of Harry Crews. Yet it seems worthwhile to note that both share a strong element of religiosity in common with West, an element which is more clearly (even conventionally) Christian in the work of West and O'Connor, much less so in Crews. O'Connor, a Catholic writer working in a deeply sectarian Protestant South, introduces a characteristic note of grace among her grotesques, a metaphorical beam of light that irradiates otherwise twisted, hopeless lives. West likewise allows his characters some kind of transfiguring, Christlike passion. But Crews is an artistic Antaeus, being entirely pagan and earthbound, for whom the religious experience is never transcendent, always tied to violent exercise, being a version of heightened fury not bliss: much blood is in evidence, none of it wise, the violent always bear it away, and good men are very hard to find. If Crews is an important contemporary writer, and I think he is, he serves to remind us that the old outrage sleeps on under the chrome-plated New South, deeply rooted as ever in defeat and frustration, a kind of red-clay kraken that may yet rise again. (pp. 621-26)

> *John Seelye, "Georgia Boys: The Redclay Satyrs of Erskine Caldwell and Harry Crews," in* The Virginia Quarterly Review, *Vol. 56, No. 4, Autumn, 1980, pp. 612-26.*

JACK MOORE

Harry Crews subtitles *A Childhood,* his book of autobiographical reminiscences, "the biography of a place" because, he explains, "the biography of a childhood necessarily is the biography of a place, a way of life, gone forever out of the world." . . . Place is the terrain created by Crews's imagination. It does not dominate that quirky imagination, but it provides a land upon which he can construct the odd blend of intense realism and uproarious, sick, dreamy fabulation that is the secret blend of his artistry. Crews's manic-depressive world of comic, sexual, and sometimes something like spiritual highs and pit-bottom lows (the low of the failed soul finding out there isn't any Hell and no God around, only death and small-town Georgia) is held in place partly by the terrain that stretches in his mind from one story to the next. (p. 46)

The territory of Crews's South is generally an unlovely and bitter land, though it is a land he fears and respects and not a place (or places) that he mocks, as he ordinarily does the fabricated world of towns and cities and empty civilization that mankind has jerrybuilt upon it. In *A Childhood* the land of his youth, around Alma, in Bacon County, Georgia, is depicted usually in terms that would make Thomas Wolfe's Old Catawba seem like a Norman Rockwell paradise.... (p. 47)

A Childhood is autobiographical, but perhaps all biography is simply another version of fiction. The work serves as a revealing introduction to most of Crews's novels since it displays nakedly many of the ways in which, in his earlier novels, he uses the land and the city; in *A Childhood* he writes that "everything everywhere in the city was tainted." His first published novel, *The Gospel Singer*, deals with similar physical and spiritual territory. Tracing the rise, fall, and possible popular apotheosis of a Georgia evangelist from a place so small it can hardly be called a town, the book is Crews's most obviously, though not necessarily his most intensely, religious novel. True religion and not just religious imagery is an important element of Crews's fiction, much of which traces some kind of religious quest or other for salvation or atonement, though for what (other than being simply human) is not always clear. In *A Childhood* Crews writes, "Hell was at the center of any sermon I had ever heard in Bacon County," Hell and "God and heaven and damnation and the sorry state of the human condition."

Enigma, the chief locale of *The Gospel Singer*, also seems like Hell. Like Crews's childhood place, it is also inescapable. Enigma, Georgia, is also a real town that can be found on a good road map. It is one of those places you suspect no one has ever been, and were you to drive through it, chances are you would probably doubt that it existed after you left. Like so many of the other small places Crews writes about in Georgia (that can also be found on good maps), if you saw it you would sense that it momentarily materialized around the road because there has to be something there beyond the cement or macadam other than void. But Crews knows the inside of these places, and he opens them up in all their rank depravity (though again, in alternative reality, they may very well be the quiet, loveliest little villages of the plain). One of Crews's fairly constant techniques is to insist upon the reality of his places, partly by using real though strange place names like Enigma—or Mystic, Georgia, in *A Feast of Snakes*—and then to distort the reality of the place into one of his warped fables of "the sorry state of the human condition." But unlike Erskine Caldwell, with whom Crews is sometimes compared because they both seem to work the same region with the same comic and violent and sexual sense of the grotesque, traces of a God, though perhaps a fearsome and even sadistic God (the Ultimate Sumbitch), remain throughout Crews's land. Crews is a religious novelist, and Caldwell, despite *God's Little Acre,* was not—he has not that resonance throughout his work though he has a socio-political awareness Crews lacks. Even Faulkner has not, it seems to me, Crews's religious mania, for, though there is strong religious symbolism in Faulkner's work, it often seems (though beautifully crafted) more part of his artistic than of his spiritual identity. The Southern writer whose mean, sacred land Crews's setting seems most like, is Flannery O'Connor, whose mind traveled along some of the same dark highways as Crews's. (pp. 47-8)

Naked in Garden Hills, like *The Gospel Singer,* possesses a strong sense of place and a religious orientation that Crews pursues under the surface of his story in painful allegorical detail. The novel's chief locale, Garden Hills, Florida, has been created by the mysterious Jack O'Boylan, who bought the land without ever seeing it, but who, Crews writes with satirical, pseudo-biblical phrasing, "looked, and saw that it was real good" on a geologist's report. O'Boylan sets men to work reshaping the land into a model industrial community, and long after he has left like a departed god, men still work the place, why, "Nobody knows! Nobody knows!" Only "Jack O'Boylan knows, but he's not here and he's not telling." The book is like a parody of the creation myth, a sort of disjointed allegory where you feel that parallels were worked out and then one list slipped from the matching set of cultural associations just enough to throw the identifications haywire but not so much as to destroy the structure of seeming correspondences. This technique suggests that such correspondences are arbitrary anyway, since the original story is a sham itself, or an artificial construct. Thus, creation becomes a "shaggy dog story" because it is pointless beyond the activity of itself. Things can fit anywhere....

O'Boylan's dreams for the land are based upon geologists' reports that it is rich in phosphates. Bulldozers move the earth into hills, an enormous plant is constructed, the unemployed are given tasks, Buicks are bought, and, ultimately, the town of Garden Hills is constructed from prefabricated houses—at the bottom of a twenty-five acre hole produced by the removal of phosphate soil for the factory in which the town's inhabitants work. "The earth trembled" with machines and the factory "increased of its own will." And then, all was silence. The factory stopped running, closed. The geologists had erred. The land was profitless.

What remains is the place of the novel, a land mainly without hope, a collection of failures, mostly. The land was bad before the fall, and after wards it is worse. (p. 51)

What to do after the fall is the problem of the novel, how to exist in the nothingness that is Garden Hills, a dead white world whose veneer of civilization is once more made of junk....

Crews seems ambivalent about the possibility of honest hope in such an existence (and who can blame him?). There is a spot of green in Garden Hills: "The Jack O'Boylan Reclamation Park," mass-produced in Peoria, Illinois, and transported by a fifty-truck caravan. The park has grass, flowers, trees, a well and sprinkler system that rains each night.... Unfortunately for the hopes of the people, the green pasture never grows any bigger, though neither does it shrink and disappear. The park is another joke, of course; it has been turned into a roadside lunch stop, and, if things work out, will be part of a planned tourist attraction (trap). Still, it is green and moist and there.

The attraction itself is another ambiguous feature of the local landscape. Planned by an ex-Phosphate Queen (Crews has a charming regard for beauty contest winners that he expresses in several books) who, tacky as her imagination may be, refuses to quit hoping. All indications suggest it will be an even more bizarre highway stop than such legendary American shrines (counterparts of Mont St. Michel and Chartres) as "South of the Border" in South Carolina or "Harold's Place" in Reno. Dolly, the Phosphate Queen, appears to have a desire to live fully and no respect whatsoever for the integrity of Garden Hills, which she splotches blood red, even its weeds, with garish paint slopped from the side of the old factory. What she will create on the land seems terrible and obscene—the Fat

Man in a disco cage suspended over a dance floor—but it also seems alive. Perhaps this is all the people of Garden Hills can hope for, living over the excreta of dead organisms (the phosphate) between Tampa and Orlando. (p. 52)

Karate Is a Thing of the Spirit is Crews's first novel to take place entirely in an urban context. Land is therefore no force in the book, but place is still significant. Most of the book's action occurs in a narrow strip of territory north of Miami including Dania, Hollywood, and Fort Lauderdale.... Although the northern part of Florida is Southern (centrally), the southern counties of Broward and Dade (roughly from Miami to Fort Lauderdale) he mentions in the book are really not. So it is significant to note that Crews selects as his locale a place where the traditions one would expect to obtain, do not, and where there is, in place of the old rich (and perhaps rank) Southern culture, a variety of cultures, many of them as new and practically as thin as the parking lots and roads which are among their chief architectural features. It is perhaps even significant that he uses somewhat smaller and definitely off-center places such as Dania and Hollywood, which lack Miami's lush, glittery formica-top byzantine quality. That he is precise about the roads that crisscross these cities is only natural since the roads in a sense are the cities, are what has replaced the empty land that the cities once were. The bumper-to-bumper, deafening traffic Crews describes seems a constant element of the landscape, like the sun always hot and burning straight down at noon....

This is a country of hot parking lots and bright, bleak motels—the novel's Tara is called the Sun 'n Fun Motel. Here train the karateka the book's hero is trying to join. They practice in a dry pool that perhaps parodies the old sacred fount Joseph Campbell memorialized in his *Hero with a Thousand Faces*. It is no wonder that people are no longer in touch with themselves, except perhaps to smear on more suntan lotion.

How you get in touch with yourself (but not become narcissistic) and how you properly get in touch with the people around you, how you bear to live in a terrifying world, seem to me generally the big questions Crews is always getting at in his novels. *Karate Is a Thing of the Spirit* contains a lot of kung-fu muck that perhaps is meant to be wisdom about how these questions are answered.... The point of the novel is that the old gods have surely gone, and we are miserable if we cannot find new gods to sustain us in a paved-over, super-highwayed universe trashed with motels. (p. 54)

Oddly, there is a loveliness to the real area Crews has chosen as the novel's locale, one that only rarely is noticed in the book, probably both because the beauty would be unsuitable to the symbolic environment Crews wished to wrap around his characters and because in reality that loveliness (the huge, usually blue sky, the big clear moon—the "Moon over Miami" really is splendid—the clean-looking ocean) has been in part squeezed out by junk piled on top of dredged-up sand and drained-away hammocks....

What John Kaimon discovers from the karateka and from the miraculous beauty queen and karate master he is raped by and impregnates, such as the new joy he can feel enduring pain, tells him apparently more than he knew before and maybe brings him closer to what his hero William Faulkner knew. But ultimately he leaves the karateka and their motel and presumably the urban society that is violent and dangerous like the land, but, unlike the land, unworthy of respect and inadequate to sustain piety; he lights out on the road. He is one of

the survivors in Crews's fiction, and, as the epigraph to *A Childhood* states, "Survival is triumph enough."

Crews's remaining novels expand and deepen his use of land and city to illuminate his characters' search for some way to deal with the generally terrible life and place they find themselves in. Whether the later novels are darker than the earlier ones is debatable. The apocalypse at the end of *The Gospel Singer* seems as agonizing in its way as the slaughter concluding *A Feast of Snakes,* and the cruel but respected terrain in the former novel neither more nor less frightening than the snake-filled hills of Mystic, the locale of the latter work. Always Crews packs his books with incidents central to basic American myth (though not the ones usually discussed in textbooks), as, for example, the archetypal sexual fantasy he describes in *Car:* a high school cheerleader tupped by the star fullback who had scored also four touchdowns that day, screwed in his "Vette," the American post-adolescent dream car. Always America is packed with the junk of our cheapened civilized life, and often the land offers as an alternative something wild and dangerous not to love, exactly, but to respect because somehow a spirit—even if a destructive, evil spirit—resides in it. (p. 55)

The Gypsy's Curse is the least place-centered of Crews's novels. The book concerns Marvin Molar's search for something fulfilling in life, a search made complicated by his physical grotesqueness (his body is exceptionally powerful but his legs are wasted, and when he gives shopping mall demonstrations of his strength and agility he tucks them like skin flaps under his buttocks).

Areas such as Tampa Bay, Ybor City (in Tampa), Clearwater Beach, and Tarpon Springs, all in close proximity in Florida, are locales for the book's action (though an important minor character is from Bacon County, Georgia), but none is used extensively, either as symbol or physical place. (p. 57)

The area [Crews] writes about could be practically anywhere, except that it is warm and has beaches. Perhaps that is his point about the sameness of life in most of America, a land where housewives can buy fake ballerina slippers (as does the juiceless wife of Russell Muscle, the weightlifter) anywhere, at any Woolworth's, in any shopping center. The vision of the novel is Marvin's vision, not necessarily Harry Crews's, and Marvin sees little value in the land.... For Marvin there is no spirit or force in the land around him for him to fear or respect, and at the end of the book no one alive that he can both need and love (he kills the woman in whose "lap" he has found such bliss). In his concluding words he says he is heading for a prison that perhaps his awful body has directed him toward all along, but a prison it is possible that he, through his own limited and warped vision—in part, a vision reflected back from how the world sees him—has helped to construct.

The Gypsy's Curse is also about how close Crews feels love and violence are. *A Feast of Snakes* concerns the proximity of lust, violence, human terribleness, the nothingness of existence, and so many other Crewsian horrors it almost becomes a parody of Crews, but, as *The Sound and the Fury* escapes parody, so does it. Seemingly in complete innocence Crews prefaces his book with the disclaimer that "this is a work of the imagination.... Even though there is a real Mystic, Georgia, the town by that name in this book is, itself, an entire fiction." On the map and in the heart Mystic is not far from the Enigma of *The Gospel Singer*. Football may have replaced religion, more people than just the singer are humping away at sex, mountains may have replaced the swamp, but the moral terrain is still the same. The land is strong and grim. (pp. 57-8)

Meanness is a way of life and so is football in Mystic, though some bring their meanness from faraway places like Tifton or Cordele or Gainesville. The alternative to this hard land is the same sad, dull world of *The Gospel Singer:* Coca Cola signs, the television on all day, Jim Beam drunk from half-pint bottles, a twirl-off between graduates of the Dixie National Baton Twirling Institute (headed by "Mr. Baton," Don Sartell, one of the greats undoubtedly listed in *Who's Who in Baton Twirling,* a resource book I hope Crews has not invented).

What is one to do to exist in this land, in these worlds? Most screw or drink or play football for excitement. Some engage in combinations of the three. Filled with beer, Joe Lon, the novel's protagonist, strikes his straddle-legged cheerleader ex-girlfriend in bed "from behind like she'd been a tackling dummy." But Joe Lon has not been able to go to college to prolong his years of mindless stardom playing football, a brutal game of "joy" and "celebration," and so for most of the time he is left alone on the land selling bootleg whisky to Negroes and dying of despair. He is dying in one sense of his own limitations, but in another way his failure is, as Crews sees it, I suppose, mankind's failure, the failure of all ultimately who will one day have no more fun, no more sexual bliss to cover momentarily the nothingness out there, the time when status goes and identity goes and sooner or later the body goes, and despair settles in like a dense fog throttling what used to be the soul, when the screwing is over.

A Feast of Snakes ends with an act of madness and is pervaded by madness. The land itself or what has been made of it is crusted with madness, as snake festival tourists swarm over the surface of hills, hunting out snakes, burning them up from caves, clubbing them, penning them. One of the acts of history that obsesses Crews occurred when Charles Whitman climbed up the library tower at the University of Texas and methodically killed twelve people walking across the University square. We all face, he says in *Blood and Grits,* our own Texas Towers. "To deny that you have your tower to climb and that you must resist it to succumb to the temptation to do it, to deny that is done at the peril of your heart and mind." The day of the snake hunt Joe Lon climbs his tower and discovers what he has all along wanted to do in this world of despair. After he kills four people with shotgun blasts, the snake hunters attack him as they had the snakes and throw him into the snake pit. "He fell into the boiling snakes, went under and came up. . . . Snakes hung from his face." The snakes are part of the land of which Harry Crews always writes. Traditionally they are evil, but in *A Feast of Snakes* they seem no less horrible than the hunters who pursue them. They are a force on the land we should not forget, and in Crews's novels they inhabit a place that we should fear perhaps as gods are feared, or as they once were feared when they inhabited the land.

I have ignored or given minimal attention to much that is important in Crews's fiction—in terms of his themes, his characterization, and his superb use of comedy, for example—to focus upon how he uses place in his novels. I have tried to indicate that the South he has written about so far is usually the South of very small towns in rural Georgia or areas (often urban) in the Sunbelt South that are without significant history in the Old South of popular myth. These places lack the regionality of the locales he uses in and around his Bacon County home terrain but seem quintessentially American in their kitsch-ridden superficiality. Raw nature in his books may be harsh

and usually is unlovely and cruel. It is not Faulkner's land of pre-lapsarian beauty and fertility cursed by the South's sins of pride and slavery (though he obviously admires Faulkner as a writer), nor it is completely the hard, red gullies of Erskine Caldwell's despiritualized territory (though Crews also admires Caldwell). Crews's land is ordinarily a tough place in which to make a living, but it is also a wild place of more than physical potency, a place where spirits would dwell (though not benign spirits) if our earth possessed anywhere remnants of some godly force. It is a place of snakes and hawks. What man has created instead of it, the reclamation parks, the strips of beach and highway north of Miami, the car terminals like Jacksonville, have nothing godly residing in them as places. Their cultures are material and comic and shallow and secular. Perhaps people are drawn to them for these reasons, and because the Bacon Counties are not, after all, particularly happy places to be. (pp. 58-9)

[Place] in Crews's fiction is carefully designed to help dramatize that world from which God seems to have departed, leaving sin and vengeance behind. His Southern fiction typically erases or suggests only faintly in the background the South's beauty; instead, Crews stresses the harshness and ugliness of its terrain, which is usually a bleak and bitter and unproductive land, burned by the sun and bursting only into muck with the rain. But Crews does not view this natural landscape merely as a barren place of toil. The land contains a powerful force to be feared, a wildness to be respected, an almost godlike cruelty. If God exists, he is probably best represented by the land. If He no longer exists, the remains of His punishing spirit may still reside in the land—and possibly in the hearts of the people who inhabit the land and who seemingly have nothing else to replace God with. Usually this land is out of the way. The cities are in the way, in a newer, tawdry South without rich traditions, loaded with junk and blank with parking lots and despiritualized lives. No fear or respect is owed these urban places.

Crews's major characters living in either place are unhappy, though frequently viciously funny. Like the characters in Graham Greene's novels (and Greene is one of Crews's favorites), whether they know it or not, they are trying to find substitutes for God. On a less portentously theological level, they are trying to make do, to cope, to love, desperately to blot out the nothingness of life and the everywhereness of death. Some, like Dolly in *Naked in Garden Hills,* appear to succeed, but at a tremendous cost of diminished values. Others, such as the protagonists of *Car* or *Karate Is a Thing of the Spirit,* seem to find at least temporary hook-ups with loving, similarly needful women. But in each of these books the finally coupled lovers swirl away down the highway much like the fabled sweethearts in Keats's "Eve of St. Agnes," who fade romantically into a beautiful storm. Others, such as the Gospel Singer or Marvin Molar or Joe Lon, drown in violence, their own or that of others they have induced.

Blacks suffer along with whites in both the country and city locations Crews depicts. Like Willalee in *The Gospel Singer,* they are similar to whites in believing in false saviors—they have not, as they seem to have in Faulkner, cornered the market on true piety. They are often victimized, although occasionally they display, as does Pete in *The Gypsy's Curse,* a fool's greater wisdom. They also try like Jester in *Naked in Garden Hills* to escape the same pits of failure as the whites, and, again like Jester, they can succeed in the sense that at least their dance of doom can take place in a jazzy discotheque. In other words, in many ways Crews treats his black characters the same way he treats his whites. He constantly satirizes characters who are black, but he performs the same operation upon his whites. In earlier novels such as *The Gospel Singer* he employs traditional stereotypes in focusing on razor-toting, high-yellow, loving "niggers," but even then he also demonstrates awareness of their brutal dispossession from society.

In his most recent books, *A Feast of Snakes* and *A Childhood,* he continues to employ these stereotypes, but with increased perception of the reality of blackness underneath the mask of behavior some blacks have been forced to assume. Partly because the values dominating Crews's books are the values that dominate his white characters, his fiction so far doubtless would be awarded no medals for promoting racial understanding or portraying black characters positively. Doubtless, too, Crews does not perceive those goals as consistent with his concept of the writer's job, which is to tell stories that show what we are like by placing us in extreme situations where we are pushed to the brink and beyond. (pp. 65-6)

> Jack Moore, "The Land and the Ethnics in Crews's Works," in A Grit's Triumph: Essays on the Works of Harry Crews, *edited by David K. Jeffrey, Associated Faculty Press, Inc., 1983, pp. 46-66.*

FRANK W. SHELTON

In the mid-1970s [Crews] expressed an interest in writing about himself directly rather than in the disguised mode of fiction. The results were *A Childhood,* a series of articles published in an *Esquire* column called "Grits" which appeared fairly regularly from 1975 to 1977, and longer essays published in such magazines as *Esquire* and *Playboy. Florida Frenzy* is the second collection of his nonfiction pieces, the first being *Blood and Grits* (1979). There is a good deal of overlap between the two volumes; *Florida Frenzy* includes thirteen essays (all having to do with some aspect of Florida), five of which were previously published in *Blood and Grits.* The earlier volume is much wider ranging, consisting of seventeen essays covering a greater variety of subjects.

Aside from *A Childhood,* a moving and beautifully written autobiography, the two volumes of articles are the best introduction available to the personality of Harry Crews, for regardless of the ostensible subject of an essay, one focus is always Crews himself. Many of the articles were originally published in *Esquire,* an original champion of the New Journalism, and Crews, though often dealing with characteristically Southern subjects, dramatizes himself in somewhat the same way a journalist like Hunter Thompson does. He does not remain aloof or detached from his subjects but like Thompson shows how they have an impact on him personally. In **"The Car,"** a treatment of the role of the automobile in contemporary culture, he describes himself painting his automobile twenty-seven times, saying, "I went a little nuts, as I am prone to do, because I'm the kind of guy who if he can't have too much of a thing doesn't want any at all." Like Thompson, he will frequently present himself as either drunk or high on drugs, suggesting that he is not immune to the insanity around him. (pp. 132-33)

Everyone Crews writes about becomes a Crews character, odd and given, like him, to extremes of action and attitude. It may be that he brings out this facet of others, or perhaps he has been able to choose his assignments so that he writes only about things and people that appeal to him. Of course, an

alternative explanation might be that he is fudging the truth a bit, for some of the events and people could have been lifted directly from his novels. . . . Crews would assert, I think, that his pieces are true to the essence of an experience, if not to every literal fact or detail.

He presents in his nonfiction a world at once violent and absurd and seeks value therein. The absurdity is often manifested by tourists, through whom Crews satirizes what has happened to the modern South, as he often does in his fiction. In **"The Wonderful World of Winnebagos,"** for example, he encounters a man and his son who are determined to hit a golf ball off of every scenic overlook in the Shenandoah National Park in Virginia. He witnesses other kinds of absurdity as well. During the same walk along the Appalachian Trail he meets Jake Leach, a lawyer whose life was shattered when, at age five, he witnessed the hanging of a circus elephant. In the first instance, Crews's reaction is outrage, but in the second he feels a kind of sick and horrified pity. The people he seems to admire most are genuine and down to earth and remain what he calls "grits." He seems to have little respect for sophistication or even for formal education. One of his best pieces, which appears in both *Florida Frenzy* and *Blood and Grits,* is **"Tuesday Night with Cody, Jimbo and a Fish of Some Proportion."** Focusing on two Good Old Boys who are close friends but who are in constant violent competition with one another, Crews describes and evaluates them:

> Both Cody and Jimbo worked with their daddies on two of the biggest watermelon farms in North Florida, the watermelon capital of the world. Years of tossing thirty-pound melons up to a man on a high-sided truck from first light to first dusk had given them bodies so keyed up, coiled, and ready to strike that if they weren't actually heaving melons, they literally did not know what to do, how to act. The problem resolved itself in random violence full of joy and love masquerading as anger. Nobody ever said it, but everybody knew it. It was his knowledge that gave the senseless, meaningless, childish moments late at night a certain and very real dignity.

Crews will often find dignity and meaning in violence. One of his favorite topics is ports: drag racing, horse racing, hawk training, and especially cockfighting and dogfighting, two subjects covered in *Florida Frenzy.* He admits, "I love blood sports. Not a particularly admirable trait, but one that I've always had and one that I've never tried to suppress or find the reasons for." (pp. 133-34)

Several of his more interesting pieces (not included in *Florida Frenzy* but in *Blood and Grits*) are his lengthy portraits of people done on assignment. Crews admits he is a terrible interviewer because he is not self-effacing, but the value of these pieces is his personal responsiveness to his subjects. : . . Especially in **"Television's Junkyard Dog,"** his long piece on Robert Blake, the rebellious star of "Baretta," Crews, through an almost total identification with Blake, conveys more about himself directly than he does in any other piece of his writing except *A Childhood.* In fact, this essay is essential to anyone wanting to understand the life and fiction of Harry Crews.

His nonfiction as a body, interesting in itself, is valuable for the light it sheds on his fiction, since finally his greatest importance is as a novelist. His interest in sports can definitely be seen in the novels. Further, his essay **"The Car"** has direct application to *Car,* as does **"The Hawk Is Flying"** to *The Hawk is Dying.* Crews holds nothing back in anything he writes. Even clearer in the nonfiction is his stance as a particularly modern

Southerner, situated uncomfortably between two worlds. One part of him remains deep in the Southern soil of his ''grit'' childhood and wants to remain there. But given his adult experiences, especially teaching for many years at the University of Florida, another part of him is firmly situated in modern urban America. The personal tension many of the essays convey arises from this divided allegiance, which is what makes Crews a particularly important contemporary Southern writer.

The pieces in *Florida Frenzy* and *Blood and Grits* above all are readable and reveal a unique perspective on the modern South, as does his fiction. No article in either collection is mere routine journalism; Crews could not write that if his life depended on it. It is hoped that the availability of *Florida Frenzy* will whet readers' appetites and encourage them to explore those works where his artistry is more profoundly on display, *A Childhood* and the novels. Then Harry Crews will receive proper recognition as a unique voice in contemporary Southern letters and one of the best novelists currently writing about the South. (p. 135)

Frank W. Shelton, "The Nonfiction of Harry Crews: A Review," in The Southern Literary Journal, *Vol. XVI, No. 2, Spring, 1984, pp. 132-35.*

DAVID K. JEFFREY

A Feast of Snakes (1976), Harry Crews's eighth and, in my view, best novel, chronicles four November days in the life of its protagonist, Joe Lon Mackey, a former high school All-American fullback in Mystic, Georgia, who, two years after his graduation in the book's present time, finds himself no longer Boss Snake of the Mystic Rattler football team but rather the manager of the town's annual rattlesnake roundup, for which he is preparing as the novel opens. Although invited to more than fifty colleges and universities, Joe Lon has never played college football because he is unable to read. . . . Joe Lon is trapped in Mystic and surrounded with reminders that his own glorious days are past; as the novel opens, he watches the majorettes prance and football players practice, telling himself again what he tells himself ''about ten times a day: *That's all right. By God, I had mine.*'' As the novel progresses, however, his life is increasingly not all right. It fills with drunkenness, bullying, sex, and blood, and it finally collapses into madness and murder, ending when an irate mob throws him into a snakepit filled with rattlers. Yet, at the same time Crews tells Joe Lon's brutal story, Crews writes an intensely funny book; he elicits from the reader considerable sympathy for the murderous illiterate who is his protagonist, and he provides insights into his own sense of the nature and causes of his protagonist's violence and the violence which pervades Joe Lon's world.

As the novel opens, Crews outlines the sorry state of Joe Lon's life in a series of brief and vivid scenes: Joe Lon standing in the end zone bleachers, watching Hard Candy Sweet, majorette and sister of Berenice Sweet, his former girlfriend, soon to return from the University of Georgia for the rattlesnake roundup and promising (or threatening) to see him when she does; Joe Lon living in ''a constant state of suffocating anger'' with his wife Elfie and two unnamed male babies in a doublewide trailer which smells as if she's ''been cooking baby shit,'' as Joe Lon says, and where he beats her and otherwise treats her ''like a goddam dog,'' as he recognizes; Joe Lon howling in frustration and pain as he drives to the shed-like store where he and two black helpers deal whiskey and moonshine illegally and plan

the logistics of setting up Johnny-on-the-spot chemical toilets for the roundup participants; . . . finally, late that night, Joe Lon bringing whiskey at the house of his deaf father, Big Joe, a deacon in the Church of Jesus Christ With Signs Following, who—in one room—trains the best pit bulldogs in Georgia by strapping them to an electric treadmill with weights on their lower jaws and running it until the dogs drop and who—in another room—keeps Joe Lon's lunatic sister, Beeder, in bed now for several years watching television and who, when Joe Lon looks in on her, lifts a piece of excrement from her chamber pot and puts it into her hair. All in all, not anybody's idea of a good day.

These events introduce the novel's two major images and its central analogue; too, the events prepare the reader for the novel's terminating violence.

The first of the major image clusters in *A Feast of Snakes* has to do with excrement, which permeates the world of the novel from Mystic, Georgia, to Vietnam, as Donald Johnson has noted [in his essay ''The Athlete's Hand Filling Up: Harry Crews and Sports'']. Metaphorically and vulgarly, for example, Joe Lon has ''shitty younguns'' and his trailer reeks of their stink; Buddy threatens to ''slap the shit'' out of Lottie Mae but ''catch[es] some shit'' when Lottie Mae castrates him, rendering him ''shit out of luck''—and dead. As Beeder Mackey remarks, using an expression that appears in four of Crews's novels, ''Daddy would say to wish in one hand and shit in the other, see which one fills up first.'' Appropriate here, the expression indicates that Joe Lon's ideals, his hopes and dreams for his future, even for his life, are severely limited by the reality which excrement images. As both Norman O. Brown and Ernest Becker have noted, anality reflects the tragedy of man's dualism, for the two dimensions of his existence—his body and his self—cannot be reconciled, given the body's continual reminder of man's link with nature. . . . Lacking the excitement and immediacy of sport, the promise of his youth, Joe Lon's life has filled, metaphorically and literally, with excrement, reminding him of the impossibility of transcendence. His wife can spend half her life washing out baby diapers, Joe Lon can import chemical toilets all the way from Cordele, Georgia, but their efforts will not avail against the tide of ''shit. Human shit in quantities that nobody could believe,'' as Joe Lon correctly predicts. By the novel's third day, as one of Joe Lon's friends phrases it, ''Mystic, Georgia, has done tore its ass.'' The Johnny-on-the-spots are overflowing and the participants have turned into a primordial mass, the kind of mean and angry mob Crews portrays at the conclusion of several of his novels to mirror man at his most bestial. Here again Crews uses excrement metaphorically as an image of the mob's rancor and nastiness; here, his excremental vision, like Swift's, functions as social commentary and social satire, a vulgar and realistic reminder of man's animality and his final end.

The novel's second and related major image cluster has to do with snakes. Real snakes abound in Mystic, the ''best rattlesnake hunting ground in the world.'' Rattlers are killed for meat, their rattles woven into mosaics, their skins used to fashion wallets, belts, shoes, and underclothes. Metaphorically, Joe Lon has been Boss Snake and, years ago, has lain with Berenice Sweet in an empty snakepit where she imagines a cold bath of snakes, snakes in her blood, crawling through her heart, hanging from the world's throats, while being serviced by ''the Boss Snake of all,'' Joe Lon's penis. At the novel's conclusion, of course, her bizarre sexual fantasy is realized literally, when the mob throws Joe Lon into another snakepit and rattlers hang "from his face." Buddy Matlow's transformation of *his* penis into a snake, using a snake-headed prophylactic with a diamondback pattern to do so, has a similarly catastrophic conclusion, though one which has a certain rough justice. He makes the mistake of exhibiting his serpentine member to Lottie Mae the night after he has threatened her with a real rattler and raped her; she has retreated into a madness resembling Berenice's sexual fantasy, for snakes now sleep inside Lottie Mae, wear her skin like clothes, grow in her hair, move in her stomach. When Buddy threatens her again with a snake, she strikes his lap with her razor; the result, as she tells Beeder, is "That snake shrunk up and died like magic," as Buddy himself does. Sex seldom has happy issue in Crews's novels, and here it is just no fun at all.

If snakes symbolize male power and threat here, they also function in another traditional symbolic way throughout the novel, as emblems of religious evil. The first words of the snake-handling preacher, Victor, emphasize this function: "The great dragon was cast out," he says. "The old serpent called the devil and satan which deceiveth the whole world. He was cast out into the earth and his angels were cast out with him." Lucifer and his angels seem to have lighted not merely on earth but, more specifically, in Mystic, Georgia. . . . Mystic's frank glorification of the snake differs from Victor's snake handling, since Victor, as Joe Lon's father says, "strings diamondbacks in his hair like a lady strings ribbons. I seen'm kiss a snake and a snake kiss him. He's been bit in the mouth. He's been bit everwhere. It ain't no more'n a kiss from his ma. He follers where God leads him." Believing in the reality of evil, which the snakes represent, Victor experiences "great joy" in handling them, hoping, by doing so, to come to terms with and triumph over them for the glory of God; thus, the snakes that hang from his face indicate his attempt to control evil. Such a hope, such an ideal is as unlikely to be fulfilled in the novel's world as wishing in one hand, and the snakes which hang from Joe Lon's face at the novel's conclusion indicate the more likely triumph of evil.

While the major images of the novel indicate Crews's sense of man's life as filled with excrement and evil, the book's principal analogue—dogfighting—suggests his sense that life is a constant and losing battle. Many of the novel's characters—none of them much given to literary matters—do recognize various aspects of the analogy. For example, Lottie Mae and Beeder, listening to the "ragged beating" of Big Joe's treadmill, "like the beating of an enormous erratic heart," equate the dog's labors on the machine with man's own labors in life; they believe Big Joe, like a kind of god, will eventually tie everyone onto his machine, and they recognize that he uses the treadmill not so much to exercise his dogs as to find out how much punishment they can take. Unlike the function of a poem, the function of the pit bull is not to be, but to be mean. No wonder Big Joe names all of his dogs Tuffy.

When Old Tuffy grows too old to fight and too old to procreate, Big Joe sharpens the fighting skills and blood lust of the dog's son by allowing the younger dog to destroy his father. Here Crews's analogy operates most clearly in the various Oedipal contests between Joe Lon and his friend Willard, the current Boss Snake, and between Joe Lon and Big Joe. Willard, of course, is out to break Joe Lon's old football and trade records and the two friends come close to attacking each other physically at least three times during the novel. Big Joe and Joe Lon seem to be contesting which one can drink more and which

can be more brutal to his wife; it is no real contest, for Big Joe has driven his wife to suicide. The difference between Joe Lon and either Willard or Big Joe is that neither of the latter, Joe Lon's friend or his father, seems hampered by even a modicum of sensibility, the smallest distaste for his lot, while Joe Lon, of course, suffers throughout because of his. (pp. 45-9)

While kneeling in the dirt exhibiting Tuffy, Joe Lon is confronted by a series of people, each bearing bad news: first, Willard announces Buddy's death; then, Elfie tells him he's shamed her in their bed with Berenice the previous night; then, Berenice admits she's told both Elfie and Shep, her fiance, that she and Joe Lon have had sex the night before; then, Shep tells him Buddy died spouting blood from his crotch; then, Victor begins loudly to preach; and then, Joe Lon begins to howl and loses consciousness. Hours later, recovered from his spell of madness, he begins to comprehend:

> it was not any one thing that scared him. It was everything. It was his life. . . . Everything seemed to be coming apart. He could see the frayed and ragged seams of everything slowly unraveling . . . everybody coming to him in the pit, barking and barking at him, and the overwhelming feeling that he was going to be in there the rest of his life with everybody he'd ever known filing past to tell him how he'd failed.

That night, after watching Tuffy die, he puts himself "carefully on the bed" and goes "carefully to sleep, a deep, dreamless sleep," because he knows and accepts

> for the first time that things would not be different tomorrow. Or ever. Things got different for some people. But for some they did not. There were a lot of things you could do, though. One of them was to go nuts trying to pretend things would someday be different. That was one of the things he did not intend to do.

The next morning, when Joe Lon sees Victor strip to the waist, take up some snakes, and begin "singing on about good and evil," he recognizes what thing he did intend to do, what he has "planned to do all along," what thing has "lain rank and fascinating in his brain" since the night before. He swings his shotgun down from its rack, blows a hole in Victor's chest, shoots away the deputy sheriff's face, then Berenice's neck, and finally the nearest snake hunter, all the while feeling "better than he had ever felt in his life. Christ," he thinks, "it was good to be in control again." Seconds later, the mob has thrown him among the rattlers. (p. 49)

Joe Lon's first three victims are by no means random targets; he murders characters who represent religion, law, and love; his fourth, a random and unnamed victim, images the faceless mob. These characters represent the forces, if not the very people, aligned against Joe Lon from the outset of the novel. His slaughter of them, therefore, has its logic and at least literary appropriateness. I do not interpret his act as mad, as Jack Moore does, and my sympathy for Joe Lon, apparently unlike Frank W. Shelton's [see *CLC*, Vol. 23], is mixed with horror. Both Moore and Shelton support their interpretations by citing in evidence Crews's essay **"Climbing the Tower."** In that essay, Crews meditates on the mass murder of twelve people in 1966, when Charles Whitman climbed to the top of [a tower] . . . and began shooting. An autopsy provided the most comforting explanation of Whitman's behavior, for the coroner discovered a tumor in Whitman's brain stem, and psychiatrists attributed to that physical imperfection Whitman's murders. Crews will have none of it; he states that "all over the surface of the earth where humankind exists men and women are resisting climbing the tower. All of us have our towers to climb.'' Crews also seems to link the collapse of this resistance to ''an atmosphere of perpetual failure. . . . All of us whose senses are not entirely dead realize the imperfection of what we do, and to the extent that we are hard on ourselves, that imperfection translates itself into failure.'' Moore uses the essay to argue by analogy that both Joe Lon and Charles Whitman, recognizing finally that their very lives are failures, climb the tower in despair and commit mass murder out of desperation and madness. In a recent essay on violence, however, Crews argues that some men use violence to avert their descent into madness. For such men, ''locked into social circumstances that result . . . in a kind of raging frustration,'' violence is a ''release,'' an ''outlet,'' an ''escape''. In Crews's view, the violence of such men does not make them either mad nor ''bad, it only makes [them] human.'' (p. 50)

Crews notes, Joe Lon ''like[s] violence. He like[s] blood and bruises, even when they [are] his own.'' For him there is ''a certain joy'' in brutality. ''The brutality on the football field, in the tonks, [is] celebration. Men were maimed [there] without malice, sometimes—often even—in friendship''. For Joe Lon violence seems to serve several functions: in its heightened intensity it provides escape from frustration and the mundane; it celebrates man's physicality and by so doing asserts life itself; it thus reveals to him a central truth about mankind and about his culture. . . . If theorists of violence veil this truth in their rational, sociological, or historical explanations, Crews tries to reveal that truth in his novel. If Crews comes close to agreement with any of these theorists, he comes closest to the theory of Konrad Lorenz. Lorenz argues that rational responsibility forms the most effective inhibitory mechanism against violence and that man's cultural forces, erected throughout history as stopgaps against violence, have been largely ineffective. It is impossible to test Lorenz's argument in favor of rational responsibility against *A Feast of Snakes,* or indeed, against any of Crews's novels, for his characters are hardly rational people; they think, if at all, with their muscles, their loins, and their blood. Yet Crews does pay particular attention to the cultural forces of his region, to the manners of his people. . . . In *A Feast of Snakes* he focuses on the fragility, corruption, and awesome cruelty of those forces.

Love, for example, which might otherwise bind man and woman, bind family, bind community—love in the novel's world is ''a scabrous spot of rot, of contagion, for which there [is] no cure. Rage would not cure it. Indulgence made it worse, inflamed it, made it grow like a cancer.'' In the novel's world, love has pitched its mansion in the place of excrement, as the reader discovers during the brutal and comic scene during which Joe Lon and Berenice fornicate. Love has driven Joe Lon's mother to suicide. It has driven Beeder insane. It drives Buddy Matlow to rape and leads to his castration. At least in part, love drives Joe Lon to adultery, buggery, and murder. Nor does the law sustain or restrain mankind. Its representatives, significantly, are an amputee/rapist (Buddy), an ineffectual, whining buffoon (Luther Peacock, the deputy sheriff), and a body-builder and karate champion (Duffy Deeter, a lawyer, who takes more pleasure in fighting than in torts). Finally, religion does not sustain. While Joe Lon believes ''in the total mystery, power, and majesty of God,'' he also believes that he is guilty of some unnamed and unknowable crime for which his life is a punishment, and God's representatives in Mystic, Georgia, Big Joe the deacon—harsh, unloving, and brutal—and Victor the

preacher—bizarre and monomanical—offer Joe Lon no promise of salvation or even relief.

Joe Lon's slaughter of Berenice, Luther Peacock, and Victor at the novel's apocalyptic conclusion represents, then, an assertion of the corruption and fragility of man's cultural forces, while the elation Joe Lon feels during this cataclysm asserts the essentially violent primordial nature of man. Joe Lon's murder of the nameless snake hunter, on the other hand, represents his (and, I suspect, Crews's) loathing for the faceless, mindless, anarchic animal, its ''teeth bared,'' to which man reverts when those cultural forces are destroyed, while the mob's murder of Joe Lon both asserts and reinforces Crews's sense of man's true, bestial nature. (pp. 52-3)

In sum, the image clusters, central analogue, and final scene of *A Feast of Snakes* makes clear Harry Crews's sense of contemporary man as trapped in a bizarre and fallen world. In such a world, man's cultural forces do not sustain him but rather disguise from him the truth of his condition and his reality. Only violence reveals that truth and provides an escape from madness and the mundane. (p. 53)

> *David K. Jeffrey, ''Murder and Mayhem in Crews's 'A Feast of Snakes','' in* Critique: Studies in Modern Fiction, *Vol. XXVIII, No. 1, Fall, 1986, pp. 45-53.*

CHRISTOPHER LEHMANN-HAUPT

Harry Crews is a founding member of what might be called the shopping-mall-Gothic school of Southern writers, whose imaginations inherited Faulkner's Snopeses instead of his Compsons. Mr. Crews hasn't published a novel since *A Feast of Snakes* came out 10 years ago. Earlier there were such bizarrely hilarious works as *The Gypsy's Curse, The Hawk Is Dying, Car* and *Karate Is a Thing of the Spirit,* among others. In the meantime, he has produced a harrowing account of his growing up on a south Georgia farm, *A Childhood,* and a collection of his journalism, *Blood and Grits.*

So it's good to see him back in print with a new novel, *All We Need of Hell,* a fable about an overdriven man who is redeemed by the author's unusual vision of friendship and love.

Duffy Deeter, the novel's mesomorphic, Type A protagonist, is an extreme version of a certain archetypal American male. Love-making with his mistress is for him a physical competition accompanied by fantasies of death, to be followed by a bicycle sprint through the streets of Gainesville, Fla. because ''nothing centered a man like pain.'' He ''often thought'' that sexual intercourse ''ought to be included in the Olympics judged on difficulty and variety of positions and how smoothly the positions were integrated. The ultimate dance. Nothing could be faked.''

Duffy resents his wife, Tish, for buying useless furniture, and holds his son, Felix, in contempt for living on candy bars and television. When his law partner, Jert McPhester, tries to engineer his humiliation on the handball court by setting him up to play against a pro football player named Tump Walker, Duffy absorbs a vicious blow to the head and then lays Walker out with ''a perfectly executed Okinawan roundhouse reverse, leading with the heel of his right foot, to Tump's head. . . .''

Duffy is living on the edge, and when Tish throws him out of the house—for making their son work out on an exercise machine to the point of vomiting—he goes over it. . . .

If *All We Need of Hell* ran according to Harry Crews's earlier fictional form, Duffy's misadventures would lead him to some bizarre or even ghoulish fate, to the punch line of a wildly inventive sick joke. But something new has been added in the interval since the author's last published novel. Just when things look darkest for Duffy, Tump Walker, the football player, shows up again and proceeds to teach Duffy the values of forgiveness and friendship.

There is something decidedly forced and even sentimental about this turn of events, and we wouldn't accept it from most novelists. We won't even take it from Harry Crews, really; we come away from the novel regarding it as a distinctly lesser effort. Still, we can't help forgiving him for it. There's still such a vividness to his characters. There's still such ease to his prose.

So we are charmed when the jive-talking Tump suddenly becomes a role model for Duffy's son, the slothful Felix. We are warmed when, at the story's ending, everyone winds up happily eating in the huge apartment Tump Walker got as part of the deal when he was traded from the Philadelphia Eagles to the Miami Dolphins. . . .

Tump tells his new friend: "You're a good man, Duffy, but you're willful. I got a feeling you missed a whole lot of good things in your life because you decided too much ahead of time." We accept Mr. Crews's sudden dive into cracker-barrel philosophy because he still has the power to make us smile and even laugh out loud.

> *Christopher Lehmann-Haupt, in a review of "All We Need of Hell," in* The New York Times, *January 12, 1987, p. C19.*

BEAUFORT CRANFORD

As Part Two begins in Harry Crews' 1976 novel *A Feast of Snakes,* Duffy Deeter is having sex with a young woman named Susan Gender. Duffy is thinking of Treblinka and Dachau, "about those showerheads and the wonderful gas spewing out into the children."

Duffy is distracting himself with such thoughts so he can keep hammering away at Susan, who is much less his lover than his victim.

As Harry Crews' 1987 novel *All We Need of Hell* begins, Duffy Deeter is having sex with a young woman named Marvella Sweat. Duffy is thinking of Treblinka and Dachau. What Marvella says to Duffy, what Duffy says to her, and what Duffy thinks—all of it is practically identical to what Harry Crews wrote years earlier in *A Feast of Snakes.*

Just what in the blue-eyed world is Harry Crews doing? A chapter of *All We Need of Hell* appeared in Crews' paperback anthology *Florida Frenzy* as "The Enthusiast," but I can't think of another case in which an author lifted a section from one novel and dumped it whole-hog into his next. . . .

Harry Crews has written a slew of exquisite fiction—brilliant and bitter stuff like *A Feast of Snakes,* or brilliant and moody stuff like *The Gypsy's Curse* (1974). He has also, in novels like *Car* (1972) and *The Gospel Singer* (1968), chewed at hypocrisy, materialism and conceit until they hollered. He has also, in *A Childhood* (1978), written a moving book of autobiography. He has also, in the collection *Blood and Grits* (1979), proven himself a splendid essayist and magazine writer.

Fine. Anyone who has read Harry Crews already knows he's an artist, and too bad for those who haven't; most of his previous books can't be found.

But *All We Need of Hell* can be. And if Duffy Deeter, who managed to emerge unscathed from *A Feast of Snakes* (no small feat), is anything, he is certainly an enthusiast. He is a world-class idiot, too.

Duffy thinks he thinks of other people, but what he really thinks is of other people doing what he says they should do. . . . His wife Tish, about whose past he thinks in ways most people think of racehorses, is ready for divorce; his young son strikes him as nothing more than a sluggish glob made of candy bars.

To top it off, Duffy's law practice isn't going well, and his partner's having an affair with Tish. All our raging Duffy wants to do is get out of Gainesville, Fla.—and fast.

So we follow Harry Crews into the jungles of doubt and despair that he has explored so often and so well, waiting for the customary hideous but cleansing surprise.

But a surprise of another sort awaits. And though it is pretty and bright, it is not easily stomached. Not precisely because we readers of Crews suddenly find ourselves on alarmingly cheerful ground, though it is that; more because it smacks of sheer absurdity, given what has preceded it in this novel. There is even a messiah of sorts, a tough black pro football player and coke-head named Tump, who leads Duffy Deeter and his family into the paths of self-knowledge and hope.

I am accustomed to being shocked wide awake by Harry Crews' eloquent use of violence and pain, and by the howling demons he can dredge up from the deeps of human souls. But in context, the long denouement of *All We Need of Hell* is a different kind of shock, much like a sudden infusion of sugar. And even after a lot of thought, it's still clear to me that one time around is all I need of *that.*

> *Beaufort Cranford, "Harry Crews' Surprise from Hell," in* The Detroit News, *February 1, 1987, p. 2H.*

RUSSELL BANKS

The title of this excellent, edgy novel [*All We Need of Hell*] is from Emily Dickinson: "Parting is all we know of heaven, / And all we need of hell." It decribes the predicament faced by Duffy Deeter, a 40-year-old lawyer in Gainesville, Fla., who has deliberately parted from the world around him. It's a familiar world, rotten with greed, sloth, materialism and mendacity, as it has always been, but it's the Sunbelt version, and Duffy is a Yuppie with soul, or so he intends. He's hip and up to date. Instead of joining a rural commune and making pots, he has, in a sense, turned his life into a health club, turned control of his body—initially a mild form of protest—into a private cult. Locked inside his body, as it were, he lives as much in heaven as in hell. . . .

Duffy is a physical performer, but for an audience of one, the only audience worthy of appreciating the performance. He runs against the stopwatch, lifts weights against a machine, measures the pain of a four-hour workout like a connoisseur at a wine tasting. This typically 1980's and solipsistic way of expressing disapproval of the corrupt society he lives in isolates Duffy as well from the people he is closest to, including his law partner, his wife, son and mother, and even his mistress, who is supposed to be an ally. (p. 9)

[Duffy plays a game of handball] against one Tump Walker, a black professional football player for the Miami Dolphins, and here begins his spiritual education. Tump—as much an athlete as Duffy, if not more so, and just as repelled by hypocrisy—nonetheless bears toward the fallen world a huge, good-humored affection. He's the guru of wholesome acceptance, perhaps the only person, by virtue of his being black, intelligent and an athlete of supreme ability and discipline, able to force Duffy to question his assumptions. The Karate Kid Goes South.

But not before Duffy resists. He forces his son Felix, aged 9 and fat and mournfully chomping a giant sized Baby Ruth, to work out on the Universal machine, until the sad lad sickens and vomits, causing his overprotective mother, Tish, to rebel at last against Duffy's mad obsessions with fitness, health, Zen koans, karate, performance and control. She expels him from their overdecorated, upwardly mobile ranch house to his specially modified Winnebago camper (it has weight room over the bunk room, among other things), freezes his assets, files for divorce and begins an affair with his now ex-law partner Jert.

Duffy tries to remain above it all—runs on a cinder track outside a small-town high school, trying to do a 4:30 mile—but soon finds himself, in spite of his principles, angry, hurt and lonely, and before long he is fighting his way back to his son and wife and, by inference, to the rest of the world he has parted from. His counselor and model in this quest is Tump Walker, and some of the funniest and most affecting parts of the novel are the scenes in which Tump shows Duffy by example how to talk and deal with a 9-year-old boy. . . .

Plotting is not this book's strong suit; the episodes are more or less heaped up, so the novel is structured incrementally rather than dramatically. Nor is Harry Crews a particularly fine writer. His prose has the qualities he says Coach Jake Gaither of Florida A. & M. required of football players: "Ag*ile,* mob*ile* and hos*tile.*" He's a comic moralist, Swiftian at times in his ferocity and wit, more in the tradition of Flannery O'Connor than, say, Eudora Welty. Like many Southern male writers, he portrays violence as an expression of helplessness and frustration, but unlike many of them he refuses to sentimentalize it as a more or less harmless form of bawdy, late adolescent behavior. His greatest gift is his ear for speech, black and white, urban and rural, New South and Old, for not only can he hear the differences in speech patterns between Birmingham, Tupelo and Gainesville, he can make you hear them, too. Beyond that, there is in all of Harry Crews's work the sheer pleasure of reading a man who is not embarrassed by his own sense of moral outrage. (p. 11)

Russell Banks, "Duffy Deeter and the Guru of Wholesome Acceptance," in The New York Times Book Review, *February 1, 1987, pp. 9, 11.*

ALLEN SHEPHERD

[Crews's ninth novel, *All We Need of Hell* provides] slender inspiration for those who have waited in hope since 1976 when his eighth, *A Feast of Snakes,* appeared. It is not very far into *All We Need of Hell* that one is pointedly reminded of its predecessor, in that Duffy Deeter, a supporting character in the earlier work, has now been promoted to the rank of principal hero. Resemblances extend well beyond familiar characters, however, for the opening pages of *All We Need of Hell* derive

almost word for word, with minimal alteration, from the beginning of Part Two of *A Feast of Snakes.* (p. 627)

A good many of the better details later in *All We Need of Hell* also derive from *A Feast of Snakes.* (p. 628)

All of Crews's novels are of necessity tragicomedies; all of them, even the least inspired, are illuminated by flashes of brilliance; and all of them, even the most successful, are marred by stylistic lapses and self-indulgent grotesqueries. Unhappily, *All We Need of Hell* is among the author's least inspired.

Early in the novel Crews writes a promising sentence: "He [Deeter] tried to look savage." What the sentence seems to promise is that Crews will not take his hero too seriously nor expect us to. Wrong on both counts. The kind of man Deeter is and the kind of situation in which he finds himself are generic Crews, though Deeter's code embodies machismo raised beyond parody. In *A Feast of Snakes* he was, fairly simply, a lawyer from Gainesville, Florida, and also a small-sized, middle-aged stud and weight lifter whose subsidiary skills included karate, handball, pool, and marathon running. From one of the largest and strongest of the All-American natives of that novel he earned genuine if grudging praise: " 'Jesus,' said Willard to Joe Lon, 'ain't it nothing that little sucker cain't do?' " Not much, no, but he is principally an out-of-town observer. By the time Deeter has arrived in *All We Need of Hell* he has become truly formidable, adding bicycle racing, rock climbing, white-water canoeing, and rodeo performing to his *curriculum vitae.* He has lost five pounds but not aged a bit.

Deeter seems to be a recapitulation of many—almost all—earlier Crews male models. Thus his fierce commitment to self-discipline and craftsmanship, and his reluctant recognitions that the body, however powerful, will finally give out and that the spirit, bereft of wholeness, will continue to hunger. Thus, too, his guilty sense of failure and despair about his family, his certainty that his life has gotten fatally out of hand, and his belief that neither love nor work will recover health or happiness.

Crews attends seriously to only two characters: only for Deeter and Tump Walker is there any pretense of development, of multidimensional human particularity. Walker, in his *Feast of Snakes* manifestation, was Joe Lon Mackey's mentor and "one of the great high-school [football] coaches in the country"—who had, he claimed, "boys all over this country. Playing on six pro teams, coaching two." Coach Walker's physical presence and turns of speech have been deeded in *All We Need of Hell* to Jert McPhester, Deeter's law partner, but his name and mentorship have gone to a large black Miami Dolphins running back whose firm friendship and devoted concern for Deeter, though not explained, serve to bring the novel to a happy (and, for Crews, atypical) ending.

The bonding of Deeter and Walker accomplishes more than could reasonably be expected, given the novel's other characters and their circumstances. Deeter's wife Tish is a confection of purple hot pants and see-through blouse with platinum hair and long red fingernails and beautiful feet and other things, whose defining characteristic, aside from her growing distaste for her spouse, is her tendency almost daily to buy more large pieces of furniture. Though one can sympathize with Tish as she listens to her husband's Zen koans in the backyard by the pool and coexists in the same house with this "constant and voracious eater of garlic," she is nonetheless a very minor figment of Crews's not-very-covertly misogynistic imagination.

The first of two other significant women in Deeter's life is one Marvella Sweat (pronounced Sweet?), a nubile excheerleader from Alabama, presently a brilliant philosophy grad student at the University of Florida, a cocaine addict, and a sex partner on Deeter's payroll. Alarming numbers of people gallop in and out of her apartment, which Crews uses as if it were a sitcom set. Toward the other end of the chronological spectrum is found Deeter's mother, for whom he has done the appropriate filial thing by setting her up in a commodious condo. Her substance, in sum, is discoverable in two comic turns which she several times performs: she is unexpectedly foul-mouthed and she keeps goldfish in large numbers, half of which at any moment are likely to be dead.

Beyond Tish and Marvella and Mrs. Deeter are four males who signify somewhat more and whose relation to Deeter embodies the novel's central thematic concerns: McPhester and Walker, plus Deeter's overweight son [Felix] and deceased father. (pp. 628-29)

The true Tump Walker of this volume is allowed to surpass Deeter unscathed, except for absorbing a karate kick (set up by McPhester) on a handball court. In Tump Walker (*Jerome* to his mother) we see Crews's first attempt at a major black character—who turns out to be someone we can believe Deeter would take to. He is bright, genuine, and articulate; he is an enemy of hypocrisy, a generous man, a memorable athlete, and a practitioner of healthful accommodation. He admires old mothers, knows better than to marry younger women, and shows Deeter how to talk to and be with the nine-year-old Felix.

But the bonding of these two, or three, is dramatized in a fashion sometimes affecting but usually suspect. What is suspect is the way the change in Felix is presented. A fat, lethargic, disdainful television addict—who favors his mother, resists Zen instruction, and vomits on his father's exercise machine—becomes within a single page a wisecracking jock and a devotee of fitness, full of the requisite arcane statistics but respectful still of his not-very-old mother. What is happening to him is clear enough: a mother's boy is becoming a father's boy as

Felix recasts himself in the model of Tump Walker. The problem is that Crews doesn't offer us sufficient cause to believe any of this.

The fourth consequential male is Henry Deeter, Duffy's enigmatic and long-dead father, a World War II fighter pilot who was unbalanced by his experience and filled the house with model airplanes which he and his young son flew on daily missions. After Duffy's own somehow analogous experience, he still loves, imagines that he understands, and is no longer ashamed of his father. Thus three generations of Deeter males are squared: Henry, Duffy, and Felix.

At novel's end Walker brings Deeter and Tish together again. Both make gratifying confessions, have good cries, and go to bed for the best sex in years. Afterward Tump asks, "See how everything works out?" and Duffy responds, "Yeah, I *do* see."

Looking back over the novel, what we see is a plot that is often extemporaneously haphazard, features characters few of whom aspire above cliché, and is set down in a style which is notably erratic, sliding from biting to banal and evincing a tone which is often sentimental. The nature of Deeter's malaise, as climactically diagnosed by Dr. Walker, offers us the knowledge that, "You're a good man Duffy, but you're willful. I got a feeling you missed a whole lot of good things in your life because you decided too much ahead of time." Loosen up and cool out, says the moralist.

Crews's good work is very good, but this novel isn't it and it is well to say so. Little as it may appear from the preceding pages, I honor Crews's best work—which includes the novels **Car** and **The Hawk Is Dying** and **A Feast of Snakes,** plus his autobiography, **A Childhood**—and am thus perhaps readier to resist the least distinguished, in which category **All We Need of Hell** is certain to be located. (pp. 630-31)

Allen Shepherd, in a review of "All We Need of Hell," in The Georgia Review, *Vol. XLI, No. 3, Fall, 1987, pp. 627-31.*

H(arold) L(enoir) Davis

1896-1960

American novelist, short story writer, poet, essayist, critic, and translator.

Considered an important contributor to the development of Western American literature, Davis examined the effects of environment and lifestyle on individuals who explored and settled the Western regions of the United States. Eschewing the heroic dimensions of much Western writing, Davis focused on the contrast between reality and myth in the annals of the American frontier by portraying the physical, emotional, and moral hardships suffered by settlers and by featuring young protagonists whose discontent conflicts with the optimism of previous generations. Possessing an irreverent wit that elicited comparisons to Mark Twain, Davis has received praise for realistic characterizations, use of authentic Western American vernacular, and evocative descriptions of landscape.

A descendant of early pioneers, Davis engaged in various occupations as a youth in Oregon. His experiences as a printer's apprentice, sheepherder, cowboy, deputy sheriff, and surveyor provided him with first-hand knowledge of the daily existence of many Northwesterners and supplied him with material for his writings. In 1919, while serving in the United States Army, Davis began composing verse. His early pieces were published in *Poetry* magazine and attracted praise from Carl Sandburg and Robinson Jeffers. During the 1920s, at the suggestion of H. L. Mencken, Davis shifted his literary focus from poetry to prose, and by 1928 he was writing mainly short fiction. Davis published his first novel, *Honey in the Horn*, in 1935. Set in Oregon during the early 1900s, *Honey in the Horn* is the picaresque story of a young sheepherder's relationship with an itinerant horse trader's daughter and his conflicts with the local sheriff and an escaped outlaw. By studying the customs, occupations, and values of Northwest settlers, Davis presents an ironic portrait of the pioneers' indelible spirits. Described by critics as a blend of folklore and history in which Davis successfully employs colloquial Western idioms and provides detailed descriptions of Oregon's flora and fauna, *Honey in the Horn* was awarded the Pulitzer Prize in fiction.

Davis's next novel, *Harp of a Thousand Strings* (1947), centers on the fictional experiences of three American pioneers and their unusual encounter with French revolutionary leader Jean-Lambert Tallien and his wife, Thérèse Cabarrus de Fontenay. Described by Mary McGrory as "[a] parable of love, vengeance and ambition," this book explores parallels between events of the French Revolution and the founding of an American wilderness town. In *Beulah Land* (1949), Davis presents the adventures of a young pioneer couple as they journey across the United States in search of the ideal dwelling place. An examination of several types of love, *Beulah Land* has been interpreted as a symbolic portrait of the settlers' will to endure. *Winds of Morning* (1952) is a story of initiation and disillusionment involving the relationship between a young deputy sheriff and a wise old pioneer. Set amid the Northwest territory's Columbia River Valley, this novel explores the corruption of a frontier town by contrasting the beauty of the Western landscape with the depravity of the human spirit. In *The Distant Music* (1957), Davis portrays the lives of several generations

NYT Pictures

of settlers as they witness the social and economic changes that accompany their town's growth. In this novel, Davis alludes to the growing discontent and failure of many frontier communities.

While best known for his accomplishments as a novelist, Davis also published several volumes of short fiction, including *Team Bells Woke Me and Other Stories* (1953) and *Kettle of Fire* (1959). His poems are gathered in *Proud Riders and Other Poems* (1942) and *The Selected Poems of H. L. Davis* (1978).

(See also *Contemporary Authors*, Vols. 89-92 [obituary] and *Dictionary of Literary Biography*, Vol. 9.)

H. L. MENCKEN

[*Honey in the Horn*] begins to glow with joy on the very first page, and until Mr. Davis tires of it at last, and shuts it down with scant ceremony, it remains *scherzo* in the grand manner. But if you translate *scherzo* too literally and think of it as meaning only farce, then you will be mistaken indeed, for this book is in essence perfectly serious, and what Mr. Davis essays to do in it is not merely to recite an amusing story about a herd of stupid people, but to penetrate, as far as may be, to the secret of the American pioneers. It is thus history as well as fable, and social document as well as history, and in all three aspects it is very good stuff.

Mr. Davis, of course, is too young by a century to have known the pioneers when they staggered down the western slope of the Alleghenies to the central plains, and there proceeded laboriously to hatch their immortal Abe Lincolns and John Browns; he is even too young to have seen the second wave of them undertake their dismal scramble up the eastern slope of the Rockies. But he was a boy in Oregon at the time their last forlorn guard was baffled by the rollers of the Pacific, and what he saw in those days he made a note of, and now reports with [gusto]. . . . The result is a narrative of really extraordinary merit. It moves with steady, regular step, heading as precisely as a parallel of latitude across a confused and difficult terrain. It throws up characters as prodigiously as a police court, but in even the least of them there is not a glass eye or a wooden knee. Above all, it is beautifully written in sound American, and yields nothing at all to the stylistic quackeries now prevailing.

There is a young fellow named Clay Calvert who appears on page 11 and then dodges in and out of the story to the end, and in the course of it he breeds casually with a girl named Luce, the daughter of a wandering horse trader, but it would be an error to think of Clay and Luce as its hero and heroine, or even as its principal figures. They are no more essential to it than Huck is to most of *Huckleberry Finn*. Its real hero is the sempiternal pioneer, half knave and half child, and its heroine is the uncomely and irrational female who followed him on his witless peregrinations, dragging his dishpans, swallowing his hallucinations and spawning his scurvy children. Here we have the last canto of the great American saga, howled idiotically at the imperturbable ocean. They plowed up and polluted the plains, and they turned the helpless mountains inside out, but when they got to the western shore a little line of breakers hauled them up.

What is the story? There is no story. A couple of men are killed, another is lynched, whole families die out, and others somehow arise out of nothing and get a toe-hold on the cosmos, but fundamentally nothing whatever happens. The wanderers are all pretty much the same at the end as they were at the beginning. They have sweated and panted through a series of hostile deserts, and panted and sweated over a series of even more hostile hills, but they have learned nothing useful and forgotten none of their cherished principles, all of them palpably untrue. Sinking down exhausted like so many badly used mules, their gear worn out and dissipated, their gastric juices baffled by inedible food, and their women reduced to revolting scarecrows, they yet hang to the theory that milk and honey must be gurgling from great casks and carboys over the skyline. So next day at dawn they start out again, sweating and panting some more, and so on for week after week and month after month, until Mr. Davis, having exhibited them sufficiently for his purpose, humanely pulls down the curtain.

It would have been easy for him to have made their chronicle a mere exercise in ribaldry, for they invite burlesque at every step. Not a few of them, in fact, scale the very heights of the comic; they are almost as laughable, even in their agonies, as a bishop caught in *flagrante delicto* or a bull chasing its tail. But Mr. Davis somehow resists the temptation to stand off and cackle at them. His fine irony does not miss their humors, but he never forgets that when they skin their shins it hurts, and

that an ideal blowing up stings and bruises them as much as it would a metaphysician. He wastes no tears upon them, for they have none to waste upon themselves, but the tragedy implicit in comedy is never forgotten, and now and then there is an evocation of overtones that must be described, I suppose, as a kind of poetry. . . .

It would be silly to say that this is a first novel of promise. It is, in fact, the achievement of an extremely competent journeyman, with little to learn from most of his contemporaries, at least in this great Republic. He has a large experience of writing behind him, both in prose and in verse, and he was doing notable work at least so long ago as 1929. In every line of his book there are the proofs of well directed, painstaking and thoroughly informed skill. There is not an amateurish moment. You may not like the story, but you will have to strain desperately to argue any part of it down.

H. L. Mencken, "History and Fable and Very Good Stuff: Prize Novel Penetrates the Secret of the Early Pioneers," in New York Herald Tribune Books, *August 25, 1935, p. 1.*

MARY McCARTHY

Honey in the Horn is not a fantasy; its boy-girl plot is unrolled in straight, realistic fashion; yet in its use of hyperbole, its full-blown, homely metaphors, its poker-faced humor, it bears a plain family resemblance to the tall tales Mr. Stevens used to tell. As a novel it is a flat failure; its virtues are those of a folk tale; its value is anthropological.

The period of Mr. Davis's novel is the early nineteen hundreds; the setting is the state of Oregon, from the homestead farm lands in the east, through valley hop fields and mountainous grazing land, to the Indian fishing villages on the coast. As comprehensive as an encyclopedia article is Mr. Davis's study of the customs, characters, and occupations of the Oregon settlers. Imbedded in each chapter are chunks of historical information. There are dissertations on agriculture, on hunting and fishing, on Indian tribal customs; and a million varied human specimens are on display, earmarked, well catalogued, like livestock at a country fair. Storekeepers, sheriffs, harvest hands, strike-breakers, Indian bucks and squaws and whores, wagon trains of migratory settlers, gamblers, horse traders, gun-toting desperadoes elbow each other for space in these hard-packed pages. It is from these myriad thumbnail characterizations, in which each individual, though briefly glimpsed, is so highly colored that he seems like the hero of a minor saga, from the literal descriptions of flora and fauna, from the occasional bright nuggets of rustic philosophy, that the novel gets its modicum of life. Unfortunately, this blend of folklore and history is presented not for its own sake but simply as a backdrop for a faltering, mystery-romance story involving a pair of lovers. The heroine is a beautiful, savage, straight-shooting adolescent; the hero, a morose, untutored boy of seventeen, whose character is so amorphous that it persists, at odd moments, in merging with that of the author. These personalities, thinly imagined, indistinct, are too weak to support the mass of detail with which the book is stocked, and what might have been an entertaining non-fiction portrait of early Oregon becomes a tiresome, maladroit novel. The unflagging, chest-thumping virility of Mr. Davis's style does nothing to give his book either distinction or interest although his prose transcription of the Western drawl is occasionally amusing. (p. 249)

Mary McCarthy, "Tall Timber," in The Nation, *New York, Vol. CXLI, No. 3660, August 28, 1935, pp. 248-49.*

THE TIMES LITERARY SUPPLEMENT

Mr. H. L. Davis's *Honey in the Horn,* awarded the Harper Prize for 1935, is a novel which irresistibly demands to be described as racy of the soil; for that is not only its intention but its achievement. There seems almost an element of piety in the author's original aim—subsequently modified—of including "a representative of every calling that existed in the State of Oregon during the homesteading period" of some thirty years ago: but if the design tends to make his story at times a little slow-paced it does not diminish the interest and entertainment for the reader who is prepared to take it at its own rate. The story is in fact somewhat desultory. The young sheep-herder, Clay Calvert, unwillingly smuggles a "gun" to the outlaw, Wade Shiveley, who is in gaol. Fearing the consequences, he rides away on Wade's horse and makes for the mountains, but falls in with a horse-trader and his daughter Luce. Clay and Luce join their wandering lives, and presently attach themselves to a train of settlers shifting from the coast to the grass country inland. Wade turns up again, to cause trouble not least for himself, and Clay, separated from Luce, tries his hand at a number of jobs in a number of places before they come together once more in a seemingly final relation. These principals have all character and interest of their own, but their adventures are also plainly a framework for displaying the varied life of the place and time—harvesters, hop-pickers, cattlemen, storekeepers, small-town estate agents, Indians, aged pioneers and many other such types, living still to a surprising degree in genuine frontier conditions remote from cities, railways and even roads.

Mr. Davis cultivates a generally effective if rather limited colloquial style, and his rough humour is distinctly in the Mark Twain tradition, as, for example, in the engaging story of the man who fell into a vat of molten iron: "and the company, by way of showing its sense of bereavement, had the whole three-ton ingot carted out to the cemetery and interred with appropriate ceremonies, several large floral pieces from officials and fellow-workmen, and a full set of honorary pall-bearers assisted by two donkey-engines." The neat placing of the final item will possibly help to suggest a certain subtlety and restraint even in the author's broader effects.

A review of "Honey in the Horn," in The Times Literary Supplement, *No. 1752, August 29, 1935, p. 536.*

STANLEY YOUNG

[*Honey in the Horn*] represents a full-blooded picture of a relatively untracked part of our historic past, of Oregon during the homesteading period, 1906-08. Reading it is somewhat like looking at an old family album with orange plush cover and gold filigree, turning the pages slowly and jocosely attributing all sorts of hearty traits to the craggy exteriors within, and then finding that our most robust imaginings were true.

Mr. Davis has assembled hearsay and legend and first-hand fact to make a gallery of frontier Americans like none other on earth. And he has done the very difficult technical thing of interesting us, without any plot to speak of, in the primitive ways by which his eccentric old settlers extract from the land

just enough to live on, developing in excess only a "mutual oppositeness of character." This "oppositeness" gives the figures distinct, masculine dimensions and yet places them well beyond the era in which, pretty generally, novels of the Far West were peopled only with noble pioneers, gentlemanly rogues and restless-eyed young men with the land-fever.

Still more obviously, this author's astonishing knowledge of the unroseate but hearty realities of the more settled sides of everyday frontier existence—of sheep-herding and hop-picking, of wheat-ranching and horse-trading—makes Owen Wister's deliberate romances of the Wyoming of the same period, with all the pat, red-blooded, "when-you-call-me-that, smile" implications, appear even more sentimentalized than we had imagined. The heavily applied lavender of *The Virginian* is to *Honey in the Horn*'s plain human stuff just about what the tinted tale of *The Deerslayer* is to La Farge's *Laughing Boy*.

As for technique in the larger sense, the present work takes on a linear picaresque form which allows occasion to describe a variety of conditions and experiences in the Oregon of the early Nineteen Hundreds. In and out of Shoestring Valley we follow the aimless wanderings of Clay Calvert, "a drip-nosed" but "hard-mouthed young hell fry" of about 16, who becomes a fugitive largely through a misunderstanding and is obliged to keep traveling, a jump ahead of "justice" in the person of the Sheriff, from one cross-grained old buck to another, leading a hand-to-mouth existence lightened only by his shy meetings with Luce, the itinerant horse-trader's daughter. Luce, as with most of the pioneer women of this story, is of a steadier cut of character than the average man. There is one fleck of suspicion upon her, however, when Clay discovers in her wagon a well-used rifle to which she will not admit ownership. This incident, plus the fact that Clay will never tell her why he is a fugitive, casts a shadow over their relationship and makes for most of the surface suspense of the story.

Around Oregon with the roving Clay goes an "unsociable little pint of willow-juice," a fish-eating Athabascan Indian boy of 13, who for a time shares the adventures of the road but with somewhat less loyalty than the conventional picaresque companions—the Sancho Panzas and Parson Adamses and Partridges, who followed their heroes with an energetic readiness to risk their necks at all unlikely moments.

Generally speaking, however, the liveliest power of this novel does not derive from the mere invention of incident but rather from the vigorously humorous characterization. We have suggested that Mr. Davis gives a more authentic picture of the West than some of his predecessors because he has not glorified his characters into conventional, sun-tanned supermen. He does not refrain, however, from touching up his portraits in a different way. Whether he tones them up or down, he certainly tends to exaggerate their oddities, to display them with the finely distorted humor of the born raconteur, and thereby to raise them to somewhat romantic and legendary proportions even while supporting their day-by-day activities with carefully observed realistic detail. (pp. 3, 16)

Mr. Davis never involves his characters in any of the sordid bucolic moods which might be expected from the rather oversimple logic of their natures. The wonder of it is, we become so beguiled by the author's strapping interpretations that even when the characters display the most outrageous traits—as they generally do—we somehow feel that they are not only memorable creations but even a little lovable. This feeling grows until at the end of the story the tougher they come—the mustier, the fustier, or the crustier—the more indulgent we are.

Unfortunately, some of the best characters drop out early in the story never to reappear. Of course this is the weakness of the picaresque form. If the characters do reappear it is seldom plausible and if they don't we are often disappointed. The author has stated in a prefatory note that he "originally hoped to include in the book a representative of every calling that existed in the State of Oregon during the homesteading period" but that he gave up the idea. And well he did, for it is still a little evident at points that we are being urged along. This abruptness would not matter if the author had introduced us less toothsomely to Geary and Old Simmons and Uncle Preston and Luce and Captain Waller and the mysterious girl with the guitar. It is hard to lay them all aside forever simply to cover a little more Oregon territory.

The central character, Clay Calvert, the only person who has an extensive physical place in the story, remains the most shadowy creation of the work. We know less of his half-formed motives and desires than of any of those whom he meets. He is neither an unmitigated rascal nor a strong character. He remains somewhat blurred to the end, especially in his casual reactions between the time of his separation from Luce, under most trying circumstances, until he emerges from the saloons of the Columbia River towns to find her again.

But even if the slender framework of the story were to collapse entirely, which it never does, the gift of reporting vividly the daily prairie events would keep us reading as long as Mr. Davis cared to go on. . . .

When it is not such close description which holds us, it is certain homely judgments on life that creep into the generalized narrative. Undoctored, unpsychoanalyzed, common-sense ideas that get said with a smacking kind of racy American speech and Yankee exaggeration that is entirely removed from any likeness either to the overplain cult of the simple or to more abstract expression. . . .

Plainly this is a book which demands quotation. For page after page it reveals the most original usage of unvarnished, robust Americanisms known to me, and it presents in its characters the salt of the back regions of Yankee earth—a cantankerous, hard-bitten folk with a direct way of acting and a spare, earthy manner of speaking which is reproduced throughout with full flavor.

Though perhaps bearing no direct social implications, nor achieving in form the balance and restraint of the more classic American novelists who have worked the Western scene— effects such as Willa Cather achieved with the Kaeterlings of Iowa and the pioneers of the Nebraska tableland, or as Rölvaag did with the somber people of the Dakotas—still this work gets a place in the memory not far from them simply because of its irrepressible robustness. In a way this novel is a kind of American *Anthony Adverse*, on a smaller and livelier circuit, with a group of characters that could be found no where else under the sun. And it says in picturesque speech things Anthony never could have. It is wholly an American thing. Whichever way we look at it, Mr. Davis's first novel is honey in the literary horn. (p. 16)

> *Stanley Young, "Pioneer Portraits in 'Honey in the Horn',"* in The New York Times Book Review, *September 1, 1935, pp. 3, 16.*

PETER MONRO JACK

H. L. Davis is a poet-novelist and neither is separated from the other. His Pulitzer Prize novel, *Honey in the Horn,* had overtones of poetry. His poetry has a strong strain of prose. It is mainly regional: the landscape, nature, characters, experi- ence of the Far West, from Oregon to Mexico. Mr. Davis divides [*Proud Riders and Other Poems*] into pastoral and nar- rative. It is a good distinction with a tradition of pastoral poetry from Virgil to Spenser and of narrative from Chaucer to Mase- field. Actually Mr. Davis does not make the distinction clear in his own work. His poems are almost always in a mixed form of description, characterization and storytelling. The best of the "pastoral" poems, **"The Gypsy Girl,"** is a narrative. Mr. Davis's sense of nature is really a sense of people, and people make stories. The pregnant gypsy girl who makes offers to him is far more direct than the natural description that tends to clutter his verse with words, like this:

> Our fire of dead willow-branches lights beyond the tilled ground
> And the boat-path where plowhands camp.

I feel this is the beginning of a short story; and that if it had been written as a short story it would have been done better. It would have been simpler or more complex. As it is, it is compound (in the grammatical sense), an increase or addition of phrases without the emphasis that prose would be forced to give them.

A true pastoral, however, is **"New Birds,"** which begins:

> Now all of the snow's gone from the high desert, now the frost
> Lets go of the ground except in the deep draws, we find
> And recognize and enumerate new birds.

But this, I think, is indebted to Horace's ode *Diffugere Nives* (Houseman translates it: "The snows are fled away"). The enumeration of the new birds is not Horace, though. It belongs with Whitman's pleasure in making catalogues of things instead of making a poem of them. . . .

In his narrative poems he reminds me of the vigor and color and sentimentality of Bret Harte. Decent, desperate and dis- reputable people tell their stories of crop campers, steel gangs, Mexican sheep-herders. The violence of hard work mixes with the eroticism of the brothel. Mr. Davis could compete with Bret Harte, Kipling or Robinson Jeffers. There is character- ization in his verse. The question is whether there is character to his verse. At the moment, I think, it is too much of a mixture of a poet-novelist.

> *Peter Monro Jack, in a review of "Proud Riders and Other Poems,"* in The New York Times Book Re- view, *April 26, 1942, p. 4.*

JAMES HILTON

Twelve years have passed since Mr. H. L. Davis won the Pulitzer Prize with his novel, *Honey in the Horn,* and readers will find some but not all of its high qualities in a long-awaited successor, *Harp of A Thousand Strings.*

It is not an easy novel to read. Characters are introduced ab- ruptly, there are random divagations that seem to have little to do with the main narrative, and the writing, always of a schooled intelligence, makes no concessions to the reader who is un- prepared to use his own. Compounded of unequal parts of history, legend and fiction, the story is told from odd and changing angles—as odd as the names of its three American characters, Commodore Robinette, Melancthon Crawford, and old Jory the Indian (formerly known as Apeyahola). More than a century ago these three settled down, after troubled and adventurous lives, in the wilds of the Osage country. Having become principal land owners in a place they had seen grow from a mere trading post, they wished to give it a new name; so each wrote his selection on a slip of paper without consulting the others. To their astonishment they found they had all chosen the same—that of a woman they had met years before, for a few hours in a foreign city, and had remembered ever since.

The woman was none other than Therese Cabarrus de Fontenay (we are not told which part of her name was utilized); and here we step right into history, for she was the wife of the French Revolutionary leader, Jean-Lambert Tallien, who sent countless aristocrats to the guillotine during the Terror. Therese was almost one of them; but Tallien fell in love with her, and she made good use of that fact, to the extent at least of saving the lives of many of her friends. How far she softened his tyrannical nature and how far she merely imposed upon it the tyranny of his infatuation for her, makes a congenial theme for the novelist, though a difficult problem for the historian. After bringing about the fall of Robespierre, Tallien became for a time all-powerful, and Therese queened it over Paris; then he fell out of favor, and she deserted him for a rich banker, whom later and in turn she deserted for a prince. One might well suspect that she combined mercy with shrewdness. Anyhow, she is the heroine of *Harp With a Thousand Strings,* and two-thirds of the book consists of her husband's story of his life and love. He tells it to the three already-named Americans whom he meets by chance in a waterfront warehouse where they have taken refuge during the American bombardment of Tripoli in 1801; and in the same warehouse, also by chance, the three Americans have their one memorable glimpse of the fascinating Therese.

It will be seen that Mr. Davis is not afraid of coincidence; indeed, the plot of his story is somewhat top-heavy with it, as well as, by any analysis, complicated and at times even cumbersome in a gossamer sort of way. The real merits of the story lie elsewhere—in the subtle (occasionally oversubtle) delineation of character, in the play of an intricate mind over an intricate situation, in the scrupulous assessment of human motivations and in [the] writing. . . .

To one reader, at any rate, [his descriptive] . . . passages are a just reward for the rather hard concentration that a total intake of Mr. Davis's story requires, as well as welcome proof that he still possesses the lyric quality that made *Honey in the Horn* memorable. Or, to put it another way, one senses that however sound may be his understanding of French history, his feeling is for the American scene; so that *Harp With a Thousand Strings* is at an enchanting best on that note.

James Hilton, "A French Woman Remembered," in New York Herald Tribune Weekly Book Review, *November 2, 1947, p. 4.*

MARY McGRORY

A parable of love, vengeance and ambition as exemplified in the career of Tallien, the French revolutionary leader, set within a framework that is a jocund contradiction of the shallowness of American human history, *Harp of a Thousand Strings* relates the fall of Robespierre to the founding of an American prairie town. Mr. Davis illuminates the continuous flow of events, not in the "for want of a nail" sequence but in the transference of a motivation from a beautiful French noblewoman to three

desperate American refugees, who are brought together in a North African warehouse for one night during the war with Tripoli. Thérèse de Fontenay is confronted with the full score of the deaths committed in her name by Tallien. Her final betrayal of him is deftly underlined. While the three Americans listen to his teaching, it is her beauty which they remember, and immortalize, in the wilderness of America.

Tallien's reminiscences of his rise from provincial law student to Citizen President of the National Convention are an object lesson in the irony of human affairs. Editor of *L'Ami des Citoyens,* he is importuned by Anne-Joseph Theroigne, a rabble-rousing virago, to lead the Sections of Paris in the storming of the Tuileries, thus insuring his ascendancy over the people. Yet when it comes to a choice between her and the Countess de Fontenay, he literally hurls Anne-Joseph to the mob. In bargaining for the Countess' safety, he imperils his own; finally, to insure her liberation from prison, he engineers the coup d'état which ends the reign of the extremists under Robespierre.

This recital of expediency, intrigue and terror is detailed in the North African warehouse; it is heard out with some impatience by the three Americans, who are detained thereby from pursuing their separate ends: Commodore Robinette, whose "lifelong affliction" had been women, has hopes of winning advancement by giving information about the shore batteries to the American Navy; Indian Jory, longing to rejoin his wife in Georgia, and Melancthon Crawford, who nurses a dream of revenge on the people of a Pennsylvania village. The years are to make of them satyr, murderer and thief—and they live to regret that they did not heed Tallien. But it is the Countess, who unveils her face and gives them her seal which is to be their talisman in the ruin of their expectations.

Mr. Davis' virtuoso style, biblical in its cadences, is a continuous joy. When he describes the three founding fathers in their dotage, it is in the garrulous, inventive, mirthful ramblings of a frontier tale. As the scene shifts to France, the language takes on an epigrammatic, paradoxical elegance. Making no attempt to reproduce the idiom of the age, Mr. Davis writes dialogue that is like a chant with its insistence on one fatal word. It is an index of his severity that while Tallien's whole public life is directed by his passion for Thérèse, there is not a single love scene in the book.

In revitalizing the intangible rather than the intimate aspects of the past, and in proposing that a dream can possess the unlikeliest of men, Mr. Davis has attempted a theme that is worthy of his creative art. Its oblique execution is fraught with symbolism illuminated by his speculations on the absurdity of human behavior; its appeal is almost purely intellectual.

Mary McGrory, "From World to World," in The New York Times Book Review, *November 16, 1947, p. 18.*

RILEY HUGHES

Mr. Davis has interlocking stories to tell [in *Harp of a Thousand Strings*], though they come together for no more ostensible purpose than do lines consorting on the same plane. What have three American adventurers, a Naval officer of quixotic honor, an articulate Indian, and an inarticulate young man of unreflecting action, to do with M. Tallien, sometime head of Republican France? Tallien, Carlyle's "red-gloomy Tallien," holds them for the fraction of an evening in Tripoli. He tells them the story of his public life; they pass into the night; they carry a part of the story, that symbolizing his greatest defeat, into their own destiny. A small American town, a settlement which does not know the story of its three founders, is the unlooked-for result of that shadowy evening. What does any of them get for it, what but "a deepening sense of life poured out lavishly, sometimes frantically, and waste and emptiness in return for it?"

It is hardly reasonable to ask what this story is "about." Surely it is not simply the story of the growth of the American West. Nor again, despite the fact that most of these pages recount with immediacy of sight and sound and sense Tallien's days of power in France, is this merely the story of that country's Revolution. Partly it is a parable on the uses of power, on the fact that chief of all things men use is other men. "I keep thinking," says the countess whom Tallien long ago rescued from the guillotine—she is speaking of him and of another unconscious pawn in her life—"they represent what it has cost to keep me alive." Each, then, represents, in varying ways, the cost it all has been to another.

For more than anything else, *Harp of a Thousand Strings* is what the novel was intended to be: a study of moral choices. Tallien's decision, with its gray mixture of motives, to rescue the countess was no final thing; it merely brought about other choices. When he is faced with what seems to him the most anarchic choice of all, when his enemy the young marquis elects death rather than escape and dishonor, Tallien must momentarily learn that right will is the chief harmony of order. Choice becomes a link with meditation; action adds a line to the pattern undiscerned and all but undiscernible.

Harp of a Thousand Strings is one thing more. It is prose of a rareness in our time. It is prose in contemplation, commentary. It is prose that has life around it and in it. (pp. 378-79)

Riley Hughes, in a review of "Harp of a Thousand Strings," in Commonweal, *Vol. LXVII, No. 15, January 23, 1948, pp. 378-79.*

HAMILTON BASSO

Mr. Davis, who will be remembered for his fine *Honey in the Horn,* a novel dealing with the early migration to the West, took the title of his new book [*Beulah Land*] from *Pilgrim's Progress.* The few people alive who have read John Bunyan's morality tale will remember that the Land of Beulah is the happy, peaceful place where the pilgrims lay over until they are summoned to the Celestial City—this side of Paradise, as it were. Like Bunyan's book, Mr. Davis's novel is the story of a pilgrimage, but his pilgrims are two young people who are looking for a terrestrial home, not a heavenly one. This requires quite a search. It takes them on one of those prodigious treks that people made during the earlier days of this country's history (the time of the novel is from around 1840 to just after the Civil War), and one of the best things about Mr. Davis's chronicle is that he makes it as believable as any of the accounts of journeys that, in diaries, journals, and other writings, have come down to us from the period.

Because of its geographical scope, the novel meets one of the prime requirements of the adventure story—a lot of territory in which to move around. Starting out in the Cherokee country of western North Carolina, the two young people—an impulsive, trigger-tempered half-Indian girl named Ruhama and a devoted, superstitious, Indian-bred foundling white boy called

Askwani—go cross-country to the Mississippi, down it to Natchez, up it to Illinois, then westward across Missouri and Kansas, and south to their own Beulah Land, in what was the Indian Territory. They are accompanied for part of the journey by Ruhama's father, Ewen Warne, to whom Askwani is deeply attached, and by an Indian woman, Sedaya. Mr. Davis's novel is, however, essentially the story of the two young people and their long, hazardous journey.

I found it interesting nearly all the way. Besides the ability to write of the past without sounding like a historical novelist, Mr. Davis has a quiet, irreverent humor, and one passage in the book, describing a backwoods wedding, is almost as hilarious as anything in Mark Twain. I also liked the parts that have to do with life as it was then on the Mississippi (one or two pages give Mark Twain another run for his money); the chapters about Natchez in the time when it wasn't all garden clubs, old mansions, and visits to the azalea displays; and, most especially, the story of Ruhama and Askwani crossing the prairies on their way to the Indian Territory.

There were times, however, toward the end of the book, when I felt that the author's power of invention was showing signs of strain. This is understandable, considering what it had been through, but after his earlier pages, filled with all kinds of high, well-managed excitement, it did make the final chapters seem a trifle thin. I didn't care for his ending, either—one of Ruhama's and Askwani's daughters turns up on the arm of a British dignitary at an inaugural reception in Washington (yes, our protagonists settle down long enough to have a couple of children)—but I may be going out of my way to find fault. (p. 84)

Hamilton Basso, "The Great Open Spaces," in The New Yorker, *Vol. XXV, No. 15, June 4, 1949, pp. 84, 87-8.*

THOMAS HORNSBY FERRIL

In *Beulah Land* Davis's historical awarenesses and artistic stubbornness achieve a fine balancing-out. In my opinion it is a very important book, qualitatively equal in every respect to *Honey in the Horn,* but preceding it chronologically and embracing a wider geographical and social field, moving, as the story does, from North Carolina to Oregon in the period immediately preceding, including and following the Civil War.

Davis has written as compelling a love story as I have read in a long time. Not the love and passion that have been perverted by bosomy historical romances. In that sense there's not a single love scene in *Beulah Land,* and while there are a few erotic episodes, they are incidental.

The love themes come through Davis's lean vernacular, never emotional, and so integrated as perhaps to elude the person who reads for distraction, but they are all here: love of one's land, love of one's people, love for one's country, of one's social system, marital love, forbidden love, parental love, treacherous love, filial love, love of every separate kind—and what love can lead to in times of unrest and transition. Some of the love themes are interwoven with conscience and duty, some come in back-handed and, if a summary be attempted, Davis seems to be saying that love can maim and even destroy more often than it can save its possessors. It takes stubbornness and stamina to last love out but if you can, there's a sort of victorious salvation in it.

Beulah Land is a story of the Western faring of the men and women who settled America: from North Carolina down the Tennessee and Mississippi rivers to Natchez, then up to Illinois, across Missouri and Kansas, down to Indian Territory and, finally, to Oregon. It opens in the Carolina mountains in 1851 when the last remnants of the once-powerful Cherokee Nation—an advanced people with their own constitution, schools, books, farms, industries and deep sense of freedom—are being herded by freedom-loving white men to the far-off country where Oklahoma is now.

We meet these Cherokees in the rundown hamlet of Crow Town. Here lives a white man, the town herder, Ewen Warne, very resourceful if somebody prods him into it. With Warne is Ruhama, his eleven year old half-Cherokee daughter. The mother is dead and his other daughter, Elison, lives over the mountain with the Cargills, a hot-tempered white family. Ruhama's playmate is the forlorn Askwani, a white orphan reared by the Indians and Indian in every trait. The Indian woman who is out for Warne, and gets him, is Sedaya who wants to go West to rejoin her own people whom she has betrayed.

If Warne has compunctions about pulling out, he now has no choice, for in trying to recover his own daughter Elison from the Cargills he kills a Cargill, beginning a feud which is not to end until Warne is destroyed and the last Cargill dies at the hands of Askwani in a remote battle of the Civil War. It is the two youngsters, the half-Indian Ruhama and the white Askwani, who carry the tale to Horse Heaven in Oregon. At first they are held together only by their love for Warne and their obligation to recover the lost sister. When Warne dies, although they have to stay together, they are emotionally separate and Ruhama marries young Savacol whom she had met on a river boat. But as it turns out, it had to be Askwani after all. "I don't want to leave you," she says. "I don't know how I can. There ain't anything to me except what's yours."

Davis's knowledge is astonishing. Were I not carried along by the story, I could read *Beulah Land* for facts alone: life on the river flatboats, life in the Deep South, the beginning of mechanized farming in Illinois, customs of the cattle trade, political and religious mores, medical therapies, superstitions, Indian lore, gambling, prostitution, the ways of the wagon trails, the social composition of the pioneers—he knows every bird, beast, tree and flower, every soil and landscape. It all works, not toward realism in the accustomed sense, but toward integrity within the illusion of the novel, enabling him, when he feels like it, to tell tall tales that would tickle Cervantes. You take it as gospel truth that one of the Cargills can knock over a cow with his fist and that young Savacol can teach a quarter-horse to jump the starter's gun by watching the hammer instead of waiting for the sound. His lyric use of the concrete image is poetic and sometimes frightening, as in the passage where the sick Ruhama, her cart horse dead, is left alone in the wilderness for days, hemmed in by wolves and great cream-white buzzards. "Only a dead animal could have stood it."

Through his wide knowledge of man and nature, Davis becomes a philosophical ecologist in that the behavior of his people, however magnificent or petty the immediate motive, is always conditioned by the total environment, physical and spiritual. Free will and circumstances are forever at odds, yet within the choices which must be tolerated, since they cannot be controlled, man edges things his way—to the end that Beulah Land finally reached by Ruhama and Askwani, if not the blissful paradise promised in the old gospel hymn, possesses its particular kind of peace and grace, symbolizing enough

pioneer triumph of trial over error to fortify our faith in America's todays and tomorrows.

Thomas Hornsby Ferril, "The Men and Women Who Settled America: H. L. Davis' Passionate, Inevitable Tale of Their Western Faring," in New York Herald Tribune Weekly Book Review, *June 5, 1949, p. 1.*

HORACE REYNOLDS

[In *Beulah Land*] Mr. Davis writes with detailed knowledge of pioneer America. He knows the little things which do so much to re-create time and place. He knows that the movers across the prairies found, ready for eating, wild plums and wild raspberries, simlin squashes and a species of turnip which the French had named *pomme-blanche;* that occasionally they were able to procure wild honey for sweetening from bee hunters. He tells the reader how the hawks killed the turkeys on the open prairie, and the habits of the javalina, a wild dog which one observer has described as "a ball of hair with a butcher knife run through it." He is aware that "when a horse is unable to see that his work is accomplishing anything or moving toward any visible end, he loses heart and spirit." The flora and fauna of pioneer America, what the pioneers saw and heard and did as they moved westward—these are the good things in Mr. Davis's novel.

As an attempt to represent the consciousness of pioneer men and women, the book is not successful. Not one of the main characters—neither Ewen Warne, a white herder for the Indians, whose talent for solving problems in mechanics foreshadows America's technological skills, nor his half-Indian daughter Ruhana, nor Askwani, the white boy with an Indian name, whom she eventually marries—no one of these ever comes clearly into focus. They remain representations, not individual men and women. Mr. Davis is unable to particularize feeling, give it a home in an individual. It is a pity that Mr. Davis here lacks the dramatic sense, the ability to create character and suspenseful action, for he has, in addition to his knowledge of America's past, integrity, sincerity, and a feeling for beauty. As it is, he is historian rather than novelist.

The book is dull reading because it lacks animation and the momentum of rolling story, because Mr. Davis has not been able to personalize his knowledge of what our ancestors thought and did. The best thing in the book is the account of the wagon journey across Kansas to Indian Territory. The Tennessee River chapters are less convincing. One finds it hard to believe that people floating down the Tennessee in the 1850's wouldn't notice Muscle Shoals and the small but rapidly growing town of Paducah at the mouth of the Tennessee. Surely these are two things which would have had a place in their minds. Also both they and Mr. Davis seem unaware that to get from the Tennessee into the Mississippi you have to float down some forty-six miles of the Ohio River.

Horace Reynolds, "The Re-creation of Time and Place," in The Christian Science Monitor, *June 14, 1949, p. 18.*

FANNY BUTCHER

Almost as seldom as city dwellers see the sun set like a shimmering golden ball is there a book like H. L. Davis' *Winds of Morning.* It is a tale of the old west, but it is as unlike the conventional western as it differs from the conventional love story.

It is as much about nature as it is about man, and yet it is as different from most books in which nature is a principal character as it is unlike usual tales of mystery, altho it has a mystery to solve. It is an "original"—both poetic and earthy, humorous and a little sad, tender and as realistic as the stars or man's passions.

Technically it is a basic story almost covered with incidental tales, all highly pungent. It is filled with a philosophy of reality, not of theory, with that most uncommon of qualities—common sense—and at the same time with a kind of idealism which only the very wise have. It is full of homely observations about man and his ways, as well as about nature and hers. It is a story that is as meandering as life itself, but, like life, with its own inevitable pattern.

To many [readers]. . ., it will be primarily either a tale of the old west before it was spoiled by too much civilization, told with a gamey sense of humor, or a remarkably sensitive picture of the great outdoors with the colors of the coming of the spring, the feel of a cold wind on a sun baked face, the smell of a fire in the pine woods, an infinitude of earth's ways known by the five senses.

The plot of *Winds of Morning* is no precious one, however. In it men murder and hate as well as love and are foolish as well as wise. But whatever men (or women) do they do in their own way, not the way the story books have taught us. The characters as well as the plot are all originals.

The excrescences to the main story are all earthy tales. The main characters, the young deputy sheriff who tells the story and an old man whom he has in custody, are both unintentional idealists, but certain that they are uncompromising realists. The old man is the source of most of the irresistible (if unconventional) philosophical wisdom in *Winds of Morning*. He is also the axle on which the wheel of the plot turns.

If it is impossible to classify *Winds of Morning,* it is even more impossible to be sure that every kind of reader will enjoy its (to this reader) irresistible simplicity, its both subtle and earthy humor, its slow, meandering pace, its often hilarious wisdom, its uniqueness. For often the very quality of being different, unclassifiable, contradictory, is for many readers a repellent instead of a lure. *Winds of Morning* is an insidious book, tho, and I suspect that even those who think they won't will enjoy its tang.

> *Fanny Butcher, "An Unclassifiable, Meandering, Wise Novel of Old West," in* Chicago Sunday Tribune Magazine of Books, *January 6, 1952, p. 4.*

A. B. GUTHRIE, JR.

A western in a sense and a mystery in a sense, *Winds of Morning* is much more than either or both of these. It is a persuasive and mature work, honest to experience, wide in its embrace. It is great fun to read. It is such a book as seldom comes along.

The narrator and co-protagonist is Amos Clarke, an under-age deputy sheriff, who stumbles on a killing, in the middle Nineteen Twenties, fails to make a case in court and at the Sheriff's orders unwillingly agrees to get out of town until the acquitted and vindictive defendant cools off. So people won't talk, the Sheriff tells him, he can haze a bunch of loose horses into the open back country where they won't be getting on the railroad tracks.

Clarke dislikes the assignment as much as the retreat, particularly since his only helper will be an old herder by the name of Hendricks who has come back to the neighborhood after leaving it suddenly for some reason years before. Hendricks, Clarke figures, will turn out to be a rickety ancient in need of a nurse.

Hendricks turns out to be no such thing. He's not young, to be sure, but he's able-bodied. More important is that he is thoughtful and generous and salty, possessed of an old-timer's recollections of the once-young country, articulate, with an old man's hard-considered and often striking judgments. He likes Clarke and Clarke likes him. As they worry with the horses, his past unfolds and involves itself with the present, with tight squeaks and shootings and mysteries and sorrow and murder. But it is the man one remembers, the rich, provocative character. It is the relationship between the young man and the old—between a hard-boiled innocence and a sore and heavy knowledge.

It needs to be added quickly that this is not the down-beat piece the last lines may seem to imply. It is robust, earthy, full of kick. It is the nice contrast of tickle and trouble that living is. Its use of Western idioms is accurate, expert and altogether wonderful. Its dialogue is a delight. So are Mr. Davis' recreations of the Western scene. . . .

Mr. Davis has elected to write in the first person. That method allows him to volunteer comments, without seeming to intrude, on a number of subjects he has ideas about. I imagine he found a great satisfaction in saying them. And I'm sure the reader—should I say especially the male reader—will find a great satisfaction in seeing them said. Part of the time I was laughing in sympathy; part of the time I was nodding amen.

But first-person narrative casts one shadow on illusion. Why should any character, unless he's a writer, why should this deputy sheriff in particular, be telling a story? In the present case I was bothered a little, too, by the fact that the young deputy writes (or talks) far too well and wisely for his years and station. Though the reader may surmise as much, he isn't actually informed until the end that the tale is told long after the events.

But these are trifling criticisms. Mr. Davis knows the West as well as he knows the art of storytelling. He knows both very well, indeed.

> *A. B. Guthrie, Jr., "Robust, Earthy, Full of Kick," in* The New York Times Book Review, *January 6, 1952, p. 5.*

HORACE REYNOLDS

[*Winds of Morning*] is a story of action in the Middle Columbia River country of the Northwest in the 1920's. Its two main characters are Old Hendricks, who was a homesteader in the days when the Northwest was young, and young Amos Clarke, a boy of nineteen, who has grown up in the country to take what casual jobs it offered: timekeeping on the railroad; tagging fleeces for the Mexican shearing crews; finally, when the story opens, a stretch as deputy sheriff for the county. Practically all the action takes place out of doors, in the wind, rain, and sun of a high-country spring. The talk between the two men, who are at least two generations apart, provides vocal counterpoint for the action of herding horses and making camps.

This yarn exploits the resources of the Western, both pulp and film, Indians, bad men, sheriffs and shots stalk and sound through its pages. But the handling is very different. In this book both Busick and the vagrant Mexican are as far from the Western's conventional villains as the sheriff and his young deputy are from their prototypes.

They are illustrations, too, of Davis's belief that the country has changed less for the worse than its people, who find leisure harder to take than their forbears found work. As this country is finding out, prosperity is a telling test of character. The book revels in the scenery of the Western movie, the beauty of the latter's appeal to the eye. It draws, too, on the suspense of the mystery, for there is a shooting, the solution of which is suspended and delayed, but it, too, is miles from the conventional unravelings of the whodunits. . . .

The best thing in this book is the speech. Old Hendricks is worth listening to for manner as well as matter. When he would say, "Don't cross your bridges before you come to them," he puts it into such gallus terms as, "Don't pull all the stretch out of your suspenders ahead of time." He has the saltiness of utterance possessed by men who have worked outdoors all their lives and learned their words from doing, not from books and newspapers. Behind the salty metaphor of his talk lies keen observation. There's sweat and laughter, sunshine and wind in it. It characterizes the region better than all Amos's perhaps too lengthy descriptions of its sights, sounds, and colors.

The old homesteader has lived long enough to learn that it isn't what one takes from life that counts but what one gives, a simple lesson but one which can spell the difference between misery and happiness. "It ain't what you git out, it's what you put in that lasts," he tells the boy. "Some of it lasts as long as you live, and maybe after you're dead, and it's the only thing that will." It is this belief which dictates the course of the old fellow's actions. He lives to help, and the boy takes in all he says and builds it into his mind.

This duet between Old Hendricks and Amos might have had more interest and variety had the boy been made consistently to think and feel more like a boy.

But Mr. Davis speaks through Amos, tells the story in the first person of the boy, and obviously could not resist using Amos as a mouthpiece, not only for his own concern with moral values but also to express his joy in the natural beauty of the Columbia River region. Indeed he couldn't get it all in any other way: once he had chosen to tell the story through Amos, he had made inevitable the central inconsistency I am pointing out. But we are so much in accord with Amos's poetical and philosophical observations that we sit back and enjoy them, forgiving the logical violence done the character.

This is a book with a large common denominator of interest. . . . It is honest, humorous, pungent. It is history and social criticism joined to real laughter and real tears.

Horace Reynolds, "'Things Are Happening to the Western'," in The Christian Science Monitor, *January 10, 1952, p. 13.*

EDWARD WEEKS

Winds of Morning by H. L. Davis is a rare narrative in any season—I like the country it is laid in, the Columbia River valley; the characterizations, which are telling; and the style, which is supple and masculine. The story is the story of a young sheriff's assistant, Amos Clarke, who is trying to live up to the lean, hard tradition of the Northwest. He has been flimflammed by one of the big operators in this grazing country, the lawyers have made a monkey of him in court, and the jury (some of them bought) have brought in a verdict he knows to be wrong. Amos is disgusted with the law and glad to leave the courthouse on an assignment to round up some wild horses that have been loose on the railroad track. In the act he meets old Hendricks, a decent, virile guy, and before long the pair of them—the oldster and the sheriff's assistant—are drawn back into the fight against the big operator and his crooked, ugly foreman, Busick.

The book gets off to a fast start and the pace never slows. The style is the man; and the man of course is young Amos, and you share his impressions so accurately that it is not until you put the book down that you appreciate the full force of his personality and the scope and weight of his (and your vicarious) experiences. Amos wants to believe that his part of the country can recover from the corruption eating into it, and in this he is supported by his friendship with Hendricks, who knew the land when it was virgin and who has the tenacity and wisdom of experience. The book is full of good scenes—I remember particularly the dawn by the pond when Amos in his blankets identifies by the sounds the animals who have come down to drink; and perhaps the most stirring of all, Hendricks's account of how he once prospered in the young country. This is pungent Americana and a hard book to beat.

Edward Weeks, in a review of "Winds of Morning," in The Atlantic Monthly, *Vol. 189, No. 2, February, 1952, p. 78.*

DAYTON KOHLER

[Davis'] region is Oregon, more particularly the Columbia River Valley and the high grazing country, in the homesteading period and after; and he writes of this territory with a frontiersman's awareness of nature in all seasons and weathers. Landscape in his pages is a physical presence vividly re-created with details of sight, smell, and sound—sheep-camp meadows below the snowfields, rich river bottoms, clumped with wild crabapple and blackberry thickets, Coos Bay lashed by autumn gales, a waterhole where birds and animals came to drink at first dawn, frontier towns, squalid Indian villages, steamboat ports on the Columbia, the old orchards of abandoned farms, the wet-sap freshness of a sawmill clearing, the mountains after a blizzard, and the dry, dusty sagebrush country.

On occasion, Davis has left the western scene for other places—the North Carolina mountains, Natchez, Paris during the Reign of Terror, Tripoli—but always his geographical rangings are set in some clearly perceived relationship to the region which gives his work its center and its roots.

Few areas in American fiction have been more carefully examined in their sociological aspects. Sheepherders, cowpunchers, horse-traders, storekeepers, wheat-threshers, homesteaders, gamblers, prostitutes, sheriffs, badmen, Indian bucks and their squaws—all are accurately described and dramatically presented. These people are not abstractions of vice and virtue, however, as they are in popular "Westerns." Because they function in a special region and at a particular moment in history, their significance extends and deepens the implications of Davis' work, for they make up the unsifted, drifting society of an arrested frontier. They are the backwash of a pioneer movement turned back at the edge of a continent to despoil a promised land which, as they discovered too late, already lay behind them, not ahead. In addition, their trades and skills allow Davis to round out his regional pattern with a variety of relevant details: information about frontier cookery and dress, hunting lore, Indian tribal customs, backwoods politics, songs, and jokes, the routines of sheepherding, wheat-ranching, and hop-picking. A brief foreword to *Honey in the Horn* states that he had originally planned to put into his book a representative of every calling in Oregon during the homesteading period between 1906 and 1908, until limits of space and consideration for his readers deterred him.

The story of *Honey in the Horn* is simple and straightforward. Clay Calvert is a sixteen-year-old waif living at Uncle Preston Shiveley's run-down toll-bridge station in the Shoestring Valley. For his part in a jailbreak which frees Wade Shiveley, Uncle Preston's outlaw son, he becomes a fugitive in the timber country. Later Clay and a horse trader's daughter, Luce, strike off on their own and winter near Coos Bay. In the spring they join some homesteaders moving into the dry lands east of the Cascades. When Wade Shiveley reappears, the emigrants track down the outlaw and lynch him. Clay and Luce are separated, and he wanders from one job to another for a year. Clay suspects the horse-trader of murder, but, when he overtakes the trader's outfit, he finds Luce alone and her father dead. Reunited, they throw in their lot with a wagon train headed west to the construction camps of the new Harriman railroad.

It is a story of the place and time, admirably sustained by a lively chronicle of frontier life and legend. Davis has a talent for comic portraiture, and the brief yarns scattered so profusely through his first novel contain some of his best writing. (pp. 133-34)

The true center of the book is its core of irony, insight into the contrast between illusion and reality in the story of the West. The tensions of this irony give Davis' work the weight and substance of serious art. His subject is the frontier experience—a conditioning factor, even though indirectly, in the lives of most Americans, for the pioneer story has never lost its hold upon the collective imagination. Because the frontier gives shape and life to our national myth, we have preferred to see its story in romantic outline, an account of individual enterprise and heroic achievement, with little regard for the cost in economic waste, hardship, lost hopes, and eroded human values. Oregon, in the homesteading era, was a frontier over which the first waves of settlers had already passed. Although the pioneer effort had reached a dead end, its aftereffects were all too apparent. The migratory society of Davis' novel cannot rest. Holding to the illusions of their fathers, they must always be attempting a fresh start, but among them the pioneer virtues of energy and optimism have dwindled to restlessness and discontent. Deriving unmistakably from the writer's own observations on a late frontier, *Honey in the Horn* presents a contemporary's account of all that had happened before at every halt of the westward advance. (pp. 135-36)

Davis did not publish another novel for twelve years. When *Harp of a Thousand Strings* finally appeared, reviewers seemed puzzled by a work so completely different from *Honey in the Horn.* Briefly, the book tells how a western town was named. One night, while Tripoli is being bombarded by United States naval guns, three young Americans take refuge in an old warehouse. There they encounter Jean-Lambert Tallien, one time Citizen President of the National Convention, now an obscure consular official under Napoleon. During the long night they listen to his story of his rise to power and eventual ruin because

of his love for the notorious Thérèse de Fontenay. Commodore Robinette, the Indian Jory, and Melancthon Crawford, prisoners escaped from the pasha's dungeons, are an ill-sorted trio, but Tallien tells them his story because he sees each young American marked by one phase of his own life: ambition, love, vengeance. Thérèse de Fontenay, disguised, is also in the warehouse while Tallien speaks; the Americans see her face, still beautiful, for only a moment. Years later, when their natures have made them what they are, whoremaster, murderer, and thief, the time comes for them to name the frontier town they have founded. Each remembers the woman he had seen when they were young, and so out of the bloody turmoil of the French Revolution Thérèse de Fontenay gives her name to a trading post in the Osage country.

Judged by any standard, *Harp of a Thousand Strings* is first-rate historical fiction, a novel joining the events and personalities of revolutionary France to the development of the American West, the whole illuminated by a theory of history which asserts that even "obscure and unmeaning lives are not yielded to forgetfulness forever: their land still lives and they contributed by some weight of being to make their land what it is: good or bad, great or small, it all counts the same in the gathering of stories by which a land maintains its hold on life." And history itself is the thousand-stringed harp of the title, an instrument capable of endless vibrations and echoes.

Harp of a Thousand Strings is a novel over which Davis must have labored with patient craftsmanship. Its underlying theme is the reverberations of history between great events and small, a subject requiring a more calculated method of presentation than the loosely episodic form of *Honey in the Horn.* The novel is contrapuntal in design. The American frontier, the Barbary wars, and the French Revolution are introduced in turn for thematic effect, later to be alternated and combined in a pattern of variation, dissonance, and resolved harmony. Davis uses technique to uncover his subject and reduce it to a form appropriate to the sensuous, epigrammatic texture of his style. The pattern is also based on a system of triads: the three settings, America, Tripoli, and France; the three Americans, each corresponding to one of the drives in Tallien's career; the three moral choices Tallien must make, and their consequences; the three organic divisions in the structure of the novel. If the new critics had been reading historical fiction in 1947, they would have found in *Harp of a Thousand Strings* a novel to match their passionate concern for technique.

Beulah Land marks a return to the manner and material of *Honey in the Horn.* It is the story of a westward faring to Oregon in the last century, an experience commonplace enough at the time and not without heroism, although the people involved never realize that they are agents of manifest destiny. In the 1850's, after accidentally killing a backwoods bully, Ewen Warne leaves the North Carolina log village where he tended cattle owned by survivors of the Cherokee Nation. With him go his half-Indian daughter Ruhama, a white boy whom the Indians call Askwani, and an outcast squaw named Sedaya. Eventually, after Warne's death, Askwani and Ruhama make their own way to the Cherokee Agency. There Ruhama marries young Savacol, a gambler. But Savacol dies in an almost forgotten engagement of the Civil War, and Askwani and Ruhama begin their wanderings once more, settling at last in the Horse Heaven country of eastern Oregon.

Life and death, time and change, the long struggle that ends in triumph or defeat—these are the matters that count most in this novel. Like *Harp of a Thousand Strings,* it can be read on different levels. On one it is a pioneer adventure story, enlivened by hilarious or tragic detail. On a second it is an account of the patience, courage, devotion, hard work, and haphazard circumstances that made a nation. On another it is a picture of frontier society before and after the Civil War. Finally, and most important, it is a psychological study of the kinds of love possible for all in a free society and a new land—love of place, of country, of freedom, of men and women; loves devoted, kind, selfish, treacherous, cruel—and what they do to human character and lives. "There should be a place somewhere," Ruhama thinks, "in which people could love without being shamed or frightened or exterminated by it."

Narrower in scope than its predecessors, *Winds of Morning* is in some respects the best novel Davis has written. Within its compact framework he brings together the themes which have previously engaged him: the West, the past, the world of nature, the ground swell of history, the ironic contrast between appearance and reality, the imperatives of love, the necessity and consequence of moral decision. As in *Harp of a Thousand Strings,* he has his material under objective control, for he employs a narrative device which permits him to separate whatever is spectatorial and passive in his writing from the primary flow of action. In *Honey in the Horn* there are scenes in which Clay Calvert and Davis tend to merge against their common background, so that it is hard to distinguish between the hero's sensibility and the writer's. In *Winds of Morning* Davis avoids this process of interfusion by means of a narrator, a young deputy sheriff who tells his story in the first person. The point of view is deliberate and dramatic. The fact that the story is being told long after the events described allows meanings to show through which were not apparent when the action was going on. Thus action and reflection function on different planes, paralleling but never overlapping, in a quietly paced narrative displaying at every point the working of the author's skeptical, inquiring mind.

For this is what Davis offers in *Winds of Morning*—shrewd insight into men's motives and wry reflection on human behavior. The scene is the middle Columbia River country about thirty years ago. The central action, involving a young deputy, an old horse herder, a frightened Mexican boy, a ranch foreman's runaway daughter, four shootings, and two deaths, is precipitated when Amos Clarke, the sheriff's young assistant, is sent to help the old herder trail a band of horses to upper pastures in the mountains. But the action of the novel is less important than the underlying meanings it discloses. What gives the book density and weight is the way in which profound issues of modern society are presented, almost casually, in terms of human violence and of man's inescapable relationship with his natural environment. Young Clarke comes close to the central thought of *Winds of Morning* when he says:

> In the old Hendricks' younger days, there had been more value set on people. Nature had been the enemy then, and people had to stand together against it. Now all its wickedness and menace had been taken away; the thing to be feared now was people, and nature figured mostly as a safe and reassuring refuge against their underhandedness and skullduggery.

This reflection is reinforced by the basic symbolism of the novel, for Davis builds his narrative upon a contrast between the low valley country and the mountains. They are also the unreconciled opposites of a journey which symbolizes the young deputy's initiation into manhood and social responsibility, as well as his realization of what this country had meant to the men who saw it first. The valley becomes associated in Clarke's

mind with a society grown selfish and corrupt; it is the place of ugly towns and run-down farms, of bought juries, crooked dice games, cheap girls, drunkenness, brutality, greed. But as the herder and the deputy travel into the mountains, the moral climate of the book changes. There the efforts of men carry more weight in deeds of bravery, pity, and love. The setting is rough and filled with threats of violence, but it has natural beauty and is still close to the frontier past. In the mountain sequences the true moral stature of old Hendricks is at last revealed. From him the young deputy learns that men cannot exile themselves from their own pasts or their children's future. This symbolism is constant but never forced. It derives from meaningful particularity, of a place, a people, and a time, which gives a sense of universality to regional writing, and it is as appropriate to Davis' novel as the colloquial rhythms and precise imagery of his style.

Style, in fact, is one of the qualities setting Davis apart from the sagebrush romancers, who use the same materials with vastly inferior effects. Many readers have little regard for style; to them it is something finicky or precious, verbal decoration for aesthetic effect. But style is technique as well as language, and Davis must be considered as a stylist if his work is to be viewed as an artistic whole. His use of language is always expert. Serviceable, supple, it is capable of a variety of effects. Unlike the practice of many writers who cultivate style and give it the stamp of their personalities in any context, Davis' method is to fit the rhythm, tone, and imagery of his style to the requirements of scene or character. The result is stylistic evocation. (pp. 136-39)

[Davis'] literary kinship is clear. His novels, regional in setting and theme but more broadly American in spirit and significance, belong to a literary tradition going back beyond Mark Twain to the anonymous storytellers of the frontier. They shaped an indigenous art, a regional tradition complete with geography, subject matter, and a cast of characters, which gives the West a usable past, rich and moving even in its violence.

H. L. Davis is a worker in this tradition. Like Walter Van Tilburg Clark and A. B. Guthrie, Jr., he is reclaiming the realities of western experience from the writers of two-gun epics and the clichés of Hollywood. He also holds his balance true between the pitfalls of landscape mysticism and anthropological sentimentality, which have in many instances falsified the imperatives of the region. While critics have labored to sustain lesser talents among the imitators of James, Hemingway, and Joyce, Davis has quietly produced four novels of technical expertness and moral insight. The work is his own and in the native grain. Criticism, if it hurries, can still catch up with his achievement. (pp. 139-40)

> *Dayton Kohler, "H. L. Davis: Writer in the West,"*
> *in* College English, *Vol. 14, No. 3, December, 1952,*
> *pp. 133-40.*

C. V. TERRY

As a highly successful novelist, Mr. Davis has been with us for a good many years. Readers who remember *Honey in the Horn, Beulah Land* and *Winds of Morning* with affection have a rare treat in store in [*Team Bells Woke Me*]—if they missed these stories when they first appeared in such magazines as the Mencken-edited *Mercury* twenty-odd years ago. This author's range is narrow: the two stories with a non-Oregon setting that close the collection seem the least effective in the book. But Mr. Davis is a regional writer in the best sense. His sheepmen and cowhands and track workers may seem Bunyanesque at first—but so is the country they inhabit. Their creator's ear is true, his eye for detail unerring. When you have finished the shortest adventure in this book you will take leave of these strange, cantankerous men and women with real regret. Thanks to Mr. Davis' magic, they will probably seem familiar as life-long friends.

It's hard to pick favorites in a book of short stories without a dull page. Three of the very best are **"Beach Squatter,"** the diagramming of a rather shaggy widower's regeneration, after he has had family responsibility thrust upon him, almost literally, at gun-point; **"Flying Switch,"** a Walpurgis-Night adventure in a bunk-car hurtling down the divide to almost certain death with ice-jammed brakes and a crew of human catamounts inside; and **"Open Winter,"** a skillfully counterpointed variation of the old-and-young-cowboy pattern, with a herd of wild horses as the menace that turns into a blessing at the end. In all these stories, characters and setting are completely true and completely observed; the fun and drama emerge naturally from these pages. Each story breathes as cleanly as a chinook wind in spring.

At least two fine stories, **"The Stubborn Spearmen"** and **"The Homestead Orchard,"** prove that sheepmen can be as human as a horse wrangler; **"Old Man Isbell's Wife,"** an expert spoof of the Old Injun Fighter, shows that it is possible to be both an authentic hero and a bore. Yet even the bores in these stories have their human side; even the villains (and the author introduces us to some humdingers) have their redeeming qualities. **"Extra Gang,"** a moving account of the collision of a group of track-workers with a skinflint railroad-boss, is the bitterest story of the lot—but the easy irony of its telling makes the tragedy all the more real.

Two of the stories, properly speaking, aren't fiction at all. One is **"A Town in Eastern Oregon,"** a blow-by-blow satire on the life and death of a steamboat stage on the Columbia, where the protagonist is the whole community and plain human cussedness the only real villain. The other is [**"Team Bells Woke Me"**], a simon-pure remembrance of things past that still manages to pack more of the authentic West into its eighteen pages than many an overweight novel. But Mr. Davis' formula, like all good magic, defies analysis. His short turns, like his full-length books, belong at the very top of the shelf of creative Americana, Northwestern Division.

*C. V. Terry, "Those Strange, Cantankerous People,"
in* The New York Times Book Review, *May 31,
1953, p. 5.*

WALTER HAVIGHURST

The stories [in *Team Bells Woke Me*] present a gallery of teamsters, sheepherders, old Indians, young ranch hands. Usually there is a boy in the story, who has a hard but enviable life. He learns to keep his eyes open and to respect himself and to prefer that sparse and windy country to any other. The best stories are the loose ones, told with a rambling relish and in a wry and racy style. **"Team Bells"** recalls the color and racket of a wagon camp before the railroads (they came in 1910) put the freighters out of business. **"Open Winter"** shows a youth lean and toughened by the high country who wouldn't trade places with any carefree youngster in town. **"Back to the Land"** pictures the last shambling homestead rush into country already sprinkled with abandoned sagging houses amid the sagebrush.

The wary men in these stories are all on the outskirts and the defensive; if the weather doesn't get them the game warden or the government agent will. They are pasture-jumpers, hobo sheepmen, horse-traders; they make furtive camps and they keep moving, a step ahead of calamity. But the real contest is always inside them, between a man's mournful pessimism and his endurance. Mr. Davis is endlessly curious about his people—and about horses, pack rats, weather, bunkhouse conversation, the rise and fall of Western towns. Behind each man is the big spread of the country and behind each of these stories is the larger story of the changes that have come to eastern Oregon. . . .

H. L. Davis has lived in that changing world, and if he came too late to have a hand in all of it, he has heard about it all. These stories range over the whole panorama of a country and a time. But they don't include the big new reclamation projects, the latest step in that dramatic changing. A man so committed to the old wild country might prefer Capt. Bonneville's wilderness to the Bonneville Dam.

*Walter Havighurst, "Eastern Oregon, High, Wild
and Bare," in* New York Herald Tribune Book Review, *June 14, 1953, p. 6.*

FANNY BUTCHER

[*The Distant Music*] begins in 1850 with one Ransom Mulock staking out his claim to land along the beach. It ends with his grandson—another Ranse, who has been determined never to have anything to do with it—being as captured by the claims of the land [and of love] as tho he were a salmon with a barb in his mouth.

Soft springs, snow blanketed winters, hot summers, the flashing beauty of falls, follow one another in the pages—eternal background for the slow changing of a settlement into a town and for lives which reflect nature's inevitability. Oddly enough, when the book is finished, the reader has no vivid picture of any one of the Mulocks or of their wives or their neighbors, altho the background is so vivid. It is almost as tho the humans in the book were seen thru the big end of a telescope, minute against a vast landscape.

If there is one motivating force in *The Distant Music,* it is the power of "what will people say" in a community. Fear of it or disdain of gossip makes many of the characters do what otherwise would seem against their own as well as human nature. If the Mulocks had one thing in common it was that they didn't want anyone to tell them what and what not to do—their parents, their wives or their neighbors.

This reader, who thought *Winds of Morning* one of the remarkable books of its year, must confess that *The Distant Music* was hard sledding for her. There were pages of description which brought a moment in time and a place vividly alive, but there were also pages and pages of heavy narrative about characters who never seemed to come wholly alive, despite an occasional, colorful bit of pioneer talk, a rough [not so rowdy as realistic] observation. Other readers may disagree with my estimate, but I, unhappily, found *The Distant Music* a dull book.

*Fanny Butcher, "Prize Winning Author Writes Dull
Pioneer Tale," in* Chicago Sunday Tribune Magazine of Books, *January 13, 1957, p. 5.*

HORACE REYNOLDS

[The scene of *The Distant Music*] is a landing on the Columbia River, which in the last century grows from a jumping-off place to a town with railroad yards and a large box factory. Its characters, mostly three generations of Mulocks and two generations of Inmans, are defiant, cantankerous people, with gnarled, grotesque names, who yell and fight among themselves, whose touchy perversity and discontent drive them from pillar to post.

Mr. Davis fails to interest us in these people. The reader no sooner begins to know and get interested in one set of characters than Mr. Davis snatches them off the scene in order to take up the next generation. Things move so fast they have no place in our minds. . . . The sparseness of detail gives the book a chronicle-like character which Mr. Davis's use of indirect discourse does much to foster.

All through the novel one thinks, Now surely something is going to start, but nothing ever does. Only time moves on. When Lydia Inman comes on the scene, the one person her father and her brother respect, the reader thinks, Here is a woman whose quiet moral surety will influence and help these people. Here is the beginning of some sort of integrated thought and action.

But Mr. Davis no sooner interests us in Lydia—and she is the only character whose consciousness has any depth or meaning for us, the only character who speaks from a center of individual being—than he sends her away and marries her to a husband we know nothing of, and when he brings her back to close the book and speak for her tribe she no longer has any interest for the reader.

The virtues of the book lie in the descriptions of the country in various times, seasons and moods; in Mr. Davis's obvious knowledge of its flora and fauna, in Lydia's memories of what she has seen and her sister Tencey's salty speech and story; in the book's avoidance of the sentimentality of American pioneer life. But to get even this, the reader has to struggle with a craggy style, finds himself rereading sentence after sentence, doing the work which the writer should have done for him, and Mr. Davis is so determined not to idealize his settlers in one way that he proceeds to idealize them in another: he is so determined that they shall work and suffer that he neglects to allow them any play or joy.

This then is a disappointing, inconclusive book, about people whose universal discontent, I think, is more Mr. Davis's than their own, though I suppose it was failure and discontent which twisted the tails of many immigrants and set them roving.

One failure in this chronicle of a river town I feel with particular force. Anyone who has lived for some time in a valley with a navigable river in it knows how deeply the river enters the consciousness of its people: how aware they are of its moods and manners, its droughts and floods, the comings and goings of the steamboats on it; how many times they think of it every day. Mr. Davis's people are much too unconscious of the great river which brings them their goods, carries them east and west, and molds their lives.

Horace Reynolds, "H. L. Davis's Cantankerous Pioneers," in The Christian Science Monitor, *January 31, 1957, p. 11.*

RICHARD L. NEUBERGER

Ordinarily, collections of this kind, made up of magazine articles, lack a theme. They jump about like grasshoppers in a field of corn. However, the fascination nature holds for Mr. Davis is the glue that holds these pieces [in *Kettle of Fire*] together. A Boy Scout might learn how to earn merit badges from reading the chapter "**A Walk in the Woods,**" in which Mr. Davis finds significance in everything from huckleberry bushes to the hole beneath a log which once had trapped a leaping deer.

Mr. Davis assiduously avoids politics and economics, cites no election results, no unemployment statistics. His sociology is confined to the dead grass and broken flumes, which hint where a sawmill might have flourished and hired lumberjacks who long since have gone. If he deigns to mention the extensive unionization of the logging industry, it is mainly as a backdrop for telling how life in the woods has changed. And he mourns whenever intimate contact with the wilderness is diminished.

He recalls the days when huge cigar-shaped rafts of logs were towed out through the choppy mouth of Puget Sound into the strait leading to Canada. The log rafts were as long as a dreadnought: it took a stout tug to hold its own with such a tow against the tide. And, although lumber towns are supposed to be notoriously ugly, Mr. Davis claims he never has seen fairer communities.

Although *Kettle of Fire* may not lure the author back to the region of his nativity, its tantalizing descriptions of forest solitudes and vernal meadows are certain to make many others susceptible to the temptations of Mount Hood and Mount Rainier and the salmon-filled waters of Puget Sound.

Richard L. Neuberger, "Northwest Miscellany," in The New York Times Book Review, *November 8, 1959, p. 46.*

THOMAS HORNSBY FERRIL

If younger readers need introduction to Davis, or older ones further confirmation of how his brilliant mind works, *The Kettle of Fire* will be rewarding for, in this ten-chapter miscellany on the American Northwest, all the facets of his nature are manifest.

A preface summarizes some of his theories of the West; how the Civil War interrupted recognition of what was actually happening, how specious romanticization became ritualized, and why, if literally authenticity is to be realized, "a certain layer of time and history is necessary before material becomes manageable."

"A man always describes best what he knows best," writes Davis, and the following chapters are rich in interpretive description and autobiographical incident: "**Oregon,**" "**Fishing Fever,**" "**A Walk in the Woods,**" "**Puget Sound Country,**" "**The Brook,**" "**The Camp,**" "**The Forests**" and "**Sheep Herding.**"

The final piece is "**The Kettle of Fire,**" a promethean parable about a pioneer youngster who sets out to find hot embers and bring them to a beleaguered wagon train. Ostensibly a folklore narrative, the tale is really a pilgrim's-progress sort of thing, two stories deep in morality. This integration of adventure, humor and allegory has been characteristic of Davis. Time and again in his books circumstances ironically dominate intent and, through wayward, comic or tragic situations, the oblique becomes triumphant. . . .

Davis personally knows his Northwest as intimately as Thoreau knew Walden, and what Davis adds, or rather integrates, is what has come from books about every flower, berry and beast. *The Kettle of Fire* reveals Davis as poet-ecologist-historian; it is a unique realization of the meanings of that country to its people.

> *Thomas Hornsby Ferril, "H. L. Davis and the American Northwest," in* New York Herald Tribune Book Review, *November 15, 1959, p. 4.*

PAUL T. BRYANT

Little critical attention has been paid to the poetry of H. L. Davis since the early 1930s, when he abandoned writing poems for fiction. Indeed, some critics who value his novels and short stories seem unaware that he has written a substantial body of poetry. Yet for his first ten years as a writer, approximately from 1918 to 1928, he was primarily a poet. This period not only produced work deserving critical attention, but also undoubtedly had an important influence on his development as a novelist. (p. 28)

Although there may have been some uncritically romantic response to Davis's poetry as coming from the "Great West," the critical reception of Davis's work remained both favorable and perceptive throughout his years as a practicing poet. Carl Sandburg said in 1927 that Davis was the "only" poet in the Pacific Northwest, and Robinson Jeffers stated that he knew of no other modern poetry through which the countryside appears with such "Virgilian sweetness." Davis's lack of fashionable concern for current ideas, Jeffers concluded, had kept his poetry from receiving wider recognition, but he felt that this characteristic of his poetry would finally make it more durable.

The landscape, however, does not represent the heart of Davis's poems. He uses the land as it responds to the cycles of the seasons, and as it shapes and responds to the people who gain their living from it, as a basic metaphor for human experience and perception. The poetry finally deals with an internal landscape of the poet himself. By looking again through the eye of the imagination at the people and their land and their ways, the poet both praises them (naming the people and the things on the land was to Davis in itself a form of praise) and sets them in order to declare their meaning. Poetry, Davis felt, can be more a way of feeling than a way of saying; it can be something "to which speech is only incidental"; it can be emotion that carries experience "to its end in understanding." Thus Davis is not basically a poet of the West, although he uses the West in his poetry. In fact, he is not the poet of any particular physical locale. Through an emotional intensity of imagination, he gives us an internal landscape available to human experience in any time and place. He gives us not the world, nor the world as he sees it, but how the world affects the internal landscape of a sensitive and sympathetic participant in humanity. If a central theme runs through all of the poetry, it is a love of humanity and a sense of the tragedy of the human condition.

Yet from this very use of the landscape of his imagination, with its symbolic cycles of planting and harvest, river hills and salt sea spray, there is an indistinctness, a blurring of focus, as if in the prevailingly autumnal air our view of the people

and the land were partially obscured by the smoke of autumn fires or by the haze of Indian summer. Jeffers called this failure of clarity reticence, but he could not assign a reason to it. He observed that Davis had a keen, virile, decisive mind and that, "if more of that cavalry-captain decisiveness were in the poetry[,] . . . one wouldn't wonder whether haughtiness or evasion blurs the composition a little."

From the broader perspective of Davis's career not only as a poet but also as a writer of short stories and novels, the problem seems more likely to have been associated with a question of esthetic distance between the writer and the subject. (pp. 39-40)

Since Davis's landscapes are internal, he is seeking some form of negative capability by which he can remove himself, as poet, from the poem. He uses a variety of devices in attempting to achieve this: chronological distance through remembrance of past times in such poems as **"Of the Dead of a Forsaken Country,"** social distance by making the speaker of the poem an outside observer as in **"A Field by the River,"** and personal distance in identity by creating a specific persona as first-person narrator as in **"Crop Campers"** and **"In Argos."** But these techniques do not always serve; and, even when they do, Davis sometimes seems to want more distancing than they can provide. This need leads to the retrospective, indirect quality of many of the poems and to opaquely elliptical language in most. Both characteristics give the reader a sense of evasion and reticence. The ironic humor that serves Davis so well to gain esthetic distance in his fiction does not appear in his poetry except fleetingly in the last line of **"Steel Gang."**

Another factor that perhaps contributed to the problem was Davis's own complex view of life. Although he wrote about man from love and sympathy, he saw the weakness, foolishness, and evil in humanity as well as the strength, courage, and love. The ironic humor of his fiction provided a vehicle for expressing this complexity fully, but Davis never developed as satisfactory a technique in his poetry. His closest approach was in **"Gypsy Girl," "Crop Campers," "White Petal Nanitch,"** and **"Steel Gang."**

Without the freedom such distancing devices could give Davis, he is limited in his imaginative treatment of his material, even though he put supreme artistic value on the imagination: "It is worth less to repeat what men say than to show what they are; and if a man's writing is worth anything, his imagination is worth more—the last thing and maybe the only thing that is new, and that we can take his word for." This statement is significant because Davis regards poetry as an intensely human activity; the poet cannot be the fully detached and disinterested observer of the human scene, but must instead be fully involved in it.

If, as Davis said, poetry is a way through the emotions to the understanding of experience, the difficulty lay in taking the poem through to that understanding on terms available to the reader. Indirection, evasion, reticence erect no barriers to the poet's own understanding, because he knows, for example, when an ambiguity offers all of its possible meanings as part of the poem and when only certain choices will serve. The reader, on the other hand, must determine the range and function of a given ambiguity from within the poem. With a consciously reticent poet, the poem is the one place that will not provide the needed information. Providing this information within the poem, yet maintaining his own distance, was Davis's most difficult artistic problem. Until he developed the ironic humor of his prose, he did not have a reliable solution.

Toward the end of his life, Davis made light of his poetry when he wrote in his journal that his poems "never were much," but he underrated his achievement. In a little more than a decade of writing, Davis produced a body of poetry that was original, characteristic, and of artistic substance. That he did not consistently solve his artistic problems in his poetry may more likely be ascribed to the fact that he moved away from them toward the problems presented by fiction, where he did find solutions. Within this slim body of poetry, Davis has succeeded in creating a landscape that relates both to the actual landscape of his time and place in Oregon and to the inner landscape of the experience and perception of the poet himself. He has peopled this landscape with figures that are not always seen clearly, but that always have a reality and a dignity which relate them to the human experience of any time and place.

For these poems, Davis's long line and his quiet, common, and sometimes slangy language admirably suit the pastoral tone of most of his work. Perhaps his most significant achievement lies in this taking of the ordinary and making it into poetry. Without any of the mannered posing of the self-consciously proletarian poets, Davis presents ordinary people—farmers, track workers, immigrant laborers, cattle drovers, sheepherders—on the land doing their ordinary work. He resorts neither to verbal pyrotechnics nor to extraordinary circumstances to give their lives significance. He simply assumes their significance and so shows them to us that we accept that assumption. In this sense, his is a realistic Western poetry that does not rely on the traditionally picturesque and romantic elements generally associated with "Western" literature.

Davis's poetry deserves critical attention because he developed a distinctive poetic voice to express a body of experience that is both characteristic of a special time and place, and representative of universal human experience. In addition, it deserves attention as the literary apprenticeship of a significant American writer of fiction. Although the ironic boisterousness of much of Davis's fiction cannot be found in his poetry, we can nevertheless see his major themes already beginning to develop, and also the artistic significance of his ironic humor in achieving esthetic distance from his material.

Much of his prose style clearly grows out of his poetry, from which he learned to see clearly and to verbalize what he saw, and from which he learned the subtle device of praising by naming that makes his prose so vivid. Perhaps most important, the careful reader can see his sensitive awareness of the tragedy and terror of human existence, an awareness that underlies and even gives rise to the reticence and indirection of the poetry and to the humor of the fiction. Critics who have missed this underlying sad consciousness of the human predicament in Davis's fiction, and there have been several, cannot have known his poetry.

Soon after Davis began to publish poetry in 1919, he was writing review essays for Harriet Monroe's *Poetry*. By 1927, as his work began to include narrative poems, he was also experimenting with short stories and prose sketches of the people and the landscape of the Pacific Northwest. From 1929 to 1947, almost all of Davis's published work, with the exception of his first novel, *Honey in the Horn,* took the form of short stories and sketches. This period of concentration on short prose gives that prose dual significance: both as a broad form that represents some of Davis's best artistic achievement, and also as a major transitional form in which Davis began to develop some of the primary themes he was to use in the novels that represent the apex of his writing career.

The short prose falls generally into four major groups: short stories, sketches, essays, and critical writing. Although the distinctions separating these categories may at times be arbitrary, the groups have a chronological as well as a formal principle of division. Only the critical essays were written at times ranging through Davis's entire career as a writer. The other types, which were concentrated in specific periods of his life, represent stages in his development.

Most clear cut of these groups is that of the short stories, all but one of which were published in the years 1928 through 1941. Although the works classified . . . as sketches and essays frequently contain anecdotal accounts that are dramatized in the telling, only the short stories put primary interest on dramatized development of character in some unified experience that leads to a coherent effect. (pp. 40-3)

Davis began experimenting with short stories about 1927, and he first published one under his own name in 1929. With the exception of the anomalous **"Kettle of Fire,"** written in the late 1950s and published in 1959, he abandoned the writing of short stories in 1941. Between 1928 and 1941, however, Davis made a significant portion of his living from his short stories, many of which he sold to *Collier's* and to the *Saturday Evening Post,* and he began in them the development of some of the major themes he later used in his novels.

As we might except, dependence upon the sale of short stories to the "slick" magazines led to the writing of a number of formula "potboilers." These stories show Davis to have been a skilled craftsman who was capable of writing to given editorial requirements, but many of these stories are not of significant artistic merit. Of the twenty-six short stories he published (excluding sketches and essays), ten have substantial artistic value and deserve the continued attention of scholars and critics. Although the requirements of writing for the slick magazines might lead the serious writer into bad habits, against which Davis frequently cautioned himself in his journal, acceptance by these magazines did not preclude literary excellence. Even with the pages of the critically more prestigious *American Mercury* open to Davis until Mencken left its editorship, some of Davis's best short stories were published in the better-paying "slicks." (pp. 47-8)

In those stories of artistic worth, three major themes recur. The most common and significant centers around human dignity, endurance, and love for other individuals and for society. Treatments of these themes may be found, for example, in **"Flying Switch"** (1930), **"Extra Gang"** (1931), **"Beach Squatter"** (1936), and **"A Flock of Trouble"** (1941). Two of Davis's best, **"Open Winter"** (1939) and **"Homestead Orchard"** (1939), are primarily initiation stories about boys who are learning their own nature and its relationship with the world around them. Finally, in **"The Kettle of Fire"** (1959), Davis presents an ironically Promethean theme that tries to deal, not altogether successfully, with the whole range of dignity, love, endurance, initiation, and social obligation in a symbolic, mythologized pattern. (p. 49)

In his short prose works, particularly his stories, Davis developed the style and tone that were to be used in his novels: vigorous, unconventional, and effective use of vernacular, without the tediousness of heavy dialect. Davis's "Western" style most clearly contributes to a regional flavor, but the humorously detached tone growing out of that style clearly makes the vision of human life universal.

Western rural dialect is only hinted at in a few spellings (''git'' for ''get'' and ''yourn'' for ''yours,'' for example), but these are generally semiliterate rural pronunciations found in any part of the country. More characteristic and effective are the speech patterns of the characters, drawn from the tradition of Western humor, a tradition in which the cataclysmic is mentioned casually and the trivial is made mock heroic. This tradition, made familiar by Mark Twain, carries through all of Davis's prose fiction; but it becomes even more distinct in his novels than in his earlier short stories and sketches. In this mode, for example, the Woodside brothers of **"Beach Squatter"** hate paying pasture charges on their stray cattle and never do it ''without a lot of impassioned oratory and the most acute suffering,'' but when Volney Pickett pulls a gun on them, he merely ''hoisted a gun loose from a wad of haberdashery,'' without drama, suspense, or ceremony.

This oblique, ironic Western humor prevails through both dialogue and narrative in his stories, and also in his description of people; but, when he turns to description of the landscape, the tone and the style change. The land is presented with unfeigned seriousness and wonder. Davis's poetic technique of praising by naming is given full range in his detailed descriptions of flowers, weather, rivers, and topography. When the human element is removed, or is there only as ruins from the past, the presentation is direct, graphic, and serious; there is none of the ironic humor with which Davis came to present all things human. (pp. 65-6)

• • • • •

H. L. Davis is one of a few recent writers who have reclaimed the West and the frontier experience for American literature. Ultraromanticized stereotypes that had no relationship with the actual Western experience had so dominated the popular concept of the West by the 1930s that serious literary treatment of the region was neither recognized nor accepted for its real artistic merits. The result of this almost automatic stereotyping was the removal of the American Western experience from the range of subjects available to serious imaginative artists in this country. (p. 134)

A major accomplishment of H. L. Davis, along with a handful of other writers, has been to reclaim the Western experience for real artistic exploration. Davis, as well as such writers as Walter Van Tilburg Clark, Harvey Fergusson, Wallace Stegner, and Frank Waters, ran the risks and accepted the penalties imposed by the Literary Establishment on those who seek to deal seriously with the American West. Examination of the critical reception of Davis's novels suggests the kind of price such authors have paid for writing out of their own cultural heritage and experience, but their courage and persistence have begun to reopen this rich vein of essential American material for serious literary treatment. In a very useful pioneering study of some of these writers, F. E. Hodgins has concluded that Davis was one of the new writers about the West who ''have recreated in imagination a part of our American heritage that was lost to fiction'' and that, in doing so, he added a new depth and complexity to American literature. Of this group of Western writers, Thomas Hornsby Ferril in 1960 called Davis ''probably the most important writer of the modern West.'' (pp. 134-35)

Davis was a writer of considerable originality and flexibility. He did not write by formula or set pattern. On the other hand, most of Davis's work is related in some organic way with the whole body of his writing. Each of his novels, for example, builds in theme, style, structure, and other ways upon those that have gone before. Given this unity of development in Davis's writing, a few technical aspects of his work that deserve particular consideration are style, structural techniques, the uses of folklore, and the uses of the landscape.

Davis's literary style is characteristic yet supple and adaptable to a variety of purposes. Perhaps most characteristic is Davis's use of vernacular both in dialogue and in narrative. Although this vernacular is clearly the heightened product of conscious artistry, it is based on folk expressions and therefore gives an air of verisimilitude—of indigenous reality and immediacy— to his work.

A characteristic of such Western vernacular is its ever-present underlying vein of ironic humor. It is rooted in the masculine Western tradition of offhanded stoicism and understatement in the face of a harsh life and frequent danger. Strong emotions are usually concealed, or revealed only partially and indirectly, in this style. The implicit humor usually present also allows Davis to write scenes highly charged with emotion and human tragedy without becoming sentimental in the presentation. Such humor does create at times an air of aloofness, a sense of philosophical detachment that makes some critics uneasy. However, this sense of olympian noninvolvement is only on the surface; it is a device that allows the reader to supply the emotional reaction rather than forcing him to accept the author's. (pp. 136-37)

When Davis switches from dialogue and narrative to description, he uses a different prose style—one that drops the aloof indirection and ironic humor and looks instead directly at the thing described. When Davis is describing landscape, the reader is reminded that this writer began as a poet. Commenting on this obvious connection between Davis the poet and Davis the novelist, Carl Sandburg wrote, ''As a novelist he can't stay away from streaking in a poem regularly without labeling it as such.'' Davis of course was quite aware of this aspect of his style, and he employed it deliberately for his own artistic purposes. Some three years before Sandburg's comment, Davis acknowledged in a letter to Thomas Hornsby Ferril that ''The novel, even at its best, sneaks poetry over on [the reader] by disguising it as information.''

The disguise is easy to effect because of Davis's poetic style, which is itself underplayed. Davis does not give us his reaction to the landscape through evaluative adjectives: he presents the landscape itself. He tells us the colors, the sounds, and the smells; he gives us the names of the flowers and the feel of the wind; he shows us the lay of the land. The descriptive detail is both profuse and precise, and by involving all of the senses, Davis increases the impression of profusion by pressing in on the reader's perceptions by all possible avenues. (p. 137)

As a sophisticated artist, Davis used a number of structural techniques in his fiction, such as manipulation of the point of view, multiple flashbacks, grouping of narrated events into patterns, allusive use of archetypal patterns, and so on. (p. 138)

The journey as the basic dramatic structure of a novel or short story is a device often and successfully used by Davis. Unlike the traditional *pícaro*, however, Davis's protagonists parallel their physical journey with development of perception and understanding. The people and situations they have encountered along the way become more than mere focuses of incident and excitement: they become steps along the road to some final awareness or resolution for the protagonist. . . . The physical motion provides a dramatic line along which the development of the characters occurs.

Another common structural device for Davis might be called the technique of counterpoint. In this Davis uses alternating, opposing, or complementary pairs: idealist and cynic, age and youth, isolation and society, Indian and white, past and present, illusion and reality, movement and stasis. Often these contrasts provide not only the motive tension of the plot but also illustrate the contradictions of life in the West. Davis's complex view of life keeps these contrasts from becoming polarized at extremes, and the resolution of tension between them generally arrives at some middle ground. His counterpoint never presents purely black and white absolutes, but a basis for interaction and development. Such counterpoint especially fits both the times and the topics with which Davis deals in most of his fiction. His time was a point of balance in the West between the old dreams and the new realizations of reality. Davis brings into play this conflict between the old and the new not to glorify one or to discredit the other, but to seek a usable balance between idealism and cynicism, between unrealizable dreams and the passive acceptance of stagnation.

Like Hawthorne, Twain, Faulkner, and other major American authors, Davis has used folklore as a basis for significant art. The way Davis employs folk materials in his work is perhaps one of his most artful techniques, but it appears as one of the most artless. Because of some of the regional characteristics on the surface of the folk materials Davis has used, many readers have, ironically, missed the universal elements common to most folklore. Moreover, Davis uses folk materials in a variety of ways. As he observes in *Harp of a Thousand Strings,* "the stories of a land are the cumulative assertion of what it is, its character, its people, its individuality, its being." In this way, folk tales give a sense of place and of a people. They provide not only richness of context for Davis's principal story line but also rhythm for the progression of the story through illustrative diversions. These tales throw sidelights on the story, illustrate the central themes, and expose the common elements of human experience in them.

Critics have frequently cited Davis's use of folk tales as an aspect of his Realism, but such usage is not their primary function. Davis has noted that his unsentimental treatment of the West has often been praised for its faithfulness to life, to "the real thing." To Davis, such an objective is only the means to a more significant effect, for "A book should do more than catch life as it is. It should widen the reader's understanding of the possibilities of life and its meaning, whether missed or attained. . . ." This heightened revelation of the possibilities of life suggests, on the one hand, the "possible other case" of Henry James and, on the other, the artful exaggeration of the tall tale. This combination, the essence of Davis's use of folk tales, introduces the element of romance into the work with the very material for which Davis is praised as a Realist.

This paradox is resolved if the true nature of folk tales is properly understood. The stories do indeed grow out of the real experiences of real people, but the tales themselves are not simple, unembellished, factual accounts of actual events. If they were, they would merely be oral history, not tales. What these tales do, in their gradual evolution from a basis in experience, is distill the central elements of the common experience of the folk into a representative story. Part of what makes such stories representative, however, is the addition of judicious heightening. Real life seldom has the clarity, the ironic humor, or the concentration of folk tales that represent

the possibilities of the race, not the actual experience of some single individual. Although Davis's tales are never sentimental, they are romantic in the best sense since they present the possibilities of human experience in ways that seldom actually occur but that are true to the human heart.

The aspect of Davis's writing most often mentioned, and most consistently praised, is his presentation of the natural landscape, particularly when it is that of Oregon. This evocation of the scene represents both a skillful avoidance of a number of common pitfalls for Western writers and a useful technique in the development of Davis's fiction. The hazards faced by the serious writer in presenting the Western landscape have been well analyzed by Thomas Hornsby Ferril, who speaks of a "low-grade mysticism" that is encouraged by the scope and the grandeur of Western scenery. To Ferril, "The imagination, transported by enormous mountains, deserts, and canyons, endeavors to answer landscape directly and tends to disregard, or curiously modify, what might otherwise be normal considerations of human experience," even though that experience gives the landscape meaning. This distortion of the creative imagination by the Western landscape, in turn, tempts the writer to people that landscape with "men to match my mountains," supermen who become stereotyped heroes.

With the exception of a few scenes on the Columbia River and on the deserts in eastern Oregon, Davis avoids most of this problem by presenting only the immediate landscape in specific detail. He does not use grandiose panoramic pictures, for he usually presents the flowers blooming in a mountain meadow without expanding the view to the whole mountain or to the range of which it is a part. Since Davis most frequently presents his landscapes as they are perceived by one or more of his characters, he focuses on how the character is affected by the landscape, rather than on the landscape itself.

These characters generally see the landscape as a stage for the awesome continuity of the life force in both plants and animals. The coyote kills the sheep and is killed in turn. When the snow comes and covers both, the mice clean their bones under the snow. By spring, all traces of death are gone. Blossoms appear from the most gnarled and apparently lifeless wood. The irresistible cycles of nature continue quietly, regularly, in spite of the human comedy and tragedy for which they provide the setting.

Nature was an important part of Davis's writing even in his earliest poetry. It provided various symbolic associations: a river or a white bird for wildness; the sexuality of a spring, of tall, straight poplars, or of hills "in foal" with ripening grain. The cycles of the seasons, of gardening, or of farming provide patterns that suggest the seasons of life: the time of year and the weather often set the moods and establish the backgrounds of human emotions and actions. The constancy of nature and its inevitable cycles often contrast to the ephemeral affairs of humanity. The landscape thereby becomes a metaphor for the inner landscape of the people and for their sense of a passing or a passed life.

*Because of the inexorable, invariable, nonemotional procession of the life processes in nature, Davis is able to make dramatic use of the landscape in his fiction as an offset, or foil, or illustrative contrast to the human dramas played in the broad natural setting. In musical terms, we might regard the landscape as the continuo over which the characters play out their individual human melodies. In his early novels, Davis often only used the landscape as a colorfully varied background to go with the varying events of the journeys; but, with the mature mastery shown in *Winds of Morning,* Davis integrates the landscape fully into the development of the novel in much the same way as he had earlier in such short stories as **"Open Winter"** and **"Homestead Orchard."** In *Winds,* the coming of spring becomes a continuing affirmation that people are finally able to achieve. In this fashion, the landscape becomes a norm, an unwavering constant of continuity and unequivocal life force against which we may measure the whims and vagaries of the human scene, just as the continuo provides the basic chords within which the melodies of life must all be played.

Since Davis's writing was a part of the development of his own view of life and of humanity, his works represent a part of the process of solving problems, of gaining broader understanding, of resolving tensions, and of coming to conclusions. As his principal characters arrive at acceptance of some aspect of their lives, their solution most likely represents a similar acceptance for Davis; for an artist's emotional maturation must surely be reflected in that of his art. In this connection, it is interesting to note that the most prominent season in Davis's poetry is autumn, the season that casts a romantic melancholy over many of his poems. As Davis moved from poetry to fiction, and from sketches and short stories to novels, this preoccupation with autumn disappears and spring becomes steadily more prominent in his writing and more thoroughly integrated into the development of his stories and novels. In *Winds of Morning,* it has become an essential part of the novel; this change indicates Davis's steadily developing affirmation which he uses nature to express.

Through the long span of Davis's examination of the Western experience, a few major themes emerge that lie at the root of man's experience and unite it to the universal human condition throughout the world and throughout history. In fact, our understanding of these themes and of how they function in Davis's writing is the key to our fullest appreciation of Davis's artistic achievement. These thematic patterns can be summarized in six general categories: initiation, alienation, Christian patterns of sin, atonement, and redemption, the costs and meanings of love, illusion and aspiration, and the proper uses of the past.

Initiation themes, which present the development of new understanding on the part of a central character, and which occur frequently in Davis's fiction, usually involve a "father-son" conflict between an old man and a boy in his late teens. In our youth-oriented society, such a conflict is not uncommon in our literature, but Davis's treatment has notable differences. (pp. 138-43)

First, the initiation that resolves the father-son conflict involves new knowledge and deeper understanding on the part of both, not just the initiation of the youngster. Second, the positions of the two are usually reversed from the traditional association of age with experience and youth with unrealistic idealism; for, in Davis's work, the older man is usually the innocent idealist and the boy is the cynical voice of worldly experience. (p. 143)

Davis also makes use of the more traditional simple, single initiation theme in *Honey in the Horn* as well as in such short stories as **"The Stubborn Spearmen"** and **"Extra Gang."** In these, a boy in late adolescence or early manhood, perhaps one isolated from society, has an experience that helps him understand more fully the faults as well as the virtues of the people around him; and, with such understanding, he accepts them and joins society. In each case the initiation is an affirm-

ative experience, even though it may have been accompanied by some kind of loss of innocence. The experience never ends, however, with the defeated protagonist's walking away from society, alone, through the gray rain. Initiation for Davis is invariably an experience that ends isolation and brings the initiate into human society.

The theme of alienation is frequently associated with the use of initiation in Davis's fiction but not in the poetry. Nonetheless, the speaker in many of Davis's poems is an alienated observer of society who remains statically isolated. In the later fiction, however, the development of the plot brings an end to the central character's isolation and he finds ways to rejoin the human community. (pp. 143-44)

Underlying these patterns of initiation and of alienation is the basic human need for love. Every one of Davis's novels and the majority of his poems deal with the question in some significant way. Clay's love for Luce makes it possible for him to accept human society with all its guilt upon it in *Honey in the Horn*. Love is one of the three driving motives both for Tallien and for the three Americans in *Harp of a Thousand Strings*. Every variety of love—love of land, love for one's own people, love between parent and child, and love between man and woman—is explored in *Beulah Land*. The risk of each in terms of vulnerability to losses is shown to be high, but the value of love in giving meaning to life is higher.

In *Winds of Morning,* love is the important affirmation, both for Hendricks and for Amos, as the key to an acceptable future and to a meaningful acceptance of the past. Hendricks finally has to accept the full scope and meaning of his love for his daughter and, in his acceptance, his love prevails over past alienation from his children. Amos's love for Calanthe gives some value to what he has learned from Hendricks. Both Hendricks and Amos end their alienation from human society because of their acceptance of the significance of love.

In *The Distant Music,* Davis explores what happens to people when the love of land, a special piece of land, becomes the most significant emotion. As a result, love between parent and child, between man and woman, between individual and community are subordinated, lost, or rejected. Only the Inman sisters, kept on the periphery through most of the story, explore and learn the value of other kinds of love; and, in the end, Lydia, not Ransom Mulock, is fulfilled.

Exploration of the forms and consequences of love emerges as a major pattern in all of Davis's longer fiction. From the examination of the working of romantic love between Clay and Luce, this exploration broadens into more subtle and complex considerations of the other common forms human love can take. As Davis's art matured, he came to the fullest and most complex examination of the various forms in *Winds of Morning*. In each case, the novel concludes with a fulfillment and acceptance of the cost of love in pain and sacrifice. Finally, in *The Distant Music,* Davis turned to an examination of a distorted, incomplete, sterile love, but he was only partially successful. We can only speculate where this line of exploration might have carried him had he been able to continue it.

Exploring the deeper levels of human love leads Davis directly to the use of the central symbols and images of Christianity. Through the patterns of sin as a denial of love, atonement through knowledge, and redemption through acceptance, Davis is able to move to the heart of human experience and to unite the life of the American West to the stream of development of Western civilization. These archetypal Christian patterns are so useful that it is no coincidence that they form the structural core of Davis's two finest novels, *Honey in the Horn* and *Winds of Morning.*

Beyond the natural affinity between the problems of human love and the traditional symbolic patterns of Christianity, Davis finds other values in the use of Christian archetypes. The short, direct history of the American West lacks the kinds of cultural associations and allusive context so important to the serious artist. Not only is this regional history short in time, but also in numbers of people and in scope of events. The artist working with Western materials does not have the rise and fall of empires, the fully developed mythologies of a long past, nor the works of centuries of great artists on which to draw. To supply this lack and this need, Davis tried to reestablish the roots of the West in the civilizations from which its people came; and, in this effort, Christianity provided a valuable resource. (pp. 144-46)

Any fictional treatment of the American West that is true to the human experience inevitably has to deal with illusion and aspiration, for both played major roles in bringing people to the West, and the loss of illusion and aspiration was a problem for those who remained or who came during following generations. As a "realist" who does not sentimentalize either the settlers or the Indians, Davis might be expected to favor the destruction of illusion and to scoff at aspirations based on illusions. Such an attitude, of course, is not the case.

The special double-initiation pattern that Davis uses is made possible by the peculiar circumstance, already noted, in which the first generation of settlers were the idealists who expected more of the West and of themselves than either could ever achieve. The later generations were the disenchanted, the cynics who had witnessed the failure of the dreams of their fathers and grandfathers and who had thereby become the often harsh realists. This difference produced the inverted relationship with which Davis worked so effectively: the idealistic, essentially innocent old-timer, still clinging to shreds of the Adamic expectations with which he had entered this Eden: and the cynical youngster for whom aspiration and illusion were the same folly.

That neither view was sufficient is repeatedly the conclusion of the double initiation in Davis's fiction. (pp. 146-47)

Old Hendricks reiterates, as we have often noted, that what a man puts into life is more important than what he gets out; and he continues in that belief after his full initiation into the reality of the present. In Davis's fiction, this view is the one which the old idealist and the young cynic finally share. In effect, even failure, if it is due to worthy aspiration, and if it is met with dignity and courage, is not really failure at all. Remaining faithful to worthy aspiration—living, as old Hendricks suggests, according to one's sentiments—is in itself sufficient success regardless of the outcome.

From the position of the old-timer, this means accepting the likelihood of failure without becoming discouraged. From the point of view of the cynical youth, this means paying less attention to what is possible, or even likely, and focusing on what is worth the efforts of a man's life. In short, we find ourselves back at the moral center of Davis's work: doing that which one ought to do is more satisfying than doing that at which one can always succeed.

In choosing to write about the American West, H. L. Davis accepted a number of handicaps, and one of the largest of these was a paradox. Not only does the West have a very short past, with little of the allusive richness so important to an artist, but also whatever past the West does have has been so stereotypically mythologized that it is almost unusable by a serious writer of fiction. Furthermore, one of the effects of this distortion of the Western past has been to isolate it from any present reality. . . . The modern Westerner has too often lost a sense of real connection with the past, although such a connection does exist. (pp. 147-48)

H. L. Davis's task as a writer in and about the West was to close this gap in the consciousness of Americans by awakening them to the continuity of their history and their cultural development. He shows us that an understanding of our past is necessary for a healthy sense of community in the present and, therefore, that the West must not be overwooded and underrooted like Uncle Preston's apple trees, lest we blow over in every strong wind. Davis accomplishes this task by building on the felt cultural tradition of the West, the folk materials of the oral tradition already present in the consciousness of the people. With this base, he reaches across the gap in the Western consciousness and finds the connections in the formal traditions, the unities with events in the formal histories, the connections with the formal cultural heritage. The Christian tradition proves especially effective in this respect because, of all the elements of the formal European cultural tradition, Christianity was the one that survived the deculturation of the frontier. It provided the connection between the surviving folk knowledge and the thousands of years of European and Mediterranean culture that is as much the heritage of Americans as of Europeans.

By showing the unity of Western folk tradition with the experience of all humanity, Davis built the necessary cultural bridge. By persisting in writing significant literary works using Western materials, in spite of critical prejudices to the contrary, Davis was one of a few twentieth-century American writers who have opened the West for literary settlement and given us back our essential cultural unity. In this effort, H. L. Davis was an original; he did not follow any established "school" or ideology in his writing. He stayed clear of literary cliques and politics; he found his own subjects and developed his own special style for dealing with them. Yet, at the same time, he was deeply aware of the whole cultural tradition of our society and was able to make rich, meaningful use of it. As a result, his work is a significant advance for the American literary tradition. (pp. 150-51)

> *Paul T. Bryant, in his* H. L. Davis, *Twayne Publishers, 1978, 173 p.*

Charles Dickinson

1952-

American novelist, short story writer, and editor.

In his fiction, Dickinson employs a concise, understated prose style to explore the mundane personal and familial conflicts of ordinary small-town characters from the Midwestern United States. Fernanda Eberstadt called Dickinson "one of the finest and, as yet, least well-known of a growing number of regional American writers whose novels and short stories bring to life, in careful, bone-dry prose, areas of the United States which have been neglected in serious fiction almost since the days of Sherwood Anderson and Sinclair Lewis." He is often commended for his vivid evocation of place, his subtle humor, and his insight into provincial life.

Dickinson's first novel, *Waltz in Marathon* (1983), concerns widower Harry Waltz, a benevolent but illicit usurer from the imaginary town of Marathon, Michigan. When his clients refuse to repay their debts and his unbalanced son suggests that he resort to violence, Harry is forced to confront his rationalization that he "brought honor and gentlemanliness . . . to loan sharking." L. Scott Tomchak observed: "Dickinson looks deep into the soul of a man whose life is barren and monotonous and draws from it an amazing and beautiful new birth." Dickinson utilizes elements of both mystery and comedy in his next novel, *Crows* (1985). This book details student Robert Cigar's efforts to locate the body of his close friend and former biology professor, Ben Ladyship, a likeable but promiscuous man who drowned in a boating accident. Attempting to unite the teacher's disintegrating family, Cigar moves into their home and alternately alienates and intrigues family members by relating Ladyship's "crow tales"—stories about the advanced moral and judicial systems of crows which comment on relationships between the characters.

Many of Dickinson's short stories collected in *With or Without* (1987) were originally published in *Esquire*, the *Atlantic Monthly*, and other magazines. These pieces often center on small-town characters in unfulfilling occupations. The discrepancy between aspirations and actuality is a major conflict in such tales as "Risk" and "Sofa Art," which many critics deemed the most distinguished pieces in the collection. According to Alida Becker, each story in *With or Without* contains "gentle twists of humor and longing, glimpses of dreams and satisfaction and disappointments that strike wonderfully close to home."

CHRISTOPHER LEHMANN-HAUPT

Harry Waltz is a loan shark, the richest man in the fictional Michigan town of Marathon. The people of Marathon look up to Harry Waltz, but mostly because he lives on a hill that overlooks the town. Still, Waltz is a loan shark with a difference. People pay him back not because he ever muscles them, but in order to protect their good names. As Harry says at one point in Charles Dickinson's fine first novel, *Waltz in Marathon:* "I was able to talk people into believing there was noth-

ing wrong with them taking my money. *That* is the source of my fortune. I brought honor and gentlemanliness . . . and seemliness to loan sharking."

So when the ground begins to shift under Harry Waltz—when suddenly in the late 1960's his customers start defying him by not making their payments on time—it represents not only a crisis in Harry's life, but also the change in American values brought on by Vietnam, which, not incidentally, has cost Harry the life of his favorite son, a brilliantly talented musician. Harry Waltz might be said to be the prototypical American businessman, his method of operation being the old handshake system of honor. When that system breaks down, we fear what will take its place.

Harry's crisis is so effectively encrusted with the detail of the quotidian that we almost forget its symbolic significance as the novel progresses. . . .

In fact, one has to wonder if the author, too, hasn't lost sight of his story's underlying significance in the welter of domestic detail. In the face of his growing deadbeat crisis, Harry refuses to resort to violence. Yet it is violence that eventually solves his problem, so in a sense he is having it both ways. On the other hand, Mr. Dickinson may be exquisitely aware of the strain of hypocrisy in Harry's coming to terms with his crisis. The very idea of his being a principled usurer is precisely what makes Harry Waltz so interesting, just as it is their self-contradictory behavior that makes all of Mr. Dickinson's characters unusual. It isn't so much villainy they represent as a monumental ordinariness that is fascinating.

> *Christopher Lehmann-Haupt, in a review of "Waltz in Marathon," in* The New York Times, *November 8, 1983, p. 23.*

JULIAN MOYNAHAN

Waltz in Marathon, an arresting first novel by Charles Dickinson, is really two novels, a very good one carrying a pretty bad one—a sort of malign, loud-talking twin—on its shoulders. The good novel tells of Harry Waltz, a lively and good-natured 62-year-old widower living in Marathon, an imaginary town near the real city of Flint, Mich. A keenly honed, briskly paced narrative, couched predominantly in the present tense, fills us in on Harry's early years as one of the twin sons of the town's richest man, a physician. It describes his shy courtship of and eventual happy marriage to Louise Parker, the local sheriff's assistant jailer and speed typist. It expresses the joy and pride he took in a musically gifted son who died in Vietnam and his distress as another son turned out brutal and nasty. It shows his abiding love and concern for his beautiful twin daughters, Susan and Carla, both in love with the same paltry and manipulative man and entering the testing decade of their 30's as the story gets under way.

The strength of this narrative lies in its authenticity. Eastern Michigan's fierce winters of fog and ice, the miseries and satisfactions in the daily affairs of ordinary people, the distinctive and essentially egalitarian social patterns of a long established and important American region are rendered realistically and vividly but not without humor and surprise. The story comes to its touching, even joyful resolution when the widower becomes involved with a lean, white-haired Flint attorney, Mary Hale. . . .

A further distinction of Mr. Dickinson's prose is its strongly pictorial quality, making one think sometimes of Edward Hopper and the best traditions of realist American art. . . .

The bad novel in *Waltz in Marathon* also centers on Harry Waltz, but here everything is contrived, inauthentic and exaggerated, along the lines of a fifth-rate idea—the imperial American self—that continues to circulate in creative writing courses. It's not enough that Harry should be the happy genius of his household, in William Carlos Williams's fine phrase, but he must be Marathon's genius incarnate, the tallest man in town as well as the richest, the scion of a family famous for producing identical twins and one son in each generation who lives to be 100. . . .

Harry Waltz in these parts of the novel is a male chauvinist who reflects about a woman that "she dressed simply but attractively and was conscientious about her personal hygiene." And he is a hypocrite with respect to his freely chosen work, which is loan-sharking, a hypocrite not for doing it but for the rationalizations he produces about it. For like any loan shark, he charges what the market will bear, seizes automobiles and household appliances when his customers are in default. . . . Yet to hear Harry on sharking, you would think he was Santa Claus. . . .

[There] have been public hangmen who believed they performed a valuable and necessary social role. Let it be said, however, that Charles Dickinson shows remarkable promise in this work of drastically mixed quality. He should go far when he learns how to make finer distinctions between the real and the counterfeit.

> *Julian Moynahan, "Loan Shark in Love," in* The New York Times Book Review, *November 13, 1983, p. 12.*

L. SCOTT TOMCHAK

What can you make of the feelings and thoughts of an aging loan shark in love? If you are Charles Dickinson, you can make them into a masterpiece, a poetic and ethical parable, a magical exploration of the Eternal Return. Widower Harry Waltz is a twin, a son of a twin, a father of beautiful twin daughters. Harry doesn't see why he is a pariah in his hometown, yet, "Sitting in front of his house like hard-shelled candies are repossessed vehicles." A twin understands about the teaching properties of mirrors, and *Waltz in Marathon* is about what happens when Waltz finally sees himself in the mirror. . . .

[In *Waltz in Marathon*], Charles Dickinson looks deep into the soul of a man whose life is barren and monotonous and draws from it an amazing and beautiful new birth.

> *L. Scott Tomchak, in a review of "Waltz in Marathon," in* Best Sellers, *Vol. 43, No. 10, January, 1984, p. 358.*

DAVID CASTRONOVO

Harry Waltz, a 62-year-old loan shark (and protagonist of [*Waltz in Marathon*]), does business without breaking legs or hiring goons. A gentleman in his dealings, he lectures clients soberly, reminding them that they promised to pay. . . . Still bound by a code of honor and decency in the 1980's and repelled by the chaos and brutality that surround him in economically depressed times, he nevertheless is a rather hard character, "stony" in his determination and harsh towards weak people like his violent son Eugene. In fact, the very ironic tensions of the novel, quietly presented, emerge from the ways in which other people are not up to the standards of this town usurer. (p. 97)

[Dickinson] has all the narrative skill, economy of means, and delicacy of technique to succeed as a craftsman. Wherever Waltz looks, there are clever bits of reality to advance Dickinson's theme: troubled children, a shifty son-in-law who is "finding himself," friends who drift from him, a sadistic brother, agents of organized crime in Flint and clients who destroy property. But despite the good breeding and sly humor of the well-tailored story, the novel suffers from its minimalist view of people.

Dickinson's understated style—honed and polished, but flat, does not carry much emotional resonance. The men and women are believable enough, but generally lack personalities or especially arresting problems. . . . The oddly marked son Eugene is by far the most promising and well-drawn character. Raised several powers above the others by his inner torment, he seems as though he might erupt into some recognitions. In fact, however, Dickinson offers only shadowy development. In Marathon, there are a good many frustrated characters whose destinies are not drawn tautly across the structure of the plot.

The author is a writer of talent, especially in his ability to describe the external side of small-scale disorders in Marathon. But he makes the mistake of being too cool and evasive about the problems that he can identify so well. The most significant conflict lodged in the novel—that old-fashioned exploitation of Harry's sort may be less disturbing than what is ahead for America—is important, but it is here handled without anger or pity, wonder or dread. This results from Dickinson's decision to lock himself, rather consistently, into Harry's dry, thin consciousness. Even the ironic shots directed at this stony man who has a heart at least bigger than a bank loan officer's are not enough to get the novelist very far beyond the stolidity of his character. The Middle West that nurtured Hemingway, Sherwood Anderson, J. F. Powers and William Gass is certainly explored with wit and clear-eyed realism by Charles Dickinson. Yet the reader awaits fireworks. (p. 98)

> *David Castronovo, in a review of "Waltz in Marathon," in* America, *Vol. 150, No. 5, February 11, 1984, pp. 97-8.*

GEORGE CORE

In *Crows* Charles Dickinson remakes the intruder plot. Robert Cigar, the novel's protagonist, finds himself an intruder in the household of Ben Ladysmith, where he boards—under constant threat of eviction from Mrs. Ladysmith—throughout the action. Ben is missing and is presumed dead, a victim of a boating accident. But there is a chance that Ben has used the occasion as a ruse to disappear and start a new life, and so *Crows* is a mystery as well as a comedy in some of the best and largest senses of the term *comedy.* When the novel opens, Robert, out of work, is making little or no effort to find a job. Ethel Ladysmith is driving a cab to support her three children, the youngest of whom, Duke, has lost a leg in the accident. Robert seems to be finding himself—while fitfully looking for Ben's body in the nearby lake—in a very casual and leisurely fashion; but Robert, in an unexpected series of reversals, gradually becomes the head of the Ladysmith household and a successful businessman while continuing to look for the missing father, who was a lovable and humorous but irresponsible and promiscuous man. Two symbols—crows (the principal objects of Ben's research as a biologist and professor) and the lake (in which Robert dives repeatedly in searching for Ben's body)—complement and orchestrate the plot, which is tinged by pathos and irony as well as comedy as the family struggles to stay together and as each member fights to maintain his or her identity. The economy of the action, like that of [Fred Chappell's *I Am One of You Forever*], is very impressive. In both fictions action moves effortlessly and surely and never lags, and in both there is a steady pace as the momentum builds. Dickinson is especially good at presenting recurring situations and building upon them so that an apparently casual detail in an early scene gradually gathers force and meaning. (pp. xl-xli)

> *George Core, "Procrustes' Bed," in* The Sewanee Review, *Vol. XCIII, No. 12, Spring, 1985, pp. xxxix-xlii.*

CHRISTOPHER LEHMANN-HAUPT

The title of this new novel by Charles Dickinson [*Crows*] refers to the crow stories that Ben Ladysmith, a biology teacher at a small Middle Western college, was forever telling before he disappeared in a boating accident on Oblong Lake.

The crow stories are charming and touching. They're about the Smarter Crow, who saved the species by staying awake one night and discovering that crows forget everything whenever they sleep. They're about a crow who was falsely condemned and executed for murder, and a crow with a wounded wing who was saved by a vigilant female. . . .

Mr. Dickinson's novel is also charming and touching, an impressive advance from his promising first novel, **Waltz in Marathon.** In *Crows,* it is as if he had combined *You Can't Take It With You* with Margaret Atwood's *Surfacing,* yet come up with something so original that comparisons are useless. And no matter how you summarize the plot of *Crows,* something important always gets left out.

In the wake of Ben Ladysmith's disappearance, his young friend Robert moves in with his widow and three children. They don't especially want him around. They tolerate him with various forms of indifference. But Robert has nothing in particular to do with himself. His career as sportswriter has been aborted by the collapse of the local paper, and he won't live at home because he finds his parents silly and overly absorbed with themselves.

Besides, he wants to find Ben Ladysmith's body in the waters where he disappeared. . . . It doesn't seem to bother Robert when he is accused of hanging around "like death itself."

Now, if all this sounds a little on the morbid side, then so be it; part of what *Crows* is about is healing and coming to terms with death. But the novel has its droll side, too. The town where it is set is called Mozart; the newspaper was The Scale and the college's swimming team the Wolfgang. Robert's last name is Cigar, and his parents own a store called Cigar's that has failed in every line from lettered T-shirts to engraved pewter mugs. When Robert is finally forced by Ethel Ladysmith to find a job, he goes to work in a sporting-goods store where he wears a black-and-white striped referee's shirt and blows a piercing whistle at shoplifters he discovers while prowling the aisles.

In other words, Mr. Dickinson keeps us readers off-balance. When we think he's gone morbid, he gets funny. After melting us with the sentimentality of the crows, he stiffens us with brutally frank treatment of one character by another. . . .

There are no clichés in *Crows.* What pulls it all together, of course, is the anticipation of the spring season and the dive into Oblong Lake that will reveal Ben Ladysmith's rotting body and lift the curse from the town of Mozart. But it is more than suspense that keeps the novel so taut; its parts somehow tame one another. That they do is probably deeply significant; very likely Mr. Dickinson has found a new way of expressing the contradictions of small-town mid-American life—of reconciling the silliness with the passion, the pettiness with the nobility. Yet one hesitates to analyze why the recipe works for fear of letting the dish grow cold.

It's like trying to explain the crow stories. No doubt they mean something, and what they mean probably connects to the character of the biologist who invented them. Maybe they even explain how Ben's body winds up where Robert eventually finds it. But one hesitates to analyze. *Crows* is such an impossibly successful marriage that one prefers not to interrogate the couple. Let slapstick and melodrama go their happy way. Mr. Dickinson has gotten hold of something special. One looks forward to following wherever it will end up taking him.

> *Christopher Lehmann-Haupt, in a review of "Crows," in* The New York Times, *April 26, 1985, p. 29.*

DOUGLAS UNGER

Charles Dickinson's first novel, *Waltz in Marathon,* focused his sharply imaginative prose on an eccentric character in a small Middle Western town. His second novel, *Crows,* also follows an unusual small-town character, but one less sympathetically drawn; much of his story remains as locked in ice as the long Wisconsin winters during which much of it takes place. . . .

In *Crows* Mr. Dickinson attempts to interweave two major themes. The first is that of the relations between fathers and sons. Robert is estranged from his wishy-washy father and "seemed to have risen above him, borne aloft on a cloud of contempt." But he tries to assume a fatherly role with the Ladysmith children, as if to make up for his cold relationship with his own father, a childish man who is dominated by Robert's mother.

The second theme is the discovery of a personal ethic in fables—the "crow tales" Robert remembers as Ben's legacy. "In fact, crows have a very structured moral sense. They have conscience, guilt, love, devotion, dishonor. A very advanced moral code," Robert says, echoing Ben's words.

The trouble with the novel is that the themes never effectively meet. The crow tales are presumably meant to give meaning to the story but in fact rarely do. . . .

There are many passages of impressive writing as we follow Robert's transition from feckless young man to businesslike, in some ways Babbitlike, adult, the manager of SportsHeaven, a sporting goods store the size of a supermarket. Mr. Dickinson's knowledge of the northern Middle West is sharp and authentic. . . .

What most comes alive in *Crows* is [an] authenticity of landscape and of the seasonal and social cycles of a small Wisconsin town. And the authenticity suggests another theme of *Crows*— Robert would rather stay at home in the Middle West and accept whatever job he can get than face the insecurities of a strange world. This desire to remain has the potential for emotional richness, but it lies buried in uneven fables and an unconvincing story.

Douglas Unger, "Intruder in the Nest," in The New York Times Book Review, June 30, 1985, p. 9.

FERNANDA EBERSTADT

[Dickinson] is one of the finest and, as yet, least well-known of a growing number of regional American writers whose novels and short stories bring to life, in careful, bone-dry prose, areas of the United States which have been neglected in serious fiction almost since the days of Sherwood Anderson and Sinclair Lewis. *Crows,* Dickinson's second novel, set in a small lakeside town in Wisconsin, tells the story of an out-of-work sportswriter named Robert Cigar who is struggling to maintain an uneasy place in the household of his late biology professor, Ben Ladysmith. . . .

The book shifts from a cautious yet curiously charged present to recollection of Ben Ladysmith's courting habits and his "crow-tales"—solemn and ingenious fables about the enlightened judicial system and social customs of crows. The common sense and civility reflected in these tales find a pleasing correlative in the human kingdom as depicted here by Dickinson. . . .

The novel's style is cool, modest, humorous and uninflected, its action and emotional content guarded—much of the characters' time is spent simply trying to get through the winter with their souls "turned down a notch like a gas-flame."

Yet despite this diffidence, *Crows* is in fact an immensely persuasive novel, compelling in its human sympathy, in its low-keyed generosity and its feel for the ordinary, stirring in its description of college sports, of crow-hunting and ice-fishing, of the way children mourn for dead parents, of the mannered vanity and jaunty bitterness of a certain type of failed academic. It may superficially suggest something of the minimalism and willed eccentricity of plot which has characterized serious American fiction of recent years, but it is free of the cultivated disaffection with American life which lies at the heart of, say, Raymond Carver's work. Dickinson draws on popular culture without irony or contempt and portrays ordinary families with understanding. The wry and unsentimental appreciation of small-town life in a hard climate, likeable characters endowed with pluck and common sense, a quiet charge of suspense and a resolution at once happy and convincing, make *Crows* and its author a welcome find.

Fernanda Eberstadt, "Down a Notch," in The Times Literary Supplement, No. 4312, November 22, 1985, p. 1310.

KIRKUS REVIEWS

At their best, Dickinson's deceptively simple stories [in *With Or Without*] are as charming and poignant as his warmhearted novels, *Waltz in Marathon* (1983) and *Crows* (1985).

And at his worst, Dickinson sounds a lot like the trendier voices in contemporary fiction. Characters from a typical Ann Beattie story wander into **"Risk,"** where playing the game of that name, two of them sublimate and reveal their problems, mostly predictable worries about adultery. And the blue-collar couple who meet on a picket line in **"A Night In The Garden"** recall Raymond Carver's inarticulate working-class lovers. But the less self-consciously proletarian fictions collected here reveal more about the nature of work, and more about the sources of Dickinson's often singular art, than the more fashionable pieces do. . . . In **"Jinx,"** a hapless fellow who's putting his wife through a Master's degree in Actuarial Science by hauling garbage learns one day how to turn his liability—all his co-workers fear the trouble that seems to follow him—into a most lucrative asset. A wonderful pair of stories with a juvenescent point of view (**"Sofa Art"** and **"The Fire"**) displays an unusual feel for the psychological complexities of boys at play. And two previously unpublished pieces (**"Black Bart"** and **"With Or Without"**), both about good, solid people having a tough time getting by, provide a strong finish to an uneven collection.

Dickinson's quiet prose often manages to transform the little disturbances of man into the most necessary of fictions—modest tales of everyday desperation *and* affirmation.

A review of "With or Without," in Kirkus Reviews, Vol. LV, No. 5, March 1, 1987, p. 324.

ALAN CHEUSE

Charles Dickinson is a more conventional craftsman than Frederick Barthelme. The rewards of reading his stories [in *With or Without*] come a little quicker but are no less interesting than Barthelme's. A number of Dickinson's characters dwell somewhere around the lower end of society's scale—they work on garbage trucks and in factories or work as actors in provincial theme parks—and this lends his work an interesting perspective on contemporary life, in which so much focus is put on the upper end of the ladder that we don't always see how many are standing at the bottom, leaping in place.

Dickinson has a canny eye; he can create a tender but compelling voice that lends a character tone as well as visibility; and within the bounds of the conventional well-made story he can surprise us at almost every turn. This is the kind of collection that you'll read all the way through as soon as you find the time. Buying it will be like giving yourself a box of chocolates in which every piece is a coveted nut. (p. 7)

> Alan Cheuse, *"Three Collections Keep Alive the Short Story Renaissance,"* in Chicago Tribune—Books, *April 19, 1987, pp. 6-7.*

MICHIKO KAKUTANI

With or without—given that dichotomy, nearly all of Charles Dickinson's characters would place themselves on the side of the disenfranchised. They belong to the ranks of the dispossessed, the lonely, the defeated or the weary—people who have somehow allowed their favorite dreams to slip away and have resigned themselves, in the interim, to carrying out the humdrum tasks of ordinary, small-town life. No doubt many of Mr. Dickinson's people would identify with Moss in **"A Night in the Garden"** when he goes Christmas shopping and feels "like an imposter in the greedy crowds that filled the stores." . . .

In fact, for many of the people in [*With or Without*], the promise of romance, accomplishment or familial connection hangs, temptingly and unexpectedly, just out of reach, like a bright and elusive carrousel ring. Mr. Dickinson possesses something of Sherwood Anderson's sympathy for the confused denizens of small-town America; and like Anderson, he not only chronicles their frustrations and groping failures but also bestows upon many of them a vision—or at least a glimpse—of freedom, of the possibility of escape from the discouraging necessities of the daily grind.

In **"My Livelihood,"** the Bartleby-like narrator loses his position at the local dairy, decides he's really in no hurry to find another job and in the face of protests from his family, proceeds to happily pass his days at the golf course. In **"Sofa Art,"** a would-be painter who's wound up managing wholesale art exhibitions (specializing in those ubiquitous pictures of bullfighters, clowns and big-eyed kids), watches with a mixture of envy and pride as his young son shows signs of becoming an artist himself. . . .

In two novels, Mr. Dickinson has demonstrated a decided taste for parables. In *Crows,* a series of tales about birds counterpointed the narrative's central familial drama; and in *Waltz in Marathon,* a loan shark's shifting fortunes became a mirror of the changes overtaking America in the late 1960's. As for the stories in *With or Without,* many are animated by a similar awareness of symbolism—a few even take their entire form and momentum from the author's manipulation of extended metaphors.

"Risk," for one, sets up a fairly predictable scenario in which the board game Risk (played by waging wars for world domination) is meant to comment upon the characters' own chaotic relationships. Mr. Dickinson's orchestration of detail, however, is so meticulous, his ability to surprise so consistent, that

the tale never wanders into cliché but instead opens out into a sad, sweet chronicle of thwarted lives. . . .

By anchoring the larger, symbolic movements of his narrative in a welter of personal and domestic details—a "sorry string of Christmas lights" decorating a house, children scribbling the number 343 on a fence to conjure a baseball stadium—Mr. Dickinson achieves the sort of organic symmetry that makes the reader feel happily enmeshed in his characters' lives rather than painfully aware of the thematic patterning of the story.

Unfortunately, the flimsier offerings in this volume often do have the contrived feel of an O. Henry tale. In **"The Jinx"** (the story of a garbage collector who brings bad luck to his colleagues) . . . and **"Black Bart"** (the story of an amusement park actor who realizes he's in a dead-end job), the characters devolve into bad method actors who wildly gesture and emote as they carry out their designated (and all too ironic) roles. Such stories both undermine this volume and do a discredit to Mr. Dickinson—a fine writer, who's capable, as tales like **"Risk," "With or Without"** and **"Sofa Art"** attest, of a great deal more.

> Michiko Kakutani, *"The Dispossessed,"* in The New York Times, *May 2, 1987, p. 12.*

RICHARD PERRY

Charles Dickinson's first collection of stories, *With or Without,* features narrative voices that inspire trust, and language so unpretentious that occasional figures of speech surprise like unexpected gifts. The stories are about men and are mostly set in small towns. No blacks or Asians or Hispanic Americans exist here, or if they do, their presence has no impact. The outside world in general does not intrude. It's as if the author had chosen to reduce the world's power to distract by cutting much of that world away. In the resulting monochromatic settings, we watch his men participate in the dramas of their lives, unencumbered by what the rest of us know is hovering just above our heads.

But as is often the case, absence calls attention to itself, and there is a troubling sense here that something is missing. In the company of a writer as skilled as Mr. Dickinson . . . , we look for motives. Perhaps what is absent operates as a metaphor for the fact that something is missing in the men we're introduced to. Those relationships to history, work, to women and children, and to play that might in other men's lives be characterized by passion are marked in theirs by an uncertainty of purpose and a baffling detachment. They are, quite simply, emotionally marooned. We do not accuse them of having never cared; these are men who, we believe, have tried to connect and have not, for whatever reasons, succeeded. They arouse our empathy. We move among them as among a room of accident victims, wondering if any will recover, and who or what is responsible. . . .

Several stories propose that the dislocation we're witnessing results when fathers fail in the rearing of their sons. In **"My Livelihood,"** a man's refusal to get a job though his wife is pregnant with their second child is traced to a father who taught him to hate work. . . .

With few exceptions, the stories in *With or Without* present conflicts that are not resolved. What we have at the ends of these narratives is the conflict arrested, cast in relief, illuminated in such a way that we are forced to look again, to discover at some deeper level what we thought we had already known.

In **"Sofa Art,"** the story's last, economical line connects a distant father/son relationship to the inability of that father to create his art. . . . **"Bill Boston"** is a song about the powerful way that males can bond with one another; it is also a lament for a lost youth that is remembered in terms of innocence, athleticism and friendship. This story suggests that when men love best they love each other, and we think we understand this halfway through the telling. Yet when the depth of the character's loyalty and affection for his boyhood pal is revealed in the last line, the effect is stunning. . . .

Mr. Dickinson does not slip often. We come away from this collection sobered but enlightened, feeling that what is left out in these stories is meant to signal how very fragile these men are, how it is all they can do to bear what loads they have.

Richard Perry, "Board Games Are Safer Than Marriage," in The New York Times Book Review, *June 21, 1987, p. 35.*

Odysseus Elytis

1911-

(Also transliterated as Elýtis; born Odysseus Alepoudelis, also transliterated as Alepoudhélis) Greek poet, essayist, graphic artist, translator, and critic.

An internationally acclaimed poet who is considered among the foremost Greek literary figures of the twentieth century, Elytis celebrates the splendors of nature while affirming humanity's ability to embrace hope over despair. Combining his interest in surrealism with lyrical evocations of Greek landscape, history, and culture, Elytis creates poems that exalt the virtues of sensuality, innocence, and imagination while striving to reconcile these attributes with life's tragic aspects. Through his rejection of rationalism, Elytis suggests that truth resides in mystery, and he endeavors to establish parallels between the physical and spiritual worlds by blending elements of mythology, pantheism, anthropomorphism, and Christianity. Describing himself as an idealist who is unconcerned with reflecting the sensibility of his era, Elytis stated: "I consider poetry a source of innocence full of revolutionary forces. It is my mission to direct these forces against a world my conscience cannot accept, precisely so as to bring that world through continual metamorphoses more in harmony with my dreams." A recipient of the 1979 Nobel Prize in literature, Elytis was cited by the Swedish Academy for writing "poetry which, against the background of Greek tradition, depicts with sensuous strength and intellectual clearsightedness modern man's struggle for freedom and creativity."

The youngest of six children, Elytis was born in Iráklion, Crete, to a wealthy industrialist and his wife. He attended primary and secondary schools in Athens before enrolling at the University of Athens School of Law. As a youth, Elytis spent his summer vacations on the Aegean Islands, absorbing the seaside atmosphere that deeply informs the imagery of his verse. Also essential to Elytis's poetic development was his attraction to surrealism, which he developed during the late 1920s through the works of French poet Paul Éluard. In 1935, after leaving law school, Elytis displayed several visual collages at the First International Surrealist Exhibition in Athens and began publishing poems in various Greek periodicals. His first collection of verse, *Prosanatolizmi* (1939; *Orientations*), which focuses on the beauty of the Aegean landscape, is characterized by sensual imagery through which Elytis depicts humanity's integration into the physical world while emphasizing the significance of erotic forces in the progression of natural and human events. These poems also display Elytis's affinity for such surrealistic devices as the portrayal of supernatural occurrences, exploration of the unconscious, and personification of abstract ideas and natural phenomena. In his next volume, *Ilios protos* (1943; *Sun the First*), Elytis confirms his predilection for examining nature's intrinsic relationship with human spirituality. Referring to the environment Elytis establishes in his first two books, Kimon Friar stated: "In this enchanted and enchanting summer world, Elytis turned to the praise of a happy beauty, to 'summing up his green moments,' and he created youths and maidens who, for an entire generation in Greece, have become the glorification of whatever is carefree, daring,

adored and adoring, innocent, sexually awakening in childhood and early adolescence."

During the Fascist invasion of Greece in 1940 and 1941, Elytis served on the Albanian front as a second lieutenant in Greece's First Army Corps. The heroism he witnessed amid the tragedy and suffering of combat is reflected in his long poem *Azma iroikó ke pénthimo yia ton haméno anthipologhaghó tis Alvanías* (1945; *Heroic and Elegiac Song for the Lost Second Lieutenant of the Albanian Campaign*). Centering on the death of a young Greek soldier whose transfiguration and resurrection serves as an affirmation of justice and liberty, this work advances Elytis's concerns with the merging of physical and spiritual existence and pays tribute to those individuals who resist oppression and defend freedom. Following the publication of *Heroic and Elegiac Song,* Elytis ceased producing poetry for more than a decade, immersing himself in civic and cultural affairs. From 1948 to 1953, during the civil strife in Greece, Elytis lived in Paris, where he studied at the Sorbonne and wrote articles in French for *Verve* magazine. Several years after returning to Greece, Elytis published *To áxion estí* (1959; *The Axion Esti*), an intricately structured cycle alternating prose and verse that has been described by Edmund Keeley as "a kind of spiritual autobiography that attempts to dramatize the national and philosophical extensions of the poet's personal sensibility.'' Indebted for much of its tone, language, symbolism, and structure to the liturgy of the Greek Orthodox Church, *The Axion Esti* incorporates elements of Christianity and images of Grecian landscapes and culture while augmenting Elytis's concern for the spirituality of the material world with an awareness of humanity's need to accept and assimilate life's dichotomies.

The poems in Elytis's next book, *Éxi ke miá típsis yia ton uranó* (1960; *Six and One Remorses for the Sky*), reveal his efforts to reconcile elements of the dualism of human existence. In *Thánatos ke Anástasis tou Konstandínou Paleológhou* (1971; *Death and Resurrection of Konstandinos Paleologhos*) and *To fotódhendro ke i dhekáti terári omorfiá* (1971; *The Light Tree and the Fourteenth Beauty*), Elytis continues to examine the triumph of hope over despair, the union of spirit and flesh, and the richness of Greek culture and tradition. *Maria Neféli* (1979; *Maria Nephele*) is considered Elytis's major poem of the 1970s. Consisting of a series of antiphonal passages between a liberated woman, who functions as a symbol of the individual in contemporary society, and an intelligent and mature poetic persona, this work illuminates Elytis's preoccupation with humanity's ability to attain harmony amid the chaos of the modern world. Elytis has also published *O ílios o iliátores* (1971; *The Sovereign Sun: Selected Poems*) and *Selected Poems* (1982), as well as a collection of essays, *Anihtá hártia* (1974; *Open Book*).

(See also *CLC*, Vol. 15 and *Contemporary Authors*, Vol. 102.)

KIMON FRIAR

In his first two books [*Orientations* (1939) and *Sun the First* (1943)] Elýtis recalls the desolate beaches in the dazzling sun, the golden cricket husks of August in a midday sleep, the stone the scorpion wears next to his skin, the olive groves and vineyards stretching to the sea, the desolate glance that blows on stones and the deathless cacti. These poems deliberately avoid any depth of perspective or the imitative realism of Renaissance painting, for in the clear light of Greece the near and the far seem to coexist on one flat plane, as in Japanese prints. His poems may best be likened to Byzantine mosaics, and his images and words to the bright colored stones, glass, and pebbles which are the alphabet of these icons (the word in Greek also means ''images''), where each individual mosaic stone retains its brilliance, its hard, sharp outline, yet is united with other equally individual stones, not by shading or contour, but by linear design and cluster association of color. The mosaic stones Elýtis used were the pebbles, seashells, conches, grains of sand, plants, flowers, crickets, birds and clouds of the Greek landscape in an outline of horizons and rock-island formations. Perhaps because he accepted his island seascape as his familiar environment, no Greek poet had ever hymned so ecstatically the Aegean Sea or the dazzling desolation of its beaches.

In this enchanted and enchanting summer world, Elýtis turned to the praise of a happy beauty, to ''summing up his green moments,'' and he created youths and maidens who, for an entire generation in Greece, have become the glorification of whatever is carefree, daring, adored and adoring, innocent, sexually awakening in childhood and early adolescence. Early childhood receives its apotheosis in Elýtis' poetry, in his ''child with the skinned knee, / Close-cropped head / Legs with crossed

anchors / Arms of pine, tongue of fish / small brother of the cloud'' who carries the sun between his thighs. The natural destiny of these boys are the ''grapehard girls'' who are ''slowly burning because of the hydrangeas,'' who are chiseled by the wind's experience. There is Marina of the Rocks, that ''Heroine of Iambics,'' with a taste of storm on her lips, wandering all day long in the hard reveries of stone and sea, keeping a trace in the unclothed water of all its luminous days, the epitome of whatever is untouched and desired.

Elýtis created a ''countryside of the open heart'' and inhabited this dream landscape with metamorphosed boys and girls, mythical maidens with flowing hair and translucent bodies, ''seablue to the bone,'' who held and brought in their hands an innocence as though from another world, making the invisible visible, reshaping objects according to the heart's desire, exposing the secret mystery of common things in an innocence of fused emotion from which the ideal cannot be separated from the real. He entitled his second book *Sun the First* to announce that in Greece the sun is an absolute sovereign under whose refulgent gaze objects not only become cleared and cleansed but also dazzle away into a transillumination almost abstract, into an absolution of justice, an ethical nudity, a physical metaphysics. In no other poet, with the exception of Nikos Kazantzákis, has the sun and its light played such a central role. For Elýtis the sun, the wellspring of light, not only finds its true and absolute position in Greece but demands continual sacrifice in order that it may be maintained—the contributions of both the living and the dead. It is the magical sign with which he conjures away evil from the world and in whose purifying light Justice stands created and revealed. The Aegean for Elýtis is not only a geographical space, the triangle in which his own personal subconscious sank its racial roots, but is also a luminous, spiritual space where the past and present of fragmented Greece promises to repossess an ethical unity. The two poems which best represent his early manner are ''The Body of Summer,'' in which the abstract is personified by the concrete, and ''The Mad Pomegranate Tree,'' the symbol of whatever with delirious recklessness battles all that is evil and suffocating in the world.

It is true that the overall effect of Elýtis' early poems is one of hope and radiance, but there are nonetheless indications of dark clouds, inclement weather, wintry skies. Elýtis himself has never been the youths he hymns in his poetry, except in wish-fulfillment and transforming imagination. He felt impelled to describe not what life had deprived him of, but what he would have liked it to be, to transmute the ''Melancholy of the Aegean,'' (the title of one of his poems) into joy out of an ethical need for Platonic idealization. Joy was for him not so much a reality as a vision of paradisiacal perfection. For Elýtis, the poet does not necessarily express his times, but may heroically oppose them. Nor would it be correct to say that he is a poet of optimism as opposed to a Kariotákian pessimism, for hatred is also a falsification. ''Hat is for me,'' he writes, ''superfluous on the road of the sky.''

When Mussolini invaded Greece in October of 1940, Elýtis was among the first to serve in the frontline trenches as a Second Lieutenant. Out of his own tragic involvement in the war, out of his admiration for his people who reacted with a beautiful rashness over self-calculation, and out of a desire to praise all Greeks who throughout their long history have fought oppression and occupation, he wrote, in 1943, his *Heroic and Elegiac Song for the Lost Second Lieutenant of the Albanian Campaign*. In this he turned to a poetry of clarity in a need to speak of the dreadful events in which he had participated, though with no loss of fertile imagery which surrealism had bequeathed him. The Second Lieutenant of this poem is the boy with the bruised knee who has now come of age. He is the same sturdy lad who, like Robert Frost's boy climbing birches, had once "defied the peach tree leaves," or could have been found "scratching the sun on a saddle of two small branches," but who had been called upon, like so many heroes of Greek folk songs, to wrestle with Death on "the marble threshing floor." The "white gamin of the white cloud" now lies on his scorched battle coat, a bullet between his eyebrows, "a small bitter well, fingerprint of fate." At his side, as though amputation was not so much an irreplaceable severance of what had been but the promise of growth to come, lies his "half-finished arm." Turning, as he was more and more to do, to symbols in the rituals of the Greek Orthodox church, though without belief in its dogmas, Elýtis clothes his Lieutenant in the blazing light of an Easter resurrection.

During the next ten years Elýtis said a long and lingering farewell to the enchanting dreams of his youth, during which he wrote many poems and essays on aesthetic matters, but discarded them all, seeing that neither his poetry nor his theories were advancing much beyond his earlier work. During this period he immersed himself in civic, cultural, and critical affairs out of a renewed sense of racial consciousness and communal responsibility, and also traveled much abroad. Time no longer went by "like leaves, like pebbles," but became a "frenzied sculptor of men." And finally, in 1959, he published *Áxion Estí,* and in 1961, *Six and One Remorses for the Sky.* Although published two years later than the former book, the poems in *Remorses* were written between 1953-58, like pendent of jewels hung on the longer necklace of the matched precious stones of *Áxion Estí,* the light of one reflecting and illuminating the light of the others.

All the poems in *Remorses* show the poet in his full maturity, come to terms at long last with the tragic element in the world. These poems are nevertheless regrets, pangs of conscience and guilt for the lost azure sky, for the "ouranós" (the word in Greek means "heavens" as well as "sky"), for an atmosphere no longer innocent or pellucid but overcast and polluted, the embattled region where now not a single soldier or the armies of men, but all mankind struggles in the field of the universe with eternal antagonists, for the stone gods have leapt out of the metope of the sky, brandishing their lightning and thunderbolts. **"Sleep of the Valiant"** is in two versions. The first thirteen lines of each poem are the same, but the first version has a coda of three, the second of six lines. In both versions the boy with the bruised knee of the Aegean islands, and the Second Lieutenant of the Albanian Campaign have become the valiant symbols of mankind battling with the mysterious powers of the universe that are no longer oppositions of good and evil but agonizing and mystifying correlations of both. In the first version, the valiants are depicted in their tragic courage. Vultures swoop down to savor their clay entrails and their blood, but their footfalls are not annulled, and like the earlier lad "drinking the Corinthian sun / Reading the marbles," they now "read the world insatiably with eyes forever open." In the coda of the second version, the valiants wander in an ageless time, restoring "to things their true names." In a world that had rotted out of ignorance, and where men "inexplicably had committed their dark iniquities," Arete descends, whom Elýtis identifies with excellence of every kind, with Greece, with the Virgin Mary, a girl with a lean boyish body who performs miracles. She is the apotheosis of all Elýtis' Aegean girls who

now comes to the vast dark places and labors to turn darkness into light. In these poems Elýtis has finally embraced the tragic element in life, acknowledging evil as almost an equal element with goodness, but still reading the world insatiably with open eyes, with nostalgia that rises as though from the "crevices in the sleep of the valiant." And in one of the loveliest poems he has written, **"The Autopsy,"** the poet performs a dissection on himself, permitting the knife to penetrate there where "the intention suffices for the Evil." Pricked with pangs of conscience, burdened with remorse and reconciliation, acknowledging the pollution of the azure sky and the heavens, Elýtis now asserts his lyricism with a grave and somber voice, rifted with strains of the tragic.

Magnificent as are the poems of *Remorses,* they are finger exercises in comparison to the symphonic poem written concomitantly, *Áxion Estí,* "Worthy it is," a phrase that occurs often in the ritual of the Greek Orthodox Church. Elýtis had long been dreaming of an epical-lyrical poem which would combine within itself the consequences of the contemporary experiences he had undergone, the dangers and evils he had encountered, particularly in the Second World War and its aftermath, but which would, in composition, go beyond the loose structure of *Heroic and Elegiac Song.* In the three parts of this book-length poem, **"Genesis," "The Passions,"** and **"Gloria,"** all his earlier symbols derived from nature are named one by one, lovingly caressed as never before, placed in a sacred and profane hierarchy. "This then is I," he announces, "created for young girls and the islands of the Aegean / lover of the roebuck's leap / and neophyte of the olive trees / sun-drinker and locust-killer." But also, he laments, "my girls are in mourning, my young men bear weapons." Now his images take on their deepest, their most ethical meaning, for they have become symbols derived from a transfiguration of nature into spiritual essence. In his early poems Elýtis had sung of whitewashed courtyards, of whitewashed dawns, of a whitewash that bears all noons on its back, and even of casting whitewash onto the horizons to whiten the four walls of his future. Finally, in *Áxion Estí,* he has abstracted lime into the transcendent realm of Ideas when he declares, "Now in whitewash I enclose and entrust my true Laws." Here the cleansing and purifying essence of whitewash as used in Greek island homes has been transported to an ethical level of invisible Platonic *Laws,* to new Commandments by which to live, a new ascetic. "Light-years in the sky," he has written in a poem as yet unpublished, "virtue-years in the whitewash," as though there exists a measurement for ethical distances in whitewash comparable to astronomical distances in the heavens. And in **"Gloria"** all phenomena in Elýtis' personal mythology, whether good or evil, are embraced in an ecstasy of laudation, their ephemeral elements glorified in verses beginning with a "now," their eternal essence in those beginning with "aye." As he marches toward a "distant and sinless land," the poet discovers that "It is the hand of Death / that bestows Life," and that ultimately, though mankind must struggle ceaselessly for freedom and justice, for the triumph of good over evil, life must, nevertheless, be accepted in its total necessity, and concludes, with sadness and resolution, in a phrase that sums up all his orientation, that "WORTHY is the price paid."

I know of no other poem either in English or Greek with a comparable complexity of structure. Elýtis found it impossible to attempt a work of great length and spirit, one that would sum up his experience, his growth, his maturity, his awakened conscience, his national identification, without the firm foundation of an initial plan that would give him the assurance and the grandeur an epical-lyrical work involves. He found the need to create new forms, new limitations which the poet himself would arbitrarily establish so that the struggle with structure, pattern, order, meter, stanza and thematic counterpoint would create a tension, as in Kálvos, as in Pindar, that would throw out sparks, fire the imagination, deepen thought, and achieve a new freedom in which density of image and sound and a free-flowing association of images are not caged in but, on the contrary, are given wings and strength to fly to greater heights. Few better examples may be found of a poet's stubborn ability to grow and change, to reach in some regard a position almost diametrically opposite to that from which he began, and yet to retain integrally the basic component parts which from the beginning informed his personality and his temperament.

Áxion Estí is also a rich treasure house of the Greek language, for Elýtis is aware that he has been "given the Hellenic tongue," that his house, though a humble one, is built "on the sandy shores of Homer." He has kept to a strict demotic base with taste and discretion, but he has also added embellishments from all periods of Greek development, and even coined words of his own. In his entire career he has been primarily interested in the plastic use of language, manipulating words and images like a painter or sculptor. He has shaken off the tyranny of the speech of the common man together with the purified diction of the pseudoeducated, for both are strangleholds on the creative spirit. Of all Greek poets, Elýtis has shown the greatest capacity for growth, both thematically and technically, the ability to compose superb works at each stage of his development. We can rest assured that, like Yeats, he will continue to give us fine poems—of old age as he has of childhood, adolescence, and maturity. (pp. 226-30)

> Kimon Friar, "Between the Baltic and the Mediter-
> ranean, Five Modern Poets: Odysseus Elýtis," in
> Books Abroad, *Vol. 45, No. 2, Spring, 1971, pp.*
> *225-30.*

KIMON FRIAR

The two books reviewed here belong in kind to those in *Six and One Remorses for the Sky* (1961), but whereas those were more tightly knit, the images more compact and intellectualized, the poems in *The Light Tree and the Fourteenth Beauty* and in *Death and Resurrection of Constantine Paleologos* are more open, their imagery more expansive and loose, relying on apprehension by feeling rather than by the mind. They also experiment with a new form of punctuation where stanzas are printed as one continuous line and where spaces are substituted for punctuation. This permitted Elýtis—or perhaps itself induced—a looser syntactical and grammatical structure that, in harmony with content, becomes the vehicle of a more relaxed, emotive poetry than he wrote before.

He has given *Paleologos* separate publication to emphasize his lingering tribute to his Byzantine heritage and to point up the figure of king or poet as idealist fighting against odds, upholding Greek tradition, making "noon out of night—all live a radiance," one with a broken lance in his hand, the other with an unbroken word between his teeth. And in this poem is announced the leitmotif of all his work, uttered in *Áxion estí* as "worthy is the price paid," and here as "The world's an oppressive place to live through but with a little pride it's worth it."

In these poems Elýtis speaks implicitly of themes that have pervaded all his work; the inspirational and magical source of poetry; the suspension beyond time and place in revelations that come at such insignificant moments as when a child leans out his bedroom window to see how far he can sling his spittle into the back yard; the search for perfection and paradise where the world can be made over according to the heart's measure; the fact that it is man himself who creates phenomena, for "Spring even Spring is a product of man"; the exaltation not only of love but also of sexuality and lust. These are Elýtis's most sexual poems, utilizing even the image of the voyeur and the wet dream where an act is neither moral or immoral, good or evil, ugly or beautiful except as it is apprehended in the mind of the doer. "It is time," he had said in a previous poem, "for lust to begin its holy career," and in **"On the Republic"** he writes frenziedly of that Utopia where all forms of love and lovemaking may be accepted in their own beauty and morality, as diversified as "the various ways birds have of flying little by little as far as the infinite."

The sun has always been the sovereign image in all of Elýtis's poems, but here it dissolves into pure light. In *Saviors of God* Kazantzákis exclaims: "Amidst the smoke and flames, reposing on the peak of conflagration, immaculate, cool, and serene, I hold that final fruit of flame, the Light." And so here amid the transluscent branches of his own Light Tree that flourishes unwatered and untended in a back yard amid stinkweed and rubbish (like the poet himself amid the crude catastrophes of the world), Elýtis gathers under its blazing shadow all he has loved or transmuted into love: his country and her sorrows, her Aegean boys and girls, the transubstantiation of evil into goodness, into a new and higher morality, into justice. All Elýtis's poems may now be judged to be a metaphysics of light. (pp. 599-600)

> Kimon Friar, in a review of "To Fotódhendro ke i
> dhékati tétarti omorfía" and "Thánatos ke Anástasi
> tou Konstandínou Paleológhou," *in* Books Abroad,
> *Vol. 47, No. 3, Summer, 1973, pp. 599-600.*

M. BYRON RAIZIS

[*The essay from which this excerpt is taken was originally published in* World Literature Today, *Spring, 1980.*]

The strange "newness" of *Maria Neféli* should not surprise or offend us, for we must try to comprehend and appreciate it in terms of [Elytis's] artistic work as a whole. (p. 87)

In his often cited interview with Ivar Ivask back in 1975 . . . , Elytis had talked of three periods in his poetry. The first consists of *Orientations* and the collections that were produced during the hard and dark years of the 1940s. After a rather long silence appeared *The Axion Esti* (1959) and the "memory" poems from his experiences in World War II and its traumatic aftermath. In these poems of his second period a mature Elytis directly and indirectly alludes to, and employs, historic and cultural details from Greece's recent as well as Byzantine past. The third period contains his books of verse of the 1970s, his prose works and *Maria Neféli.* As he puts it himself, Elytis is not quite sure that *Maria Neféli* "constitutes a kind of *summa* of my third period just as *The Axion Esti* stands out from my second period." He adds, though, that *Maria Neféli* perhaps does "constitute the synthesis of my third period which is already finished in my mind."

In the same interview Elytis explains the basic concepts of this composition, which was then work in progress. Unlike most of the poems which, though "usually rooted" in his experience, "do not directly transcribe actual events," *Maria Neféli* was inspired by a young woman he had met in real life. His contact with this attractive, liberated, restless or even blasé representative of today's young women made him suddenly desire "to write something very different from *The Axion Esti*." This Maria then is the newest manifestation of the eternal female, the most recent mutation of the female principle which, in the form of Marina, Helen and other more traditional figures, had haunted the quasi-idyllic and erotic poems of his two earlier periods.

It must also be stressed that Maria is a product and *spiritus loci* of an urban environment. She has gone through experiences similar to those that had generated the lyrics of the Aegean climate and *The Sovereign Sun*. Other experiences, though, as well as social developments and pressures, have left their imprint on her, completely obliterating the natural suntan. This urban Neféli is the offspring, not the sibling, of the women of Elytis's youth. Her setting is the polluted city, not the open country and its islands of purity and fresh air. (pp. 87-8)

The main feature in the structure of *Maria Neféli* is the dialogue, or more precisely, a juxtaposition of parallel statements by its two dramatic characters, Maria Neféli and the Antifonitís (Responder), who stands for the Poet himself, as Elytis has indicated in the already mentioned interview. Neither character is stereotyped, simple or flat. Both are sophisticated and complex urbanites and express themselves in a wide range of styles, moods, idioms and stanzaic forms.

The first poem in the book, "**The Presence,**" is the closest thing to a dramatic exchange between the two protagonists—for the Poet is as much a key figure here as the woman herself—and acts as an introduction to the book. Its lyrical prose and verse are followed by seven poems, each with its title, spoken by Maria. All seven are introduced by the phrase "Maria Neféli says," which serves as a stage direction, as it were. Maria's poems are printed in italics. En face are printed (in normal Roman type) seven corresponding poems spoken by the Responder (Poet), each with its title and each responding or existing parallel to each of Maria's pieces. At the bottom of the last page of each Neféli and Responder poem Elytis has appended an epigrammatic dictum (of one to three lines)—a total of fourteen—most of which are of remarkable economy, wisdom and beauty. "**The Song of Maria Neféli,**" a light, fast-moving, autobiographical lyric in rhyming quatrains, concludes Part A of the book.

Part B repeats the same pattern, the only difference being that the Poet's seven pieces are printed first, followed by their seven epigrams; and these are faced by Neféli's seven responses (always in italics) and their epigrammatic codas. "**The Song of the Poet,**" a candid confessional poem in rhyming couplets, completes Part B. Its last couplet could be rendered freely as: "That's why I sent my fate to hell / and returned to myself, to my shell." The third and last Part C restores Neféli as the first speaker. Her seven lyrics and their epigrams are countered by the Poet's seven pieces and their epigrams. The final poem in this part, "**The Eternal Wager,**" serves as a kind of epilogue to the whole composition.

Readers familiar with the structure of *The Axion Esti*, "**The Monogram,**" *Six and One Remorses for the Sky* and most longer and composite poems of Elytis will easily realize that the structure of *Maria Neféli* is an ingenious architectural variation based on similar principles and numbers of symbolic or mystical significance. Three and seven, Elytis's favorite numbers, are reflected in the tripartite organization of the book (Parts A, B and C), plus the seven poem-speeches by each of the two "actors." The number of the trinity is also reflected by the three lyrics that conclude the three parts. Seven and its multiples fourteen and twenty-one are respectively reflected in the number of poems by each person in every part (7), in the number of poems in each part (14), and in the total number of speeches by each person (21) in the whole of *Maria Neféli*. Elytis's predilection for the number seven may be explained by the fact that the Pythagoreans considered it the symbol of justice. Both speakers do justice to their views by airing them seven times on each of three occasions. (p. 89)

Neféli in Greek means "cloud," a word that Aristophanes had used in his comedy *Nephelae (The Clouds)—nebulae* in Latin. Its connotations are many. A *neféli* is light, airy, foggy and floats in the sky changing shape and appearance following the whims of the winds. In Greek mythology Nephele was the mother of Phrixos and Helle, also the cloud of sadness and of death. In contemporary reality the word also applies to the cloud of air pollution that covers Athens and most big cities. It is also a fine net to catch birds, modern human birds dwelling in an Aristophanic city of birds in the clouds. In the Christian tradition a *neféli* often surrounds an angel, or describes the space where the divine dwells—something that makes a precious or holy image remote, barely visible, almost inaccessible. Finally, a *neféli* (cloud) is by definition intangible and mysterious. I do not mean to say that Elytis had all these in mind when he thought of Maria Neféli. The fact remains, however, that its meaning suggests plenty.

The first name also, Maria, must have been chosen with care. Maria is the name of Christ's mother, the only traditional mother figure whose significance in the formulation of our moral values, and the restoration of hope after Eve's transgression, is universally accepted in the West. Maria is also the commonest name for a woman in Greece and much of the Christian world. So the combination of "Maria" and "Neféli" makes a very strong mixture indeed. At the same time the qualities suggested by "Neféli" are almost diametrically opposed to those of "Maria." The young woman and lover of today is all of these. Her complexity parallels the complexity of our social and metaphysical predicaments.

"Antifonitís" (Responder), used for the Poet, is equally carefully picked. In classical Greek *antifónesis* (or *antifónema*) means "response to an address," and in church terminology *antifonía* is the reciprocal chanting of biblical verses (*antífona*) by two alternating choirs. The word is of the same root as *diafonía* (disagreement), but the meaning is different. Elytis very wisely chose "Antifonitís" to suggest his role in the poem, because his attitude is closer to that of a commentator rather than to a disagreeing opponent in an argument. *Maria Neféli* could be taken as a modern Frostian "lover's quarrel with the world," since these two love and care about each other, and their differences arise from the way they react to external stimuli offered by society.

In poem 2 of Part A the Responder longs to become a *Nefelegerétes* (Cloud-Gatherer) like Zeus, the lover of mythological Nephele. And in "**Hymn in Two Dimensions**" of Part B he confesses his "two-dimensional" love for the girl. In several other pieces his admiration of her physical appearance is implied, while in others he sounds ironic or challenged by her behavior, manners and much of what she stands for.

These two characters, antithetical as they are, complete rather than negate each other. They coexist and constitute a "whole," not a system based on a Hegelian dialectic, to be sure, but on an antiphonal device like the reciprocal chanting in the church. Both choirs sing of similar or related events, wonders and values; but each utters its own words, to its own tune. Neither is more important, and both aim at the same goal. Paradoxically, though their courses are parallel and never converge, at the end both reach the same destination. This principle dominates meaning and form in *Maria Neféli*. Its themes and truths are complementary, and so are its organic parts.

In her first poem, **"The Forest of Men,"** in a series of allusions to scientific names of flora, fauna and primitive creatures and men, Maria suggests the ferocity and jungle-like quality of the milieu where she breathes and functions. In that spirit she invites, or challenges, the Poet to follow her and adjust his behavior to the demands of that environment. The verse used is free but controlled. The epigram following her poem reads: "The law that I am / will not subdue me," thus asserting her independence. The response of the Poet, though apologetic, is positive. He accepts to follow Neféli, alluding to the failure of the world he had believed in, and to the necessity of substituting the primitive for the refined.

> Poetry, oh my Saint—forgive me
> but it is necessary to stay alive
> to cross to the other bank;
> everything is preferable
> to my slow murder by the past.

This is clearly a Poet's apologia. He feels doubts about the reality of his own existence, as well as of that of "The Light Tree," the "idol" which in the eponymous collection of 1971 had become a luminous symbol of his metaphysical salvation as an artist.

The meaning of this poem's title ("To stígma") is intentionally ambiguous, I believe. The word *stígma* in Greek may be the singular of *stígmata*, the holy marks that appeared on the palms of St. Francis of Assisi (who is mentioned in the title of Neféli's last poem in Part B), symbolizing the Saint's empathy with Christ's crucifixion. Offering this interpretation, Gina Politi writes: "The key word here is *Ananghelía* (Announcement). If the stigma is sin, it is also the seal of God, the promise of salvation by the angel bearing the news to Mary. The stigma connects the Antifonitís to another poet who received the stigmata, . . . St. Francis of Assisi."

This observation makes considerable sense in view of the context. Since, however, Elytis used the word *Ananghelía* instead of *Evanghelismós*, which is precisely the Greek for "Annunciation," one may suggest a parallel meaning which is quite secular and does not bestow on Elytis either the crown of suffering and sainthood or the Byronic stigma of Cain's sin. *To stígma* in Greek also means "the bearings," the navigational term indicating the point where longitude and latitude meet. The "Announcement" then may refer to the need felt by the Poet of "Orientations" to reorient himself, to avoid getting lost in "the forest of men" where he must follow Maria Neféli. Addressing her, he raises his reversed palm with open fingers forming "a heavenly flower," as he says, but also making the blasphemous gesture known as *múndza,* and adds: "We might have called this 'Hubris' or even a 'Star'." This Hubris-Star may give him his bearings, for he concludes addressing his friends this time: "Don't make fun of my clumsiness / for you know that these are contrary times." Through this apologetic statement and gesture of disrespect toward the sky, the Poet is probably accounting for the strange novelties that his fans will encounter in *Maria Neféli*. The Poet guided

by this "Hubris-Star" is not exactly the "sun-drinking" Elytis of the refulgent Aegean, or the inspired maker of *The Axion Esti.* He is an artist who must always change his means and manners to survive as an artist *of today*—in other words, to avoid repeating, and thus dating, himself and his work. The epigram to his poem reads: "Show such dexterous clumsiness / and lo: God appears!" Its paradox explains Elytis's predicament and, at the same time, indicates the new and only way left for survival.

The six remaining poems of Neféli bear the titles **"The Cloud," "Patmos," "Discourse on Beauty," "Through the Mirror," "The Thunder Steers"** and **"The Trojan War."** The corresponding pieces of the Poet are **"The Cloud-Gatherer," "The Revelation," "The Water Drop," "Aegeis," Hymn to Maria Neféli"** and **"Helen."** Without having to analyze each in detail, we may note the relation of each pair of poems even on the basis of what is suggested by their titles. To **"The Cloud,"** which stands for Neféli herself, the Poet responds with his **"The Cloud-Gatherer,"** connoting Zeus the lover of Nephele. **"Patmos"** and **"The Revelation"** are, respectively, the island where St. John lived and died plus the title of his holy text, *The Apocalypse.* **"The Water Drop"** of the Responder, a thing of beauty and precious coolness in today's spiritual aridity, counters Neféli's **"Discourse on Beauty." "Through the Mirror,"** a title written in English, implying the border of transition to the realm of irreality where the nebulous girl struggles to find herself, is countered by the Poet's **"Aegeis,"** which, in addition to reminding us of the Aegean milieu, is actually the geologically primeval land whose vestiges haunt the dreams and longings of the Responder. **"The Thunder Steers"** is a kind of self-analysis by Neféli; the Poet counters it with his own **"Hymn to Maria Neféli,"** whom he perceives as an Iris inhabiting our mundane world. The two final poems are about human conflict. Maria concludes hers with the telling line, "Each period has its own Trojan War." The Poet cleverly reciprocates with "Each period has its own Helen," emphasizing the cause rather than the result.

This statement-counterstatement device and technique introduces a motif. At the ends of **"The Inquisition"** and its response, **"St. Francis of Assisi,"** both in Part B, we read: "Each period has its Inquisition" and "Each period has its own St. Francis of Assisi." At the ends of **"Stalin"** and **"The Hungarian Insurrection,"** both in Part C, we find respectively: "Each period has its Stalin" and "Each period has its Hungarian insurrection." The repetition of this device strengthens the structure of the antiphonal composition and reiterates main thematic premises. I must also point out that this motif is always used in the seventh pair of poems in each part. Analogous stylistic and verbal motifs control other pairs of poems in all subdivisions and units of *Maria Neféli.* Nothing is disorganized or at random in this text about our contemporary confusion, disorientation, almost chaos. (pp. 90-2)

[The] last poem in the book, **"The Eternal Wager,"** which, being addressed to the woman, is spoken by the Poet. It consists of seven oracular stanzas of three lines each—again the mystic numbers seven and three—and refers to the future, to the time when an aged Maria Neféli will have achieved the wisdom and peace that Odysseus Elytis has already reached. The Poet wagers "That one day you will sink your teeth / into the new lemon and will release / enormous quantities of sun from within it." And the last stanza concludes *Maria Neféli* by creating a beautiful picture worthy of the sensitive "sun-drinking" painter and poet: "That at last on your own you will gradually / become harmonized to the splendor / of sunrise and of sunset."

What we have mentioned can only give a fleeting impression of the poetic wealth and contemporary thematic relevance that abound in Elytis's latest collage of words and rhythms. Impressive is also the array of verse forms he uses: fine rhyming couplets, as well as parody couplets with intentionally clumsy or facile rhymes; quatrains and other kinds of stanzas with alternating rhymes, half-rhymes or internal ones; controlled or loose free verse; lyric prose and prosaic, almost vulgar verse. The variety of styles is astonishing: whole poems or passages are dramatic, narrative, lyric, satiric, oracular, contemplative or confessional. The tone changes according to the thematic demands of each poem, from serious to light, from humorous and ironic or sarcastic to didactic. Moods in the verbal expression suggest the ever-changing moods of volatile Neféli, and of the challenged or even agonized Poet.

His language is, clearly, more elaborate and difficult than the lingo of the nebulous woman. For the first time in his career Elytis uses much unpoetic diction, even profanities and abusive terms. Cabron's word (*skatá* in Greek) is not spared either. Phrases or even whole lines in some poems are written in German, Italian, English or French. Foreign names, titles and terms are always in their original languages—this linguistic mosaic in explosion must, of course, correspond to the cacophony of tourists and jet-set Greeks heard in the streets of downtown Athens. Strangely, as people become increasingly multilingual, their talk becomes more and more incoherent and less articulate—just functional. How does all this sound to the ears of a veteran master of the Greek language? *Maria Neféli,* itself embodies the answer to this question.

All manner of allusions are found in this book: scientific, geographic, religious, artistic, literary, mythological, cultural, biblical, historical, contemporary, even commercial—all of them expertly utilized to create a keen commentary on today's lifestyle, esthetics, ideology, love, human relationships, philosophies and metaphysics by the two interacting persons in *Maria Neféli.* The trade names of cars, perfumes, cigarettes, gasoline, alcoholic drinks, air-lines—the universal words in today's "uniworld"—are used by Elytis, and are even made to have meaning and rhyme with his colloquial Greek. No translation can approximate this unique phenomenon. (pp. 93-4)

Last but not least, Elytis occasionally echoes or paraphrases ideas and images from his own poems **"The Light Tree,"** **"The Stepchildren"** and other old or recent collections, thus reminding his readers that the father of *Maria Neféli* is a renewed and reoriented Elytis of *The Axion Esti,* of *Six and One Remorses for the Sky,* of **"The Concert of Hyacinths"** and so on. This Elytis has grown and has learned to accept the good and the evil, light and darkness, ugliness and beauty, not as conflicting phenomena or values, but as coexisting and necessary manifestations in a realistic, complex urban world from which transcendence can be attempted only by means of what he calls "solar metaphysics." (p. 94)

Maria Neféli is, beyond doubt, the *summa* of Elytis's third creative period. And this original, dynamic and impressive poetic collage records and dramatizes the anguish and tragicomedy, the promise and vulgarity of our aggressive and incoherent decade, just as successfully as the *summa* of his second period, *The Axion Esti,* had distilled and preserved the agony and the glory of its own times. (p. 95)

M. Byron Raizis, "1979 Nobel Laureate Odysseus Elytis: From 'The Axion Esti' to 'Maria Neféli'," in Odysseus Elytis: Analogies of Light, edited by Ivar Ivask, University of Oklahoma Press, 1981, pp. 87-95.

GEORGE ECONOMOU

Published in Athens in 1978 and started 18 years before, *Maria Nephele* represents an important advance in Elytis' development as a poet both in its form and its subject matter. The growth that results from the setting and meeting of new challenges has become as prominent a trait of the poet's career as some of the personae, landscapes and modes that typify the body of his work. Elaborately structured like his *The Axion Esti* (1959), which figured so importantly in the Nobel citation, *Maria Nephele* relies more on colloquial language and makes greater use of the urban situation than any previous Elytis work.

The poem is divided into three main parts, each comprised of seven pairs of poems in which the personae of Maria Nephele (Maria Cloud) and an Antiphonist (the poet) "say" and "respond" to each other's convictions on subjects ranging from philosophy, poetry and love to recent political events. Each of these 42 poems is concluded with an italicized epigrammatic statement which hangs from it like a distillated drop of insight. For example, at the end of a poem entitled **"The Waterdrop"** (a recurring motif in Elytis' work) comes the line, *"In the village of my language Grief is called the Radiant Lady."* In addition, there are a prologue, two interludic songs, and an epilogue. The parts of this whole are closely, often serially, interrelated and unified through various thematic correspondences and are animated by a large number of literary and mythological references and allusions. All of this has been ably explicated and annotated by [the translator] . . . in the introduction and notes to his strictly literal version of the poem.

But the true dynamic of the poem lies neither in its structure nor in its allusiveness. It is, rather, Elytis' ability to compact and unite the work's elements into a single, comprehensive myth that makes its experience significant. In an interview published in *Books Abroad* in 1975, Elytis explained his interest in finding the sources of his neo-Hellenic world by keeping "the mechanism of myth-making" rather than the traditional mythical figures. This mechanism, mastered and exploited so effectively and lyrically in his previous work, in fact nourished *Maria Nephele* in a new way. Maria Nephele, the complex feminine mediator between the contemporary world and the poet, has her roots in Marina, the enigmatic girl of the Aegean with "the taste of tempest" on her lips in a poem Elytis published in 1939. . . . So now she comes in the form of a young radical speaking for the world-view of a new, alienated generation to lead him into a new awareness of which he forges a tribute to their mutual endurance. The mythic model that comes to mind is that of the epic journey to the other world, especially Dante's *Comedy,* when one considers Elytis' revelation that he met a young woman in real life that provided him with the basis for the mythical figure of the poem. A kind of Beatrice, she confronts and tests the poet's commitments and leads him through previously uncharted territory, forcing the poet to show the other side of himself. This territory, represented by the usually clashing world-visions of the two personae, also forces the reader to show other sides of himself through an ingenious strategy of poetic thinking: To read this antiphonal work is to become involved in the dialectic of the encounter, and the reader's interpretations must synthesize the oppositions of the two voices. (p. 8)

Maria Nephele has enjoyed an extraordinary popularity in Greece, going into a second edition nine months before the Nobel award was announced. It is still one more confirmation of Elytis' having earned his status as a chief poet of his language and people, as a world poet whose life's work makes an eloquent case for human dignity. (p. 14)

George Economou, "The Two Voices of Odysseus Elytis," in Book World—The Washington Post, September 6, 1981, pp. 8, 14.

PETER BIEN

In 1975 the periodical *Books Abroad,* edited by Ivar Ivask, honored the contemporary Greek poet Odysseus Elytis with a special issue. In 1979, partly owing to this coverage, Elytis received the Nobel Prize. Now the issue has been republished in book form [as *Odysseus Elytis: Analogies of Light*], updated as to bibliography and chronology, and with an additional essay on Elytis's most important poem completed since 1975, *Maria Nepheli.* (p. 345)

Thanks to Ivask's efforts, readers are now in a position to assess the poet's career. What they will discover first of all is a writer easily distinguishable from his two outstanding contemporaries, Seferis and Ritsos. The modern Greek literary revival seems to offer astonishing variety as well as depth— astonishing because, as George Savidis has reminded us in a short essay called *Odysseus Elytis: Roes, Esa, Nus & Miroltamity,* we are speaking of "a nation with a population equal to that of Bavaria or Ohio"! More clearly than either Ritsos or Seferis, Elytis has retraced European literature's central journey in this century: into modernism and then out of it again into post-modernism. Furthermore, Elytis's career is distinguishable from Ritsos's because it is so philosophically idealistic (not to mention bourgeois), from Seferis's because it is so devoid of existential angst. Andonis Decavalles, attempting to define the shape of Elytis's three-stage development, asks us "to think of Blake, his innocence, his experience and his eventual marriage of heaven and hell." Expanding on this, Decavalles defines Elytis's first stage as "that of an innocent, erotic youth in the arms of an Aegean blessedness. The next stage," he continues, "brings the loss of that world and its purity, the loss of youth, the ugly experience of war and the taste of death, where that early world is passionately recollected as a solace. The third stage draws from this experience the elements not only for the recovery of that lost world, but its spiritual justification and transcendence as well . . . , all this for the building of a new paradise. . . . Opposites are reconciled and unified in the light of recollection of that splendid old summer, the realm of the Sun . . . , where now Purity and a sun-like Justice are triumphant. This is the paradise within." What we also see, parallel to such a development in vision, is a concomitant technical change. Savidis cites Elytis himself in this regard: "Technique has no meaning unless it truly reaches that high level where it too becomes part of the content. And for this very reason it has to be a personal invention, not a given method." Putting together the growth in both vision and technique, we see a shape familiarly European, yet rarely exhibited so comprehensively by a single artist. What we see in Elytis's development is an evolving vision and technique that reach all the way from the tail-end of romantic aestheticism to the stoic minimalism of contemporary post-modernists, supported in the middle by the same kind of modernist robustness visible in a James Joyce or a D. H. Lawrence, both of whom share Elytis's "profane sacramentalism" as well as his worship of Sun and Eros.

Once we have pictured the shape of Elytis's overall career, we can concentrate on the individual periods without losing the forest for the trees. *Odysseus Elytis: Analogies of Light* helps us to do this while at the same time keeping before our consciousness the unified aesthetic theory that underlies the various changes. These changes are most authoritatively described by Elytis himself in the Ivask interview: "In my first period, nature and metamorphoses predominate (stimulated by surrealism, which always believed in the metamorphosis of things). . . . In my second period, including *The Axion Esti,* there is greater historic and moral awareness." He adds, however, "yet without the loss of the vision of the world which marks my first period. The world has remained for me the same down to the present day." Andonis Decavalles expands on this in an interesting way when he argues that *The Axion Esti,* while clearly the product of vision and technique impossible in the first period, nevertheless encompasses that first period and also looks forward to the third—is, in short, an epitome of the entire career in that it offers "a 'Genesis' to rebuild the universality of the Aegean world, 'the Passion' to come to terms with time and experience and set the foundation for a resurrection, and the concluding 'Gloria' singing the praise of the resulting new world of Purity and Love"—the marriage of heaven and hell. Regarding the third period, Byron Raizis [see excerpt above] sees in it "a renewed and reoriented Elytis of *The Axion Esti.* . . . This Elytis has grown and has learned to accept the good and the evil, light and darkness, ugliness and beauty, not as conflicting phenomena or values, but as coexisting and necessary manifestations. . . ." *Maria Nepheli,* the summa of this third period, presents two antithetical characters who nevertheless "complete rather than negate each other. . . . Neither is more important, and both aim at the same goal."

These are some of the ways in which the present volume enables us to trace the poet's creative growth over three definable periods. At the same time, the book continuously reminds us of certain constants. The Blakean progression from innocence to experience and then to the marriage of heaven and hell, while useful as one way of comprehending Elytis's tripartite career, may be too neat. We are made to realize how accurate Elytis is when he says that the world has remained the same for him from the start of his career down to the present day.

The constants everywhere evident in the essays under consideration could be formulated in various ways, one of which is supplied by Elytis himself in the Ivask interview. I would like to offer as my own formulation the four categories of surrealism, correspondences, imagination and Greekness.

We have already encountered Elytis's assertion that his first period was "stimulated by surrealism, which always believed in the metamorphosis of things." In France, surrealism was the most radical expression of romantic anti-rationalism, and for Elytis in Greece it became attractive specifically as a weapon against the western misconception that Greek civilization is quintessentially rational. At the same time, the aspect of surrealism that always believed in the metamorphosis of things has allowed Elytis's debunking of this western misconception to be positive rather than negative, since what he strives to put in the place of Hellenic rationalism is not chaos but mystery. Rationalism seeks to relate entities that are alike, surrealism to relate ones that are unlike, viewing objects as "signatures" of mysterious powers that seem totally incongruent with the objects themselves—in other words, opening up a system of correspondences.

Like Joyce, Baudelaire, Yeats and so many other modernists and proto-modernists, Elytis is willy-nilly a follower of Hermes Trismegistus' occult doctrine "as below, so above." After insisting "that even the most irrational thing can be *limpid*," he in effect defines the doctrine of correspondences when he continues: "What I mean by limpidity is that behind a given thing something different can be seen and behind that still something else. . . ." Behind nature, in sum, lies the world of the spirit; ". . . a line a painter draws is not limited to itself alone but has an 'analogy' in the world of spiritual values." Precisely why this faith in correspondences allows Elytis to be positive rather than negative becomes clear when we listen to the poet's assessment of Picasso. "To affirm, as does the totality of his work, that the most fertile field for our imagination is not to be found in the sublime but rather in the most humble things which surround us, means to have confidence in life itself and its innumerable possibilities." So Elytis, armed like his modernist contemporaries with a belief in mysterious correspondences, has been able throughout the various phases of his career to "strive for *something which is pure*" (his italics) and which at the same time is rooted in phenomena. As Kimon Friar says, referring to the poet's collages as well as to his poems, "For Elytis, whatever is natural is holy, and the five or more senses are sacred portals to an earthly as well as to a celestial paradise."

Imagination, third on my list of constants, is for Elytis the faculty by which we perceive correspondences and thereby reaffirm life's worth. This is the faculty which, overleaping the trap of dichotomization which gapes every time we match the profane to the sacred, effects the marriage of heaven and hell. Listen to Elytis: "If you move from what is to what may be, you pass over a bridge which takes you from Hell to Paradise. And the strangest thing: a paradise made of precisely the same material of which Hell is made. . . ." And what is the quintessential act of imagination if not the creation of a poem? Thus poetry, for Elytis, as for so many other modernists, acquires a redemptive power in a world in which "love, the senses, dreams [are] expiring from a new, unheard-of atrophy in the history of human imagination." A poem is like the sun, overcoming darkness; indeed a poem for Elytis, must be an analogy to the solar system, "complete with the same tranquility and the same expression of eternity in its totality, the same perpetual motion in its isolated component parts." Itself a marriage of heaven and hell, the poem possesses "the ability to re-create the world" if only because it regenerates in us the imagination without which we cannot have confidence in life.

Lastly in our consideration of the constants in Elytis's work, we come to Greekness. This has nothing to do with nationalism or chauvinism, Elytis assures us. Instead, "Greece represents for me certain values and elements which can enrich universal spirits everywhere." Earlier, we saw his dissatisfaction with the misconception among western philhellenes concerning Hellenic rationalism. "Surrealism, with its anti-rationalistic character," he explained to Ivask, "helped us to make a sort of revolution by perceiving the Greek truth." And what is this Greek truth, this Greekness, that Elytis perceived? He answers by speaking about Seferis: "Yes, he is somber, but he never vilifies life. He has that respect toward life which has existed in Greece ever since antiquity." This confidence in life which Elytis offers as the Greek truth involves praise of all of life's gifts, such praise becoming possible only when, liberated by surrealism, the poet is able to bring his imagination to bear on Greek reality and therefore to see through and beyond that reality to a system of correspondences. Of course, Elytis was not alone in searching out this "Greek truth" of respect toward life. Seferis, Kazantzakis, Sikelianos, Theotokas and Ritsos are part of the same movement whose ideal, as George Savidis

puts it, "was a Greek equivalent of Negritude: a new consciousness of the distinctive spiritual and natural values of Hellenism . . . expressed in forms only partly derived from Western European traditions." But Elytis, of all those mentioned, seems to have given this quest for Greekness the clearest shape. (pp. 345-49)

Peter Bien, "Elytis: Surrealism, Correspondence, Imagination, Greekness," in Western Humanities Review, *Vol. XXXVI, No. 4, Winter, 1982, pp. 345-49.*

RACHEL HADAS

Drawing on volumes published between 1940 and 1979, *Selected Poems* presents a series of sensitively chosen selections which give the reader a good sense of the work of a poet whose vision, even allowing for variation and development, displays striking unity. Transcendent, mystical, slangy, laconic, rhetorical—and he can be all these by turn—Odysseus Elytis is first of all a poet whose unique strength is the celebration of a landscape that is his protean theme, his finest invention. This terrain is both his beloved Greece and the human body, a vision rooted in the past and passionately imagined in a kind of floating, timeless present.

Grief, anger and darkness have a place in this world, but they are transient. "I wish nostalgia had a body so that I could push it out of the window!" cries the poet in **"What Cannot Come About"** (1971). In fact, nostalgia *does* have a body; in these poems, everything has or is a body or part of a body. Perhaps the most famous example is **"Autopsy"** (1960): "And so they found that the gold of the olive root had dripped in the recesses of his heart." There are many other examples. . . .

In *Selected Poems* the standard of translation is uniformly high. . . . But the poems, taken together, betray the fact that Mr. Elytis is not an easy poet to translate. Unlike the austere Seferis, he is rhapsodic in ways that defy translation into contemporary English. Torn from their polysyllabic native language, his long musical lines lose much of their grace. His images, which at their best achieve a simple, sunlit radiance, can go garish or dull in the fluorescent light of even a skillful translation. . . .

[This] translation of the book-length poem *Maria Nephele* fares worse. What is rhetorical even in Greek here teeters on the brink of farce. . . . (p. 29)

[The translator] is not wholly to blame. The sad fact is that *Maria Nephele* contains more dross than gold. The poem is characterized by the same peculiar mixture of flowing lyricism and elaborate architectonics which marks the far more successful *The Axion Esti* (1959). In that work, Mr. Elytis blended his elements so as to create a unique and striking effect. *Maria Nephele,* by contrast, seems hardly to believe in its own aspirations to complexity and profundity.

The poem is a dialogue spoken alternately by Maria Nephele and the Antiphonist—Mr. Elytis himself. The figure of Maria Nephele is based, the poet has said, "on a young girl I met in real life," whose world view "is that of the young generation of today. . . . I try to understand her." Such understanding should hardly be difficult, for at the same time Maria Nephele is "the other half of me." In the words of the poem's epigraph, "On the other side I am the same."

Maria Nephele is thus other *and* self, female *and* male, young *and* old, particular *and* universal. Reluctance to leave anything out takes its artistic toll: This "poem in two voices" is really a long monologue spoken by an indifferent ventriloquist. Maria Nephele's speeches may be on the left-hand side of the page and the Antiphonist's on the right, but the dramatic space between the two is so inert as to be nonexistent.

In fact, the only real antiphony in *Maria Nephele* is the dialogue between impatience and pleasure that the poem is liable to set off in the reader. Mr. Elytis's compulsive habit of alluding to everyone from Heraclitus to Fellini, and his symmetrical structurings of poem and response, song and epigram, can be pretentious and obtrusive. Yet his rich language is often a welcome relief from the cultural and imaginative impoverishment of much contemporary poetry. But sometimes he strains too hard for profundity, trying to load extraneous significance onto language whose truest meaning is its own clear and buoyant beauty. When such beauty is lacking, all the poet's ambitious scaffolding fails to save his lines from flaccidity. But when Elytis is most himself, the structures fall away like the earlier, discarded stages of a rocket, as the poem itself moves into the empyrean. (pp. 29-30)

> Rachel Hadas, *"The Landscape and the Body,"* in The New York Times Book Review, *February 7, 1982, pp. 29-30.*

PAUL MERCHANT

When Elytis was awarded the Nobel Prize in 1979, those readers familiar with his poems only through the Penguin *Four Greek Poets* may have been surprised. That 1966 selection presented a poet of remarkable lyrical gifts, a private, intense, incantatory speaker of charms against decay. The charms were powerful—primary colours, fruit, birds, fish, trees, the Aegean sea, sunlight, stars, the scent of herbs, girls remembered in moments of sharp ecstasy, the sun-drenched body which is both a person and Greece itself. And against all these, the enemies: darkness, chaos, tempest, evil. They are lyrics of nostalgia—beautifully made, bittersweet, minor poetry. Omitted from the 1966 selection were the two masterpieces of 1945 and 1959 which had already established Elytis as a poet of international importance.... [*Selected Poems*] prints the first of these works, *Heroic and Elegiac Song for the Lost Second Lieutenant of the Albanian Campaign,* complete, and a brief selection from *Worthy It Is,* (whose title is oddly left untranslated as *The Axion Esti,* as if in such an important matter the reader will suddenly acquire Greek). (p. 75)

It is good at last to see both sides of Elytis represented in a full-scale edition. Of the early poems the most effective are still **"Anniversary"** (**"Commemoration"** in 1966; still shorn of its epigraph from Swinburne, '... even the weariest river / winds somewhere safe to sea!') and the extraordinary symbolist flowering of **"The Mad Pomegranate Tree"**. These are confident pieces, which cross the gap between poet and reader. The *Seven Nocturnals,* on the other hand, so delicate and musical in the original, lose their poetry in this transition.... There are very few lapses [in the translation] (four winds for Elytis's five in **"Adolescence of Day"**) but there is a lack of resonance and a failure to surprise in these versions of the early poems—no doubt the price paid for literal fidelity. This seems a pity in the case of a poet whose language is always so fresh and startling. The difficulty of translation, especially of a great lyric poet, is in producing a version that people will want to read as poetry. That challenge is triumphantly met in *Heroic and Elegiac Song,* the poet's most unambiguously successful

work. The poem is a white-hot sequence of songs of loss and transfiguration, centred on the death of an officer (of Elytis's own rank) in the anti-fascist Albanian campaign. Here, writing at full pressure throughout, Elytis can be compared with the Neruda of Machu Picchu. *Heroic and Elegiac Song* is one of the key poems of the twentieth century, and it is finely translated, without gestures or false tones, in a dignified, direct manner that allows both the anger and the delight to flourish.

The Albanian experience is important also in *Worthy It Is,* furnishing, together with the German occupation of Athens, material for its horrific prose-poems, which are perfectly translated here. The other two elements of style and subject-matter, from the Orthodox liturgy and the Demotic tradition of folksong, transfer less easily, the liturgical style perhaps presenting the greatest barrier. There are precedents, however, for this kind of mixed form in English (one thinks of David Jones and Pound) although some attempt should have been made to offer at least a suggestion of rhyme when working Elytis's haunting rhymed quatrains. But this rich, difficult, allusive poem comes over with great force, and readers of the selection will want to turn to the complete poem.

In these two great war-influenced works Elytis was painfully and heroically engaged with his times. But there is a movement in the recent work towards a more arcane subject-matter and an introverted private imagery. MacDiarmid said in a 1974 interview with Walter Perrie that 'the lyric, by its very nature, cannot reflect the complexities of modern life', and these late poems are perhaps a kind of retreat.... But the earlier passions now have a tinge of sentiment, and the anger of the war poems seems to be changing into disillusion, with the old choices being replaced by more sterile abstractions. The final sequence, *Maria Nepheli,* a quirky debate between a woman and The Other Speaker about the modern world, is punctuated with aphorisms at the foot of each page, so that the weak final couplet of **"That which convinces"**,

> And something more: when it begins to rain
> Let's strip and shine like the clover leaf...

is followed by the proposition

> A sea which is a mistake is impossible.

This is the Emperor's new profundity, ringing false in the modern world of ordinary Greeks which Ritsos, for example, has always confronted so directly.

One deeply moving, delicate, conscience-stricken piece, however, **"Silver Gift Poem,"** stands out here like a talisman against despair. It has the gentle mastery, the authority that only major poets attempt:

> And yet   let us imagine children playing
>   on an old threshing floor
> which could even be in a tenement   and that
>   the losers
> Must by the rules   speak and forfeit some
>   truth to the others
> So that at last they all find themselves holding in
>   their hand a small
> Silver gift poem.

(pp. 75-6)

> Paul Merchant, *"Both Sides of Elytis,"* in Poetry Review, *Vol. 72, No. 2, June, 1982, pp. 75-6.*

ANDONIS DECAVALLES

[In] his long development as a poet, Elytis has never ceased to experiment technically, with inventive metamorphoses and revisions, but he has stayed essentially faithful to his initial conception—the notions, feelings, the world, the objectives and cause, and the insistent message. A consideration of what is new in *Maria Nefeli* offers the chance, therefore, to seek that unity of which it is a part; the search involves a challenging adventure.

First published in December 1978, about a year before the poet was awarded the Nobel Prize, *Maria Nefeli* was subsequently reissued several times, twice within a month of its initial appearance—a fact that speaks eloquently of its instant popularity. The poem appealed especially to a younger generation of readers and writers. They saw in it an illustrious, well-established, older poet who monumentally surpassed them in expressing their own contemporaneity, who embraced and gave voice to their own reality, and who, in part at least, even adopted their mode of feeling and expression.

There have been, nonetheless, old admirers who confessed surprise, reservations, even objections as to the poem's novelty which seemed to them a disturbing deviation from what they had long cherished in Elytis—if not, in fact, a betrayal of his long-established poetic creed. Novelty often fascinates even as it shocks, but the Modern Greek intellect has generally been reluctant to change, particularly as to language, because ethnic and cultural survival have, for at least two millennia, identified language with the Greek national identity. Well-known is the example of Cavafy whose linguistic and other "unorthodoxy" tooks years of struggle to gain triumphant, epoch-making acceptance in the body of Modern Greek poetry.

So, too, the example of Elytis, though not for the same reasons. When, together with his colleagues, he brought surrealism to Greece, Elytis met much opposition, even ridicule in the 1930's. His extraordinary lyrical gifts of genuine originality, with his unswerving belief in surrealism as a liberating force, and with his sunny, youthful Greekness, enabled him to acclimate that movement to his native soil. He made surrealism a powerful means of redeeming his country's poetry from mordant post-symbolism on the one hand, and Karyotakian suicidal pessimism on the other. In his poetry, the impulsive automatism of surrealism was, however, unfailingly subjected to an art which was constantly experimental yet highly disciplined aesthetically and intellectually.

Form has been one of his supreme concerns, much modulated by the rich musical and imagistic potentials of the Greek language. He soon became one of the most influential shapers of his country's modern poetic and spiritual identity that eventually attained the highest recognition at home and abroad. In its unity, the poetry of Elytis has matured through a consecutively widening and deepening of its initial foundations, by a constant renewal in answering the same universal questions posed by the poet's cultural Aegean origin, his upbringing, temperament, experience, and no less, his time. His unceasing innovations of craftsmanship and his tireless reaching for new resources have rescued his art from the danger of monotony in its recurring affirmation of life's permanent beauty and worth. In no romantic sense, his youthful, intuitive convictions gathered strength from a cultural inheritance that ranges from the world of Homer to that of Ionian ontologists and lyricists, the Pythagoreans and Orphics, and further on, the Platonists, the Byzantine hymnologists, the fathers and mystics of the Byzantine Church, some of the Modern Greek writers like Mak-

riyiannis and Papadhiamandis, and above all from the Greek folk tradition and spirit as he found them still vibrant in the Aegean archipelago.

To these resources his approach has always been impulsively lyrical rather than learned. From them the magnet of his temperament has selectively attracted and assimilated the elements which affirm the sunlit view of life in its material and spiritual, physical and metaphysical essence, elements which co-exist and are co-essential, inseparable and mutually enriching. There, evil joins good, sorrow joins joy, darkness joins light in a harmony beyond any dualistic conflict, in a totality of vision where the divinities of his mythology are predominantly the still nameless, primeval *daimons,* the powers that move the elements.

His progress has been from an apparently careless, erotic innocence, in a sunny world under the pure skies of childhood and youth, to the complexities of a world darkened by the clouds of experience. A first awakening to the beauty of nature and love passed to an increasing awareness of suffering that caused the need to recognize its inevitability and transcendence. Simplistically, Elytis has been called the optimist because he has insisted on maintaining that youthful erotic innocence as capable, if spiritually enriched, of becoming the means to combat the alienating existential negativism of the postwar West. He has remained "the same" in keeping his faith in man's capacity to discover the means to transcend life. This transcendence is the supreme function of poetry. His "first period," as he has called it, of *Orientations* in 1939, and of *Sun the First* in 1943, won him the title of "The Poet of the Aegean." It projected the world of his own birthplace and of Greek culture as a realm of eternal youth and beauty, of clarity, sanity and vigor. The Sovereign Sun, its creator, with vivifying, revelatory and purifying power reigns supreme over that world, initiating the boys and girls who inhabit that realm to Eros whose universality, creativity and sacredness unite them, through *analogies,* with the elements that surround them. In that first period, "nature and metamorphosis predominate (stimulated by surrealism, which has always believed in the metamorphosis of things)," as Elytis stated in [an] . . . interview with Ivar Ivask.

The war experience in 1941—Elytis was active at the Albanian front—the Nazi Occupation of his country and the subsequent Civil War, all brought him "a greater historic and moral awareness, yet without loss of vision of the world that marks [his] first period." The young hero who perished in the war, in the *Heroic and Elegiac Song for the Lost Second Lieutenant in the Albanian Campaign* of 1945, embodies all youth that perishes in every war; yet, the poet does not let him perish. The Aegean spirit, that of the hero's origin, and his youth itself, the youth of all times, achieves the transcendental miracle, making the hero the victor over his own death. If the individual body dies, universal youth lives on. It is destined only to learn repeatedly of life's darker side and to overcome it through the glory of light.

The major masterpiece of Elytis' second period, deemed by many as his *magnum opus—The Axion Esti*—of 1959, with its epicolyrical grandeur may be said to have its initial conception in the *Heroic and Elegiac Song.* The central meaning is much the same, but its majestic expansion required the study, contemplation and hard work of fourteen years of seeming silence that separate the two poems. Much like the major poets of Modern Greece who have preceded him, Elytis felt the need to discover and define that which lends the Greek identity its cultural uniqueness. He, therefore, studied the sources of that identity, the wealth of its cultural past, so as to raise his lyrical concept to its epic dimensions.

Much has been written about **The Axion Esti,** its nature, pattern, language, its wide variety of sources and of art; all the qualities which won the special praise of the Swedish Academy need not be repeated here. In short, in the three parts of Elytis' Aegean equivalent of the Byzantine mass, the Aegean (in fact, the Greek world as "genetically" and historically shaped by physical, psychological and spiritual elements and by intellectual and moral values) endures the war decade, as one of several experiential tests, a "Passion" of suffering brought upon it by external and internal evil. That Aegean gains from that experience the stern wisdom which helps it re-emerge "gloriously" to the promise of restitution of an earthly yet spiritual paradise where vices are transformed into virtues, and darkness into light.

These two poems seem to have set the pattern which is typical of most of Elytis' later poetry—what he has called *"a kind of meteorism . . . a tendency to mount up into the sky [or heaven], to rise toward the heights . . . a search for paradise . . . that happens all the time in my poetry."* Has the term *meteorism* been drawn from *Phaedrus,* 264D, where Plato—with whom Elytis feels much spiritual affinity—equips the soul with wings for its celestial ascent? . . . In the avowed yet modified Platonism of Elytis, the words, as carriers of a deeper perception into the essence of things, function as the wings for a *meteoric* rise, yet not quite to the realm of the gods. The rise is to a paradise that is *"another world incorporated into our own, yet it is our fault that we are unable to grasp it."* His fullest poetic rendering of that paradise is **"The Gloria,"** of **The Axion Esti.** . . . (pp. 23-7)

Criticism of Elytis' early verse has stressed the beauty of its lyrical imagery as springing from an erotically inspired *insouciance.* Criticism of his middle period, besides admiring the exquisite craftsmanship of astonishing variety, has noted mostly his way of recording historical experience as that is quintessentially summarized in five of the six so-called "Readings" in **"The Passion"** of **The Axion Esti.** Less significance has generally been attributed to the fact that the historical experience and its painful awareness were to serve the poet as a condition and stimulus for an existential deepening of the meaning of life and the human condition, their physical and spiritual, their *moral* order, and their teleological justification. On such a philosophical substratum, that poem and its major aspirations are essentially based. In that fundamental philosophical and *thymosophical* substratum, the long adventure of the Greek mind and soul has been selectively stored; there, they have been emotionally integrated and renewed so as to face the alienating challenge of our time.

Elytis always stresses the balance that must exist between man and the world. No dualism exists between them or between matter and spirit. They are held together by universal links. Such was, too, the prevalent belief among the Pre-Socratics. The enlightened mind cherishes their co-existence. . . . Also in the poem is the Pythagorean belief that "the Unlimited exists in perceptible things," and that "the soul is a sort of harmony, of attainment, a synthesis and blending of opposites" [Aristotle, *De Anima*]. Much of Elytis' physical, moral, and aesthetic world-view, as found in his verse and explained in his prose, basically echoes Heraklitos: . . . "all is one—opposition brings concord, out of discord comes the purest harmony—nature likes to hide—the hidden harmony is better than the

obvious one.'' These are central concepts inspiring much of life's affirmation. If Dante found in the mediaeval world a comparatively ready spiritual cosmology and a set of values with which to construct with mathematical accuracy his *Commedia,* Elytis needed boldness, at a time of much disparity and alienation, to combine elements that range from his favorite Pythagorean numbers to the ritualistic order of the Byzantine mass. From much of the latter's symbolism and lyrical wealth Elytis constructed his own "comedy." (pp. 27-9)

For Elytis, among modern Green writers, kindred minds are the novelist Stratis Myrivilis (1892-1969) and the poet Angelos Sikelianos (1884-1951). With Myrivilis, Elytis shares the Mytilenean-Aegean origins, the beauty and richness of vocabulary and imagery, and the sensuous warmth of feelings about life. Myrivilis' novel *The Mermaid Madonna* gives a fascinating, imaginative, legendary precedent of the pagan-Christian folk mixture that Elytis has adopted. The poet's visionary and temperamental affinities with the Lefkadian Sikelianos go far deeper; not withstanding the differences between their origins, times and experiences, Elytis is in many ways the descendant of Sikelianos in the composite traditional line. . . .

Very similar have been the elements in Greek culture which the two poets chose to draw from imaginatively, to renew and absorb, so as to provide Modern Greek cultural identity with its most powerful, most sane, most invigorating resources during times of crisis. However divergent their respective ways, both poets turned to the folk tradition because it has retained the pre-classical, mythic, ontological, visionary, pre-rational world, including its remote Oriental precedents. Both poets deemed that tradition as the most genuine in its universal, spiritually-inspired earthliness wherein man, inseparate from the physical, still shares in the divine as part of the World-Soul. Supreme in both poets is the wonder about life in its entirety, and both recognize the sensual as a necessary part of the spiritual. (p. 30)

Not to be overlooked are the striking contrasts between the two poets. In its Dionysiac yet thoughtful impulsiveness, where Delphic Apollo himself is a manifestation of Dionysus, the verse of Sikelianos, often obscure in its theoretical, complex, almost dogmatic implications, starts from a concept expressed in image. The post-surrealistic verse of Elytis, however, stems instead from the conglomerate imagery itself which, as it haphazardly discovers, reveals a concept to become its visual manifestation. The complex and learned mythical references of Sikelianos are concrete and expanded to a considerable degree; the myth of Elytis is personal and anonymous in its references—his gods are still the elemental *daimons*—suggested or implied in furtive glimpses. Only in the later verse of Elytis are his references somewhat concrete but still furtive.

Implicitly, yet insistently identifying man with nature in terms of his so-called "analogies," in a mutually shared and revealing communion between man and the Universal Soul of which man is a part, Elytis—like Sikelianos—expects man, the poet, to be the perceiver, the Orphic Phanes, the *knower,* the revealer. (p. 31)

Remarkably, but not surprisingly, Elytis' understanding of that *knower,* the imaginative revealer, seems to have a precedent in the *Katha Upanishad.* . . . There, that *knower* is defined as the mouth of death itself, as being "smaller than small, greater than great, this Self hidden in the heart of Man," actually the Soul which is "consciousness in the life powers, the light within the heart . . . the Spirit of Man dwelling in two places, both this world and the other world. The borderland between them is the third, the land of dreams.''

This definition is amazingly close to Elytis' view of man's position in the universe as the sharer of two co-existing worlds—the physical and the spiritual. Elytis also stresses the need to be aware of them, to discover them, and the transcendental function of poetry to impart an understanding of paradise as a ''borderland'' between these two worlds, a ''land of dreams'' (*vide* ''surrealism'') a land that unites opposites in a *tertium quid*, a *''third state''* as Elytis has called it. This is the state of poetry. (pp. 31-2)

Elytis here is possibly not far from Plato's idea-forms, further implying the soul's immortality and its pre-existence as recollected in that ''third state.'' In his later poetry, Elytis more fully reveals his Platonic affinities; his worship of the body and the senses certainly indicates, though not precisely, a thorough commitment to Plato's idealism. The *''third state''* is eventually embodied in the *''third heights''* which are already implicit in **''The Gloria''** of *The Axion Esti* and are specifically mentioned in *The Light Tree and The Fourteenth Beauty* and again in *Maria Nefeli.*

Their earthliness seems to gain a celestial, ''metaphysical'' dimension, much as a state of mind, a paradisical state where ''opposites cease to exist,'' a state which, ''like nature itself,'' is ''neither good nor bad, beautiful or ugly; it simply is.'' (p. 33)

In the beginning the light—these first words of *The Axion Esti* declare the genetic primacy of the light, the Greek light, of the sun which has ''its axis'' in the poet. It is the sunlight that grants the Greek world and the poet's perception, through . . . a very special *limpidity,* physical and spiritual. The Sovereign Sun of the poet's early verse acquires, during his middle period, the symbolic value it holds in Plato, that of the supreme good, enabling the viewer to perceive sempiternal truth. Yet, for Elytis, in the earthly world, the oneness is beyond the apparent dualities. It enlivens recollection . . . and stirs the imagination which—as referred to by Demokritos, Plato, Blake and Shelley, among others—is, as Elytis writes, *''nothing else but that function which knows how to render value, how to utilize memory, and how to turn to the future''* [*Open Book*].

The poet's *''third period,''* as he has named it, began in 1960, when he was in France among the foremost modernist poets and artists, particularly those with surrealist connections, and he thought of writing an article entitled, ''Towards a Lyricism of Architectural Invention and Solar Metaphysics.'' That article was never written. Yet, several statements in *Open Book* speak of the ''Solar Metaphysics'' as he understands them, certainly not a new version of Solarism as understood in ancient mythologies. In Modern Greek literature, the essayist Pericles Yiannopoulos (1869-1910) and the poet George Seferis have paid special tribute to the Greek sunlight as formative of the Greek world, soul and intellect. As already noted, Elytis attributed symbolic value to it for its ''limpidity'' wherein *''physical forces co-exist inseparably with moral and ethical values.''*

In his volume of poems *The Light Tree and The Fourteenth Beauty* of 1971, the most representative of the poet's third period, solar metaphysics has its most seminal expression. (pp. 33-4)

The Light Tree may not generally have received the attention it deserves for its individual worth and for its central place in the poetics of Elytis. Those poems, among his most personal and contemplative, also have the widest universal implications. Their concreteness contains much spiritual abstraction. . . .

Andreas Karandonis has called these poems ''a wave-like, unfolding chapter of a 'Poetic Bible''' through whose images ''we instantly communicate with the whole, a . . . paradisiac world created by the light as 'projected by the Tree,' a light melancholic or even secretly despairing.'' There is much truth in this statement. In *The Light Tree,* the mature poet nostalgically recollects his past, real and imaginary experiences, in an effort to recapture their essence, their symbolic and archetypal meaning, to evaluate them, to wonder and finally to affirm once again their precious creative value, their revelation and their wisdom as a means of interpreting and facing life. Of a life's experience, he imparts the almost quintessential residue and the lesson. (p. 35)

In its low-toned, meditative, even existential questioning, its often cryptic imagery, its deep evaluation of experience, *The Light Tree* was preceded by *The Six and One Remorses for the Sky* [or *Heaven*] of 1961. Significantly, that work was composed about the same time as *The Axion Esti* and shares some of the epico-lyrical, lucid yet often grandiose texture of that major work. *Remorses for the Sky* had already opened the way toward awareness of the poet's Solar as well as his Lunar Metaphysics. In retrospect, as he has stated, he grew aware of chance occasions in his life that were to prove decisive: his Ionian-Aeolian origin and the fact that he was the first to express it by setting into motion ''a magic mechanism as it continued to exist for him among the people of the Greek Islands.'' Another fact was that he was innately inclined *''not to express in poetry his conflict with the external world, but to shape spiritual models of an ideal life by means of the Greek language which, according to its nature, would not grin expressionistically.''*

These extended notes on the development of Elytis' mind and art are a necessary prologue to an understanding of *Maria Nefeli* as a new step in the changeful ''sameness'' of Elytis. It is rooted in the elements out of which his poetry grew, and *Maria Nefeli* is its most recent fruit. (pp. 36-7)

The dramatic structure of *Maria Nefeli* has no significant precedent in the work of Elytis. Almost exclusively a first-person lyrical poet, Elytis grants in *Maria Nefeli,* for the first time, to another voice a share equal to his own. In its first two editions the poem was subtitled ''A Scenic Poem,'' as if meant for the stage, but that subtitle was subsequently dropped. What, however, seems to be a dialogue, is in fact a series of parallel monologues of mutual awareness; the two speakers speak more *of* than *to* each other in a process of mutual understanding. Between them is an initial conflict of times and generations, of respective experiences and mentalities, which cause apparent discord. Maria Nefeli perceives an unbridgeable distance between herself and the Antiphonist; he gradually discerns deeper affinities that make them two sides of the same human coin.

Elytis has called the girl Maria Nefeli his *''other-self''*—obviously implying an inner dialectical conflict which searches for resolution through the exchange of monologues. As he informs us, Maria Nefeli was a ''real girl'' he knew, who had a distinct personality and a world of her own. He, the poet of eternal youth, has now grown old, while she is young; he is the bearer of a tradition, while she, non-traditional, lives the death of that tradition.

She is comparatively deprived of solacing beliefs, for she is the embodiment as well as the victim of change. She is the changing, fumbling, alienating present, and as such she is the challenge to him, expecting his rejuvenation. He strives to accomplish this, not through betrayal of his beliefs and principles but through their enlargement. Her challenge, which is of time and reality, clashing with his frame of mind, lends this sequence most of its power and originality.... As their arguments gradually unfold, the solacing discovery comes that *"we are just the same.... My conclusion in this poem is that we search basically for the same things but along different routes.... In her I am showing the other side of myself."*

Despite this identification, Maria Nefeli's pulsing individuality is not lessened, nor are her femininity, activism and eloquent voice—all that distinguish her from the impersonal and voiceless "girls" who recur in Elytis' verse. If they have been the beloved and beautiful creatures, the silent, inspiring muses who embody the natural elements and virtues, his *animas,* but objects rather than subjects, spiritualized in their very earthliness and sensual attraction, she is a real, powerful, vocal figure. Eros, however, is again the magnetic, procreative and transcendental force that unites her with the Antiphonist and with the symbolic femininity in his world. (pp. 37-8)

But what is Maria Nefeli's individual identity? She is a young, modern girl, the product and victim, as already stated, of our jet-set, consumer-oriented world. She has a rootless intellectualism; she is sophisticated but not learned; self-analytical and sceptical, embittered and rebellious. She is unemployed, dependent, and apparently has no purpose in life. She is, according to Karandonis, almost a corpse, a maenad, and a Sphinx. Her memory does not contain more than her post-war disheartening experiences, and she expects nothing from the future. For her there seems to be nothing but the emptiness of the present. Yet, all this is only one aspect of her; there is another, deeper dimension beyond temporaneity, which the Antiphonist strives to discover, to reveal and to liberate.

Elytis has spoken of multiple mythical significance in her double name, but various mythical interpretation of commentators are hardly convincing or enlightening. *Nefeli* means, literally "cloud" and there have been several meaningful "clouds" in the poetry of Elytis, intruding mostly as carriers of loneliness, sorrow, worry and darkness. (p. 39)

Yet, in life's Heraklitean opposites, as embraced by Elytis, there is also the other, brighter aspect of the girl as indicated by her first name—*Maria*—the most common feminine name in Greece, that of the Virgin Mary. It implies the girl's purer, angelic self as the victimized, fallen angel who, however, retains the powers of redemption and ascension expressed in the prophetic tone of **"The Eternal Wager,"** the poem which closes the sequence. In the process, the reality she initially reflects, the temporal becomes supernal. From being filled with *hybris* she becomes a *star* where the worldly reveals its otherworldliness—a characteristic transformation in the poetry of Elytis. Worldly contradiction transcends into the Pythagorean harmony of another world. Like a celestial magnet, she conquers gravity and thus gathers upon herself the qualities of the poet's highest vision. (pp. 39-40)

The Antiphonist is the mature poet himself with his long-established beliefs and accumulated wisdom, facing a new challenge in the young girl. He meets her world and her arguments with his own, and discerns the deepest bond between them, revealing her as another, the newest embodiment of life's abiding permanence among apparent changes. (p. 40)

In *Maria Nefeli,* [Elytis's] wider vision of life's physical-spiritual reality in its universal aspects gradually turns the apparent initial contradictions between the two characters into mutually complementary elements forming the axis round which their harmonious polarity revolves. Clearly, Maria Nefeli is more than herself; she is Nature, Life—both Matter and Spirit. (p. 41)

Elytis characteristically ends visions in wishful prophecy. This has expressed his *meteorism* which has earned him the title of optimist. In his maturity, he has certainly not been unaware of the contemporary crisis, of the gathered darkness that obstructs foresight of what is to come. Elytis has not been untouched by despair; it is perceptible in the lower tones of his verse. Even indignation has often been the point from which he rises toward brighter visions, at times in terms of self-defense. The challenge has caused him to enrich and broaden his initial intuitive commitment, his *sameness,* by embracing the strength he has found in his heritage. What he has found agrees with his belief in the spiritual Oneness of life beyond its seeming changeful multiplicity, in the inseparability of matter and spirit as sharing equally in the sacredness of the universe. His poetic development has been marked by the gradual rising of the initial leaven. (pp. 56-7)

Andonis Decavalles, "Maria Nefeli and the Changeful Sameness of Elytis: Variations on a Theme, an Essay," in The Charioteer, *Nos. 24 & 25, 1982-83, pp. 23-57.*

NINA ANGHELIDIS-SPINEDI

During a particularly active period in the life of the Greek poet Odysseus Elytis, the second half of 1984, a new book of his poetry was published. *Calendar of an Invisible April* is a poetic calendar that deals, day by day, with the poet's life during the month of April and part of May, presumably in 1981. A brief poem or two—never more than three and in nine cases, none—is dedicated to each day of that period. There are, in all, forty-nine poems, plus a beginning and a conclusion.

April in Greece is especially rich in meanings and events. It not only is the time of spring and Easter, both of which are represented in the present book, but also harbors other mythical allusions precious to the Greek spirit.... He obviously also incorporated into the book characters and situations that arise from his personal "mythology" (film titles, quotes from unidentified texts, unknown names, et cetera), which the active reader must guess or discover, if possible, according to his curiosity.... As happens with every hermetic work such as this "calendar," various readings and different levels of analysis are permitted. There is, however, one thing that the reader must constantly bear in mind here: although the individual poems are all self-sufficient—a sort of soul's progress—they form a unity in their totality. If the reader loses sight of this fact, he will be unable to understand what Elytis seeks to express.

The poem (now one can speak about a single poem) leads us to a meditation on death apropos of life. Elytis develops an autobiographical chronicle in which the relationship between space and time has been altered and which transcends his personal contingencies and everyday events. Throughout the book we observe Elytis's passage through this world without the guidance of Virgil. The author, not unlike such poets as Dante, Lautréamont, Hölderlin, and finally Eliot ("April is the cruelest month"), has fashioned his own metaphysical adventure, thereby providing a personal and simultaneously poetic reply to fundamental questions that men of all times have formulated. Anyone familiar with the Nobel Prize winner's oeuvre knows that this is not the first instance in which the poet has treated the subject of death. Bearing in mind too that he submits his themes to considerable elaboration, it is possible to trace, in his previous writings, the nucleus from which he develops the present work. In *Anihtá hártia* (*Open book*; 1974) he states:

> The first truth is Death. We have to find out which is the last. . . . That is why I am writing. Because poetry begins there, where the last word does not belong to Death. It is the conclusion of one life and the beginning of another, which is the same as the first, but deeper, and reaches the most distant place that can reveal the soul—there where the Sun and Hades touch each other.

This passage implicitly contains the calendar's scheme: the poet himself proposes to explore those depths, together with the reader; he will not occupy himself with the person who is inscribed in the civil registers; he is concerned with "the other one whom I do not know; but I am my own self, entire, not the half of me that walks in the streets." Therefore he endeavors to strip from death all those meanings that have been attributed to it at different times, to refine it to the maximum degree of purity in order to see through it the truth of a world that otherwise would remain veiled. . . . (pp. 54-5)

The external world in *Calendar* distantly reflects the inner world of the author by providing contrast and giving it material support. Every day seems like a station of a personal calvary— "Now, go ahead! my right hand, / when it causes you pain, paint it devilishly," Elytis exclaims in the introduction— smoothed and illuminated by the worthy beauty of his poetry. He gives lucid testimony of the progressive laceration to which his flesh has been subjected, and he does not dream of becoming eternal (22 April, Ash Wednesday) or seizing the unseizeable (25 April, Easter Saturday). He feels that it is real, actual death, still young, that has begun to work (24 April, Good Friday).

In every life there is a Holy Week during which the revelation of the sacred brings us face to face with our own death and at the same time points us toward the special moment of resurrection by means of the spirit. This peculiar epiphany can fade away within the caverns of fear, obscurity, and emptiness, or can be assumed by the protagonist. Elytis prefers the latter course: his destiny is to die, and he descends to occupy his place in the grave (26 April, Easter Sunday) in order to be

reborn afterward, under other aspects, naked before the mirror (29 April, Wednesday). Now he knows that Hades is but a carnival dance (1 May). He has overcome historical time, and a voice (Dante's perhaps) advises him that already "he is not of the earth" (3 May, Sunday). Chronological time abandons him, and the poet enters into mythical time. His contemporaries cannot understand him any more; his writing has turned legendary (7 May, Thursday). The words of the final couplet— "Everything gets lost. To everyone arrives his hour. / Everything endures. I am leaving. Now you will see yourselves"— constitute a stimulating, provocative act, not lacking in ironic tenderness, from someone who has already passed this world's test.

This latest work by Elytis has, in a certain sense, bewildered many Greek critics, not so much because of its hermetism but for its tone, which they have not hesitated to qualify as elegiac. They think they have discovered signs of pessimism in a poet generally considered "optimistic," an analysis that has not pleased Elytis. He believes that both characterizations are wrong, a result of associating his poetry's youth and luminosity too readily with joyfulness and an absence of problems. The reader who finds in *Calendar* a mournful or pessimistic tone has probably not understood Elytis's vision, which is in fact free of the very prejudices he tries to expel. It is also true, however, that the light of the Aegean Sea does not shine in this book as elsewhere in his work and that the poems are painted with an uncharacteristic melancholy. At moments we feel we are witnessing a farewell. However, a careful reading devoid of preconceptions allows us to conclude that the work is not a valediction (Elytis's long-range projects and current activity confirm this), but, perhaps, a true exorcism. The calendar's series of numbered poems offer a poetic intensity created by language that has been distilled to a level of exigency and sensibility we have come to expect of Elytis, who charms the reader as well with stylistic innovations. . . . In this way, the poet tries to overcome the unavoidable gap that exists between the historical time during which the visible April elapses, and the mythic time in which he situates the invisible. In order to make such an asynchronism compatible, he has engaged his fullest efforts as a writer without diminishing the beauty of his poems, which are comparable only to the most successful of his previous works. (pp. 55-6)

Nina Anghelidis-Spinedi, "Odysseus Elytis's 'Calendar of an Invisible April'," in World Literature Today, *Vol. 60, No. 1, Winter, 1986, pp. 54-6.*

Witold Gombrowicz

1904-1969

Polish novelist, dramatist, memoirist, autobiographer, short story writer, and essayist.

Gombrowicz's fiction and drama, particularly his acclaimed novel *Ferdydurke,* have earned him a reputation as an irreverent satirist and early proponent of existentialism. A central concern in his work is the interdependence of human beings, or what he termed the "interhuman church." According to Maria Baraniecki, this philosophy reflects Gombrowicz's belief that "[man] is . . . without independent essence, and his only identity is a combination of reactions, determined by the actions of those around him and their collective situation." Gombrowicz's interest in the "interhuman church" led him to the second major focus of his writings: the conflict between humanity's desire to attain maturity and its concomitant attraction to youthful immaturity. While Gombrowicz considered maturity inauthentic because it implies individual subjugation to the demands and expectations of others, he recognized immaturity as a characteristic of social independence. He observed: "I think I have shown by my own example that awareness of a 'lack'—lack of form, lack of evolution, immaturity—not only does not weaken, but may even give more strength." Although some critics consider his narratives abstruse and fault his fiction for its preoccupation with personal philosophies, Gombrowicz is widely heralded as one of the most influential and respected Polish authors of the twentieth century.

Gombrowicz's first novel, *Ferdydurke* (1937), is his most trenchant examination of the paradoxical qualities of youth and maturity. Containing fantastical and darkly comic situations yet written in a lucid, descriptive prose, this work explores the psyche of a thirty-year-old man who finds himself in a grammar school where he is viewed as a boy of fifteen. Although unable to accept his sudden regression, the protagonist is equally disillusioned by the adult world in which individuals perform artificial, socially required roles. At the novel's conclusion, according to Robert Boyers, "all he knows . . . is that he must cease to live for others, that he cannot forever continue to be a projection of the needs of others." *Ferdydurke* has been variously interpreted as a political allegory, a surrealist study of modern civilization, an existentialist novel, and a complex parody of several concerns of classic Polish literature. Although banned in Poland shortly after its initial publication, *Ferdydurke* met with renewed acclaim upon being reprinted in 1957 and is now considered Gombrowicz's masterpiece.

Trans-Atlantyk (1953) is a satirical account of Gombrowicz's first years in Argentina, the country to which he emigrated at the outbreak of World War II. Written in archaic Polish dialects, this novel examines life from the perspective of a Polish emigré to critique what Gombrowicz perceived as the prevailing attitudes and values of his homeland. Largely due to its colloquial narrative style and frequent allusions to Polish culture and literature, *Trans-Atlantyk* has not been translated into English. Gombrowicz's next novel, *Pornografia* (1960), again involves the interrelationship of human beings and the tensions between maturity and immaturity. In this book, two middle-aged intellectuals, one of whom is named Witold Gombrowicz, attempt to vicariously satisfy their passion for youth

© *Jerry Bauer*

by intruding into the affairs of two adolescents. According to Ewa M. Thompson, *Pornografia* emphasizes that "[youth], with its 'unfinishedness,' lack of achievement, inferiority and vague possibilities is, paradoxically, an object of desire and envy for age." Some critics consider Gombrowicz's last novel, *Kosmos* (1965; *Cosmos*), in which he expresses his belief in the arbitrariness of being, the most existential of his texts. In this work, an autobiographical protagonist travels to a rural Polish village to study for his college examinations. During his stay, he embarks on a futile struggle to organize reality by imposing form on a series of unrelated events. Although often regarded as a less successful realization of Gombrowicz's artistic intentions than *Ferdydurke, Cosmos* was awarded the International Publishers' Prize.

Gombrowicz's dramas are usually associated with the Theater of the Absurd because of their black humor, bizarre situations, nonsensical dialogue, and disjointed structure. Most of his plays explore concerns similar to those of his prose works. In *Iwona; Księżnicka Burgunda* (1957; *Ivona, Princess of Burgundia*), for example, the fiancée of a prince provokes chaos in a fairytale kingdom when her diffidence and lack of social graces prohibit her from responding in the expected manner to members of the royal court. *Ślub* (1963; *The Marriage*) dramatizes the dream of a Polish soldier in France during World War II.

In his reverie, the soldier imagines that he has returned to his hometown, where his parents are innkeepers and his fiancée is a prostitute. When a drunkard describes the soldier's father as "untouchable as a king," the inn is transformed into a kingdom and the characters into royalty. The soldier, now a prince, gradually realizes that human beings adapt to social decorum and the expectations of others. In *Operetka* (1966; *Operetta*), which parodies the conventions of opera, Gombrowicz extols the virtues of immaturity through his depiction of a young peasant woman who refuses to dress. At the play's end, the naked woman dances atop a coffin singing "O nudity, eternally youthful, hail!" George Gömöri noted: "These words sum up Gombrowicz's 'message' in a striking manner: they convey his biological optimism as well as his life-long insistence on unmasking, and on demolishing 'set' forms."

Gombrowicz also authored several volumes of memoirs in which he offers insight into his artistic and philosophical doctrines. These works were initially published as *Dziennik: 1953-1956* (1957), *Dziennik: 1957-1961* (1962), and *Dziennik: 1961-1966* (1966); a selection from the memoirs has been translated into English under the title *Diary: Vol. 1* (1988). Other works by Gombrowicz include an autobiography, *Rozmowy z Gombrowiczem* (1969; *A Kind of Testament*); two collections of short stories, *Pamiętnik z okresu dojrzewania* (1933) and *Bakakaj* (1957); and *Opętani* (1939; *Possessed*), an unfinished novel that parodies Gothic literature.

(See also *CLC*, Vols. 4, 7, 11; *Contemporary Authors*, Vols. 19-20, Vols. 25-28, rev. ed. [obituary]; and *Contemporary Authors Permanent Series*, Vol. 2.)

JOHN HEMMINGS

The narrator in *Cosmos*, called Witold for the same reason that Proust's narrator was called Marcel, observes a series of slightly off-beat phenomena which seem to point to something odd, sick or sinister in the household in which he and his companion Fuchs, an *alter ego* of his own age whom he dislikes intensely, have found temporary lodging. They come across a dead sparrow whom someone has hung with a bit of wire from the branch of a tree. A crack appearing in the ceiling of their room, in the shape of an arrow, leads them to a refuse-yard where they discover a bit of wood hanging from a length of thread tied round a brick in the crumbling wall. Clues? But leading to what? 'The world was like a moving screen that led you from one partial revelation to another.'

The world. The title Gombrowicz actually used means just this, of course, but probably more besides. 'Cosmos', say Liddell and Scott, originally meant 'order'. The Greeks applied the word to the universe 'because of its perfect arrangement'. If the world is perfectly arranged, as the optimistic ancients believed, then Witold is right in supposing that something must connect and explain a hanged sparrow and a hanged bit of wood. But if there is no such underlying arrangement, then he is, as he feels himself to be at times, 'tangled in a net of clues that led nowhere and questions to which there were no answers'. At such moments as these he experiences something of Roquentin's nausea at the sheer proliferation of unmeaningful objects crowding out the individual.... The insufferability of mere contingency is conveyed in repetitious lists of these objects, 'clumps of earth, dust, dried-up leaves, cracks',

which tease the narrator with their tedious ambiguity. Are they hieroglyphs or are they no more than things that are there? Is it cosmos or chaos?

The crisis comes when Witold, in exasperation, intervenes to insert his own blob into this hypothetical pattern of doubtful coincidences, conjunctions and configurations. He climbs a tree to spy on the young married couple, Lena and Louis, and sees the husband showing his wife a teapot, that homely, humdrum representation of the male sexual organs. After this bout of voyeurism—which reminds us that *Cosmos* dramatises, amongst much else, the smarting discomfort of immaturity—Witold catches Lena's cat, strangles it, and hangs it from a hook on the wall.

Motive? In part, of course, to 'batter his way through' to Lena: a symbolic rape. But also, to continue the series: 'three hangings were different from two, they amounted to something.' Sure enough, they amount finally, in obedience to a rhythm far deeper than cause and effect, to Louis hanging himself with his trouser-belt in the woods. And to Witold, who has discovered him there, repeating to himself: 'And now I must go and hang Lena.'

There is a passage in his still untranslated journal where Gombrowicz declares: 'My main problem, perhaps my only real problem, is myself; I am myself the only one of my heroes who really interests me.' But elsewhere in the journal we read this: 'When I write my books, I never shut my eyes to the fact that outside my little personal world there are other and different worlds.' This steady confrontation of the consciousness of self with the consciousness of 'different worlds' is something one finds in no other writer, at least not to the same degree, for Gombrowicz is a genuine original. The nearest analogy I can suggest is with Kokoschka; especially in his portrait paintings, the same irrepressible fierceness of personality spills onto the canvas, linked to the same agonised awareness of the impenetrable uniqueness of his subjects, his 'different worlds'.

John Hemmings, "A Hanged Sparrow," in The Listener, *Vol. LXXVIII, No. 2016, November 16, 1967, p. 640.*

CZESŁAW MIŁOSZ

[The essay excerpted below originally appeared in the first edition of Miłosz's History of Polish Literature *(1969).]*

A writer who was to win international renown after World War II and simultaneous acclaim from his younger colleagues in Poland, for whom he is a recognized master, even though he lived abroad since 1939, Witold Gombrowicz started out as the son of a well-to-do gentry family. To invoke one's genealogy was very unpopular in literary circles, but just because of this, he always stressed it, and such a reversal of the accepted codes of behavior has been typical of his "method." He completed his studies in law at the University of Warsaw, then studied philosophy and economics in Paris, but abandoned his budding legal career when he made his literary debut with some crazy short stories—*Memoirs from the Time of Immaturity* (*Pamiętnik okresu dojrzewania*, 1933). No less crazy were his novel *Ferdydurke* (1938) and his play *Yvonne, Princess of Burgundy* (*Iwona księżniczka Burgunda*, 1938). If we have employed the word "crazy," it is because Gombrowicz exhilarated the public with his buffoonery. In fact, he proceeded by a game of constant provocation, cornering the reader into an admission of unpalatable truths. Of a philosophical mind, but completely free from any respect for the sort of philosophy taught in universities, he had no reverence whatsoever for literature. He derided it as a snobbish ritual, and if he practiced it, he attempted to get rid of all its accepted rules.

Along with Stanislaw Ignacy Witkiewicz and Bruno Schulz, his close friend, Gombrowicz broke radically with the nineteenth-century "mirror of life" novel. His works are fables composed to communicate his thought on existence, which is too involved to be expressed in treatises; the plots he invented for his various works allude to each other in counterpoint fashion. To explain Gombrowicz, quotations from Heidegger and Sartre have been used, but there was no borrowing of ideas, only a convergence. (Sartre's books, for example, came out later.) Gombrowicz's whole work consists in a chase after authenticity, hence his fascination with adolescence. An adolescent is a set of contradictions which may be envisaged as possibilities; he can take one or another form. When he is caught by the world of adults, he assumes a form not his own but pre-existing, elaborated through mutual relationships between adults.

Ferdydurke is a story of a thirty-year-old whom a malicious schoolmaster-magician, Pimko, transforms into a schoolboy. The first part deals with the hero's adventures in high school, where the teaching is frozen into formulas repeated *ad nauseam* and where the youngsters are forced to admire such and such a great poet only "because he is great." Moreover, the youngsters, when they are by themselves, submit to a frozen convention of "boys will be boys" (dirty words, bragging, etc.). The hero, who is also the narrator, loses his battle for self-liberation, since his escape from high school "patterns" merely lands him in a Warsaw family of young intelligentsia, and this means a new serfdom: progressivism, lack of prejudices, a daring approach to sex, everything that seems to be "anti-Establishment," but, again, is frozen in forms, rules, and canons. The hero escapes a second time, with the vague hope of recovering his authenticity in the countryside, not through any union with nature but through fraternization with a fellow man who personifies primitive health, the country lad. The third part recounts a new disaster, as on the estate where the hero lives, both masters and servants repeat automatically the gestures and attitudes prescribed for masters and servants. A recurring motif in the novel is the pandemonium of a wriggling "heap" (*kupa*) of bodies as the characters throw each other to the floor in a kind of frenzy. That writhing mass is perhaps an image for the only authentic human contact. The opposition of immaturity and adulthood, authenticity and form can also be phrased as an opposition of nature and culture. For Gombrowicz, men, "those eternal actors," are shaped by each other, by their mutual seeing of each other. Man is "adapting" every instant to what is expected of him, according to his role—thus, schoolboys expect dirty words and bragging from each other. True individuality is unattainable, for man is always enmeshed in interdependences with other human beings. Gombrowicz even speaks of an "interhuman church," by which he means that we create one another; we are not self-existing. People whom we meet in a given situation infect us with their behavior, and even if we oppose that behavior, we are not free, since our very opposition is a pattern we fall into. And vice versa: if the behavior of one person, introduced into a group, differs from the group's, the discrepancy unleashes a chain of patterned reactions. Gombrowicz proves this in his play *Yvonne, Princess of Burgundy:* a crown prince walking in the park rebels against the pattern demanding that a young man run after beautiful, enticing girls. He notices Yvonne on the bench. She is

a very ugly girl who suffers from such slow blood circulation that she never utters a word, to the despair of her aunts, who chaperone her. The prince decides to marry her and brings her to the royal palace as his fiancée. There, her numb presence soon begins to act with explosive force. The dignified court, as well as the king and queen themselves, reacts to Yvonne's numbness first through patterns of irritation, then through sadistic impulses, and at last, an unboned fish is served to Yvonne in the hope that she will choke to death, which she does. The play says a great deal about Gombrowicz's method of provocation. Anything which destroys "the form" is good, but Gombrowicz has never solved his nature-culture dichotomy. By doing so he would have to concede that man can get rid of the "interhuman church." For Gombrowicz, there is always both a striving toward liberation from "the form" and a necessary submission to it, since every antiform freezes into a new form. Each book of his, however, is a renewed attempt to capture one variety of striving and to smash one more sacrosanct rule of art. In his *Diary* and in the essays built into his novels, he attacks the inauthenticity, for instance, of people who incite each other to admiration at a concert or an art exhibit, or before masterpieces of literature. Everything he published before the war voiced his scorn for phony relationships reduced to the assuming of roles. The same premeditated arrogance helped him in his subsequent exploits.

In the summer of 1939, Gombrowicz went on a cruise to Latin America and was stranded in Buenos Aires by the outbreak of the war. During the many years he lived in Argentina, he stuck to Polish, and no wonder, as linguistic playfulness is a vital part of his craft. His novel *Transatlantic* (*Trans-Atlantyk,* 1953), has an Argentinian setting but is written in a language that parodies Polish seventeenth-century memorialists. Many consider it his most accomplished work, as it brings into the open a theme underlying all his writings: how to transform one's "Polishness," which is felt as a wound, an affliction, into a source of strength. A Pole is an immature human being, an adolescent, and this saves him from settling in a "form."

For Gombrowicz himself the key to his thought is his play *The Marriage Ceremony* (*Ślub,* 1953). On its most superficial level, that of the plot per se, it presents the dream of a soldier (Henry) in World War II who, in his nightmare, returns home to confront there a debased reality—his father is a drunken innkeeper, his fiancée a whore. The idea of the play is explained by the author in his Introduction:

> Man is subject to that which is created "between" individuals, and he has no other divinity but that which springs from other people.
>
> This is exactly what is meant by that "earthly church" which appears to Henry in his dream. Here, human beings are bound together in certain forms of pain, fear, ridicule, or mystery, in unforeseen melodies and rhythms, in absurd relations and situations, and submitting to these forms, they are created by what they themselves have created. In this earthly church the human spirit worships the interhuman spirit.
>
> Henry elevates his father to the office of king so his father might bestow the sacrament of marriage upon him, after which he proclaims himself king and seeks to confer the sacrament upon himself. To this end, Henry compels his subjects to invest him with divinity: he aspires to become his own God.
>
> But all of this is accomplished by means of Form. Being united, people impose upon one another this or that manner of being, speaking, behaving. . . .

Each person deforms other persons while being at the same time deformed by them.

(pp. 432-35)

After *The Marriage Ceremony* (*Ślub*) came the novels *Pornografia* (1960) and *Cosmos* (*Kosmos,* 1965), plus volumes of *Diary* (*Dziennik,* 1953-1968). Each book developed and deepened Gombrowicz's philosophy. *Cosmos* opens up a terrifying dimension where any laws ruling human behavior as well as those ruling matter are dissolved—since they are dependent upon an observer who arbitrarily picks this and not that point of departure for a whole series of reasonings. This principle of "it might have been otherwise" applies not only to the world in Gombrowicz's novel but to his literary procedures as well. . . .

Gombrowicz's destructive talent has always been directed toward depriving the reader of his certainties and his presumed values. In *Cosmos* he cast doubt upon the very nature of the act by which we apprehend the simplest objects. (p. 436)

> *Czesław Miłosz, "Independent Poland: 1918-1939," in his* The History of Polish Literature, *1969. Reprint, second edition, by University of California Press, 1983, pp. 380-440.*

JOHN SIMON

[Gombrowicz] was that melancholy phenomenon in literature, the minor writer on to a major vision. Gombrowicz conceived of an "interhuman sphere," which he also called "Form," that represented the collective shape he saw mankind assuming. "Being united," he wrote, "people impose on one another such or such a mode of being, talking, acting. . . . Every person deforms other persons while being simultaneously deformed by them." In Gombrowicz's works, people labor to find their selfhood, but are constantly foiled by overlapping with or getting dented by others—by some fiendish collective being into which they must merge, like several water colors flowing into one another to form one ugly, off-color blob.

The idea is worthy, even important, but Gombrowicz's attack on it is often less than incisive. There is much self-indulgent doodling in both the plays and the fiction; much cleverness that fails to amuse and fine writing that fails to arouse. Thus in *Cosmos* (first published in Poland in 1965) we keep coming across such easy paradoxes as an oxymoronic hand that is "erotically nonerotic" or such characteristic conceits as "I thought hard and deeply and at the same time my mind was a blank." . . .

Cosmos is the nonstory of Witold, a summer-vacationing student from Warsaw, who finds himself in a humdrum country boarding house into which he is led by an acquaintance, Fuchs, a paranoid clerk. Both young men get entrapped in patterns: first, that of a hanged sparrow outside the Wojtys boarding house and a tiny sliver of wood hanging by a minute bit of string from the rear garden wall; then by the slightly disfigured mouth of the maid, Katasia, which keeps imposing and transposing itself on the mouth of the landlady's pretty, just-married daughter, Lena, with whom Witold falls nebulously, neurotically in love. . . .

Though the novel is, in form, the obsessive interior monologue of Witold, the author's alter ego, another character gradually emerges as dominant: Leo Wojtys, the landlord, a retired bank clerk, bored husband and father, who is revealed as a "Bergist" or "Bambergist." "Berging" or "Bamberging"—the term

may well remind us of Oscar Wilde's "Bunburying"—is to play little erotic games with oneself: with parts of one's body, foods, objects fiddled with, tirades delivered and even snatches of song. All this feeds secret thoughts, a kind of inner emigration or mental Bunburying; but it is also a form of masturbation. Indeed, *Cosmos,* a shaggy dog story, ends with Leo, unseen but heard in the dark, performing before his entourage an act of sentimental onanism, while elsewhere another of the novel's characters is unexplainedly hanging from a tree. The consequences of both acts remain untold.

And this is another difficulty with *Cosmos,* a crypto-homosexual book, in which Witold, spying through a window, is less impressed by the naked Lena than by a teapot held by her husband. The teapot, in fact, incenses Witold to the point of killing—and hanging—Lena's cat. The paradoxes, non sequiturs and obsessive preoccupation with trivia in which *Cosmos* abounds strike me as hallmarks of homosexual writing, not particularly rewarding except in the hands of absolute masters. (p. 4)

"I don't know what to say, but I shall soon find out / What I will have said," observes the protagonist of Gombrowicz's play *The Marriage*. That seems to have been the guiding principle in the composition of *Cosmos*; though for his earliest works, the novel *Ferdydurke* and the play *Ivona,* one can make out a valid claim as precursors of absurdism and the *nouveau roman,* however much Gombrowicz was to disparage the latter. Yet even if one misses in the willful weirdness of *Cosmos* Beckett's horrible jokes or Kafka's almost jocular horror, there is something haunting about a character like Leo. And in the evocation of a certain malaise of which one does not know whether it is existential or merely semantic, *Cosmos* does achieve a tenuous, cobwebby charm. (p. 38)

> *John Simon, "The Nonstory of Witold from Warsaw," in* The New York Times Book Review, *February 15, 1970, pp. 4, 38.*

BETTINA L. KNAPP

The themes that occur and reoccur in [Gombrowicz'] dramas center, for the most part, around the problem of adolescence versus maturity. The former is looked upon as a period of growth in which each individual may choose his life's course from innumerable possibilities. Maturity, on the other hand, is rejected as synonymous with a condition of stasis. Questions concerning the validity of the church as an institution also arise. Here, Gombrowicz wields his hatchet, destroying little by little the stones of man's superimposed religious edifice, but never does he harm that primal force—God. Outmoded political institutions are likewise demolished: it is the monarchy in his plays, though it could be any governmental structure which has outlived its usefulness. The importance accorded "matter" in our present society is treated: it is considered as having reached danger-level and therefore is formidable enough to crush man and drag him down into a miasma—the polluted waters of his own soul. Problems of identity, facelessness, and man's utter loneliness are frequently interwoven into the fabric of Gombrowicz' dramas, most particularly in *Yvonne* (1935) and in *Le Mariage* (1946).

Modern in all respects, Gombrowicz' theatre is antinaturalistic, antisentimental, and antipsychological. It is mystifying. His characters are not recognizable human beings, but rather one-dimensional creatures, fiberlike, enacting their phantasmagorias on stage. They are symbols, an outer expression of the author's unconscious contents. Frequently they perform like robots, assuming guignolesque stances, screeching, running, pointing fingers, unfeeling, and unable, therefore, to discover any common denominator between themselves and others. They are mercurial in their views, mocking and satirizing the world about them—like gargoyles. Their realm is macabre; their personalities discordant; their actions animal-like. They have no identity, no reality. (pp. 75-6)

Yvonne tells the story of Prince Philippe, who takes Yvonne, the ugliest, the most sullen, the most unpleasant of all beings, as his fiancée. He does so not because he is in love with her but because such an act appears challenging to him; it makes him feel his humanity. The King and Queen are, as to be expected, against such a match. Convinced he will come to his senses eventually, they do not really try to dissuade him from carrying out his intentions. As time passes, Yvonne becomes the harbinger of "strange complications" at court. Absurd suspicions, guilt, bestiality, and stupidity are generated within the hearts of the courtiers, who at the same time mock Philippe and his Yvonne. The situation worsens. The Prince and his parents now project on Yvonne their own unconscious evil traits. They cannot bear the vision. Neither can Philippe, who breaks his engagement to her and becomes affianced to a Court Lady, Isabelle. He is not aware that Yvonne has fallen in love with him, and when he does realize this, it makes little difference to him. He seeks only to rid himself quickly of an unpleasant relationship and therefore decides Yvonne must die. Philippe, his parents, and the Chamberlain decide to kill her. To commit such an act openly, they conclude, would destroy the image the masses have of them. The crime, therefore, must come "from above." They arrange a feast. Yvonne chokes on a fish bone and dies. "The royal family finds peace again."

As the play's title attests, Yvonne is the focal point of the drama. She symbolizes the negative aspects of the three main protagonists: Philippe's weaknesses, the Queen's past orgies, and the King's previous murders—the guilt to which these characters and their acts have given rise. . . . Like Lucifer, the "Light Bringer," the irritant, Yvonne, the creator of turmoil, ushers in renewed energy and with it the possibility of creativity. (pp. 76-7)

Prince Philippe is a typical adolescent who wants to strike out on his own. In his attempt to achieve independence, he rejects his parents and his entourage. Symbolically, he is seeking to dissolve the childlike subservience in which he has lived thus far, that state of "paradise" known to Adam and Eve before the Fall. Independence must be earned, and heroism of some sort is required of the initiate. Philippe has merely experienced a *desire* for freedom: no assessment of his situation has thus far been forthcoming. He acts rashly, like a petulant child, when choosing Yvonne as his mate. . . . Unaware of the strength required to battle convention, to stand the verbal assaults made upon him by the courtiers, he finally realizes that his very sanity is at stake, and whatever heroism he might have possessed suddenly vanishes. Indeed, he has now become frightened of Yvonne, who has come to represent a mirror image of certain inferior characteristics within his own psyche. . . . He is shocked, then annoyed, and finally unable to face himself (her). Rather than overcome the ordeals of youth by coping with what Yvonne represents within him as well as within society, he prefers to remain in the indecisive adolescent realm, where *choice* for future activities is still possible, where definite points of view have not been determined. Maturity, a state where an existence has been given focus, where man has *de-*

fined himself in the Sartrean sense, is seemingly tantamount to death for Philippe. The catalyzing agent Yvonne, that "Irritant," is killed at the end of the play, restoring peace to the court, crushing all turmoil, preventing thereby any type of growth process from occurring—at least for the time being. Philippe bows to public opinion and convention, and therefore never achieves a heroic or independent attitude. He will live in that *undefined* state of adolescence. (pp. 77-8)

Just as Philippe had begun feeling stifled by Yvonne's presence (a personification of his own negative characteristics), so his parents experience a similar annoyance. Indeed, they have grown to despise what she represents: "a reflection of their own imperfection." The King is overcome by feelings of sin. He has murdered and he confesses his anguish. He becomes convinced that only death—Yvonne's death—can eradicate such gnawing feelings. As for the Queen, she tries to wash the blood from her stained hands, as had Lady Macbeth. She walks about in a virtual trance at one point, reliving her past infidelities and orgies, as well as the excruciating loneliness they brought in their wake.

The protagonists of *Yvonne* do not have the moral fiber to face and confront their sordid inner world. Neither Philippe nor his parents are capable of assuming the role of murderer or of taking the responsibility for their act. If the crime is perpetrated from "above," they reason, "chance" or "God," and not they, will be its Creator—at least in the mind of their people. The royal family, therefore, will enjoy the benefits and not the blame accruing to them from Yvonne's murder. Such an escapist attitude not only stultifies the inner growth process but forces the individual to flee from himself, to live out a "blind" and *unauthentic* existence. Certainly, under such conditions (that is, the killing of disquieting forces and the inability to assume blame) peace reigns among these stolid beings, as does inactivity, and growth slumbers.

Le Mariage is a far more complex work from a philosophical as well as from a technical point of view. Though similar questions are broached (ugliness, governmental institutions, adolescence, murder), others (facelessness, unauthenticity, absolutes, heroism, the young girl) assume greater significance. (p. 80)

The play's plot is not complicated on the surface. It assumes, however, a labyrinthlike quality as it progresses. Henri, a Polish soldier during World War II, is fighting the Germans somewhere in France. He dreams of his native land and his family. Instead of *dreaming* of the charming and beautiful people he had once known and of his happy home, everything is cast in nightmarish tones. In his dream his home is transformed into a tavern; his father into a coarse tavern-keeper; his mother, into an old, bedraggled, and overly solicitous nag; and his lovely fiancée Marguerite, into a servant-girl prostitute. As the vision comes more sharply into focus, he sees his father pursued by a drunkard. To save himself, he shouts out, "untouchable," to which his pursuers answer, "Like a King." The father is then transformed in the dreamer's mind into a King, and Henri, therefore, into a Prince. Marguerite becomes the beautiful and pure girl he had always thought her to be. The marriage ceremony is going to bind them together. Preparations begin. Doubt, however, enters Henri's mind. The drunkard, now transformed into an Ambassador, insinuates that Jeannot, Henri's friend, has had a liaison with Marguerite. He then prevails upon Henri to betray his land, his father, and his church, whereupon Henri proclaims himself King and decides to perform his own marriage ceremony. After dethroning his father and his mother, he becomes dictator. His power cannot take on true meaning, he feels, unless it is sanctified by a sacrifice. Jeannot is the victim: he kills himself. Horrified by what he has asked of Jeannot, Henri cannot face his act. The marriage will not take place.

The title of the play, *Le Mariage,* is indicative of its main theme: a bond which strangulates any individual who has a lust for life. Like the state of "maturity," marriage imposes a *static* condition that precludes further choice or self-definition. In the play marriage is looked upon as a travesty, an artificial institution; religion, as a hoax; and the parent-child relationship, devoid of love and affection, as based on false values and misapprehensions. In today's society, where the collective assumes a primal role, such "old-fashioned" and withered concepts (marriage, religion, and so on) must be swept away along with the rubble of tradition.

The themes of *facelessness* and *unauthenticity,* in the Sartrean sense, also confront the viewer. The author uses his characters' inability to discover their identity or reality as a means of mystifying his audiences. The aim is to throw them off balance, forcing them to think, to probe, and perhaps to generate new points of view; also to flounder. The protagonists have fundamentally disconcerting natures; they do not know who they are, what they are, or why they act as they do. To make matters worse, they suffer from a "double deformation," as Gombrowicz has put it—forever tortured by the question of whether they create themselves or whether they are created by others, whether they are unconsciously motivated or act and speak as they do, or whether their acts are the result of a conscious desire to *become* the person others believe them to be, to turn into an image, the sum total of the characteristics imposed upon them by the outside world. (pp. 80-2)

The ambiguity implicit in the theme and concretized in the characters gives life to amoebalike personality-types on stage, the vaporous and tenuous creatures one encounters in dreams, physical at one moment, nonmaterial at others, shadowlike, living in a dimensionless world. Henri does not know who he is or what he is. Is he a soldier in France? Is he a tavern-keeper's son? A Prince? Who is his father? Any resemblance between his memories of his father and the coarse tavern-keeper he sees in his vision is certainly coincidental. The climate of irreality now turns to one of *artificiality.* Indeed, one wonders whether Henri's visions are not contrived. . . . Unable to see clearly within himself, Henri wonders whether his actions are his own or whether he is trying to identify himself with the image others have of him. He concludes: people adapt themselves to the outside world's view of them; everyone wears a mask whether aware of it or not; people are not authentic. Such unauthenticity may be due to the fact that neither subject nor object is completely independent of one another; neither plays a clearly defined role. (p. 82)

The absence of *absolutes* is another theme. Just as no stability or continuity exists in events or characters, so no absolutes exist in the world: no institution or value is permanent, either political or spiritual. Monarchical form of government symbolizes decadence in *Yvonne,* as it does in *Le Mariage.* Monarchies are proponents of class hatred, of economic inequality and injustice. Neither monarchy nor any other form of government is valid if it does not respond to man's needs. The same can be said of the church as an institution. It is a vacuous edifice superimposed upon people in order to stifle thought. Because man is fundamentally naïve, Gombrowicz implies,

any concept can be foisted upon him, whether political or religious, if the argument has sufficient emotional appeal. (p. 83)

Philippe, in the first play, sought to reject his parents and their domination by marrying the ugly Yvonne, but was unequipped to attain "maturity." He was able neither to act heroically nor to face himself at any point. Henri, sounder in personality, less fickle and floundering, accomplishes his act of rejection, installs himself on the throne, accepts or rather encourages Jeannot's sacrifice, which is designed to give official sanction to his newly acquired position of King. In the last analysis, however, he too can neither face nor assimilate his act. He is not a Roland and certainly not a Siegfried. He had not been able to take the final step, the positive action which establishes independence.

Henri differs from Philippe as a hero in still another way. Henri's first act of independence—breaking the ties with his parents—was not an act of volition, but resulted from outside circumstances: the war. Henri was forcibly torn from the environment to which he longed to return, and to which he did return, in the form of a dream. Strangely enough, however, rather than reflecting the world he had known—that state of paradise every child experiences more or less—his fantasy world became a source of anxiety and frustration. The dichotomy between the reality experienced in his memory and the realities depicted in his dream was a reflection of a division within him. He is no longer identified with the world, as he had been in childhood, when it seemed beautiful, when differentiation and discrimination had not yet been developed. He is double now: both subject and object in a vast conglomeration which is the world. The fact that he dethrones his father in his dream signifies two things: that he has cast aside a withering force . . . within society; and secondly, that he has rejected within himself an unproductive element represented by his father. The new, the energetic and positive forces within Henri's nature are now free to come into their own. The "hero" consequently is free— but to do what with his freedom?

The ritual of sacrifice becomes an important element in this drama. History tells us that sacrifices were made to kings and to gods throughout man's dominion on earth. Now Henri demands it of his friend Jeannot, for no reason; he claims: "for the sole reason that I want it this way and that such is my pleasure!" The very ambiguity of Henri's statement is an attempt to underline and to mock the rationalizations offered in explanation for other well-known sacrifices: Job's, for example, or Christ's. . . . Sacrifice, whether it be a living mystery or not, is given short shrift by the protagonists.

In *Yvonne* the sacrifice (or crime) is perpetrated "from above"; no one, therefore, assumes any responsibility for it, nor does anyone feel guilt. The characters are as oblivious to the part they have played in such a murder as they are to their role in life. Henri, however, is tortured by the sacrifice he has demanded of Jeannot—all the more since he is unable to discover the real reason for it: Was he motivated by jealousy over Marguerite or was it truly a gratuitous act? He confronts his doubt, and because of such face to face assessment of his situation, he lives, for the moment, at least, *authentically.* He sees himself as a man imprisoned by his thoughts, his past, his personality. Such an attitude, however, is not maintained any more than is any other point of view or character identity. When Henri becomes aware of the personal profit which can be gained from Jeannot's death, he speaks forth in a liturgical manner.

> Over there, some place, very far away
> Let my act be elevated to the greatest of heights!

Such a finale indicates the vast gulf which exists between the personal act and its motivations (which are never clear) and the collective interpretation of this same act. Once an action has entered the public domain, whether it be sacrificial or otherwise, it can take on the most spiritual and beautiful of meanings, or its opposite, as the case may be. The implication in *Le Mariage* is that the sacrificial act, no matter what its nature, will always be transformed by the masses into the most remarkable of events and will further deify those connected with it.

As for Marguerite, she is a complex figure, having both positive and negative female attributes. Whereas Yvonne was a composite of ugliness, Marguerite is endowed with a double aspect, comparable to the virginal and beautiful heroine, as she appears in the beginning of *Faust,* and the amoral, low-bred girl her neighbors believe her to be after her downfall. Yet she is the same person viewed under different circumstances. Henri, having passed beyond the state of undifferentiated childhood, where life seems rose-colored, is confused by the new conflict in his experience. He has not yet been able to accept life's opposing forces (good and evil, spiritual and sensual, etc.) or to integrate these into his psyche and to live creatively with them. His view of Marguerite is unstable; it is one of sliding values—as is all else in life. At first he formulates personal evaluations of her based on his experience, but he cannot hold on to them in the face of attitudes imposed upon him by the collective.

Yvonne and *Le Mariage* are reminiscent of Alfred Jarry's *Ubu Roi,* with its mordant satire, its virulent humor, its alliterations, repetitions, and crudities, its use of masks and the marionette-like quality of its characters, and its debasing and deriding of everything normally considered beautiful. Yet Gombrowicz is a strikingly original writer who has infused his poetic language with a personal brand of humanity. (pp. 84-7)

Gombrowicz has probed deeply and expressed his own reality in extraordinarily violent terms. His plays issue from feelings of bitterness, hatred, and extreme depression on the author's part. Their substance reaches down into the depths of each individual who has suffered from doubt, from the injustices inherent in man's world, and from the fear of things to come. (p. 87)

> *Bettina L. Knapp, "Witold Gombrowicz: A Faceless Theatre," in* Yale French Studies, *No. 46, 1971, pp. 75-87.*

JOHN COLEMAN

A good part of Gombrowicz's 'testament' [in *A Kind of Testament*] is devoted to the time-honoured pastime of deriding critics and explaining the genesis and intentions of his various works, but it is not the best part. For all his disclaimers, he is not averse to practising some sharp criticism of others himself: his few pages on Borges provide a characteristic mixture of insight and petulance. This irritation with the current literary scene is understandable when set in the strange context of Gombrowicz's life. Faintly rebellious son of a minor aristocratic family, he studied law, travelled, toyed with letters. A fluke found him in the Argentine when war broke out and he was to stay in Buenos Aires for the next 24 years. It may have been the making of him, this psychic and physical alienation: it was certainly the making of this book, which is superior in interest—to my mind—to those novels of his (*Ferdydurke, Pornografia*) on which I have cast a rapidly clouding eye.

The key to the man is here: "My starting point is misleadingly simple: each of us plays at being cleverer and more mature than he is." So everything is in doubt, including—as Gombrowicz is the first to admit—his own sincerity. Among series of mind-numbing paradoxes (his games with 'form' and 'Form,' his enthronement of 'immaturity,' which has its links with his avowed bisexuality), he finds room for an amazing amount of good sense about what passes for art and how we really react to it.

> *John Coleman, "Tripping Egos," in* The Observer, *February 25, 1973, p. 36.*

JONATHAN MEADES

Gombrowicz calls *A Kind of Testament* 'something like a romanticised autobiography'. He claims that he has 'embellished and dramatised [his] existence' in order to make it more readable, less tiring. It certainly doesn't resemble 'ordinary' literary autobiography—he doesn't seek to link topography to time or sense to space, he knew very few other writers (found Borges a bore, though delighted in his stories), spent years in near solitude, shunned serious personal relationships till the last five years of his life and indulged in few of the pseudo-philosophical conversations which are characteristic of the lives of the artistes. So he was left with his work, and it is this, his reflections on it, its genesis and its relationship to him, which forms the subject of this book. He at once clarifies and mystifies; at one time or another he rejects just about every psychological and explanatory system which has had any currency this century. He is equally opposed to Freud, Marx, Christianity, Darwin, structuralism, the theories of the *nouveaux romanciers,* existentialism and so on. His vituperative, mocking and sometimes rather silly attacks on these and other disciplines stem more, I think, from a hate of formalism and a scorn of 'joiners' than from disagreement with specific strictures; he considers, quite correctly, that adherence to any pre-established creed is (or should be) anathema to the artist, implying that nihilism is the only way and that it is from scepticism that art is born—however that is far too convenient a formula to find proffered here. Of course it's inevitable that many of his opinions must coincide with those of adherents to certain systems and he's always ready to acknowledge the fact whilst disclaiming any influence from those quarters. He also demonstrates, cunningly and casually, how various dicta of Freud, Marx *et al* have been embraced by a liberal establishment quite unaware of whence they sprung.

His consistent bitterness at his lack of recognition, which is hardly mitigated by a singular lack of modesty, seems at first unjustified—he was after all awarded the International Publishers' Prize and did live to see himself widely acclaimed in the West. However by a not very tortuous process I came to see that his grousing wasn't that of a whining, arrogant paranoiac—I thought at first that *A Kind of Testament* might turn out to be, like his fictions, a sort of parody, but it's not—he strikes poses, assumes attitudes in an attempt to make himself understood to an audience which is unfamiliar, to no uncertain degree, with the literary, social and ideological conventions which he mocked and which at the same time provided him with a starting point. His bitterness is really that of a man who resents the paucity of his native culture and who knows that he cannot take on another like a ready made coat or sculpted foundation garment but has to create his own. It is the bitterness of the self-made man who grew up in a slum and regrets the privations of his youth but at the same time realises that making his fortune made him.

Jonathan Meades, in a review of "A Kind of Testament," in Books and Bookmen, *Vol. 18, No. 12, September, 1973, p. 107.*

GEORGE GÖMÖRI

Authenticity is the central problem in Witold Gombrowicz's writing. He was grappling with it throughout his life and it was around this problem that his entire work crystallized. (p. 119)

He was born in 1904 on his father's estate at Maloszyce, in Southern Poland. Although he received what might be called a conventionally 'good' Catholic education in Warsaw, he soon began to flout the conventions of his class and challenge the cultural establishment of those days. In a conversation with Dominique de Roux Gombrowicz explained that in his formative years his personality was developing on three different lines. On the face of it he was a polite, sometimes sarcastic but, basically, nice young gentleman from a good family; at the same time he developed a taste for intellectual scrutiny which led to early emancipation from Catholic dogma and traditional class-prejudices. While such a development was not, in itself, unusual, in Gombrowicz's case there was still another factor—his biological urges and appetites. In the long run, it was this that proved the most decisive. Adolescence is a painful experience for most people, but it is hard to imagine in what ways a state of *permanent adolescence* would affect one's personality, what stigmas and deformations would result from a young man's inability to grow up. As far as we can see, this was the main problem bedevilling the young Gombrowicz. Later on [in *A Kind of Testament*] he confessed that much of his time as a student was spent in a hopeless quest for sexual experiences below his social status—there are unmistakeable allusions to this obsession in the short story **"The Kitchen Stairs"**—and that at the age of twenty-nine he was still living on his father's money. He managed to overcome his chronic immaturity and resulting 'inner disorder' through writing. His aim was, above all, self-therapy. The title of Gombrowicz's first collection of stories, *Memoirs of a Time of Immaturity* published in 1933, indicates two things: that the author was aware of his immaturity and that with the projection and structuralization of his 'sickness' he hoped to overcome and relegate it to the past.

In these years Gombrowicz was striving for liberation through Form, authenticity through creation. His first stories, none the less, pinpointed something different: the lack of authenticity in human behaviour. In most of these early stories people appear in masks, they act out now conventional, now strangely unconventional roles which reveal the power of Form and the baseness of the characters' secret desires. The sophisticated aristocrats in **"The Feast at Countess Fritter's"** (**"Biesiada u hrabiny Kotłubaj"**), turn out to be cannibals; well-mannered young men reveal their nature as sadistic maniacs, turning nice young girls into revolting masochists. Striking and disturbing, ironic and inventive, Gombrowicz's early stories provide no solution to his problem—in them non-authenticity or alienated human response is 'cured' with fantasies and absurd acts (such as the 'verbal rape' in **"The Memoirs of Stefan Czarniecki"**), in other words, with devices which make the solution authentic only from the narrator's rather arbitrarily chosen point of view. Neither self-degradation, nor the imaginative humiliation of others (however false or non-authentic they may be) can create authenticity. (p. 120)

[Gombrowicz's first novel, *Ferdydurke,*] is a brilliant inventory of various kinds of 'immaturities' as well as the saga of the struggle that the immature individual puts up against 'mature' forms. The novel consists of five parts, two introductory and philosophical, and three narrative. Joey, the hero, is a thirty-year-old but still floating, unsettled individual, whom Mr Pimko, the schoolmaster, visits in his home and by the sheer force of his schoolmaster's authority transforms into an adolescent. As in a bad dream, Joey is thrown back into the cockpit of fermenting immaturity, the grammar school. Schoolboys are, of course, biologically immature, but their education, a mishmash of lofty truisms and meaningless formulas, only increases and perpetuates their immaturity. In *Ferdydurke* one cannot get the better of immaturity even outside school, whether in the household of the 'progressive' Youthfuls or in the conservative country house where Joey's uncle lives. The hero-narrator is disgusted with his own greenness but cannot accept the barren and fake maturity of the grown-ups and the rules laid down by 'mature' society. This inability to come to terms either with oneself or with society is the attitudinal axis of *Ferdydurke,* while the protagonist's elaborate but futile attempts at self-liberation provide the absurd but amusing plot. . . .

In *Ferdydurke* form takes precedence over ideology, ideals are undermined by biology, and language is shown to camouflage rather than to reveal reality. Without realizing it at the time, Gombrowicz [according to Andrzej Mencwel] created here a *general structural model* of the human situation and of inter-human relations in our century. Man is not authentic, because he is dependent on others; because he is constantly influenced and shaped by the opinions, attitudes and actions of others, including the self-appointed guardians of social and cultural values. This restriction is particularly strongly felt by creative people. (p. 122)

Is it only people who shape us by their positive or negative opinions? No, it is also Form in general and forms in particular. Social, psychological and cultural patterns are imposed upon us as soon as we have made our first steps in the nursery and there is no sensible way to liberate ourselves from the domination of these forms. Artistic creation in itself is no remedy against them (the artist is also judged and classified by others); they can be overcome for a short time through an act of self-liberating violence. When forms become too constrictive, man tries to break out of them—all narrative parts of *Ferdydurke* end in such a break-out attempt, in a 'heap' of bodies, a *mêlée.* Forms can also be manipulated; art itself is a skilful manipulation of forms. The law of analogy and a longing for symmetry can be more powerful motives in human action than political or economic interests. Not only do people manipulate each other; forms also manipulate them. Gombrowicz's two post-war novels, *Pornografia* and *Cosmos,* are both stories of elaborate manipulation of people by forms impressed upon them by others.

[*Ferdydurke*] is a grotesque novel packed with striking psychological observations and interesting philosophical propositions. On the basis of his first novel and his later *Journals* we could try and define Gombrowicz's philosophy. It is fundamentally existential, a distant relation to Heidegger's and Sartre's existentialism. Gombrowicz shares with Heidegger a special concern for authenticity; also, like Heidegger, his work is directed against those cultural schemata which falsify contemporary man's life and make it inauthentic. In school 'one' behaves like a schoolboy, in visiting respectable people 'one' behaves like a visitor of respectable people, and so on. Heidegger rejects this impersonal 'one' (in German *man*) as an inauthentic mode of human existence and so does the author of *Ferdydurke,* though for rather different, less philosophical reasons. More than one critic has compared Gombrowicz with Sartre. . . . The famous Sartrean dictum 'Hell is other people' certainly finds its (perhaps less explicit) parallel in Gombrowicz's work, the two writers agreeing on the point that this 'hell' is nevertheless very necessary, for we exist as civilized human beings only by virtue of and thanks to the mediation of others. On the other hand, Gombrowicz does not hide his differences with Sartre. He finds Sartre's political engagement irrelevant and irritating; in his view the artist is a private person who should be left in peace to pursue his own goals. Also, in the *Journals* Sartre is referred to as a 'liberating force' for the French: it was he who had extracted them from their 'pompous petty-bourgeois universe'; in the following passage, however, Gombrowicz goes on confessing that he cannot agree with 'at least half of his [Sartre's] deductions in *L'être et le néant'*. He cannot stand the 'dry, cerebral, speculative and anti-artistic' side of Sartre's thought; according to him the Frenchman is sinning against life itself, he is blind to the biological *Urgrund* of existence. Not surprisingly, Sartre's rigid rationalism is just too much for a man who admires not only life, but also *youth* in all its immaturity and unpredictability.

'Youth' in Gombrowicz's vocabulary stands for a number of things, such as inferiority and potentiality, imperfection and beauty. So when he says 'Man is suspended between God and youth', he means that though the artist is striving for power and perfection (God), he is attracted by beauty and imperfection. Fascination with youth may be a constant theme in Gombrowicz's work, yet it is usually subordinated to such antinomies as 'maturity-immaturity' or 'form-formlessness'. Most of his writings have erotic undertones; though here the word 'erotic' needs further clarification. It does not mean descriptions of sensual love or licentiousness and *Pornografia,* for example, with its deliberately misleading title, must be a sore disappointment for the collector of blue literature. Gombrowicz's eroticism is amazingly diversified: it entails sado-masochism, a Hellenistic fascination with form and pure symmetry, exhibitionism, fetishism, even homosexuality. Nevertheless, it is important to stress that none of these erotic interests appear in his writing directly; they are merely suggested through symbols and allusions; they are all part of Gombrowicz's creative neurosis.

The human body has a particular significance for Gombrowicz. This is clear not only from certain, by now famous, phrases from *Ferdydurke,* as 'mug' (*gęba*), 'bum' (*pupa*), and hence 'fitted with a bum' (*upupiony*), or the congenial 'rape through the ear' (*zgwałcenie przez ucho*). In fact, in almost every novel or play of Gombrowicz a part of the body is singled out to play a central, symbolic or magic-hypnotic part. *Ferdydurke* is certainly composed on the basis of this principle—the school is the kingdom of the bum (*pupa*), the house of the super-progressive Youthfuls emanates a cult of the schoolgirl's calves (*łydka*), while the country house reflects the superiority of gentlemen's faces over peasant mugs (*twarz* VS. *gęba*). The same principle applies in later writings where different parts of the body continue to have special significance. . . . (pp. 123-24)

Gombrowicz wrote three plays in all, of which *The Marriage* is the most impressive, in spite of the success of *Princess Ivona,* a schoolboyish satire on human nature in the vein of Jarry's

Ubu Roi. The Marriage has much more intricate composition and dramatic depth than *Ivona*; it is also open to more interesting interpretations. As in the case of *Ferdydurke,* this play can also be approached from different standpoints; it is partly true that here Gombrowicz showed the destruction of traditional norms which were both the cause and the consequence of the Second World War, and that his play expressed a real historical situation. All the same, this assessment ignores a basic truth about *The Marriage,* namely, that it is 'a scenic demonstration of the power of the word'. Words have a curious autonomy; they create new reality and the dramatic action follows from and provides a running commentary to utterances. The Father proclaims his untouchability, so he will be untouchable. Henry suggests that his friend Johnny should kill himself to prove his loyalty, and because Johnny states aloud that he would (to cheer up Henry), he eventually does kill himself. The mysterious power of words is realized by Henry who intends to manipulate them to his own ends: 'Words liberate certain psychic states in us . . . they shape us . . . they create new forms of reality between us'. Words can do almost any trick except one: they cannot give back to Henry's bride, Molly, her lost innocence and create a situation in which the past is undone.

Apart from words, symmetries and analogies are also at work, artificially 'staged' situations can lead to decisive dramatic action. The Drunkard who at the end of Act II associates Molly with Johnny by establishing an artificial, symbolic link between them is aware of this—by making this link he successfully arouses Henry's jealousy for which Johnny will pay with his life. Although the play is supposed to be Henry's dream, within the drama his function is symmetrical to that of the Drunkard's: they are both priests of a new cult, celebrating a strange and dark 'humanly human' mass (that of Godless human creativity). However firmly Henry believes in the holiness of form born out of the 'interhuman' sphere, for all his absolute power he cannot be God, and the new 'religion' that he creates cannot fill the gap that had opened up with the destruction of the old. Man, alienated from his own past, is crushed by the weight of his new responsibility. (p. 125)

[The mood and the situation of *The Marriage*] have a compelling force of their own. They affect man's freedom, although he is free to act in a way which appears to him 'logical' or 'natural' in the light of his inhibitions. Gombrowicz who believes that 'to be human means to be artificial', does not mind sounding artificial, if this preserves his freedom. In fact, Henry declares his boundless desire for freedom in a muddled, wildly meandering monologue which culminates in a series of negations: 'I reject every order, every concept / I distrust every abstraction, every doctrine / I don't believe in God or in Reason! / Enough of these gods! Give me man!' The problem of this existentialist-anarchist rebel against the Old Order is not only his loneliness and rejection of yesterday's values, but also his lack of direction—he is groping toward the future through forms alien to him. *The Marriage* may be interpreted as a modern mystery play. As the author puts it: 'The ultimate tragedy [in this play] is based on the terror of man who sees that he is being formed in a way which he had not foreseen— by the discrepancy between man and form.'

If *The Marriage* is the tragedy of man trying to impose his will upon history, Gombrowicz's last play, *Operetta* could be called the tragicomedy of historical change. The genre indicated in the title was chosen by Gombrowicz because of the ultimate theatricality of the operetta, with all its singing, dancing, and masquerading; moreover, the make-believe world of frivolous and bored aristocracy symbolized the *ancien régime* exceedingly well. In *Operetta* Gombrowicz did more than travesty the idiocy of French or Austro-Hungarian operettas: in the guise of an operetta he gave a shattering critique of the 'forward march of history'. (p. 126)

Act I introduces us to the world of the *ancien régime* which hides its brittleness and inauthenticity by incessant 'dressing up'. (This mania is wittily illustrated by the wishes of the Baron who intends to seduce a girl not so much to undress her but to dress her up.) The social masquerading reaches its apogee during a masked ball given by Prince Himalaya, a glittering event reduced to chaos by the machinations of Count Hufnagel and the rebellion of the lackeys. The scene is plunged into darkness and Act III takes place in the ruins of Prince Himalaya's castle. The wind of history is blowing. The old order has been overthrown but the revolution is still going on, Hufnagel, the leader of the revolution galloping on top of his theoretician friend, the puking Professor. The notables of Acts I and II are turned into things: the Prince pretends to be a lamp, the Princess a table, and two elegant barons reappear as village idiots. . . . Finally, everyone's attention is riveted on a coffin brought on to the stage by the two baron-idiots; the body in the coffin is that of Albertine, the girl whom both barons had wanted to seduce at the beginning of the play. Suddenly Albertine wakes up and rises from the coffin in all her naked splendour. The play ends on this note, amidst general rejoicing: 'O nudity, eternally youthful, hail!'

These words sum up Gombrowicz's 'message' in a striking manner: they convey his biological optimism as well as his life-long insistence on unmasking, and on demolishing 'set' forms. Politically, Gombrowicz is not on the side of the aristocrats but he is not a supporter of the 'gallopers' either. The storm of history was perhaps inevitable; still, its results are questionable, for social revolution merely changes the parts in the same play, it fits people with new 'mugs' and new, rather dubious identities. The clothes and masks have changed but there is one thing that has remained the same—man's biological destiny, his birth, life and death, his nakedness. Albertine is obsessed by nudity and in the end, when all garments and pretences have been shed, it is she who emerges triumphant. If we regard the first act of *Operetta* as a 'thesis', and the second, culminating in the rebellion of the lackeys an 'antithesis', the conclusion of the play reveals the anti-authoritarian and apolitical 'synthesis' proposed by Gombrowicz—it is youth and nudity, the biological brotherhood of all human beings. (pp. 127-28)

Until now I have been discussing those works of Witold Gombrowicz which present his antinomies in the most characteristic and artistically most accomplished manner. *Trans-Atlantic*, written in the late forties, is missing from my survey for the simple reason that, while I agree that it belongs to the core of Gombrowicz's *œuvre*, its discussion would have raised issues beyond the scope of this essay. . . . As for *Pornografia* and *Cosmos*, two novels to follow *Trans-Atlantic*, neither of them is as exciting and provocative as *Ferdydurke*. (p. 128)

Yet *Ferdydurke*, *The Marriage* and the three volumes of the *Journals* (and to some extent *Operetta* and *Trans-Atlantic*) remain important achievements of a writer who managed to transform his 'hump', his weakness, into a source of strength; who challenged and forced not only his Polish, but many of his European, contemporaries to rethink their values and their attitudes to form. He showed modern man's quandary: he is in the pull of conflicting cultures, torn between 'superiority' and

'inferiority', striving for power and wisdom but admiring the dynamic immaturity of youth, dreading the penetrating influence of 'others' but celebrating the mass of 'the interhuman'. Gombrowicz's work has been and certainly will be interpreted from different standpoints, the truth-content of his statements can and should be scrutinized, but already at this point we can agree with him that he has been a liberating force: 'Declaring everywhere . . . that man is higher than his products I provide freedom which our cramped soul needs today very much indeed.' Those who free people from bonds cannot 'comfort hearts', and there may be some who resent Gombrowicz's attacks on authority and ruthless probing of the human soul; still, it is hard to imagine modern literature without his superb mockery, his verbal thrust and his gripping, powerful antinomies. (p. 129)

George Gömöri, "The Antinomies of Gombrowicz," in The Modern Language Review, *Vol. 73, No. 1, January, 1978, pp. 119-29.*

EWA M. THOMPSON

[*Trans-Atlantic*] in Polish is *Trans-Atlantyk,* a new usage. It brings to mind the adjective *transatlantycki,* transatlantic, yet the author wished the title to mean *Across the Atlantic:* a look at Poland from across the Atlantic. This is the most Poland-oriented of Gombrowicz's books—in the same sense in which Faulkner's novels have the South as their central hero. Paradoxically, this is also the only novel of Gombrowicz which narrates events that do not take place in Poland. Its place of action is Argentina.

Trans-Atlantic, written with a sense of humor which ranges from benevolent to gently satirical, is a delightful Rabelaisian account of Gombrowicz's first years in Argentina. It is also a serious study of the change of heart concerning his heritage which the narrator undergoes under the influence of a foreign milieu.

Trans-Atlantic has been called a novel for convenience's sake; in fact, it is written in the style of the old Polish *gawęda,* a literary genre which imitates spoken, rather than written, narrative. The narrator in *Trans-Atlantic* tells the story in a manner similar to that used by *raconteurs,* as opposed to writers. His sentences are spoken sentences, full of exclamatory words, unfinished phrases and the spelling which follows pronunciation instead of orthography. The speaker practices what Northrop Frye calls associative speaking—the slightly incoherent way of stringing sentences together in a casual conversation. This kind of narration brings forth the elements of intonation and natural turns of phrase which often disappear from written texts. The speaker in *Trans-Atlantic* is an actor as well as a narrator: his rhythms of speech and abundant colloquialisms require reading aloud. *Trans-Atlantic* is one of those prose narratives which should be performed rather than read. (pp. 79-80)

Gombrowicz's use of this archaic genre reflects his desire to turn Polish readers' attention away from largely derivative nineteenth-century literature toward the worthwhile and neglected parts of Polish cultural heritage dating back to the Renaissance and the baroque period.

The linguistic experiments of *Trans-Atlantic* have a similar purpose. They bring forth similarities between baroque Polish and contemporary peasant dialects, thus suggesting that peasants have kept alive at least a small portion of the baroque heritage whereas the educated class abandoned it altogether.

Trans-Atlantic is the most inventive work of Gombrowicz from the point of view of language. The narrator mixes archaic Polish and contemporary peasant dialects, capitalizes words in the middle of a sentence creating unusual intonations, and uses archaic and peasant phraseology to describe situations and events calling for standard Polish. The dialects of Polish have preserved many features of seventeenth-century speech, e.g., a single conjugation for the first person plural in present tense (seventeenth-century Polish has *zapalemy, wstydziemy, prowadziemy* and so do contemporary dialects). Thus in many cases Gombrowicz's archaisms sound like the speech of uneducated people and vice versa: his renditions of peasant speech bring to mind seventeenth-century literary Polish. (pp. 81-2)

Trans-Atlantic conveys the state of mind of a Pole facing both East and West. This attitude has much in common with the attitude of any minority person (national, racial, or psychological) confronted by his or her minority culture and the prevailing culture of the time. In such a situation different people behave differently, and Gombrowicz demonstrates many such behavior patterns in the book.

He starts his settling of accounts with his heritage by satirizing it. In the first part of the book, the Polish characters are shown in their most stereotyped poses and actions. The narrator describes a number of people who can be said to play the game of "we also can" and "we also have that." The Polish ambassador to Argentina tries very hard to show his hosts that Poland has produced many great men and that the courage and bravery of her citizens are remarkable. Members of the Polish community in Buenos Aires flatter one another by mouthing patriotic slogans and recollecting the past glories of the nation. They are extremely sensitive to being slighted at cocktail parties they attend; whenever feeling they do not receive proper attention, they begin to play the "we also have that" game with increased energy.

The characters continue to respect old class divisions while engaging in ego games with the outside world. The aristocratic baron looks down upon his partners in business, Ciumkała and Pyzdral (both of these are peasant names), who in turn resent the baron and purposely embarrass him by their coarse behavior. They do so individually, however, rather than through any feeling of solidarity for one another. The irony of the situation is that no one here can live without the other: the skills of the refugees are closely interconnected. Instead of recognizing this and seeking a *modus vivendi* transcending differences of background and habit, they try to put down their partners at every opportunity. A similarly absurd situation takes place in the mysterious basement where the Knights of the Order of the Spur secretly gather. Their only occupation is the thrusting of spurs into one another's legs and watching the expression of pain on the face of the victim. They imagine that by so doing they "keep the faith" and further the national cause. (pp. 83-4)

The narrator is only partially aware of all these ruses. He records the behavior of people without fully understanding it. The reader is expected to see farther and deeper than the narrator and share with the author an enjoyment of the situational ironies. The narrator, however, is observant enough to understand that there is something profoundly wrong with the attitude of the characters he describes, and that it is probably a good idea to break away from the ways and habits of his minority group. His first step is to refuse to return to Europe with the same passengers with whom he arrived. He remains in Argentina and tries to start a new life instead. His second step involves becoming responsive to suggestions and arguments of Gonzalez, who becomes a guide in the narrator's exploration of the psychology of his minority group. Why, asks Gonzalez in his conversations with the narrator, should one always honor the father before even considering the son? Why should the safe ways of fatherland be always preferred to the uncertain explorations of the sonland? What makes it inadvisable to take risks in self-development?

Gonzalez's questioning applies first of all to the citizens of eastern Europe who have been asked to do much more for their fatherlands during the last two centuries than the citizens of western Europe during the same period. It also applies to those who hesitate between personal development and loyalty to their own national, racial or minority group. In short, behind the political question lies the psychological one. As Gombrowicz states it elsewhere, is the attitude of the hobo preferable to that of the miser? The miser chooses the safe way; he piles up his treasures in a secret place and forgets about the world in contemplating them. The hobo recklessly sets out on a journey whose destination is uncertain. The Knights of the Order of the Spur are the misers who sit in the cellar contemplating values they profess. Gonzalez encourages the narrator to be a hobo and press forward at any price. The miser's fate is predictable: he will wither away with his riches. The hobo's fate is unsure: he may perish even more miserably than the miser, or he may find in his travels riches that will surpass those of the miser. Misers usually try to induce everyone to live the way they do—and so do hobos. Gonzalez suggests that a minority person has no choice but to elect one or the other of these attitudes. Either be the hobo or the miser, either the father or the son. There is no third choice.

Does the narrator follow this suggestion? The plot of *Trans-Atlantic* ends inconclusively, with an outburst of laughter in which all adversaries participate. Matters are not brought to a point where what route the narrator has chosen becomes clear. The plot also turns out to be a poor guide in this respect. The narrator sympathizes with both parties, and is only too glad to declare a truce between the warring sides. At the end, we witness a moment of tolerance instead of a "night of the long knives." This seems not to be the answer to Gonzalez's impassioned pleas, however. Indeed, a look at the structure of the book shows that author Gombrowicz has more to say on the subject than narrator Gombrowicz. (pp. 84-5)

Trans-Atlantic has parodic structure. Its verbal acrobatics and mockery of the most stereotyped Polish attitudes are but the surface of a more ambitious aim—to parody Adam Mickiewicz's *Pan Tadeusz* (1834) and Henryk Sienkiewicz's *Trilogy* (1888). The parody is accomplished by a recasting of these latter two works in baroque phraseology and mode of being.

When he began writing *Trans-Atlantic,* a conviction began to ripen in Gombrowicz that original and vital elements of Polish culture were rooted in the baroque period rather than in the romantic or post-romantic one. He began to believe that an undercurrent of Polish culture ran through baroque exuberance, detectable in a lack of inhibitions and enjoyment of life's unsophisticated pleasures. The melancholy patriotic pathos of the romantics is an element alien to it. While most Polish thinkers and artists paid this element homage, it remains, he felt, an artificial ingredient in the Polish way of being. Consequently, Gombrowicz's ambition was to bring this state of affairs out into the open and to challenge Polish cultural consciousness by doing so. He wanted to reawaken the baroque sensibility and do away with what he perceived to be romantic fallacy. In order to accomplish this, he bypassed the nineteenth century altogether, returning to the seventeenth century for his models of language and the narrator's way of looking at events. His *Trans-Atlantic* is wordy like the seventeenth- and eighteenth-century Polish narratives. It relies heavily on the device of metonymy as opposed to romantic metaphor. Its characters think and behave in a way which makes them akin to the world of [the seventeenth-century Polish author Jan Chryzostom] Pasek rather than that of Mickiewicz or Sienkiewicz. (pp. 85-6)

• • • • •

The *Journal* (*Dziennik*) is the most enjoyable of Gombrowicz's works. It is also the longest and most spread-out in time: 750-odd pages written over a period of fourteen years. Gombrowicz published it in installments in *Kultura* where many readers took it to be a nonfictional piece, the diary of a writer who spoke frankly about himself and forms of cultural life around him. . . .

Even a casual reader, however, easily discovers that the *Journal* is not to be equated with an extended entry in a biographical dictionary. Its speaker is stylized, dressed up to resemble Gombrowicz, but not identical to the writer. He is much more open than authors of journals meant for publication usually are. But still, his frankness is selective. In addition Gombrowicz occasionally reverts to techniques of fiction, recording imaginary conversations between the speaker (named Gombrowicz) and some other person . . . , describing himself in the third person, giving a fictitious account of an event in his life—the entry describing the speaker's trip to Europe after twenty-four years of involuntary exile—which contains excerpts from "Events on H.M.S. Banbury." Sometimes there are two speakers, one being a cool and ironic commentator on the actions of the other, an emotional and insecure person. (p. 101)

These examples indicate that deciding the identity of Gombrowicz's speaker is not a simple matter. He is not Gombrowicz recording spontaneous remarks about matters at hand, yet he obviously is somehow close to the writer. He does not fit into the existing categories of the literary characters, the journalistic persona, or the author addressing his readers, but most closely approximates the voice of an interviewed author who takes his interview seriously.

The speaker, then, represents a special case of the reduction of the author's personality. The reduction is undertaken to highlight a cause: the *Journal* as a whole can be likened to the old Polish *zajazd* (raid) of one nobleman on another. Gombrowicz fights for a cause, and he presents all the aspects of himself—emotional, intellectual, factual—which are relevant to this cause. The rest is never mentioned.

What cause does Gombrowicz champion? His purpose here is to demonstrate how the public and private personalities of people differ, how man is formed by the things he himself as well as others say about him. Gombrowicz believed that our perceptions of others, especially public figures, are ridiculously distorted, and set up for himself the task of demonstrating this through an example. The public figure he seeks to demystify is himself, and he performs the task with considerable lack of concern for his own psychological comfort.

The beginning of the *Journal* is a direct attempt to lay bare the pretensions of a writer. . . . (pp. 101-02)

What follows is a running commentary on cultural, social and political events interspersed with the incidents of self-praise and scheming in the speaker's life. This purposeful baring of the seamy side of the speaker's personality cannot but alert the reader to the fact that "serious" views expressed in the *Journal* may have been refracted by petty concerns of the speaker and so should be approached with scepticism. This method of building up doubt in the reader is characteristic of Gombrowicz. It goes back to the self-deprecatory humor of the Middle Ages and Renaissance, and has been evident in other works of Gombrowicz. It is particularly striking in the *Journal* because of the proximity between the writer and the *Journal*'s speaker.

Nowhere in the *Journal* can one find a passage where the speaker tries in all seriousness to present himself to best advantage. He takes great pains not to identify himself with his achievements or slip into the role of a Great Writer. . . . Gombrowicz deplores the rigidity of a modern code of behavior which forbids men of some achievement to show their weaknesses in public. He maintains that at a certain level, everyone is unfinished and immature, yet people who publicly communicate with others pretend that this level of immaturity does not exist in them. (pp. 102-03)

The *Journal* gives the reader a sense of intimacy almost impossible to achieve in print. In this sense, it is a pre-Gutenbergian work. It talks to the reader the way a teller of tales talked to his audience in the dim interiors of a medieval chamber. There are hardly any calendar dates in the *Journal,* and daily entries are separated by the notations of the days of the week. . . .

At the end of his *Journal,* writer Gombrowicz appears disarmed, his authorial imperturbability destroyed, his sophistication in doubt, his fake certainties openly exposed. The reader realizes that unlike most public figures he meets in life, this particular person is unsure of his views and tentative about his knowledge. The waverings of the personality Gombrowicz conveys in the *Journal* are one of his great literary achievements. The intensity and persistence of his search and the frankness with which he records his setbacks make the *Journal*'s speaker the most memorable of Gombrowicz's characters. (p. 104)

Ewa M. Thompson, in her Witold Gombrowicz, *Twayne Publishers, 1979, 171 p.*

BLAKE MORRISON

Witold Gombrowicz's *Possessed* is [an] overt piece of harking back. Subtitled "A Gothic Novel," it has all the stage effects of the genre: a massive, mist-surrounded castle containing untold riches; a haunted room and unsolved murder; spooky Transylvanian forests; and a cast that includes a mad prince, a decrepit housekeeper, a professor, a clairvoyant and an indeterminate number of possessed souls. . . .

There is also—and it's here that Gombrowicz begins to adapt the Gothic trappings to his own ends—a doppel doppelganger. Hired as her tennis coach, the low-born Walchak remarkably resembles the talented, bewitching Maya Okholowska—and the resemblance is something which everyone, including Maya's jealous fiancé, can't help but notice. As the pair become embroiled in intrigues first at the nearby castle and then in Warsaw, a struggle between the forces of good and evil emerges. And a question: what is it that Maya and Walchak have to do with another case of double (or even treble) identity, that of the prince, his dead bastard son Francis, and a local farmer called Handrycz? Rather as he might with a thriller, the reader is able to anticipate a good many of the twists and turns; but the ending is strange and ambiguous. . . .

Possessed does little on its own to explain why Gombrowicz should have been hailed as a master of European fiction. But his exploitation of the genre is highly skillful and the plot (though the phrase is unfortunate in view of all the strangulations that take place) thoroughly gripping.

> Blake Morrison, "High Seas of Passion," in The Observer, *April 6, 1980, p. 39.*

MICHAEL IRWIN

Possessed is a minor production—a Gothic novel published pseudonymously as a newspaper serial in the summer of 1939. Gombrowicz apparently did not acknowledge authorship until shortly before his death. The reticence is understandable: it seems possible that he wrote the work largely to make a fast zloty.

Merely as "a Gothic novel", however, *Possessed* has a lot to be said for it. The story begins with Walchak, a young tennis coach, arriving at a remote country house where he is to give tuition to Miss Maya Okholowska. Quickly a strange affinity is established between them—an affinity that seems to exacerbate the worst impulses of both. Eventually they sense a connection between this unhealthy relationship and a haunted room in the enormous castle nearby, where a crazed old prince lives in terror-stricken seclusion, oppressed by some guilty secret. And so forth. At first the narrative is deftly and imaginatively developed: the book offers fast, suspenseful reading. Gombrowicz relishes the traditional nonsense of the genre. . . . About the halfway point, however, the story-telling becomes wayward and jerky. Several of the main characters depart to Warsaw for a vaguely-defined period of time. Even an entertaining murder cannot compensate for the dissipation of the claustrophobic confinement that any Gothic tale needs if it is to achieve true rotten-ripeness.

The story recovers much of its energy in the later chapters where the action centres once more on the country house and the castle with its haunted room. In fact the narrative is moving quite powerfully towards a juicy conclusion which will make sense of all that has gone before—when it stops. It seems necessary for a reviewer to stress a point that is made neither on the cover of this volume nor in the introductory note: this is an incomplete work. The incompleteness could presumably have been an authorial jest. Alternatively it may have had something to do with the fact that the final instalment of the serial version apparently came out on August 30, 1939. In either case the publishers say nothing about the matter—an omission that may irk those members of the public who purchase what they reasonably assume to be a complete narrative. . . .

[It] is impossible to see *Possessed* as a "serious" work. One or two themes, one or two formulations—"She tried to stir her heart into feeling the emotion she was exhibiting"—are characteristic of the author's work, but only in a trivial way. Granted his preoccupations, the idea of "possession" of the usurpation of personality, is one that he might well have turned to account. Certainly he would have been unlikely to see the frivolousness of the genre as inimical to serious comment of some kind. The inference must be that *Possessed* was no more

than a light-hearted, perhaps no more than a half-hearted, technical exercise.

> Michael Irwin, "Gothic Remains," in The Times Literary Supplement, *No. 4022, April 25, 1980, p. 463.*

EWA THOMPSON

Possessed is worth reading on two counts: as a fast-paced mystery story, and as an example of the importance of contexts. Let me explain the first point: an old and haunted castle; a mad prince whose son committed suicide years ago; a local beauty in love with her tennis coach, both of them possessed by the evil spirits who also take part of the castle hostage; and, unexpectedly, a happy ending. There is enough suspense here based on an intimation of the supernatural to satisfy a casual reader's demand for entertainment.

Possessed also has something to offer a student of literature: when it first began to appear in installments in a Warsaw newspaper, it was meant to have an explicit ending where all the details of the final strange discovery would be explained by the narrator or the characters. But Gombrowicz never wrote the final installment owing to the outbreak of World War II. To a nineteenth-century reader, the book would have seemed unfinished. But the plot gets far enough for the contemporary reader to guess the ending, and this makes the novel much more interesting than it might first seem. I expect that *Possessed* will soon occasion a scholarly article on how contexts become texts, and on how impossible it is to distinguish between the two.

> Ewa Thompson, in a review of "Possessed," in World Literature Today, *Vol. 56, No. 3, Summer, 1982, p. 539.*

GARY INDIANA

Whenever Witold Gombrowicz is mentioned, we hear of his unjustified obscurity: perhaps no great writer of this century has been so obdurately and celebratedly obscure. Although much of his work was made available in English by Grove Press in the 1960s, Gombrowicz never greatly profited from America's short-lived appetite for arcane Euroculture. He was a bit *too* weird, devoted to gnarled, foggy themes. His books heavily alluded to pedophilia and queerness, but lacked recognizable pornography. No one chose to play Sartre to Gombrowicz's Genet. Only in the '60s, the last decade of his life, was he celebrated, in Europe, as a "world-class" author. His American audience remains negligible. . . .

In his novels, Gombrowicz travels under his own name as an adult narrator who craves the unformed, open-ended existence of Youth. Until 30 we become more and more alive, he believed, and after that we become more and more dead. Young people live in a different sort of time, and should have a different language from the old. Gombrowicz's novels reveal the terrible secret that maturity consists of choosing a mask to wear through the rest of one's life, while chaos worries the edges of every gesture, every glance, every word. What people instinctively want is exactly what the social order forbids them. Inside everyone lives a horribly awkward, amoral child, picking its nose and plucking the wings off flies, while the grownup exterior politely passes the salt.

These ideas festered within Gombrowicz deeply enough for the books they produced to transcend the simple Freudianism they suggest. He worked them up elaborately in his journals, articulating a private cult of *life* before *art.* . . .

Gombrowicz's distaste for the literary world had little of Lawrence's celebration of Instinct and sweaty loins about it; he was a snob by training, self-indulgent to a fault, and simply difficult to get along with. . . . [Through his journals, published serially between 1953 and 1968 in the Paris-based émigré journal *Kultura*], he involved himself in polemical brawls with Camus and Sartre and Cioran, aired his acid views on politics, and explained his own work with the obvious conviction that he was making Literature. Yet there is something deflationary of the literary enterprise, indeed of any enterprise, inherent in Gombrowicz's thought. His practice of stripping off the surface of human activity to uncover grotesque inadequacies reduces any decent intention to empty histrionics.

When he savages Neruda in his journals, or Camus's *L'Homme révolté,* the reader gets an unpleasant mouthful of the inferiority complex Gombrowicz cultivated into a world view. He is quite astonishingly vicious and, more disquieting, what he writes is true. . . . Gombrowicz's journal registers every little blip of his consciousness. It is not so much an emotional record as a philosophic one. His clinical candor about himself has the same abrasive quality as Genet's sublimely stupid confessions, with the added irritation that Gombrowicz is an intellectual. Like Genet, Gombrowicz led an unusually rangy existence, with the filter of class ripped off the lens, so to speak. He sees through everybody and carries a large grudge.

Writing of himself, he assumes an inevitable failure or insufficiency. Poland is a secondary, provincial culture; as a Polish writer, he measures himself against the suffocating perfection of "the big cultures." He wants to write like Goethe, Shakespeare, and Dostoyevski (and, though he never mentions him, like Chekhov), but "as a Pole and an artist, I was doomed to imperfection . . ." He describes Poland as "a country of weakened forms"; his early works dismantle these wobbling structures with fierce adolescent glee.

In three recently reissued novels, *Ferdydurke, Pornografia,* and *Cosmos,* Gombrowicz's narrators are creatures of overpowering passivity, living quietly desperate lives until some external agent, usually a maniac, propels them into a diseased paradigm of social order: a situation forms around the hero, like a calcinating fungus. The question becomes when, and how, a state of benign or virulent inanity will mutate or crack into something worse.

Unlike the later novels, *Ferdydurke* belongs to fantastic literature. An absurd premise is elaborated through a sequence of broad exaggerations, none of them believable. Gombrowicz's novels seldom connect very closely with the literature of verisimilitude, despite the naturalism of the later ones. The narrator in each case shows a psychotic detachment from the world of others, though he passes as an ordinary, if unusually laconic, presence, a sort of ambulatory piece of furniture.

It's an odd first-person tactic. Imagine one of Joseph Conrad's speakers abruptly intervening in his tale as a full-blown sociopath. Gombrowicz's confidence trick is to place a reasonable-sounding madman among lunatics who *sound* crazy. (p. 23)

Ferdydurke begins like a dust-coated Existential saga of uselessness-between-world-wars, with the narrator recounting his terrible dream.

> By a regression of a kind that ought to be forbidden to nature, I had seen myself at the age of fifteen or sixteen, I had reverted to adolescence . . . it had seemed to me that the adult, the thirty-year-old who I am today, was apeing and mocking the adolescent that I was then, while the adolescent was mocking the adult; and that each of my two selves was thus taking the rise out of the other.

The dream comes true, an inversion of the 19th century coming-of-age novel. A deranged second-form master, Professor Pimko, kidnaps Johnnie from his Warsaw flat and forces him to attend grammar school. Life begins running backwards. Johnnie remains 30, but no one seems to notice. The school is a Wilhelmine hangover where students are drilled in Latin and Polish classics. It teaches infantile submission to authority, received ideas, nationalism, "tradition"; these things are all represented by infantile adults. In *Ferdydurke,* childishness is an inescapable condition, the logical product of a national backwater. Poland, Gombrowicz implies, forever at the mercy of pushy neighbors, is an adult reduced to helplessness, a process replicated in each of its citizens. Since life offers no real choices, people can only repeat inanities. (pp. 23-4)

For an American reader, one of the unintended ironies in this satire of education is that however idiotically it reads, its 13-year-olds are already better educated than most American college graduates. There's a similar irony about Gombrowicz's complaints against the provincialism of Warsaw in the '30s, which was radiantly cosmopolitan compared with New York or Los Angeles. But this too had its dark side, its desperate wish to be something else—a mania for "advanced" Western cultural products like G. B. Shaw and Greta Garbo. The curse of profound insecurity hangs over everyone in *Ferdydurke*—the progressive-minded Youthful Family, prattling at breakfast about the abolition of the death penalty, the promise of modern science, and birth control; the puberty-haunted boys striking vapid poses of idealism and depravity in the schoolyard; the seedy aristocrats who regularly whip their servants and don't know how to tie their shoelaces. Gombrowicz even throws in a village of human dogs, peasants regressed to all fours.

Ferdydurke's characters are overtly monstrous, like Dostoyevski's creatures who chatter freely about their murkiest urges. Gombrowicz's people, though, are more or less oblivious obsessives, nearly automata. Only Johnnie notices the fixations of others as well as his own; this enables him to manipulate people into catastrophic self-exposure.

The stock epiphany of a Gombrowicz novel comes when an assortment of cohabiting delusions uses up all the available oxygen and starts emitting an explosive gas. People suddenly regress into puddles of infantile craving, baby talk, uncontrollable libido, murderous enthusiasm. This process is set into motion by the narrator's erotic frustrations, which warp off into eccentricities, little tamperings with the gestalt that bring out the adult baby in the others. Gombrowicz uses submerged desires as the basis of plot: his protagonists want certain unimaginable icky things to happen, and the sheer force of this want charges banal reality with a greasy kind of sexual ominousness. There is a constant struggle of surfaces against the powers of subjectivity.

In *Pornografia,* the hero's companion, a one-time theater director named Frederick, possesses a charismatic ability to inflict self-consciousness on other people. (p. 24)

The spectacularly charmless, mute heroine of *Princess Ivona* makes others intolerably conscious of their defects—so much so that they band together and murder her. In *Pornografia,* the propeller of odium is a voyeuristic wish, i.e., the desire of Gombrowicz and Frederick to effect an "ideal" sexual act between Karol and Henia, who repeatedly fail to interest each other. The adults then contrive to unite the young in an act of killing. As it happens, a Resistance leader who's lost his nerve is stranded at the house. Orders come through to assassinate him. None of the adults has the nerve to go through with it . . . but getting the kids to do it makes it sexy. . . . By joining a politically "responsible" liquidation to the fulfillment of Byzantine perversity, Gombrowicz dramatizes his notion of politics as a mask for ennobling wormy souls. Or as he puts it in *A Kind of Testament:* "In the end both the ideas of 'higher synthesis' and 'higher analysis' become mere pretexts for the pure pleasure of action. As, I assume, does Fascism or Communism."

In fact, none of Gombrowicz's characters is capable of behaving well, unless out of fear of behaving badly. Absolute rectitude is an absolute masquerade. The saintly Amelia, mother of Henia's plodding fiancé and patroness of war refugees, inexplicably attacks an adolescent intruder by sinking her teeth into his leg and stabbing him with a kitchen knife. On her deathbed, her attention strays from the crucifix to the face of the atheist Frederick, erasing a lifetime of piety at the very moment when it should have come in handy.

The irrepressible cruelty of Gombrowicz's work is one of its chief attractions. His narrators feel boredom and twisted lust, with no intermediate emotions cluttering their sensibilities. Fetishism replaces human involvement. The protagonists fixate on body parts, inanimate objects, insane connections between random phenomena. Gombrowicz's speciality (unique in the modern novel, as far as I know) is to make a universe of paranoid symbols coincide with external reality—not in the manner of Gogol's *Diary of a Madman,* or Nabokov's *Pnin,* where the blurring of inside and outside makes the difference between them obvious, but as if a layer of collective psychic topsoil had suddenly blown off.

Gombrowicz is greatly preoccupied with the friction between Form and Chaos. Humans secrete form, rather like beeswax. I behave like this because you behaved like that; the form of our relationship is collaborative, and unique to ourselves. As an extreme refinement of Sartre's line between existence and essence, Gombrowicz defines the interhuman world of form as a theater of ultimately arbitrary actions, with no intrinsic moral or philosophical underpinnings. We may believe we do things, for example, for high-minded reasons, but "high-mindedness" is simply a habitual response we've learned from other people. If we're Communists we will exploit people with one polemical excuse, if we're Fascists we'll use another, if capitalists still another. The fact of exploitation remains untouched.

In this sense, Gombrowicz's books proceed like mathematical formulae, seemingly open to chance and the unpredictable volition of their characters, but the terms set in motion at the outset can only produce one solution. These novels are wholly incredible, but written in a light, casual style that makes them seem almost plausible. *Cosmos* is the most extreme exercise in arbitrariness: the plot develops out of certain stray features

of the landscape, insignificant visual obstructions, a hanged sparrow, a block of wood, a set of bedsprings, things that knit together for no discernible reason. Witold and Fuchs arrive at a country house, they rent a room, the maid has a hideous scar on the side of her mouth. They've noticed a sparrow hanging from a tree, and now this strange mouth . . . it must mean something, and what about that crack in the ceiling, the one that looks like an arrow, pointing into the yard? What's it pointing at? A rake, resting at an odd angle against a tree. The rake seems to be pointing to the garden wall. (pp. 24-5)

The clues present themselves because Witold is bored stiff in the countryside and finds himself attracted to the family's married daughter, Lena—whose mouth somehow recalls the scarred mouth of the servant, and the wire mesh of the ashtray used at the dinner table, and a bit of cork sticking to the lip of a winebottle, and so on. We see him desperately trying to infuse meaning into the static desuetude of the house, the yard, the surrounding woods. Nothing adds up, nothing materializes. . . .

But it must mean something, so Witold strangles the family cat and hangs it from a tree in the yard. Now the clues lead directly to this vicious, mysterious killing. . . .

This is "the pure pleasure of action" gone considerably haywire; what's remarkable in this black stream of a book is its sudden change of course. Once the cat is strangled, Witold's obsessively gathered, private symbols take on palpable significance for the others. His dread and insanity become theirs, their little tics inflate into hysteria, and the sleepy world of another middle class family bites the apocalyptic dust. The cat hanging will now lead to a human hanging, with a logic everyone can see.

For Gombrowicz, chaos isn't simply the action of desire on reality, but an *a priori* condition of things. Complicity influences the shape of reality with infinitely greater force than the individual. Moreover, individual will is not straightforwardly "desirous," but devious and strange to itself, complexly mediated, displaced. The displacement of desire creates the grotesque form of the world.

Like Céline, Gombrowicz maps the foggy territory of delusion, the chasm between what people think they are and what they really are. His work is necessarily cold, sinister, and cruel, the song of a chronic malcontent determined to squeeze a good laugh from the horror of existence. Gombrowicz's novels suggest obvious 20th-century affinities—with Malaparte and Junger as well as Genet and Céline. But the writer he most resembles is Tommaso Landolfi, another Russophile fantasist devoted to a life of action rather than literature. Landolfi's obsession with roulette and Gombrowicz's relation to the experience of exile have a similarly romantic, literary tinge. Both writers display an uncontrollable modernity, a revulsion against contemporary life quite typical in modern literature. In Céline, this revulsion reaches down to the level of syntax. In Landolfi and Gombrowicz, it produces that mimicry of classical form which links their works to Goethe, Kleist, Turgenev, and Chekhov, like a bridge of ice between the centuries. (p. 25)

Gary Indiana, "Heart Like a Heel: The Classy Creepiness of Witold Gombrowicz," in VLS, No. 55, May, 1987, pp. 23-5.

Günter (Wilhelm) Grass

1927-

(Has also written under pseudonym of Artur Knoff) German novelist, essayist, poet, dramatist, nonfiction writer, editor, and scriptwriter.

Among the most significant and controversial authors to emerge in Germany after World War II, Grass established his reputation with the novels *Die Blechtrommel* (1959; *The Tin Drum*), *Katz und Maus* (1961; *Cat and Mouse*), and *Hundejahre* (1963; *Dog Years*), collectively known as *The Danzig Trilogy*. These books graphically capture the reactions of German citizens to the rise of Nazism, the horrors of war, and the guilt that has lingered in the aftermath of Adolf Hitler's regime. Influenced by Surrealism, German Expressionism, and such disparate authors as Bertolt Brecht, Herman Melville, and Alfred Döblin, Grass combines naturalistic detail with fantastical images and events. His exuberant prose style and blend of diverse stylistic techniques, through which he makes extensive use of black humor, satire, and wordplay, have prompted comparisons to the work of James Joyce, Laurence Sterne, and François Rabelais.

Grass's imagination and artistic sensibilities derive largely from his childhood experiences. Some critics have suggested that his fiction often centers on perversions of youth as a result of his own Nazi indoctrination and the advent of war during his adolescence. Several years after the Nazi takeover of Danzig, his native city, Grass became a member of the Hitler Youth. Drafted as a Luftwaffe auxiliary in World War II, he was wounded and captured during the German defense of Berlin in 1944. Following the war, Grass studied painting and sculpture at the Düsseldorf Academy of Art. He later joined "Gruppe 47," a prestigious association of German writers formed after World War II. This group published much of Grass's early poetry in the literary journal *Akzente* and awarded him the prestigious annual "Gruppe 47" prize in 1958 for his first novel, *The Tin Drum*.

The Danzig Trilogy is considered Grass's most distinguished achievement. This work depicts the effects of nazism on everyday life in Danzig through its examination of such themes as loss of innocence, individual responsibility, and national guilt arising from Germany's wartime atrocities. George Steiner reflected critical opinion when he remarked of *The Danzig Trilogy:* "It is not Grass's enormous success that matters most. . . . It is the power of that bawling voice to drown the siren-song of smooth oblivion, to make the Germans—as no writer did before—face up to their monstrous past." As the first book of *The Danzig Trilogy, The Tin Drum* earned Grass international acclaim and popularity. The protagonist of this novel is Oskar Matzerath, a precocious dwarf who had willfully stunted his physical growth at an early age to protect himself from the chaos and destruction of his era. Described by H. Wayne Schow as "an achievement of imaginative and technical brilliance," Oskar is portrayed as a wild, erratic, and adaptive personality who vividly recounts the traumas of Hitler's rule while playing a tin drum from his cell in a mental institution in the late 1950s. Rich in allusions to mythology and the New Testament, *The Tin Drum* combines fantasy with realism and

Fay Godwin's Photo Files

prose with poetry to produce what Anthony Burgess proclaimed "a big, bawdy, sprawling triumph."

Cat and Mouse, the second book of *The Danzig Trilogy,* relates the story of Joachim Mahlke, an alienated Danzig youth whose oversized adam's apple, or "mouse," leads him to seek social acceptance through athletics and, later, the Nazi military. Despite his heroic accomplishments, Joachim remains an outcast at the novel's conclusion. While some reviewers considered this work's allegorical and symbolic content obtrusive, others praised Grass's sensitive rendering of Mahlke's guilt and self-torment. In *Dog Years,* the final book of *The Danzig Trilogy,* Grass employs the disparate perspectives of three narrators to describe the forces in German society between 1917 and 1957 that led to the emergence and subsequent fall of nazism. Central to this novel is the relationship between Walter Matern and his half-Jewish friend, Eduard Amsel. Juxtaposing Matern's childhood defense of Amsel from a gang of ruffians with his vicious beating of Amsel after Matern has become a Nazi stormtrooper, *Dog Years* returns the focus of the trilogy to postwar Germany, where Matern, now vengeful and guilt-ridden, stalks the German countryside, infecting the wives and daughters of his former Nazi peers with venereal disease. While some critics considered this complex novel excessively didactic and occasionally abstruse, most praised Grass's satirical skills and poignant examination of how the German language became defiled by fascist rhetoric.

Grass's later novels have been less popular with readers than the books of *The Danzig Trilogy* and are sometimes faulted for failing to assimilate ideological digressions within their fictional narratives. Often addressed to Germany's younger generation, these works explore the futility of simplistic solutions to contemporary conflicts. In *Örtlich betäubt* (1969; *Local Anaesthetic*), Grass discourses on the Berlin student uprisings of the 1960s. The central scene of this novel depicts a confrontation between a teacher and an admired student who threatens to publicly burn his pet dachshund to protest the use of napalm in the Vietnam War. *Aus dem Tagebuch einer Schnecke* (1972; *From the Diary of a Snail*) combines fiction and autobiography with a factual analysis of snails, which Grass characterizes as apt symbols of slow but persistent democratic change. Written in the form of a diary, this book also records Grass's involvement with the Social Democratic campaign during the 1969 West German elections. *Der Butt* (1977; *The Flounder*) spans several historical periods and blends scatological humor with ideological discussions to address the divergent roles of men and women throughout civilization. This novel derives from the fairy tale "The Fisherman and His Wife," in which a magical flounder rescinds wishes granted to a fisherman after his wife insists that she be designated as God. In Grass's work, a group of feminists attempts to put the magical flounder on trial for his past conspiracies with men. Criticism of *The Flounder* ranged from charges of misogyny to praise from those who considered the text an endorsement of feminism. John Simon called the book both "the first major satirical feminist novel" and "the first major satirical anti-feminist novel. For in it Grass scrupulously makes both men and women equally ridiculous in their more fanatical isms."

Grass's next novel, *Das Treffen in Telgte* (1979; *The Meeting at Telgte*), set during the final days of the Thirty Days War, describes the fictitious gathering of twenty seventeenth-century German writers who seek to reconstruct their homeland through a purified language and literature. Their intentions closely parallel those of Grass and other members of "Gruppe 47." *Kopfgeburten; oder, Die Deutschen sterben aus* (1980; *Headbirths; or, The Germans Are Dying Out*) is a blend of travelogue and fiction inspired by Grass's travels through Asia in 1979 and by his negative reaction to West Germany's 1980 elections. In this book, Grass discourses on such topics as the reuniting of East and West Germany, the declining birth rate of the West German populace, and the emergence of neo-Nazi organizations. Grass also imagines the creation of a film in which a young couple debate whether or not to raise a child in an unstable world. John Leonard described *Headbirths* as "part fiction, part travelogue, part screenplay, and part political pamphlet . . . , a wise, sad, witty mess." The narrator of Grass's recent novel, *Die Rättin* (1986; *The Rat*), is troubled by apocalyptic dreams in which a talking rodent, known as she-rat, sardonically documents the history of political and ecological ignorance that has led to humanity's demise. While some reviewers faulted the book's exhaustive length and esoteric allusions, Eugene Kennedy deemed *The Rat* "a disturbing modern-day book of Revelations written in dream language by an artist who draws easily on the enormous resources of his unconscious to render a bleak and not-so-bleak vision of what is really at stake in the world."

In addition to fiction, Grass has written poetry, dramas, and essays. Although English-speaking critics generally consider his poetry of lesser significance than his prose works, Grass's verse is well-regarded in Europe. The tone of his poems has shifted from ebullience and playfulness in such early volumes as *Die Vorzüge der Windhühner* (1956) and *Gleisdreieck* (1960) to a more restrained examination of moral and political issues in *Ausgefragt* (1967). *Selected Poems, Gesammelte Gedichte* (1971; *Collected Poems*), and *In the Egg and Other Poems* (1977) include representative verse from various periods in Grass's career. Several of Grass's plays have been linked with the Theater of the Absurd for their startling imagery, black comedy, and bleak view of society and existence. These dramas, which employ diverse theatrical techniques to create what Martin Esslin called "poetic metaphors . . . for the stage," are considered powerful statements but have achieved only modest popular success. Grass's plays include *Hochwasser* (1957), *Noch zehn Minuten bis Buffalo* (1957), *Onkel, Onkel* (1965), and *Die Plebejer proben den Aufstand: Ein deutsches Trauerspiel* (1966; *The Plebeians Rehearse the Uprising; A German Tragedy*). Grass's essays on political topics are collected in *Über das Selbstverständliche: Politische Schriften* (1969). *On Writing and Politics, 1967-1983* (1985) features previously published articles on literature and contemporary German society. Grass has also worked as an editor with Heinrich Böll and Carola Stern on *L-80*, a German literary journal.

(See also *CLC*, Vols. 1, 2, 4, 6, 11, 15, 22, 32; *Contemporary Authors*, Vols. 13-16, rev. ed.; and *Contemporary Authors New Revision Series*, Vol. 20.)

CHRISTOPHER LEHMANN-HAUPT

[In *On Writing and Politics: 1967-1983,* Mr. Grass] seems to be divided into two parts like his country and to be waging a kind of cold war within himself.

It isn't simply that the book is divided in two, one section being "On Writing" and the other being "On Politics." The division in Mr. Grass goes deeper than that. One half of him is witty, intellectually playful, anti-ideological, an observer of history who after all his experiences "with time and its contrary course," has inscribed "a slow-moving animal in my escutcheon and said: Progress is a snail." The other half of him is shrill, ideological, polemical, an oversimplifier of history who seems to contradict his insistence that "there is no such thing as a jumping snail."

One part of Günter Grass has written thoughtful essays on Franz Kafka and Alfred Döblin, the author of such nearly forgotten books as *Wallenstein, Mountains, Oceans and Giants,* and *Berlin Alexanderplatz* whom Mr. Grass embraces as his mentor and entices us to rediscover. . . .

The other part of Mr. Grass sees the world as black and white. It demands that writers must be politically engaged, if only because of the history of the cold war. . . .

Now many readers will insist that there is no contradiction between the two parts of Günter Grass that seem to be set in opposition here. They will argue that these essays simply reveal him as a deeply contemplative man who has been forced to engage himself politically by the crisis of the times. . . .

This may be so. But even if it is, I submit a subjective defense of my division of all Grass into two parts. One is interesting to read and the other is not. It is, for example, highly absorbing to follow his elegant historical analysis in **"Erfurt 1970 and 1891,"** an address delivered in Baden-Baden in 1970 in which Mr. Grass tries to show how a 19th-century congress held by the Social Democratic Party ultimately led to the geographical division between the two Germanys today. It is, for another example, gratifying to encounter Mr. Grass's dismissal of the television series "Holocaust," for failing to reveal anything about the roots of German anti-Semitism, and to watch him try to redress the failure by examining the history of Heinrich Heine's unfinished story "The Rabbi of Bacharach." These essays are engaging and enlarge our understanding of European history.

It is, by contrast, boring to read Mr. Grass on technology, industrial waste, missile arms and the imminent arrival of the end of time. It is boring because what he has to say has been said so many times before, and worse, it's disturbing to find it boring because if what he says is true, as it well may be, then we ought to be awakened to the threats instead of numbed by their repetition.

Fortunately, there is more of the interesting side of Günter in *On Writing and Politics* than there is of the boring side. The interesting side engages the reader and makes the time spent with it seem worthwhile. As for the boring side: For better or for worse, one forgets it almost as quickly as one reads it.

> *Christopher Lehmann-Haupt, in a review of "On Writing and Politics: 1967-1983," in* The New York Times, *June 17, 1985, p. 17.*

DOUGLAS PORCH

Forty years ago this May the war in Europe ended. . . . German reaction to the 12 or so years of Nazi power have run the gamut from an outright denial that the Holocaust happened (admittedly a fringe view), to those who point out that ours is a murderous century and that, in any case, Allies who engaged in a strategic bombing offensive whose only purpose was to kill women and children, or who implemented a Stalinist Terror whose victims at least doubled in number those of Hitler's camps, are hardly in a position to deliver the Sunday sermon to the sinful.

Not surprisingly, Günter Grass adopts none of these arguments [in *On Writing and Politics: 1967-1983*]. He admits to enjoying the luxury of claiming an age exemption and to having committed no crime against humanity more serious than that of attending the weekly meetings of the Hitler Youth. Nevertheless, he is puzzled by memories of pastors and priests in his native Danzig who prayed for the victory of the German armies and for the health of the Fuehrer, but who never once wished God's mercy on the persecuted Jews, whose gaunt, burned-out synagogue stood only a few hundred yards away.

Grass finds the explanation, not in human bestiality, but in the fragmentation of responsibilities, the subdivision of the human conscience into narrow networks, the bureaucratization of moral values so that loyalty to superiors and the implementation of orders are elevated into the *imperium* of human virtue. His vision of Hell is that of Kafka and Orwell—a world directed by bureaucratic machines whose many-layered structure of responsibilities means no responsibility at all. In Grass' view, those who stood aside and did nothing are as guilty as Eichmann himself.

None of this is especially original. But Günter Grass' arguments are offered from fresh perspectives and in a language which, so far as I can tell, is splendidly translated. His hu-

manity saves him from pessimism. The writer must be *engagé* for it is he who struggles against the "transparent society" of data banks, listening devices, an unlimited faith in technological progress, and ideological powers who claim exclusive possession of the truth but who, in the end, leave behind "only the muck of a new bureaucracy"—the class that Marx forgot. Traditionally, the writer has left to future generations the assessment of his work. However, for the first time in the history of our species, the writer can no longer assume the existence of posterity. All the more reason, therefore, to cry out, to protest, to bring men to their senses. We are in trouble, he tells us, but we are not dead yet. (p. 9)

> *Douglas Porch, "Strategies for the Balance of Power," in* Book World—The Washington Post, *August 11, 1985, pp. 9, 14.*

JON COOK

For Grass, the facts of history are not something which once happened but have ceased to matter. They surface in the everyday world of family life, in the questions that his children ask him about what the Germans did to the Jews during the Second World War. Grass's answer was to write *From the Diary of a Snail* and one of the essays in this collection [*On Writing and Politics: 1967-1983*], **"What Shall We Tell Our Children?"**, describes how that book came to be written. The essay reveals that Grass's subjects choose him as much as he chooses them. His children's questions provoke a chain reaction. Seemingly disparate circumstances connect together like stars in a constellation. An unfinished story by Heine about the fate of the Jews in Germany; Grass's own memories of his childhood in Danzig and the enigma of his ignorance about the fate of the Jewish community which was almost literally round the corner; the 1969 elections to the German Parliament in which the beneficiaries of Nazi crime were still active: these are inescapably political circumstances and for a writer like Grass they are the demands and questions which provoke him to new ways of telling stories.

Writing and politics are therefore inextricably connected. Everyday life is saturated with political reality. In recollecting his own Danzig childhood Grass recognises how family intimacies and personal friendships were all shaped by the unfolding of Fascism. Writers can choose to evade these facts or confront them. Evasion means contributing to a collective amnesia which allows people to pretend that they haven't done what they've done. Grass sees the contemporary state of Germany as a compound of denials. Against these denials what he discovers is that the leaders of both the Catholic and Protestant Churches did know and, almost without exception, they refused to tell. The responsibility of the writer is not to forget. At one level this means dredging up the facts that have been deliberately discarded. But it also means lodging these facts in a narrative which will not itself become an evasion or denial, a way of remembering which is in reality a means of forgetting.

English readers may be tempted to see the concerns of these essays in terms of a position which is not their own. Grass is, after all, a German writer caught up in the particular anguish of his nation's recent history. Fortunately, we are allowed no such comfort. The future weighs heavily on Grass's writing and the future which preoccupies him is not local or national but global. In one essay, **"Racing with Utopias,"** he juxtaposes the futuristic fantasies of Alfred Döblin with his own record of a journey through Japan, Thailand and Indonesia. Döblin's fantasies begin to coincide with contemporary fact. Governments conspire in mad acts of environmental destruction in the name of scientific progress. The Fascist reality continues, although by another name, as the many live terrorised lives so that the few can continue to profit. . . .

In this situation, writers work in an increasingly narrow margin. For the first time the simple existence of a future is no longer secure. The traditional certainty that a writer's work might be received by posterity has gone. But Grass does not simply acquiesce in this gloomy reality. Against it he offers the arts of peace which we find so difficult to learn. He contributes to these arts by the tone of his own writing: witty, sardonic, refusing to be overtaken by the pace of events. And if his own writing is the record of great terror, there is firmly lodged within it another history of acts of human solidarity and courage which keep a vestige of hope alive. Grass does not flatter us but he doesn't lecture us either. His inventiveness continues to represent an insubordinate democratic impulse which is not simply of his own making.

> *Jon Cook, "And When They Ask Us," in* New States-
> *man, Vol. 110, No. 2843, September 20, 1985, p. 27.*

D. J. ENRIGHT

'Writing is not biting your nails or picking your teeth. It is a public activity.' This quotation from Günter Grass's 'teacher,' the novelist Alfred Döblin, sets the scene for these 13 essays and addresses [collected in *On Writing and Politics: 1967-1983*]. Grass himself repudiates with ease the arguments against the coupling of literature with political activity—that the style of the latter corrupts the style of the former, that power and intellect are incompatible. He repudiates them with suspicious ease. . . .

Possibly the best piece ["**Kafka and His Executors**"] concerns Kafka and the Kafkaesque nature of bureaucracy. All ideological systems are subject to 'one international order,' bureaucracy: the idea is commonplace, but Grass refreshes it through the lightfooted seriousness of his treatment. And a wry humour pervades his account of the attempts by a Marxist conference in Czechoslovakia, in 1963, to rehabilitate Kafka and reclaim him for communism by freeing him from the metaphysical mystifications imposed by bourgeois capitalist critics. The conference was less successful in getting Kafka out of trouble than in getting the participants into it. . . .

Our Promethean world yields ironies in plenty: a photocomposition printing plant in Jakarta specialising in pictorial wrapping paper (the paper itself having to be imported), which 'only makes shopping more expensive in an impoverished country'; in an Indian famine area, large quantities of food burned as an offering to whatever gods may be in the hope of averting future cyclones.

The essay in which these Asian ironies feature is more than alarming. Grass repeats the commendation, arising out of his 1969 campaign for Willy Brandt and the Social Democrats, of the snail and its gradual, mild amelioration as opposed to the various stallions who at various times have galloped under the colours of 'historical necessity' or some other grandiose flag. Undeniable though its metaphorical virtues are, the snail isn't a very exciting creature to write about. And despite his insistence on 'the slow, parliamentary way,' in effect Grass looks more like an apocalyptic stallion, a mirror image of the 'literary

rhapsodist' for whom revolution seems to promise 'spectacular gestures.'

He is fairly spectacular in his diagnoses of guilt and despair and his prophecies of doom; the problems, as he describes them, seem well past solution. In his speech on receiving the Antonio Feltrinelli Prize he announces that the book 'formerly made to last for ever' is now 'beginning to resemble a non-returnable bottle.' It isn't yet certain that we do not have a future, but 'already we have stopped reckoning with one.' His next book, he says, will have to include a farewell to the damaged world and to us. Great stuff, this, for writers; not so great for people who read it.

The most hopeful essay—on writers and trade unions, who 'both invoke the concept of brotherhood'—is also the least persuasive. While conceding that if they allow writers into their ranks, it is the unions who run the greater risk, Grass is in favour of admitting writers to the Printers' and Paper Workers' Union. They have much to offer: their precision and love of story-telling, their trained memories, their obstinate restlessness, their pleasure in criticism. . . . Surely writers can do all that, can do their best or their worst, or as much as they are allowed to do, without unionising themselves? Grass points to no *need*—outside the somewhat poetical 'existential bond with paper and the printed word'—for the operation.

The thought occurs that he is altogether exceptional in, among other things, his political intelligence; we cannot easily visualise a union of Grasses. He is a good short-order historian, adept in characterising the past; his novelistic gifts make him a vivid writer about politics, but how well they would serve him as a politician is another matter. In day-to-day politics, the imaginative considerations of men of his quality would be cast aside for fear of clogging up the works. . . .

Grass's novels live, and will go on living; his references to the Greek military dictatorship, one of his *loci classici,* already require a footnote. It is Salman Rushdie, in his introduction, who sounds or at least amplifies the note of optimism. 'What this work says is: We aren't dead yet,' and where there's life, there is, with all its arduous concomitants, hope. Possibly he has Grass's fiction more in mind than these dealings with what we call the real world.

> *D. J. Enright, "Snail's Pace," in* The Observer,
> *September 29, 1985, p. 22.*

RICHARD H. LAWSON

Grass's second career in politics, reflected in numerous addresses, essays, open letters, and polemics, was based consistently on advocacy of both causes and candidates, but never on his own candidacy, or even his availability, for political office. Avoiding the designation "politician" in its usual opprobrious sense, one notes that in his political writings as in his political activities Grass shows a development from idealistic amateurism to pragmatism, followed, finally, by a tempering of active involvement.

In pursuing this second track of his two-tracked career, Grass is essentially a trailblazer. The German tradition has been to separate and compartmentalize intellect and power in a rigid manner. Accordingly a career as a writer or artist effectively precluded even dabbling in, let alone actively pursuing, politics. There have been partial exceptions: Heinrich Heine's quixotic social advocacy; Goethe's career in the grand ducal establishment in Weimar long before the emergence of democracy in Germany; Thomas Mann's uncomfortable role in exile politics after the violent disappearance of democracy in Germany.... Günter Grass has been the latter-day pioneer in breaking the taboo, in reducing if not leveling the conceptual barrier. Not surprisingly, in doing so he has provided a prominent target for critics on both sides of the lowered barrier—literary critics as well as political critics.

Like his poetry, and unlike his fiction, Grass's political writings are only partially available in English. Still, a reading of what is available will yield rich rewards for the reader of English in an increased understanding and enjoyment of the fiction. In Grass's case, the one genre implies the other, and of course, in Grass fashion, the implication may run in either direction. To be a writer, Grass says, is to be an engaged writer. His engagement in both senses is an unabashed political love affair with democracy. It is a demanding, sometimes exhausting affair, but like Walt Whitman, whom he frequently quotes, his constant song is to democracy: "Of thee I sing!" Subsequently he modifies democracy to "evolutionary democracy."

Grass's self-proclaimed political bench mark of 1961 was prophetic of what was to come: in the one instance support of Willy Brandt, then mayor of West Berlin, and the Social Democratic party (SPD); in the second instance outrage at the repression practiced by the Communist dictatorship in East Berlin and East Germany. From early on Grass had no love for Konrad Adenauer, the then much-praised Chancellor of West Germany and leader of the Christian Democratic party. When Adenauer, who led an avowedly Christian political party, permitted himself invidious references to Willy Brandt's bastard origins, a furious Grass lent his writing and editing talents to behind-the-scenes work in behalf of Brandt and the Social Democrats. (pp. 69-70)

Grass's third bit of political involvement in 1961 consisted of a rather whimsical and self-conscious public appeal to vote for the SPD. The appeal was his contribution to a pocket book edited by Martin Walser under the title, *The Alternative, or Do We Need a New Government?* ... The "Government" in Walser's title is that of Adenauer, whom of course Grass attacks sharply. But the little essay is more interesting for its revelations of Grass, the literary writer, as a political novice. It is laced with personal and personal-literary references, some of the latter almost too coyly clever. For example: "Not that I'm claiming that Oskar Matzerath votes SPD."

In 1965 Grass took part in the parliamentary election campaign on the broadest possible front. As he notes with effect: fifty-two cities, fifty-two speeches. He is still a free-lancer, however, still looked at with as much reserve as gratitude by the SPD organization. After all, their famous supporter was also in many eyes infamous as a blasphemous and pornographic author.... And the writer inside the political activist is still clearly evident in his use of anecdotes, his allusions, and his difficulty in getting down to the nitty-gritty characterizing operational politics.... [In one] speech, **"The Issue,"** delivered in the summer of 1965, Grass is still quoting from Walt Whitman. But toward the end he denounces in plain terms Adenauer's reluctantly anointed successor, Ludwig Erhard, and lauds Erhard's opponent, Willy Brandt, and the Social Democrats. Then, as if not entirely comfortable with plain advocacy, he reverts to Whitman.

Political critics were not slow to denounce "the tin drummer," as they called the literary invader, on the grounds and in the manner that Grass surely knew they would. He continued

doggedly, fazed but not defeated by criticism and hisses. One of his more memorable speeches from that same summer is his **"Song in Praise of Willy,"** in which his resentment at the savaging of Brandt finds eloquent and ironic expression. (pp. 71-2)

In his praise of Brandt, Grass touches especially on two points that hold lasting significance for Grass, and that within a few years emerge interrelatedly in his life and his literature in a most ironic way. First, he declares that if the professional politicians and political establishment of the SPD continue lukewarm toward Brandt and continue to play safe, traditional politics, they will continue to drive the most gifted youthful members out of the party and into the arms of splinter leftist groups. Second, referring to the workers' uprising in East Berlin on June 17, 1953, he maintains that Brandt was the first person to protest the falsification of that uprising into a national revolt.

That workers' uprising in East Berlin, and Bert Brecht's refusal to support it, comprise the thematic basis of Grass's play, *The Plebeians Rehearse the Uprising,* which he was trying to write in the same year he campaigned for Brandt. As to Grass's early perception of the disaffection of youth with the SPD and youth's consequent desertion, radicalization, and protest, it proved all too accurate an indicator of what was to come.... [In] 1967 an invasion of radical students was a factor in the disbandment of Group 47. In 1969 Grass published *Local Anaesthetic* and premiered *Max: A Play,* in both of which he finds the student radicals to be somewhat self-indulgent and in any case pursuing completely ineffective methods to effect reform. Of course they denounced him, probably in most cases not even aware that he had pleaded their cause at its very inception.

On September 19, 1965, the Christian Democratic party won the parliamentary election; the SPD lost. Three weeks later Grass received the Georg Büchner Prize.... Instead of a polite acceptance speech, Grass delivered "to an audience of the defeated" a bitter assessment of the campaign conducted by the SPD, as well as of the condition of West Germany, not forgetting in the process his own fifty-two speeches on the road to defeat. This speech is entitled **"On the Self-Evident,"** which in the German original becomes the title of [*Über das Selbstverständliche: Politische Schriften*], the first collection of Grass's speeches and essays to be published as a book. Grass is tired of anecdote, tired of his opponents' slanders. (pp. 72-3)

[It] takes just one more disillusionment in the grubby arena of politics to make Günter Grass abandon his last remaining literary illusions about politics. That disillusionment was the so-called Great Coalition, entered into on December 1, 1966, by which the Christian Democrats and the SPD joined in the governance of the country. Willy Brandt accepted the vice-chancellorship. Kurt Georg Kiesinger, who had been a Nazi from 1933 to 1945, became Chancellor. Grass, still adhering to the not necessarily literary notion that politics could be made consonant with morality, was aghast. He attacked on several fronts, not excepting the SPD itself, whose principles seemed to him severely compromised if not indeed bartered.

He immediately dispatched an open letter to Willy Brandt, in which he again raised the all too ominous matter of the desertion of the young from the SPD.... Grass continued to attack Kiesinger frontally and unremittingly in both literature and speeches. In **"The Pinprick Speech"** of January 29, 1967, Grass asks pointedly, "Can a Nazi become Chancellor?" The embittered reply: "If he has repented, yes, certainly." (pp. 74-5)

In 1969 Grass, fervently dedicated to ending the Great Coalition, again played an energetic role in the parliamentary elections. This time his approach is distinctly more pragmatic. . . . And this time his speeches are almost purely political, inspirational only on a political basis. At this point Grass seems to be a practicing, realistic politician. The SPD wins, and Willy Brandt, still his friend, becomes Chancellor.

In late October 1969 Grass delivered a lecture at a writers' congress in Belgrade, Yugoslavia, entitled **"Literature and Revolution, or the Idylist's Snorting Hobby-Horse."** If the title is fanciful, the first sentence of the speech is plain: "To begin with, I am an opponent of revolution." He goes on to declare his aversion to "the absolute demands, the inhumane intolerance" of revolution. . . . The mechanism of revolution is the same whether the revolution is of the left or of the right. Even the role of literature suborned by revolution is of the same pattern, whether left or right: Brecht's hymns to Stalin are not essentially different from the philosopher Martin Heidegger's obeisances to the Nazis. For his international literary colleagues in Belgrade, Grass makes use of plentiful literary references and insights. In his Belgrade address one can see a harbinger of his celebrated "return to literature," which presumably began slightly more than two years later with preliminary work on *The Flounder*. It may be questioned whether the rise of the political man necessarily has to coincide with an eclipse of the writer. For already in a May Day speech of 1970, given in Baden-Baden, Grass is picturesquely employing the basic metaphor of *From the Diary of a Snail*, published in 1972. (pp. 75-6)

In 1972 Grass again took to the political stump for Brandt and the SPD. Brandt was returned as Chancellor. In March 1973 Grass announced in a speech that he regarded his own political work as completed and that he proposed to withdraw from the front ranks. He had never entertained any ambition to hold office himself because he was and is content in his own profession, which he describes as "being a writer and remaining an illustrator." And, with occasional exceptions, his emphatically dual role ended. He worked on *The Flounder*. (p. 77)

> *Richard H. Lawson, in his* Günter Grass, *Frederick Ungar Publishing Co., 1985, 176 p.*

G. P. BUTLER

Grass is said to have described [*Die Rättin*] as a "catastrophic book". Perhaps "chaotic" would be more appropriate to its narrative, but certainly catastrophies, actual or imminent—above all the fast-approaching Big Bang ("der Grosse Knall"), which man will not survive—are its principal theme; and to find fault with such an author's ways of handling such material, particularly when, as here, his stances and his apparent purpose are beyond reproach, may be thought a trivial pursuit. But *Die Rättin* does leave you wondering whether, having chosen prose fiction (interlaced with poems) as his medium, Grass would not have been wise, on this of all occasions, to make the accessibility of his messages a higher priority than before. His established readership, though massive, can still only be a small proportion of those who need persuading—and whom he might reasonably aspire to persuade—that, for instance, the destruction which threatens every one of us, and which has already taken place in the nightmarish, rat infested settings of *Die Rättin*, will come about because of man's lack of fear: "In the end, people were too cowardly to be afraid." And yet it is above all for that predictable proportion that Grass has mixed this bitter concoction too.

Ideally, therefore, newcomers will have prepared themselves for *Die Rättin* by reading, at the very least, *Die Blechtrommel* (1959; *The Tin Drum*, 1962) and *Der Butt* (1977; *The Flounder*, 1978): Oskar Matzerath, now pushing sixty, and his multi-skirted grandmother, Anna Koljaiczek, now celebrating her 107th birthday, are among the figures from that first novel whose lives we are assumed to be acquainted with; and the feminist world of the talkative turbot (or flounder, as the English has it) which caused the last major stir in the author's constituency is also to the fore once more. Beyond that, watch out for, say, allusions to his play *Hochwasser* . . . , and bear in mind that of course when the term "Kopfgeburt(en)" appears, or the name Döblin occurs, or that of a particular "Filmemacher" (presumably Volker Schlöndorff) is omitted, each such passage constitutes a nudge to the knowledgeable—to those in the know about the nudger.

Beyond that again: access to *Die Rättin* is naturally further restricted by a range of more commonplace, less obtrusive assumptions about readers who, though the nudging is not for them, may wish to persevere even so, and whom Grass must this time surely wish to reach. If they are Germans—better still, West Germans—and remember the early 1950s, they will have a head start. . . .

Such readers can also perhaps be expected to understand why the brothers Grimm are described, rightly, as "two upright men . . . prepared, if need be, to resign", and why Rumpelstiltskin hesitates to sign his name; . . . they may indeed need no telling who Ludwig Bechstein, Musäus and Hauff were, and be entertained by much of the hide-and-seek they are called upon to play. But fun for the few (or the many, for that matter), of this or any other, less rarefied, kind, however ample and appropriate in Grass's work thus far, has so little to do with the overall mood of *Die Rättin* that even its most obvious function, as light relief, is hard to acknowledge. And when you find yourself literally laughing—as every now and again you still may, at Grass's irony, wit, inventiveness—the laughter is likely to be reluctant, uneasy at best.

Germany's dying forests, fears for the ecological balance of the (western) Baltic, and the anticipated demise of the fairy-tale, crushed by modern barbarism . . . : these three [concerns] give rise to the mingled and extensive subplots which—in addition to the news of Oskar *et al*—leaven the twelve-chapter story of the rat, the dreamt exchanges between her (its sex seems important to Grass, hence the coinage "Rättin") and the first-person dreamer who retails them. The talk is about how and why the world as we know it ended for humankind (the narrator is out of this world, strapped into a space-capsule); about how rats survived the Flood and put paid to the dinosaurs, and what might actually have happened in Hamelin in 1284; about life on the still just conceivably habitable earth, when *homo sapiens* has perished . . . , when the *rattus norvegicus* dominates the scene, when "Watsoncricks"—part-man, part-rat—develop, take over and perish in their turn . . .

Why rats? Well, for one thing they have shown themselves to be perhaps the most resilient of all mammals. . . . The revulsion with which the man in the street—let alone his betters—will generally respond to these creatures no doubt enhances their appeal to the author: Grass's renowned ability to shock yet fascinate, though no longer displayed with the Rabelaisian vigour of his heyday, could hardly have been focused on a more suitably repellent scenario.

One wishes that the focus had been sharper. The prospect of annihilation, seen as certain unless current ingrained values change radically and fast, and emphasized by the ghastliness of an imagined aftermath which could have no chronicler in fact, is quite enough to worry about in one book; to voice other worries alongside it, however cleverly, and however legitimate they may be in other contexts, is to run the risk of trivializing both it and them. Yes, if you try to go down in the woods today, you may indeed find that the original big surprise and its setting have been blotted out by the effects of acid rain or troop manoeuvres; and all such damage, the threat of any such loss, is deplorable and should be resisted. But ultimately these are competing items of urgent business in a world which can still agree priorities; the threat of extinction is *hors concours*. Of course, as much of **Die Rättin**, including the despair of the final poem, shows (''I dreamed that I might hope again'', but no—what we are left with is ''the rats jeering / when the last hope, too, had been squandered''), Grass is one of many who do not need to be told that. But the optimal packaging of momentous truisms calls perhaps for less sophisticated resources, wiles and tools than he can now marshal.

> G. P. Butler, ''The End of the World, and After,'' *in* The Times Literary Supplement, *No. 4331, April 4, 1986, p. 355.*

FRANCIS KING

[Apocalyptic dread] has inspired Günter Grass's **The Rat**, as it has also inspired Martin Amis's brilliant collection of stories, *Einstein's Monsters*. . . . Along with this apocalyptic dread, as though a patient were suffering from typhoid and malaria at one and the same time, there is also, in Grass's case, an ecological one. This ecological dread takes the form of the conviction that, while we are waiting to destroy each other with intercontinental missiles, we are already destroying our natural habitat with the aerosols that we launch into the ozone layer, the waste that we dump into our rivers and oceans, and the pesticides that we spray over our fields.

Unfortunately, when a dread becomes an obsession, it can also become a bore. No one could claim that Amis's book is a bore, but it is difficult to see how anyone could claim that Grass's is not often one. As the same point is made over and over again, often in precisely the same manner, the reader is likely to find himself exclaiming: 'Yes, yes, I agree with every word you say, but I do wish you wouldn't go on and on saying it!' . . .

The ferocious energy of this book is undeniable. To read it demands a comparable energy. It can best be compared to an ant-hill, in which the reader finds himself constantly lost, directionless, in one murky, labyrinthine corridor after another.

> Francis King, ''Two Dreads Are Better than One,'' *in* The Spectator, *Vol. 258, No. 8294, June 27, 1987, p. 37.*

EUGENE KENNEDY

In this dazzling book [**The Rat**], Günter Grass, like the magician Merlin who appears in its pages, touches his wand to the Waste Land of the contemporary imagination and sets it blooming vigorously.

If most science fiction writers are mechanics of our uncertain future, Grass is a bold and sure artist letting go here in an evocation of the ''post-human era'' that arises from his poetic vision of the present. Just as George Orwell wrote in *1984* of what he could see clearly in 1948, Grass offers us tales, constructed like Chinese boxes, that spring from his grasp of life in the '80s. This is not a book about what *may* happen; it is a novel, built on our profound need for fable, about what *has* happened to western civilization.

It begins simply, almost cozily, in the Grass' own home in a Christmas season that, despite its essentially old-fashioned comfort, is made drastically different by the fulfillment of the author's wish to receive a rat for a present. The Christmas rat watches him at his work. ''She plays with my fears,'' he writes, ''she can feel them.'' And so he begins to dream of her, this rat whose hypnotic presence he cannot escape. . . . And the reader, as if in a skiff pushed by an unseen hand into the current, is carried into the dream universe of the book itself.

As in all dreams, past and present overlap, the living and the dead converse, symbols abound, and the experience, in part confusing and in part searing, may be more vivid than the bright world of everyday consciousness. (p. 1)

In the course of the narrative Grass delivers scalding, ironic attacks on the leadership that has already led us into the post-human era of the fuguelike narrative. . . . If the dream, as the author later says, is one he yearns to escape, it is because it reflects the nightmare of contemporary geopolitical arrangements.

Grass sees the death of German forests as the death of fairy tales, for the latter take place always in the former. Where else can people be so frighteningly lost or joyously found? How can we preserve our humanity if we destroy the environment that is its natural medium? Our heritage is preserved in narrative; we lose ourselves if we lose that and its power to knit the generations together. Grass' elaborate but deft juggling of themes—he scatters ideas prodigally—compel our attention, for he is speaking to all that is richest in our natures and to the wrongheadedness through which we are destroying it in the name of protecting it.

Some of the most powerful passages in this dense and demanding book center on the political folly that leaves the great nations lumbering toward Apocalypse, buckling under gleaming shields of armor, stumbling unfreely toward Doomsday. Grass' bitterly sardonic examination of a world that loses its freedom by betting everything on security are among the most provocative in modern literature. . . .

This complex novel is a disturbing modern-day book of Revelations written in dream language by an artist who draws easily on the enormous resources of his unconscious to render a bleak and not-so-bleak vision of what is really at stake in the world. We can only save ourselves and preserve our freedom by cleansing, as Blake long ago said, the doors of perception. We cannot survive in the world by demolishing the imagination in which we espy, store and pass on that which is most sacred and wonderful about men and women. (p. 9)

> Eugene Kennedy, ''The Age of the Rat,'' *in* Chicago Tribune—Books, *June 28, 1987, pp. 1, 9.*

JANETTE TURNER HOSPITAL

This exhilarating exhausting, maddening, brilliant, funny and profoundly disturbing novel [**The Rat**] is about the end of mankind, the end of plot, the end of syntax, the end of language.

Words about the end of language?

This has always been the central philosophical and artistic dilemma for Günter Grass; how can the truth be told when language is as worthless as the postwar Deutsche mark? What shape can the novel have when "words stumble into their hole" and writers, according to Franz Josef Strauss (leader of the opposition in the German elections of 1980), are "mere rats and blowflies"?

Mr. Grass has given us a gallery of famous sidesteppers of the language impasse: a dwarf with a tin drum, a talking fish and now an impassioned and visionary She-rat. In the age of logorrhea, his novels (mutating in form and syntax along with his hominoid protagonists, writhing like indomitable victims of some linguistic Chernobyl) are passionate attempts "to put off the end with words" even as words themselves must be scraped free of the counterfeiter's muck.

In *Headbirths,* that exquisite little novel-travelogue-philosophical tract of 1982, the author was explicit about the problem:

> In 1945, Germany was not only militarily defeated. . . . National Socialist ideology had robbed the German language of its meaning, had corrupted it and laid waste whole fields of words. In this mutilated language, writers, handicapped by its injuries, began to stammer more than write . . . only stammering could assert itself.

The stammerer of [*The Rat*] . . . is a pet Christmas rat in a cage beneath the tree. Like the protagonist in *The Flounder,* who was "only contemporary for the time being," the Christmas rat is all rats: from the ones left off the ark by Noah, to the Pied Piper's rats, to the lab rats of modern science, to the apocalyptic She-rat of the sci-fi video track, to the hominoid rat of the posthuman era. The rats know how to survive. It's the Bikini reflex—the one that got the vermin back onto that atoll in next to no time—so that when rats abandon the sinking ship, it is truly doomed. . . .

There's comfort, of a sort, from the She-rat: "Free at last from humans, the earth is reviving, filling again with creatures that creep and fly. The seas are breathing again. The air seems rejuvenated. And everywhere time is on hand, an inexhaustible supply of time."

Only time and the rats and the reruns—and the lone observer in the sci-fi track. "Someone . . . is dreaming us in installments," he weeps (with a nod to Borges). "In His flashbacks, thanks to the divine lust for publicity, we survive"—and in the leftover fairy tales and the gibber of writers, those "rats and blowflies," who—in video flashback—"talk the human present into existence."

"I thank you, ladies and gentlemen," says the narrator addressing the empty Bundestag of the ghost city of Danzig-Gdansk (spared by the art-loving neutron bomb), "for your eloquent absence."

All flesh is Grass, and this is the year of *The Rat.*

> Janette Turner Hospital, "Post Futurum Blues," in The New York Times Book Review, *July 5, 1987, p. 6.*

JAROSLAW ANDERS

"At Christmas I wished for a rat, in the hope, no doubt, of stimulus words for a poem about the education of the human race," begins Günter Grass's new novel [*The Rat*], his first major work since *The Flounder*. As soon as this didactic purpose is stated, and the Christmas wish granted, it turns out that the human race is sadly unfit for any education, as unfit as it has always been since man set foot in the author's native land, the Kashubian shores of now Polish Pomerania. (p. 29)

In *The Rat* no less than the whole of humanity is taking leave, both with a bang and a whimper, to be replaced by a new civilization of rats—the chosen tribe that comes to rule an earth liberated at last from man's unwelcome presence. In a manner befitting such a valedictory occasion, Grass's novel reassembles some of his favorite characters and themes, to allow them halfhearted and finally futile attempts at new beginnings. Oscar Matzerath of *The Tin Drum* is now a successful video producer turning 60. . . . The painter Malskat is a master forger of Gothic frescoes; but nobody dares to challenge their authenticity, since their appearance on the whitewashed and burned out walls of the Lübeck Cathedral is presented as a "miracle" by the authorities. . . . The Flounder, too, still speaks from the depths of the polluted Baltic Sea, or at least his presence is felt by six feminists on a maritime ecological mission. (pp. 29-30)

The author-narrator plans to produce in cooperation with Oscar Matzerath, a video film in which a group of fairy-tale characters organizes a conspiracy to save Germany's dying forests by subverting all the industrial civilizations and installing the Brothers Grimm as the leaders of a new government. It soon becomes evident, however, that we are trapped, together with all the novel's characters, in a dream, a nightmare really, in which the author-narrator, marooned in a space capsule, is forced to listen to his Christmas rat's endless exhortations against human perfidy and to the gruesome details of the inevitable end of the human race.

Despite the accumulation of realistic, grotesque, and surreal events and images, one has the odd feeling that very little happens in Grass's book. One of the reasons, perhaps, is the familiarity and the predictability of most of what actually does happen. Of course the women on board the research vessel will endlessly complain about the arrogance of men, while patiently knitting sweaters for them. Of course the painter Malskat will be punished, not for his forgeries but for trying to reveal the sham. Of course the fairy-tale characters, together with their forest, will be trodden into the ground by the ever-triumphant military-industrial complex. Of course the world will end in an apparently accidental nuclear exchange. And of course that holocaust—which will destroy . . . nearly all of life on earth—will spare the rats and some other low (and therefore innocent) creatures, and Grass's native Danzig-Gdansk, as his monument of unfulfilled and unreciprocated nostalgia. . . .

Grass's rats speak in a tone of moral superiority. Yet they present, perhaps deliberately, a most ambiguous alternative to human ignominy. Their strength is a purely biological instinct for survival—a tribal instinct that calls for endless sacrifices of individuals for the good of the species. "Stop being individual 'I's' and become a collective 'we,'" advises the She-rat in one of her moments of compassion. Indeed, when more details are filled in, the kingdom of rats begins to resemble a totalitarian utopia, where all individuals learn to act and feel as a single body. . . .

Against the author-narrator's weak protestations, and more frequently with his silent consent, the rat's voice rises in wrathful judgment, rejecting and ridiculing the whole of human history. But it is a voice (as the author himself remarks) that speaks exclusively in "didactic generalities." . . .

These crude generalities amount to little more than the clichés of two decades ago, to a parody of the radical indignation of the '60s. Men were created brothers, yet they hurt and kill each other; reason should bring self-improvement, yet we turn it into power; we were given the planet to share, yet we wallow in greed and pollute our environment. Nuclear weapons in particular figure prominently as proof of human insanity. There are also suggestions that the world would be a better place if we allowed women to take it over and to create a peaceful and nurturing civilization. And, as if to strengthen the impression that his bleak vision of humanity is desperately seeking a political cause, Grass interrupts his narrative with long poetic passages—presumably fragments of the "poem about the education of the human race"—that unerringly convey a sense of adolescent regret and confusion. . . . (pp. 30-1)

Of course, Grass being Grass, we are not allowed to take it all too seriously. There is subtle mockery of the feminists, the ecologists, the punk rebellion, the Swedish protesters. But the mockery is too subtle, and too little. Finally Grass's clichés are not a means of reaching for something more genuine and more original. His novel is completely dependent upon its platitudes for its imagery and its moral teaching. No illumination, nothing surprising or paradoxical, should be sought in *The Rat*. No mystery is hidden beneath its surface, no sudden reversals, no exploration of contradiction, no bold revelation of a new thought on a familiar opinion. There is nothing, in short, that makes this contribution to the literature of moral anxiety artistically compelling and intellectually credible.

Günter Grass's reputation as a moralist is based primarily on his early novels *The Tin Drum* and *Cat and Mouse*. They were interpreted as indictments of war and Nazism. Their characters, children growing up in German-Polish Danzig on the eve of the war, appear as victims and as judges of their society, but also as the embodiments of that society's ugliest and most disturbing aspects. Their physical and moral deformities are both the product and the indictment of the evils inherent in history and in individual lives.

A closer look, however, shows that the war, and more generally the totalitarian madness, played only an indirect role in Grass's novels. The heroes' self-appointed, rather manipulative innocence, their programmatic immorality, and their destructive urges were less a rebellion against the corruption of the "adult" world than the expression of a painful ambiguity about their own childhood. The strength of these early books really derived from a struggle between nostalgia and disgust for those allegedly arcadian years. . . . [This conflict] provides at least a partial explanation for the young protagonists' "outsiderness," and for the irrational negativism with which they confront the apparent normality of life after the war.

In his later works, especially *The Flounder*, Grass employs that same irrationalist perspective of offended innocence as a legitimate tool of moral evaluation. His *portes-paroles* assume animal forms to stress the distance that separates them from the world they put on trial, and perhaps also to liberate them from the inevitable relativism that results from any involvement in human affairs. From that comfortable position they denounce and castigate humanity, practically uncontested by any opposite view. But their hectic soliloquies and their apocalyptic prophecies, always unmitigated by a sense of the relative character of their own position, are the signs of a moral irrationalism that tends to elevate instinctive responses to the rank of general principles.

The main characteristic of this moral irrationalism is the absence of any sense of proportion and relation between things. All forms of evil, real and imagined, become equally ominous. Such a leveling undermines any serious moral reflection. In Grass's later novels, as in his political writings, we see more and more a powerful impatience with distinctions, an impatience that allows him to maintain his moralizing tone while carefully avoiding real moral and political issues. (p. 31)

Toward the end of [*The Rat*], Grass makes an interesting experiment. He retrieves the condemned human world; he allows his characters to complete safely their missions and to continue, for a while, their uneventful lives. Oscar Matzerath celebrates his 60th birthday. . . . Finally we witness a tender reunion between Oscar and Maria, his adolescent love and the mother of his brother-son; there are intimations that at this late point in his life, with the Kashubian chapter of his childhood closed, Oscar Matzerath may finally start to grow.

But swiftly the nightmare returns. *The Rat* ends on the familiar hysterical note. Having taken the name of the (unflinchingly non-violent) Polish "Solidarity," the rats relentlessly exterminate their humanoid kin. "Thus mankind's foulest idea has been expunged. Its last monstrosity has been exterminated. What those iron letters say, we have practiced, man has not. Nothing capable of survival bears witness to him." We have reached the end of the line. There is nothing more to say or to deny. Even hope, as we are told, is a delusion, a cruel joke played by humanity on itself.

Still, surprisingly, somebody tries to voice an objection. It is none other than Herr Matzerath himself, the "angel of innocence, who took part in everything without taking part." "Too much apocalypse," he protests to the narrator. "Decreeing the end of the world as if you were God Almighty. You and your everlasting last tango." He has a point. (pp. 31-2)

Jaroslaw Anders, "Floundering," in The New Republic, *Vol. 197, Nos. 2 & 3, July 13 & 20, 1987, pp. 29-32.*

TOM CARSON

Since his rambunctious popular heyday in the '60s, Günter Grass's books have pushed further in two contradictory directions. For the future, he's written enormous elaborations on quasi-Joycean mythic schemas, in which chunks of extraordinary writing, like the great "Father's Day" chapter in *The Flounder,* are immured in pages justified only by the need to work out the conceit. At the same time, the duty he feels to address the present—abroad if not here, Grass taught a literary generation what it means to be a public writer—has produced a series of what amount to situation reports, bundling fragments of autobiography and political argument together with improvised, deliberately unfinished fictional reveries.

The Rat finds the balance between the two. Literary and topical at once, comprehensive but loose, it's probably his most fulfilled novel since 1970's *Local Anaesthetic*—the book that marked the end of his explosiveness as an international force, but which holds up as one of the best fictional explorations of what the counterculture was all about.

With Grass, a lot depends on the central image he hangs each novel on—especially in his later work, where his choice of material is determined ever more exclusively by its fairy-tale suggestiveness, while fairy tales and fables become his dominant modes. The hook for *The Rat* is a wonderful one. The caged rat Grass finds as a gift under a Christmas tree—a memorable picture all by itself—gets anthropomorphized in his imagination into "the She-rat of my dreams." . . . The book's suspense is whether her matter-of-fact implacability will prevail over the broken stories, shards of hope, and alternate memories the author conjectures to counter her. . . .

The most insightful touch, funny and bleak at once, is that the rats, having triumphed, still look up to the old oppressor who's been shown to be inferior to them—some struggle to walk on two legs, others worship human artifacts like a collection of blue plastic Smurfs in industrious poses.

When the She-rat gives him room, Grass's own stories proliferate, each surfacing briefly, being rejected for another, then picked up again. . . .

On a technical level, all this is beautifully interwoven: random tales begun by Grass turn out to pay off in the She-rat's alternate narrative, stuff like that. But not until the book's done do you realize how much ground has been covered, how many correlatives found, from the Greens as Hansel and Gretel to rats as the tenacious, persecuted best in us. The women on the research ship, though Grass keeps this muted, are clearly identified with women from Grass's own past—what a lovely way to think of one's former loves, all sailing away together to an imaginary land. He doesn't have to spell out the connections; the premise that the world might be ending makes these voyages, remembered deceptions, and dreamlike stavings-off cohere emotionally anyway.

Much in *The Rat* suggests that Grass sees the novel as a summing up, if not necessarily a final one. His imagination hasn't softened, nor has its alertness to the world. . . . [The] weary, persistent humanist in Grass now calls the shots: all his fabulism is aimed at expressing his most earnest concerns as baldly as he knows how. He's direct enough to include a wrought-iron Solidarnoṡc logo among the artifacts the rats find worth saving. His She-rat complains that Noah tried to exclude her kind from the ark; Grass thinks novels now should be arks, and he's found room in *The Rat* for everything he knows whose preservation might help keep his own kind afloat.

Tom Carson, "Grass Menagerie," in The Village Voice, *Vol. XXXII, No. 44, November 3, 1987, p. 62.*

Spalding Gray

1941-

American monologuist, dramatist, short story writer, and actor.

Gray has won critical acclaim for his autobiographical monologues, in which he transforms the banalities and sometimes embarrassing intimacies of his personal life into larger reflections on contemporary society. Described by Don Shewey as "a hybrid of performance artist and stand-up comedian," Gray sits at a desk on a barren stage and improvises from a prepared outline. His performances have elicited comparisons to the work of such contemporary comedians as Woody Allen and Lily Tomlin and to the writings of Mark Twain. While some critics view Gray's monologues as immoderately self-indulgent and superficial, many applaud his insights and storytelling expertise. David Hirson observed: "Gray's revelations tap into a collective worship of the mundane self: he titillates our narcissistic impulses by a titanic display of his own."

Gray's work as a monologuist grew out of his experiences as an actor during the 1970s with such East Coast experimental theater companies as the Performance Group and the Wooster Group. Gray considers the acting theories of Performance Group director Richard Schechner instrumental in the development of the stage persona he has brought to his monologues. According to Gray, Schechner "emphasized the performer, making him more than, or as important as, the [dramatic] text." Through the influence of Schechner and Wooster Group director Elizabeth LeCompte, Gray created the intimately autobiographical character "Spalding Gray," whom John Howell described as an "astonished, bewildered man-child trying to understand the 'real' world."

Gray began presenting his monologues in 1979 at the Performing Garage, an off-Broadway theater. In his first two works, *Sex and Death to the Age 14* and *Booze, Cars, and College Girls,* Gray interweaves his childhood and college experiences with such events as World War II, the dropping of the atomic bomb on Hiroshima, the polio epidemic, and the Cuban Missile Crisis. The first piece humorously evokes the conflict between Gray's sexual awakening and his strict Christian Science upbringing, while the second records his misadventures as a student at Emerson College. In *India (And After),* Gray relates the events which led to a nervous breakdown he suffered in 1976 after touring India with the Wooster Group. *In Search of the Monkey Girl* documents his encounters with sideshow performers at the 1981 Tennessee State Fair. *Interviewing the Audience* is an improvisational piece in which Gray invites members of his audience to participate.

Gray earned widespread recognition with *Swimming to Cambodia,* an account of his experiences as an actor in Roland Joffe's motion picture *The Killing Fields.* While the film details the atrocities committed by the Khmer Rouge in Cambodia following the Vietnam War, Gray's monologue, according to J. Hoberman, "effortlessly brings together the movies and Vietnam, sex and drugs, the end of the '60s and the end of the world. Modest, ironic, subtle, it's everything *The Killing Fields* wasn't." *Swimming to Cambodia* was filmed under the direction of Jonathan Demme. In his recent performance piece, *Terrors of Pleasure,* Gray details the misfortunes which arose

© Judith Bachmann

following his purchase of a dilapidated country estate in the Catskill Mountains. This work also includes an account of Gray's adventures in Hollywood, where he attempted to procure a role in a television series in order to fund the renovation of his house. Gray's monologues are collected in *Swimming to Cambodia: The Collected Works of Spalding Gray* (1985) and *Sex and Death to the Age 14* (1986).

In addition to his work as a monologuist, Gray collaborated with Elizabeth LeCompte on the avant-garde dramas *Sakonnet Point* (1975), *Rumstick Road* (1977), and *Nyatt School* (1978). The first two plays examine the mental illness and suicide of Gray's mother and their effect on his personal life, while the third is a satire of T. S. Eliot's drama *The Cocktail Party.* These works were collectively performed in 1979 as *Three Places in Rhode Island.* Gray has also published *Seven Scenes from a Family Album* (1981), a collection of short stories that reveals the emotional instabilities and superficialities of a suburban family.

THOMAS LASK

Out of what must have been a shocking experience, the suicide of his mother, and the need to explore the reasons for such an act, Spalding Gray, in collaboration with Elizabeth LeCompte, has composed (to use their word) *Rumstick Road* a play that is partly a documentary and partly a series of counterpointed happenings that resemble bits from silent movies.

Working with the answers supplied by Mr. Gray's grandparents, father, a neighbor and a doctor who treated his mother—all of which he captured on tape—the authors have fashioned a number of scenes, each revealing a side of the mother's illness. . . .

With the help of colored stills, shown large against the back wall, an elaborate sound system and such aids as a salmon-colored tent, the authors have used the tapes in various and sometimes enormously effective ways.

In the best of them, the confessions of the grandfather, with his New England twang, are heard over the music of Bach's great, unaccompanied Chaconne for solo violin as the figure of a woman bends and shakes in a paroxysm of grief and madness against the enlarged color slide of her home. It is frightening and moving at the same time, and a superb, imaginative use of four really disparate elements.

In another scene, by contrast, only the question-and-answer response of the son and the doctor are heard. And the doctor is revealed as vapid, shallow, and smug, the last person one would want to entrust with the mental well-being of a loved one.

What emerges from these probings is the unwillingness of those questioned to admit that each somehow might have contributed to the death of the mother. . . . The speakers are coolly rational in the most callous, unfeeling and, in the end, most repelling way.

In spite of the effectiveness of individual scenes, *Rumstick Road* is, at this moment, strangely bloodless. It is a play with an obvious point of view, but it hasn't quite made up its mind how to express it. The authors appear caught between their desire to let the play unfold as a documentary and their attempt to shape it to a desired end.

For a work with such potentially explosive and mentally jarring material, it is too neutral. The audience leaves this hour-and-a-half exercise not feeling anything strongly one way or the other.

Thomas Lask, "'Rumstick Road' Examines the Death of a Mother," in The New York Times, *April 5, 1977, p. 38.*

MEL GUSSOW

[*Nyatt School*] opens academically and ends apocalyptically. The middle is elliptical and perhaps could only be clarified and rescued by the Marx Brothers.

The root of this performance piece, written by Spalding Gray and Elizabeth LeCompte . . . , is T. S. Eliot's *The Cocktail Party,* a most unusual source material for the artistic indelicacies of the present company.

[The audience] is perched on steep bleachers, facing a precipice. On the edge, seated at a long, narrow table is Mr. Gray—in front of a phonograph and a stack of long-playing records. . . . He leads us through an apparently autobiographical account of his early life as an actor, which included an appearance in summer stock in a production of *The Cocktail Party.*

Selecting from the recordings, he plays a stretch of laughter from *The Cocktail Party* and also a sampling of Alec Guinness (the psychiatrist in the original production) tripping through a tongue-twisting thicket of words.

Mr. Gray, fussily and absentmindedly, offers sidelong comments on Eliot, Guinness and his own misadventures on stage. He does this with the dry milquetoast humor of a Bob Newhart. Soon he is participating in a stagy reading of a scene from *The Cocktail Party.* . . . He inscribes quotation marks in the air to indicate dialogue that should be stressed. This is a deft and occasionally amusing parody of pedantry.

Then a Dr. Kronkheit-style vaudeville skit takes place in a room on the floor below the bleachers—we look down from our precipice. Mr. Gray is now the proprietor of an antic hospital and in league with an assistant. . . . To the tune of raucous, repellent music, he supervises a burlesque, anatomical examination of a female patient. . . .

The scene is meant to be funny. Instead it is silly and labored, as is a subsequent episode about a giant chicken heart that is about to take over the world.

The evening becomes increasingly hallucinatory, an explanation that does not alleviate our growing discomfort. In this piece, the authors lack the precision and the transporting imagination of Richard Foreman or Lee Breuer. This time the Performance Group offers mild shock and tepid sensation.

Then the scene is set for a party. A quartet of children, dressed up like adults (they look as if they had raided their parents' closets) and wearing wigs and masks, arrives and play-acts a portion of *The Cocktail Party.* . . .

However, just as we begin to find some enjoyment in the exercise, Mr. Gray returns to his long table, where he and his adult colleagues begin to gouge, burn and smash the phonograph records. . . . The wanton destruction makes us realize that *Nyatt School* is not really an ironic commentary on *The Cocktail Party,* but a savage assault on phonograph records.

Mel Gussow, "'Nyatt School'—Misadventures of an Actor," in The New York Times, *May 13, 1978, p. 14.*

RICHARD EDER

In his trilogy of plays, *Three Places in Rhode Island,* Spalding Gray deals with autobiography, but . . . his real subject is memory, not documentation.

The two plays I have seen, *Rumstick Road* and *Nyatt School* [along with *Sakonnet Point*] . . . operate on memory with a whole variety of instruments, most of them finely sharpened and powerfully employed.

Letters, interviews and spoken memoirs are used in combination with dance movements, music, surreal tableaux, slides and pantomime. The tone varies from straightforward searching to brilliant absurdity; comic and sometimes tragic distortion is used to expand the possibilities of narrative recollection with a sense of dream, nightmare or fantasy. . . .

A great deal is attempted: to make memory live not only for the rememberer, Mr. Gray, but also for the audience. Feelings about one particular past are not merely described and portrayed but—or at least this is the attempt—also transmitted. Lazarus is not simply being recollected; he is being revived and made to walk among us. . . .

In *Rumstick,* Mr. Gray appears as narrator, interrogator and actor in the scenes that evoke his search for the past. . . .

Mr. Gray's voice is heard—sometimes directly, and sometimes on tape—telling about the house he lived in, and interviewing his father and his two grandmothers about his mother and his childhood. The voice of one of the grandmothers wavers affectingly between recollection and forgetfulness; it shimmers like the past itself.

The father's voice is full of anguish; not so much in his narration of his wife's suicide but in his rejection of Mr. Gray's persistent attempt to explore the meaning of her hallucinations. For him, they were a matrix of memory; for his father, they were pure pain. . . .

There is some absurdist humor in *Rumstick.* . . . Most of the absurdity though, is reserved for *Nyatt School.* . . .

Nyatt School's absurdity is often very funny, and frequently spectacular. It gets out of hand, though; its serious purpose is too private, and its connection with Mr. Gray's themes is lost. It is entertaining but less successful than *Rumstick Road.*

I spoke of Lazarus earlier: In many ways, the achievement of Mr. Gray and his collaborators in making a dead past live is as spectacular as that of resuscitation; and like that one, it has its elements of failure.

But it is a brilliant and engrossing work; one whose abstraction and complexity are at the service of genuine emotion, and whose artistry in execution is such that even its conceptual misfirings are splendidly theatrical.

Richard Eder, "Operating on Memory," in The New York Times, *December 19, 1978, p. C7.*

CARYN JAMES

[In Spalding Gray's *Seven Scenes from a Family Album,* unrestrained] impulses of mind and body pierce the banal surface of suburbia to reveal the complex underside of a middle-class family.

The seven fantasies glance at the lives of Ted, Jean, and their son Jessie. The emphasis on sex, death, and family brings to mind Gray's autobiographical performance pieces, but this thematic continuity is less significant than the calm artistic authority Gray's experience in theater lends his fiction: *Seven Scenes* offers a mature command of narration, rhythm, and imagery. Narrative voices and points of view shift easily among the characters. Poetry merges with prose. Dialogue which intentionally echoes clichés gives way to language bluntly descriptive of physical detail or lyrical with a nostalgia for lost hope and romance. The confrontation of these elements produces tension, humor, and some dazzling moments of emotional power.

In the most satiric scene, **"A Christmas Letter from Ted and Jean Just To Catch Up and Let You All Know How We All Are . . . Doing,"** Ted writes about falling in love with Jean's legs, "the way they went up into her cheerleader outfit," and remembers their weekend dates, "shaving her legs by candlelight." In later scenes, after Jessie is born, Gray's vision of the vapid marriage becomes darker, more imagistic, full of adult desires and fears.

"Go Wake Jessie Up. We Are Going to the Beach!" begins as a family breakfast time conversation. Soon, sex and language drive the characters so far beyond control that Ted literally

bites into Jessie's flesh, nearly devouring his child. . . . The acceleration of language and accumulation of images reflect Ted's voracious need to possess Jessie. From the extreme depths of parental love, emotional cannibalism becomes physical reality. . . .

Throughout, Gray's critical distance from the characters' deadened lives is balanced by a sympathy with the substance of emotions. That he maintains this balance while controlling such a variety of styles and techniques, and does so with no pretentiousness, no self-conscious technical tricks for their own sakes, makes *Seven Scenes* extremely impressive.

Caryn James, in a review of "Seven Scenes from a Family Album," in The Village Voice, *Vol. XXVII, No. 5, January 27-February 2, 1982, p. 42.*

JOHN HOWELL

The *Art in the Anchorage* events took place in one of the Brooklyn Bridge "anchorages," the cathedral-like stone halls in which the Bridge's cables are moored. Spalding Gray proposed to interview several preselected subjects about experiences connected with the Bridge; he faced off with each guest, one at a time, in conventional TV-talk show set-up on a stage erected at one end of the hall on the Brooklyn side. And nothing of much interest happened for over two hours. Gray has successfully interviewed members of his audiences before (the guests were "ordinary people," and came up when invited from the audience), using a variety of selection methods ranging from on-the-spot requests for volunteers to preselection. In this particular show, however, he was a wandering questioner, and his subjects—an elderly Brooklyn laborer, two young women artists—were likable but tedious raconteurs. Only near the end of the long session did some lively, unexpected humor pop up. Gray asked for volunteers with urgent Bridge stories and got two energetic conversation partners who seemed to enliven his interest.

Was this uneventfulness the fault of the flimsy conceit? Was Gray not on the ball? Were his guests simply not the best choices? All of the above, I'm afraid, and more—with such improvised gabfests as Gray's there's usually something to watch irrespective of the success or failure of the project as a whole, but here, despite the occasional witticism, even the unusual process of spontaneous public discourse didn't add up to much. (pp. 77-8)

John Howell, in a review of "Art in the Anchorage," in Artforum, *Vol. XXII, No. 3, November, 1983, pp. 77-8.*

CLARISSA K. WITTENBERG

Gray's monologues are far from straightforward narratives. They dart and switch and capture details in a mosaic fashion to create a larger whole. In *Travels Through New England* he refers to his childhood in Providence, Rhode Island, his early adulthood working in Provincetown and his later years traveling and doing monologues. No story is simple and all are economical. The night I saw him work I was extremely tired and a little unreachable, and he seemed a little unable to really pull out the personal coloring that had made his work so special in the past. The strain of a one-man show seemed to tell. Nevertheless his narrative was so special that the evening remained valuable. He has a particularly American, say Mark Twain-like humor, and it was particularly evident in his description of visiting a recreated Pilgrim village in Massachusetts.... He talks of superannuated hippies, of a woman in a small Vermont village who made life masks of all 360 some residents and of the new immigrants who work in the Polo mill making suits for Robert Redford to wear to the Academy Awards ceremony. He is affectionate and acid at the same time and not a little self-mocking as well.

Gray is a master at stripping down to the basics of theater. Seeing him perform is valuable in being reminded of the elements of theater. He sets a high standard.

> *Clarissa K. Wittenberg, in a review of "Travels Through New England," in* Washington Review, *Vol. XI, No. 1, June-July, 1985, p. 9.*

DAVID GUY

[*Sex and Death to the Age 14*] is a collection of six of [Gray's] monologues.

It is obvious that sincere convictions lie behind this book, a belief on Mr. Gray's part that his truest talent lies in this kind of performance, that there is more substance in the simple telling of stories than in more self-conscious art forms. There is also a belief that the real truth in life lies in its most banal and embarrassing moments, that to pretty such things is up is to falsify them.

Unfortunately, I simply don't find these stories interesting. They seem disjointed and incomplete; they wander aimlessly; they make no point. ["**Sex and Death to the Age 14**"], for instance—which certainly sounds promising—concerns the deaths of a number of Mr. Gray's pets, a few episodes of early sex play and Mr. Gray's discovery of masturbation. "**Booze, Cars, and College Girls**" includes a long series of adolescent drinking stories and mentions every car Mr. Gray ever owned before it gets to its more interesting third subject, but then not much happens with the college girls either.

I have no doubt that Mr. Gray has a love of the banal and boring that borders on the mystical. But as long as people have been telling stories they have been embellishing them, not because they want to be untruthful, but because they believe a higher truth can be found in an artful lie. Also, of course, because when they did not embellish, they noticed their listeners starting to nod off.

> *David Guy, "From the Heart," in* The New York Times Book Review, *May 4, 1986, p. 32.*

MEL GUSSOW

[Gray's] new monologue, *Terrors of Pleasure*, is a hilarious tale of his harrowing quest for home ownership, a milestone on the perilous road to becoming a grown-up....

Terrors of Pleasure begins in Krummville, a tiny town in the Catskill Mountains, where the actor-author has decided to set up housekeeping. First he must find a house to keep and, as his tale unfolds, it is a *Candide* comedy about a city dweller who becomes a self-made rube.

All he wants is to be landlocked on Shady Valley Road in what appears to be an idyllic red bungalow, but, as he discovers, dreaming is merely the tentative prelude to home owning....

For our edification, he plays a taped telephone message from the man who is trying to sell him the house. Listening to the

self-defensive salesmanship, Mr. Gray smiles sardonically—after the fact. "Would you buy a house from this man?" he asks, and before the audience can shout back in unison, "Not on your life!" he confesses, "So I bought the house."...

To pay for the renovation of his home, Mr. Gray takes the only possible recourse known to actors. He flies to Hollywood to seek a fortune and the monologue merrily loops off on a satiric account of the idiocies in lotus land and the search for "spiritual materialism."

Because of his newly acquired celebrity, he is now a candidate for leading roles on sitcoms and in made-for-television movies, opposite actresses such as Patty Duke and Farrah Fawcett. Naturally he is rejected for everything, including an appearance on the Johnny Carson show.... In performance, he is told, he projects a "quality of thinking."

That very quality, of course, enriches his stage monologues. Through a look or a comment, he offers intelligent analysis. Though the narrative is entirely centered around Mr. Gray himself, it never suffers from self-pity or self-indulgence. He remains the antihero in his own fascinating life story, the never ending tale of EverySpalding.

In his earlier one-man shows such as *Sex and Death to the Age 14,* and *A Personal History of the American Theater,* Mr. Gray amusingly strung together anecdotes on such subjects as theater, romance and travel. But in *Terrors of Pleasure,* as in *Swimming to Cambodia,* he has a single roller coaster of a story to tell. The narrative has dramatic cohesiveness as well as comic insight, building to a climax that would have been appreciated by Don Quixote. For Mr. Gray, the whole world is his windmill and his siege, his terrors, become our pleasure.

> *Mel Gussow, "Spalding Gray," in* The New York Times, *May 15, 1986, p. C19.*

EDITH OLIVER

Having been raised on Ruth Draper, I tend to steer clear of monologuists, so my first exposure to Spalding Gray... [was] in *Terrors of Pleasure*.... Mr. Gray, a lanky, personable fellow, tells us, in a most informal way, about his purchase of a house in the Catskills—a house with no foundation, built upon clay. Everything that can go wrong does so, and the contents of the piece soon become an inventory of humdrum rustic catastrophes. In order to recoup his losses, he goes to Hollywood and almost lands a role opposite Farrah Fawcett. The material is so scuffed, so threadbare from overuse, that it is impossible to tell much about Mr. Gray though not to wonder why he thought it would be interesting. That is the strongest opinion I'll venture so far.

> *Edith Oliver, in a review "Terrors of Pleasure," in* The New Yorker, *Vol. LXII, No. 14, May 26, 1986, p. 87.*

ROBERT BRUSTEIN

[Spalding Gray's *Sex and Death to the Age 14*] is the story of his childhood in Barrington, Rhode Island, and his evolution into sexual awareness behind the stern, repressive backs of his Christian Science family.... Gray recounts his early experience of animal deaths with the same awed innocence with which he tells of his mother washing his "tinkler" ("I never knew it could be pleasurable until much later when I got to do it myself"). It is intriguing how this "normal" small-town childhood—the familiar bucolic material of so many plays and movies—could be so full of dread and ignorance. Kenneth Tynan once wrote a parody of *Our Town* that had the Stage Manager musing on lynchings and Jew-baiting, but Gray reveals that if Thornton Wilder ignored these social issues, it was because they were virtually unknown in New England villages: "I never saw a black, a Jew, or a double bed until I moved to Boston."

What Wilder really omitted from his small-town portraits, however, were the erotic components, and Gray generously fills in the lacunae. Telling of his first book of pornographic photos—it showed a man putting his semi-erection into a glass of water being drunk by a girl ("Did our parents do this in order to have us?")—then of a friend who amused himself by displaying his rectum, then of his petting sessions with Judy Brooks ("What?" asked an outraged friend. "You touched the place she pees out of?"), and finally of his first ejaculation after masturbating with a Davy Crockett beaver cap, Gray creates an erotic history of early adolescence that does for New England Protestants what Lenny Bruce and Philip Roth did for New York and New Jersey Jews. (pp. 36-7)

> *Robert Brustein, "One-Person Shows," in* The New Republic, *Vol. 195, No. 1, July 7, 1986, pp. 36-8.*

SEAN FRENCH

Most readers will close [*Swimming to Cambodia: The Collected Works of Spalding Gray*] knowing more intimate details about Spalding Gray than they do about virtually anyone apart from themselves.

In performance, these stories, compulsively communicative, must be hypnotic. The memories of his Rhode Island youth are in the Sawyer/Caulfield mould, but presented as if straight from the subconscious: "**Sex and Death to the Age 14**" and "**Booze, Cars and College Girls**" are like two hymns to the inexhaustible appetites of the American male. Most of Gray's teenage years seem to have been spent masturbating with one hand while tipping alcohol down his gullet with the other.

His encounters with college girls are more lyrically described. At college he preserved the entire set of a student production of *The Misanthrope* to use as firewood in his apartment. He would feed this to the fire and watch the flames reflect off the naked body of the love of his life. Unhappily, when the fuel ran out, so did she. . . .

Spalding Gray's stories are not shaped; they pour out with the thrill of improvisation. The big moments are rather small: when he visits Thailand to play a small part in *The Killing Fields*, his thoughts on the Cambodian horrors are commonplace. But when he tells the tale of his existence on the fringes of the movie, his failed attempts to go commercial in Hollywood, or his disastrous exercise in homebuilding in the Catskills, he is enthralling, the Scheherazade of the avant-garde.

> *Sean French, "Monologorrhoea," in* The Observer, *February 15, 1987, p. 24.*

NICK KIMBERLEY

[In *Swimming to Cambodia: The Collected Works of Spalding Gray,* I was] hoping to find links with that important tendency in post-war American writing towards performance, writing whose presentation on the page already suggests a score. I was thinking in particular of the poet David Antin, who has also evolved a monologue form, partially improvised, in which a private poetic language expands to embrace every aspect of the public.

Such hopes were thwarted in the reading of the pieces in *Swimming to Cambodia,* all developed as performance monologues and only transcribed when performances had defined their shape. On the page, we of course miss the nuances of gesture and intonation which illuminate, perhaps even change their meaning. But we gain the chance to stop the spiel and think about what's being said. I haven't seen Gray perform, but am prepared to believe he's persuasive, capable of winning over the most sceptical audience. On the page, he simply comes across as a cartoon version of the self-dramatising, all-American alternative culturist. From primal screams to Bhagwan Shree Rajneesh, from Perfect Moments to tripped-out fantasies, he lazily spews up the world in an endless burble of 'me-me-me'.

Performance art as a genre consistently risks self-dramatisation: the audience is forced to watch personal dilemmas, reactions, opinions presented as drama. But the best performance art goes beyond self to something mythic, not the trivial which obsesses Gray. Of course, there's something ironic here; but what a feeble weapon irony is if its aim is merely to guy performer and audience's stoned complacencies: Cheech and Chong did that more wittily nearly 20 years ago. Gray trots around the globe, the archetypal tourist trying to make himself at home; and then, worse than showing us his slides, he proceeds to talk about his trips endlessly.

The two-part ["**Swimming to Cambodia**"] piece is typical; it relates the author's experiences filming in Thailand for Roland Joffe's *The Killing Fields,* in which he had a part. Gray generalises outrageously about the Thais, who, we're told, 'have a word, *sanug,* which loosely translated, means "fun". And they never do anything that isn't *sanug*—if it isn't *sanug,* they won't touch it.' Worse still, Gray almost *celebrates* the fact that millions of dollars are being spent so that European and American actors and audiences can anguish in safety about the plight of suffering Cambodia. The contradictions never seem to occur to him; he happily swims around in the warm sea, looking for the Perfect Moment that will tell him it's time to go home. If none of the other pieces here is so smug, none of them suggests, either, that this is a voice offering any sort of opposition—to anything. (pp. 29-30)

> *Nick Kimberley, "Padded Sell," in* New Statesman, *Vol. 113, No. 2918, February 27, 1987, pp. 29-30.*

LYDIA ALIX GERSON

Ostensibly, [*Swimming to Cambodia*] is a fever chart of Gray's work on the film, *The Killing Fields,* and as such is an impressionistic, introspective revelation. Yet in interweaving his experience from his film work in contemporary Cambodia, his knowledge of the genocide that took place under Pol Pot, and his understanding of life in contemporary America, Gray outlines a continuum of atrocity between the American and Asian continents.

The monologue, ranging freely in time and space, is comprised of fractured, discontinuous episodes. The several stories do not seem to be moral equivalents, moving as they do from urban nuisance to Cambodian genocide. Yet this technique serves to force parallels between domestic and international outrage—and, perhaps more importantly, to point up their connection. Within the same hour and a quarter, the audience is treated to a numbing span of contemporary and historical events. . . . Gray reports all noncommittally; none of his tones trill in outrage. Nor does he state any of the obvious conclusions. The positioning of the pieces makes the historical point.

Although the moral issues raised in *Swimming to Cambodia* are of global significance, somewhere embedded in all this narration is a specific indictment of the United States for creating the requisite conditions for atrocity in Cambodia. The unspoken question in the piece seems to be: what kind of nation have we become to bestow automatic moral probity upon a Pol Pot simply because he answers to the tag of non-Communist? (pp. 96-7)

The monologue also focuses on the expendability of human life in a more quotidian context. Gray's upstairs neighbor makes incessant noise into the wee hours. Neither civility nor threat has dampened her enthusiasm for nocturnal riot. Over the course of time, the woman has become, in fact, progressively more offensive. Frustrated, Gray heaves an empty beer bottle through the offender's window. The action nearly precipitates a battle to the death with the woman's allies.

The unifying theme of the piece seems to be the relative value assigned to human life. In Pol Pot's Cambodia, there was no value assigned at all. In Pat Pong, Bangkok, bodies are fractionalized according to a schedule of escalating fees for prostitution. In New York City, human life may well be worth the price of a beer bottle.

This disparity confuses Gray, and it is at this juncture that sociological comment becomes ontological reflection in his piece. What has become of the cultural fraternity that existed in Gray's native Boston where a phone call appealing to mutual civility could accomplish détente? With the lack of a consensually defined humanism, we have lost a common notion of humanity and with it, all sense of proportion. We live in a world without moral compass, a world in which small outrages rank with large ones simply because we have lost all sense of scale in evaluating human affairs. . . .

If at times [Gray] lapses into the routine of a stand-up comic, it is because such *kitsch* is the only relief to the anomie which *Swimming to Cambodia* relentlessly expounds. (p. 97)

> *Lydia Alix Gerson, in a review of "Swimming to Cambodia," in* Theatre Journal, *Vol. 39, No. 1, March, 1987, pp. 96-7.*

J. HOBERMAN

Nearly as austere as Gray's stage production [of *Swimming to Cambodia,* the film version] opens with the solitary star crossing Grand Street on his way to the Performing Garage. Gray climbs up on the stage, and that's where he stays, seated at an aggressively spare desk, with nothing for company but a glass of water and a Ronald McDonald notebook. . . . Except when preempted by a handful of one-minute clips from *The Killing Fields*, Gray is never offscreen. His face is the landscape, his gestures a sort of ballet.

The film, which seamlessly compresses the three hours of *Swimming to Cambodia*'s two parts into less than 90 minutes, is remarkably faithful to the feel of Gray's stage presence. Only rarely does Gray attack his material with a camera-amplified surplus of gusto—and the same is true of the camera itself. . . .

Gray's monologue in *Swimming to Cambodia* effortlessly brings together the movies and Vietnam, sex and drugs, the end of the '60s and the end of the world. Modest, ironic, subtle, it's everything *The Killing Fields* wasn't. On those terms, the film is a success—and yet, given the richness lurking in this material, [director Jonathan] Demme's self-effacing technique may have been too cautious. . . .

In the film's final minutes, Gray's farewell to paradise is juxtaposed with the evacuation chaos from *The Killing Fields*— shots of choppers, kids waving in slo-mo. Here everything officially comes together: the imperial ego and the imperial state, the expulsion from Eden and Cambodia Year Zero, poignance and horror, Hollywood and Wooster Street. But because the film has remained so linear, the effect seems mechanical. The elements slip by each other without engaging. It's the perfect moment that doesn't happen.

> *J. Hoberman, "American Gothic," in* The Village Voice, *Vol. XXXII, No. 11, March 17, 1987, p. 51.*

DAVID DENBY

[In the film *Swimming to Cambodia*], Gray talks fast—faster than an evangelist working a country fair, faster than a standup comic in Las Vegas, or a late-night-TV appliance salesman, or a patient on an analyst's couch trying to make himself interesting. Gray, who bears a fleeting resemblance to all those American types, gives the impression of someone trying to express everything he's ever felt or thought—*at once*, before it flies away. *Swimming to Cambodia* is a filmed theatrical event—Spalding Gray sitting in front of an audience, with only such props as a wooden desk, a notebook, and a couple of maps and a pointer. The talk, which carries the whole show, is meant to mesmerize and surround. And it does. . . .

[Even] though *Swimming to Cambodia* has been recorded on film, it's not finished or definitive, and never can be. The piece is an unruly living thing, an enacted comic autobiography in which Gray's embellishments and reflections on his experience and sometimes his non-experience) necessarily change over time. . . .

The "Spalding" we hear about in this monologue is an unassuming, fallible, not entirely timid man, a "passive-aggressive unconscious coward" who nevertheless stays open to the vibrations of paranoia, cruelty, and pleasure passing through the air. He ventures after whores yet prizes the security of his girlfriend back home. He's given to mystical episodes yet worries about his career. He is not a hero, except in his ability to take things in. "To record one must be unwary," F. Scott Fitzgerald wrote in his notebook. Gray is a recording angel. But of a unique kind. He has some of the intellectual and emotional qualities of a good writer, yet he's essentially an actor. He experiences something in order to perform his recollection of it.

This actor absorbs and re-creates not just the attributes of a single character but the full dimensions of experience—what happened, what he felt when it was happening, and what he feels now, recollecting the moment. He's acute, as well, on those self absorbed moments when vision fades and only the fuzz of consciousness seems real. Jokes, absurdities, metaphysical speculation of a grandiose or trivial nature, all fall into place in an easy, spontaneous rhythm. His narrative method is circular; the meanings arrive in pieces, renewed and enlarged over time. Although he always comes back to himself, he cannot be accused of narcissism or monomania. Before our eyes, his ego shreds. We look at him and see the sunlight, the ocean, the characters. He performs himself re-creating life. (p. 82)

There are parts of Gray's temperament that I don't much care for. He has an awed, hippie-intellectual side, a fondness for tripping back and forth between dream and reality, or rather, between the dreaminess of reality and the reality of dreams, all of which reminds me of some sixties gurus who have fortunately taken to the hills. What's best about him is the side that's unmystical and hard-edged—his visceral apperception of the strength of evil and absurdity and the necessity of pleasure.

The monologue climbs on the wings of his sexual avidity. Aloft, he flies in streams of sensation, passing through areas of delight and misery. At times, as he talks of a sex show in Bangkok, or a day at the beach, the spontaneous dialogue between ease and unease, euphoria and dismay, carries echoes of Twain, Henry Miller, Vonnegut. Even when I don't care for Spalding Gray (and most of the time I do), I know I'm listening to someone with a first-class mind and unique narrative talents. (pp. 82, 84)

David Denby, "*My Dinner with Spalding,*" in *New York Magazine, Vol. 20, No. 12, March 23, 1987, pp. 82, 84-5.*

TERRENCE RAFFERTY

[Spalding Gray is] not really an actor. In his published monologues, *Swimming to Cambodia* and the collection *Sex and Death to the Age 14,* Gray seems casual and unfocused: the language of his autobiographical rambles isn't especially vigorous, the insights are less than dazzling and the structure is nearly invisible. But he isn't really a writer, either. And no, he's not a comedian: his stories are comic, but the timing is desultory and the punchlines don't always arrive. Being not quite an actor, a writer or a comedian puts Gray . . . in the peculiar catchall bin labeled "performance artist," along with all the not-quite-dancers, -musicians, -playwrights and -conceptual artists who do something unclassifiable and do it in public.

When this sort of art works, it's partly because of the formal ambiguity. Keeping us unsure of what he's up to, engaged in defining and redefining what he *is,* is the performance artist's substitute for conventional theatrical technique: he remains a moving target, darting in and out of recognizable categories, as a way of holding our attention. Gray, like everyone in his not-quite class of performer, runs the risk of merely frustrating us: if we get tired of projecting possible identities onto his bland, ordinary-guy persona, his art just vanishes into thin air. What he practices is autobiography as conjuring trick—now you see it, now you don't—and it's delicate work. The storyteller keeps pulling his life in and out of his hat, and if it's not done with magical lightness, this game of appearance and disappearance can reduce our consciousness to a slow, dull flicker—the way the world looks when we're blinking to fight off sleep, the way a movie looks when the projector's running down.

It's done, of course, with mirrors. "I'm convinced that all meaning is to be found only in reflection," Gray writes in the preface to the text of *Swimming to Cambodia,* and he clearly means it. In his monologues, he presents such a placid and enigmatic surface that the audience can see almost anything in

him: critics' descriptions have included references to Woody Allen, Mark Twain, Shelley Berman, Andy Warhol, Lily Tomlin, Norman Rockwell, Frank (*My Life and Loves*) Harris, Johnny Appleseed, Bob Dylan and *My Dinner with André.* Gray can't be held responsible for every outrageous comparison, but there's surely something in his method that invites these desperate attempts to find a trace of the familiar glancing off the flat, primitive tableaux he sets before us. Sitting behind his no-frills desk, droning on about an unremarkable middle-class boyhood, some standard collegiate sexual exploits, banal picaresque adventures on cross-country drives and his halfhearted shots at settling down in a relationship or a career or a house in the country, Gray seems to draw his audiences into a kind of complicity with his artlessness. His persona, in all of his stories, is that of a guy who's just muddling through, making it up as he goes along. The point of his narratives is always how blobby, undefined and malleable his identity is—he's forever trying and failing to "take a stand" or "go for it"—so he reflects our bewilderment in his presence right back at us. And the experience of watching and listening to this halting autobiographer becomes sort of cozy, reassuring. His life is as trivial, his responses as shifty and incoherent, as our own: we're all amateurs here.

If you're in the right mood—feeling inept, befuddled, insecure—Gray's ingenuousness can be appealing. But the studied naïveté of his persona can also get pretty tedious: credulousness and boyish ineffectuality aren't necessarily all that charming in a 45-year-old man. In one of his monologues, Gray describes himself to a Hollywood producer as "a Huck Finn-Candide-type who gets into all these weird situations," and while this is clearly a joke, it's hard to avoid the feeling that, on some level, Gray really is trying to universalize his shlemiel persona—to make us see him as the representative white middle-class American male of his times, a mythic innocent. Most of Gray's monologues allow us to ignore this implication—he's too diffident to insist on it—and just laugh at the jokes, but it's crucial to *Swimming to Cambodia.* The story of Gray's experiences in Southeast Asia as an actor in *The Killing Fields* is too long and detailed, its backgrounds too real, for us to take it as simply another installment in his dizzy chronicle of his life and times. The jokes here have a darker tone than usual, and aspire to metaphor: making a movie that reflects one of the most horrifying episodes in recent history, the Khmer Rouge takeover of Cambodia, Gray's playing a bit part (and not playing it very well); with images of death and destruction all around him, Gray remains detached, dithering on the fringes of the action like Stendhal's Fabrizio at Waterloo—drinking, getting stoned, having minor personal crises and trying to arrange what he calls a "Perfect Moment" for himself. This relentlessly self-ironic monologue means (insofar as its intentions can be fathomed) to examine the consequences of Americans' innocence and self-absorption, to question even Gray's cherished democratic-amateur values, the cultivated immaturity that leaves amiable bozos like him helpless on the sidelines while the pros engineer atrocities.

This would be a whole lot more convincing if the construction of Gray's piece showed any real transformation of his aesthetic principles, if we felt his determination to fight fire with fire, to counter the artful lies of American politics with artful truths of his own—to turn pro at last. But *Swimming to Cambodia* is at least as shapeless and ramshackle as his other work, as random in its effects, and even longer. And Gray can't quite bring himself to give up his mirror relationship to the audience. His irony about himself is a little half-hearted; his bumbling and incomprehension, his aging-hippie stabs at spiritual transcendence still elicit warm chuckles of recognition. The stuff *Swimming to Cambodia* is supposed to be about is just too serious for Gray's limited resources, and he falls back on what's worked for him before, the narrative sleight of hand and the mild boyish charm. In the film of *Swimming to Cambodia*, Gray, seated at his desk with graphics (Asian sunsets, a map of Cambodia) flashing on a big screen behind him, often seems like a local newscaster who's been handed a bulletin about the end of the world but keeps up his happy-talk with the weatherman.

Fortunately for Gray, there's a real pro on hand in this movie: its director, Jonathan Demme.... There's no ambiguity about what Demme is—he's only a director, an artist who seems in perfect command of his material. He can't fully make up for what's lacking in Gray, but his work here reminds us, as Gray himself can't, that there's some value in craft. Without him, *Swimming to Cambodia* would stop making sense a lot earlier than it does. (pp. 518-20)

> *Terrence Rafferty, in a review of "Swimming to Cambodia," in* The Nation, *New York, Vol. 244, No. 15, April 18, 1987, pp. 518-20.*

DAVID HIRSON

For almost a decade, Gray has been delivering monologues which chronicle his life from early childhood to the present.... Dressed in a plaid shirt and seated behind a small table, he addresses the audience directly, referring to an outline but altering or re-structuring material as the spirit moves him. This technique lends each performance a quasi-improvisational air which Gray feared might be lost in transferring his monologues to the page. 'None of them had been written down,' he says, 'they always came together in front of the audience.' [*Swimming to Cambodia: The Collected Works of Spalding Gray*] however, confounds expectations. Instead of their impact being diminished, the monologues have every bit as much vitality in print as they have on stage. If we miss the manic energy of a Spalding Gray performance, there is ample compensation in the unhurried, discursive way his stories expand to fill a volume. Also, these seven pieces taken together yield insights into Gray's character: a significant point for a man who so desperately wants to make himself known.

Who is he? Gray's autobiographical monologues should answer that question, especially since they pretend to a level of frankness where apparently anything goes.... [His] confessions for the most part show him to be endearingly neurotic or naive or outrageous. There is no real risk involved. Discussing private matters from psychotherapy to early experiments in masturbation ('we called it Madam Palm and her five lovely daughters'), he is always very funny, but not daring in the way he seems to think he is. 'I pride myself on telling the truth,' he says. The truth Gray tells, however, has at least one eye on the audience at all times. His desire to please decides the range of his honesty, and the result is the subtlest of poses: that of the ingratiating, 'self-defeated shlub' guy whose sense of alienation is no different from yours or mine, and in whose misadventures we inevitably recognise ourselves. His themes covet general appeal: growing up (**"Sex and Death to the Age 14"**,) travel (**"Nobody wanted to sit behind a desk"**, **"47 Beds"**), home-ownership (**"Terrors of Pleasure: the House"**) and **"Booze, Cars and College Girls"**. The place where his identity actually resides is difficult to make out....

Gray's quest for a totally pure experience—what he calls the 'Perfect Moment'—is frustrated by a crippling self-awareness. He seems incapable of enjoying anything without in effect saying to himself, 'Here I am, Spalding Gray, enjoying this,' and his entire life is observed as if it were happening to somebody else. 'SPALDING! BE HERE NOW!' a friend urges him at one point. Only for a split second in Oregon does Gray admit to feeling 'in the right spot at the right time'; otherwise, whether seeking Perfect Moments in America or Thailand or Greece, he is unshakeable in his conviction that life is *really* happening wherever he is not, and usually in the place that he has just left.

This haunting sense of inauthenticity propels him through a revolving door of therapies, drugs and religions, all of which only heighten his aesthetic distance. An initiate kneeling before Bhagwan Shree Rajneesh at the guru's ashram in Poona, Gray confides, 'I really wanted to ask him "Where are the orgies?"' and he adds: 'I was the only one in the ashram in beige.' The self-consciousness which he aims to banish shows him how farcical he looks, or how morbidly distanced from himself he has become....

Incessantly reminded of his own existence, he remains completely unconscious of *who* he is: or rather, he is convinced that he is nobody at all, a self with no firm identity. WASPy, doughy, middle-of-the-road Spalding plods along, torn between 'going for it' as an actor in Hollywood and joining the Peace Corps (he does neither), chronically indecisive, unassertive, impressionable and apolitical ('I've never even voted in my life'). The monologues search his past for clues. They reveal that this sense of nonentity extends even to his physical being....

Gray struggles in vain to get any sort of purchase on identity.... Hired by Roland Joffe to play a small part in *The Killing Fields*, he comments that the man on whom his character is based is a continent-hopping, devil-may-care Princeton graduate whose six languages include Khmer. 'I graduated from Emerson College,' Gray says, 'and am still wrestling with American.' What are actors, he wonders, compared to these dazzling ambassadors and foreign correspondents and cinematographers who treat 'the whole world as their stage'? 'They're no one,' he concludes: 'They're conduits. They're not as threatening as Real People.'

Having to 'make-believe' as his profession only aggravates Gray's sense of personal inauthenticity. He is doubly bound by pretence. Camel cigarette ads taunt him with their depictions of natural, swarthy fellows tacking sloops or racing dune buggies—living life to the lees! He marvels at their ability to be out there all alone, 'Where a man belongs!': but he consoles himself with the realisation that 'they're not alone, of course, someone's there with a camera, and that makes me feel a little better.' Gray heaves a sigh of relief because he cannot imagine a life unwitnessed. There would be no point....

Relentless self-consciousness and lack of identity constrain him to 'act himself' all the time. It is a short and logical step for him to 'act himself' on stage, where those unreal experiences may be redeemed. Telling about life 'eroticises' it. In front of listeners, the sham evolves into an authentic centre of attention.... In our presence, at least, he appears to be somebody, maybe even one of the Real People....

What rescues these pieces from pure (if entertaining) self-indulgence is the consistency with which they do, in the end, communicate a 'representative piece of reality'. Gray's stories show an America which is in the throes of a narcissistic identity crisis not unlike his own. There is a man in Santa Cruz whose living-room is distinguished by a 'huge home-made deprivation tank'; a doctor in South Dakota whose novel methods of weight loss include administering the larvae of tapeworms to his patients; a 'pilgrim Twilight Zone' in Plymouth, Massachusetts whose inhabitants re-create the 1627 colony by assuming the language, dress and identities of the original families. . . .

Wherever he looks, Gray discovers Americans in various stages of self-creation. He is not alone in his longing for identity. It is a condition to which the narcissist in everyone responds, and Gray, an extremely gifted storyteller, exploits that fact in his monologues. Recording the minutiae of his experiences, he forces each of us to recognise our obsession with the banal details of *our* lives: even, perhaps, to revel in them. 'The Perfect Moment,' he says, 'is like falling in love . . . with yourself.' In this way he dignifies, through the telling, matters which can only be of personal significance: the names of childhood friends and high-school teachers, for example, or of streets where he has lived, his father's Bloody Mary mix, the Ponderosa Steak House where his girlfriend Renée has her period. Private memories are made acutely specific: his brother Rocky, he says, used to take him 'into the bottom of the bed—he called it Noss Hall, a foreign land under the blankets'. Gray's revelations tap into a collective worship of the mundane self: he titillates our narcissistic impulses by a titanic display of his own.

David Hirson, "Just Be Yourself," in London Review of Books, *Vol. 9, No. 14, July 23, 1987, p. 27.*

John (Clendennin Burne) Hawkes (Jr.)

1925-

American novelist, short story writer, dramatist, poet, editor, and critic.

Hawkes is regarded as an important writer of experimental fiction whose literary concerns primarily involve the realm of psychic and imaginative processes. Employing complex patterns of language and imagery while emphasizing the sadistic and darkly humorous aspects of unconscious impulse, Hawkes creates what have often been described as visionary landscapes of the mind. Characterized by disjunctions of time and space, gothic scenes of random brutality, and vivid sexual imagery, Hawkes's fiction is intended, in his own words, "to expose, ridicule, attack, but always to create and to throw into new light our potential for violence and absurdity as well as for graceful action." Concerned with portraying the hallucinatory and paradoxical extremes of existence, Hawkes eschews the conventions of mimetic fiction while focusing on themes related to love, death, cruelty, fear, sexual repression, and desire. Although some critics fault Hawkes's obsession with unorthodox subject matter and his reduction of narrative to isolated and unassimilated events, most praise his lyrical prose style and comic inventiveness while noting the mixture of fascination, terror, and compassion frequently evoked by his writings.

Born in Stamford, Connecticut, Hawkes spent his early adolescence in Alaska where, he stated, he "acquired a permanent preoccupation with the alien nightmare landscape of darkness, rain, high wind, mountains, fragments of glaciers, distant bears, wild strawberries, one-legged Indians and the terrifying ruins of abandoned mining towns." By 1940, Hawkes had returned to the eastern United States, and in 1943, he enrolled at Harvard University. In 1949, following two years as an ambulance driver for the American Field Service in Italy and Germany during World War II, Hawkes completed his education at Harvard and began publishing fiction.

Hawkes's early writings focus on the brutality of war, the repression of individual freedom by social institutions, and emotionally unfulfilling sexuality. Through their surrealistic portrayals of decomposing civilizations, these works present a bitter indictment of modern existence. In his first major novel, *The Cannibal* (1949), Hawkes depicts a chaotic world on the verge of annihilation through an obliquely related series of images and fragmentary sketches that evoke the ravaged landscape of Germany in the aftermath of World War II. Imprisoned and dominated by their surroundings, the inhabitants of this hostile environment have become depraved conspirators in their own corruption and in the decline of society. Like much of Hawkes's early work, this novel features imaginative verbal structures and displays little concern with plot progression or character development. Hawkes's next novel, *The Beetle Leg* (1951), revolves around the events following the accidental death of a construction worker who is buried alive while building a dam. Set in the arid desert landscape of the western United States, this bleak, surrealistic parody of conventional regional literature presents the American West as a barren wasteland populated by somnambulent characters who are oblivious to their capacity for brutality and devastation.

In his third novel, *The Lime Twig* (1961), Hawkes constructs a sardonic parody of the detective novel as a pretext for his exploration of violence, sexuality, and desire. Set in England during and after World War II, *The Lime Twig* is ostensibly concerned with the consequences of a respectable middle-class couple's attempt to steal a famous race horse. Considered a demanding and difficult work, *The Lime Twig* is noted for displaying a more coherent plot and more consistent characterization than his earlier books. *Second Skin* (1964) continues Hawkes's subtle shift toward more traditional modes of discourse, departing from the multiple points of view utilized in his earlier fictions. In this novel, Hawkes manifests his increasing concern with the struggle between the forces of Eros—the erotically motivated desire for life—and Thanatos—the longing for death. Although consisting primarily of the narrator's memories of his violent and death-oriented past, this book introduces a life-affirming quality which derives from the power of the protagonist's imagination to transform his bleak existence. Noting Hawkes's focus on his narrator's psychic development, Carol A. MacCurdy observed: "Beginning [with *Second Skin*] . . . , Hawkes's emphasis changes. Rather than concentrating on the depiction of a dark, powerful world, he begins to stress modern man's reaction to chaos."

Hawkes's triad of novels, *The Blood Oranges* (1971), *Death, Sleep, and the Traveler* (1974), and *Travesty* (1976), has furthered his reputation as a central figure in contemporary literature. In these works, as in *Second Skin*, Hawkes subordinates the external environment to the interior atmosphere of the psyche by presenting characters whose lyrical, sensuous, and imaginatively created worlds are intended to offset reality's threatening forces. Unlike his previous work, however, Hawkes's trilogy reveals that the imagination simultaneously offers freedom and annihilation. *The Blood Oranges* is an account of an American couple living within the narrator's imagined erotic locale of Illyria. Their seduction and destruction of another couple uncovers the selfishness and vanity of the protagonist's vision. *Death, Sleep, and the Traveler* involves the narrator's journey through the depths of his unconscious in the form of an uncharted ocean cruise. Focusing on the central character's preoccupation with sexuality, this novel alternates between antithetical settings that are ultimately used to equate sex and death. In *Travesty,* Hawkes reduces his setting to the confines of an automobile that is being driven by the narrator. Racing through the night along a rural road in southern France, the car is destined for a deliberate and fatal collision with a distant stone wall. Delivering a fragmented monologue on the aesthetics of death and sex, the protagonist consciously chooses the creation of death over an acceptance of life in his pursuit of the ultimate imaginative experience. While farcical in their improbable situations and gross incongruities, these novels poignantly explore their protagonists' attempts to experience and control reality, reflecting humanity's desire to impose order on chaos. Carol A. MacCurdy suggested: ''The artist-figures in the triad are victimized by their own radical pursuit of freedom as it resides in the creative imagination and by their rebellion against life's limitations. The inherent irony, of course, is that in combatting death (stasis) art leads to the same inevitable result.''

In his later works, *The Passion Artist* (1979), *Virginie: Her Two Lives* (1982), and *Adventures in the Alaskan Skin Trade* (1985), Hawkes unites the external landscapes of his earliest fiction with the disordered interiors of *Second Skin* and his triad. *The Passion Artist* focuses on sexual repression as the primary source of humanity's inability to live imaginatively. In this novel, Hawkes creates a static and devastated cityscape that is disrupted by an inmate uprising at a penal institution for women. The prison functions simultaneously as the embodiment of modern civilization's repressive forces and as the chamber that confines the male protagonist's deepest fears as well as his singular opportunity for achieving understanding and freedom. In *Virginie: Her Two Lives,* Hawkes alternates his story and setting between a low-rent boardinghouse in Paris at the end of World War II and a castle in the French countryside in 1740. Narrated by an eleven-year-old protagonist who is portrayed as the personification of erotic innocence, this novel suggests that every society and each individual possesses the capacity for both sexual freedom and degradation. *Adventures in the Alaskan Skin Trade* is a psychological study of the effects of subconscious irrationality on human behavior. Revealed as the childhood memories of the forty-year-old female narrator, this book examines such thematic concerns as guilt, myth, failure, cruelty, masculinity, and the relationships between fathers and daughters.

In addition to his novels, Hawkes has also published a volume of poetry, *Fiasco Hall* (1943), and a collection of one-act dramatic works, *The Innocent Party: Four Short Plays* (1966), which contains *The Wax Museum, The Questions, The Undertaker,* and *The Innocent Party.* His short fiction is gathered in *Lunar Landscapes: Stories and Short Novels, 1949-1963*

(1969) and *The Universal Fears* (1978). *Innocence in Extremis* (1985) is a novella which includes characters from *Adventures in the Alaskan Skin Trade*.

(See also *CLC*, Vols. 1, 2, 3, 4, 7, 9, 14, 15, 27; *Contemporary Authors,* Vols. 1-4, rev. ed.; *Contemporary Authors New Revision Series,* Vol. 2; *Dictionary of Literary Biography,* Vols. 2, 7; and *Dictionary of Literary Biography Yearbook: 1980.*)

ARTHUR C. DANTO

John Hawkes is the Cellini of contemporary fiction, a demonic artificer of works in verbal virtu. The surviving masterpiece of the legendary goldsmith is the great saltcellar of Vienna, an extravagant and mannered ornament almost ironically disproportionate to its residual domestic function as a holder of the king's condiment. So with the intricately filigreed exercises in narrative architecture typical of Mr. Hawkes: they are achievements in the craft of pure imagination and disproportionate to any of the residual uses to which literature might be put. Indeed, they are typically based on premises so impossible that there is no way they could be realized outside the precincts of imagination and so no way they could be utilized for anything except art. . . .

This characterization of Mr. Hawkes's writing is reinforced by the format of *Humors of Blood & Skin,* in which excerpts from his various novels, together with four pieces of short fiction and an extract from a work in progress, are ranged as though in a gallery of gems, exhibited as so many specimens of hammered gold and gold enameling, with helpful explanatory display cards set in front of each. In these he describes those experiences in his life that provided the occasions for his fictions, which are transformations of them through so many strata of imagination that even the ''autobiographical'' novel in progress turns the author into a little girl who is to grow up to be mistress of a lucrative brothel. (Mr. Hawkes earns his livelihood as a teacher of writing.) So it is about as confessional as everything else, which is to say scarcely at all. In addition, Mr. Hawkes furnishes for the unfamiliarized reader outlines of the settings in which the displayed pieces were originally embedded.

It is surprising how little these writings gain in intelligibility from either kind of context. They seem so suspended in their Tiffany-window spaces as to feel complete, and one cannot distinguish the excerpts from the short fictions, or truncated novels from fragments of fully achieved ones. It is as though each part were a whole unto itself, which is perhaps inevitable, given the impossibility of the containing structures and the fact that no part implies the existence of any other. . . . The parts of his novels are held together by the energies of ruthless artistic will rather than by any inner narrative urgency.

On the other hand, seeing all of Mr. Hawkes's work assembled in retrospective juxtaposition enables us to understand things about individual works that may have been concealed from us on isolated readings. These works might, for example, have seemed to be about what in fact only occasioned them, as *The Cannibal* of 1949 (which, incidentally, gains immensely by being extracted from) must have appeared to be saying something about Germany and about defeat. Certainly, in that cascade of astonishing images with which the book begins, of dismemberment, death, deprivation—the debris of *après-guerre*—Mr. Hawkes seems to have worked up a picture of the frozen hopelessness of the nuclear winter. But bit by bit the imagery becomes too opulent, motivations become too dotty and oblique, the enactments too abstractly symbolic, and in the light of the total corpus, *The Cannibal* now seems to have used Germany much as Mr. Hawkes has used his material throughout, only as something to process into fiction, like those almost incidental experiences—a chill draft, a distant bark—that set a dream going.

Current literary theory offers us the conception of the self-contained work, a theory given an abrupt generalization in the thought of Jacques Derrida, for whom, since everything is text, there is nothing outside the text. Happily, Mr. Derrida's theory collapses the moment one seeks to apply it, but the more limited theory of literature he has inspired is almost perfectly confirmed by Mr. Hawkes's work—it is as though they were made for one another. But in fact, the theory is as unfair to Mr. Hawkes as it is to that wide body of texts that do mean to be about something outside themselves. For he has striven to achieve an autonomy of imagination, and it diminishes him to say that to be a text at all is already to be self-contained. His achievements match his considerable gifts, but both are limited. In the end, even with a genius like Cellini, the goldsmith's art is one of constrained amazement. When the last page has been turned, one has the sense that despite the nightmare extremity of the episodes one has been driven through—execution, torture, rape, cannibalism, dismemberment, to be sure, betrayal, incest, disappearance, suicide, incineration, madness, sickness, starvation, abandonment, ritual cruelty—and despite all the sex-shop gear of chains, chastity belts, whips, pincers, frilled panties, needles, ropes, pistols and dungeons, one has thought, mostly, about the marvelous prose.

In one of his pieces, a man says: "You can't even smell it, boy. No ashes. No smoke. Nothing. It's just a reflection—a reflection of some fiery nightmare. Don't you see"? The narrator responds: "Sure. If that's what you want. But I prefer a little more than weeds and discoloration." These fictions are reflections of fiery nightmares. "The beauty of the nightmare," Mr. Hawkes writes, "is that it inevitably shows forth some unattainable ideal." Because unattainable, the ideal extends the nightmare, and if you too prefer a little more, you must read elsewhere. Mr. Hawkes has the power to do, gorgeously and as art, what most of us can at best do drably and as dream—transform incident into phantasm. For connoisseurs of this rare craft, the refined rewards are frequent and the pleasures subtle and the charms undeniable.

Arthur C. Danto, *"Gems without Their Settings,"* in The New York Times Book Review, *November 25, 1984, p. 3.*

JACQUELINE AUSTIN

Adventures in the Alaskan Skin Trade has one major flaw which runs straight down the center—the protagonist could not be who she says she is—but that does not make it any less vivid or intriguing. There is a double dialectic here: yarning versus dreaming, naturalism versus supernaturalism. And how many times a year does there come along a novel which could have been sired by Jack London and Flannery O'Connor, which would be equally at home on the bookshelf next to Dylan Thomas . . . Eskimo myths . . . Xavier Hollander . . . Freud?

The heroine, a sort of inverse Eve, fits right into Hawkes's pantheon of seducers, icemen, and Oedipi. Sunny (Jacqueline Burne Deauville for long) is an all woman woman, dragged up to Alaska at the age of five by her larger-than-life father, "Uncle Jake," on a search for his personal icon—a totem pole topped by an image of Lincoln. Now it's the '60s, and Sunny, all grown up, has more than fulfilled her early promise by becoming the proprietress of Gamelands, an oddball whorehouse. Gamelands is a retreat in more ways than one: a gleaming trailer park set in the middle of an Alaskan wilderness. At the gate is Sunny's answer to her father's search: a totem pole on which naked women ecstatically climb toward a statuette of Uncle Jake. At Gamelands, sex is lusty and guilt-free, the fifth of nature's elements; it is anything but neurotic:

> Sex is my favorite word. It's a nice word, a cute word, a tiny green snake stiff in the mouth. . . . The smallness and closeness of the ear is drawn to that sound as no other. No sooner does anyone say it— sex—than you want to put your ear to his mouth. . . .

This preoccupation with language, with verbal rhythms, certainly brands Sunny as a Hawkes creation. With her 24-carat heart, six-shooter taste in clothing, and 39-year-old "nubile" body, as well as her exalted speaking and thinking style, she is sometimes a classic male fantasy figure, more often than not. Sunny concentrates on making much out of the English language, flying her airplane, interpreting and refining her bad dreams, and trying to determine the nature of her truest, deepest feelings about the past. All of these endeavors are linked to handsome Uncle Jake, whose major aim in life, besides being an American-style Canadian Mountie and entrepreneur, was to tell the best stories in and around Juneau.

Sunny has inherited Uncle Jake's propensities and verbal exhibitionism along with the sweet charms of her pallid, flowerlike mother. Mostly she dreams about her father and, while finding these dreams horrible, relishes and retells them. I wanted to adore Sunny. In the first half of the book she (and the conceptual morass surrounding her) was enthralling, but then she began to annoy me. Why is such a strong woman so hung up on her father, well beyond the age at which she plausibly would have begun to resolve her conflicted feelings? Why does such an idiosyncratic woman fit so patly into nauseating stereotypes? Granted, *Adventures* is an exploration of myth and stereotype; yet, like many a dedicated anthropological essay, it overmuch becomes one with its object of study. Sunny, the construct, does not do Sunny, the character, full justice.

At the book's beginning, haunted by the nightmares, she has just about decided to pack it in and go to France. Later, the nightmares become fact: a female incarnation of Uncle Jake descends from the Hawkean Valhalla to take over Sunny's boyfriend as well as Gamelands. . . .

This woman, Marty, has arms like "a Brahmin cow," breasts jutting like crags from the ocean, a square jaw; she swills champagne as if it were light beer and is covered with the scars of a bear's embrace. She is larger than life, certainly larger than Sunny, and she epitomizes the swallowing of Sunny by nightmare images of Uncle Jake. if it hasn't become clear that *Adventures* is structured on fictional levels, each of which raises the ante and prepares for the next, by the time Marty fades away she has exposed the book's endoskeleton. The only person who can upstage Marty is, of course, Uncle Jake himself: *Adventures* climaxes not when Marty takes over Gamelands, but when Sunny discovers exactly how, and when, Jake died.

In the rush of structures and discourses and levels of language, Sunny is occasionally lost. Some of the things she says are absurd, while meaning, I think, to be mythic and resounding. "In sex I have found my father's gold mine" is a statement so literal that it sounds comic, and what woman would refer to her own breasts as "fulsome"? Still, Sunny's mind is, at foundation, of neuter gender, genuine emotions, and maximum intelligence; she has not been treated by Hawkes with condescension. She is a worthy attempt to turn archetype into reality. Her secondary sexual characteristics are admirable, and, more important, she's a good sport, as ready to hike up a mountain or enjoy a good belly laugh as to moon about Daddy or entertain a client. And her dreams, such as the one which opens the book, tend to be marvels. . . .

In its attempts to blend subconscious and conscious realities, surrealism and superrealism, *Adventures* massively but unselfconsciously comments on the nature of fiction. It has many of the same concerns as the "metafiction" of the '60s, without falling into the obnoxious abstractions of that form. This is because it sticks close to its sources, and approaches them from the inside, rather than skating around on their surfaces. Jack London's Alaska has been absorbed and transformed in *Adventures,* but not discarded; Mark Twain's naturalism and humor, particularly that of *Life on the Mississippi,* and in its dark incarnations, of *Huckleberry Finn,* have been used, with love, keeping their original impulses intact.

For the primary source, and for the title, Hawkes has turned to another autumn writer, Dylan Thomas, whose *Adventures in the Skin Trade* was perhaps the prototypical nightmare novel. Opening as young Samuel Bennett destroys his parents' house and never finishing, with excursions into drowning, seduction, cutting loose the moorings, coffin images, ludicrous sex, and race, *Adventures in the Skin Trade* prefigures Hawkes's *Adventures* not in plot, but in feelings. When Samuel has to go about London with the bottle stuck on his finger, when he fantasizes in a lunchroom about a woman aged 38, when he sinks in the bathtub after meeting Polly, these are all nightmare moments hooked into a dark and queasy reality: Samuel is not so sunny, and neither, at heart, is Sunny. Jake may find his icon, and Sunny may exorcise hers, and nothing beats death so well as living in the present, but as Sunny knows, and Hawkes seems to say time and again, winter's just around the corner, and spring may never come.

Jacqueline Austin, "Seductive Reasoning," in The Village Voice, *Vol. XXX, No. 38, September 17, 1985, p. 45.*

BOB HALLIDAY

Longtime admirers of John Hawkes' fiction who have had trouble with his past two novels can relax: his new book, *Adventures in the Alaskan Skin Trade,* is one of his very best. (p. 5)

Readers who pick up the novel will get yanked in so quickly that they may forget who it is they're dealing with: a writer whose true subject is the irrational reality that lies under the surface of things. In this case, the surface is the adventure-packed memoir of an Alaskan whorehouse madam with the unlikely name of Sunny Deauville. Underneath, it is a psychological study of a disturbed father-daughter relationship, so powerful and acute that it bears comparison with Christina Stead's great *The Man Who Loved Children.*

Like Sam Pollit, the demonic father in Stead's novel, John Burne Deauville, Sunny's father, is an irresistibly magnetic figure. After bringing his wife and daughter to Juneau in 1930, he chases around after adventure, casting his family in whatever roles he finds necessary to fulfill his fantasies, and disappears without a trace in 1940. Sunny narrates all of this from the standpoint of 1965, when she is 40 years old and desperately trying to leave Alaska, the land of her father's disappearance, and travel to France, where he was born.

A large portion of the novel is made up of Sunny's retellings of her father's accounts of his adventures, spun out to family and friends each time he returns home. The tales themselves are whoppers: killing giant bears, pulling teeth for suffering Indian chiefs, rescuing prospectors driven mad by mosquitos, but it quickly becomes clear that Sunny's feelings will not permit her to recount his narratives accurately. She is possessed by her memories of her father, wounded by his unexplained disappearance and abandonment of her to a degree she can't begin to express directly, and her portrait of him is grotesque with the distortions wrought by 25 years of tortured and unresolved speculation about him. He emerges as a kind of spring-wound incarnation of the Boy Scout Oath, a monster of manly virtue and relentless self-conscious moral purity, who speaks a laundered macho idiom straight out of boys' adventure fiction as he unconsciously destroys those who are closest to him.

From the outset, John Deauville sets up impassable barriers between his family and himself. He is especially creative in using nicknames to undermine natural relationships: his daughter becomes Sunny; his wife, Cecily turns into Sissy, and he himself "a few months prior to going to Alaska . . . renicknamed himself Uncle Jake . . . My father, then, was Uncle Jake. I was not allowed to call him Father. I was never allowed to call him Dad. Especially was I never allowed to call him Dad." . . . He is also ambivalent in his perception of pain in those who love him. He never becomes aware of Sissy's crushing unhappiness in Alaska, and even though he suffers mightily as she is being treated for a toothache, he fails to observe the symptoms of the heart disease which will kill his wife after five years in the unhospitable territory.

Although Uncle Jake is a handsome and dashing man, he is so oblivious to sexual identity that he spends years in the vicinity of a Juneau hotel swarming with prostitutes without ever realizing that they are anything other than friendly women who know how to give a warm greeting if you meet then in the corridor. He knows how to mix a wicked punch, but will never touch anything stronger than ginger ale, and emphatically forbids family and friends from sipping even a beer. He never questions the presumed natural inferiority of American Indians, one of several firmly held prejudices that Sunny records without comment.

Her judgment on all of this is her chosen style of living, which is in effect a gigantic reaction against Uncle Jake. In response to his puritanism she construct the Alaska-Yukon Gamelands, a kind of theme park brothel which caters to the supermales which populate Sunny's Alaska. After her father's disappearance she wastes little time in sacrificing her virginity to an Indian named Sitka Charley, and she has no aversion at all to alcohol.

But his rejection takes a toll. Fight it as she may, Sunny is still Daddy's girl. The first word of her memoir is "Dad," despite the injunction, and throughout her account she unwittingly romanticizes her father extravagantly. Her account of his courtship of Sissy, for example, is an elaborate paraphrase of the Cinderella story, complete with malicious sisters and fateful footwear. More poignantly, he haunts her dreams. Even those who know the surrealist methods of Hawkes' first novels will be amazed at the power of the nightmares he creates for Sunny: tight formulations of failures and guilt which embrace the reader with the suffocating pressure of real dreams. In each of them she rather impassively watches Uncle Jake die a gruesome death as he requests her help with equal impassiveness.

All refer to his request that "when I go—when it's my turn to go—you're the only person I want at my funeral. Not even [my partner] Fran, Sunny, just you." Sunny can never really move on until she participates in some form of funeral for him, even if it is just an understanding of his disappearance. Such a revelation does occur, and it forms the crux of the novel, heralding Sunny's liberation from her guilt and acceptance of herself.

Sunny is a fascinating character, and she keeps the book constantly and vigorously alive. Some of her reminiscences jolt with their perverse originality, such as her account of how the most virile of her lovers was stolen by the astounding Martha Washington, an amazon aviatrix and adventuress whose penny-dreadful life succeeds in all the areas where Uncle Jake's fails. But Hawkes' greatest success in *Adventures* is the depth with which he permits the reader to understand Uncle Jake despite the narrator's various blindnesses. He passes the fact of Uncle Jake's vast vulnerability right over Sunny's head to the reader, showing the deep scars left by the neglect, the suicide of loved ones and other forms of emotional abandonment which had been part of his upbringing. (*Innocence in Extremis,* a long story by Hawkes in the current issue of *Conjunctions* recounts an incident from Uncle Jake's childhood that makes a passing but important appearance in the novel.) Uncle Jake's compulsive bravado and unintentional cruelty come to seem inevitable and pathetic. One episode dealing with his fear of heights is particularly wrenching, as is a hint midway through the book that he already foresees his end.

But Hawkes captures his Alaskans alive; he never makes the book hold still for a session of character analysis. It zips along like the page-turner it is, and it is only in retrospect that one really appreciates its profundities. *Adventures in the Alaskan Skin Trade* is the most moving and accessible novel yet from one of the most distinguished of American writers. It should be with us for a long time. (pp. 5-6)

Bob Halliday, "Father and Daughter," in Book World—The Washington Post, *September 29, 1985, pp. 5-6.*

JACK BEATTY

Adventures in the Alaskan Skin Trade refers to nothing outside itself; it sets off, as you read it, none of those anticipations of significance you expect of serious fiction; it lacks the tug of profundity that pulls you through a book and amounts to a promise from the author that behind his story is his real subject and your task as a reader is to crack the narrative code disguising it: Imagine *Moby-Dick* as just—as only—what Hemingway called it, "a fish story," and you have a model for understanding this often gorgeous prose poem to Alaska and to male camaraderie. . . .

[Sound] and rhythm, the music of writing, is what Mr. Hawkes is interested in here, not in plot, character, psychology, society,

history or the cosmos. Not even in sex, for every word in this book could be reproduced in a family newspaper; and although the narrator is a prostitute, the sex scenes are few, and they are handled obliquely, more as poetic than as carnal transactions. And yet, as in Nabokov's elaborate word puzzles, there are moments of beautifully conveyed emotion in this novel. It is as if the author permits himself to stoop to what Nabokov called "human interest," the bastard satisfactions—cognitive and moral—of the realistic novel, only rarely and then only after the most exquisite refinement of the effect. It is the literary equivalent of nouvelle cuisine, and, as a meat and potatoes, not to say ham and egg, reader, I found I wanted something more.

Though sex is Sunny's profession, "father-love" is the subject of the tale she has to tell. Sunny's father is an adventurer nicknamed Uncle Jake ("I was not allowed to call him Father. I was never allowed to call him Dad"), who leaves a comfortable life in Connecticut, in 1929, to journey to Alaska with his wife, Sissy, and Sunny. . . . The novel opens with Sunny, in 1965, reviewing the last decade of her father's life, after he got to Juneau. Even though Gamelands is prosperous, she is thinking of leaving Alaska for France, where the Deauvilles came from in the late 19th century, for she is stalked by visions of her father pleading with her to save him, and she wants desperately to escape from these torments over a man 25 years in the grave. At the end, Sunny decides to stay in Alaska ("So here I am, an Alaskan woman feeling good in her skin in Alaska") because of what she learns from one of her father's friends, Sitka Charley, about his mysterious death, while on one of his adventures, in 1940.

Uncle Jake is one of those men whose lives would be unendurable if they had the merest spark of imagination. He seems to be modeled on a figure like Frank ("Bring 'Em Back Alive") Buck. While Sissy cries herself to sleep every night from fear and loneliness, Uncle Jake lives a life of pure adventure. He had not been in Juneau a day before he had found what every adventurer must have, a partner, Frank Morley, the owner of a gun shop and a man who gives his aging heart to Uncle Jake, plucky, hale, hearty, blind to danger, alive to duty, a hero of constancy and uprightness. Sometimes alone, sometimes with Frank Morley or a bush pilot friend, Rex Ainsworth, and sometimes with Sissy and Sunny, Uncle Jake (who seems to have no means of making a living) makes a career of rushing to the aid of people in distress in the remote wilderness. . . .

Why is Uncle Jake an adventurer? Mr. Hawkes does not provide a clue. The dissection of motive is not his game. This is a boy's book of adventures as seen by a not very credible girl. As a woman, though, Sunny is a man's dream—an ideal listener. Along with Frank and Sissy and Sissy's friend Hilda, she expresses her love for Jake by hearing out the stories of his adventures with a rapt attention. It is in the depictions of this quality of love as listening that a real toad or two pops up in Mr. Hawkes's imaginary tundra and the reader is moved, stirred in his feelings for life, not merely in his feelings for art. These moments, precious as they are, are few. The tall tales crowd them out.

John Hawkes's prose carries a charge of intensity beside which the ordinary run of writing seems pathetically underfelt. There are, moreover, images and whole scenes in this novel that have clearly sprung from an artist's imagination, strange, haunted and wonderfully expressive. But in the end, *Adventures in the Alaskan Skin Trade* is too claustral, too confined in its range of reference, for all its size too small. It is like a giant brown bear that casts no shadow; or, better still, like Alaska itself—cold, grand and all but empty.

Innocence in Extremis is an outtake from *Skin Trade,* whose publisher may have adjudged it a digression damaging to the art or, more likely, to the already slim commercial appeal of the mother text. *Innocence* details a visit to the Deauville ancestral estate in France, undertaken by Uncle Jake's family and retinue of servants in 1892, when Jake was a small and chaste American boy. It includes two marvelously done scenes of high eroticism. One depicts the crushing of the estate's harvest of grapes by a group of village virgins, their unembarrassed flesh exposed to the greedy eyes of an array of aristocrats seated in plush Empire chairs. Their performance is introduced and orchestrated by the "Old Gentleman," Jake's rakish grandfather, whose amatory adventures throw a late but welcome light not only upon Sunny's choice of profession but also upon Jake's own lust for adventure of a more innocent sort. The other scene is the mating of a mare in heat, a copulation staged and savored by the wanton old man. *Innocence in Extremis,* would have provided the makings of a fine erotic comedy for Jean Renoir, the French film director. It is an inspired visual piece of writing. . . .

> *Jack Beatty, "Uncle Jake and the Mosquito-Crazed Prospector," in* The New York Times Book Review, *September 29, 1985, p. 9.*

RICHARD GILMAN

John Hawkes's new novel [*Adventures in the Alaskan Skin Trade*] is much his longest, his most conventional in substance and manner, and by a wide margin his worst. The book comes wrapped in deception, from the title and dust jacket (a painting of a long stockinged female leg thrusting a spike-heeled shoe through a set of deer or elk or caribou horns), which promise erotic exploration and discovery such as have been among Hawkes's stocks-in-trade, to its description by the publisher as a "psychological thriller of stunning depth and perception." There's not a thing erotic about the book. It offers a few mild thrills of a physical kind but none of a psychic nature, and its perceptions are so far below Hawkes's usual level as to make you wonder what calamity of the literary imagination has struck here.

To dispose of the narrative, or plot, first. Jacqueline Deauville, called Sunny (pun), is taken . . . in 1929 from Connecticut to Alaska, the result of a sudden decision by her father, John, who for unexplained reasons insists on being called Uncle Jake. He is a peculiar fellow, full of grandiose and, as it turns out, sterile ambitions; flamboyant and puritanical at the same time, he needed, Sunny tells us, "some vastness to smile upon." The mother, Sissy, is a woman who has "spent her poor wronged life clinging to music and femininity." She dies in 1935 and Sunny, now ten, is raised by Uncle Jake and several other "colorful" characters, who give her an education in frontier, largely masculine existence.

The story ends in 1965 with Jake having disappeared and Sunny working as the proprietor of the Alaska-Yukon Gamelands, an elaborate whorehouse about whose activities, unfortunately, we're told next to nothing. In the same way we're informed that Sunny's motto is "Heed Hedonism," that "sex is [her] favorite word," and that a bumper sticker on her jeep reads "sworn to fun, loyal to none," but nothing in the novel bears out any of this.

Although Sunny is the narrator, the book's protagonist is clearly her father. This is where the trouble begins and stays centered, for protagonist literally means "first contestant," more subtly the character in whom psychic struggle or moral suffering is chiefly played out, and for the life of me I can't determine what struggle or suffering Uncle Jake is undergoing. One possibility, if a thin one, is suggested by Sunny's frequent disparaging references to his exuberant and ham-fisted machismo. He lives, she says, "among the dark shadows of male certitude," has "mannish *mannerisms*," and offers "false flourishes of manhood."

If we add the facts that his own father was a sexual innocent while his grandfather seems to have been a satyr and that the family has fallen from rather high estate, becoming progressively more effete, Hawkes may mean that Jake is working out some male destiny designed to cut through, resolve, or transcend his psychic and moral inheritance. Alaska, huge, raw, infinitely *possible*, almost nothing at the time but future, would then be a fertile setting for such novelistic action.

But what undermines this desperate thesis of mine is that Alaska isn't so much a setting as a subject, and one that's treated by Hawkes, astonishingly, in a manner reminiscent not of Faulkner and the South or of Edith Wharton and New York but of Michener and Texas or Hawaii. We learn what Juneau was like 50 years ago and how it got its name. We're told that the word "mush" as an order to sled dogs comes from the French "marche," to "go," and that bannocks-cakes are made from flour and glacial water. There are tales of the exploits of bush-pilots and the perils of their work, stories of crazed Indians and giant marauding bears, and futile searches for precious metals. It's as though Hawkes, one of the most oblique, gifted, and rigorous of our literary stylists, a writer for whom language has always been paramount and physical reality mainly a ground for verbal invention, wants to prove now that he can spin a yarn with the best of them.

Within my longtime admiration for Hawkes's work there have been pockets of irritation, annoyance at the way his imagination sometimes archly attenuates itself, occasional discomfort at the strain of cruelty he can exhibit. But I've never come close to being embarrassed by his writing the way I am by this novel. By turns flaccid or forced, sentimental, cute, *false*, it almost never affords delight or even satisfaction. A mildly arresting line like this—"I woke . . . to the blank consciousness from which the genie of unexpected life leaps forth"—is so rare as to reinforce one's conviction that the book is a huge aberration in Hawkes's career. (p. 44)

> *Richard Gilman, "Empty Vastness," in* The New Republic, *Vol. 193, No. 2, November 18, 1985, pp. 44-5.*

IRVING MALIN

This significant novella [*Innocence in Extremis*] ends with the paragraph: "Their return crossing was the worst Atlantic crossing in nineteen years." I stress the word "crossing" because Hawkes, as usual, is interested in the energies and strategies of movement, transformation, juxtaposition. His title is, of course, a clue to the process.

Jake, the adolescent American, visits France with his extended family—including the mistresses of his lecherous father—and he believes that he will be a routine voyager. He soon discovers that he cannot merely view spectacles, static objects. He unconsciously—and then consciously—participates in the dream-like, surrealistic scenes. Thus his innocence crosses the border, the edge.

When Hawkes describes the ride of a mysterious girl on a horse or the crushing of grapes by village virgins—these events occur in a classical subsconscious—he gives us the odd gesture, the incongruity.... Hawkes believes that life is opposition between symmetry and incongruity. The "balance" of experience is tense, ready to explode. His sentences, although apparently "classical" and "congruous," threaten us because we wait (as does Jake in "real life") for the sudden jump, the off-center, descriptive detail.

Jake loses his innocence. He learns that he must be constantly alert so that he can appreciate all events. He accepts the "crossings" of life. Therefore he reflects Hawkes's style (or vice versa). Hero and author merge in an eerie manner.

I suggest that this novella is one of Hawkes's most brilliant works because of the compressed balance, the deliberately controlled incongruities. It will not be easily forgotten; it is a dangerous, beautiful, final *crossing*.

> *Irving Malin, in a review of "Innocence in Extremis," in* The Hollins Critic, *Vol. XXII, No. 5, December, 1985, p. 12.*

ARTHUR WALDHORN

Although less than a hundred pages long, *Innocence in Extremis* has the familiar ingredients that either enthrall or repel (and nearly always confuse). Hawkes machines the most ingenious and baneful tropes currently being shaped in American fiction. His landscapes seem surreal and hallucinatory; the natural and man-made objects that fill them feel and smell of the overripe and the rotten; and the violators and victims who flesh out his often nightmarish scenes lend support to his asserted goal "never to let the reader off the hook, never to let him think that the picture is any less black or that there is any easy way out of the nightmare of human existence."

Possibly intended as a prelude to *Adventures in the Alaskan Skin Trade,* this short novel about an adolescent is selfcontained but, read along with its much longer companion, it provides useful insights into the youth's subsequent failure as husband and father. Uncle Jake is a 12-year-old in the early Fall of 1892 when his father brings the family to visit the ancestral Deauville estate in Chantilly, France.... The ritual passage fails to draw Uncle Jake from boyhood to manhood. What Uncle Jake sees and suffers at Chantilly includes a stasis that may freeze him forever in the extreme innocence of the title—his only refuge from corruption he can neither understand nor abide.

And yet, nothing grisly or unnatural happens. A light-hearted (one might even venture "innocent") hedonism plays across the surface. "We live," says the Old Gentleman, Jake's grandfather, "only to honor our horses, our women, and our grapes." The Deauville motto is "Nothing Too Much," its creed, "Ours is a morality of excess." Both the father and the grandfather trivialize sex with their servants and secretaries. Uncle Jake's mother, while expressing outrage at the Deauville's immoderation, secretly anticipates a possible bout of sex with her father-in-law. At first glance, then, the operative mode seems to be akin to Ingmar Bergman's gentle irony in *Smiles of a Summer Night,* those special smiles reserved for "the simpleton and the incorrigible." But although irony abounds in *Innocence*

in Extremis, it has turned sour and acerb, the smiles indecorous and lewd.

Although he says and does nothing, Uncle Jake is responsible for the shadows that darken the mood. A wholly passive spectator, he embodies inviolate innocence ripe for desecration. His grandfather, a benign but determined sadist, orchestrates the rites. In each of three brilliantly evocative episodes, the Old Gentleman undertakes to awaken desire in his grandson. In the first, he displays Jake's beautiful 14-year-old cousin in an exhibition of horsemanship erotically designed "to bring to absolute fruition the beauty of the young girl and her steed." Jake is awed by her skill, admiring of her beauty, but unsullied by lust. A few weeks later, the Old Gentleman offers Jake a festive pageant of naked village girls treading vintage grapes in a trough. Among them—and the fairest of all—is his cousin: "My gift to you," the Old Gentleman whispers to the now aroused but abashed, confused, miserable, and speechless boy.

Not a word of Jake's is recorded. He merely looks, listens, nods, and recoils. Yet his silence explodes eloquently into an incoherent stammer at the climax of the Old Gentleman's third and final staging: Jake and his cousin watch a stallion mount a brood mare in heat. By the time Jake sails for America soon after (he will endure yet further an unsettling encounter with his grandfather's mistress and with a broken-necked corpse), he will have shored against the ruins of his lost innocence only "emptiness, silence and injured pride."

Innocence in Extremis is more accessible than much of Hawkes's fiction. Its narrative line is straightforward, its structure clear and firm, its images readily (too readily?) comprehensible. What Hawkes fails to resolve, however, is an ambivalence he engenders in our response to Jake's plight. Although the Old Gentleman's sadism is undeniable, he has done little more than dramatize for his favorite grandson scenes of commonplace eroticism. Jake's fourteen-year-old cousin, for example, is not shattered by these revelations about the animal side of human behavior. On the contrary, she gracefully and joyfully participates in the rituals. Does this signify her corruption? Hawkes fails to let us know. Like many of his readers, Hawkes seems trapped in a characteristically American paradox—between an urbane acceptance of sensuality and an agonized, Puritanic rejection of its destructive impact upon unsoiled, Edenic innocence. *Innocence in Extremis* affords readers an engrossing introduction to Hawkes's concerns and his craft. It should also encourage them to pursue their study of Jake in the companion volume, *Adventures in the Alaskan Skin Trade.*

> *Arthur Waldhorn, "Introducing Hawkes," in* The American Book Review, *Vol. 8, No. 4, May-June, 1986, p. 12.*

CAROL A. MacCURDY

The verbal "pictures" in John Hawkes's novels are unforgettable, provocative visions that have perhaps more impact on the reader than any other element in Hawkes's fiction. Descriptions of a slumbering insane asylum, an arid desert inhabited by giant snakes, an abandoned lighthouse amidst sharp, black rocks, a lyrical Illyria of no seasons, an anchorless, drifting ocean liner, and a car streaking toward destruction are all powerful images that dominate such other fictional elements as plot, character, or theme. Rather than exploring a subject or pursuing the location of "truth," Hawkes wishes to enthrall, capture, and enchant the reader with the intensity of his vision. He chooses not to offer an accurate representation of an independent, pre-existing reality but insists on the creation of, in his words, "a totally new and necessary fictional landscape or visionary world." (p. 318)

These worlds are the end result of the creative process, the repository of Hawkes's unconscious, as well as the source of his writing. What has not been well understood is their essentiality to Hawkes's aesthetic and their development in technique and focus. Hawkes's imaginary worlds have evolved since he first published in 1949, and these changes reflect the four distinct phases in his literary career: 1) the use of visionary landscape tied to specific locales; 2) the use of landscape projected out of first-person perspectives; 3) the use of landscape totally contained by psyches; and 4) the return—with a difference—of the visionary historical landscapes found in phase one. A study of Hawkes's fictional landscapes demonstrates his continual development as a writer and also clarifies his evolving world view.

Hawkes's insistence on constructing private landscapes results in early works of "nearly pure vision." Any reader of **"Charivari,"** *The Cannibal* (1949), *The Beetle Leg* (1951), *The Owl* (1954), *The Goose on the Grave* (1954), or *The Lime Twig* (1961) will attest to their visual brilliance as well as their difficult narrative. Little sense of plot progression emerges; instead one finds stunning set pieces that dazzle the imagination while disorienting one's perceptions. These absolute visions produce surrealistic, dreamlike effects.... In **"Charivari"** a cat talks to a seamstress; marauding dogs board a passenger train and become paying customers in *The Cannibal*; and a giant desert snake strikes out the headlight of a vacationing family's station wagon in *The Beetle Leg*.

War dominates the landscape of Hawkes's novels between 1949 and 1964. Set in post-World War II England, Germany, and Italy, these locales seem standard World War II fare, yet Hawkes's hallucinated vision makes the desolate backgrounds not places but nightmares. Rid of most signs of civilization, the primitive landscapes seem timeless reminders of war's horrors, a world void of reason and doomed to annihilation. In *The Cannibal* Hawkes bestows upon Germany a completely fictional, nonexistent town, *Spitzen-on-the-Dein*, a setting that epitomizes his warscapes, especially those in *The Owl* and *The Goose on the Grave*. *Spitzen-on-the-Dein*, "shriveled in structure and as decomposed as an ox tongue black with ants," is a debris-ridden village stripped of any civilizing influence. Using the metaphor of a vulture or carrion bird, Hawkes pictures the town as a giant slumbering fowl: "The town, roosting on charred earth, no longer ancient, . . . gorged itself on straggling beggars and remained gaunt beneath an evil cloaked moon." This fatalistic picture suggests inevitable human extinction, as do most of Hawkes's early war-ravaged landscapes.

All of Hawkes's fictions from **"Charivari"** to *The Lime Twig*, whether or not they are war-related, present such apocalyptic landscapes bereft of life-sustaining energies. Tony Tanner suggests that Hawkes's "landscapes of desolation and decline . . . point to the progress of entropy quite as graphically as the landscapes of Burroughs and Pynchon." Indeed, each setting in the early work conveys nothing but waste and death. In *The Cannibal* nature itself has become mutant or exhausted; this wasteland yields only "twisted stunted trees," "bleached plants," acidic earth that burns human flesh, and cows that scratch for food with hare's teeth. In such a desiccated landscape man likewise is depraved, as illustrated by the Duke's eating of the young boy. Entropic landscapes underscore not only man's fall from innocence but, more important, his plunge

into nightmare. For example, in *The Beetle Leg,* Gov City and its inhabitants live in the shadow of obliteration as the manmade dam drifts forward, promising again the Great Slide. Instead of being tamed, the American frontier is hostilely swallowing up impotent cowboys. In *The Owl,* the medieval town, Sasso Fetore, meaning "Tomb Stench," is a barren fortress of violence, sterility, and death. In *The Goose on the Grave,* a grim, war-scarred Italy leaves an orphan exposed to the degeneracies of failing Western culture. Clearly, the terrain of a world in shambles, with such breaches of nature and violations of humanity, comments on the condition of modern man.

These ominous settings not only suggest the state of their inhabitants but also dominate them. Environment controls and circumscribes human action. In *The Cannibal* the characters seem doomed to recapitulate the history of their war-ravaged world. In *The Owl* the townspeople of Sasso Fetore are subject to the Owl's inhuman demands just as their town is dominated by his iron fortress. In *The Beetle Leg* the great silent desert renders minuscule the clustered human communities. And in *The Lime Twig* Michael and Margaret Banks, children of war and lodgers of Dreary Station, seem destined to collapse with the dreams of a lost generation. Imprisoned by such hostile landscapes, people become aimless creatures somnambulating across a geography that determines their behavior. Even the social institutions created to give order inevitably contribute to the general collapse. All the institutions in *The Cannibal*—the asylum, University, and nunnery—are doomed to failure. Their commitment to the preservation of social order ensures ruin because in this world the apparent order is war. Rather than impeding the surrounding world's decline through the imposition of controls, the existing social institutions accelerate it. Any effort to control chaos promotes only an entropic decline into deathly uniformity and stasis. Both modern man and his environment, therefore, promote entropy, which, according to the second law of thermodynamics, results in an ultimate state of inert uniformity. Neither nature nor man is benign and ordered; an incipient chaos rages in both.

Because both man and his environment are identified with the potentional for destruction, no clash between life-sustaining and death-oriented impulses occurs. Humanity is just as corrupt as the surrounding world.... As a result, characters appear flat, the narrative remains impersonal, the structure is circular, the images are death-ridden, and the settings are imprisoning. A tensionless, inert universe reigns. Largely deterministic, these dark hallucinatory landscapes suggest Hawkes's early world view.

Beginning in 1964, Hawkes's emphasis changes. Rather than concentrating on the depiction of a dark, powerful world, he begins to stress modern man's reaction to chaos. Trapped in a wasteland, isolated, full of anxiety, and unable to communicate, man falls back upon himself. Because his external environment is not congenial to the self, he marks off the "inner" world from the "outer" world and turns inward. Starting with *Second Skin,* Hawkes demonstrates the change by using a first-person point of view. This shift in narration affects the presentation of landscape and signals a new direction in Hawkes's fiction. The earlier works' sense of stasis and impersonality gives way to subjective fictions with a dramatic form. (pp. 319-22)

Instead of presenting dark, authoritarian worlds, Hawkes offers settings that serve the narrators' storytelling by dramatizing their struggle with life and death. The "plot" of *Second Skin* and *The Blood Oranges* consists of the narrators' creating lyrical landscapes in sensuous detail to offset the world's threatening forces; settings are not solely besotted with the forces of death. Discussing *Second Skin,* Hawkes acknowledges for "the first time, I think, in my fiction that there is something affirmative. . . . I got very much involved in the life-force versus death." The resulting tension between these two primal forces changes the topography of the novels after *The Lime Twig* as Hawkes increasingly structures his novels through the use of two contrasting settings. . . . In these later works Hawkes's settings express structural importance as they dramatize the narrator's struggle with Eros and Thanatos.

In order to convey this inner conflict through the novel's landscape, Hawkes uses purely imaginative settings. Searchers with maps will not locate Skipper's floating island or Cyril's mythical Illyria of no seasons; likewise, Allert's whereabouts are unknown. Skipper, Cyril, Allert, and Papa create their territories. Because of their destructive pasts and their inability to make sense of the surrounding confusion, the narrators concentrate the enormities of their existence, consciously shape them into a manageable environment, and transform the brute chaos into a fictional but consciously patterned world. . . . The memoirs of these first-person narrators are fictional projections of both mythical worlds and identities desperately trying to regain a sense of self. Stimulated by a fear of hostile forces as well as a desire for a serene, pleasurable existence, Skipper and Cyril creatively resist the excruciations of life and actively produce a reality that is consistent with their psychological and creative needs. Their fictional landscapes thus offer them self-preservation, aesthetic satisfaction, and freedom—the freedom to create a world and an identity to their liking. Skipper can be an artificial inseminator of cows, and Cyrial can be a sex-singer in Illyria. As Hawkes says to John Kuehl, "what we all want to do . . . is to create our own worlds in our own voice."

Hawkes's first-person narrators produce their fictional landscapes primarily out of a pastoral impulse. Like many American heroes, these characters withdraw from society with its deterministic limitations, guilts, anxieties, and enslavement to time. Rejecting society's boundaries and the burden of history, the mythical American hero journeys into a domain where an unspoiled beauty offers psychic renewal. Hawkes's characters share the same desire for security, repose, freedom from the flux of time, and the opportunity for a spontaneous, instinctual life. However much they may yearn for an unbounded, timeless world, such an idyllic pastoral setting is unavailable in the contemporary world. The American fables of the redemptive journey into the wilderness told by Cooper, Thoreau, Melville, Faulkner, and Hemingway now arouse mere nostalgia. (pp. 322-24)

Even though the inherited symbol of a pastoral retreat or an American Eden may evoke an ironic response, the urge for a world remote from history, where nature and art are held in balance, still exists. For Hawkes, however, the possibility for the establishment of such a pastoral ideal is through the aesthetic imagination. The landscapes themselves hold the opposing forces of life and death; it is therefore up to the narrators to create a fictive order. In essence, the narrator's creation of a fictional landscape has become the surrogate for a pastoral ideal, for within this self-created world paradoxes can be aestheticized and therefore made tolerable. In the realm of supreme fiction man can escape the flux of time and the dualism between internal and external reality. Hawkes's narrators thus attempt to become Adamic heroes in the garden of their memoirs.

In *Second Skin,* Skipper's memories of a past filled with death and violence make up much of his "naked history." His early childhood lived out at his father's mortuary, his wartime experiences, and his stay on the infernal black island, site of Cassandra's suicide, all suggest a world dominated by death. In many ways this fictional world remains as death-oriented as the earlier novels, for the cruel landscapes formed by Skipper's imagination compose most of the novel's structure. Until Skipper reaches his unnamed wandering island, the landscapes he travels harbor nothing but inexplicable malice. The affirmation in the novel comes not from Skipper's environment but from his redemptive imagination. Experiencing both psychic extremes—of Eros and Thanatos, as illustrated by the two alternating islands—Skipper chooses life over death in an act of creative will. Even though death exists on his peaceful island in the form of a cemetery, he illuminates the dark graveyard with candles to produce an "artificial day" and "to have a fete with the dead." Not denying the presence of death, he creatively resists it and instills life (creative passion) into the resistant forces of nature.

Likewise, the narrator of *The Blood Oranges,* Cyril, tries to restore his shredding tapestry of love from his pastoral retreat of Illyria. Choosing the seacoast of Shakespeare's *Twelfth Night* as his locale, Hawkes signals the reader that Cyril's country resides in his imagination, like Skipper's floating island. According to Hawkes, Illyria "actually consists of an arid landscape" that Cyril transforms into his own erotic idyll. . . . Skipper's and Cyril's pastoral worlds are not restricted to a terrestrial landscape but spring from their imaginative vitality; the two narrators vigorously pursue the creative act. The fictional landscapes of *Second Skin* and *The Blood Oranges* consist of the narrator's interior world where the restrictions of time and space are nonexistent, where the imagination reigns freely, and where the pleasure principle is enshrined. (pp. 324-25)

Following *Second Skin,* each succeeding novel in Hawkes's triad—*The Blood Oranges* (1971), *Death, Sleep & the Traveler* (1974), *Travesty* (1976)—goes a step further in banishing the rational external world to concentrate on the interior journey into the psyche. Hawkes's narrators reflect this process of reduction; external landmarks and events becoming increasingly removed from the novel's world. In the triad, Hawkes reduces landscape to private, solipsistic underworlds dominated by the narrator's unconscious needs and fears. Whereas Skipper consciously uses his imagination in a redemptive act of creativity, the other narrators increasingly pursue a destructive course. In *The Blood Oranges* Cyril wreaks havoc on his terrestrial paradise by attempting to force others into his tapestry of love. In *Death, Sleep & the Traveler* Allert floats in his anchorless ship on his own psychic waters until he is so remote, detached, and obsessed that he exists solely in his dreams. And in *Travesty* Papa confines himself to the interior of his car as he speeds toward suicide and murder. As Hawkes charts the narrator's inner migration, the destination becomes increasingly ambivalent, for the unconscious simultaneously offers freedom and annihilation.

The characters' complete isolation in their own inner landscapes emphasizes the danger of such imprisonment. Like characters in the early novels, they too are imprisoned by their environments. The difference is that they are ensnared by projects of their own making. No longer casualties of outer forces, they have become victims of their own internalization—victims of their own psyche. The artistic imagination when impelled by a disturbed psyche can shape a diminished or nightmarish world rather than a coherent one. According to Frank Lentric-chia, ''the telling sign of such self-destructive consciousness is its monolithic, absolutizing character'' where ''single vision reigns.'' Only in Skipper's *Second Skin* do the conflicting forces of life and death coexist. This healthful reconciliation results from the creative mind's ability to transform the un-intelligible into a fictive order.

In contrast to Skipper's ''naked history,'' Cyril's tapestry, which is also an artistic design, is in shreds; Illyria is coming apart at the seams because of Cyril's singleness of vision. Ironically, his tapestry, rather than weaving together the op-posing threads, unravels to reveal the polarity in his pastoral scene. When Hugh, an alien to Illyria, comes over the moun-tains and brings with him the repressive forces of civilization, Cyril is unable to incorporate Hugh's ''alien myth'' into Illyria. Hawkes suggests that Hugh is not the only character guilty of subverting life into a rigid order. Cyril's effort to raise sexual activity—a natural process—to an art form promotes disaster. Although his sexual theorizing is an attempt to compose the merging paradoxes, no erotic harmony results. Insistent on the supremacy of his vision, Cyril fails to balance the paradoxes of Eros and Thanatos. *The Blood Oranges* therefore remains Cyril's version of a failed pastoral.

Another narrator who struggles to create a world that will sustain his imagination is Allert in *Death, Sleep & the Traveler;* his imagination, however, leads him to demons. As an artist, Allert's aesthetic achievement lies solely in the creation of his dreams, but no lyrical affirmation resides in his nightmares. Allert's descent into his psyche is enacted on a large scale when he takes an uncharted ocean cruise. The novel consists of his interior journey into the oceanic depths of his uncon-scious and his subsequent effort to aestheticize the emerging terror. The narrator's location is unidentified; his detached voice speaks from a void, suggesting his isolation, deprivation, and possible madness. The story he tells alternates between two fictional landscapes—one the frigid northern world where Al-lert, Peter, and his wife Ursula form a ménage à trois, and the other a southern world of sun and sea where he journeys with Ariane and Olaf. Hawkes once again uses antithetical settings, but unlike the opposing islands in *Second Skin,* representative of Eros and Thanatos, these two landscapes contain both sex and death and ultimately make them synonymous. (pp. 325-27)

Like other figures in American romance who journey into their psychic wilderness in pursuit of their dreams, Allert also in-vestigates the font of his dreams and risks the dangers of an-nihilation. Whereas *Walden, Moby-Dick,* and *Huckleberry Finn* offer a chance of temporary return to pastoral simplicity, Allert remains exiled in his dream-world. Psychic renewal is possible only when the exile is impermanent. Allert remains an aimless traveler who drifts between two worlds. Unlike Skipper, he does not trade one world for another or, like Cyril, attempt a faltering reconciliation between the two. Hawkes implies that Allert's voyage has led him not to freedom and a world of total possibility but to denial of life. His pursuit of his imagination brings destruction. While on board the ship, Allert kills Ariane by dropping her into the ocean and then kills himself by re-maining lost in the waters of his psyche. *Death, Sleep & the Traveler,* according to Hawkes, ''mixes the night sea journey with a real descent into the realm of death; the narrator is accused of murder and suffers his own psychic death.'' Allert, nevertheless, refuses to admit his culpability. His final words are ''I am not guilty.'' Claiming innocence with these last words, he denies not only his guilt as a murderer but also his guilt as an artist.

Whereas Allert refuses to admit that his pursuit of artistic illusion has reaped devastation, Papa, the narrator of *Travesty,* consciously chooses death over life. He makes death his chosen art form. Delivering an uninterrupted monologue on the aes-thetics of death, Papa careens through the night, hell-bent on suicide. Hawkes reduces the novel's landscape to the confines of the car, making it synonymous with the narrator's mind; the ride itself suggests another interior journey into the imagina-tion, like Allert's ocean voyage. Yet a difference remains. Allert floats on his psychic waters, and as he heads for oblivion, he takes notes. Papa, on the other hand, is at the steering wheel, directing imminent destruction. Rather than merely drifting to inevitable annihilation, Papa argues for the conscious design of death, a planned execution, not a ''submission to an obliv-ion.'' For him death is an artistic experience to be immortalized in the landscape of the novel. For him the ultimate artistic experience is the creation of death—a final union of paradoxes where creator and creation are one. This fatal design is the perfect composition, a ''tableau of chaos.''

Just as Skipper values his occupation as artificial inseminator, Cyril, his tapestry, and Allert, his dreams, Papa likewise values artifice over reality. When he rages toward the final purity of creation, he seeks illusion over the raw material of life. His pursuit of death is, therefore, not only an imposition of form on chaos, but also a creation of something outside of life: ''that nothing is more important than the existence of what does not exist; that I would rather see two shadows flickering inside the head than all your flaming sunrises set end to end. There you have it, the theory to which I hold as does the wasp to his dart.'' Although a comic exaggeration of artistic pursuit, Papa's statement nevertheless espouses Hawkes's belief in the artist's need to defy the world around him and ''to create from the imagination a totally new and necessary fictional landscape or visionary world.'' This dictum is echoed in Papa's italicized words: *''Imagined life is more exhilarating than remembered life.''* This belief, which all Hawkes's narrators hold, explains their monomaniacal insistence on the artistic act that inevitably leads them into their own psychic underworlds. Like Narcis-sus's plunge into the waters of his own reflection, Papa's car ride is a metaphor for the absolute artistic experience. Hawkes suggests that such a romantic endeavor must be fatal. The artist-figures in the triad are victimized by their own radical pursuit of freedom as it resides in the creative imagination and by their rebellion against life's limitations. The inherent irony, of course, is that in combatting death (stasis) art leads to the same in-evitable result. As Papa says in his closing words, ''there shall be no survivors. None.'' *Travesty* thus ends with the final fictional landscape—the destructive vitality of man's psyche.

Because *Travesty* presses landscape to the lowest limits of psychic isolation, some critics suggest that Hawkes has nowhere to go—no other worlds to explore. John Graham, for example, says: ''In *Travesty* the progression into an isolated world of language goes so far that, without a new start, Hawkes may next offer a blank page.'' *The Passion Artist* (1979) and *Vir-ginie: Her Two Lives* (1982) mark Hawkes's ''new start.'' Pub-lished by Harper and Row, instead of New Directions, and written for a larger audience, these two novels are his most accessible to date. Rather than reducing the fictional world to the confines of his narrator's interior landscape, Hawkes opens up his last two fictions by presenting a character in an external world. With *The Passion Artist* Hawkes returns to the distancing of a third-person narrator and to a landscape set in a European location. Although *Virginie: Her Two Lives* has a first-person narrator, she is an eleven-year-old girl who functions mainly as an innocent companion to the novel's central artist-figures Seigneur and Bocage. Not a direct participant, Virginie offers some distance on the proceedings. Besides this change in narrator, the novel also takes place in a specific locale—Paris and the countryside of France. With both these novels Hawkes returns to landscapes tied to verifiable settings, as was true of his early fiction.

The world expressed in *The Passion Artist* in many ways resembles Hawkes's early fictional landscapes, but with a difference. In *The Cannibal, The Goose on the Grave, The Owl,* and *The Lime Twig,* the violence of war, the repression of social institutions, and the sterility of sex all combine to present a damning portrait of the modern world. *The Passion Artist* evokes a similar world view. Like *Spitzen-on-the-Dein,* the "city without a name" embodies the sterility of modern civilization with its gray buildings, desolate parks, and preponderance of institutions. Such a portrait of society is a given in Hawkes's work, but his artistic energy no longer seems engaged in conveying this bleak world's chaos; his emphasis has changed. Rather than offering surrealistic descriptions of a decomposing world, as he does in his early fiction, Hawkes suggests this town's minimalism in his prose. . . . Hawkes's language reflects the listlessness of the static landscape instead of countering it with a Dionysian form of verbal energy.

In *The Passion Artist* Hawkes is not content with just presenting landscapes of apocalypse and doom. In a 1979 interview he implies that his fictional worlds have developed. Referring to the anonymous European city in *The Passion Artist,* he says, "We are archaeologically on top of the buried city of Spitzen-on-the-Dein, and ironically, the new world is bleaker, deader than the world of *The Cannibal.*" . . . The human negation illustrated by the unnamed city's sterility is not tied to war and irrational violence, as in the earlier fiction, but to the repression of the "domain of the psyche." True, the conflict between authoritarian, life-denying order and creative irrationality has permeated all of Hawkes's works and been evidenced in the novels' landscapes. In the early fiction the conflict is characterized by entropic landscapes wrecked by war and in the later fiction by landscapes more and more disordered by the destructiveness of the narrator's own psyche. With *The Passion Artist,* however, Hawkes brings together these two domains—by presenting both a civilization in collapse and an interior excavation into the psyche.

The Passion Artist focuses on sexual repression as the source of a culture's authoritarianism and man's enslavement to a life bereft of imagination. Dominating the entire city's landscape is a woman's prison, La Violaine, a symbol epitomizing the sexual deprivation of modern civilization. The incarceration of women characterizes this society. Konrad Vost, the middle-aged protagonist, parallels his deficient surroundings with his rigid self-control and sexual celibacy. When a prison riot at La Violaine breaks out, Vost and other male volunteers enter the prison to quell the riot but instead participate in it. Hawkes suggests through this eruption the dangers of confining not only unruly sexuality but also all disruptive needs lodged in the unconscious. La Violaine, like Hugh's dungeon, is emblematic of man's culturally repressed unconscious ("the domain of the psyche"). Similar to other gothic enclosures that confine nightmares, the prison embodies Vost's worst fears as well as his only chance of tapping life's mysteries.

At this point *The Passion Artist* is reminiscent of Hawkes's other post-1964 fiction. Although not filtered through a first-person narrator, the landscape becomes internalized and Hawkes

mirrors Vost's "disordering": "the prison had exploded, so to speak; interior and exterior life were assuming a single shape." His "disordering" takes place in two locales: inside the city's prison itself and in an old stable in an outlying marsh. Playing on the age-old distinction between the "city" and the "country," Hawkes dichotomizes the forces of civilization and nature, illustrating the central conflict between repressive consciousness and the irrational, imaginative unconscious. The dichotomy between "city" and "country" is also clear in *Virginie: Her Two Lives,* with the presentation of Paris in 1945 as opposed to the rural French countryside of 1740. Even though a character does not travel from one experience to another, in this novel Hawkes juxtaposes the city and rural settings to dramatize the conflict.

Like Allert's voyage and Papa's ride, Vost's trip from city to marsh is a journey into the interiors of self. The turn inward is immediately characterized by the squalid nature of the landscape itself and by the return of Hawkes's visionary use of language. . . . Like the entropic decay of *The Cannibal*'s landscape, this marsh actively decomposes all signs of life and "was in itself a morgue." Walking deeper into its dark formlessness, Vost finds a stone enclosure of "wet rocks" and "slimy roughness." Womblike in its warmth, yet repulsive in its filth, this obviously sexual symbol is nature's analogue to civilization's prison. A recurrent symbol in Hawkes's fiction, this chamber of sex and death subjects the character to unexplored psychic terrors (just as the lighthouse does in *Second Skin,* the dungeon in *The Blood Oranges,* and the ocean liner in *Death, Sleep & the Traveler*).

Likewise, the entirety of *Virginie: Her Two Lives* takes place in such disordering interiors. The novel alternates between a low-rent flophouse in postwar Paris and a castle of erotic decadence set in the French countryside of 1740. Within either one of these interiors lies the possibility of the ultimate in both sexual expression and complete degradation. In the Paris salon five trollops in various stages of undress cavort with a tattooed boxer and an old man, under the behest of Becage, a greasy cab driver. Although the group frolics congenially, the atmosphere is deathly because of the mute presence of Maman. Upstairs the "bedridden effigy" of Maman lies paralyzed in a dark, camphorous bedroom. In the countryside chateau of 1740 five French beauties live in the elegant simplicity of a castle with stone corridors, vaulted windows, and courtyards and in the pastoral beauty of shepherds' huts, haystacks, and poplars. Yet within this rural tableau, which Virginie describes as "the very domain of my purity," Seigneur oversees acts of bestiality and self-abasement. The landscapes themselves, whether plebeian or aristocratic, as well as the experiences within them suggest paradoxical extremes—of terror and freedom—and relate to the epigraph by Heide Ziegler: "beauty is paradox."

Captives of these dark interiors, Vost and Virginie, like all of Hawkes's characters, are caught in nightmares of sex and violence. Whether external microcosms of an entropic modern world or internal representations of a narrator's psyche, all of Hawkes's landscapes imprison the characters. In *The Passion Artist* Hawkes externalizes the imprisonment as a symbol not only of a repressive world's confinement of the individual spirit but also of the individual's enslavement to his own submerged unconscious. After Vost's journey into the marsh, it is therefore fitting that he is brought back to prison. His release, ironically, comes from imprisonment. By being held captive in the darkness of his own interior, Vost is forced to experience the ambivalences present in the unconscious—the terror and the freedom.

For the first time in Hawkes's fiction the paradoxes evident in the landscape, to which the main character is subjected, are ultimately transcended. Not an artist-figure like Skipper who transforms one world into another, Vost reconciles the ambivalences in his unconscious. Freed from the imprisonment of self, he achieves the ultimate artistic experience through sex (not death), the "willed erotic union" of the self and the other, the creator and the creation, and thus achieves momentarily what all of Hawkes's first-person narrators try to create in their fictional landscapes. Unlike Allert, who merely dreams it, or Papa, who aesthetically designs it, Vost not only confronts but attains the actual experience. The possibility of achieving such freedom exists in Hawkes's world, both in *The Passion Artist* and *Virginie: Her Two Lives*. (pp. 327-33)

The cost of such freedom is great. In Hawkes's world authoritarian order and erotic vitality inevitably collide in violent disruption. Vost is shot as he emerges from the prison gates, and Virginie perishes in flames. On the other side of completely integrated psychic experience is annihilation. Thus Vost achieves "his final irony" and in death discovers "for himself what it was to be nothing." Virginie also is destroyed after finally consummating her relationship with her creator-father. As the Beckett epigraph suggests, "Birth was the death of her." In the Paris sequence her Maman sets fire to their abode, and in the other sequence Virginie joins her creator (Seigneur) being burned at the stake. The novel begins and ends with apocalyptic flames.

Despite the paradoxical extremes present in Hawkes's fictional landscapes, they ultimately all move toward death—whether it is the destruction inherent in a repressive world or in an irrational mind. The triad shows the danger of tapping the irrational; *The Passion Artist* shows the danger of denying it. Believing in the necessity of pursuing demons in order to exorcise hidden fears responsible for the external world's bleakness, Hawkes follows his characters into their inner recesses. From these interior journeys into man's psyche have emerged lush landscapes of exotic sexuality and lyricism as well as the darkest, most horrific nightmares imaginable. These emerging ambiguities come from Hawkes's own plumbing of his unconscious, from which spring his visions. In an article, Hawkes writes: "my own imagination is a kind of hall of 'whippers' in which the materials of the unconscious are beaten, transformed into fictional landscape itself."

Hawkes probes his unconscious not only to stimulate his own artistic visions but also to express his belief that from this pursuit comes balance. Only by excavating the interior depths where the irrational, imaginative, and erotic lie can man ever achieve harmony. Not denying the significance of sanity or rationalism, Hawkes pursues unreason, which is too often denied, in an effort to forge a union: "Yes, of course sanity is important. But basic harmony, serenity, and a rational equilibrium can be achieved only out of a workshop of the irrational."

Always interested in pursuing the nightmare, in assaulting the conventional world, and in creating what did not exist before, Hawkes uses the device of fictional landscape so necessary to his creative vision as well as his aesthetic. Explaining his travels down the dark tunnel from which emerge his singular works of brutality and beauty, he writes: "For me the writer should always serve as his own angleworm—and the sharper the barb with which he fishes himself out of the blackness, the better." Hawkes makes no promises about what will be retrieved from these depths, but the resulting landscapes testify to his unremittingly creative vision. (pp. 333-34)

Carol A. MacCurdy, "A Newly Envisioned World:
Fictional Landscapes of John Hawkes," in Contemporary Literature, *Vol. 27, No. 3, Fall, 1986, pp.*
318-35.

Wolfgang Hildesheimer

1916-

German dramatist, short story writer, novelist, biographer, scriptwriter, essayist, critic, and librettist.

Regarded as Germany's foremost dramatist writing in the manner of what Martin Esslin termed the Theater of the Absurd, Hildesheimer is also esteemed in Europe for the clarity and intellectual credibility of his diverse prose and nonfiction works. Employing a witty, sophisticated style sometimes compared to that of Lewis Carroll and Thomas Mann, Hildesheimer often embraces the absurdist tendency to emphasize the meaninglessness and futility of existence and to restructure rather than imitate reality. According to Hildesheimer, the purpose of literature is "not to turn truth into fiction but to turn fiction into truth: to condense truth out of fiction." Hildesheimer established his reputation during the 1950s with plays and stories that feature urbane criticism of German society and satiric portrayals of characters who are victimized by their own pretensions and by universal forces. Often associated with "Gruppe 47," a prestigious circle of German writers formed after World War II, Hildesheimer was awarded the Georg Büchner Prize in 1966.

A German-born Jew, Hildesheimer received his preliminary education at Frensham Heights School in England. In 1933, to escape Nazi persecution in his homeland, he immigrated to Palestine, where he studied interior design. Four years later, he traveled to London to receive instruction in the field of graphic arts. During World War II, Hildesheimer served the British government as an Information Officer in Palestine, and after the war, he was an interpreter at the Nuremberg trials in Germany. Although he began his literary career in 1950 with a series of sardonic, intellectual radio plays, Hildesheimer first attracted significant international attention for his premier collection of short fiction, *Lieblose Legenden* (1952; revised and expanded, 1963). The stories in this volume offer a combination of surreal and satiric observations on German culture and language. In "The End of the World," for example, an isolated group of bourgeois intellectuals become so involved in a garish musical recital that they fail to notice their private island settling into the sea. According to Roderick H. Watt, Hildesheimer's primary intention in these stories "is to appeal to, and play on the quasi-cultured, precious tastes of the socially and culturally pretentious élite which is the target of his satire."

In his famous speech, "Erlanger Rede über das absurde Theater," Hildesheimer attempts to define characteristics of the Theater of the Absurd and identifies his own dramas with the surreal tradition exemplified by the works of Eugène Ionesco. For Hildesheimer, "the 'absurd' play becomes a parable of life precisely through the intentional omission of any statement. For life, too, makes no statement." In the one-act dramas *Pastorale; oder, Die Zeit für Kakao* (1958), *Landschaft mit Figuren* (1958), and *Die Uhren* (1958), which are collected in *Spiele in denen es dunkel wird* (1958), the stage lights gradually fade to emphasize the finite limits of human imagination. *Pastorale* concerns a group of elderly singers who engage in pretentious and inane discussions about art and business matters while autumn changes to winter and several characters die. In *Landschaft mit Figuren*, a similar group of pompous individ-

uals pose for painted portraits but are soon overcome by old age and death. The painter then packages their corpses and sells them to an art collector. *Die Uhren* centers on a couple obsessed with the past who purchase a multitude of clocks and gradually become part of their machinery. The futility of attempting to escape everyday existence is further explored in Hildesheimer's full-length drama, *Die Verspätung* (1961). In this play, an elderly professor dies after failing to locate a rare primeval bird from which, he contends, humanity is descended.

Although he used the term "novel" to describe his first full-length prose work, *Paradies der falschen Vögel* (1953), Hildesheimer rejected traditional narrative in his later fiction, contending that "[the] novel has no reality for me now, fiction stands for fiction. But writing signifies: translating a personal preoccupation into style. In which case, why construct a pseudo-reality, with its heroes and hams?" Hildesheimer termed *Tynset* (1965) a "prose narrative," since it contains little conventional plot or action. When the insomniac narrator of this work attempts to find sleep by perusing a volume of railway schedules, he discovers that his efforts lead instead to reflections on the mythological connotations of place-names and to an imaginary world of his own design. In *Masante* (1973), which Hildesheimer identified as a traditional novel, another narrator troubled by insomnia undertakes an excursion to a remote desert village in hopes of finding sleep and attaining an absolute state of mental clarity. He is unable, however, to escape the excruciating awareness of time and space that symbolizes his own inadequacy.

Hildesheimer attracted international attention for his next major work, *Mozart* (1977), which combines critical explication and biography while examining the life and music of Wolfgang Amadeus Mozart from a cultural standpoint. Hildesheimer rebukes previous Mozart scholars and biographers for imprecise methodology and subjective judgments, offering instead an analytical approach and examining such physical evidence as personal correspondence, handwriting analysis, and short biographies of select historical figures who may have influenced the composer. Despite his conclusion that Mozart's life and work elude explication, Hildesheimer was commended for his creative theoretical approach. Hildesheimer described his next work, *Marbot: Eine Biographie* (1981; *Marbot: A Biography*) as a "speculative biography." This work centers on Sir Edward Marbot, an imaginary nineteenth-century French critic whose incestuous relationship with his mother, combined with his incompetence as an artist, results in his unprecedented ability to analyze great works of art from a psychoanalytic perspective. The book, which features fictitious excerpts from Marbot's criticism as well as photographic reproductions of real historical portraits that Hildesheimer presents as actual paintings of Marbot and his family, was praised for its unique blend of realism and illusion. Christian Grawe called *Marbot* "a fine example of precise poetic imagination, a cleverly contrived biography situated between reality and fiction, a highly entertaining book on a highly intellectual level."

Often considered an astute critic of literature, art, and music, Hildesheimer has also experimented with a wide variety of literary, journalistic, and artistic genres. He has translated into German the works of such authors as George Bernard Shaw, James Joyce, and Djuna Barnes, and he has written a libretto for the radio opera *Das Ende einer Welt. Mitteilungen an Max: Über den Stand der Dinge und anderes* (1983) is a volume of light, sardonic essays written to commemorate the seventieth birthday of Hildesheimer's friend and colleague, internationally respected author Max Frisch. *The Collected Stories of Wolfgang Hildesheimer* (1987) includes representative short fiction from throughout his career.

(See also *Contemporary Authors*, Vol. 101.)

MARTIN ESSLIN

The Theatre of the Absurd has struck a responsive chord in the German-speaking world, where the collapse of a whole civilization, through the rise and fall of Hitler, has made the loss of meaning and cohesion in men's lives more evident than elsewhere. The major dramatists of the Absurd have been more successful in Germany than anywhere else to date. Yet so total has been the vacuum left by Hitler that it has taken a long time for a new generation of dramatists to arise. . . . Nevertheless, the breakthrough of a new generation of writers has started.

Wolfgang Hildesheimer (born in 1916), one of the first German dramatists to take up the idiom of the Theatre of the Absurd, spent the war years, significantly enough, in exile abroad, and is still an Israeli citizen. Originally a painter, Hildesheimer started his career as a dramatist with a series of witty and

fantastic radio plays—picaresque tales of forgers, grotesque Balkan countries, and Oriental romance. The step from this type of intellectual thriller to the Theatre of the Absurd seems a natural development. Hildesheimer regards the Theatre of the Absurd, as he has pointed out in a brilliantly argued lecture on the subject ["**Erlanger Rede über das absurde Theater**"], as a theatre of parables. Admittedly,

> the story of the prodigal son is also a parable. But it is a parable of a different kind. Let us analyze the difference—the story of the prodigal son is a parable deliberately conceived to allow an indirect statement (that is, to give the opportunity to reach a conclusion by analogy), while the "absurd" play becomes a parable of life precisely through the intentional omission of any statement. For life, too, makes no statement.

Hildesheimer's collected volume of the plays that illustrate his conception of the Theatre of the Absurd has the title *Spiele in denen es dunkel wird (Plays in Which Darkness Falls)*. This is literally the case. As each of the three plays unfolds, the light fades. In *Pastorale, oder Die Zeit für Kakao (Pastorale, or Time for Cocoa)*, some elderly characters disport themselves in a strange syncopation of dialogue concerned with business matters and stock-exchange deals, with artistic and poetic overtones (a mixture very characteristic of the tone of West German society today). As the light grows darker, summer turns into autumn and winter, and death overtakes the president of a big company, a consul, and a mining engineer.

In *Landschaft mit Figuren (Landscapes with Figures)*, a painter is shown at work painting the portraits of a group of equally empty and pretentious characters—a great but aging lady, her gigolo, and an elderly tycoon. Here to the characters pass from middle to old age before our eyes until they die, are neatly packed into boxes, and sold to a collector—so that the characters themselves have become their own portraits. As this work proceeds, a glazier is putting new panes of glass into the studio windows. It is through them that the light gradually becomes dark. But at the end the painter and his wife are as young as they were in the beginning, and as they are left alone, the mauve panes of glass fall to the ground and the stage is once more bathed in light.

The glazier appears again in *Die Uhren (The Clocks)*, but this time the panes of glass he puts into the windows of a room inhabited by a man and wife are jet black and impenetrable. As the work proceeds, the couple relive scenes from their life together; toward the end a salesman comes who sells them a profusion of clocks of all kinds. And at the final curtain the man and his wife are inside the clocks, making ticking noises.

These dramatic parables are impressive poetic statements, even though they are far from being free from rather obviously drawn analogies and somewhat facile conclusions. (pp. 193-95)

> *Martin Esslin, "Parallels and Proselytes," in his* The Theatre of the Absurd, *Anchor Books, 1961, pp. 168-228.*

HELMUT HEISSENBÜTTEL

[*The essay excerpted below originally appeared in the journal* Die Welt der Literatur.]

Tynset is the name of a railroad station in Norway—at least, according to Wolfgang Hildesheimer's novel [*Tynset*]. A man who cannot find sleep, or whom sleep cannot find (is there any difference?) tells us how, lying in bed of a winter's night, he blindly reaches for a book on his night table. His hand first lights on a telephone book, then on a volume of timetables of the Norwegian State Railways of 1963.

The man reports:

> I am reading the timetables. . . . Of Elverum and Tynset I know nothing. They sound rather promising, but Elverum, because of its neuter ending, perhaps less promising than Tynset. Tynset has a "y" in it, and where we find a "y," we sometimes find a real secret, though often only mythology. Yet Tynset does not have the ring of mythology, at least not as much as Röros.

This much the reader learns at the start about the name Tynset. Every statement that appears is completely factual. After all, where can we find more reliable facts than in timetables, particularly if their credibility is further enhanced by detailed information, such as that we are dealing here with State railways in the year 1963? Even that brief meditation on the vowel 'y,' by showing us the difference between a real secret and mythology, leads us back to the flat statement that Tynset does not have the ring of mythology. And yet the impression left by this passage is one of pure invention. In a world where facts can be recorded, these inventions seem even further removed from reality. The passage forms a world of its own invented by a narrating "I" who is vainly seeking sleep.

From the very beginning we do not know whether this "I" invents his own world because sleep will not come, or whether sleep shuns him because he cannot stop inventing such a world. But is this pure invention? Doesn't memory play a part? Is he not recalling incidents that must have occurred in a world with which the reader is familiar?

One thing is certain: this tale maintains perfect balance between its own creations in words and sentences and its other elements that—at least regarding the narrated happenings—can be related to a tangible world. Its landscapes, reminiscences, episodes and anecdotes are extremely realistic. The house in which the sleepless man lies down to rest, or wanders about, emerges almost with the clarity of a hallucination. Episodes that must be regarded as imaginary have the weight of a chronicle of historical events.

At the same time, however, nothing that is recounted has any relation to a realistic and identifiable set of experiences; everything is related only to itself. (pp. 122-23)

[Certain] names acquire thematic lives of their own, as when the first-person narrator reports that he had wakened some strangers in the middle of the night and had forced them to flee by telling them that all was discovered. Here, too, we see flashes of the real world. Persecutors who sought concealment driven from their hiding places. But where memories of former friends, deported or murdered, seem to establish a link with reality, the novel again becomes a series of fables invented by a sleepless man.

At this point we can't help asking: Who is the narrator, the sleepless "I" who creates for himself an imaginary world? The first answers that come to mind only evade the question. To begin with, it can be pointed out that this "I" is always consistent, always faithful to himself; he never abandons his role—a role that one might be tempted to call wise, melancholy, serene except that the almost terrifying precision and the merciless accuracy that the "I" displays forbid the use of such adjectives.

Undoubtedly it can also be said that the narrator's "I" is not the author, even that references which could be autobiographical are definitely not based on Hildesheimer's own life. Then who *is* the narrator? A third personage? Should we regard the fantasies of a sleepless night as a stage monologue? How should we characterize the actor? Is it even possible to characterize him? Apparently not. . . .

[In *Tynset*], Hildesheimer has given us a work of fiction which accomplishes what Max Frisch set out to do in *Mein Name sei Gantenbein:* a novel that analyzes an experience. Frisch himself failed, producing only an obscure and depressing picture of private suffering. Hildesheimer's book is real literature. This incomparable tale attains the heights, where it stands alone. (p. 123)

> Helmut Heissenbüttel, "'Longtemps Je Me Suis Couché . . .'," translated by Konrad Kellen, in At- las, Vol. 10, No. 2, August, 1965, pp. 122-23.

RAINER TAËNI

Most new plays which are at present being discussed in Germany may be considered to belong, in one way or another, to the general category of the Documentary Theatre. . . . [Documentary Theatre] does by now have a kind of history in Germany. Its successes have tended to overshadow certain other plays written in a different style which may yet prove to be no less important. This may be said in particular of some plays with a pronounced affinity to the so-called Theatre of the Absurd written by Wolfgang Hildesheimer and Hans Günter Michelsen.

Of course I am well aware that "absurd" in recent years has become somewhat of a catchword, a popular if none too meaningful phrase frequently used in an attempt to label that which cannot easily be pinned down, grouping together what may in fact be as different as the work of Beckett and Ionesco. Yet there is a certain limited sense in which the term may be, and indeed has been, defined clearly in such a way as to offer some valuable insight into the nature of what it may designate.

No such definition may justly fail to take note of the essential difference between "absurd" and "grotesque". The plays of Dürrenmatt, for example his *Physicists,* or Max Frisch's *Firebugs* are certainly grotesque in the extreme, yet they are not absurd. "Grotesque" implies being out-of-shape, distorted, stylised in a grossly exaggerated way—yet elements of alienation to which the term, used in this sense, may be applied can be found, not only within the "Theatre of the Absurd" but in most other kinds of drama. . . . The term "absurd", however, implies something more as well, implies illogical features, something contrary, contradictory to Reason.

In his justly famous *Erlanger Rede über das absurde Theater,* a speech given in 1959, in which he attempts to define the nature of the Absurd in drama, Hildesheimer does allow for this difference. To him, the "Theatre of the Absurd is a parable about the strangeness of man in the world. Hence its playing serves to estrange. It is the ultimate and most radical consequence of estrangement." The absurdist author perceives absurdity as the normal, natural state of the world. His play will therefore aim to transport its audience . . . "into the realm of the Absurd, make it feel at home where, in the opinion of the author, it is indeed at home already without knowing it: in the 'questionableness' of life which holds no message nor meaning." This kind of drama does not merely point to certain aspects of our world which may be considered absurd (or grotesque, for that matter) but in it the world is represented as fundamentally absurd in its totality. The feeling that such is its "normal" state is what the author aims to communicate to his audience. Accordingly, where he employs symbols, he will also do so to this end only. A play which constitutes a parable on a specific (for example, a political) situation thus ceases to be truly absurd in this sense, as Hildesheimer points out with regard to Ionesco's *Rhinoceros*—just a political grotesque in which certain absurd elements of stylization are employed. Nor, Hildesheimer insists, is experimentation with the Absurd possible. An author not truly convinced of the inherent absurdity of the world will obviously not be able to convince his audience. (pp. 76-7)

A genuinely and most convincingly Absurd play . . . is Hildesheimer's *Nachtstück*. The same may be said also of the first two plays of Hans Günter Michelsen, *Stienz* and *Lappschiess*. These three works illustrate the wide range of different possibilities that is left after excluding all mere experimentation in meaninglessness. They also show something else (already evident in particular in the work of Beckett): that in order to be considered truly Absurd, a play need by no means necessarily be funny; secondly, that it does not *have* to make use of a great number of surrealist elements (considered by Hildesheimer as "secondary attributes of the Absurd")—and, finally, that its characters are, like those of expressionist drama, largely abstractions, not individual characters in the ordinary sense, but mere types like "the Man", "the Major", "the Girl", etc., only occasionally bearing short names.

Nachtstück opens on a note of complete realism. The setting is described in some detail: a bedroom in Victorian style, with numerous empty medicine bottles standing around all over the place. The hero is simply called "A Man who Wants to Sleep" and, superficially, the play deals solely with his efforts to find rest. These efforts consist partly in his taking strong doses of sleeping pills, partly in the observance of a complex ritual which he has evolved through the years and which is composed of such apparently unnecessary items as checking whether the light in the bathroom has been turned off, or locking the door of the room (of which the Man knows, "it isn't necessary . . . After all, the front door has already been locked"). Yet, as he says with regard to Number Four on his list ("looking under the bed"): he cannot do without it. After all, it is not the actual security which counts, but the feeling of it. And the ceremonial seems to him indispensable for the precise reason that the unexpected is always more likely to happen than the expected: so that invariably that which is most unlikely, by virtue of having to be expected, becomes the most probable.

We may laugh at this man, and much of the play is very funny indeed. His situation certainly seems grotesque, but it does not strike us as absurd even though there is a certain element of surrealism in his narrator of the four terrible experiences of his life which have caused his sleeplessness and necessitated his taking ever stronger doses of pills. They are: a concert of "angelically pure" choir boys; a procession of 715 Cardinals being carried in litters through the streets of Rome; the spectacle of 3,000 generals' widows silently goose-stepping through Paris in a march of protest; and finally, an assembly of at least 4,022 balded Senior Public Servants in a medieval castle singing the last movement of Beethoven's Ninth.

Now the fact alone that in these shattering experiences we recognize a kind of personification of the whole range of commonly accepted values of our Western world—this in itself is

obvious enough and none too important. It is easy for any playwright to invent symbols, in particular, symbols of absurdity—what matters is the power of these symbols to affect the audience. True: it is only to the unreligious, unmilitary, unpolitical person that these things which have struck terror into the heart of the Man will appear devoid of any meaningful function, and therefore utterly preposterous. But does not this today apply to the majority of people? Long before we come to sympathize fully with the Man's attitude towards these "values" we have already come to perceive in his particular efforts to find sleep a reflection of our own, of Man's, universal concern for peace and security in a world where both are continually threatened. This makes it all the easier to accept also the Man's narration of his shattering experiences as something more real than mere phantasies. Moreover, the events in the play actually prove the Man to be right in his assumption that it is always the improbable which is most likely to occur: despite his apparently pointless precautions these prove to be not only necessary indeed but at the same time ineffectual. It is a point of subtle irony brought across by Hildesheimer very convincingly: in the end the suspected burglar does very improbably lie under the bed.

The figure of the Burglar thus serves to underline in theatrical terms Hildesheimer's point that the world is absurd, while vindicating the Man in the eyes of the audience as having been somewhat of a "realist" after all. At the same time the Burglar undoubtedly represents normalcy as against the Man's hypersensitivity. He remains cool and collected throughout. He is quite unimpressed by the Man's threats of calling the police and, when tied up in a chair (which has been standing carefully prepared for this sole purpose), simply begins patiently to loosen the knots until he has freed himself. The Man's narration of his horrifying experiences leaves him utterly cold even though he seems to accept its truth. He has, for instance, "nothing against Cardinals" but plainly states that he would have known how to deal with the situation: "In these situations one has to shoot."

I have not mentioned that the Man who Wants to Sleep is also plagued by certain mysterious 'phone-calls which may be taken to symbolize theatrically both his isolation and his difference from "normal" men. Knowing that the calls are "never for me", he usually silences the telephone with a pillow whenever it rings. When he does answer it, the caller invariably has dialed one of two numbers similar to his own: he either wishes to speak to a firm of Organ Builders, or he dictates a set of figures which the Man dutifully notes down, but the meaning of which he is unable to comprehend. Nevertheless, this lack of comprehension seems not to be shared by anyone else: he may himself dial any number at random and dictate those very same figures to whomever answers—they will always be accepted without question or surprise. The Burglar, after the Man has finally fallen asleep, handles both types of 'phone-call with unperturbed ease. He is not only in full possession of all technical details concerning the building of organs, but even able to suggest the most suitable instrumental combinations to impress different kinds of church-goers and actually increase church attendance; and as far as the mysterious numbers are concerned, he seems to understand even why they suddenly change from five sets of figures to only four.

It is here that we, the spectators, will begin to feel that this representative of "normal" man who functions within his world as this world functions for him, who manages to appear in a locked room, who knows all the answers. . .—that he in all his undauntedness and efficiency is really the uncanny figure in this play. This shows Hildesheimer to have been successful in making us feel "at home" in the absurd (because utterly incomprehensible and unpredictable) world which threatens a man's sleep. We not only sympathize with, but even seem to understand the Man who Wants to Sleep, whereas we finally look askance at his opponent for whom life presents no problem. After having smashed up the room, the Burglar sits down to a breakfast of sandwiches and hot coffee he has brought with him, muttering as he munches contentedly:

> No reason to worry. Everything's flowing (*he takes a sip from his flask*), everything's running and sliding smoothly (*he chews*), interacting (*he swallows*) and pushing itself into place—(*he gives a brood smile*) all by itself.

Yet the audience is left wondering, amazed, if anything, at this kind of brazenness. (pp. 77-9)

[In *Nachtstück,* absurdity] is revealed as a fundamental condition of life itself. Having once been brought to accept the world of Hildesheimer's and Michelsen's plays, it will be, if at all, only with a considerable effort that we as audience will be able to distance ourselves from this recognition. This fundamental involvement, which no clever construction of intricate parables on the theme of meaninglessness could in itself ever achieve, is in each case attained without even a great many elements of overt surrealism. It is to be considered as a measure of the quality of these plays, ensuring them of an important place among the works of the Theatre of the Absurd. (p. 83)

> *Rainer Taëni, "W. Hildesheimer and H. G. Michelsen: The Absurd Play as Mirroring a Fundamental Condition of Reality," in* Komos, *Vol. 1, No. 1, March, 1967, pp. 76-84.*

THE TIMES LITERARY SUPPLEMENT

Anxiety, stasis, indecision, an almost masochistic self-doubt and self-examination—these are the thematic strands which bind and unify *Masante,* Wolfgang Hildesheimer's first prose narrative for eight years. In *Tynset* the first-person narrator discovered, focused on and then finally abandoned the project of making a journey to the isolated Norwegian village of the title, the book following every twist and turn of his meandering thoughts, recollections and fantasies during a single sleepless night. "Prose narrative" because Hildesheimer explicitly rejected the term "novel", for *Tynset* had no plot, no action in a conventional sense. "The novel has no reality for me now, fiction stands for fiction. But writing signifies: translating a personal preoccupation into style. In which case, why construct a pseudo-reality, with its heroes and hams?" Now in *Masante,* the author, or his publishers, seem to have relented: "Roman" appears on the jacket, but not on the title page.

Tynset was a refuge, a goal for the narrator's cosmic aimlessness, "a haven in a sea of confusion". Now he has actually undertaken a journey, from his villa in Italy, Cal Masante, to an anonymous inn, a former caravanserai, "a point on the edge of the desert": to Meona . . . , one of those places you find by jabbing a pencil into a map blindfolded. It is on the tension set up between these two locales and what they represent—a tension expressed in Hildesheimer's original plan to call the book *Meona*—that *Masante* is based.

Why has the narrator gone there? Besides a desire to press the German intellectual's archetypal *italienische Reise* to its extremity—Meona is the "southernmost and easternmost counterpart to Masante"—he hopes to escape from an oppressive sense of time, from an overpowering sense of place—pitiless reminders of his own inadequacy. But in his quest for abstraction, for nothingness—that perfect nothingness existing between bits of matter which he sought through his telescope in *Tynset*—he finds that even such a seemingly neutral spot as Meona is too dense, too rich. . . .

[Like *Tynset*], *Masante* is given an almost unrelenting intensity by the narrator's associative interior monologues. He indulges his own subjectivity, letting his thoughts rise and flutter and fall—the wind is a constant presence—picking up threads, to unravel some and discard others. To reproduce this digressive and parenthetic play, Hildesheimer has divided the text into heavily indented lapidary paragraphs, units of thought; with spacing to indicate complete breaks and new beginnings; full points for neatly rounded thoughts; dashes for untidy cuts and leaps; commas for mental enjambments.

What does the narrator's voracious mind feed on? On whatever presents itself. Alain and Maxine, his host and hostess; the local policeman; the inn, and the objects it contains . . . ; and, of course, his own past: all parade before the lens of his mind's eye, in fugal patterns; all mere pretexts for his reflections. But it is the nightmare of the pursuers or persecutors (*Häscher*) that obsesses him most, with their sinister names—Globotschnik, Perchtl, Fricke, Kabasta.

A difficulty peculiar to the postwar German conscience is finding a way of considering, let alone coming to terms with, the grisly traumas of recent history. Although never made absolutely explicit, we are left in no doubt that the "pursuers" are in fact the Nazis. Identifying narrator with author would be simplistic, but it is worth noting that Hildesheimer, who fled to Palestine in 1933, had first-hand experience of some prime specimens of Nazism as a simultaneous translator at the Nuremberg Trials. And clearly the anxieties besetting modern German historiography are paralleled in the author's scepticism about novel-writing, in the traditional sense of fictionalized history—a scepticism many of his contemporaries of course share. The German word for "story" and "history" is the same: *Geschichte*. Hildesheimer plays on this ambiguity; hence the constant interventions, equivocations, inconsistencies in the narrative—to show the futility of searching for the Truth.

This futility is equated with (is identical with?) the narrator's attempt to get away, to face himself in a (so he had hoped) timeless and spaceless environment. . . .

Yet it is not people and places as such that he is trying to escape but the inescapable—himself, his memories of the past, his perceptions of the present. These are at the root of his impotence: "When am I going to come to the point? Never, of course, I should have learnt that by now. Never." . . .

As in *Tynset,* only a few hours have elapsed, the narrator's rambling consciousness has returned to its opening motif. And Hildesheimer's taut, beautifully clear and simple prose—a counterpoint to the book's loose overall structure—may be regarded as much a musical as a literary experience. . . . *Masante*—with its resonant names, both melodious and discordant, its staccato passages, its jolting key-changes, its fugues—is a prose tone-poem. Longer and less concentrated than *Tynset,* it is perhaps not as well sustained. Nevertheless, Hildesheimer has fashioned a perfect vehicle to express unashamed subjectivity; so it is understandable that the reader should feel the bewilderment, the amusement, the embarrassment and even the occasional tedium of a privileged eavesdropper on another mind.

"Landscape without Figures," in The Times Literary Supplement, *No. 3715, May 18, 1973, p. 545.*

STUART PARKES

[The term "theatre of the absurd"] requires some clarification when used in connection with German playwrights. A number of critics have made the point that German dramatists have seemed to take over the techniques of the French theatre of the absurd without having statements of comparable intensity to make. A number of differences are immediately noticeable; the petty bourgeois setting, the sense of the author's involvement found in French absurd plays are often missing. By contrast, German absurd plays often come closer to direct parable; indeed the leading German dramatist of the absurd, Wolfgang Hildesheimer, has said that every absurd play is a parable. His theatre stands, therefore, somewhere between the French theatre of the absurd and Brecht. This parabolic element is particularly clear in *Pastorale* (staged 1958), where a strange quartet of singers assemble in the open air and talk a mixture of business and artistic jargon. As summer turns to winter and two of them die, the connection between bourgeois business and cultural life and death and decay is shown. The message is stressed by the title Hildesheimer gave to the cycle of plays to which *Pastorale* belongs: *Spiele in denen es dunkel wird* (*Plays in Which Darkness Falls*). The difference between the Brechtian parable and Hildesheimer's plays is that the latter suggest no solution to human problems. Hildesheimer's contention is that the whole world is absurd. This seems to be the idea behind the play *Die Verspätung* (*The Delay*: staged 1961). A professor comes to an almost depopulated village in an attempt to discover a bird, from which he claims man is descended. At the end of the play, he thinks he does sight it, but it is an illusion. He sinks down dead. Hildesheimer points to the futility of all human efforts to find any meaning in life, whilst stressing the 'absurdity' of existence through the setting of the play. What lies behind Hildesheimer's conception of life becomes clearer in *Nachtstück* (*Night Play*: staged 1963). It is the sense of having been born too late, of having no new outlet because everything has already been done. The chief figure in the play, simply called a Man, lies unable to sleep in a room full of pictures. These, together with the grotesque visions he has of marching cardinals and civil servants, represent the burden of cultural and social traditions. (pp. 139-40)

Stuart Parkes, "West German Drama Since the War," in The German Theatre: A Symposium, *edited by Ronald Hayman, Oswald Wolff, 1975, pp. 129-47.*

MARION FABER

It is tempting to describe Hildesheimer's *Mozart* in musical terms: it is contrapuntal, with several themes. First and foremost, it is a biography of Mozart; but in addition to the narrowest sense of that term, it is an examination of the cultural phenomenon Mozart. It attempts to explore the relationship between the figure of Mozart and his music; further, it examines the phenomenology of music in general. Within the large biography are mini-biographies of people central to Mozart's life, each illuminating some aspect of the main figure. The book is a theoretical speculation on the nature of genius—and, in ad-

dition to everything else, it is a criticism of earlier biographies, a questioning of the method and perhaps the very act of writing biography. Its overt intention is to challenge and correct biographical clichés, thereby *widening* the gap between the historical Mozart and our preconceived image of him.

This particular theme is my interest here, the biographical-critical aspect of Hildesheimer's work. Because of the wealth of biographical data about Mozart, Hildesheimer feels it is not for him simply to repeat chronologically the well-known, bare facts of Mozart's life. . . . In an age predicated on psychoanalytical insights, on a phenomenological skepticism, Hildesheimer's work is as much an attempt to dispute, eradicate, expose, and challenge former biographies of Mozart as it is a biography per se. Incisive criticism of the method and practice of biography is a fundamental structural element of his book. (One could also profitably examine Hildesheimer's criticism of *musicological* method, but I will confine myself here to biographical criticism alone, however forced the distinction.) Hildesheimer is writing a self-conscious biography, and in its self-conscious preoccupation it approaches meta-biography, akin to what Lionel Abel has called meta-theatre. (pp. 202-03)

[In his preface to *Mozart,* Hildesheimer addresses his first criticism to] the romanticization of the hero. Hildesheimer is attacking the notion that Mozart's greatness, his sublime musical achievement was recompense for his material suffering, that his suffering "paid off, so to speak." But for whom? As opposed to those who see Mozart's painful life as glorious, Hildesheimer's conscious intent is to emphasize its degradation—the fact that "an inconceivably great mind" went through much of his life and to his grave unrecognized and unsaluted by virtually everyone in his society, especially by those with power (Haydn being the notable exception).

Hildesheimer's second target is the nationalization of the hero (which is of course related to romanticization). Hildesheimer quotes Bernhard Paumgartner, who attempts to make Mozart into an Austrian folk hero, despite the indisputable fact that in Austria Mozart suffered a humiliating lack of recognition, and despite the fact that Mozart hated his native city Salzburg and the Viennese as well.

Hildesheimer does not, however, confine remarks of this nature to the preface alone. Rather, his *whole work* is informed with this kind of critical comment; at times Hildesheimer's chief aim seems to be critical rather than synthetic. In this sense, his is a negative, "neinsagende" biography. Almost more important than establishing the facts and relating the events is the exposure of his predecessors in biography.

Both nineteenth and twentieth century biographers are constant references throughout the work. Hildesheimer mentions how Franz Niemtschek, Mozart's second biographer, used reports from dangerously biased sources, Mozart's wife Constanze, for example. Thus the information that Mozart preferred playing billiards most of all in the company of his wife, coming, as it does, from the wife herself, is open to question. (pp. 203-04)

Not only does Hildesheimer expose Mozart's contemporaries and near-contemporaries . . . , he is every bit as severe on authors of his own time. He sees them primarily as descendents of the nineteenth-century, their critical biographical methods stemming directly from a romantic habit of mind. For a non-German audience, then, the point of his criticism is perhaps less urgent. (p. 204)

Hildesheimer also attacks the rationale, the didactic nature of biography. He notes that the subliminal intention of biography has been to "admonish." The biographical subject has to be a model for others to emulate. Thus the political partisan tries to make Mozart into a radical politician. The Catholic biographer tries to make Mozart into a good Catholic. Or, in a related kind of persuasion, biographers who feel inadequate and helpless in the face of death, need, according to Hildesheimer, to portray Mozart as a man "half in love with easeful death." The biographer who cannot make his peace with death tries to pull himself up by his model's bootstraps. In all these cases the great genius has to be a great human being as well.

The ultimate object of Hildesheimer's criticism is the mythification of the biographical subject. He admits that the urge to turn a man into a myth may be irresistible: referring to Giesecke, the unacknowledged co-author of *The Magic Flute* libretto, he notes that biographers tend to ignore him and concentrate on Schikaneder as sole author, out of the need to mythologize one single figure, a need, he writes, that "is as old as monotheism." But Hildesheimer is resolved to combat this need by revealing it in others. The myths abound. (pp. 205-06)

In summary, then, Hildesheimer's biography is a critique of the subjectivity and mythologizing prevalent in the work of his predecessors. Of course, his own work is also an attempt to overcome that which he criticizes. What methods does he employ to *counteract* the tendencies he deplores? How successful is his attempt to overcome them?

Hildesheimer's methods are many. He has examined Mozart's handwriting in manuscript to try to discover signs of emotion in the very ductus of Mozart's strokes, to use graphology as an insight into character. He describes portraits of Mozart, trying to find a common essence behind the external features, and exposing here, too, romantic euphemisms. In both attempts, he must ultimately acknowledge failure.

He refers at great length to Mozart's letters, taking them not at face value, but handling them with the critical tools of a man of letters familiar with eighteenth-century epistolary formulae. As he himself notes, his other tool is psychoanalytical insight. Thus he contends that Mozart did not experience his mother's death as *object loss* (it was not a devastating event in his emotional life). He carefully analyzes the relationship between Mozart and his father. And from letters written to Constanze during Mozart's stay in Leipzig, he reconstructs the "erotic compatibility" that made their marriage a relatively happy one.

He uses Mozart's music as a key to the man, as well. But one of his achievements is that he avoids the trap of trying to explain or understand Mozart's music *through* the biographical context in which it was written. He does not look for causal connections between Mozart's emotional life and his compositions. . . . Furthermore, Hildesheimer's biography never loses sight of the fact that it is his *music,* not his life, makes Mozart great. That his life need not, indeed cannot, be that example of perfection that is his music. In what is perhaps the most original and convincing aspect of his work, Hildesheimer emphasizes the unsocial side of the genius, the eccentric Mozart, whose pranks often have an air of desperation. Might his phenomenal mental preoccupations have made him an exasperating dinner guest?

Another of Hildesheimer's methods is to test the statements of contemporaries for veracity. He tries to siphon off the fantasies

of witnesses from that which "can hardly be invented." Inevitably, however, and despite his critical tools, his must also be an act of subjective judgment, in that his own personality must also be at work when assessing credibility and determining what is essential. In the end, Hildesheimer, too, cannot (and should not, some would add) avoid the subjective element in his own work.

Hildesheimer admits that he too knows "wishful thinking." Characteristically, he also exposes this side of his mind in its biographical work. But at times he is not so clear about this subjective element. For despite his caution, he is actually relying on his own superior powers of imagination to identify with Mozart and his situation. He asks that we trust him in a tremendous act of "Einfühlung" (identification) on his part, too, as much as with any other biographer.

For example, he follows his criticism of those biographers who see Mozart's welcoming attitude to death as a model by writing that Mozart "belonged to those who accepted death as their inevitable destiny without wasting any words about it." Mozart didn't worry about death, Hildesheimer contends. Is this not every bit as great a projection? Does not the reader tend to think that the author, too, is a man who does not worry about death? Is he not projecting *his* values onto Mozart?

He contends that it was not his mother's death, but his own freedom, Mozart's newly-acquired independence that made the year in Paris important for him. Here, too, Hildesheimer's subjective value system is at work, for he can never know Mozart's real reaction to his mother's death. His views on Mozart's Catholicism are another case in point: how can we be *sure,* as Hildesheimer seems to be, that Mozart thought of a church only as a "place where an organ stood"? His scepticism about Mozart's love for his mother and sister is also based purely on intuition. Even though Hildesheimer is probably right in seeing Mozart's epistolary protestations of love as mere formulae, he cannot really conclude anything definitive about Mozart's true sentiments, for, as he himself often points out, Mozart's letters do not express them.

Thus Hildesheimer is putting together the pieces of this puzzle according to his own insight and imagination. His is a powerful, acute imagination, and the image of Mozart that we derive from his book may well be closer than others to an accurate one (accuracy being Hildesheimer's professional goal). But it, like all the rest, is shaped by subjectivity, no rhapsodic, naive subjectivity, it is true, but analytical subjectivity.

In its integrity, however, it is convincing. One might liken the technique behind its integrity to the *Verfremdungseffekt* (alienation effect). The machinery, the flies and wings of Hildesheimer's biographical stage are brightly lit. His criticism of biographical method is part and parcel of this technique. His is a *self-consciously* subjective biographical meditation on Mozart, a meta-biography, and can claim for that reason an advantage on its biographical predecessors. Indeed, the subjectivity and mythification that he criticizes in the work of others may result from a want of this kind of alienation in their technique. In Hildesheimer's work, reason is to brush away the cobwebs of easy emotion. Yet, as in Brecht's Epic Theatre, the alienation techniques of Hildesheimer's biography also elicit an emotional response, one more rigorous, tempered by critical judgment. (pp. 206-08)

Marion Faber, "Wolfgang Hildesheimer's 'Mozart' as Meta-Biography," in Biography, *Vol. 3, No. 3, Summer, 1980, pp. 202-08.*

CHRISTIAN GRAWE

Among Hildesheimer's [short fictions collected in] *Lieblose Legenden* there is an engaging little story entitled "**1956—ein Pilzjahr.**" It is the fictional biography of Gottlieb Theodor Pilz (1789-1856), who made it his purpose in life not to promote art but to prevent it. He convinced Schumann that four symphonies were enough, persuaded Rossini to give up composing and turn to cooking instead, et cetera. What makes this story so charming is the skillful merging of a fictional character and the actual personalities of a cultural period.

In his latest book [*Marbot: Eine Biographie*] Hildesheimer has exploited this particular talent of his on a larger scale. Again he has chosen the first half of the nineteenth century, and this time he has even included portraits of the fictional hero and his family together with pictures of real persons and appropriate paintings. The book is the biography of a young Englishman, Sir Edward Marbot (1801-30), relating his encounters with European celebrities (Goethe, Byron, Berlioz, Delacroix) and his travels. The book also contains excerpts from Marbot's writings on fine art. He is the "inventor" of Freudian art analysis—seventy years before Freud. . . .

Just as Marbot searches for the repressed drives behind the great paintings—and some of his interpretations are indeed most impressive—Hildesheimer searches for the repressed drives behind Marbot's theory. He discovers two things: a frustrated desire to be a great painter, for which he has only very limited talent; and an incestuous relationship with his mother, which he severs when he goes to Italy. Marbot committed suicide at the age of twenty-nine, Hildesheimer suspects, because he could not explore his theory any further. . . .

In *Marbot* Hildesheimer pursues his literary investigation into the mysteries of artistic creativity, and thus the book sheds light on his book about Mozart as well. It is interesting to note that he has chosen a (real) musician and a (fictitious) enthusiast of fine art, not a literary figure. *Marbot* is a fine example of precise poetic imagination, a cleverly contrived biography situated between reality and fiction, a highly entertaining book on a highly intellectual level.

> *Christian Grawe, in a review of "Marbot: Eine Biographie," in* World Literature Today, *Vol. 56, No. 4, Autumn, 1982, p. 676.*

RODERICK H. WATT

The purpose of the following textual interpretation is first to elucidate the function of the implied reader of the satirical stories [collected in Hildesheimer's *Lieblose Legenden*]. Such an analysis suggests that the real reader envisaged by Hildesheimer is such as to render ineffectual the intended satire. We can show that these stories are written for, directed against, and can only be properly appreciated by, a very limited public. This readership consists of people with a very high level of formal education, who are at least quasi-cultured, and are certainly characterised by philistine pretensions to the social prestige attached to a public display of culture. In short, it is the group sometimes contemptuously referred to in German as the *Bildungsbürgertum*. But this intended readership, identifiable through a study of the implied reader, is exactly the social group satirised in the stories. Whatever their shortcomings, such readers are certainly educated and literate enough to appreciate the consummate artistry of Hildesheimer's work while

dissociating themselves from, and thus ignoring and thereby neutralising, its satirical purpose. (p. 62)

The aspiring satirist has always been confronted with the problem of navigating a safe course between the Scylla of artistic virtuosity and the Charybdis of crudely effective propaganda. . . . One could argue paradoxically that if the razor is too keen, if the satire is too subtle because artistic virtuosity is pursued for its own sake, then that satire is blunted and ineffectual. This is precisely the conclusion towards which this article works, namely that in Hildesheimer's *Lieblose Legenden* the artist triumphs at the cost of the satirist.

With one exception, all the stories in the 1962 edition of *Lieblose Legenden* are, to a greater or lesser degree, relevant to a study of Hildesheimer's satire of the middle-class, pseudo-cultured philistine. The exception is "**Schläferung.**" . . . Dedicated to, and written expressly for, Hans Magnus Enzensberger, this story has no satirical intention and reveals the mutual admiration and respect of one artist for another. Of the other stories, most were first published between 1950 and 1952 and were collected in book form in the first edition of *Lieblose Legenden* (1952). (pp. 62-3)

In general, Hildesheimer's strategy is to appeal to, and play on the quasi-cultured, precious tastes of the socially and culturally pretentious élite which is the target of his satire. We can illuminate the narrative tactics which he employs to this end by examining the various devices he uses to write the implied reader into the text. . . . In *Lieblose Legenden* we can identify and isolate four principal narrative techniques which serve this purpose. They occur in a richness of variety which makes the selection of illustrative examples positively embarrassing, and a representative sample will have to suffice.

The first of these four main narrative devices is the use of casual asides such as *bekanntlich* ["as everyone knows"], *natürlich* ["naturally"], *selbstverständlich* ["of course"] and similar phrases which appeal to the complicity of, and thereby postulate the participation of, a certain kind of reader in the reading process. Such phrases exploit the cultural solidarity of an identifiable social group, assuming the common fund of experience, the shared spectrum of values and sensibilities characteristic of the snob, socialite and "culture vulture"— Nietzsche's *Kulturbanause*. (p. 63)

In "**1956—ein Pilzjahr**" Hildesheimer refers briefly to the unproductive period in Beethoven's creative life, "die *bekanntlich* von 1814 bis 1818 währte", a detail of musical history not likely to be known to anyone but the specialist. A similar, although more ironic identification of the implied reader by an appeal to his specialised knowledge can be found in "**Bildnis eines Dichters**". Here the author describes how the main character assumes the traditional pose of the *Dichterfürst* [literally, "poet-prince"], sitting in a high-backed armchair with a rug round his legs. . . . (p. 64)

Hildesheimer's second means of writing his implied reader into the text is to exploit the use of proper names, and he does this in three different ways. Firstly and most obviously, he satirises the habit of dropping names as a distinctive form of snobbery. Secondly, he not only pillories this weakness, but also plays on it to identify the implied reader as the target of his satire. This is most clearly seen in those stories where he deliberately uses fictional and non-fictional or historical names in the same context. Within the fictional world of the narrative all the names clearly have the same truth-value, but for the literate reader with any cultural pretensions there is a provocative combination of fictional names and recognisably genuine ones drawn from history. Such a reader is tempted, challenged even, to indulge and display his erudition by distinguishing the fictional from the non-fictional and thereby betray the very vice of name-dropping which the author is satirising. Thirdly, Hildesheimer uses the names of historical figures, whether implicitly or explicitly stated, as a code or form of shorthand decipherable only by the cognoscenti, a small, highly educated and well-read élite who alone can respond to, and appreciate the cultural allusions and resonances associated with such names.

The satire on the social snobbery of name-dropping, whether as practised by fictional characters or by the implied reader, is so obvious and prevalent as to require no further comment except to draw attention to one refinement which can be exemplified from **"Das Ende einer Welt"**. Here the narrator repeatedly uses the definite article to suggest that certain names are, or should be, familiar to the cultural initiates of the world created in the story. (p. 65)

In **"Das Ende einer Welt"** there is a typical combination of real and fictional names. We find fictional characters such as Herr von Perlhuhn; a Fräulein Dombrowska, who seems modelled on Isadora Duncan; [and] a choreographer whose name, Basiliewky, may be inspired by that of Diaghilev.... Yet alongside these obviously fictional and occasionally grotesque names we find explicit references to Abraham-a-Santa-Clara, Jean-Paul Marat, Jean-Philippe Rameau, Antoine Watteau, and implicit references to Béranger and Puccini. The story cannot be fully appreciated unless all such references are fully understood. The same is true, to a greater or lesser degree, of virtually every story in the book, but especially of **"1956—ein Pilzjahr,"** which makes almost encyclopaedic demands of its reader. This particular story is accessible only to the reader who can respond to the cultural resonances of names such as: Mozart, Heine, Rembrandt, Caesar, [and] Freud.... Any reader who enjoys successfully registering all the relevant associations of these names, and many university academics, especially Germanists, would be particularly susceptible to this, comes perilously close to identifying himself with the target of Hildesheimer's satire.

Finally, with reference to Hildesheimer's exploitation of proper names to specify his implied reader, we can study some examples of how he uses such names as a socially, educationally and culturally conditioned code. In **"Das Ende einer Welt"** the narrator avoids a lengthy description of a scene deliberately intended to conjure up the atmosphere of the Rococo by comparing it to a picture by Watteau. The reader who does not know who Watteau was and what his pictures look like will obviously be at a loss here. (pp. 65-6)

The next two narrative techniques to be discussed define the implied reader of *Lieblose Legenden* even more precisely, suggesting that Hildesheimer focuses his satirical attention on those readers who have not only social, but also academic pretensions. Frequently he plays on cultural allusions, especially literary *topoi*, which will be appreciated only by such readers. (pp. 66-7)

Two stories, **"Bildnis eines Dichters"** and **"Die zwei Seelen"**, play ironically on Goethe's "Zwei Seelen wohnen, ach, in meiner Brust". In the latter story Hildesheimer also recognisably parodies a procedure overworked by both German writers and critics, namely analysing one individual's personality in the light of characteristics inherited from parents of conflicting temperaments and talents. Hildesheimer develops such an analysis at considerable length, only to reject it out of hand in the last sentence of the relevant paragraph. (p. 67)

[It is primarily] Hildesheimer's repeated satirical parodies of the turgid, pseudo-scientific jargon of many would-be-critics and scholars in the liberal arts which identifies this group as the implied readers of *Lieblose Legenden* and therefore the prime target of the book's satire. For any reader with pretensions to literary scholarship, the most telling piece in this respect is **"Ich schreibe kein Buch über Kafka"**, a story first published in 1951, when the boom in Kafka studies was just beginning. This story pillories the minor academic who seeks out a minor literary figure on whom to write a major work, and is an effective satire on the mass of published "scholarship" produced by the "publish for publishing's sake" mentality. The narrator is in the process of writing the definitive biography of one Ekkehard Golch, the biographer of Samuel Johnson's biographer, James Boswell. In other words, the narrator is working at three removes from the primary figure of interest, Johnson himself. The narrator's aspirations to immortality are, in turn, based on his hope that some day someone will devote a book to him in his capacity as Golch's biographer! The smug arrogance and quasi-scientific pretensions of a small-minded academic are effectively parodied.... [The satirical point] is largely lost on any readers except those who already dwell in, or at least on the periphery of, the hallowed groves of academe.

In **"1956—ein Pilzjahr"** Hildesheimer parodies the rash of distracting footnotes and cross-references which so liberally besprinkle the pages of certain academic publications, and the information which he offers in this way is naturally even more ostentatiously trivial than usual. **"Bildnis eines Dichters"** tilts at the literary feuds and diatribes between rival writers and critics, while **"Aus meinem Tagebuch"** and **"Westcottes Glanz und Ende"** deflate the pompous pretentiousness of the art critic. The last of these stories contains a particularly ludicrous aesthetic evaluation of a tattoo on a lady's back. (pp. 68-9)

All the evidence adduced above points to the conclusion that Hildesheimer expended a considerable degree of effort and ingenuity in identifying the implied reader of *Lieblose Legenden*, and therefore the real reader and intended butt of his satire, as the middle-class pseudo-intellectual with academic leanings and philistine pretensions to the social cachet attaching to a public display of culture. But this is precisely the reader who can enjoy the art of Hildesheimer's satire while dissociating himself from its critical intent. Jonathan Swift's words from his preface to *The Battle of the Books* (1704) seem peculiarly apt here: "Satire is a sort of glass, wherein beholders do generally discover everybody's face but their own; which is the chief reason for that kind of reception it meets with in the world, and that so very few are offended with it."

We might even reason that the greater the ingenuity Hildesheimer invests in the art of his satire, above all in identifying ever more precisely the implied reader as its intended target, the less effective that satire becomes. There is a strong case for suggesting that in *Lieblose Legenden* the author eventually sacrifices satirical effect to literary virtuosity, thereby becoming something of a refined cult for initiates and cognoscenti, the very sort of readers he intended to expose and criticise. (p. 69)

Roderick H. Watt, "Self-Defeating Satire? On the Function of the Implied Reader in Wolfgang Hildesheimer's 'Lieblose Legenden'," in Forum for Modern Language Studies, *Vol. XIX, No. 1, January, 1983, pp. 58-74.*

GERT SCHIFF

[In *Marbot: Eine Biographie,* Hildesheimer] purports to resuscitate a forgotten figure in English nineteenth-century art and letters; a writer whose achievement—as was the case with Beckford, Byron, Swinburne, Wilde, and many others—was in some way linked to sexual "deviation." According to Hildesheimer, the work of Andrew Marbot has passed largely unnoticed because his ideas were too novel and radical for his own time. For this short-lived amateur art historian was the first scholar ever to have searched for the psychological roots of artistic creation, thus anticipating some of the discoveries of the psychoanalytical theory of art. . . .

[Many facts regarding Marbot's life], Hildesheimer explains, were known from an earlier biography by an American, Frederic Hadley-Chase (1888). . . . Hildesheimer, however, does not conceal his pride in his own research, which produced, among other interesting details, Marbot's hitherto unrecorded interview with Goethe. He tells us with some excitement how his own view of his subject changed dramatically when a descendant of the tutor's heirs put at his disposal all of Marbot's manuscripts, including his private papers. For then Hildesheimer realized that there had been a secret behind Marbot's busy intellectual life and aloof manner. His premature insights had been conditioned by his own extremely vulnerable psychic disposition. The trauma that drove Marbot to the point of becoming, as it were, a Freudian long before Freud was an incestuous relationship with his mother. . . .

Hildesheimer reconstructs this life with empathy, tact, and authority. Numerous excerpts from Marbot's writings add greatly to the book's interest, as do the illustrations. (p. 43)

But, alas, upon consulting a few books and museum catalogues, one finds the Delacroix lithograph represents not Andrew Marbot, but one Baron Schweiter. . . . According to the National Gallery of Scotland, the female portrait by Raeburn is not Lady Catherine Marbot, but Mrs. Scott Moncrieff. . . . And in case anyone wants more proof: there is no trace of the Marbot and Claverton families in the *Dictionary of National Biography,* nor does the National Union Catalogue list titles such as Marbot's *Art and Life,* or a biography by Frederic Hadley-Chase.

Hildesheimer has invented his hero, his hero's writings and Victorian biography. He has added the illustrations as representing the characters of his story. And one can only congratulate him on their selection: each looks exactly as the character it is meant to portray should look. He is as shrewd in his verbal commingling of fact and fiction. In many places he works with the most unabashed interpolations. . . . The "excerpts" from Marbot's writings, inevitably in German, are often interspersed with short phrases from the English "original," as if to clarify the meaning in passages difficult to translate. In impeccable scholarly fashion, Hildesheimer sifts the evidence or makes conjectures about missing information. He takes issue with his uncritical predecessor, Hadley-Chase, he rages against the tutor's sloppy editing of Marbot's writings, and he refers repeatedly to a forthcoming modern edition that will include the private papers. (pp. 43-4)

The result of so much cunning is a sustained illusion of authenticity. Nevertheless, the book is not a hoax, for it lacks deceitful intention. It has the format of a novel, it has no

footnotes, and Hildesheimer himself suggests that he is writing a fictitious biography. He uses the pretense of authenticity as a mode of representation, as a narrative device. But to what end?

In his other works Hildesheimer seems to enjoy using hoaxes, practical jokes, and mystification. Readers of his short stories and his two previous novels may remember how, in *Tynset* (1965), the narrator relates how some time after the war he used to frighten presumptive Nazi criminals with anonymous nightly phone calls saying, for instance, "The cat is out of the bag, you'd better get out!" In *Masante* (1973) the narrator approaches a young lady in the Musée Condé under Piero di Cosimo's portrait of Simonetta Vespucci; in order to please her, he invents the biography of the Renaissance beauty, characteristically including incest. . . . Yet in *Marbot,* Hildesheimer does not seem to intend to mystify or to parody scholarship. . . . (p. 44)

His true intention becomes clearer if one reads two statements of his literary creed. The first is a lecture, **"The End of Fiction,"** delivered in 1975 in Ireland; the other is the introduction to his great book [*Mozart*] (1977). In both he argues that it is no longer possible to write traditional fiction. Not only are all conventional plotting devices exhausted; but no hero—whether he is the writer's alter ego or not—can be taken as representative of our time because the "anomalous machinery" that determines our destinies transcends his, or any other person's experience. "Today, villainy is worldwide, its syndicates elude fictionalization, they appear as a near-abstract principle." In his novels, the "anomalous machinery" appears in haunting visions. In the 1975 lecture, however, he doubts whether a writer can still take his stand vis-à-vis the world by means of language. Only action—or silence—are appropriate.

The modern writer is, of course, free to write a true biography, i.e., to revive a historical figure. . . . Still, he will never be able to present the full truth about a historical character—least of all when he is dealing with genius. Hildesheimer relates movingly how in his struggle with Mozart he was always faced with the impenetrable "strangeness" of his subject.

It was therefore understandable that he should resort to a fictitious biography. For only if he created a hero and put him into a socio-historical setting could he hope to gain perfect control over the character in his interaction with "his" time. Only in a mind of his own making could he read as in an open book. In this way, Hildesheimer can be said to have attempted in *Marbot* what he believes is the highest goal of literature: to transform fiction into truth.

That his imaginary hero anticipates insights of much later aestheticians and psychologists does not undermine the credibility of the story; for the plot is, as we have seen, based on the very premise that Marbot is ahead of his time. The question whether his views and discoveries are in keeping with the spirit of the 1820s is irrelevant. . . . Nor should the historically conscious reader raise his eyebrows when Marbot's speculations adumbrate the mechanism of repression, or the function of art as wish fulfillment and catharsis. Poets and sages of all times have intuitively grasped fragments of that strange knowledge which Freud systematized. (pp. 44-5)

It becomes clear that the lengthy "excerpts" from Marbot's writings are meant not only to illustrate the genesis of his theory, but also to reflect his desperate attempts to come to terms with his trauma. Marbot wants to understand himself; hence his search for the unconscious roots of artistic creation, and his insistence that the content of a work of art is not its subject, but the artist himself and his inner life. He does away with normative aesthetics because he rejects the moral norm. His interpretations of paintings are not just artful evocations of the visual facts, but self-revelations. . . . As Hildesheimer writes, Marbot "substituted active libidinous execution by theoretical penetration into the art of its representation, and into the secret of creativity. However, this object-displacement led him beyond the spiritual heights of pure, disinterested knowledge; it led him on the other side down again into the psychic depth of the death wish."

Ever since his separation from his mother, he has been moved by a longing for annihiliation. Only artistic creation of his own can help him over her loss; but he is not an artist. As "biographer," Hildesheimer can reflect upon the sources of his character's behavior to an extent inadmissible in ordinary fiction . . . ; thus he analyzes the incest in its pathological, ethical, and romantic aspects. The two come together on the eve of Andrew's Grand Tour; their affair has its precarious blossoming after the death of his father. They part in order to spare the younger children the consequences, but they remain obsessed by each other. . . .

Marbot finds confirmation of his despair in the poetry of Leopardi and in the philosophy of Schopenhauer; but he objects that both lack consequence. Why does Schopenhauer, evangelist of the renunciation of the will to live, reject suicide? Why is Leopardi, in spite of his misery, still alive? Through a series of especially poignant events, Hildesheimer traces Andrew Marbot's growing resolution to commit suicide.

What are we to make of this sad life? It is hard to resist reading this book as a reflection on the deep absurdities of experience. If we play Hildesheimer's game, we can also say that Marbot's life at least has not been lost. For who could ask for a sweeter resurrection? (p. 45)

Gert Schiff, "The Man Who Wasn't There," in The New York Review of Books, *Vol. XXX, No. 8, May 12, 1983, pp. 43-5.*

MICHAEL TANNER

[*Marbot: A Biography* and *Mozart*] are both biographies, though of an unusual kind. *Marbot* tells us a considerable amount about a person who didn't exist, though he is surrounded by others who did. *Mozart* tells us very little indeed about the most remarkable artist who has ever existed. Both books are puzzling in crucial respects, and considering them together has added to rather than lessening my bewilderment. . . .

[Hildesheimer] produced *Mozart* in 1977 and *Marbot* in 1981. Though it is the earlier book which can't get under way without extensive broodings on the task of the biographer in general and Mozart's in particular, it is the later book which, eschewing selfconsciousness on that front, gives a clearer indication of what Hildesheimer expects of a biographer. Or perhaps not. Whereas Mozart's biographer is unquestionably Hildesheimer, using always the authorial "we", and often to very irritating effect, the biographer of Marbot is a persona, and one who happily uses the first-person singular. We don't find out much about him. . . . And it is difficult to know to what extent he is to be viewed critically. He is an extremely naive Freudian, but then so is Hildesheimer. Both have heard of the Oedipus complex, and Marbot's biographer occasionally refers to object transference; but there their use of, and so far as one can gather,

their knowledge of psychoanalysis ends. Marbot's incest with his mother—the crucial event of his life—is described as "the fulfilment of a burning mutual desire than which scarcely anything more illicit and sinful can be imagined." . . . Such gaucheries incline one to think that Hildesheimer is indulging in a laborious joke, but that idea is contradicted by the fact that the biography of Marbot is deemed worth writing because he was the first modern critic, in that he regarded individual works of art as valuable above all because of the insight they give into the recesses of the mind that created them, and he therefore provided a blueprint for Hildesheimer's activities in *Mozart*. For Hildesheimer not only loves Mozart's work, he regards him as the supreme critical challenge because of the eternally insoluble riddle: How could that man have written those works?

The biographer of Marbot is not, of course, faced with any such riddle. If the reader of *Marbot* asks why it was necessary for Hildesheimer to invent him, the answer is: because he didn't exist. He plugs what Hildesheimer clearly regards as a wanton hole in cultural history, his alleged depth-psychological forays validating later critical procedures. The last entry in Marbot's notebooks, before he committed suicide, is "The artist plays on our soul, but who plays on the soul of the artist?" and his biographer comments "With this question Marbot's notebooks end. He was the first to ask it. We are still waiting for the answer." But who does "we" refer to? Not, at any rate, to the vast majority of contemporary critics, whose apparatus is so sophisticated that they are likely to be unmanned by such a Marbotian passage as this from *Mozart:*

> Hardly any serious student of Mozart can have avoided playing this game of key speculation [ie, What is the characteristic emotional tone of works in G minor, A major, C minor, E flat, in Mozart?], for it is fruitful and open to all; everyone can play and, by sharing his experience, can consider himself a winner. There would be losers only if some witness were found to swear that Mozart wrote the andante of the G minor Symphony, for example, in high spirits, in a great creative moment, feeling himself capable, in a truly imperious way, of mediating for the listener the experience of a tragic feeling. . . .

Not only is the idea that the ultimate criterion for establishing the tone of a passage is the author's word absurd, but the dangers of circularity for anyone engaged in an enterprise such as Hildesheimer's are plain: one validates one's claims about the work from what the author says about it, and then writes one's biography of the author's soul from what one has found in his work.

Oddly enough Sir Andrew Marbot, in the numerous passages on works of art quoted from his notebooks and letters, never seems inclined to do any such thing. The brilliantly perceptive remarks (which of course demonstrate that Hildesheimer is a superb critic of painting) about Mantegna's frescoes in Mantua, Giotto's in Padua . . . , Rembrandt's portraits, especially his self-portraits, neither claim nor infer anything about the artists, nor are the artists called in to explain or determine the character and quality of their work. Marbot's interest in the wound and the bow is frequently stressed by his biographer as having its source in his own wound—his relationship with his mother, and the necessity of its termination—and his lack of a bow: he valued artistic creativity above all other things, and knew himself to be totally devoid of it. Like many people in the same predicament, he was insatiably curious to know what it would be like, in detail, to be an artist. But that curiosity seems, in spite of a great deal that his biographer says, to have left his critical faculty intact. Marbot also emerges as an acute psychologist, of Byron, for example, and of Schopenhauer.... But he is also shown as being acute enough to know that the gap between art and artist is often very considerable, and not something to make a fuss about.

A fuss is exactly what Hildesheimer does make about Mozart. During the heavy breathing of the opening pages he derides many previous biographers for sentimentality and comic Romantic pseudo-connections. No one is insignificant enough to escape his contempt.... Not only can we agree that "We cannot take this seriously". I don't see why, in a serious book, we should be asked to take it at all. Hildesheimer immediately continues:

> In Mozart's rather deliberate objectivity we see that unique element, the absolutely puzzling.... Mozart's music reproduces the depth of the experience for us without the experience; as the expression of the absolute it does not reach the experience itself, nor does it want to. Everyone understands Mozart's music differently. In reality, no one understands it, but the little we do understand is enough to suggest the rest, which we are left to interpret.

If that's the kind of thing you like, this is the book for you. It seems to me that in this passage Hildesheimer fails to understand, because he doesn't want to—it would short-circuit his investigations—that he has resolved the "absolutely puzzling" in saying that "Mozart's music reproduces the depth of experience for us without the experience". Not that that is the last word on the subject, but it's an excellent start. By reproducing the depth of experience, Mozart leaves his listeners free to fill in their own content—what answers, in *their* experience, to the deep expressiveness of Mozart. In that sense, there is nothing to understand: Mozart's music is pellucid, and anyone who finds it problematic, whether or not he is inclined to invoke the bizarre category of the "absolutely puzzling", does so because he is bewildered by being able to gaze through so transparent a medium at what has most disturbed him in life....

However, if we confront what Mozart's music achieves with what we know of his life, a new rash of problems breaks out. It isn't in the least surprising that, faced with the phenomenon of his art, people have sentimentalized his life, nor that that in turn should give rise to the backlash which we find in its crudest form in Peter Shaffer's unspeakable play *Amadeus,* and in a somewhat more sophisticated version in Hildesheimer's book. Both here and in *Marbot* he is enormously concerned with his subject's letters.... The relationship of Mozart to his letters is taken to be much more devious: his pathetic begging-letters are alleged to contain elements of exaggeration, calculating self-pity and disingenuous self-exculpation. Their structure is compared to a stilted *opera seria* aria, with invocations to cruel deities and so forth. Such deconstructions are often clever, and will have their appeal, but in general they are only supported, as is a great deal else throughout the book, by volleys of "perhapses", as the author himself admits at the outset. His discovery that Mozart's most moving letter ... is an accurate paraphrase of a popular work of philosophy by Moses Mendelssohn, doesn't impress me as much as it does him. That Mozart didn't originate its sentiments or phraseology doesn't make it any less sincere. But Hildesheimer is a relentless moralist; Marbot is more fortunate, his biographer usually insisting—he has lapses, as we have seen—that he has a duty to abstain from moral criticism. Hildesheimer reads like a converted sentimentalist, scandalized to find that his hero,

who gave more to the world than any other person has done, was a moral mediocrity....

So in Hildesheimer's view there is Mozart himself, the great unknowable; his letters and reported behaviour, unreliable guides to his true nature; and his works, many of them transcendently great but mysteriously independent of that hidden self. That means that we can only expect from this book illumination of the works; and sadly I didn't find any. Even when he is dealing with the operas, where he might be expected to be at his best, he has nothing insightful to say....

Hildesheimer neither fulfils Marbot's criteria for being a good critic, nor practises criticism as well as Marbot himself. Plagued with the selfconsciousness of an age which produces vastly more "serious" criticism than art, he is only able to achieve critical insight when he adopts a persona. I look forward to the promised publication of Marbot's complete notebooks, from which, in the all-too-brief biography, we are only given tantalizing extracts; but not at all to any further furrowed-browed performances from Hildesheimer *sich selbst.*

Michael Tanner, "Between Art and Artist," in The Times Literary Supplement, *No. 4201, October 7, 1983, p. 1074.*

JOHN SIMON

Wolfgang Hildesheimer's *Marbot: A Biography* is a marvelous hoax; would that it were as marvelous a book. Mr. Hildesheimer ... [has made Sir Andrew Marbot] out of whole cloth. But it is quality cloth: fine batiste, sheer enough to let us see through it the spirit of the age and some of its prime embodiers, yet firm enough to take in an unwarned reader of considerable sophistication.

Andrew Marbot is the scion of Northumbrian Catholic gentry, educated by a worldly Jesuit chaplain in literature and languages, and by his maternal grandfather, Lord Claverton, a former ambassador to Italy and art collector, in the fine arts. He despises his unintellectual father, but is enthralled by Lady Catherine, his beautiful and refined mother.... Andrew will grow up an inveterate lover of art and infatuate lover of his mother. Oddly enough, it is the latter passion that, upon his father's death, is consummated, but though he would give up everything (he does give up God) for it, his mother, equally impassioned, renounces it after two years for the sake of her religion and her younger children; to one of them Andrew cedes his estates as he goes off into permanent exile on the Continent....

All along Marbot keeps discovering more and more old masters and makes pert and pertinent comments about them, in letters to his tutor, mother and friends or in noteboooks he keeps for possible publication. His special heroes are Rembrandt and Shakespeare, certain Flemish masters, Tiepolo and Watteau, and, far-sightedly, Turner, in defense of whom he writes the only article printed in his lifetime....

The dazzling mini-essays we also get [in *Marbot*] are, alas, too long to quote. Continually, Marbot searches for "the relationship between the artist's creativity and his command over his own life," not for "the event depicted but the painter who made it happen." At the same time, however, he champions painting of "such truth and dignity" that we can ignore "the abstract concepts from which the idea sprang." "Nature," he recognizes, "is the subject of beauty, but not its embodiment," and, in a passage that mysteriously occurs only in the American edition (the passage . . . is not in the published German text), we find him even presaging abstract art. (p. 11)

The literary-biographical-historical sleight-of-mind is carried out magisterially. Mr. Hildesheimer, who has lived in England and various other countries, is at home in the world of all the arts as well as in the art of worldliness. . . . In the German edition the author interlards his text with parenthesized passages in English, supposedly as Marbot wrote them and not susceptible of perfect German rendering. . . . The book is illustrated with paintings of its main characters and photographs of their abodes, which, though phony, are powerfully persuasive. (pp. 11, 30)

These and similar devices are always ingenious and sometimes amusing. The disquisitions on incest and other Freudianly tinged observations are sober and delicate enough to be inoffensive even if not particularly enlightening. The pronouncements on art, whether Marbot's or the author's comments on them, are often criticism of true distinction. There are vivid opinions on sundry subjects, from cookery through poetry. . . . (p. 30)

Perhaps the best things are the dizzyingly deft sketches of renowned figures. . . . Unfortunately, such pungency and penetration are seldom extended to the main fictional characters, and the reader often feels that he is being led through the story blindly, by a remarkably intelligent seeing-eye dog miraculously gifted with speech.

Since Marbot is forever worrying the mystery of creation—the cause and quiddity of the artistic impulse—it may be licit to wonder what made Mr. Hildesheimer, who began as an engaging fabulist and fantasist . . . , discard fiction as fiction for fiction costumed as biography—or, in the case of his *Mozart,* naked biography? As he said elsewhere, he considers the possibilities of fiction exhausted. He seems, consequently, to have transferred his concern to what caused it, or any form of art, to be created and how this was done, when it still could be done. But on this he does not shed conspicuous light; indeed, the book ends with Marbot's last diary entry: "The artist plays on our soul, but who plays on the soul of the artist?" It is a question, Mr. Hildesheimer tells us, that Marbot "was the first to ask. . . . We are still waiting for the answer."

Regrettably that last sentence is a mistranslation. It is faintly hopeful. The German says, "The answer is still outstanding," which sounds much more discouraged. (pp. 30-1)

As a whole *Marbot* is smaller than the sum of its parts, but collectors of incidental felicities will not emerge from it empty-handed. Some may even glean from it a secret significance, which one of its characters, Count von Platen, expressed in two famous verses that are not quoted in this book. "Who with his own eyes has gazed on Beauty, / Is already forfeit unto Death." It matters little whether that beauty is the forbidden one of the mother's body or the elusive one of artistic perfection. (p. 31)

John Simon, "A Passion for Art and Mother," in The New York Times, *October 9, 1983, pp. 11, 30-1.*

DOUGLAS BLAU

To write that this biography [*Marbot*] is actually a novel is redundant, for the biographer's art—like that of the critic and historian—is one of transmutation and misrepresentation, of fashioning believable lies. Whether substantiating fiction or interpreting fact, biographers can only hope that readers will think them realists rather than fabulists and will overlook the distortions and gaps.

That there is no real difference between knowledge and speculation, between history and myth, is the premise of Wolfgang Hildesheimer's portrait of an early 19th-century English connoisseur . . . — a book that reads as a satiric attack upon the academic positivism that [Hildesheimer claims] "plagues the art-historical and biographical trades." . . . A revisionist not wanting for wit, Hildesheimer advises his readers to suspect that all information is simply conjecture disguised. Distrust the declarative! is his battle cry.

What, then, can we believe about the life and work of Hildesheimer's subject, art critic Sir Andrew Marbot (1801-1830?)? Following his chronicler's advice, we must assume that Marbot is not his own creation so much as that of his describer. . . . Accordingly, the true hero of this novel is Hildesheimer, who arranged Marbot's meetings with Goethe, Byron, Shelley, Schopenhauer, Denon, Delacroix, Zelig, Wordsworth, Turner, Berlioz, Blechen, Blake, Corot; Hildesheimer, whose character respectively dismisses St. Augustine as "a man whose chief claim to fame was his perfect use of the pluperfect tense," refers to Vasari as "that assiduous originator of legends," and faults Dante for his dependence on faith; Wolfgang Hildesheimer, fabulist, realist, *fictionateur.*

Every sentence in his period-piece, his immaculately constructed ruse, seems a *double-entendre* or the product of subterfuge; the result is reflexive fiction with a self-reflecting hero whose verisimilitude is as easily accepted as it is denied. Sir Andrew Marbot is painted as part pensive Hamlet, wondering whether it would be better not to be, and part wandering Oedipus—not blind but self-exiled for his incestuous infidelity. (pp. 21, 23)

In order to illustrate his own belief that the words "art" and "life" are synonymous, Hildesheimer writes of Marbot's actions and theories as if they were inxtricably intertwined. Thus Andrew looks at art as if looking at himself through his biographer's eyes: he considers paintings independent of their social context, outside history. Obsessed with his mother, this art critic investigates "the source of creation." Believing that a work's "true meaning" can be grasped only by understanding its maker's "unconscious impulses," Andrew tries to devise a scientific way to objectify the motivations of (in his own Romantic term) the artist's "soul." Had he succeeded, Marbot would have been able to do what Hildesheimer has done: write of a psychological concept as if it were concrete.

In a sense, *Marbot* is similar to the story of Pinocchio: an omnipotent narrator tells a lie—a puppet can become a man—then sends his central character off on a quest for truth. Yet in no way does the tone of this novel resemble that of a fairy tale, for Hildesheimer needed to use a realist's voice to demonstrate that objectivity is a literary conceit. It is to his credit that the biography's illusion of authenticity does not depend on the genre's well-worn tricks: faithfulness here is not the result of a careful rendering of minute peripheral details or of placing Andrew in rooms with illustrious proper nouns; nor is it created through the use of documentary images . . . or accuracy with dates. Rather, Marbot's plausibility is owed to the author's crafty use of the conditional phrase—to his unwillingness to feign infallibility, to this authority's open confession that his method is inherently flawed. Hildesheimer's false honesty is disarming and urges us to believe . . . that truth lies in the convincing use of a subjective voice. (p. 23)

Douglas Blau, in a review of "Marbot: A Biography," in Art in America, *Vol. 72, No. 2, February, 1984, pp. 21, 23.*

MONA KNAPP

In honor of Max Frisch's seventieth birthday, friends and colleagues collected sundry essays for the festschrift [commemorative volume] *Begegnungen.* Wolfgang Hildesheimer's contribution that that occasion is reprinted [in *Mitteilungen an Max: Über den Stand der Dinge und anderes*]. . . . Hildesheimer's work is distinguished not only by cultivated intellectualism and scintillating wit, but by its sheer diversity. It includes virtually every literary and journalistic genre, and even the graphic arts, as demonstrated here by six original pen-and-ink drawings.

The purchaser of this handsome booklet, hoping to find revelations regarding "the state of things," will be vastly disappointed. It is a flippant compilation of wordplays, associations and jokes of the *Kalauer* species. Hildesheimer opens with free prose variations on Hölderlin (**"Hälfte des Lebens"**) and Rilke (**"Herbsttag"**) that will insult the most tolerant reader—they are lowbrow, shallow and at times outright silly. Next come musings on whether it is not more blessed to receive than to give after all, what hell might be like, . . . et cetera. But these profound themes do not hold the author's interest, and he soon moves on to more practical matters: for example, might it not be that not only many, but in fact all cooks spoil the pudding? . . . And, even more vital, how is one to fill the empty hours before boarding the elevators labeled "For 6 persons only" while waiting for five more people to show up? Difficult questions indeed.

Through all this, the narrator remains exceedingly pleased with his own wittiness and with his stance of educated ennui. Laconic references to identity crisis, or to the impossibility of having been born someone else, say nothing whatsoever of relevance to Frisch's works. But that is apparently not the point here. For readers too poorly read to catch all the puns, a glossary is provided, containing originals of all the poems, quotations and terms parodied.

If Hildesheimer is trying to satirize Frisch's recurring themes and "everyday metaphysics," the attempt most definitely fails. . . . The book's only redeeming feature is its esthetic makeup, with lovely print on thick, eggshell-colored paper.

Mona Knapp, in a review of "Mitteilungen an Max: Über den Stand der Dinge und anderes," in World Literature Today, *Vol. 58, No. 3, Summer, 1984, p. 413.*

CHRISTIAN GRAWE

Wolfgang Hildesheimer's thirteen speeches delivered over a period of twenty-five years [and collected in *Das Ende der Fiktionen: Reden aus fünfundzwanzig Jahren*] are thoughtful, precise, elegantly formulated, and make for most enjoyable reading. They are also very informative in that they shed much light on the author's literary development, ideas, convictions, interests, and—last but not least—personality . . . , which comes across as honest, modest, and humane. Two speeches are written in English (translations supplied by the author), and one is a personal statement titled **"Mein Judentum,"** which adds a

reasoned voice to the recent discussion by German Jews (e.g., Fleischmann, Broder) about their heritage.

Hildesheimer outgrew his surrealism of the fifties and sixties and, after two autobiographical novels (*Tynset,* 1965; *Masante,* 1973), turned to biographical writing. This, however, is not the straightforward, matter-of-fact kind which he calls "Dokumentenbiographie." Rather, he incorporates in subtle ways the sur-realistic elements with reality, thus creating "spekulative Biographie," which amounts to a new form of fiction, even though Hildesheimer would not call it that. He indicates that for him there will be no return to traditional fiction (hence the title of the book) and that he regards the contemporary novel as trivial. In his view, the function of literature is "not to turn truth into fiction but to turn fiction into truth: to condense truth out of fiction." . . .

The concept has so far resulted in two major works: a biography of a real person, Mozart, and one of a fictional character, Marbot. In *Mozart* (1977) Hildesheimer employed his artistic imagination to rescue the composer from the fragmentation of partisan biographers. . . . [The protagonist of] *Marbot* (1981) is a would-be artist turned art critic whose life story Hildesheimer sets in the real world of the romantic period. Thus, in the first case, reality inspires speculation, and in the second, speculation is merged with reality. In [*Das Ende der Fiktionen*] Hildesheimer elaborates on both projects and adds a new piece to the Marbot mosaic: a speech titled **"Schopenhauer und Marbot."** When one considers Hildesheimer's attempts to create a new reality which encompasses fact and fiction, it is not surprising that he is fascinated by the question of objectivity versus subjectivity.

Hildesheimer speaks of fellow writers with sympathy and insight. The exception is Thomas Mann, who, Hildesheimer believes, never even attempted "to establish any relationship or parallele [*sic*!] with our time" and who produced "high class reading matter without problems"—surely a misjudgment of spectacular proportions. How a Jewish German can ignore the relevance and urgency of *Das Gesetz* is beyond me.

Christian Grawe, in a review of "Das Ende der Fiktionen: Reden aus fünfundzwanzig Jahren," in World Literature Today, *Vol. 59, No. 3, Summer, 1985, p. 425.*

PUBLISHERS WEEKLY

[*The Collected Stories of Wolfgang Hildesheimer*] are less conventional stories than *jeux d'ésprit,* after-dinner performances, fanciful jests told in a mocking tone. In **"The End of the World,"** the guests at a soirée given on her artificial island by the Marchesa Montetristo . . . are too engrossed in a recital of rococo music performed by musicians dressed in period costumes to notice that the island is sinking. Music and talk of music is a recurrent strain, jokey, sometimes amusing and always sophisticated. . . . The playful tone is that of a literary intellectual and man of wide culture who has no stomach for philistines and charlatans. The targets of the satiric barbs are perhaps too obvious, and the humor is often rather broad in the Teutonic manner, but these pieces are nothing if not civilized.

A review of "The Collected Stories of Wolfgang Hildesheimer," in Publishers Weekly, *Vol. 231, No.16, April 24, 1987, p. 61.*

DAISY ALDAN

"I listen to [a] vaguely imagined song that sings itself," says a guitarist in one [tale in *The Collected Stories of Wolfgang Hildesheimer*], and that inaudible song suggests the immaterial world that lies beyond the familiar and is the constant concern of this author. These intensely witty works presume a reader with a background in German Romanticism who would have literary insight into the multilayered references they contain. . . . [Hildesheimer] holds the mirror up to the conventions that reveal their hollowness and absurdity—conventions Saul Bellow has identified as "the ideal constructions" of contemporary behavior. Like Mr. Bellow, Mr. Hildesheimer is adept in the use of hyperbole and caricature while depicting himself as a spectator who values the nonmaterial. Whether the author is describing the inundation of an Italian island owned by the Marchesa Montetristo . . . , or the hilarious biography of Gottlieb Theodor Pilz, who became distinguished for "the works which never came into being," subtleties of meaning repeatedly emerge. The stories (there are 19 here) develop organically, expanding, flowering, resonating. Outstanding among them are **"The Garret,"** a small poetic masterpiece in which a young man eliminates the last support of a fragile structure and founders in the rubble, and **"Missives to Max,"** a clever intertwining of maxims that have become clichés of contemporary thought. The narrator writes to his friend Max that he is working on "a metaphysics of everyday life," and that may be said to be what these tales contain. . . . These magical stories are especially welcome in a time when works of raw reality and not the "real" proliferate.

> *Daisy Aldan, in a review of "The Collected Stories of Wolfgang Hildesheimer," in* The New York Times Book Review, *May 10, 1987, p. 20.*

RAYMOND E. LINDGREN

[*The Collected Stories of Wolfgang Hildesheimer*] serve as a good introduction to [Hildesheimer's] work. They are an interesting potpourri, often focusing on human failure or on some strange event: an owl's being carried to Athens to perch on the Parthenon, an endless party, the ultimate in gruel reduced to a blob in the bottom of a pan, and finally, in **"Missives to Max,"** a clutch of clichés that ends in the nothingness of self. A moral: Life is a dismal trial, better finished quickly and quietly, for we are all mediocre in person, thought, and deed—except perhaps Hildesheimer.

> *Raymond E. Lindgren, in a review of "The Collected Stories of Wolfgang Hildesheimer," in* Library Journal, *Vol. 112, No. 9, May 15, 1987, p. 97.*

PAUL STUEWE

The modern European tradition of deadpan absurdity, exemplified by Kafka and Calvino, has another stellar recruit in Wolfgang Hildesheimer. . . . [Pieces in *The Collected Stories of Wolfgang Hildesheimer*] offer small-scale versions of the same sort of dedicated pursuit of outrageous ideas: an acclaimed musician yearns for a career as an insurance agent, party guests maintain proper decorum while their host's island sinks around them, and an artist progresses from canvas to shrubbery to human skin in the search for an ultimate form of expression. A few of these fictions are merely clever, but the majority sparkle with a degree of wit and imaginative inventiveness that puts them at the very top of their literary class.

> *Paul Stuewe, in a review of "The Collected Stories of Wolfgang Hildesheimer," in* Quill and Quire, *Vol. 53, No. 9, September, 1987, p. 86.*

David Huddle

1942-

American short story writer and poet.

Huddle's works are set in such diverse locales as rural Virginia, Vietnam, and New York City. According to John Engels, "[Huddle's] characters are, like himself, expatriates, and each measures himself by the degree to which he has deviated from what is right and good, and delivered himself over to the humiliations of evil." For example, the story "Rosie Baby," in Huddle's first book, *A Dream with No Stump Roots in It* (1975), centers on the disillusionment of an American soldier in Vietnam who is forced by the conditions of war to betray his moral values. Huddle's penchant for introducing surreal elements into ordinary situations is reflected in the collection's title story, in which a man becomes obsessed by the fear that the roots of a tree stump will grow through the floor of his house and strangle his wife and baby. John Engels asserted: "This is a profound and moving book. It ascribes an unfashionable dignity to man, and his moral dimension."

Huddle's second short story collection, *Only the Little Bone* (1986), contains seven tales relating significant episodes in the coming of age of two brothers. Six of the tales are set in a small Virginia factory town. One critic commented: "The scrupulous avoidance of pyrotechnics, the quiet, steady tone, captures the lives of a family—parents, grandparents, children— in small, revealing gestures. This is how life was in the small town of Rosemary, Madison County, Virginia; how it looked and felt, and how memory transforms it into legend."

Huddle has also written a collection of poems, *Paper Boy* (1979). The first part of this volume describes experiences and idiosyncrasies of residents of a small Virginia town during the 1950s as seen through the eyes of a paperboy. In the second half, the youth leaves home to become a soldier in Vietnam. In a review of this collection, Susan Wood noted: "For Huddle, memory is a kind of sacrament, rescuing people and places and events from insignificance, and this makes for a wonderfully outward poetry full of real speech and real people, vivid detail and emotion deeply felt and truly rendered."

(See also *Contemporary Authors,* Vols. 57-60.)

ROWE PORTIS

Huddle's stories [in *A Dream with No Stump Roots in It*] present a surface that is disturbing enough in itself, and they reveal below this an undercurrent of troubled fantasy. . . . [Three stories]—including **"The Interrogation of the Prisoner Bung by Mister Hawkins and Sergeant Tree,"** about as good a story as anyone has written about the war in Vietnam—depict Americans being brutal in Asia or pious in Africa. . . . Huddle's grim stories bring to mind the early work of Harry Crews or Tom Topor; serious readers of fiction will find them rewarding.

Photograph by Donna Kaplan. Courtesy of David Huddle.

Rowe Portis, in a review of "A Dream with No Stump Roots in It," in Library Journal, *Vol. 100, No. 12, June 15, 1975, p. 1240.*

JOHN ENGELS

[*A Dream with No Stump Roots in It*] is a collection of short stories by a young Southern writer from whom, as they say, we will hear more. Huddle is a Virginian who now lives in Vermont, having got there by way of Vietnam, Germany, and New York City. His characters are, like himself, expatriates, and each measures himself by the degree to which he has deviated from what is right and good, and delivered himself over to the humiliations of evil. Huddle is one of the few writers—young or old—who is willing to profess artistically a belief in a hierarchy of loves, values and choices, to acknowledge sin and the possibility of its expiation. There are ways in which he resembles, for me, Bernanos, Mauriac, Powers, and Greene in his steadfast concern with man as his own spiritual adversary on a battlefield which offers, unequivocally, damnation and salvation.

I hasten to add that Huddle is also unequivocally pessimistic about man's ability to win out over the Devil; but there is nothing stoical about him. His great dignity is that he assumes personal responsibility for his failures, and takes full credit for whatever small triumphs he may achieve. There is never a hint of self-pity in the stories: for me the most characteristic image is that of Carson, the hero of **"The Proofreader,"** having himself a bowl of clam chowder and crackers while he interestedly listens to his wife and another woman discuss his most intimate failures and virtues. If evil is truly ubiquitous and dominates human experience, it is equally true that men fight to be good, and measure their worth by how well they succeed.

Huddle's characters are always discovering—like Luther, a fundamentalist missionary who finds himself well over his head in the midst of an African sex cult—how far they have come from where they have been. Most of them have been in a place that has strongly inculcated a sense of personal responsibility, a fundamental ethic that the author believes in as strongly as he believes in the inevitability of transgression. Everybody sins in this book, and knows it, and is humiliated by it. The word *shame* crops up over and over throughout the collection. (p. 132)

The hero of **"Rosie Baby,"** an American soldier guarding a garbage dump in order to keep the Vietnamese scavengers from discovering classified materials, is broken by his realization that his belief in love, honor and friendship is helpless in the face of the more powerful orders that prevail. He betrays the people whom he has befriended. (p. 133)

There is, finally, the *persona* of [**"A Dream with No Stump Roots in It"**] who "makes a stump out of an oak tree" and then becomes increasingly obsessed with the roots that remain, and cause him to dream of "strangulation, of roots coming up through the floor of my house to choke my wife and sweet baby . . ." His wife is troubled and does not understand: he tries to burn the stump and fails; he goes out one night into the yard and thinks: "There are worms and moles too . . . and I took off my [pajamas] tops and bottoms and laid myself down on the earth in the cold and wet. I wished it would rain."

He is seen by the milkman and the paperboy and finally discovered by his wife.

> What are you doing out here? Like Christ, like Lazarus, I rose, shamefaced, gathering my pajamas, looking at the imprint my body had made, a place of matted grass perfectly the shape of my body there on the lawn. I wanted to tell her, there are worms, there are moles, there are roots, but instead I said, I am ashamed, I am deeply sorry, and I slunk past her through the doorway.

To recognize the danger and try to prevail against it, and to find ourselves powerless to effect the good is despair. We are subdued, or prevail to the degree that we are wrong or right. Huddle does not feel we have much chance, that we risk ridicule and shame, and that most of what we believe is rooted in another place and time, and is irretrievable. (pp. 133-34)

This is a profound and moving book. It ascribes an unfashionable dignity to man, and his moral dimension. The writing is characterized by simplicity, directness and, of all things, eloquence. The characterization is strong and open. The formal balance of the stories is apparent without ever being obvious, and the stories are notable for their willingness to be resolute.

This is a strong first collection. (p. 134)

John Engels, "Of Sin, Damnation, and Salvation," in The Carleton Miscellany, *Vol. XV, No. 2, Spring-Summer, 1975-76, pp. 132-34.*

ROCKWELL GRAY

David Huddle's collection of stories *A Dream with No Stump Roots in It* takes its memorable title from a final two-page dream fragment in which the author recounts a fantasy of uprooting a stubborn stump left in his lawn after the tree was cut down. Whether this title piece is meant to stand for the book as a whole I cannot say. Perhaps it provides an organizing rubric for the five principal pieces in the collection, two of them set in Viet Nam, two in New York City, and a fifth in a quasi-surrealistic and wildly fantastic Africa, where an American missionary comes to bring religion to the natives.

Huddle's stories oscillate between being heavily pointed and diffuse. The longest of them, **"The Proofreader,"** is by turns absorbing and aimless. Its central figure . . . is, like most of Huddle's characters, an uprooted and aimless soul. He falls in for one day with a lovely but vaguely drawn young woman who meets him sipping gin on a park bench in New York City. We follow the two of them through meandering episodes aimed to point up the dingy life of Carson Moore, who has drifted from a lackluster childhood in a small North Carolina town to an ingrown middle age in the City. Moore is going nowhere—that much is patent. He returns from his day's adventure with Leslie to his dreary marriage and idle ways. If we are to assume, as Huddle appears to suggest, that he is somehow better and wiser for a day that culminated in his wife's confessional conversation with the blithe spirit from the park, there is still little to be garnered from this final return, slightly refreshed, to the old routine. The story is a warmed over version of the "displaced soul" or "dangling man" motif by now so well worked in modern American fiction.

The two tales set in Viet Nam (**"The Interrogation of the Prisoner Bung by Mister Hawkins and Sergeant Tree"** and **"Rosie Baby"**) take a certain power from the situations they portray in life behind the lines of a deeply absurd war. But again the characters and the action are almost formulaically familiar and do not begin to embody the potentially devastating raw material of their setting. Finally, **"Luther,"** the dreamlike account of a young Protestant missionary's capers in Africa, though it successfully employs a flat, vaguely Midwestern tone of first-person narration to heighten the sense of an absurd world, does not have anywhere to go. If it is Huddle's purpose to suggest that none of us is going anywhere in particular, he has done that successfully enough, and the concluding dream of a smooth lawn and suburban life divested of annoying stump roots may then appear the appropriate sign for these pale life-stories entangled in the knotty world Huddle tries to portray. (pp. 461-62)

Rockwell Gray, "Varieties of Innocence," in Book Forum, *Vol. II, No. 3, 1976, pp. 459-62.*

SUSAN WOOD

This first book of poems [*Paper Boy*] by a writer who has also published a number of much-admired short stories strikes me as a bravely unfashionable book. It is a welcome one in the face of the sometimes tired descriptions and excessively private voices in the prevailing "poetry of nuance." What makes Huddle's poems different is the narrative that informs them; taken together, they tell the story of a boy growing up in a rural community in the '50s, of his family, his friends, of what he sees and hears as he delivers the newspaper to the townspeople, a cast of fascinating characters. For Huddle, memory is a kind of sacrament, rescuing people and places and events from insignificance, and this makes for a wonderfully outward poetry full of real speech and real people, vivid detail and emotion deeply felt and truly rendered. . . .

Paper Boy reads like prose but has the quickness and illumination of poetry, marking Huddle as an original and distinctive American voice.

> Susan Wood, *"Discovering New Voices,"* in Book World—The Washington Post, *August 19, 1979, p. 8.*

R. BRUCE SCHAUBLE

[*Paper Boy*] immediately calls to mind Masters' *Spoon River Anthology*. Like Masters, Huddle has re-created life in a small town by describing the adventures and idiosyncrasies of its inhabitants; but whereas in the *Spoon River Anthology* the point of view shifts to a new speaker in each poem, in this book the town is seen through the eyes of the man who was once the town's paper boy.

The poems, which deal primarily with events in the early 1950s, are short, witty, and down to earth. As various characteres appear and reappear in the situations described, the fabric of life in the town is woven before one's eyes. The predominating tone of the book is one of nostalgic amusement, captured in the small but central events in the lives of the citizenry. . . . The one complex poem in the collection is a telescoping in 14 short segments of the years from 1960-1970, during which time the writer left home, went to Vietnam, and returned only in time to witness his grandfather's death and funeral. It is a powerful sequence, and it emphasizes the strength and value of the traditional small town relationships as personified in the figure of the grandfather, whose presence lends considerable emotional weight to this thoroughly accessible and enjoyable book of poems. (pp. 23-4)

> R. Bruce Schauble, in a review of *"Paper Boy,"* in Kliatt Young Adult Paperback Book Guide, *Vol. XIII, No. 6, September, 1979, pp. 23-4.*

DAVE SMITH

There is no question in my mind that David Huddle's first collection, *Paper Boy,* aims at defining reality. His book, a kind of *Spoon River Anthology,* authentically explores a rural Virginia town complete with eccentric characters, set-jawed relationships, civil decay, small jobs, first loves and true fights, and Death. It is very like fiction, like Southern fiction: dedicated to the psychological imprisonment of people whose lives are demeaned, abused, and yet impacted with the tonnage of explosive possibility. These stories are human and grit true as facts and we believe that in spite of everything wrong back there they throve; but they are only stories, not enough for poetry. The poem about strikers getting shot for their action cannot be allowed to end ''things like that / can happen anywhere.'' Poetry's truth is greater than fact. Huddle's lack of music, his nonchalance within words, trivializes rather than illuminates reality. These are poems only in their resort to lineation and simile. We are drawn through them not by poetry but by fiction's suspense; the language is too inert to engender either transcendence or transformation of factual and local detail. Everything comes to seem thereby predictable and stereotypical, truly formulaic: in honky tonk world we cannot have *real* emotional responses to *real* people. Everything is a joke, especially the stud-colloquial, pseudo-intimate, leering and

winking narrator, but a joke just one boot short of vision. Huddle has necessary tools, an eye for realistic detail, a sense of dramatic organization, a feel for moments of crisis that go to the heart of what it means to be alive; he can be interesting and readable. In fact Huddle is rarely a bad writer, but as poet he has no ear and is mediocre. His poems are, I would say, semi-tough prose anecdotes. (p. 40)

> Dave Smith, *"One Man's Music: Some Recent American Poetry,"* in The American Poetry Review, *Vol. 9, No. 2, March-April, 1980, pp. 40-3.*

KIRKUS REVIEWS

[*Only the Little Bone* contains seven] interlinking stories about growing up in (and growing away from) a small factory-town in Virginia, carrying the lives of two brothers into marriage and early adulthood.

In the childhood summer of **"Poison Oak,"** Reed Bryant and his brother Duncan are given swimming lessons (by their mother) in a local river, while their father goes daily to his job as manager of the carbide factory in Rosemary, Virginia. Pleasures for the reader here are numerous, not only in the graceful ways the author evokes time and place, but in his unobtrusive suggestion of danger underlying the homely surfaces of things; by story's end, it's understood that a sexually malicious farmhand has rubbed the inside of the mother's bathing suit with poison oak. **"Summer of the Magic Show"** is equally rewarding in its whole, as Duncan goes to college, loses his girl, and briefly reveals his own streak of sexual malice. . . . Less successful is the shallower **"Save One for Mainz,"** which takes Reed to his culturally naive GI days in Germany. And the bottom falls out in **"Dirge Notes,"** a bloated, Faulkner-rhetorical piece on the death of a grandfather. . . .

Overall, a couple of slumps along with some very bright work, making a reader look forward to what Huddle might do next.

> A review of *"Only the Little Bone,"* in Kirkus Reviews, *Vol. LIV, No. 8, April 15, 1986, p. 568.*

MEREDITH SUE WILLIS

David Huddle's excellent new book of linked short stories, *Only the Little Bone,* is not just another tale of growing up south of the Mason-Dixon line. Its real interest, even when the narrator is still a young boy, lies in the depiction of the lines of power within the family, the community, the industries that support the community—and of the kind of men these institutions produce. . . .

The writing . . . throughout is multilayered and always controlled. Moreover, there is an interplay among the stories that enriches the book as a whole. Only rarely does Mr. Huddle misstep, and I suspect that the flaws seem greater than they are in contrast to the accomplishments of the rest of the book. One story, **"Dirge Notes,"** is marked by a taint of sentimentality over the death of a beloved grandfather, and another, **"Save One for Mainz,"** about a soldier in the period of the Vietnam War, hinders the reader's engagement by a certain lack of generosity toward the characters. . . .

Otherwise, there is one solid success after another. The last piece, the title story, is a reprise of themes and techniques. Told in the present tense, **"Only the Little Bone"** appears at first to be a boy's vivid impressions of day-to-day life during a polio epidemic, when he is kept within his own house and yard. The atmosphere is close with the child's observations of nature and family discord. Then, smoothly, skillfully and with complete authority, the author widens his field of view to include that of what the adult Reed will become. This stunning shift allows Mr. Huddle (who is also a poet) to have this story resonate with scenes from earlier pieces. An automobile breaks Reed's leg, becoming once more the metaphor for dangerous rites of passage. And the grandfather reappears as the chief carrier of the family trait of "flawed competence."

This quality, of course, is emblematic of more than the Bryant family. The final lines of the book extend the field of view as far as possible. This boy, this man, his family, his town and his nation represent human history writ small, writ large, written by a gifted artist.

Meredith Sue Willis, "A Gene for Flawed Competence," in The New York Times Book Review, *September 14, 1986, p. 40.*

JUDITH KITCHEN

[Discovering] the meaning of the individual moment in the larger, lived life seems to be at the heart of David Huddle's story sequence [*Only the Little Bone*]. Quietly told, with a loving attention to detail, these seven stories follow Reed Bryant from childhood into adulthood. The setting is a small town in rural Virginia with at least the vestiges of old traditions—a structured society in which every child knew who, and what, he was. Reed's father manages the carbide plant, works hard, and has some prestige in the town. His grandmother mourns a lost "status" (she no longer has the help she was accustomed to), and his mother wears her natural superiority with grace. All this we discover through Reed's eyes, so that this unifying point of view, along with the specificity of setting and characters, might make the book seem like a novel, with each story serving as a "chapter." But it refuses to act like a novel. The stories are discrete. And finite. There are gaping holes between them, leaving us with nagging questions about characters who appear, pique our interest, and then disappear again. We piece together this fictional life much as in our individual lives we piece together the tales of a new acquaintance until the cumulative knowledge adds up to friendship. In the end, this is an exercise in memory (flawed, distorted, incomplete as it may be) and the use of memory to explore rather than to explain. We can't help feeling that Huddle (or Huddle as Bryant) wants to understand not only his own life, but the lives of those he knows best, and that the only way to do this is to wade in, to make it real all over again.

Because memory is what this book is "about," Huddle's fiction asks more than it answers. The big question is *why*—why one event stands out while others recede, why one moment seems to take on added significance in retrospect. Huddle is careful to let us sense the adult behind each story—an adult sensibility suspecting that significance will reveal itself only if he can approach the event exactly *as it seemed at the time*. Yet the reader is allowed to re-experience the event, along with Reed, without the heavy hand of hindsight. We look as through a window, seeing with the eyes of memory itself—the moment rendered cleanly, almost without adjective or adverb to come between it and its recollection. The first story ["**Poison Oak**"], for example, recounts the summer Reed's mother suffered from recurring poison oak. Eventually we see that something more is happening to her—something having to do with class and circumstance. But the boy is too young to understand, unable

to piece together what he knows or intuitively senses. The imagery is of shadow—an adult, shadowy life that is not available to the boy. Even now, seen through adult understanding, the facts are hazy; only in the retelling does he allow us to conclude the unthinkable that he declines to articulate.

As Reed grows up, he begins to perfect his powers of observation. The reader is increasingly drawn into the Bryant family and treated to their foibles. . . . But it is Reed who interests us most. We watch him grow from the recognizable younger brother through several phases (including an unpleasant macho year in the army, stationed in Germany) to become the man we suspected he'd be. We believe in him with a parent's ferocity. We don't like everything we see, but we do understand most of it, and the rest we write off with indulgence. So it is that we love the not-quite-lovable man who drives South for his grandfather's funeral, so jealously guarding that lost relationship that he cannot, or will not, share his grief with his young wife or his older brother. Yes, we find ourselves saying, that is what it's like. And we realize how the clear prose that lets us see *into* but not *around* the life has allowed us to gain this perspective.

In the center of the book is a long story/novella, "**The Undesirables**." Here we watch Reed come up against community mores, and against his father. Reed moves from one side of the playing field to the other, joining the legion of men who use women and then the even larger legion who have had to challenge their fathers on the way to manhood. The scene captures, with a certain glee, the pissiness of adolescence. . . . (pp. 209-11)

The final story, "**Only the Little Bone**," rearranges the sequential pattern of the book, weaving itself back through the previous stories, picking up threads and adding new dimension to what we have already read. Told in present tense, it is technically different from the rest of the book. Reed relives his seventh summer—a summer when, because of a polio scare, his mother confined him and his brother and cousin to the back yard; a summer when, in a rare moment of freedom, Reed breaks his leg in a bizarre accident while trying to retrieve his Roy Rogers scarf. The memory is so intense—so alive—that the events happen again for writer and reader alike. What might otherwise be merely another childhood anecdote is transformed by the change of tense and by the story's placement at the end of the book, so that the story sheds light on earlier events, demonstrating again the layering effect of memory. Cars (a source of power, status, and threat throughout the book) become the instruments of freedom and of danger. The reel rolls backward—no wonder Reed felt worried when his father steered the car at him in the driveway, no wonder he used the same trick to assert his independence and his anger.

At this point, the adult behind the story asserts himself; he comments, assesses, finds meaning, adds a perspective to extend the story beyond its natural limits. The story pushes past closure to enable Reed to connect his present and his past by discovering the gene for "flawed competence"—the inevitable "screw-up." Thus he is able to resurrect his beloved grandfather. And because Reed can recognize something of his origins in their shared propensity to make small but telling mistakes, he is able to take these bits and pieces of *a* life and feel *all* lives. His history is our history. (p. 211)

Judith Kitchen, "The Moments that Matter," in The Georgia Review, *Vol. XLI, No. 1, Spring, 1987, pp. 209-14.*

Randall Jarrell

1914-1965

American poet, critic, novelist, translator, essayist, and author of children's books.

Jarrell is among the foremost figures of what critics have labeled the "Middle Generation" of American poets. This group, which included such noted authors as Robert Lowell, John Berryman, and Delmore Schwartz, displayed in their verse the influence of the Modernist movement of the first half of the twentieth century as exemplified by T.S. Eliot and W.H. Auden. While borrowing from the Modernists the theme of cultural decline, however, the Middle Generation poets adhered to no set artistic credo and developed styles as original and diverse as their Modernist predecessors. Jarrell's poetry is frequently divided into three distinct periods: his early verse is derivative of Modernist experiments while utilizing the heavily metered lines and metaphysical themes typical of Fugitive poetry of the post-World War I era; his volumes published after World War II reflect the alienation and loneliness of both children and adults during the war; and his later compositions, often rendered in colloquial language, display his extensive knowledge of psychology, philosophy, and children's literature, especially the German märchen, or folktale. Affirming his status as a preeminent contemporary poet, Suzanne Ferguson noted: "Jarrell's gifts were basically a far-ranging, inquisitive, continually testing intellect; a strong perception of the ironic incongruity of men's ideals with their way of living; a sure feeling for the moral and psychological crises men have in common; and a messianic vocation to show others what he learned and saw in the world."

Much of Jarrell's work is informed by his personal life. Born in Tennessee, he was later raised by his grandparents in Hollywood, California. The family's proximity to the center of the United States film industry helped nurture Jarrell's interest in the relationship between fantasy and reality. He later attended Vanderbilt University, where he earned an undergraduate degree in psychology and a graduate degree in English while studying under such prominent Fugitive poets as John Crowe Ransom, Robert Penn Warren, and Allen Tate. Although he never completely adopted their tenets, Jarrell often employed the forms and philosophical content characteristic of the Fugitives. After teaching English at Kenyon College and the University of Texas, Jarrell enlisted in the Army Air Force during World War II and spent most of his tenure as a flight and navigation instructor. He resumed his academic career following his discharge in 1946 and taught at numerous American colleges and universities. In his later years, Jarrell was beset by physical and emotional problems that resulted in at least one suicide attempt. He was killed when struck by a car while walking near his home in Chapel Hill, North Carolina.

Jarrell first received critical attention for "The Rage for the Lost Penny," a selection of poems collected in the 1940 anthology *Five Young American Poets* and reprinted in his initial collection, *Blood for a Stranger* (1942). Critics often note that the formal structures of Jarrell's early poems resemble those of Allen Tate, to whom *Blood for a Stranger* is dedicated, and W. H. Auden. Many of these pieces focus on the moral and cultural bankruptcy Jarrell perceived to exist in the twentieth

century, while other compositions, including "Children Selecting Books at a Library," examine relationships between art and life, childhood and adulthood. Jarrell's next two volumes, *Little Friend, Little Friend* (1945) and *Losses* (1948), continue to examine serious themes while revealing a more relaxed style. Reflecting his impressions of World War II, such frequently anthologized pieces as "The Death of the Ball Turret Gunner" and "Eighth Air Force" are noted for their vivid images of the effects of war and are widely considered among the best poems inspired by World War II. Hayden Carruth asserted: "[From the first, Jarrell] wrote with ease.... When the war came he already possessed a developed poetic vocabulary and a mastery of forms. Under the shock of war his mannerisms fell away. He began to write with stark, compressed lucidity."

Jarrell's verse following World War II focuses on more esoteric intellectual themes and reflects his fascination with German culture. *The Seven-League Crutches* (1951) and *The Woman at the Washington Zoo: Poems and Translations* (1960), the latter of which won the National Book Award for poetry, examine the paradoxes and contraries of an increasingly commercial society. In one of his most famous pieces, "A Girl in a Library," Jarrell's narrative persona structures a dialectic between educated and uneducated states of mind as well as between past and present cultures. "The Woman in the Washington Zoo'' and ''Seele im Raum'' utilize the dramatic monologue form to develop sympathetic psychological portraits of lonely middle-aged women. *The Lost World* (1965) features autobiographical poems inspired by Jarrell's childhood that both emulate and parody the style of Marcel Proust's *Remembrance of Things Past. Selected Poems, including The Woman at the Washington Zoo* (1964) and *The Complete Poems* (1969) solidified Jarrell's reputation as a writer of great technical skill who was capable of adapting intellectual abstractions into lucid verse.

Jarrell is also admired for his accomplishments in fiction and criticism. His novel-length prose work, *Pictures from an Institution* (1954), which derives from his experiences as a faculty member at Sarah Lawrence College, is often cited as one of the major satires in contemporary literature. The title of this work, a reference to Modest Mussorgsky's famous musical composition *Pictures of an Exhibition*, has been the subject of much critical speculation. Sylvia Angus commented: ''[The structure of *Pictures from an Institution*] is internal, as harmoniously conceived as music, the parts interwoven as carefully as those in a toccata and fugue. The music begins with the entrance of the serpent into Eden and ends with her departure. . . . Jarrell explores with gaiety, insight, and all the brilliant verbal devices of the poet those who live in the garden.'' Jarrell's criticism is considered by some critics his most significant contribution to twentieth-century literature. The volumes *Poetry and the Age* (1953), *A Sad Heart at the Supermarket* (1962), *The Third Book of Criticism* (1969), and *Kipling, Auden, & Co.: Essays and Reviews, 1935-1964* (1980) collect many of Jarrell's witty, perceptive, and often acerbic opinions of modern writers. *Randall Jarrell's Letters* (1985) also features numerous examples of his literary preferences.

(See also *CLC*, Vols. 1, 2, 6, 9, 13; *Children's Literature Review*, Vol. 6; *Contemporary Authors*, Vols. 5-8, rev. ed., Vols. 25-28, rev. ed. [obituary]; *Contemporary Authors New Revision Series*, Vol. 6; *Contemporary Authors Bibliographical Series*, Vol. 2; *Something about the Author*, Vol. 7; *Dictionary of Literary Biography*, Vols. 48, 52; and *Concise Dictionary of American Literary Biography, 1941-1968*.)

FRANCIS STEEGMULLER

[*Pictures From an Institution: A Comedy*] is a searching novel about a mean lady novelist writing a mean novel about a college where she is spending a year teaching creative writing. It portrays a savage, lethal-tongued bluestocking, pitilessly intent on pinning down her colleagues as specimens for her already gruesome collection, while remaining insensitive to much that Randall Jarrell, as narrator, finds genuine and fine in the community.

Mr. Jarrell is on the side of the angels. His is a divine meanness, and he exposes his female writing devil punitively, matching her stream of poisonous wisecracks with a series of coruscating cracks of his own worthy of Dorothy Parker at her most hilarious and deadly. This double display of sacred and profane meanness on the same bill makes the show well worth the price of admission.

Pictures From an Institution is a rarity in being a work of prose fiction written by one who not only possesses obvious culti-

vation but is also a distinguished practicing poet. The language is pure and inventive; the ''seething of metaphors'' reaches points of considerable beauty. And when Mr. Jarrell deals with the witch and her victims—and with a subsidiary witch (the college president's wife) and *her* victims—he is a brilliant satirist. His fireworks crackle and dance around the ladies and their stooges, lighting them with lurid, searing flashes; the reader squirms, laughs aloud, and asks for more. ''She is a *truly* witty woman,'' a character cries out impulsively about the dangerous heroine. Mr. Jarrell is a genuinely witty man.

It is scarcely surprising that in a performance of such kaleidoscopic brilliance the elements of coherence and staying-power should to a certain extent be sacrificed. Mr. Jarrell is less convincing in displaying his ''good'' values, which remain throughout the book in a kind of splendid isolation. The good and the bad do not clash dramatically—they are merely juxtaposed; and more generally the book lacks conventional novelistic architecture.

Both the title and subtitle perhaps indicate Mr. Jarrell's awareness of this. But even though the total picture remains, for all the vividness of detail, somewhat blurred, the author achieves unique effects by highlighting with his poetic torch some virulent corners of human behavior.

Francis Steegmuller, ''Streaks of Meanness,'' in The New York Times Book Review, *May 2, 1954, p. 4.*

LOUIS O. COXE

Mr. Jarrell, disarmingly, calls [*Pictures From an Institution*] a ''comedy''; the publishers, with an eye to the audience, call it a novel, and the reader must pay his money and take his choice. All questions of genre or mode apart, one faces at last the old question; what did the author intend? What is his attitude and what should ours be? From the first hard, witty, malicious thrusts to the last elegiac diminuendo Mr. Jarrell takes us through the antic gallery of types at Benton College, and the trip makes us, if not the angels, weep and laugh at moments when we do not grind our teeth in irritation at Mr. Jarrell.

Roman à clef, we mutter after the first sentence, and having identified the President and others satisfactorily, we move on to the novel thus unlocked. And the riches of absurdity disclosed obviously tickle Mr. Jarrell to the feeling that he has been an attendant lord in a scene of high comedy and low farce. The chapter called ''Art Night'' is the showpiece of the book and a delight to read; how familiar it all seems and how shrewd the sensibility that shows it to us. The empty undergraduate painting, the sculpture—''It's ugly but is it Art?'' And of course the dance-group, the presentation of *The Spook Sonata.* All in all, it's a wonderful evening, a guided tour of the progressive women's college. Mr. Jarrell doesn't miss a trick.

There, one begins to think, the trouble lies; he misses and leaves out—nothing, at least nothing that can make his people and their world of Benton grotesque, heartless, inhuman. If there is a central character, it is the ''I'' who narrates, Mr. Jarrell himself, who would, one is sure, be the first to admit the obvious. At opposite poles in the scale of humanity are Gottfried Rosenbaum, the Austrian-Jewish musician, and Gertrude Johnson, the acid, vicious novelist-in-residence at Benton. . . . Others fill up the gallery, all types and all drawn with wit, a vivid sense of the absurd, and an ear for the cliché.

What an ear for the cliché! After fifty pages of *Pictures,* this reviewer felt as though he could never speak or write again, so hopeless did the chance of avoiding the damning cliché, the banal reaction, the suppositious insight that turns bromide in solution. Mr. Jarrell has mercy on few of his characters, the Rosenbaums and Constance excepted; above all he has no mercy on the reader, for who can match his wit, his analysis of motive and character, above all his learning? To match the latter one would have to go to graduate school and Take Everything, to resort to one of Mr. Jarrell's pet ironic devices, the Derogatory Capitalization. He suffers from total recall; one hopes everything he knows is in this book; otherwise the reader must feel that in such speculation madness lies. From analysis of the fictitious music of a post-Berg school to breezy reference to matters of Thomistic theology, from Milton to Einstein, from Capability Brown to Grimm's fairy tales, in German—German dialect! One wants to cry out, "Stop you have made the point. I know nothing. Nothing at all. I'm sorry I ever thought I did."

Humanly, the book troubles the heart. Why all the apparatus brought to bear on these odious vermin? Why destroy President Robbins with the main battery of a battleship when the first witty knife-thrust has done the job to perfection? Why belabor poor Gertrude; we know all there is to know of her in the first fifty pages; after that her subacid comments cease to amuse and she either bores us or we begin to wonder why it seems so particular with Mr. Jarrell. Much of what he ascribes to the destructive female novelist comes home to plague him. Everything must be at someone's expense, and feeding hands exist to be bitten. Despite the farce, the wit and the absurdity, Mr. Jarrell has written no comedy but a very revealing study of the antipathy of the writer to a patron, any patron, and in this peculiarly modern case, the patron is the academy. One cannot avoid the feeling that Mr. Jarrell has stabbed Benton with ingratitude, for all he may try to make up for it in the final pages.

This alone would trouble us little; more important, Mr. Jarrell cannot create character. His people, fools and knaves and geniuses, the good guys and the bad guys, are as flat, black-and-white fictions as the folk in a play by Arthur Miller. For one thing, we never know what they look like though we know Gottfried is big and Constance beautiful. We get little sense of world, of where we are, of a density of life. Only the truly creative novelist can give us these things and Mr. Jarrell has sense and tact enough to call this no novel. Under the wit we feel a void aching away for substance to fill it, and neither the devastating portraiture nor the wide spread of allusion can fill it, for the picture is indeed *la vie morte*.

There is no plot. We pass through the academic year, concentrating on the high spots. Mr. Jarrell's method is to pick up sets of characters, talk about them, then move on to others; occasionally he brings several of them together, as at Gertrude's ghastly party. Juxtaposition, contrast, parallelling—all these devices are effectively used. As for the satiric method, for all the amusement it affords, its secret becomes obvious after a few pages: take a cliché, reverse the crucial term, and there you are. Mr. Jarrell is a poet and brings a sensitivity to language to bear on his ironic study. He overdoes it. The structure will not bear the load of play with words. Oscar Wilde got away with it in an epigram. Perhaps he did the same in *The Importance of Being Earnest*. G. B. Shaw had the last word, though; he called that play "heartless." The moral judgment dooms Mr. Jarrell's book equally. (pp. 19-20)

Louis O. Coxe, "Groves of Academe," in The New Republic, *Vol. 130, No. 19, May 10, 1954, pp. 19-20.*

ANTHONY WEST

The dust jacket of *Pictures from an Institution,* a first novel by Mr. Randall Jarrell, the distinguished critic and poet, raises the liveliest expectations. On it, Miss Marianne Moore refers to the "mighty task" Mr. Jarrell has undertaken, and Mr. William Carlos Williams promises the reader a visit to "regions seldom disturbed by most modern writing." To say that what follows is disappointing is an understatement, since it turns out to be a novel about a lady novelist on a college faculty who is writing a book about her college. A higher purpose is also involved, but this is the essential fabric of the thing, and it arouses in this reader, at least, the sort of dismay aroused by those oils in which the artist is discovered solemnly painting himself, the back of his canvas, and his easel, as he sees them in a looking glass on his studio wall. This kind of picture is, like the feature story in a magazine about the preparation of a feature story for the magazine, a petition of bankruptcy, indicating that the workshop set up for the artist's convenience has become a cell from which he cannot escape. In this cell, the painter mentally starves to death, first eating his props, his easel, his models, and himself, then falling back on paintings "about" the problems of painting, serving up the bones of compositions as abstractions and formal patterns, and at last turning to painting paint itself, which leads him to produce pictures that deal solely in pure color and texture, and then in the qualities of the material used. Mr. Jarrell's novel is down a parallel road; he is writing about another writer at work, but he is primarily concerned with problems of writing.

The theme of *Pictures from an Institution* is an attack on one kind of writer by another kind. Gertrude Johnson, Mr. Jarrell's major figure (one could even say villainess), is passionate by temperament and a born partisan, and it is impossible for her not to take sides on an issue. At the same time, she subscribes to the school of writing that stems from Flaubert and Chekhov, a school that induces in some people, when face to face with its products, the unease Henry James felt when he read Flaubert. James expressed this unease in a memorable critique in which he said that he felt Flaubert was a defective writer because he wrote without pity and without natural warmth, and accused him, with an unusual roundness, of not liking anyone. James was so wrapped up in his own aesthetic, which involved being for or against people on the basis of their sensitivity or their lack of it, and the delicacy or indelicacy of their behavior, that he was unable to appreciate Flaubert's, which involved being for or against ideas in the abstract classical manner, as well as being wholly objective about people's behavior. The sentimental heart demands some pity for poor Mme. Bovary and recoils from Flaubert's point-blank statement of the truth that she had made her own messy bed and must lie in it. Flaubert was against messy behavior, but he did not believe that it was his function to state his attitude; that was to be done by taking a situation and working out its logical consequences. Whether Mme. Bovary is nice or nasty is beside the point; what is important is that Bovarysm leads inevitably in a certain direction.

Mr. Jarrell's villainess sees the progressive college of which her creator is so broadly tolerant as a fortress of Bovarysm, and her intuitions inform her that educated liberals as a caste are her Mme. Bovary. She is concerned not with whether they are nice or nasty but with reporting on their behavior and on the ironic contrast between it and their dream of being the liberal guardians of the sacred groves of humanism. The question of temperament obtrudes here, because Mr. Jarrell's principal character is so violent a partisan of the values of humanism that the novel she is writing about her fellow-workers on the faculty does not seem merely cold, as Flaubert's novels seemed cold to James; it seems filled with an actual hatred of the people whose timidities, incompetences, uncertainties, and petty venalities she is describing. She makes their inadequacy on the side of the angels as evil as the wickedness of the enemies of academic freedom and humanism.

Mr. Jarrell springs to the defense of the college and its faculty his villainess is pillorying, and in doing this he has constructed a comedy of incomprehension. He represents Gertrude Johnson as a woman deaf to all she does not choose to hear. . . . (pp. 93-4)

All this, enormously diffused, is James's complaint against Flaubert; Gertrude is showing a lack of warmth and an inability to love. But one sees her side of the case when Mr. Jarrell introduces the characters who are supposed to be lovable. Gottfried Rosenbaum, a faculty man who is a refugee from Mittel-Europa, is among those toward whom Gertrude is as the deaf adder. . . . (p. 94)

Of course, if one were thus authoritatively assured of Rosenbaum's kindness and cleverness—by God himself, apparently—it would no doubt argue a want of heart to say one couldn't stand him. But Mr. Jarrell then lets us have a good look at Rosenbaum in action:

> He had once ended a long half-hour's political lecture—conversation, the speaker would have called it—by saying to the speaker: "Nijinsky said, *Politics is Death*. Is that right?" The man looked at him speechlessly, and he [Rosenbaum] said: "Is that right? You say politics *is* in English? *Is*, not *are*?"

Hearing Dr. Rosenbaum, who left Austria as the Nazis were coming in, being elfin along these lines might have persuaded Gertrude Johnson to consider the light glinting on his spectacle frames and to recall one of the most moving and most terrible of the photographs that came out of the concentration camps—the one of the room in Maidenek where were piled up the thousands upon thousands of spectacles taken from the Rosenbaums who were not lucky enough to get to America before they were fed into the crematorium ovens. But the passage is the essence of intellectual Bovarysm, and it is just that kind of deadly silliness which Gertrude is to describe so passionately and so lucidly in her novel. In the face of its bland idiocy, it is difficult not to share her passion and to mutter to oneself, "I can't *stand* that Gottfried Rosenbaum." Mr. Jarrell takes pains to be explicit about the virtues of Rosenbaum and his circle in building his case against Gertrude, yet the more he does so, the more rational and sympathetic her passion seems.

Now he is talking about Rosenbaum's wife, and a student who admires both the Rosenbaums:

> And of all the singers I have ever heard she was the most essentially dramatic: she could not have sung a scale without making it seem a part of someone's life, a thing of human importance.
>
> (p. 97)

It loooks as if the question is being begged, and in disagreeably woolly language. It is pure Bovarysm to pretend that a singer can do that much by singing a scale. An equivalent statement, "She could not have recited the alphabet, or intoned the Arabic numerals, without making them seem a part of someone's life, a thing of human importance," would show it up for what it is. It presents a ludicrously gross claim for the artist's powers on the one hand, and on the other hand it debases the creative process to a matter of feeling intensely and getting a response.

To make the notes of a scale "a thing of human importance," it is necessary to do something much more complex and much more exacting than "making it seem a part of someone's life." The final exhortation, too, comes from the realm of bluff. The scale, once it has been turned into a song, is supposed to say, "Believe, believe, my heart . . . that life is uncreated and will not be destroyed." The considerable practical advantage of this creed is that it resembles a forthright declaration of some kind while it commits one to absolutely nothing.

Gertrude is aroused to indignation at the Rosenbaums and the other inhabitants of the sacred groves dedicated to the higher learning and teaching precisely because of their addiction to such noncommittal all-weather creeds. The question is not whether one believes in life but whether the zone of order that has been hacked out of chaos with enormous effort, where aesthetic speculation can be carried on and where it has meaning, can be kept in being. There is no doubt that it is in danger and that we are unhappily living through one of those periods in which it is as important to create or to defend the conditions of life under which art can exist as it is to create the works of art themselves. It is not enough to believe, in a soupy, emotional way, in life, which cares no more for man and his works than it does for stones and fish; it is necessary to believe in man and in certain rational concepts of human behavior. When it comes right down to it, one is for Gertrude, for her single-minded passion for what she believes to be right, for any gaucheries and excesses into which her passion may lead her, and not for those refined abstainers who stand sniggering behind their hands on the sidelines while precious things go by default. (pp. 98-9)

Anthony West, "The Sacrosanct Groves of Academe," in The New Yorker, *Vol. XXX, No. 18, June 19, 1954, pp. 93-4, 97-9.*

MARTIN GREENBERG

I don't know when colleges first began to give courses in creative writing (as distinct from English Composition): the practice was already established when I went to school. Those who taught these courses were generally young writers themselves. Literature profited from this arrangement by a spate of short stories about the relations of instructor and student written by the former—it certainly did not profit from the students' side, at least in any observable way, the results of writing courses, like the results of psychoanalysis, being impossible to ascertain with any assurance. Since then more and more writers have been invited to join teaching staffs, especially by the progressive colleges, and another genre of story promises to arise in which the writer-teacher bites the hand that fed him for a semester or so.

Randall Jarrell's gallery of *Pictures from an Institution*—it is not a novel—is in this genre. He snaps amusingly at the institutional hand of Benton, a progressive college half of whose "campus was designed by Bottom the Weaver, half by Ludwig Mies van der Rohe." But, as we shall see, when his teeth do close on its fingers it is only to forbear and merely scratch the skin. Mr. Jarrell's book contains an innovation. *Pictures from an Institution* is not only a case of biting-the-hand, but also of the biter bit: the chief person satirized is a fellow writer-teacher, Gertrude Johnson, who is herself writing a satirical novel about Benton—a woman, we are told, who greatly admires Swift but cannot understand why he suddenly went soft on the Houyhnhnms.

Mr. Jarrell has a well-deserved reputation for wit; he lives up to it, he more than lives up to it, in this book, fulfilling and overfulfilling his quota on every page. He is best, however, with the formidable Gertrude, whose great fault as a writer was that "she did not know—or rather, did not believe—what it was like to be a human being." When the suffering president of the college (a former Olympic diving champion, a sort of enlightened stuffed sport shirt) remarks, with forced good nature, that Gertrude's bark is worse than her bite, the author comments: "This was foolish—Gertrude's bark *was* her bite; and many a bite has lain awake all night longing to be Gertrude's bark." I am tempted to hail this as, at last, the American epigram: American in its farfetchedness and humorous overstatement, and yet neat and contained as an epigram should be. We have had the tall story; this is the tall epigram.

But the whole book is not as good as its parts, the chapters are not as good as the paragraphs and sentences. The *mots* and metaphors collect like pebbles in a heap; at the end there is just the heap of sparkling pebbles. But why isn't a lot of wit good enough? The trouble is with the form of the book. *Pictures from an Institution* is not a novel, as I have said, but it arouses some of the expectations of one. It starts like a story, but there is none—just the machine-gun rattle of witty definitions and descriptions. Its people start out like the people of a novel, but then get defined right off in a *mot;* their types are summed up neatly enough, but their life is missed, and the meaning is the same at the last as in the beginning. What was wanted, perhaps, was a kind of form that fulfilled itself in this play of witticism and epigram; but what exactly this form might be I do not know.

On Benton, the college itself, Mr. Jarrell is least satisfactory.... The truth is that the author has hardly more to tell about Benton's liberalism than that it is absurd—"the absurdities of Benton were so absurd." Benton's liberals are just reactionaries turned inside out, and vice-versa: "In the world outside one met many people who were negatives of the people of Benton: exact duplications, but the whites and blacks reversed. They were people who thought anything but calendars and official portraits Modern Art, and spoke of it with exasperated hatred; people who wrote to the Chicago *Tribune* to denounce it for the radical stand it had taken on some issue...." This is to miss the huge gap separating the prejudices of reactionaries—a sort of unquestioned sense of things—from an ideology of cultural and political self-righteousness; it is, also, to miss Benton.

On this point I find Mary McCarthy's *Groves of Academe* a much superior book.... Mr. Jarrell, I am afraid, lacks [McCarthy's] satiric understanding of the liberal ideology. In the end he forgives Benton its absurdities, for he has no other grounds for mocking it, and absurdity is a fault that the charitable and loving—as opposed to the malignant and unloving Gertrude Johnsons—can easily forgive. There is more than a touch of unction here. "I felt that I had misjudged Benton, somehow—for if I had misjudged Miss Rasmussen so [the absurd sculptress-in-residence who specializes in welding "root-systems of alfalfa plants," but suddenly produces an inspired work], why not the rest of Benton?..." This is the moral of the book, but it rings false. How does Mr. Jarrell know that Miss Rasmussen's piece of sculpture is great? He just looks at it and knows. But we know that the perception of greatness comes harder than that. In the same way, the loving kindness with which the author accepts Benton and the world at the end, in studied contrast with Gertrude Johnson's inability to love,

strikes one as complacent and false. Love, too, comes harder than that. It isn't there just because Mr. Jarrell, who knows the right thing to say, says it's there. (pp. 424-26)

Martin Greenberg, "A Tall Epigram," in Partisan Review, *Vol. XXI, No. 4, July-August, 1954, pp. 424-26.*

PATRICK F. QUINN

With its opening paragraphs, *Pictures From an Institution* establishes itself as a kind of mordant memoir about some people on the faculty of Benton, a women's college of so progressive a character that in one advanced art class (sculpture) the students used blowtorches, and, "in their goggles and masks, looked wonderful, like race-track drivers about to give a *Nō* play." This gag occurs towards the end of the book, but Randall Jarrell is something of a blowtorch-writer and the verbal acetylene flares early and often. In the first chapter the heat is put on Dwight Robbins, president of Benton, and on his wife Pamela. The writer in residence at the college, a novelist named Gertrude Johnson, is seared briefly and then put aside for lavish attention later on. Intermittently there are some cooling-off periods in the novel, for Jarrell knows that a competent satirist must avoid a wholly negative attitude. He should affirm something, too, have something *positive* to offer. And so in the dull, conscientious stretches of the book we meet the sane people: the composer Gottfried Rosenbaum, his wife Irene, their protégée Constance Morgan, and their friend the narrator, a good and guileless man. But at no point does one ask What happens next? The question is, rather, What will Jarrell *say* next, and how well will he do it? The usual things that solidify a novel—story, characters, ideas—are only subsidiary details in this book. They function dimly as props, provide some illusion of context, while front and center in the reader's interest is a verbal performance, as the author demonstrates what can be done with the felicitous and feline phrase. This is the insidious attraction of the book. It is not a well-made novel, scrupulous about point-of-view, structure, pace, and other niceties, nor did Jarrell attempt to make it one. He presents the book as a "comedy", which it sometimes is; and in fact the only really bad joke in the book is one contributed by the publisher. An announcement is made on a fly-leaf that *Pictures From an Institution* is a work of fiction, and hence any resemblances to an actual institution or to actual persons must be regarded as imaginary. More make-believe is packed into this bit of legal fiction than exists in all the pages that follow. There might be some point in thus advertising the book as a *roman à clef* if it were more of a *roman*, and if the *clef* were not so easily available. What Benton's real name is, who President Robbins and Gertrude Johnson are—these questions are scarcely interesting since they are so readily, almost instantaneously, solved.

A darker mystery is why the publisher saw fit to surround the book with so large a cordon of appreciative first readers. Half of the dust jacket is used as a billboard for testimonials from Wallace Stevens, Jean Stafford, and some nine others, making up a formidable claque. All this fanfare is offensive. It makes the game look "fixed". No writer, certainly not Randall Jarrell, needs so many sponsors, even for his first novel. And the novel itself is one that neither deserves nor solicits such elaborate protection. One might as well arrange a coming-out party for a king cobra. "Witty", "brilliant", and so on, the book obviously is. But how anyone can speak, as James Agee and Eric Bentley do, of its "humaneness", and of its being rooted in "enjoyment and love" is more than I can make out, though I made a special effort to watch for these qualities. They are not conspicuous in the following: "If I tell you that Mrs. Robbins had bad teeth and looked like a horse, you will laugh at me as a cliché-monger; yet it is the truth." Usually the prose is more adroitly calculated than this; but when Jarrell forgets himself and lets go, as he does in this sentence, the attitude revealed is simply one of naked spite. (pp. 460-61)

Patrick F. Quinn, in a review of "Pictures from an Institution," in The Hudson Review, *Vol. VII, No. 3, Autumn, 1954, pp. 460-61.*

C. E. MAGUIRE

The novel, *Pictures from an Institution,* justifies its title. This is another—but not *just* another—of the novels which have resulted from the recent discovery that members of college faculties, and perhaps especially college administrators, are also people. This discovery was made not by the faculty or the administrators or even the students, but by the "creative" writers imported by these institutions to teach their art to the young. Jarrell inserts into his story one of these artists, Gertrude Johnson, who has come to Benton to write her novel (her eighth) and shamelessly regards all her associates as Material. Gertrude's novel, if it ever saw the light, would probably much more resemble Mary McCarthy's *Groves of Academe* than Jarrell's book, for Gertrude casts the proverbially and glacially cold eye on her surroundings, whereas Jarrell is helpless before the helplessness of even so reptilian a character (no, a *person*) as Gertrude Johnson, or so mechanized an administrator (or grown-up little boy) as the President, Dwight Robbins, or such a Convention-of-Sociologists-in-person as Jerrold Whittaker.

One way of distinguishing between the novel and the poems would be to consider Jarrell as writing the novel with his mask on, and the poems with his mask off, but saying very much the same thing, although a previous acquaintance with the poems helps enormously in detecting the overtones of the novel. As a matter of fact, the whole body of Jarrell's writing so far is interlaced with like themes, ideas, quotations and even characters. A simple—perhaps too simple—way of checking Jarrell's chief preoccupations is to trace these repeated themes and quotations and people, or types of people, through his work, treating the whole body of it as if it were one of those mosaic or thematic organizations he mentions.

The structure of *Pictures from an Institution* encourages one to do just this. It is not a story in any sense, except that two of the characters have a beginning, a middle and an end of their career at Benton; but is it the story of Gertrude Johnson and how she used Benton? or of Constance Morgan and how she found the Rosenbaums? Neither of these is engaged in an action, even in Francis Fergusson's explanation of the term; for Constance, though she grows—or does she?—in Perception, has no conscious Purpose and no noticeable Passion; whereas Gertrude, as the author sees her, has plenty of Purpose, and creates obstacles to supplement those which nature has provided for her, but her Passion never leads to any Perception. If I have to choose, I should say Constance is the central character, but she does nothing except listen to the Rosenbaums and to records of *la musique sérielle et dodécaphonique,* and, offstage, file and type and stamp envelopes in the President's office. While she does this, the author, with sometimes loving and sometimes horrible fascination, presents to the reader all the fauna of this almost incredible institution, placing each

group in a detailed family background and physical setting, and watching them all affect one another. They never change. They merely progressively reveal themselves. And behind the *dodécaphonique* chaos of this animated jigsaw puzzle rumbles the "old St. Bernard's voice" of Dr. Rosenbaum quoting Goethe: "Man would not be the best thing in the world if he were not too good for this world." The author again, in **"Girl in a Library,"** quotes this at Tatyana Larina; and it is the nearest I have come, in Jarrell's writing, to the expression of a unifying theme. This is the ultimate in value he has reached so far; and most of his work is a kind of ballet in which he confidently or fearfully or despairingly approaches this belief, or else tosses it aside or pretends to toss it aside in exasperation or mock exasperation, as if undecided whether it is man's fault or someone else's that he cannot reach out to something for which he is *not* too good. In his most serious moments, as in the poetry, and in many of the sections of the novel devoted to the Rosenbaums, he is concerned with the meaning of life in its ultimate aspects. At other, lighter moments, he is concerned with comparing the American view of life with the European and trying, without any real satisfaction, to justify the American. (pp. 181-82)

C. E. Maguire, "Shape of the Lightning: Randall Jarrell," in Renascence, *Vol. VII, No. 4, Summer, 1955, pp. 181-86, 195.*

SYLVIA ANGUS

[The essay excerpted below originally appeared in the Southern Review, *Summer, 1966.]*

In an issue of the *New York Review of Books* several months ago, the poet Robert Lowell has a long and affectionate essay on his friend, the late Randall Jarrell [see *CLC,* Vol. 2]. It traces Jarrell's life, discusses his personality, and treats in considerable detail the excellence of his poetry. Two sentences only are devoted to Jarrell's one novel: "His novel, *Pictures from an Institution,* whatever its fictional oddities, is a unique and serious joke-book. How often I've met people who keep it by their beds or somewhere handy, and read random pages aloud to lighten their hearts." One is left with the uncomfortable sense that Lowell wished he did not have to comment at all on his friend's one fictional excursion. "Joke-book." This is a destructive epithet, the more astonishing because it stands alone in a sea of praise and poetic perceptiveness.

Lowell's attitude is additional evidence of the remarkable degree to which Jarrell's novel has been undervalued and misunderstood by the reviewers. It has been seen almost exclusively as a tour de force of wit—and it *is* probably the most consistently and devastatingly witty book of our generation. Nearly every line in it is instinct with light and sparkle, an overflowing of intelligence which makes one grope back toward *Tristram Shandy* in an effort to find suitable comparisons. No one, however, seems to have noticed that the book is a multilevel creation of enormous subtlety and depth, musical in structure and moving simultaneously on psychological and on allegorical levels. (p. 266)

[In *Pictures from an Institution: A Comedy,*] Jarrell has gathered together a galaxy of characters which is at once a humorous cross section of college "types," a sensitively understood group of individuals, a collection of interlocking, contrapuntal motifs, and a group of allegorical archetypes quite clearly representing the mythic vision of heaven and hell. It is a remarkable achievement, perhaps most unusual in that it is illuminated throughout with a coruscating wit which has blinded reviewers to all else. Perhaps only James Joyce in our century has had the brilliance and audacity to use the tool of wit in treating so fundamentally large and somber a subject as the condition of man in our time. The lines in Jarrell's book, as in *Ulysses,* are jewels, but they could never make up a joke book because the essence of their wit is that they are indissolubly wedded to the characters they formulate. (pp. 266-67)

It would take a monograph to explore completely all the rich allusiveness of *Pictures from an Institution,* for Jarrell was not only a sensitive, perceptive, and comically gifted man; he was also an unusually erudite one, whose novel offers a happy hunting ground for the tracking down of allusive and elusive references.

Jarrell's novel, it seems clear, has suffered critically from its wit as Adlai Stevenson's political career suffered from his wit. There is an assumption, which even our most astute minds seem unable to overcome, that if one is witty one cannot be profound, or, as Benton's president might say, "sincere." *Pictures from an Institution* has suffered both from reviewers who didn't understand it at all, like Anthony West, and from reviewers who thought it was terribly funny and nothing more, like Francis Steegmuller. West in an influential *New Yorker* review begins by saying he is disappointed in Jarrell because he has written a book about an author, a situation he compares at great length to a man looking at himself in a mirror looking at himself in a mirror [see excerpt above]. This implies the absurd suggestion that the artist who uses himself as material is on the wrong track; that Thomas Mann, Henry James, James Joyce, Thomas Wolfe, Gide, and a host of others, would have been *sounder* if they had written, say, historical novels instead of all those self-centered portraits of the artist. But this is scarcely less outlandish than West's reaction to the main characters. He dislikes Gertrude because she is *inhuman,* but he prefers her to Rosenbaum, because he is *too human.* He offers, as a critique of the humane and compassionate Rosenbaum, a philosophical position which is his own and quite opposed to Jarrell's. Speaking of Rosenbaum, he says: "It is not enough to believe, in a soupy, emotional way, in life, which cares no more for man and his works than it does for stones and fish; it is necessary to believe in man and in certain rational concepts of human behavior." But the essence of Gottfried is precisely that he goes beyond the narrow, people-oriented view which dwells on its own rationality because it fears the broad comprehensiveness of the world. Gottfried is immensely—though never soupily—understanding of people, but he believes in a broader concept, in a process of life which is often sad and oftener absurd, but he cannot hate it. If this "yea" to life is what West refers to as "soupy," then it seems plain that West's own position is close to that of the redoubtable Gertrude whom he prefers: "She had never had a nightmare; this was her nightmare. She looked at the world and *saw,* and cried out, her voice rising at the end of the sentence into falsetto: 'Why, it wouldn't fool a *child*!' "

Steegmuller, with far less space at his disposal in a *New York Times* review, does at least offer homage to Jarrell's wit [see excerpt above]. Unfortunately he is so overwhelmed by the pyrotechnic display that he misses everything else. He says, for instance, "It is scarcely surprising that in a performance of such kaleidoscopic brilliance, the elements of coherence and staying power should to a certain extent be sacrificed." This is a startling sentence. Staying power, the ability to keep up the fireworks is precisely one of the remarkable qualities of

the book. Jarrell, furthermore, is the most lucid and coherent writer to be found anywhere. One can only suspect that Steegmuller means, perhaps, "cohesion," because he says, a few lines later, that "the book lacks conventional novelistic architecture." What "conventional novelistic architecture" means is a bit difficult to determine if one searches for it in some novels which have been called great, say *Tristram Shandy,* perhaps, or *The Immoralist,* or *The Stranger,* or *Herzog.* To demand "conventional" architecture is to ask for dead form. Presumably, Steegmuller means that Jarrell's novel lacks structure.

In a sense this remark is justified. *Pictures from an Institution* does lack the plot development of much customary fiction. The book is not architectural. It is musical in form and therefore somewhat obscure to readers who do not expect this.

Jarrell was deeply interested in music, as the book itself makes clear. That he saw his book in musical rather than architectural terms seems evident from the title he gave it. *Pictures from an Institution,* like Moussorgsky's *Pictures at an Exhibition,* is a series of portraits, but they are interwoven, contrapuntal portraits, balanced and moving in relation to each other, as well as in relation to his several levels of development. Each portrait is conditioned by the fact that it is of a human being interacting with other human beings against the theme (in the bass) of Benton College, USA. But all of these characters exist on a triple thematic level. We see them as riotously funny stereotypes of humanity; as separate, sentient, and suffering individuals; and as allegorical figures in a mythic drama. It is a complex musical score Jarrell has composed—intricate, full of recurrent motifs, grace notes, and distant echoes. (pp. 269-70)

Jarrell, himself, did not write—perhaps could not, almost certainly would not—write Gertrude's kind of book. Nothing much happens, but this is not the same thing as saying that *Pictures from an Institution* has no structure. Its structure is internal, as harmoniously conceived as music, the parts interwoven as carefully as those in a toccata and fugue. The music begins with the entrance of the serpent into Eden and ends with her departure. In between it paints the good, the wise, the innocent and the foolish as Jarrell explores with gaiety, insight, and all the brilliant verbal devices of the poet those who live in the garden. The lack of typical architecture in his book is not a flaw. It is a perception.

Jarrell's book has been assessed in a number of curiously limited ways.

It has been codified as a "college novel," one of those dubious categories which equate the substance of a work with its locale. Benton College is, of course, a locale, but its inhabitants are as universal as Everyman. One might as well call *Remembrance of Things Past* a French bourgeois novel and feel that one has thereby summed it up and explained it. The life of the college conditions some things about the characters; any locale must. But the characters are fundamentally of the world; they are human beings wherever they live and they portray humanity to the degree that their creator was capable of understanding human life. Jarrell was deeply capable. The book has also been seen as a malicious exercise in wit at the expense of very specific people. This narrow view has provided numbers of people with amusing after-dinner conversation of the "You know who *Gertrude* is, don't you?" variety. It has been seen as a joke book, stuffed with wit to beguile a weary hour. It has been seen as a clumsy exercise in fiction by a poet with no sense of architecture. It has even been seen as mushy emotionalism by a woolly-headed romantic.

Pictures from an Institution is far more complex and profound than any of these views suggest. It is a study of a group of people by a man of insight and vision, who saw how strange and wonderful humanity is and who could not help but laugh, and could not help but understand. It seems likely that this warm, brilliant, and compassionate novel will, more than his poetry, be the work by which Jarrell's creative stature will be judged. (p. 271)

> Sylvia Angus, "Randall Jarrell, Novelist: A Reconsideration," in Critical Essays on Randall Jarrell, edited by Suzanne Ferguson, G. K. Hall & Co., 1983, pp. 266-71.

KARL SHAPIRO

[*The lecture excerpted below was delivered at the Library of Congress, Washington, D. C., on October 17, 1966.*]

Our generation—the generation of Jarrell, Wilbur, myself, Roethke, Lowell, Schwartz, Bishop, Ciardi, Berryman, Kunitz, Nemerov, Whittemore—one is almost inclined to add Merrill, Lynch, Pierce, Fenner, and Smith—our generation lived through more history than most or maybe any. We lived through more history even than Stendhal, who fell, as he says, with Napoleon. We were reared as intellectuals and fought the Second World War before it happened and then again when it did happen. We witnessed the god that failed and helped trip him up. We predicted the Alexandrianism of the age and like everybody else we throve on it. We drove our foreign cars to class to teach. And we bit the hand that fed us, but not very hard, not hard enough. The hand went on signing papers. Once upon a time we were all revolutionaries of one stripe or another, but when we got married and settled down, with tenure, we talked technique instead of overthrow. Half of us stopped rebelling and not because of middle age. The age made it so easy to be a poet, or to survive on lobster, the age gave in so sweetly to our imprecations, the age so needed us to help it hate itself, this spineless age ended by softening the backbone of poetry.

Dylan Thomas was the anti-symbol of our group, that Dylan who died after he saw the faces of mice in the Bristol crystal. It was Thomas who taught poetry to stop thinking, and we resented that! Though we were not all drunks and suicides, we had our goodly share. But all of us felt the rot of institutionalism in our bones. Jarrell got it down in a novel, the kind of novel the age demanded, the exposé of sensibility. Jarrell's novel *Pictures from an Institution* is so brilliant that it defeats itself as a fiction; it becomes a hornbook of avant-gardism, sophisticated to the point of philistinism. Jarrell is misleadingly philistine, say, about Modern Art of all varieties. It is because he is impatient with failure or imperfection or goofing around with the Muse. But this impatience of Jarrell's is also a veritable lust for perfection; and both the impatience and the philistinism are what you might call Texan. *And yet*, what Jarrell does to Gertrude, his anti-heroine in the novel, is almost beyond belief. Can anyone be that worthy of hatred? One wonders what Gertrude thought when she read her portrait. Gertrude is one of those savage Southern female novelists who leaves the world in terror of the art of fiction.

The setting of the novel is Benton, a very expensive higher education academy only six versts from Sarah Lawrence or

Bennington. Benton's President Robbins doesn't fare any better than the loathed Gertrude, and the only lovable character in the book is a German-Jewish composer-in-residence named Rosenbaum. Jarrell attacks avant-garde institutionalism and everything it implies by immolating President Robbins and all his kinfolk in the way Gertrude might. He attacks dehumanized letters in his lip-smacking crucifixion of Gertrude. True humanity, true culture, true wisdom are preserved in the broken-English Rosenbaums. (pp. 203-04)

I am not reviewing the novel, but I give it a central place in Jarrell's work as a kind of negative plate of the poetry. The empty intellectualism of America is pinpointed at Benton: the author says, "Nowadays Benton picked and chose: girls who had read Wittgenstein as high school baby-sitters were rejected because the school's quota of abnormally intelligent students had already been filled that year." Jarrell, not quite a Des Esseintes, suffers from a disillusionment of America which all our best artists share, suffers from the disappointment at the failure of the healing-powers of poetry in this nation. Benton—American higher education—is only a rarer kind of custom-built Cadillac. One can almost begin to see the coat of arms emerging on the enameled door. One is already afraid of who is inside. He says, lapsing into what he thinks: "Is an institution always a man's shadow shortened in the sun, the lowest common denominator of everybody in it?" It is bitter to answer yes, but so it is in the modern Institution. (pp. 205-06)

> Karl Shapiro, "The Death of Randall Jarrell," in Randall Jarrell, 1914-1965, Robert Lowell, Peter Taylor, Robert Penn Warren, eds., Farrar, Straus and Giroux, 1967, pp. 195-229.

SUZANNE FERGUSON

Renouncing plot in its title, *Pictures from an Institution* remains true to its promise. Its major characters neither act nor develop; its putatively major events are reported but not dramatized; in the events that *are* dramatized—a dinner party, a funeral, the "Art Night" of a women's liberal arts college—nothing of consequence happens, and no causal relationship among these events is established. Most of the chapters are named for particular groups of characters, but vignettes and anecdotes about other characters appear in each one. The numerous aphorisms—used both for description and for narration—and allusions seem to project aspiration for a permanent place in a rhetorical *Book of Records* rather than a history of the novel. In some notes toward a lecture now in the Berg Collection of the New York Public Library, Jarrell wrote, "My book has no plot, no action, no sex, no violence, . . . no sweep, no scope." Antinovel? Metafiction? In part, no doubt, for it persistently calls into question the project of representing "life" in a novel.

Yet, for all the fun it has at the expense of the conventions of the realistic novel and of that peculiarly narcissistic subgenre, the academic novel, *Pictures from an Institution* is also a mock-epic prose poem in which Randall Jarrell attempts to come to terms with several of his life-long obsessions. On its title page he calls the book a "comedy"; it is also a meditation upon American character, American education, and the nature of good and evil in modern culture. Its structure reflects a dialectical opposition of two impulses in Jarrell's character: to judge and to love, damn and praise.

In setting out to write a prose fiction of some length, Jarrell apparently recognized two demands that he could not adequately fulfill by writing poems or essays: to confront very directly his experiences as a teacher in postwar American colleges and to allow his own ambivalent feelings toward the aspects of human nature and culture revealed in that setting to work themselves out in a series of confrontations of character and situation. In these confrontations, or juxtapositions of "pictures," Jarrell tests his own values and conflicting attitudes.

In *The Poetry of Randall Jarrell*, I remarked the deep core of didacticism in Jarrell's work, his tendency to want to teach his audiences—readers and friends as well as pupils—his enthusiasms in the world of the arts and in the arts of living: sport, philosophy, psychology [see *CLC*, Vol. 2]. In suggesting that a motivating impulse of *Pictures from an Institution* is the impulse to teach its audience, I do not mean to imply that it is an "apologue," arguing like *Rasselas* or *The Confidence Man* some reasoned, abstract world view. Yet there is more than a hint of apologue (and its inversion, satire) in the book's coyly self-conscious rejection of plot, in its extended analytical descriptions of the characters, in its consideration of abstract issues of national character, the relations of life to art, the relation of good to bad art, the follies of progressive education. If, on one level, the book is a compendium of all Jarrell's enthusiasms (usually referred to specifically, by name) and an indictment of his bêtes noires (usually attacked in general), on another level *Pictures* appears to be Jarrell's own struggle with a demon, the demon of judgment which constantly demands discriminations among high and low, good and bad, wise and foolish, sophisticated and ignorant, as the fundamental human activity.

As a critic and professor, Jarrell's task was to discriminate between good and bad art. To him, the good in art was not only beautiful but accurate in its observation of life: True with a capital *T*. The value of "great" writing or painting or music resides in truth-telling about the human experience, truth-telling about reality and wishes, as well as in excellence of style. In his criticism, Jarrell did not hesitate to rank Kipling, Christina Stead, and others among the very good but not the very best of writers after weighing precisely both their artistry and the depth and accuracy of their vision. Reading his poems and his novels, we sense that he made such judgments not only in his criticism, but that, either from instinct or training, he habitually measured not only art but the whole quality of life with similar clear-eyed and austere standards. However, Jarrell knew, too, that while we need such evaluations, we also need sympathy, compassion, and forgiveness for our sins. The judge of others needs these things not least among mortals, as Jarrell shows in his characterization of Pilate in **"Eighth Air Force."**

In *Pictures from an Institution*, Jarrell presides over his own case against the world and himself, finding both to be reprehensible and lovable. His ideal characters, the Rosenbaums and Constance, are both strong and weak, sweet and bitter (or, in Constance's case, sweet and bland); but even his "worst" characters, Gertrude Johnson and President and Mrs. Robbins, are allowed at least touches of humanity and affection. While the chief targets of satire in the book are the essential folly and stupidity of progressive higher education and the ignorant self-righteousness of those who complacently perpetuate that folly, in the world of Benton College the greatest evil is finally unkindness. Here as in the world of Jane Austen, the worst crime is the humiliation of the weak and defenseless, whether out of unthinking hubris or the deliberate but misguided desire to reveal the "truth," to teach someone a lesson. In satirizing

hubris, the satirist himself becomes self-righteous. Considered from different perspectives, Truth itself has limitations, means different things even, at different times and to different persons: hardly a discovery, but an observation that Jarrell instinctively found difficult to accommodate, since his desire so clearly was that the true and the good should be one and eternal in a paradise never to be lost.

What his character Gertrude does in "smoking" heads for her novel is in a sense what Jarrell also does in presenting most of the characters and themes of his novel. The difference, we are asked to believe, is that Jarrell sees also good in the beings whose follies and blindnesses he impales, whereas Gertrude sees only the folly and blindness. . . . In Jarrell's judgment, however, Gertrude is not what she thinks she is, and so, although her ignorance of peoples' better nature and her snobbish aggressiveness are made fun of, her wit, her affection for Sidney, and her own vulnerability to loneliness are seen with sympathy, even admiration.

Jarrell's struggle between judgment and unjudging love is most strongly reflected in the main metaphoric pattern of the book, in which Benton is an earthly paradise whose inhabitants seem mostly unaware that they are threatened with loss as they enact the roles of humans tempted (some not very strongly) by the apples of knowledge. Into this Eden comes a cynical Satan, Gertrude Johnson, expecting and sometimes tempting "these mortals" (in the title of her most recent book) to prove their folly, God, repeatedly invoked in seemingly playful and conventional ways, remains remote from the activities, allowing Gertrude free rein for "going to and fro in Benton and . . . walking up and down in it." Her chief opponent, in terms of values, is Gottfried Rosenbaum: "If a voice had said to her, 'Hast thou considered my servant Gottfried Rosenbaum, that there is none like him in Benton, a kind and a clever man,' she would have answered: 'I can't *stand* that Gottfried Rosenbaum'." Although she cannot tempt him, she baits him, to her own discomfiture. Complementary patterns of allusion and metaphor repeatedly emerge—from Jonah as from Job, from the story of St. George and the Dragon, from *Comus* and *Faust*. In these as well as other allusive motifs—those evoking *Der Rosenkavalier*, "The Witch of Coös," "Hansel and Gretel," "Lucifer in Starlight," *The Ghost Sonata* (which Jarrell calls *The Spook Sonata*)—the themes of knowledge and ignorance, judgment and forgiveness, pride and foolishness press into the surface of the narrative.

Jarrell's ambivalence about judgment appears prominently in his narrator's relationship to Gertrude, whom M. L. Rosenthal has seen as "discharg[ing] the hostile and supercilious side of Jarrell's critical intelligence." A poet-teacher, as Gertrude is a novelist-teacher, the narrator frequently agrees with Gertrude's judgments about other characters' failings, although he disassociates himself from her acerbic desire to find evil in everyone. Like Gertrude's, his observations of the Bentonites come from a devilish "going to and fro in Benton and from walking up and down in it." The narrator is basically an observer rather than a participant in life, a type seen with suspicion in American fiction from Brockden Brown to Fitzgerald. It is in his voice that the most trenchant criticisms of progressive education are sounded; and with Gertrude, he condemns the trivia and silliness of "Art Night." Unlike Gertrude, however, he believes in the possibility of good in people and thinks that he has found it in Constance and the Rosenbaums, whom Gertrude loathes and slanders because they do not fit her debased conception of human nature. He shows his ability to appreciate the good in the unlikeliest places when he admires Miss Rasmussen's wonderful statue "The East Wind," although he has trouble recognizing the good when it appears in the context of grotesque exaggeration and physical gracelessness, as in Flo Whittaker: "after you had been with [her] you didn't know what to do—honesty and sincerity began to seem to you a dreadful thing, and you even said to yourself, like a Greek philosopher having a nervous breakdown: 'Is it right to be good?'"

Jarrell is ambivalent, too, toward Benton, where the system of progressive education leaves its students ignorant of facts but learned in social consciousness. Though Benton displays only too clearly the absurdities of postwar progressive colleges, it is repeatedly seen as a kind of paradise. . . . In this paradise, or lotus-land (one hardly knows which), the students are prepared for *Life,* its apologists claim, but Jarrell-the-narrator knows that is not so. . . . Education at Benton consists largely in developing the students' sense of guilt—guilt for their own privileged position in society: "Many a Benton girl went back to her nice home, married her rich husband, and carried a fox in her bosom for the rest of her life." Having "sloughed off the awful protean burden of the past: of Magdalenian caves and Patmos and palm-leaf scriptures from Ceylon; of exiles' letters from Thrace or the Banks of the Danube; of soldiers' letters from the Wall—the Roman Wall, the Chinese Wall." Benton's students have no cultural experience to enrich their imaginations and comfort them in times of trouble. To them the Blatant Beast is "Something in a long poem that none of *you*'ll ever have to read," as both Gertrude and the narrator tell one of them; to Jarrell, clearly, that is a loss not only to the student but to the general richness of society.

This kind of criticism, and there is much more, is typical, in content if not expression, of conservative reproaches against progressive education, not just in college novels, but in the real world. Atypical, and almost surprising in Jarrell, whose own standards are distinctly conservative, is the equanimity with which the misprision is accepted. His satire of "Benton"—Sarah Lawrence, primarily—is decidedly benign. (pp. 272-76)

Clearly, although they shelter many producers of "art," both students and teachers, the groves of academe are not seen by Jarrell as the nurturing ground of great artists. Even here, however, one may be struck by lightning. Miss Sona Rasmussen, the Finno-Japanese "potato-bug" sculpture teacher—to appreciate whose aesthetic theories "you would have had to be an imbecile"—abandons her welding briefly at term's end to carve from a railroad tie something astounding. . . . This quasi-magical transformation demonstrates a key principle of Jarrell's critical faith: that there is a grace beyond craftsmanship that paradoxically makes the work of art *live.*

Gertrude's novels will never be so transfigured precisely because their impulse is so rational, so "scientific": "Gertrude dissected to murder." Her novel about Benton invites comparison with Jarrell's novel about Benton. Obviously, hers will also be highly crafted. Unlike his, it will have a plot because though she usually has minimal plots, she senses that "a plot that could have supported the First National Bank" will be necessary to give plausibility to the improbable characters she has taken from the life. One Bentonite, Jerrold Whittaker, is too implausible to use at all: "Seventy or eighty years ago I could still have got away with him, but nowadays—not a chance! He's just too good to be true. . . . My readers wouldn't believe in that man for a minute." Jarrell's novel, since it is telling

the "truth," lacks plot: as his narrator points out to Gertrude, nothing happens at Benton. He can also use too implausible characters such as Jerrold.

The thematic dialectic of judgment and love is reinforced structurally, in *Pictures,* by a dialectic of verisimilitude and artifice. Despite the fact that they are composed of a tissue of witty apothegms, Jarrell's characters mostly have the air of being drawn from life; and since its publication *Pictures from an Institution* has always had the reputation of being a *roman à clef.* (pp. 278-79)

The anecdotes are close to home; the descriptions, wildly exaggerated and impossibly elegant in their rhetoric, are nonetheless homely in content. (p. 279)

The "pictures" from the institution are not simply portraits, however, as Jarrell makes clear in his chapter titles, the first five of which name pairs or groups: "The President, Mrs., and Derek Robbins"; "The Whittakers and Gertrude"; "Miss Batterson and Benton"; "Constance and the Rosenbaums"; "Gertrude and Sidney." These may be regarded as "conversations" in the painterly sense, not because the characters named in the titles converse in a literal way but because their portraits are juxtaposed so as to reflect upon each other in complementary and contrasting ways. The remaining chapters, "Art Night" and "They All Go," suggest a broader canvas but still no motivated action. The activity, such as it is, goes on in the readers' minds as they attempt to come to terms with their own need to judge these characters, this institution.

In the lack of developed dialogue or a sustained plot, Jarrell makes a virtue of necessity. His poems and children's books confirm the suspicion that he could not—any more than Gertrude usually can—construct a traditional plot, possibly because he saw human affairs in terms of accident and of forces beyond human control. The characters of the novel, like those of the poems, are isolated individuals whose most successful means of communication is the mutual perception of works of art. Jarrell builds his composition of individual figures and groups with minute, deliberate strokes upon strokes, like Seurat with his bathers or his Sunday-afternoon-relaxing bourgeois. Like painted figures, the characters are caught in movement but static, monumental in the changing but unchanged landscape of Benton. Their significant personal affairs are kept deliberately offstage: we witness neither of the terrible quarrels between Gertrude and President Robbins; we are not privy to the Rosenbaums' decision to "adopt" Constance. Yet these are virtually the only events—other than Gertrude's realization that she could not get along without Sidney—that the book offers in the way of incidents that might have formed the basis of a plot. (The usual business of academic novels—academic politics, hiring and firing, the seduction of students by teachers and vice versa—is mercifully absent.)

The structural pattern that emerges from the juxtaposed portraits is not static, however, for it portrays the tension of opposites constantly merging with and being reflected in each other as Jarrell alternately scourges and praises his characters. The unself-conscious complacency that will later be associated with the Benton faculty and students in general is first seen in President Robbins, who early on is characterized as "an institution," but an institution somehow like St. George, since he must battle the dragon, Gertrude, to preserve the faith. Gertrude's skepticism is her destructive—but perhaps also purgative—fire. Not only a figure of the Satan of Genesis and Job, Gertrude is also "the witch" who leaves "the forest" at the end of the narrative; but there are other witches, too—Else, Mrs. Robbins, Fern Whittaker (Flo and Jerrold's nasty daughter), and, surprisingly, Irene Rosenbaum. Indeed, it appears that any wise woman has witchlike qualities. Those who lack them are saintly and somewhat monstrous innocents: Miss Batterson, Flo, Constance, Sylvia Moomaw.

The male characters also present a configuration of oppositions. There are the basically institutional sorts who display only brief moments of humanity; in addition to Dwight Robbins, these are Jerrold Whittaker and the memorably null "Head" of the large public university English department which hires away Miss Batterson—an expert on Cowper who is thought by most who hear that name to be an expert on Cooper. Their opposites are the flawed humans, Gottfried Rosenbaum and the narrator, who by constantly compromising their own values manage to live in harmony with the institutions. Comparable with the female innocents is Sidney, Gertrude's possession "as a baby is its mother's." The two snake-loving boys—Derek Robbins, in most respects so ordinary, and John Whittaker, brilliantly precocious—form a gratuitously implausible juxtaposition that makes fun of Freudian interpretations of behavior and the conventions of fiction even as it keeps us keyed into the theme of a lost paradise.

The book is shot through and through with images figuring the motif of the "fall" into knowledge as a recognition of mortality. Wisdom seems, inevitably, wisdom about what is wrong with things and people. To bring wisdom, as Gertrude does, is to bring evil: truth makes people unhappy, not free. Gertrude's "truths," derived from the principle of extrapolating the worst possible motives—to her, greed or sex—are seen as relatively trivial truths if not actual mistakes in the face of the more profound recognition of aging and the drift toward death experienced by the narrator, by Rosenbaum, and once, fleetingly, by Gertrude herself. (pp. 280-81)

After knowledge, there is forgiveness. Out of the clash of personalities and values, Jarrell salvages affection for the humanity represented in his "pictures" and brings his dialectical structure to a resolution. Like Gertrude, the narrator has "misjudged" Benton, and he feels a willingness for it to misjudge him in return. "I signed with it a separate peace. There was no need for us to judge each other." As the narrator, so the author: after impaling the errors and asininities of progressive education on a thousand barbs of aphorism, after dissecting the "wicked" inhabitants of the institution with his comic scalpel, Jarrell makes a separate peace with the world of his novel in the benign and sunlit atmosphere of its close. He seems to have arrived at the benediction Constance remembers from St. Augustine and applies to Rosenbaum: "I want you to be." This statement, introduced so early in the novel, is a touchstone to which the narrator returns several times in the course of his story and, implicitly, at the end. Emerging from the tensions of opposed judgments, Jarrell-as-narrator accepts Miss Rasmussen's one miracle, as a sign from the Providence that rules the world as the novelist rules the novel, and decides to love. (pp. 282-83)

> *Suzanne Ferguson, "To Benton, with Love and Judgment: Jarrell's 'Pictures from an Institution'," in* Critical Essays on Randall Jarrell, *edited by Suzanne Ferguson, G. K. Hall & Co., 1983, pp. 272-83.*

KATHE DAVIS FINNEY

The fiction of a lyric poet automatically raises questions about its motivation. What need prompts a poet to write a story instead of a poem? Why does the craftsman of the minute particular extend himself to the painful length of a *novel*? Randall Jarrell seems to have felt the narrative impulse particularly strongly: even apart from the strong narrative line apparent in much of his poetry, he compiled five anthologies of fiction, wrote four storybooks for children (one almost novel-length), and, most conspicuously and popularly, wrote the wonderful novel *Pictures from an Institution*.

Jarrell's discussions of fiction, as well as his fiction itself, make apparent that his motivation has to do with his interest in a problematic raised by all art, but one which fiction makes most explicit: the relation between fiction and reality. As narrative fiction is traditionally the mimetic genre, its forms have seemed appropriate to raise explicitly the question always implicit in the art of fiction-making: what is real ("really" real), and how do we know? How accurate are our perceptions; what reality do they have? How much do we the perceivers—and more, we the conscious inventors—invent our own realities in the act of perception.

Jarrell's contemporary and friend Delmore Schwartz articulated in "The Isolation of Modern Poetry" (1941) the popular notion that the alienation of the modern poet is what accounts not only for his obscurity, but also for his limitation almost exclusively to lyric forms, rather than to narrative or dramatic forms. Since the time of Blake, explains Schwartz, it has become "increasingly impossible for the poet to write about the lives of other men." The only available subject has come to be "the cultivation of his own sensibility," including his own life and other poetry. . . . The real merits of this argument are less important than the fact that it, or the idea it expressed, was widely accepted. With many of his contemporaries, Jarrell was very consciously the inheritor of a historical and cultural condition of dispossession, his sense of alienation exacerbated by personal circumstances, including a broken home, as well as by his academic training and the pressures of a reality that included the Depression and *another* war. But the very events which intensified the sense of dispossession he shared with the preceding "Lost Generation" made it impossible for him to accept that generation's solutions. "The middle generation," as John Berryman dubbed his contemporaries, or "The Last Generation," in Schwartz's parodic phrase, fought not only against their own alienation, but also against the lyric closure and formalist aesthetic which were its artistic correlates, and the solipsism which was its logical conclusion. The older poets had integrated the personal with the social and the philosophical in the pursuit of the impersonal; the younger ones pursued the same integration to the point of personal revelation.

Jarrell reacted against an autotelic idea of art and the related complex of values not in simple opposition, however, but dialectically, opposing only by assimilating and transcending. He began deep in "the modern tradition." Not merely highly intelligent, but also highly intellectual (and highly educated), Jarrell used his learning to search for a way of writing and being that would go beyond the merely learned: intellectual, rational, conventional. He both celebrated and deplored our book-bound condition, what we have since learned to call intertextuality. Not yet quite appalled by a Borgesian vision of the infinite library, he composed works full of other works, presenting and nostalgically seeking authority for his own authorship while at the same time illustrating the benighted state of those who live by books (or words, or ideas) alone.

Both an avid reader and a merciless critic of the poets of the "high modernist mode," Jarrell was also the student and friend of such critics as John Crowe Ransom, Allen Tate, Robert Penn Warren, R. P. Blackmur, and others of the best and best-known codifiers and apologists of those poets and of New Critical aesthetic values.

He shared Schwartz's interest in philosophy, though always partial to its most literary manifestations (e.g., Goethe). He was deeply read in European literature in general, almost obsessively so in German. And Kafka in particular struck a deep chord in Jarrell's being, perhaps partly because of *his* father-preoccupation, as well as other obvious affinities. Jarrell quotes and refers to Kafka often in his introduction and essays and is especially fond of citing Kafka's dream narratives as examples of pure story.

Most importantly, the psychological knowledge which had been news to the generation of the twenties was for the middle generation a matter of established fact and serious study. Jarrell's bachelor's degree was in psychology, and he knew Freud in particular deeply and well. Freud seemed to address Jarrell's personal problems in his preoccupation with the role of the father, as well as his psychological version of the myth of the Fall and the sense of loss that it explains. Most of all Freud was important, to Jarrell as to the literary world in general, for *The Interpretation of Dreams*. Freud not only redefined "mind" so that it was no longer equivalent to consciousness, but by the same token he asserted the reality of the mental world. As Edward Said points out, "The *Interpretation* deals as much with the nature of psychological reality as with the meaning of dreams." He adds, "the book's fascination lies in the fact that Freud does not choose between illusion and reality until the very end," and discusses the way in which Freud himself used techniques developed by late nineteenth- and early twentieth-century writers to deal with the inadequacy of language as mimetic. Dream, as a window on the unconscious, depicts a reality equal to if not profounder than that of the waking world. "There is a reality behind the outer reality," Jarrell says in *Pictures*; "it is no more real than the other, both are as real as real can be, but it is different." The artist as the bringer of this subterranean truth to the public can be understood then as both alienated and essential (as Edmund Wilson, for instance, explained him by means of the Philoctetes myth in *The Wound and the Bow*, published in 1931).

This complex of factors and influences caused Jarrell to question both internal and external realities in ways he could best deal with in fiction rather than poetry. His narratives took Jarrell toward a postmodernist solution to the problems of dispossession, though he did not quite arrive there. He sought a nondualistic formulation of man's place in the world, and rejected—or tried to reject—the dichotomies of subject and object, life and art, without finding a fully satisfactory formulation for his insights. He explored at least tentatively the idea of the shared human world as constitutive of human reality (including personal identity), but the idea was not clearly articulated or fully developed enough to serve as a real or personally enabling solution.

Though moving beyond the high modernist aesthetic meant moving toward narrative, Jarrell could not go back to traditional narrative any more than he could retreat to mere subjectivism or expressionism. Consequently his fiction is post-Joycean, though not obviously so: short on plot, heavily autobiographical (as Schwartz said it must be)—if only in disguised form—with fictionality itself as one of its subjects. Jarrell wrote, that is, a fiction moving strongly in the direction of what we now call metafiction.

In his essay **"Stories,"** Jarrell reflects upon the word *story:* it means, he says, both history ("truth") and fiction. "A story, then, tells the truth or a lie—is a wish, or a truth, or a wish modified by a truth." But after Freud the opposition between truth and wish is no simple one. "The truths that he systematized, Freud said, had already been discovered by the poets; the tears of things, the truth of things, are there in their fictions." Reality may stand in opposition to the pleasure principle, but "truth" does not necessarily lie with reality: "The wish is the first truth about us . . ."

By embodying the truth of wishes, story both clarifies and expands our selves. In *Pictures from an Institution,* the family-lyless girl Constance, "adopted" by the Rosenbaums, finds an emotional correlative of her life in the Grimms' fairy tale (entirely "unrealistic," of course) "The Juniper Tree." Weeping "in joy for herself and her happiness and in grief for her own stupidity and the world's," she ends "no longer conscious of the world except as the brimming margin of herself, a boundary that was not a boundary." Jarrell was, Karl Shapiro says, "the poet of the *Kinder* and the earliest games of the mind and heart." And his motive for writing children's stories was likewise, I think, his own wish to convey the archetypal or psychological primal truth of wishes. (pp. 284-87)

Pictures from an Institution, written for adults, presents by contrast the surface of "the outer reality." But just as Gertrude Johnson, the novelist within the novel, writes books which are unquestioningly read as experimental, though their "grammar, syntax and punctuation were perfectly orthodox," so Jarrell, in *this* apparently conventional novel, is preoccupied with the metafictional concerns of the "reality behind the outer reality." For adults, the primary access to the "reality behind" is through art, and the forms and functions of art are a major concern of the novel. The "pictures" are, like the bat-poet's, portraits of a series of individuals, but seen socially: in pairs or in groups, and within their institutional setting. (That the nature of the institution is not specified in the title is of course a commentary on academics, or maybe is even more general: we are all institutionalized in some sense.) The institution is Benton, a "progressive" women's college. Characters, and scenes in which they are variously (and artfully) combined, are juxtaposed as, quite explicitly, contrasts among alternative realities, and the novel has as its profoundest theme the problematic nature of "reality."

Pictures is a novel of one day, though that fact, established on the first page, is so little insisted upon that it can go unnoticed until the last page. Without a plot in any conventional sense (the chronology of the day is not significant, nor significantly pointed to, and no structuring conflicts are presented and resolved), the novel is exquisitely patterned as a minuet. But not obviously so: Jarrell seems to regard plot as inversely proportional to action, in that plot is the artificial imposition of pattern upon the events of life. Precisely because nothing happens at Benton, Gertrude can write there her first novel with "a real Plot," "a plot that could have supported the First National Bank." Jarrell's own structure is not such a Plot, but rather a series of arrangement of characters, or "pictures" of those characters. (p. 291)

Kathe Davis Finney, "The Poet, Truth, and Other Fictions: Randall Jarrell as Storyteller," in Critical Essays on Randall Jarrell, *edited by Suzanne Ferguson, G. K. Hall & Co., 1983, pp. 284-97.*

J. D. McCLATCHY

It is usually said, and with good reason, that Randall Jarrell was the best poet-critic of his generation, a literary journalist with impeccable taste and perfect pitch, and an intelligence so discriminating and convincing that his eloquently argued opinions about the major modernist poets still shape the way we read them. And a glance over his other work—his novel, his translations, his books for children, his many reviews and occasional essays—shows him to have been a man of wide interests, one who wrote from his enthusiasms: sports cars, Russian novels, German music, Donatello and tennis. His greatest enthusiasm was writing, and as [*Randall Jarrell's Letters* makes] clear, he *worked up* his style, as if it were his backhand.

In a sense, it was the back of his hand that distinguished his style. Thurber's sobriquet for Alexander Woollcott might also be used of Jarrell in his criticism: Old Vitriol and Violets. He was famously cruel in his judgments, but rarely inaccurate. "When we read the criticism of any past age," he once wrote, "we see immediately that the main thing wrong with it is an astonishing amount of what Eliot calls 'fools' approval'; most of the thousands of poets were bad, most of the thousands of critics were bad, and they loved each other." Yet as Robert Lowell remarked, "Eulogy was the glory of Randall's criticism." He did not have a critical mind on the order of Eliot's or Blackmur's, but his proper scorn and his quicksilver praise enlivened the state of criticism in his day, which was, he said, "astonishingly graceless, joyless, humorless, long-winded, niggling, blinkered, methodical, self-important, cliché-ridden, prestige-obsessed, and almost autonomous."

What makes his writing so vivid, and his opinions still so forceful, is his style. He thought in images and wrote in phrases, and thereby seemed not merely to describe an author's intention but to embody it. To characterize William Carlos Williams's attitude toward formal verse, he wrote: "If you have gone to the moon in a Fourth of July rocket you built yourself, you can be forgiven for looking askance at Pegasus." He speaks of the "iron spontaneity" of the beatniks, or of the disciples of Yvor Winters, says that they "wander, grave weighing shades, through a landscape each leaf of which rhymes, and scans, and says softly: And the moral of *that* is . . ." The one thing it seems that Jarrell could *not* write was a dull book, but Mary Jarrell, his second wife, has now published one in his name.

It would have been a dull book in any case. The simple, and sad, truth is he was not an interesting letter writer. Even so, Mary Jarrell's selection (less than a fifth of those letters preserved) is lumpy, and her apparatus overdone. In effect, she wanted her running commentary to provide a biography of sorts. While often informative, it is rarely illuminating. Very much the *veuve abusive*, she is so intent to brighten the image of Randall Jarrell that she only casts a greater shadow over it—over his erotic life, his last days (with their apparent insanity and ambiguous end), his instincts and motives, the sources and drives of his genius. She is a jaunty and sometimes an amusing memoirist, but she is no judge of people and is often careless about facts.

As Weldon Kees once observed about Randall Jarrell in company, "The thing that rather puts one off about him is his way of hoarding his wit for his writing." And he did not lavish it on his correspondence either. Though there are exuberant and plangent exceptions here, details and ideas lovingly touched on, his letters tend to be stiff, practical, at times downright telegraphic. In 1951 he happened to read his own letters, a hundred of them written to his first wife, Mackie, and returned by her after their divorce. "Well, I have been reading them," he writes, "and enjoyed it *very* much, I have to confess. There are some terribly funny parts, and some rather well-written

ones. I was struck with how (relatively) cheerful and determined I managed to stay, at least in the letters. Sometimes I'd be amused at what the letters didn't say." One has the sense indeed that a lot has been left out, and much made determinedly cheerful. The letters to his mother have been lost, those to his best friend, Peter Taylor, withheld. They may have shown a different side of Jarrell, but I doubt it. Except in his poems (and there in a fictive guise) he was not very forthcoming about his emotional life, nor did he have any of the bad habits that make for an interesting letter writer. He was unsocial, prissy, withdrawn, alternately haughty and silly—which is to say, extremely shy. He could not bear small talk, low gossip, or vulgarity, and was bored with the Literary Life. He did not like to travel, preferred the company of cats, cultivated a dull routine: his idea of bliss was to sit with a milkshake and read *The Wind in the Willows*. There was more than a little of Charles Dodgson in his character. And maybe some of Alice herself. His poem **"A Girl in a Library"** remains his best ironic self-portrait as "an object among dreams."

When he wrote a letter for publication, on the other hand, he was suddenly brilliant. Perhaps it could be said that he wrote well only when he was in love. In print, or on the podium, he was in love with himself, with his own powers of quickening sympathy and withering contempt. And in his private letters he is best when he is in love with a young woman or an older man. Edmund Wilson said Jarrell was "essentially an adolescent," and he seemed to crave, for his closest relationships, parents he could fawn on (Wilson was one, along with John Crowe Ransom and Allen Tate), rivals to buck against, or women to preen before. Far too much space in this book is taken up with letters to his two wives (to his first while he was in the Army, and to his second while courting her) and to Elisabeth Eisler, a young Austrian woman with whom he was infatuated. Women brought out the best in him—his poems—and he had a great deal of the right kind of understanding of them; he himself said that he had a "semifeminine mind." But they also brought out the worst—a cloying, sentimental tone that pervades his love letters and results in a kind of romantic twaddle. It does not make Jarrell look like a fool, it merely makes him look like the rest of us. A letter to Lowell criticizing Delmore Schwartz might as well be describing himself: "some queer segmentation of his personal being into an objective part with taste and another part with nothing but adolescent self-absorption."

The book falls roughly into four parts, or periods of Jarrell's life. The first, from the mid-1930s until the war, contains the letters of a young writer eager for a career and not above some flattering to promote it. His marriage and the publication of his first book gave him confidence, even the self-confidence to be patronizing. From the start he has a true wit's way of turning fate into a phrase, as when in 1939 he writes, "I felt quite funny when Freud died, it was like having a continent disappear." During the war he was stationed at Air Force bases in Texas and his letters to his wife show a desperate boredom. Except when he mentions his reading and writing, they are as tedious as his duties were.

It is the next section, covering the five-year period after the war, that is the heart of the book. Jarrell was then at his liveliest, writing his best poems, busy as literary editor of *The Nation*, recognized and powerful as a critic. His letters to Robert Lowell at this time are extraordinary and suggest why Lowell later said of Jarrell that he made others

> feel that their realizing themselves was as close to
> him as his own self-realization, and that he cared as

much about making the nature and goodness of some-one else's work understood as he cared about making his own understood.

Lowell was then writing the poems that came to be *Lord Weary's Castle,* and not since Pound functioned as Eliot's ideal reader and blue-penciler has a poet been so well served. Jarrell's letters are a constant and buoyant source of what any writer most needs: praise ("they are some of the best poems anybody has written in our time, and are sure to be read for hundreds of years") and useful advice ("the last stanza is good but you could use that somewhere else. It's too mannered a poem, both form and content. All this might be wrong, but I'm sure this isn't"). No doubt he was such a perceptive critic of Lowell's poems because he sensed their similarity to his own; as he said, their work shared "the same core of sorrow and horror."

About his own poems he has little to say, and again that may be an effect of his instinctive, self-protective shyness, his difficulty with intimacy. His reticence is a great disappointment. Another is the second half of the book, most of it what he called his "very scrappy, spotty, low-pressure" letters to his friends, and gushy domestic rambles to Mary Jarrell. These are the years of his teaching in North Carolina—a profession he loved and claimed was "the next thing to hereditary wealth." A sedentary life, it depended on books and visitors: "Elizabeth Bishop left last night—nice, but unhappy and not knowing what to do with her life. She left a typewriter, a large box of Eskimo baskets and sculpture (she'd been in Labrador) and a sweater—I look in corners occasionally, for *her.*" Of books and music he has rousing opinions: "The trouble with the *Kindertotenlieder* is that it sounds as if those children had always been dead; and it's enough like *Das Lied von der Erde* to make you think the children must have been half-Chinese." And about writers he is best when waspish: "Auden certainly is becoming a sit-by-the-fire-do-my-embroidery and to-hell-with-the-muse poet, isn't he?" Or this: "I wish all the San Francisco poets would eat all the University poets and burst, so that Nature, abhorring a vacuum, would send one plain poet or cat or rat to take their place."

If he has little to say about his own poems, we do learn what a lot of trouble his novel, and his publishers, gave him. And his uncompleted projects, hashed out in these letters, are as intriguing as anything he finished. We learn that he had signed a contract to write a book about Hart Crane for the "American Men of Letters" series. He took notes for a study of T. S. Eliot's work, never written. He planned to edit an anthology of modern poetry with Lowell. And he wanted to write a play, but "it's rather like joining some church—I need to believe in plots first."

Toward the end of his life he was less interested in literature itself than in the culture of which it is part. But all along he had felt that the best poems "seem life first and poetry second." It is precisely those connections and priorities that enriched his poetry and steadied his criticism. (pp. 597-98)

More's the pity, then, to see this clear-eyed man sink into a clinical melancholia which dimmed his powers and enthusiasms. Mary Jarrell's account of the last year of the poet's life is disheartening. He didn't seem to have the strength to fight his bouts of mental illness. "It was so queer," he told his wife, "as if the fairies had stolen me away and left a log in my place." He may have sensed his own sinister depths years before he finally succumbed to them. I come back to his description of his poems, of their "core of sorrow and horror."

If that was at any time what he saw when he took the measure of his own mind, we are not permitted a look at it in these letters. Certainly it seems to account for his having backed away so violently from Lowell's manic episodes: fear, not fastidiousness, drove him. In any event the stunned and suicidal poet is not the image we take away from this book, however diminished the man may seem by our disappointment with his letters. The man as he emerges here writing to Berryman and Moore, to Bishop, Hannah Arendt, Adrienne Rich, and above all to his friend Robert Lowell, is the one we remember. And that man is the wise child. (p. 598)

> *J. D. McClatchy, "The Wise Child," in* The Nation, *New York, Vol. 240, No. 19, May 18, 1985, pp. 597-98.*

DAVID KALSTONE

[*Randall Jarrell's Letters: An Autobiographical and Literary Selection*] contains little of the strange, the essential, Jarrell. Social exchange was less his medium than the heady air of poetry. As he wrote to his first sweetheart, in a rare autobiographical aside: "I've lived all over, and always been separated from at least half of a very small family, and been as alone as children ever are. As long as I can remember, I've been so different from everybody else that even trying to be like them couldn't occur to me." Letters from Jarrell's youth and to his family have evidently not survived to be included in this edition. In letters to others he never mentioned them. . . .

Except for the letters to his two wives, Mackie, from whom he was divorced in 1951, and Mary, the editor of these letters, the correspondence is not intimate or much preoccupied with the dailiness of life. Jarrell takes little interest in exploring and extending relationships. He didn't use letters for self-analysis or gossip, as Virginia Woolf did. Nor did he write the kind of breezy, affectionate literary gazette for which Robert Lowell was noted. Nor was he drawn to descriptive styles, like those startling detailed presentations of the world that were Elizabeth Bishop's way of assimilating herself to the felt strangeness of life.

When the Jarrell correspondence begins he is a brilliant young student and instructor at Vanderbilt and Kenyon. His letters to Allen Tate, to Edmund Wilson at *The New Republic,* and to Robert Penn Warren at *Southern Review* are staccato reports and requests by a young man eager to place his essays and poems. It is only when these somewhat unfocused letters are read beside his real work—the poetry and the criticism of the late 1930s and early 1940s—that we recognize his iron determination to establish and champion new kinds of poetry and criticism, which he would call, too loosely, in an influential essay on Robert Lowell, "post-modern."

However grateful he was, and however dependent on John Crowe Ransom, Tate, and Warren, his letters to and about them define attitudes strongly critical of theirs. At Kenyon, in fact, he had been something of a maverick: a reader of Auden, a leftist in the midst of southern agrarians, and largely unpopular with his fellows. (p. 33)

For Jarrell there was always the sense that the New Critics were too self-consciously "manly," arbitrary, inflexible—and too dogged by the burden of Eliot and historical modernism. When Tate criticized the "limp" meters of Jarrell's poems, the latter replied that it was "the defect of a quality. . . . I'd rather seem limp and prosaic than false or rhetorical. I want to be rather like speech." "False and rhetorical" was, of course, a rebuke to Tate, whose work the younger poet felt too stiff, lacking in the ability to identify itself with anything "non-Allen." "Allen never feels the need of any *motivation* of violence—violence is to him, perhaps unconsciously, an intrinsic good." Warren, too, "manages his life by pushing all the evil in it out into the poems and novels," and not sufficiently mixing it with the good. Jarrell was looking for meters and forms that accommodated more of the human voice and its contradictions—hence his attraction, from early on, to dramatic monologues.

It was at this stage in Jarrell's career that the single most riveting encounter in these letters takes place. Robert Lowell had already published (in 1944) *Land of Unlikeness,* a book much indebted to Allen Tate and shadowed by Tate's forms and violence of tone. Lowell was in the course of revising the book, adding and deleting poems, for what would become his first commercial volume, *Lord Weary's Castle,* the book that brought him lightning fame. He and Jarrell had known one another, contrary to some of the sentimentalizing legends, in an uneasy and antagonistic friendship at Kenyon. Jarrell showed little interest in Lowell's early work, and in letters to Tate and Warren barely mentions them. "There are five or six poems by Cal Lowell (original and goodish, though perfunctory and queer) in the latest *Sewanee Review.*" But Jarrell's interest was truly piqued when he saw Lowell revising himself away from Tate. Lowell was to become *the* example of the new poet for Jarrell, and he lavished letters and suggestions at a time when Lowell most welcomed them. Few poets can have received such detailed scrutiny and such trustworthy counsel from a contemporary. (pp. 33-4)

"I think your biggest limitations right now," Jarrell wrote [Lowell],

> are (1) not putting enough about *people* in the poems—they are more about the actions of you, God, the sea and cemeteries than they are about the 'actions of men'; (2) being too harsh and severe—but this is already changing very much for the better too, *I* think. Contemporary satires (which you don't seem to write any more) are your weakest sort of poem, and are not really worth wasting your time on; your worst tendency is to do too-mannered, mechanical, wonderfully contrived, exercise poems, but these you don't do much when you feel enough about the subject to start from a real point of departure in contemporary real life.

Jarrell reiterated his feeling, both in his letters and in a landmark review of *Lord Weary's Castle.* . . . There are no peaks of critical involvement as exciting as these in the remainder of this volume of the letters, except for some engaging critiques offered to Adrienne Rich after her early work appeared. (p. 34)

Jarrell enjoyed educating the women he knew. He sent long reading lists to Elisabeth Eisler, a young Austrian with whom he had a platonic affair during and after the Salzburg Seminar in 1948. He also seemed to take a tutorial pleasure in the long series of courtship letters to Mary von Schrader, who became his second wife in 1952. There are other flashes of Jarrell the critic from time to time: of Peter Viereck, for example, "He's the only man I know who *couldn't* write an anonymous letter—he even signs bombs." There are few, but striking, portraits of writers: tonic insights into the troubled R. P. Blackmur, whom he came to know at Princeton; a glimpse of Auden. . . . Most memorably there are encounters with Robert Frost. . . . (p. 35)

One day this collection is bound to be superseded. Mrs. Jarrell was seriously hampered in her efforts because Peter Taylor, a close friend of her husband since Vanderbilt days, did not release their correspondence for this edition. Whether those letters will tell us more about the Jarrell who wrote the poems, and about the darkening of his last years, is a moot point. The lonely strain always audible in his poetry clearly surfaced in his life as he began to suffer manic-depressive illnesses in the 1960s. His friends—Lowell and Taylor among them—described his death in 1965 as a suicide. Mrs. Jarrell, in a lengthy day-by-day commentary on Jarrell's last hospitalization, presents it as an accident in which he was run down by a car while taking an early evening walk. The coroner judged it as accidental, or as the doctor in charge of the autopsy put it, there was "reasonable doubt about its being suicide." There are few clues in the letters, but from Jarrell's writing habits we do not even expect them. The real Jarrell is elsewhere—in the poems and in the privacies he never chooses to explore with the correspondents he addresses in this book. (pp. 35-6)

> *David Kalstone, "A Critic Apart," in* The New Republic, *Vol. 192, No. 22, June 3, 1985, pp. 32-6.*

PATRICIA BEER

[*Randall Jarrell's Letters*] tell us as much about his generation as they do about himself and are therefore doubly welcome. The biographical commentary provided by editor Mary Jarrell, the poet's second wife, is skilfully organised, highly informative and quite startlingly detached. (p. 25)

[Jarrell] stood out as a most distinctive individual. Both he and his wife state categorically that he was not gregarious. But he very often speaks as though there were a flock somewhere around: from his greetings in an early letter ('Give my love to Cenina and Cleanth and Tinkum and Albert') to later letters in which he writes to Robert Lowell about how Blackmur did a wonderful review of Trilling in *Kenyon Review,* to John Crowe Ransom about how he can hardly wait to see Robert Penn Warren's long poem *Brother to Dragons,* part of which Ransom is printing in *Kenyon,* and to Warren about his nomination of John Crowe Ransom for the Academy of American Poets award.

One of the things at which Jarrell excelled them all and for which he became widely known was the ferocity of his criticism. In 1948, when he was first teaching at the Woman's College of the University of North Carolina (where eventually he was to end his career), the whole question of how he could be as cruel as he was, if he was, received a thorough airing in his letters as well as in print. The review he wrote for *The Nation* of Conrad Aiken's *The Kid* concluded: 'There is something a little too musically ectoplasmic, too pretty-pretty, about Mr Aiken's best poems; but one longs for them as one wanders, like an imported camel, through the Great American Desert of *The Kid.*' This review, mildness itself by the standards of at least two British hatchetmen, provoked a violent response from Aiken, in which he spoke of attempted murder and of Jarrell as 'this self-appointed judge and executioner', suggesting that he was 'condemned in advance to condemn in advance, and therefore to look with glee for faults about which he can be funny rather than with love for virtues that can be praised'.

This particular accusation was one that Jarrell had already denied, in a letter to the *New Republic* some years before, in connection with Aiken's work, and he denied it again now, in a letter to the *Nation.* Not everybody was convinced. John Berryman roundly said: 'He was immensely cruel, and the extraordinary thing about it is that he didn't know he was cruel.' But, he explained, Jarrell hated bad poetry so much, he could not realise that human beings wrote it.

From his letters it appears to have been not quite like that. Robert Penn Warren said of him in his student days 'He was overwhelmed by the spectacle of human dumbness', a comment which he was to echo in a wartime letter to his first wife: 'If this world were cleverer I'd be happier.' His attitude seems to have been not so much arrogant delight that he was brighter than other people as sadness that they were stupider than himself. If this is so it makes marginally more amiable his otherwise appalling remark about his students: 'The average North Carolina girl talks as if she were an imbecile with an ambition to be an idiot.'

In a youthful letter to Edmund Wilson, Jarrell declared his belief in a very precise difference between poetry and prose: 'A poem doesn't exist till it's written but prose is what you think or say anyway.' This is intelligible, not to say simplistic; but it is infinitely arguable, and the argument is relevant to *Randall Jarrell's Letters*. So many poems, sent with letters, are included in this collection and the material presented in prose is so often treated simultaneously in poetry that Jarrell's dictum is being put constantly to the test.

To take an example: in 1943, during his months of military training at Chanute Field, Illinois, Jarrell spent a short leave visiting the University of Illinois. While there he wrote a poem 'The Soldier Walks Under the Trees of the University' and this he sent to his wife within hours of its being written. To read it now embedded in the surrounding letters is to recall the advice traditionally offered to adult actors about the dangers of appearing with children and animals.

The poem has a weary composure and a predictable philosophy which may well be part of war but which make it come across as something you might think or say anyway. Whereas Jarrell's prose descriptions of army life and the occasional respites from it—in Texas and Arizona as well as at Chanute—steal the show: energetic, unrehearsed, almost blurted out, as though they had not existed before they were written. And so, except for the occasional self-conscious *mot,* do most of the other letters. Jarrell's dividing line may have fallen in the wrong place or he may have been mistaken as to what was on which side of it. (pp. 25-6)

> *Patricia Beer, "Randall Jarrell's Cruelty," in* The Listener, *Vol. 115, No. 2947, February 13, 1986, pp. 25-6.*

MICHAEL HOFMANN

[*Randall Jarrell's Letters*] are as attractive as Jarrell's celebrated reviews and as the poems in his last, best book, *The Lost World*. What they share is quickness and agility of mind, an unlikely grace, forthrightness without coarseness, a magnetic attraction towards goodness and love of life. All these go into the characteristic Jarrell tone, and it seems as wicked to call the poems infantile as to find the reviews malicious. . . .

The *Letters* are full of Jarrellisms: expressions of excitement like "Gee!" or "crazy about", and of rejection, like "dumb" or "dopey". There are his imaginative conceits, acute and slightly florid: a vintage bottle of *Spätlese* "like a raisin's daydream", his loneliness at Princeton, "If I had a lion I'd be just like St Jerome." His prodigious cultural range is a source of more mirth and peculiarity: "One sees lots of criticism by

William Carlos Williams these days, but very little by Baby Snooks; it's an unjust world." (Mary Jarrell explains who Baby Snooks was.) . . . There are innumerable occasions in these letters of such motiveless joy in expression; as we saw, even Oscar Williams could serve as one. How could anyone be accounted malicious who was capable of ending a review: "And now I have so little space, and so much enthusiasm, for Adrienne Cecile Rich's *The Diamond Cutters* that I can only make boiling and whistling noises like a teakettle"?

At times, Jarrell thought writing reviews was as futile as raining into the sea: it remained as salty as ever. Perhaps it was even worse than that, it made the waves reach for the sky. . . . For Jarrell, though, it was always the expression of enthusiasm that was most important, and this is carried on just as much in the letters as in the reviews. There are detailed considerations of their poems addressed to Lowell, Elizabeth Bishop and Adrienne Rich, as well as the far more rapid and generalized promulgation of preferences to other correspondents. He gave a page-long reading-list to an Austrian friend. He found himself defending Robert Lowell to a Sister Bernetta Quinn, who preferred Jarrell's own work. If by now his modern canon—Frost, Stevens, Williams, Moore, Bishop, Lowell—seems classically obvious and unarguable, it is worth bearing in mind that it wasn't at the time, that the sea really *was* salty. Mary Jarrell's short footnotes bring this out rather more than her husband's letters; he was, as he says himself, "cheerful and determined" in them. She, though, is free to point out that an anthologist "chose neither widely nor too well", or to inform us that "The year Jarrell nominated Bishop, the Poetry Society of America prize went to Joyce Horner."

As a correspondent or a confederate, Jarrell is wonderfully bracing: staunch, exuberant, witty and serious. He has the gift of being genuine, without being dull or lavish or incredible. . . . He none the less kept his independence, rejecting, for instance, Lowell's prose-memoir "91 Revere Street". ("'What's wrong with it?' And Jarrell said, 'But it's not poetry, Cal.'") He could be impatient and intolerant, but never immodest. . . . [Jarrell's] is a mind of rare responsiveness and tenderness, capable of detecting Auden in the work of his contemporaries, even when absorbed indirectly, and at very low concentrations; and of worrying at a sight or sound or taste in a poem, even if it means overturning a whole life to find it. . . . In dedicating this book to her husband and his generation, some alive, mostly dead, Mary Jarrell quotes two lines from one of his poems: "For all we said, and did, and thought— / The world we were", omitting the line preceding, "There is no one left to care". In the event, she is right, and he is wrong. It is impossible not to care for that lost "world we were", so vividly brought to life in these letters, beautifully edited to constitute a mixture of biography, autobiography and group portrait.

> *Michael Hofmann, "The World He Was," in* The Times Literary Supplement, *No. 4345, July 11, 1986, p. 759.*

JOHN BAYLEY

It was once observed by J. B. Priestley that the literary life in England was 'a rat-race without even a sight of the other rats'. English authors on the whole prefer to work on their own and find their friends outside the confraternity—indeed, because of this preference, there is hardly such a thing as a confraternity. 'Very bad—very good, too,' as Conrad's Stein would say. With us, both the best and the worst writing seems unconscious that anything else is being written. Writing in America, on the other hand, is a joint pioneering venture, undertaken in a spirit, if not exactly of co-operation with other authors, then of mutual comment and criticism, malice or kindliness equally supportive. In the vast contingency of the American scene, writers must cling together.

The truth is brought home in the prolonged minutiae of Marianne Moore's criticism and in the small talk of [*Randall Jarrell's Letters*]. Both have great collective charm, giving the effect of looking through the glass into a well-matured aquarium. . . . In 1946, Jarrell served a year as Literary Editor for the *Nation,* doing so well at matching books and reviewers that John Crowe Ransom said he deserved a Pulitzer Prize for it. 'Not since Poe had an American poet laid down the law in quite such a carnival spirit.' In those days of talented amateurs the Eng Lit business was still the Gay Science. Used by Nietzsche, and as a title for his book on criticism by the Victorian reviewer E. S. Dallas, that phrase goes back to the troubadours, beloved of Ezra Pound: and there is a troubadour spirit in both these American poets, the collective spirit that Pound did so much to foster. More and more, he appears as the presiding genius not only of 'Modernism' but of modern American literary culture.

In the aquarium with Jarrell, to be more precise at the Bloomington, Indiana School of Letters, one of his several groves of academe over the years, were Jacques Barzun, R. P. Blackmur, Alfred Kazin, Lionel Trilling, Delmore Schwartz, Allen Tate, Kenneth Burke, Robert Fitzgerald, Leslie Fiedler and John Crowe Ransom—this last its founder as a school of literary criticism 'to teach those who teach it'. Marianne Moore, in Brooklyn, had a quieter time, but was just as much in touch with them all through friends and books. All the critics were poets and all the poets critics. There were giants in those days, and their daily voices are audible in these reviews and letters in a way that they are not in their other writings, as these survive time. Time here is very local, very much in the past, and that is its fascination.

Marianne Moore's best poems are beyond its grasp, but about Jarrell's one cannot be so sure. Of this query he was himself acutely aware, and it may have contributed to his mysterious death—accident or suicide—struck by a car when walking on a main road. The tone and import of his letters are as bland as apple pie, and their reader has no sense of the tensions and traumas that led him to mental hospital. It may partly be the reticence expected of a Southern gentleman, a quality to be admired, which makes a change of wives seem as smooth and effortless as the gears on the sports cars Jarrell so much fancied. Mary Jarrell has done a loyal and meticulous job, her comments on friends and situations are humorously vivid: but she also leaves the surface of the literary life quite undisturbed. There is no trace here of the competitive insight which produced the memorable portrait of Gertrude in *Pictures from an Institution,* that coruscating but already time-haunted novel which allegedly put Mary McCarthy on the spot. Jarrell himself discounted this, claiming hardly to know her: but Philip Rahv at *Partisan,* who knew her much better, politely declined to print any of the novel, and Jarrell replied by sending him no further articles or poems. Gertrude is certainly his idea of the archetype of the American woman writer, and in this, as with other matters, his vision may now appear out of date.

There may indeed be a certain ominous correlation between the bland friendliness of these letters and something easy—too

easy—in the texture of his poems. It has been said that of the big three—himself, Berryman and Lowell—Jarrell is the likeliest to survive as a poet, if only because the other two are so much more all of a piece with their poetry. Jarrell, like his master John Crowe Ransom, seems to stand outside his. Ransom has so much style that in his case this does not matter, but in Jarrell's it does. His poetry has the unpersonal friendliness of his letters—he was an excellent instructor who loved to teach—as if it were there to illustrate the academic and cultural process, rather as Gertrude in *Pictures from an Institution* illustrates the willpower of the American cultured female. Himself a dedicated and totally competitive intellectual who was also an expert ball game player, Jarrell seems to have suffered from the lack of a private identity, including a sexual one. In spite of what Robert Lowell called his 'upsettingly brilliant air of knowing everything', he also 'gave off an angelic impression'. 'His mind, unearthly in its quickness, was a little boyish, disembodied and brittle. His body was a little ghostly in its immunity to soil, entanglements and rebellion.' At one time Jarrell and Lowell shared an attic together in the Crowe Ransoms' house, and Jarrell's detailed comments on his friend's early poems are the best things among his letters. They are founded on the New Criticism, on Empson and on Jarrell's own highly Empsonian master's thesis on Implication in A. E. Housman, but they display, too, a remarkable impersonal insight. Not every critic in 1945 would have said of Lowell that 'you write more in the great tradition, the grand style, the real *middle* of English poetry, than anybody since Yeats.' At the same time Jarrell was telling all his friends that Christina Stead's *The Man Who Loved Children* was 'one of the best novels I have ever read'. There is something endearing about that.

The impression of a disembodied intelligence remains, as strong in the letters as it must have been in life. Observing that he had 'the most glittering IQ you ever met', William Barrett at *Partisan Review* said of Jarrell that 'one would be unlikely to take him for a poet at all, so intensely cerebral did he appear to be.' In New York Jarrell's nervous defensiveness intensified this impression—'uneasy with New York intellectuals, he felt perpetually challenged, whereas he in his nervousness was the challenging one.' In a letter to Lowell at the time of the Korean War Jarrell included a poem 'I just wrote' called **"A War"**:

> There set out, slowly, for a Different World,
> At four, on winter mornings, different legs . . .
> *You can't break eggs without making an omelette—*
> That's what they tell the eggs.

Like the still more famous **"Death of the Ball Turret Gunner"**, this makes us admire its wit rather than moving us; and even the wit has to be set up too methodically—the first two lines and the rhyme are there only to explode the joke. No one could accuse Jarrell of being an unfeeling intellectual, but the poetic wit is just the same as the poetic sentiment in **"Girl in a Library"** and other poems: both are competing, as it were, in different matches in the tournament, and all set to win in both. There is no doubt that the wonderfully monstrous Gertrude in *Pictures from an Institution,* is really a kind of self-portrait, like Flaubert's of Madame Bovary, based on Jarrell's knowledge of his own will. At the same time there is something extremely likeable about him, and his need to give and receive affection, and this comes through in all the letters. (p. 18)

John Bayley, "Knives, Wounds, Bows," in London Review of Books, *Vol. 9, No. 7, April 2, 1987, pp. 18-19.*

Bob (Garnell) Kaufman
1925-1986

(Also wrote under pseudonym of Bomkauf) American poet and novelist.

An important yet largely unheralded innovator of the 1950s Beat movement, Kaufman employed the improvisational style, harmonic structures, and argot of avant-garde jazz musicians as well as the rebellious, irrational spirit of Surrealism and Dada to create verse that influenced such poets as Allen Ginsberg and Lawrence Ferlinghetti. Like other Beat writers, Kaufman repudiated conventional morality, espousing nonconformity, spontaneity, primitivism, and Eastern philosophies. Kaufman is credited with playing a crucial role in disseminating the Beats' values in Europe, where he established a much stronger critical reputation than in the United States.

At age thirteen, Kaufman entered the United States Merchant Marine, where a shipmate introduced him to many classic works of literature. During the 1940s, he attended the New School of Social Research in New York City and met Allen Ginsberg and William Burroughs. Kaufman and several writers who later formed the Beat movement settled in San Francisco in the late 1950s; there, with Ginsberg, John Kelley, and William Margolis, Kaufman founded *Beatitude* magazine. Kaufman's initial literary efforts consisted of improvised poems recited in San Francisco's jazz clubs, coffeehouses, and streets. Kaufman so valued spontaneity that he rarely wrote down his work, and many of his published poems were transcribed from performances recorded by friends. His first book, *Solitudes Crowded with Loneliness* (1965), includes the poetry broadsides *Does the Secret Mind Whisper?* (1959), *Second April* (1959), and *Abomunist Manifesto* (1959). This volume had little impact in the United States but was lauded by critics in France, who christened Kaufman "the American Rimbaud." Kaufman's contempt for modern American society and what he viewed as the government's hypocritical, cold war mentality surfaces in "Abomunist Manifesto," which incorporates wordplay, satire, prophecy, irony, and surreal images in a series of lists reminiscent of the poetry of Walt Whitman. Several poems in *Solitudes Crowded with Loneliness* also pay tribute to such artistic nonconformists as Albert Camus, Hart Crane, and Guillaume Apollinaire.

In 1963, in response to the assassination of President John F. Kennedy, Kaufman took a Buddhist vow of silence and retreated from society; he neither wrote nor spoke for twelve years. However, *Golden Sardine* (1967), edited from fragments of Kaufman's manuscripts, was published during this period. The poems in this collection, which are largely incomplete, explore such familiar Beat concerns as the necessity for dissent, rejection of mainstream society, the anguish of existence, and the importance of aesthetic truth. Kaufman broke his silence and resumed writing on the day the Vietnam War officially ended in 1975. The poems written between then and 1978, which comprise part of *The Ancient Rain: Poems, 1956-1978* (1981), display Kaufman's growing interest in politics, religious mysticism, and black consciousness. In 1978, Kaufman again withdrew from writing and society, emerging only rarely before his death.

(See also *Contemporary Authors*, Vols. 41-44, rev. ed., Vol. 118 [obituary]; *Contemporary Authors New Revision Series*, Vol. 22; and *Dictionary of Literary Biography*, Vols. 16, 41.)

DUDLEY RANDALL

Bob Kaufman, author of *Solitudes Crowded with Loneliness*, is the son of a Martinique Negro woman and a German Jew, but instead of confining himself to purely Negro protests he voices the wider protest and rejection of the Beats—Ferlinghetti, Corso, Ginsberg, Kerouac, with whom he started the San Francisco renaissance. His long lines are not loose improvisations, but have a firm structure provided by parallelism, repetition, and catalogue. In his fondness for experimenting with words he reminds me of the Elizabethans, especially John Lyly. He has their play on words in **"Hollywood:"**

Horrible movie-makers making horrors that move . . .
Legions of decency borrowing their decency from the Legion.

He has their love of paradox:

"Ginsberg won't stop tossing lions to the martyrs."

To these qualities he adds neologisms: ''oleomarginality,'' ''stereoriginality,'' ''hi-finalities;'' his modern heroes—Parker, Mingus, Holliday, Crane, Dylan; sexual images; and surrealism.... (pp. 52-3)

Sometimes I feel, as with Lyly, that the verbal elaboration is too great for the content, or the originating feeling. His best poems occur when the technique is less strained, or the content or feeling is stronger. They include **"Bagel Shop Jazz," "Dear John," "A Remembered Beat,"** and **"War Memoir:"**

> What one-hundred-percent redblooded American
> Wastes precious time listening to jazz
> With so much important killing to do?...

One of the high spots of the book is the famous **"Abomunist Manifesto"** with other Abomunist papers which alone, with their wit and mockery, make this a book to buy, re-read, and enjoy. (p. 53)

> *Dudley Randall, in a review of "Solitudes Crowded*
> *with Loneliness," in Negro Digest, Vol. XV, No. 3,*
> *January, 1966, pp. 52-3.*

BARBARA CHRISTIAN

Little has been written about Kaufman's life; I know little of the facts that are invariably used to describe a life. What I know I have found in his two published volumes of poetry: *Solitudes Crowded With Loneliness* (1965) and *The Golden Sardine* (1967). These two books project the philosophy of the Beat poet, of the man who challenged middle-class American values in the Fifties, when many Black and white intellectuals were yet to see the connection between the incredible blandness of American life and the destruction America as a government and as a propagandist idea symbolized.

Like Ginsberg, Joans and Kerouac, Kaufman's poetry began to take hold on the Lower East Side—the fringe of New York City, of America—where artists, poor people and exiles from the mainstream gathered. Along with these and other poets, Kaufman was a part of that outlandish, rebellious element of American life which emerged in the midst of Eisenhowerian conformity and mediocrity. (p. 21)

Much of Kaufman's poetry is inherently critical of America, protesting its scurrilous ways, calling attention to its bloodthirsty appetite. Passionately, Kaufman reviews its past, illuminates its present, projects its future while he measures the reality of America against the myth it broadcasts. **"Benediction"** ... is one of the most damning poems written about America, damning not because it uses invective, but because it uses well-placed irony so effectively:

> Your ancestor had beautiful thoughts in his brain.
> His descendants are experts in real estate.
> Your generals have mushrooming visions.
> Everyday your people get more and more
> Cars, television, sickness death dreams.
> You must have been great
> Alive.

> **"Benediction"**

The poem concentrates on both racism and imperialism, on America not only as a threat to the American Black and the American poor, but to the entire world as well.... More than 10 years after Kaufman wrote [**"Benediction"**], Blacks had just begun to appreciate how far-reaching was America's oppressiveness. In fact, Kaufman's poems seldom allude exclusively to the plight of the Afro-American. His poems always

couple domestic racism with American criminal behavior abroad. He attacks the basic values of America, seeing the race problem in its midst and its behavior toward the rest of the world as reflections of the country's internal corrosion.

America's tentacles, which tamper with the world's psyche, are the various forms of its media—the means through which meta-messages are subtly imprinted on the mind. Like LeRoi Jones in the Fifties, Kaufman takes great pains to warn us of the termite eating at our spirit. His media poems are set against the background of the West, Los Angeles and San Francisco, for in this wild rootless land, recently taken from the Indians and Mexicans, medialand constructs its images. The lie of the media is tucked away in the West, heavily camouflaged by the glitter of the sweet life. Remember, Kaufman cries, that Hollywood actually represents:

> Five square miles of ultra-contemporary nymphomania
> Two dozen homos, to every sapiens, at last countdown
> Ugly Plymouths swapping exhaust with red convertible Buicks.
> Twelve year old mothers suing for child support,
> Secondhand radios making it with wide-screen TV sets,
> Unhustling junkies shooting mothball fixes, insect junk,
> Unemployed pimps living on neon backs of
> Unemployed whores.

> **"Hollywood"**

Ironically, Hollywood makes its bait under the name of Art, and in so doing insults the craft of Bob Kaufman. Kaufman retaliates. In ending his poem to Hollywood, he salutes it as ''the artistic cancer of the universe'': ''I want to prove that L.A. is a practical joke played on us by superior beings on a humorous planet.''

Kaufman not only attacks Hollywood, he senses that the ambitious movers of medialand are efficient, having capsulized their product into a portable machine. TeeVee, the machine par-excellence of hypnosis, has created a land of drugged people:

> The younger machines occupy miles of dark benches,
> Enjoying self-induced vacations of the mind,
> Eating textbook rinds, spitting culture seeds,
> Dreaming an exotic name to give their latest defeat,
> Computing the hours on computer minds.

So Hollywood, in essence, is plugged into the homes of America, and is yearned for by the hungry people of the planet as a drug to ease their pain. For Kaufman, Hollywood and TeeVee are manifestations of America's emptiness and decay, just as the Bowery drunks are evidence of her falseness.

As one reads more and more of Kaufman's poetry, this attitude toward America prevails. Her only saving grace comes from those she casts off: for example, from the Black whose music, grace and mores keep her going. **"War Memoir"** ironically plays on this theme, for in its imagery, the poem juxtaposes the technical stuff America creates for destruction alongside jazz, a music which absorbs everything, even technology, making it into a thing of beauty.... (pp. 22-5)

Jazz as a protest music permeates Kaufman's being—its modal variety and flexibility adapts itself to every situation. And in the late Forties and early Fifties, Jazz as taken higher by Charlie Parker expressed the alternate route that America's outcasts could take. Kaufman soaks himself in Parker's music, in bop strains of electricity and blood-rhythms. One of his poems, **"Walking Parker Home,"** is studded with those intricately carved word-jewels of a genuine poet in communion with a master musician:

> In that Jazz corner of life
> Wrapped in a mist of sound
> His legacy, our Jazz-tinted dawn
> Wailing his triumphs of oddly begotten dreams
> Inviting the nerveless to feel once more
> That fierce dying of humans consumed
> In raging fires of Love.

Jazz is the subterranean music, existing as its protests, developing as it rejects, becoming fuller as it strips away the debris of rot.

To continue to maintain and authentic existence in the face of so much falsehood and decay is a long, hard fight. Charlie Parker heroically conquers American decay with his music. Kaufman expresses the psychic loneliness of a man who is plagued by his environment and turns in on himself. His psyche cannot always stand the loneliness imposed upon him. . . . There is loneliness throughout many of his poems, not just the loneliness that might come from solitude, but an even more devastating psychic loneliness that can come only from knowing so few people who share his perceptions. Such loneliness haunts a man who sees more than the people of his time. Images of dissolution, of being unable to come up from under, burst from these poems as if they, the poems, are the writer's only companion. The absence of any widespread awareness about the visions Kaufman breathed, and the lack of any expansive Black cultural context certainly contributed to Bob Kaufman's loneliness. He was a decade too early—or rather he had to suffer alone so that others in later years could create together.

The extreme objective correlative of this loneliness in our society is the prison. Kaufman's **"Jail Poems"** protest both America's injustice and succinctly, painfully reveal his own psychic prison—the real prison from which he cannot escape. Surrealist images, dada symbols jet-stream through these poems. And Kaufman is magnificently graphic in rendering this loneliness, for he knows the mind often perceives what it cannot logically express. Certain states are irretrievably beyond logic. . . . As we discuss the plight of political prisoners today, our minds are now ready for the **"Jail Poems"** of Kaufman. The prison cell is an appropriate symbol for America's way of life and can trap the man who opposes America more through his life-style, than because of any specific act.

Living with the present, living existentially, lies at the core of the Beat philosophy, and necessarily befuddles, thwarts a life-style based on systemization. Kaufman was well-acquainted with the formal outlines of existentialism, as his **"Poem to Camus"** indicates, but he felt that existentialism itself had become too codified.

The **"Abomunist Manifesto"** picks up where existentialism left off. Like (Richard) Wright in *The Outsider*, Kaufman realizes the limits of all *isms*, the eventual decay of all systems. Kaufman's anti-philosophy, Abomunism, is finally as much a put-down of itself as it is of anything else. The very name makes serious fun of *isms*, manifestos and the like, transforming sense into nonsense, turning reality upside down. Signed ''Bomkauf,'' the manifesto was duly written in legal, political structure. There are ''Notes'' and ''Further Notes,'' ''Craxions,'' a glossary, an anthem, founding documents, and even a newscast. . . . Defined as ''a rejectionary philosophy founded by Barabbas and dedicated to the proposition that the essence of existence is reality essential and neither four-sided nor frinky, but not non-frinky,'' Abomunism derides logic, philosophy,

academic and political jargon, and whatever manifestations exist in response to the need to systematize the world. Commercialized religion, as a major form of systemization is singled out for commentary by the Abomunists. (pp. 25-7)

The **"Abomunist Manifesto"** creates a world counter to mainstream American life; in effect, it is a blueprint for a revolutionary way of life. It does not purport to know the right way to live; rather, it gives the Abomunist guidelines for avoiding the snares of systematic living, while thwarting the system itself. In some ways, it is the precursor of the hippie and professional revolutionary life-styles. Kaufman saw that in order to live with any kind of freedom, and to be able to fight American mediocrity and destructiveness, a life-style rooted in protest must be invented. In effect, this manifesto is the creation of an alternate community, one in which Kaufman might have been able to function.

Kaufman's poetry, his **"Abomunist Manifesto,"** are all the result of a new language, a new mode of perceiving. In striking at the lifeless English language, Kaufman creates a new language, linked to Jazz. His poems, along with those of Ted Joans, use Jazz's concept of improvisation as their stylistic core. Casting aside traditional and even more avant-garde forms and images such as the recent breathline, Kaufman plays with word rhythms and dada images:

> Smothered rage covering pyramids of notes spontaneously
>   exploding
> Cool revelations / shrill hopes / beauty speared into greedy
>   ears
> Birdland nights on bop mountains, windy saxophone
>   revolutions

> **"Walking Parker Home"**
> (p. 28)

But where is Bob Kaufman?—the Black poet who challenged the American life-style with his own, who fought with the pen as passionately as many do with weapons or rhetoric, who pointed the way to the painful visions Blacks lived through in the Sixties: political prisons, the need for an alternate life-style, America's rottenness, the sacredness of jazz. He wanders the streets of San Francisco, mostly unknown and forgotten, considered mad by many, cared for by few. As his books circulate, the question of responsibility, the responsibility that Black cultural organizations have to protect such a man, screams to be heard. If we do not care to sustain our own wise men who suffered, sacrificed, were attacked and assaulted, then can we really speak of ''nation-building''? Who will look to Bob Kaufman—if we don't? (pp. 28-9)

> *Barbara Christian, ''Whatever Happened to Bob Kaufman,'' in* Black World, *Vol. 21, No. 11, April, 1972, pp. 20-9.*

ROCHELLE RATNER

The Ancient Rain collects early unpublished poems, plus new poems written from 1973 to 1978 after a self-imposed ten-year vow of silence. In the early work, Kaufman's imagination, self-effacing humor, and inventive language prove him a pure poet in the same way the early Corso was one. The new poems form a unified sequence, highly political, embracing a new-found black consciousness, yet without forsaking the surrealistic use of image. Even if not as impressive as the earlier work, these poems make a conscious attempt at vision; it was that vision, one senses, which forced the poet into another vow of silence in 1978.

*Rochelle Ratner, in a review of "The Ancient Rain:
Poems, 1956-1978," in* Library Journal, *Vol. 106,
No. 5, March 1, 1978, p. 562.*

RAYMOND PATTERSON

What ever happened to Bob Kaufman, the San Francisco Bay
area's legendary beat poet of *Solitudes Crowded with Loneliness*
and *Golden Sardine*? For anyone who cares—and Kaufman is
a poet who always managed to make one care—*The Ancient
Rain: Poems 1956-1978* may provide an answer. Certainly we
are encouraged by those words in **"Small Memoriam for Myself,"** the poem which ends the first section of this long-awaited
third collection: "No blend of grief can cause the death of
laughter now."

Readers familiar with Kaufman's poetry know that there has
been grief enough in his life. . . . Yet grief—"America, I forgive you . . . I forgive you / Eating black children, I know your
hunger."—was but the ground from which he launched, in
Solitudes Crowded with Loneliness, his dazzling solo flights—
now bitterly rebellious, now wistful, whimsical or hilarious—
in the be-bop jazz tradition of Black American music, borrowing its technique to elaborate and improvise themes that were
to become identified with the poetry of the Beat Generation:
alienation, hipsterism, the saving grace of jazz, drugs and Eastern philosophies, a contempt for conformity, materialism and
consumerism, and a sense of the absurd, heightened by Hiroshima and the atomic bomb—"We witness God's divorce,"
"we cry jazz historical tears," "The wind is in charge of our
lives / Tonight," "alone in a lemming world," "In a universe
of cells—who is not in jail?"

"I acknowledge the demands of Surrealist realization," Kaufman announced in *Solitudes,* but it is to the jazz tradition that
he owes his melodic line and rhythmic pattern—jazz, with its
improvisational mode and acknowledgement of "standards"
against which to work out one's lyric identity. . . .

In *Golden Sardine* the beat themes persist, but the range is
narrower, the indignation deeper, perhaps from a growing
awareness that "A terror is more certain than all the rare desirable popular songs i / know. . . ." But like the heroic jazz-
man, he must face the terror, and so "CARYL CHESSMAN IN-
TERVIEWS THE P.T.A. . . ." is played over again as "The
Enormous Gas Bill At the Dwarf Factory. A Horror Movie to
be Shot with Eyes." "Night Sung Sailor's Prayer" is later
heard as **"Plea."** In *Sardine* the theme of "dropping out" is
sounded repeatedly, and the book ends with an angry, transcendent letter from Kaufman to the San Francisco *Chronicle*
denouncing a conspiracy against him. Then followed a ten-
year period of silence in which Kaufman "neither spoke nor
wrote."

The Ancient Rain: Poems 1956-1978, the collection for which
the foregoing is intended as a preface, breaks that silence and
reminds us how essential Bob Kaufman's work is to any assessment of the poetry of the Beat Generation. Consisting of
poems, many of which were transcribed from a tape recording,
The Ancient Rain divides into "Poems 1956-1963" and "New
Poems 1973-1978," the more recent work including several
long poems, notably **"The American Sun"** and the title poem.

"Poems 1956-1963" makes it abundantly clear that Kaufman
was an accomplished poet even two decades ago at the outset
of his career. He was preeminently "THE STAR JAZZER IN
TRANSIT, ON FLUTED BARS OF BLACK / LIGHT," the work ahead

of him (we now see) simply the revision and elaboration of
themes through a kind of dialectic. . . .

We are not puzzled by seeing Picasso, Miro, Van Gogh, El
Greco, Rimbaud and Lorca included in Kaufman's pantheon.
Indeed, such serendipity is characteristic of the beat sensibility.
But above all it is Federico Garcia Lorca of **"The King of
Harlem"** who dominates "New Poems 1973-1978" with its
prophecies, **"The American Sun"** and **"The Ancient Rain."**

Immediately following a brief Lorca-inspired poem that tells
us "THE SUN IS A NEGRO," we encounter **"The American
Sun"**:

> THE AMERICAN SUN HAS RISEN,
> THE OTHER SUNS HAVE LEFT
> THE SKY, THE POEM HAS ENTERED
> THE REALM OF BLOOD.

And we are given a vision, only slightly redeemed by irony,
of destruction: "THE AMERICAN SUN / BRINGS DEATH TO ALL
ENEMY / EMPIRES," those empires being Russia, Ireland, England, France, China, Japan and "More to Come."

Also less than Kaufman's best work is **"The Poet,"** a shorter
poem using the refrain, "A FISH WITH FROG'S / EYES, / CRE-
ATION IS PERFECT." The following are typical sentiments: "THE
POET KNOWS HE MUST / WRITE THE TRUTH, / EVEN IF HE IS /
KILLED FOR IT. . . . THE POET LIVES IN THE / MIDST OF DEATH /
AND SEEKS THE MYSTERY OF / LIFE. . . ."

What is one to make of this, weighed against so much solid
achievement? **"The Ancient Rain,"** the final poem in the collection, its title reminding us of William Blake, raises the
question again: "The Ancient Rain wets people with truth and
they expose / themselves to the Ancient Rain." "The Ancient
Rain is falling all over America now."

What is one to think—or feel—about "Washington standing
at Appomattox," "Crispus Attucks . . . falling before the British / guns on Boston Commons," or the declaration, apparently
without irony, that "Crispus Attucks will never fight for Russia"? It is not enough to say that Kaufman is rendering history
as myth and is not obligated to be factual or rational. Are we
being asked to read **"The American Sun"** the way one reads
Blake's "America: A Prophecy"?

Kaufman is by far a better poet than he appears to be in the
weaknesses noted here—weaknesses that are outweighed by
many fine poems which deserve praise and serious attention.
His work speaks not only for a generation of beat poets but
for all poets who declare with Ephesians: ". . . our contention
is not with the blood and flesh, but with dominion, with authority, with the blind world-rulers of this life, with the spirit
of evil in things heavenly." Bob Kaufman's *The Ancient Rain*
makes this clear.

*Raymond Patterson, in a review of "The Ancient
Rain: Poems, 1956-1978," in* The American Book
Review, *Vol. 3, No. 4, May-June, 1981, p. 12.*

KEN KESEY

Yeats went out to a hazel wood, because a fire was in his head.
Bob Kaufman went out into the burnt black streets of the
apocalyptic wino dawn, because of that very fire. Neither poet
went out there seeking extinguishment, or ease, or even illumination. They had illumination enough. What they sought
were shadows, hollows in the landscape of the soul, to throw

their light into. Now they are old with wandering, through hollow lands and hilly lands. But they will not rest.

And they are bound to a restless end. . . .

To have seen Bob Kaufman, occasionally mumbling in bee-tlebrowed distraction on this street or that around San Francisco during the Sixties and Seventies, one would have bet cash against the chances of his reaching thirty, or forty, let alone 55! yet he goes mumbling on, like ol wandering Angus Yeats. And, as the years pass, he begins to take on the permanent quality of old leather and polished mahogany . . . as though he might mutter ferociously on there at the corner of Grant and Green for centuries, gnarly and inscrutable, like a kind of cigar store Indian that increases with value as it hardens and cracks. . . .

So it is not as astonishing today to hear that a new work [*The Ancient Rain: Poems, 1956-1978*] of Bob's is being published as it would have been five or even ten years ago.

The talk around the expresso set used to be "Kaufman? He's fried, and I do mean fee-*ride!* Gazonga! Cross off Bob Kaufman." But those who stuck close, like Eileen Kaufman and Tony Seymore, knew that Bob was still working, fried or not, still working because he had no choice but to still be working. . . .

[There] is something astonishing and remarkable about these new poems; there is a change in Bob's position as a poet. Two changes, actually. First, he is more overtly black than in any previous collection—not bitterly black, or boisterously black—simply black, as a phenomenon . . . and, second, he is more American. Patriotic, even; patriotic and at the same time paradoxically apocalyptic. He sees our nation not so much as an accomplishment of Democracy as an Act of God, perhaps even the final act and it is this new viewpoint that strikes so much new fire into what would otherwise be merely more old run-down literary conventions. Listen to the patriotic peal of this old Beatnik's poetry, simultaneously clanging out alarm and encouragement like the rashest revivalist on an Independence Day dais:

> The Ancient Rain is falling all over America now.
> The music of the Ancient Rain is heard everywhere.
> The music is purely American, not European. It is
> the voice of the American Revolution. It shall play
> forever. The Ancient Rain is falling in Philadelphia.
> The bell is tolling. The South cannot hear it. The
> South hears the Ku Klux Klan, until the bell drowns
> Them out. The Ancient Rain is falling.

> The Ancient Rain does what it wants. It does not
> explain to Anyone.

> *Ken Kesey, in a review of "The Ancient Rain: Poems, 1956-1978," in* The American Book Review, *Vol. 3, No. 4, May-June, 1981, p. 13.*

ALVIN AUBERT

In writing about Bob Kaufman one thinks immediately of the interface of Afro-American mainstream America thinking or attitudes or stances, whatever, in regard to Afro-American writers and writing. The focal issue is Afro-Americans as writers in a hostile environment. Afro-American writers trying to create and publish in an inhospitable literary tradition, mainstream literary America.

Bob Kaufman, his life and writings—or perhaps more accurately, his poem making self—provide something of a "field"

for such considerations, for he is the ultimate suffering servant in our midst, the archetypal American literary votary in the peculiar temple of U. S. literature. Jew and Gentile, African and European converge in him, literally. He is a metaphor, but foremost (as we tend too often not to remember in considering such matters) he is a human being, preeminently so; witness his peculiar agony. Note the yearning expression in the vatic title poem [of *The Ancient Rain: Poems, 1956-1978*] "Ancient Rain," for the time when "All symbols shall return to the realm of the symbolic and reality become the meaning again." In the same poem, as it turns to focus on that other suffering servant/scapegoat, the Spanish poet in New York Garcia Lorca, Kaufman describes a "Federico Garcia Lorca sky, immaculate scoured sky, equaling only itself," as it assails the symbolic mode, forcing it to declare its own inadequacy in a manner reminiscent of Pablo Neruda's dilemma in achieving an appropriate metaphor in "The children are bleeding in the street like—" until Neruda arrives at the epiphanic reversal: "The children are bleeding in the street like children." (p. 155)

There is a yearning in Kaufman's life and work that the term *nihilistic* does not quite get at. Its expression is best comprehended, despite that other yearning spoken of earlier, in metaphorical terms, in the figurative receptivity one generates in viewing the poet's life and work as continuous, fused, a perspectivity that is rarely encouraged in literary America. The life and works of Bob Kaufman permit this perspective in a way that few other (if any) U.S. poets do, and this fact has a great deal to do with the type of poet Kaufman is. The only other U.S. poets (other than Whitman) I can think of in this way are Thomas Merton and the Afro-American poet Jean Toomer. Toomer's poem "Song of the Son" might have been written for, or by, Kaufman, reflecting the kind of interchangeable sensibility that it does. The poet/persona of Toomer's poem becomes a Rilkean-Orphic singing tree, "An everlasting song, a singing tree, / Caroling softly souls of slavery. . . ." A corresponding figure appears in Kaufman's poem "Private Sadness," in the speaker's perception of himself as in some way imprisoned within himself, a "mere human tree," desiring ". . . the fall / To eternal peace / The end of All." The soul of America and of the world—The World Soul—is a prime concern of Kaufman's, but particularly, in the words of W. E. B. DuBois, "the Souls of Black Folk," ontologically speaking. . . . For DuBois, Afro-Americans comprise "two souls, two thoughts, two unreconciled strivings; two warring ideals in one dark body, whose dogged strength alone keeps it from being torn asunder." Kaufman the man and the poet partakes of this peculiar weakness/strength, the saving Afro-American duality. It is his grounding, an aspect of which for him is the poet's right to choose his own way of life and dying, defining *for himself* the terms of his own infinity (and identity), giving him the man and god ordained will and the clarity (illumination) to say: "I see the death some cannot see, because I am a poet spreadeagled on this bone of the world." He who suffers earns the right to speak, is ordained to speak, and the substantiality of that utterance is so because it is informed, *in formed*, by the man/poet's suffering. Such a speaker is, with Lorca, "At once . . . at the great sun, feeling the great sun of the center," sensing, that is, the source of all life and suffering.

There is an ironic edge to Kaufman's yearning that "reality become the meaning again," although one questions the applicability of a term like "irony" to a poet like Kaufman, for irony is a characteristically Western world terminal mode, motivated in great part by the essentially European impulse to construct absolutes, paradigms, dichotomously assigning things to their places, boxing them in, as Jean Toomer would express it, so that "people" can set about the business of running the world, ordering and subverting it. Irony being a terminal mode, Kaufman might want to banish it along with the symbol. I introduce the subject of irony here as an attempt to locate that which, as mentioned earlier, the term *nihilistic* barely accounts for. The quality I have in mind here is seen in Kaufman's self-effacing tendency, which is directly related to his yearning for "green," the green of Lorca, primaveral. Feeling "the great sun of the center" and "Hearing the Lorca music in the endless solitude of crackling blueness," the poet/speaker says in the title poem **"Ancient Rain"** that he "could feel myself a little boy again in crackling blueness to kiss out my frenzy on bicycle wheels and smash little squares in the flush of a soiled exultation." There follows the passage quoted earlier about the Lorca sky, "immaculate scoured . . . equaling only itself." A world void of symbols, in other words, is a world of innocence, prelapsarian, to use the Christian theological term, where the human being and human values are permitted to embrace in a way they are prevented from doing in the dichotomizing embrace of the symbolic and ironic modes. (pp. 156-57)

Kaufman's poems declare his Afro-Americanness, his Blackness. What we get so much of in the little that has been written about him is Kaufman the local color figure, only incidentally "born in New Orleans of mixed Black [mother] and Jewish parentage." If not the local color figure, the tragic mulatto of stereotypical notoriety, the invention of Euro-Americans. When in **"[I Want to Ask a Terrifying Question]"** the speaker of the poem declares:

> My back is moonburned,
> And my arm hurts,
> The blues come riding,
> Introspective echoes of a journey,
> Truth is a burning guitar,
> You get off at Fifty-ninth Street forever

we are to take no particular note of "The blues" as a cultural reference, for after all, didn't Allen Ginsberg invent the blues? Then there is the assertion (in **"Fragment From Public Se-**

cret"): "EVERY TIME I OPEN MY BIG MOUTH / I PUT MY SOUL IN IT." And it is, after all, the Garcia Lorca of Harlem, "Harlem's king," that engages Kaufman, the Lorca who might, in the words of Kaufman's poem **"Dear People,"** protest the

> Buying diamonds
> Off the backs of
> South African Negroes
> The wax bitches
> Are well dressed tonight,
> Dear people,
> Let us
> Eat jazz.

(p. 158)

To conclude, Kaufman knows precisely *what* he is, if not *who*. His work declares it, which is not to say he rests easily in the knowledge, for the tension of a highly specified uncertainty reverberates throughout. . . . In addition to knowing what he is and his use of that knowledge as a leverage in his quest of who he is, Kaufman is a poet of broad sympathies, capable of projecting a vision of unity, cosmic and social, that few of us can—partly out of the fear of sentimentality and of lapsing into cliché. The speaker of **"Like Father, Like Sun,"** invoking the love of Lorca, declares that:

> America is a promised land, a garden torn from naked stone,
> A place where the losers in earth's conflicts can enjoy their
>   triumph
> All losers, brown, red, black, and white; the colors from the
>   Master Palette.

And lest we think we know Kaufman better than he does himself, heed number II of his series of **"Bonsai Poems,"** in which he takes to task:

> All those well-meaning people who gave me obscure books
> When what I really needed was a good meal.

(pp. 158-59)

Alvin Aubert, "When What I Really Needed Was a Good Meal," in Callaloo, *Vol. 7, No. 3, Fall, 1984, pp. 155-59.*

Tommaso Landolfi
1908-1979

Italian short story writer, novelist, poet, dramatist, translator, and critic.

Among the most innovative stylists in modern Italian fiction, Landolfi has been compared to Edgar Allan Poe, Franz Kafka, and Jorge Luis Borges for his extravagantly imaginative nightmarish tales, his use of fantasy, and his preoccupation with language. Marked by irony and macabre humor, Landolfi's writing usually features characters who are unable to communicate effectively or discover love, faith, or spiritual grace. A versatile, idiosyncratic writer who considered his work understandable only to intellectuals, Landolfi incorporated an authoritative knowledge of Italian, Russian, French, and German languages and literatures in his fiction and poetry to amplify the implications of his themes. Sergio Pacifici observed: "Like Kafka, Landolfi moves in an extraordinary, surrealist *milieu*, a restless world whose fabric is not woven of events and action . . . but of fears and expectations, of anxiety that is never successfully turned into anguish."

During the 1930s, Landolfi became involved with the Italian literary movement of hermeticism, which developed a highly metaphoric and obscure poetic idiom. Although not overtly political, Landolfi's works of this period were considered by government censors to contain anti-Fascist sentiments, and he was incarcerated for a brief time preceding World War II. Following his release, Landolfi lived the remainder of his life as a recluse. Although he was a respected writer who won several prestigious literary awards in his native land, only a small portion of Landolfi's work has been translated into English. These pieces appear in three volumes: *Gogol's Wife and Other Stories* (1961), *Cancerqueen and Other Stories* (1971), and *Words in Commotion and Other Stories* (1986).

Landolfi's first book, the short story collection *Dialogo dei massimi sistemi* (1937), displays his obsession with language. The title story, "Dialogue of the Greater Harmonies," concerns a man who becomes demoralized when he learns that his poems, written in a nonexistent language which he mistakes for Persian, are untranslatable. "The Two Old Maids," the surreal, farcical title story of *Le due zittelle* (1945), one of Landolfi's most respected volumes, involves two spinsters who become distraught when they discover that their pet monkey has been sneaking into a church and mocking the ritual of the Catholic mass. A debate ensues between priests, nuns, and the two women about sin, cruelty to animals, the intolerance of authority, and various spiritual issues.

After 1950, Landolfi moved away from carefully crafted stories toward freer, more symbolic narratives. In *Cancroregina* (1950), he experiments with science fiction, particularly in the long title piece, "Cancerqueen," which consists of the diary of a solitary pilot lost forever in space. The pilot, who agonizes over the appropriateness of his words even though he knows no one will ever read them, proves to be an unreliable narrator, and the story can be read on several levels. The short stories in *A caso* (1975) exhibit Landolfi's increasing preference for tales rendered almost entirely in dialogue. These works feature such characteristic topics of Landolfi's work as emotional in-

adequacy, physical disfigurement, suicide, death, love, and the relationship between illusion and reality. Assessing the pieces collected in *Words in Commotion and Other Stories*, a compendium of short stories from various phases of Landolfi's career, Annapaola Cancogni noted: "Landolfi's fiction brings us face to face with that nether world of phantoms and fears that we constantly . . . repress in the name of 'reality' and that he controls by sheer linguistic rigor."

Some critics contend that Landolfi's first novel, *La pietra lunare* (1939), is his masterpiece. This work revolves around a boy's infatuation with a half-human, half-beast female who enjoys an intimate rapport with nature. The boy is one of many male characters in Landolfi's work who is haunted by females or by specters with feminine qualities. Landolfi's other writings include *Rien va* (1963) and *Des mois* (1967), literary journals written in the form of diaries that are renowned for their stylistic originality and insights into literary matters and for reflecting his eccentric view of life. Landolfi also composed two volumes of poetry, *Viola di morte* (1972) and *Il tradimento* (1977), and several dramas.

(See also *CLC*, Vol. 11 and *Contemporary Authors*, Vol. 117 [obituary].)

RICHARD KOSTELANETZ

Landolfi's [tales in *Gogol's Wife and Other Stories*] take a bit of effort, sometimes even several rereadings, before one gets a firm grip on the keys that unlock their pleasures.

He is a master of the symbolic tale in which, as in Kafka, strange happenings become stand-ins for literal facts. For instance, [the title character of **"Gogol's Wife"**] is described as a balloon. This is a symbolic way of saying that she had the appearance of a balloon, and in the course of the story Landolfi succeeds in making the metaphor more real than the literal fact. . . .

Sometimes the technique of symbolism can be used for a devilish purpose, as in the author's tour de force, **"Wedding Night."** Here he describes the bride's deflowering in terms of her encounter with the family chimney sweep, full of soot and dark animal energy. The underlying story is quite well masked—until one realizes that all the odd details have ulterior meaning.

Of a different quality is the short novel, **"The Two Old Maids,"** which is, to my mind, the most extraordinary piece in the book. On the surface, Landolfi tells of a pet monkey who escapes from his cage to prowl through a nearby convent, devouring the consecrated host and, in an unforgettable scene, going through the motions of saying the mass while drunk on sacred wine. For his "crime," one of the maids later kills him with a hatpin.

One cannot miss the symbolic resonance Landolfi infuses into the story as the monkey takes on, first, the spirit of the Devil and, then, the outlines of Christ. Soon the reader realizes that in this monkey tale the author has created a commentary on the significance of Christ's death. Like another equally neglected European novella, Miguel de Unamuno's "St. Emanuel the Good," Landolfi's **"The Two Old Maids"** is a deeply religious short novel. It belongs among the minor classics of our time.

Though several of these nine stories are unquestionably superb, the collection itself, drawn from 25 years' work, is uneven. The themes of two pieces escape this reviewer's persistent effort. Others, such as the overworked "diary of a madman" formula, are all too obvious and predictable. (Inexplicably, his best story in this vein, **"Cancroregina,"** translated many years ago, is not included.) Yet Landolfi's best stories place him firmly among the most important contemporary Italians.

Richard Kostelanetz, "Fantasy Becomes More Real than Fact," in The New York Times Book Review, *January 5, 1964, p. 6.*

SUSAN SONTAG

[It] would be a mistake to think of Landolfi as a twentieth-century recluse devoted to writing imaginary nineteenth-century short stories. His sensibility is of an entirely modern order, intellectually playful, sardonic, and riddled with disgust. With whom might one compare him? The already semi-official tag, "the Italian Kafka," is not very apt, I think. Something of a cross between Borges and Isak Dinesen would be more accurate: Landolfi has something of the perverse ingenuity of the one, and the solemn romanticism of the other. It is likely, however, that he is a greater writer than either. For he is less claustrophobic, less febrile than Borges; and his use of irony never becomes sentimental, or merely arch, as so often happens in the work of Dinesen. Although, like Borges, Landolfi is a

prolific translator—he has done mostly Russian writers (Pushkin, Gogol, Turgenev, Dostoyevsky, Tolstoy, Chekhov, Bunin, Lermontov), as well as some non-Russian writers such as Hofmannsthal—he does not use his culture in an obtrusive way. While Borges proposes the idea of bibliomania and a mostly imaginary erudition as the equivalent in his stories of a sensuous surface, Landolfi's stories have a nude, fable-like character, virtually placeless and timeless. Nevertheless, it does not seem surprising that both men are professional translators. Both the monstrously recondite fantasies of Borges and the more abstract tales of Landolfi are written in a markedly homeless, cosmopolitan literary style.

At least five of the nine stories in [*Gogol's Wife and Other Stories*] are very short, and minor in scale. The weakest of this group, I think, is a frigid and rather contrived horror story told in letter form called **"Pastoral."** The best of the very short tales, a mere four pages long, is **"Wedding Night,"** a delicate, finely imagined story about the end of sexual innocence. But Landolfi is at his best at a greater length. He is brilliant at impersonation, at the first-person narrative about a strange or marvellous event to which the narrator was a privileged though inept witness. And he is also a master of the fully dramatized narrative. The longest story in the book, **"The Two Old Maids,"** really combines both talents. While related by one of those diffident, clerkish narrators so common in nineteenth-century fiction, it has a vigorous, straightforward plot. Two dreary spinster sisters discover that at night their beloved pet monkey steals out of their apartment to defile the altar of the adjacent convent, and they formally try the blasphemer and execute him. The theatrical climax of the story is a rancorous debate between two priests whom the sisters have invited to assist them in judging the poor monkey. The other long story—to my mind the best in the collection after **"Gogol's Wife"**—is entirely different. It is called **"The Death of the King of France,"** and is written in a complex, oblique prose, broken into five sections like the movements of a piece of music. Much of the "narration" consists of chains of images, presented as equivalents to the emotional states of the characters. The climactic scene is a long aria rendering the orgiastic fantasies which accompany the onset of menstruation in a twelve-year-old girl.

In Landolfi's stories there are none of the elaborate figures of motives and scruples which provide the spine of a Kafka story. Landolfi is a more objective, a more gothic writer. In fact, the situations which he relates in his stories really make an anti-psychological point. In a typical Landolfi story, the mind is confronted with a brute fact; the mind circles around this fact, unable to penetrate it. One of the brute facts which recur in Landolfi's stories is the bulk and mystery and repulsiveness of the physical body. In **"Gogol's Wife,"** the writer inflates his rubber wife through the anus with an air pump. In **"Pastoral,"** all the inhabitants of a village hibernate for the winter in hideous fetid bags which hang from the ceiling. The offending monkey in **"The Two Old Maids"** must be killed because he urinates on the convent altar. In **"The Wedding Night"** the dogged labors of the chimney sweep cleaning out the kitchen fireplace offer the young bride a lurid analogue to her own imminent defloration. And **"The Death of the King of France,"** which was (Landolfi mentions in a note) originally titled "W. C.," begins and ends with its hero, whose name is So-and-so, straining on the toilet.

Like physical indecency, the intellectual dilemmas which are the subject of some of Landolfi's other stories also have the character of irrefutable, arbitrary facts. The fairly long story,

"Dialogue on the Greater Harmonies" (whose idea is one Borges would surely have loved), is about a man who has learned a non-existent language thinking that he was studying Persian, and now unhappily finds himself the only person who can speak this language which is very beautiful and which he loves deeply. His despair is that the poems which he writes in this language happen to be untranslatable. A brief tale on a parallel theme, **"Giovanni and his Wife,"** relates the pathetic fate of two passionate music lovers, so wildly out of tune that they cannot produce a single note recognizably, yet who, when they sing together, always and unfailingly agree on how to sing each note. One day the wife bursts a vein in her breast while singing, and dies, leaving her husband bereft of anyone to understand him musically. Both stories are meditations on the arbitrariness of concord and discord, sameness and difference.

What, of course, makes Landolfi's stories unlike the short stories mainly being written today in England and America is not his morbid wit or his eccentric notions of disaster. It is rather the whole project of a basically neutral, reserved kind of writing. In such writing, the act of relating a story is seen primarily as an act of intelligence. To narrate is palpably to employ one's intelligence, the unity of the narration, characteristic of European and Latin American fiction, is the unity of the narrator's intelligence. But the writing of fiction common in America today has little use for this patient, dogged, unshowy use of intelligence. American writers mostly want the facts to declare, to interpret, themselves. If there is a narrative voice, it is likely to be immaculately mindless—or else strainingly clever and bouncy. Thus, most American writing is grossly rhetorical (that is, there is an overproduction of means in relation to ends); in contrast to the classical mode of European writing, which achieves its effects with an anti-rhetorical style—a style that holds back, that aims ultimately at neutral transparency. Landolfi belongs squarely in this anti-rhetorical tradition. It will be a pity if these stories are shelved as the latest high-class Italian culture import. Landolfi's methods seem to me an entirely viable alternative to the fatty but not very nourishing practice of fiction in America today. (pp. 15-16)

> *Susan Sontag, "Gogol's Grandson," in* The New York Review of Books, *Vol. 1, No. 11, January 23, 1964, pp. 14-16.*

THOMAS G. BERGIN

Landolfi has no apparent concern with social problems, although he has been writing since the late Thirties and I think his technique of malicious mystification is partly another example of the intellectual's devices to elude and mock the Fascist line against which many writers of his generation rebelled.

The substance of his stories is not based on a town, as Pratolini's epics tend to be, or on a region, as Vittorini's work focuses on Sicily. Landolfi's *paese* is his own odd psyche, which inhabits the frontier between nightmare and illusion. He has been called "the Italian Kafka," but such is not quite accurate.

It should not be denied, however, that Landolfi has his own special brew. **"The Two Old Maids,"** published originally by itself in 1946 and the longest story in [*Gogol's Wife and Other Stories*], illustrates his formula. It is about a pair of unappealing spinsters whose only joy is their pet monkey; he reminds them of their departed brother. Unhappily, the monkey is a sacrilegious beast given to eating the Host and drinking the wine in

the tabernacle of a near-by convent. For this crime he is "tried" by the two sisters and their spiritual adviser. After an ardent defense of simian attitudes and, incidentally, human freedom by a rather unstable young priest, justice is done.

It is a little fable meant to be at least two-thirds successful. Which two-thirds will depend on the reader. Likewise, **"The Death of the King of France,"** having nothing to do with France or kings of any kind, is a study of arachnephobia which would be morbid if it weren't so willfully sardonic. The other seven selections are considerably shorter, but the mixture is consistent, regardless of the size of the bottle. **"Gogol's Wife"** is perhaps judiciously chosen to lead the reader into the Landolfi trap. Who could resist the appeal of a rubber wife, inflatable to the proportions desired?

Landolfi is somewhat heartless and explicitly aloof from the vicissitudes of his characters, whom he regards with fairly consistent contempt. Herein lies the secret of his individuality; it is what keeps him from being a writer of the first rank but it is what assures him a certain endurance.

> *Thomas G. Bergin, "Pretensions Punctured," in* Book Week—The Sunday Herald Tribune, *February 2, 1964, p. 17.*

THOMAS LASK

The characteristics of the stories gathered in **Cancerqueen** are evident enough, but far from easy to convey. [Landolfi] is a sharply observant writer, for example, and his descriptions of a dolce vita party, of a dog worrying a rodent, of a man contemplating the killing of his woman companion, have a geometric exactness and clarity that no realism will surpass. Nevertheless, these details are put to other uses. It's what he does with them that distinguishes his fiction. And it is here that any easy characterization of his work falters.

The forms of his writing suggest that he is a man who should be read on more than one level—to use a handy phrase that is happily losing its popularity. And with a little ingenuity it is not hard to do so. **"Stefano's Two Sons"** says as much about the relation of the artist to society, to his family as does Thomas Mann's "Tonio Kroeger." One of Stefano's sons is the child of his loins, the other the child of his imagination. To which does he owe a greater allegiance? Stefano tries to avoid making a choice by being fair to each. But the result is that both turn out to be monsters—malformed, sterile, repulsive. In another story, **"The Sword,"** Renato, the hero, a relict of an aristocratic line, comes upon a miraculous sword among the dusty heirlooms in his possession—a sword so sharp, so quick that it cleaves in twain anything it touches. Renato proves its efficacy by testing it on all the old objects around him. He wants fame and fortune and the sword, he is sure, will now bring them to him. But of what use is such a razor-edged weapon today? In the end he turns it on the innocent and defenseless. It does not require a deep thinker to draw a dozen morals from such a tale.

The long title story ["**Cancerqueen**"] also leaves itself open to weighty interpretations. The narrator is in a space ship going around the earth, and trailing the ship outside in space is the body of a man he has murdered. How did he come into such a predicament? Earlier he had been visited by the murdered man, who had escaped from an asylum, but who protested that he was not mad. On the contrary, he had constructed a space ship that could take both of them on a voyage to the moon.

After surmounting a number of earthly hazards, among them eluding the keepers looking for their sometime patient, the two set off for the moon. But the escapee, as it turns out, is mad (is the author saying that one can construct a space ship and be mad at the same time?) and has to be disposed of.

In the course of their differences, the machinery is tampered with and the space vehicle is deflected from its route to circle the earth forever. This course correction, as it might be called, brings some new perspectives to the survivor. The earth begins to appear less and less vile and the activities and strivings of mankind take on a dignity. Don't assume that the author agrees with the judgments of his luckless mariner. He may be commenting sardonically on man's notions of his own heroism.

But although Landolfi's stories can be read in this symbolic fashion, I agree with Raymond Rosenthal, whose translations by the way are exemplary, that it would be wrong to do so. The point in each of his stories, sometimes more than one, is to be found in the story. It does not have to relate to what is outside of itself. . . .

No, Landolfi's stories do not require metaphysical probings, but a recognition of his fictional gifts: an ability to render scene and character, animal, or man, with an etcher's exactness; an acute awareness of the psychological vagaries of man and considerable narrative strength. . . .

In an attempt to place them in a familiar niche, critics have compared Landolfi to Isak Dinesen; Borges; Kafka. They'll all do. **"The Sword"** is a Dinesen story from start to finish. And there are parallels to Borges throughout. But, essentially, Landolfi is himself; astringent, intellectual, sometimes brittle, a writer not everyone will like, but one every serious reader of fiction should notice.

Thomas Lask, "On the Edge of Realism," in The New York Times, *July 30, 1971, p. 31.*

LEONARD MICHAELS

[In **"The Mute,"** the opening story of *Cancerqueen*], a very serious murderer, in jail, says, "I killed a fifteen year old girl. I must try to convince myself that I am not guilty," and he undertakes a description of the crime in order to analyze its development in his thoughts and feelings. Among them he hopes to come upon his innocence. Sophistication looking for innocence in depravity is a joke; but it is also a kind of search that characterizes a great literary tradition, often associated with Byronic heroes, and it is nothing to laugh at in Landolfi's story.

The girl lives in the murderer's description. She is lovely and as silent now as she was then (she was in fact a mute). Her presence makes his self-examination, with its moral intention, noisy, hideous and crazy. He feels these difficulties, accuses himself of naivete, and persists. Soon he relives the murder in which every instant becomes more unspeakable with every spoken self-dissecting reflection. He particularly remembers that because nothing else seemed right, he used a razor. Appropriately, the instrument of intellect, and very gruesome; but in literature we are often edified by strange pleasures.

The murderer cannot, however, distinguish literature from life, which is unfortunate for the mute, lovely girl, though it is exhilarating for him. She enjoyed reading poetry. He must live it. She dies. He plucks sentimental heartstrings. And his music

is gorgeous—sensual, mysterious and ghastly enough for all good Germans.

Landolfi's other stories tend also to be about the limits of human perspective and the infinite disease of self-consciousness, especially the two famous symptoms—romantic love and literary art—both of which are salient in his murderer. He is an excellent choice for the overture of *Cancerqueen*. It is thereafter apparent that regardless of how Landolfi renders his themes—fantasy, allegory, philosophic-dramatic dialogue or the conventions of naturalism—he is capable of intellectual and imaginative brilliance. **"Gogol's Wife,"** the tile story of an earlier collection, introduced English readers to Landolfi's wit and originality. Several stories in *Cancerqueen* are comparable to **"Gogol's Wife,"** but the excellence of the collection is in variety.

One kind of story, lavish in description and mood, is lusciously gothic—like Poe—but, brainier than Poe, Landolfi is more interesting in grand, self-inflicted desecrations of the soul; another kind of story is merely charming and light; in yet another kind the author's literary competence becomes his subject, and art and life confront one another as the antagonisms of ingenious, dazzling myths which are reminiscent of Hawthorne's allegories of heart and mind.

For Landolfi, as for other self-critical artists, the demands of form are not less than everything, and heart is destroyed—by life, mind, art, by the fear of writing junk, and sometimes heart destroys itself as a way of protecting its integrity. In the first story a razor does the job; later it is a sword; finally, it is a gun.

Landolfi's versions of this ancient slaughter are grim and frequently, funny; but *Cancerqueen,* as the title suggests, is not a funny book. It will best gratify a catholic taste, because its effects are as various as its stories—subtle, delicious, discomforting, and mixed in what might be called witty-grotesque. (pp. 5, 10)

I alluded to Byron, Poe and Hawthorne, and indicated the widest and narrowest context I can think of for *Cancerqueen.* In conclusion now, a fleeting comparison too obvious not to make.

Landolfi has been compared to Kafka, and scholarship assures us that Kafka laughed aloud when reading his stories to friends. Where would we be without this clue? Both are masters of the witty-grotesque. (Not "black humor," which is often applied to the giddy-grotesque.) It is, however, unimaginable that Landolfi's work will be equated with neurosis and one day admired as prophecy. It will live in its variety and art, and so will Kafka's unless he is indeed the prophet of our final terrors. Then nothing will live. Literary questions about feeling and art will no longer be mooted. They will go the way of Landolfi's mute. The pun says how difficult it is to be serious in a literary way. *Cancerqueen* intimates the pun and gives drama to the idea. It is remarkable for civilized speech among doubts and fears, for being sensitive, witty, and thoughtful in matters of despair. (p. 14)

Leonard Michaels, "Great Self-Inflicted Desecrations of the Soul," in The New York Times Book Review, *August 1, 1971, pp. 5, 10, 14.*

RONALD DE FEO

The characters in [*Cancerqueen and Other Stories*] are, for the most part, restless, obsessed beings, compelled to possess and to destroy, plagued by fantasy, curiosity and conscience. They can't seem to find peace. Their everyday lives are vague. We know little about how they exist, where they reside, what they did before they imprisoned themselves—for their obsessions have reduced their worlds, narrowed their emotional and intellectual range. They are not hysterically insane, but rather quietly, subtly mad.

Landolfi's work is like Poe's in its stifling intensity and perversity. The reader is not kept at a safe distance from the maniacal protagonist but is thrust into his limited world, made to share and understand—even condone—his particular obsession, however repulsive. In **"The Mute"** we enter the mind of a man who has murdered a 15-year-old mute girl. While he waits in his cell for his executioners, the murderer tries to convince himself that he is innocent of the crime—innocent in the sense that he really had no choice but to kill. The girl's handicap, he explains, made her more desirable, for as a mute she seemed more helpless, childlike and innocent. The trouble was that she became for him *too* innocent. He could not bring himself to possess her in a natural way. She deserved something better. He slashed her to death. While all of this may not sound logical in synopsis, it does make a kind of sense in the story itself. Landolfi almost convinces the reader—as the narrator almost convinces himself—that the murder was a necessary act, the only means of relieving a tortured mind. Like Poe, Landolfi builds up so much frustration and tension that the reader begins to weaken under the strain and finds himself cheering on the madman, saying, Yes, go ahead, kill her, get it over with.

Murder in this case and in other violent Landolfi stories . . . is an insanely logical final step, relieving both narrator and reader. At times, however, murder is the first step, altering a character and his world. In **"Hands,"** we have a kind of minor murder. Federico, who lives alone in a large deserted house, is determined to kill a mouse he has discovered in the storage room. He and his old hunting dog vigorously pursue the elusive and seemingly indestructible creature. Only after an unnaturally frantic and violent struggle do they succeed in killing it. At first Federico is relieved, but soon the act begins to trouble him. The murder is described in great detail. In fact, it takes up a good part of the story. Landolfi magnifies it for a number of reasons. He is saying that no death or act of violence is really inconsequential. He wishes to shake us and have the crime haunt us as it will haunt Federico. This can best be accomplished through meticulous, memorable and rather disgusting detail. . . . The accumulation of such absurd, loving description also produces another response in the reader—he tends to smile at it all. For Landolfi, who is an extremely subtle and witty artist, seems to be mocking the very genre in which he is working, the blood-curdling horror tale which Poe approached with so much seriousness. (p. 698)

Some of Landolfi's characters are writers, like the Stefano of **"Stefano's Two Sons,"** whose fictional son becomes more important to him than the child of his body. Other characters could very well be writers, given their imagination and curiosity, and the ability to record their experiences and transform them into art. The narrator of **"Cancerqueen"** is an unsuccessful gambler who accompanies a mad inventor on a journey to the moon. The trip is described vividly and at length, but the reader simply cannot accept the account as fact, cannot take the narrator seriously. The reader begins to suspect that the narrator has, in fact created a work of fiction in order to relieve his troubled mind. We know that he has murdered a

man. But has he murdered the mad inventor, as he claims in his journal, or is the victim someone else, someone we do not know? The narrator says that he is lost in space, with the moon above him and the earth below. Is this state symbolic of his detachment? The inventor's corpse drifts outside the spacecraft, following it, haunting it. Does the image represent a haunted conscience? **"Cancerqueen"** is a puzzling, ambitious story that invites the reader to speculate. It may simply be a parody of the science fiction tale, but with a writer as clever as Landolfi, one suspects that there is much more to it.

Throughout this collection we are in the presence of an erudite and original writer, an artist who is in full control of his material. The stories are superbly constructed. I've mentioned Poe in connection with Landolfi, but while both writers are wildly imaginative, Landolfi sees the comedy in the terrifying situations he creates and we laugh with him, not at him (as often happens with Poe when he is purple or plain silly). He writes beautifully. . . . (pp. 698-99)

The previous Landolfi volume, *Gogol's Wife and Other Stories*, was only a teaser compared to the present book. Landolfi surely is one of the great modern Italian writers, along with Svevo and Gadda, and a major figure in contemporary fiction. *Cancerqueen* is brilliant, different and refreshing without being self-consciously "experimental." We are drawn back to all superior works of art. I have already returned to *Cancerqueen*. (p. 699)

> *Ronald De Feo, "The Author of 'Gogol's Wife'," in* The Nation, *New York, Vol. 213, No. 22, December 27, 1971, pp. 698-99.*

GERALD WEALES

Certainly, despite recurrent themes and artistic mannerisms, one does not come away with the feeling that [*Cancerqueen and Other Stories*] is governed by a central attitude, plainly not the "profound existential anguish" that [translator Raymond] Rosenthal sees in the author. What I find at work in Landolfi is a professional story-teller, one who uses the traditional materials—loss, death, cruelty—sometimes to explore man in his greatest pain, at others simply to play games with the reader. Although there is some variety of style in the book (a few of the stories are simply dialogues), the basic Landolfi mode is a slow, deliberate narrative, rich in detail, beset with digression . . . which explores the philosophic meaning of events even while they are being recounted. I prefer those stories in which the disintegration of the narrator is the explicit (**"Cancerqueen"**) or implicit (**"Week of Sun"**) subject and in which Landolfi's sense of grotesque invention is given fullest play. Sometimes, as in **"Night Must Fall,"** a similar mechanism is used with great skill but without—at least for me—the same commanding interest. A number of the stories are fairly straightforward fables, and they tend to be successful within that vein. In **"The Sword,"** for instance, the hero, having sliced up most of the furnishings in his castle, manages to cleave his beloved from guggle to zatch, using the weapon which he "should have brandished in defense of the good or at least to gain his happiness . . . to destroy the dearest thing he had on earth." A number of the stories, finally, are more superficial than surface. **"The Calculation of Probability,"** for instance, is a lady-or-tiger exercise in which the gambler, having ascertained that he has a fifty-fifty chance of failing, hangs himself in the last sentence and thus leaves the reader dangling. **"A Family Chat"** uses a scifi setting to make a mild satirical point about the uselessness of talk on earth, but the whole story collapses on the last page; in an attempt to explain *talk* to his son, telepathically one assumes, an intergalactic father struggles to define unfamiliar concepts such as *sound* and *atmosphere* and then blows the carefully constructed conceit by comparing the earth people to "our magpies." These weak examples aside, there are enough good things in *Cancerqueen* to please any reader whose tastes run to the fabulous. (p. 724)

Gerald Weales, "Fiction Chronicle," in The Hudson Review, *Vol. XXIV, No. 4, Winter, 1971-72, pp. 716-30.*

ISABEL QUIGLEY

The short stories of *A caso* . . . are almost short plays, being almost entirely in dialogue: radio plays, perhaps, depending on aural rather than visual qualities and generally with an air that makes them read (or sound) as if they had been switched on in mid-sentence from nowhere in particular for an audience of uneasy eavesdroppers in the dark. Reading then recalls those eery moments when, through some technical quirk, a pocket radio that is expected to give out a blare of news or pop music instead turns up the police swapping local information in off-duty voices, car to switchboard and back; flat but curiously exciting, occasionally involving places one knows, people one recognizes. As reader one feels almost intrusive, a tape stealing sounds in silence and obscurity: a narrator hardly obtrudes.

The stories deal directly with feelings and, mostly in murmurs, build up from nothing to something through dialogue that seems almost weirdly recognizable. Signor Landolfi is particularly good at the sounds that, in Italian, match particular gestures, movements of fingers or eyebrows, shrugs of this sort or that. . . . You feel the personality in talk and, through the talk, all this underlying language of the body, the presence of something communicable in other ways than the ordinarily linguistic. . . .

Signor Landolfi is busy seeming artless, a mere taper of talk; but, like the electronic wonders that do the taping, he has plenty of expertise, technical skills that make the awkward seem easy, that give the casual air he seeks to the most strenuous of efforts. The title *A caso* has the right sort of flipness for a book that seems to suggest—or to want to suggest—it was blown together by chance rather than design. But the designer is there, of course; not so much puppet-master pulling strings in a sweaty box as computer programmer with his feet up, munching sandwiches yet grandly in control.

Themes are played with, touched upon, dropped; large themes (death, murder, suicide, love, impotence, physical handicap) treated lightly, almost jokily. In one story, a man driven to suicide hires a professional killer and pays him a large sum to kill him within a year. The killer will do it painlessly, he will be dead before he knows it; so he starts barring the house, trembling at noises, even falling in love and making plans for an impossible future. Finally, when he loses both girl and money, he longs for death once again, by which time he and the killer have become friends of a sort and besides, the large sum he paid for his death will, if restored to him, set him up again and make death unnecessary.

Shorter stories have less complex action: there is the theme of appearance versus reality, variously treated: in one story, a girl called Rose, who claims to be a hermaphrodite; in another, a girl who is marvellously enticing when dressed and turns out to be horrific when naked. In several there is the theme of inadequacy, of sexual ambiguity or impotence, and of physical beauty masking it. In one of the best, two innocents learn to make love, talking themselves, as it were, into ecstasy. In another, there is the now familiar technique of "making up" the story as it goes along, arbitrarily naming the characters in action, introducing a mephistophelean voice in italics to steer what is thought and what happens this way or that; at the same time using talk of a melting realism that, in descriptions of nymphets, recalls no one as vividly as Nabokov. Two of the stories seem to me failures, and several confusing half-successes; but the book makes a whole because Signor Landolfi's voice, mostly through other voices, is so clear and true, so much in tune with the present.

Isabel Quigley, "In Mid-Sentence," in The Times Literary Supplement, *No. 3842, October 31, 1975, p. 1310.*

ITALO CALVINO

[The Introduction by Italo Calvino excerpted below was originally published in a 1982 collection of Landolfi's stories, Le più belle pagine di Tommaso Landolfi, *which was edited by Calvino.]*

[Landolfi] had that great gift for capturing the reader's attention and inspiring his awe (he inherited a taste for the "shocking" story from the masters of "black romanticism"); but it was his own acumen, panache and incomparable wealth of verbal resources that made for his highly affective writing). Yet his reputation for being an impractical and peculiar character gave credence to the conviction—which still holds true today—that his writing is only for "a select few." (p. ix)

In a work like Tommaso Landolfi's, the first rule of the game established between reader and writer is that sooner or later a surprise will come: and that surprise will never be pleasant or soothing, but will have the effect of a fingernail scraping glass, or of a hair-raising, irritating caress, or an association of ideas that one would wish to expel from his mind as quickly as possible. It is no surprise that Landolfi's closest literary forebears, Barbey d'Aurevilly and Villiers de L'Isle-Adam, title their story collections *The Diabolical Women* and *Cruel Stories*.

But Landolfi's game is even more complex. Starting with a simple but nearly always wicked, obsessive or lurid idea, an elaborate story takes shape, related by a voice that usually appears to be an ironic counterpoint of another voice (just as a great actor has to alter his own diction ever so slightly to define a character); or it may pretend to be, say, a parody of another piece of writing (not by any particular writer but by an imaginary author whom everyone has the illusion of having once read) which, in fact, is ultimately immediate, spontaneous and faithful only to itself. In the verbal spectacle that unfolds, theatrical effects are precisely paced, but they can also turn into the most fickle fancies imaginable.

This is the kind of story Landolfi writes when he wants to employ his inventive versatility and his fixed ideas to construct some precise mechanism, or to set up a calculated strategy. But on other occasions, many other occasions, another mood prompts Landolfi to strip the act of writing of any pretense of constructing a complete, easily accessible and enduring story and instead he substitutes a careless gesture, a shrug or grimace, like someone who knows that the creative process is a waste, insubstantial and meaningless.

The extent to which Landolfi adopts this attitude is proved by this statement (in *Bière de pécheur*): "Could I ever really write at random and without design, thus glimpsing the chaos, the disorder in my own depths?"

"At random": the same phrase becomes an existential program in the story **"Mano rubato": "Living at Random"** is then the title story (in **A caso** [1975]). But this insistence, which could be seen as some kind of aspiration toward automatic writing in literature and as an apology for the "gratuitous act" in life (thus validating the surrealist tag others inevitably labeled him with), takes on another dimension in the above-mentioned story. Here he shows the impossibility not only of a random murder but also of a narrative developed outside of some logical framework.

Actually, chance was a god to which Landolfi showed feverish devotion even though he was constantly led to doubt its existence and power. If an absolute determinism dominates the world, chance is rendered impossible and we are condemned to our fates, without any hope of escape. (pp. ix-xi)

That this problematical relationship with chance was so essential for him should come as no surprise, considering his great passion for gambling. After observing him on various occasions at the roulette table (he spent a good part of his last years at San Remo, and I knew that I had to go to the casino to see him), I had the impression that he was not a good player for the very reason that he played "at random" without any strategy or design (or at least it seemed so to me), instead of following one of those forced patterns or systems with which shrewd gamblers attempt to capture and trap the shapeless fluidity of chance.

It is likely that I was the one who understood nothing. What could I know of the imperatives and illuminations which move a gambler by vocation (or damnation?). I, whose only rule would be minimal risk were I to gamble. Perhaps in his passionate relationship with chance, which was both a courtship and challenge, he alternated between strategies too sophisticated to ever be revealed to anybody else and a "rapture" of dissipation in a maelstrom where all losses lead back to the loss of oneself, which is the only possible victory. Perhaps chance was the only way for him to test nonchance. And since nonchance par excellence is the most absolute thing, in other words, death itself, chance as well as nonchance are two names for death, the one fixed meaning in life.

In fact, when I saw him manipulating the chips on the green felt (and reflected on the words "at random," which kept going through my head like a motto), I came up with a comparison between Landolfi the player and Landolfi the writer. For, in both, there was the use of a rigorously determined form or formula which might stave off chaos and contain it, on one hand; and on the other hand, a gesture of supreme nonchalance which scorns any work or any value because the only basis for any action or discussion lies in the equation chance-chaos-nothingness-death; and the only possible stance toward that is ironic and desperate contemplation.

But another possible link between gambling and literature—what part need and what part the unknown play in both—has already been explored by Landolfi himself. In the story **"La dea cieca e veggente,"** a poet drawing upon words at random ends up writing *The Infinite* and wonders (like that Borges character who considers himself author of Don Quixote) if this is really his own work or Leopardi's. Seeing that he has been lucky in stumbling upon highly improbable combinations, the poet decides to test his gifts in a game of roulette; the results are disastrous and he loses everything. The game of chance refuses the order which poetry can attain, being an impersonal system or preserving—thanks to its internal mechanisms or probable combinations—the secret oneness of the individual.

Governed as they are by necessity and chance, man's actions always disappoint his demand that they influence events to suit his will. For this reason, Landolfi's relationship to literature, as to existence itself, is always twofold: It is the gesture of someone who commits himself wholly to what he does, and at the same time throws it all away. This also explains the interior split between his dedication to formal precision and the indifferent detachment with which he abandoned his completed work to its own fate. After throwing himself into his work and enjoying it, he lost interest in the completed book to such an extent that he didn't even bother to correct the proofs. (pp. xi-xiii)

The "real Landolfi" . . . is one who prefers to leave something unresolved in the work, a margin of shadow and risk: the Landolfi who squanders the stakes that he puts on the table and then swiftly withdraws them with the horrified gesture of a gambler. (pp. xiii-xiv)

Landolfi's relationship to himself, if one traces it throughout his writing, reveals an egotism of the most complex and contradictory nature. One moves from the narrative theater where he rages against himself and the world, to a direct and open autobiographical vein where moderation and control reveal the suffering. And tracing this same continuum of psychological constancy, we begin with his memories of boarding school at Prato and end with one of the last sketches published in the *Corriere della Sera*, **"Porcellina di terra,"** which has never before appeared in book form.

At this point I will not delve into the question of how much of his internal torment was real and how much of it was theatrical: the simple fact that he wanted to entertain his readers or himself by parading his suffering "I" redeems his stance, whether it is egocentric or all an impersonal game. Likewise, it would be pointless to establish whether the obsessions and phantoms of his sexual imagination are purely fictional or correspond to some pulse in his unconscious: in his exhibitionism he seems to leave himself open to psychological interpretation (and thus, using the story **"A Woman's Breast"** as a point of departure, [the critic Elio] Sanguinetti traces a constant sexual phobia, or more precisely a fear of the female sex, throughout his work; at the same time, the absence of interior censure weakens such an interpretation since it would suggest that the real unconscious lies elsewhere).

Any exploration of what Landolfi really *says* has yet to be made. Because while he claims to have "nothing to say," he always follows the thread of the discussion at hand. Eventually his philosophy will be unraveled from the knot of questions without answers, contradictions, proclamations and provocations surrounding him. If our intention here is simply to pass on the pleasure of reading Landolfi superficially, that is because it is the first necessary step. And it is also only superficially that we are pointing out his taste for fake "treatises," fake "conferences" and fake "moral works," though not without noting that at some point we might establish that they were "fake" only to a certain degree; that there is a thread linking Leopardi and Landolfi, a similarity between the two rural villages where they lived and the two paternal dwellings, between their youths spend laboring over paper, and their invectives against human destinies. (As for the dialogues, which Landolfi writes frequently, especially recently, I must say that I like them the least of all his writing. If I can trust my own superficial reading, they seem written in a much less successful vein . . .). (pp. xv-xvi)

It is too easy to say that what Landolfi writes is always a mask of emptiness, of nothingness, of death. One cannot forget that this mask is nevertheless a whole concrete world, full of meanings. A world made up of words, naturally. But of words which are significant precisely for their richness, precision and coherence.

Take an emblematic text like **"La passeggiata."** The sentences are constructed from incomprehensible nouns and verbs, much like Lewis Carroll's experimental ''Jabberwocky,'' in which words from an invented lexicon have make-believe meanings. If it were the same thing, there would be no new amusement or gratification. However, if the reader only takes the trouble to consult a good old Italian-language dictionary (Landolfi used the Zingarelli), he would find all the words there. **"La passeggiata"** is a text with complete meaning; the author simply set up a rule to use as many obsolete words as possible. (He himself couldn't resist the temptation to reveal this secret in a later volume, thus poking fun at those who had not caught on.) So Landolfi the ''mystifier'' becomes the ''demystifier'' par excellence: he gives meanings back to words which have lost them (and instead of leaving the common reader in the wrong, he takes the trouble to patiently explain what he has done).

But Landolfi's inquiry into language had begun long before this. The title story in his first book (*Dialogo dei massimi sistemi*, 1937) [published in *Words in Commotion* as **"Dialogue of the Greater Systems"**] contains a discussion of the aesthetic value of poetry written in an invented language that only the author (and maybe not even he) can understand. I don't think it is mere hyperbolic irony that the story and volume are decorated with such an illustrious title. It is as though Landolfi wanted to point out that beyond the text's paradoxical humor (and beyond the satire, which clearly arises from the then-predominant philosophy of Croce), the problem that concerns him is one of language as a collective convention and historical inheritance, and of the individual and mutable word. And this is the first document which reflects a concern—a concern no less serious or rigorous for its acrobatic tone—which will appear in all of Landolfi's work right up to **"Parole in agitazione"** **"Words in Commotion,"** that crystalline little fable from his last book (*Un paniere di chiocciole*, 1968) about the ''signifier'' and the ''signified.''

I can't account for the sources of his knowledge; certainly, one couldn't say that linguistics (much less DeSaussure's structuralism) were the order of the day in European literary culture when he was educated. And I would doubt that he gave it serious thought even later when linguistics became a ''pilot discipline.'' And yet, everything he writes about it seems to have such scientific ''exactitude'' (in terminology and concept) that it could be used as a text in the most up-to-date university seminars.

From Landolfi's stories and diaries, I think one can extrapolate a linguistic theorization whose basic assumptions are innate mental structures (see his reflections on his child's first attempts at speaking in *Des mois*), the arbitrariness of linguistic symbols, and most importantly, the nonarbitrariness of language as a system, a historical creation and cultural stratification. . . . (pp. xvi-xviii)

The poet's individual and unpredictable work is only possible because he has at his disposal a language which has rules with established uses, a language which functions independently of him. Landolfi's reasoning always revolves around this point (in conversations as well). I remember the first time I talked to him twenty-five years ago, he somehow ended up discussing language and dialects, and he refuted my argument that we could have a literary Italian with its roots outside of the Tuscan dialect.

In any case, it isn't the avant-garde's innovative thrust which prompts Landolfi's acrobatics. On the contrary, he is a conservative writer in that particular (and even metaphysical) sense that the gambler cannot but be conservative because the immutability of the rules guarantees that chance will not be abolished with every throw of the dice.

His most faithful critic and companion (up through the Florentine years), Carlo Bo, has written many times that Landolfi was the first writer since D'Annunzio who could do whatever he wanted with the pen. At first the comparison between the two names astonished me: even if both came out of the mold of the nineteenth-century dandy (like Huysmans' des Esseintes), D'Annunzio had gone in the direction of the erotic-euphoric, while Landolfi tended toward self-irony and depression. Indeed, their personalities, their literary presences, their relationships to the world were diametrically opposed. But reconsidering it, I realized the real common element between them was something else. It could be said of each of them (and of them only) that they wrote in the presence of the entire Italian language, past and present, and that they made use of it with a competent and knowing pen, as if they could draw abundantly and derive continuous pleasure from an inexhaustible patrimony. (pp. xviii-xix)

It seems to me that all language, including ''dead words,'' is a part of life for Landolfi, but precisely because death is only steps away and on every side. . . . [In] Landolfi there is a dramatic power that springs from the consciousness of the living man. Isn't the moral of the diaries (*Rien va* and to an even greater extent *Des mois*) really the fact that all his negative meditation unfolds before the imposing presence of life, represented by Minor and Minimus [the nicknames Landolfi used to refer to his daughter and son], that is in his acceptance—despite everything—of a vital continuum?

The physicality of existence is constantly present both in his imagination and in his reasoning. A death urge—fear and attraction—imposes itself upon his thoughts at all times, but is ultimately represented by bodily emotions. The disembodied abstraction of the philosopher's mind is not for him. His problem is with the body's fixed, physical and palpable presence, his own as much as others', which provokes in him tumultuous reactions such as horror and homicidal cruelty. However, these are merely the extreme points of a gamut which includes all emotional possibilities.

This might explain why real reflection—and the need to keep a diary—begins for him when he feels he must come to terms with a new ''biological'' fact—paternity in his mature years, which suits neither his ways of being nor the predictable roles in his repertory. And even here he allows the whole gamut of possible attitudes to spring forth without denying any: from the most open tenderness to the rapture of sadistic infanticide (though the latter is actually less frequent). And it is the experience of the relationships between human beings—one's fellow man felt as a physical closeness—which will determine the course his ideas take, and not the other way around.

(This also explains the meaning of the before and after in his "erotic" fantasies: the accounts of attraction and repulsion, spells and aversions are remarkable precisely because they are erratic and open-ended.)

And death then? Can one create a palpable image and experience of it? In the romantic and symbolist writers, the main theme of fantastic stories was ghosts, the living dead, that uncertain boundary between the world-beyond-the-tomb and our own world. Landolfi reaches far and wide in that repertory and apparitions from the beyond are not lacking in his two major novels, *La pietra lunare* and *Racconto d'autunno*. However, I would say that the world of the dead never comes into the foreground in the shorter stories from which I made my selection; for him, the obsession which overrides even that of death is the pathology of living. The dominant theme of necrophilia in Poe, with whom he is often compared, is not to be found in Landolfi. We find only the complementary theme of the anxiety of a mistaken death and premature burial, as in the story **"Le labrene"** [**"The Labrenas"**], but it is a subtle pastiche and ironic homage to the master.

Death and nothingness, which are often named but seldom represented, belong therefore to the restricted number of abstract concepts in Landolfi's always concrete world, a concept that represents a necessary boundary, a breath, a rest from this world so dense with existence, so loaded, so intense . . . Landolfi's real nightmare is that nothingness does not exist. His two books of poetry (*Viola di morte* and even more *Il Tradimento*) often return to this theme which is expressed in a passage in *Rien va:*

> Existence is a condemnation without name and without redemption; there's nothing to be done against it. And perhaps it is only hope—our need to catch our breath, as if from the sharp pain of a wound—that allows us to imagine a state outside of existence; a nothingness. My God, perhaps everything exists, has existed and will exist in eternity. There is nothing we can do against life but live it, just as there is nothing to do in a closed, suffocating, smoke-filled room but go on smoking.

(pp. xx-xxii)

Italo Calvino, in an introduction to Words in Commotion and Other Stories *by Tommaso Landolfi, edited and translated by Kathrine Jason, Viking Penguin Inc., 1986, pp. ix-xxiii.*

MARY HAWTHORNE

Most of the pieces in *Words in Commotion* (only two of which have been previously translated), as well as the introduction by Italo Calvino, are taken from the 1982 Italian edition that Calvino edited [*La più belle pagine di Tommaso Landolfi*]. He explains that his selection, spanning 40 years of Landolfi's work, reflects an attempt to reintroduce Landolfi . . . in all his colors—which, it must be said, are usually the murky noncolors of disturbed dreams.

Even in translation (this is, by the way, a very graceful one), Landolfi's mastery of irony and narrative seduction is readily apparent. Without delay, he piques our curiosity and draws us effortlessly into his strange, unsettling landscapes. . . .

It doesn't take long to figure out that we are being toyed with, in fact manipulated, often cynically, by narrators who appear insane, sadistic, pathetic, despicable—or even likable. A peculiar intimacy between reader and narrator is established through Landolfi's frequent use of the confidential, confessional first person. The narrator of **"The Eternal Province"**—himself a bitter, self-mocking victim—while languishing on the bed in his hotel room one hot afternoon, notices a spider web drifting from the ceiling. He becomes fascinated by its fragility and by the complete mastery he holds over its existence. "My breath was an atrocious inquiry and its contortions were its impotent answers. . . . With one brutal breath I could nail it to the ceiling, blow it out for good." Suddenly, the idea of finding a real victim—a woman he can manipulate and torture to take his revenge on all women—takes obsessive hold. The narrator finds his victim, naturally, and just as naturally refuses to explain how things "end." He tosses us this bone instead:

> In any case, don't ask how it ended: everything ends badly. Even when the human creature rises above his sick nature and overcomes his instincts, his madness, his transience; even when he raises himself, establishing a reign of brotherly love, joy, and freedom, and seemingly returns to his origins and accepts a contrary fate. And even when he joins the others who have been redeemed and ascends to the place he belongs, the home of the spirit . . . even then, everything ends badly, if only because wherever there's fuel there's fire.

Occasionally, Landolfi's stories end fantastically or whimsically, but mostly they *do* end badly, or at any rate perversely. They may close with an ironic rhetorical question or with the kind of cavalier remark that thinly masks a terrible impotence and despair. All the same, we are led on; we want to read these stories in the way we want, say, to visit the House of Horrors. But *Words in Commotion* also exhibits Landolfi's quirky, original sense of play and imagination. . . . In **"The Kiss,"** the notary D, a bachelor who's terrified of women, realizes, after turning out the light and going to bed one night, that his lips have been grazed with a kiss from some intangible, amorphous being. In **"Words in Commotion,"** the narrator, brushing his teeth, spits out, "instead of the usual disgusting mixture," mutinous words that demand new meanings. Nonetheless, these stories generally leave you feeling dejected and distraught; Landolfi's brutal grotesqueness can make for painful, unpleasant reading. **"Maria Giuseppa"**—a tale of the sadomasochistic relationship between a master and his female servant—is a particular case in point. (Disturbingly, the objects of Landolfi's cruelty are nearly always women.)

Calvino notes that Landolfi has traditionally been hostage to the notion that his work is for only "a select few." . . . It's unlikely that *Words in Commotion* will change Landolfi's reputation significantly, if at all; his vision is too bizarre and discomforting.

Mary Hawthorne, in a review of "Words in Commotion and Other Stories," in VLS, No. 49, October, 1986, p. 4.

ANNAPAOLA CANCOGNI

Words in Commotion and Other Stories contains 24 stories, only two of which have previously appeared in the United States. The editor and translator, Kathrine Jason, has justly included two "dialogues" from other sources to provide the

American reader with a broader sample of Landolfi's verbal acrobatics, his troubling masks.

"I felt a sort of religious and superstitious love and terror of words back then," Landolfi writes in **"Prefigurations: Prato,"** an autobiographical fragment. "Words were practically my only reality. Therefore, I would have even been ready to close my eyes to the objects which my companions' words, I can't really say designated, but inferred or dragged behind them like mishaps, but not to the words themselves! And in the end, whatever reality added up to, couldn't those words evoke terrible things?"

Yes. As the mature writer eventually discovered, words can erase the confines between reality and illusion and, fusing the two realms, give shape to the unknown, the unexpected, the merely probable. "Labrena"—its mere sound is enough to transform the common gecko it designates into a quasi-mythical monster whose "round, bulging, glittering eyes" eventually lead the narrator of the first tale, **"The Labrenas,"** to a premature coffin—or is it a straitjacket? The shred of a spider web shivering at the slightest variation in his breath gives the narrator of **"The Eternal Province"** the idea of similarly subjugating a young woman. Maria Giuseppa is a scrawny, ugly, old servant: what imp of the perverse drives her spiteful master to taunt her, torment her and finally covet her all the way to her grave? And why does the blood on the blade that murdered the young girl of **"The Provincial Night"** never dry?

Landolfi's fiction brings us face to face with that nether world of phantoms and fears that we constantly, and more or less successfully, repress in the name of "reality" and that he controls by sheer linguistic rigor. "Could I ever really write at random and without design, thus glimpsing the chaos, the disorder in my own depths?" he wonders in **"Bière de Pécheur,"** the fictional journal of a gambler quoted by Italo Calvino in his introduction [see excerpt above] but not included in this selection. And, indeed, one of the terrible things words can evoke is the void and the chaos they normally conceal but can suddenly disclose when they get out of control, as in the title piece, **"Words in Commotion,"** or when they lose their conceptual framework, as in **"Dialogue of the Greater Systems."**

Landolfi's name is often associated with those of Poe, the 19th-century French writers Barbey d'Aurevilly and Villiers de l'Isle-Adam and, of course, Pushkin, Gogol and Dostoyevsky, the Russian masters he translated into Italian. But if he certainly deserves a prominent place in the pantheon of the fantastic tale, his place in Italian literature is much harder to define: there he has the ambiguous privilege of being unlike anybody else, of having no recognizable forebear with the sole and subtle exception of the major 19th-century Italian Romantic, Giacomo Leopardi. It is probably to Leopardi that one can trace what most distinguishes Landolfi from his foreign precursors: a particular vocal quality that blends the stormiest Romantic accents with classical suavity—the Latin conceit (or is it Tuscan hubris?) that comes through in his unwillingness to commit himself to any conclusion, in the way he deliberately passes up the "last word," as a gambler would, almost despite himself, forever delay the denouement of his game. For Landolfi, literature, like gambling, must remain an ultimately gratuitous act, a metaphysical challenge.

Annapaola Cancogni, "Confronting Phantoms," in The New York Times Book Review, November 30, 1986, p. 37.

LIZ HERON

Spiked with literary and philosophical conundrums, full of pastiched gothic perversions and surreal fantasies—premature burials, grotesque bodily transformations and mutilations—in some respects Landolfi's writing bears immediate comparison with the labyrinthine hypotheses of Borges. But its linguistic and narrative tripwires are sprung with a shocking, punitive ferocity, then often cut loose as an idea is taken to its cruel extreme and carelessly abandoned. Landolfi plays cat and mouse [in *Words in Commotion and Other Stories*] though not only with the reader or the fictional character but, apparently, with himself, or rather the idea that possibilities for existential freedom are open through words. He looks always through the darkest of glasses, harbouring cosmic pessimism in even the most delicately poetic of his conceits, like the tale of the werewolves who kidnap the moon (in which he most resembles Calvino, who introduces this volume).

The collection aims to make a 'difficult' but important writer posthumously more readable. Landolfi remains enigmatic, at an ever-ironic and often distasteful distance. But his wilfully foreign voice is insistent and memorable.

Liz Heron, "Like One Possessed," in New Statesman, Vol. 113, No. 2919, March 6, 1987, p. 38.

JOHN BAYLEY

Like Nabokov and Borges, Landolfi seems implicitly to claim a special status, a status arranged and protected by the admiration of his fellow-authors. They view him with affection as an odd bird, a writer's writer; and one, incidentally, who is nobody's rival, never in competition for a public. He was, self-consciously, a magic writer, and magic is based on violence. Barbey d'Aurevilly and Villiers de L'Isle Adam, with their tales of cruelty and diabolical women, are obvious predecessors. In his introduction to *Words in Commotion*, Italo Calvino writes of Landolfi's "black romanticism" [see excerpt above]. He specializes in the obvious giveaway, revealing allegory or Kafka-like symbol, which is then collapsed into pointlessness or cliché. **"A Woman's Breast"** imagines a beautiful girl with hideous and sinister breasts, a romantic fantasy which Shelley, among many others, would have been familiar with, and which goes with Landolfi's closet misogyny. Like most black jokes, his tale is memorable; and technically interesting for the way in which the climax is muted into a few Gogolian musings on the sadness of life. "It would seem that we must be contented with joys that are not only ambiguous and twisted, but even fleeting." All one can say of that is that it is better than the simple shock ending, as in **"Chicken Fate",** where two chicken farmers find themselves trapped in a wire run and surrounded by fowls as tall as trees.

Landolfi is not in the first class. But his stories are typical of what is sometimes claimed as a modern revival of the form, a revival based on "tall stories" and the tricks that can be played with them. Tall stories are cruel in their nature, like fairy stories. You happen to disturb a witch who thereupon turns you into a frog. **"A Woman's Breast"** begins with the man accidentally saving the girl from being run over. Insisting that she is in his debt, she says she must grant him a favour; so, after some embarrassment, he asks to kiss one of her nipples. And so on. The heartlessness of tall stories is in perfect accord with modern critical techniques: in fact the author's device and the critic's recognition of it are virtually one and the same thing. Landolfi "uses" a tone for an effect which in

Gogol is absolutely natural and moving. He gives the impression of parodying an imaginary author—a composite, say, of Ambrose Bierce, Kafka, Paul Bowles and Julio Cortázar—whom the reader cannot identify but feels he must once have read. This is the ultimate use of the fashionable dictum that all literature comes out of other literature in a perpetual spiral, and it seems to be the basis of the "new" short story. Anything goes, including the "poetic" effect, provided we can see where it comes from, and how it has been manipulated; provided there is nothing about the story which is inexplicably moving. [Anton Chekhov's] "The Lady with the Lapdog" would seem very old-fashioned stuff in the context of short stories today. Any distinction between tall and true has disappeared. (pp. 317-18)

John Bayley, "The Tall and the True," in The Times Literary Supplement, *No. 4382, March 27, 1987, pp. 317-18.*

James Laughlin

1914-

American poet, editor, nonfiction writer, essayist, short story writer, and translator.

Best known as the founder of New Directions, an innovative publishing house dedicated to experimental literature, Laughlin is also an admired poet whose characteristic short, unrhymed lines and colloquial diction reflect the influence of the writings of William Carlos Williams. Structured according to what he termed ''prosody of the eye,'' indicating that each line must not vary more than three spaces from the length of the opening line when typed, Laughlin's poems derive tension from a contrast between technical discipline and free-flowing cadences. By interweaving English with foreign phrases, similar to the techniques of T. S. Eliot and Ezra Pound, Laughlin displays a classical and cosmopolitan sensibility while infusing his poetry with verbal texture and allusive depth. Generally regarded as a romantic poet, Laughlin combines confession and candor with satire and wit, producing lyrical reveries and meditations on such topics as love and loss, innocence and experience, desire and fulfillment, society, and politics. Although faulted for evincing sentimentality and for employing a poetic style that some critics consider prosaic, Laughlin has been praised by such literary figures as Donald Hall and Hayden Carruth for his lyricism, acute observations, and sensual descriptions.

The son of a wealthy steel company executive, Laughlin was born in Pittsburgh, Pennsylvania, and attended private boarding schools in the United States and Switzerland before enrolling at Harvard University in 1933. Disappointed with the quality of Harvard's English faculty, particularly their resistance to modern literature, Laughlin was granted a leave of absence during his sophomore year to travel to Europe. Using a letter of introduction from one of his teachers, Laughlin visited Ezra Pound at his retreat in Rapallo, Italy, and entered his ''Ezuversity,'' a curriculum which involved listening to Pound's extended monologues on a variety of subjects, reading books from his personal library, and writing poems for him to examine. Pound's assessment that Laughlin would never be a writer and his directive to ''do something useful'' prompted Laughlin to return to Harvard and initiate New Directions. In 1936, with financial support from his family, Laughlin published the inaugural issue of *New Directions in Prose and Poetry*, an annual anthology of experimental writing. Including works by Pound, William Carlos Williams, Wallace Stevens, Elizabeth Bishop, Marianne Moore, E. E. Cummings, and Henry Miller, this volume established New Directions' policy to publish outstanding works of literature regardless of their commercial viability. Despite years of financial loss, Laughlin and New Directions have maintained their commitment, resulting in a catalog of publications by some of the most important figures in American and European literature during the twentieth century.

Laughlin's own poetry, which he initially distributed chiefly among friends and associates, received wider recognition following the publication of *In Another Country: Poems, 1935-1975* (1978). Featuring pieces from such early volumes as *Some Natural Things* (1945), *A Small Book of Poems* (1948), and *The Wild Anemone and Other Poems* (1957), *In Another Coun-*

Photograph by James Percival. Courtesy of James Laughlin.

try is highlighted by the long title poem, an account of a brief romantic interlude between an American boy traveling in Italy and a local Italian girl. Illustrative of much of Laughlin's verse, this piece is concerned with love and loss and displays multilingual techniques. Noting Laughlin's blending of English and Italian in the poem, Penelope Laurans observed: ''Here is an old technique of modernism, a favorite trick of Eliot's and Pound's, utterly inverted for use in a different way, not to make the poem larger through historical allusion but simply to convey intimate experience more immediately.'' *Selected Poems, 1935-1985* (1986) is divided into five sections and is characterized by short lyrics, experiments with longer lines, homages to various poets, and poems that make use of both English and foreign phrases. Much of Laughlin's early verse has also been published in the bilingual editions *Certaines choses naturelles* (1963), *Die haare auf grossvaters kopf* (1966), and *Quello che la matita scrive* (1970). *The Owl of Minerva* (1987) gathers material that has been published in various literary periodicals since 1984.

In addition to his poetry and his work with New Directions, Laughlin has also collaborated on a book about skiing, translated poems by Virgil, and published *Gists and Piths: A Memoir of Ezra Pound* (1982).

(See also *Contemporary Authors,* Vols. 21-24, rev. ed.; *Contemporary Authors New Revision Series,* Vol. 9; and *Dictionary of Literary Biography,* Vol. 48.)

CHARLES TOMLINSON

James Laughlin is one of those very few poets you can describe as modest and not mean either that they are pleasantly negligible or that their art is a showcase for inverted egotism. For the better part of twenty years Laughlin has brought out his own little books of verse [including *Certaines choses naturelles*] without availing himself of that system of promotion which, as a leading publisher, he could so readily have commandeered. The reason there have been so few notices of his work is simply that he has refrained from sending around review copies—ask any magazine editor. Laughlin seems to have looked on verse as a kind of *jeu,* and though lightly, not irresponsibly. Indeed, there have been times when, as in *The Publishers to the Poet,* he has felt the need to apologize for and to himself:

> Right hand blush never
> for left handed brother
>
> action and thought are
> children of one mother

That "left handed brother" is typical of his effects and a phrase which expertly condenses his general concern—the humiliations of relationship and the need for it, whether it be domestic or social; the inevitability that the generations and the nations will violate one another. It's all there in **"Step on His Head,"** a piece in which the poet's children do precisely that, though—for the moment—the head is only a bobbing shadow. . . . (p. 125)

Miss Moore, using as illustration Laughlin's **"Above the City,"** has registered her approval of his absence of commas. "Nothing," as she says, "can be more stultifying than needlessly overaccented pauses" (*Predilections*) and those expressively unfolding, unpunctuated lines of **"Step on His Head"** provide the perfect justification. (pp. 125-26)

In **"Technical Notes,"** Laughlin tells us that

> Milton
>
> thought rhyme was vulgar I agree
> yet sometimes if its hidden in
>   the line a rhyme
>
> will richen tone . . .

Time and again, Laughlin exemplifies this in a gamut ranging through wry fantasy (**"The Hairs of My Grandfather's Head"**), love poem (**"Hard and Soft"**), and domestic incident (**"Letter to Hitler"**). He can touch on rhyme lightly or he can harmonize densely. . . . (p. 126)

Laughlin's movement—he forces us to watch for it carefully, to feel it out on the lips as we follow the sampler-like arrangement of his unpredictable lines—has an originality which entitle him to a place (he didn't get one) in Donald Allen's *The New American Poetry* with its emphasis on the projective line. Laughlin had it twenty years ago when academic-baroque was in: already he had learned from Williams without becoming Williamsesque and exhibited a Creeley-like hold on the short poem before Creeley had established his own mode. Robert Lowell, a very different poet from Laughlin, bears witness to this early and unacknowledged breakthrough and also to the context in which it took place: "When I was a freshman at Harvard," writes Lowell, ". . . our only strong and avant-garde man was James Laughlin. He was much taller and older than we were. . . . He knew the great, and he himself wrote deliberately flat descriptive and anecdotal poems. We were sarcastic about them, but they made us feel secretly that we didn't know what was up in poetry" (*Hudson Review,* Winter 1961-62).

Despite their differences, Lowell seems to have learned something from Laughlin: a remarkable family poem, **"Easter in Pittsburgh,"** and one about Laughlin's uncle, **"The Swarming Bees"** (the first appeared in a 1945 collection, the second in a 1948, and both are reprinted in the admirable *Selected Poems* of 1959), sound for the first time a note that we are to hear again, deeper perhaps and more splendidly and violently orchestrated, in Lowell's *Life Studies.*

The beauty of [*Certaines choses naturelles*] . . . is that it not only justifies "left handed brother", but proves him a minor masters in the poems I have already quoted. There are many others (**"Confidential Report,"** **"What the Pencil Writes,"** **"Another Fragment,"** **"Prognostic,"** **"The Empty Day,"** for example) that ought to be present in any representative anthology of modern American poetry. Laughlin's "plain brown bricks / of common talk American talk" with "one Roman stone / among them for a key" make for an excellent domestic architecture. (pp. 127-28)

> *Charles Tomlinson, "A Natural Art," in* Poetry, *Vol. CV, No. 2, November, 1964, pp. 125-28.*

PENELOPE LAURANS

Laughlin's poems [in *In Another Country*] have a genuine claim as original versions of the American style that he has helped to make famous. As one would expect, they derive from the lessons of Pound and the example of Williams, but they are not mere copies. In point of view, diction, and tone, they are purely and determinedly American, but they exploit the particular bent of their Americanness in a fresh and original way. . . . (p. 297)

Laughlin's method in [**"Go West Young Man"**], as in all his poems, is to measure lines by counting typewriter spaces—that's right, *typewriter* spaces. Impossibly constricting as this may sound in theory, in practice it is only an extension of that free verse convention which substitutes the "cut" of line endings for the formal controls of rhyme and meter. Here the strict delimitation of the lines forces boundaries on a poem without freighting it with any of the attendant weight of tradition that rhyme and meter carry with them, and the rhythms of the poem are created by the way the poet plays with the room he has. As in other Laughlin poems, the typewriter spaces in this one replace all punctuation, inside and outside the lines, except for final periods. But this lack of punctuation helps to free the offhand, easy, amused voice which is at the center of the poems and which, in this one, enables the poet both to lightly mock and to celebrate the American style, a style which allows us to judge Ken and Stan at the same time that we feel an affectionate complicity in what they represent.

The special advantage of this voice, a natural voice, partly inspired and controlled, one might say, by the modern writer's mechanical muse, the typewriter, is perhaps first that it provides a restraint, a counter for the feeling which might threaten to make the poems—almost all of them love poems of different kinds—balance on the edge of the sentimental. American scenes, American faces, descriptions of American family and children, all brimming with the lyricism of the bittersweet pain of love, and love lost, turned aside, or never fully expressed, take some of their power from a mode which restrains sentimentality or coyness with easy colloquialism and plain speech. ("Nothing, nothing," as Pound said, "that you couldn't, in some situation, actually *say*.") Even the high lyric mode is subjected to control by the lines which do not allow the emotion to break through but force it to press against the limitations they provide. . . . (pp. 298-99)

Since these poems gain their strength partly from the fact that they indicate more than it seems possible they can be saying in so few and such contained lines, the weakest of them are those in which everything there is to say seems instantly revealed. There are a few which offer a moral point—one on Viet Nam, another on T.V., which force their slightness upon you because there simply is not enough resonance in them. It is easy to see, however, from the best of them, what so startled and transfixed Robert Lowell when, as a freshman at Harvard, he first saw Laughlin's and then Williams's poems and suddenly understood a different possibility for poetry, the possibility of a narrative voice so simple, straightforward and natively innocent, so unpoetic and full of the plainness of American speech that it throws into relief the complexity of experience it is capable of describing. . . . The power of ["**Cynthis in California**"] . . . is the nostalgia it shares for an American type it understands all too well, a nostalgia which is conveyed through a diction that seems almost too straightforward for what it is presenting. The situation is sophisticated and subtle. The presentation of it is so direct as to point up the subtlety. The poem distances sentiment by assuming impersonality, talking almost as if this were an intriguing case study—although the beginning of the poem makes clear that the poet is more implicated than he completely allows. This is the kind of poem Laughlin often writes, one where the shortened lines and utter plainness of report obliquely restrain depths of implication that are present.

There is one long poem in this book more openly expressive than the others and somewhat beyond the others in scope and ambition. It is called "**In Another Country**" and gives the book its title, referring not only to the Italian setting of this poem, but also to the country of youth, of another world, almost another age, lost now except to memory. The poem tells the story of a love affair with a young Italian girl in pre-war Italy. Parts of the poem are in Italian, sometimes two or three lines at a time, but the words are all the words of a simple Italian girl, and they are incorporated into the poem in such a way that even the reader who knows no Italian would never be at a loss to know, at any particular point, what they essentially mean or imply. Here is an old technique of modernism, a favorite trick of Eliot's and Pound's, utterly inverted for use in a different way, not to make the poem larger through historical allusion but simply to convey intimate experience more immediately. The Italian gives the poem an authentic, magical quality, the cadences of it evoking the first sweetness of an innocent love, one that could only happen "in another country." . . . (pp. 300-01)

Penelope Laurans, "In Another Direction," in Poetry, Vol. CXXXV, No. 5, February, 1980, pp. 297-302.

MARJORIE PERLOFF

In Another Country is a very partial—and many would say not the best possible—sampling of Laughlin's poetry. One doesn't mind the elimination of such topical World War II poems as "**Song of the GI's and MG's**" or "**Stuttgart: In A Nightclub**" or "**Letter to Hitler**," but it is a pity that so few of the love poems are included, for James Laughlin is, first and foremost, a love poet. The theme is announced in Laughlin's *ars poetica,* "**Technical Notes**." . . . (p. 196)

A Small Book of Poems, in which "**Technical Notes**" first appeared, is dedicated to "Bill Williams: Any way you look at him—writer or man—in his time: none better." Superficially, "**Technical Notes**" looks like a Williams poem, with its short unmetered and unrhymed lines and lowercase letters, its studied avoidance of "poetic diction" in a favor of the "plain brown bricks / of common talk American talk," and its *faux-naif* insistence that "a poem / is finally just / a natural thing." But these are surface likenesses just as the declaration of homage to Catullus is a Poundian gesture that probably doesn't go very deep.

The verse form, for one thing, is entirely Laughlin's own invention. From Williams, he may well have learned the importance of typographical arrangement, the precise placement of words and lines. But in Laughlin's case, a faith in "the typewriter as the symbol of the twentieth century" led to the strict counting of the characters (both letters and spaces) per line as the poet's "limiting metric." As Laughlin explains it to Robert Fitzgerald:

> The rule is that in a couplet any second line has to be within three spaces of the line preceding it. Now that is unquestionably the most artificial metric that the mind of man has ever devised but it suits me. I'm able to get from it the kind of tensity I want between a free-flowing prose cadence in the poem working against the strict architectural discipline of this narrow column of lines.

To which Fitzgerald responded: "It's no more arbitrary than four iambic feet. It makes for a tension between the visible form and the speaking voice carried through it. The eye limiting the ear I remember your saying once. The eye and the ear contending in the line."

So much for the poem being "just / a natural thing." The discipline of counting characters per line (in "**Technical Notes**," the first tercet has the count 31, 32, 16, and no subsequent tercet deviates more than three spaces from this norm) looks ahead to the typographical format of John Cage's lecture poems or Jackson MacLow's *The Pronouns.* It creates a fixed grid within which the "free-flowing prose cadence"of Laughlin's conversational speech is contained. Thus the opening sentence of "**Technical Notes**" ends with the word "bowl," but the verse form demands at least four more spaces in line 3, and so we get the line "in his bowl love," which gives the tercet a secondary meaning: love, it would seem, is made up of equal parts of acid and honey. (pp. 197-98)

Laughlin's love poems, by contrast [with Williams' explorations into the nature of sexual desire itself], concern the longing for a particular desirable woman, the joys of possession, the fear of loss, the bittersweet memory of love's pleasures. Here is "**The Cave**":

> Leaning over me her hair
> makes a cave around her
>
> face a darkness where her
> eyes are hardly seen she
>
> tells me she is a cat she
> says she hates me because

I make her show her pleasure she makes a cat-hate

sound and then ever so
tenderly hands under my

head raises my mouth into
the dark cave of her love.
                    (1966, *In Another Country*)

Not woman as a flower as in Williams' "Queen Anne's Lace,"
nor woman as a Greek goddess as in the *Cantos,* nor, for that
matter, woman as the ground and anchor for the otherwise
unstable self as in the love poems of Robert Creeley. For an
American poem, **"The Cave"** is curiously devoid of Puritan
self-consciousness; its speaker feels no guilt, only pleasure at
entering "the dark cave of her love." Readers who want their
poems to yield psychological complexities may accordingly
find this and its companion poems disappointing. But if one
studies Laughlin's verbal and phonemic structures, the intri-
cacy of his lyric becomes apparent.

We may note, to begin with, the witty transformation of the
word "cave." In the opening couplet, it is the familiar hair-
tent of the pre-Raphaelites enveloping the lovers. Then the
"cat-hate / sound" the woman utters in her "pleasure" makes
a cave of her mouth. But not until we reach the "bottom" of
this head-to-not-quite-toe portrait does the cave reveal itself to
be the sound-alike cunt. The foregrounding of personal pronouns, both nominative and genitive, intensifies the poet's
stress on gradual arousal: "she" and "I," "her" and "my"
are seen as coming together in the hate-pleasure of love. Again,
the interweaving of vowel and consonant sounds (leaning-m*e*-
s*ee*n-sh*e*-tenderl*y;* m*a*kes-c*a*ve-h*a*tes-m*a*kes; t*e*lls-th*e*n-*e*ver-
t*e*nderly; ov*er*-und*er*-*e*ver-pleas*ure;* h*er*-h*air*-h*ar*dly-h*a*tes-h*a*nds;
c*a*ve-l*o*ve) enacts the sexual union of the lovers. In a text made
up almost exclusively of monosyllables, many of them repeated
("cat," "hate," "makes"), words like "leaning," "darkness," and "pleas- / ure" stand out. The only trisyllabic word
is, appropriately, "tenderly."

The effect of lineation itself is best understood if we transpose
"The Cave" into prose:

> Leaning over me, her hair makes a cave around her
> face, a darkness where her eyes are hardly seen. She
> tells me she is a cat. She says she hates me because
> I make her show her pleasure. She makes a cat-hate
> sound and then, ever so tenderly, hands under my
> head, raises my mouth into the dark cave of her love.

Here we lose what Laughlin calls "the limitation that the eye
places upon the ear." For instance, when we read

> Leaning over me her hair
> makes a cave around her
>
> face a darkness where her
> eyes are hardly seen. . . .

"her" is twice separated from the noun it modifies so that we
are aware of the woman as female presence rather than as a
person with eyes and a face. The chiasmus of "her hair"—
"hair / her" contributes to this impression. And when we look
at successive line endings, we find the sequence *hair, her, her,
she, she.* Or again, the line unit "sound and then ever so"
qualifies the "cat-hate / sound," and the buried rhyme "show" /
"so" / "into" looks ahead to the last line of the poem as does
the vertical placement in the first couplet of "over" / "cave."
In Laughlin's verbal landscape, "A man and a woman / Are
one" as they never are, for that matter, in Williams' "Love

Song," where the "you far off there" remains distinct from
the "I" who "lie[s] here thinking of you."

Laughlin has written many such seemingly simple but exquisitely wrought love poems, but few in which the lover attains
so great a measure of satisfaction. Generally, the "I" is deprived of his beloved; she is in another country, or she hasn't
written to him, or she is just a girl seen somewhere (in a cafe,
on a plane) who doesn't so much as notice him. The poet
makes no attempt to analyze his relationship with women; nor
does he speculate on the politics or metaphysics of love. Rather,
he wants to capture the moment when a particular emotion
crystallizes, when feelings of longing or deprivation transform
his existence. (pp. 199-201)

At times, the poet tires of playing Orpheus to his Eurydice; he
longs for a nice cooling-off period in a warm cozy place. **"It's
Warm Under Your Thumb"** is a charming poem about such
regression. . . . (p. 203)

Here each stanza (the outer lines have c. 23 characters, the
inner 17) is like a little thumb print, and the speaker's comic
posturings ("perish the baubles," "It's written that the crav-
ings of a heedless man . . . grows within him") are nicely
deflated by the deadbeat flatness of the first and last lines.
Between "I guess I like it here" and "I think I will just stop
running," the poet waxes bold and brave, spouting metaphors
about golden bowls and Maluva creepers. But what he really
wants, at least at this moment, is playfully designated by a
series of monosyllabic words that end on *m—sum-, him, from,
warm, thumb.* All these point to the unnamed center of the
poem, the womb to which this slightly weary lover longs to
return. But perhaps not for long. There is always the renewed
interest provided by, say, a "diagonal girl" (**"Hard & Soft"**),
who, "when she is deep in / hard talk," knocks her cigarette
ash "quick over her shoulder" in a particularly soft and fetch-
ing manner, calling to mind the "milky way" and "stars stars /
stars."

Thus "love / is my subject & the lack of love"; it is eros that
makes **"What the Pencil Writes"** become a poem. When
Laughlin engages in social or political commentary, he is, I
think, much less acute. Such early attempts at satire as **"Highway 66"** fall flat. . . . This poem fails to come alive because
the poet does not identify in any way with the "little people"
he writes about; he stands to one side, somewhat superciliously
nodding his disapproval of their tawdry California dream. Again,
when Laughlin tries to make a political statement, as in a recent
poem on the Vietnam War, he tends to lose his Objectivist
cool, his "down-to-earthiness," as he himself calls it.
(pp. 203-04)

[The] poet condescends to his material as well as to us. It is
the voice that speaks to us from the Prefaces of the early
volumes of the *New Directions* annual, declaring, for example:
"The economist (at least *one* economist!) has the right answer
to the paradox of poverty amid plenty, but he is confronted by
such a solid wall of static thinking that he cannot force his
ideas across" (1936). Homage to Pound may have helped to
make Laughlin the great publisher that he is, but it was possibly
detrimental to his poetry, just as Williams is perhaps least
interesting when he tries, in the "Without invention" passage
of *Paterson II,* to imitate the Usura Canto. It would seem that
"the Americans" are not nearly so congenial a subject for
Laughlin as is one particular American: the poet himself.

The showpiece of the new collection is the title poem, which
appears here for the first time. **"In Another Country"** is a

very long poem for Laughlin; its thirty-two quatrains recount an autobiographical tale that could have easily been sentimental and trite. American boy (eighteen) travelling in Italy meets local girl (fifteen). They are immediately attracted to one another, go swimming together, make love, and try to talk a bit across the language barrier. The idyll soon comes to an end: the boy departs on the train, leaving behind a weeping lovesick girl. It is the purest of pure Hollywood romances, and yet, with the possible exception of the final quatrain with its hard-boiled conclusion: "the train / stopped at Genova and they / made her get off because I / couldn't buy her a ticket," **"In Another Country"** is curiously affecting and believable.

Partly, the charm of the poem depends upon its careful delineation of the cultural frame within which "love" takes its course. The euphonious Italian phrases that introduce each section—*tesoro, Credere!, Giacomino!, Genovese, Tornerai?*—are set in opposition to the flat, almost laconic description of what happens. . . . (pp. 205-06)

Throughout the poem, the girl's speech is rendered in Italian (sometimes followed by translation into English, sometimes not), partly to give us the precise nuances of her reactions, but also to pinpoint the central difference between her culture and the poet's. . . . The word *tesoro* (echoed by "the *golden test*icle *of a god*") introduces a baroque note that points to the central conflict between the apparent freedom of the lovers to do as they please and the artificial stability of pre-World War II Fascist Italy, with its signposts bearing words like OBBEDIRE! COMBATTERE! and its sham *ordine*, whereby the railroad crossing is closed off ten minutes before train time. Leontina, as the girl is called, submits to the imposed order of her society (*mamma m'aspetta alla casa*), but her assent is only superficial like the "Sunday dress" she wears in the parting scene. Indeed, just as the noisy crowd at the railroad junction obeys (OB-BEDIRE!) the ten-minute rule, all the while laughing, shouting, and treating the law as "a big joke," so Leontina's real law is her own instinct.

In this gracefully decadent world of bogus *ordine*, the young Dante meets his Beatrice "*com' allora / al ponte* only neither of us / was shy." The poem wisely makes no attempt to justify or "explain" the boy's conduct, nor does it suggest that he is in any way morally culpable. By the same token, Leontina is distinguished by her curious blend of Romantic excess and down-to-earth pleasure: she enjoys loving and being loved without the slightest coyness or guilt. From the speaker's point of view, such openness places her firmly "in another country"; it is implicit throughout that, back home, girls don't quite respond in such an unaffected, whole-hearted manner. So the central love scene in the "hidden grotto" which is the young girl's "se- / cret place," is both magical and very real. . . . Again, the effect depends upon the subtle contrast between operatic gesture (*O Giacomino Giacomino / sai tu amore come lui è bello?*) and the erotic realities of "here," "touch me here," "does that feel good?", "lie still / *non andare via* just lie still lie still."

The narrative begins at a railway crossing and ends, appropriately, with the lover's departure on the train. The story ends sadly, with the girl begging not to be left behind. . . . But, reading these lines, one does not feel that the girl has been cruelly used. The expansive florid gestures (*tornerai amore mio*) will, one surmises, sooner or later find a more suitable object. The poem's tone is bittersweet; it records a moment of very special but also very improbable happiness. Laughlin's

presentation of that moment is pointed and direct: he is attentive to word, gesture, expression, physical fact:

> and at the cove she changed
> behind a big rock into her
> suit it was white and tight
> too *ti piace*? she asked you
>
> like it?

Here the modulation of t's and long and short i's (beh*i*nd, a*t*, b*i*g, in*t*o, sui*t*, *it*, wh*i*te, *t*ight, *t*oo, *t*i, p*i*ace, l*i*ke, *it*) creates a "limiting metric" that carefully controls the casual flow of the narrative. And this tension is sustained until the end.

Ezra Pound, we recall, had told the young Laughlin to learn the "three Don'ts" of Imagism, that is, not to forget "the three propositions (demanding direct treatment, economy of words, and the sequence of the musical phrase)." One could argue that, in these terms, **"In Another Country"** belongs squarely in the Imagist tradition: its author does "go in fear of abstractions"; he does not "retell in mediocre verse what has already been done in good prose"; and he "realize(s) that the natural object is always the *adequate* symbol."

But of course the tone is quite different from the Imagist drive to be "free from emotional slither." The sensibility exhibited in Laughlin's poems has less to do with Cavalcanti and Catullus—Pound's heroes—than with a late nineteenth-century writer like Chekhov. When I try to find analogues for such love poems as **"In Another Country," "The Cave,"** or **"Hard & Soft,"** I think of Vershinin, bidding farewell to Masha before his regiment departs, or of the middle-aged Gurov waiting breathlessly in the lobby of the grubby provincial theater for a glimpse of the "Lady with a Pet Dog" with whom he had a liaison at Yalta. (pp. 206-08)

Marjorie Perloff, "A Portrait of the Publisher as Poet," in Parnassus: Poetry in Review, *Vol. 8, No. 2, 1980, pp. 194-209.*

ROBERT B. SHAW

Quite apart from his own poems, modern literature is in debt to James Laughlin. By founding and maintaining his publishing house, New Directions, he gave poets such as Pound and Williams consistent access to an audience. Of Pound and Williams he has been not only a faithful publisher, but, as [*Selected Poems, 1935-1985*] shows plainly, an artistic disciple. The advantages and drawbacks of such discipleship are intriguing to consider.

Certainly Laughlin has adapted many of the qualities that attracted him to his two masters with diligence and wit. From Williams he has learned compression and ease of common speech. His most usual verse form, a line whose length is determined by counting typewriter characters, owes something to the same source: in its taut compactness the appearance of these poems on the page is Williams-like. From Pound Laughlin has inherited a number of cultural icons to venerate and a taste for weaving other languages in with his own to produce an interesting verbal texture while pursuing allusive depth. Other influences ranging from Catullus to Cummings hover in the background, as might be expected of writing which operates for the most part in two modes: love poetry and satire.

As a satirist Laughlin is economical and on target. He has a sharp eye for various forms of American ghastliness, and he devastates simply by setting down what he notices. (p. 96)

Such poems may not be momentous, but they have a distinctive tang which to me seems largely missing from the love lyrics. The persona and his attitudes there are conventionally self-centered and predictable. The women come and go without displaying personality as the lover ruminates upon satisfactions or disappointments. The tone, so coolly gauged in the satires, seems often to veer to one or another extreme: either the speaker is nervously flippant or self-consciously exalted like one of Pound's troubadors. This latter manner can be quite lovely— as is an address to one "lady of brightness & / the illumined heart // soft walker in my blood / snow color sea sound"— but the work seems, more often than not, too finely spun. In such cases, Pound's stylized eroticism has put Laughlin in a spell and muffled a voice which is, as he demonstrates elsewhere, more naturally humorous and robust. In other respects, too, Laughlin follows Pound's example too slavishly. His macaronic poems rarely come off well; the Greek and Latin tags are harder for him to accommodate in brief, epigrammatic pieces than they were for Pound in the vast, unrolling tapestry of *The Cantos*. Some of these poems are diminutive in an uncomfortably studied way: we feel as if we are witnessing some curious alchemical process whereby a Poundian canto is reduced to the size of a postage stamp. It may be that Laughlin would not have written much at all without having the model of Pound to emulate, but clearly some effects of the influence have been negative. His best poems are pithy, cunning, and inventive, leaping free of the penumbra cast by his master. They deserve to be better known. (pp. 97-8)

> *Robert B. Shaw, in a review of "Selected Poems, 1935-1985," in* Poetry, *Vol. CXLIX, No. 2, November, 1986, pp. 96-8.*

GEORGE DICKERSON

James Laughlin's verses [in *Selected Poems, 1935-1985*] are either centered on his personal feelings—his need for love, his frustrations at life's diurnal trivia—or on intellectual games with another writer's work.

In **"Some Natural Things,"** the largest and opening section of this volume, Mr. Laughlin's linguistic philosophy rests on unadorned simple speech that for the most part shuns the enrichment of poetic image, metaphor or simile and employs direct statement that is all too often prosaic. . . .

As a result of this philosophy, poems about lost love, for example, become badly overstated and suffer from an excess of sentimentality. . . . Many of these poems are restricted to the same linear pattern, with the start of a thought or idea arbitrarily placed at the end of one line and then carried over into the next and so on until form becomes monotonous.

Mr. Laughlin thinks of Catullus, Ezra Pound and William Carlos Williams as his masters, but in a section entitled **"Stolen Poems"** he borrows awkwardly from them without mastering their influence. Here he relies heavily on macaronics and centos.

Mr. Laughlin protests that composers are allowed to play around with others' work, so why shouldn't poets do the same? And, indeed, they have practiced centos for millenniums. The risk is that, unless you do it well, it is better not to do it at all. For example, in his **"Camino de Amor,"** Mr. Laughlin takes Machado de Assis' wonderfully philosophical line "Traveller, there is no road, the road is made when we walk on it" and

revises it as "there was a road and there is / a road to be found and taken."

At other times Mr. Laughlin "steals" a line with some effect, then ruins his own otherwise decent poem with overstatement that looks out of place next to the brilliance of the stolen line. This happens in **"She Seemed to Know."** Mr. Laughlin utilizes well Pound's sensual "rescription" of Propertius, "In a gleam of Cos / in a slither of dyed stuff," then follows it with several lines of his own that diminish the power of both the stolen line and the poem's last line and a half. . . .

Other sections of Mr. Laughlin's book include poems he has written entirely in French, **"Long-line Poems,"** and poems written by his alter ego, Hiram Handspring. Some of these last poems demonstrate Mr. Laughlin's capability for wit, as in **"Take Off Your Socks!!"**; "Go live in an igloo, rubbing noses with an eskimo / She probably won't mind if you keep your socks on." . . . But in the long run, the reader wishes Mr. Laughlin's muse had given him better service. (p. 30)

> *George Dickerson, "Essences and Sentiments," in* The New York Times Book Review, *November 2, 1986, pp. 28, 30.*

CHARLES MOLESWORTH

I begin with the code word *minor* not only to set firmly the context and scale of James Laughlin's poetry, but also to raise the question of how we are to read lyrics that invite simple pleasure as their central reaction. Laughlin chooses not to wring the neck of rhetoric, like some symbolist cook stirring the broth of modernism. Yet he is the thoroughly modern, down to his wry, even tender relation to the past. Nor does he intend to mix sapphires and mud in order to clot the axles of alienation. Yet he is a plaintive lover, a political dissident, even a bit of an ethical miscreant. He knows that he prefers "to build with plain brown bricks / of common talk American talk" a poetry of simple desires, complicated only by memory and a sophistication that propels his heart even while it confuses him. He is one who cultivates the plain style as well as the "trobar clus," a parodist who loves his models.

That Laughlin is both would-be troubadour and one who cherishes the American grain is not a limiting contradiction, but rather the heart of a paradox that sets the terms of his scale. Laughlin has deep feelings but no extreme habits of language. He admires "the wild anemone / the daring flower," and he is a compleat sensualist. But something chastens him. Call it the thread of memory, the sense of folly, or even the distancing effect of his master Catullus and the tension of the "odi et amo." To love and hate in the same breath, the same occasion, the same person is to start a lesson in human folly. The lesson can produce mystical transport, or benign disenchantment. It is partly a question of scale. Laughlin experiences the disenchanting joys of the flesh as only someone can who has also keenly felt its sorrows. Laughlin is, despite or even because of his scale, one of our most Latin poets. (pp. 1, 9)

[*Selected Poems, 1935-1985*] has a remarkable consistency of sensibility, despite the varied sections: **"Some Natural Things"** (mostly short Catullan lyrics); **"Stolen Poems"** (homages to various poets, most in the Latin European tradition); **"American/French Poems"** (more than tourist-level French, but less than Mallarmé); **"Long-line Poems"** (prosy, "naked" stretches of satire and reflection); and **"Funny papers by Hiram Handspring"** (puckish poems reminiscent of Ferlinghetti). The satiric bent that is evident in the last two sections is present throughout the volume in greater or lesser intensities. Laughlin is never solemn, though he can be serious. I found that two revolving and unfolding pleasures recurred as I read through all these poems. The first was the pleasure of watching the expression of direct emotion confront but never challenge its own limits. Here a typical poem might be **"Easter in Pittsburgh,"** an autobiographical account of how a young heir to a steel magnate's fortune encountered religion and the class struggle in industrial capitalism. As the workers at his father's plant go on strike, the boy has "to learn a long psalm," partially in punishment for breaking the bathroom mirror. The poem flirts with the themes of *ressentiment* and repression, but sees them always with an innocent, almost Blakean eye.

The second pleasure, like the first essentially a controlled pleasure, came from the poet's level of consciousness about the very fictiveness of his own writing. The book opens with a poem called **"The Person,"** and tells how someone, who "lives in some other / sphere," writes the poems while Laughlin is left to wonder about his identity. But we know from the start that we will never explore this mystery fully—there will be no equivalent to Williams's "Desert Music" or Duncan's "Opening of the Field." In a plain style that never courts demystification, nor indulges in depth psychology or the darker arts, Laughlin can almost casually offer his comparisons. His lover's legs propped against the wall remind him of Nerval's ruined tower. A child waiting for a play to start is viewed allegorically as an innocent waiting for some political utopia: "I want to see the / lights go on and have // the people walk around / & talk & laugh & sing!" An old drunk man is seen through the same lens that pictures a young boy, spoiled by neighbors and kindness. These and other comparisons are easy, that is to say ease-ful, not glib, but presented as if they either offered their own justification, their own music, or else not.

Laughlin's plainness of speech and the plaintiveness of his sensibility lead him into a gentle satire, more Horatian than Juvenalian, with perhaps a shadow of Martial. The foibles of the modern world are his focus, whether in the form of a cardiac autoscope which allows people to track their own heart problems, or how to behave in a bubble bed ("What if my long toe-nails pierced the sac and I / made a big mess in the . . . guestroom?"), or relating how a drunk Gregory Corso called him late at night to ask if Laughlin might will him his teeth when he died. (Poets make strange demands on their friends.) Laughlin can see beautiful women as windmills to be tilted at, but he can also see himself as guided by an Eros more like Sancho Panza than Leporello, himself more Quixote than Giovanni. He has a telling poem where he fantasizes skiing without skis. It's an appropriate emblem of his playful desires and self-image.

Laughlin's scale is minor by one measure, but his poetry is harmonious and integrated because he knows his own scale and has learned to live within it. This may be his most unmodern trait, but it is nevertheless the chief source of what pleasures he has to offer. But like all valuable and successful minor writers his work rests on an affinity, a closeness, a rhyme with at least one of the great themes and subjects. For Laughlin that subject is the richness of memory. As he says at one point, "Memory must be my comforter, he gave me so much to remember." The "so much" includes not only his own personal loves and pleasures, but political honesty and the greatest works of the major writers. When we consider that, we realize that even a minor scale can offer full-blown values. Laughlin is worth reading, and becomes, in his own way, a memorable poet. (p. 9)

Charles Molesworth, "More Quixote than Giovanni," in The American Book Review, *Vol. 8, No. 6, November-December, 1986, pp. 1, 9.*

Deirdre Levinson

1931-

Welsh-born American novelist and short story writer.

In her two novels, *Five Years* (1966) and *Modus Vivendi* (1984), Levinson makes use of personal experience to portray characters whose lives are altered by unpleasant circumstances. *Five Years* depicts the political turmoil Levinson encountered in South Africa between 1957 and 1962, when she taught English at the University of Cape Town. The protagonist of this work travels from England to South Africa in order to ''find common cause with all mankind.'' She becomes disillusioned, however, after joining a revolutionary organization whose attempts to politically reeducate the populace and undermine the repressive government are thwarted by internal dissension. Conor Cruise O'Brien maintained: ''The reality of apartheid reaches one, drily, without rhetorical accompaniment, through a personality which feels it as a permanent assault.'' In *Modus Vivendi,* protagonist Queenie Quesky mourns the loss of her infant son, to whose death she may have contributed by using amphetamines during her pregnancy. A British teacher at a New York university whose scholastic experiences are based on Levinson's years as an instructor at New York University and Queens College, Queenie must endure her bereavement while earning little money, raising a daughter, and attempting to save her marriage to a professor addicted to drugs. Carolyn See described the world that Queenie inhabits as ''hideously familiar to those who've spent time in it: a nightmare academia.'' Levinson has also contributed short stories to the journal *Commentary*.

(See also *Contemporary Authors*, Vols. 73-76.)

CONOR CRUISE O'BRIEN

The narrator of *Five Years* is Jewish, Oxford-educated, received into the Catholic Church, and different. . . . [*Five Years*] is a short book, laconically and brilliantly written, full of suffering and horror, simultaneous with comedy. . . . [The narrator comes to South Africa from England and] joins a revolutionary group, the Africa People's Organisation. She falls in love with an African colleague at the University, Boris. Boris is a member of the Organisation, but incurs the disapproval of its respected and intransigent leader, Mr French. Mr French's doctrine asserts the present primacy of political education of the masses, insistence on nothing less than full democratic rights, abstention from premature actions, avoidance of helping Liberals. Boris sins by marching in an academic procession in protest against the closing of the University to non-white students. This—being a protest on behalf of the small minority who might qualify for university admission—is contrary to the Organisation's all-or-nothing anti-Liberal policy. Boris fails to translate an Organisation pamphlet . . . condemning strike action. Worse still, he actually helps the strikers. . . . [At the] inquiry Boris also gives the names of witnesses to the police violence. 'Sabotage,' said French. 'He gives the Liberals the help they need to get the government out and the United Party

in.' French's theory is that the crafty Liberals—the 'imperialists'—are in the long run a greater danger than the Verwoerd government—the 'fascists', whose 'crude methods of oppression' tend to bring about 'unity of the oppressed' and pave the way for 'successful revolutionary action'.

Politically, the narrator does her best to accept the French doctrine. In practice, however, she can neither break with Boris nor wholeheartedly belong to the Organisation: 'I lacked sufficient intellectual and moral energy to combat my long Liberal English education at its long Liberal English roots.'

The great strength of the book is that the conflict of emotional and political loyalties which here turns around Boris and the Organisation is central to the character and life-history of the narrator. Her strong affection, suspicion of affection, need to repudiate affection, are as evident in her relations with the Jews and with Oxford as they are with Boris, and work in the same way. She feels the pull of the particular, the fell attraction of Burke's 'little platoon'. She is convinced of the necessity to transcend this, and move away from Oxford, as from Zion, toward, as she says, 'universal brotherhood'. The trouble about the universal, however, is that it is much harder to identify than the particular. What movement is really bound towards the universal, what faces represent it? The narrator of *Five Years* judges them by their fruits, and the more unpalatable these are the surer she is that their claim to represent the universal is well-founded. Thus, speaking of the time of her conversion, she says of Jesus: 'I detested him personally but he was on my side—the side of total inclusiveness' (she does add 'and Western civilisation' but I think that has to fall by the way). Her adherence to Mr French and his circle seems similarly motivated.

His was 'a hard, hard little organisation'; he and his wife are doctrinaire, arid, over-bearing. That is how manna tastes. Poor Boris reeks of the fleshpots of Egypt. These characteristics seem to throw the narrator politically off the scent. Mr French, for all his steel-minded airs, is no Lenin, not even a Kautsky. His obsession, under Verwoerd, with the Liberals reminds one of the Stalinist slogans during Hitler's rise: 'social fascists are worse than fascists.' His theory about the relative potential utility to the working class of Verwoerd's 'crude methods of oppression' is unsupported by evidence. If it can be claimed that Boris is 'helping the Liberals'—by providing evidence of police brutality—the French policy of withholding such evidence clearly helps Verwoerd. Indeed the whole logic of this policy means keeping Verwoerd with his 'crude methods' in power until the Organisation is strong enough to overthrow him. Given the relative strengths of the Organisation and of what Verwoerd represents, it is small wonder that both Boris and the narrator decide to leave South Africa.

Five Years is 'an experience of South Africa'. The reality of apartheid reaches one, drily, without rhetorical accompaniment, through a personality which feels it as a permanent assault. The present reviewer was left shaken by this experience more than by any book about South Africa which he has read. It is clear that Miss Levinson must continue to belong to what she calls 'my own dialectic—my source and the protest it engendered', in life, in politics, and probably in Africa. My fear would be that if she enjoys writing she may turn against that too, as being of the fleshpots. I hope she will remember that for her readers her manna is bitter, and salutary.

Conor Cruise O'Brien, ''Digging,'' in New Statesman, Vol. 71, No. 1840, June 17, 1966, p. 885.

THE TIMES LITERARY SUPPLEMENT

Mr. Truman Capote is not the only one to turn fact into fiction. [In *Five Years*] Miss Levinson has done something similar, in that she has taken a real situation as it exists today in South Africa and as she experienced it there, and has simply fictionalized herself and the other characters in the book in order, presumably, to help herself to objectify her feelings about the situations.

Miss Levinson, or her heroine-narrator, tells us early on that she has come to South Africa because, herself Jewish, she wished to be "of the universal brotherhood and publicly to find common cause with all mankind". In an attempt to aid that part of mankind which is being pushed around in the Republic, she joins a revolutionary organization. Plunged into the realities of life and the unrealities of much of the organization, she finds the moral problems involved are even more complex than she had at first envisaged.

Five Years is by no means just a well-meaning tract in disguise. Miss Levinson has as much talent as she has conscience and compassion; that is to say a very great deal. Quite apart from its subject matter, her book can be read as an engrossingly well-written, serious novel by a new author whom we are sure

to hear of again. Her concern is with people, and she will not exhaust it easily.

A review of ''Five Years,'' in The Times Literary Supplement, No. 3358, July 7, 1966, p. 600.

PUBLISHERS WEEKLY

How one woman goes on living in the face of tragedy, guilt and despair is the theme of this powerful [novel, *Modus Vivendi*]. Levinson's acute intelligence and mordant humor make it a significant, memorable narrative. Queenie Quesky Ansell (her origins are the London slums via Jewish immigrant parents; her husband is a perennially insecure professor; they live in New York) has been a fighter all her life. Sharp-minded and tart-tongued, she married Eli to her own surprise, had a daughter and then a son, who died after a few weeks of life, of a congenital heart defect. Queenie's heart is sick, too, for in the first trimester of her pregnancy, exhausted by her duties at home in addition to a full-time teaching job and overtime classes to pay the bills accumulated by the feckless Eli, she took pep pills in a desperate attempt to find the energy to face each day. The pills were easy to come by since Eli has been getting high on drugs for years. Eli's quintessentially guilt-imparting Jewish parents are responsible in part for his angst; and Queenie's self-esteem has also been damaged as a result of her upbringing. She survives her year of bereavement as she has survived other troubled times that strengthened her character, but she is a changed woman, irredeemably bitter, unsparingly realistic. Her distinctive, vibrant narrative voice propels the chronicle and makes us care about her and think about the implications of her accommodation to a life forever altered by dark knowledge and emotional pain.

A review of ''Modus Vivendi,'' in Publishers Weekly, Vol. 225, No. 23, June 8, 1984, p. 56.

CHRISTOPHER LEHMANN-HAUPT

[In *Modus Vivendi*, Queenie Quesky recalls addressing her students] on the occasion of their immersion in Shakespeare's sonnets.

> ''Inasmuch as we are undoubtedly among the last representatives of the posterity that wears this world out till the ending doom,'' she says, ''and inasmuch as it must follow that even the poet's pow'rful rhyme, eternal lines, black ink, virtue of pen cannot outlive all life, it behooves us, as among his last readers, therefore to read him well.''

So literature is the real heroine of this fiercely eloquent, ironic novel about a woman trying to put herself together again after the death of her baby son. Queenie would drown her students in literature just as she once nearly drowned herself in water when, growing up as part of a tiny Jewish minority in a Welsh village, she devised for herself "a training course in adamantine endurance, inflexible courage" to distinguish herself from her three sisters, "docile little girls, undifferentiated, undifferentiable, sifting and pouring and whisking and stirring and bowing and scraping in abject servility."

She would inundate her students with words just as she overwhelms us readers with prose so affecting that it's almost lonely to leave it. A spell is broken when it ends. You feel abandoned to the trickle of your own consciousness. You want to go back and reimmerse yourself in Deirdre Levinson's roiling, rolling sentences, her mordant, angry humor. . . .

Unfortunately, *Modus Vivendi* does end—too soon, too abruptly and on an uneasy note that leaves you feeling that something is out of joint. Why, you want to know, does Queenie endure so long the inept, drug-addicted Eli, this man who half-amuses and half-infuriates her, and whom she beats and attacks with knives, and ultimately blames for the death of their son?

Why, you wonder, does Dr. Spinney have to be such a caricature of a psychiatrist with his comic-book questions about Queenie's sex life and her femininity? ("But don't you find thinking, well, hard and thrusting: Is there no place in your scheme of things for the open and yielding?") Why not make him a match for her corrosive intelligence and her insistence that women do not come in parts, not even private parts?

Why does her pain and anger seem excessive, even in the face of her argument that a baby dying of heart failure doesn't know that it isn't a developed personality yet? Maybe the trouble is that her rage is too close to the anger of her childhood, when she could forgive neither her father for disdaining his female children nor her mother for wanting her to be a cliché of femininity.

In any case, Miss Levinson . . . can't forestall these questions any more than great literature, despite Nietzsche's assurances, can make Queenie's existence bearable for her. At the end of this brilliant but flawed novel, Queenie recalls an uncle's brick memorial to Lithuanian Jewry that contains a photograph of a concentration-camp wall with Yiddish words written in blood saying "Jews Revenge":

> What words, I'm thinking, as, waving the children goodbye, I go down into the subway, forward to my school, would I bite through the flesh of my finger to write on the wall?

> Out of the subway, into the bus, out of the bus, up the street, through the gates, into the classroom. Into the classroom, to teach the young things facing me there the Sonnets again, as if the Sonnets save, as if that were what I would write on the wall.

As if she would write with the blood flowing from her finger that Shakespeare's sonnets can save. As if. But she doesn't believe it for an instant. And you wonder what she really would like to write with her bitten and bloody finger.

> *Christopher Lehmann-Haupt, in a review of "Modus Vivendi," in* The New York Times, *August 6, 1984, p. C22.*

ANNE TYLER

It's generally supposed that people with an extraordinary gift for words will write extraordinarily good novels. That seems a tautology, in fact. Then you read Deirdre Levinson's novel and you wonder. Deirdre Levinson is positively spilling over with words—rich, yeasty, learned words. But *Modus Vivendi* is a strangely dense and muffled book.

Written in the first person, it's the account of Queenie Quesky, an Englishwoman married to an American and teaching at a university in New York. Queenie's month-old son has died of a heart defect that was almost certainly caused by her taking pep pills during pregnancy. But she took the pills because she had to keep working, since money was scarce and her husband—given to near-suicidal tranquilizer binges—was in danger of losing his job. All this Queenie tells us reflectively, almost randomly. In tone, the book resembles a diary that's meant to be read by a friendly outsider.

She reminisces about her childhood, which she spent consciously training herself to be strong and fierce and impervious. She speaks of her marriage to Eli and the birth of her daughter Poppy. She recalls her son, whom she still mourns so deeply that she can barely go through the motions of living. And then, as the book moves beyond his death, she describes adopting a Vietnamese orphan, and enlisting the help of a bizarre psychiatrist, and gradually regaining a sense of hope. (p. 3)

Struggling to teach her classes after her baby's death, she is "dumbstruck, snorting, impotent," and "pinioned, lockjawed, mammering," and "yerking at the texts like a thrall on an assembly line." She eulogizes the seamy, vibrant sights of city slums till you wonder what idiot could ever prefer the country. She calls up so vividly the exhaustion of early pregnancy that the reader longs for bed.

Deirdre Levinson has a special talent for single-stroke characterization. Eli's catastrophic ineptness and Queenie's pugnacious spirit come through at a glance. More remarkable still, their baby emerges just as clearly, with his "benign countenance," his "kind, alert dark eyes," his "tall hairy little man's body," and finally the expression of "doubt or flickering anxiety" as his heart begins to fail him. There's not a chance that even the most callous reader will call Toto "only" a baby, and therefore unworthy of full-fledged mourning.

Paradoxically, though, it's the book's language that's the problem. For every apt phrase, for every startling, powerful adjective, there's a sentence so turgid that our eyes glaze over. Queenie doesn't say anything as straightforward as, "I was pregnant"; she says she acquired a baby carriage "on long-term loan, due for tenantry come January." She doesn't say, "I wasn't sure what kind of marriage I wanted"; she says, "The ranks of wifehood yielded no precedent suiting my purposes, no guiding star lighted my married way." (pp. 3-4)

There are times when the overblown style is deliberate, a form of humor; for this is often a very funny novel in spite of its subject matter. But at other times it seems more of a tic. It serves to obfuscate, to pad the truth. By the last page, we feel we've been cheated out of many of Queenie's experiences. What about her decision to adopt the Vietnamese orphan? Or the process by which he becomes the light of her life? Or her oblique relationship with Eli, or the resolution of her grief? None of this is made concretely visible to readers. We're left with a peculiar combination of irritation and hopefulness, for while *Modus Vivendi* ends as a kind of broken promise, it introduces a writer who could work wonders if she ever decides to step forth from behind those long, thick paragraphs. (p. 4)

> *Anne Tyler, "Caught in the Web of Words," in* Book World—The Washington Post, *August 26, 1984, pp. 3-4.*

CAROLYN SEE

Like a little girl who has been told ten thousand times to stand up *straight* and does; like a girl whose mother's switches flay her ankles but *won't* cry out; like an orphan who makes a virtue of malice, so does the prose style of *Modus Vivendi* go. Deirdre Levinson's novel is "women's material": life and death seen, not by whole countries scorched to ashes, but one infant boy suffocating—done to death by the negligence of his mother. Mrs. Levinson has been trained. Her learning, her defiant excellence in performance, turn a novel of "men and women" into something as harsh and implacable as an Icelandic saga.

Queenie Quesky's life plays out in a world almost impossible to explain to an outsider, but one hideously familiar to those who've spent time in it: a nightmare academia. . . .

Queenie, who's always felt—no matter how much her parents, and now her husband, disregard her—that she's extraordinary, a Cleopatra floating down the Nile, a visionary on a quest, is in worse trouble now than ever. She's the mother of one child, pregnant with a second and teaching for peanuts in a private school, while her husband mopes along forever with his endless dissertation:

> Dully, from the uttermost depths of my desperation,
> I said, "I can't go on." As if it weren't on his express
> recommendation that I was increasing our family, as
> if I weren't pregnant for both of us, "If you can't,
> you can't," he dismissed me through gritted teeth,
> snapping in two the coat hanger he held in his hands.

Wretched Queenie, wife of a scholar, does go on. Her husband has found solace in a veritable salad of pills: uppers, downers, and anything he can get his hands on. Queenie, just for a month or so, avails herself of a little speed, to cut through the torpor of pregnancy and the numbing depression of teaching sonnets to ingrates. By the time she feels better, the damage is done. Her beautiful son looks healthy at birth but is dead within weeks, victim of his mother's "carelessness."

As one who's taken her integrity for granted if nothing else, Queenie remembers with wrenching nostalgia her days as a single girl when she and a companion would tour Europe— "roofless nights, hungry days no object, pilgrims bound for the shrines of art." Now she must face the fact of her own complicity in this death, and more than that, her fall from grace as a member of the human race. Her sin has been dullness. Central to the whole book is the question of why she's stayed with such a low-life klutz, a doughy bully who tells her to shut up at parties, and "bombs out" for days at a time. How could a Queen take up with and stay with such a man?

Her husband's name here is Eli Ansell: Eli, teacher of prophets, and Ansell, that "best friend" in E. M. Forster's novel of unhappy marriage, *The Longest Journey*. Ansell's disconcerting habit was then, and is here, in *Modus Vivendi*, not just to tell the truth but *be* the truth. Queenie's husband, then, is part of her quest, one horrid answer to many of her questions.

Don't think that art will save you! That's Eli Ansell's silent comment on their life, on all life. "Art" and literature have been Queenie's only weapons. She's not beautiful, she's not loved, but she's smart: "Self shrinks, shrivels; soul faints with shame. What arms could I bear, in what furnace forge them,

against this steamroller . . . this spirit-breaker?" This outburst, for instance, against her mother, invokes Old English, John Skelton and Gerard Manley Hopkins, but doesn't do much about her mother as such. "His heart will never leap up at the sight of the rainbow," Queenie tells a psychiatrist about her dead son, but the doctor doesn't care about Wordsworth and her son is still dead.

Mrs. Levinson dances with the language, recapitulating the history of English Literature in 106 pages. She makes outrageous jokes, she sees that her heroine triumphs, or at least fights reality to a draw. If a grumpy reader might question some of the implicit assumptions here: that suffering, injustice, hatred, poverty are here to stay on this earth; that the best of us are—at some level—murderers, and that melancholy correlates directly with intelligence and sensitivity, Mrs. Levinson makes a good case for this morose point of view.

Eli Ansell, that lord-husband, is Queenie's cross to bear, her children—even the dead Toto—are soothing narcotics, tickets to the future, a theoretically better world. Meanwhile, "art" is what we've got for now: "Into the classroom, to teach the young things facing me there the Sonnets again, as if the Sonnets save, as if that were what I would write on the wall."

Carolyn See, "Queenie Quesky's Fall from Grace," in The New York Times Book Review, *September 2, 1984, p. 11.*

MARY HAYNES KUHLMAN

[*Modus Vivendi* is a] sad story—but it's not depressing or boring, thanks to the verve and humor of Levinson's sophisticated, passionate style, with its great sentence variety, accurate images, even a delightful undercurrent of wit and wordplay. And while Queenie's story is as unusual as it is short, the poignant details illuminate basic human problems. Women (who get pregnant) and parents (who forever risk great suffering should anything happen to their child) can identify with Queenie's dilemma and grief. Yet not only women, or parents, have to find a never-easy balance between conflicting commitments, as between personal life and professional career.

So Queenie, who sought fame and glory, then love and happiness, has to accept her limitations and losses. We know that this unusual woman will find, not a way to change the past, not an end to all sorrow, but, indeed, a modus vivendi.

Mary Haynes Kuhlman, in a review of "Modus Vivendi," in Best Sellers, *Vol. 44, No. 8, November, 1984, p. 288.*

Sara (Louise) Maitland

1950-

English novelist, short story writer, nonfiction writer, and biographer.

In her fiction, Maitland combines Christian beliefs with feminist ideals to address problems faced by contemporary women in a male-dominated society. She focuses on female protagonists whose crises challenge their sense of identity, underscoring their situations through allusions to biblical and mythical women who faced similar difficulties. Her short stories also examine themes relating to women while taking place in a variety of cultural settings and time periods. Neasea MacErlean stated: "[Maitland] is a first class writer of fiction, not a camouflaged theorist. Writing about women has directed her attention particularly to the effects on character of repression and frustration. Two main routes emerge for the journey from captivity to release, one through violence, the other through love."

Maitland's first novel, *Daughter of Jerusalem* (1978), concerns a woman who is unable to bear children. During the course of the story, the protagonist undergoes humiliating medical examinations, endures pressure from her feminist group to join their pro-abortion campaign, copes with her husband's obsessive desire to father a child, and confronts a doctor's suggestion that her infertility might be psychosomatic. Sister Anna, the protagonist of Maitland's next novel, *Virgin Territory* (1984), becomes emotionally and spiritually traumatized after learning that a nun in her South American convent has been raped. While Sister Anna recuperates and undertakes a historical research project in London, she begins a quest for self-knowledge which Maitland symbolizes through several conflicting voices in Anna's mind. According to Jane Rogers, these voices "represent the unforgiving Old Testament God demanding sacrifice and unquestioning obedience; the irresponsibility of childish madness (. . . personified in Caro, a brain-damaged three-year-old Anna helps to look after), and . . . women who have rejected men—radical lesbians."

Maitland is also respected for her short stories and nonfiction works. Of her first collection of stories, *Telling Tales* (1983), Richard Martin noted: "There are the obviously feminist fictions of contemporary women, there are the legendary, mythic tales that relate to feminist concerns, and there are those which retell established personal stories of the past." Maitland's recent volume, *A Book of Spells* (1987), includes both fabulistic, symbolic tales and straightforward stories addressing contemporary feminist themes. Maitland's nonfiction books include *A Map of the New Country: Women and Christianity* (1983), a historical survey of the role of women in Christian churches and the responses of various denominations to feminism, and *Vesta Tilley* (1986), the biography of a celebrated music hall performer. In addition, Maitland has collaborated with Aileen La Tourette on a collection of short stories, *Weddings and Funerals* (1984), and with Michelene Wandor on a novel, *Arky Types* (1987).

(See also *Contemporary Authors*, Vols. 69-72 and *Contemporary Authors New Revision Series*, Vol. 13.)

Photograph by Leonie Caldecott. Courtesy of Sara Maitland.

HERMIONE LEE

Sara Maitland would probably not like to be thought soft, but though she has written an intelligent and likeably energetic study of a feminist who wants, but can't seem to have, a child, *Daughter of Jerusalem* needed to be more austere: there's not enough distance between narrator and heroine. Too many garrulous, naïve attacks on sexist institutions (like maternity wards), too many bursts of purple, particularly in the embarrassing passages about Famous Barren Women of History, overload what might have been a lively, and often is a quite funny, first novel. . . .

[The difficulty faced by Liz, the protagonist], in maintaining both her integrity as a feminist and a rational sense of her own needs makes a very interesting predicament. But . . . the novel is, alas, still-born.

Hermione Lee, "Marriage à la mode," in The Observer, October 22, 1978, p. 35.

JOHN NAUGHTON

Daughter of Jerusalem is one of those books which take rather too seriously the obligation to explore contemporary obsessions and developments. The subject this time is feminism and the dilemmas it creates for radical women who also want some of the more traditional things—like motherhood. . . . [The heroine, Liz], is married to an ex-gay, and wants badly to have his child. But she repeatedly fails to conceive, and the (male) medics can find no physiological reason for her failure. Eventually, it is suggested that the trouble may be, er, um, *psychological*—to wit, a kind of subconscious rejection of her femininity. The book is about Liz's response to this suggestion over a period of (would you believe?) nine months, and has a suitably ambiguous ending. But it is rather too self-conscious in execution, with a conceptual structure which frequently oozes out into the dialogue. People may sometimes *write* like Ms Maitland's characters talk; but they never *talk* like them. (p. 659)

> *John Naughton, "Leavisites in Yorkshire," in* The Listener, *Vol. 100, No. 2586, November 16, 1978, pp. 658-59.*

SUSAN KENNEDY

Despite the noisy publicity heralding the test-tube baby, a society which is seeking to solve the problems of population growth pays little attention to the subject of barrenness. Sara Maitland tackles it head on in this extremely intelligent and enjoyable first novel [*Daughter of Jerusalem*].

In many ways hers is an extraordinary achievement. She has found a vocabulary for what is, after all, an intensely personal experience—the monthly pattern of menstruation—without making Liz's obsession with the workings of her body cloying or claustrophobic. Combining lyricism with humour and toughness, and with a striking use of simile, she offers a series of stimulating images of the female biological make-up. Not everyone will be able to share the intensity of her interest; but Liz's moving experiences as she undergoes exploration by laparoscope and X-ray will leave others with renewed respect for the mysterious complexities of their own bodies.

Liz is likable and intelligent, a London literary agent . . . who possesses in fairly large measure the ability to laugh at herself. She certainly needs it. Once a week she attends her women's discussion group—the glimpses given here tend to confirm an outsider's misgivings about such events. Each of the others, blinkered by her own particular angle on the feminist struggle, underestimates Liz's growing despair. . . . Understandably, her marriage to Ian is under strain already, made all the more complicated by his former homosexuality. The implications of Dr Marshall's suggestion that the root cause of Liz's infertility is psychological threaten to bring the whole thing crashing down.

For Liz is already carrying around a great burden of guilt: that she was in process of losing her virginity the night her father suffered a fatal stroke; that, trying to punish him, she turned her time at Oxford into a promiscuous gallop from bed to bed. Some of this comes rather too neatly tailored, and some of Liz's implied assumptions—that gays are a great deal more sensitive than straights, for example—can be irritating. But Sara Maitland has the gift of making the reader care about what she is writing about, and already possesses an enviable assurance and range of technique, equally evident in her subtle uncovering of Liz's slow realization that, after a lifetime of jealousy and suspicion, she actually rather likes her mother, as in her re-creation, in some powerfully written passages, of the pain of those biblical symbols of barren womanhood, Rachel and Elizabeth, as well as of the glory of Mary's triumph over

the biological facts. Three short stories published in 1974 in Faber's *Introduction* series revealed Sara Maitland's interest in woman's historical role, an interest these passages echo. *Daughter of Jerusalem* shows her overwhelming concern for the contemporary situation, and shows, too, how rewardingly she has been able to extend herself in the longer format of the novel.

> *Susan Kennedy, "The Biological Bind," in* The Times Literary Supplement, *No. 4000, December 1, 1978, p. 1404.*

PUBLISHERS WEEKLY

Skillfully and sensitively written, with a mature grasp of psychological subtleties and a keen perception of character, Maitland's first novel [*The Languages of Love* (published in Great Britain as *Daughter of Jerusalem*)] deals with a barren woman's obsession to have a child—a traditional theme here given a contemporary twist. Liz Smith is a liberated feminist and a successful London literary agent, married to Ian, a man with a past he is trying to forget. Both crave children; Liz's inability to conceive has become the focus of their lives. . . . [Maitland] examines the pressures on childless women imposed by society and even by their well-meaning friends, and she accurately exposes the tensions that can threaten the foundations of a marraige. There are the requisite flashbacks to Liz's childhood to partially explain the psychological blocks that seem to be the only barriers to conception. Only a stagey device evoking biblical women (Mary, Sarah, Delilah) and the way they dealt with sexuality and motherhood (or the lack of it) doesn't ring true. Otherwise the novel, which won the Somerset Maugham Award in England, is an absorbing experience.

> *A review of "The Languages of Love," in* Publishers Weekly, *Vol. 219, No. 5, January 30, 1981, p. 62.*

MONICA FURLONG

The Church was the last of the great institutions to remain ignorant of feminism. Until the Seventies (and maybe until now) not only did it retain its sexist assumptions and sexist language intact, but it resisted even the knowledge that it made a poor showing in its attitude to women—it remained sublimely indifferent to the fact that there was even a problem. . . .

In the Church of England attempts to introduce feminist insights produce chidings about 'divisiveness', and any protest automatically evokes the adjective 'strident'. . . .

Even the Free Churches, who are supportive of women to the extent of making them ministers, discriminate against them in other ways—[*A Map of the New Country: Women and Christianity*] tells of a Baptist woman minister forced to give up her pension rights on marrying and 'everywhere women ministers face longer periods of unemployment, lower salaries, less opportunity to shoulder full responsibility and less likelihood of appointment or selection to leadership positions within ecclesiological structures.' . . .

In this beautifully researched and intelligent book Sara Maitland has mined jewels of interesting material about women in the churches. She tells the extraordinary history of the missionary societies, many of them founded by women desperately trying to find a role for themselves within the churches, and often subsequently annexed by men. She looks at the very interesting history of women's organisations within the churches, using two of them—the Women's Guild of the Church of Scotland and the Episcopal Church Women of the USA—for detailed study. She shows how on the one hand church organisations were a godsend for intelligent women otherwise allowed to be little but domestic toys—they learned how to handle money, how to speak in public, how to take part in meetings. All such organisations, however, have had a hard fight (the Scots are still at it, it seems) to free themselves from clerical domination, and to retain the right to dispose of their own funds.

One of the most interesting chapters of the book—Women in the Bureaucracies—shows how sexism operates within the office structures of the churches. It is devastating about the way Church House, the bureaucracy of the Church of England, hides how it relegates women to secretarial and cleaning jobs by claiming to operate Civil Service methods (in themselves sexist).

Is the Maitland picture one of total gloom? Far from it, because, in a growing awareness of their own power, Christian women have begun to work together with a new energy and high spirits. . . .

Sara Maitland, who minds a great deal about the exclusion of women in the churches, does not want women to be ordained, partly because she fears they will get drawn into the clericism of the status quo, partly because (quoting Mary Daly) she says it would be like black people deciding to join the leadership of the Ku Klux Klan. Perhaps because I belong to an organisation working hard to get women ordained I find this tricksically highminded on the one hand, and scaringly paranoid on the other.

I prefer another insight of the book. The Body of Christ, says the writer, is a pregnant body, pregnant with new birth. Throughout history, one group after another, often a despised group, representing the Other, have been midwives to new birth. 'Now it is women who after centuries of repression (of talents, symbols, values and authority) are demanding their place in the body that sought to exclude them. The demand that women are making of their churches and of the world is . . . the prophetic voice crying in the wilderness for a return to God, to adventure and to hope.'

Monica Furlong, "A New Voice," in New Statesman, *Vol. 105, No. 2711, March 4, 1983, p. 25.*

RUTH McCURRY

[It] has been only recently that [discussion of feminism and Christianity] has been opened up in Britain, by the publication in 1981 of Susan Dowell and Linda Hurcombe's *Dispossessed Daughters of Eve*, now unfortunately out of print. Sara Maitland's [*A Map of the New Country: Women and Christianity*] is just the successor that was needed—it is fuller, and weightier; she has had more opportunities for thorough research on both sides of the Atlantic, and she has been able to cover more and different areas.

In a disarmingly personal preface Sara Maitland establishes her feminist credentials; she then proceeds to a businesslike survey of the history of women and the Church—its ideas on, and practice of, ministry, the position of nuns, the issue of women's ordination, the Churches' bureaucracies and religious language and spirituality—which is impressive in its scale and its interdisciplinary competence. She does not attempt, as her predecessors did, to apply Christian insights to feminism in return.

The Church has tragically lost much wisdom by undervaluing the contribution that women can make to its beliefs and preaching; the reason for this is explored in the first chapter:

> There now seems to be an emerging consensus that the root of the problem is a very ancient Christian heresy. Dualism . . . means splitting the wholeness of God's creation into divisions labelled "good" and "bad". . . . Feminist theology perceives that dualistic splits are the cause, not just of sexism, but of racism, classism and ecological destruction.

This idea is well worked out throughout a book which in itself is an attempt to overcome the dualistic division between a woman's beliefs as a Christian and her experience as a woman. Only once does this attempt fail, and dualism reassert itself: on the question of women's ordination. This is the key issue, the one which comes up in connection with every aspect of Christian feminism. Nearly every page of this book illustrates its crucial nature and on nearly every page the case for women's ordination seems powerfully put. . . . Yet on this point the author loses her nerve. Suddenly she confesses to her own "'conservative' ecclesiology" which does not allow her to believe in women's ordination. In a few pages she goes back on all the rest of her book.

The following chapter, however, on women in the bureaucracies, cannot be praised too highly. Sara Maitland opens up a critique that has not been attempted before, putting in a unified context such issues as how the Churches' funds are invested (and whether the Churches should have investments at all), whether the Church is an equal opportunities employer, why no trade union is recognized at Church House. It is in the next chapter, on language and spirituality, the author paints the happiest and most positive picture—of the joy and poetry and humour of women's spirituality, of the sisters' capacity to play and dance, to make pillars out of up-ended pews and create art out of junk.

Ruth McCurry, "Sisters and the Cloth," in The Times Literary Supplement, *No. 4176, April 15, 1983, p. 384.*

JEANNE AUDREY POWERS

Some are called to be trailblazers or pioneers; others to be cartographers; the rest of us in the wilderness of the institutional church require maps of the journey. Sara Maitland, Christian feminist and British activist, records the terrain [in *A Map of the New Country: Women and Christianity*] by moving back and forth between Britain and the United States, as she herself did physically in preparing this book.

Maitland's chapters focus on all the right issues: male dominance in the Christian tradition, women acting together in missionary societies and contemporary networks, the ordination of women, Roman Catholic women's religious communities, women in the bureaucracies, inclusive language and feminist spirituality. A discussion of intersections between the women's liberation movement and the renewal movement in the church culminates each historical tracing. Many readers will find Maitland's efforts to maintain a radical stance in both streams stimulating and encouraging. Others who have never understood the difficulty will find this map illuminating.

The author's comprehension of some of her subjects is superb. Her accounts of the roots of sexism in the church and the unique gifts that women bring to an understanding of ministry read with the freshness of insight. . . .

Maitland does not do so well, however, when her "very, very English" perspective collides with American diversity; though she has done an enormous amount of homework for this book, an understanding of the church scene in the U.S. still seems to elude her. Though she attempts to intersperse other viewpoints, her self-described "conservative ecclesiology" and Anglo-Catholic bias are obvious. Her anger at church bureaucracies bristles on every page, but she has collected little data from the Protestant traditions. She seems unaware of the "quota systems" that operate formally or informally in many denominational national staffs or of the "political clout" that some women who have not compromised their principles do have. In a political or personnel analysis, dismissing such women as "tokens" is not good enough. The United Methodist Church's Women's Division or the executive office of its Commission on the Status and Role of Women, for example, model roles for women that fit Maitland's vision of mutual ministry, prophetic leadership and the empowerment of the laity. . . .

There is indeed a "new country" out there, but Maitland may have tried to chart too much territory.

> *Jeanne Audrey Powers, in a review of "A Map of the New Country: Women and Christianity," in* The Christian Century, *Vol. 100, No. 19, June 8-15, 1983, p. 590.*

ROGER LEWIS

Sara Maitland's *Telling Tales* are ululatory fables about womankind. The battle of the sexes started as soon as Adam missed his rib and altercations have occurred ever since when his sons punish the daughters of Eve for not giving it back. Sara Maitland's book, nevertheless, transcends the limitations of having to view men as the enemy—creatures who pinion their women with psychological cruelty—and manages to work well as an exercise in the macabre.

In **"Natural Freaks"** an adolescent daughter is repelled by her mother's pregnancy. She sees the mountainous belly as grotesque whereas the mother extols its beauty. These observations are made while visiting Potter's Museum of Curiosity, a Victorian freak show with its tableaux of taxidermised creatures in little costumes and mummified monsters in glass jars. The conjunction of anthropomorphism with the secret inside the mother's womb has an almost gothic bizarrerie. The most alarming tale [**"The Tale of the Beautiful Princess Kalito"**] is an account of binding the feet of Oriental girls to keep them petite. Underneath the perfumed socks is the stench of putrefaction. This represents fettered femininity, woman imprisoned; but it is also excellent as literature.

> *Roger Lewis, "Pinball," in* New Statesman, *Vol. 106, No. 2728, July 1, 1983, p. 27.*

NEASA MacERLEAN

[*Telling Tales,* a] collection of sixteen excellent short stories, mostly about women, takes us from Ancient Greece to the present day, from the Arctic to South America and from murder to near-selfless generosity.

That Sara Mailand is known as a feminist author should not deter any potential readers. She is a first class writer of fiction, not a camouflaged theorist. Writing about women has directed her attention particularly to the effects on character of repression and frustration. Two main routes emerge for the journey

from captivity to release, one through violence, the other through love. . . .

Whilst several of the stories are triggered by historical and mythological figures . . . , Ms Maitland also describes moments in everyday contemporary life that suddenly sharpen into crisis: an adolescent girl beginning to scream in a museum, a woman suffering a miscarriage and a divorcee triumphing in her independence.

The techniques are as varied as the settings, and as satisfying. None of these tales is disappointing or repetitive. Many are disturbing, most are uplifting, and all are highly stimulating. . . .

> *Neasa MacErlean, in a review of "Telling Tales," in* Books and Bookmen, *No. 336, September, 1983, p. 37.*

MICHELENE WANDOR

Sara Maitland's first collection of short stories [*Telling Tales*] is an extraordinarily challenging one. Her greatest strength is that she can confidently take on the tone of a traditional storyteller, and infuse that reassuring and conventional form with the insights and horrors of a contemporary perspective—part of which is strongly and overtly feminist. . . . The fierceness of her contemporary perspective, however, means that these are never tales in which good triumphs over evil; indeed, her subversive art is to question any fixed system of values which is based on men's oppression of women, or any simplistic assumption that women are free of conflicts among themselves. Some of the stories touch on the fine line between great passion and madness; all of them hold the gothic and dangerous, the taboo, in the secure constraints of a poised, cool and classical style.

> *Michelene Wandor, in a review of "Telling Tales: Short Stories," in* British Book News, *November, 1983, p. 709.*

JANE ROGERS

The virgin territory of Sara Maitland's title [*Virgin Territory*] includes a number of areas: the virgin territory of Sister Kitty, a nun in Santa Virgine in South America, which is invaded by rape; the virginal minds of her conventual sisters which are darkened by the horror of the assault, so that Sister Kate's anger drives her to political extremism, and Sister Anna finds herself unable to eat and prone to uncontrollable tears. Sent on compassionate leave to London by her Mother Superior, Sister Anna is torn and driven by the conflicting voices of "The Fathers", who represent the unforgiving Old Testament God demanding sacrifice and unquestioning obedience; the irresponsibility of childish madness (also a kind of virgin territory, personified in Caro, a brain-damaged three-year-old Anna helps to look after), and the virgin territory of women who have rejected men—radical lesbians. . . .

For Anna freedom from inner torment can only come through identifying her own territory: standing up to, and rejecting, the voices of The Fathers, and discovering her own relationship with "the country of the Mothers". This is a female source of power and deity, linked with her own natural mother (missing since childhood), the Virgin Mary, Mother Nature, and the history of Amazonian tribes of powerful women. She plans a journey back to the Amazon jungle, "the womb", where she will find herself and become "either a radical lesbian or a contemplative nun".

One of the successes of the novel is that these alternatives do not seem incongruous: we accept that Anna could become either of these things in the course of becoming a free woman. Masculine domination, violence and exploitation within the church—in the name of religion—are shown all too clearly to be the same as the evils of patriarchy which Karen [a lesbian teacher] and her friends reject. This success is achieved, however, at the cost of many of the ingredients that would make the novel enjoyable to read. From sentence to sentence, and chapter to chapter, it is hard work. The drama and conflict take place within Anna's head, between the voices of The Fathers, Caro, and Anna herself. The Fathers and Caro employ insistent and repetitive arguments couched in short sharp hammer-like sentences which become both tedious and predictable well before the end of the book. . . .

External events are not confidently described, and apart from Anna, the characters remain shadowy and implausible. The novel lacks a surface: it is all cerebral conflict, sticky grey matter, without enough skull and face to contain it.

> *Jane Rogers, "Sticky Matter," in* The Times Literary Supplement, *No. 4258, November 9, 1984, p. 1289.*

NEASA MacERLEAN

When Sister Katherine Elizabeth was raped Sister Anna came close to having a nervous breakdown. Sent from their missionary convent to London, to recuperate and to rediscover her vocation, Sister Anna finds herself, at thirty-five, free for the first time to make her own decisions. But before she can choose her path forward, Sister Anna must reconcile the past.

To explore this question of a woman's freedom, Sara Maitland has set up a book of extremes [in *Virgin Territory*]. Sister Anna, a quick learner as far as secular language is concerned, soon understands one cause of her doubts, "If God was not going to protect his holy Virgins, what the hell was the point of becoming one?" Yet, questions like this one, which can be answered fairly easily in the mind, have also to be answered by the heart and the body. Emotional guilt and physical desire, more than intellectual anxiety, disturb Anna's once straightforward life of "professional loving". (pp. 34-5)

Ultimately, Anna is still unsure of which road she will take, "I will end up as a radical lesbian or as a contemplative nun!" but she is starting to find the sides of herself that a life of selflessness had denied or distorted.

Sara Maitland is undoubtedly setting herself up to be written off immediately by some potential readers as predictable in her feminism and absurd. Certain aspects of the book, like Sister Anna's language, "Well fuck you sweetheart", may seem unconvincing, especially to non-feminists and laymen. Many criticisms may be made of the novel (rather patchy, somewhat inconsistent, using types to express themes), but it is, nevertheless, a challenging and joyful book by an extraordinarily gifted writer. (p. 35)

> *Neasa MacErlean, in a review of "Virgin Territory," in* Books and Bookmen, *No. 351, December, 1984, pp. 34-5.*

VALERIE SHAW

[The] plot of *Virgin Territory* seems to offer more distress than entertainment. . . . But *Virgin Territory* actually bludgeons the reader with feminist issues far less than the rather sensational plot line suggests, and Sara Maitland . . . manages to broaden the interest of her book into an examination of the whole question of commitment, religious and secular. Anna's struggles with her conscience as both Karen and the disabled child Caro challenge her previous view of life are forcefully rendered, and the dilemmas in which she finds herself are made real enough. The alternatives seen as available to modern women (chastity, motherhood or lesbianism) are, however, presented much too schematically to convince readers that the concept of virginity is being explored as profoundly as Sara Maitland hopes it is; and when Anna finally steps 'freshly outside her own conditioning, out of her carefully constructed skin', the gesture seems to belong more to the novelist, anxious for an open ending than to the fictional character. Stylistically, too, the book tends to be over-insistent, employing too many repeated phrases and sudden switches of tense in an attempt to maintain a sense of crisis.

More discreetly, Sara Maitland uses imagery, some of it drawn from myth, to convey the ideas and events that haunt Anna, and in general the passages describing the heroine's memories and inner turmoil are more successful than those using the form of dialogue. Karen's slangy hectoring of Anna is at odds with the lyricism cultivated elsewhere in this novel, which seeks to ask questions rather than to preach and which is at its best when the answers are made to appear most elusive. (pp. 48-9)

> *Valerie Shaw, in a review of "Virgin Territory," in* British Book News, *January, 1985, pp. 48-9.*

RICHARD MARTIN

The subtleties of language matter to Sara Maitland; she is a writer for whom the tale is almost everything but for whom the medium is of immense importance. And Sara Maitland is a passionate and sincere feminist. And having said that, one might think, one has said all. But far from it, for Ms. Maitland is also a convinced socialist and, last but by no means least, a practising Christian. All these elements are present in her work, but above all one is aware of the dedicated teller of tales.

This was already apparent in her first novel, *Daughter of Jerusalem* . . . , which was more than the story of a young woman desperately anxious to have a baby and thus to overcome the fears that she is barren; or more than a discourse on the problems of relating homosexuality to a heterosexual ambience. It was more, too, than an examination of the problems of one woman faced with the complex problem of female plurality. The novel incorporated into its structure re-creations of the histories of heroic and fruitful women from the Bible: Sarah, Delilah, Jael, Deborah, Mary Magdalene, Rachel, and the Virgin Mary. The retelling of the familiar, the injecting of old stories with new vitality, this is Sara Maitland's very own and peculiar talent. . . .

[*Telling Tales*[establishes without doubt Sara Maitland's claim to a place in the forefront of contemporary British short fiction writing. The sixteen stories represent the various fields of interest to which Ms. Maitland has devoted herself in the dozen or so years since she graduated from Oxford. There are the obviously feminist fictions of contemporary women, there are the legendary, mythic tales that relate to feminist concerns, and there are those which retell established personal stories of the past.

The first group is, to my mind, the weakest—as though Sara Maitland is at her most vulnerable as a writer when still betrammeled by the world in which she actually lives. The subject matter of these tales tends to be almost too programmatic: the obligatory lesbian story, the token tale of divorce (**"The Loveliness of the Long Distance Runner,"** and **"No Way Out but Through"**). However, having said this, one has to admit that one of this group—the obligatory pregnancy story, **"Blessed Are Those Who Mourn"**—is an example of Sara Maitland's writing at its innovative best. It is the tale, simply told, of a miscarriage at twenty weeks. The reason why this story emerges so powerfully is that the author relates the events of "spontaneous abortion" in an almost detached, matter-of-fact style and yet contrasts them at the same time to a nobler tradition of death by juxtaposing passages describing ancient and cross-cultural funeral rites. (p. 13)

Sara Maitland's most convincing talents as a writer are reserved for the mythic legend, the totally fictionalized story told from outside in the uninvolved manner of the traditional teller of tales. As a result, she persuades the reader of the authenticity of a whole new range of shared myths of the atrocities of male dictatorship, the unnatural sufferings of women, and the need for understanding, spontaneity, and sheer courage. The best example of this in the present collection is undoubtedly **"The Tale of the Beautiful Princess Kalito,"** which is set in a fabulous China of the past, in which the aristocratic lady is subjected to the indignity of having her feet bound in order to satisfy male-invented canons of female beauty. The indescribable ordeal and the resulting putrefaction of the flesh of the foot is contrasted to the passive, doll-like prettiness of the Lady Kalito and the sweetness of the ritual washings and perfumings of the assaulted members. . . . The story closes with the Princess's attempted moment of revolt; hearing the gay singing of the unbound working women in the cherry orchard, she decides that she will free herself of the confines of her noble life and go out to share the sweet, melodious air. She removes the bandages and attempts to walk from the room, but is overcome by the pain involved and screams in response to the sheer agony of the ordeal. Sara Maitland's true ability as a writer lies in the way in which she manipulates the close of the story by inserting herself in her fictional persona as narrator between related events and the reader. Thus she focuses attention on the temporal dimension of the myth as part of a contemporary tradition, and in so doing achieves the metamorphosis from gothic tale to feminist statement on the traditionalized subservience of women. . . . (pp. 13-14)

"Art," as Sara Maitland wrote [in her contribution to *Tales I Tell My Mother*, a collection of essays by various feminist writers], "permits types of expression to some writers which could not be manifested by them in any other way." In this story, as in a number of others in this collection she demonstrates the truth of this statement for herself. As also she makes us realize just how the aim of fiction is to "convince or beguile the reader into agreeing that this is how things are (or were or could be)." (p. 14)

Richard Martin, "Tradition, Myth & the Feminine,"
in The American Book Review, *Vol. 7, No. 5, July-*
August, 1985, pp. 13-14.

SALLY JORDAN

In *Virgin Territory*, her fourth book, Sara Maitland tackles the thorny topics of women, religion, the Church, and the patriar-

chy. That sounds a bit daunting, and, indeed, the novel is not easy reading. Densely textured and both psychological and theological, it is sometimes difficult going. Maitland is so skillful as a writer, though, that her story is well worth the reader's effort.

The protagonist of the novel is Anna, a woman in her thirties who has been a nun since she started college. . . .

The actual plot of *Virgin Territory* is slight. It consists mostly of Anna's internal struggle and her relationship with two people she meets in London who become important in this struggle: Caro and Karen. Caro is a brain-damaged child Anna volunteers to work with; Karen is a lesbian feminist writer and teacher Anna meets at the British Museum. Both represent choices Anna could make—choices upon which the Fathers sternly frown.

The Fathers are the voices of the patriarchy, voices that Anna, in her near-madness, actually hears. They berate her for her worthlessness, threaten her with terrible consequences if she is disobedient, quote and misquote Scripture at her. Caro has another voice in Anna's mind. She sings of disobedience, of darkness and chaos, of the pleasures of being dirty and defiant. (p. 38)

Karen becomes a third force contending for Anna. Her voice exists objectively, outside Anna's mind, and as she seems to keep the other voices away she is at first a help and a comfort to Anna. She pulls Anna in another direction, however, when she falls in love with her and Anna finds herself keenly attracted in turn. The sway of these forces and Anna's fight for her sanity and salvation form the content of *Virgin Territory*.

Such an abstract and internal story must be well-written if it is to be bearable, and fortunately Maitland is a gifted writer. The novel is painful to read at times, and it requires concentration, but it is always engrossing. Maitland adroitly makes real Anna's spiritual and mental breakdown, and she moves smoothly between visionary scenes of the Fathers' and Caro's voices and more concrete ones which help ground the book and make it accessible. Her characters seem believable and her use of language is generally graceful and fresh.

Some reviewers have called *Virgin Territory* didactic, and to some extent it probably is. Its strong feminist perspective is certainly evident, but Maitland has not written a polemic or parable. She avoids easy answers and the all-organized-religion-is-hopelessly-sexist-and-must-be-rejected analysis that could be the predictable conclusion of a book like this. She is willing to admit complexities. She also avoids the tempting solution of turning Karen into a *dea ex machina* who sweeps Anna away from the repression of the nunnery and takes her off to live a life of feminist freedom. Karen is an appealing character and it's easy to understand Anna's attraction to her, but it's also clear that Anna is very young emotionally and not ready for what Karen has to offer.

Virgin Territory is at times dark and disturbing. The character of Caro is particularly well-drawn and haunting. Fiercely defiant, she resists the exercises her parents and Anna force upon her to make her "normal"; she demands to be loved as she is, dirt and drool and all. Her mother, when she gives birth to a new, undamaged child, ultimately cannot do this. Anna can, and in so doing learns to love some of the unacceptable, chaotic parts of herself. (pp. 38-9)

Virgin Territory would probably not be to everyone's liking. It's frequently troubling—Anna's stirring sexuality is disturbingly mixed with masochistic guilt, and disturbing also are the accounts of the tortures that some of the female saints and mystics Maitland mentions inflicted on themselves—and it's sometimes repetitive and hard to read. It raises some difficult questions about religion and about human nature. But I, at least, found it absorbing and worthwhile. It's good to find a strongly feminist work which is well-written and honest enough to avoid glib solutions. And the characters seem believable and are easy to care about. (p. 39)

Sally Jordan, "Maitland's Newest: Worth the Effort," in Sojourner, *Vol. 12, No. 2, October, 1986, pp. 38-9.*

LESLIE DICK

Latin American magic realism comes out of a context of Catholicism and, like the Catholic religion, it relishes the darker side, the obscure, diabolic or even dangerously evil. Sara Maitland's new collection of stories [*A Book of Spells*] is relentlessly English, feminist and Anglican, making her version of magic realism a wonderful thing, a sort of magic realism on the vicarage lawn. She is also a (self-proclaimed) moralist and, perhaps inevitably, each of these stories contains a moral lesson, neatly packaged to take home and keep. Sara Maitland insists on white magic, always illuminating, always hopeful, angry possibly but never despairing, and always clear—she makes her meanings available to us in writing that is never indeterminate or opaque.

Some of these stories are fairy tales for feminists, using that simple, radical reversal in which we're invited to see things from the Wicked Stepmother's point of view, making her cruelty to Cinders understandable, everyday, though no less painful for both of them. Various good witches make their appearance, part of a feminist mythology of the wise woman aiding the young girl to discover the 'strong woman' in herself, witchcraft presented as a mythic version of the power of female friendship.

Other stories consist of sustained flights of fancy and imagination, following identical twin acrobats to the top of the nearly finished Eiffel Tower, or a young man's transformation into a woman and a seal. There's a lot in common with Angela Carter in her *Nights at the Circus* phase but, where Angela Carter's source springs from the wild delights of surrealism, which is always against nature, pagan and artificial, Sara Maitland finds magic in *this* world: gardens, children, the English countryside, churches, 'ordinary life'. None of the above quite has the cutting edge or style of the avant garde—which might tempt one to dismiss her work as well-intentioned whimsy, but it's more complicated than that. First, she writes very well, and the power of the writing takes you places you might not choose to go. Second, there is nothing whimsical about her theology: a vigorous critique of patriarchal aspects of Christianity combined with a passionate sense of God as 'careless, random, extravagant, indiscriminate'. She describes the Church as like the Great Novel, a traditional form to structure the amazing chaos of the world.

In *A Book of Spells,* interrupting stretches of sustained imaginative prose, the author herself, down to earth, keeps appearing. There are lots of little messages from her, as if pinned all over the book: a preface and an afterword, a witch's spell on the dust jacket and Marlowe's *Faust* as epigraph: ''Tis magic, magic that hath ravished me.' She refers to Annie Dillard's *Pilgrim at Tinker's Creek* in no less than three different places, as if enthusiastically admonishing us to go find and read that book. She even speaks up inside the stories themselves: to tell us how difficult it is to write this bit, or how perhaps you might not get the point if she describes it this way, or why she refuses to write this part from *his* point of view as she'd intended. . . .

Sara Maitland's presence within the text—her matter-of-fact voice, her faith, her insistence on hopeful possibility—gently disrupts the settled expectations of this resolutely heathen reviewer, magically transforming even the vicarage lawn.

Leslie Dick, "White Magic," in New Statesman, *Vol. 114, No. 2945, September 4, 1987, p. 29.*

LIZ HERON

Sara Maitland, working within a similar domestic topography [as Fay Weldon in *The Hearts and Lives of Men*], ventures even deeper into the fairy-tale land of staple gender myths. In one of her stories in *A Book of Spells,* Cinderella's stepmother notes the vogue for fictional role reversals: 'There's this thing going on at the moment where women tell all the old stories again and turn them inside-out and back-to-front—so the characters you always thought were the goodies turn out to be the baddies, and vice versa'. Simplistic stuff like this cuts no ice with the stepmother; her version of the fairy-tale—Cinderella's dog-like refusal to fight back—comes as a lesson in the perils of too much female virtue.

Given that Maitland's writing is a variety of feminist didacticism, as indeed is Weldon's, it's interesting to see how she negotiates the goodies and baddies trap: women as always right and often wronged. As the stepmother insists, it's more complicated than that, and her perverse polemic is saved from any earnestness by a final sting of down-to-earth humour. Maitland is good at ironies and disruptive incongruities, at handling shifting points of view—as in her biblical triptych of Hagar, Sarah and Abraham. Likewise, her own authorial perplexities of viewpoint have a candour that's illuminating, though only when inserted with economy.

It's an uneven collection. Maitland writes with panache; its reverse side is a lack of punctiliousness, and her passionate sense of injustice sometimes overbalances into sentimental whimsy or too schematic remedial fictions that stick over-literally to an agenda of wrongs to be righted.

When she abandons it for more imaginative and ambiguous fantasies, the writing soars, carried along by graceful and vigorous lyricism. Didactic writers have to be optimists, after all, if not utopians. In **"A Fall From Grace"** and in a story about benign, elderly witches—who nourish a child's sense of power by taking her seriously—Maitland's women really do fly.

Liz Heron, "Three Wishes," in The Listener, *Vol. 118, No. 3029, September 17, 1987, p. 25.*

Sarah Gertrude Millin

1889-1968

South African novelist, short story writer, biographer, nonfiction writer, autobiographer, essayist, and editor.

Millin is considered among the most significant South African writers of the first half of the twentieth century. Her novels take place in the settlements, farms, small towns, and cities of South Africa and portray conflicts among European settlers as well as their relationships with such native groups as the Kaffirs and the Hottentots. Employing realism and irony, Millin wrote of tragic events in the lives of farmers, miners, missionaries, and their families. Her treatment of the evils and social dilemmas that arise from miscegenation are a pervasive theme in her work. Informed by her views that support racial segregation, Millin's fiction has fallen into critical disfavor in recent years. J. M. Coetzee explained that while her works are "neglected nowadays because her treatment of race has come to seem dated and even morally offensive," Millin's ideas "are not a hotchpotch of colonial prejudices but the reflection of respectable [nineteenth- and early twentieth-century] scientific and historical thought, only barely out of date in her time; further, her emphasis on race is at least in part a response to formal problems that face any colonial writer working in the medium of the novel."

Early in her literary career, Millin was regarded as a vivid interpreter of the history and customs of South Africa, and she was consistently praised for her unsentimental, concise, and forceful narratives. Her first two novels, *The Dark River* (1919) and *Middle Class* (1921), focus on the disappointments and disillusionments of unfulfilled characters. The former work concerns hardships endured by miners and their families, while the latter examines conflicts among members of a middle-class family in Johannesburg. With the publication of her next novel, *The Jordans* (1923), Millin gained recognition as an important South African author. Set in Johannesburg, this work centers on a rebellious young man who struggles to escape his mundane family life. Critics praised Millin for the power she achieved through her realistic and dispassionate descriptions and characterizations. *God's Stepchildren* (1924), Millin's best-known and most controversial novel, begins in 1821, when Reverend Andrew Flood, an English missionary, goes to South Africa to convert the Hottentots. Flood marries a woman from the tribe, and the remainder of the novel chronicles the tragic lives of three subsequent generations of this mixed marriage. Regardless of whether the descendants are of light or dark skin, they suffer the pain of ostracism and self-hatred throughout their lives. Widely praised by critics for its clarity and insight, *God's Stepchildren* was a best-seller in both South Africa and the United States. In recent years, however, several critics have condemned this novel's racial views.

Millin's next few novels are character studies that detail significant events in the lives of ordinary people. *Mary Glenn* (1925) deals with snobbery among the inhabitants of a provincial South African town that models its class structure on that of London. *The Coming of the Lord* (1928) details the tragedy that arises when a small-minded isolated community encounters an unusual religious revival. Both *The Sons of Mrs. Aab* (1931) and *Three Men Die* (1934) center upon characters

driven by greed to perform unscrupulous acts. The protagonist of *The Sons of Mrs. Aab* is so desperate to leave the poverty-stricken mining settlement where he was raised that he fraudulently insures his retarded brother's life, naming himself as beneficiary, and is tempted to commit murder when the sickly boy does not die. The seemingly virtuous heroine of *Three Men Die* poisons her first two husbands and her only son in order to secure enough money to live in luxury. Millin's next novel, *What Hath a Man?* (1938), relates the frustrations of an idealistic upper-class Englishman who travels to South Africa and attempts to improve that country's social conditions.

Millin's later works depart from her focus on ordinary conflicts and events. *The Herr Witch Doctor* (1941; published in the United States as *The Dark Gods*), for example, reflects her antifascist and anti-Nazi sentiments. This novel revolves around a South African tribe beset by internal political problems that are exacerbated by German missionaries who try to convert them to nazism. The missionaries succeed in gaining influence over the tribe's witch doctor, who stages a gruesome ritual murder. *The Burning Man* (1952) is a historical novel based on the life of Johannes van der Kemp, a debauched eighteenth-century Dutch minister's son who converted in midlife to the Church of Scotland and journeyed to Africa to serve as a missionary. Millin recreates the era of British conquest by including descriptions of the trading scene in Cape Town, the anarchic tendencies of Boer soldiers in the hinterland, the Hottentot slavery issue, and the threatening approach of the hostile Kaffirs. Millin's next novel, *The Wizard Bird* (1962), details black insurgency in Central Africa. This book depicts an African tribal leader who is educated in England but, under the guidance of a witch doctor, uses savage means to obtain independence for his people. Millin's last novel, *Goodbye, Dear England* (1965), employs dual narratives to relate the devastating effects of World War I on a middle-class English family.

Millin is also well known for several works of nonfiction. *The South Africans* (1926; revised and reissued as *The People of South Africa*, 1951) is generally recognized as a definitive study of the people and politics of South Africa. *Rhodes: A Life* (1933; reissued as *Cecil Rhodes*, 1938) and *General Smuts* (1936) are biographies of South African leaders. *War Diary* (1944-1948) is a six-volume history of World War II. *The Night Is Long: The Autobiography of a Person Who Can't Sleep* (1941) and *The Measure of My Days* (1955) are autobiographical works.

(See also *Contemporary Authors*, Vol. 102, Vols. 93-96 [obituary].)

KATHERINE MANSFIELD

To read *The Dark River* is . . . to listen to a solo for the viola. Running through the book there is, as it were, a low, troubled throbbing note which never is stilled. Were that note more deliberate—not louder, or more forced, but, musically speaking, firmer—it would be a great deal more effective. This low, throbbing note is essential to Miss Millin's novel; and we must be very certain it is there, for though the story plays above and below it, that which gives it significance and holds our attention is the undertone. Perhaps a novel is never the novel it might have been, but there are certain books which do seem to contain the vision, more or less blurred or more or less clear, of their second selves, of what the author saw before he grasped the difficult pen. *The Dark River* is one of these. Very often, when Miss Millin just fails to make her point, we feel it is not because she does not appreciate the point that is to be made, but because she is so aware of it herself that she takes it for granted on the part of the reader. It is a fascinating, tantalizing problem, how much an author can afford to leave out without robbing the characters of the "situation"; but that is not quite Miss Millin's difficulty; she has rather misjudged a little what she has "put in."

The scene of the novel is South Africa, and the first nine chapters describe the life of John Oliver, diamond digger. It may seem, as the story unfolds itself and is found to be not so much concerned with John Oliver as with the Grant family, and Alma Grant in particular, that these chapters are disproportionately long, but Miss Millin knew what she was about when she wrote them. They give a sudden view of a country and of an experience that the Grants could not understand, even though they lived in its very midst. But the heart of the book is Alma Grant and how she, who seemed so made for life, somehow just missed life, just missed the fineness of everything. This girl waiting, at first because she could so well afford to wait—the best was bound to be kept for her—and then gradually realizing that, after all, others had pushed in front of her, they were choosing and taking and sharing, until

there was nothing for her—nothing but Van Reede—is an unusual and fascinating character.

Katherine Mansfield, "Orchestra and Solo," in The Athenaeum, *No. 4686, February 20, 1920, p. 241.*

THE NEW YORK TIMES BOOK REVIEW

Although *The Dark River* is a first novel, it shows little or nothing of crudity. It has faults of construction, but these faults are such as are made all but unavoidable by the nature of the theme. . . . [We] are occasionally annoyed by being, so to speak, forcibly removed from the society of some individual in whose fortunes we have become greatly interested, and taken to watch those of another. But this defect is small in a book which has so much to recommend it. *The Dark River* is well written, in a clear and vigorous style, it is interesting, it gives that sense of reality which makes us feel that we are actually observing the lives and fortunes of a group of living people. Moreover, it has the rare quality which distinguished Arnold Bennett's *The Old Wives' Tale*—it gives an effect of the passing of time, the slow, inexorable progression of the years and the changes they bring, often imperceptibly, always definitely. All these merits are independent of the background, yet this background is an important factor in the book. For the scene is laid in South Africa, and the life there is vividly and interestingly described.

First we are shown the settlement well named "Lost Hope Diggings," whither John Oliver drifted in 1902. He belonged to a respectable English family, and was himself one of those weak, well-meaning men who do so much mischief in the world. . . . The opening of the book describes his first meeting with Hester Grant, when he was a young man full of hope and physical strength, and she was a girl of 16, and then tells of his slow, steady degeneration. Down he went, and down, to the depths he had once scorned. He was living with a drunken Kaffir woman and the four woolly haired children she had borne him, when the World War came. It thrust upon him the chance he had never had the courage to go and seek for himself— the chance to get away from Lost Hope Diggings and from those of whom he was ashamed. He went, fought bravely enough, won a commission and presently went to Muizenberg to recuperate from a wound in the leg. There he again met Hester, now a woman of 28.

John Oliver, the plausible weakling and moral coward, who yet would have greatly preferred to be a clean and honorable man, is admirably drawn, but the psychology of Hester, the "unwanted woman," is perhaps even better done. . . . There were three of the Grant sisters, Alma, Hester and Ruth, and each is portrayed at full length, with her thoughts and feelings, the outward events of her life, and the adjustments, both of mind and of living, forced upon her alike by temperament and by circumstances.

From the diamond diggings at Lost Hope the story moves to Cape Town, where the Grants lived, thence to the gay seaside resort of Muizenberg, then to Kimberley, to Johannesberg, and to the diggings at Steytler's Rush, a place even more forlorn than Lost Hope. All these places are clearly set before us, with their widely differing ways and atmospheres, so well set before us that, were the human drama of which they are but the background less real and less interesting than it is, they would of themselves suffice to make the book worth reading. . . .

The novel is leisurely, but it does not drag; it has in it nothing of the sensational, nor of the sugary flavor which pervades so much of our fiction, but it has reality. Most of us have known an Alma, the delightful girl who little by little faded into a gentle, wistful woman with no especial place in the world; and many of us have either known or guessed at the existence of a Hester, fiercely resentful of her own lack of attraction. *The Dark River* is a notable novel.

A review of "The Dark River," in The New York Times Book Review, *January 2, 1921, p. 28.*

THE TIMES LITERARY SUPPLEMENT

[*Middle Class*] tells the story of the Wendovers, a family living in Johannesburg. Mr. Wendover is a trite little book keeper with a passion for economy. Mrs. Wendover, we are told, is a "stormy spirit" with a sense of beauty and a dislike of housekeeping. They meet in their children, but their children outgrow them. Frank, on his return from Cambridge and the war, marries and begins to aspire socially. Tessa is a rebel, and shows it by marrying secretly Bob Rivers, a Labour leader. Her rebellion, however, does not stand the shock of the discovery that Rivers was a married man before he met her, and that his first wife is alive. Nor do Rivers's democratic principles hold out against prosperity. . . . Middle-class tradition weighs heavily on Tessa, and ultimately shows her her own heart. Miss Millin describes the Wendovers with care. She has the gift of catching a likeness, but to make a living human being something more than this is needed.

The development of a character, its attitude to other characters and to the things that happen to it, must grow naturally from the character itself. And here Miss Millin fails to convince us. The whole relationship between Tessa and Bob Rivers, for instance, seems to us unreal. Miss Millin describes it, but it does not evolve, as all real things must evolve, inevitably from the people themselves. Again, we are told that Rivers's convictions change, but we are never conscious of the hidden working of the mind which such a change must mean. It is indeed the inner process which all through her book Miss Millin is too apt to ignore; and since it is always the inner process which explains life, we are left feeling that the main link in the chain is missing.

A review of "Middle Class," in The Times Literary Supplement, *No. 1039, December 15, 1921, p. 843.*

J. P. COLLINS

[*Middle Class*] is a clever study of a middle-class household in Johannesburg. Robert Wendover, the father, was of the type generally recognised as worthy but unsuccessful. He was careful and frugal, and it was the fetish of his life that one-fifth of his small income should be saved. It was altogether a somewhat grim and cheerless household. . . . When [daughter Tessa's] chance of escape presented itself she seized it with unconventional promptitude, and when she came back from her holiday at Cape Town she presented herself to her astonished parents as Mrs. Robert Rivers, the wife of a notorious young labour agitator. The study of Rivers is the best thing in a book that is rather strong in characterisation, and gives us a very clever analysis of disguised egotism and selfishness. Rivers's ethics were of the most elastic description, and the fact that he had a wife in England troubled him but little till the secret was discovered. Circumstances in due time made Rivers a propri-

etor and speculator, and his radical tenets slipped from him like a mantle. It was characteristic of the two that while to Rivers prosperity and the death of his first wife seemed to make all things clear, to Tessa they brought revulsion and the determination to lead her own life.

J. P. Collins, in a review of "Middle Class," in The Bookman, *London, Vol. LXI, December 25, 1921, p. 97.*

THE BOOKMAN, LONDON

The Jordans is a story of extraordinary power and strength; rugged, realistic, sordid in parts, tremendously alive. The people in this remarkable book are as far removed from the usual "fiction characters" as the poles are apart. There are few books that would not seem somewhat anæmic if read immediately after *The Jordans*. And yet it is simply the story of the Jordan family, and their little world in South Africa. There are vivid word pictures of the diamond fields in 1871, and of Johannesburg, where young Daniel Jordan is born and brought up. Daniel, with his reserve, his pride, his egotism, his pluck, is not altogether likeable, but he is very human. Charlie Jordan, his brother, a born rebel who, although terribly ill, becomes the men's leader in the great Rand strike which was so nearly successful [in 1922], makes an excellent foil to Daniel. . . . These two alone would be the making of a book. But add to these [the other Jordan family members] . . . ; and Benjamin Jessel, the millionaire who adopts Daniel; and Celia, the girl Daniel loves and loses, and finds again when he has outgrown her, and no longer wants her; and Celia's family: with such a gallery as this, described in their creator's sympathetic, dispassionate manner, the book is lifted clear out of the ordinary rut. The author has dared to give her story a gloomy ending—but one feels it is the right ending, and no other would have been possible. *The Jordans* places Sarah Gertrude Millin among writers of to-day who really count.

A review of "The Jordans," in The Bookman, *London, Vol. LXV, Autumn, 1923, p. 58.*

THE NEW YORK TIMES BOOK REVIEW

Whoever needs to be convinced of the terrible effectiveness of genuine realism has only to read *The Jordans*. It is an exemplification of the paradox that nothing is more subtle than perfect simplicity. At first reading, it appears to be just the simple story of far from extraordinary people told with the utmost simplicity, but then comes the realization that here is a more impressive and soul-disturbing exposition of man's incompetence in the art of living than a highly emotional indictment of society could ever be. Readers who enjoy a first-rate novel concerned with life as it is and those who want a veracious picture of South Africa will be well repaid for the time they devote to *The Jordans*, but it is no book to pick up when seeking diversion and relief from the travail of existence. (p. 14)

Daniel and Charles are the outstanding members of the family, although they are as unlike as their experiences with life were to be. The former has pertinacity and intelligence, almost too cool a head, while the latter is the embodiment of undirected force. (pp. 14, 19)

Almost any one would want to escape such a family as the Jordans. The father went out from England in the early days of the rush to the diamond fields. . . . In his first months out he threw away through lack of vision his opportunity to make a fortune and a partnership with a man who was to be one of the big figures in South Africa. . . . His career was a steady descent down hill. . . . [Daniel] possesses many of the necessary qualities. He is the best of the Jordans, but he is a Jordan in more than name. As his kinship with them causes him grief and humiliation throughout his life, so the common heritage leads him to pettiness when, by rising to the occasion, he could triumph. As we leave him, he stands forth for the first time worthy of himself.

A simple enough story, devoid of momentous events and situations, but not one that can be forgotten soon. Not for an instant has Sarah Gertrude Millin departed from the rôle of narrator. She writes dispassionately, impersonally, without any emotion or emotional appeal, but it is creative writing, not reporting of photographic realism. Her characters are living, flesh-and-blood individuals, and Johannesburg becomes a city we might know personally. (p. 19)

A review of "The Jordans," in The New York Times Book Review, *November 4, 1923, pp. 14, 19.*

THE TIMES LITERARY SUPPLEMENT

God's Step-Children is the name with a nice touch of imagination about it given by Mrs. S. G. Millin to the coloured people of South Africa, aboriginals and half-castes, and those more tragically white in spite of the betraying streak of colour in their ancestry. . . .

The book, beginning with the Rev. Andrew Flood, who goes to Africa as a missionary in 1821 and takes lawfully to wife one of the blacks among whom he is labouring, covers four generations. The Rev. Andrew lives with the tribe, and gradually sinks to their level of physical degradation without bettering them spiritually. He has two children, and with Deborah his daughter and her descendants the story runs on. Deborah has a son by a casual affair with a Boer, and calls him Kleinhans. The son fancies himself so white that he will be accepted as a Boer, and he is most brutally undeceived. He marries a half-caste girl, and has a lovely and nearly white child called Elmira; and with her tragic life the greater part of the story deals. Kleinhans is farmer to an Englishman, Lindsell, a nervous, selfish type of man seeking health in South Africa, and bored by his wife and dullish little girls. From the first he takes an interest in the brilliantly lovely little Elmira, and through him she is sent to a convent with white children, and learns to dread discovery and to pray for a white marriage. Dramatically enough her origin comes to light, and she too eats the bitter bread of the half-caste. The curse of the colour streak is that each generation despises the father that begat it and disclaims its parentage. . . . Barry, the son of an old man and of mixed blood, is feeble and old-fashioned and terror descends on him when he learns of the colour bar. It haunts his life in Cape Town, whither his step-sister takes him after the death of their father; and he is only able to forget it when he goes to Oxford and finds relief in the comfortable indifference of England to the colour question. Barry, so nearly white, has the most pitiful history of all; and Mrs. Millin scarcely solves his problem or the problem of the book by making him go as a missionary to his mother's people to atone for the sin of having married an English wife and called another child into being. Like his great-grandfather, the Rev. Andrew Flood, he too may become the parent of dark-skinned children and start another set of tragedies.

[*God's Step-Children*] is full of fierce feeling and is written with swiftness and certainty, and evidently from lifelong observation of South African life. Besides the colour studies there are equally sure pictures of Europeans and of the various grades of whites; and the unhappy relationship between the half-caste timorous boy and his elderly warped step-sister is painful and powerful. A book that strangely holds the mind after the end is reached.

A review of "God's Step-Children," in The Times Literary Supplement, *No. 1163, May 1, 1924, p. 266.*

JOHN W. CRAWFORD

Mrs. Millin could readily be forgiven, even if the opening chapter of *God's Stepchildren* led to much less than the startlingly beautiful epic of compact simplicity which is developed in the succeeding pages. It is a triumphant first chapter, and is deceptively complete in itself. It is so satisfying that it induces a second of fearful hesitation lest the rest of the book be an anti-climax. Yet it invincibly states a situation and unleashes an impetus that will not be quiet until the last page. The attention of the reader is sluiced into the irresistible drive of Mrs. Millin's narrative. Each separate episode is such a gem that it demands to be read aloud, yet it is rigidly subordinated to the sweep of the design. Cumulative suspense is as competently handled as in a first-class detective story, yet the whole deposits a richly personal vision of life.

The underlying conception of *God's Stepchildren* is an inexorable visualization through an essentially religious temperament of the conditions and consequences of the inevitable conflict between two racial civilizations, the white and the black, against the mysterious, ageless background of South Africa. The Rev. Andrew Flood, going to the heart of the jungle in 1821 to preach the gospel to the Hottentots, is the initiating circumstance of a genealogy, stretching over a century, which crystallizes the biological and social implications of the fluid yet enduring battle between the natives and the invading English and Dutch settlers. The Rev. Andrew is a sort of Don Quixote of the whole foreign missions movement; he puts literally into practice the eighteenth century ideal of equality, even to the point of marrying a Hottentot.

The Rev. Andrew is a tragic comment on the force of Mrs. Millin's observation: "That was the worst of impulses. They trailed their inconvenient and persistent effects after them." He cannot, however, lightly be dismissed as of those unfit who presumably figure in miscegenations. If he were merely a negligible degenerate the whole structure of the novel would fall to the ground. The Rev. Andrew is a complicated being, and his decision results from an inescapable convergence of motive. Long before his blind fanaticism has prevailed over the scruples of his brother missionary, a hundred miles away, and he is, before the horrified eyes of the reader married to the savage, his pathetic ridiculousness has caught at the reader's throat. It is certain, when the white girl rejects him and the natives maintain a spirited raillery of dialectic toward his mission, that the two failures will be merged by the Rev. Andrew into those humiliations and sufferings which form the base of his religion. The imagination of the Rev. Andrew has done more than compensate for a harassing incongruity between his actual and his desired position before the world; it has impelled him toward a stark identification, albeit unconscious, of his own sufferings with the passion of the Christ. The Rev. Andrew then, for all his ineffectual absurdity, stands at the peak of the white civilization, just as that earlier creation, Don Quixote, exemplifies at once the strength and the weakness of the medieval ideal of chivalry.

The Rev. Andrew lives to welcome home his light-skinned daughter, carrying the son of a Dutch farmer. The other child has gone back to the Hottentots and already is the father of innumerable blacks. The reality of the Rev. Andrew's sublimely idealistic impulse presses its iron into his soul, so that he checks his daughter's boasting over the light skin of her child with: ''There can be no more white children for us.'' He has made his disillusioned surrender to the windmills against which he tilted, and he has previsioned the harvest of racial prejudice which he has sowed for his own.

Mrs. Millin concentrates upon the fortunes of those in whose divided natures the aspiration toward the white blood is uppermost, yet the darker shadows are ever present. Her emphasis partakes of something of the nature of biological selection, as of the fittest in each generation, as well as evinces a sure artistic feeling for significant drama. The bearded grandson, looking like a tanned Boer, and his almost white wife transmit by a supreme effort all their yearning toward a higher cultural level to the first girl, whose election as their instrument is made concrete in the still paler pigmentation. Her repeatedly frustrated escape is at length consummated in a union with an elderly eccentric Englishman; their son is a final victory for the white blood. His emergence at the Rev. Andrew's starting point is flavored with a slight physical resemblance to his remote ancestor, and with a rebirth of the Rev. Andrew's religious fervor. A sequence of events obliges this tender, quixotic boy to return to the settlement of Canaan and struggle as his forefather did with the heathens. This immortal living force that even more than the Rev. Andrew's progeny is the central figure of the novel, and that seemed to body forth a vividly confirming corollary to the biological ideal of slow upward progression, has turned and swallowed its own beginnings like a serpent. . . .

The tempered detachment of *God's Stepchildren* lends its panorama of a century of South African life a mellow, clarified forbearance; sensational incidents fall into accurate perspective. Yet the reader is helplessly involved in the affairs of these struggling, suffering, aspiring characters. Mrs. Millin has recognized the fundamental duality of actor and spectator of each of us; her magic of absorption of the reader's being is so thoroughgoing that this divided self is witnessing and experiencing an organic existence of its own with the insistently provocative materials she has provided.

The scene is South Africa, and the situation exploits the varying degrees of friction between the blacks and the whites. Mrs. Millin has so exactly conditioned her setting and her drama that they could do no other than qualify the circumstances which she enumerates. Yet their total impact is such that a universal application is indicated. If it were only a tale of South Africa, or merely a subtle study of the interplay of race and color, it would still be a distinguished performance. . . .

This is a book to read and to treasure and to fight over and to contend with. It cannot be laid aside, once it is started; it cannot be readily forgotten once it is finished. It is fertile incitement to endless and delightful discussion. It is thoughtful and witty and stimulating and exciting and profoundly stirring. It is apt to unsettle rooted (it was inadvertently spelled ''rotted,'' which might stand as unintentional satire) convictions, to force a ''revaluation of old values,'' and to increase, rather than dispel,

those disintegrating doubts which seem so much a spirit of this age. Yet it is not depressing to a robust and healthy organism. It seems to say, with refreshing doggedness and gallantry, life may be a sorry gamble, yet we may ''win at the turn of the game.''

God's Stepchildren brings to focus all the nebulous spiritual and material quests of this every-day now; it is a classic of our own times. It apparently brings to bear all the equipment of modern learning and science upon the problem of observing human conduct, yet the record shows no trace of tedious analysis. The chronicle of the Rev. Andrew Flood and his progeny is there, all there, inevitably there, without an excess word or syllable. It had to happen so, and there is nothing to do about it except to enjoy *God's Stepchildren* and offer praise for Sarah Gertrude Millin.

> John W. Crawford, ''Black Blood to the Third and Fourth Generations,'' *in* The New York Times Book Review, *February 1, 1925, p. 11.*

H. L. MENCKEN

[*God's Stepchildren*] is a sociological study more than a novel—a searching and mordant treatise, often brilliant, upon the effects of racial mixtures. . . .

[Mrs. Millin has] a truly astonishing capacity for narrative. Her story starts to move on the very first page, and there is not a sign of slackening to the end. Nothing is unnecessary; nothing is without its appositeness and its effect. One is dragged along by it as by some external and irresistible force; it is immensely engrossing and unflaggingly readable. In brief, the story of the Rev. Andrew Flood, a missionary, and of the corruption of his blood. Flood goes out to the Cape in 1821 to convert the Hottentots, and discovers to his dismay that his Christian theology simply amuses them. They detect embarrassing discrepancies in Holy Writ; they are full of devastating criticisms of Christian ethics. Flood decides that he must attack them in some dramatic and overwhelming manner. The Hottentot damsel, Silla, is conveniently at hand. What if he should marry her? Wouldn't her fellow savages respect him and give ear to him then? Moreover, isn't she tempting otherwise, with her youthful bloom and wriggly hips? So Flood persuades a reluctant and horrified fellow missionary to join him to her by book and bell, and proceeds at once to consummate their union.

The rest of the story is the chronicle of their descendants. They have a daughter, Deborah, and in due time she succumbs extralegally to a wandering young Boer, one Hans Kleinhans. The issue is a son, and Deborah names him simply Kleinhans: it is both his given name and his substitute for a surname. Kleinhans, growing up, sprouts a blond beard, and decides to move over into the white race. But when he tries it at Kimberly the alert Nordics of the mines detect the imposture, and he gets a beating that cures him of his aspiration. Then he marries a half-caste girl, Lena Schmidt, alias Smith, and they have a large family. One of their children, Elmira, is very beautiful, and almost white. She is sent to school by Adam Lindsell, her father's employer, but an illness reveals her black blood, and she is turned out. Eventually Lindsell, who has no color prejudice, marries her, and they have a son, Barry. In this Barry the tragi-comedy comes to its last act. The fanaticism of old Andrew Flood, after three generations of quiescence, flares up. Barry has taken holy orders and married an Englishwoman. Now he resolves to expiate the evil of both sides of the house. ''This is my vow,'' he says. ''For my sin in begetting him I am not to see my child. And for the sorrow I share with him I am to go among my brown people to help them.'' It sounds melodramatic, and even maudlin. But there is surely nothing maudlin in Mrs. Millin's story. How many novels have been written around the tragedy of mixed blood! But how many of them do you remember? Here is one, I believe, that will stick longer than the others. It is an extremely artful, knowing and moving piece of work. (pp. 507-08)

> *H. L. Mencken, in a review of "God's Stepchildren," in* American Mercury, *Vol. V, No. 20, August, 1925, pp. 507-08.*

MILTON WALDMAN

Stated baldly in synopsis, the plot of **Mary Glenn** suggests the most sentimental of popular novels. The heroine is a snob of low birth living in a South African town; she marries the ineffectual scion of a good English family in order to dazzle the circle on whose fringe she hangs, after refusing a young farmer of good but unexciting prospects; the latter espouses her friend on the rebound and prospers greatly, eventually becoming the economic saviour of Mary and her husband. The situation is solved and the unhappy twain brought together by the death of their son, who has been shot in error by his father while on a hunting expedition.

But if Mrs. Millin puts her people in sentimental or sensational situations she sees them neither sensationally nor sentimentally. It is a valuable gift, this, to concoct plots with all the potential thrills of a best seller while adhering steadily to the line of truth where character and human relations are concerned. It is a gift that has been vouchsafed to most of the great English novelists, and explains perhaps why *Oliver Twist* or *The Return of the Native* can be read with keen interest by a large and unexacting portion of the fiction-loving public. In **Mary Glenn** this feat is particularly pronounced. None of the characters are in themselves of a sort to enlist sympathy, neither the snob, the passive ne'er-do-well, the stodgy, respectable farmer nor his dowdy, commonplace wife. Yet so rapid and intense is the action, so swift and penetrating the exposition of these people's characters, achieved on the wing as it were, that only urgent demands of time could conceivably cause a reader to lay the small volume aside before its conclusion. Part of this effect of speed is due, no doubt, to the author's brave technique—the *fortissimo* opening, containing the urgent and unexplained appeal to the Van Aardts to come at once: the unrolling of the necessary previous information during the rapid motor ride over the veldt, and the almost immediate entry upon the climax, the search for the missing boy.

But this technique, although useful in obtaining excitement and compression, exposes one grave fault in Mrs. Millin's method—her jerky, undistinguished, monotonous style. It is an exceedingly delicate matter to present past events; the pluperfect and past conditional tenses do not lend themselves to easy writing, and most authors choose to avoid them whenever possible. Mrs. Millin does not, and although her method may make for gains in intimacy and even verisimilitude, it loses in flow and balance. . . . That this indirect, awkward, nervous fashion of exposition is not evidence of total inability on the authoress' part to write well can be seen from several passages at the end of the book, where the torrential stream slows down and broadens out to its peaceful end. . . . There is so much matter in this little book that it might well have been longer; Mrs. Millin would, I think, have improved on her own fine achievement

by a less intransigent insistence on compression and a more generous concession to the graces of style. (pp. 542-43)

> *Milton Waldman, in a review of "Mary Glenn," in* The London Mercury, *Vol. XII, No. 71, September, 1925, pp. 542-44.*

THE NEW YORK TIMES BOOK REVIEW

Out of material that might well have gone toward a rereading of the time-tried Cinderella legend, Mrs. Millin [in her novel **Mary Glenn**] has fashioned the tragedy of a snob set into a comedy of manners. Mary Glenn has all the attributes of a fairy-tale heroine: good looks, talent, kindness to her mother, and lack of recognition for her virtues. In the absence of the all-powerful godmother, Mary resorts to her own imagination to create for herself a Prince Charming, and a social status in keeping with her ambition. . . .

In Mary Glenn's case, the chimney corner is the low estimation of her importance which is entertained by her fellow-townsmen in Lebanon, South Africa. Mrs. Millin pictures the ludicrous attempts of the little ''mushroom'' town to pattern itself upon a picture-paper London, and to ape a social stratification which bears all the marks of authenticity except the organic right to exist. Mary knows it for what it is, yet cannot quiet her envy and her craving for its recognition. Mary is at length accepted, after her striving has left her empty-handed and stricken low. The condescending compassion of her inclusion by Lebanon is one more turn of the knife.

Since it is to London that her little world looks, Mary also grasps at London, or rather at the young Englishman strayed to Cape Town. He is her ''face card''; all too late, she realizes that manners and accent, ''face,'' are indeed everything this poor weak mortal has to offer. It is one more instance of the contrast between Mary's aspirations and her achievements which substantiates the splendid visioning of fundamental irony on Mrs. Millin's part. The very instrument to which Mary looks for her salvation is the agency of her complete and ultimate diminishment. Mary's return, after five years in England, is indeed a beginning of a new order. Her husband and her son, Jackie, her new English accent, and her dressing for dinner are outward signs of an access in grace. Mary's pathetic little show drags her lower, eventually, than if she had brought her family in the actual rags of their bankruptcy. Mary's only hope, her only ''pawn to fate,'' is the engaging young aristocrat, her son, Jackie.

A superfluous gesture of depreciation of herself comes in time, beneath the successive shocks of humiliation, to assume the malignant growth of a canker of self-hatred. Mrs. Millin seems tacitly to intimate that a failure of honest pride in self is a defect amounting almost to a cardinal sin. It is this for which Mary must appear to have suffered retribution, this rottenness of self-contempt, rather than Mary's trivial prettifications, her harmless poses, her sadly futile efforts toward a superficial grandiloquence. Those are merely effects, external evidence of a deeply rooted falsehood. Mary's castigation is of a terrible sublimity, an unbelievable, far-reaching, ethical appropriateness; it is very slightly short of the austere calibre of the Old Testament; Mary might be of the blood of David, mourning in self-abasement and true humility for her lost Absalom, the sprightly Jackie. . . .

While the climax brings a complete and overwhelming reversal of the situation for Mary, Mrs. Millin is too courageous, too penetrating in insight, and too uncompromising to leave Mary utterly dejected. Resilience, the return of balance, the unquenchable course of life swings back to sweep Mary onward, perhaps a little less resistant this time.

Mary Glenn is, incidentally, an able comment on the malaise of British colonials. One of Mary's deficiencies is an unseeing oblivion toward her material surroundings, an insistence upon the superfluous ameliorations of a purely imaginary London. Mary, and possibly many colonials with her, sickens for an unattainable never-never land. Mrs. Millin's new book is a thrilling and swiftly moving tale in itself. It is the most vivid picture of South African life which she has yet given. It is further a significant and provocative stimulus to the question of current standards. The distance Mrs. Millin has covered between her first novel, *The Dark River*, and *Mary Glenn* is alone indicative of a noble and responsible talent. She has attained to compassion without softening to sentiment; she has acquired assurance of judgment without becoming clever, and she is simple without resorting to formula. She is one of the notable writers of this generation.

> *"Snobbery in South Africa," in* The New York Times Book Review, *January 31, 1926, p. 9.*

THE TIMES LITERARY SUPPLEMENT

Mrs. Millin, who can so well depict the South African country and character, has not made very much use of either in her new novel, *An Artist in the Family,* but has concentrated her efforts on the portrait of a very tiresome young man whose likeness has been drawn many, many times before. Theo Bissaker is selfish, dishonest, vain, entirely without affection, and a parasite upon his impoverished parents; but we are asked to believe that his winning smile and his personal charm were such that no one could resist him. Whether his painting was worth anything at all is left to conjecture, and whether he sincerely believed in himself is not quite apparent, but he liked painting, and paint he would. His father and mother farmed in South Africa, and did very badly out of it, even when their elder son, Tom, brought his more modern ideas from an agricultural college to help them; but they were immensely ambitious for Theo to go to Cambridge and become a barrister. When they had given him twelve hundred pounds, and Tom had made his contribution too, they learned that Theo had deceived them for nearly three years; that he had not been near Cambridge but had been playing about in various art schools; and that, far from being at all likely to repay them at any time, he was now on his way home penniless and suffering from lung trouble.

The story is written with restraint and simplicity, and Mr. and Mrs. Bissaker are figures of reality, particularly angry, anxious Mr. Bissaker, disappointed and contemptuous but unable to smother a queer admiration for Theo's very ineffectiveness. . . . There is a glimpse of South Africa that is interesting in the account of the mission station and the nearly white teachers shocked and flattered by Theo's patronage. The end of the book is melodrama, quietly handled it is true, but disconcerting to admirers of this writer's earlier novels with their sincerity and force.

> *A review of "An Artist in the Family," in* The Times Literary Supplement, *No. 1357, February 2, 1928, p. 78.*

PERCY HUTCHISON

In *An Artist in the Family,* Mrs. Sarah Millin adds a not unworthy successor to *God's Stepchildren* and *Mary Glenn.* The story is not notable, and it does not, in spite of the jacket "blurb," certify the author as just a step below the immortals. Mrs. Millin has a hard climb ahead of her ere she reach the heights. But *An Artist in the Family* has many solid literary virtues. The author has marshaled a cast of characters each of whom is an individual, and has set them off one against another, has sent them clashing one with another, in a manner that is impressive for its naturalism.

Life among the English-speaking populace in East Africa is, one gathers, much like life everywhere. In the smaller towns folk are conservative, a trifle smug. The Bissakers are such a family. They own a farm near one of the towns of the veldt. They have two sons, the elder a solid citizen, like themselves; to be depended on to act sanely, to work industriously, to love his wife and to bring up his children thoughtfully. The younger son, Theo, has the more alert mind, is more original of ideas, and early shows artistic talent. The father, ignoring this, at considerable sacrifice, sends the youth to Cambridge to study for the law.

Theo, it appears, did not matriculate; in fact, he scarcely invaded the university grounds. Instead, he betook himself to Italy to paint, and sent letters to his parent via a friend in Cambridge, so that they should bear the deceiving postmark. Also, he nearly contracts tuberculosis, in consequence of which, at doctor's orders, he returns to Africa; and fully and legally contracts matrimony, or rather, more than fully, the girl being already the mother of a child, and an illegitimate child at that.

Mrs. Millin's purpose in this somewhat fantastic array of episodes is to establish Theo as a romantic egotist set in a world of realities which he in no wise comprehends, and with which he is temperamentally and actually at variance. The girl he has married from pity and a fanatical notion of chivalry, not from love. She is a witless creature; and actually Theo hates her. This woman Mrs. Millin places in conflict with Theo's mother, equally selfish, but through the higher motive of her maternal affection for her son, and contrasts her with the wife of Theo's elder brother, an over-virtuous female with a distinctly rationalistic turn of mind, the only person in the book, one is moved to remark in passing, thus completely endowed. . . .

And still Theo goes on, believing that he is destined to be one of the world's great artists, and through his egotism ruining all, including himself. (p. 2)

The novel comes to a fantastic and wholly unperceived ending. Theo, believing his mother's life threatened, resolves on a sacrifice as unnecessary as it is ill conceived. Love is not the motive. . . .

What Theo's extraordinary deed is the reader will be left to discover for himself; and the story will not be etched in further. The question of critical interest lies in what Mrs. Millin has attempted to do rather than in what she has done. The attempt is a study of the artistic temperament, with its frequent corollary of overweening egotism. Many having come into contact, perhaps painful contact, with its human expression. Her thesis is, we venture to say, Does art justify the giving of so much pain? But is the thesis sound? Has not Mrs. Millin, in the character she has drawn, posed so extreme an example as to make her conclusion particular and not general? In other words, is not Theo a maniac—in a mild way—and is not the book a study, not of the egotism of art but of egotism per se? We believe it is, and as such it is a consistent document, but belonging rightfully in the realm of morbid psychology.

And that being the case, the present writer would have preferred the story done in a somewhat different manner. Mrs. Millin, in *An Artist in the Family,* writes objectively; the acts of her characters claim attention rather than the motivation behind the acts. Yet Mrs. Millin has a Henry James theme, and she handles it not in the manner of Henry James but in the manner of one engaged only in telling a story. To some, of course, this may not seem a disadvantage. The reverse, perhaps. By adopting it, the author attains to the dramatic more frequently than would otherwise be the case. And the book has more of clarity than it could have had in the Jamesian manner. (p. 18)

> *Percy Hutchison, "Sarah Millin Studies the Artistic Temperament," in* The New York Times Book Review, *March 11, 1928, pp. 2, 18.*

JOHN R. CHAMBERLAIN

The art of Sarah Gertrude Millin is so perfect as to seem almost mechanical. Her situations dovetail so marvelously, her characters act and react upon one another with such precision and so in line with the ironic progression of the story, that one can only sit back and wonder at the grasp this South African writer has on all the essentials of novel writing. Moreover, her artifice does not lead one to snort out the epithet, "carpentry," for she has a sure knack of delineating people of any class or race, whether man or woman, and she makes her story spring inevitably from character. Her one lack is not that of an artist; it is that of personality.

And is it a lack? The Flaubertians would not say so. For, like the author of *Madame Bovary,* who deliberately kept himself out of his work, Miss Millin lets her drama take its course without intruding herself into the book. It is true that she makes comments of a vaguely cosmic sort, but they are of such universal acceptance that they seem merely inserted to aid the progress of the narrative. What she does not do is to color her book with whatever prejudices she may possess; one could not take her novels and, following the psychoanalyst, reconstruct Miss Millin from them. That is why those who like their novels for what they reveal about the personalities of the creators do not rank Miss Millin among the greatest of earth.

Nevertheless, it is a first-class novelist who wrote *The Coming of the Lord.* (p. 4)

The whole trouble hinged upon an epileptic negro, a theologian who had learned in Baptist America to swallow his Bible whole. This theologian, Aaron, has his adherents, whom he had baptized the Levites. For six years they had been visiting the height beyond the town of Gibeon annually. The seventh year being the Sabbath, in which the Rev. Aaron confidently expected from biblical evidence that the Lord would appear unto the Kaffir Levites, bringing glory and food for all, the 2,500 followers had bivouacked beyond the town, kraaled their cattle and sat down in indolence to wait the heavenly day.

The presence of the "niggers" on the height was disturbing to Arnold Duerdon. . . . Major Duerdon, a handsome, well set up, socially graceful man with the subtlety of a 6-year-old, had failed as a lawyer, but he excelled at arranging tournaments and organizing the Vigilants, who were to watch the Kaffirs.

There was an old Jew in Gibeon, Old Nathan, a shopkeeper whose sole diversion was his weekly game of chess with the

German, Dr. Diethelm. Dr. Diethelm had lost his son in the war. The son had fought with the English, but that had not prevented a partisan rabble from wrecking the doctor's consulting room. Dr. Diethelm had a fair practice, but his heart was eaten with rancor. And when Old Nathan told him that Saul Nathan, a living son, was returning to Gibeon to practice medicine, it meant the temporary end of the friendship and the chess. Dr. Diethelm could not stand intimacy with a man whose son was there as a flesh and blood comfort.

Dr. Saul Nathan came back. He was of a mind to join the Vigilants, because he yearned for acceptance, even though Old Nathan considered the Vigilants as creating trouble by their very existence. So Saul went to the Duerdon home, there to meet Hermia, Arnold's capable wife. Hermia, who was the Duerdon breadwinner (she did it by singing and acting as "Our Gibeon Correspondent"), engaged Saul in casual talk. It transpired that she agreed with Old Nathan in a low estimate of the Vigilants' usefulness. Saul, his spirit leaping to a respect for Hermia and a desire for her friendliness and companionship, went away without seeing Arnold. He had decided against the Vigilants.

What followed seems inevitable, the way Miss Millin tells it. Saul and Hermia walk and talk together. Arnold likes Saul—his first liking for a Jew—in spite of the young physician's refusal to join the Vigilants. And meanwhile old Dr. Diethelm is stewing in rancor, an emotion that boils over when Arnold tries to force him into working with the Vigilants. "You warn me about the Kaffirs," says Dr. Diethelm. "I warn you about your wife. Your wife and the Jew."

The words, released in venom born of misunderstanding that began when the British sacked the old doctor's consulting room during the World War, have all sorts of consequences. (pp. 4, 20)

With Saul dead, the pitiful, inoffensive, fundamentally likeable Saul, and with the Levites wiped out, Gibeon is able to settle down to its normal rote. The Duerdons are reconciled, and Dr. Diethelm resumes his chess with Old Nathan. The irony of the book is the greater because none of its tragedy was necessary; that is, none of it would have been necessary had the responsible actors been endowed with reasonable intelligence. The triumph of *The Coming of the Lord* lies in Miss Millin's compassionate understanding of people of small minds as well as of people of intelligence; she populates a region that is recognizable as a living section of earth. She has done the undernourished backwater community, with its human pettiness, better, we judge, than any one since Ibsen wrote *An Enemy of the People.* (p. 20)

> *John R. Chamberlain, "Mrs. Millin Offers an Ironic Tale of Human Pettiness," in* The New York Times Book Review, *September 30, 1928, pp. 4, 20.*

THE TIMES LITERARY SUPPLEMENT

In *The Coming of the Lord* Mrs. Sarah Gertrude Millin once more induces in the reader a momentary suspension of disbelief. It is not more than momentary; that is one of the things which distinguishes Mrs. Millin and the other good realistic novelists from the great creative writers. For with a great imaginative work disbelief remains, in that particular instance, finally suspended; we can never quite escape from its spell. Even a little genius can hold us; but let that fiery bond be lacking and, the book closed, we are back again in our everyday incredulity.

So it is with this chronicle of a religious revival and its reactions on a group of individuals. The small Transvaal town of Gibeon is menaced, or believes itself menaced, by the coming of the Levites, a fanatical Kaffir fraternity, to the Heights just outside the town.... And so the Levites straggle up, 2,500 of them, to await the Lord's coming, and Duerden, the militant solicitor of Gibeon, falls to drilling his Vigilants, and the Government, having wheedled in vain, begins to threaten, and, having threatened in vain, sends mounted police and aeroplanes and a machine-gun to dislodge the tiresome black believers from their tabernacle on the Heights. But before this the Levite pilgrimage has had its psychological effect on the inhabitants of Gibeon. Saul Nathan, the doctor, son of an old Jewish storekeeper, has refused to join Duerden's Vigilants because he hopes his refusal will please Duerden's wife; and between the two, the cultured, introspective woman and the young Jew, has grown up an intimacy which may kindle to more than spiritual heat. Old Dr. Diethelm, the German, too, has refused to join the Vigilants, because his son died fighting against Germany, because his sacrifice has been ignored, above all because he wants to annoy Duerden. But at last he goes too far in his desire to annoy Duerden; he warns the arrogant, stupid, well-meaning man of the friendship between his wife and the Jew. It is the signal for a series of psychological explosions, the last of which coincides with a civil explosion....

We are left, then, where we began, since Saul, when the book opens, has not come back from England to complicate his father's existence, and since Hermia Duerden returns after his death to her husband. And in another sense we are left where we began, because Mrs. Millin, despite a sympathetic study of the two old men, Diethelm and Old Nathan, succeeds only in interesting us and not in making her characters part of our emotional experience.

A review of "The Coming of the Lord," in The Times Literary Supplement, No. 1393, October 11, 1928, p. 730.

THE TIMES LITERARY SUPPLEMENT

What will please the reader particularly in Mrs. Sarah Gertrude Millin's novel **The Fiddler** is its simplicity and directness. It would have been easy to ruin this episode—for it is not more—by sentimentality or by piling upon it a mass of corroborative detail. Mrs. Millin proves that, in a novel, concentration is one of the most telling factors.... Janet Mars running away by night with Matthew Harkness, the first violin at the hotel at Lourenço Marques, was ... the witness of an unpremeditated crime. When the drunken car-driver, in the middle of the bush, demanded an extortionate addition to the agreed fare to Johannesburg and threw Matthew's violin out on to the ground, Matthew shot him in blind rage. The worthless life he ended was a secondary matter; the primary matter was that he abruptly ended an illusion. We have to accept the illusion, Jennie Mars, a model wife, was carried away, and not even against her better judgment. She found that she had no judgment and no conscience. This, her first passion, seemed a thing outside normal life at her husband's side, to which she would go back. It was irresistible. She existed outside her old self, a young girl again, more virginal than before.

Mrs. Millin makes us realize this break of continuity in the woman's existence, inexplicable but not abnormal: and she

contrasts the woman's unreflecting self-abandonment with the surrender, not without misgiving, of a weak and cautious man. Harkness, though vain and a fascinator of women, cared, at heart, only for safety. Luck had been against him, or he would have been sheltered with the wife and family to whom he was attached. Janet, not a great passion, carried him off his feet: the murder and its consequences brought him to the ground. His only thought is to concoct a good defence, to be acquitted and to go home. With painful directness Mrs. Millin traces every step of his spiritual degradation as he awaits arrest and trial. Janet, for all the bitterness of realization, remains noble till the end.... She perjures herself to free him, and still loving him and not blaming him she relapses, as he had done, into protecting arms.... So ends a story which, though slight, is a work of art.

A review of "The Fiddler," in The Times Literary Supplement, No. 1435, August 1, 1929, p. 606.

JOHN CHAMBERLAIN

Sarah Gertrude Millin is one of the most self-effacing artists in the world. Her novels are uncluttered with the prejudices and the personal interests that find their way into the work of most writers of fiction; her characters live in their own right, for she succeeds phenomenally in separating them from herself. Her sense of drama is sure: she has the command of the expert over the mechanics of fiction, and, luckily, she does not let this technical ability defeat her ends. For, however her novels may dovetail, however much she may depend on a blow from fate to start or resolve a train of events, she never forgets that her characters must not violate their own rhythm and integrity....

In **God's Step-Children** and **The Coming of the Lord** she has done work that is more important in the sociological sense; these books not only succeeded in creating a living array of people, fine as well as petty, but they dealt with far-reaching problems of racial conflict and religious hysteria. In **The Fiddler** she has done something of the limited scope of **An Artist in the Family,** choosing for one of her characters a sensitive, vacillating, artistic nature much like the painter, Theo Bissaker, of the latter book.

The story Miss Millin has to tell in **The Fiddler** is not exactly new in any sense. But the treatment of the problem in altering affections, adultery, unpremeditated murder and flight is such that the antique triangular arrangement is forgotten. Miss Millin has selected a situation growing out of old motives, but the important thing is that she has understood these motives. Amid all the perils that lie in wait for those who tread their way through seductions, elopements, unexpected murder, and jail and court room incidents, this South African novelist moves with certainty; the psychology never seems wrong.

From Jennie Mars, the English girl who is married contentedly enough to an elderly Nyasaland tobacco planter, to Matthew, the sentimental, romanticizing and emotionally unstable fiddler, the characters are appealing. Not one of them is wholly good, not one is wholly bad; and they contain within themselves the elements of their destruction. You like them, not for reasons of nobility or personality, but because you understand and pity them....

[From the point where Matthew murders a taxi-driver] Miss Millin's sure understanding of human psychology stands her in good stead. Matthew can't bear insecurity; the fact that he is a murderer eats away his passion for Jennie, and the remainder of the book is a matter of making the most of the emotional conflicts of Jennie and the fiddler as they fluctuate between pity and dislike, tenderness and hate, comradeship and cruelty.

Miss Millin writes nice, short sentences. There is fervor in them, but it is fervor held in vigilant restraint. This artistic watchfulness of Miss Millin's saves her again and again from sentimentality. Her one lack, as we have said elsewhere, is a lack of talent for poetry, a lack of profusion in imagination, of that elusive element of personality. Some like it in the novel; some don't. Personally, we are always grateful when a little of it is thrown in to round out the measure.

> *John Chamberlain, "Miss Millin Revitalizes an Old Story," in* The New York Times Book Review, *August 4, 1929, p. 7.*

WINIFRED HOLTBY

Mrs. Millin is a realist. Her novels have something of the austere and disciplined solidity of classic work. They show moreover a suggestive technical development from the more loosely woven, ambling domestic narratives of her early writings, to the controlled and masterly compression of *Mary Glenn, The Coming of the Lord* and *The Fiddler.* She always has a profound and steady insight into the deeper springs of human action, a rather sober sense of humour, and that quality which Jane Austen possessed in its highest degree of endowing small details of daily life with intense significance and interest. Her home is in Johannesburg, and she writes mainly of the Transvaal, though *The Dark River* deals with outlying diggings, *Adam's Rest* was on the Cape side of the Vaal River, and the tragedy of *The Fiddler* takes place at Lourenço Marques and in Swaziland, though it might equally well have happened anywhere. She deals with middle class people, with the quiet domestic life that will suddenly flare up into drama or tragedy. In *Mary Glenn* and *The Fiddler* the tragedy is wholly personal; in *The Coming of the Lord* and *The Jordans* it is partly political. Her best known, though not perhaps her best novel, *God's Stepchildren,* treats the colour question with the same impartial, objective, penetrating, unemotional justice that she brings to the problem of the artistic temperament in *An Artist in the Family,* or the sorrows of snobbery in *Mary Glenn.* Once she wrote a book which was not a novel. *The South Africans* is a brilliant, compressed, graphic survey of South Africa to-day. She has chosen her own method; her ability for selecting the illuminating detail has stood her in good stead. Nobody else could have picked the way so wisely, so justly and so humorously among the chaotic confusion of controversial detail in which any historian of South Africa must be involved.

Mrs. Millin's work stands by its intellectual strength, its integrity, its justice. She is one of the most interesting of modern realists. (pp. 280-81)

> *Winifred Holtby, "Writers of South Africa," in* The Bookman, *London, Vol. LXXVI, No. 456, September, 1929, pp. 279-84.*

THE NEW YORK TIMES BOOK REVIEW

Adam's Rest marks a new and not altogether successful departure for Sarah Gertrude Millin. In the past this South African writer has generally worked her sense of drama and her keen perception of irony for all they were worth, and her inability to give us a really profound interpretation of life has been compensated by sure-footed craftsmanship.... *Adam's Rest* offers none of the sharp conflicts, none of the arresting juxtapositions, of the former Millin stories. It is a novel of life in a South African village called Adam's Rest—one of those towns which might yield up an Emma Bovary or a Hedda Gabler. But in the present case no Hedda, no Emma, is offered; instead we get the parallel life stories of two sisters whose days wear themselves away by attrition, and there is no real attempt by either sister to break through the vicious circle of the uneventful and the boring. (p. 6)

Janet, the younger sister, marries a good-natured, optimistic, thoroughly lazy soldier who is billeted in Adam's Rest during the Boer War. It is her one flare-up, and the rest of her life, including the realization of the failure of her eldest son to achieve his early promise, is mildly dispiriting. Janet lacks the capacity to suffer greatly, and she does not question much; therefore her life is lacking in real significance. Her sister, Miriam, is somewhat different. She has her standards, and the spectacle of miscegenation disturbs her. It is as if the sight of white men and half-caste women giving themselves to each other had built itself into her fiber and caused her to fear what, between two persons of the same race, is regarded as entirely normal. Then, too, the daily presence of her aunt, Laura, whose disfigured face is a symbol of enforced negation, complicates the feeling caused by the proximity of the half-breed. As a result of her inhibited nature Miriam is never really able to accept anything. All she can do is to waver between a desire to sacrifice herself in some noble cause, and a wish to get more out of life than the daily round. Her feeling for her husband is not love; but she never reacts from its tepidity in a way that leads to drama.

No doubt Miss Millin has achieved just the sort of effect she intended in *Adam's Rest*. There are moments of feminine insight (as when Miriam toys with a consumptive artist because her husband takes her for granted), and there is no little skill in presenting the uneventful as the uneventful. But for a novelist who is capable of *The Coming of the Lord* to so limit her scope is rather distressing. In *Adam's Rest* Miss Millin's material has betrayed her. (pp. 6-7)

> *"Dispiriting Lives," in* The New York Times Book Review, *September 7, 1930, pp. 6-7.*

FRED T. MARSH

The theme of the passionate, high-strung individual in conflict with an environment that has but recently grown out of a pioneer stage, one in which the harsh, forceful code of a former fighting generation has become a mere set piece of social superstitions, is a favorite with novelists who deal with the social side of living in the so-called newer portions of the globe.... Mrs. Millin, in all of those of her books which I have read, pursues this theme as it manifests itself in South Africa with unflagging devotion. In [*Adam's Rest*] she shows greater depth and restraint than hitherto. She dissects her Miriam pitilessly enough in the early chapters—pitilessly, I say, since the character is only that of a superior child and young girl and adolescent with quite normal fancies and day dreams—but she avoids the hammer-and-tongs vindictiveness against both the sensitive and the stupid which made *An Artist in the Family* such an abominable book. She is not so well satisfied with a merely clever and oftentimes superficial analysis of emotion-stuffed figures.

Adam's Rest is the name of a village in the Cape Colony. Mr. Lincoln, an ineffectual, grey—later to become white—little gentleman, is the apothecary in this village. Aunt Laura, a vividly sketched character, a shy woman, who as a young girl had been disfigured in an accident, is glad to keep house for him in this secluded corner of the world. Mr. Lincoln has two daughters. Janet is pretty, matter-of-fact, satisfied with her fate so long as things go well. But Miriam is—well, different. She has imagination, vague ambitions and desires. She feels that at Adam's Rest she is cut off from all that she longs to get out of life. But Miriam is intelligent. She knows she has no special talent. So her wild flights of fancy end neither in follies nor in frustration. Instead she marries the one man among her acquaintanceship whom she should have married. She makes a charming hostess and a wise wife and mother. The novel covers the greater part of Miriam's life, follows haphazardly the fortunes of the other members of her family and of such outsiders as play a part in her life. It ends shortly after Janet, who married a soldier during the Boer War, loses her son, a talented youngster whom Miriam loved more than she did her own daughter, in the World War. . . .

The Crofts, an ambitious family of mixed blood, are divided among themselves. Those whose skins are light enough "keep white," refusing to associate with colored folk outside their own family, avidly seeking white friendships. Some of the children marry white men. But people like the Lincolns, though they may stop and talk with them, may not walk with them. Even Miriam, whose heart bleeds for the Kaffirs, will have nothing to do with such people. And for certain special reasons she comes to hate all the Crofts who seem to be always in her path.

The stories of the Croft family and the Lincoln family run side by side without ever fusing. Mrs. Millin does not seem to aim at a perfect unity or, better, completeness. She leaves many loose threads lying about. Miriam's husband bores her, one imagines, so he remains a shade, a sort of Sir Charles Grandison of his time and place. Janet's stupid, unsuccessful husband amuses her, so he is done to perfection. Janet, herself, sinks out of the picture from what had been an important niche, and little Isabel, Miriam's daughter, comes up out of nowhere to develop into a tennis champion and marry a biologist. But Mrs. Millin continues to show those bits of deftness, even of inspiration, in character reading which has always given her work a note of real distinction.

Fred T. Marsh, "Conflict with Environment," in New York Herald Tribune Books, September 14, 1930, p. 4.

THE NEW YORK TIMES BOOK REVIEW

The story of **The Sons of Mrs. Aab** is a good one . . . and attests the increasing maturity of Mrs. Millin's art. It displays a remarkable complexity of character and motive and contains a variety of figures ably handled and clearly defined. There is Mrs. Aab, the large, determined, hopelessly unattractive daughter of a prosperous farmer, who deserts her respectable family to marry the shiftless and disreputable Nicholas Aab and to live with him in the remote mining settlement of Sheba. She descends to the social level of her handsome husband, to the class of the "poor whites," without apparent regret. After the death of Nicholas Aab Mrs. Aab carries on, supporting herself by sorting bantams, the small, flawed stones from the diggings.

There are her two sons, survivors of her brood of seven children. Gideon, the elder, is a clever and ambitious boy, anxious to leave Sheba and make his way in the world. Hercules, the younger, is a Mongolian idiot, living on through childhood and adolescence into maturity in defiance of the doctor's prophecy, his infantile bronchial trouble, and the influenza epidemic. These are the figures of the principal plot; the subplot concerns the fortunes of Fanny King, a sex-starved school-teacher secretly in love wih a handsome drunkard, George Redmarsh, and destined finally to marry Gideon Aab.

In the realm of the grotesque the picture of Hercules, the idiot boy, represents a veritable triumph. Cherished by his mother and protected from the harshness of life at the expense of his brother, he becomes the central figure in the conflict of Gideon's life. Gideon hates Hercules because he is a monster and because of the wrong to himself that he symbolizes. He shrinks with loathing from the animal-like devotion with which Hercules fawns upon him. And against his will he pities him. Working futilely in the worn-out diamond mines of Sheba, and wasting his small earnings to buy comforts for Hercules, Gideon raged against his fate, against the circumstances which had deprived him of education and freedom. When he found that he could, fraudulently but with a good chance of success, insure Hercules's life in his own behalf, he grasped at the opportunity. Fraud or none, Gideon felt an essential justice in this plan to get back his own from the uncomprehending Hercules. Begun almost by accident, the plan grows into the dominating motive of Gideon's life, cripples his enterprises in other directions, tempts him to murder, and brings him to ultimate ruin.

The world Mrs. Millin describes is a world dominated by accident, a world in which fate is no more than blind chance, carrying some men to honor and fortune and ruining others without justice or logic. There is no right nor wrong, no reward nor punishment, save in the minds of the helpless victims of destiny. Unfortunately, Mrs. Millin has not been wholly impartial in her portrayal of this world. There are no beneficent accidents, and the proportion of malignant accidents is rather too high for complete verisimilitude. Then, too, she displays a certain inconsistent taste for melodrama and coincidence. The deus ex machina never actually arrives, but she gives one reason constantly to expect him.

A review of "The Sons of Mrs. Aab," in The New York Times Book Review, August 30, 1931, p. 6.

L.A.G. STRONG

The Sons of Mrs. Aab errs a little on the side of over-arrangement. Mrs. Millin's characters carry in them, it is true, the seeds of their own destruction; but we feel that Mrs. Millin put them there.

Caroline, gaunt, big-boned, fell in love with a "poor white" named Nicholas Aab, and in defiance of her parents married him. Turned out, she came to the little mining town of Sheba, and the hardships of a digger's livelihood. Her first son, Gideon, throve; but the next to survive was the seventh, Hercules, a Mongoloid idiot. Caroline clung to his life and brought him to maturity. Everyone and everything she sacrificed without scruple to the needs of the gentle, mooncalf creature: and Gideon learned to hate him bitterly. Taking advantage of the local doctor's drunkenness, he persuaded him to certify a fraudulent application to insure the idiot's life. The application was accepted; and the day when he should claim full benefit became the one hope of Gideon's dreary existence. The hope sustained him through ill-luck, through the fiasco of his marriage to poor Fanny, through his slow degradation, to the day when, half out of his mind, he listened to the evangelist Carey and arranged to go the roads with him, consigning his mother and Hercules to the care of separate institutions. How Caroline frustrated the plan, and how, in ultimate misfortune, Gideon lost his benefit from the insurance, completes his grim and moving story. The story of Fanny runs parallel. The severe little school teacher fell in love with the remittance man, George Redmarsh, a drunken loafer who knew how to make himself agreeable to women. He went away, and she remained faithful to her memories even after the day she met him, reclaimed, rejuvenated, about to marry a thoroughly nice young girl. Fanny never loved Gideon. She was just another of the things in his life that went wrong.

Tragedy demands a certain stature in the characters, a certain necessity in what they suffer: and here, as we suggested, Mrs. Millin's novel falls short. The misfortunes in her story seem too often arbitrary, and except for Caroline the characters are under-sized. There is nothing wrong with Gideon except that, as a "poor white's" son, he lacked vitality. He deserved success. Even his vices were petty. It may be argued, too, whether a Mongoloid idiot is a fair ingredient. There *are* such births, and no one knows the reason. They occur, in infinitesimal percentage, to normal parents: and for this very reason it is difficult not to feel that the infliction of Hercules upon Caroline is, as the schoolboy said, "put in to make it harder." The real bother is that *The Sons of Mrs. Aab* is so good as to suggest perfection, and make one resent anything that comes between. (p. 650)

> *L.A.G. Strong, "Round the Compass," in* The Spectator, *Vol. 147, No. 5394, November 14, 1931, pp. 650, 652.*

MARGARET CHENEY DAWSON

It is hard to define the fascination and indubitable power of [*Three Men Die*]. It has a plot that could easily have been frilled and fancified into a pretty good detective story, but in Mrs. Millin's hands it is nothing of the sort. . . .

Thus it happens that we see something rarely met in fiction: the development of a criminal character and actions deep in the tissue of normal living. There is no sordid or melodramatic background. The successive crimes are not particularly skillful. No marvelously quick-witted detective makes astute deductions. Such queerness as creeps into the people enacting this drama is only that of various temperaments reacting to an unrecognized stimulus.

Julia is the heroine and villainess, Johannesburg the scene. We get a brief but revealing sketch of Julia's life before her marriage in 1909 to Alexander Bishop. There is her childhood in Rhodesia, not unusually significant, except that her father's clumsy loss of a small fortune gave her a chance to measure exactly the space between cozy security and the teetery edge of poverty. . . .

By the time she was seventeen she was engaged. But after waiting six years for her young man to make his farm pay, she was more chagrined than bereaved when he died of black-water fever. At his death bed she found herself devoid of appropriate feeling. She could and did, however, think with satisfaction of the small legacy she was to receive from him. Her emotions

at this time and her cool recognition of them must have taught her a dangerous lesson.

Yet it is not so simple as that. Even after the convulsive death of the mild little Bishop man who was Julia's first husband, you might wonder whether anybody but fate was at fault. For it becomes clearer as you go on that Julia cannot be judged solely as an avaricious woman, or a standard type. Afer all, money is a means to her. What she really wants is to make life toe the mark. Hers is the determination of many a strong character and is not necessarily, perhaps not often, linked with viciousness.

And so it is with a kind of suspense that cannot be satisfied by a peek at the last page that we read of the deaths of a second husband and finally of her son Johnnie. Incidentally, Johnnie's slow progress from normality to maladjustment under the pull of a subconscious tension is brilliantly, though very simply, shown. Yes, we know the end. But we do not lose interest, even after we have closed the book. For all this has been made vivid to us not as a plot, but a highly possible deviation in the behavior of real people.

> *Margaret Cheney Dawson, "The Making of a 'Criminal'," in* New York Herald Tribune Books, *October 7, 1934, p. 5.*

WINIFRED HOLTBY

Sometimes when I read Mrs. Millin, I wonder why anyone admires Mr. Hemingway. For years now—ever since she wrote that brief, stark, beautifully moulded tragedy, *Mary Glenn*—she has been practising the laconic austerity, the dry abrupt statement, the assurance which demands neither embroidery nor mitigation, so much admired by transatlantic critics, but she has been doing it without violence, without brutality, without the affectation of illiteracy which is so much the momentary vogue. . . .

[Mrs. Millin] neither describes nor explains; she asserts. But her assertions are so precise, balanced, aimed so exactly at the very bull's-eye of her intention, that they completely fulfil her purpose. They do not glow with the incandescence of suggestion; they do not re-echo—as certain of E. M. Forster's sentences re-echo—in the mind with vibrations which change and deepen as memory prolongs them. But what she says, we accept, without contention and without misgiving.

Three Men Die is the story of a woman poisoner. It is told with quiet, spare detachment, without pity or repulsion. Julia, the Rhodesian nurse who comes to work in Johannesburg, is competent, attractive and courageous. Men like her. She is "game"; she does not lose her head. But after she has taken her training she returns to Rhodesia to find the lover, for whom she has waited and worked during six hard years, dying of blackwater fever. Two aspects of this tragedy impress her. He has, in dying, left her his small savings, and she feels, as she sits beside his deathbed, no great sorrow. The association of death with profit and with lack of grief is not stressed by Mrs. Millin, but throughout the story we feel that early incident affecting and partially explaining everything. Julia's attraction, her economies, her impatience with physical and temperamental weakness, her zest for life, her ruthlessness, her danger, become more and more convincing. . . .

Julia's acquisitiveness was part of her implacable instinct for life. She must be rich in order that she might live more abundantly—even if she bought her abundance at the cost of three other lives.

This is not Mrs. Millin's best book; but it achieves, brilliantly and economically, exactly that which it sets out to achieve. It is an impressive performance.

> Winifred Holtby, "A Woman Pioneer," in The Lon-
> don Mercury, Vol. XXXI, No. 181, November, 1934,
> p. 84.

V. S. PRITCHETT

It is the general vice of the English novel to evade the intellectual; but it reflects, therein, the English attitude to life. . . . [It] must be confessed that if by a fluke we do produce a primarily intellectual novelist he is not normally of the first rank. Our best lies elsewhere; yet how much better than our common ruck of amiable novelists is our occasional intelligent "sport." Such a one is Mrs. Sarah Gertrude Millin. It is true that when you put her down, with Mr. Maugham, among their colleagues across the Channel, there is a heavy drop in stature. They both seem a pair of unhappy, embittered, and isolated souls who are less remarkable for their brains than for not fitting in; but still, on our side, they are not a little striking. It is a pleasure to see the intellectual dissection of moral types and issues done in English at all, and if in the following lines I pull [*What Hath a Man?*] to pieces, it is because Mrs. Millin has, so to speak, made it worth my while.

What Hath a Man? is a character study of an Englishman of the educated class, who, hating both his parents, goes out to Africa on an impulse of idealism which has been aroused by a speech of Cecil Rhodes and becomes for the rest of his life a Government servant. From his childhood, when he lived as an only child with his elderly, cold, hard-headedly sceptical father and his younger dim mother, Henry Ormandy lives a scared, isolated life. . . . A bad marriage, ill-health, and the repetition in his relationship with his son of the same father-son difficulty which he had had in his time, completes his life-story. (pp. 647-48)

In fitting him with a psychological strait-jacket, Mrs. Millin has seen that it is necessary to make Henry Ormandy come into contact with important issues. He comes across not only religion and sex but the building of a country. He remains essentially, however, a minor character, as he remained a minor official. He is one of those tall, good-looking, intelligent English types of the upper classes whose faces look clear and serene at first glance, but which soon reveal the inner panic and incapacity. He is the kind of Englishman D. H. Lawrence hated and, not unnaturally, Lawrence's hatred gave considerably more life to such characters than the searching, tabulating fairness by which Mrs. Millin deals with Ormandy. Impartiality, one of her characters observes, is not necessarily truthfulness (she is a veritable surgeon among the viscera of meaning), and the anatomy of Henry Ormandy is done only in one grey tone. His evident masochism is lightly treated, though it must surely have been nightmarish. And what is stated to be austerity looks like meanness.

It is the weakness of the intellectual dissection of character that it dwarfs and flattens the subject. All the people in this book receive the harder or fainter imprint of the same rubber stamp. Ormandy is not contradictory human nature, but a pattern all of a piece. Mrs. Millin is so identified with Henry Ormandy that she justifies his view of other people—women, for ex-

ample—on every page. He says they are bitches, and bitches she makes them. This is monotonous as well as special pleading. She is merely raising frigid game for frigid intelligence. It is a limited sport. Only twice, in fact, does she warm; once in the human and vivid portrait of Rhodes, and again when a German woman sets out to seduce Ormandy in Rome. For the rest she falls back upon irony and pity, and indeed she knows the halting, broken movements of these emotions as only the cruel writer can. Despite these severe limitations, hers is a striking book. (p. 648)

> V. S. Pritchett, "Sarah Gertrude Millin," in The
> London Mercury, Vol. XXXVII, No. 222, April, 1938,
> pp. 647-48.

PERCY HUTCHISON

It is written in the Book of Ecclesiastes: "For what hath a man of all his labor . . . wherein he laboreth under the sun?" And it is this question which Sarah Gertrude Millin attempts to answer in this profound and subtly woven novel of England and Africa [*What Hath a Man?*]. . . . Mrs. Millin, who was the author of the African novel *God's Stepchildren*, has also done a biography of Cecil Rhodes. And *What Hath a Man?* might well be termed the fictive biography of one who, while fired by Rhodes's vision of empire, nevertheless follows a dream far more exalted. Henry Ormandy's "crusade" for an Africa where whites and blacks would jointly rule, living in peace and friendliness, not killing one another in their lust for power, was a futile one. But is not a crushing materialism equally futile in the end? We seem to hear Mrs. Millin say that it is.

The tale, which is an absorbing one, apart from any ulterior significance, begins in London. The father of Henry, a wealthy and ruthless stockbroker, cannot understand the sensitive child he has begotten. As the boy grows older he can understand him still less. Eton and Oxford, of course; a cultural canter. And then, the brokerage business, with wealth piled on wealth; perhaps a marriage into the aristocracy and a creditable and solid English life. One recognizes the picture. It has been presented scores of times. The boy, and long before he enters Oxford, is, however, in rebellion against it all. His desire is to be an artist; yet he has the discernment to perceive that his talents are not sufficient to make him an authentic artist, and he abandons the idea, although never relinquishing his ideals of beauty.

Henry's parents are what once were called Dissenters. And the lack of color, the lack of warmth, in the services he has been compelled to attend as a boy throws him over to Catholicism. Keeping him true all his life to the faith he has adopted, the author is nevertheless at pains to make it clear that Ormandy was more lured by the mysticism of Catholicism than by its dialectic. The difference, for the novel, is important, for herein is the key to Henry's career. Spurning his father's wealth, inspired by the thought of the ancient Crusaders, he secured an appointment in Africa. In other words, he sees his life as a mission, a latter-day crusade. . . .

Mrs. Millin, we take it, is less concerned with drama than she is with life, specifically with life's overtones. Born and reared in Africa, she knows both the native and his white overlord. But she is not primarily involved either in the attrition of races or in the African scene. She looks upon this country in which her lot has been cast as the crucible in which are tested the souls of mankind. Africa, in this novel, is for her the wine press of the Lord, in which every Cecil Rhodes and Henry Ormandy is a ripened grape to be fermented at last into the full-fruited wine. Her interest is in watching man play out his destiny, and wherever she stations her characters, that is her stage. *What Hath a Man?* is, therefore, universal. . . .

The ending of the novel I shall not touch upon. But, as I have sought to make evident, the power of this unusual novel is not in the story told. *What Hath a Man?* is searching, grave, sincere. Mrs. Millin is not much concerned as to how the world is going; but she is greatly concerned over the way men may go. She neither praises nor condemns. Nor does she prognosticate. Hers is the laboratory method.

> *Percy Hutchison, "Mrs. Millin's Tale of a Crusader," in* The New York Times Book Review, *May 29, 1938, p. 6.*

KATE O'BRIEN

The Herr Witch Doctor is a very serious, indeed a desperate, book. It is written, as is usual with [Millin], with all possible coldness, sobriety and attention to facts; it is compact of a pitiless kind of pity that, extenuating nothing and offering none of the bribes of imaginative grace, claims nothing less than full consideration; and, that given, it establishes in us an anxiety that does not pass when the book is closed—anxiety before the unravelable stupidities and vices of man, which are deadly platitudes, of course, but are here assembled with terrible, cold vigour in one small report of the doings of black man and white. It is impossible to read or reflect upon Mrs. Millin's book with other than a heavy heart; it is impossible to derive the coldest comfort from it—save perhaps in the reflection that the thing has been so well done. The pathology is good indeed—but where are the physicians?

The story is intricate. It revolves round the internal politics of an African tribe dwelling in a northerly corner of the Union, close to the border of what was once German South West Africa. The regent of the tribe, backed by the witch doctor, proposes to block the lawful succession to power of the young chief, and the two are subtly encouraged in this by the local German "missionaries," whose job it is to win the Bagamidri tribe to worship of the "new white god," Hitler. In this nucleus of Nazi work we are shown the whole Nazi plan for Africa—the years covered by the story are 1934-39—but are also shown its utter cruelty, its complete imperviousness to every value not dictated by Berlin. The succession to the chieftaincy is nothing save to the tribe, but the emotions and manoeuvrings it creates help the Germans to gain command over the vain, dangerous mind of the witch doctor, winning him to curiosity about white magic and "the white god." . . .

Meantime against all the flood of ignorance, innocence, greed and cunning, two helpless figures stand—vainly set on helping the black people. One is himself a black, a brother of the two warring chieftains. He is educated, and has all his life been intoxicated by dreams of Prester John, and of there one day arising another Prester John, who will restore all Africa to the Africans, and teach them how to be free, proud and self-reliant. The other, to some extent his mentor, is an Englishman with some black blood in his veins—a curse which seems to defeat his most courageous moods, and to be, apparently, for those who possess it, a profoundly unmanageable affliction, alike when they confront black men and white. Not all the Christianity of this clergyman, nor all his love of his humblest black brothers, can eradicate his unresting self-consciousness—and

his nerves render him useless both against native weakness and German strength. The book ends in sharp irony, with the conversion of "Prester John" to Nazi ideals, and the immediate practical defeat of these by the Union's declaration, in September, 1939, that it stands with England and the democracies. [*The Herr Witch Doctor*] is not an entertainment, nor is it, by usual standards, a very good novel. But it is a cold and terrible document, and it stirs up anxieties from which it is only idiotic to flinch.

> *Kate O'Brien, in a review of "The Herr Witch Doctor," in* The Spectator, *Vol. 166, No. 5886, April 18, 1941, p. 432.*

THE TIMES LITERARY SUPPLEMENT

[In *The Burning Man*] Mrs. Millin has chosen a difficult subject, but after a shaky start she proceeds to a satisfactory conclusion. Johannes van der Kemp was a Dutch gentleman, born in 1747; as an officer in the Dutch army he lived a life of debauchery until compelled to resign his commission for marrying beneath him; in middle life he experienced conversion, took orders in the Church of Scotland, and was sent to the Cape as a missionary to the natives. No author is equally at home in every part of the world, and the first 50 years of van der Kemp's life, in Holland and Great Britain, are not drawn with the vividness of the later episodes; but in Africa the book comes to life.

The period is that of the British conquest, and all the complicated factors of the tangled situation are excellently described; the cosmopolitan traders of Cape Town, the anarchic freedom-loving Boers of the hinterland, the enslaved Hottentots, and the menacing approach of the warlike Kaffirs. The Boers, remembering the Civil Law which ruled in Holland, feared that if their slaves were baptized they would automatically become free; that was not the English Common Law, which made no provision either for slavery or enfranchisement; but it lay at the root of their hostility to the missionaries. Johannes was bothered, in addition, by a personal problem; he was incapable of the celibate life, and it is in reference to St. Paul's advice to such persons that the author calls him *The Burning Man*. His Dutch wife had been drowned, in an accident which her husband survived; that, of course, filled him with a sense of guilt; in South Africa he must marry, so he married a black woman. He then tried to found farming settlements where Hottentots might live in freedom, though for lack of practical ability these settlements failed. The point is that Mrs. Millin makes a genuine and living character out of the hero of these disjointed adventures, and in addition, because she writes with deep knowledge of the South African mind, this interesting evocation of the past is made very relevant to the modern world.

> *"Evoking the Past," in* The Times Literary Supplement, *No. 2639, August 29, 1952, p. 561.*

ROBERT LOWRY

Historically true, *The Burning Man* reads with the rolling incantation of a biblical story. "Oh, God, let me, let me alone, and not thy Son, suffer for my wickedness and so be cleansed," cried a 19-year-old Dutch minister's son one day in 1766. Yet tall, blue-eyed Johannes van der Kemp went right on sinning. He shocked his father by calling himself a deist, quitting medical school for an army commission, and setting up housekeeping with another man's wife. One afternoon a waterspout upset his sailboat and Johannes, no swimmer, saved himself while he watched his wife and child drown. Then, to save his own soul by saving others, he joined the London Missionary Society and sailed for South Africa.

He got a cool welcome. The descendants of the Voortrekkers shunned him for his uncompromising attitude about racial equality. The natives questioned his God while they accepted his beads. He set up one grass-hut missionary school after another in the wilderness, and outraged blacks and whites alike by marrying a native girl. Though his converts were few, his influence went far. When he died of a stroke in 1811, he was remembered as a political conservative who had sown a radical seed of nonsegregation that was already troubling the new ''democratic'' government.

Mrs. Millin's style is lush at times, but more often her phrasing is frugal and her viewpoint is distant. Fueled with a true and tragic story, but lacking high-test fiction's hot immediacy, her book burns less than her burning man.

Robert Lowry, ''Between Two Worlds,'' in The New York Times Book Review, *November 23, 1952, p. 52.*

R.G.G. PRICE

With everybody writing novels about race relationships and most of the good ones being on the same side, anybody putting the case for the white settler needs to show at least the minimum forensic qualities of smoothness, pace and grip. *The Wizard Bird,* which takes the ''scratch an educated native and find a witchdoctor's dupe'' line, ignores any need for holding the reader with a glittering eye, a disappointment from one of South Africa's leading novelists. It is full of single sentence paragraphs which give it a portentous jerkiness. These do not add a dimension to the African tragedy, as they are obviously intended to, but make the novel read like a book dropped from the *Apocrypha* for lack of demand.

The rejection of the young Oxford-trained ruler of a tribal area by the family of his white anthropologist friend makes him revert to savagery and, under the sway of a witch-doctor, he tortures and kills. The garishly improbable story contains one or two vivid splashes of blood-coloured action but neither arouses a suspension of disbelief nor leads the British-based optimist to reconsider his liberal assumptions. The witch-doctor, the key figure, is no more than a stand in an ethnological museum covered with feather cloak and necklace of bones. (pp. 841-42)

R.G.G. Price, in a review of ''The Wizard Bird,'' in Punch, *Vol. CCXLII, No. 6350, May 30, 1962, pp. 841-42.*

THE TIMES, LONDON

In *The Reeling Earth* Mrs. Sarah Gertrude Millin wrote of Mr. Charles Chaplin that to her mind he was ''not a satirist at all, but a sentimentalist—an inspired comic without wit . . . finally, a man without taste.'' That, at a time when nothing except the most inflated superlatives would do for *The Great Dictator,* argued a certain toughness and independence of mind, and it is not surprising to find, in *The Wizard Bird,* that she has brought to the deep and difficult problems involved in black insurgence in Central Africa the same refusal to follow the easy, conventional line.

Mrs. Millin, to put it another way, is not so much concerned with rights and wrongs as with differences, and it is her will-

ingness to recognize differences, as long ago Mr. E. M. Forster did in *A Passage to India,* that distinguishes her novel. Ngogo, the witch-doctor, performs unspeakable rites, to help Chibisa, the African educated in England, to obtain independence for his people, and Chibisa participates in them. Mrs. Millin, with a great experience of Africa, sets that fact down, and all the rest, the relationship of Chibisa to his white friends and supporters, is subordinate to, and revolves round it. Mrs. Millin allows her dislike of politicians who fly in from London for a weekend and make speeches implying that they know all about everything to shine through her pages and her habit of setting down colons and following them with direct, didactic statements stops *The Wizard Bird* from being a novel of any great aesthetic pretensions. The knowledge and imagination—imagination harnessed to commonsense—it contains, however, constitute a more than adequate compensation.

A review of ''The Wizard Bird,'' in The Times, *London, May 31, 1962, p. 16.*

EZEKIEL MPHAHLELE

When Sarah Gertrude Millin's *God's Stepchildren* became a best-seller in the United States in 1925, the catharsis of it must have rubbed the white Americans the right way. Here's the tragedy of mixed blood, and we're in it too, brotherman, they must have thought. A shattering guilt complex set in: not over the white man's rotten treatment of the blacks, but over his 'sinfulness' that produced the Afro-American. Mrs. Millin was trying to show that miscegenation between black and white is an evil thing, evil, she thought, because it produces a degenerate race in social and political conditions that outlaw mixed marriages. She certainly succeeded in setting off physical and emotional reactions in me that do her no credit.

The missionary, the Rev. Andrew Flood, marries a Hottentot woman in order to prove something: that he regards blacks and whites as equal in the eyes of God. He hopes his non-white converts will better understand Christ's Gospel when he has married one of them. The members of his congregation often ask him awkward questions about the Gospel, but there are some who haven't the slightest intention of taking the missionary's word seriously or being converted. There is no indication that any of these Hottentots are capable of any deep thinking about religion and the meaning of existence.

Naïvely, the missionary abandons his European standards of cleanliness, again in order to prove that God doesn't make any distinction between black and white.

Mrs. Millin tells us that the community in which Flood has come to work are a very indolent, *dagga*-smoking crowd who thrive in dirt. They are also addicted to witchcraft. In fact, they regard Flood as a fool rather than as a brother. He degenerates. 'He was himself in many ways a savage,' and he dies a miserable person.

No doubt, the author means to tell us, Andrew Flood has by marrying a 'Hottentot' decided the fate of future 'Colored' generations. One by one these characters crumble; external conditions have no influence on character any more, and Sarah Gertrude Millin cannot save her characters. Deborah, Flood's daughter, cannot go straight, although she grew up under another missionary at some other station—Mr. Burtwell, who lived normally. To satisfy her animal instincts, we are told, she falls in love, first with a Hottentot, and then with another man. We are treated to such generalizations as: 'She (Deborah) had, *as most half-caste children have,* a capacity for imitation' (my italics). Deborah's learning ability reaches a limit, because 'inevitably the point would be reached where a solid barrier of unreceptivity would hinder all further mental progress.' Another label. Again, 'native children arrived at their full capacity very early—at fourteen or fifteen they would begin to falter, to lag behind, to remain stationary while their white competitors went ahead.' Adam Kok, half-caste leader of the Griquas and Hottentots, with whom Deborah and her son, Kleinhans, subsequently go to live, is described as a 'leader of shamefully born savages and fugitives and outlaws and emancipated slaves.'

'In that community where work was universally despised' Kleinhans is said to be by nature a husbandman. 'Heaven knows what germ in his distant white ancestry had quaintly chosen to establish itself in Kleinhans' character.' He hates the 'meek, dark bearers of shame.'

Kleinhans is not accepted by whites in spite of his conscious efforts to live down his 'colored' blood by engaging in money-making projects. A group of whites beat him up. Those qualities which his white ancestry is supposed to have brought with it collapse in him. No, they never go beyond the ordinary level, these half-castes, the writer suggests. No firmness of character at all! Kleinhans ends up as a farm manager and marries a 'colored.'

Elmira is born of this marriage. She is sent to a European school to 'try for white.' For himself Kleinhans admits defeat: he cannot cross over; but his children must not go to an African school. Elmira is thus offered as a pathetic sacrifice, and we see her walking on a very tight rope in that school for whites. It snaps by accident, and her personality crumbles. It is her illness which brings her parents to the school to see her. Her real identity is unveiled. She never puts up a fight during her stay in the school. Shame has done it again; she is ashamed of her parents. But more than that, the accident of color, which forms the motif of the whole novel, has brought about the inevitable collapse of Kleinhans and his wife, Lena. (pp. 141-43)

Lindsell, who has been responsible for Elmira's schooling, undertakes to marry her. She must do it; not because she loves this old man, but because she is a creature of circumstance, and, like all the rest, a slave to a hereditary fate.

For the first time in the story, someone in the Flood line—the last in the line—starts thinking about color and mixed blood in a manner no other fictional character before him has done. This is Barry, Elmira's son by Lindsell. In Cape Town, Barry looks around him and thinks how unambitious and unenterprising 'colored' folk are. A black man, he observed, can scale up as far as an English or Scottish university even without the political and social privileges enjoyed by the colored man. And still the 'colored' man remains behind. (pp. 143-44)

Someone tells Barry that an ancestor of his once blundered into a marriage with a Hottentot. Because of this, a line of 'colored' children had been born, each one of them continuing the 'evil.' Barry must see that he does not repeat the blunder. He tries to fight back, but he fears his blood and is harassed by a sense of inferiority. He succumbs to the suggestion, and decides to be a minister of religion. 'It would be some recompense for what his ancestors had done.' This is the millstone to which his character is tied.

Barry's experiences at Oxford and later as a soldier in the First World War have a wonderful effect on him: they seem to broaden his vision and the color issue is no longer an obsession with him, just as it isn't in Europe. He marries an English woman and returns home. When she is expecting a child, he is nagged by the same person as before into telling his wife the truth about his colored blood. His nightmare is not softened when he goes back to his folk to see his dying mother, Elmira. The sight of her, his great-grandmother and all other 'colored' folk living in poverty and misery decides Barry to start missionary work for their uplift. He gives up his English wife.

We are made to understand that Elmira's slavish acquiescence to Lindsell's demands is the same as that of her grandparents, of her parents, of her tribe—that 'unluckily born,' grovelling, defeated breed of 'God's stepchildren,' 'who must always suffer.'

Sixteen years after *God's Stepchildren,* Sarah Gertrude Millin continues the story of Barry Lindsell in *The Herr Witchdoctor.* Barry is still atoning for his forefathers' miscegenation. He fails, and is aware of his failure as a missionary. But being born for failure, he does not get our sympathy. He has the grand opportunity of returning to his family—his wife and child—but he rejects it. 'Had he ever in his life stopped crying: "Don't let the brown people take me."' (pp. 144-45)

Aaron, the leader of the Levite sect in Mrs. Millin's *The Coming of the Lord* is another fate-driven creature. He is a religious fanatic and no one can reason with him. 'God will fight on our side,' is his stock reply to all who beg, persuade, order, urge him to leave the Heights where he has established his town against Government regulations. For the rest, the Levite masses are described as people who love an idle life, the implication being that they mean to enjoy themselves on the Heights while they wait for the coming of the Lord—the Revelation.

The Levites are forced out by the authorities. Once again, character tumbles down to an inevitable end.

Again and again in Sarah Gertrude Millin's novels we see non-whites driven or goaded by a fate. Her works reveal in turn Mrs. Millin's strong will and an uncompromising tenacity to her ideas and ideals. She succeeds best when she does not impose her own will on her characters, e.g., in her volume of short stories, *Two Bucks Without Hair and Other Stories.* These are intimate portraits of Africans in one predicament and another. Particularly striking are those of her servants, chief of whom is Alita, the domestic.

Alita is always fighting other people's battles, trying to stretch her meagre wage a long way to provide for a number of dependants. Her grown-up son and daughter are always creating responsibilities which she is ever ready to shoulder. And in the typical African fashion, she claims her daughter's illegitimate child as hers and does not feel ashamed of her daughter or grand-child, no matter how wayward the daughter is.

Although she takes a deep interest in Alita and her children, such as only few South African whites are capable of, Mrs. Millin records objectively the emotional twists and turns that she observes in her workers and her own failures and successes in handling Africans. Her beliefs do not stand in the way of character development at all. (pp. 145-46)

Sarah Gertrude Millin is a historian as well as a novelist. Hers has been a prolific writing career in both fields. One cannot help but feel that the ever-present element of fate that weighs so heavily on her fictional creations comes of her strong sense of history, a desire to place things within the spectrum of cause and effect. And who knows, there has probably been a tug inside her between a love of history and an ability to write fiction. And then there is that other and overriding factor which must always confront the serious South African writer as long as politics maintain their present drift: the need for a writer to come to terms with himself in relation to his position as either one of an underdog majority or as one of a privileged minority. Within this context the urges to preach, protest, hand out propaganda, to escape, sentimentalize, romanticize, to make a startling discovery in the field of race relations, to write thrillers, and other urges, all jostle for predominance in the writer. A practicing critic is just as apt to be angry and impatient in a set-up like this as the writer is, particularly when as I am compelled to do, the critic identifies himself with the underdog characters of his color. Because of this, I may appear to be unduly hard on Mrs. Millin. (pp. 146-47)

> *Ezekiel Mphahlele, "White on Black," in his* The African Image, *revised edition, Praeger Publishers, 1974, pp. 125-93.*

NADINE GORDIMER

[As] a white, English-speaking intellectual [Sarah Gertrude Millin] was so totally untypical of the evolution of the intelligentsia in South African society that there is a strong case for placing her right outside the development of South Africa with which her span ran parallel. Without exception, white, English-speaking South African intellectuals with any claim to as fine a brain as hers have found revulsion against racialism to be the touchstone of their mental and spiritual development. South African writers, from the days of Olive Schreiner and William Plomer, were among the first and have become the most vociferous opponents of the colour bar. Sarah Gertrude Millin alone developed the other way: she ended her long life as a passionate defender of apartheid, and a tragi-comic pariah among her peers in South Africa and abroad.

How did it happen? How did this brilliant woman, who sensed so accurately the danger of fascism that she went to London to add her voice to the anti-appeasement group, come to admire Vorster? How did this proud Jewess, who was obsessed with horror and fury during the Nazi persecution, justify a pathological prejudice against blacks? . . .

Why did a woman with a writer's insight never examine her own attitudes? Why did she never seek the experience of relationships with blacks who were on her own intellectual level? Finally, why did she feel no empathy with, indignation at the suffering she had witnessed, only condemnation?

Even before her death, she was not so much forgotten as deliberately shunned, as a writer. Her position is like that of Céline in France after the Second World War. What are we to do about her? Can literary judgment ignore the moral convictions, or lack of them, of a writer? Can a traitor be a good writer? The validity of a writer's insight implies that his level of achievement as an artist cannot, in a society living an institutionalized lie, be assessed without relevance to that terrible state. One cannot look at form without content. The reverse is also true. Today, no young black writer and very few white ones would admit that Sarah Gertrude Millin wrote well, that her prose has—as Katherine Mansfield said [see excerpt above]—a "low throbbing note" of individual power. She is dismissed as a bad writer.

The fact is that she was, at her best, a remarkably good writer with a repugnant and twisted personality, and in the end the consequent degeneration of mind and spirit destroyed the writer. A world away from the literary movements of her time, she was working, in the 1920s, towards the same kind of simplification of prose that that other Gertrude, in Paris, was teaching Hemingway. But Sarah Gertrude's thorn was a thorn was a thorn. It is a supreme irony that, her crop stuffed with colour prejudice, she had, in spite of herself, the writer's instinct to choose wonderful themes for exposing it. The novel that brought her acclaim in America and England, *God's Stepchildren,* was taken in those countries to be an indictment of the status, for coloured people, implied in the title; the Nazis (she was indignant to discover, because she managed to loathe German racialism while keeping her own intact) hailed it as a moral tale about the sin of interracial marriage, a *Rassenroman.*

Like the great Balzac before her, who unwittingly exposed the hypocrisy of bourgeois life while himself a political reactionary, she had given away the big lie in her society, and in herself.

> *Nadine Gordimer, "A Brilliant Bigot," in* The Times Literary Supplement, *No. 3989, September 15, 1978, p. 1012.*

DAVID RABKIN

That the decade of the 1920s were a period of exceptional creative upsurge is a commonplace of modern English literary history. The impact of the First World War is often advanced as a cause. It has less often been observed that the period was exceptionally fruitful in South African literature, too, in quality if not in quantity. The years 1924-6 saw the publication of [Pauline Smith's] *The Little Karoo* [and] *The Beadle,* [Sarah Gertrude Millin's] *God's Stepchildren,* and [William Plomer's] *Turbott Wolfe,* which together form a very substantial segment of what is valuable in South African prose fiction in English. (p. 78)

God's Stepchildren was immediately popular, recognised by South Africans as the plausible and articulate ejaculation of their racial nightmares. . . . Mrs Millin's work was immediately successful, running into several editions, and being translated into many languages. (p. 79)

Yet in critical estimation . . . *God's Stepchildren* [has followed] a steadily descending curve. The change reflects changing attitudes towards the question of race in the English-speaking world; a novel which was enthusiastically promoted by the Nazis as a lesson in the evils of racial impurity must today have a serious question mark placed over it. (Ironically, as a Jew, Mrs Millin was an ardent opponent of Nazism.)

Sarah Gertrude Millin was born in 1889, and spent her early years in the Kimberley area, along the banks of the Vaal. One of South Africa's most prolific authors, she wrote sixteen novels, as well as two volumes of autobiography and numerous works of non-fiction and essays. Her early novels recount life along the Vaal river, and the theme of miscegenation is powerfully present from the very beginning. Mrs Millin has herself identified this pre-occupation with her childhood experience:

> Nothing in my young life has shocked me more than the wickedness of miscegenation: the immediate shame and the way it filled the world with misery.

Nevertheless, it is in *God's Stepchildren* that Mrs Millin first presents this theme in a systematic (one might almost say, schematic) way. (pp. 79-80)

God's Stepchildren is a frankly racialist novel, of a type common enough in its time, but probably quite rare today. It reflects the general theories of race popularised in the age of Empire, and instilled into the youth of the time by numerous schoolboy adventure tales. For Mrs Millin the spectrum of pigmentation, from white to black, is equivalent to the spectrum of mental development, from the fully human to the animal. The browns occupy a rank just above the apes, whom they resemble in many ways. Thus the Hottentots are 'monkey-like people', 'in the main, stupid and indolent', while their Coloured descendants 'often remained to the end of their days gamins by disposition, imitative and monkey-like', as well as being 'too often . . . small and vicious, and craven and degenerate'. Small wonder that Barry is ashamed of his ancestry, or that his maternal grandfather, Kleinhans 'despised a man in proportion as he was brown'. But this too, this self-hatred, which, if Mrs Millin's racial theories were accurate, is only a rational view, is interpreted by the author as evidence of her characters' degeneracy.

In other ways, too, Mrs Millin's novel reflects the racial theories of the time. Thus the 'backwardness' of the coloured races is accounted for by a theory of arrested development, according to which the young black person develops more quickly than the white, but reaches a peak of ability sooner and at a lower level. This theory determines the characterisation in the novel, as will be seen below. The early precocity, followed by mental stagnation, is closely linked in the novel with the early sexual maturity supposed to be general among African peoples. In a peculiarly unpleasant way the two notions are thought to bear out the animality of the non-white.

If, in *God's Stepchildren*, all black people are thought of as inherently inferior to whites, nevertheless Mrs Millin reserves a special *frisson* for the person of mixed race. He is thought to combine 'the worst of both races' and to be rejected by both alike: 'Whatever else the black man might be, he was, at least, pure'. That Mrs Millin herself accepts these ideas, and is not merely exhibiting them as typical attitudes is very clearly demonstrated in the section where she steps out of the narrative structure of the novel to discuss race. The following passage generalises the theory in national terms:

> In other parts of South Africa, among the Zulus, the Pondos, the Swazis, the Damaras, and other such tribes, the people were big, and black and vigorous—they had their joys and chances; but here, round about Griqualand West, they were nothing but an untidiness on God's earth—a mixture of degenerate brown peoples, rotten with sickness, an affront against Nature.

Here is a fitting argument for selective genocide. It is not surprising that Hitler's ideologues found *God's Stepchildren* a worthy work of literature.

On the evidence of such ideas, it might be expected that Mrs Millin's attitude towards the act of miscegenation itself would be simply negative. It is negative indeed, but a curious duality runs through her attitude, expressed most clearly, perhaps, in a remark quoted from [*The Night Is Long*, her] autobiography. There she refers to two aspects of miscegenation, 'the immediate shame and the way it filled the world with misery'. Thus the white man who has intercourse with a black woman is committing a shameful, sinful act *whether or not* a child is born as a result. This is the sin, which is to be visited upon even the fifth generation, though Mrs Millin does not tell us which commandment the act violates. Instead she tries to give substance to her shame of sin by depicting the misery it brings to successive genrations.

Nowhere does Mrs Millin suggest or imply that the unhappiness felt by the offspring of mixed relationships is caused by the prejudices and racial animosity shown by white South Africa towards its black fellows. On only two occasions does she refer to the existence of non-racialist ideas about multi-racial societies. At the very beginning of *God's Stepchildren* she refers to Andrew Flood's British conviction of the 'essential equality of all human beings'. In large measure, the novel itself is intended as a refutation of this proposition. Towards the end of the book, Barry's English wife responds to his confession of 'black blood' with a surprised 'Is that all?' It is very unlikely that Mrs Millin endorses this comment, because some pages earlier Mrs Lindsell's remark is heavily qualified by the reflection that the 'ordinary person' in Britain was unconcerned with colour, 'did not think of it, or brood over it, or consider it, *or understand it*' (my emphasis). Moreover, Mrs Lindsell's *sang-froid* does not survive long, and soon she is demanding that Barry take her back to England, where she 'need not see these brown creatures'. At most there is in Sarah Gertrude Millin a hesitation about endorsing race discrimination *in principle,* i.e. as a universal law, but there is little moderation in her general contempt and distaste for Coloured people, which can be discerned in the tone and imagery of her narrative, as well as in its explicit pronouncements. It is certainly true to say, as the Czech critic Vladimir Klima remarks [in *South African Prose Writing in English*], that Mrs Millin was 'too much frightened by miscegenation' to 'present any real analysis' of the phenomenon.

The deficiency of analysis in the novel is supplied to some extent by the strong note of fatalism that runs through the narrative. Mrs Millin's novels in general conform to a fatalistic and often pessimistic outlook on life. *God's Stepchildren,* with its structure based upon the passage of generations, and its great need to compress events and reflection, necessarily moves at a cracking pace. Birth, parturition, and death are viewed in a detached way:

> As, without protest, the stars ran along their endless course, and woman went so many months with child, and seeds burst into life through the earth, and death came swishing along, so, with the same abandoned sense of fatality, Elmira accepted her function as Adam Lindsell's wife. . . .

Similarly her comment on the death of the first Mrs Lindsell, after she has catalogued the ways in which the surviving family adjust their attitudes towards the deceased, is a curt 'And life went on'.

Two secondary themes bear out the general fatalism which the novel displays. There is the theme of heredity, which, in addition to the 'attenuated dark stain' borne by successive generations, is expressed in Barry Lindsell's physical and emotional resemblance to his remote ancestor, Andrew Flood. The second is the attack upon liberalism, indeed upon all attempts to reform the world; it is the main content of Part One of the novel, 'The Ancestor', which condemns as futile and mischievous naïvety Flood's attempts to communicate upon equal terms with his aboriginal flock. . . . (pp. 82-4)

They despised him utterly, and his religion. The belief that any social or political concessions offered by the whites will be abused by the blacks is, of course, a stock South African response to the liberal proposition. Sarah Gertrude Millin reinforces the 'logic' of this response by making the Rev Andrew

Flood a wholly unattractive and unconvincing proponent of liberalism. The emotional life of the character is so shallowly conceived by the author that he appears to the reader as little more than a vague succession of sighs and blushes. Mrs Millin does not give liberalism a chance.

Such are the main features of *God's Stepchildren,* as far as content is concerned. . . . In its central theme the novel touches on a concern which is crucial to the South African novel, and became its main pre-occupation in the twenties, largely through the influence of this book. (pp. 84-5)

Plot in *God's Stepchildren* is the enactment, through four generations, of a proposition which is fully developed in the first section of the novel ('The Ancestor'). The sequence of events is determined by the need to change the historical backdrop periodically, from the trek of Adam Kok's Griqueas to the Diamond Fields and on to suburban Cape Town. Fundamentally, the options open to the descendants of Andrew Flood do not change or develop. Actual mechanical development of the plot is therefore necessarily a matter of chance, as is the discovery of Kleinhans by Adam Lindsell. Yet for all her fatalism, Mrs Millin is unable to imbue the twists of her plot with the sense of an inevitable Hardyesque tragedy (something she would perhaps like to do), for the essence of her proposition about miscegenation is that it is a *voluntary* act of evil, all the consequences of which are implicit in what she herself called the 'immediate shame'. The narrative developed by Mrs Millin is thus full of incident but barren of events. That is why she is able to develop an essentially irrelevant interest in the circumstances of the Lindsell family, without any distraction from the main topic. Indeed the main topic, since it is quite static, must needs be defined by contrast with the surrounding scene. Many things happen, in *God's Stepchildren,* but little changes. (pp. 90-1)

[Character] is largely incidental to the purposes of *God's Stepchildren.* Mrs Millin attributes immutable qualities to the races and, with minor distinguishing variations, applies them to her variously coloured characters. The method is, of course, more noticeable in the black characters, who are developed only to the extent that they are required to embody the author's thesis. Kleinhans, who according to the plot of the novel must have been a man of some force of character, makes virtually no impression on the reader. In contrast Adam Lindsell, whose character is developed with some care (at least we are told a lot about it) plays no significant part on the action which is either the product of his unique personality or a stimulus to its further development.

Mrs Millin's technique illustrates clearly the weaknesses of naturalistic character depiction. Her representative figures are designedly average, 'ordinary people' whose portrayal involves no revelation of principles moral or social, but merely fills in outlines laid down by the author by other means. They are therefore of little interest.

Sarah Gertrude Millin did not 'discover' the problem of colour. Nor was William Plomer the first to satirise South African racial attitudes. The importance of these writers in the development of the South African novel lies rather in their identification of the colour question as the central moral issue of South African society. Thus, both Olive Schreiner and Pauline Smith, while not excluding the question of colour from their range of discussion, saw it as an area where the moral issues which they were concerned with should be brought to apply. It was not for them the testing ground of morality that it constitutes, for the first time, in the writings of Mrs Millin and William Plomer.

Another way of putting it is that the awareness of colour is the dominant imaginative process at work in these novels. From their opposed points of view, both Mrs Millin and Plomer are writing from an impulse that originates in the awareness of colour. The segregated imagination has as its *starting point* the division of the races.

Such an awareness has been a dominant trend in South African fiction in English ever since the twenties. (pp. 92-3)

In her essay, "The Novel and the Nation in South Africa", Miss Gordimer remarks of the colour question:

> . . . it still is *the* question. It's far more than a matter of prejudice or discrimination or conflict of loyalties—all things you can take or leave alone: we have built a morality on it. We have gone even deeper: we have created our own sense of sin and our own form of tragedy.

If, as Miss Gordimer implies, the tragedy is a bogus one, then the whole course of the South African novel since *God's Stepchildren* may well be a diversion. But writers cannot choose the ground of their creativity. The segregated imagination will become an anachronism, some time in the South African future. For the white South African novelist writing in English it has, since the twenties, been an unavoidable path. For the critic the criterion has therefore been similarly predetermined. How honestly has the writer charted the path? How far has he been able to see beyond it? (pp. 93-4)

David Rabkin, "Race and Fiction: 'God's Stepchildren' and 'Turbott Wolfe'," in The South African Novel in English, *edited by Kenneth Parker, Africana Publishing Company, 1978, pp. 77-94.*

S(idney) J(oseph) Perelman

1904-1979

American humorist, essayist, dramatist, scriptwriter, and autobiographer.

Along with James Thurber, Ring Lardner, and Robert Benchley, Perelman is one of the most esteemed humorists in twentieth-century American literature. His essays and sketches, most of which were originally published in the *New Yorker,* display his sophisticated prose style, whimsical imagination, and talent for parody, wordplay, and social satire. Among his topics of ridicule are the entertainment and advertising industries, popular fiction and film, rural life, and foreign culture. Frequently, however, Perelman himself becomes the object of humor, as he reveals personal foibles which render him the hapless victim of a complex, turbulent society. Although critics have sometimes faulted him for failing to underscore his humor with insightful observations, Louis Hasley maintained that Perelman's ''failure to engage us at the level of serious ideas allows us to enjoy the crazy roll of his dice without being concerned over the ethics of the management.''

Perelman began his literary career at Brown University, where he worked as a cartoonist and later as an editor of the *Brown Jug,* the campus humor magazine. After leaving Brown in 1925, Perelman worked for four years as a cartoonist for the popular weekly journal *Judge* before joining the editorial staff of *College Humor.* Selections of his work for these publications were posthumously reprinted in *That Old Gang o' Mine: The Early and Essential S. J. Perelman* (1984). During his stay at *College Humor* and his early years with the *New Yorker,* to which he began contributing sketches in 1930, Perelman developed the two-thousand-word format and extravagant prose style for which he became famous. He regarded Robert Benchley, James Joyce, Max Beerbohm, and George Ade as important influences on his writing, which Peter De Vries described as ''polyphonic. . . , ingeniously blending high literary allusion, slang, show-biz hype, Yiddishisms, unabashed puns, canyon leaps of the imagination, fantastic coinages of proper names, all compacted into a manner at once densely droll and featherlight.'' Perelman's sketches for the *New Yorker* and other popular magazines were collected in numerous volumes, including *Strictly from Hunger* (1937), *The Dream Department* (1943), *The Ill-Tempered Clavichord* (1952), *The Rising Gorge* (1961), *Baby, It's Cold Inside* (1970), and *Vinegar Puss* (1975). Perelman employed the sketch format throughout his career and never ventured into longer fiction. However, to appease many of his critics, Perelman produced several full-length humorous works chronicling his travels in the United States and abroad. These books include *Westward Ha!; or, Around the World in Eighty Clichés* (1947), *The Swiss Family Perelman* (1950), and *Eastward Ha!* (1977).

Perelman was also a noted dramatist and scriptwriter. While critics applauded his skill at creating spirited dialogue and noted the buoyancy of individual scenes, they frequently cited Perelman's inability to sustain humor as a significant fault in his plays. Perelman's works for the stage include *All Good Americans* (1933) and *The Night before Christmas* (1941), written with his wife, Laura Perelman; *Sweet Bye and Bye* (1946), with popular caricaturist Al Hirschfeld; and *One Touch of Ve-*

nus (1943) and *The Beauty Part* (1962), with Ogden Nash. As a scriptwriter, Perelman is best known for the two screenplays he authored for the Marx Brothers—*Monkey Business,* in collaboration with Will B. Johnstone and Arthur Sheekman, and *Horse Feathers,* with Bert Kalmar and Harry Ruby—and for his film adaptation of Jules Verne's novel *Around the World in Eighty Days,* for which he and coauthors James Poe and John Farrow received an Academy Award. Four chapters of Perelman's unfinished autobiography are included in *The Last Laugh* (1981), and his personal correspondence is collected in *Don't Tread on Me: The Selected Letters of S. J. Perelman* (1987). In 1978, Perelman received a special National Book Award for his contribution to American letters.

(See also *CLC,* Vols. 3, 5, 9, 15, 23, 44; *Contemporary Authors,* Vols. 73-76, Vols. 89-92 [obituary]; *Contemporary Authors New Revision Series,* Vol. 18; and *Dictionary of Literary Biography,* Vols. 11, 44.)

ROBERT VAN GELDER

Most people who write funny pieces produce slowly because they baby themselves into thinking that it is necessary to have an idea before starting to write. For example, a Frank Sullivan feels better if he has some such idea as dinner at the captain's table on a Staten Island ferryboat, or a Christmas gift from an elevator man. A Robert Benchley likes to quarrel with a pigeon before starting to work. A James Thurber thinks how strange it would be if a cop found a man down on all fours at the edge of a roadside at night trying to prove whether human eyes gleam in the darkness the way a cat's do, and when he has thought of that for a while he is all set to face his typewriter. They are all builders, craftsmen who work as carefully as poets in Indian Summer.

S. J. Perelman is more like a brewer making bock. He doesn't build. He scatters. He feels no need for ideas, as his writings [in *Strictly from Hunger*] very clearly show. When the fit is on him he just leans up against a wall or the side of a sty, and writes. The choice of topic is of no interest to him or any one else. The secret of his success all lies in a couple of hundred laughs. If he can average two hundred laughs in a piece a thousand words long he thinks he is doing fine.

His stuff is very up and down in quality. Sometimes the laughs he draws come up from the toes of his readers. At other times they are just snorts. But, anyway, there is always action.

His weakness is that his material is generally impossible to quote. Only one member of a moderately chummy family is likely to read a Perelman book. You read his book and laugh over it and some one else on the porch says: "I wish you'd stop that. You make me nervous." Now if you were reading Parker or Benchley or Thurber or Sullivan, you would say what the joke was.

But with a Perelman book in your hands about all you can answer in defense is: "This fellow talks about being drummed out of the Boy Scouts," or, "This one starts: 'Now that Autumn is here again, every Tom, Dick and Harry will be waking up in the morning and asking himself the question, "Poisonous mushrooms—yes or no?" In every mossy dell, in every nook or cranny, these delicious little edibles are springing up.'" And such answers seem to rouse no desire to beg to be next for the book. It's the general spirit that gets you—always adding, if and when it gets you at all.

> *Robert Van Gelder, "Mr. Perelman's Thoughts While Hungry," in* The New York Times, *August 8, 1937, p. 5.*

MIRIAM BORGENICHT

Though Robert Benchley, in his introduction [to Perelman's *Strictly from Hunger*] describes the author as having cornered the dementia-praecox market, the book steers reasonably clear of absolute mania. It is gibberish, to be sure, but premeditated gibberish by which Mr. Perelman fools his readers into going along with him—and then lets the ground drop out from under their feet. Mr. Perelman's properties include the non-sequitur, the intentional malapropism, the blank irrelevancy, the wild hyperbole; but his most popular device is carrying the figurative to its literal conclusion. "The whistle shrilled, and in a moment I was chugging out of Grand Central's dreaming spires," he writes, while the reader leans back, unsuspecting. "I had chugged only a few feet when I realized that I had left without the train, so I had to run back and wait for it to start." . . .

[Anything] serves him as a starting point—from which he often gets nowhere and sometimes does not even start off at all. The impression of so much wandering is rather uneven. Occasion-

ally it falls into the banal by way of literary exercises and quips whose point can be guessed before they turn the corner; more often (as in **"Red Termites,"** the travesty on Red-baiting), it reaches peaks of comic distortion which cover really fine satire. Taken in one gulp, all this waggishness is likely to put a strain on even the most faithful Perelman addict. But absorbed in judicious teaspoonfuls, it is calculated to disturb the sanity of any reader.

If the Marx Brothers represent madness, then Perelman (who has been writing their scripts) is their prophet.

> *Miriam Borgenicht, "Perelman (S. J.)," in* The New Republic, *Vol. XCII, No. 1187, September 1, 1937, p. 108.*

TIME, NEW YORK

Peculiar to this century is a form of wit inadequately known as screwball. Its method is free association, its state of mind is somewhere between a power dive and a tail spin. It has close affinity with hot jazz, surrealist painting and the deranged poetry of Rimbaud. It calls for an exquisite sense of cliché and mimicry, and a nihilism which delights in knocking over-crystallized words, objects and gestures into glassy pieces that cut each other. Most advanced living practitioner of this form of wit is James Joyce. Perhaps quite as richly gifted in it, if far more inhibited in using it, are Groucho Marx and Sidney Joseph Perelman.

Dawn Ginsbergh's Revenge (1929) was written, much of it, while S. J. Perelman, who had graduated from Brown University in 1925, was working for the now *Judge*. It had an abundant, frenzied incandescence that promised either 1) to burn out, or 2) to become as brilliant and sure and destructive as anything in U. S. satire. Perelman did not burn out, but he has cooled off. . . . [For] seven years he has been writing pieces for *The New Yorker*. **Look Who's Talking,** like **Strictly From Hunger** (1937), is a collection of these pieces and several from other periodicals.

Nearly all of them are frank, formularized potboilers, a virtuoso's improvisations on minor themes. Tempered to the genteel tastes of *The New Yorker*, these pieces seldom hold a Roman candle to real **Ginsbergh** fireworks. Yet they are also as hard, sharp, bright and cold as a display of surgical instruments; and sometimes they do genuinely surgical work. (p. 66)

[If Perelman] continues at the level of his last two books he will have to be spoken of as one more greatly endowed U. S. author (Twain, Lardner, Crane, Melville, Wolfe, Faulkner, Fitzgerald, Hemingway) who never quite became what seemed to be in him to become. But like all of those he will have delivered enough. (p. 67)

> *"Surgical Instruments," in* Time, *New York, Vol. XXXVI, No. 7, August 12, 1940, pp. 66-7.*

OTIS FERGUSON

S. J. Perelman is one of the *New Yorker* standbys; but it's seemed the last few years, and it seems double in the twenty-four collected skits of **Look Who's Talking!** that his wind is short and he's swinging at everything. All these essays run to a general formula: Perelman digs up a *Harper's Bazaar* or an advertising campaign or a fad of the moment; a hotel courtesy folder, a comic strip, a pulp, a serious book, a promotion layout—God knows where the poor man's nightmares must take him—quotes it, kids it, pretends to gibber in the coalbin, ad-libs new situations or further catchwords, and gets out in 1,500 to 2,000 words. The topics always need a good ribbing, if they need anything; they usually get it. And nice titles: **"You Should Live So, Walden Pond," "Hello, Operator? I Don't Want a Policeman," "Mercy, the Cat's Got into the Budget."** If I were a publisher I could say, "He wields the scalpel on the foibles of our civilization," and you could slap my face. . . .

There are some really mean and funny pieces here all right—**"Ye Olde Ivory Tower," "Somewhere a Roscoe . . . ," "Abby, This Is Your Father"** (one of the best), **"Down with the Restoration!"** (probably *the* best). In these the method works; you not only agree and approve, but remember. It isn't so much that the ones in between the best and the out-and-out busts are merely so-so, or even that they leave a little grit in your teeth, being clever till it hurts but never with warmth or compassion or anger. It's simply that the practising humorist needs for his success to be the fool of heaven; and that in too many cases heaven is looking the other way. (p. 421)

> *Otis Ferguson, "The Business of Being Funny," in* The New Republic, *Vol. 103, No. 13, September 23, 1940, pp. 421-22.*

WOLCOTT GIBBS

Nobody operating a typewriter these days is funnier than S. J. Perelman, a definitive authority on the life and times of Mr. Sherlock Holmes; the author of many brave and tender books, including perhaps my favorite title in modern literature, *Dawn Ginsbergh's Revenge;* and the greatest living exponent of the free-association method as applied to humor. The Perelman system has a misleadingly simple air, causing many to suppose that all he has to do is sit down and let his mind frisk lightly from one thing to another, like a mountain goat, and consequently that any damn fool can write good nonsense. This is somewhat like saying that all the gifted people who tell dialect stories at dinner parties ought to be actors, and it is a great mistake. . . . At its best, the Perelman nonsense has a very strict discipline and logic of its own, and as a form of social and literary criticism it is frequently a good deal more instructive than a lot of stuff you'll find in the *New Republic.* He is very, very good, and he also knows more about style than some I could name who make a fancy living going around and annoying undergraduates with lectures about it. All this, very reluctantly indeed, leads up to the problem of why *The Night Before Christmas,* on which he collaborated with his intelligent wife, isn't quite the play we all hoped it was going to be.

The comedy . . . suffers from some strangely indecisive acting in its principal roles and its director hasn't contributed much in the way of invention or pace, but I'm afraid the Perelmans can't be regarded entirely as the victims of an unfortunate production. The idea of a gang of small-time crooks and con men taking over a Sixth Avenue luggage shop for the purpose of tunnelling into a bank vault next door ought to be funny, and quite often it is, but the total effect is disappointing. The authors are wonderful at thinking up isolated bits and pieces of fine nonsense, but, unlike the same material in the hands of Mr. Kaufman or Mr. Abbott, these are never made a structural part of the play, essential to its movement. . . .

[There] is something about Mr. Perelman's active mind that makes routine exposition a little dull for him, because the parts of his play that deal with young love and other necessary but tedious complications seem more or less perfunctory, as if he

had written them off rather rapidly, conceivably on a train. Altogether, in spite of such pleasant, ingenious moments as the one when a safecracker crawls into a magician's trunk and noisily disappears, and another when a salesman from a luggage company demonstrates a lady's hatbox that is also an umbrella, *The Night Before Christmas* hasn't quite the shape or substance it is likely to need to get along in a highly competitive profession, or racket.

> *Wolcott Gibbs, "Much More in Sorrow," in* The New Yorker, *Vol. XVII, No. 10, April 19, 1941, p. 29.*

TIME, NEW YORK

[*The Night Before Christmas*] is not a bedtime story. It is a mottled Sing Sing folk tale of a silver-haired confidence man past his prime and a slop-house plug ugly who pair up to crack a bank vault for Christmas. They buy a tired Manhattan luggage shop next door to the bank and start tunneling. Obstructed by unwanted customers, garrulous neighbors, former penmates, they dynamite, not the vault, but a near-by cafeteria, while Santa Claus stuffs their stocking with a cop.

The screwball wit of S. J. Perelman strangely enough fails to make this wacky plot rock his audience back on their seats with the clanky shock of his offstage writings. The play's isolated episodes, bald-faced gags, screwy curtains are sometimes hilarious, but they fail to bind together into effective farce. . . .

[Perelman's] best book (of four) was his first, *Dawn Ginsbergh's Revenge* (1929). On its jacket was the blurb: "This book does not stop at Yonkers." *The Night Before Christmas* does.

> *A review of "The Night Before Christmas," in* Time, *New York, Vol. XXXVII, No. 16, April 21, 1941, p. 61.*

STANLEY WALKER

S. J. Perelman, bon vivant and farmer, may be the funniest man in America. There is a highly respectable set of connoisseurs who think so. He has dash, imagination, inventiveness and a mighty neat turn of phrase. Some compare him with Robert Benchley, some with Frank Sullivan, some with the early Corey Ford, and some with Stephen Leacock. All unnecessary. Mr P. wears no man's collar. He is amusing in his own right: let the others do their stuff and he can be counted on to do his.

This little volume [*The Dream Department*] is a collection of Mr. Perelman's sketches, most of them parodies tinged at times with burlesque, which have appeared over the last few years in *The New Yorker.* This Mr. P. will see something in a newspaper or in some obscure magazine that arouses his sense of derision, and he will immediately swing into action. . . .

Mr. P. is one of the craftiest, slyest, most accomplished writers of nonsense now practicing. But can the customers stand a whole book of it at one dose? It is a moot point. Many of us are geared for only one laugh of the Perelman brand a week. However, there is no compulsion about reading this book at one sitting. One chapter every few days ought to turn the trick.

> *Stanley Walker, "Gaily Crazy," in* New York Herald Tribune Books, *January 31, 1943, p. 14.*

BEATRICE SHERMAN

Mr. Perelman is not a nature lover—nature faker would be more like it. His particular brand of jittery and joyful madness seems to be the slap-happy result of overexposure to books, magazines and advertisements. Give him a grubby little item in an obscure magazine, or a shiny big ad in one of the slicks, and his lunatic and ludicrous imagination grabs it, plays with it, worries it, until it has developed into a thing of monstrous hilarity.

It seems that he cannot look at a printed or color-engraved page without being haunted by the grotesque and fantastic possibilities that lie behind it, seen through the Perelman distortion lens. He can write in crazily humorous fashion along other lines (see **Dawn Ginsbergh's Revenge**) but in **The Dream Department** most of the skits in the collection are hung on the peg of some printed peculiarity. . . .

For good measure he is not above inventing a learned quarterly review, just for the fun of it. In **"Swing Out, Sweet Chariot,"** he cites the autumn issue of *Spindrift* in which he avers he was reading an exciting serial called "Mysticism in the Rationalist Cosmogony, or John Dewey Rides Again." With a thin air of veracity he maintains that his newsdealer was unable to supply him with the next number containing the doings of the Morningside Kid, so he had to be contented with a copy of *The Jitterbug,* which set him off on a sizzling critique and interpretation of the favored fiction of young rug-cutters. The line between fact and fancy for Mr. Perelman is very hazy, practically non-existent. . . .

The range of subject-matter is wide, from goldfish to snakes, from hard liquor to petrified men, from foundation garments to Christmas decorations. And practically all of the sketches are fantastically funny. Even the titles are temptingly funny. For instance, **"P-s-s-t, Partner, Your Peristalsis Is Showing,"** or **"A Pox on You, Mine Goodly Host."**. . . None of them ought to be missed by any Perelman fan.

S. J. Perelman can be carping, coy, niggling, extravagant or, downright tough. In any mood his stuff is lunatic and delightful.

> Beatrice Sherman, "S. J. Perelman's Unlikely Statements," in The New York Times Book Review, January 31, 1943, p. 3.

RUSSELL MALONEY

[Perelman's] writing is hundred-proof humor, with none of the facetiousness that the usual funny writer throws in to make things easy for the home folk. Reading a two-thousand-word Perelman piece is, in fact, quite a workout; not unlike tangling with a judo expert. The reader is tripped up by his own clichés, expressions he has hitherto accepted as having some sober meaning, while the Professor stands by, not even breathing heavily.

There is no very exact word for the kind of pieces Perelman writes. He invented the form and, so far, nobody else has come along who can handle it as well as he. His work might be described as little two-thousand-word clumps of free association, touched off usually by some irrational or outrageous aspect of modern life. . . . What he does is postulate the logic of whatever nightmare situation he has uncovered, then project another similar situation, no less logical but calculated to send the average borderline case screaming to a psychiatrist. . . .

Keep It Crisp is· [his] latest collection. It's no better and no worse than the earlier ones, which is to say it's superb. (p. 4)

Perelman is the only objective humorist of our generation. The typical contemporary funny writer is the pseudo-neurotic, the man who can't cross the street without holding somebody's hand and who makes his living by confessing this in print. Perelman is just a good writer. He knows more about words and their functions, probably, than man is supposed to know. He knows too much to be seriously impressed by any words in any combination.

A little more ignorance, a little less perception, and Perelman would be a great stylist. As it is, he's a nihilist. He starts a paragraph with the conventionally deprecatory "I may be wrong," then, wearying of the tawdry pose even before his sentence is completed, continues, "and always am." (pp. 4, 25)

Now and then Perelman takes a few days off and writes the year's best parody. *Keep It Crisp* includes his version of a Raymond Chandler mystery story, which stands on the same peak of perfection occupied by ["**Waiting for Santy**"], his earlier parody of an Odets play. Two of the pieces touch lightly but firmly on the not-so-lovable quirks of wartime advertising. And just as a *tour de force,* Perelman has written that piece about going to the dentist, a piece as old as dentistry (or humor; whichever came first). Good, too.

In all Perelman's writing there is a Proustian feeling for time and place. That the places he chooses to mention are all out of bum novels makes his performance no less impressive; the fascinated reader is yanked from the London docks to Spion Kop, from Park Avenue penthouse to an opium den. . . .

Looking for grim aspects of comedians is something out of a past era, but it has to be said that Perelman prose is a pure distillate of big-city jitters. Lewis Mumford might as well have been talking of Perelman rather than Joyce when he said, "He shows the mind regurgitating the contents of the newspaper and the advertisement, living in a hell of unfulfilled desires, vague wishes, enfeebling anxieties, morbid compulsions, and dreary vacuities; a dissociated mind in a disintegrated city; perhaps the *normal* mind of the world metropolis."

After which, in simple justice to Perelman and his publishers, it should be simply and candidly stated that *Keep It Crisp* is a hell of a funny book. (p. 25)

> Russell Maloney, "From Park Avenue to Opium Den," in The New York Times Book Review, August 25, 1946, pp. 4, 25.

THOMAS SUGRUE

[As a writer Perelman] is a superb craftsman; his knowledge of words is a constant source of wonder, his use of them a continuous joy. His parodies of the styles he encounters in other writers are subtle as the bonds of love; there is no telling when a line or a phrase will tear loose the supports of a set of tricks from which, almost unconsciously, we have been suffering overlong. The whole area of our foolishness is always his target, the selection of a certain point is technical. The gun is loaded with buckshot; anything in the vicinity is apt to be hit.

[*Keep It Crisp*] is full of these random bullseyes. A coy note in Clementine Paddleford's food column results in the best parody of contemporary mystery fiction trends that has appeared or is likely to appear. An unintended contiguity of sentences in *Life* magazine brings on a take-off of J. P. Marquand's novels, which alone is worth the price of admission. . . .

There are twenty-five essays in *Keep It Crisp,* each a complete absurdity in itself. There are no illustrations or introductions to hamper the reader, nothing but a remark on the dust jacket that herein Mr. Perelman "offers a brand-new carnival of his inspired waggeries." Since it is a customary sadism for publishers never to let authors see the dust jackets of their books until publication, this may be a mild revenge for a piece beginning on page 127 which undertakes to analyze the Fruit-of-the-Month Club but ends up with an author's eye view of a publisher. But waggeries or no waggeries, it is a genuine Perelman. . . .

> Thomas Sugrue, *"Delicious Absurdities: Keep It Crisp,"* in New York Herald Tribune Weekly Book Review, *September 8, 1946, p. 4.*

LISLE BELL

The binding of **Listen to the Mocking Bird** is canary yellow with panels of bluebird blue. The end papers are shrimp pink. The jacket is red. The Hirschfeld drawings are black on blue, green, orchid, orange and yellow.

Mr. Perelman's text is also colorful. It has to be colorful to stand up against a spectrum like this, but he is equal to the situation—a humorist who knows his pigments and hues to the line. He doesn't slap the paint on with a wide brush; his wit is not for murals, but neat and pointed, somewhere between Stephen Leacock and Robert Benchley, we should judge. . . .

Some of the brightest chapters were inspired by Mr. Perelman's habit of browsing through the advertising sections; he chips little specimens of copy from Macy's, Russeks, the Pequot Mills and other mother lodes of merriment.

About a third of the space is devoted to *The New Yorker* series called **"Cloudland Revisited"**—a reexamination of torrid classics in the harsh light of maturity and the Kinsey report. He rakes over the embers of Elinor Glyn, Warner Fabian, E. M. Hull, Maxwell Bodenheim and others, and it is a joy to follow the rake's progress. . . .

Despite the wild, owlish aspect in Hirschfeld's caricatures, this writer can wield a satiric snickersnee that is lethal without spilling blood. He leaves the scene of execution unspattered, and the victim doesn't realize that his head has been severed until he attempts to turn it.

> Lisle Bell, *"Mother Lodes of Merriment,"* in New York Herald Tribune Book Review, *October 2, 1949, p. 4.*

JOSEPH WOOD KRUTCH

The schizophrenic or surrealist school of American humor seems to have been invented by Donald Ogden Stewart in the twenties, widely popularized by Robert Benchley, and brought to full development by S. J. Perelman. Serious students of our culture will probably point out that it is a phenomenon of social disintegration, that at least two of its most accomplished exponents had or have left-wing sympathies, and that the "I" of Mr. Perelman's essays seems to be a maniac visited by occasional

moments of semi-lucidity in the course of which he realizes what it was that drove him mad.

For those who prefer a purely literary analysis it should be said that he is a master of the relevant irrelevance; of the brilliant cliché ("to capture on film a small but significant segment of the life around me"); and of the transparent misconception ("'A really crackpot notion,' she admitted, confusing the word with 'crackerjack' with typical feminine disregard for the niceties of slang"). (pp. 379-80)

[*Listen to the Mocking Bird*] hardly breaks new ground or reveals unexpected facets of his genius, but all the characteristic virtues are there. Included among other things are several dramatic fantasies for which the *donnée* was some advertisement like that of Macy's Bureau of Standards, which gave as its reason for rejecting a certain bathing salts for weight reduction the discovery that it would dye the user blue if he happened to get a few drops of iodine mixed in. There is also a series describing the adventures of the author's soul in revisiting such literary masterpieces of his youth as *The Sheik, Black Oxen* and *Flaming Youth*. . . . On the subject of Hollywood Mr. Perelman's observations seem to me rather more effective than the solemnities of Huxley and Waugh. To those who don't like him I can recommend at least the admirable tolerance of his remark apropos of "Graustark": "Chacun a son goo." (p. 380)

> Joseph Wood Krutch, *"Mr. Perelman's Essays,"* in The Nation, New York, *Vol. 169, No. 16, October 15, 1949, pp. 379-80.*

RICHARD MANEY

Mr. Perelman might well have called [**The Swiss Family Perelman**] *Ordeal by Ptomaine.* Violating longitude and latitude alike as he and his brood ranged the earth, Mr. Perelman survived vapors, megrims, swindles, humiliations, *vins du pays,* Bels gin, persecutions and a mynah bird in his defiance of the Kipling precept "he travels fastest who travels alone." In the discharge of his furious quest by land, sea and air, our intrepid hero invariably found his fellow passengers low varlets or scurvy knaves, their habits and manners ever at odds with the Code Perelman. Dutch bureaucrats outraged him, as did his mate as she added to their ever-mounting tower of luggage with tribal knickknacks the purchase of which tended to beggar the master. From the day they sailed West on the S. S. President Cleveland, "the largest single object our children had ever been called upon to take apart," until they collapsed in their Washington Square apartment months later only to learn that the building was about to be razed, the Perelmans survived a succession of horrors that would have been the undoing of a less fearless covey.

But all the indignities of travel—the culinary plots they survived, the official rebukes they endured, the ravages of clime and insect life over which they triumphed, have proved so much grist to the Perelman mill. **The Swiss Family Perelman** enlarges upon these multiple outrages in a fashion that only so vivid and irreverent an enlarger as Mr. Perelman can manipulate. Under its surface wit and levity **The Swiss Family Perelman** boils with protest at many of the injustices of the world.

> Richard Maney, *"Longitude, Latitude and S. J. Perelman,"* in New York Herald Tribune Book Review, *November 26, 1950, p. 4.*

REX LARDNER

[Perelman is] a master of the mellifluous, prosy sentence that leaves you, at the end, high and dry, like a mess. He may be also said to be a successful wooer of Synecdoche, the Muse of Small and Great Irritations, for his second book of voyages, called, shrewdly enough, *The Swiss Family Perelman*, is a gallimaufry of harrowing descriptions of battles with the elements, and with merchants, waiters, fellow-passengers, Mrs. Perelman, and custom officials, to name a few.

In Mr. Perelman's first account of his travels, the reader will recollect, the gentleman was accompanied by Al Hirschfeld, the artist; in this book he seems to be accompanied by his wife and two curiously oriented, precocious children. . . .

The idea had been, Go to Siam and save some money; but that exotic land (reached after quick jaunts to Los Angeles, Hollywood, Manila, Hong Kong, Banda Neira and Macassar), was full of disenchantment—crowded, steamy, and shot with inquisitive policemen. So, buying up firecrackers, tins of lychee nuts, and the mynah bird, the troupe emplaned for Calcutta and points west. Istanbul, Ireland, and Copenhagen were well received by the author, but in other places he was sorely tried. In England he had trouble mastering a peculiar traffic rule, in Paris the mynah bird felt seedy (but recovered after the ministration of the staff clinician of a Paris hospital), and in Rome Mr. Perelman thinks he overtipped. In short, this is a book for everybody.

> Rex Lardner, "The Bedeviled Perelmans," in The New York Times Book Review, *November 26, 1950, p. 24.*

JOHN MALCOLM BRINNIN

Anyone who has followed the career of S. J. Perelman since the publication of his *oeuvre première,* **Dawn Ginsbergh's Revenge,** has been privileged to witness the growth of a master in the process of marking out and stocking his own inviolate preserve. Perelman has created a genre, established a set of formulae and confirmed a point of view adding up to something as individual as a trade mark. In this new collection of anarchic hilarities [*The Ill-Tempered Clavichord*], the only curbs on this reader's delight are two. The first is a tendency to maintain at all costs, especially at the cost of comedy as *situation,* a barrage of precision-tooled language so thickly studded with allusion and so rapid as to produce monotony. The second is his self-indulgent reminiscence into the extra-curricular reading of his puberty, resulting in those long-winded pieces he groups under the title, **"Cloudland Revisited."** These latter are a sad waste of a lavish and otherwise resourceful talent. . . .

Like most funny men, Perelman inveterately sees himself as the victim, especially of the absurdities in *Harper's Bazaar, Printers' Ink, Modern Screen* and other journals that report activities on some margin of Civilization As We Know It. He reads with a complete suspension of disbelief—and then writes as if reality might never again close in. He is perhaps unique in that he can be pop-eyed and analytical at the same moment. He threads his way, ferret-like, through the pint-sized horrors of modern civilization (*and* Roget's *Thesarus*) with the adroitness of a Jean Valjean or a Harold Lloyd. "*Personne ici* except us chickens," he tells us, and we almost believe him. Yet a thousand disguises still cannot conceal his sane and liberal intelligence. Because we have confidence in that, we allow him to take us anywhere—from the "**Nesselrode to Jeopardy**" to "**Nirvana Small by a Waterfall.**" (p. 26)

> John Malcolm Brinnin, "Virtue of Freshness," in The New Republic, *Vol. 127, No. 23, December 8, 1952, pp. 26-7.*

MORRIS FREEDMAN

This most recent collection of S. J. Perelman's essays [*The Ill-Tempered Clavichord*], though small like all of his volumes, makes, as usual, exasperatingly slow reading. On each page you have to plow through a syntax and vocabulary as self-consciously baroque as Sir Thomas Browne's. More than one sketch at a sitting cloys your senses. Not that Perelman isn't the funniest American writer still actively working: the fantastic cavorting of his imagination is as ridiculously hilarious today as when he wrote scripts for the Marx Brothers. But the strain, the near violent tension of a Perelman production leaves you limp.

Like a hockey goalie, Perelman lets nothing get by him—no foible of language or life—without taking a swipe at it. Never relaxed or off-hand like Benchley or Thurber, or urbane like E. B. White, or casual like Will Rogers, he insists on taking personally all lapses from grace in writing or living that impress themselves on him. He is derisive, sour, nihilistic, uncharitable, in short, as he himself suggests in the title of this latest book, ill-tempered, a Boys' High humorist permanently engaged in a crazy imitation of a retired Pukka Sahib growling at the decay of standards.

Part of his acerbity is the result of his seldom working directly from life. His wit is exegetical; it lives largely off the writing which sees experience through the weird prisms of advertising agencies or Hollywood publicity offices. But reality nevertheless underpins his burlesque. He is always contrasting the implausibility of advertising and cheap culture with the unexpected but convincing tawdriness that reality, however carefully manipulated, inevitably takes on. It is the pull between the two kinds of distortion—Perelman's of reality, the other of a manufactured tinsel ideal—that we find the fun.

In thus rooting himself, however remotely, in life, Perelman is nearer to the earthy traditions of Twain and Will Rogers than most contemporary American funny men. But he differs even more significantly from Cantor, Berle, Durante, Benny, Hope, Skelton, Jessel, Sophie Tucker, and some of the syndicated columnists and occasional contributors to the mass-circulation magazines. . . . One way or another, they all peddle personality; they insist on attention to their very bodies, emphasizing baldness, stoutness, proboscity. . . . (pp. 208, 210)

Perelman is not, to be sure, so impersonal and anonymous as Sid Caesar, perhaps the finest of modern performing comedians and satirists; Perelman does use himself, but the "I" of his sketches seems factitious, a way merely of introducing the note of autobiography required by current written satire. Nor is he as spontaneously ebullient as Groucho Marx, with whom he shares, among other talents, a wonderful facility for shrewd and surrealistic punning. But like both Caesar and Marx, he bases his humor on the exploitation of technique rather than just personality or "material."

I don't suppose any recent writer outside of Joyce and possibly Beerbohm has shown a greater responsiveness than Perelman to the effect of written language—the flow of a sentence, the meaning of a word. And his consciousness of the multiple possibilities of communication is positively Talmudic. . . . It is this prodigality that is so tiring. The sustained cerebration in some of his sketches is almost of the kind required for playing or watching chess, or for reading a particularly ungraceful New Critic's explication of a poem. Between sessions with Perelman you have to keep returning to the everyday world of sloppy communication and sloppy feeling to catch the full character of his astringency.

At the bottom of Perelman's criticism of life and language is the traditional serious, self-satisfied, snobbish Jewish contempt for foolishness and the works of thick heads. It shows up mediocrity and idiocy by brilliant "showing off," taking it for granted that criteria—whether in doing or living—must be preserved. . . . One becomes most impatient with Perelman when he expends his elaborate strategy and enormous fire-power on some minute pip of a target such as the lush prose of an inconsequential trashy novel of the 1920's, totally forgotten now, perhaps never really known.

Perelman's sprinkling of Yiddish throughout his essays suggests that he is slyly talking for the family—made up not necessarily of those who know Yiddish by inheritance, but of all the metropolitan sophisticates who read the *New Yorker*—where, with rare exceptions, his work appears—and who may be presumed by virtue of their civilized sense of inclusiveness to have picked up a smattering of the secret language. The Yiddish is just another device in his repertory, a part of the jargon of insiders. (pp. 210-11)

In the following exchange, from what I found the funniest skit in the book, **"A Hepcat May Look at a King,"** Perelman indicates his own awareness of the hidden fraternities in our society. Two Oriental potentates are besieging a booking agent's office after Michael Todd's *Peep Show* used songs written by Bhumibol, the King of Siam (which, for the skeptical and uninformed, actually happened).

> BHOPAL: Mind you, I won't say this Bhumibol ain't an able administrator, but he don't know a beguine from a cakewalk. The kid is absolutely devoid of rhythm.
>
> KAPURTHALA: He's a Buddhist, that's why. A downbeat don't mean a thing to a Buddhist.
>
> BHOPAL: I'm surprised a showman like Todd would fall for that type air.
>
> KAPURTHALA: Eight to five he's a Buddhist, too. All those guys stick together.

Perelman *aficionados* mayn't really stick together, as Buddhists probably don't, but like their Mexican and Spanish brethren they do know that they all enjoy watching a superb matador dispose of the bull. (pp. 211-12)

> *Morris Freedman, in a review of "The Peeve as Humor," in* Commentary, *Vol. 15, February, 1953, pp. 208-12.*

LEWIS NICHOLS

S. J. Perelman must be one of the most assiduous readers of newspapers and periodicals on record. On the prowl for a subject, he turns over the pages, eyes some innocent frailty and is off like a pinwheel. Puns, gargantuan metaphors, plausible impossibilities—also a style—are there, tossed in without haggling. Before he returns to earth again the result is pretty funny indeed.

This autumn's collection of fireworks is *Perelman's Home Companion,* its proprietor, explaining in a foreword that most of the pieces come from earlier books no longer available. So be it, as long as he is here again, available. Ever meet an old college friend and decide to have him to dinner? Ever leaf through catalogues in which publishers list their coming wares? Mr. P. has done both, and the one should bring needed caution to reunions, the other drive much of publishing underground. . . .

Spring beckons to Mr. Perelman, causing him to latch onto a couple of pulp magazines called *Ideal Love* and *Gay Love Stories.* The findings? All the males of the stories therein are "six feet of lanky, bronzed strength"; all the females are glamorous, and "when these golden lads and lasses have at one another, they produce an effect akin to the interior of a blast furnace." End, spring.

So it goes, with Mr. Perelman not drinking and getting into trouble, Mr. Perelman receiving some letters from his dog, Mr. Perelman trying to jack up and cover his car for the winter. Since this last is the result of the lust for someone else in the house for bargains—whatever they cost—it should everywhere ring a loud bell.

Back to the foreword: Mr. Perelman declines to discuss the nature of humor. What is it? Well, it can be Mr. P. in there slugging for the stands. Sometimes he fans, but doesn't Ted Williams?

> *Lewis Nichols, "Fireworks and Frailties," in* The New York Times, *October 30, 1955, p. 4.*

HERBERT KUPFERBERG

Perusing this most companionable of Companions [*Perelman's Home Companion*], one is struck with the rapidity with which Mr. Perelman reduces the peruser to a state bordering on idiocy. The author will take note, let us say, of a brief paragraph in a society gossip column wherein a young heir learns that his fortune stems from chain-store profits. Mr. Perelman reflects on this event so vividly that in a moment we are transported to the Park Ave. triplex of Mr. and Mrs. Milo Leotard Allardyce DuPlessis Weatherwax, whose furnishings include a bust of Amy Lowell by Epstein and a bust of Epstein by Amy Lowell. And there it is that young Rapier Weatherwax learns where his money comes from, a revelation that makes gossip column news seem more picayune than ever.

It should be mentioned that, to obtain the maximum effect, *Perelman's Home Companion* should be taken in large and steady doses, for it has a remarkably cumulative effect. . . . But taken in sequence they demolish one's risibility threshold completely.

But who needs a risibility threshold in a split-level home? The important thing is that *Perelman's Home Companion* is not to be confused with ordinary humor books. This one is funny.

> *Herbert Kupferberg, "Thirty-Six by Perelman, and All Under One Roof," in* New York Herald Tribune Book Review, *November 6, 1955, p. 6.*

JOHN WAIN

I gather that Perelman's importance as a satirist is recognized in America; it isn't, yet, in England, where his conventional standing is simply that of an adroit 'crazy' humorist, associated in most people's minds with the Marx brothers more than with anything else. Recently, on a visit to England, Perelman was interviewed on the radio by three men at once (this technique of setting on the victim in a mob is spreading among interviewers), and their questions revealed a staggering lack of perception, especially with regard to this question of seriousness. None of the three seemed to realize that they were dealing with a satirist, a man who has selected definite targets and peppered them with something a good deal heavier than the buck-shots of the orthodox *feuilletoniste*. Some of his targets are within the area that could be broadly described as aesthetic; offences against taste, whether literary, architectural or gastronomic, always call for at least a flick from Perelman's lash; but often (surprisingly often, when one comes to read him in bulk) he directs his satire at something bigger and more tangible. Certain figures of fun, and very venomous fun at that, appear over and over again. The employer who keeps his subordinates in a continuous state of panic and mutual suspicion, for instance, is a great theme of Perelman's, all the way from Sanford Claus, head of 'the biggest toy concern in the world,' in his early parody of Odets, **"Waiting for Santy,"** to Fleur Fenton Cowles, 'to-day's editorial thunderhead and the most dynamic personality in the postwar publishing world'. The techniques differ; Santy goes into the workroom on December 24th with, 'Boys, do you know what day to-morrow is?' Gnomes *(crowding around expectantly):* 'Christmas!' Claus: 'Correct. When you look in your envelopes tonight, you'll find a little present from me—a forty per cent pay cut. And the first one who opens his trap—gets this.' *(As he holds up a tear-gas bomb and beams at them, the gnomes utter cries of joy, join hands, and dance around him shouting exultantly.)*

Here the joke is more at the expense of the social-protest drama of the 'thirties than at anything of flesh and blood; Mrs Cowles ('I guess I'm just professionally intolerant of stupid people. . . . It's one of my biggest faults, but I can't help it') is made the subject, or perhaps we should say the peg, of a very devastating satirical piece (**"The Hand that Cradles the Rock"**). (pp. 535-36)

Of course, if all Perelman's more satiric pieces were concerned with this theme of people cringing before the boss, we might deny him the status of a satirist and call him merely a writer who has worked in Hollywood and carries the inevitable scar-tissue. (It is impossible to read far in Perelman without coming across a hostile reference to Hollywood.) But there are other recurring targets. People who see a 'Red' behind every move toward reform, for instance. (p. 538)

Outside of dialogue, almost every sentence he writes echoes the inflated style of late-Victorian and Edwardian writing. It is not so much this or that author who is suggested as the whole anonymous style of the period between 1860 and 1914. Sometimes Perelman steps up the pomposity, turning the effect from simple imitation into parody, but usually he copies faithfully the rhythms, cadences and vocabulary of his chosen period, and the joke lies in the incongruity of context. On a visit to the Sphinx, for instance, recounted in **Westward Ha!,**

> All I bore away from the encounter was a nose burned the colour of an eggplant and a fearsome case of bloat induced by drinking seven bottles of soda pop in quick succession. Some anonymous genius has had the inspiration to pitch a soft-drink stand a few hundred feet away, or possibly it was even part of the original statue; in any case, I never expect to recapture the gratitude I felt for that pitiful patch of shade.

In those few lines we can see the style teetering on the edge of parody ('bore away from the encounter') but on the whole keeping to what we might call straight Perelmanese (the rueful joke at his own expense, recounted with fanatical precision of imagery), until, in that last sentence, it plunges straight into the language of the Edwardian tale of adventure. Every intrepid traveller, every retired Colonel, every tanned, pipe-smoking man of few words who settled down, his hair greying at the temples and his joints stiffening, to write the story of his adventures in Africa or India, must at some point or other have said, 'I never expect to recapture the gratitude I felt for that pitiful patch of shade.' It took Perelman to transfer the formula to a soft-drink stand by the side of the Sphinx. And by doing so, he accomplishes two things. First, he turns the already droll tale of his adventure into a parody of the retired colonel's narrative, thereby giving us, so to speak, another gift inside the same package; secondly, he shows a streak of yearning for an age which had more leisure, dignity, stateliness. There is no doubt that Perelman's compulsion to introduce Edwardian phraseology really points to an affection for it, just as his constant references to the masterpieces of literature and art represent an instinctive recoil from the shoddy and the pretentious which make up the target for his satire. Only a man steeped to the very eyebrows in the fiction of an older day would find his pen so continually reproducing its rhythms. (pp. 538-39)

What gives this prose its vertiginous quality is the lightning juxtaposition of irreconcilables. The Edwardian adventurer 'dined famously' off a cold bird and a bottle of hock; the Perelman-figure dines famously off a charmburger; the effect on the reader is a rapid jolt from one world to another, and of course depends on his having some familiarity with both. When a generation arises, as it is probably arising at this moment, that has never read yarns in which the hero 'chooses his wardrobe with some care' and 'dines famously', half of Perelman's magic will be lost. Only half, because he has wisely not invested his whole comic capital in this parody; there will still be the quick-fire dialogue, the rubbery vocabulary that twists itself out of shape, the metaphors that suddenly leap into grotesque life, and so on. (pp. 539-40)

Still, the element of parody and re-creation, the constant echo from a past that was fading before Perelman wrote a line, is what claims one's attention; it is, after all, the thing that distinguishes Perelman from other humorists. Edwardian prose, the gloomy magnificence of a lost age of dignity, flavours everything he writes. He is like a living man wandering in a world of ghosts, uttering spells which call them up and then finding himself unable to talk to them. And in this he joins hands with many of the most characteristic writers of our century. It is instructive to compare a piece by Perelman with, say, Mr Eliot's *The Waste Land.* In each case, the building is sharply contemporary, but the bricks have been taken from the ruins of an older building, and the impact depends on the reader's awareness that this is so. Eliot's quotations from the classics, woven into the structure of his poem in the same spirit of ironic juxtaposition as the musical quotations that occur in a jazz-man's improvisations, are—for all their different intention—the exact counterpart of Perelman's dizzy rain of parodied fragments. In each case, the impression left by the writing is one of sharp-witted mockery tinged with deep pessimism.

The technique of *The Waste Land* is primarily cinematic. . . . And perhaps it is not irrevelant to point out that Perelman, with his years of work in Hollywood, is more directly a child of the cinema than Eliot, just as his relationship with jazz is more direct. . . . In the last analysis, what all these jazz and cinematic techniques are doing is something quite easy to describe, though not easy to do. The aim is always to create an art which will hold dissimilar elements in some kind of unity, however precarious. That is the search of the characteristic modern intelligence as applied to art. Thomas Mann once remarked that in our time the traditional categories of comedy and tragedy had crumbled, leaving the grotesque as the dominant mode. Certainly a work like his *Felix Krull, Confidence Man* is a gigantic piece of grotesque art. The modern man lives in a world of shattered structures; artistically and intellectually, the bombs have already gone off, and we are trying to pick up the pieces and fit them together in a new way. And this applies not only to the fragments we find outside ourselves but also to the ones within. Perelman's art, like that of Eliot, is an art stretched to cover moods and attitudes that sometimes lie a long way apart. Perelman's joking does not exclude melancholy; it includes it, as everyone can feel. (pp. 540-41)

As an American writer, working steadily from the mid-'twenties to the late 'fifties, Perelman has lived through a series of social and intellectual earthquakes, which are faithfully recorded in his work. One feels that he devised his strange, kaleidoscopic style because he felt the need of a new way of writing, one that would mirror the restless dance of incongruities that so disturbs the European visitor to America. The whole modern world suffers from this disease; once industrialism has put an end to the world of hand industries and local materials, there is no reason why cities, for instance, should grow up in a homogeneous style; but for obvious reasons America, and particularly the West, suffers most. Perelman is clearly very sensitive to this continual jangling and discontinuity. Sometimes he rounds on it with a blast of pure satire (as in the wonderful piece **"Second Class Matter,"** but at others he seems to be trying, as most artists have tried in the last thirty years, to devise an idiom that will come to terms with it. (pp. 542-43)

S. J. Perelman could never be anything but an American writer. He has the restlessness, the unflagging zest of novelty, which gives American art, as well as life, so much of its glitter. And he is also American in his haunted awareness of Europe. In some American literary and artistic circles, it is the fashion to pretend that European culture was a passing fad of the American people, the product of mere self-consciousness and insecurity, and can now safely be dismissed. In Beatnik society, for example, it is better not to admit that you have ever heard of Shakespeare or Mozart, assuming that you have heard of them. Perelman has no such illusion. He knows, and every page that he writes shows it, that America has been a vast consumer-market for the European artist for three solid centuries, much too long to start pretending overnight that it never happened. His work reveals a mind deeply imbued with, and appreciative of, a traditional and therefore European-tilted culture; an American mind, wrestling with the problem of creating a new world, buoyant, energetic, and yet often dubious of the materials that are to hand and looking round for assurance that the old timbers, should they be needed, are still there. In a time like ours, such a mind will probably seek expression either in poetry or in a wild, imaginative humour. For they, after all, are the two kinds of writing that most nearly meet. (pp. 543-44)

John Wain, "A Jest in Season: Notes on S. J. Perelman, with a Digression on W. W. Jacobs," in The Twentieth Century, *Vol. 167, No. 1000, June, 1960, pp. 530-44.*

NORRIS W. YATES

Perelman resembles the Lardner of the plays in his frequent use of a dramatic framework; Leacock, Benchley, and Joyce in his talent for parody and monologue; and the Marx brothers in his controlled wildness of incident and metaphor. . . . Moreover, Perelman also stands in the mainstream of American humor by virtue of his frequent contrasting of the Little Man with the crass and venal executives, salesmen, ad-writers, and movie-makers who harass him—those who might be called the *lumpen* middle class. In Perelman's version of the elite versus the mob, the archetype who represents the elite is defeated and disturbed, but he is still a battler against odds for his sanity, as have been the protagonists of such diverse humorists as Mencken, Benchley, White, Cuppy, and at times, Ogden Nash.

Once in a while Perelman uses Jewish dialect, and at such times he belongs to a branch of a once important but now dying tradition: dialect humor based on the uncouth English of immigrant minorities. In the twentieth century this tradition was represented earlier by George V. Hobart and his "conversationings" of Mr. and Mrs. Dinkelspiel; the stories by Montague Glass about Potash and Perlmutter, and later by the work of Milt Gross with his "Nize Baby" series; Arthur Kober with his tales about Bella Gross and her family; and Dr. Leo Rosten (Leonard Q. Ross) in his stories about H*Y*M*A*N K*A*P*L*A*N.

Perelman's use of Jewish dialect is most frequent in **Dawn Ginsbergh's Revenge,** where he employs many Yiddish words or Yiddish-English turns of phrase in puns or in bits of parody—"If you must vex somebody, why don't you go home and vex the floors?" Other examples are, **"What It Minns to Be a Minnow,"** and "It was a veritable fairyland as we drove homeward in the cutter with the bells tinkling and Irma's cheeks red like two apples her cheeks were red." In his later books Perelman limits this dialect to an occasional Yiddish word, like "momzer," "zoftick," or "nebich," and to a few Yiddish turns of English phrases, as in the title, **"You Should Live So, Walden Pond."** He uses a good many Jewish proper names, and the total effect of these devices is to suggest the forced and incongruous merging of the most resistant elements in the Anglo-Saxon and Jewish cultures. This incongruity has been a fertile source of humor to writers for the Yiddish theater, and a historian of that theater could doubtless find that it contributed as well to Perelman's development.

Those who see only despair and insanity in Perelman's humor have not looked hard at his major type-figure. The Little Man may be pushed toward the gulf, but he rarely loses his sense of values—values which the author behind the mask emphatically shares. (pp. 334-36)

More commonly, Perelman speaks in the first person from behind a narrator's mask the nature of which can be indicated by the proposed title of this narrator's memoirs—*Forty Years a Boob*—and by the apter title of one of the author's books—*Crazy Like a Fox.* Perelman's wise fool might be called the Sane Psychotic, in view of the fantastic images that swirl in this figure's consciousness and suggest insanity to the unwary reader. These aberrations plus the egotism of the Sane Psychotic make him a clown, but behind the clown's mask and among the dancing images lurk the same values found in Benchley's bumbler—integrity, sincerity, skepticism, taste, a respect for competence, a striving after the golden mean, and a longing for better communication and understanding among men. These values are found too in Mr. Dooley, Abe Martin, and Will Rogers, despite the enormous difference between the unpolished dialect of the crackerbarrel and the dazzling vocabulary of Perelman's narrator. The neighborhood oracle and the college graduate may define some of these values differently, but they agree that the values do exist and can be defined.

To further disarm the reader, Perelman uses the familiar technique of tempting him to laugh at the narrator. In an introduction to *The Best of Perelman,* "Sidney Namlerep" pokes fun at his own conceit, which is all too typical of that found in authors. . . . "Sidney Namlerep" is only somewhat more of a self-burlesque than are Perelman's other narrators, but if they represent the author's faults in exaggerated form, they also present the values he strongly feels—in underplayed form. These narrators—or rather the narrator, for they are all one—the narrator carries a torch for sanity and good taste, but the author half hides that torch by making the carrier "foolish" in the sense of making him neurotic to the point of insanity. (pp. 336-38)

Perelman's interest in psychological imbalance is partly expressed through an atmosphere of nightmarish zaniness which he achieves by loading his prose with wildly incongruous contexts, often superimposed one upon another in highly condensed form. Sometimes he does this superimposing by means of puns, especially in his titles—**"To Sleep, Perchance to Steam," "A Farewell to Omsk," "It Isn't the Heat, It's the Cupidity."** Sometimes he does it through telescoping two or more well-known quotations, titles, clichés, or catch-phrases, some of which are altered almost but not quite beyond recognition. Again his titles furnish examples—**"Short Easterly Squall, With Low Visibility and Rising Gorge," "I Am Not Now, Nor Have I Ever Been, a Matrix of Lean Meat," "The Yanks Are Coming, in Five Breathless Colors," "No Starch in the Dhoti, S'il Vous Plaît."** "Free association" is a misleading term for this technique, because Perelman's superimposition of contexts is not really free but is rigidly controlled; anyhow, this incongruous juxtaposition on a larger scale is exemplified in the following passage from **"Amo, Amas, Amat, Amamus, Amatis, Enough:"**

> The other day I surfaced in a pool of glorious golden sunshine laced with cracker crumbs to discover that spring had returned to Washington Square. A pair of pigeons were cooing gently directly beneath my window; two squirrels plighted their troth in a branch overhead; at the corner a handsome member of New York's finest twirled his night stick and cast roguish glances at the saucy-eyed flower vendor. The scene could have been staged only by a Lubitsch; in fact, Lubitsch himself was seated on a bench across the street, smoking a cucumber and looking as cool as a cigar.

The simple act of waking up and looking at the plaza outside is fused with the notion of rising to the surface of a pool, also with the idea of cocktails ("laced") and with the actual remnants of what nice people have been feeding the pigeons. Other realistic details about the scene are given in language that parodies the popular sentimentalizing of the season. Suddenly introduced into the scene is an object with only a farfetched and hypothetical relationship to that scene—a well-known producer of movie comedies, whose actions are indicated in two trite but ludicrously mixed metaphors. The composite picture is an incongruous blend of the relevant with the irrelevant and of precise detail with worn-out phrases, all for the purpose of satirizing at least three different phenomena: overemphasis on spring, writing in clichés, and the triteness and artificiality of certain situations in films.

Sometimes the blend of incongruities is achieved by the use of a phrase or statement simultaneously in both a literal and a figurative meaning. . . . A variation of this literal-and-figurative usage is the occurrence of a word or phrase in a figurative but commonplace and accepted sense followed without warning by a switch to one or more usages of that same word or phrase which are extraordinary. Thus, "The color drained slowly from my face, entered the auricle, shot up the escalator, and issued from the ladies' and misses' section into the housewares department." Here Perelman uses "color" first in a hackneyed, commonplace fashion and then in a sense highly unusual.

Perelman's respect for James Joyce becomes more understandable as one recalls that Joyce too made basic use of the superimposition of multiple contexts and for this purpose developed the pun into a major artistic device, especially in *Finnegans Wake.* Perelman's use of stream-of-consciousness also suggests Joyce, and at least once, in **"Pale Hands I Loathe,"** Perelman specifies that in imagining the stream-of-consciousness of a business executive, he is using "the kind of tackle Mr. Joyce employed on Leopold Bloom." Another piece, **"Scenario,"** is a monologue composed of the trite language of movie-makers as it might be heard on a dozen different sets and read in any number of publicity releases during the making of a dozen different but monotonously similar historical "epics." In its blend of violence and triteness, **"Scenario"** suggests the Walpurgis Night episode in *Ulysses,* an episode Perelman has called "the greatest single comic achievement in the language." . . . The influence of Joyce is clear enough, but one recalls that Perelman's violent yoking of associations also owes much to the techniques of the very movie-makers that he satirized, especially the technique of montage, in which fragments of two or more pictures are combined in space by the superimposition of one upon another, partially or entirely, so that highlights of each and all may stand out and other details of each shot may be glimpsed through the intervening details of the other pictures. A variation in time of this technique is the rapid succession of shots of extreme brevity. In humorous writing, the equivalent effect of either technique might be called Perelmontage.

Perelman's prose reflects a civilization which is dizzying in its speed, complexity, and disorder, and staggering in the sheer, oppressive *quantity* of things and forces with which it bombards the average consciousness. The use of multiple contexts is one way of indicating this quantity; the use of contexts that are also incongruous is a way of suggesting both complexity and discord.

"Things close in," Walter Mitty says, and the apparent derangement of Perelman's Little Man likewise arises from the closing in on him of forces that invade and corrupt his personality and impel him toward neurosis. But he hasn't yet given in completely. The fact that his resistance is sometimes wrongheaded often obscures his essential good sense in really important matters. His reaction to dentistry, for instance, resembles that of Benchley's narrator, but the fear and trembling of both characters is neurotic only insofar as it is carried beyond the "normal" dislike of having dental work done. When it is so carried, this reaction makes Perelman's man look pretty foolish, but his equally extreme reaction to bad taste in advertising and in window display includes rational and humanistic reflections that should give pause to all who pretend to mental and political health. He observes, in a shoe-store window, the skeleton of a human foot wired to a hidden motor that makes it move. The sight makes him want to rush home and lie down, and as he thinks about it later . . . , he realizes that, "That little bevy of bones had been oscillating back and forth all through Danzig, Pearl Harbor, and the North African campaign; this very minute it was undulating turgidly, heedless of the fact the store had been closed two hours." Are his reactions neurotic? Possibly, but the display itself is more neurotic, and the meditation on how (during days of "horror, despair, and world change" as Dorothy Parker had put it) this bit of grotesque commercialism has as much or more of permanence and "stability" as most higher and worthier phenomena—this meditation lifts the narrator's reactions above the level of mere neurosis.

Perelman's dental patient reacts to persecution with a desire to escape and an aggressive desire to retaliate, though the aggression actually manifested is the merely negative act of refusing to go back to the dentist again. Patterns of withdrawal and aggression are common in the disturbance of Perelman's main character. Withdrawal may be manifested by an overpowering desire to flee, physically, from the scene of one's torment. Discomfort and poor service on the Santa Fe railroad's "Super Chief" cause Perelman's man to slide down an arroyo, crawl up a mesa, and hide behind a mesquite bush until the train has left. A magazine column of hints on how to consume more conspicuously sends this moderate consumer into a mad flight from Brentano's basement into "the cool, sweet air of Forty-Seventh Street." . . . Both aggression and flight, the latter manifested as a suicidal urge, appear in his reaction to Maxwell Bodenheim's erotic novel *Replenishing Jessica*: after referring to himself as "hysteroid," he reports that, "Unlike the average hypnotic subject, the central character was fully conscious at all times, even while asleep. He ate a banana, flung the skin out of the window, flung the book after the skin, and was with difficulty restrained from following."

The aggressions of Perelman's narrator run the gamut from futility to violence. He will wear a cord to hold up his pants rather than use a Talon fastener. The style of a certain female fashion-analyst causes him to fling the New York *Times* from him with a force that demolishes a lamp. An ad that represents food as articulate . . . stimulates him into planting a microphone and a tape recorder in the refrigerator. Then, beset by hallucinations about what has been "recorded," he rushes to the refrigerator, intent on throwing out the contents. Small wonder that his wife locks herself in the henhouse. The skeletal foot in the shoestore window leads him to propose bombing the store, anarchist fashion, and to anyone who follows the advice given in a book on *How to Crash Tin-Pan Alley* he will gladly give a "just reward"—two hundred lashes with a blacksnake whip.

Obviously Perelman's Sane Psychotic is less sane and more psychotic than the Little Man of some other writers. But does the fault lie in the man or in his environment? His need for "a good five-cent psychiatrist" arises from his reading about the possibilities for getting a fatal shock from an electric blanket. Is this man sicker than the men who make and advertise such gadgetry? A certain store clerk gradually comes to feel that he is being watched by a mannequin. So he is—by a movie director hidden in this dummy. However, because the clerk thinks he must be going mad, he does go mad. This narrative grew out of an actual suggestion by a film critic that scenes could be shot in stores and other places of business with concealed cameras, and it has political implications concerning censorship and snooping. Perelman is suggesting that such tactics on the part of movie-makers—or anybody—would in-

vade the right of privacy of the unfortunate citizens thus photographed, as well as drive them batty. (He has yet to give full expression to what he probably thinks about "Candid Camera.") The clerk's "hallucinations" are all too real; the aberration is that of a society which would countenance such spying. Through his narrator, Perelman mocks the weaknesses of himself, and by implication, of his readers, but he is also insisting that his own irrationalities should not be abetted and compounded by those of society and its mass media. If they are so compounded, what (he implicitly asks) is left for the harassed man of sensitivity but aggression and / or withdrawal?

Escape to the country has not helped Perelman's man much. In *Acres and Pains* and in shorter pieces dealing with life in Bucks County, Perelman (or rather, his double) shows that he has, on the whole, merely added to his troubles by becoming a part-time farmer. He says, "In a scant fifteen years [of country living] I have acquired a superb library of mortgages, mostly first editions, and the finest case of sacroiliac known to science." This little "exurbanite" has been affronted or victimized by the climate, by the soil, by workmen, by the natives, by fellow exurbanites, by architects, by machinery, by house servants, by ghosts (or so he thinks), by pets, by his own elaborate plans, by cruel chance and malign fate. (pp. 341-48)

In his two travel books, [*Westward Ha!* and *Swiss Family Perelman*,] Perelman's narrator shows his affinity with the wise American fool of Mark Twain's *Innocents Abroad* and with dozens of other equally shrewd but parochial tourists, including the narrator in Cobb's *Europe Revised*, the Old Soak of Don Marquis, and at times, Sinclair Lewis' Sam Dodsworth. Perelman as tourist refuses to see anything new or exciting in foreign parts; when he isn't recalling the dirt and the heat, or the discomforts of travel and the obnoxiousness of his fellow travelers, he is insisting that the fabled sights of far countries are no more exciting than various commonplace scenes at home. Perelman's traveler describes his first sight of China as "a sullen range of hills disturbingly similar to those we had left behind in Southern California." Just as Mark Twain had compared Lake Como unfavorably with Lake Tahoe, Perelman's man finds the scenery about Chinwangtao "reminiscent of the less attractive suburbs of Carteret, New Jersey." The Oriental night club where the deposed Emperor of Annam, Bao Dai, took his pleasure "turned out to be a somewhat sedater version of Broadway's Roseland. . . ." Of all the Oriental cities he saw, only Bangkok impressed him, and of all the great sights, only the Taj Mahal.

In the *Swiss Family Perelman* this wiseacre has his family along, and his problem becomes one of getting the little woman and two children past such perils as the ship's menu, their fellow passengers, friendly foreigners, and assorted sights on shore. In the fashion of Lardner, Day, Benchley, and Thurber, much emphasis is given to father's attempts to preserve his ego from demolition by his family when things go wrong, as they usually do. The wife's comments at one dismal moment are typical:

> "Did I ever tell you," she went on, "that in order
> to marry you, I jilted an explorer?"
>
> "Honestly?" I asked. "What did you tell him?"
>
> "I wish I could remember," she murmured. "It sure
> would come in handy."

The rich cultural allusiveness of Perelman's discourse should not blur the basic traits which establish as his central figure a superior type of American, a man of sensitivity and intelligence who remains ordinary in the sense of sharing the faults and foibles of most of his countrymen, and of humankind. His normal quota of foolishness is exaggerated into psychosis for the purpose of satirizing the madnesses of this man's environment. Whether he appears as writer, exurbanite, traveler, or mere consumer of mass media, this type exercises his reason and taste in pointing out the disorders of his civilization. In so doing, he re-enacts the revolt of the consumer hoped for by Walter Weyl in 1912, and in spite of irrational responses to some of these disorders, he fights to retain his loosening grip on ideals of clarity, honesty, common sense, and the right to his own personality—which includes the right to be foolish and undignified in his own way, not in the more effectively lethal ways forced on one by an environment madder than he. He still knows the good, though he cannot always will that good which he knows or do that good which he wills.

He is a shade better off than "Miss Lonelyhearts" in the novel of that title by Perelman's brother-in-law, Nathanael West. "Miss" Lonelyhearts goes completely to pieces in his disordered environment, but Perelman's narrator retains a measure of sanity in a world which suffers from what Erich Fromm has called "the pathology of normalcy"—a world where even visions of the Hereafter include "time clocks, Kardex systems, and for all we know, conferences in which ghostly Corona-Coronas are chewed." In such a world, the faith of Perelman's narrator in the decency of at least a small number of human beings may seem fatuous but it will not down. That faith saves him from the fate of West's anti-hero—that faith, and a sense of humor. (pp. 348-50)

> *Norris W. Yates, "The Sane Psychoses of S. J. Perelman," in his* The American Humorist: Conscience of the Twentieth Century, *Iowa State University Press, 1964, pp. 331-50.*

V. S. PRITCHETT

[*The essay excerpted below was originally published in* New Statesman, *November 24, 1967.*]

The huge advantage of American humour, as one sees it in S. J. Perelman, is in the punishment of character and the use of language. Unlike Thurber who has been much admired by [the English], Perelman is not an understater who suddenly throws out an almost spiritual blossom. He drops ash into the dessert. Perelman either grew up with burlesque or soon got caught up in it. Immediate action is his need. An idea has to seize him. His very best things have come out of grotesque experiences in Hollywood; or when, not having enough time to read Palgrave's *Golden Treasury,* he has had to feed on the advertising columns of glossy papers. One gets the impression that English humorists snub the commercials, whereas an American like Perelman regards them as part of the general awful meal that makes us what we don't want other people to be. Having acquired a stomach of zinc, he knows it's his duty to swallow the poison, like someone who feels it a duty to see what cyanide does to the system. As a character, he is a harassed detective, stuck in some lobby, chain-smoking, pedantic, always in disguise, with the air of one about to follow footprints and tracking something down. He is Groucho Marx's more sensitive alter ego, the con-man's shadow. (pp. 189-90)

Perelman's speciality, like O. Henry's and Mark Twain's, is Fraud. He looks at the landscape and it is gashed and billboarded with the poetic news that here someone made a killing and cleared out quickly. The inner life of a grey Puritan culture is dramatic, gaudy and violent; fraud, in the sense of the double-think, double-appearance or fact and the image that palms them off, is basic. . . . Chicken Inspector No 23 Perelman of the Fraud Squad surveys the field of conspicuous waste, the biggest fraud of the lot, with a buyer's hypnotised eye. He is the un-innocent abroad; at his best in the subjects of showbiz, he is a tangy raconteur, though I find him less speedy when he turns his idea into a script with dialogue. This is odd since he has been one of the finest script writers in the funny business; indeed, remembering the Marx Brothers, a genius. He is above all a voice, a brisk and cigary voice, that keeps up with his feet as he scampers, head-down upon the trail; in his own words 'button-cute, rapier-keen and pauper poor' and having 'one of those rare mouths in which butter has never melted'. He has a nose for non-news. For a long time the English humorists have suffered from having achieved the funny man's dream; they have either gone straight for the information or have succumbed to the prosaic beauty of their own utterance. They are 'facetious' without being Boswell. Mr Perelman is not entirely free of the English vice. I have caught him adding an unnecessary, 'I said with hauteur' or 'I said with dignity'. This weakness he may have picked up on his annual visits to those fake cathedral closes of ours in Savile Row. (The metaphor is his.) But he does not wear thin. (pp. 191-92)

> *V. S. Pritchett, "S. J. Perelman: 'The Con-Man's Shadow'," in his* A Man of Letters: Selected Essays, *Random House, 1985, pp. 188-92.*

DOUGLAS FOWLER

From the early 1930s until his death in 1979, one of the most interesting and accomplished of American comic voices was that of S. J. Perelman, and of all the writers who have attempted to create an American comic perspective in those years Perelman's efforts may have been the most distinctive and the most likely to weather the future. This is a large claim to make about a writer who has deliberately imposed upon his work severe limitations as to its focus, intentions, and technique, and I would immediately agree that it would be a mistake to claim for Perelman "major" status: he never undertook the novel form or the serious discursive essay; his pieces never show personality in a process of growth or change; his intention was solely to amuse and delight for almost fifty professional years. He worked in balsawood, not marble, and we cannot find in his work any direct attention to our most urgent human concerns—life, death, sexuality, loss, choice, freedom, power, moral dilemma; we cannot expect it to show us ourselves. Perelman was a toymaker; a professional toymaker, perhaps one of the most gifted who ever lived by that craft. But it would be a misleading mistake to confuse his craft with portraiture, architecture, or the manufacture of weapons—with that of the novelist, the theorist, or the satirist. Literary people are too quick to try to attach serious moral purposes to Perelman and to assume that because we know he was a man who found the world a dangerous and disappointing place (and he told us again and again that he did), his comic writing must in some way embody that truth. Must it? The rhetorical shape of that question has already alerted you to the fact that I believe otherwise. . . . In a study he calls *The American Humorist: Conscience of the Twentieth Century,* Norris W. Yates claims that behind Perelman's facade of cartoon and parody "lurk the same values" that a Stoic philosopher or a Scoutmaster would applaud: "integrity, sincerity, skepticism, taste, a respect for competence, a striving after the golden mean, and a longing for better communication and understanding among men'' [see excerpt above]. We might well come to agree that Perelman the man was the very embodiment of every virtue listed, but in coming to appreciate him as an artist we may find such a catalog confusing and inadequate. An artistic truth can be complex and full of contradictions, and it might not be entirely flattering to the artist and his audience, either.

Perelman was a master technician with prose and a remarkably skillful comic strategist, and he did the small things he chose to do with wonderful precision. But like most creation which celebrates its own form over its own content, Perelman's work has become famous as a style and yet largely ignored as a mode of sensibility. (pp. vii-viii)

Perelman was always playful and he always worked in small forms, and so, although his name has become a label, a descriptive adjective, the distinctiveness of his achievement has never been closely defined. He continued a tradition; he had influence; a tradition continues from him. When the British-born critic Martin Green came to read Salinger and Nabokov, he discovered in both "a style characterised by its exuberant and recondite vocabulary, highly literary and highly technical at the same time, lavish of foreign phrases, commercial terms, academic turns of speech . . . its images . . . extremely clever, its manner consistently self-conscious, its effects all variations on a theme of exaggeration," and that the America described in *Lolita* and *Franny* is "most unlike the broad shafts of sunlight bathing the broad and noble cornfields in ordinary poetic descriptions of America." What Green recognized in that urbane and self-conscious artificiality is Perelman's influence and Perelman's sensibility, for . . . one of the most uniquely American of writers turns out to be everything we have supposed an American writer is not: Jewish, playful, urban, artificial, an exquisite stylist, erudite, shrill, small, and negative. For a culture that has been calling *Moby-Dick* its greatest epic and Hemingway its archetypal artist-hero for the last fifty years, the idea of Perelman as a lens for looking into an important aspect of national sensibility may seem almost indecent: and yet it is true, just as it is true that Gogol's voice contains and explains as much of Russia as Tolstoy's, or that Lewis Carroll's voice is as real to the English experience as Hardy's, or that Ambrose Bierce's eerie and morbid gothicism is as central to the American experience as William Dean Howells's yea-saying. (pp. viii-ix)

Douglas Fowler, in his S. J. Perelman, *Twayne Publishers, 1983, 172 p.*

PETER De VRIES

[With the publication of Perelman's *That Old Gang o' Mine: The Early and Essential S. J. Perelman*], all the oeuvre relevant to professorial study or reader pleasure has been brought between covers. It contains fifty-five pieces and over a hundred cartoons written and drawn by Perelman during the salad years immediately following his graduation from Brown, in 1925. . . . The contents may not make a lasting contribution to the gaiety of nations, but they do offer up the fascinating embryo of a writer whose mature work does. Even in the sketches spun out on the obvious college-humor level of the era we see the wild free association, anarchic word-play, maniacal non sequiturs, preposterous names, and surrealist juxtapositions prescient of the accomplished pyrotechnician to come. While most of it is thus period rather than vintage, plenty of vintage stuff appears. "I have Bright's disease and he has mine" is here, and not as a

line in a story, which many devotees who quote it as their favorite gag think it is, but as the caption to a cartoon.

That's one of the chief surprises—Perelman as the cartoonist he first was. As an artist he was quite good, principally in the woodcut tradition of the day, although, Perelmanesquely enough, the captions rarely have anything to do with the pictures, parts of which, to extend the absurdity, have nothing to do with each other. (pp. 88-9)

There seems one marked difference between the early cutup and the mature craftsman we know. The former is frequently pulling the reader's leg, if not the rug from under his feet, in an unending series of unpredictable twists and turns, while the latter tends more to invite the reader to join him on mockouts of his innumerable targets, which as often as not, of course, include himself. There is a more exhilarating joyride from the master in full control of that polyphonic style, a prose ingeniously blending high literary allusion, slang, show-biz hype, Yiddishisms, unabashed puns, canyon leaps of the imagination, fantastic coinages of proper names, all compacted into a manner at once densely droll and featherlight. "Wit lasts no more than two centuries," Stendhal pontificated. Humor has an even shorter life span, so that the statistical chances of a humorist's outliving his own stuff are great—hardly a consoling thought to anyone but executives of life-insurance companies. Most perishable of all is topical humor, but the best of Perelman's improvisations in that category manage to transcend the journalistic springboards from which he does his high diving, and the brand of wit with which he executes his aerial acrobatics gives him at least a fighting chance against Stendhal's aphorism. (p. 89)

Peter De Vries, "Perelmania," in The New Yorker, *Vol. LX, No. 26, August 13, 1984, pp. 88-91.*

D. KEITH MANO

Someone should protect dead writers from people who collect and publish their juvenilia. (Did that sound like a dirty word? Did to me.) This is S. J. Perelman material [in *That Old Gang o' Mine*]—almost lost, but no such luck—taken from *Judge* (1925-1931) a national college-humor review. I fell asleep over it four nights running, sitting. As [editor] Richard Marschall (the culprit himself) has written: "No wonder his pieces were never more than article length—such roller-coaster rides in short trips were exhilarating; longer assaults on our assumptions would have been exhausting." So what did the damn fool do? Right, he put together a 160-page assault. I mean, some people never learn.

Not that PERELMAN is without IMAGINATION—good GRIEF, if only he WERE now and then, I wouldn't need to wear this darn GOALIE'S MASK. His associative mind boiled quite off: I'd rather read Hegel while smoking Utah mushrooms. Each sentence, each paragraph, is in danger of capsizing. A railroad track with two thousands switch frogs per mile—pun, allusion, idiomatic quirk, whatever, can shunt sense off, good-bye. It's almost as if SJP didn't trust his ability to manage sequential narrative. Like a middle-rank abstract painter, he stumped criticism with surreal images instead of committing himself to some judgeable coherence. I imagine he does have a swell ear (this at age 21 to 26) for cliché and the popular written genre—but that might be rather hard to estimate accurately in 1984. It is all more intense and unrelieved than *Foxe's Book of Martyrs*. And you can put my name in there, too, now.

Perelman began as a cartoonist—a dreadful one. . . . The artwork has less animation than cuneiform—by 1925, I guess, they hadn't invented sight gags yet. Oh, you say, humor must be down below, in his caption. Yah, but the text (an egregious pun without fail) is totally unrelated to whatever was drawn up above. Picture of mother and son: caption, a pun about cows. So there. All this, mind, is intentional—kind of, "Oh, so you expected to laugh, did you?" drollery. Perelman adds a tag line mocking his own precious witlessness. "And they shot Lincoln, just think." Or "Stand back, boys, a woman has just fainted." I do believe they call this "zany" humor. A word that can cause me to run from the room. Zany means so mindless that mindlessness itself is both punch line and double take. Or so they hope. (pp. 52-3)

That Old Gang o' Mine has antiquarian interest: fun to note what made people laugh in 1925. The plumbing was also pretty primitive back then. It's ten after five, Boss, can I go home now? (p. 53)

> D. Keith Mano, "Perelman's Book of Martyrs," in
> National Review, New York, Vol. XXXVI, No. 21,
> November 2, 1984, pp. 52-3.

CHRISTOPHER LEHMANN-HAUPT

So much print, and only the *selected* letters of S. J. Perelman? This is not credible coming from a writer who was known for bleeding words, who once described himself as "an introvert nail-chewer who has to lock himself into an iron maiden, preferably sound-proofed, to even answer a dunning letter." Yet sure enough, here is [*Don't Tread on Me: The Selected Letters of S. J. Perelman,*] a crowded half-century's worth of Mr. Perelman's correspondence to friends and enemies, family members and lovers, the famous and the obscure, with identifying footnotes in case we've forgotten (or never knew) who the recipients were.

And the words invariably flow smoothly, whether joshingly or vitriolically. No signs of bleeding here, except by those who've been hatcheted. . . .

In fact, so incandescent is Mr. Perelman's prose that we begin to wonder if he's going to reveal anything about himself. . . . The volume's editor, Prudence Crowther, who became a close friend of her subject during the last year of his life, admits in her preface: "Tenderness, for example, gets short shrift; so does ribaldry. He could be eloquent in both, but to gain the cooperation of certain correspondents I have acceded to some editing by other hands." The letters, then, "constitute a species of autobiography, starting in 1928 and ending only with Perelman's death" in 1979.

A species of autobiography, yes, but it leaves out much of what Dorothy Herrmann revealed in her 1986 biography, *S. J. Perelman: A Life* [see Herrmann's entry in *CLC*, Vol. 44], of his unhappy marriage, of his wife's sufferings, of his children's troubles and of his own emotional difficulties and remote personality. A careless reading of these letters might make it appear that except for the intrusion of Hollywood—in particular that "sinister dwarf" Mike Todd, who paid Mr. Perelman more than he could refuse for writing the screenplay of *Around the World in 80 Days*—life was mostly traveling abroad, writing funny pieces for *The New Yorker,* and lambasting Lillian Hellman for various reasons.

Still, the clues are present if you want to see them. There is almost no mention of his wife, Laura (except when he sends her a letter while traveling), but there is always at least one woman he is writing to on whom he appears to dote, the last of them being the editor herself. There is not a single letter to his son, Adam, and though he writes at length to his daughter, Abby, his prose is more dutiful than spontaneous, and he seems to miss her obvious call for help by taking literally her teenage complaint, after reading *Crime and Punishment*, that something must be wrong because it "deeply affected me." His chilly response: "The answer is that nothing is wrong with you because it deeply affects everyone." . . .

Maybe it's not entirely fair to read these letters in one hand, with an admittedly interpretive biography in the other. But even without the evidence Ms. Herrmann cites, it's easy enough to sense the turbulence beneath the glittering surface of the letters. "In general, I feel that any exegesis of humor is both fatal and dull," Perelman wrote in 1942, submitting a specimen to an anthologist, "but if I show some slight preference for this piece, it is because of its underlying note of desperation. It marks a troubled period when I almost gave up writing to become a charwoman. I'm still not sure I made the more profitable choice. . . ."

He made the profitable choice so far as posterity's laughter was concerned. But as well as desperation he invested rage and a certain amount of hatred in the enterprise. *Baby, It's Cold Inside,* he called one of his late collections. Baby, it sure was, to judge from the iciness within these letters. Baby, it was cold inside. And the barometer was falling.

> Christopher Lehmann-Haupt, in a review of "Don't
> Tread on Me," in The New York Times, July 2,
> 1987, p. C24.

MORDECAI RICHLER

Inadvertently Ms. Crowther's cuts [in *Don't Tread on Me*] sometimes make this collection read like a Perelman parody of a dead literary man's correspondence. "And I can't tell you how exciting is the prospect of again seeing that roll of toilet paper — — uses as a face." "Your vignette of — — and the arty-tarty set with their 'dear old sausage' talk, etc., made my blood run cold." "The guest of honor was — —, accompanied by that indescribable harridan, his wife." . . .

The publishers, sneaky smart, quote Paul Theroux's introduction to *The Last Laugh,* Perelman's posthumous collection, on the jacket flap. But I doubt that Mr. Theroux ever saw these selected letters or he couldn't have written, "When Perelman's letters are collected, as they surely deserve to be, they will comprise the autobiography he promised and began, but never got around to finishing. . . . He was always more personal and ruminative and risqué in his letters than he was in his stories."

The letters certainly did deserve to be collected. They are interesting, charming, sometimes beautifully written, but they are also evasive, no substitute for the autobiography, and the only really risqué one in the bunch is a letter sent to Paul Theroux. Perelman was involved with many women over the years. According to his biographer, he was fond of sending them playful, decidedly erotic letters; the only one I've seen is not included in *Don't Tread on Me,* but appears in Dorothy Herrmann's book [*S. J. Perelman: A Life*]. . . .

Mind you, he took a dim view of John Updike's writing about sex. . . . He also seemed to disapprove of Philip Roth and Susan Sontag, among others, but he could be generous. He admired V. S. Naipaul, Kingsley Amis, Bernard Malamud and Norman

Lewis, and was largely responsible for the grant awarded to Joseph Heller by the National Institute of Arts and Letters in 1963. *Catch 22,* he wrote, was "an extraordinary piece of work."

There's a lot of juicy stuff in the letters for *New Yorker* buffs. For openers, Perelman addressed the editor who succeeded Ross not as "Mr. Shawn," or even "William," but as plain "Bill," which I should have thought was only God's prerogative. Followers of the recent upheaval at *The New Yorker* will be amused to discover that Mr. Shawn's promotion astonished Perelman. "I was bowled off my pins to learn of Bill's ascension to the wheelhouse," he wrote to the fiction editor, Gus Lobrano, in 1952. "I suppose I had taken it for granted that if anyone were chosen for the post, it would be you, and I am still trying to puzzle it out. I of course know nothing whatever of the subterranean currents at the office, but at this distance it occurs to me there must have been an unexpected upheaval." Only five years later he wrote, "As for a certain 20-cent magazine called *The New Yorker,* I had another volcanic run-in with them which has effectively convinced me that by and large, that chapter of my life is closed.... Its whole character has changed; none of the vivacity, the gaiety it used to have is apparent any more."...

The selected letters range from 1928, a year before Horace Liveright published Perelman's first collection, *Dawn Ginsbergh's Revenge,* to the year of his death. Some of them, as you might expect, are very witty indeed; others sink in a sea of complaints. The correspondence reveals the breadth of Perelman's friendships. There are letters to T. S. Eliot, Groucho Marx, James Thurber, Raymond Chandler, Ogden Nash, Malcolm Cowley, E. B. White and many editors and lady friends, but, astonishingly, not one to his son, Adam, who was in and out of trouble with the police.

Equally astonishing, in all the letters written between 1939-45 there is hardly a reference to World War II. However, in 1947, Perelman did write a chillingly prescient letter about Indochina, as it then was, to Gus Lobrano from Bangkok.... Later letters establish his intense dislike of witchhunters and "that fearful s.o.b. Nixon." In 1952, there is a clearheaded view of Adlai Stevenson. "There isn't a shadow of a doubt that Stevenson is a literate, cultivated man with as sharp a sense of humor as any politician in American history has ever displayed, but he is most certainly not the Abraham Lincoln many have persuaded themselves he is."

Several threads run through the 51 years of correspondence—complaints about money problems, an arduous work load, hatred of Hollywood and endless bickering with editors and publishers. Through the years Perelman protested again and again about being hard pressed for money.... In the early days he was obliged to write knee-slappers for Jimmy Durante, patter for a seemingly ungrateful Larry Adler, the harmonica player, and later to churn out so-so pieces for magazines he considered beneath him. "I have about 3 weeks clear before I start on my 3rd *Redbook* piece on Las Vegas."

Perelman didn't object to being sole recipient of an Academy Award for the screenplay of the forgettable *Around the World in 80 Days,* though he was only one of the three writers entitled to credit for the script. But in later years he deeply resented being associated in the public mind with the Marx brothers, having been one of a group of writers responsible for the incomparable *Horse Feathers* and *Monkey Business.* In 1976, when a publisher wanted to include extracts from his Marx

brothers scripts in Perelman's next book, he wrote to his British agent, Deborah Rogers, that he was "sicked and tired of my endless identification with these clowns...." (p. 31)

There were endless quarrels with publishers, Perelman convinced that they were all inept scoundrels who admired other writers on their lists more and were out to sabotage rather than promote his books. Typical was a letter he wrote to Donald Klopfer, at Random House, in 1947. "To the best of my information and what I myself have seen since I left New York, no advertisement for *Keep It Crisp* has appeared anywhere since early in December." Later he would have the same complaint about a number of British publishers and about Simon & Schuster, whom he threatened to quit for Doubleday.

On the evidence of last year's biography and the letters collected by Prudence Crowther, the immensely talented S. J. Perelman was insufferably self-centered, a grouch, more than somewhat paranoid, a skinflint, a relentless womanizer and a remote and indifferent parent at best....

If he never risked going after the entire beast, but was content with short takes, snapping at its heels, a miniaturist to the end, well then, he was superb at what he did. Time will clearly pardon S. J. Perelman, pardon him—as Auden wrote of Paul Claudel—"for writing well." Prudence Crowther, in her affectionate introduction to *Don't Tread on Me,* writes that Perelman once told her that someone had called out to him as he was crossing the street in the middle of the block, "Be careful—we need you."

Yes, indeed. (p. 33)

> *Mordecai Richler, "The Road to Dyspepsia," in* The New York Times Book Review, *August 9, 1987, pp. 1, 31, 33.*

STEVEN H. GALE

[A brief review of the elements of Perelman's style] is valuable as a means of providing a unifying overview of Perelman's canon because that stylistic sum is greater than the technical parts, because his style is in itself interesting to analyze, and because for most scholars that style is the *sine qua non* for studying his work in the first place.

The attention concentrated on Perelman's use of language is in no way meant to belittle humorous writing or the social functions of his humor; his work is read for enjoyment and to commiserate with a kindred spirit in a vindictive world. Nevertheless, while his work may not be read for its philosophy or grand thoughts, among the numerous elements that contribute to and are characteristic of Perelman's writing, it is useful to start a study of his style with a look at his subject matter. The thematic content of his prose is important, of course, because to a large degree this determines his style and his audience (which in turn influence the author's style).

Ironically, as might be expected with a writer of comedy, Perelman was not studied by scholars during his lifetime, nor is he remembered now for any special or significant thematic hobbyhorse.... There are certain topics and themes that recur regularly in Perelman's work, yet they are seldom developed to any great extent, and they tend to be less significant than the questions about life, death, and the nature of reality that are usually expected to be addressed in great literature. Perelman observes and comments on the surfaces of life. Even on those occasions when he is concerned with cosmic questions, he does not choose to delve very deeply. (pp. 175-76)

At the base of his writing is a sense of perspective, an ability to see ridiculous or amusing aspects in *quotidian* experiences through his wire-rimmed glasses. This is coupled with a talent for communicating his discoveries to his audience so that they can share in the laughter. Catastrophe (the Depression, the Coconut Grove fire, politics, World War II, Korea, Viet Nam) is avoided. . . . (pp. 176-77)

As an author, Perelman is a society writer rather than a writer about social concerns. His topics are not politics but everyday subjects—films, books, travel, appliances, advertisements—topical but timeless only in the strictest sense of the word in that they represent annoyances of the kind that will always plague mankind, not because they address the largest questions about the nature of existence. . . .

If the critics are right, Perelman's goal in using humor has been met. Ogden Nash writes that Perelman "exposes the fool in his folly not through reduction, but through magnification to the absurd, so that the subject stands larger than life and twice as ludicrous, foot in mouth and egg on his chin, hoist by his own assininity" so that "the rest of us" have "a happy chance to laugh at some of the perfect asses in this imperfect world." (p. 177)

Norris Yates [see excerpt above], Walter Blair, and Hamlin Hill place Perelman in that current of the mainstream of American humor typified by the writers for *The New Yorker,* particularly those of the 1930's and 1940's such as Thurber and Benchley, who created a composite Little Man figure, even if each author's creation was slightly different. What the Little Man characters share is an unsuccessful rebellion against "ancient standards." They are average men, victims of an illogical outside world epitomized by that frightful generic monster, woman. Perelman's art and contribution to the Little Man genre is to use that persona as a vehicle for expressing his essential attitude toward modern life, an attitude at once jaundiced and hopeful, expecting the unexpected as well as the expected, and encyclopedic while self-centered. Sex frequently appears in Perelman's writing, but almost always it is alluded to suggestively, not blatantly. It is mentioned, but not seen or realized. It is in the background, but only wistfully. Often the Perelman persona or protagonist observes a woman lasciviously, seemingly like a male chauvinist, yet it is the naive, and certainly ineffectual, lasciviousness of a schoolboy that controls the observation. The longing is not dirty—it is sometimes slightly amazed, and it is doomed to remain unfulfilled. Like comedian Rodney Dangerfield, Perelman's Little Man character "don't get no respect" from the opposite sex. Thus, some of the humor in the stories comes from seeing how the hero will bungle a budding relationship through his lack of experience and misunderstanding of how to behave suavely. The very things that he does and says to impress the woman are better designed to make him appear foolish to her than as an object of sexual desire. One of the ironies that the Perelman persona/protagonist ultimately must face, though, is that even if he does everything exactly right, as unlikely as that would be, the woman probably will not find him attractive anyway. (pp. 177-78)

The ways in which the Little Man fails in his romantic quest are humorous in themselves, and the expectation of failure permits the distancing that allows both Perelman's persona or protagonist and the reader to laugh at the humor in the situation.

The Perelman persona is interesting in other situations, too. He/she exists in a world tinged with fantasy. The world is near enough to normal to be familiar, but the persona—self-described as broad shouldered, with rugged good looks or the feminine equivalent and possessing special abilities—introduces an unreal quality. The character is what one would wish to be, not what one is. Yet the character cannot be blamed entirely for succumbing to delusion because Hollywood, advertisers, and magazines like *Harper's Bazaar* not only incite such delusions, they actively foster them. Hence, Perelman is provided with a brace of targets; the sources of delusion and those gullible folks who allow themselves to be ensnared by the illusions—himself and his readers included. . . . Alone, and slightly insane in a mad, mad world, the protagonist is subdued and humiliated as well. Given the modern world surrounding them, Perelman's readers can identify with his personae easily. Blair and Hill chastise Perelman for not extending himself into the arena of satire, thus permitting his audience to escape "any message" by virtue of being overcome by "waves of banter, frivolity, and whimsy." These scholars miss an important point, though. Perelman's persona is beaten, but he is not vanquished. Humor offers hope, ultimately, and Perelman's Little Man wanders away from the scene of the accident dazed, but not defeated. He will rise again, grin slightly crooked but in place, to face whatever dragons or windmills await him tomorrow. And, as he waddles Chaplinesquely out of sight, the Perelman protagonist may be a little dusty, but there is a jauntiness to his step as he rounds the corner and disappears into the sunset. At bottom, a sense of humor and, finally, a refusal to take himself seriously become survival traits. (pp. 178-79)

If Perelman's themes do not excite scholars, his mastery of the English language and his manipulation of prose for comic effect have continually drawn praise, and his ability was such that he could apply his style to practically any topic and produce humor. (p. 180)

Any analysis of the humorist's work must begin with an acknowledgement of his use of clichés—some of which appear straightforwardly in his prose (that is, they are used as though they are literally true), some of which are used figuratively, and some of which combine the literal and the figurative, starting in one mode and finishing in the other. Next is the wide range of allusions that flow through his writing like a vein of rich ore. Tracking down all of these allusions would provide a scholar with a life's work. The possibility that the "arcane knowledge" involved in Perelman's myriad references to "cultural figures and styles long past, obsolete words, [and] architectural oddities" might limit his audience is answered by the writer's contention that "I write pretty much for myself. If, at the close of business each evening, I myself can understand what I've written, I feel the day hasn't been totally wasted." A more valid answer might be that while the allusions are an important and omnipresent element of Perelman's style, the success or failure of a piece does not depend entirely on the recognition of all of the allusions incorporated in the piece. Allusion is only one element, one that adds to the knowledgeable reader's enjoyment, to be sure, but the less well-informed reader will still find plenty to be amused by even without this added fillip. Thus, although allusions are an elitist element, they do not prevent Perelman from being a popular writer.

Related to clichés and allusions are the constant puns, and Perelman's felicity with puns is enhanced by his immense vocabulary and extensive storehouse of cultural tidbits. Many of his puns evolve out of clichés or allusions. Even the very titles of the humorist's articles and book-length collections serve to exemplify this aspect of his style. While many are puns (*A Child's Garden of Curses,* not verses), almost all of his titles rely on the reader's exposure to a wide range of sources to be able to identify the allusion, some of the sources being fairly esoteric (*The Ill-Tempered Clavichord,* taken from Johann Sebastian Bach's *The Well-Tempered Clavier*). At the same time, the titles provide evidence of the author's awareness of current customs and events in modern society (*Listen to the Mocking Bird* and *Baby, It's Cold Inside* are based on contemporary song titles).

Finally, there is another foundation upon which Perelman's humor and style rest that usually appears in unobtrusive ways but which serves as a solid underpinning and is always there. This is the Yiddish background, partially derived from American-Jewish culture as a whole and partly from the Yiddish theater specifically, that provides the device of the *shlemiel* and the stratagem of the *shpritz* . . . that is mentioned by Yates, alluded to by Ward, and discussed in some detail by Fowler. (pp. 183-84)

As was the case with the Yiddish tradition, there are some tangential associations between Perelman's writing and another sub-genre, the American frontier humor tradition. He was well aware of the major authors and works in this tradition, having read many of them during his youth. Most obvious of the connections between his writing and that of his predecessors in the tradition is his fondness for the most outrageous hyperbole delivered in a perfectly straight-faced manner. His attention to the details of life around him might lead to his being classified a local colorist, even though his wide-ranging eye did not confine him to some readily identifiable location such as the "down East" of Seba Smith but rather made him a local colorist for a nation because he concentrated on those elements that transcend county lines and are national in character—films, advertising, and the like. Ultimately, then, the stylistic similarities are interesting because they are similarities and may represent some minimal influences, not because they are indicators of any conscious or well-defined embracing of the tradition. Perelman, and the humorists whom he emulated, can write their kind of humor because the tradition exists, but this does not make them part of the tradition. Particularly in his early pieces at Brown, for instance, Perelman's style was derivative, echoing the humorous journalistic style of the time, and throughout his career he incorporated into his writing those elements that he enjoyed and could use effectively. But, like other major authors, he converted those elements into something identifiably his own, and he rose above the traditions from which he borrowed. (p. 185)

Perelman aptly records the reactions of an American everyman to the world that surrounds him. This is brought out in another link with the American humor tradition, the attitude that he expresses about the rest of the world during his many travels. Almost unceasingly Perelman compares wherever he is at the moment with somewhere in the United States, and the comparison is seldom favorable for the foreign locale. His attitude carries over from physical geography to local custom and inhabitants, too. If he were a little more assertive, he might seem an Ugly American, though it is not in his character to be jingoistic. But, too many things conspire to trip him up or allow him to be taken advantage of, so instead of blatantly parading his disdain for things not American, he spends most of his time ducking. This happens to him at home, too, of course, but at home he understands some of the motives that lie behind whatever is assaulting him, whereas when he is abroad things simply seem to be in the nature of the place and as an outsider he is destined never to comprehend that nature, just to suffer degradation at its hands. There is definitely a kinship between Perelman's travel volumes and Twain's *Innocents Abroad.* (p. 187)

The use of one final device should be addressed, that of including real or imaginary excerpts from magazine or newspaper stories as a means of initiating a short story (**"Nesselrode to Jeopardy,"** which utilizes a quotation from *Time,* is one of the dozens of pieces in which this stratagem is employed). . . . [Some] critics bewail the frequency with which Perelman turns to this device, and they find it heavy-handed besides. However, such a practice is one of the humorist's trademarks, and it became one because it is effective. Beginning a piece in this manner introduces the subject matter, elicits a sense of authority, sets the scene, implies the author's attitude toward his topic, and generally saves time by letting him avoid the otherwise necessary background explanations. (p. 188)

Perelman's polishing of his "lapidary prose" is often mentioned by students of his work. He has said himself that "easy writing makes hard reading.". . . As do many professional writers, Perelman kept files of items and ideas that he might be able to utilize as a stimulant for his imagination. . . . [In an interview with Myra MacPherson] Perelman recounted a tale of how one idea struggled on to paper:

> "In 1953 I went to East Africa and I had with me a floppy Panama hat. It was a little large. In the East Africa Standard I read about a Norfolk jacket woven in the Scottish highlands, worn by a man his entire life and passed off to a son. I folded it up and used it to tighten the band."
>
> Dissolve: Perelman is back in the United States, takes the hat to be blocked, picks up the hat weeks later, finds the article, retires to a bar, reads it there, then weaves a story about his own Norfolk jacket that was borrowed by the late John O'Hara.
>
> (**"The Rape of the Drape"**).
>
> Total time: 15 years.
>
> "That's the longest I've held a piece. The whole point of comic writers is no matter how hard you work, you must give a sense of vivacity, lightness and speed."

That Perelman could keep an element of a possible story alive in his mind over this extended period of time and finally bring it to fruition is an indication of several things. It illustrates the strength and breadth of his intellect (first, keeping one element in mind, and then seeing how it relates to another item), it demonstrates his attention to detail, and it shows his patience and willingness to keep after something until he is satisfied that the result meets his high standard. This incident reveals something of the nature of the man behind the humorist and helps explain why his work surpassed that of other authors and why he was so successful for so long. (pp. 188-89)

Steven H. Gale, in his S. J. Perelman: A Critical Study, *Greenwood Press, 1987, 232 p.*

Kenneth Rexroth

1905-1982

American poet, translator, critic, essayist, dramatist, editor, and autobiographer.

A controversial author who participated in several twentieth-century literary movements, Rexroth was considered by many critics among the finest contemporary poets of nature and erotic love. He wrote much of his verse in what he termed "natural numbers," a style that replicates idiomatic American speech through classical precision, careful syllabic modulation, lucidity, and directness. A wide range of intellectual and literary interests, including science, religion, and Oriental philosophy, inform Rexroth's poetry. Although his belief in pacifistic anarchy, his bohemian lifestyle, and his opposition to materialistic mass culture and the literary establishment often led critics to associate Rexroth with the libertarian avant-garde, his poetry is traditional in form, supportive of conventional American values, and frequently makes use of standard meter to render profound insights from ordinary experience.

During his youth, Rexroth became interested in classical literature and post-World War I avant-garde art movements. He specialized in abstract modernism as a teenager at the Art Institute of Chicago and also became involved with the "Wobblies," or Industrial Workers of the World, before deciding to write poetry in the early 1920s. Influenced by William Carlos Williams and the second Chicago Renaissance, Rexroth challenged prevailing modernist theories early in his literary career. He repudiated T. S. Eliot's and Ezra Pound's contentions that the true artist is impersonal, asserting in his essay "Poetry, Regeneration, and D. H. Lawrence" that poetry is "vision . . . the pure act of sensual communion and contemplation." Rexroth's poems of the 1920s and 1930s, many of which are collected in *The Art of Worldly Wisdom* (1949), make use of literary techniques derived from cubism and other avant-garde art movements as well as stylistic innovations introduced by Gertrude Stein and James Joyce. This volume contains *A Prolegomenon to a Theodicy,* a long, enigmatic poem written between 1925 and 1927 and first published in 1932 in Louis Zukofsky's *"Objectivist's" Anthology* that offers a dream of human transcendence through love. Morgan Gibson described this piece as "a kind of 'Paradise Regained,' beginning with extreme despair and ending with a vision of Christian apocalypse." During this time, Rexroth refined his intellectual principles through involvement with labor groups, leftist politics, jazz musicians, and a professor who introduced him to the works of eighth-century Chinese poet Tu Fu. His subsequent verse displays the simplicity of expression and close observation of nature central to the Oriental aesthetic.

In his first volume of poetry, *In What Hour* (1940), Rexroth unifies the disparate styles of his early verse through a meditative sensibility. This volume contains elegies to his first wife, Andrée Rexroth, who died in 1940, as well as poems on such topics as nature, the Spanish Civil War, and the execution of Sacco and Vanzetti. In his second collection, *The Phoenix and the Tortoise* (1944), Rexroth links his search for transcendent love with anarchist and pacifist ideals while advocating a belief that individuals must assume complete responsibility for their actions. *The Signature of All Things: Poems, Songs, Elegies,*

Translations, and Epigrams (1950) exhibits straightforward and accessible love lyrics and a more intense exploration of spiritual transcendence through communion with nature and humanity. The title poem of *The Dragon and the Unicorn* (1952) recounts Rexroth's travels in cold war Europe and his return to the United States. In this lengthy, episodic work, Rexroth presents Marxist critiques of both Soviet communism and American capitalism and consumerism.

In the late 1940s and 1950s, Rexroth served as mentor to many of the poets associated with the Beat generation, a group of post-World War II writers who attacked artistic and moral conventions. Although he helped found the Poetry Center at San Francisco State University with Lawrence Ferlinghetti and Allen Ginsberg and sponsored poetry readings to jazz accompaniment in San Francisco and New York City, Rexroth later denounced Beat literature for its general lack of artistic discipline. His most famous collection from this era, *In Defense of the Earth* (1956), contains "Thou Shalt Not Kill," a caustic elegy for Dylan Thomas and all artists destroyed by materialistic societies that critics generally consider Rexroth's strongest protest poem. This volume also includes expressions of Rexroth's personal and artistic principles, laments for lost love, and autobiographical verse. The title poem of *The Homestead Called Damascus* (1963), reputedly written in the early 1920s but not published in its entirety until 1957, is an extended philosophical piece in the symbolist style chronicling the quest of two brothers for a perfect form of love and their attempt to escape from what Morgan Gibson called "the bourgeois-Christian-Classical tradition in a state of decadence." Despite Rexroth's opposition to the basic tenets of modernism, reviewers of this collection noted strong stylistic and thematic resemblances to T. S. Eliot's *Waste Land.*

Although Rexroth was faulted throughout his career for contentiousness, most critics have maintained that his later poems, many of which evidence his immersion in Oriental culture, demonstrate a more confident and serene philosophical outlook. Major works from this period include *Natural Numbers: New and Selected Poems* (1963), *The Collected Shorter Poems of Kenneth Rexroth* (1967), for which Rexroth won a National Book Award, *The Heart's Garden/The Garden's Heart* (1967), *New Poems* (1974), and *The Morning Star: Poems and Translations* (1979). Characterized by spare syntax, rich imagery, and a serenity often missing from his early work, the poems in these volumes reflect Rexroth's search for mystical enlightenment through sensuous examinations of nature and love. *The Morning Star* features "The Love Songs of Marichiko," a sequence of poems presented as translations in which Rexroth examines passion and eroticism through the persona of a young Japanese woman. A posthumous collection, *Selected Poems* (1984), contains verse drawn primarily from the latter half of Rexroth's career.

Rexroth is also the author of *Beyond the Mountains* (1951), a tetralogy of stylized verse plays that incorporate characters derived from Greek tragedy with stylistic elements of *noh*, a form of Japanese drama that blends dance, poetry, music, and mime. *An Autobiographical Novel* (1966) is a portrait of Rexroth's personal and intellectual growth as a young man. Rexroth's essays, renowned for their iconoclastic views on literary, cultural, and political topics, are collected in such volumes as *Bird in the Bush: Obvious Essays* (1959), *The Alternative Society: Essays from the Other World* (1970), *American Poetry in the Twentieth Century* (1971), *The Elastic Retort: Essays in Literature and Ideas* (1973), and *World outside the Window: The Selected Essays of Kenneth Rexroth* (1987). Rexroth's numerous translations of Spanish, French, Greek, and Latin poets also earned him wide critical respect, and his renderings of Japanese and Chinese poetry are regarded by many critics as among the finest contemporary English translations of Oriental verse.

(See also *CLC*, Vols. 1, 2, 6, 11, 22; *Contemporary Authors*, Vols. 5-8, rev. ed., Vol. 107 [obituary]; *Contemporary Authors New Revision Series*, Vol. 14; *Dictionary of Literary Biography*, Vols. 16, 48; *Dictionary of Literary Biography Yearbook: 1982;* and *Concise Dictionary of American Literary Biography, 1941-1968.*)

GILBERT SORRENTINO

[*The essay from which this excerpt is taken was originally published in* Poetry, *June, 1964.*]

Rexroth has come a long way from the long, youthfully philosophical poem, **"The Homestead Called Damascus"**; and the selections from *Natural Numbers* testify to the stopping places along that way.

Rexroth is the kind of poet you take or leave. There's no way that I can see of shrugging him off, or of selecting poems which seem "strong" or "best." He is an honest-to-God classicist: his poems are totally free of bric-a-brac; his images are direct and simple and found only when his movement seems to demand them—that is, none of his poems are built around the image. Along with this, there is an almost cavalier disregard for the niceties of the poetic line, the metres move easily and casually, and rhyme is eschewed in work as early as **"Homestead."** He really wants to get something off his chest, this Rexroth; and his *Natural Numbers* is a sweet, honest book, taking you from *The Art of Worldly Wisdom* (1922) through the *New Poems* (1957-1962). He certainly can't teach you anything in terms of technique, and he is not one to turn a nice phrase; but he can say something like

> At midnight I make myself a jug
> of hot white wine and cardamon seeds.
> In a torn grey robe and old beret,
> I sit in the cold writing poems,
> Drawing nudes on the crooked margins,
> Copulating with sixteen year old
> Nymphomaniacs of my imagination.

—and if it isn't Villon, still, it is good work. What makes a simple fragment like that excellent is the same kind of classically oriented imagination which moves us in the naked, simple lines that end Catullus' fifty-eighth poem, "nunc in quadriviis et angiportis / glubit magnanimos Remi nepotes." This sort of imagination has been regarded with suspicion for a long time now, and many of the reflections in *Natural Numbers* can scarcely be called poetry unless one allows Rexroth his devotion to this unadorned art.

To hold **"Homestead"** alongside the later poems is to see that Rexroth was a young poet to be seriously considered when he wrote it; but he was obviously deep in books, he rigs a philosophical framework on which the lines are hung, the poem is a three-way "dialogue" and an attempt to tie together Rexroth's knowledge of ideas and the world by the use of unconvincing "poetic" voices. Poems like this suffer terribly at the hands of reviewers, perhaps rightly so; but Rexroth has published this almost as a pleasantry, the poems of *Natural Numbers* giving it stature as bibliography, background. The older Rexroth would never write anything like it, although it contains excellent fragments. . . . I, for one, am glad that Rexroth abandoned the philosophical frame some time ago and has steadily moved toward a "purer" poem. He is capable of writing some of the strongest and surest verse of our era in the next decade or so. "Rexroth is no writer in the sense of the word-man. For him words are sticks and stones to build a house—but it's a good house." That was William Carlos Williams in 1944. Now, twenty years later, Rexroth is still no word-man—and his house is still a good one. (pp. 81-3)

> *Gilbert Sorrentino, "Kenneth Rexroth: A Good House," in his* Something Said, *North Point Press, 1984, pp. 81-3.*

THEODORE ENSLIN

There is much work from Kenneth Rexroth's sixty years of practice that I would not care to talk about. For one reason or another it is not available to me, and I see no very good reason why it *should* be. I make no value judgment. But when it comes to the vast body of translation from Chinese and Japanese which has concerned him for many years, I feel no such reservations. To me, these *are* Rexroth, and I treasure them for many reasons. Further, there are those original poems of his, so much in the same vein, the same language, that it is often impossible to know, unless one is familiar with original texts, whether it is Rexroth through finite literary antecedence, or Rexroth who views his actual experience through the same lens, though from his own place in time. How thoroughly oriental that is!—and from my point of view, how admirable! A continuity, in which the universal concerns of life are always to be celebrated—so very old—so very new. Development need not be dramatic, nor in our terms, progressive. The life blood is warm and fresh; its chemical salts are as old as the galaxies. It is once more an affirmation akin to Pound's *Make It New,* and in some ways I would feel that Rexroth's major translations are superior to Pound's on just these grounds. It is desperately important that we feel around us that erotic anticipation that the eighth-century Chao Luan-Luan gave then, and that Rexroth recreates in his version of "Creamy Breasts," or similarly the heartbreak in Li Ch'ing-Chao's "Spring Ends." We do not move away from such concerns any more than we do from the purity of a Bach cantata, or Mozart's "Ave Verum." These are the constants that nurture our lives, given back to us once more in the antiphonal reminder which is high art. So Rexroth is present always in a dual role, that of the faithful translator (which does *not* mean necessarily a rigid adherence to original syntax) and the creator who understands the spirit of the original because he himself has entered it. I do not question his scholarship or competence, partly because I trust him through the sincerity of the new text he gives, and partly because I do not feel myself competent in the original languages, which I feel is far less important at this stage of trust. Except for pedantry, who can care whether one ideogram or another is exactly rendered, so long as the life of the whole is? In other words, we are concerned with life itself, not with a comment (no matter how brilliant that might be) upon it.

It is important in these terms to have a collection of women's poetry from 300 B.C. to the present, and how admirably *The Orchid Boat* illustrates that continuity! . . . Rexroth's concern with the feminine is everywhere convincing—delicate—without an element of mawkishness. Of the several readily available contemporary translations of Li Ch'ing-Chao, I find his [*The Complete Poems of Li Ch'ing-Chao*] by far the most satisfying. Together, these two books are enough to make anyone's reputation—and that reputation, not by hearsay, but the actual experience of what is offered. To add the third, the recent *The Morning Star* [a collection of poetry and translations], is to round a curve. I am by no means scanting the many other translations, any one of which is an enrichment for our time, but there is little point in piling up more superlatives. In *The Morning Star,* that rooted ambivalence—what is/is not translation by definition—is amply demonstrated. I feel that there is a need for such work, and that many of us, even though we may not know it, hunger for what is to be found in it. James Wright said, "I believe it is [Rexroth's] love poetry that matters most in the end. He is a great love poet during the most loveless time imaginable." And I heartily concur. It is ridiculous to say more. (pp. 301-03)

Theodore Enslin, "Of Ageless Celebration in Our Time," in Parnassus: Poetry in Review, *Vol. 9, No. 1, Spring-Summer, 1981, pp. 301-05.*

ELIOT WEINBERGER

Born in another country, Rexroth would have served as the intellectual conscience of the nation: a Paz, Neruda, Mac-

Diarmid, Hikmet. But here, as he wrote, "There is no place for a poet in American society. No place at all for any kind of poet at all." So in his life, and at his death, he was largely seen as a crank, a colorful American eccentric who once spiced occasional magazine copy and three well-known romans-à-clef. (p. 47)

Rexroth briefly embraced the Beats (despite his famous disclaimer, "An entymologist is not a bug") as he had so many movements: the Wobblies, the John Reed Clubs, anarchism, the Communist Party (which refused him membership), civil rights, the hippies, feminism—most of which posed a far more serious threat to institutional America than the Beats. But as a political thinker and activist, he essentially belonged to "the generation of revolutionary hopelessness." More than any other poet, Rexroth's work records that history of disillusionment: the massacre of the Kronstadt sailors, Sacco and Vanzetti, the Spanish Civil War, the Hitler-Stalin pact, Hiroshima, the Moscow Trials. . . . Yet he clung to the vision of brotherhood exemplified by the various American Utopian communities whose history he wrote. His 1960 essay, **"The Students Take Over,"** was dismissed by an academic critic as "mad" for "announcing a nationwide revolution among students on behalf of national and international integrity." By 1969 *The Nation* would write, "What is most viable in the so-called New Left is in large part the creation of Rexroth and Paul Goodman whether the movement knows it or not." As always in Rexroth's life, the initial reaction stuck, while the fact that he was proved right has been forgotten: "When a prophet refuses to go crazy, he becomes quite a problem, crucifixion being as complicated as it is in humanitarian America."

His enemies were the institutions (the U.S. and Soviet states, the corporations, the universities, the church) and their products: sexual repression, academic art, racism and sexism, the charmlessness of the bourgeoisie, the myth of progress, the razing of the natural world. He was an early champion of civil rights, and his essays on black life in America are among the few that have stayed news. He was the first poet whose enthusiasm for tribal culture was not picked up from Frazer, Frobenius or the Musée de l'Homme, but rather from long periods of living with American Indians. And he was—almost uniquely among the WASP moderns—not only *not* anti-Semitic, but an expert on Hassidism and the Kabbalah.

Most of all, he was America's great Christian poet—a Christianity, that is, which has rarely appeared in this hemisphere: the communion of a universal brotherhood. And he was America's—how else to say it?—great American poet. Rexroth, alone among poets in this century, encompasses most of what there is to love in this country: ghetto street-smartness, the wilderness, populist anti-capitalism, jazz and rock & roll, the Utopian communities, the small bands at the advance guard of the various arts, the American language, and all the unmelted lumps in the melting pot.

As a poet, he had begun with **"The Homestead Called Damascus,"** a philosophical dialogue and the only poem worth reading by an American teenager, and then veered off the track into a decade of "Cubist" experiment. Had he remained there—like, say, Walter Conrad Arensberg—he would be remembered as a minor Modernist, less interesting than Mina Loy and far inferior to his French models, Reverdy and Apollinaire. But by the publication of his first book in 1940 [*In What Hour*], Rexroth had abandoned the Cubist fragments of language—while retaining the Cubist vision of the simultaneity of all times and the contiguity of all places—to write in a sparsely adorned

American speech. (''I have spent my life striving to write the way I talk.'') It was a poetry of direct communication, accessible to any reader, part of Rexroth's communitarian political vision, and personal adherence to the mystical traditions of Christianity (the religion of communion) rather than those of the East (the religions of liberation).

The poetry: political, religious, philosophical, erotic, elegiac; celebrations of nature and condemnations of capitalism. His long poems of interior and exterior pilgrimage are the most readable in English in this century. Though he wrote short lyrics of an erotic intensity that has not been heard in English for 300 years—worthy of the Palatine Anthology or Vidyakara's *Treasury*—he belonged to the tradition of chanted poetry, not to lyric song. For some critics, the poems were musically flat, but William Carlos Williams claimed that ''his ear is finer than that of anyone I have ever encountered.'' The way to hear Rexroth is the way he read: to jazz (or, in the later years, koto) accompaniment. The deadpan voice playing with and against the swirling music: mimetic of the poetry itself, one man walking as the world flows about him.

Curiously, his effect on poetry in his lifetime was not as a poet, but as a freelance pedagogue and tireless promoter, as energetic and inescapable as Pound: organizer of discussion groups and reading series and radio programs; responsible for bringing Levertov, Snyder, Rothenberg, Antin, Ferlinghetti and Tarn to New Directions; advocate journalist, editor and anthologist. Though Gary Snyder can be read almost as a translation of Rexroth; though it is difficult to imagine Ginsberg's ''Howl'' without the example of **''Thou Shalt Not Kill''**; though everyone has read the Chinese and Japanese translations, which sold over 150,000 copies; it seems that few, even among poets, have read **''The Phoenix and the Tortoise,'' ''The Dragon and the Unicorn,'' ''The Heart's Garden, The Garden's Heart,'' ''On Flower Wreath Hill,''** or more than a scattering of the short poems.

The result is that Rexroth at his death was among the best known and least read of American poets. It is a sad distinction that he shares, not incidentally, with the poet he most resembles, Hugh MacDiarmid. (I speak of MacDiarmid's reputation outside of Scotland.) Except for MacDiarmid's Marxism and Rexroth's Christianity, which are mutually exclusive, both were practitioners of short lyrics and long discursive and discoursive poems, both were boundless erudites, and both are formed out of the conjunction of 20th century science, Eastern philosophy, radical politics, heterosexual eroticism, and close observation of the natural world. (pp. 47-50)

I suspect that the neglect of Rexroth and MacDiarmid is due to the fact that both are, at heart, outside of (despite their affinities with) the ''Pound-H.D.-Williams tradition.'' Their spiritual grandfathers were Wordsworth and Whitman: the life of the mind on the open road. . . . MacDiarmid may have been sunk by his galactic vocabulary, but Rexroth? One guess is that Rexroth was ignored because, by writing poetry that anyone who reads can read, he subverted the system: the postwar university-literary complex. Poets, especially the advance guard, driven to the fringes of society, have developed an unspoken cultishness: a secret fidelity to the ''unacknowledged legislator'' myth and a tendency toward private languages that are mutually respected rather than shared. The university professors, for their part, enjoy the power of ferreting out the sources and inside information, being the holders of the keys and the decoder rings. . . . Rexroth blew the circuits by presenting complex thought in a simple language. The English Dept. has no

use for ''simple'' poets, and American poets tend to have their simple poets Chinese.

Whatever the reasons, there is no question that American literary history will have to be rewritten to accommodate Rexroth, that postwar American poetry is the ''Rexroth Era'' as much (or as little) as the earlier decades are the ''Pound Era.'' And it will have to take into account one of the more startling transformations in American letters: that Rexroth, the great celebrant of heterosexual love (and to some, a ''sexist pig'') devoted the last years of his life to becoming a woman poet.

He translated two anthologies of Chinese and Japanese women poets; edited and translated the contemporary Japanese woman poet Kazuko Shiraishi and—his finest translation—the Sung Dynasty poet Li Ch'ing-chao [*The Complete Poems of Li Ch'ing-Chao*]; and [in **''The Love Poems of Marichiko''**] he invented a young Japanese poet named Marichiko, a woman in Kyoto, and wrote her poems in Japanese and English.

The Marichiko poems are particularly extraordinary. The text is chronological: In a series of short poems, the narrator longs for, sometimes meets, dreams of and loses her lover, and then grows old. Although Marichiko is identified as a ''contemporary woman,'' only two artifacts of the modern world (insecticide and pachinko games) appear in the poems; most of the imagery is pastoral and the undressed clothes are traditional. The narrator is defined only in relation to her lover, and of her lover we learn absolutely nothing, including gender. All that exists is passion. . . . (pp. 50-1)

The Marichiko poems, together with the Li Ch'ing-chao translations, are master works of remembered passion. Their only equal in American poetry is the late work of H.D., ''Hermetic Definition'' and ''Winter Love''—both writers in their old age, a woman and a man as woman. I see Rexroth's final transformation as a transcendence of the self: As Pound recanted *The Cantos* and fell into silence; as Zukofsky ended ''A'' by giving up the authorship of the poem; Rexroth became the *other*. (p. 51)

Eliot Weinberger, ''At the Death of Kenneth Rexroth,'' in Sagetrieb, *Vol. 2, No. 3, Winter, 1983, pp. 45-52.*

GEORGE WOODCOCK

My own relationship with Kenneth Rexroth, like that of many other people, was so largely within a context of the politics of the unpolitical that when I began this article I did not realize how largely implicit, in his poetry at least, I would find the expression of his political stance. Rexroth's attitude—an idiosyncratic but completely authentic kind of anarchism—was publicly stated and well known, yet not so much written of as spoken and lived. After publishing *An Autobiographical Novel*—that strange and inventive memoir largely of the America before the great wars—in 1966, Rexroth seemed to sustain no further interest in writing about his own life, so that there is little available in narrative form about his activities after 1927, the year in which Sacco and Vanzetti were executed. . . .

Rexroth was then twenty-two, and he . . . ended *An Autobiographical Novel* by remarking, ''One book of my life was closed and it was time to begin another.'' That second book was lived and never written, though in many ways it was the more interesting and certainly the more fulfilled part of his life, the time when he wrote the best and the most of his poetry, the time of stormy friendships and devoted fatherhood, the time when he became a literary presence in San Francisco, on the picket lines as well as in the emergent west coast literary world. . . . (p. 73)

Rexroth began his *Collected Shorter Poems* (1967) with the epigraph: ''A self-contained system is a contradiction of terms. QED.''. . . In prose, as in verse, Rexroth is never at his best when he speaks in abstractions, and for this reason, even as we examine the explicit political statements in his poems, we cannot ignore the deeper connotations that may lie in more concrete and less direct suggestions offered elsewhere in the *forêt de symboles* that his poetry often becomes.

Turning to the poems themselves, one finds already in the early works written in the 1930s and published in *In What Hour* (1940) the peculiar counterpointing of the individual and the general, symbolized in the affairs of men and the affairs of mountains, that runs through Rexroth's work from beginning to end, so that one might almost say a man in the mountains is his crucial image of human enlightenment. In a simple way one finds it in a poem called ''Hiking on the Coast Range.'' Walking, the poet remembers that it is the anniversary of the killing of two pickets in the San Francisco general strike, ''Their Blood Spilled on the Pavement / of the Embarcadero.''. . . [He views] the blood that flows in the veins of all living things as it flowed out of the veins of the slaughtered strikers, as ''the source of valuation. . . .''

> The measure of time, the measure of space,
> The measure of achievement.
>   There is no
> Other source than this.

In this way the mythology of revolt is subsumed in the wider reality of nature.

There are other poems of *In What Hour* where the approach to revolt is more direct, but still seen in a heroic and elegiac way, and sometimes leading on to the naively golden vision of hope that always irradiated the sense of doom which clouded the outlook of the Thirties. . . . (pp. 76-7)

This kind of easy vision does not occur often even in the early poems of *In What Hour*. More typical, and certainly more characteristically Rexrothian is ''Autumn in California,'' that ''mild / And anonymous season,'' when Rexroth, idling, calls ''the heart to order and the stiff brain / To passion,'' and thinks of what at this moment is happening in Nanking ravaged by Japanese planes and Madrid besieged by Franco's troops. His vision holds two young men talking in a room in Madrid of all the pleasure of a world they have left for war and perhaps for ever. . . . There is no hope in this vision: only the commitment to the extreme situation, the existential pride, and beyond it, as in the writings of Camus, the benign indifference of the universe. . . . (pp. 77-8)

Moving out of the Thirties, *The Phoenix and the Tortoise* (1944) contains a long and loping speculative poem that bears the volume's title and a series of accompanying shorter pieces. ''The Phoenix and the Tortoise'' presents the poet sleeping out of doors, by the seashore this time, though the mountains impinge on his musings, and reflections on history, fragments of political theory, speculations on the human condition mingle with his half-waking perception of the immediate world. The urgency, the activity of the preceding volume are diminished. The disillusionment, the sense of the futility of militancy in the present time that, as we have seen, characterize the later *Dragon and the Unicorn,* have set in. As the poem nears its end what it emphasizes is ''history's / Cruel irresponsibility'' and the human condition as ''tragic loss of value into / Barren

novelty.'' Yet this, in the spirit of losing one's life to save it, becomes paradoxically the ''condition of salvation.''. . . The salvation seems to lie in intimate human communion and a life in harmony with nature, represented, always, by the mountains.

Yet the sense of the revolutionary tradition and all that at its best it represents in integrity and self-abnegation survives here and there in the shorter poems of *The Phoenix and the Tortoise*. ''Again at Waldheim,'' in keeping with the generally elegiac tone of the poetry in this period, is set in the Waldheim cemetery in Chicago where so many celebrated American anarchists were buried, and the poet asks, in this time of war and horror,

> What memory lasts, Emma, of you,
> Or of the intrepid comrades of your grave,
> Of Piotr, of 'mutual aid,'
> Against the iron clad flame throwing
> Course of time?

And what he answers means that even if the memory may fade, the gesture, the stance, is its own justification, perhaps even its own eternity. (pp.78-9)

The rather sour disillusionment of *The Dragon and the Unicorn* was the prelude to a shifting into a more generalized rebellion—social and cultural as well as political—which emerges in *In Defense of the Earth* (1956), a volume whose very title seems to anticipate the environmentalist movement of the next decade, for which Rexroth was a pioneer. Perhaps the most striking feature of this volume is the outpouring of anger and denunciation against the contemporary world and its materialist culture in the long poem, ''Thou Shalt Not Kill,'' a passionate, almost hysterical lament for the death of Dylan Thomas which bears some remarkable resemblances to Allen Ginsberg's ''Howl.''. . . (p. 80)

In such a piece Rexroth's link with the Beat poets becomes quite evident, though it is ironical that their much inferior poetry became better known than his. But this did not prevent Rexroth from sharing the sudden sense of hope we all experienced in the later 1960s, when anarchism seemed to be created anew by the young. The acrimony towards fellow radicals and the generally elegiac mood of his political poetry during the 1940s and 1950s seemed both to vanish as Rexroth turned largely to prose and began to celebrate, in collections of essays like *The Alternative Society* (1970), the renewal of poetic and political vigor. . . . [Rexroth speaks] in enthusiastic terms of ''a time of wholesale overturn, a transvaluation of values at least comparable with the revolutionary years around 1848. . . .'' But there is another side of him that pulls up short to question whether the outcome will necessarily be good. The dark forces, also, are more powerful than they ever were before. . . . (p.81)

Rexroth's thought accords with the general anarchist tradition which rejected nineteenth century socialism's uncritically optimistic acceptance of open-ended material progress as a viable goal and substituted what one can describe as critical pessimism, which is by no means the resignation that accepts the worst as inevitable, but a positive state of mind that sees the worst as a threatening option and therefore assesses realistically the chances of evading it. Such a view, in Rexroth as in his comrades in the tradition, does not regard the future as necessarily better than the past. . . . The good life, in the present or in the past, is not to be based on affluence, less on luxury. . . . A rough cabin in the mountains, as Rexroth's Cordillera poems demonstrate so eloquently, a modest apartment in the city as his life declared, can be the center of experiential wealth if one is prepared for it. . . . [In] our time, as Rexroth remarked, all the important works of art "have rejected all the distinguishing marks of the civilization that produced it."

Such a view of man's role in society is not merely a complete "politics of the unpolitical," to use Herbert Read's fitting phrase; it also implies a fellowship with the environment and it accords with Rexroth's poetry about man in his relation to nature, so splendidly exemplified in his mountain poems and linked to a sense not only of the unity of all living beings but also of their symbiosis with the inanimate forces of nature, a symbiosis that can be broken only at grave peril. (pp. 81-2)

> *George Woodcock, "Rage and Serenity: The Poetic Politics of Kenneth Rexroth," in* Sagetrieb, *Vol. 2, No. 3, Winter, 1983, pp. 73-83.*

MORGAN GIBSON

According to Kenneth Rexroth's theory and practice, poetry is vision. In his work, "vision" has several meanings that are not systematically related; but they seem to me to pertain to phases of a creative process of consciousness. "Vision" sometimes means contemplation, in which Rexroth communed with nature and those he loved, and in which he periodically had oceanic, ecstatic experiences of realization, illumination, and/or enlightenment. In such experiences, perception, conception, imagination, and feeling—especially love—were clarified, purified, and radically expanded; so he also claimed that "vision is love." Sometimes "vision" refers to the act of poetic communication, evolving from interpersonal communion and re-creating community. Sometimes it means philosophizing, sometimes world view; so when I refer to Rexroth's world vision I mean to include all aspects of vision as he experienced it and philosophized about it—personal and transpersonal aspects in universal community. His vision is both immanent and transcendent, sensuous and abstract, non-verbal and literary. It is both conservative—in reviving and uniquely synthesizing Jewish, Christian, Classical, and Buddhist traditions of spiritual realization—and revolutionary in its vigorous position to the prevailing impersonality and alienation of modern society, technology, and culture. His vision is uniquely his, yet is also universal in its scope and validity, because it realizes the person in world community. His world vision reveals his, and our, "Being-in-the-World," as Heidegger put it.

"Poetry is vision," Rexroth asserts in **"Poetry, Regeneration, and D. H. Lawrence,"** "the pure act of sensual communion and contemplation." Does he mean all poetry, or the best of it? He certainly means the poetry of Lawrence, Yeats, Blake, Whitman, poetry that he translated by Tu Fu, Li Ch'ing Chao, Sappho, Reverdy, and his own. He means by "vision" the essence of poetry, the quality that makes it true poetry, the quality often ignored by critics who emphasize form, structure, construction, technique, or, worse yet, identify artifice as poetry itself. Craftsmanship is important in Rexroth's own poetry and in all poetry that he values, but as a means to an end rather than as an end in itself. Communication of what? Visionary experience: vision itself. And what is that?

He defines poetic vision as an *act*, a dynamic transformation, rather than as passive reflection; and it is a *pure* act, unlike impure acts of ordinary experience that lack unifying aesthetic concentration. There may be a suggestion that poetry is a purifying act, as in Aristotle's idea of catharsis; but poetry does more than purge impure emotion, in Rexroth's view, for *communion* indicates that poetry is an intimate experience of mutuality, a sacramental act of commemoration, in which we are

mystically united with others, and perhaps with reality as a whole. Such communion is *sensual,* for delightful sounds of language, and sometimes the beauty of calligraphy, typography, and other aspects of a text bring us into the imagined world of the poem, which has sensual as well as abstract features also. So poetry is a *contemplative* act, arising in deep, clear, open-minded, loving awareness. The text and form of the poem indicate, signify, or reveal the visionary act which is the essential poetry. (pp. 85-6)

Rexroth insisted that vision was personal, the experience of a "true person" in community. "The universalization of the human soul, the creation of the true person," was evident in the life of Albert Schweitzer, for example. Such a person is neither a self-made man, nor someone who simply loses himself in work or meditation. He or she loses ego, but not the whole person, which is realized creatively in community. Rexroth takes himself for granted as an integral person instead of condemning himself as a sinner or striving to change himself into a different person.

Because vision is personal, Rexroth typically stands undisguised in his poetry, and his prose also, instead of concealing himself behind an impersonal literary construction—a mask, like Yeats, or an "objective correlative," like Eliot. Rexroth's personalist poetics is diametrically opposed to the aesthetic theory of Stephen Dedalus, who argued in Joyce's *Portrait of the Artist as a Young Man* that the true artist, "like the God of the creation, remains within or behind or above his handiwork, invisible, refined out of existence, indifferent, paring his fingernails." On the contrary, Rexroth openly participates in his creation, which is never distinct from his personality and experience. His poetic theory and most of his practice challenge the impersonality of much modern literature and criticism, particularly as Eliot dogmatized in "Tradition and the Individual Talent": "The progress of an artist is a continual extinction of the personality. . . . The poet has, not a 'personality' to express, but a particular medium, which is only a medium and not a personality. . . ." Rexroth's "progress" as a poet was radically subversive of Eliot's principles, for Rexroth's work was a continual revelation of personality, the realization of self. He was not exhibitionistic, like Rimbaud or Byron, nor confessional, like Lowell or Sexton, but told his life directly to others, in his most characteristic poetry and autobiographies. (pp. 86-7)

Visionary experience—essentially formless—sometimes takes form; but *a* vision is not vision, as Rexroth carefully points out in *The Heart's Garden, The Garden's Heart:* "visions are / The measure of the defect / Of vision." Because true vision is clarified consciousness—not hallucination, dream, or fantasy—Rexroth's poetics is opposed to Surrealism and Dada, as shown in his cubist poem, **"Fundamental Disagreement with Two Contemporaries,"** Tristan Tzara and André Breton. Similarly, Rexroth refused to identify true vision with the drug highs of the Beat Generation, and he doubted that Allen Ginsberg's and Jack Kerouac's frantic searches for vision in *Howl* and *On the Road* got them beyond confusion. For according to Rexroth, vision is habitual clear-mindedness. . . . (p. 89)

In defining poetry as personal vision, Rexroth meant that it arises out of contemplation and communion to become communication. So he can also, without contradiction, define poetry as "interpersonal communication raised to the highest power." "It communicates the most intense experiences of very highly developed sensibilities," he wrote in one of his most important essays on poetics, **"Unacknowledged Legis-**

lators and **Art pour Art."** Here he emphasizes, as always, the *personal* origin of poetry, and its communication not predominantly of feeling or thought, but of whole *experiences:* "A love poem is an act or communication of love, like a kiss." Such communication has a strong ethical value, reminiscent of Matthew Arnold's "criticism of life"; or, in Rexroth's words, "As time goes on and the poem is absorbed by more and more people, it performs historically and socially the function of a symbolic criticism of values. . . ." So love poems and nature poems become criticisms of a dehumanized society based on the alienation of people from one another, from their own nature, and from nature as a whole. But such moral and intellectual functions of poetry are never separated from its emotional, psychological, and spiritual aspects, for it "widens and deepens and sharpens the sensibility. . . ."

Rexroth felt that Chinese and Japanese poetry, in general, communicate experiences of such "highly developed sensibilities" more directly and purely than most European poetry because "most poetry in the Western world is more or less corrupted with rhetoric and manipulation . . . with program and exposition, and the actual poetry, the living speech of person to person, has been a by product." This extraordinary statement suggests one reason for Rexroth's turn from cubism, prevalent in his theory and practice between the World Wars, to the direct address of "natural numbers," which became his predominant mode.

In Rexroth's view, communication rests upon some preunderstanding, arising from communion and community. A message is not transmitted by means of a text, from sender to receiver; rather, meaning evolves from pre-established community, some kind of mutual existence and mutual interest. Out of I-Thou, meaning comes. Unless you and I share consciousness, we can understand nothing. True communication, through poetry and other arts, helps us realize our "mutual being."

In emphasizing vision, Rexroth may seem to underplay craftsmanship; but in fact he was a meticulous craftsman in both poetry and prose, and his criticism of literature places a high value on artistic technique, not as an end in itself—as in **"Art pour Art"**—but as a means of communicating experience. (pp. 90-1)

Rexroth's own craftsmanship is impressive, and his prosody deserves a long study. He wrote some rhymed quatrains and limericks as well as a few unpublished sonnets, but most of his work is in free verse and in quantitative (syllabic) patterns that are intricately melodious: for example, the nine-syllable lines of most of **"The Homestead Called Damascus,"** and the seven-syllable lines of most of **"The Dragon and the Unicorn"** and **"The Heart's Garden, The Garden's Heart,"** of parts of *Beyond the Mountains,* and many shorter poems. Patterns of chanting, derived from American Indian, African, and other preliterate cultures, combine with cubist techniques in *A Prolegomenon to a Theodicy.* And vowels and consonants are deliberately patterned to enhance the melody of much of his verse, as he explains in his preface to *The Signature of All Things*— a method that he seems to have learned in part from Japanese poetry.

Rexroth's poetry is in three modes. It is most often in the direct statement and address of "natural numbers," in the normal grammar of actual speech. Symbolism characterizes **"The Homestead Called Damascus,"** 1920-25, but this mode was then abandoned. And cubism or objectivism was practiced mostly between the World Wars and collected chiefly in the latter half

of *In What Hour* (1940) and *The Art of Worldly Wisdom* (1949— though some appears later).

In his youth, Rexroth wrote symbolist poetry which evolved into **"The Homestead Called Damascus,"** his first long philosophical poem. This precocious, musical poem of the traumatic spiritual quests of two brothers is full of symbols and myths of decadence, sacrifice, and fertility. . . . The poem echoes Stevens, Yeats, Aiken, Proust, Henry James, French symbolist poets, anthropological scholars such as Frazer, Weston, Harrison, Cornford, Murray, and the strongest influence of all: T. S. Eliot, whose *The Waste Land* had swept Rexroth into such enthusiasm that he at first had believed it to be a revolutionary poem—compatible with his anarchistic opposition to bourgeois civilization—and only later came to the conclusion that the poem was thoroughly reactionary in its aesthetic and world view. Its symbolist style was not compatible with his emerging aesthetic theory and practice of cubism and later of direct utterance, so he wrote nothing else like **"Homestead"** and did not publish it for over thirty years. Moreover, symbolism— suggesting a transcendent Reality remote from immediate experience—grew from a metaphysic opposite to his idea of immanence—that the "Holy is the heap of dust" and is not symbolized by it. Nevertheless, the poem is a remarkable achievement that deserves to be read for its own sake, for the sensuousness of its sound, the complexity of its characters and their interactions, the suggestiveness of its imagery, and its philosophical implications.

As early as 1920, Rexroth was writing cubist as well as symbolist poems; but though they were published in little magazines from 1929 on, the earliest cubist poems were not collected until 1949, when they appeared in *The Art of Worldly Wisdom.* That volume includes, along with short poems, the long cubist reverie, *A Prolegomenon to a Theodicy.* . . . This long poem boosted Rexroth's international fame as an Objectivist, but he preferred to describe himself as a Cubist. . . . (pp. 91-3)

In *American Poetry in the Twentieth Century* (1971), Rexroth sorted out Objectivism, Cubism, Surrealism, Dada, and other movements which Eugene Jolas had characterized as The Revolution of the Word. . . . Rexroth promoted and practiced the cubist aesthetic, theoretically and practically, in his own paintings, poems, essays, and translations from the French.

The direct, definite reconstruction of the objective world distinguishes Cubism from the dreamy suggestiveness of Symbolism and Surrealism. **"In the Memory of Andrée Rexroth,"** the agonizing elegy opening *The Art of Worldly Wisdom,* is a memorable example. . . . According to Rexroth, such cubist poems

> are intended to be directly communicative, but communicate by means similar to those employed by the cubists in the plastic arts or by Sergei Eisenstein in the early great films—the analysis of reality into simple units and the synthesis of the work of art as a real parallel to experience.

He goes on to relate his own cubist poems to the work of Walter Arensberg, Gertrude Stein, Walter Lowenfels, and Louis Zukofsky as well as to similar French poetry and the songs of American Indians and other pre-literate people. And in the 1953 preface to *The Art of Worldly Wisdom,* he explains that he stopped writing this way because even the Avant-garde did not try to comprehend his cubist poems, and he discovered that he could communicate his experience more effectively by writing the way he spoke, in normal syntax. (pp. 93-4)

Rexroth's most characteristic and successful mode of poetic communication might be called "natural numbers," a term used as the title of one of his books, referring to poetry that stylistically approximates, in syntax and diction, actual speech of person to person. From about 1920 on he wrote translations from Greek, Chinese, Japanese, and Latin in this mode, starting with translations of Sappho. . . . The classical directness and clarity of such ancient poems, mastered through the art of translations, infused his original poems as well. Among the earliest of these is the sequence of love poems for Leslie Smith, entitled **"The Thin Edge of Your Pride,"** dated 1922-26, and ending:

> You alone,
>
> A white robe over your naked body,
> Passing and repassing
> Through the dreams of twenty years.

In the same years, he was writing symbolist and cubist poems, and he became famous for his cubist poems before poems in "natural numbers" began to appear in periodicals in the mid-1930s. Rexroth speaks through such poems as if a listener is present, so the poem is an intense, dramatic speech-act, typically expressing love or friendship. Even if a listener does not seem to be present, in poems of meditation and lone reminiscence, for instance, the voice remains so intimate that the reader becomes Rexroth's *confidant*. In autobiographical poems such as **"A Living Pearl"**—beginning, "At sixteen I came West, riding / Freights on the Chicago Milwaukee / And St. Paul . . ."—and contemplative poems in the mountains, such as **"Lyell's Hypothesis Again"** and **"Toward an Organic Philosophy"** the words draw us towards him as if we were sitting beside a campfire under the stars, listening to him talk.

Direct address is also evident in the revolutionary rhetoric of the poems in the first half of *In What Hour,* the anti-war memorial for Dylan Thomas, **"Thou Shalt Not Kill,"** the ethical speculations of **"The Dragon and the Unicorn,"** and the dramatic tetralogy *Beyond the Mountains,* about the collapse of ancient Greek civilization (and our own) and influenced by Japanese *Nōh.* "I have spent my life striving to write the way I talk," Rexroth wrote in *An Autobiographical Novel,* his finest prose. Even when technical terms from the sciences, philosophy, politics, and theology enter his prose and poetry, along with literary and historical allusions from the major civilizations, there is a natural flow of living speech, an acceptance of the Tao—the way things naturally are—except in the symbolist and cubist poems, in which language has been willfully reconstructed.

The evolution of Rexroth's chief mode of poetic communication, "natural numbers," from lyrical, elegiac, and satirical to dramatic forms, supported and was supported by his ideas that "actual poetry is the living speech of person to person" which "communicates the most intense experiences of very highly developed sensibilities." His friend William Carlos Williams, with whom he had many affinities, believed that "you have no other speech than poetry." This idea implies, I think, that poems are derived from the poetic flow of living speech, that poems are realized orally, that texts are indications of oral performance like scores of music, and that the oral performance of poetry—which Rexroth practiced and promoted extensively—unites poet and audience in community. Rexroth's and Williams' approach to poetry counteracts the idea that poetry is fundamentally on the page or in the mind as an object of impersonal, analytical study, or that poetry is some kind of artificially constructed arrangement of words that no one would ever conceivably say to another. When Whitman heard America singing, he too must have thought of poetry as "actual speech."

The idea cannot mean that all actual speech is poetry, but that poetry cannot be poetry unless it is vital communication, actualized in speech from one to another. Certainly the idea would have been readily acceptable to the ancient Greeks, who thought of poetry as music—delightful sounds that unite performers and audience.

Rexroth implies that not everyone can communicate poetically, for few people have "very highly developed sensibilities." In this respect, he seems dependent on Wordsworth, who defined a poet as "a man speaking to men—a man, it is true, endowed with more lively sensibility, more enthusiasm and tenderness, who has greater knowledge of human nature, and a more comprehensive soul, than are supposed to be common among mankind." Despite a fundamental agreement about the poet's nature and function, however, the poets seem to have a slight disagreement: for whereas Wordsworth thinks that a poet is innately endowed with a great sensibility, Rexroth suggests that sensibility can be "very highly developed" to the qualitative magnitude necessary for true poetry: so poets may be made as well as born. (pp. 95-7)

*Morgan Gibson, " 'Poetry Is Vision'—'Vision Is Love':
Kenneth Rexroth's Philosophy of Literature," in*
Sagetrieb, *Vol. 2, No. 3, Winter, 1983, pp. 85-99.*

DONALD GUTIERREZ

Nature in Kenneth Rexroth's verse is approached for various ends—as a context for love and sex, an inspiration to contemplation, a stabilizing contrast to the overwhelming corruption of twentieth century societies and experience.

But perhaps Rexroth's most memorable treatment of nature occurs when, without violating its integrity or particularity, he engages it to suggest certain philosophical ideas about the character of reality. These ideas in turn are arresting because, in the midst of the turmoil of large cities, wars, and social evil and misery, they remind us, to quote Rexroth quoting the nineteenth century English scientist John Tyndall, of "the obliquity of the earth's axis . . . which runs through creation, and links the roll of a planet alike with the interests of marmots and men.' " (**"Fall, Sierra Nevada,"** in **"Toward an Organic Philosophy,"** in *The Collected Shorter Poems of Kenneth Rexroth,* 1966). Rexroth is particularly sensitive to that "roll of the planet" and its place in human sensibility and the "phenomena" of society.

His conception of nature is not Tennyson's "Nature red in tooth and claw." Nature in its malign or destructive guise figures little if at all in his verse, although his sense of the radical evil of *human* nature is sharp indeed. Thus the nature of earthquakes, volcanic eruptions, hurricanes, and animals preying on each other is seen primarily in Rexroth's social poetry, converted into a polemical verse attacking human society and institutions (as in his jeremiad on the death of Dylan Thomas, **"Thou Shalt Not Kill"**). But the natural environment itself is not allegorized into a Ted-Hughes landscape of primal human ferocity and terror. As a result, there is something old fashioned yet strikingly immediate about Rexroth's nature poetry.

Rexroth's most characteristic nature poetry embodies the ancient Oriental sagacity that nature and its phenomena *are* themselves. This outlook does not mean that nature is not translated into other meanings in Rexroth's verse, but it does place more stress on the literal reality of nature than is common among 20th century poets. This philosophic literalism emerges from the clarity, particularization, and deceptive sense of artless art of his poetry, qualities to which the frequent use of declarative sentences and the virtual absence of metaphors also contribute. Rexroth's ''artless'' art endows the nature verse with both a smooth-surfaced, anti-allegorical ''finish'' and a distinctive authenticity of utterance. This poetry aspires to the difficult paradox of not meaning, but being, while implying a significant if non-discursive reality.

A Rexroth nature poem is often comprised of a movement from one crisply precise detail of knowledgeable observation to another. Frequently the result is a gradually brimming significance or an overt climactic realization. Set usually in mountain areas in central California or near the San Francisco Bay area, this verse registers an uncommon order of reality.

''**Fall, Sierra Nevada,**'' the poem that ends with the Tyndall quotation, is thick with specific details of place, flora, fauna, and weather. Located in the Sierra Nevada range in eastern California, the poem specifies landmarks, peaks like Ritter and Banner, an adjacent eastern range (the White mountains), and the salt flats of Nevada. Specific types of birds are mentioned (hermit thrush, chickadees, hummingbirds, a golden eagle, an owl—caught in two beautiful lines, ''The ventriloquial billing / Of an owl mingles with the bells of the waterfall''). Also mentioned are constellations like Scorpion and the Great Bear, planets like Jupiter and Venus, time (''This morning,'' ''At noon,'' ''All day,'' ''At sunset,'' ''In the morning''), weather (''cloud shadows,'' ''distant thunder,'' ''far-off lightnings,'' ''Rain is falling,'' ''a small dense cumulus cloud''), and frost. In addition, a range of specific colors and shades is connected with all of these terrestrial and celestial details: gold, alpenglow, burnt peaks, dark sedge meadows, white salt flats, whitebark pines.

These do not comprise all the details (or even categories of details) in this 45-line poem, but they will suffice to give an idea of the texture of concreteness and specificity typical of a Rexroth nature poem. Rexroth writes with a highly accurate sense both of his specific surroundings and of the character of those surroundings over a period of time (in this poem, 24 hours, from morning to morning). There is no romantic heightening through self-indulgent emotion or a merging with nature. Rather, the descriptiveness is so precise that it creates an intense external reality, a kind of objective super-reality: ''Just before moonset, a small dense cumulus cloud, / Gleaming like a grape cluster of metal, / Moves over the Sierra crest and grows down the westward slope.'' The poem cites a specific time of day, a literally accurate description of a cloud, followed, to intensify its reality, by a crystal-clear simile about it, and an exact description of its direction and what it passes over. The entire poem exists on this almost preternatural level of descriptive clarity, lending its climactic statement of the interrelation of all earthly life a numinosity that transcends its factual base.

Sometimes, the ''purpose'' of a Rexroth nature poem will become overt, as in the moving Tyndall quotation from ''**Fall, Sierra Nevada**'' about the common earthly interests of ''marmots and men.'' In some poems the climax might be an elegy for a dead loved one, as in one of the three elegiac ''Andree Rexroth'' verses, which ends with ''all the years that we were young / Are gone, and every atom / Of your learned and disordered / Flesh is utterly consumed,'' or an erotic vision experienced through the sheer concentration of beauty of a unique site, as in this high moment from ''**Incarnation**'' in which ''Rexroth'' has descended from a climb in the mountains and sees

> . . . far down our fire's smoke
> Rising between the canyon walls . . .
> And as I stood in the stones
> In the midst of whirling waters
> The swirling iris perfume
> Caught me in a vision of you
> More real than reality . . .

What is beautiful about the beloved is intensified by, and merged with, the beauty of the landscape. . . . (pp. 405-08)

But the point in ''**Incarnation**'' goes deeper than an association of beauties. The clear, exact description symbolizes a heightened state of being. This condition is partly brought on by temporarily living in mountains which causes the vivid sense of the physical environment to also intensify one's sense of the ''Other''. In this sort of ''nature-and-love'' verse, sexual intimacy takes on an unusual vividness. Depictions of natural surroundings become a revelation of relationship with the beloved and of the almost magical simplicities of existence, as in the post-coital ''**Still on Water,**'' ''A turtle slips into the water / With a faint noise like a breaking bubble / There is no other sound . . . ,'' in which the description also reflects the serenity of the lovers.

In one of the other ''Andree Rexroth'' poems (simply called ''**Andree Rexroth**''), Rexroth writes movingly about the experience of nature before and after the death of his first wife:

> Now once more gray mottled buckeye branches
> Explode their emerald stars,
> And alders smoulder in a rosy smoke
> Of innumerable buds.
> I know that spring again is splendid
> As ever, the hidden thrush
> As sweetly tongued, the sun as vital—
> But these are the forest trails we walked together,
> These paths, ten years together.
> We thought the years would last forever,
> They are all gone now, the days
> We thought would not come for us are here.
> Bright trout poised in the current—
> The racoon's track at the water's edge—
> A bittern booming in the distance—
> Your ashes scattered on this mountain—
> Moving seaward on this stream.

Although the poem has a clear-cut time structure of present-past-present, this arrangement achieves powerful emotional effects through precise descriptive and imaginative representations of nature. These effects are enhanced by an implicit contrast of the speaker alone in nature in the present and (through retrospection) together with his beloved in the same place ten years earlier. The poem opens indicating that it is spring again. If ''Now once more'' is the most minute of hints of a deeper sorrow to be broached, the ''I-know-that'' syntax of lines 5-7 enlarges the intimation of something lacking in the present, despite the continuing brilliance, beauty, and force of nature (the ''emerald stars'' of the buckeye branches, the ''rosy smoke'' of the budding alders, the melodious thrush, the vitality of the sun).

By line 8, however, it becomes increasingly clear what the veiled dissatisfaction with nature and with the present in the preceding lines means. Lines 9-12 amplify this dissatisfaction. The speaker and his wife had been so absorbed in each other and in the physical surrounding as to assume that the present would never end. The present itself was a future the lovers thought would never occur, but, like a vision of hell, it has come to pass. What this is emerges in the penultimate line of the poem: the death of Andree Rexroth.

This death—the culmination of the poem—is made heart-rending by the shock of its revelation, and by the fact that what had implicitly made nature "perfect" or "complete" in that idyllic past is now mere ashes. With oblique irony, nature continues to take its course (trout ready to leap, racoons hunting for fish, the huge bittern making a mating call). By indicating that Andree Rexroth is now a part of nature, Rexroth not only evokes lines from one of the most poignant of Wordsworth's Lucy-Gray poems ("Rolled round in earth's diurnal course, / With rocks, and stones, and trees"), but transcends that allusion by the pronounced context in the poem of adult love. The beloved is now a part of the nature that, at one time, had supported and beautified her relationship with the speaker, a part moving implacably towards final dissolution in the ocean.

Rexroth doesn't melodramatize his lament. Nature is—objectively—just as beautiful now as it was in the past when Andree Rexroth was alive. But of course it is no longer for him the beautiful surroundings it once was. This loss is apparent in the laconic syntax of the last five lines with its series of dependent verbal clauses, the decisive ashes line, culminating in the present participle of the last line, and the quietly mournful sense it gives that more than the beloved's ashes are "moving seaward." Through the restraints imposed by an acute fidelity to the realities of the natural environment, a fidelity reflecting his love, the loss of his beloved, and the quality of their relationship, Rexroth in **"Andree Rexroth"** embodies an exquisitely quiet sadness reminiscent of the Oriental poetry he so admired. (pp. 408-10)

[**"Time Is the Mercy of Eternity,"**] like much of Rexroth's nature verse, displays sharp, clear description. But one discovers several complicating factors in this . . . ambitious poem. There is an introductory statement about time antithetical to the mystical meanings in the title, a motif of visual recession and "mirroring," a symbolic distinction between the purity or clarity of mountain life and the confusion and corruption of city life, and a symbolic and climactic use of the image of a crystal that responds to the idea of time introducing the poem.

"Time is divided," Rexroth begins, "into

> Seconds, minutes, hours, years,
> And centuries. Take any
> One of them and add up its
> Content, all the world over
> One division contains much
> The same as any other.

Time (or "times") is an indistinguishable element that cannot give experience or phenomena character or identity, and thus value. Time in this sense is *not* the mercy of eternity; rather, it is a value-neuter quantity. Yet the poem does not reach the opposite mystical apotheosis of the title through such traditional devices as "problem-solving," narrative, surprises or shocks, retrospection, or a vision of God. Instead, it develops a heightened sensitivity, through acute response and descriptive integrity and through the elements of complexity mentioned above, towards the details and events in the natural surrounding, ascending to a mystical realization.

Rexroth is encamped on a narrow ledge with a steep drop first of 500 feet, then of another 1000 feet to a river. Beyond his ledge-camp are physical elements that also become media of the transformation of reality—first, "shimmering space," then the recessiveness of "fold on / Dimmer fold of wooded hills," beyond which, in the final medium of "pulsating heat," lies the San Joaquin Valley, the flatland of "life and trouble." The world of commerce is described shortly after as the "writhing city," burning in a "fire of transcendence and commodities," a condensed, ironic allusion to St. Augustine's lustful Carthage and to Karl Marx's chapter on commodity fetishes in *Capital*. Yet even in 20th century Carthages and Babylons, realization, "the holiness of the real," is possible, love creating a mode of genuine transcendence for the "experiencer" and the lover. But this short meditation on the city, the flatland far off, suggests for "Rexroth" or the viewer a different kind of transcendence, experienced climactically through inhabiting this "higher" life of mountain, canyon, and sky over a period of several weeks.

In the latter part of [**"Time Is the Mercy of Eternity,"**] two revelations occur, both suggesting an original perspective on life through a unique conception of the centers of reality. The first arises in a scene in which Rexroth is looking at a deep pool in early evening. He describes some of the water creatures—frogs, hydras, water boatmen. . . . This leads to a deepening awareness:

> I realize that the color
> Of the water itself is
> Due to millions of active
> Green flecks of life.
> . . . .
> The deep reverberation
> Of my identity with
> All this plenitude of life
> Leaves me shaken and giddy.

What has made this pitch of identity with nature possible is being in the midst of it ("alone / In the midst of a hundred mountains"). But like the "cloud" of midges, it is the union of the object with the articulated experience of the object that gives both a reality more forceful for being experienced in solitude. Indeed, part of the cogency and serenity of Rexroth's nature verse stems from his skill in making his persona and its experience credible. There are no self-doubting Prufrocks here, no involuted discussions of the reality of object and subject. The object is fully "there" because of a fidelity of objective description mirroring a harmony and repose in the poem's speaker.

The second vision concludes the work, and presents a process of simplifying one's needs similar to a definition of the contemplative Rexroth makes in *The Dragon and the Unicorn* in which, by putting aside appetite and the wish for consequence from possibility, one can develop a "disinterested / Knowledge of himself, of / The simplest things, knowing them / As really perspectives into / The others." This conception is made concrete in the final 22 lines of **"Time."** Conveyed through a metaphor of the crystal, it hardens objective and subjective reality, the contemplative and the "object" of contemplation, as two crystals—"At last there is nothing left / But knowledge, itself a vast / Crystal encompassing the limitless crystal of air / and rock and water." This semimonist condition is reached, after a transcendence of flatland mentality and divisiveness, through a residing in nature that Rexroth develops for several pages. The speaker consequently is "Suspended / In absolutely transparent / air and water and time," which in turn creates in him a "crystalline being."

Why the crystal metaphors? The stripping of the qualities of one's moral history, of "personal facts, / And sensations, and desires," that has occurred during "Rexroth's" immersion in nature, results in a purity or clarity of being that reflects "this translucent / Immense here and now" of the Object or physical surrounding. The crystalline "knowledge" attained, closely relating the natural elements to human existence in a concentration of serene and almost selfless repose, leads to the two "crystals" being "perfectly / Silent. There is nothing to / Say about them." Such is the language of a transcendence free from the pressures of the pantheistic deity one usually finds in pious nature verse. If this is a dialogue (those "others" Rexroth alludes to in the passage defining the contemplative), it is definitely a secularized "I" and "Thou." Part of the authority of **"Time"** and of Rexroth's other meditative nature poems derives from the basic implication that natural phenomena can, if sufficiently experienced, meet the deepest human needs. (pp. 413-15)

Even Rexroth's "pure" nature verse can surprise with the quiet force of its *literal* significance, a quality in part due to his habit, as mentioned earlier, of declarative directness, highly lucid description, and sparse figuration. In **"Clear Autumn,"** a poem from a short verse series called **"Mary And The Seasons,"** from the 1956 collection *In Defense Of The Earth,* Rexroth describes a mountain setting in which fallen leaves suggest an illumination: "New-fallen / Leaves shine like light on the floor." The light motif is not stressed; rather, it has its place amid the humming of low-flying insects, the quiet clustering nearby of Holstein cattle vistas, the floating buzzards. Yet even here a sinister image of human menace is suggested in a glimpse of "long white scrawls" in the air, the "graffiti of genocide" left by jet bombers too high to be visible.

If the fallen leaves suggest an order of naturalness separate from the captivity and menace of the human world of purpose, the final image of nature in **"Clear Autumn"** is strikingly original and delicate. Following the reference to the jets, the concluding scene opens with a description of the air as glittering with "millions of glass / Needles, falling from the zenith." We learn that this aerial miracle is

> . . . the silk of a swarm
> Of ballooning spiders, flashes
> Of tinsel and drifting crystal
> In the vast rising autumn air.
> When we get back everything
> Is linked with everything else
> By fine bright strands of spun glass,
> The golden floor of October,
> Brilliant under a gauze of light.

Rexroth has taken an unusual (and unromantic) instance of natural life, and expanded it into a symbolic image of an almost supernatural order and interconnection. The ethereal simplicity and visual uniqueness of the image also constitute its suggestive power.

Rexroth states in another poem-series, **"Aix-en-Provence"** (**"Spring,"** from his 1964 book *Natural Numbers*), that nature is primarily and ultimately itself:

> Now the buds
> Are round and tight in the dim
> Moonlight, in the night that
> Stretches on forever, that had
> No beginning, and that will
> Never end, and it doesn't mean
> Anything. It isn't an image of
> Something. It isn't a symbol of

Something else. It is just an
Almond tree, in the night, by
The house, in the woods, by
A vineyard, under the setting
Half moon, in Provence, in the
Beginning of another Spring.

Also implied in these lines is an anti-symbolic, anti-teleological esthetic and philosophy.

A similar attitude underlines the ballooning spider webs of **"Clear Autumn."** No less effective for not being tendentious, this unique image primarily *is* its meaning. The "rightness" of the spider-web image resides not in its symbolizing of nature's innate order or "artful handiwork," but in its embodiment of the sheer autonomy of nature as seasonal unfoldings, the reign of Tyndall's "oblique axis" again. Reigning, but not obliterating. Some of the complexity of Rexroth's conception of humanity and human society in the nature verse arises from his acknowledgement of the potency of organized human murderousness and destructiveness. But within the trances and meditations of mountain life, the reality of the presences of nature is uppermost. The spiders and their magical spun glass will soon disappear, as will that particular autumn and that "golden floor." But they persist in the mind and in art as an illumination of earthly existence, "brilliant under a gauze of light." (pp. 416-18)

In the wilds, humanity confronts change, limit, and death in such forms and contexts that . . . fundamental life conditions become acceptable, even graced, if we are alive to the large place of our existence in the physical environment. And there is the radical, if quiet, implication that the "objective" environment, sufficiently appreciated, becomes subjective, a part of ourselves. The natural surroundings are a mirror and "crystal" of the reality of ourself and those others whose proper interrelation Rexroth's verse and prose define as community.

From reality to realization. One beholds in Rexroth's nature poetry not a romanticization of the natural environment, but a recording of it so "crystalline" as to capture a legitimate splendor in the earth, in earthly life, and thus in the potential of human life here and now. (p. 421)

> *Donald Gutierrez, "Natural Supernaturalism: The Nature Poetry of Kenneth Rexroth," in* The Literary Review *(Fairleigh Dickinson University), Vol. 26, No. 3, Spring, 1983, pp. 405-22.*

GEOFFREY O'BRIEN

Reading the poems of Kenneth Rexroth gathered [in *Selected Poems*] is like returning to an ancient and permanent state of mind that one had unaccountably forgotten about. Critics found it easy to forget about Rexroth for most of his long and productive career, so that even today this central figure—a lyricist who can stand with Ungaretti and Reverdy and Takamura—lingers on the sidelines of the reputation market. Maybe at the time it looked easy to write so simply and clearly . . . or to rely on the force of directly stated feeling. . . . Rexroth wrote great love poetry, great nature poetry, great philosophical poetry—and as this collection shows, he did it with unbelievable consistency. The relaxed, discursive rhythms of the early meditative epics tighten gradually into the concentrated brilliance of *New Poems* and *The Silver Swan.* In its final phase his work evolves toward seamless joy needing no commentary. . . .

> *Geoffrey O'Brien, in a review of "Selected Poems," in* VLS, *No. 31, December, 1984, p. 7.*

CLAYTON ESHLEMAN

[*Selected Poems* is] a 140-page selection of [Rexroth's] poetry, and the first thing I want to say about it is that it is about half the size that it should have been. My hunch is that New Directions imposed a 140-page frame on editor Bradford Morrow and that he is not principally responsible for three glaring defects of the book:

1—Rexroth wrote a great deal of highly experimental "Cubist" poetry in the '20s and '30s, some of which anticipates non-referential, technique-dominated poetry today and represents a Surreal outpost of Objectivism. Only a five-page section from one of these works is included, and it is unsatisfactorily placed at the end of the book, as if to not interfere with the reader's initial reception of the poetry.

2—Rexroth also wrote several original middle-length poems, one of which should have been included in its entirety (in contrast to heavily edited excerpts).

3—The last 22 years of his highly active publishing career (1956 to 1978) are represented by only 16 pages! Against the 106 pages for the early years, these pages drop the *Selected Poems* into a nose dive, and will possibly alienate a first-time reader because they offer a withered, weightless image of the mature and elderly Rexroth.

As is, the *Selected Poems* portrays Rexroth as having done his finest work (leaving out the experimental writing) in the late '30s and the '40s. It opens with a selection from his first collection, *In What Hour* (1940). These are the strongest poems in the book. In such pieces as "Requiem for the Spanish Dead," "Autumn in California" "August 22, 1939" and "Toward an Organic Philosophy," Rexroth blended the presence of his first wife, Andree, a lovingly observant relation to wilderness and an optimism (qualified by inclusion of European Fascism) that revolution would change the world into a poetry profound, specific and available.

After the poems from *In What Hour,* the most engaging are elegiac evocations of Andree Rexroth, who died in 1940. (p. 1)

In contrast, his poems to his third wife, Marthe, concentrate on the conflictual and sublime aspects of the couple's sexual tuning in a way that turns nature into a metaphor for Rexroth's projection of Marthe's bravura sensuality. In his introduction, Morrow proposes that such poems as "Between Myself and Death" and "Marthe Away" are "the most original and persuasive synthesis of transcendent metaphysical and erotic verse written by an American poet this century." My candidate for such a claim would be Hart Crane's "Voyages." In Rexroth's work, the elegies for Andree Rexroth, with their clear and receptive language, seem to match Morrow's words more effectively than the more one-dimensional and darkly edged evocations of Marthe. (pp. 1, 10)

At the point Rexroth stopped being an experimental poet and began to write in an idiomatic, conversational style, a certain passivity toward language began to make itself felt, as if the revolution was "out there," an act of "outward ceremony" (Blake's trenchant phrase) and not the ongoing experimental and visionary revolution of the word. In the middle-length poems, there is often a dichotomy between tart observation and windy or gray philosophizing. Given his identification of revolution with social change, Rexroth "naturally" became disillusioned, and such a state of mind, in his case, resulted in a slackened language.

An exception is the nine-page "Thou Shalt Not Kill," the model for Ginsberg's "Howl" and Rexroth's requiem for his own lacerated hopes. It has an impact (brought to a finish by Rexroth's own borrowing from Lorca's "Lament for the Death of a Bullfighter") that Ginsberg's more Bolero-like "Howl" lacks. . . .

The central image of Rexroth's poetry is that of the erudite wanderer, a kind of "ro-nin" or masterless warrior, whom academic critics suspect because his poetry does not need their commentaries. For writers and readers who still believe that the soul of the poem is summoned by engagements that braid the ancient with the surface of the present—with how it feels, smells and responds to prodding—Kenneth Rexroth will remain a quintessential American author. (p. 10)

> *Clayton Eshleman, in a review of "Selected Poems,"* in Los Angeles Times Book Review, *March 31, 1985, pp. 1, 10.*

LINDA HAMALIAN

Many of Rexroth's early poems [in *Selected Poems*] possess the cubist, surreal quality that shaped his paintings, a kind of writing that peaked for him in the late Twenties when he wrote the poems that appear all together in *The Art of Worldly Wisdom* (not published until 1949) and Louis Zukofsky's *An "Objectivists" Anthology.* . . . Rexroth abandoned this technique afterward for a style he had been developing earlier in "The Homestead Called Damascus," his first long poem, begun in his adolescence.

> My parents had their life, it was not
> Your soft dark tragedy. It was not
> Anything like it. Saffron twilights
> Over the gas lit horse drawn city.
> Purple and gold above the desert.
> When they were sad, they shut their
>   mouths tight.
> When God spoke to Job from the whirlwind
> He refused to answer his questions—
> On the advice of his attorney.
>   . . .
> And now the sun has set and the strange
> Blake-like forms fade from our memories.
> The sky was deeper than a ruby.
> The hoarfrost spreads over the marshes
> Like a mandolin note over water.

This is a poetry of direct statement and clear images, a poetry that grows out of precise observation of the physical world yet leaves space for rumination and abstraction. At the same time, the work is infused with a passion for love and sensuality. . . . (p. 13)

Though he assimilated the sense of writers who influenced him, writers as different as H. G. Wells, Jakob Boehme, John Gould Fletcher, Tu Fu and Sappho, his poetry continued to function as a vehicle that permitted him to record his spiritual yearnings and philosophical inquiries. While he perceived the natural world as sacred and a paradigm of peace and harmony, he was profoundly disturbed by a social and political climate that indicated to him the shrinking possibilities for a world community. The execution of Sacco and Vanzetti, the Moscow trials, the Spanish Civil War, the internment of Japanese-Americans during World War II worked their way into the poetry. His disillusionment grew with the years. . . .

[In *Selected Poems,* editor] Bradford Morrow gives us a book that reflects Rexroth's evolving style, philosophy and political commitment. Only a person intimately connected with the work, and devoted to the writer would have been able to pick and choose so well. His introduction neatly provides us with biographical background and suggests various critical and interpretative approaches to the work. Unfortunately, because of space restrictions, he was not able to include any selections from Rexroth's popular translations of Chinese and Japanese poets.

I sense that Morrow was guided in his choice by at least two beliefs. One is that Rexroth was a man of deep compassion and commitment, a man who loved and suffered. Another is that Rexroth was frequently ahead of his time, yearning in the Twenties for fresh idioms and fewer boundaries between art forms, confronting the dilemmas created by the social and political crises of the Thirties and beyond, and paving the way for the fusion of Eastern perspective with Western pragmatism that can be found in so much poetry of the present moment.

A careful perusal of this book reveals that Rexroth was more than a creator of first-rate verse that succeeds in balancing aesthetics and politics, love and nature. He was a man of talent and imagination whose life reflected the more passionate and dedicated aspects of the literary life in the United States circa 1920 to 1980. (p. 14)

> Linda Hamalian, *"Compassion and Commitment,"* in Book Forum, *Vol. VII, No. 2, 1985, pp. 13-14.*

DAISY ALDAN

The editor of [Rexroth's] posthumous *Selected Poems,* Bradford Morrow, has sensitively chosen representative works from sixty years of writing and has arranged them chronologically, with the exception of excerpts from two early long works, **"The Homestead Called Damascus,"** written when the poet was a teen-ager, and *A Prolegomenon,* a lengthy cubist work composed not long after. Perhaps one should read those two last poems in the volume first, for they already contain the images which were to become lifetime symbols and provide a key to the style and structure that were to follow. Here we note the syllabic, flowing line, from which Rexroth never swerved, and also the keen attention to details, which he continued to transpose into imagery.

The four major themes of Rexroth's poems seem to be philosophical meditations, nature experiences filled with universal and mystical concepts, socially conscious outcries against "man's inhumanity to man," and love. Poems such as **"The Dragon and the Unicorn"** are full of insights, observations, journal notes, and philosophical musings, a panorama of life experiences in perception, individual reaction, thought, and feeling, a journey in every sense of the word. **"A Lesson in Geography"** brings together observations of nature juxtaposed with echoes of lives lived, always related to the great constellations and the ordered weaving of the planets. . . . Then there is the awesome **"Requiem for the Spanish Dead,"** through whose words one's senses awaken to shrillness, chill, and the airplane that will bomb into nonexistence the "unwritten books, the unrecorded experiments, the unpainted pictures, the interrupted lives lowered into the graves." Rexroth questions, "What is it all for, this poetry . . . / Put together with so much pain?" In **"Toward an Organic Philosophy"** he answers by quoting Tyndall: "The chain of dependence which runs through the creation, / And links the roll of a planet with the interests / Of

marmots and men." Another answer lies in love raised to the level of a sacrament: "Only in a secret place is the key. May human love perfect itself." (pp. 109-10)

Here is a poetry book which may offer years of thoughtful enjoyment to a reader. *Selected Poems* places Kenneth Rexroth among the important American poets of this century. (p. 110)

> Daisy Aldan, *in a review of "Selected Poems," in* World Literature Today, *Vol. 60, No. 1, Winter, 1986, pp. 109-10.*

SAM HAMILL

What Rexroth understood better than any poet since Ezra Pound (and, indeed, better than the inventor of Modernism himself), is that poetry is not disembodied, it is not something that takes place on the page of a text, but is rather the articulation of human experience as close to perfection as human articulation can be. He resembled Pound in fact in many ways: his appetite for knowledge (not simply information, but knowledge) was insatiable; his acceptance of personal responsibility for the course of history, as an active participant in the course of history; his passion, both personal and public. But unlike Pound, Rexroth sought out and enjoyed the company of common working people, ranchers and cobblers and auto mechanics. Unlike Pound, the embodiment of justice, according to Rexroth, could not be separate from the physical and emotional expression of compassion, so much so that the figure of Kuan Shih Yin (in Chinese, "who listens to the world's cries"), in Japanese *Kannon,* figures prominently in virtually all of his later books. Like his own favorite poet, Tu Fu, Rexroth was a deeply religious poet who included rather than excluded the world's religions. Unlike Tu Fu, he was a poet of erotic love without peer in his lifetime, perhaps without peer in the American language. . . .

The *Selected Poems* contains some of the most beautiful and powerful poetry of the last forty years. The poems of social involvement (i.e. **"Requiem for the Spanish Dead"** and **"For Eli Jacobson"** etc.) are tender and personal, just as the "personal" poems of love and of nature become poems of tremendous social consequence. There are also some poems that are at once funny and profound. . . . (p. 11)

Rexroth also combines the study of science with personal experience as no one before him ever did. Reading Lyell's nineteenth-century study of geology, he composes a poem, **"Lyell's Hypothesis Again,"** (another poem for Marie Rexroth née Cass) that looks hard at the "ego, bound by personal / Tragedy and the vast / Impersonal vindictiveness / of the ruined and ruining world, / . . ." and concludes:

> We have escaped the bitterness
> Of love, and love lost, and love
> Betrayed. And what might have been,
> And what might be, fall equally
> Away with what is, and leave
> Only these ideograms
> Printed on the immortal
> Hydrocarbons of flesh and stone.

He was among the first of our poets to recognize the complex utter interdependence of things, as well as the transparency of our lives and indeed of all the world as we, superficially at least, perceive it.

Anyone interested in Rexroth should also be directed to the later books. Unfortunately, the *Selected Poems* includes but one poem and a fragment from *Natural Numbers* (1964); four small poems from *New Poems* (1974); three short fragments from the major poem *On Flower Wreath Hill* (1976); three fragments from *The Silver Swan* (1978); and but seven of the sixty brief **"Love Poems of Marichiko"** (1978). In all probability, this is due to limitations of space. (pp. 11-12)

The later books are, after all, the culmination of a lifetime's dedication and achievement. Excluded from the *Selected Poems* are some of the most beautiful poems of erotic love ever composed in any language. . . . We live in an age in which the poetry of mature erotic love is out of fashion. Our poets tend to prefer the cool cerebral play of Stevens to the naked jig of Dr. Williams. . . . Rexroth himself read, of course, all the poets, and was especially fond of Ivor Winters, although he often quoted Winters's line, "Emotion in any situation must be as far as possible eliminated," following it with a guffaw. (p. 12)

Perhaps we will eventually have the *Complete Poems*. Such care did Rexroth take with his work that I have seen in his library every edition of his poems clearly penciled with typographical errors corrected, some minor revisions made, and footnotes written into the margins. On a recent visit to his widow, I even came across a small stack of hand-made typewritten errata slips he made upon publication of *In What Hour* (1940). A *Complete Poems* with generous and accurate notation would make this most accessible of post-Modernist poets available even to the high school and undergraduate readership he loved and deserved.

One can for now only hope that Rexroth will begin to receive his due. Perhaps he can attain in death that which he so richly deserved in life: just recognition as one of the major poets of American letters, a pioneer, a great teacher beyond the scholia, an original mind that has touched so many serious poets in our country (and abroad) in the second half of this century. While many of our more widely popular poets exhibit an incomparable vulgarity of the soul and a dangerous ignorance of history and tradition, while even our critics such as Helen Vendler preach (in the NY Times *Book Review*) that we have nothing to learn from the poets who survived [the] Holocaust, while our entire culture aspires to a world monoculture that excludes nature and mistrusts true beauty and embraces the musty mini-tragedies of the office, Rexroth points the way back toward an aesthetic that not only encompasses nature and history and beauty, but embraces the three as aspects of the one, the same. (p. 13)

> *Sam Hamill, "Kenneth Rexroth's 'Selected Poems',"*
> *in* The American Poetry Review, *Vol. 15, No. 3,*
> *May-June, 1986, pp. 9-13.*

GEOFFREY O'BRIEN

"He was not an academician but a creative artist, a bohemian intellectual, and a man who was largely self-educated. These are all great virtues, but not to modern critics." When Kenneth Rexroth wrote in these terms about Ben Jonson, he doubtless realized that he was describing himself. One of the advantages of being that kind of free scholar is that you can choose your own canon of masterpieces rather than submitting to the preselected and predigested. Such eternal outsiders as Ezra Pound, Henry Miller, and Basil Bunting all proffered their own versions of the World's Great Books, indelibly quirky lists that elevated H. Rider Haggard or the Welsh bard Heledd to the pantheon. *Classics Revisited* is Rexroth's version, a hand-tailored alternative to Dr. Eliot's Five-Foot Shelf, mixing the obligatory (Plato, Shakespeare, Tolstoy) with more personal

choices: Apuleius, Hitomaro, Tsao Hsueh-Chin, Restif de la Bretonne. Rexroth capsulizes each book (there are 60 in all) in a little three-page essay; the brevity lets him pare what he has to say to an expressive minimum.

It must have been an exhilarating project, to spell out one's lifelong vision of literature in a series of mini-lectures, even for such a good gray humanist bastion as the *Saturday Review*. In the '60s, when these essays first appeared, the *Review* was admirably civilized but tended to wrap literature in an aura of benign dullness. Dullness, however, was never Rexroth's strong point. Writing for a general audience, he adopted a tone geared for an imaginary common reader: an active, uncloistered person who just might find Machiavelli or Whitman relevant to his immediate surroundings. This was not talking down but an expression of Rexroth's sense of literature as ordinary, practical, suffused with the energies of a communal rather than hermetic reality. . . . Rexroth's awareness of the tragic dimension of human life is always modified by an outdoorsy enthusiasm, a keen taste for the humblest pleasures, which leads him to Japanese classical poetry or to Walton's *Compleat Angler*.

The book evokes another ordinary pleasure: that of sitting up all night with an old friend, ranging over all climes and centuries, until the universe seems to fit cozily in a single room. . . . Rexroth conjures up a lifetime of reveries and sense impressions, fleshing out the remote past with his own experience. When he writes that "Tu Fu brings to each poetic situation, each . . . complex of sensations and values, a completely open nervous system," he might once again be speaking of himself. His opinions are valuable not for their definitiveness but for their freshness and ardor. Whatever he observes is not a petrified artifact but part of a continuing process. The histories of Livy or the pranks of Rabelais are intimate events, and Rexroth responds to them as he would to news of a friend.

In *Classics Revisited* one can enjoy the company of an old-fashioned anarchist gentleman, convinced that "organized society is a lethal fraud" but awake to the beauty which sometimes emerges from it. He is neither a propagandist nor a pulverizer of icons; writing in old age, he is still amazed by simple delights. He finds his role model in Montaigne (whom he likens to "the indifferent Bodhisattva or Taoist sage devoted to government by inaction"), but he retains a wistful fondness for an adventurer like Marco Polo, with his "ecumenical mind" and "international sensibility." Rexroth was one of the inventors of the idea of a counterculture, but he wanted that culture to be well stocked with ancient riches. The books he loved he saw as emanations of living feeling, lines of communication miraculously kept open.

> *Geoffrey O'Brien, "The Old and the Restful," in*
> The Village Voice, *Vol. XXXI, No. 31, August 5,*
> *1986, p. 47.*

PUBLISHERS WEEKLY

[Rexroth] saw the modern poet as the enemy of the privileged and the powerful, since poetry is disruptive to rigid systems and ideas. In these pieces [collected in *World Outside the Window: The Selected Essays of Kenneth Rexroth*], he finds ties between Dylan Thomas's lyrics and Charlie Parker's saxophone solos, reads D. H. Lawrence's free verse as an odyssey of personal salvation and portrays Rimbaud as a capitalist adventurer. Twenty-seven essays bristle with Rexroth's wit and wide-ranging intellect. Whether he is unravelling the close links between Jewish mysticism and Gnostic sects, or satirizing the hippies' sell-out to conspicuous consumption, Rexroth challenges conventional dogma and makes startling connections.

A review of "World Outside the Window: The Selected Essays of Kenneth Rexroth," in Publishers Weekly, *Vol. 231, No. 13, April 13, 1987, p. 62.*

RAY OLSON

Rexroth was a genuine polymath—self-taught!—and beyond that, one who could interrelate all he knew and relate it to "the world outside the window." These abilities inform his poetry but are most brilliantly evident in his prose, much of which he dictated without reference to notes or sources—so astonishing was his memory, not to mention his command of grammar and syntax. He always addressed, albeit in varying degrees of formality, the nonacademic intellectual like himself, assuming his readers shared his clear-eyed, voracious intelligence and relish for lucid, authoritative communication. . . . Ranging over world literature, religion, art, jazz, and Western society, the 27 essays [collected in *World Outside the Window: The Selected Essays of Kenneth Rexroth*] explore such diverse subjects as gnosticism, classical Japanese poetry, the Beats, alienation, student revolt, [and] co-optation. . . .

Ray Olson, in a review of "World Outside the Window: The Selected Essays of Kenneth Rexroth," in Booklist, *Vol. 83, No. 17, May 1, 1987, p. 1329.*

WALTER WARING

[The pieces collected in *World Outside the Window: The Selected Essays of Kenneth Rexroth*] represent the antiestablishment stance of the "West Coast Movement" as formulated by one of its leading partisans. Although the essays span a period of 40 years, most treat topics commonly associated with the 1960s. Beyond their polemics, they express important ethical and artistic concerns and interests that remain unresolved, ranging from **"The Function of the Poet in Society"** (1936) and **"Who Is Alienated from What?"** (1970).

Walter Waring, in a review of "World Outside the Window: The Selected Essays of Kenneth Rexroth," in Library Journal, *Vol. 112, No. 9, May 15, 1987, p. 86.*

DONALD GUTIERREZ

Near the end of his career Kenneth Rexroth "translated" a body of 60 poems entitled **"The Love Poems of Marichiko."** The poems are dedicated by Rexroth to one Marichiko, a Japanese poetess, and by Marichiko to Rexroth. However, according to Eliot Weinberger [see excerpt above], Rexroth really did not translate these poems—he wrote them himself. If this contention is true, then the Marichiko poems, subtle and evocative as they are, evoke further subtleties. Rexroth is pretending to be a woman writing love verses to her (perhaps) male lover.

This complicated artistic ruse contains implications which will be explored later, for they allude to a deeper significance surrounding this network of verses. Indeed, the verses *are* a network. Rexroth himself asserts that "They form a sort of little novel. . . ." They also contain many verses that can readily stand by themselves in the long tradition of pithy, direct, yet evocative Oriental verse. But much of the real power and thrust of the series reside in its "plot," a story of an intense and

heightened love that comes to an end as inexplicably as it begins. Paradoxically, Rexroth's fabrications become in the prism of his art a reality all the more authentic for being "made up," exotic, and, by implied gender ambiguities, sexually polymorphous. The rise and fall of the love narrative have the simultaneous abstractness and specificity of the eternal universal mysteries of being in love and being left loving and unloved.

The Marichiko poems are nothing if not intense, passionate, and specific. The poetess, or, at least, the woman lover, reveals at the very beginning a dangerous vulnerability to love:

> Sick with love,
> I long to see you in the flesh.
> Love cuts through my heart
> And cuts my vitals.

These lines . . . proffer absolute love with a vengeance. . . . (p. 21)

Verse 9 introduces a powerful yet sensitively oblique eroticism that recurs throughout this series:

> You wake me,
> part my thighs, and kiss me.
> I give you the dew
> Of the first morning in the world.

The introduction of the nature image "dew" covers this act of cunnilingus with the metaphoric gauze of early-morning atmospheric activity. But it does more than that: this intimate act is so intensely experienced as passion that it is put, apocalyptically, on the level of the beginning of the earth itself. The image and act are a stunning hyperbole of the absoluteness of this love, an absoluteness, that, like most human absolutes, is, ironically, subject to change.

In the light of the entire series, poem 14 takes on an ironic poignancy. Of course this could be said, I feel, *erroneously*, of all the poems that indicate affirmation of the relationship. But #14, because it is based on the image and motif of passion as burning, possesses a special poignancy. A celebration is under way. The Chinese character for "great" bursts high in the air, "And at last died out." An analogy is made with the love of the narrator, who also "burn[s] with passion." Then she has a realization: "It's life I am burning with," which everyone in the crowd also burns with:

> They are all burning—
> Into embers and then into darkness.

Her delusion is that, like the large flaming "character" and like all the other "burning" humans in the crowd, her flame, her passion, her love relationship will not dim into embers, then go dark and fade out: "I am happy. / Nothing of mine is burning." Rereading the whole series, one reads a poem like this doubly, as a moment of intense experience of and faith in the permanence of love in the present, and as part of a stream of time in which change and flux are all—or almost all—and thus controvert that faith (though not necessarily the experience).

In #17 the motif of contingency, of the unexpected, even of death, emerges for the first time:

> Let us sleep together here tonight.
> Tomorrow who knows where we will sleep?
> Maybe tomorrow we will lie in the fields,
> Our heads on the rocks.

The idea of death recurs in #31:

> Someday in six inches of
> Ashes will be all
> That's left of our passionate minds.

The final poems in the series hedge this verse with acute irony on a second reading. At this juncture, however, death seems to be the only force that could alter or destroy this particularly intense love, which can even achieve the subtle epistemological equation of #20:

> Who is there? Me.
> Me who? I am me. You are you.
> You take my pronoun,
> And we are us.

This pronominal "jeu d'esprit" has an edge to it because the verbal play contains a sexual element. If her lover takes her pronoun, and the pronoun (as line two indicates) is "me," then her lover not only takes her pronoun and is one with her, but takes her sexually as well. The whole verse resolves itself in a two-in-one unity that is both grammatical and sexual, one order of meaning re-enforcing the other. The cleverness, even the touch of a metaphysical-verse mot, is, as observed earlier, tempered by the context of the whole series, in which the "grammatical" and "epistemological" bliss of the poem are encompassed by hints of unhappiness and of, finally, utter grief.

But the ending of the love is still some way off. Before that, one encounters some of the most passionate, even agonizingly sexual poems in the lot. . . . #24 exhibits a reciprocal passion astounding in its intensity and absoluteness:

> I scream as you bite
> My nipples, and orgasm
> Drains my body, as if I
> Had been cut in two.

Although there are many thousands of love poems in the culture of love literature, one seldom finds a poem of this stark, over-powering sexuality. Often love verse is shrouded in, or even gelded by, convention of decorum, erotic disguise or displacement, or other modes of shielding readers from exposure to naked sexual sensibility that would seem (to some) either pornographic or simply too extreme. If pornography is defined either as a desire to titillate or (D. H. Lawrence's definition) a wish to degrade sexuality, then #24 is certainly not pornographic. Rather it represents one of the peaks of sexual-*love* sensation in the whole series. Indeed, the poem almost verges on violence that perhaps foreshadows the violence the relationship itself will undergo later. "Cut in two," which implies violent death, also implies a broken heart; that kind of extremity of love sensation harbors danger—something (much) ventured, possibly much, perhaps everything, lost. Poem 24 seems to be one of the peak poems which, by virtue of some special force or intensity, stand above the rest of the Marichiko verses, either gathering in the force of all the surrounding, buttressing verses, or directing implications and prefigurations back and forth throughout the series, like verbal beacons. Poem 25, also an intensely erotic poem, though not "violent" in the mode of #24, also seems to project above most of the verses, and to erect itself in what Lawrence called the Now:

> Your tongue thrums and moves
> into me, and I become
> Hollow and blaze with
> Whirling light, like the inside
> of a vast expanding pearl.

Any potential indecency or offensiveness in this fairly graphic depiction of cunnilingus is transformed by the last three-and-a-half lines in which the sexual stimulation generates a condition of body mysticism. This . . . is not meant to cosmeticize or moderate the intense eroticism of the opening line and a half. Rather, the body mysticism elevates the eroticism in a manner typical of much of Rexroth's love verse, in which a sexuality is exhibited for its own sensual integrity and as part of a "natural religion" of erotic love free of Puritanic repression on the one hand, and pornographic sensationalism on the other.

Certainly, sexuality represents a significant component in some religious or mystical experiences, and if religious experience can be sexual, sexual-love experience can likewise be religious or mystical. There is a body spirituality here all the more striking for not being put in conventional (at least, Western) religious terms. Within the dramatic context of the whole series, the poem, with its simile of erotic sensibility likened to a "vast expanding pearl," is another motif of the ostensible infinity of this love relationship. The woman may "blaze with a whirling light," but the light will go out. (pp. 21-2)

I don't wish to suggest a simplistic or Christian moral in these poems—that Marichiko-Rexroth is implying that an occasionally arrogant or self-centered love leads to the punishment of a disastrous end of the relationship. As the narrator, whether "Marichiko" or "Rexroth" or a dramatized persona distinct from either of them, is presenting first-person experience, "her" outlook has authority—though not complete authority; *that* is invested in **"The Love Poems of Marichiko"** as an art work rather than as a biographical love document. The authority *her* statement possesses is that of the substantial authenticity and force in her exaltations, expostulations, ecstasies, and agonies during the course of her love experience. The authority it lacks is what the reader, having read the whole series of love verses and thus the whole account, knows (and understands) that the narrator does not, until it is too late. We do such "double" reading of literature all the time. In #30 (and elsewhere), we can exult in the narrator's proud joy, but not entirely, knowing that misery, termination of the love, and a death-in-life lie ahead for her. . . .

Most of the poems from #34 to the revealing #46, indicate anxiety, unfulfilled expectation, anguish, bitter disappointment. Poems 37 and 38, which form a single experience, indicate a tense, tremulous, night-long waiting for the lover by the ardent and tormented narrator. At best, she can only dream of her/him now, the word "dream" ironically recalling her dreams of her lover in poem 15, when his recurrent presence made the dreaming easy.

More pain, grief, and anguish lie ahead. In #43, we have a poem of a phase in love affairs that one could call The Lonely, Hopeless Wait. A series of images occur: the sound of crickets, of midnight temple bells, of wild geese, but "Nothing else"— the lover doesn't materialize, and the relationship appears to be falling apart.

The final phase of the series has been reached—not the climaxing of love in death found in such Western tragic-romance literature as *Tristan and Isolde,* but the harsh termination of love being something like the end of life itself. Thus the final poems almost bear the status of post-mortem effects. . . . (p. 22)

In the second half of this century, we have become so sheltered by the mass media from the whole gamut of love experience, especially when the final phase is in a dark key, that it can be difficult to properly appraise love literature in which suicide, death, falling out of love, scorn, or even hatred terminated both the relationship and the narrative—that is too unpleasant, too stark. Yet of course life has been and is like that.

This train of thought suggests a mimetic standard for love literature. Yet love literature by its very nature tends to be removed from the commonplace and diurnal, and thus from the main avenues of the mimetic. To be sure, there are recognizable patterns or processes in a love story that seem "true to life"—the extremities of feeling, the tension of expectation, fears and dangers (sometimes) of discovery, the sense of living two existences at once—ordinary, biological life, and the subjective logic of the love experience. But those very processes, because generated by the dynamic arc of love, soar, or seem to soar, above the usual life rhythms and routines.... The point at which negative love experience and phenomenal reality meet can generate an extreme intensity or force in a work of art, especially if the rendition of the love has been profound, powerful, or sensitive. Such, I feel, is the case in the Marichiko poems.

Why would a male poet pretend to be merely the translator of a verse series (supposedly written by a woman) that he actually wrote himself? And why would he, as the actual poet of the sequence, write from a woman's perspective (not to mention that of an *Oriental* woman)? This need not be a suspicious activity. Male novelists enter the bodies and minds of their women characters all the time (if not always convincingly) as part of their fictional enterprise, even in cases where a sexually dramatized woman is the protagonist or the narrator, as in Molly Bloom's soliloquy at the end of *Ulysses* or Lawrence's Ursula Brangwen in *The Rainbow*.

Yet I think the special character of the Marichiko-poems narrative, its trajectory from ecstasy to abandonment and grief, originates in Rexroth's own life, which possibly intimates something significant behind these Marichiko poems. It used to be said by friends, acquaintances, and enemies of Rexroth that he was a man given to promiscuity. Judging by Rexroth's two valuable autobiographical books, *An Autobiographical Novel* and *A Life*, volume 2 (not yet published) there is little evidence of this.

However, from Rexroth's San Francisco period, which begins in the mid-1920s, one has heard so much talk in the Bay Area about his erotic interests in any woman who attracted him ... that some truth probably adheres to the reputation for promiscuity. (pp. 22, 44)

I don't wish to imply that such wonderful Rexroth poems as **"Lyell's Hypothesis Again," "When We With Sappho,"** or **"The Old Song and Dance"** and others were not sparked by real love in the relationship obtaining at the time. But underneath the good periods there might have been guilt and rancor and even a self-hatred accumulating like a nemesis out of that long 10th-century Oriental narrative he loved, *The Tale of Genji*. And the way, or one discernible way, he supplicated

his demons of remorse or hatred was to celebrate his wives and his loves in exquisite love poems. But this was not enough.

I submit that Rexroth, as his consummational gesture of redemptive homage to the wives and lovers he might have wronged or betrayed during his life, felt compelled to go one step further, he would "poetically" *become* one of them, and let it be known through "their" eyes and mind *and body* what it was, in the most memorable and sustained verse he could conceive, to be loved and left by a man. In an authoritative way, this sort of "fiction" is the ultimate empathy, at least for a poet. This kind of homage to a lovelorn woman, rather than undermining any love relationship he might have had with a real Marichiko, would honor that relationship as well, yet, ironically and ominously, perhaps indicates *its* fate too.

Thus, there is a significant, richly ironic sense in which the *male* lover in the Marichiko poems is the real author of the series, to the extent that the Marichiko experience implies the career of some of Rexroth's own loves and infidelities. In the very act of embodying the experience in all its nuances of ecstasy and misery, the *male* poet (here both Marichiko's lover and Rexroth, who in a sense are one and the same) enacts a profound commiseration—the total artistic empathy of sexual identification with the betrayed and bereaved woman.

The experience of love enacted in the Marichiko poems raises the question, in view of the misery it depicts, whether the bliss is worth the misery. Such a question overlooks the status of the work as art. The totality of representation, of embodied love experience, is the basic or final criterion. Does one refuse to fall in love if he knows it will end sadly or even disastrously? There is no indication, until the ending, that "Marichiko" could know this. And, as I urged earlier, decisions of this sort are not readily made.... The poems are important in part because they convincingly dramatize the inevitability of love, whatever its outcome. The character of the passion—whether of ecstasy or of grief—is overwhelmingly authentic, and achieves superiority as art because of its succinct and powerful embodiment of the fullness of love—even when completion of that experience means a forlornness equivalent to a kind of death.

In some Oriental philosophies, good and evil are viewed as ultimately being the same, a quite different idea from the attitude of Western ethical thought that evil is "needed" to test or develop good. Part of the profundity of Rexroth's Marichiko poems is that he probes the Eastern attitude in regard to joy and misery in love in a manner transcending judgement or commentary. The experience of love is reduced here to the bareness of bone. The feeling of such reduced and condensed extremity constitutes the "tragic" achievement of the Marichiko poems, except that the sheer thrust of the mercilessly impassioned experience evokes an art as intensified life that is art of a high order indeed. (p. 44)

Donald Gutierrez, "Practicing Safe Sex?" in San Francisco Review of Books, *August, 1987, pp. 21-2, 44.*

Elmer Rice

1892-1967

(Born Elmer Leopold Reizenstein) American dramatist, novelist, autobiographer, nonfiction writer, scriptwriter, essayist, short story writer, and director.

Best remembered for *The Adding Machine* and the Pulitzer Prize-winning *Street Scene,* Rice was a prolific and versatile dramatist whose multifarious output included expressionistic and socially realistic plays, romantic and satirical comedies, melodramas, tragedies, and farces. Along with such prominent playwrights as Eugene O'Neill, Clifford Odets, and Robert Sherwood, Rice is considered a significant contributor to the maturation of American theater during the 1920s and 1930s. His early reading of works by George Bernard Shaw and Henrik Ibsen inspired his lifelong concern for drama committed to social reform. In Rice's words, his work advocates "freedom of the body and of the mind through liberation from political autocracy, economic slavery, religious superstition, hereditary prejudice and herd psychology." Although his plays met with varying degrees of critical and commercial success during his career, Rice earned praise for his innovations in stagecraft and his command of dramatic structure and technique. Robert Hogan observed: "As a consistently experimental playwright, [Rice] is rivalled in our theatre only by O'Neill; as a master of every kind of plot structure he probably stands alone. He has had his failures, but he has done, at one time or another, almost everything consummately."

Born and raised in New York City, Rice aspired as a youth to a career in law and entered New York Law School in 1908. While working as a clerk after graduation, he became disillusioned with the legal profession and eventually left his position to pursue his interest in writing for the stage. Rice scored an unexpected success with his first drama, *On Trial* (1914), a melodramatic murder mystery celebrated for introducing the flashback technique of film to the theater. He achieved this effect by creating a pivoting stage, which allowed the courtroom testimonies of witnesses to be enacted for the audience. This play earned Rice more than $100,000, affording him the financial independence to devote himself to writing and the study of drama. While much of his subsequent work elicited little critical attention, *The Adding Machine* (1923) has been the subject of frequent revivals and is now considered his most ambitious drama. Among the first examples of expressionism in American theater, this play relates the story of Mr. Zero, a bookkeeper with twenty-five years' seniority who murders his supervisor after he learns that he is to be replaced by an adding machine. Executed for the crime, Zero finds himself in a mechanistic heaven where he is again deemed unnecessary. Anthony F. R. Palmieri praised *The Adding Machine* as "the first important American drama to focus on the dehumanization of the American middle class as victim of a mechanized and quantified society."

Rice's next major success, *Street Scene* (1929), exhibits his skill at creating realistic drama. Set outside an inner-city tenement, around which the play's disparate story lines evolve, *Street Scene* examines the interrelationships of the building's multiethnic inhabitants while evoking what Brooks Atkinson called "the elusive, centrifugal mood of New York City—the

brutality as well as the patience and pity." Deemed one of Rice's most significant achievements, this play also marked his debut as a director, a position he occupied for many of his subsequent dramas. During the 1930s, inspired by the critical response to *Street Scene* and his growing prestige as a dramatist, Rice increasingly involved himself in public issues. As a member of the American Civil Liberties Union and director of the Federal Theater Project, he spoke out against censorship in the arts and political injustice in the United States and abroad. In 1938, Rice founded the Playwrights' Company, an association of distinguished New York dramatists organized to support independent, uncensored theatrical productions.

Rice's plays of the 1930s evidence his fervid interest in political and social topics. Although critics frequently objected to the didactic elements of these works, they respected Rice's commitment to a drama of social relevance. In *The Left Bank* (1931), Rice denounces cultural stagnancy in the United States by depicting two discontented American couples vacationing in Paris. *Counsellor-at-Law* (1931) examines ethical issues within the legal profession, and *We, the People* (1933) exposes the economic deficiencies of capitalism by documenting the deepening plight of a Depression-era family. *Judgment Day* (1934), in which Rice attacks fascism within the context of a courtroom melodrama, is based on the covert Nazi burning of the German imperial parliament building, an action Adolf Hitler imputed to communists in order to gain public support. In his next play, *Between Two Worlds* (1934), Rice juxtaposes the theories of communism and capitalism by delineating an encounter between a Russian revolutionary and an affluent young American woman.

Following a four-year retirement from playwriting, during which he publicly protested against conservatism in commercial theater and what he perceived as a lack of insightful drama criticism, Rice returned to the stage with *American Landscape* (1938). In this play, the younger members of wealthy lineage attempt to dissuade their grandfather from selling the family estate to a Nazi-backed corporation. *American Landscape* was the first of Rice's works to be produced by the Playwrights' Company. *Two on an Island* (1940) is a romantic comedy detailing the efforts of an aspiring actress and a struggling dramatist to succeed on Broadway, while *Flight to the West* (1940) portrays a young Jew who questions his pacifistic beliefs when he learns of Nazi atrocities in Europe. *A New Life* (1943) depicts a child custody battle between a nightclub singer whose husband is missing at war and her wealthy, influential in-laws. Rice's last notable achievement for the stage was *Dream Girl* (1945), a comedy about a romantic young woman whose daydreams shelter her from the realities of her mundane life. Rice's later dramas, which include *The Grand Tour* (1951), *The Winner* (1954), *Cue for Passion* (1958), and *Love among the Ruins* (1963), received largely mixed reviews and are considered among his least significant works.

In addition to his plays, Rice authored three novels: *A Voyage to Purilia* (1930), *Imperial City* (1937), and *The Show Must Go On* (1949). The first of these works is a fantasy that satirizes the artificial romanticism of Hollywood films; the second is a naturalistic portrait of an aristocratic Manhattan family; and the third examines theatrical life in New York City. Rice also wrote *Minority Report: An Autobiography* (1954) and *The Living Theatre* (1959), a nonfiction account of contemporary theater.

(See also *CLC*, Vol. 7; *Contemporary Authors*, Vols. 21-22, Vols. 25-28, rev. ed. [obituary]; *Contemporary Authors Permanent Series*, Vol. 2; and *Dictionary of Literary Biography*, Vols. 4, 7.)

CLAYTON HAMILTON

At the very outset of the current season, a great success was achieved by a youth of twenty-one whose name had never before been heard of in the theatre. Like Lord Byron, this new playwright awoke one morning to discover that he had grown famous overnight. His name—which is familiar now—is Elmer L. Reizenstein; and the title of his play . . . is *On Trial*.

The most remarkable feature of the success of *On Trial* is that it is emphatically a success of art for art's sake. The piece has been accurately described by the youthful author as "an experiment in dramatic technique"; and its instantaneous and huge success affords a hitherto unprecedented indication that our public has grown sufficiently interested in the technique of the drama to welcome plays whose strongest bid for favour is their technical efficiency.

Until this indication of a turning of the tide in favour of stagecraft for the sake of stagecraft, it had been generally agreed among observers of our current drama that popular success depended more on subject-matter than on technical dexterity. (p. 181)

But the subject-matter of *On Trial* is scarcely interesting in itself. The play has no theme; and the story that it tells is not sentimental or pretty or timely or even novel. A profligate induces an inexperienced young girl to spend a night with him at a road-house by promising to wed her on the morrow. The next morning the girl's father appears at the road-house, accompanied by a woman who is already married to the profligate. The villain runs away, and the girl is taken home by her father. Shortly afterwards, her father dies; and some years later, the girl meets and marries an honourable man. A daughter is born to them, and they develop a very happy home. It appears that the heroine was justified in concealing from her husband the misfortune that had befallen her before she met him. But the husband meets the profligate in the business world, is befriended by him, and even borrows money from him. This money he repays in cash; but the profligate takes advantage of the accidental renewal of acquaintance with the heroine to force her to yield to him again, under threat of allowing the past iniquity to be exposed. The husband, discovering the recent intrigue, seeks out the profligate and shoots him dead. A few moments before the shooting, the private secretary of the profligate has stolen from the latter's safe the cash that had just been paid him by the murderer; and it therefore appears to the police that robbery was the motive for the murder. The husband seizes on this circumstantial evidence to shield his wife and child from scandal. He confesses himself guilty of murder for the sake of robbery, and asks only to be sent to the electric-chair. But the court insists on assigning counsel to defend him; and the defendant's lawyer, by calling the wronged wife to the stand, makes clear the real motive for the shooting. The private secretary of the dead man is also called as a witness; and when the defendant's counsel succeeds in forcing him to confess that it was he who had rifled the safe and that this robbery had had no connection with the murder, the jury agree at once in acquitting the defendant.

It will be noticed that this story is entirely traditional. At no moment does it exhibit any note of novelty. It is sound enough, indeed, to seem worthy of retelling; but no one can deny that it is trite. The characters concerned in the story are also true enough to life to warrant their revisiting the glimpses of the footlights; but they are neither original nor likable nor particularly interesting. Why should the public flock to the theatre to meet a man who leads a girl astray, or another man who shoots him dead? Why should the public still shed tears over a wronged wife, and a child who remains pathetically unaware of a scandal that has destroyed the happiness of her parents?

From questions such as these, it should become apparent that Mr. Reizenstein was dealing with a story that by no means contained, within itself, the elements of sure success. Did he succeed, then, because of any trick of writing in his dialogue? The answer is, emphatically, no. The test that can be said of the writing of *On Trial* is that it is direct and simple and concise; but the dialogue is utterly devoid of literary charm and of that human richness which is akin to humour. Hundreds of plays which have been obviously better written have failed at once, in recent years, upon our stage. Why, then, did *On Trial* capture the public by assault?

The reason is that Mr. Reizenstein utilised the novel device of building his story backward. This device was interesting in itself, because it had never been employed before on the American stage; and Mr. Reizenstein's employment of it was made doubly interesting by the fact that he revealed, in this experiment, a technical efficiency that is truly astonishing in the first work of an author with no previous experience of the stage. Instead of inventing a story and then deciding how to tell it, this adventurous young playwright started out with an idea of how to tell a story in a novel way and then invented a story that would lend itself to this predetermined technical experiment.

We have observed already that the story of *On Trial* is rather commonplace; but Mr. Reizenstein has made it seem, in Browning's phrase, both ''strange and new'' by revealing it from the end to the beginning, instead of from the beginning to the end. Instead of starting out with motives and developing them to their ultimate expression in facts, he has started out with the accomplished facts and then delved backward to reveal the motives which had instigated them.

In the first act of *On Trial* we see the murder committed on the stage. In the second act, we see enacted an incident two hours before the murder which makes us aware of the exciting cause of the subsequent event that we have previously witnessed. But it is not until the third act, which reveals in action an event that happened thirteen years before, that we are permitted to discover and to comprehend the motives which ultimately culminated in the shooting that we saw in the initial act. By telling his story backward, from effect to cause, the author has added an element of theatrical suspense to a narrative which otherwise might have been dismissed by the public as an oft-repeated tale. (pp. 181-82)

> Clayton Hamilton, ''Chronological Sequence in the Drama,'' in The Bookman, *New York, Vol. XL, No. 2, October, 1914, pp. 181-86.*

THE NEW YORK TIMES

New York last night was treated to the best and fairest example of the newer expressionism in the theatre that it has yet experienced. The verdict, of course, depends upon the personal reaction on the sensibilities of the observer.

He will see and hear, this observer, in *The Adding Machine*, . . . what starts out to be the short and simple annal of one of the great and glorious unsung of life, not too far above the submerged tenth, of a person, at times symbolical and at other times intensely personal, known simply as Mr. Zero.

For twenty-five years, day in and day out, excepting only national holidays and a week in the summer, this Zero has added figures. Figures to the right of him, figures to the left of him, volleyed and thundered from 9 to 5, six days a week, half Saturdays in July and August.

He married, this Zero, what must have been a sweet, moist-eyed, trusting bit of a girl, with infinite faith and pride in his tale of what lay just beyond this necessary beginning as a bookkeeper. But the days became weeks, the weeks became years, and the years decades—and still Zero is no further than his task of adding figures, and the little slip of a bride has become an ill-tempered, nagging, slovenly woman, bitter in her disillusionments and sharp with her tongue at him who is the cause of them.

Comes then, in the language of a great art, the twenty-fifth anniversary of Zero's career with the firm, of Zero still adding figures as he did a quarter of a century before. And at the close of the day's work his employer appears, notifies him that adding machines are to be installed, machines so simple that they can be operated by high school girls, and informs him gently but firmly that his services are no longer required.

For one mad moment all the figures he has ever added whirl madly in the Zero brain—and when he is again aware of the world he has stabbed his employer through the heart with a bill-file.

At his trial he becomes partly articulate—he tries to convey something of what the years of drudgery, endless, aimless drudgery, have done to him. He is sentenced to death and executed. . . .

The part of the fable just outlined runs through two of the play's three acts and four of its seven scenes. One of these early scenes, in particular, displayed a novelty and power that will long keep it in the memory of the beholder. It is simple enough—Zero and a female Zero are reading and checking figures to each other, in a dreary and monotonous sing-song, and as they work they think aloud and show their inmost, sacred selves, but theatrical as the device sounds in cold print, it was weirdly effective and gripping on the stage.

At the beginning of the play's third act and fifth scene at least some part of the audiences will not feel able to carry through. For one thing, this fifth scene, whatever its author's intent may have been, is coldly and gratuitously vulgar. . . .

Mr. Rice's graveyard . . . served as the locale for a scene almost literally from Mr. Schnitzler's *Reigen*—with, it seemed, no reason for the enactment of the scene save that the author willed it so. Certainly there was nothing in the behavior or thoughts of any of the characters that brought it on.

Past the inevitable expressionistic graveyard, the action moves to a pleasant spot in the Elysian Fields. Here Zero is given ample opportunity to catch up with some of the repressions and suppressed desires of his former life, but he turns his back on them at the last moment for fear of being considered not thoroughly respectable. What this scene, and the next and last, are meant to convey is vague, perhaps purposely. Certainly they were not offered as things of beauty by themselves.

At this writing, with the final curtain not yet decently cold upon an expressionist heaven dominated by a gigantic adding machine, the last act remains curious, vague blur, not, however, without excellent moments of satirical observation. It is, nevertheless, by far, the weakest part of the play.

> '''Adding Machine' Replaces Poor Zero,'' in The New York Times, *March 20, 1923, p. 24.*

LUDWIG LEWISOHN

Expressionism has two chief aims: to fling the inner life of the dramatic figures immediately upon the stage; to synthesize, instead of describing, their world and their universe into symbolic visions that shall sum up whole histories, moralities, cosmogonies in a brief minute and a fleeting scene. If this form of art is to be effective and beautiful, it must be very sensitive and very severe at once. . . . In expressionism the antecedent intellectual grasp of your entire material must be firm, definite, complete. Everything must be thought out and thought through. This is what, despite moments of the highest brilliancy and glow, Mr. Eugene O'Neill did not do in *The Hairy Ape*. This is what, in a harder, drier, less poetical vein, Mr. Elmer Rice has actually succeeded in doing in *The Adding Machine*.

Mr. Rice's vision of the world may infuriate you. There were people behind me . . . who first grumbled and then cursed politely. You cannot miss it; you cannot withdraw yourself from its coherence and completeness. Examine his play scene by scene, symbol by symbol. The structure stands. There are no holes in its roof. It gives you the pleasure of both poetry and science, the warm beauty of life and love, the icy delight of mathematics. I am aware of the fact—critics should make this confession oftener—that my profound sympathy with Mr. Rice's substance necessarily colored my reaction to his play. Not, however, to its form, not to the heartening fact that here is an American drama with no loose ends or ragged edges or silly last-act compromises, retractions, reconciliations. The work, on its own ground, in its own mood, is honest, finished, sound.

What Mr. Rice has to tell us is not new. But creative literature, I hasten to add, need not have novelty. What Edgar Lee Masters, Sinclair Lewis, Sherwood Anderson, Zona Gale, what the whole new American literature of moral protest has told us, is also told here. This particular world of ours deliberately hides or chokes with dust and ashes the very sources of human life. It has made fetishes of ugliness and monotony and intolerance. It has given to these fetishes high-sounding names. It is wedded to denial and has made a pact with death. From the intolerable repressions of Mr. Zero's life flares one explosion of the nerves. But it is an explosion of the sickened nerves only. Slavery is in his soul. He is, in reality, doomed to add figures, doomed to chant in unison the pack-formulae so terribly and hauntingly projected in the third scene. He cannot stay in the Elysian Fields with Swift and Rabelais and the great company of the confessors of life and light. He cannot hear the music which is the music of life. The place is not respectable. It is no place for him. He "beats it"—beats it back to an eternal adding machine, back finally to an earth where slavery is his eternal portion and hope an ironic delusion. Mr. Rice is terribly bitter, terribly relentless. . . .

It is clear . . . that there has been here an imaginative collaboration between dramatist and producer. . . . And the results are extraordinarily telling and beautiful. There is, for instance, the place of justice to which poor Zero is brought. The tall windows are crooked; the railing is crooked. But the lines are not crinkled. To the perverse vision they may seem straight. They lean diagonally. The judge is petrified. He is literally of stone. The mob cries "guilty"; a dead heart deals out mercilessness and calls it justice. Not all the scenes are as finely conceived as this. But all have been designed by an imagination packed with close thinking, profoundly akin to the imagination that shaped the play itself. . . . [The] strange eloquence of this play and production . . . constitute, without question, one of the major achievements in the entire field of the American arts.

> *Ludwig Lewisohn, "Creative Irony," in* The Nation, *New York, Vol. CXVI, No. 3013, April 4, 1923, p. 399.*

STARK YOUNG

Expressionism, evidently, from *The Adding Machine*, is a theatrical method by which any means whatever, whether actual or ever seen or heard, may be used to reveal the content of a dramatic moment, to hit up the high lights, to give us the very soul of the incident. Whatever else he gets from Mr. Rice's play the dreariest fool can now understand expressionism as a theatrical method. (p. 164)

The Adding Machine, in so far as it is anything but theatre, tells the story of a poor, dry respectable creature, merely Mr. Zero, who for twenty-five years has sat at a desk adding up checks, without an advance in salary, with no change of any sort except the drying up and souring of his wife. In the first scene Mr. Zero lies in bed while his wife gets her personal chores done, laces up her corsets, rolls her hair in curling kids, rails at her husband's nonentity and the uptown movies, and takes off her stockings. In the next scene the clerk who loves him and who has grown faded with him, sits opposite Mr. Zero calling off the checks. Their thoughts, their retorts, their dust and ashes of emotion, appear as they go on through to the sound of the whistle that ends the empty sum of the day. The boss comes to say that Mr. Zero will not be needed longer, adding machines are to be installed; and at that Mr. Zero goes wild and kills the boss. Next comes a party at the Zeros', in places a very amusing contrivance of the dramatist's, where Messrs. One, Two, Three, Four, Five, Six come with Mrs. One, Mrs. Two, Mrs. Three, Mrs. Four, Mrs. Five, Mrs. Six, all sizes and kinds of men and women but all dressed alike, all equally stale, all of a moron public, all ending their newspaper platitudes that pass for conversation by rising and singing My Country 'Tis of Thee, Sweet Land of Liberty! Then the officer comes for Mr. Zero. The trial scene then appears, as Mr. Zero sees it. He pleads his case and is found guilty. Then the graveyard, and Mr. Zero rises from his grave to talk with a man who has killed his mother. Then the Elysian Fields, and Mr. Zero, to his surprise, finds himself there with the matricide and with his old deskmate, who has killed herself to follow Mr. Zero out of the world. They talk, Mr. Zero and the woman, they have now a chance of being forever together, they hear there at last the music that only those may hear who belong to the happy place. But Mr. Zero, unable to bear the idea of not being respectable—he is a married man and the same throughout eternity or what will people say?—runs off. Finally he is exhibited with a gigantic adding machine, happy in heaven with sum after sum, punch after punch, till, unexpectantly, he is sent back to earth again for another try at life.

Set out like that, *The Adding Machine* sounds like no small expression of life and life's drab progression through mere number and incident, its slovenly half-said dreams, its sin against the spring and surge of vitality in human beings. As a matter of fact *The Adding Machine* has very little to say about any of its incidents. There is no central idea to the play except in a sort of reflected sense, a clutter of facile recollections of *Main Street, Liliom, Peer Gynt, From Morn to Midnight*, Bernard Shaw, Schnitzler and a lively, impertinent and often vulgar journalism. There is no guiding taste throughout the play and no security of intellectual cultural attack. There is no controlling beauty or poignancy that might serve to excuse the most unequal variation, in insight or in pathetic sympathy or in accuracy of observation, that arises in almost every scene as the play gets on toward its more or less unmeaning denouément. But there are well written moments here and there in *The Adding Machine*. Some of the conjugality of the first scene is sharp and jolly. The first five minutes where Mr. Zero meets the man who has killed his mother with the carving-knife is done with great effect. The scene at the adding desk, between the assistant and Mr. Zero, is safe and sure, obvious but successfully put and true. And the scene where Mr. Zero talks with the woman in Elysium, the first two thirds of it, up to the place where he gets respectable and runs away, is beautifully and movingly written. And the whole play shows an unusual theatrical instinct, as Mr. Rice's *On Trial* did, external mostly but with a sharp eye for business and making matters hum.

But what seems to me interesting as regards *The Adding Machine* is this—a thing that hovers around so much of the world of art though it is not often so happily illustrated as here in Mr. Rice's play—it is a success gained by exploiting for extraneous purposes a method that in itself has a revealing and inner necessity for being. I mean to say that expressionism in so far as it has any reason for existence at all and in so far as it is a distinct method of dramatic writing, must exist or can be employed solely because it is the only means by which some section of experience can be fully revealed. It exists because it is the only form that suits the artist's state of mind, his soul. Any method, if it happens to be a fresh or unfamiliar form, will trouble the public somewhat, since the dialect used is not yet easily understood. The public tends to resist it, to jeer or strain away from it, to suspect it of some decadent evil. But if you take the method more or less to itself, without any bother of content to be got at, if you play up the method's novelties and tricks, in other words dramatize the method's character and ways, you may get something highly diverting and easy. "Commercialize" is the word many people use for this. But "commercialize" does not express what Mr. Rice has done. What he has done is to write a play not so much about life as about expressionism. He gets up a theatre piece in which we see what expressionism does through seven scenes. In art every true use of any method is a mystery. It is a means of drawing out the mystery of men and events. It happens as life happens, some of it knowable, some of it alive miraculously and unknowably. Its truth appears, as life appears, through its being necessary and inevitable and mysterious. But in *The Adding Machine* Mr. Rice makes it clear that this method of dramatic art is only a game like any other game—which of course every art method is up to a certain point—he lets all play at it together from the outside. He uses the expressionism not so much to reveal as to entertain. What another man might struggle to force into a revelation of his state of soul, the author of *The Adding Machine* brings smartly to market. (pp. 164-65)

Stark Young, "Marketing Expressionism," in The New Republic, *Vol. XXXIV, No. 435, April 4, 1923, pp. 164-65.*

R. DANA SKINNER

Elmer Rice, the author of *The Adding Machine,* has [in *Street Scene*] brought into the anaemic and languishing theatre of the season a play of extraordinary sweep, power and intensity, which catches up with amazing simplicity and sincere feeling the ragged, glowing, humorous and tragic life that pours in .and out of one of those brown-stone apartment houses hovering on the upper edge of the slum district of New York. It has its brutal moments and its coarse ones. But they are never brutal or coarse from the sophisticated viewpoint so many authors assume today, and behind every incident and every character you feel the pity and the understanding of a playwright who has glimpsed a great truth—that no matter what may be the pressure of one's environment, the only true power to meet the life of today must come from within the individual.

The gripping illusion of *Street Scene* quite beggars verbal description. You cannot convey through words alone what the theatre, at its best, conveys by sound, color, motion and a subtly sustained mood. Nevertheless, a brief outline of what happens is necessary to an understanding of Mr. Rice's real achievement. The curtain rises and shows us the front of an old-fashioned brown-stone apartment house set in the lamp-lit gloom of a hot summer evening. Abraham Kaplan is sitting in his shirt sleeves by the open window of the ground floor apartment. The German wife of an Italian music teacher is trying to catch a breath of air from the opposite window. People are passing and repassing, bedraggled, heat-tortured persons. . . . Slowly you begin to learn who the various people are that inhabit this grim building—the burned-out, slatternly widow, the Jewish radical, the Italian musician, the burly stage hand and his wife and children on the second floor, the woman on the third floor about to have her first baby. And so it goes, in a slowly weaving pattern, intensely human, never overdrawn and never failing, in depicting a type, to add to that type, a touch of individual characterization. As the various inhabitants of the house seek air on the street you begin to sense the possibility of drama in their lives. Mrs. Maurrant, the stage hand's wife on the second floor, has become pretty well exhausted in the struggle to get a kind word from her burly husband. Her son, Willy . . . is getting definitely out of hand. Her daughter, Rose, clerk in a real estate office, threatens to become involved with a married man who wants to put her on the stage. The neighbors have seen Mrs. Maurrant talking rather too often to the bill collector from the milk company. Is she playing with fire? Frank Maurrant is growing suspicious—his wife is growing reckless. But when the Buchanan baby arrives on the third floor, it is Mrs. Maurrant who spends the night with the mother and takes charge of the situation. Another family in the building is about to be dispossessed. Life is becoming very real and complex in this gathering place of humanity. (p. 348)

The next morning Frank Maurrant is going to Hartford for the try-out performance of a play. The bill collector drops by. The children go to school. . . . Mrs. Maurrant lets the bill collector come to her apartment. Frank Maurrant, much the worse for drink, comes back. The brown-stone beehive suddenly comes to life. Frank Maurrant rushes upstairs, shots are fired, a moment later the frantic crazed body of the milk collector crashes through the second-floor window calling for help. He is dragged back in the room. Police. Ambulance. Crowds. Frank Maurrant escapes. Tragedy in the midst of the commonplace. . . . And during all this, the sheriff and his men proceed with the business of dispossessing the Hildebrand family and dumping their furniture on the sidewalk. Life goes on.

There is a third act the same afternoon. But you can hardly call it an act when it is merely the continuing, surging drama of frightened, awestruck people who somehow keep right on about their ways in the very shadow of death. Frank Maurrant is finally captured. He has a last word with his daughter. He must have been clean out of his head, he tells her. He is not sorry for himself but the pleading eyes of his dead wife hover before him. In various ways the neighbors help Rose Maurrant. Tragedy has matured her suddenly. Even her office manager becomes a sincere friend for the moment, seeking nothing but the chance to help. . . . Rose goes off. A couple come looking for a vacant apartment. Life in the brown-stone will go on being what it has always been.

It is perhaps hard to believe that from incidents as varied and scattered as these, Mr. Rice could create an enthrallingly vivid sense of reality, poignancy, cowardice, despair and courage. But he has succeeded in an overflowing measure. It is, if you like to label things, an intensely realistic play. No detail is omitted in the production which might lend photographic realism—even to the loose rubber heel of the Scandinavian janitor. Yet I think anyone who sits through this play will realize that Mr. Rice has only used realism as a means to an end. He is telling a universal story of a city. The same kind of things, differing only in degree, might happen (from the newspapers we know they do happen) in the wealthiest or in the lowliest quarters of the city. Behind a marble front, they would happen with a less merciless exposure. That is the only difference. When all is said and done, Mr. Rice's highest achievement is in painting this vivid panorama without creating a sense of despair. Human beings are to be pitied for what they bring on themselves, but they are not mere automatons crushed under the giant footsteps of environment. Once more we come back to that brief illuminated moment when Rose Maurrant says that the force to meet life must come from within. Suffering—yes. Despair—no. Life is pretty much what we make it and the fault lies in ourselves if we make a poor job of it. In spite of the brutal frankness of a few scenes, I cannot help the feeling that the undertone of this play is honest and true. It comes vastly nearer being ''a great American play'' than the much vaunted *Strange Interlude,* or in fact any of those plays of recent years which seek to explain life from the mud flats of pessimism. (pp. 348-49)

The enthusiastic response of the audience is one of the best indications I have seen that the public automatically welcomes honesty and sincerity on the stage when it is coupled with masterly achievement. (p. 349)

> *R. Dana Skinner, in a review of "Street Scene," in*
> Commonweal, *Vol. IX, No. 12, January 23, 1929,*
> *pp. 348-49.*

STARK YOUNG

In a setting . . . cleverly realistic without being foolishly so and photographic without idle intrusions of dusty neighborhood detail from Ninth Avenue, where [*Street Scene*] is laid, we see the story unwind itself entertainingly, with an amiable pace and plenty of time for the talk of the apartment house people as they go in and out, with engaging colors drawn from the contact of diverse nationalities, Jews, Germans, Irish, Italians and 100 percent Americans, and with a due complaisance and tidy willingness to please. There is a genuinely expert economy in the way in which the life of the Maurrant family is conveyed to us, and an economy of means that is even finer in the portrait of the wife's career, this doomed Anna Maurrant, whose husband is brutal and indifferent in his treatment of her, is given to drink, is full of principles and ideas of what a family should be and what his own has got to be, he'll see to that.

The inmates of the apartment house, then, go in and out, linger about the doorstep in the stifling summer heat, sit at their windows, gossip of their children and each other, of the little husband on the third floor who acts as if he were having the baby instead of his thin little wife, of the Hildebrand family whose head has disappeared and who are about to be dispossessed. And through the whole texture of conversation they weave the thread of this pale woman's tragedy on the second floor, the visits of the milk collector that they have all observed, the spreading scandal about Mrs. Maurrant. Idly and emptily they are doing her to death, but it is all a part of the day's chatter and the neighborhood news. We see Rose, her daughter, and the married suitor, who wants to take her from the job in

his office and set her up in an apartment and a place on the stage; we see Maurrant himself, a member of the stage-hands' union, a drinker, sullen and bullying. Meanwhile, Mrs. Jones has something to say about everything, takes her husband, George, to task, and her dog, Queenie, to walk, and professes complete ease of mind about her children, one of whom is a hulking thug and the other almost a tart.

From that on, the play takes its course, clearly foreseen. (pp. 296-97)

So much for *Street Scene,* then, which on one plane of consideration is pleasantly entertaining. On another plane, where you take the play seriously and where you ask yourself whether for an instant you have believed in any single bit of it, either as art, with its sting of surprise and creation, or as life, with its reality, *Street Scene* is only rubbish, or very close to rubbish. For me, who was not bored with it as an evening's theater, it is something less than rubbish, theatrical rubbish, in that curious, baffling way that the stage provides. The presence of living beings in the roles engages us, and gives a certain plausibility to whatever takes place, and a certain actuality to any character whatever. But is it possible that anyone who could understand the values of the first act of *Anna Christie,* for example, or a play of Chekhov's, could fail to see that the last act in *Street Scene*—to take the most evident let-down—is empty and made up? The girl has found her mother shot, seen blood, at the hospital she has seen her mother die without speaking, she has seen her father caught and torn and bleeding, the Jewish boy, who loves her so much, offers to leave everything and go away with her, and she stands there making a little speech about dependence on one's self, and so on and so on, while nurses with perambulators have appeared and various persons come prowling around at the scene of a murder, and the obvious life goes on, amusing remarks from odd characters, and the rest of it—obliging journalism in sum. It must be a very elementary principle that the essential idea of a work of art goes through it, and that the themes and conceptions to be expressed must lie inherently in the substance of it, and that they are to be expressed in creation, not in superimposed sentiments.

Must we gloomily conclude that what most human beings like in the theater is a farrago of living matter with the sting taken out of it? If this Anna Maurrant's life and death really bit into us, cost us something, instead of providing a mere thrill and the comfort of pseudo-thought afterward, would we not wreck the stage for rage when we see how little this matter has stung the dramatist? One of the ways we know a work of art is by the cost of its unity in kind, in the same way that the soul within him, determining his form as he comes into the world, prevents a man's having the bulk, strength and peace of an elephant. One of the ways we can tell an artist is by the extent to which reality puts the fear of God into him; a painter of no worth will paint you anything from Napoleon crossing the Alps to an old mill in Vermont, but a real painter trembles before the mere character of human hands and the problem of their conversion into the unity that is his style. Is it any wonder that Ingres, in his despair at the success of the second-rate, threatened to paint an Allegory of Mediocrities? (pp. 297-98)

> *Stark Young, "Street Scene," in* The New Republic,
> *Vol. LVII, No. 739, January 30, 1929, pp. 296-98.*

FRANCIS FERGUSSON

[In *The Left Bank*], Rice's main idea seems to be that American artists and writers should live at home, instead of on the Left

Bank, like John Shelby, his conceited protagonist. . . . In support of this thesis he shows us not only how conceited and futile Shelby is, but how discontented is his wife. . . . And then he brings on Waldo Lynde . . . and his wife Susie. . . . It is obvious from the first that these pairs are going to trade mates, and so, at the end of act three, they do. . . .

It is of course evident that Mr. Rice is not dealing with the very real problem that beset Henry James, Hawthorne, Eliot, Pound, Whistler, Sargent and other American artists. What he seems to be trying to do is to say that American writers in Europe are liable to mix up their married relations and become promiscuous; but all of the Left Bank scandals he shows could be matched in plenty of fast business sets in our own suburbs. He seems to say that an American writer, in Paris, is reduced to reviewing and translating to keep alive; but doesn't he know thousands in the same pickle in New York? And if it is a question of "rootlessness", what is more rootless than a New York writer? In short, Mr. Rice has nothing to say about his people that wouldn't be equally true of Americans in many other circumstances; and as for the real differences between this country and Europe, which are essential for understanding the real problem, he never even bothers to ask what they may be.

Francis Fergusson, in a review of "The Left Bank," in The Bookman, *New York, Vol. LXXIV, No. 3, November, 1931, p. 302.*

EUPHEMIA Va RENSSELAER WYATT

There is no more deteriorating influence in everyday life than an unmade bed. Varying forms of untidiness may be as unpalatable but nothing to us more odiously connotes moral laxity. To be confronted with the hideous bedroom of a cheap French hotel for two hours and a half—with the bed unmade through at least half that period—is the aesthetic treat which Elmer Rice provides [in *The Left Bank*] for his ill-used audience. Should he retort that it is exactly the proper setting for his story, we can only agree; but then, we could dispense with the story. There may be Americans in Paris who are as slovenly in their habits and manners, as devoid of standards as his characters, but must we be condemned to wake with them in the morning, brush their teeth with them, comb their hair with them, dress with them, drink with them, swear—swear a great deal with them and be privy to their very anomalous going to bed? . . . Compared with *Street Scene*, the realism of *The Left Bank* is unimportantly exact and deliberately unsavory. In fact, it is both dull and vulgar. (pp. 210-11)

Euphemia Va Rensselaer Wyatt, in a review of "The Left Bank," in The Catholic World, *Vol. CXXXIV, No. 800, November, 1931, pp. 210-11.*

JOHN HUTCHENS

The Left Bank discloses Mr. Rice once more as a playwright not content with the touch-and-go conventions which the majority of his colleagues are only too happy to adopt and happier to have succeed. Nor is he satisfied to present his material until he has thought it through in the means at his command. Lacking the general theatricality of *Street Scene*, *The Left Bank* has the same surprising simplicity of conception, the same distrust of the time-worn symbols thought necessary to "step up" an interesting subject of discussion. In *The Left Bank*, for instance, Mr. Rice is saying that the American in Paris can be an obtuse

young man with a fixed idea that his own country has no meaning for him. If only because he declines to say this dogmatically, a surprising conviction attaches at once to his point of view. Our theatrical Americans in Paris have heretofore been pretty romantic fellows or else complete caricatures, and here is one who is neither. When John Shelby is not writing a biography that will never be written, he is making easy love and passing the days in an aura of fraudulent freedom. His wife longs to quit their futile attempt at a life they never can share, to go home and assume the simple responsibilities for which her husband has no strength. Their points of view are at a deadlock when another American couple drops in, a fatuous, sentimental woman and her husband, an ordinarily sensitive and sensible man. And it is precisely there, where the play takes the expected course and the four people pair off according to what they have brought to the situation, that the virtues of Mr. Rice's simplicity are manifested. . . . In dialogue that is living speech, the lives of four people have been redirected and moulded, and, though the play is of ideas rather than events, you have not been lead through the intrusive formalities of a stage argument. In a day which cherishes the drama's fast moving surfaces, it is an accomplishment not to be dismissed lightly. (pp. 983-84)

John Hutchens, "Anchors Aweigh: Broadway in Review," in Theatre Arts Monthly, *Vol. XV, No. 12, December, 1931, pp. 975-91.*

RICHARD DANA SKINNER

In contrast to *Street Scene*, which was universal, Elmer Rice's latest play, *We, the People*, is of a particular day and mood. It is vibrantly of the present moment, almost hysterically so at times. It is a play of angry and ironic protest against the broader aspects of social injustice in times like these and also against special and particular forms of injustice and hypocrisy. Hot fury runs through it like a fever, the more so because delusions are often mixed with realities and half truths with honest statements of fact. The delusions and half truths concern chiefly the inner motives of some of the leading characters. The honest facts relate to happenings recorded with tragic monotony in every edition of every newspaper—self-respecting and thrifty families brought by trip-hammer blows to utter poverty and starvation, meager profits scraped from the bent back of human misery, greed unconsciously committing suicide before the very eyes of millions it has thrown out of work. In days when the voice of the Vatican has been raised again, "after forty years," in a terrible indictment of economic cruelty, no fair-minded person can question the facts. Where Mr. Rice forfeits strength is in going beyond facts to individual motives, in imputing conscious hypocrisy to those who are often merely the product of a system and a tradition, in giving all the inner goodness to the economically oppressed and all the cynical wickedness to the alleged monsters of great wealth.

We, the People is an episodic play of twenty scenes recounting the ever-increasing tragedy of the Davis family and those with whom the lives of this family are linked. . . .

The outline recital of some of the major events in this play must inescapably give the impression of high exaggeration and of a totally unnecessary piling up of miseries. But you must remember that Elmer Rice is one of the very best of our American playwrights. He brings to this panorama of our social system all that quick sense of the theatre and all that ear for telling speech which made *Street Scene* one of the best realistic plays of many years. *We, the People* is no ordinary propaganda play. It is full of expert characterization, of clearly etched scenes with swift incisive action, of dialogue that, for the most part, has authentic tang and flavor. The play is never dull. Artistic restraint has been used in many scenes that might easily have become maudlin or unbearably gloomy. There is true comedy mixed with much of the biting irony. The dramatic unities are surprisingly preserved. In fact, the heaping up of all possible misfortunes on one family is a direct result of this effort to view a national scene through a limited field. Nor can we question the fact that in the last two years, as seldom before in our history, calamities have come in droves upon single families. . . .

Mr. Rice has the objective facts to support the incidents of his play, enough even to justify the accumulation of disasters over a single home. It is in the subjective inferences of the play that we find the debilitating blight of prejudice. If Mr. Rice could only see it, the tragedy of the present day is all the more appalling and fantastic because of the frozen habits of mind, of the inertia, and because of the only half-conscious motives of those who are helping to achieve the suicide of greed. Deliberate hypocrisy would be far easier to deal with. Blindness and a numbed conscience make far worse enemies to combat. They plunge headlong against a threatening doom as if driven by an evil fury. They are in fact, and could easily be made to become in a play, an integral part of a universal and sweeping tragedy. By thinning down these life forces, Mr. Rice has opened the way to many objections, to detailed argument, and to manifold defense mechanisms. He has missed the note of high tragedy entirely. Nevertheless, the play provides a stirring experience, and makes an appeal, no matter how prejudiced it may seem, to the fires of self-examination which are slowly kindling beneath the agony of our day.

> *Richard Dana Skinner, in a review of "We, the People," in* Commonweal, *Vol. XVII, No. 15, February 8, 1933, p. 411.*

JOSEPH WOOD KRUTCH

Elmer Rice's sociological drama *We, the People* is an indictment pure and simple. The twenty scenes which pass rapidly across the stage . . . summarize vividly the case against contemporary society and conclude with a series of speeches directed straight at the audience. No previous effort of the same sort has been anything like so ambitious, and none has been, within its limitations, so effective. The most convinced defender of the status quo could hardly fail to feel the force of the indictment, and several times the audience broke out into mingled applause and hisses. Here are clarity, logic, and an intense sincerity, plus a very unusual gift for dramatic writing.

And yet, if the truth must be told, a certain sense of disappointment is mingled with the admiration one feels. It was to be hoped that Mr. Rice would do more than state a strong case strongly; it was to be hoped that he would be technically inventive, that he would advance the art of the sociological drama by making it more satisfactory as drama. But that is exactly what he has failed to do. Perhaps it would be unfair to say that *We, the People* is merely "bigger and better" in the conventional American sense. But it would be, at least, to state a part of the truth. The play stands out because it is ambitious, elaborate, and complete. It is not essentially new, original, or inventive. Like all the other plays of its kind it is interesting almost wholly because of its subject matter. No one could

possibly call it a good play after it has ceased to be relevant to existing conditions, and it will be admired precisely to the extent that the individual spectator happens to be on the author's side.

Great propaganda must manage in some way to hold even those who do not want to hear, and that *We, the People* will fail to do. If he is honest with himself, even the most delighted spectator will realize that he is thinking chiefly of what the play is going to do to his opponents rather than of what it is doing to him. . . . We expect of a drama that it shall tell us something we do not know, give us some insight we did not have, or, if it deals wholly with the familiar, that it shall arouse and then discharge our emotions in some effective way. If it does none of these things, we may still "approve" as we approve *We, the People*; but we shall remain, nevertheless, unsatisfied. (pp. 158-59)

> *Joseph Wood Krutch, "The Prosecution Rests," in* The Nation, *New York, Vol. CXXXVI, No. 3527, February 8, 1933, pp. 158-60.*

THE WORLD TOMORROW

It is not often that a play comes to Broadway which gives the devotee of the theatre so clear a picture of contemporary life and so sharp a criticism of the iniquities and injustices of the present social system as Elmer Rice's *We The People*.

The play is a tragedy depicting the dismal facts of present-day life and the misery which results from unemployment, wage cuts, home evictions, police brutality and the cowardly use of guns by industrial concerns against their protesting unemployed workers. The tragedy is not carried through to its ultimate climax but closes rather with an appeal to "we the people" to restore ancient and honored American rights. If one were inclined to make any criticism of this excellent play it would be that the ending sacrifices drama for propaganda a little too obviously and destroys the sense of the tragic by a political exhortation which does not add power to the play.

Elmer Rice is a master in giving the outlines of a total social situation. Just as his *Street Scene* gave the hearer full insight into the lower middle-class life of New York, his new play surveys the entire American scene; and there is hardly a detail in the various factors and forces which enter into the present situation which is left out. Competent and careful craftsmanship was required to make a whole of these component parts, artfully presented in twenty different scenes. Every social group of American life is depicted in the play. . . . Though these characters are all types, they do not lack personal uniqueness. Together they present a total picture of the American scene which is strikingly penetrating and complete. It might be added that a parson finds a place in the drama, and he is neither a fool nor a tool of reaction; he is an honest fellow without radicalism but driven by religiously oriented common sense to ally himself with the radicals. Perhaps that character together with the radical professors in the play does justice to the fact that both the church and the university are actually supporting non-conformist economic and social thought through a small but sincere minority.

The play echoes current American history besides portraying various types in our contemporary situation. The Mooney case and the Sacco-Vanzetti trial are hinted at; the scene in which the college president is drafted by the bankers to run for the Presidency suggests memories of Colonel Harvey and Woodrow Wilson; the student revolt against compulsory military training is included, and the bonus march on Washington comes into the picture. One might even guess that Eliot White's radical church activities suggested Rice's parson.

It is to be hoped that every organization which is interested in arousing the American public to the seriousness of our economic and social problems will give this play genuine support. It deserves to have a long run on Broadway.

> *A review of "We the People," in* The World Tomorrow, *Vol. XVI, No. 8, February 22, 1933, p. 176.*

JOSEPH WOOD KRUTCH

[In *American Landscape,* Rice] is attempting, with something less than full success, to get out of the bad habits into which he allowed himself to fall. He, goodness knows, never went in for either mysticism or snobbery, but he did . . . get so much interested in "explanation" that he lost the power to create human beings and lost it for the simple reason that human beings had ceased to concern him except in so far as they could be treated as sociological abstractions. The new play, though far less intemperate and confused than most of his recent work, grows out of a thesis, and it often seems prosy and dull because its personages so obviously have little life of their own. It is hard to believe that a writer who, even in such minor plays as *Counselor-at-Law* and *The Left Bank,* revealed an almost uncanny gift for catching the rhythm of everyday speech and imitating the gestures of men and women could write dialogue as lifeless as most of that in the present play; and the fact that he can do so should stand as an awful warning to the artist who confuses artistic seriousness with seriousness of any other kind. With everything Mr. Rice here has to say I have the profoundest sympathy, but there is no use in pretending that his essay is much more than an essay or that it gains much by calling itself a play. (pp. 700-01)

> *Joseph Wood Krutch, "Prodigals' Return," in* The Nation, *New York, Vol. 147, No. 26, December 24, 1938, pp. 700-01.*

GRENVILLE VERNON

In intention at least Elmer Rice's [*American Landscape*] is admirable. It shows too that Mr. Rice has abandoned his somewhat jejune attitude toward social questions, and has emerged a believer in the American tradition of democracy. In *American Landscape* he no longer genuflects before the altar of the Kremlin. In his play he takes a typical New England manufacturing family, the head of which is about to sell the business in order to live in peace, away from the harassings of labor unions. But his family objects to the business getting out of their control and so do his ancestors who founded the business. The latter arrive in their habits as they lived, and without the slightest trouble become part of the family councils. Mr. Rice evidently thinks that in New England people not only believe in ghosts, but are not surprised when they appear—even when two of them are Moll Flanders and Mrs. Harriet Beecher Stowe. It is right here that Mr. Rice shows the weakness of his method. . . . Mr. Rice is distinctly a prosaic writer, a realist of the realists; fantasy is not for him. And fantasy above all else is needed in *American Landscape.* But at least let us raise our hat to Mr. Rice's intention.

> *Grenville Vernon, in a review of "American Landscape," in* Commonweal, *Vol. XXIX, No. 10, December 30, 1938, p. 273.*

JOSEPH WOOD KRUTCH

The island in question [in *Two on an Island*] is Manhattan itself, and the two who serve as hero and heroine are a boy and a girl arriving simultaneously from the hinterland. They do not actually meet until the last act, but they are, as the author points out, representatives of that great company completing the strange circular migration begun by their forefathers when the latter set out to conquer those great open spaces from which the new generation is returning for a new conquest. Through their eyes we see what is the real subject of the play— the panorama of metropolitan life sketched in broad, bold, and telling strokes. . . .

Mr. Rice has provided a series of delightfully telling vignettes, and the combination is perhaps the most successful attempt ever made to state in theatrical terms the humors of O. Henry's Bagdad on the Subway. Mr. Rice's mood is, indeed, almost as unashamed in its humorous romanticism as was that of the author of "The Four Million." O. O. McIntyre would have loved the play, and it is only the author's shrewd observation and shrewd craftsmanship which lift it above the level of the familiar heartbreak-and-glamour style of contemporary romance. But it is above that level because, even when Mr. Rice uses a method almost broad enough to suggest the cartoon, the sharpness and directness of his observation, together with his extraordinary gift for recording the speech of real people, give the thing a sincerity and a verisimilitude wholly delightful. The theatrical method which he employs has been all but discredited by "advanced" playwrights who have used it as an excuse for laziness and ineptitude, but Mr. Rice has rehabilitated it partly by the crispness of his atmospheric scenes, partly by the knowingness with which he has alternated them with the more fully developed scenes involving his hero and heroine, most of which are written with great vigor and originality. Take, for example, that in which the heroine is all but seduced by the illustrator for whom she is posing. Obviously this scene is inevitable in any such story. One is ready to assume that it could not be other than stereotyped and banal. Yet actually it is neither. . . . [This is] perhaps the best single scene in the play, freshly humorous as well as pathetic.

With *Two on an Island* Mr. Rice, I think, resumes his place among the best of our comic writers, along with the Messrs. Behrman, Barry, and Kaufman. . . . Neither the comic insight nor the wit of Mr. Rice is like that of any of the others, and it rests, one might say, on a broader base, derives from the spirit of a larger mass of people. It is not merely that his favorite characters are landladies, taxi drivers, and the like, persons whose knowingness is combined with an innocent unsophistication. It is also that the whole flavor of his writing is more robust, more earthy, less narrowly local, and less highly specialized in spirit if not in manner. Of the four he is the most inclusively American, and without him the quartet would represent far less completely than it does the comic spirit of this nation.

> *Joseph Wood Krutch, "Bagdad on the Subway," in* The Nation, *New York, Vol. 150, No. 5, February 3, 1940, p. 136.*

C. V. TERRY

[*Dream Girl*] is one more illustration of the magic an old hand can work with old hat, if the hand is expert enough. Mr. Rice is a veteran craftsman who knows his job: his story of the wool-gathering heroine who cannot quite separate romance and reality has been told with greater poignance and depth, but it has rarely been told more expertly.

This time, the wool-gatherer is a book-store proprietress, and the three objects of her dreaming are her sister's husband (who is quite as emotionally immature as she), a rich wolf who plies her with those extra luncheon stingers that sometimes spell disaster, and a plain-spoken book reviewer who goes on to better things before the final curtain. Mr. Rice keeps his little circus moving at a gay tempo throughout. In the printed play the tempo seems a bit truer than the taste, now and again, and some of the fun has an obvious ring. But Mr. Rice is a showman who writes for the theatre rather than the library: students of the comedy-fantasy form can learn much from his easy fluency in the medium.

> *C. V. Terry, "Broadway Bookrack," in* The New York Times Book Review, *July 21, 1946, p. 8.*

HENRY POPKIN

Elmer Rice's work, as represented in [*Seven Plays*], repeats the familiar pattern of most successful American dramatists of our day: the painstaking mastery of conventional technique, a brief period of originality, and then a slow hardening into run-of-the-mill attitudes expressed in run-of-the-mill forms—varied at the proper times with a social-conscious period and a patriotic period. What lends special interest to this pattern as it has appeared in Elmer Rice's career is the exceptional brightness of the hope he inspired but never fulfilled.

With his early play, *The Adding Machine,* Rice established himself as the interpreter of the "average man"; with each succeeding play he became more surely identified as the one American playwright who had most deliberately committed himself to presenting what is typical in American life. (Not even George Kelly has been as explicit as Rice in calling attention to the representativeness of his subjects.) By contrasting his humdrum bourgeois types with a few "different" individuals—foreigners, artists, radicals, and Jews—Rice guaranteed that his emphasis upon the average would not be lost. But even as he furnished more and more details about these alternatives to the dull average, he grew increasingly fond of the average itself, and, finally, in his latest plays, he has ardently glorified the typical, which has now become the *normal,* to be defended against the abnormality of imagination and intellect.

In *The Adding Machine* Rice reduced the average to its purest form, Mr. Zero. Taking full advantage of both the freedom and the restriction of expressionism, he exhibited Mr. Zero in all the nakedness of his simple mind, his fear of freedom, his resentment of those unlike himself. Mr. Zero never manages to be anything but an efficient machine, whether he is at the office adding columns of figures or at home parroting the small talk of his social class. The dramatist's job was peculiar here, in that he did not attempt to make this automaton into a fully realized individual; on the contrary, the perfection of Mr. Zero's characterization rests in his never being more than a type. But surrounding the central portrait of Mr. Zero are the dim shadows of gayer attitudes toward life, never clearly shown but only suggested: the buoyant dreams of his co-worker, Daisy Devore; the free ways of the girl whom he has had arrested for indecent exposure; the satiric tradition of the two clergymen whom the play makes residents of the Elysian fields, Swift and Rabelais; and—dimmest of all, but most significant for Rice's later work—the vague figures of the exotic strangers whom Mr. Zero resents and whom he recognizes only when he gives expression to his bitter hatred of Jews and Negroes. (p. 283)

For Rice, the dichotomy between Babbittry and Bohemia provided his most fruitful subject—and his favorite character type, for in most of his subsequent plays he has been trying to improve on his portrait of Mr. Zero. And yet, all his later studies of the typical American nonentity reveal only that he was right the first time in *The Adding Machine,* that this type is best seen in isolation, and that trying to portray him in the plural rather than the singular only multiplies Zero; in art, as in arithmetic, multiplying Zero produces only zero.

We find many Zeros in *Street Scene,* since this is the first play in which Rice created a cross section of American life. Mr. and Mrs. Zero may here be disguised by Italian, German, Swedish, and Irish accents, but these characters are obviously not intended to be exotically different foreigners; they have been Americanized, in the worst sense of the term. . . . These Zeros, like their prototypes in *The Adding Machine,* are anti-Semites, but they are more fortunate in having the victims of their prejudice close at hand. On the other hand, the Kaplans are the exotic foreigners *par excellence,* the perfect foils for the assorted Babbitts of the cast; they are the very incarnation of radicalism, culture, irreligion, and everything else the Zeros find abhorrent and dangerous. It is in the case of these "good" people in particular that Rice often seems to be offering labels (Whitman, Beethoven, Karl Marx) instead of characterization, but the rest of *Street Scene* is quite successful both as melodrama and as critique of Zeroism.

Counsellor-at-Law, the next major play, again employs the Jew as a symbol of individuality and intelligence. The banality of Zeroism is here represented not by the flotsam of the lower middle class but by the would-be aristocrats of the Social Register. We observe the offensive behavior of a Jewish lawyer's Gentile wife, her incredibly nasty little children, and her effete boyfriend, who are put side by side with the warm-hearted, warm-blooded friends of the lawyer's youth. This latter group contains a cross section resembling that of *Street Scene,* but in *Counsellor-at-Law* the Irish and Italians are "good" and interesting, not "bad" and dull as in *Street Scene.* By this time the distinctiveness of the foreigner has evidently come to be regarded as a good thing almost for its own sake; the only profound difference between the two social classes here depicted seems to be between foreign stock and native stock. (p. 284)

Judgment Day stands apart from the rest of the *Seven Plays,* since it is the only one with a European locale. It fits the pattern of the dramatic representation of Zeroism, for, in fascism, it shows the attitudes and loyalties of Zeroism made law. This is a development for which we were prepared by Lippo's admiration for Mussolini in *Street Scene.* What seems particularly significant in this connection is the way the little men, the Zeros of this far-off Slavic land, fall into line. But in *Judgment Day* the issues are made too clear and perhaps a little too easy to judge by the device of creating (partially) imaginary circumstances in a (partially) imaginary country, argued out in a very disorderly courtroom. This technique recalls the similarly melodramatic disorderliness of Rice's first produced play, *On Trial*.

While *Judgment Day* revealed Rice's opposition to legalized conformity abroad, some other plays of the years preceding suggested a more genial attitude toward the homegrown American variety. In several of these plays the commonplace American is idealized at the expense of the unattached dissident. The Americans of *See Naples and Die* are victimized by a scheming Russian nobleman. In *The Subway* an innocent girl of a conventional family is ruined by an artist. In *The Left Bank* the wife of an expatriate decides that America is better than Paris. An American girl, in *Between Two Worlds,* is seduced by a Russian film director. The villains of two later plays, *American Landscape* and *Flight to the West,* are again foreigners; in both instances they are Nazis. . . . In all six of these plays immediately preceding and following *Judgment Day,* our sympathy is sought for the plain American, who no longer exhibits the uglier signs of Zeroism, and sympathy must be withheld from the foreigner, the artist, and the expatriate.

Two artists—a playwright and an actress—are the chief characters of *Two on an Island,* but they are as commonplace and wholesome, as unconcerned about their art, as if they had just stepped out of the Hardy family; they are as typical as their names—John Thompson and Mary Ward. In this cross-section play, the only "representative" individuals whom we are encouraged to dislike are the flighty rich girl (repeating a theme of *Counsellor-at-Law*), the radical (reversing a theme of *Street Scene*), and the cynical Jewish theatrical producer. *Two on an Island* seems intended as a happy vindication of "normality": it's fun to be just folks. *Dream Girl* is a firmer step in the same direction. . . . With *Dream Girl* the development of Rice's values has come full circle. More explicitly than in any other play, Rice here enthrones the standards of Mr. Zero and at the same time rejects the "sensitive" artists. . . . (pp. 284-85)

I suppose it all proves that if one lives with Mr. Zero long enough, one gets used to him and even comes to the conclusion that he is not such a bad fellow after all. In explaining this change, we must observe that the obvious formulas do not apply to Rice. This man's head has not been turned by success. We need only recall that, following *Counsellor-at-Law,* his hit plays became very infrequent. Furthermore, Rice's disdain for his audience and his critics is well known. . . .

The most convincing explanation of Rice's friendlier attitude toward Mr. Zero is very different. Surely the Depression, the New Deal, and the rise of dictatorship abroad furnish sufficient reason for this change, sufficient to make any interested, liberal author sympathize with the average man's distress (in *We the People*), compliment his political acumen (by implication at least, in *A New Life*), contrast him with his less wise or less fortunate brothers abroad (in *Flight to the West* and *American Landscape*), and finally, in an excess of love and fellow feeling, credit him with every virtue, including many which he does not possess. Whether or not Rice intends it to be so, this attitude belongs to the new religion of the common man. The Supreme Being of this new faith, the common man himself, is almost Mr. Zero, for he is man stripped of all his distinctive, distinguishing qualities. He is a vacuum which sentiment must fill with evanescent virtues. What he is never is the concrete individual whose self-assertiveness once caused tyrants to tremble and despotisms to fall—the concrete human being who is at once the beginning and the end of democracy and art. (p. 285)

Henry Popkin, "Elmer Rice: The Triumph of 'Mr. Zero'," in Commentary, Vol. 11, No. 3, March, 1951, pp. 283-85.

RICHARD WATTS, JR.

Elmer Rice provides a sentimental journey through France, Switzerland and Italy in his latest play, *The Grand Tour.* . . . Since Mr. Rice is a dramatist of intelligence and integrity, his new work possesses the sort of sensitive sincerity that must be admired and respected. Nevertheless, although travel is said to be broadening, I am afraid that his account of an idealistic school teacher's European pilgrimage is a rather slender fable that never quite manages to achieve more than a mild glow of wistful romance.

While it certainly is not Mr. Rice's intention, I must confess that at first I found his play a trifle deceptive. At least, I thought that *The Grand Tour* started out as if it meant to be an amiably satirical story about American innocents abroad. The intelligent but naive teacher, whose father had left her some money, shows up at a tourist office to arrange for her eagerly awaited first journey to Europe. . . .

When the young lady meets on shipboard a handsome, sad and fairly mysterious American banker, whose wife is divorcing him, the scene seemed set for a happy romance between the wistful travelers. At this point the play shifts from its realism and goes in for a highly impressionistic account of the innocents' tour of Paris and pilgrimage to Chartres, in the course of which Mr. Rice gives quite a bit of guide-book information on history and architecture. By the time the voyagers have reached Montreux, however, it is clear that other matters are afoot. . . .

[While] she is in Rome, the young lady finds that the handsome banker, in addition to being an embezzler, is still in love with his ex-wife, whereupon, if you will forgive me for giving away so much of the plot, she sacrifices both her fortune and her love for him. It is no doubt quite splendid of her but it doesn't make for the most stimulating of romantic tragedies.

It is my impression that, for the type of dramatic travelogue which Mr. Rice apparently had in mind, a great deal more variety, depth, vividness and pungency in the writing were demanded than are to be found in *The Grand Tour*. Instead, despite its sincerity and moments of wistful charm, the play is, on the whole, curiously sparse and lacking in dramatic or emotional force. It kept seeming to me that the author was intending to show some interrelation between the shifting European background and the American lovers and was achieving only a mild sentimental spree.

Richard Watts, Jr., "A Trip to Europe with Elmer Rice," in New York Post, December 11, 1951. Reprinted in New York Theatre Critics' Reviews, Vol. XII, No. 27, 1951, p. 146.

BROOKS ATKINSON

[In *The Grand Tour*] Elmer Rice breaks the heart of an enchanting school teacher from Connecticut. Before the final curtain comes down he also breaks the spirit of some theatregoers. For the first half of *The Grand Tour* is a slight but tender travelers' tale. . . . And the second half is as tasteless as a pulp magazine thriller. Stereotyped in writing and plot, it is no fair gauge of the mind and character of one of our ablest playwrights.

That sort of conclusion is more than commonly regretful. For the introductory scenes are original and promising. They tell the story of a New England schoolteacher who is starting off on her first tour of Europe with the money from her father's life-insurance. . . . [She] is a beguiling creature—conventional in her habits, but valiant and humorous and full of pertinent knowledge.

Mr. Rice has written many more powerful acts in his time. But the first half of *The Grand Tour* catches him in a particularly engaging mood. The touch is light; the tone is gay and discursive; the writing reflects Mr. Rice's own fondness for travel. He is not snobbish about his tourist. No doubt he, too, likes the savory facts and figures of the wonders of Europe and the simple delight of being away.

So far, very nice indeed. But now comes the plot, and that is done in a less imaginative vein. Inevitably, Mr. Rice's school teacher falls in love, although it is less inevitable that she has to fall in love with a Minneapolis bank embezzler. That experience brings out the noblest qualities in her character. But it drains all the magic out of *The Grand Tour.*

Money is a terrible thing in almost any department of life. But it is the bogey man of the drama, for it brings everything down to a dead level. In the case of *The Grand Tour* it very rapidly destroys the innocent romance of an attractive first act, and traps Mr. Rice in some tawdry writing. . . .

Too bad that such a promising grand tour gets bogged down in a second-rate bank embezzlement. Both the schoolteacher and the audience deserve more fun on their holiday.

> *Brooks Atkinson, in a review of "'The Grand Tour',"* in The New York Times, *December 11, 1951. Reprinted in* New York Theatre Critics' Reviews, *Vol. XII, No. 27, 1951, p. 147.*

RICHARD WATTS, JR.

Elmer Rice has taken the *Hamlet* theme, given explicitness to its Freudian suggestions, and come forth with a taut and compelling modern drama called *Cue for Passion*. . . .

[While] I think it has troubles with its final resolution, it is a steadily absorbing play, which happily restores the veteran Mr. Rice to the ranks of the valuable American dramatists.

Since this is becoming a season given to paraphrases of the famous tragedy of the Prince of Denmark, it should be emphasized immediately that *Cue for Passion* is no slavish or overwrought imitation. The basic situation is there, and so are various recognizable characters and incidents, but Mr. Rice has turned them to his own purposes, freely and creatively, to give us a play which stands on its own feet as it tells with straightforward dramatic power the story of an introspective young man, who returns to his broken home with dreams of vengeance.

Young Tony Burgess comes back from two years in Asia to his family's country house in Southern California, where, during his absence, his father had been killed, presumably in an earthquake accident. He finds that his mother has married an old sweetheart, and the boy's tormented mind is filled with suspicion of treachery and murder. Convincing himself that he is devoted to his father's memory and that his mother is at least

guilty of the grossest infidelity, he is tortured by bitterness, hatred and ideas of retribution. . . .

Having suggested that I have a few reservations in my admiration for the play, it is time for me to state them. It is my impression that Tony Burgess is made too relentlessly savage and supercilious. After all, even Hamlet had a moment in which he spoke with kindliness of Polonius. It also struck me that the final revelation about the man who had married the boy's mother is not convincingly presented. And the final scene is just a bit of a letdown. But these objections are minor in view of the general forcefulness and intensity of the drama.

> *Richard Watts, Jr., "Hamlet in Southern California,"* in New York Post, *November 26, 1958. Reprinted in* New York Theatre Critics' Reviews, *Vol. XIX, No. 23, 1958, p. 192.*

GERALD RABKIN

If S. N. Behrman questioned the appropriateness of comedy in an age of crisis, Elmer Rice questioned the very credentials of drama itself. Unlike Behrman, Rice was not committed to a specific dramatic genre; he was not faced with the problem of accommodating harsh social realities within the context of a frivolous form. On the contrary, he had demonstrated his ability to utilize such divergent forms as expressionism, naturalism, melodrama, and farce. The dilemma which confronted Rice in the mid-thirties was more fundamental: could American drama, as represented on Broadway, rightfully claim the virtue of seriousness, or did formal and economic exigencies render it, in fact, subliterary? (p. 237)

That Elmer Rice should, in the thirties, raise his voice in protest against the conditions that Broadway imposed upon the dramatist is particularly revealing; for Rice, throughout both his previous and subsequent theatrical career, presents us with a body of work which is perhaps unique in American drama in its inconsistency, its alternation of seriousness and conventionality. On one hand, we have such serious plays as *The Adding Machine, The Subway, Street Scene, We the People,* and *Not for Children;* on the other, such conventional Broadway products as *On Trial, Cock Robin, Wake Up Jonathan,* and *The Grand Tour.* (pp. 237-38)

Rice's analysis of the deficiencies of the dramatic genre—as revealed in the introduction to and the play *Not for Children*—considers economic pressure as but one of the factors which prevent the drama from fulfilling its serious potential. Indeed, although Rice condemns both the "idle and frivolous amusement seekers" and "the artist who . . . panders to the tastes of the ruling class," he does not offer the familiar revolutionary corrective. The lot of the dramatist is not necessarily happier in those countries where the philosophy of individualism is not in favor and where the machinery of the theatre is under governmental control or regulation. (p. 239)

The difficulties which assail the serious dramatist are not merely economic, but inherent in the dramatic form itself. The dramatist cannot present his vision of reality directly to the audience, as can the painter or writer; he must work through the cooperative efforts of a series of transmitting artists: the actor, the director, the scenic designer. The physical limitations of his playhouse impose specific restrictions on the scope of his imagination. He is bound by temporality, by the necessity of creating a theatrical illusion instantaneously; he is never permitted to ignore the collective psychology of his audience, and, as Rice points out, "the collective behavior of a crowd varies greatly from the customary private behavior of the individuals who compose it." Thus the playwright is denied the artistic prerogative of expressing himself seriously upon political, racial, economic, religious, or sexual problems, for "doubts and heresies which are freely held and expressed by hundreds of thousands of individuals are greeted by an audience with the frightened hostility of a panic-stricken herd.

These several factors, which combine to rob the drama of its requisite creative freedom, present the playwright with his "real dilemma": "Like every other artist, he is interested in projecting reality as he sees it. But he finds himself dependent upon an interpretative medium which is essentially artificial, conservative and conventional.

Rice attempted to give this dilemma dramatic form in *Not for Children* (1934), the very title of which revealed his conviction that most American drama was infantile. The play attempts to combine Shavian intellectual comedy and Pirandellian illusionism, unfortunately not very successfully; for in using the device of having two characters both comment upon and participate in the stage action, Rice has not succeeded in balancing these dual functions; the commentary, rather than the participation, becomes the play's *raison d'être*, and one emerges with the feeling that perhaps Rice might have dispensed with the "play proper" entirely. Unfortunately Rice does not demonstrate either Shaw's ability to make ideas work theatrically, or Pirandello's skill in balancing illusion and reality. What concerns us, however, is not so much the esthetic success of *Not for Children* as its assertion of Rice's belligerently antitheatrical attitude. It may be noted that even at the moment of his most intense disillusionment with drama, Rice feels compelled to express this disillusionment dramatically.

In *Not for Children* Rice personifies his esthetic dilemma in the personages of Ambrose and Theodora, who function as a dual chorus in commenting upon the play proper, which is a Behrmanesque comedy of manners. Theodora presents the protheatre point of view, while Ambrose upholds the negative. (pp. 239-41)

[It] is soon apparent, from the sheer weight of dialogue if nothing else, that Rice is in sympathy with Ambrose's point of view. It was not a time for delight, rest, or reassurance. The theatre stands condemned, in Ambrose's words, "because it is so essentially false. Because it is so unrelated to reality. Because its emotions are so hollow, its characters so two-dimensional, its speech so hackneyed, its intellectual pretensions so ludicrous, its puppets so mechanical, its philosophy so trite". . . . Rice's moral is unequivocally stated in a play specifically aimed "not for children": "The more nearly a play is good theatre, the less likely is it to be a reflection of reality. In short, the theatre and life are antithetical".

Obviously Rice, in this last statement at least, surrendered to overstatement born of his reaction against the triviality of the commercial theatre. As a firm admirer of Shaw, Ibsen, Hauptmann, he could scarcely uphold the proposition that the theatre and life are necessarily antithetical. The significance of the polemic from our point of view lies in Rice's vehement assertion of the serious playwright's dilemma: if he wishes to comment seriously upon the world of which he is a part—and for Rice, as others in the thirties, this inevitably implied social comment—can he do so in the context of a frivolous theatre? Lawson threw his energies into criticism and political work; Behrman effected a tenuous balance between frivolity and seriousness. Rice was too much a man of the theatre to forsake it, and he, too, effected his theatrical compromise.

But theatrical compromise was nothing new to Elmer Rice. His work, as we have indicated previously, is supremely inconsistent. It is curious that his fervent condemnation of the commercial theatre should come from one whose talent has always been best expressed within its confines. It is at the *craft* of the theatre that Rice has always excelled; although he has been equally at home in many dramatic forms, this formal experimentation seems less the result of a desire to expand the bounds of conventional drama (as in the work of O'Neill) than the delight of the craftsman in demonstrating his technical facility.

Rice's eclecticism may be observed in his use of expressionism (*The Adding Machine, The Subway*), naturalism (*Street Scene*), sophisticated comedy (*The Left Bank*), psychological drama (*Cue for Passion*), allegorical fantasy (*American Landscape*), and the list may be extended. Perhaps the most persistent (and the most commercially successful) of Rice's forms has been the courtroom melodrama; he has continually exploited his legal background for theatrical purposes. *On Trial, It is the Law, For the Defense, Judgment Day,* all derive their form from the courtroom trial; and *Counsellor-At-Law* owes much of its success to its behind-the-scenes revelation of the life of a big-time lawyer. Except for the courtroom melodrama, Rice has scarcely employed the same dramatic form twice. Such versatility is not only admirable; it is almost unique. Most dramatists have been content to develop facility in but a few forms, usually moving logically from one to another. Ibsen, Strindberg, and O'Neill pass from realism to symbolism when they have, from their point of view, exhausted the possibilities of the former. But Rice fails to afford the dramatic critic any such orderly development. It is difficult to find in the sum total of his work the consistent dramatic vision which informs the work of the major dramatists. As with many other minor writers, his significance appears to be seismographic; *The Adding Machine, We the People, Flight to the West,* and *Cue for Passion,* seem less the work of a consistent artistic personality than the faithful reflection of the intellectual climate of the twenties, the thirties, the forties, and the fifties.

But it is not merely the change of viewpoint which makes a critical evaluation of Rice's work difficult. The very issue which he raises in the thirties concerning the seriousness of drama must be considered in our critical judgment, for Rice himself has continually vacillated between seriousness and conventionality, many of his plays springing, in his own words, from "no nobler impulse than a realistic desire to make a comfortable living." Although this mundane consideration need not, of course, invalidate a work of art, an examination of the bulk of Rice's work soon reveals that much of it is unworthy of serious consideration. Yet the serious core remains as a worthy contribution to American drama. Indeed, in *The Adding Machine* Rice succeeded not only in absorbing the form of expressionism, but in creating a character, Mr. Zero, who came to epitomize the contemporary antihero. And in *Street Scene* he drew a slice of New York life with such fidelity and compassion that it is still convincing.

If Rice's salient virtue is indeed seismographic, there can be no denying that his serious plays of the twenties reflect the contemporary concern with the dehumanization of man by society. In *The Adding Machine* (1923), *The Subway* (1929), and *Street Scene* (1929), we find variations upon that not uncommon theme of the age, reflected elsewhere in such plays as

Lawson's *Roger Bloomer*, Sophie Treadwell's *Machinale*, Kaiser's *From Morn to Midnight*, and Toller's *Masse-Mensch*. In each of the plays man is crushed not so much by an oppressive social system as by the sheer weight of modern industrial civilization. From a social point of view, it is significant that Rice poses no political alternatives. We do not find the sense of class division which informs the early work of John Howard Lawson. Zero, Sophie, Mrs. Maurrant are destroyed by a dehumanized society. Zero is dwarfed by the gigantic adding machine he finally is condemned to operate; Sophie by the mechanical monster which hurls itself through manmade subterranean caverns; Mrs. Maurrant by the huge tenement which denies her the elemental freedom of privacy. (pp. 241-44)

Rice's serious plays of the twenties, then, accurately reflect the prevailing fear that machine civilization was succeeding in dehumanizing mankind. It is not surprising that most who presented this indictment should, with the onset of the Depression, turn towards political radicalism, for their initial attack was essentially a gesture of protest. The villain became not the machine, but the owner of the machine, and mankind's victimization was seen, not as an immutable fact of the law of social evolution, but rather as the deliberate act of an exploiting class. (p. 247)

[From] the thirties onwards, Rice has been *un homme engagé;* he has been perennially involved with social and theatrical questions, and has consistently registered his protest against encroachments upon civil liberties. He has, moreover, been involved in various attempts to provide an alternative to Broadway. In 1933 he proposed the establishment of a People's Art Theatre which would "attempt not only to set the leaven of art at work in the masses but to drag the artist into the forum, face to face with his times." Rice's proposed theatre would have a social base; every play to be presented would be judged not only according to its dramatic and literary merits but also according to its social value. (p. 248)

In what manner were these social concerns reflected in Rice's dramas of the thirties? His concern with the seriousness of drama is consistent with the articulate protest born of his renewed social conscience. But Rice could not fully ally himself with the revolutionary theatrical movement; he could not, for example, turn toward the composition of proletarian plays. Although infused with social indignation, he could not acquiesce in the communist solution. He has continually voiced his suspicions of the adverse effects of doctrine upon art. And yet he is compelled to involve himself with social issues. Each of his plays of the thirties (except *Not for Children* which, as we have seen, is concerned with the fundamental problem of the legitimacy of the dramatic form) has at its core a social problem. *We the People* is Rice's most slashing attack upon the social chaos bred by the Depression; *Judgment Day* condemns the Reichstag fire trial and Nazi injustice; *Between Two Worlds* presents the conflict of the old social order and the new; and *American Landscape* affirms American liberalism's answer to fascism and social injustice. (pp. 248-49)

Not restricting himself to class, he penetrates [in *We the People*] into the inner sanctums of big business and big education, as well as into the factory, the school, the farm. He attacks, from a basically Marxist point of view, every social abuse that he can discover: the plight of the worker dispossessed by unemployment; the tenuous economic position of the white collar worker; the impoverishment of the farmer; the use of the Jew, Negro, and foreigner as economic scapegoats; the inability of young people to live a normal life because of lack of money;

the relationship between war and economics; the failure of organized religion to provide adequate social answers; the impact of the failure of the banks; the denial of academic freedom to dissenters; the connivance between the police and the ruling classes; the shooting down of demonstrating workers; the conspicuous consumption of the rich while the poor starve. If his fervor is vitiated it is because of the furious indiscriminateness of his attack, for no sooner does he raise one social issue than he must counterpose another. Consequently, from a dramatic point of view, he presents rather than demonstrates his indictment.

There can be no denying, however, the implication of his attack. *We the People*—two years before *Waiting for Lefty*—is almost an agit-prop; but it differs from the communist agit-prop in that its call to action, despite the catalogue of social evils which the play reveals, is not revolutionary. The play represents, rather, the aroused liberal's cry of protest against social injustice, against the misery of the poor. (p. 250)

[The] two social conditions in the thirties which forced many individuals to commit themselves politically were the Depression and the rise of fascism. It is appropriate, therefore, that Rice should follow his militant call for social justice in *We the People* with a bitter attack upon Naziism in *Judgment Day* (1934). Protest did not force, however, formal consistency upon the playwright; the form of *Judgment Day* in no way resembles that of *We the People*. In fact, Rice uses the familiar form of the courtroom melodrama in order to present his indictment. In the machinations surrounding the burning of the German Reichstag in February, 1933, Rice had, in real life, a plot replete with melodramatic intrigue and chicanery. He even had a ready-made hero, Georgi Dimitroff, the Bulgarian communist whose defiance of the mock-trial electrified the world. And he also had a happy ending, because the Nazis, still insecure in their political position in 1933, were not able to ignore either the facts of the case or the pressure of world public opinion, and so freed the defendants. In fact, the difficulty with the play is that Rice's re-creation (he set the play in an undesignated Balkan country and changed various details of the actual case) pales in comparison with the documentary facts.

At the end of *Judgment Day* Judge Slatarski, one of the few presiding judges who will not bow to totalitarian pressure, shoots Vesnic, the thinly-veiled version of Adolf Hitler, and cries, "Down with tyranny! Long live the people!" This act, coupled with the surprise appearance of a character presumed dead, unfortunately melodramatizes a situation which, in reality, was already replete with sensation. The act of wish-fulfillment in destroying the Hitler figure serves to remove the entire play from the realm of actuality. Rice thus damages his indictment by making the very real facts of the case appear equally incredible. (pp. 251-52)

Yet even if the actual facts of the case were more dramatic than Rice's presentation, *Judgment Day* was an effective weapon against Naziism. Scheduled productions in France and Holland were cancelled at the insistence of the Hitler government, and in Norway performances were prevented by rioting by the Norwegian Nazis. Rice's indictment was obviously strong enough to arouse fascist ire. (p. 252)

Rice, like many liberals of the time, respected the communists for their anti-fascist fervor and made common cause with them on many issues. But he, like Behrman, distrusted their dogmatic intensity. Again like Behrman, he was attracted to Marxist ideals, but repulsed by Marxist methods. Rice, as *We the People* indicates, strongly felt the need for a new social order to replace capitalism, but he was unwilling to throw out the baby with the bath. As a convinced libertarian, he could not deny basic freedoms even to those he detested. Thus in *Between Two Worlds* (1934) he presents the clash of representatives of the old world and the new, and suggests the need for a rapprochement which would combine the social fervor of Marxism and the individual liberties of capitalist democracy. (p. 253)

In *Flight to the West* (1941) Rice chronicles the end of an era. Again he presents a cross section of contemporary types within a confined locale; but unlike *Between Two Worlds* this time the journey takes place on an airplane bound from Europe to the United States. In the earlier play the two worlds presented were a malfunctioning capitalism and a resurgent communism; in *Flight to the West* the two worlds are simply the world of slavery and the world of freedom.

Rice articulates the liberal's dilemma in the face of incipient world conflict. Although he has been nurtured on the concept that war was essentially an imperialistic device for the obtaining of new markets, now there seemed no alternative to the fascist threat. . . . The rapes of Finland and Norway and France have changed all that. Since the young liberal, Charles, has seen the horror of aggressive war at first hand, pacifism no longer seems tenable. But if the young man is confused by the change in his views demanded by the world situation, the old liberal, Ingraham, finds it necessary to revise the intellectual convictions of twenty years. . . . (pp. 257-58)

Ultimately, however, in the course of the plane journey, in which the Nazi consul, Walther, reveals clearly the imminent danger of the fascist threat, both Charles and Ingraham have their confusion dispelled. There can be no compromise with evil; one cannot do business with Hitler as the businessman, Gage, suggests. The only answer is to combat him in the name of liberty. Symbolically, Charles, who is Jewish, throws himself impulsively in the path of a bullet intended for Walther, thus affirming the free man's defense of the individual, however much he may be detested personally. Ingraham's final advice to Charles and his pregnant wife is that they should not fear to bring a child into a world torn by strife. In fact it is upon their children that the future of mankind depends: "Bring your child into the world with . . . a faith in the future and in the eventual triumph of sanity and decency. Because your faith and your courage will help make it come true".

The thirties had demanded seriousness, and Elmer Rice, acutely attuned to the intellectual vibrations of his age, had responded. Yet his dramas of the decade survive less as works of art than as social documents; he was never quite able to forge a form which could dramatize rather than present his social convictions. Did the deficiency lie in the fact of his commitment or in the simple lack of art? Surely one cannot escape the feeling that ideas lie on top of his work, that they are never fully imbedded in the fabric of the play. Only in *The Adding Machine* has he been successful in fully integrating form and idea; and in that case he had before him sturdy European forbears. But Rice demands respect for the fervor with which he involved himself in the conflicts of his age. One senses that at heart he recognizes his esthetic limitations, but continually yearns to transcend them. A talented craftsman, he has continued to demand that American drama rise above facile craftsmanship. A paradox: but we are richer for its being posed. (pp. 258-59)

> Gerald Rabkin, "Elmer Rice and the Seriousness of Drama," in his Drama and Commitment: Politics in

the American Theatre of the Thirties, *Indiana University Press*, 1964, pp. 237-59.

ANTHONY F. R. PALMIERI

The coming-of-age of the American theater begins with the emergence of Eugene O'Neill as a playwright of consequence. He was the first to win critical acclaim in the world theater. But no theater achieves world stature by the exploits of one man alone. The heights that O'Neill was scaling were soon to be attempted by other gifted American dramatists. And if none of these was surpassing the master himself, they were at least staking out new and promising territory. Perhaps the most underrated of this group of playwrights, which along with O'Neill was responsible for the sudden maturation of our drama, is Elmer Rice. Though in prolificness and durability as a playwright Rice outdoes his fellows, and though his impact on our theater, aside from the mere writing of plays, probably surpasses that of any of the others, he has been the subject of only two books and of one doctoral dissertation. Such are the vagaries of critical and academic fashions. Clearly, Rice deserves more attention. (pp. 192-93)

About the time when O'Neill was sitting in on Professor Baker's Drama 47 class at Harvard and some years away from his first Broadway production, Rice was already on the boards with a hit [*On Trial*] that broke with tradition by introducing the flashback technique to the American theater. In itself, this might have been no startling innovation, for very likely Rice borrowed the technique from the movies. But certainly his effort to break new ground must have encouraged other playwrights, perhaps even O'Neill himself. (p. 193)

Indeed, it might be argued that at Rice's best only O'Neill is his superior. In prolificness and versatility he is unmatched by anyone but that giant of our theater. . . . His list of credits cannot be denied. Moreover, throughout his career Rice remained an innovator.

For example, in 1923 he gave the world *The Adding Machine.* Granted that in such expressionism O'Neill had preceded him—with *The Emperor Jones* in 1920 and *The Hairy Ape* in 1922—still Rice's play was very different from these. It was the first important American drama to focus on the dehumanization of the American middle class as victim of a mechanized and quantified society. Furthermore, Rice uses the aside in *The Adding Machine* as a means of revealing the inner and secret thoughts of his characters, a technique that O'Neill did not attempt until *Welded,* produced a year later, in 1924, and one that he did not fully exploit until *Strange Interlude* in 1928. . . . Then in 1929 came the naturalistic *Street Scene,* a play so radical in its departure from accepted formulas for the American theater, and so demanding in its stage devices and in casting, that it very nearly failed, for practical reasons, to get on the boards. Today *Street Scene* is recognized as one of Rice's masterpieces. Then, with *We, the People* in 1933, Rice experimented with something like audience participation. In this departure he might have encouraged Odets to try something similar in, for example, *Waiting for Lefty* (1934) and possibly Wilder in *Our Town* (1938). *A New Life* (1943) brought yet another innovation: Rice's was the first drama to feature a childbirth scene in full view of the audience. Even in his declining years Rice remained *avant garde.* In his 1954 drama, *The Winner,* he cast a Negro in a role in which the racial problem was not a factor. And that was another "first" in the American theater.

Nor does the tally end here. No American playwright was more abreast of the times than Elmer Rice. For example, when the work of Freud, Jung, Adler, and company made psychoanalysis important to an understanding of individual persons and of the human condition, and when many native playwrights began to reflect at least something of this new psychology, Rice was one of the first in the field. Admittedly, O'Neill beat Rice to the draw in *Diff'rent*, a 1920 study of sexual frustration, and again in *The Emperor Jones*, a dramatizing of Jung's "collective unconscious" that reached the boards in the same year. Still, in *Wake Up, Jonathan* (1921) Rice and his collaborator, Hatcher Hughes, treated changing concepts of child psychology. In both *The Adding Machine* (1923) and *The Subway* (1929) Rice handled repressed sexuality, and he employed the oedipal motif in *Black Sheep* (1923). (pp. 193-95)

Clearly, in his subject matter and themes Rice was often enough ahead of his fellow playwrights. (p. 195)

With the coming of the Great Depression, Rice turned his attention, as did many other playwrights then, to the sickness of his country, to the two major concerns of the period: social and economic injustice. He had, however, as far back as 1916, in *The House in Blind Alley,* attacked the indifference of society to the evils of child labor; and in *Street Scene* he had counted up the human costs of the lower-middle-class environment. Now, once again, Rice comes to grips with the social and political ills of an era. In plays like *We, the People, Judgment Day, Between Two Worlds,* and *American Landscape*—these four done between 1933 and 1938—he used the stage in behalf of social and political reform. In these ventures Rice surely holds his own among contemporaries like Maxwell Anderson (*Both Your Houses* [1933] and *Winterset* [1935]), Lillian Hellman (*Days to Come* [1936]), Clifford Odets (*Waiting for Lefty* [1934] and *Awake and Sing* [1935]), and Sidney Kingsley (*Dead End* [1935]). Moreover, Rice is the first American playwright to recognize and reveal the menace of Nazism, which he does in *Judgment Day;* Clifford Odets's one-acter, *Till the Day I Die,* was not staged until one year later, in 1935. And in *American Landscape* he is the first to deal with the Nazi threat emanating from within our own society, for Lillian Hellman's somewhat comparable *Watch on the Rhine* follows Rice three years later, in 1941.

Though he made no fetish of novelty or innovation for their own sakes, throughout his career Elmer Rice was regularly in the vanguard. Sometimes—one thinks of *The Iron Cross, The House in Blind Alley, Street Scene,* and *Judgment Day*—he was so far ahead of the crowd that he appeared to be alone. Even as his career approached its end, his keenness of insight and the breadth of his social interests did not diminish. (pp. 196-97)

None of this is meant to argue that, next to O'Neill, Elmer Rice is the greatest figure in American drama. Granted, the quality of his work is uneven. . . . Nevertheless, Rice should not be denied his rightful place among those few who in the first half of the present century brought the American drama to worldwide recognition.

One paradox is that perhaps Rice's greatest strength is related to his chief failing. That is, like Shaw, he would use the theater as a platform for discussing the ills and self-deceptions of society. His impulse was that of the reformer, not merely in the art of dramaturgy, but also in the actuality of the real world. Sometimes he slid too easily into the didactic or the propagandistic. For all that, his better plays are very little dated.

One aspect of his struggle was to maintain his integrity as a serious artist and yet somehow make his way on commercialistic Broadway. Few other dramatists of Rice's stature hit this double-edged problem so head-on. For everyone he fought the good fight against conditions that at best are uncongenial to and at worst destructive of genuine creativity in playwriting. His directorship of the New York Federal Theatre Project and his helping to found the Playwrights' Company are only two passing episodes in a long and strenuous career. Because he took his own art seriously, he strove to improve the quality of the theater, to widen its appeal, and to improve the working conditions of all those involved in it. Always something of a crusader, Rice has had an impact on American drama and on American life that goes beyond the mere writing of plays and extends to the very heart of that theater and that life. To borrow from the title of one of his last published plays, Rice himself had many cues for passion. In speeches, articles, interviews, books, and in his dramas, he attacked the status quo of Broadway; he struggled against censorship in all the arts; he was always the enemy of bigotry, intolerance, social and political injustice; he championed freedom and dignity for the individual. In his vision of America, Rice was committed to the tradition of liberalism, in the best sense of that problematic term. The American theater indubitably has been a little healthier and American society a little better because a youngster named Elmer Leopold Reizenstein one day decided to give up the practice of law and make the stage his career. (pp. 197-98)

Anthony F. R. Palmieri, in his Elmer Rice: A Playwright's Vision of America, *Fairleigh Dickinson University Press, 1980, 226 p.*

(Eleanor) May Sarton

1912-

(Born Eléanore Marie Sarton) Belgian-born American poet, novelist, autobiographer, journalist, author of children's books, and scriptwriter.

A prolific author who is respected for her poetry, fiction, and autobiographical writings, Sarton often dwells upon such concerns as the joy and pain of love, the necessity of solitude for creativity and identity, and the conflict between body and soul. Influenced by her early exposure to both European and American cultures and her interest in such European poets as Rainer Maria Rilke and William Butler Yeats, Sarton evidences a literary sensibility that is regarded as diverse and astute. Sarton's verse is often introspective and displays her penchant for natural imagery and refined language. Although some critics fault her rigid adherence to traditional forms and her tendency to lapse into melancholy and didacticism, others praise the passion, insight, and graceful language she exhibits in her poetry. Sarton's novels, which explore various topics, including aging, the failure of communication, and the relationship between love and artistic commitment, are commended for their rich descriptions of place and atmosphere and their reflective prose. Sheila Ballantyne stated: "[Sarton is] a seeker after truth with a kind of awesome energy for renewal, an ardent explorer of life's important questions."

Sarton's first published verse appeared in *Poetry* magazine in 1929. Her initial collection, *Encounter in April* (1937), displays her skill with varied poetic forms, including short lyrics, meditative pieces, free verse, and Shakespearean sonnets. In "A Letter to James Stephens," from her next volume, *Inner Landscape* (1939), Sarton suggests that an artist's dedication to the creative process may require isolation and independence from others. This concept has served as both a literary theme and a personal directive throughout her career. In *Inner Landscape*, as in her first book, Sarton makes use of a wide range of poetic forms and examines love, art, and personality while employing landscape as an increasingly dominant image. During the next decade, Sarton lectured extensively at colleges and universities throughout the United States. The poems in *The Lion and the Rose* (1948) detail her visits to different regions of the country and explore such topics as social unrest, native American culture, and feminist issues. *The Land of Silence and Other Poems* (1953) reflects the tranquility and spirituality Sarton experienced in her travels through the American West during the early 1950s. *Cloud, Stone, Sun, Vine: Poems, Selected and New* (1961) contains thematically linked verse from previous volumes as well as new pieces, including "A Divorce of Lovers," a complex sequence of twenty sonnets in which Sarton combines ordinary and decorative language to detail the end of a love affair.

A Private Mythology (1966) was inspired by Sarton's visits to Japan, India, and Greece during the early 1960s. The poems in this volume evidence her experiments with such forms as free verse and the Japanese haiku as she searches for spiritual peace and reveals a sense of humor rarely present in her previous work. The pieces in *A Grain of Mustard Seed* (1971) comment upon global violence and injustice in commensurately harsh language and imagery. This volume also contains reli-

© 1987 Nancy Crampton

gious poems, many of which suggest the need for faith in solving world problems. In *A Durable Fire* (1972), Sarton reaffirms her belief in the importance of grace and spirituality through a variety of verse forms. Most of Sarton's poems in *Halfway to Silence* (1980) and *Letters from Maine* (1984) contain observations on domestic matters and the landscapes of New Hampshire and Maine.

Sarton's first novel, *The Single Hound* (1938), features a confused young writer who becomes more confident in himself and his artistic abilities through his friendship with an older, established female poet. In this work, Sarton introduces one of her most important themes: the conflict between physical passion and artistic commitment. Like *The Single Hound*, which takes place primarily in Belgium, Sarton's next three novels also utilize European settings. *The Bridge of Years* (1946) focuses upon a Belgian family struggling to maintain their principles despite the moral disintegration engendered by World War I and the fascism of the pre-World War II era. *Shadow of a Man* (1950), set mostly in France, details how a young man of American and French parentage gains self-knowledge through his association with a longtime friend of his recently deceased mother. *A Shower of Summer Days* (1952) is a study of an Irish woman whose extraordinary beauty has brought her both happiness and sorrow.

In her next novel, *Faithful Are the Wounds* (1955), Sarton explores political topics and human relationships through an examination into the suicide of Edward Cavan, a liberal Harvard professor and victim of governmental persecution whose death prompts various reactions from his associates. In *Mrs. Stevens Hears the Mermaids Singing* (1965), considered by many critics her most important novel, Sarton clearly reveals her beliefs concerning the inspiration and commitment necessary for artistic creation. This novel revolves around the ruminations of acclaimed poet Hilary Stevens as she prepares for and gives an interview about her career. Throughout this novel, Sarton raises such provocative questions as whether a woman can be a successful artist while maintaining a family, what compels an author to write, and how personal emotion can be transformed into art. *As We Are Now* (1973) examines American attitudes toward the elderly by focusing upon Caroline Spencer, a former teacher confined to a nursing home whose independence is shattered by the dehumanizing treatment of the institution's staff. At the book's conclusion, Caroline burns down the home as an act of defiance. In *A Reckoning* (1978), Sarton examines different attitudes toward death through an account of a woman's battle with terminal cancer. *The Magnificent Spinster* (1985) contains discourses on such topics as social conscience, aging, feminist issues, friendship, and the nature of art.

Sarton has also garnered critical praise for her autobiographical works. *I Knew a Phoenix: Sketches for an Autobiography* (1959) relates her childhood and youth up to the publication of her first collection of verse. In *Plant Dreaming Deep* (1968), Sarton recounts her purchase of an old farmhouse in rural New Hampshire and details the responsibilities of being a homeowner, emphasizing the importance of a stable domestic life and her need for solitude in relation to her literary career. *Recovering: A Journal, 1978-1979* (1980) is an account of Sarton's emotional and physical recovery from cancer that further underscores the importance of love in her life. *At Seventy* (1984) chronicles the daily events of Sarton's seventieth year.

(See also *CLC*, Vols. 4, 14; *Contemporary Authors*, Vols. 1-4, rev. ed.; *Contemporary Authors New Revision Series*, Vol. 1; *Something about the Author*, Vol. 36; *Dictionary of Literary Biography*, Vol. 48; and *Dictionary of Literary Biography Yearbook: 1981*.)

SHERMAN CONRAD

To read any book of first poems is to be present at a program of impersonations. It is the devotee's peculiar pleasure to name each mime correctly, to estimate the skill in the mimicry, to catch the moment when the performer's ability exceeds his mask and the individual, the new person is revealed. *Encounter in April* affords ample opportunity for these enjoyments to those who have been interested in Miss Sarton's scattered publications here and in England. (p. 229)

[A] good part of Miss Sarton's poems are love sonnets, the best of which are perhaps the first and fourth in the sequence ["Encounter in April"]. But to achieve the high polish which these sonnets possess it has been necessary for the poet to employ a good many pre-fabricated emotions, just as the sonnet form itself lends a ready-made gloss to the verse. The result is that the whole performance inevitably calls up Millay, *et* *al.*, in their second April moods, and Miss Sarton's sonnets seem to stem from literary rather than personal emotions.

The free, unrhymed lines of the poems in the middle sections of the book are somehow much more effective. This is not a derogation of metrical forms, though how to make a sonnet a poem rather than just another sonnet is one of the most baffling poetic problems there is. These less rigid poems (such as "Japanese Papers"), because of a lack of sufficient composition in language and mood, can also come to nothing, drifting away rather than remaining like perfectly cut agates in the mind. But such poems as "The Trees" . . . and "Kew" . . . show an eye at once simple and sophisticated, individual in its observations and feminine in the sense that Edith Sitwell and D. H. Lawrence are such.

The finest piece of work in every way is a lyric in ten fluid parts, "She Shall Be Called Woman." Its theme is a girl's first putting-on ("a shift, And she was trying it for the first time") of her mature body ("this shape of a pear, This heaviness of a curving fruit"). There is a delicate physiological nearness here that recalls Kay Boyle's best prose.

> She looked down
> at the naked hand
> and wept.
>
> the mesh
> the exquisite small hairs
>
> this delicate savage
> this was her hand,
> a present someone had given her. . . .

This genuine sensibility and emotional necessity motivating Miss Sarton's poem impart to the lines an "unresistant, completely rhythmical" form which is beautiful and satisfying in every way.

This poem seems to me to reveal that secret access that women have into the core of their sensations and feelings. And it is certainly from that heightened consciousness that their best and unique work always comes. It is to be hoped that Miss Sarton's future writing will take its departure from this point. (pp. 229-31)

Sherman Conrad, "First Discoveries," in Poetry, *Vol. L, No. IV, July, 1937, pp. 229-31.*

ROSE C. FELD

May Sarton is twenty-five years old, she is a poet and *The Single Hound* is her first novel. Embraced in these few words lies the fact that youth which carries the gift of song within its heart must carry also the burden of its pain. It is not strange, therefore, that in this volume one is enmeshed in beauty of words which reach into the inner chambers of human fears and confusions. A poet should be young enough to soar and his story should be old enough to have a meaning for all. In *The Single Hound* this union between youth and age is gently consummated.

It is a simple tale that May Sarton tells, the story of two poets, one a little old lady in Belgium whose creative life is over and the other a young man, lost in the conflict between the word written in anguish of spirit and the impulse that gives it wings. . . .

Doro is the important one in the story. With fine, masterly strokes, May Sarton paints her in all the beauty of her sensitive clairvoyance and her physical fragility. Her country knows her as a poet and has paid homage to her, but in her heart she feels that the words that have given her fame are poor things compared to the rich silence that nurtured them. Years before when her first volume of poetry had appeared, she had written,

> Before, when people talked around me, I listened, child that I was, and possessed my thoughts, possessed them alone in rapture and in fear, without wanting to understand or that any one should understand me. Now I have wanted to say everything. I have stammered. I have dared. And I have said nothing, nothing.

This she wrote in her diary in 1903, long before Mark Taylor was born. When he is twenty-five, a poet lost in the confusion of a world that stands at grips with shattered ideals and illusions, he comes upon the poems of Jean Latour and in their clarity and uncompromising transparency recognizes the person who can help him. So great is his need of kinship and peace that he decides to go to Ghent and find this Belgian poet. . . .

It is Doro, the Jean Latour, he comes to seek in trembling and in humility, who brings him peace. He had feared to find in the unknown poet an imposing, frightening man and discovers her to be a tiny, aging woman with large gray eyes whose depths hold knowledge greater than personal love. From the first moment he felt that "like her poems, she was transparent. She could accept the truth. She could accept the heart." And she, for her part, feels that having known this poet who, at the close of her days, has come to speak to her in language built out of the poignant pressure of her own youth she can face death without fear. "That is why one is a poet," she thinks, "so that some day, sooner or later, one can say the right thing to the right person at the right time." That she will soon die, she is certain, but warm within her lies the knowledge that this darkly glowing youth speaks in golden accents of personal integrity because of the strength she has given him.

It is not for the story that one will remember and reread this book but for the beauty of characterization of one poet who is ready to die and one who is beginning to live. And let not the word "poet" estrange those who fear that it may bring them to land alien to their feet. The things that May Sarton writes of will speak in a familiar tongue to all human beings who have known the terror of walking in darkness and the joy of finding a hand that can light the way even though it be for solitary journeying.

> *Rose C. Feld, "The Heart of the Poet, in Youth and in Age," in* New York Herald Tribune Books, *March 20, 1938, p. 5.*

JANE SPENCE SOUTHRON

Only a poet and, perhaps, only a young poet could have written this beautiful and distinguished first novel [*The Single Hound*]. In it May Sarton has created a little world of some half dozen people and she has given them rich, bountiful life, not only pregnant with meaning for this present instant of time in which she has placed them, but deeply rooted in that humanity which is ageless.

They are not ordinary people but a little society of unusual individuals such as are likely, at any stage of civilization, to gravitate together through interest in the reception and exchange of ideas. . . . Against a background of huge sky from which the "small flat country [of Ghent, Belgium] . . . took on grandeur" she sets a charming little house and an enchanting garden; and it is there Mark Taylor, a young poet, finds the inspiration that is to turn his feet from a wilderness of sick doubt to a path of assurance and difficult but straight endeavor.

Mark's struggle begins for him in England, where the young men who are his friends are concerned, variously, in trying to puzzle out what part they can best play in the muddle of the time. To most of them action of some sort, preferably violent, is the answer. Mark's greatest friend becomes a Communist and goes off to Spain. Mark's irresistible impulse is to "withdraw, think, be silent" for a time; but he is ashamed of it and the poem he writes during three months of isolation is a conscious effort to fight his individualistic inclinations.

And then, headlong, love comes into his life, at sight, for an artist married, in supreme contentment, to a man who adores her. The story of Mark's mad passion for Georgia Manning is of the stuff of tragic poetry; the evanescent tragedy of poetic youth. It is a stark, plain tale with a rush of fire in it. Neither here nor elsewhere is there a sense of poetry gone astray into prose. What we have is the packed meaning and economy in word and phrase that poetic discipline demands and insures.

The house in Ghent is the home of three women who, forty-odd years before, had been girls together. Brilliant and fascinating girls; now, at 60 or so, brilliant and accomplished women with the charm inseparable from distinction. Dorothée (Doro) Latour, a poet, had won romance and lost it because of her integrity. Claire Mentel, a writer of stories, had buried happiness with her husband; but serenity is left to her. Annette Le Coq, lover of children and a born teacher, achieved delight and scattered it around her by virtue of an invincibly sunny nature. Now they run a school; and a more delectable one it would be hard to imagine. . . .

The dominating idea of the novel is the influence of mind on mind through books. The great dead writers, "the adorable dead," as Doro calls them, "had comforted and nourished her far better than any one alive." When she had long given up writing poetry the chance reading of her poems sent Mark hot haste to Ghent to find the "Jean Latour"—Doro's pen name—who had said the things he himself had hardly dared release from his subconscious. The results, to the young poet, were momentous. There was not alone the spiritual intimacy with Doro and the two gay spirits who made up, with her, a perfect trio of friendship; but there was Doro's help given, out of the experience of her own life, because she understood him; so that he comes to realize even the value of abnegation. Her judgment on his poem is one that we may take to be of vital significance to the book's ideology. "I have never been able to believe," she says, "that from a depersonalized, universalized being anything really human, any living form of art could be born." As the story ends, Mark Taylor's career begins.

This is not, like so many first novels, to be regarded as autobiography disguised as fiction; but it is personal. Here, as in her poems, May Sarton's aim is to arrive at what she calls "transparency." She has, also, in *The Single Hound* exemplified a way of life and enunciated a literary creed. Her second adventure along the road of literature has taken her far—encouragingly far—ahead.

> *Jane Spence Southron, in a review of "The Single Hound," in* The New York Times Book Review, *March 20, 1938, p. 6.*

PERCY HUTCHISON

The workmanship that has gone into the making of [the poems in *Inner Landscape*] . . . is beyond cavil. Done with something of the eighteenth-century care for the sedate, unemotional line, [Miss Sarton's] poems suggest the even lawns and precise gardens of the time of Queen Anne and the first of the Georges, before the turbulence of the romantic movement rushed in from the left to bewilder and overturn a strictly ordered world. Nevertheless, there is at the same time more emotion beneath the surface of Miss Sarton's dignified verses than was common to eighteenth-century poetry. The result of this slightly paradoxical combination is interesting. Let one try to visualize a butterfly imprisoned within a cake of ice and one will have a fairly good parallel to the poems.

And in selecting [*Inner Landscape*] for [the title of] her book Miss Sarton has to some degree acknowledged the accuracy of this critique of her poetry. Though the medium through which the reader may gaze on that landscape is translucent, nevertheless he may see it only through an interposed medium; the poet does not let him come into actual contact with her soul. Miss Sarton uses words more often to conceal than to reveal. And if it must be said in all frankness, while not abating a whit my appreciation of May Sarton's closely clipped lines, I do find her extreme reticence a bar to whole-souled enthusiasm. Lyric poetry, at its best, should look before and after; and although the poem itself need not pine for what is not, it should so tease the imagination of the reader that he is carried beyond the limits of the poem itself. Because her verse fails in this, *Inner Landscape* falls short of lyric poetry's high office, which is to stimulate emotion and arouse imagination. To be sure, there is much trivial verse written which may to some degree step up the pulse rate; and May Sarton's verses are well outside this category. But we do wish her lines had more color; that she had not kept her Pegasus so strictly under curb.

> *Percy Hutchison, "The Butterfly Imprisoned in Ice,"* in The New York Times Book Review, *March 5, 1939, p. 5.*

THE TIMES LITERARY SUPPLEMENT

[Although in *Inner Landscape* Sarton's] dominant theme is "a human heart, a human passion" and her mode intimately feminine, she submits both to the control of "impassioned reason" and her verse is as intensely formed as it is felt. Sometimes, indeed, her craftsman's passion to create "ice out of fire" results in a style simple indeed, but too consciously cultivated. But generally it is a true expression of the experience which includes in the landscape of the heart not only the world of inner feeling but the "outward forms of light." The poems entitled **"Summer Landscape"** for example, look outward as perceptively as **"Conception,"** which precedes them and is perhaps the most remarkable in the volume, looks inward. And, whether in her love sonnets or her lyrics, she plays a subtle counterpoint between the actual and imagined worlds. Her verse suggests comparison with that of Elinor Wylie or Edna St. Vincent Millay and certainly does not suffer by it.

> *A review of "Inner Landscape," in* The Times Literary Supplement, *No. 1947, May 27, 1939, p. 318.*

FLORENCE HAXTON BULLOCK

Had Miss Sarton merely written with serene and rich understanding (as she has [in *The Bridge of Years*]) the story of the Duchesnes, an interesting and ebullient Belgian family who lived in a country house on the outskirts of Brussels during the morally devastating period between the wars, she would have produced an immensely worth while and charming novel. But her further purpose—brilliantly accomplished—was to give at least one concrete and convincing answer to the often-asked question: What could any single individual, or any one family, have done against the on-rushing tides of Nazi-minded inhumanity and prejudice that were sweeping along toward total war? In its full-textured entirety *The Bridge of Years* is Miss Sarton's answer—an answer that is extremely tonic in its implications. For the novel shows how one intelligent, morally well grounded European family built up its strength to endure, consciously made its psychological preparations to resist, the moral typhus that swept over fortress Europe.

At the beginning of the novel, spring, 1919, Paul Duchesne, young, clear-thinking husband of the vigorous and happy-natured Melanie, a philosopher and writer by profession, was already taking an extremely pessimistic view of the future: he could see no hope whatever ahead for the peace of the world. And because his intelligent eyes had looked so deep into the abyss, Paul found it difficult to get on with his writing. What he had to say, the world at that time was quite unwilling to hear.

Melanie understood this—with her loving and intuitive heart if not, perhaps, with her head. Herself an artist and creator rather than a thinker, Melanie's response was, as always, action. Continuing to adore her irascible husband and to keep her sensitive five-year-old daughter Françoise on a nearly level emotional keel, Melanie bore Paul two more lovely and promising daughters, ran their big country house and garden . . . , and went daily into the city to preside over the troubled destinies of the Maison Bernard, a fine old furniture factory and shop which Melanie had inherited from her mother. The department store competition of cheap machine-made furniture from postwar Germany was threatening the Maison Bernard with extinction. But the practical Melanie, with Paul's judgment to back her, was able to modify the Maison's old-fashioned methods to make survival, even a small growth, possible. And on the civic side the vigorous young wife offered effective leadership in an organization designed to help young ex-soldiers solve their problems as she had helped Jacques, the young son of her old friend the gardener, to solve his.

Meanwhile family life at the Duchesnes developed healthily. . . . Young Françoise gave up an unfair advantage in a competition for the stage designs for a Paris production in order to work whole-heartedly with a group of her fellow students in a little truck-borne road company; Colette turned her back on young love, so tender, so easily hurt, so difficult to relinquish voluntarily, because the young man on whom she had fixed her romantic yearnings turned Jew baiter, and Solange— but enough. The young people growing sensitively aware of the nasty fingers of Fascism and anti-Semitism reaching into their own country, felt the debilitating effect of the phony war of 1939-'40. And then, quite suddenly at the last, the Germans invaded Belgium. The Duchesnes heard their neighbors' cars and trucks, loaded with goods and extra petrol, go rumbling off toward France. In another day or two at the most they would have to decide in family conclave whether they should follow. All the interwoven events of the novel up to this point are the preparation for that decision. When the decision was finally made they all felt with Solange that "somehow now they were safe and had escaped a great peril."

If you get a sense from my report that *The Bridge of Years* presents a self-righteous family wrestling with moral ideas, overtly doing good in a wicked world, I shall have grossly misrepresented Miss Sarton's delicately lovely novel. Its style is limpid, unpretentious, beautifully expressive, and its content is beyond all things warmly and humanly emotional.

> Florence Haxton Bullock, "Pilgrim's Progress of a Family: 1919-1940," in New York Herald Tribune Weekly Book Review, April 21, 1946, p. 5.

CATHERINE MAHER

[*The Bridge of Years*] opens in the first spring after the end of World War I and closes in the spring days of 1940, when an invading German Army is again on Belgian soil. Outwardly concerned with the homely pattern of daily life in a Belgian middle-class family, May Sarton's main object in *The Bridge of Years* is an analysis of what went on in men's minds and hearts during this period between two wars. Her novel, if not brilliant, is always interesting, competently written and distinguished by its honesty and its broad plane of inquiry. . . .

The Bridge of Years could be called a war book, though most of it is concerned with years we were optimistic enough to term peaceful. These Belgians, all of them, feel the necessity for self-searching, against the day when, as in 1914, they will have only their faith to live by. The Duchesnes and their friends are all attempting to find and hold that state of equilibrium, for through it alone they see a hope for survival in war.

> Catherine Maher, "Self-Searching between Wars," in The New York Times Book Review, April 21, 1946, p. 26.

M. L. ROSENTHAL

The first poem in May Sarton's *The Lion and the Rose* is called **"Meditation in Sunlight."** The title would be apt for the volume as a whole, for almost the entire range of her verse is open country. She admires, almost deifies, Dante and Eliot, yet her shadows suggest no horror, being merely points where the eye pauses on a sunny landscape. "Time," she writes, "is light not shadow," and her best images, usually, are bright and warm—as when, to describe the birth of love, she says that "the apple blossoms foamed, Under my window." When she does use darkness in a central image, it is to suggest passionate life, conscious and intense.

Her lyric talent shows up best in the love poems . . . and in the semi-imagist pieces of the section named **"Theme and Variations,"** where she attempts a symbolic identification of self and landscape in a pure, formal statement of essential values. Many modern poets have gone to graduate school with Yeats, but Miss Sarton is one of the few "influenced" in the right way. . . . The other poems, which often present deftly worded but strongly felt arguments for various wholesome ideas, seem in general less telling. The crucial wit, intellectual toughness and colloquial edge of that "aged man" are missing and without them one follows him at great peril. The problem becomes clearest in such poems as **"Place of Learning," "The Work of Happiness"** and **"Navigator,"** which, for all their attractiveness, are never quite free of that hint of sentimental dilution that tends to drive the reader's good emotional coin out of the market.

> M. L. Rosenthal, "The Mysterious Art of Singing Words," in New York Herald Tribune Weekly Book Review, July 4, 1948, p. 6.

FRANCIS McCARTHY

Miss Sarton's poetry is most successful when its content is religious and its method most parsimonious. Though her craftsmanship is usually scrupulous and deft in the handling of detail, her conception of poetry, and of the poem, is one that lends itself too readily to the wastefulness of the flat, didactic statement and not readily enough to the economy of suggestion. Some of her poems [collected in *The Lion and the Rose*], notable among them **"The Window"** and **"The Magnet,"** achieve effective concentration and a genuine fusion of thought and emotion within the bounds of a single image. Less successful are the loosely articulated structures of **"My Sisters, O My Sisters"** and **"To the Living."** Both compositions contain much genuine insight, but the one resembles a perceptive essay and the other an eloquent editorial.

Miss Sarton's central theme is the primary importance of the life lived "in inwardness." To her, religion, humanism and democracy are traditionally the faiths which have upheld the dignity of the human spirit and hence are the only soil out of which can spring a better and more creative future. This belief (most movingly conveyed in the excellent **"Celebrations"** and **"Return to Chartres"**) is basic to **"American Landscapes,"** a group of descriptive interpretations of what various significant American locales have contributed to define or to deny the democratic faith.

In unfortunate contrast to the achieved tension of the religious poems is the limpness of those in the group entitled **"Work of Happiness"**—the task of creating and the delight of enjoying beauty. Like most poems too conscious of "beauty" and of the necessity for being beautiful, the world they reflect seems that of the ivory tower: a realm in which attractive people are engaged in having sensitive perceptions in the midst of beautiful objects. When, in another group of poems, Miss Sarton attempts to cope with the horrors of contemporary barbarity, the voice trained to sweetness cannot compass the tones of "savage indignation."

> Francis McCarthy, in a review of "The Lion and the Rose," in The New York Times Book Review, August 15, 1948, p. 18.

JEAN GARRIGUE

May Sarton's *Shadow of a Man* makes too free with the novel form. Here is the lyrical novel, or the novel of sensibility oversimplified. There is in it a general atmosphere of right thinking and good feeling about life and about, specifically, what a young man in the progress of his soul (from Boston to France and back) ought to do with life (and how he can cut himself from the silver cord); but being a novel of sensibility without, actually, a real situation, its wisdom and cultivation of spirit do not come to grips with any of the problems suggested by the education of the hero. He, being at odds with family and culture, must learn how to love, must learn what it is he wants to do with his life and talents. He learns: a French mistress, about his dead mother's age, and the *plein air* of Paris happily instruct him, so that he may return to the job and the girl at home. A young man is *found*, who had been *lost*. But all this spiritual enterprise is told from the surface, too glibly. At worst, [*Shadow of a Man*] is woman's-magazine writing; at best, it treats of serious matters too easily.

> Jean Garrigue, in a review of "Shadow of a Man," in The New Republic, Vol. 122, No. 19, May 8, 1950, p. 20.

EDITH H. WALTON

When Persis Adams Bradford [a character in May Sarton's *Shadow of a Man*] dies in Boston, she leaves behind her a second husband and a grown son, Francis—child of her earlier marriage to an unusually gifted Frenchman. Francis is difficult and tormented. With everything, apparently, in his favor, including a background of wealth, he is at odds with himself, his stepfather, his surroundings, his strangely mixed heritage. Although he had never been able to achieve intimacy with his extraordinary mother, her death leaves him rootless and bereft. . . .

Thus cursed and lost, Francis goes to Paris, where he soon embarks upon an affair with an older woman, Solange, who was formerly a friend of his mother's. The experience—an intense one—is ultimately wounding, but it teaches Francis how to love, how to discard his repressions, and how to come to terms with his heritage. When he returns to America, he is not only able to adjust himself to his rather conventional Brahmin background, but he is able to seek out the girl who for years has been waiting for him, and whom he has hitherto been incapable of loving.

May Sarton is also a poet, and there are passages throughout her novel which are full of lyric charm—as, for instance, her descriptions of Paris and of Chartres. Moreover, her book is sensitive, perceptive, alive to delicate shades of feeling, and unquestionably sincere. Miss Sarton, however, takes her curiously immature hero a bit too portentously; he doesn't seem as attractive and as interesting to the reader as he quite obviously does to his creator. Francis, I am afraid, seems often merely spoiled, and one neither fully grasps what originally caused his difficulties, nor does one believe that they could have been solved quite so easily. Nevertheless [*Shadow of a Man*] is a provocative and on the whole an appealing book.

Edith H. Walton, "Brahmin Waif," in The New York Times Book Review, *May 14, 1950, p. 20.*

ROSE FELD

Four human beings and an antiquated stone house in Ireland are the characters in [*A Shower of Summer Days*]. To say that the house is the scene where the action takes place is wrong, for as Miss Sarton develops her theme of emotional disturbances and discoveries, it is the house which sounds a constant major note of changelessness and security.

After twenty years of living in Burma, Violet Dene Gordon and her husband, Charles, come back to Dene's Court, Violet's ancestral home in Ireland. To Violet, a woman of fifty, the house is both a sanctuary that holds peace and a place haunted by still lacerating memories of guilt. Here it was that she and her younger sister, Barbara, had grown up in the security of family tradition; here it was that she, with her renowned beauty and charm, had destroyed the first love her sister had known. That it was done casually, without malice and with rejection of the reward, deepened rather than lessened her crime. Barbara had again fallen in love and gone off to America with her husband, but the wound of personal defeat and inferiority had never been healed.

With a touch at the same time delicate and penetrating, Miss Sarton explores the heart of a woman who knows that her beauty has been a two-edged sword that has brought her both happiness and pain. She knows that she has used it consciously to draw people to her, to live in an atmosphere of admiration and love, of personal power. It has brought her happiness in the thirty years of her marriage with Charles, but continually threatening that happiness is the fear that her beauty is fading. With consummate art, Miss Sarton does not make of Violet a weak or superficial person. She is not a silly aging beauty but a charming and beautiful woman who becomes increasingly aware of the dubious fruits of a gift she has treasured.

To Dene's Court, shortly after the arrival of the Gordons, comes Sally, twenty-year-old daughter of Barbara, sent to Ireland for the summer to keep her from marrying a young actor with whom she is in love. Rebellious, resentful, coltishly awkward, the girl, who feels the house is a prison, charges the air with conflict.

With seemingly trivial incident, with almost casual accent, Miss Sarton develops the effect of the girl's presence on the two members of the household. Outwardly, there is no drama; there are no moments of high tension. But seeking Sally's love, needing it honestly, Violet sees Charles attracted by the girl's youth. Caught in memories, caught in fear, she knows that in her own way, without betraying herself too much, she must protect herself, her marriage and the girl. It is in the final pages that Miss Sarton brings her theme into full orchestration. Here it is that the subterranean drama rises to the surface; here it is that the continually stirring portrait of Violet receives the final strokes that raise it to magnificence.

Rose Feld, "Shimmering and Melodic," in New York Herald Tribune Book Review, *August 26, 1952, p. 6.*

JOHN NERBER

Miss Sarton ranks with the very best of our distinguished novelists. *A Shower of Summer Days* establishes once and for all her unmistakable authority. . . .

To the enchanted and sad Irish springtime of Dene's Court, Violet and Charles Gordon return after thirty years abroad. To Violet, a Dene, and mistress of Dene's Court, it is a poignant homecoming, filled with the delicate tensions of a memorable youth when, as the acknowledged beauty of the countryside, she held rural court, and from which she departed, married somewhat below her due. Too, there is the memory of the younger, resentful sister, Barbara, defeated and lost in the brightness of Violet's beauty (who, nevertheless, managed a brilliant American marriage, escaping at last). Finally, there is Charles, philandering Charles, who must be eased into the life of the house as gently as a foot is eased into a new shoe.

They are scarcely settled before Violet's niece, Sally, arrives from America, sent by Barbara in order to nip an unfortunate affair with an actor. The novel recounts the precarious balance of their relationship, what happens when Sally's lover flies over for the week-end and falls under Violet's spell.

It is Violet, the mansion looming behind her, in whom, and through whom the novel is focused. She is flesh and blood, and she is legendary, filled with the intuitions and reticences of the tantalizing women of history, yet her full essence is yielded to the reader without loss of the basic mystery, the fabulous creature quality. It is a measure of Miss Sarton's craftsmanship that Violet is never reduced to the novelist's mercy. Violet is complete. There is nothing more for Miss Sarton to say, and this reader is compelled to that feeling of awe which the accomplishment of first-rate literary creation inevitably brings forth.

John Nerber, "The Shabby Great House," in The New York Times Book Review, *October 26, 1952, p. 4.*

BABETTE DEUTSCH

One could wish for something of the salty quality of Mac-Neice's work in Miss Sarton's [*The Land of Silence and Other Poems*]. Her technical competence is clear, and her sensitivity to the interplay between public and private life finds expression that is always graceful and often penetrating, as in the final lines of **"The New Tourist"** who feels "His camera become heavy / As an albatross." What, then, is missing? Language as exquisitely appropriate as the rhythms, the sparkle of wit that would redeem the softness of the verse. There is a tendency to more statement than the poem requires, and a peculiarly feminine quality well illustrated in the sonnet sequence. This sometimes lapses into the conventional or into a tone almost embarrassingly personal. It is barely saved by its candor and its clever craftsmanship. Because of the virtues in Miss Sarton's performance, its lacks are the more regrettable. They seem to be largely due to her being insufficiently severe with herself. (p. 280)

Babette Deutsch, in a review of "The Land of Silence and Other Poems," in The Yale Review, *Vol. XLIII, No. 2, December, 1953, pp. 276-81.*

LOUISE BOGAN

May Sarton begins, in her fourth volume of verse, **The Land of Silence,** to show signs of an insight "into the life of things." The collection is too long, and in part rather conventionally "literary," but at least a dozen poems exhibit her mature power of recognizing the heart of the matter and of expressing it in memorable terms.

Louise Bogan, in a review of "The Land of Silence," in The New Yorker, *Vol. XXX, No. 2, February 27, 1954, p. 115.*

EDWARD WEEKS

May Sarton's new novel, **Faithful Are the Wounds,** is by all odds her best. It is a clearly lit, impassioned story of the American Liberal and of what he has been living through recently. Edward Cavan, a Harvard professor, is the pivot of the book about whom revolve the controversy, the anger, and the remorse. He has achieved a national reputation by what he has written on American literature and by the brilliance of his seminars. Edward's dilemma, which in the end destroys him, is like that of so many of his intimates. An ardent Socialist who took his cue from the Fabians, and in particular from Beatrice and Sidney Webb, he has lived to see his dream become a spotted reality. He has seen Communism snuff out the Socialists in Czechoslovakia, and Wallace, whom he fiercely supported, misled by the Progressives. He has seen opinion, even among those he loved, swing back toward the center of a new Conservatism, and all this has made him infuriated and unyielding. He feels walled in, and when he can no longer get through to those he used to trust, he kills himself.

The novel, then, is the cause and effect of Edward's suicide, and the elucidation of the tragedy is relayed to us by Edward's sister Isabel, whom he had long ago shut out of his bachelordom. Isabel, the elegant, well-cared for wife of a San Francisco

surgeon, had been incapable of following her brother in his quest for the Liberal ideal, and it is only when the disaster has called her to Cambridge that she begins to relate the boy she had worshiped as an older brother to the famous scholar now so cruelly in the headlines. The truth about the mature Edward is conveyed to Isabel by his Cambridge friends, and it is she who again and again supplies the missing links going back to his family.

Isabel's portrait is as finely drawn as Edward's; despite her poise and apparent complacency she is capable of deep feelings, and these are aroused in her encounters with [Edward's close friends] . . .—they share with her a sense of communion and affection, rare to find on the printed page. The story takes its pulse from these people with their fighting principles and their candor; and while at times Isabel finds them childishly passionate, she also realizes how deeply they are committed to her brother. . . . Edward, the angry idealist, the scorner of compromise, who had fought so long against the extreme Right that he could not tolerate the enmity of the Left, is a figure who will walk in our imagination long after the book has been put down. (pp. 74, 76)

Edward Weeks, "Grief and Loyalty," in The Atlantic Bookshelf, *a section of* The Atlantic Monthly, *Vol. 195, No. 5, May, 1955, pp. 74, 76.*

PAUL PICKREL

[*Faithful Are the Wounds* is] close enough to an historical instance to raise serious doubts about the taste of the undertaking as a whole and to occasion extraliterary speculation about some of the details. But on literary grounds alone the book is open to certain reservations. We never get to know the professor; we are never admitted to his mind; in the end we do not know why he committed suicide. Miss Sarton impatiently brushes aside the objection that nobody commits suicide out of a general political malaise, yet she hedges enough to show that she is ready to consider other explanations. We see the whole thing obliquely, through various friends of the professor. That would be all right if the novel were an attempt to explore the ambiguity of such an event in its public effects, but the book is up to something else: its object is to show that the professor was right. Right about what? On the evidence presented we simply do not know.

The best thing about **Faithful Are the Wounds** is its fine evocation of the setting, Boston and Cambridge. Too much of the dialogue is the dispirited exchange of discouraged liberals; it is accurate enough but not necessarily for that reason suitable for preservation between covers. The book badly needs the depth of satire. Everything is taken very seriously, and with the same degree of seriousness. There is some unconscious humor in Miss Sarton's supposition that the use of the mind is an activity limited to the banks of the Charles. (pp. 637-38)

Paul Pickrel, "Outstanding Fiction: Some Political Novels," in The Yale Review, *Vol. XLIV, No. 4, June, 1955, pp. 634-40.*

ELIZABETH JANEWAY

The Birth of a Grandfather concerns the interrelations of a family, which is a good thing for a novel to be about; and it is an inaccurate title only because the reader is going to be at least as interested in Frances, the prospective grandmother, as in her husband, Sprig Wyeth. The scene is Cambridge, Mass.

(not Boston!), and an island off the coast of Maine, where the Wyeths have had a summer home for fifty years. The cast of characters includes three generations: Sprig's father, aunt and uncle; a second generation consisting of Sprig himself, Frances, his sister and various friends; and, from the third generation, Sprig's son and daughter and the Irishman (Harvard Irish) whom the daughter married.

Miss Sarton's theme is the gear-shifting that often happens in the middle of a marriage, in the middle years of life. Paralleling this internal adjustment, the middle generation must take on its shoulders the weight that the older people are now unable to hold. At the same time, they must watch the steps their children take into adult responsibility as they set out in their turn on marriages and careers.

This is a serious and sensible theme, and Miss Sarton writes about it with sincerity and accuracy. But there are two things I miss. One is force. The other is quite possibly related: this novel rather gives the impression of floating in space, of not being tied down to everyday life in the Nineteen Fifties as experienced by ordinary people, and I have the feeling that a little more energy in its presentation would have given it a firmer foundation. The air of Cambridge and of third-generation summer homes is a bit rarefied and not entirely familiar to all of us. We need the explication of a John P. Marquand, the brilliant unravelling of social relations of a James Gould Cozzens, to place the Wyeths and their milieu, to make their emotions immediately understandable and moving. Miss Sarton's presentation is never inaccurate, but it is oblique. It is fleeting.

This is not a "woman's novel," a lending library favorite; it is much too precisely observed, truly told and serious minded. But it is limited to much the same material as these contrivances, the feminine world of family and home. What is worse, the delineation of its male characters is weakened by what may well be a conscientious scruple; a refusal (since one is not male) to try to see these characters in male terms, because such an effort would involve invention almost in the sense of falsification.

For a novelist as finely observant, as capable, as Miss Sarton, such scruples are nonsense. Of course a woman-writer must begin by seeing the world through a woman's eyes, but she can go on from there just as far as her talent will carry her. If women are to write novels at all (and it's certainly late in the day to try to distract them), the duty is laid on them to use that common humanity in the case of all their characters. After all, men have had very little trouble doing the other thing, from Richardson and Defoe right down to the present.

Elizabeth Janeway, "Shifting the Gears," in The New York Times Book Review, *September 8, 1957, p. 4.*

WHITNEY BALLIETT

The Birth of a Grandfather is May Sarton's best novel. If it is not a perfect one, it is because it is too solemn, too flat-footed. Miss Sarton's prose curiously lacks the sinew and tension that distinguish her best poetry, and at times even slumps into such battered phrases as "lost in thought," "drunk with tiredness," and "he screwed up his eyes." Some of the exciting intensity a novelist can achieve by mercilessly rubbing together opposing thoughts and actions is here, as in her other books, but it is eased by a thin lubrication of sentiment that time and again allows the genuine feeling one senses beneath to slip away. Nevertheless, *The Birth of a Grandfather* is a neat, thorough examination of a unique race—the Yankee aristocrat. Much of it is set in present-day Cambridge, Massachusetts, where nineteenth-century men of leisure like Miss Sarton's hero, Sprig Wyeth, still take the air on Brattle Street. Wyeth, who is fifty, lives on money inherited from his father. Although he is far from being the celebrated New England miser, the money has atrophied him. He has spent his life as a minor philanthropist, in toying with landscape gardening, and on never-finished translations of Greek plays. Worse, he is a shy, graceful, stubborn man who has never been able to give of himself. For the first time, he is forced to the test; he must either enter into true human relationships by compromising with others or, having come so far, slowly begin to close up like a dying leaf. The test is not easy. He must give in to a reasonable wish of his son's, whom he has always dominated. He must accept the premature death of his best friend, whose outpouring spirit has always been a crutch for his own selfishness. He must accept the demands inherent in the birth of his first grandchild. Above all, he must at last turn to his wife, who for all of their marriage has cheerfully sown her considerable love on stony ground. Miss Sarton patiently isolates in Wyeth the curious and always astonishing warring selves that make up the old-line New Englander—the tough Northern hide vs. the wild, almost Latin temperament. Yet the split that appears in the outer Wyeth at the end of [*The Birth of a Grandfather*] is, in a way, a betrayal of the very stubbornness and faithfulness to self that the true Yankee has made virtues of. Wyeth's unbending is a victory for kindness. But it is also a victory for sentiment. Like many weaker men of his age, Wyeth is going a little soft. (pp. 184-85)

Whitney Balliett, "One Hard, One Soft," in The New Yorker, *Vol. XXXIII, No. 33, October 5, 1957, pp. 181-85.*

RICHARD RHODES

Kinds of Love is one of those books a reviewer has trouble deciding how to take. The work of an accomplished and prolific poet and novelist, it is yet flawed in style and flabby in content. A family novel thick with characters, it yet does not bring the reader in to share the depth of those characters' experiences. It reads like a book intended for a private printing, in the sense that Miss Sarton assumes by her style that we already know, somehow, the people and events she portrays. And that assumption—not, presumably, deliberate—makes shallow what might have been profound.

The novel, Miss Sarton's 13th, is set in a small New Hampshire town much visited over the years by summer people. Christina and Cornelius Chapman, elderly and long-standing summer people, have retreated to Willard following Cornelius's partly crippling stroke and have resolved to winter there for the first time. Around them and around their house swirl the events of the story, events surprisingly unmoving. The town will celebrate its bicentennial the following August, and each of the central characters in *Kinds of Love* will have a part. . . . What the town was and is becomes important to everyone there as the long New Hampshire winter wears on.

For Ellen Comstock, an impoverished widow who lives in the town with her son but who has been a lifelong friend of the wealthy Christina, Willard is a life to be got through proudly but bitterly. For her son Nick it is a natural world rapidly being destroyed by bulldozers and hunters. When he attacks the road agent who is directing the bulldozing, he is taken off to the state mental hospital he has visited more than once before as a casualty of World War II. For Christina and Cornelius, Willard becomes a place to grow old in gracefully. However, when they discover the winter life of the town they find themselves stirred anew by compassion for its residents and fresh knowledge of the complexity of human life. For Joel Smith, a long-haired Dartmouth dropout, Willard becomes a haven amidst the society he has learned to detest—but a haven which he must leave for military service and a more practical view of the world.

There is more, much of it potentially fascinating: the final saintly days of Jane Tuttle, a tiny spinster schoolteacher who has given direction and love to many of the young people in the story; Old Pete, the town's jack of all trades and resident philosopher, losing a leg to frostbite while he sleeps off a drunk in his unheated cabin; the evolving marriages of the Chapman children and the strength they find in their wise parents; the speech Eben Fifield, retired diplomat and Willard native, makes to the surprised and then pleased crowd at the bicentennial celebration.

But Miss Sarton leaves us on the outside, as if she, and we too, are summer people. Perhaps the flaw is that she tells us of feelings rather than showing us. Or the tendency not only of the Chapmans but of many other residents to speak in "shant's" and "old boys" and "do you knows," as if they were fresh from a drawing-room comedy. The effect of the prose is to tantalize and frustrate: one imagines what the story might have been if these people were real, but with the exception of Ellen Comstock they simply don't come alive.

> *Richard Rhodes, "How the Summer People Learned to Pass the Winter," in* The New York Times Book Review, *November 29, 1970, p. 56.*

THE NEW YORKER

[In *Kinds of Love* we] watch with fascination as Miss Sarton builds her huge portrait of a joyous and generous spirit who is doomed, even in old age, to suffer the pain of bewildered love.... Christina wants to be loved, not only by her own people—those of her family and of her clan—but by everybody in sight, and, what is more, she wants proof of love from everybody, in sight and out of sight. The proofs are given easily enough, but in Christina's keen intelligence there is enough self-doubt to enable her to sense the reservation between herself and many of those she would like to call her own, and this sense of alienation afflicts her most sharply when she and her husband, Cornelius, return to their big summer establishment in Willard, New Hampshire, and prepare to spend their first winter there.... With complete success, Miss Sarton portrays Willard under a double spell—first, the spell cast by the spectacular winter weather, and, second, the spell of Christina's longing, a longing that never tires and that continues to hold her story in tension after the ice and snow are gone and forgotten.

> *A review of "Kinds of Love," in* The New Yorker, *Vol. XLVI, No. 44, December 19, 1970, p. 143.*

HENRY TAYLOR

The merging of political and other human realities in a sensibility that may previously have separated them creates interesting tensions in *A Grain of Mustard Seed*.... Miss Sarton

has long been recognized as one of our most accomplished writers, but her poetry has too often been taken for less than it is. Her earlier work may sometimes have been weakened by the easy moral which can arise from minute observation of nature; but in her seventh book, *A Private Mythology* (1966) she began to move toward more deeply earned utterance, in a more personal voice. [*A Grain of Mustard Seed*] speaks firmly in that voice in many poems, some of which approach Roethke's power of sympathy with nature. Too few of the several public poems here arise from that kind of sympathy; there are ballads about segregation, for example, which seem to strain against self-consciousness. Nevertheless, Miss Sarton continues to try new areas of discovery, and each of her recent books has shown a mastery over something which appeared tentative in an earlier book. She is still fighting the isolation which has helped her find her best poems so far; when she comes to terms with the right balance of isolation and involvement, she will have mastered what seems tentative here. Meanwhile, there are many poems here which remind us that she is, at the same time, a well-established poet and a vitally developing talent. (p. 372)

> *Henry Taylor, "A Gathering of Poets," in* Western Humanities Review, *Vol. XXV, No. 4, Autumn, 1971, pp. 367-72.*

JOSEPH PARISI

[In *Halfway to Silence: New Poems* Sarton] speaks of poetry as "craft that may sometimes harness strange powers, / Those airs above the ground that banish time," and her frequently formal verses aspire upward, often offering inspiration and "uplift." Much of her verse is rhymed, and its tone is likewise old-fashioned. In their feminine sensibility (with all the negative connotations of the phrase), Sarton's short lyrics—usually of love, tinged with melancholy or self-pity but touching consolation, too—are reminiscent of Sara Teasdale. But unlike the work of that master technician, Sarton's poems lose poise through awkward rhythms, strained effects, and occasionally jarring diction that can mix literary allusion with psychological jargon. Amid much praise of nature, there lingers more than a hint of the hothouse here, a perfumed atmosphere where the obviously "poetical" has a penchant for implicit moralizing. Still, readers with a taste for the traditional and familiar may find rewards in Sarton's often skillful reworking of the perennial themes.

> *Joseph Parisi, in a review of "Halfway to Silence: New Poems," in* Booklist, *Vol. 77, No. 1, September 1, 1980, p. 26.*

MANLY JOHNSON

[The poems in *Halfway to Silence*] carry on what we know from *The Collected Poems 1930-1973* as the journal of a life. Some celebrate people and places; others record a deeply personal response to jealousy, pain and anger. They continue Sarton's customary orchestration of vowels and control of form....

That these poems come after a long drought signals a new phase, though they are not so different in style, manner or form from the earlier poems, except for two or three. The last one, "The Muse," is like the preceding entries from "A Winter Notebook"—spare and direct. If not yet that "crude honesty" which Sarton sees as her hope for poetry, nor herself yet that "great, cracked / Wide-open door into nowhere," which is wisdom, she seems to have located the door in a north wall, opening onto "winter joys." In that phrase about the door, at any rate, is evident the kind of magical evocation of sound from consonants that she has always been able to command from vowels.

Sarton's father was Belgian, her mother English, who moved to New York when their daughter was a small child. She could not determine for many years whether in her heart she was European or American. The cultural ambiguity was settled by an odyssey through the land in 1939-40, reading poetry at colleges and writing—her discovery of America and commitment to it. But the ambiguity remains in her poetry, a matter both of culture and of style. These new poems exhibit the sometimes too meticulous clarity and precision that derives more from French than English, a depth of feeling under glass, except for the occasional granitic outcropping that comes apparently from New Hampshire, the land that has taken over her imagination.

Her first role in the theatre, which after three years she gave up for poetry, was in *Peter Pan*, as a wolf, whose eyes she made to glow with the aid of a flashlight. Showing through in some of these poems is a glitter sparked by something elemental that could become wild. Poetry has had several wild old men. May Sarton be our first wild old woman.

> *Manly Johnson, in a review of "Halfway to Silence,"
> in* World Literature Today, *Vol. 55, No. 2, Spring,
> 1981, p. 319.*

SHEILA BALLANTYNE

It seems natural to discuss May Sarton's 17th novel, *Anger,* in the context of the work that immediately preceded it—her remarkable book *Recovering: A Journal 1978-1979*—so linked, at times so nearly identical, are their major themes.

Anger is the story of a marriage of opposites: between the opera singer Anna Lindstrom, half-Italian, half-Swedish, artistic, passionate and verbal, and Ned Fraser, a Boston bank president who insists on making love with the lights out and achieves tender communication only with his dachshund. These two characters are the medium through which Miss Sarton voices her concern about intimacy, repression and self-knowledge....

In *Recovering* Miss Sarton focused on three personal traumas: an unfavorable review of her previous novel, *A Reckoning,* the failure of a recent love relationship and the effects of her cancer surgery....

If *Anger* is to be evaluated within the context which nourished, if not dictated, its themes, there is a deeper question to be considered. Miss Sarton was especially dismayed that the reviewer saw dormant lesbian themes in work that was not explicitly homosexual, and she equated the reviewer's exploration of those themes with McCarthy-era "guilt by association," feeling herself accused. Yet in the journal as elsewhere, Miss Sarton focused largely on women, and tangentially on lesbian relationships. Still, she bristled in the journal at what she regarded as reductionism: "The vision of life in my work is not limited to one segment of humanity . . . and has little to do with sexual proclivity." (p. 14)

It seems especially appropriate to consider the origins of a work when the author has made a point in a published journal of her private conflicts concerning that future work. Near the end of *Recovering* Miss Sarton reflects:

> I have the wild hope that by the end of the summer I may begin to make notes for a new novel. The journal has proved beneficial in one way, that here I am able to think and speak about women honestly. It is hard to do. I sometimes sit here and think for an hour before I can bring myself to say certain difficult things, difficult because they are not things most people want to hear. But the big block between me and a new novel has been the pressure to do that in fiction.

If *Anger*—being the novel published directly after the journal—is that work, then one must conclude that Miss Sarton backed off the challenge. While one can't say that such a change of perspective would have made *Anger* a less distanced, more believable novel, it is certainly a possibility.

In the journal Miss Sarton complained of her loved one's inability to respond, to be openly affectionate:

> What I long for with those I love is not so much to be understood as to be accepted warts and all. . . . I have sometimes felt in this past year that I have become at least for one person important to my inner life, a carrier of the plague . . . the plague being feelings. She herself is so afraid of feeling . . . she has come to see me as the enemy. . . .

This is the very problem we now encounter in Ned, *Anger*'s prototypical "repressed" male. At the other end of the spectrum, Miss Sarton's struggle in her journal to balance the emotional forces in herself—"I know that what makes me a person often hard to live with . . . (all those tears and rages) are what makes me a good writer"—reappear as the central drama of the character of the fiery Anna, who insists, "I am whole. . . . I'm not two people, one good and beautiful, the other bad and ugly. . . . You have to take the whole person."

There is something curiously artless in the direct, untransformed transposition of Miss Sarton's personal concerns (described with mastery and feeling in the journal) to the characters in her novel; some of the very phrases she has used in the former often seem to leap unaltered onto its pages. The novel has a peculiar lack of power for all its "right" and genuinely compelling themes. In the journal she included a marvelous quote from Pirandello: "One cannot choose what he writes—one can only choose to face it." It appears that *Anger* is not the novel she would have written had she faced the many cues that sprang repeatedly to mind throughout *Recovering*.

If, as Miss Sarton has indicated, the theme of incapacitated love is an important one—being universally shared by both sexes—it deserves to be treated comprehensively rather than by drawing on the usual stereotypes (feeling women, repressed men) to represent it. If certain women are incapable of feeling, as Miss Sarton so poignantly stated in her journal, why assign this incapacity to yet another male in a novel meant to examine this problem? Speaking of *Anger* in a recent interview in *Ms.* magazine, Miss Sarton claimed, "I didn't make the main characters be two women because then people would have said 'Oh, that's what women do together, they fight.' Now people can say: 'Oh, a man, a woman, and anger—it's universal.' Someday emotions that are universal will be taken as such." That "someday" won't be an immediate reality so long as important novelistic choices are dictated by what "people would have said."

"So many people write me that the journals and memoirs and the poems are the better part of my work," Miss Sarton wrote early in *Recovering,* recognizing as she must both the enormous scope of her work and the number of people who have been reached by it. When considering this, it is clear that May Sarton's best work, whatever its form, will endure well beyond the influence of particular reviews or current tastes. For in it she is an example: a seeker after truth with a kind of awesome energy for renewal, an ardent explorer of life's important questions. Her great strength is that when she achieves insight, one believes—because one has witnessed the struggle that preceded the knowledge; her discoveries do not come cheap. (pp. 14, 37-8)

Sheila Ballantyne, "Something Helpless that Needs Help," in The New York Times Book Review, *October 17, 1982, pp. 14, 37-8.*

LINDA BARRETT OSBORNE

In whatever May Sarton writes one can hear the human heart pulsing just below the surface. She is a novelist of great sensibility, and many of her characters share with her the ability to apprehend and express strong emotions, almost, at times, as if any withholding would not be honest, would fall short of their capacities as human beings. In *Anger,* her 17th novel, Sarton gives us Anna Lindstrom, a mezzo-soprano whose art is inextricably bound with her tempestuous feelings, and through Anna's marriage to Ned Fraser, a repressed, formal man, explores with mixed results many of the themes of her past books.

In several ways Anna and Ned are embodiments of the classic communications dilemma of our times, the war between the person who needs to convey his emotions, and the one who feels assaulted by them and can not convey his own. These differences are intensified by their backgrounds. She, the woman, is half-Italian, a singer; he, the man, is upper-class Bostonian and a banker. . . .

Ned is drawn to Anna because of the beauty and purity of her voice, and by the warmth of her personality. She feels secure with him, and is also touched by his inability to talk about the feelings she thinks of as natural. But soon after their marriage, the tension begins, and within two years they are both threatened, edgy, and argumentative. Ned is infuriated by Anna's violent moods and her insistent attempts to draw out his feelings, and responds with a cold resistance. She is dismayed by his inability to be warmly affectionate or communicative, even to say "I love you," and feels circumscribed and punished because "his silence is violent, too."

Anger is the only strong emotion Ned can express, and when they do fight, it is often he who attacks while Anna tries to defend and explain herself. "I think you are two people, Jekyll and Hyde. One is a great personality, a lovable, beautiful woman. . . . The other is a screaming peacock . . . a wilful witch who cannot be criticized without an outburst, totally self-indulgent," Ned tells her. And Anna responds, "I'm whole. . . . I cannot compartmentalize myself. . . . I'm not two people, one good and beautiful, the other bad and ugly. . . . You have to take the whole person." And later she says, "You ask me to censor myself all the time—I am becoming the prisoner of your ethos, and it is making me ill."

This passage of dialogue conveys many of the concerns of the novel, as well as its flavor. Reading *Anger* is like spending the evening with friends who are sniping at each other, who consistently, painfully hurt each other, almost despite themselves, and disconcert others with this revealed aspect of their intimacy. It is a very tense experience, and the language is

often surprisingly literal, less balanced and poetic than in Sarton's other work. . . .

Although the language can be limiting, the ideas developed in *Anger* reach beyond the conflict of men and women and consider the deeper questions of personal, emotional, and artistic growth. Anna's strong feelings are related to her art, the creative force which sustains and enriches her singing and gives it character. It is one of the ironies of the book that the voice which attracts Ned should become the instrument for intruding upon him, but it is one more way that Sarton shows the connection of art to life. As in other Sarton novels, self examination and the willingness to change are also essential if one is to go forward, to do the work of creating himself as a full human being. The violence and rage which is so frightening to Anna, even as she feels it is important, and which can be damaging to relationships, also hold the power to shape personal growth. In such a setting, someone like Ned must seem stunted and sad, and when Anna finally gets him to feel and express pain, centered around his father's death, there is no question that this is a good and necessary step toward self knowledge and development.

If *Anger* shows the way that two people of very different but aggressive temperaments battle together, it also asserts the importance of openly expressing deep feelings so that growth in both the marriage and the partners' individual lives is possible. These are certainly contemporary concerns, but they are not new to Sarton. . . .

Anger benefits from being read in the context of the other novels, as something more than the exploration of a relationship which holds few surprises for those who read about men and women today. To see it as part of the body of Sarton's work amplifies and enhances the book, and gives it a resonance it might otherwise not have.

Linda Barrett Osborne, "Wars within the Walls of Marriage," in Book World—The Washington Post, *December 12, 1982, p. 11.*

SUZANNE OWENS

Sarton's 'private' writing offers a continuity of form and idea that clearly deserves consideration as literary art apart from its relationship to her substantial body of fictional prose and poetry. It is particularly evident in two subjects which inform her memoirs and journals: the creation-recreation of "home" and the nature of solitude. As literary explorations, the Sarton journals and memoirs record a life-philosophy working out through daily experience filtered through a particularly sensitive and attuned consciousness. . . .

For Sarton, events remembered in *I Knew a Phoenix* (1959) take on a certain legendary quality through memory, particularly as she recalls scenes from childhood. It is in this volume that we begin to read of her intense identification with houses as homes and as constructs of remembered family life. (p. 53)

The sketches of *I Knew a Phoenix* move freely between the very distant past (her parents' lives) and her childhood, each chapter reading as a portrait of one person or of an event. *Plant Dreaming Deep* (1968) is a sequential narrative-memoir of Sarton's move to rural New Hampshire and of particular interest to the later journals for the development of the central presence of the house as character. We immediately recognize that "home" and "house" are, naturally, metaphors of particular importance to Sarton's life as an artist, thus continuing a thread from the sketches. The opening chapter of *Plant Dreaming Deep,* in fact, is titled ''The Ancestor Comes Home,'' an examination of heritage and the quality of the past in the present. Hanging an oil portrait of a distant Belgium ancestor in her Nelson, New Hampshire house, Sarton makes clear, ''I knew I was performing a symbolic act, and this is the way it has been from the beginning, so that everything I do here reverberates, and if out of fatigue or not paying attention, I strike a false note, it hurts the house and the mystique by which I live.'' In moving to the village of Nelson and buying an ancient farm house to restore, Sarton was searching, it seems, for her real American roots separate, though not entirely divorced from, the lives of her parents.

As a memoir of that first year in Nelson, *Plant Dreaming Deep* details the typical daily chores and responsibilities Sarton took on as householder, but there is always attention given to even the most physical of experiences as philosophical or metaphorical keys to understanding the artist's life. In choosing to purchase an old, run-down house in need of rehabilitation, Sarton notes that she ''saw the house as becoming my own creation within a traditional frame, in much the same way as a poet pours his vision of life into the traditional form of the sonnet.'' But her analysis is not just a truth recognized in hindsight; the point of the entire memoir seems to be the documentation of a life consciously constructed as an expression of the writer's *work*—that is, of literary work. And there were spiritual features of the Nelson house which could only come from connections between Old World and New. (pp. 55-6)

The memoir is important in relation to the later journals because it is the beginning of Sarton's conscious and detailed exploration of that ''metaphysical frame'' and, most important, of ''self.'' Indeed, the title of the first journal, *Journal of a Solitude* (1973), follows from a comment we read in *Plant Dreaming Deep:* ''People often imagine that I must be lonely. How can I explain? I want to say, 'Oh no! You see the house is with me. And it is with me in this particular way, as both a demand and a support only when I am alone here'.'' Sarton's sense of self, of the physical-metaphorical nature of house and home, of even the condition of solitude are expressed most clearly in *Plant Dreaming Deep.* The memoir sets up conditions and questions which the later journals meet head on. (p. 57)

Journal of a Solitude (1973) is a brooding work, but as readers we should be aware that the daily and scrupulous recording of life through journal writing may be a much darker work than the memoir softened by memory. The memoirs had not been entirely untrue, of course, but the screen of memory can filter out the harshest of details, even when the writer does not intend to. Sarton's choice of the journal as the next form for her private writing was, in a sense, a means of 'correcting' herself, of altering the 'false' image of her life which she was afraid she had created in *Plant Dreaming Deep.* . . . Sarton had taken solitude to be the subject of her journal and it is through an examination of her episodes of depression, anger or frustration that she believed the ''true'' image of her life would become clear. We are reminded at the beginning of *Journal of a Solitude,* for instance, that ''there is nothing to *cushion* against attacks from within, just as there is nothing to help balance at times of particular stress or depression.'' In Sarton's terms, solitude was a condition of living, not a temporary predicament and often became the source of acute distress. When an elderly couple approached her door hoping to be able to meet her, for example (''friends of the work'' as Sarton labels her readers), Sarton was horrified to find herself pouring out her troubles to

them, perfect strangers: ''Here the inner person is the outer person. It is what I want, but that does not make me any less absurd.'' So *Journal of a Solitude* becomes an unpredictable work. Just as Sarton seems completely enmeshed in days of dark humor and high tension, she breaks into gentler considerations of small details, as she did on one October morning: ''the ash has lost its leaves and when I went out to get the mail and stopped to look up at it, I rejoiced to think that soon everything here will be honed down to structure.'' A memoir might have lost such a detail, but the moment fixed in the daily record of the journal provides a distraction from inner turmoil for both writer and reader.

Because the journal form so often catches the writer at unpredictable moments, experience is never expressed as a final evaluation; it is more likely to be built up of recurring emotions and predicaments, underscoring the truth ''that nothing stays the same for long.'' At times, the journal becomes a collection of essays devoted to topics prompted by daily experience, a way of stripping away restraint in acceptable form.

Other subjects are daily concerns of the journal, housekeeping and gardening in particular. The continuity these responsibilities bring to Sarton's days as a woman living alone carry over into the writing. She writes, for instance, of her need for structure in daily physical activity; but the journal is structure too. Both hold together the emotional fragments the woman alone must face. . . . Writing is at least a contrast to the physical demands of the house and grounds, and the journal is the best literary construct for that part of her life. Solitude is a beginning, but simple physical isolation is an ambivalent condition— at times refreshing and at times intensely disturbing. Sarton comes to understand her ''separateness,'' that is, her isolation as a solitude in a spiritual sense: ''We are aware of God only when we cease to be aware of ourselves, not in the negative sense of denying the self, but in the sense of losing self, in admiration and joy.'' Attention to life in even its smallest details through writing becomes a kind of dissolution of self. It is a positive experience that leads to revelation. . . . (pp. 57-9)

In 1973, May Sarton moved from Nelson to York, Maine, where she took up residence in a house on the coast. Two journals have been published since that time: *The House by the Sea* (1977) and *Recovering* (1980). While the dark period in Nelson heralded a need for change, Sarton found her new proximity to the sea inspiring as a clear break from old associations and sorrows. The new home and land required special attention, particularly gardening. A new landscape (the rocky shore and sea) required new perceptions. The first of the Maine journals is a ''happy'' book overall as new beginnings and new hopes shape the writer's work. *Recovering* is a far different record—quite literally the account of a mental and physical recovery from life-threatening illness. Taken together, these journals do not so much 'complete' a story as bring it full circle. . . . The move was not abrupt; Sarton was coaxed to Maine by friends who knew of the house called ''Wild Knoll'' and, as Sarton explains, she really ''had two years in which to dream myself into the change.'' ''Home'' is an imaginative construct, and the shift of scene from New Hampshire to Maine brought about a new need for documenting, of telling again the story of home and house. (pp. 61-2)

In New Hampshire, the job of creating home became a job of restoration and rebuilding. The physical reality of the house itself loomed over much of the daily chores and carried over into the writing. ''Wild Knoll,'' a spacious house set back from the shore and surrounded by woods, pulled the writer's focus further away from the confines of house and yard; from Sarton's front door, a direct path meanders through tall grasses (the "wild knoll") and runs headlong into the rocky surf below—a stunning sight. . . . The landscape is cathartic, a touchstone for emotions as well as a filter for the worst of them. The poet's eye turns outward. . . . What grew so deeply inward during the writing of *Journal of a Solitude* was [in *The House by the Sea*] pushing the limits of private space as far as the eye could see. Outer and inner landscapes joined in her sense of personal boundaries. In fact, during the early months of the new journal, Sarton expresses herself in metaphors clearly drawn from the new surroundings. . . . Sarton's image of the self pulling away from land to "tighten up, go inward" is a drawing away from the house on land. The eye looking out to sea from the doorway of "Wild Knoll" is now the eye casting off from the rocky surf, leaving the house behind. Perhaps a subtle substitution is evident here: the house at Nelson with all its painful associations is really the house on the knoll. Sarton's voyage inward through the new house is a drawing away from the past towards the sea, which is inspiration and the return of poetry.

In *The House by the Sea,* solitude, isolation, aging and death are bound up together. What we witness in this particular journal is the process by which a fear or anxiety is recognized, weighed, contemplated and finally connected to other values. We see the idea rising from a natural context—a daily chore, a piece of news arriving with the mail, a memory sparked. While Sarton may feel quite definitely one day that aging is partly a cutting off from the past (because old friends are gone and seem to have taken the past with them), she can sincerely explain some time later, "I do lead two lives, the past and the present, and sometimes the past is far more vivid than the present." There is always room in a well executed journal for backing up, retracting, modifying or just ignoring what's been claimed before. If *The House by the Sea* can be summed up as a work, one would have to note its fluctuations between what it hopes to be and what it reads as being. (pp. 62-3)

The House by the Sea continues the great subject of solitude as a condition of life and as a focus of literary materials while it chronicles a year of life engrossed with new beginnings, new adjustments and—as we learn by the end of that year—new appreciations of aging and death. *Recovering* (1980) is quite literally the tool Sarton used to mend a physically and emotionally shattered life—'recovering' as a means and an end. In fact, *Recovering* begins with a recognition that the journal as a literary form may be Sarton's particular talent and her most valued activity as a writer. There is an urgency in the opening of this record (dated December 28, 1978): "I had thought not to begin a new journal until I am seventy, four years from now, but perhaps the time has come to sort out, and see whether I can restore a sense of meaning and continuity to my life by this familiar means."

Routine writing—that is, daily recording of experience—quickly organizes itself. Sarton, whose reasons for publishing her private work had shifted through the years, now felt that laying herself bare on paper was "the only valid medicine against the flu, old age, depression." Day after day, the journal charts a course of despair. . . . The reader is caught, quite dramatically, on the threshold of a personal disaster that Sarton senses but cannot, of course, foresee clearly. Sarton, as the character of her story, seems to be using her journal as a kind of countdown to—what? There is design to the entries: daily chores and daily troubles combine to assert, again and again, that the writer is doomed. The "disaster" follows:

Friday, June 8th

> Saw Dr. Dow yesterday and, as I have suspected for some time, I shall be going into the York hospital on the seventeenth for a biopsy, followed at once, Dr. Dow believes, by a mastectomy of the left breast. It is no surprise, and in some ways a relief, for I know that the amount of suppressed rage I have suffered since last fall *had* to find some way out . . . I look on the operation as a kind of exorcism. Something had to give, as they say.

Of course, it is not as simple as that. Sarton realizes soon after the operation is over that the physical pain could not and did not alleviate the emotional turmoil and that she had not emerged "like a phoenix from the fire, reborn." The journey back to a sense of self and well-being would start all over again.

But the journal continues. It is, as before, a medicine that the writer (and reader, of course) knows cannot be ignored. The writing, in fact, begins to serve a purpose other than that of a simple cathartic exercise or reinforcement for creativity. In these particular circumstances, the journal becomes a witness to the transformation of despair into hope and renewal. The reader, carried along, becomes a witness too. (pp. 64-5)

Recovering is not simply a book of revelations, nor is it entirely a "success" story. Sarton confronts the fact of her physical "mutilation" as evidence "that the door has closed forever on passionate communion with another human being"; at the same time, she "would like to believe when I die that I have given myself away like a tree that sows seeds every spring and never counts the loss, because it is not loss. . . ." Whatever failures she was experiencing that year as a lover (a relationship was ending) and as a woman stricken by cancer, her writing continued to connect her to something beyond and outside the self—her readers certainly, but more importantly to the larger conception of literary identity. It might be true to say that Sarton's desire to "give herself away" in work was a kind of intentional self-effacement to counter physical deterioration. There was still anger to deal with, and fear, but the focus of the journal was on gut-level pain, so that various issues were forced out in the open that remained shadowy in the earlier works. The journal becomes an attempt to resolve the past or at least clear away patches of old grief. . . . (p. 66)

Acceptance—of self, of the past, of the future—is the final movement of *Recovering*. Sarton begins again to "center" her life as autumn approaches. Her "revelations" are provocative, and rather than shutting doors on issues they reorganize Sarton's (and the reader's) perception of her solitary life. One of the deepest understandings she comes to is a new truth about her relationship with the unnamed former lover:

> To see a person for himself or herself, not for one's feelings about them, requires wisdom, and I must assume that it is part of the ascension of true love beyond the initial passion and need. . . . How does one achieve perfect detachment? Partly perhaps by accepting the essence of a being for what it is, not wishing to change it, accepting.

Sarton's mood is somber but the reader recognizes that detachment is a quality she is trying to develop not only towards her former lover but for herself as well. It is a huge step towards the restoration of well-being. . . . Sarton's final achievement in *Recovering,* and, indeed, throughout the course of her published memoirs and journals, is not a resolution of the rage, despair, confusion, and darkness of the many days, weeks and months of writing. The great art of private writing as a literary experience is exactly what Sarton concluded—enlarging the perimeter of the intensely personal into the universal. The universal value of such reading is a recognition that one not only experiences life in such ways as these volumes record, but that one survives, "recovered" and renewed. (pp. 66-8)

Suzanne Owens, "House, Home and Solitude: Memoirs and Journals of May Sarton," in May Sarton: Woman and Poet, edited by Constance Hunting, National Poetry Foundation, Inc., 1982, pp. 53-68.

GEORGE BAILIN

In the preparation of a manuscript which is intended to give accurate impressions of some of the writings of May Sarton, one feels very much like an inexperienced, untraveled adventurer who has arrived at a grand vista. From the place where he suddenly finds himself standing, he sees it all: the mountains, the high peaks, the sharp drop in the valley wall, the stretch of desert, and perhaps above all, the clarity and the color of it quickly outstripping his first stumbling words. He quickly is aware of the fact that he cannot say very much that will convey what he has seen, yet others back home want to have, and deserve to have, some comment on his travels. His first impulse then is to say: you must see this. Then he resigns himself to the fact that what he has seen is after all quite out of his reach, out of his powers to describe. And so he begins to write. Something like this, one supposes:

There is everything here.

There is passion which seems suprahuman, there is pulverizing joy, poem after poem. But there is also pain here, a falling, a darkness to match that bright light which was just seen. This is the play of brilliance and of gloom in the mind of May Sarton as the world changes, as the situations change. There is hope, tall statements of certain aspirations that tower beyond the clouds. But there are stretches of aridity and realistic, sober awareness that such hope is not justified. There is that surge of emotion and strength that rises in May Sarton when she knows, because she has felt it in her nerves and her muscles, that she alone hears the distant voice of the human community. Therefore, she senses that on occasion she is speaking for all the men and women who ever lived, who ever dreamed for that which all of us long: peace and plenty and assurance and love; and there is also the abrupt awareness equally true, but on another day, at another time, that there is no one, that she is alone. She knows that each person is called on to live at least two lives: that of the individual being as well as that of the member of a nation called humanity. That these are separate roles, irreconcilable, necessary, demanding. (pp. 263-64)

May Sarton says somewhere that she prefers poetry to fiction writing since it is in poetry that she is permitted to explore her feelings, while in the fiction she is enabled to delve into her thinking. She is well aware that intuition as highly developed as hers can find, does discover, in a sonnet, what many a scribe has labored after futilely in a large opus. And yet her fiction has strength, is vibrating with creative energies and vivid lessons that seem somehow or other to have eluded even wiser men than this writer. One feels sure sooner or later that the body of her work, the novels and the tales which she has written will come to receive the praise that is their due. It seems to this reviewer that the fiction is sometimes overlooked not for any weakness of its own, not because there is any lack in it, but because the clarity of the line, the care of the plotting, the creation of the characters, all of this issues from a conscious-

ness that is unhurried, that is filled with dignity, that is meticulous about its vision of reality, that is moving harmoniously. One can then understand that this 20th century with its haste, its taste for the violent, a hunger after the bizarre, its peculiar and distorted understandings, can and does easily miss the beauty and the proportion in well-crafted writing. That her novels are not more celebrated is an indictment of our times. (p. 264)

[It appears] that May Sarton can be best understood, most carefully judged, most thoroughly enjoyed, when one knows these things: that May Sarton is primarily a Platonist, that she is a consummate intellectual who values, even overvalues the powers of the mind . . . , that she is, in the best sense, a utopian, as was Thomas Browne, Sir Francis Bacon, even John Milton, because each had a vision of paradise, that she is in large measure a mystic, although the present scene cannot, does not escape her attention. She is a mystic with roots in the real world. Of course, these are sweeping comments, and perhaps they are not always supportable. They may be in some cases shown to be faulty. However, if these large generalizations are permitted to be used as keys to her work, we shall be able to penetrate her writings more fully, with more intelligence, with more pleasure than would otherwise be possible. (p. 265)

May Sarton has taken on herself the job of making deductions about this cosmos in which we live, she has taken hold of the thread which she finds in her hands, and with courage, vitality, with an incredible hopefulness, follows where it leads.

It has already been stated that May Sarton is a Platonist, and Platonism is a complex of ideas, whose doctrines state that the enduring realities are Ideas, while the relative world, the world of time and space, is ephemeral by comparison. (One is astonished to see in May Sarton's work that her high art, the fusion of her passion with the people, the times, the events through which she has lived, begin to take on the qualities of the Idea, that which is lasting. Indeed it is a measure of her skill that she is able to do what Keats did in some of his very best work.) The sects of the modern world, the various institutions, the Christian ethic, for all its breadth, are too narrow to hold her. Her spiritual posture is a dynamic, one that moves and grows as it assimilates experience, as it enlarges by using each happening to nourish the perspective being built. She is an avid explorer of spiritual life. And by this, we mean the vast, the very widest sense of spirit imaginable. And beyond. However, she is also a physical being. These opposites make for the most fruitful tension.

Let us have an example or two of her spiritual dialectic. We can find that in her very first work, when she was in her twenties or thirties. We refer to the poem, **"A Letter to James Stephens."** May Sarton writes that he told her these things:

> . . . Forget your love, your little war, your ache.
> Forget that haunting so mysterious face
> And write for an abstracted beauty's sake. . .
> Your job is to draw out the essence and provide
> The word that will endure, comfort, sustain a man.
> This is your honor. This should be your pride.

This is an artist who all her life has been concerned with an abstracted beauty, not merely as language, not as tenuous thought, not as some impossible ideal, but where possible, in the here and now, a temporal form, a spatial location, a concrete demonstration of beauty, a nexus in which heaven and earth, so to speak, would be joined.

With some careful thought, one concludes that such a position as this is perhaps not tenable. All the more reason for Sarton to take it! She is not one to be bound by logic. She is willing to be burned in the fires of prudence and reason if it must be, but she will not take a backward step. She believes, and one may find in this same poem proof of it, *that the very act of writing a poem* which is generated by the afflatus of spirit, by the fires of passion, of passionate conviction, is magical, is potent, is the effective and transforming prayer:

> "... My honor (and I cherish it for it is hardly won)
> Is to be pure in this: is to believe
> That to write down these perishable songs for one,
> For one alone, and out of love, is not to grieve
> But to build on the quicksand of despair
> *A house where very man may take his ease*...."

The italics are mine, but the magic is Sarton's. What a daring. What a supreme madness! What a utopian! Is this not the innocence and the power of the child? And May Sarton is, among other personae, the everlasting child, as we shall see. She is the perennial innocent, the harmless, the loving, the inquisitive, the injured, the wide-eyed and loving child. Thank goodness for her prolonged youth! (pp. 265-66)

One should not think, one cannot believe reading her verse, and going through her journals, that May Sarton does not have a good grip on the "real world" and, conversely, one dare not assume that this space-time universe does not command her fullest attention. (p. 268)

May Sarton from the first was a hunter for happiness. In her adolescence we find evidence of her experiments with love, in her poem **"First Snow,"** from *Encounter in April* (1937).... Of course May Sarton knew love, knows it in all its forms, there is ample evidence. And of course from the first, she could detect the flaw, the thin crack, the slight wavering. She looked for solidity and for companionship. But it was not there. In her twenties there is further testimony of a similar sort, perhaps even stronger, more alarming, always filled with truth.

In **"Summary,"** which appears in *Inner Landscape* (1939), she writes this: "In the end it is the dark for which all lovers pine..." and "In the end it is escape of which all lovers dream." But the corrosive insight comes here, it appears to this writer:

> ... They are found to believe
> That love endures and their pain is infinite
> Who have not learned that each single touch they give,
> Every kiss, every word they speak holds death in it....

What could be more clear?

But May Sarton is a celebrant of this world too! She enlarges it with her praise, she enjoys it with her mind and her body, she toasts it with her wine, though she clearly sees what it is, and what it could never be. (pp. 270-71)

In times to come, when chroniclers of the twentieth century turn their attention to the motivations behind writers, when they look at the soul, the psyche of our times, and when they want to find an artist who outlined them, whose hopes and whose thinking give a full picture of what it means to be a living, sentient writer of this part of human history, they will be able to find much of their problem solved by reading and re-reading Sarton.

Not only is she a poet, not only does she write novels and journals, but she holds herself up for all to see, large, clear. She examines her thinking in the open, so that one can see what a writer is, what is being accomplished, why, how. This artist reveals herself fully, and outlines the spirit of the times as well. (p. 272)

Sarton has not only looked within. Only? As if that were not enough! But she has looked without as well, to friends, to colleagues, to other cultures and nations also. And some of the most impressive writing has come from that searching in those places. She has looked, for example, in her poem **"Indian Dances"** in *The Lion and the Rose,* to the native American Indian, his magic and his dances.... She is impressed with the dignity and the stateliness of the Indians who are at one with the forces of the universe, who do not suffer from that veneer which some call civilization, a polish that often abrades the skin and suffocates the self. In her poem **"Santos: New Mexico"** she talks about a release that is known to the spontaneous and unschooled dwellers of the desert:

> We must go down into the dungeons of the heart,
> To the dark places where modern mind imprisons
> All that is not defined and thought apart,
> We must let out the terrible creative visions ...

Yet it is not an acceptance of the old tribal ways, or of the old Christian myth (in this same poem) that Sarton is after, but rather a new departure, a new way of seeing our time and our space, a perspective that will be individual and unique, and by its very nature not susceptible to collective approval or rejection. It is the uncovering of the self in each of us, for it is an energy that wants to grow. (pp. 273-74)

Earlier I wrote that though Sarton is a mystic, she has her roots in the real world. And so it is. As a matter of fact, her mysticism, at either end, touches spiritual truth. There is the contact with the abstract reality that lies behind the world of sounds and sights, but there is the immanent reality that is seen when she looks carefully at the objects, attends carefully to the events that take place before her. She finds much to admire, much to worship, in this natural scene. For this essayist, the visual splendors Sarton writes about reach their peak in her volume called *A Private Mythology* (1966). (p. 276)

Her whole voyage around the world is here, done with bold strokes, with precision. In **"Birthday on the Acropolis,"** the look of the Greek sky is captured: "Stepping out from the plane / To stand in the Greek light / In the knife-clean air. / Too sudden, too brilliant? Who can bear this shining? / The pitiless clarity? / Each bone felt the shock." The world of the senses is loved and appreciated: a cup of tea, a bright cloud, a small bird; the small and the large are at home in the world of May Sarton. It is a rare hospitality, where all receive their due, where none is a stranger. The pressure of her invention is able to invest the passing moment, what appears trivial, with the fullness of permanence. Each small scene becomes a tableau in the mind of the reader; long after one has put the books down, there are reverberations. (pp. 277-78)

She intimates, as she writes, as she muses over the scenes outside her windows, what is there that is not important? What is there in this world that is not burning with the sacred fire, which cannot communicate to us that blaze, that holy ignition, if only we will sit still and look and listen, and give that absolute attention? She has read Simone Weil, and she knows as did Weil that the complete, the whole, the detached and compelled attention is the same as prayer. Sarton worships the visible and that which is not visible as well. She contemplates her life. It is a gigantic effort, one which we are not likely to see again soon. And it is a gaze which is indifferent to what is being said in the schools of poetry, it is a listening that does not stoop to the local gossip of smaller thinkers. She is a Thoreauvian for our time, more charming, more frail, equally intelligent, equally bright. (p. 278)

For this writer, May Sarton is one of the great ones of our time. She shows consistent power, and continuing genius. Not because she is white hot in every line that she ever wrote, not because each novel is one which smashes the audience with unfailing power and magical, magnificent spectacle. Not at all. Precisely because the writing is detailed, faithful, complete, meticulous, and honest, and because the work is passionate, inquiring, brimming with the joy and sorrow of life on this planet, because she is one of us, she is our voice and our spirit. When have we last seen such a lively intelligence? Do we have the time, the patience, the love to examine and to listen, to cherish the art that we have here before us? Judging her, we are ourselves being held up to the light. And the implications of that inquiry connect with our own selves, our own unfoldment or lack of it.

To this essayist, it is as though a small girl named May Sarton sat one day in a window seat in her house and opened a book of poems by John Keats, and read, re-read the lines:

> Heard melodies are sweet, but those unheard
> Are sweeter; therefore, ye soft pipes, play on;
> Not to the sensual ear, but more endeared,
> Pipe to the spirit ditties of no tone . . .

And May Sarton has been listening to that unheard song, and she has many times merged with it, letting it seize her, living in it, speaking of it, growing with that music which is at the core of our own being, that silent truth, the quiet existence, that ineffable love and beauty which are the elements of this superb writer's own life. One day all of us will say, and will show, how grateful we are to have her among us. (pp. 279-80)

> George Bailin, "A Shining in the Dark: May Sarton's Accomplishment," in May Sarton: Woman and Poet, edited by Constance Hunting, National Poetry Foundation, Inc., 1982, pp. 263-80.

JOSEPH PARISI

[In **Letters from Maine: New Poems** Sarton again] displays the sensitivity, charm, and craft that distinguish her many other volumes, though the tone here is decidedly autumnal. Beginning with a series of "letters" recalling a brief but intense love affair that has sadly passed, she returns to nature for frequent inspiration and hope. Particularly touching are her several descriptive meditations on the sea and coastline and the many reflections that make up her sequence **"A Winter Garland."** Mortality is much on her mind, but in considering last things she also concentrates upon making the very most of each present, precious moment. If the style and formal structure of these verses is unapologetically old-fashioned, what Sarton has to say is of perennial interest and worth hearing again.

> Joseph Parisi, in a review of "Letters from Maine: New Poems," in Booklist, Vol. 81, No. 12, February 15, 1985, p. 818.

JOSEPHINE HUMPHREYS

May Sarton has for decades been writing about the inner lives of thoughtful women. In an almost frightening number of nov-

els, journals and volumes of poetry (over 40 at last count), she has indefatigably kept up what amounts to a lifelong investigation of women in work and in love. . . .

At age 70, Cam [of **The Magnificent Spinster**] is writing her first novel, and she has a specific purpose—"to celebrate an extraordinary woman." Jane has just died; she was Cam's seventh-grade teacher and lifetime friend. Fiction, Cam thinks, will serve her purpose better than memoir or biography because it will free her "from the struggle with minute detail, with dates and facts," and let her make an "imaginary reconstruction" of Jane's life. "I want to make her come alive," Cam says.

From the day she first entered Jane's history class, Cam knew Jane was no dull "old maid." She had passions—for politics and theater and language, for her family's summer cottage, for her teaching position. She had a "passionate interest" in the League of Nations. But her passions did not extend to men. As far as Cam can tell, Jane never had a love affair. One early friendship with a young man was "innocent and deep" and suited both parties. Maurice thought he might never marry; Jane was certain she would not. . . .

Her deepest friendships were with women. The work of a dedicated schoolteacher, as May Sarton convincingly shows it, can be not merely hard but killing. Jane's friendships sustained her as teaching gradually wore her down and, finally, betrayed her. But Cam doesn't know the details of Jane's closest friendship, with her colleague Marian Chase. Of the summer Jane and Marian spent together in England, Cam says only that the trip turned out to be a disaster. "Whatever went on between those two will never be known and perhaps should not be, but Jane told my mother that after a month Marian had closed the door against her completely, and refused even to speak at meals."

Cam backs off from the closed door. "I . . . am not a good enough novelist," she says, "to invent episodes that never really happened or that I can only imagine as having happened." But wait. May Sarton is the real novelist and a good enough one to invent episodes. She could certainly tell what went on between those two. Her narrative reluctance here doesn't make sense; it handicaps her own narrator, who can only add to the list of Jane's virtues. Jane was full of life, extraordinary, glamorous, innocent. But Jane isn't shown with the sort of detail that enlivens.

Cam thought that in writing a novel she would be free from the struggle with detail. But a novel should be one long struggle with detail, not of dates and facts but of difficult scenes, of character caught off guard. Words like "passionate" and "glamorous" are the opposite of detail. They become in a novel almost useless, the vocabulary of eulogy.

If Cam fails as May Sarton's narrator, she succeeds as a character. She is "more vulnerable and more conflicted" than Jane. Her family life is a mess. She has no inherited fortune, as Jane did, so work is more than her passion, it is her food. While Jane was apparently without sexuality, Cam has had to come to terms with her love for a woman, Ruth, a love that has brought her both comfort and anguish.

In a scene with her snake of a father at the Harvard Club, during which he shows more interest in the hashbrowns than in his daughter's plea for understanding, and in a later scene when Ruth dies, there is evident in Cam what was missing in Jane. It is the magnificence of the ordinary, and it is more striking, in these brief glimpses, than all of the extraordinary Jane.

Josephine Humphreys, "Inventing Women," in The New York Times Book Review, *October 27, 1985, p. 26.*

VALERIE MINER

The Magnificent Spinster, May Sarton's forty-second book, is a model and metaphor of her literary life. A rather magnificent spinster herself, Sarton has had an iconoclastic and prolific writing career, publishing seventeen previous novels, fourteen books of poetry, eight volumes of non-fiction and two children's books. This complex new novel is provocative in itself and as a mirror of past work, reflecting such classic Sarton issues as social conscience, aging, women's autonomy, friendship and the nature of art. . . .

Sarton's books are infused with a European urbanity, a Yankee sternness and a *raffiné* pugnaciousness. . . . She was nominated for two National Book Awards in 1956, but since then has fallen out of fashion among members of the literati too busy being clever-clever to appreciate the brilliant simplicity of her style and the passionate courage of her ideas. Some reviewers have even criticized her for being closeted in her writing, forgetting that she lost a couple of jobs in 1965 because of the lesbianism of *Mrs. Stevens Hears the Mermaids Singing.* But readers have long applauded her traditional narrative approach, her direct, accessible language as well as her examination of moral development. And readers keep her books alive. (p. 7)

I, like many of her diverse readers, am sparked by the honest, fervent and disciplined practice of her art. The new novel is a satisfying reconsideration of former themes and a journey into new territory.

What is familiar in *The Magnificent Spinster* is the cherished New England setting and the nature of the two protagonists—charming, cultivated women of elegant determination. The book opens as Cam Arnold, a retired history professor, is beginning to write a novel about her beloved teacher and lifelong friend Jane Reid, who has just died. Cam's book requires extensive research into Jane's life as well as hours of contemplation of her own life.

Born in 1896, Jane grows up with four sisters in a wealthy Boston family complete with a British nanny. After graduating from Vassar, she goes to France to assist with World War I orphans. She returns to Cambridge to teach elementary school and to work as a community activist. Throughout her life, Jane exudes a radiant talent for friendship.

Meanwhile, Cam matures under Jane's light, attends Vassar, sets off for Europe, comes back to teach history at a small college near Boston and continues to flourish in Jane's friendship. Sarton is at her best shaping the distinctive temperaments of these friends—balancing Cam's rash enthusiasm with Jane's grace—and in revealing how the women complement and confound each other.

It is the private greatness of Jane and Cam that distinguishes *The Magnificent Spinster.* The book's power lies not in the characters' high drama, but rather in the quality of their deeply engaged days. Cam is practicing a sort of feminist history, recovering the worldly contributions of an "unpublic" public woman. . . . Jane chooses a single, singular path which would

be better understood and appreciated by subsequent generations.

Inspiration for *The Magnificent Spinster* came from Sarton's own primary school teacher, Anne Longfellow Thorp, to whom the book is dedicated. And it is perhaps this proximity which accounts for the novel's one serious fault: Cam's portrayal of Jane is overly reverent and sentimental. Sometimes we are told about Jane, rather than being permitted to see her in person; Cam (or Sarton) presumes an intimacy between Jane and the readers she has not quite created.

In contrast, Cam's own character is vital and idiosyncratic. I suspect Cam's prominence in the novel was a second thought. Sarton said in a lecture on "The Design of the Novel" (given at Scripps College in 1963), "Characters, if they are alive at all, prove to have an existence of their own, insist on breaking out of too arbitrary formulations. A character may change the whole tone of a novel by its intrusion, by its radical thrust up from the subconscious." *The Magnificent Spinster* turns into a story about Cam as well as about Jane and about the two of them together.

Although Sarton's books could hardly be called political novels (with the exception of *Faithful Are the Wounds*), most of them are set in the framework of an acute social conscience. Here, for instance, we find Cam challenging sexism among her contemporaries and fighting fascism in the Spanish Civil War. We see Jane helping Germans reconstruct their lives after World War II and then returning to contribute to the Cambridge Community Center. Jane confronts Boston racism—and her own bigotry—through her growing friendship with Ellen, a Black woman who directs the Center. Jane, fuelled with asexual passion, is at first shocked when her cousin Jay confides he is homosexual, but ultimately comes to his defense in a court case. Throughout *The Magnificent Spinster,* lesbian attraction is acknowledged without the throat-clearing fanfare of more didactic lesbian novels. Cam and her lover Ruth share a tender, satisfying life.

Understated social context marks other Sarton novels—in the examination of the dreadful treatment of old people in *As We Are Now;* in the consciousness about rights of the dying in *A Reckoning;* in the exploration of academic ethics in *The Small Room.* (pp. 7-8)

[In *The Magnificent Spinster*] Sarton reclaims the word "spinster" with an ardor worthy of Mary Daly, who writes in *Gyn/Ecology,* "She who has chosen her Self, who defines her Self, by choice, neither in relation to children nor to men, who is Self-identified, is a Spinster. . . ." For anyone dismayed by the current feminist infatuation for motherhood, it is refreshing to read a novel in which the women do stand on their own. Being spinsters allows Cam and Jane to give to their communities with time and spirit unavailable to those who have chosen to reproduce and live in cloistered families.

Jane spins a web of allegiances with friends and colleagues, "Yes, with a hundred delicate threads binding a hundred lives to hers. . . ." This is a novel about friendship in which the profound connections are companions and comrades and confidantes rather than lovers. We follow Jane's friendship with Cam, with Ellen, Frances, Marian and Lucy. This thread of sustaining personal loyalty seams together other Sarton fiction and journals like *The House by the Sea* as well as her poetry. . . .

One of the subplots involves the search for an appropriate biographer for Jane's illustrious grandfather, yet another writer.

"'But heaven knows,'" says her cousin Jay, "'no biography tells the whole truth. It is truth filtered through someone's mind . . . someone of another generation, often, as in this case—the whole ethos has changed.'" Cam offers a more benign view of the biographer: ". . . in fifty years no one will exist who remembers Jane Reid. I want to celebrate her. I want to make her come alive for those people who never knew her." Jane is Cam's muse as well as her mentor. *The Magnificent Spinster* is a startling portrait of Cam as a woman coming into her own as an artist at the age of 70. . . .

That art is a challenge and blessing to the artist is a common Sarton theme. Writing Jane's story has the same distilling satisfaction for Cam that "serving Bach" has for Anna in *Anger* or composing poetry has for Hilary in *Mrs. Stevens Hears the Mermaids Singing*. . . .

[*The Magnificent Spinster*] is an intricate, yet accessible experiment in form; a testimony to independence; an enlightening portrayal of old age; a celebration of friendship and an engrossing story. (p. 8)

> Valerie Miner, *"The Light of the Muse,"* in The Women's Review of Books, *Vol. III, No. 3, December, 1985, pp. 7-8.*

Vernon Scannell

1922-

English poet, novelist, autobiographer, scriptwriter, editor, and critic.

Scannell is respected for his unaffected traditional verse in which he examines themes relating to war, violence, and mortality as well as such domestic issues as marriage and aging. Grounded in human experience and adhering to established forms, Scannell's poetry chronicles in a wry anecdotal style the ordinary setbacks of what he terms "the walking wounded" of contemporary society. Anthony Thwaite commented: "Scannell is at his best as a sardonic, bruised reporter of experience, the man with a slow wink and a fading black eye." Eschewing abstractions, Scannell employs economical, straightforward diction, and the accessibility of his verse has made him a popular poet in England.

Scannell's works are informed by several difficulties he endured as a young man. While recuperating from a severe wound he suffered as a soldier in France in 1944, Scannell became demoralized by military life, and following the Allied victory in Europe, he deserted the army. In addition to holding numerous odd jobs, Scannell was a professional boxer, an occupation he often depicts in his novels and which he employs as a metaphor for life in several poems. In 1947, Scannell was arrested for desertion and was ordered to spend time in a mental institution before being discharged by the army. These experiences and other significant events in Scannell's life are detailed in two autobiographical works, *The Tiger and the Rose* (1971) and *A Proper Gentleman* (1977).

Shortly after his discharge, Scannell published his first volume of poetry, *Graves and Resurrections* (1948), which contains bleak poems influenced by the apocalypse poets of England. In *A Mortal Pitch* (1957), his first book to gain significant critical attention, Scannell employs crisp phrasing, adheres to traditional rhyme patterns and metrical arrangements, and examines topics relating to war, teaching, and marriage. These features recur in such later volumes as *A Sense of Danger* (1962), *Walking Wounded: Poems, 1962-1965* (1965), and *The Winter Man* (1973), which are generally considered his most accomplished collections of verse. In a review of *New and Collected Poems, 1950-1980* (1982), Alan Brownjohn linked Scannell with such poets as Gavin Ewart, Roy Fuller, and A.S.J. Tessimond. Brownjohn characterized their work as "a poetry which embraces the immediate, wears and describes the scars of ordinary living, is plain (including plain frightened and plain indignant) about life and death and moral problems, rarely intricate, rarely delicate, always absorbing in its firm yet friendly insistence that the here-and-now of modern urban existence is what almost all of us have to fit into for most of the time."

In his novels, Scannell employs unaffected language, ironic humor, and pathos while examining many of the themes contained in his verse. *The Face of the Enemy* (1961) concerns aging, adultery, and the pressures of modern urban life; *The Big Time* (1965) focuses upon a boxer who is exploited by a wealthy man; and *Ring of Truth* (1983) examines issues relating to boxing and human relationships. Scannell has also written

several radio plays and coedited the anthology *Not without Glory: Poets of the Second World War* (1976).

(See also *Contemporary Authors*, Vols. 5-8, rev. ed.; *Contemporary Authors New Revision Series*, Vols. 8, 24; and *Dictionary of Literary Biography*, Vol. 27.)

ROY FULLER

[Vernon Scannell] needs all the help he can muster to make his poems memorable, for his thought is apt to be rather commonplace. Several of these pieces [in *A Mortal Pitch*], **"How to Fill in a Crossword Puzzle"**, **"Gunpowder Plot"** and **"Schoolroom on a Wet Afternoon"**, are already quite well known through anthologies and they undoubtedly contain neat ideas, resourcefully worked out. But when one takes them apart one sees that their basic notions are literary in the pejorative sense and their construction lacking in distinction of language. Mr Scannell's book can, however, be read with pleasure and whatever he has to say is at least uttered in clear and unpretentious tones.

Roy Fuller, in a review of "A Mortal Pitch," in London Magazine, Vol. 4, No. 5, May, 1957, p. 93.

DONALD HALL

Most of the verse written, published, and broadcast in our years is simply pale and incompetent, with gloomy flashes of felicity. Vernon Scannell's *The Masks of Love* seems to me a typical contemporary collection. **"The Masks of Love"** is the best; it is a 'good idea for a poem', and most of its words are adequate in their sarcasm, but at the end it falls into a stale familiarity, and nothing happens. From the height of this near-miss, we fall all too frequently to the spectacle of clichés dancing in a ring.... In most of these poems, the author seems unaware that he is using metaphor; 'labour' is 'crowned with love' in a poem to which the regal metaphor is irrelevant (to say nothing of the familiarity of the phrase). Scannell's metre is sloppy; inadvertent alexandrines wander hopelessly among the pentameters. In short, Scannell lacks art. There are poem-length thoughts but no poems here. In **"Letter to a Poet"**, Scannell praises poetry as able to 'Convey what prose could not express / Without a loss of vividness'. Now this is merest cliché, but it raises again the question of relative standards. I wonder if contemporary prose, vivid or not, allows such phrases as 'youth's ebullient song', which Scannell uses? I suspect that it is easier to get away with bad writing if you call it poetry. Later in his **"Letter to a Poet"**, Scannell writes, 'Thus with the poem: it's common sense'. Alas, one needs a bit more than this solid, British, middle-class virtue.... (p. 302)

Donald Hall, "Habits of Language," in New Statesman, Vol. LIX, No. 1511, February 27, 1960, pp. 302-03.

THE TIMES LITERARY SUPPLEMENT

In [Jenny] Joseph's *The Unlooked for Season*, ... the best poems plunge the reader into a mass of particular observations. The scene-setting is often so scrupulous as to seem obsessive.... Mr. Scannell [in *The Masks of Love*], too, has an eye for detail; but his role is active, his approach more worldly than Miss Joseph's, and his poems are neater, more ironical.... The strong, often violent, movement of much of his work puts the element of control at a premium.

The conclusion of **"The Lynching"** illustrates this, and a good deal else, about Mr. Scannell's poems. It is after the hanging; the men responsible are riding home as though pursued by Furies. The vocabulary is rough and energetic: the "speed", "lunge" and "drag" of the lynchers contrasting violently with their "deed" which "Beneath the non-commital dark / Star-punctured sky ... hung still / And black". This is what follows:

> And in the town the white wives in their white
> Nightgowns listened to the clock
> And with their wide-eyed fingers plucked
> Those gowns which, fastened at the neck
> And neat at feet, need not be roughed that night
> To prove their husband's manhood, or the lack.

This is the kind of writing that really stops one short. One can only call the quiet underlining of the comparison between the hanged man and the wives ("fastened at the neck / And neat at feet") unemphatic emphasis. It also reveals a quality which Mr. Scannell and Miss Joseph have in common: their ability

to speak through images. On the whole these are superbly integrated poems.

"Eye for Detail," in The Times Literary Supplement, No. 3075, February 3, 1961, p. 76.

RONALD BRYDEN

[Vernon Scannell's novel, **The Face of the Enemy,** is] a modest anti-idyll of two middle-ageing lovers who meet in a seedy Paddington drinking club where war-derelicts huddle to recapture the golden days of their youth, heroism and value. It betrays the occasional slackness of a poet using what he considers an inferior medium, but manages to smelt from drab materials a touching, dignified statement about the human need for allies against oblivion. (p. 330)

Ronald Bryden, "Adrift in England," in The Spectator, Vol. 207, No. 6950, September 8, 1961, pp. 329-330.

THE TIMES LITERARY SUPPLEMENT

That well-known figure, the ex-R.A.F. officer with a moustache which juts out like the wings of his aircraft, is the central feature of Mr. Scannell's [**The Face of the Enemy**]. He is well known because he—and his army wartime comrades—still appear in the pubs all over England today in their duffle coats. These brave men won the war, but after it they obtained little enough recognition....

Mr. Scannell has had the excellent idea of doing these men justice, in a novel which is as charitable as it is satirical. On the one hand, he laughs at the pretensions of these old warriors who are for ever harping back to the days of their glory.... On the other hand, he reveals, in a most moving passage at the end, that these men, most of whom appear stupid, bitter (inevitably) and bigoted, are the salt of the earth.

He does it in the following way. These men, whose common plight keeps them permanently together, respect only one thing, "to have had a good war". They have a little club in London, "The Combined Ops", where they meet almost every evening, to get drunk and nostalgic over their gins and beers. A few female characters add colour, and hate a coward even more than the men do. Then suddenly it is revealed that one of their number—a member of "The Combined Ops" club—was court-martialled during the war for desertion in the face of the enemy. How this very human and well-drawn character solves the problem, thanks to the woman he loves and, in the last resort, to the decency of the ex-warriors of "The Combined Ops" club—each of whom has been drawn as no more than a *miles gloriosus*—is the theme of this well-written novel.

"Forgotten Heroes," in The Times Literary Supplement, No. 3109, September 29, 1961, p. 641.

RICHARD MAYNE

Vernon Scannell's subject [in **The Dividing Night**], adultery in the stockbroker country, sounds dispiritingly unambitious, especially by comparison with his last year's **The Face of the Enemy:** but in fact his theme is once more that of man's reluctance to accept the cruel joke of growing middle-aged. His hero is a married publisher just under 40 who starts an affair with a neighbour's greedy and voluptuous wife.... The background is London and the commuter's countryside, the settings are roadhouses, parked cars, and a squalid bungalow known to local bar-props as the Orgy Shed. Never has vice been made so unattractive, even by Graham Greene. Deception is followed by discovery, worry by remorse and resignation; but if this sounds dull I'm misleading you. The whole thing has harrowing authenticity. (p. 914)

Richard Mayne, "I Morti nelle Piazze," in New Statesman, Vol. LXIII, No. 1632, June 22, 1962, pp. 913-14.

JOHN DANIEL

The Dividing Night has the compelling reality one expects from a poet. John, a middle-aged publisher, finds in his own village the embodiment of every man's dream: a nymphomaniac. While his wife is visiting Mummy in Yorkshire he has a furtive, heady affair with her. But for John (public school, 'a Puritan without a religion') guilt and remorse become more than the words he imagined, and his perfect mistress is a little too perfect for his fuzzy, Calvinist conscience. It sounds like lending-library stuff. In fact, Mr. Scannell has achieved the near-miracle of making middle-class people human and of writing a very good novel about them.

John Daniel, "Cold Facts," in The Spectator, Vol. 208, No. 6991, June 22, 1962, p. 834.

ANTHONY THWAITE

Almost half the poems in *A Sense of Danger* are worth reading more than once, and if that sounds a very pale recommendation it isn't meant to be: I quite often come across poems that are worth reading once but with which I'd hardly want to live. **"The Telephone Number," "Dead Dog," "My Father's Knee," "An Old Lament Renewed,"** have that combination of interest and skill which is so rare to-day; too often one finds either the first or the second but not both. Scannell's *forte* is the anecdote, often commonplace and banal in itself but organised—seldom forced—into a poem with real depths. This he shares with Larkin, from whom I think he has learned; that sense of

that emptiness
That lies just under all we do

is made more powerful by the concreteness of detail, the exactness of observation. *A Sense of Danger* is an impressively achieved book. (p. 83)

Anthony Thwaite, "Voices and Personalities," in Encounter, Vol. XIX, No. 1, July, 1962, pp. 81-4.

JOHN MONTAGUE

To judge by his new book, *A Sense of Danger,* Vernon Scannell seems almost too real to be true, the typical contemporary English poet, his 'whole terrain a wintry cabbage patch.' His favourite method is the anecdote, told with skilful spareness (a training as a novelist, as Hardy found, is the best way to learn the poem-as-story). I say English because of his refusal—honest but obstinate—to elaborate: compare his **"Dead Dog"** with Richard Wilbur's poem on the same subject. The American poet's dog glitters even in decay, while Scannell's is a mongrel, 'ordinary as bread.' . . .

The trouble with the anecdotal technique, of course, is its tendency to slip into an O. Henry slickness (**"Incident in a Saloon Bar"**). Scannell's saving grace is that you feel the

poems, however neatly turned, are necessary to him, gestures towards sanity. For this trim landscape is haunted by the baby-faced psychopath, the raped girl 'like a fallen glove.' This obsession widens in an *ubi sunt* lament for 'the enormous dormitory' of the dead, and a poem on **"The Great War."** What terrifies in the latter is the way time has transmuted suffering into a romantic travelogue. . . . (p. 193)

John Montague, "Menaced Mildness," in The Spectator, Vol. 209, No. 6998, August 10, 1962, pp. 193-94.

THE TIMES LITERARY SUPPLEMENT

Mr. Scannell's poems [in *A Sense of Danger*] . . . spring out of, or embody realistic story-situations; the ordinary-looking man embarrassing everybody by weeping quietly in a saloon bar; the middle-aged suicide who is taking a belated revenge on the grown-ups who snubbed him in his childhood; the poet himself looking at an old address book, the telephone numbers, the addresses, now mostly meaningless, of ten years ago; the disillusioned schoolmaster remembering his own schooldays. The tradition is Hardy's, both in the honest homeliness, combined sometimes with a certain stiffness of language, and the taste, in incident, for a combination of the violent, or fateful, and the drab. . . . Mr. Scannell seems a little uncertain in his handling both of diction and rhythm, as in the rather wobbly and cacophonous lines,

and I must strangle anger
Impatience and despair when she is late
Though at her going this joy will terminate

But the sense of situation gives these poems a distinct grip.

"Poems of Truth," in The Times Literary Supplement, No. 3158, September 7, 1962, p. 674.

IAN HAMILTON

Vernon Scannell's speciality is the suburban fable and much of his subject matter [in *A Sense of Danger*] seems to have been drawn from a pious reading of his local newspaper; it is the beast in us that brings that sense of danger to our breakfast tables. But the case-book psychopaths who populate these glibly compassionate anecdotes have no more complex a presence than would be permitted them by the tabloids their author claims to despise. One suspects that Scannell has not had to stray too far from the breakfast table—physically or emotionally—to arrive at his neat position on, for example, **"The Incendiary"**—a typical situation, in which 'one small boy with a face like pallid cheese' causes a fire which is 'brazen, fierce, huge, red, gold, and zany yellow' and costs Farmer Godwin 3,000 guineas. . . . It is not unfair to suggest that a responsible press report of the plain facts of the incident would carry a good deal more imaginative conviction than the brawny dispensing of antitheses which makes up this poem; the boy could be simply small, the fire fierce, and the price 3,000 guineas and nothing important would be lost. One would still not have a poem, to be sure, but at least one's view of the facts would not be diffused by a mediocre interpretation of their middle-class significance.

This tendency to agitate a promising enough situation on to the level of florid rhetoric and then deflate it with a cosily aphoristic 'solution' pervades Scannell's book and where he is not doing this he is simply being 'moderate'. . . . Less literary self-consciousness and more direct and concentrated observation would help, of course, but there is little in this book to raise one's hopes. (pp. 84-5)

Ian Hamilton, in a review of "A Sense of Danger,"
in London Magazine, *n.s. Vol. 2, No. 8, November,*
1962, pp. 82-5.

THE TIMES LITERARY SUPPLEMENT

[*The Big Time*] concerns a tycoon named George Melville, who is obsessed by the idea of turning his naturally brilliant discovery, Ray Willis, into "a perfect fighting machine" and eventually into heavy-weight champion of the world. His overriding motive is not money but the lust of creation: "Do you know the story of Frankenstein?", the narrator of the story, Bill Crane, pertinently asks. And Melville's pretty young daughter, Jill, points out that her father regards his protégé as "a gun or something. Something he aims at other boxers and they fall down." So they do, to begin with. Willis obediently wins the A.B.A. championships and knocks out his first professional opponents with astonishing ease. But though he is malleable, touchingly naive and not very bright he is, of course, also very much of a human being. He tires of the relentless training routine imposed on him by Melville, and he falls in love, innocently and idealistically, with Jill. Moreover, as a boxer he has a "fatal flaw"—he cannot take punishment—and when, on his way to the top, he is for the first time hit really hard (by an opponent technically far inferior) he "takes a dive" and is counted out. He runs away both from Melville and Jill and eventually finishes up doing rigged bouts in a fairground booth.

It will be seen that this story has points of similarity to Budd Schulberg's *The Harder They Fall*—in both cases, for example, the narrator is a hard-bitten, soft-at-the-centre boxing journalist capable of higher things, but incapable, it appears, of a normal mature relationship with the woman who loves him. But although Mr. Scannell's book has plenty of boxer's know-how, vividly conveyed, and occasional flashes of poet's insight . . . the novel lacks the crude energy and force of Budd Schulberg's. This is chiefly because the potentially interesting characters are for the most part only picked at, while the women do not come to life at all. The outstanding exception is the narrator, whose exploitation of his woman friend Mary neatly counterpoints that of Melville in respect of his boy-wonder, and whose blend of egotism and wry self-distaste is effectively communicated: but besides being a rather unlikable person he somehow throws an air of discouragement over the book as a whole.

"Too Softly They Fall," in The Times Literary Supplement, *No. 3294, April 15, 1965, p. 289.*

GAVIN EWART

Mr Scannell is a straightforward poet, and in many ways a good one. Poetry exists to tell the truth—about things, people, ideas. Exercises in technique may give a lot of pleasure . . . but in the end what we want most from a poem is an 'illumination' of experience.

Personality and entertainment value are also involved, and Mr Scannell has a lot of both. For this one can willingly forgive the occasional roughnesses [in *Walking Wounded: Poems, 1962-1965*] ('Though the so long scream ripped from another throat than mine', 'Enraptured paean, by which they set small store', 'Windscreen and chrome flash desperate messages'—

why were they desperate?) and even a bad rhyme in a final couplet:

> Till fatigue or error dragged him down,
> An ordinary man on ordinary ground. . . .

On the other hand his words often have the air of being carefully—and well—chosen . . . and the thought is above the average for poetic thought. . . . (pp. 93-4)

Among these 42 poems at least eight are of considerable merit: **"Act of Love"**, **"Walking Wounded"**, **"Since Donovan Died"**, **"This Summer"**, **"The Old Books"**, **"Tightrope Walker"**, **"Ruminant"**, **"My Three Hoboes"**, **"Moral Problem"**. **"A Case Of Murder"** is not quite good enough, somehow, to carry the violent emotion it is meant to bear. Weakest of all is the old hat motive-guessing game that goes on in **"Millionaire"**. . . . **"The Caller"** is another poem where the very-much-expected occurs. These poems inhabit the real world; they concern life as it is lived today. And they are, in the very best sense, 'consolatory'. (p. 94)

Gavin Ewart, in a review of "Walking Wounded,"
in London Magazine, *Vol. 5, No. 10, January, 1966,*
pp. 93-4.

THE TIMES LITERARY SUPPLEMENT

[In *Walking Wounded*] Mr. Scannell gives the appearance of working harder [than Francis Hope] for his effects, though, to be fair, his range is wider. He shares with Mr. Hope a somewhat ruthless urge to moralize and a weakness for a flat ending, but he does not seem to achieve as much as the younger poet, in spite of a vigorous and not unsympathetic attack on "up-to-date" and difficult subject-matter. Mr. Scannell's real failing is glibness, a confident facility for metaphor and colourful argufying. And this, too, screws those flat last lines into hair-clutching banality, simply because most of the time Mr. Scannell is going through lively motions and one really does wait for the pay-off. There are perhaps some lurking Dionysiac notions of an ex-Maverick to be found in this hit-or-miss method. What is needed is some restraint, some exactness and purity of language.

"Movement's Wake," in The Times Literary Supplement, *No. 3337, February 10, 1966, p. 104.*

THE TIMES LITERARY SUPPLEMENT

Vernon Scannell's *Epithets of War* veers . . . towards an over-demonstrative display of what are, for the most part, stalely conventional responses to the fighting. . . . Too many of the poems read like bad Sassoon: the volume, lacking any consistent set of concerns, ekes out its sparse subject-matter (the inevitable poem from a crippled survivor, a poem about a cigarette and a poem about itself) with a slack and careless use of rhythm.

"Soldiering On," in The Times Literary Supplement, *No. 3525, September 18, 1969, p. 1021.*

ALAN BROWNJOHN

Vernon Scannell's **"Walking Wounded"** . . . was one of the best poems to come, very late, out of the Second World War. In the sequence which gives [*Epithets of War*] its title he has not managed to repeat the success: these are very routine run-throughs, much less interesting than some of his shorter, wryly self-scrutinising pieces—though here, too, *Epithets of War* is a rather hit-or-miss collection. That bluffly world-weary mood (seen here in **"You, too, can have a body"** and **"Death in the Lounge Bar"**) he has done before, and often done better. Scannell's extrovert, no-nonsense standpoint, his approachability, his alert eye for everyday detail, are attractive. But only in one or two places here does he marshal these resources to achieve something telling on a more touching or disquieting note: **"The Moth"**, **"A Quaint Disorder"** and **"View from a Wheelchair"**. . . .

Alan Brownjohn, "Physical Jerks," in New States-
man, Vol. 78, No. 2014, October 17, 1969, p. 540.

ANTHONY THWAITE

As a poet, [Scannell] has never had his due. Starting off with some innocuous but over-ripe verses in the little magazines during the late 1940s, he seemed to plot on for years, copiously there, but uncertain, incorrigibly minor, a figure on the scene among dozens of others in the pages of *Poetry Quarterly* and *Outposts*. Yet a few poems in the late 1950s showed there was something altogether more individual and striking in him: a knack for catching a mood, or more often an incident, and transmitting it economically and directly. And the knack developed. There are 10 or a dozen poems in *A Sense of Danger* (1962) and *Walking Wounded* (1965) which stand among the best of their decade. Such poems as **"Gunpowder Plot"** and **"Hide and Seek"** crop up over and over again in such places as school anthologies, yet somehow Scannell hasn't been properly noticed except on this educational circuit. . . . Now the *Selected Poems*, coming together with *The Tiger and the Rose*, give a chance for justice to be done.

The autobiography [*The Tiger and the Rose*] makes an immediate appeal, and some of its virtues are the virtues of Scannell's poetry: he is straightforward, masculine without being aggressively tough, circumstantial, unphoney. His reflections on the nature of his experiences jar a little, and made me impatient for him to go on again with the experiences themselves, which he describes with a marvellously clean and clear accuracy. The character that emerges might seem to be *l'homme moyen sensuel*, but the facts of life are so extraordinary that they belie such a view. A shifting, rackety, provincial childhood in an ill-matched, poor family; a squaddy's war in North Africa and Normandy, ending with a wound and followed by desertion; on the run, doing odd jobs, holed up in Leeds and being a sort of unofficial underground student at the university English department there; racapture, a court of enquiry which remanded him for a psychiatrist's report (supposedly because he wrote poetry), discharge, more odd jobs—including spells as a professional boxer—and unqualified teaching in dim and dubious private schools; sporadically, the literary life . . . It is a picaresque grand tour, far from the more usual read-English-at-Oxford-now-lectures-in-English-at-Warwick encapsulation; and Scannell tells it all quite unassumingly, even self-deprecatingly. At least once the reader's involvement becomes as painfully immediate as the autobiographer's: in the account of the birth and death of his handicapped son Benjamin, where the force is all in the restraint.

The Tiger and the Rose is not one of the great 'poetic' autobiographies: it is an odd, erratic life plainly recorded. The poems have a plainness too, the plainness of a man who recognizes very well all his illusions, is battered by his experiences, and is rueful, amused, wryly romantic, unaffectedly

honest. Unlike the tightrope walker of his poem, Vernon Scannell, while being 'An ordinary man on ordinary ground', has 'trained the common skill' until it holds our attention and compels our admiration; 'snarled up', it may be, but plain about the snarls. (pp. 368-69)

Anthony Thwaite, "Plain Tales," in New Statesman,
Vol. 82, No. 2113, September 17, 1971, pp. 368-69.

THE TIMES LITERARY SUPPLEMENT

Saying that an autobiography "reads like fiction" often means that it is overloaded with detail and conversation derived more from invention than from memory. In contrast, Vernon Scannell's *The Tiger and the Rose* has the clear, shrill ring of truth; yet it, too, reads like fiction. This is largely because of its construction, for the author begins right in the middle of his story at the point, in 1945, where he deserted from the army. From here he follows his adventures in London and, later, in Leeds, where he supported himself by tutoring ("one pound a week and no ration-book"), became Northern University boxing champion, and was finally run down by the police in 1947.

So far the course of the book has been rather like that of a typical novel of the 1950s or early 1960s—brisk, ironic, rather detached, hurrying on down or up or along. But now the author jumps back to the traditional country of the poet's memory. In a series of sharp snapshots, he gives us glimpses of his childhood at Ballaghaderreen in Ireland, at Beeston, near Nottingham, where he became a cinema fan (but did the silent films really have captions at the *foot* of the screen?), and at Eccles, in Lancashire. Eventually, he rejoined his parents at Aylesbury, where he left school, learnt to box, and at eighteen, following a noted precedent, lost his virginity to a woman of twenty-six. The chapter which follows—four or five superbly told episodes, some of which were later worked into poems—suggests that Mr Scannell might have written one of the best books about the Second World War, but a wound brought an end to his war experiences and an end, also, to this part of his autobiography.

The story now leapfrogs on to the time of his discharge, after court-martial, in 1947, and this device immediately rouses expectancy. Two separately drawn lines have converged on the same point: what is going to happen next? What *is* going to happen, of course, is that Mr Scannell turns into a poet, and though this, in itself, is no disappointment, in the context of the book it seems rather unexciting after the prize-fighting, mine-laying and police-dodging which have gone before. . . .

The trouble is that it is obvious from the start that this particular match will end in a draw, for both tough and sensitive are in gear in Mr Scannell's stylishly practical technique. The last part of the book is lively and interesting, with accounts of literary pubs, rigged prize-fights, and all the feints and side-skips of bread-and-margarine journalism, but it does go on perhaps a few rounds too long. For the central event in the second half of the author's story is really the writing of the first half, and three-quarters or more of his book is a brilliantly entertaining demonstration of how to master a craft.

"Match Drawn," in The Times Literary Supple-
ment, No. 3629, September 17, 1971, p. 1108.

PETER PORTER

We should have been given Vernon Scannell's Collected Poems and not just [*Selected Poems*]. Nothing in Scannell's poetry would be foreign to Hardy or Edward Thomas, but he goes about tradition in his own way. He specialises in the scena from experience, which sometimes degenerates into the equivalent of an O. Henry ending banging into place, but truth to detail justifies his large poetical personifications and his affection for the full romantic line. Scannell has selected well from the poems he wrote before *Walking Wounded*: none is more powerful than the grimly orthodox **"An Old Lament Renewed"**.

Peter Porter, *"Melodious MacBeth," in* The Observer, *November 21, 1971, p. 33.*

DOUGLAS DUNN

Vernon Scannell's *Selected Poems* is . . . welcome, although, viewed in quantity, his poems reveal the monotony of rhythm common in post-modernist poets upholding nineteenth-century metrics. Effortful blank verse, quatrains, moralised narratives and monologues occasionally rhymed—Mr Scannell has a wide enough range to sustain interest in a volume of this length; although his subjects are limited to variations on marriage and war, both are large enough to be going on with. But his cadences are deadeningly iambic, and the main interest is supplied by story-telling. There are some good local effects:

> The evening brings
> A smoky sadness to the mortgaged lawns,

which, despite its derivation from Eliot of the *Preludes,* goes some way towards compensating for the tiredness of rhyme and language in a poem like **"Silver Wedding"**, with phrases like ''A black wind grieves'', and ''Youth's ebullient song.''

War is a recurrent obsession, cropping up in metaphors in poems about something else. Scannell has a claim to be considered among the best of the British Second World War poets. He had direct experience of the fighting, and although this is a substantial presence in *Selected Poems,* it is only because the two poems drawing from this experience are his best. The real thing comes across unmistakably in **"Walking Wounded"**, where the plight of the unspectacularly hurt is ominously dramatised. (pp. 69-70)

Douglas Dunn, *"King Offa Alive and Dead," in* Encounter, *Vol. 38, No. 1, January, 1972, pp. 67-74.*

MICHAEL SCHMIDT

At 49, Vernon Scannell is perhaps a little young to be recalling his past in autobiographical terms, dividing his life into alternating ''Then'' and ''Now'' chapters, the former descriptive and the latter gleaning aphoristically the lessons of youth and of a varied and at first glance rich life.

Mr Scannell more than once justifies [*The Tiger and the Rose*] by saying that the man he is bears little relation to the man he was except in name. He sees the act of writing autobiography as—to a degree—trying to find continuity between distinct identities. Possibly this is what makes this sometimes entertaining book so strangely unsatisfactory: that in tracing incidents—from Irish childhood, through a boxing career, military desertion, battle, etc. (in no chronological order)—Mr Scannell does not at the same time reveal his own maturing process towards his present identity. This anecdotal autobiography does not show the development of a poet, nor does it reveal a mature outlook—it shows the poet's journey through space and time externally. (p. 80)

There is a failure of irony, too—the humour is largely heavy-handed. And the first character we meet, the military intellectual and gentleman's gentleman, is observed—as are all the people Mr Scannell dislikes—not with ironic humanity, but with a scorn which is unpleasant. He fails, in his response to people, to experiences, to himself, to place them in a context where their full nature, their tragedy and comedy as well as their annoying quality to him, are visible.

The ''Then'' chapters are, nonetheless, very interesting reading. The style is not too self-conscious, and Mr Scannell's descriptive ability, especially in writing of the war and of his response to the birth and death of one of his children is excellent. One balks at the style in the ''Now'' chapters, with Mr Scannell, by his own confession usually writing in a hungover state. . . . Throughout the ''Now'' passages, except at the end of the book, there is a forced heightening of style, a bringing into play of unnecessarily latinate vocabulary, of extended syntactical constructions which tend to weigh down Mr Scannell's lessons from life.

There is not enough of Scannell as a child; nor does he explore why he was more interested as a youth in boxing and poetry as modes of identity, not modes of expression. He does not assess the various psychological tensions which have led to his poetry, and though he points out the Georgian origins of his work, he goes no distance at all into his literary beliefs or—in depth—tastes. (pp. 80-1)

Michael Schmidt, *"Is and Was," in* Encounter, *Vol. 39, No. 3, September, 1972, pp. 80-1.*

PETER PORTER

"The Soldier's Dream" in Vernon Scannell's [*The Winter Man*] is the kind of poem I should like to see him writing more often. In this densely metaphorical piece, Scannell allows the deeper layers of his imagination to contemplate the sights and sounds of his constant recall of war. After war, he seems to suggest, its memories haunt one in more personal areas of destruction; none so dark and lethal as love. . . . Other poems in *The Winter Man* are almost as good: **"Cold Spell," "Charnel House, Rothwell Church"** and **"End of a Season"** among them. Scannell has always been the poet of uneasiness, of the generous colours of life stained by autumn darkenings, and this tone is conveyed in his new book more effectively than ever before.

Some poems here are too long-winded, some grindingly formal and his besetting fault of over-use of adjectives has not abated, entirely, but there is an amplitude of emotion and a power of statement which is very welcome.

Peter Porter, *"The Transit of Venus," in* The Observer, *November 4, 1973, p. 39.*

ALAN BROWNJOHN

The fears one had about a poetry so steadily that of the ordinary sensual man as Vernon Scannell's were simply that it would end up repetitiously sensual and unfailingly ordinary. No need to worry. *The Winter Man* is arguably his best book yet. He hasn't changed his material or his poetic personality: just found new ways with old subjects, achieved an increasing technical confidence, and written more movingly and interestingly than before. True, the most ambitious poems here—**"Comeback"** and **"The Winter Man"** itself—aren't altogether successful. In the end, or before the end of these two longish narratives, the tension disperses, the rhythms slacken, they break down into something like (quite good) short stories. It's in the poems set in the usual Scannell territory—love and sex, in marriage and out of it, war and its psychological aftermath, the wry contemplation of death—that he is displaying a new variety and a new forcefulness of statement.

There has always been more of a detached intelligence at work in Scannell's verse than his various familiar personae—the boozer, the libertine, the soldier tired of heroics—have suggested. In this volume it shows itself in the very clever edge given to ostensibly light or casual poems like **"Five Domestic Interiors"**; or **"The Discriminator"**, where delicate choices in feminine beauty are seen as a matter not of taste but of the fastidiousness that comes with simply ageing. On another level, it's there in the ingenious organisation of visual imagery to produce disturbing effects in a poem like **"Cold Spell"**.... On another level still it emerges in the fine Jacobean effect at the end of **"Charnel House, Rothwell Church"**, where the speaker suggests his wife take a skull to her pillow while he is absent.... These are the darker notes. **"Polling Day"**, offering two cheers for democracy, sees Scannell both cheerfully and seriously giving his ballot paper the awkward reverence Larkin gives to his suburban church, and voting with a 'cross, illiterate kiss'. And all in all, *The Winter Man* represents a most encouraging advance. (p. 916)

> *Alan Brownjohn, ''Scars,'' in* New Statesman, *Vol. 86, No. 2230, December 14, 1973, pp. 916-17.*

THE TIMES LITERARY SUPPLEMENT

"Picnic on the Lawn" is one of the most successful poems in *The Winter Man,* which is Vernon Scannell's best volume to date. Three women compare fantasies; those of the two mothers are exotic projections of liberated woman, while the childless third wishes simply to be like them in their experience of the present moment.... This sort of poem, where truth and pathos are evinced from the suggestions of a very slight situation, is notoriously difficult to bring off without sounding sugary or contrived, and it says a great deal for Mr Scannell's delicate judgment and dramatizing skill that he avoids both pitfalls. The piece shows extreme shrewdness in ordering significant physical detail; the deftness and economy with which the scene is set and the action interlinked are the result of a fertile image-making power working comfortably within its limits.

Mr Scannell is most successful when working like this; there is a tendency in certain poems to load every rift with ore. And it is not always ore: in **"Confessional Poem"**, an otherwise witty and apposite piece, the reader is at one point urged to ''shed no liquid salt''—a truly monstrous piece of poetic diction that shouts from the page. But this is one extreme of a style that time and again proves itself superbly on the senses, and is often most effective when deploying a sort of paramilitary force of images drawn from war and the ring. There are excellent poems, in fact, directly or allegorically about these subjects, among them the long monologue **"Comeback"**, **"Battlefields"**, **"War Cemetery, Ranville"** and **"The Soldier's Dream"**. Elsewhere death and irony slug it out as vigorously as ever.

> *''Keep It Short,'' in* The Times Literary Supplement, *No. 3751, January 25, 1974, p. 77.*

THE SPECTATOR

Nearly twenty years separates Vernon Scannell's first published poems, *A Mortal Pitch* from his new collection *The Loving Game* and, as the titles of the books suggest, he continues with his baleful view of life as rough sport—getting rougher in middle-age. If his themes haven't changed much neither has his style; he has not really developed his poetry but he has succeeded in perfecting it. There is no good reason why he should feel obliged to coax himself out of a finely executed if unrevolutionary style just to prove his modernity. So one wonders why he makes an issue of his new faint rhyme scheme (men/rib/spin) by bothering to name it, pretentiously ''triadic rhyme.'' True he uses it with great effect in some of his best poems but by drawing attention to it as innovatory he seems to lack the courage of his own conservative convictions....

Mr Scannell is at his best when writing about love's failures and the ensuing contraction of the heart. In [**"The Loving Game"**] and **"Wicket Maiden"**, among others, he shows himself to be the most accomplished poet of prosaic love writing today. *The Loving Game* is his most consistent volume to date and with it he undoubtedly emerges as one of the best poets of his generation—candid, resilient, lyrical.

> *N.C., ''Shorter Notice,'' in* The Spectator, *Vol. 235, No. 7694, December 13, 1975, p. 766.*

ANTHONY THWAITE

Vernon Scannell is at his best as a sardonic, bruised reporter of experience, the man with a slow wink and a fading black eye: happiness (as he almost suggests in **"Amities"**, one of the poems in his new book) doesn't suit him, which is perhaps why *The Loving Game* has made less of an impression on me than his last three or four books. Not that it is markedly more cheerful than the Scannell of old, but some slackness seems to have got into his language.... Among the gently joking [poems] I liked **"Wicket Maiden"** and (though long anticipated by Anthony Powell et al) **"Right Dress"**; but the authentic voice I have admired for a long time came through with its proper melancholy in **"An Anniversary"**.

> *Anthony Thwaite, ''Reporters of Experience,'' in* The Times Literary Supplement, *No. 3855, January 30, 1976, p. 108.*

SIMON CURTIS

[To] those who prefer significant communication to self-expression Vernon Scannell's *Collected Poems* demonstrates much that is right with the plain presentation of mood and reflection, linked to incident and episode; poems that limit themselves to saying something clear. He belongs to a fraternity of poets who have ''soldiered on'' independently, without great praise or fuss: F. T. Prince, Charles Causley, Norman Nicholson, X. J. Kennedy, James Simmons, Stanley Cook, and (in his early work) Tony Connor. To call them ''mainstream'' writers only goes to show how diverse and colourful are the currents that compose the stream.

''Soldiering on'', because there is something soldierly about Mr Scannell's metre and stanza-forms: well marshalled, in step, blunt, even ''veteran'', plain at times to a fault. ''Keeping the step'' courts the danger of flatness, and he does not always avoid the trap of predictability, especially in his first collection *A Mortal Pitch* (1957). The formal poet needs a good ear and the ability to modulate a clinching line or climax. . . . Yet these early poems of Vernon Scannell have shape, and are at least well made; careful apprentice work. (By saying this, I do not mean that he is a poetical Sardou, playing for a stock-response.) Among them, **"Gunpowder Plot"** is the most notable—simple, but effective.

Masks of Love (1960) shows a development of range, from the chill of **"Lynching"** to the suburban failure dramatized in the **"Simon Frailman"** sonnet-sequence. . . . The title-poem of this book is a good one and **"Two Appearances"** moves with a Gravesian twist of irony—but with Scannell's voice, not Graves's. Later successes of this witty kind are **"Act of Love"**, **"Moral Problem"**, **"Polling Day"**, **"The Rivals"** (with its understated icy ending) and **"Wicket Maiden"**.

In *A Sense of Danger* (1962), **"Incendiary"** stands out, while the 1965 collections, *The Walking Wounded* and *Epithets of War,* show Vernon Scannell on top form. . . .

In *The Walking Wounded* Vernon Scannell shows a talent for the dramatic monologue; one thinks of the tradition of Victorian monologue writers. **"Old Books"** and **"Pearless Jim Driscoll"** may be taken with **"Comeback"**, about a boxer, **"Defrauded Woman"** and the ballad **"Captain Scuttle"** from *Epithets of War.* These five monologues stand among his best poems, all worth anthologizing. . . . The scope created by fictional dramatization allows the poet to escape from the confines of the subjective but still be personal. Other memorable poems by Scannell include **"Eidolon (Phantom) Parade"**, a moving and grimly humorous elegy for comrades fallen in the Second World War, and the more recent **"Mystery at Euston"** with its image of a girl who is predestined to be exploited as a prostitute coming up alone to the big city. . . .

A last section of new poems concludes appropriately with **"A Partial View"**, an unpretentious, meditative poem, reflecting generally on the evil and good in human beings (**"**manichaean**"** is the sort of word Vernon Scannell would not use). This poem puts one in mind of George Orwell's sentence about Dickens: "If man would behave decently, the world would be decent". It is a world, as Mr Scannell describes, in which a five-year-old can have his penis cut off by motor-bike yobs, while adults are victims of political torture. Art, though, may build "small barricades against the confusion": in music and in language, you can

> find yourself, with almost no surprise,
> Accepting everything, rejoicing even
> That all is as it is, not otherwise;
> Though when the music fades and meanings blur,
> The hordes remass, you turn again to her
> To whom you might conceivably be true
> As she, against the odds, might be to you.

The refusal to be deceived by a life that, all in all, despite its horrors, he relishes; the plain, unadventurous imagery (music fading, hordes remassing); the rhythm; the resolute sticking to statement rather than defining some symbolic landscape: these make **"A Partial View"** a touchstone for the appreciation of Vernon Scannell's work.

The personality behind these poems is an engaging one. **"Incendiary"** catches well Vernon Scannell's unsentimental understanding: the boy fire-raiser "with face like pallid cheese / And burnt-out little eyes", comes from a loveless home, and the poem reflects how "frightening" it is. . . . There is of course the danger that the generalized "home-truth" will seem

to some homely or homespun or even trite; but this poem, read as a whole, makes its point well.

Vernon Scannell has an instinctive sympathy for "losers", and a sense, too, that winners have their secrets and regrets: his **"Comeback"** monologue and his war poems testify to this (Mr Scannell himself was both boxer and soldier). He is a natural democrat, but a reflective and disabused one. There is not an obscure line in the whole of his *New and Collected Poems*.

His themes have been suggested above: fatherhood, soldiering, fear, death, wry bitterness at aging, love in many aspects, the vulnerability of seemingly-strong characters; episodes such as bonfire night, hide and seek, incidents told by raconteurs in pubs or those that might be found in a local newspaper; scenes whose backcloth is the railway station, the schoolroom, the bar, the bedroom; images resolutely ordinary—the kite, the "dizzy branch of fun" about to crack under the children, tenderness concentrating the "burning-glass of gratitude and awe", the "blurred and stumbling cul-de-sac of booze" of those who try to escape life. Ordinary to a prosy fault? In the poems I have named, I do not think so. And a boxer-poet is after all extraordinary.

      Simon Curtis, "In the Middle of the Ring," in The
      Times Literary Supplement, *No. 4036, August 1,
      1980, p. 876.*

ALAN HOLLINGHURST

Vernon Scannell has brought together [in *New and Collected Poems, 1950-1980*] all those poems which he wishes to preserve and added an Introductory Note in which humility and pride rub against each other. He admits to some failures in an impressive way, cutting out 'poems which on re-reading seem to be quite obviously false, banal or inept' . . . and hopes that readers will find things in his work 'that will, in Doctor Johnson's words "enable them the better to enjoy life or the better to endure it"'. This concept of poetry as something publicly accessible, pleasurable and morally consoling is clearly important to Scannell, as is his personal exploration of experiences which have mattered to him, and the result is a body of work of easy appeal and genuine and likeable personality. His manner is ideal for making the domestic ruefully amusing and for telling tales of clear moral application. He moves ably between the worlds of pugilism, drinking, lust, marriage, sexual unhappiness, melancholy and self-caricaturing ageing. He is funny and ironical; but he is not numinous, and his poems are unlikely to haunt the reader. This is partly as a consequence of their being well-made, formal and unambiguous, envisaging poetic success in a readily available clarity: this indeed is their achievement and their limitation. When Scannell attempts a larger subject, as in **"A Partial View"**, a new long poem on violence and war which closes the collection, the power and sophistication of response are clearly inadequate to his extremely serious theme. (p. 18)

      Alan Hollinghurst, "Good for Nothing?" in New
      Statesman, *Vol. 100, No. 2579, August 22, 1980,
      pp. 17-18.*

ALAN BROWNJOHN

Both Vernon Scannell and Gavin Ewart are heirs to that gentler sort of English modernism which paid its respects to Eliot (though not to Pound, or any insistently American or European modernism), took root in the early Auden and most of MacNeice, and branched out in individual ways in the work of poets like Roy Fuller and the late A. S. J. Tessimond. It is a poetry which embraces the immediate, wears and describes the scars of ordinary living, is plain (including plain frightened and plain indignant) about life and death and moral problems, rarely intricate, rarely delicate, always absorbing in its firm yet friendly insistence that the here-and-now of modern urban existence is what almost all of us have to fit into for most of the time.... [Most of Scannell's poetry in *New and Collected Poems, 1950-1980* is] about the blunt and ordinary alarms of mortality.... [Recollections] of the war, the sense of the precariousness of present security, and the indelible knowledge of violent impulse in himself and others surface continually in the later writing. Scannell considers formal discipline to be an important and necessary accompaniment, and the later Ewart finds it an essential challenge: in this emphasis they both appear to look back to a *pre*modernist stage.... (pp. 64-5)

Scannell has been firm in combing out what he considers the weaker poems in the seven previous volumes represented here (the first, *Graves and Resurrections,* from 1948, has gone altogether), and the instinct is right. *A Mortal Pitch* included three poems which have won a place in the affection of his admirers—"Posthumous Autobiography", "Gunpowder Plot" and "Four Dead Beats to a Bar"—but only the second of these wears really well. These early poems, well on into *The Masks of Love* (1960), were drawing something of an expected romantic veil, conventional for the period, over the real issues.... It's not as uncommon as is supposed for poets to find their true voice in middle age, and by the time he dons the persona of "Simon Frailman", Scannell has it splendidly.... He is the poet of the profound and *ordinary* fear of death, the bluff extrovert caught "Howling for Love", the Don Juan of middle age who has known war, and indeed inherited it.... Scannell is ... insistently rooted in the present moment.... And yet, by one of those mysterious, inexorable and beneficent rules which govern the poetic composition of poets as practised and prolific as he is, when a compelling theme and a well-chosen form coincide, the result can be startlingly moving and beautiful, not at all ordinary. As often as not it's the war themes with Scannell—the finely-handled climax to the marching pentameters of "Walking Wounded", or the carefully modulated half-rhymes of "The Soldier's Dream" where he goes over the ground of a famous war poem of Keith Douglas with (dare one say it?) more compassion and more gripping effect. (pp. 65-6)

Alan Brownjohn, "Going Concerns," in Encounter, Vol. LV, No. 5, November, 1980, pp. 64-7.

DICK DAVIS

Vernon Scannell's is a ... robust talent—his tone [in *Winterlude*] tends to be one of colloquial, man-to-man, saloon-bar chat rather than mawkish inwardness (the more lyrical poems are usually the least convincing). He has a Jonsonian belief that 'a good poet's made, as well as born' and the sense of mastered craft (the first poem, "Mastering the Craft" compares boxing and poetry) his poems give is a constant pleasure. The risk such craft-conscious poetry runs is that it can at times seem glib, both in form and content—many of the poems draw to what appears a slightly too smug, even bullying, close. The saloon-bar analogy is again apposite, as if when a poem ends Scannell is waiting for his interlocutor's confirming 'H'm, makes you think doesn't it ...' But the poetry is well-made and continually interesting. (p. 27)

Dick Davis, "Vision and Anger," in The Listener, Vol. 107, No. 2759, May 6, 1982, pp. 26-7.

PETER PORTER

Winterlude is ... almost entirely made up of hits. [Scannell] now employs his enriched style more discreetly: it is not so much high as opulent, as in the line 'pure song, ophthalmic dew.' By risking being more arbitrary and decorative, he gains real spoils of originality.

His favourite device of realism rinsed by irony appears in many of these poems. In "War Movie Veteran" he parodies the aficionado of Hollywood styles of killing, but appreciates that reality (war) can be made to go into art, even to the satisfaction of those who have experienced the real thing.

Peter Porter, "Unheeded Howls," in The Observer, June 6, 1982, p. 30.

GEORGE SZIRTES

Masks of Love, Walking Wounded, A Proper Gentleman: the titles of some of Vernon Scannell's earlier collections suggest a British version of John Crowe Ransom's "Captain Carpenter", who "rose up in his prime" and rode out to meet a succession of disasters. Like Carpenter, Scannell adopts a code of honour which seems consciously anachronistic, one based on laws of conflict, dynastic in Carpenter's case, pugilistic in Scannell's. Scannell's autobiography, *The Tiger and The Rose,* described how this strange mixture of practical man of action and sensitive loner came together to create the erratic, lyrical, sour, tough formalist poet. His boxing background has remained prominent, a kind of "singing school" accentuating both the romance and discipline of conflict. *Winterlude* begins with a poem outlining techniques of poetic survival in the terminology of the boxing ring, and maintains the tone throughout: one is constantly made aware of winners and losers of various kinds, particularly losers who, like Captain Carpenter, led with noble chins....

Passion in the winter of life dominates the poet's thoughts: passion as conflict, both with one's partner and with time. This is a view with an honourable tradition, expressed by Donne, Marvell, Suckling and many others. Crabbed age has its defences. Scannell's "Juan in Limbo" oozes disgust with sex, at least with its prologues of sweet-talking.... And at the heart of the most integrated and loving love poem there is the echo of the Beast himself, tamed by Beauty....

Away from the private sphere with its delights and its agonizing, Scannell's world is refreshingly unliterary and unclever. It is primarily urban and hard-bitten, sometimes too much so. The erratic in Scannell occasionally makes him buttonhole us in a Mean Streets manner. War veterans perhaps have a right to display their wounds, yet in practice it is usually more effective to allow the audience to assume them. But this should not distract us from Scannell's achievements, which are considerable. He is rarely ungraceful, he can deal with complex and powerful emotions, he has a coherent view of the world and an impeccable understanding of his social and historical milieu. And when sheer poetry creeps up on him he can respond with great sensitivity. ("Learning", for example, develops the *donnée* of a misunderstood cry in the streets into a marvellous evocation of early puberty.) He is, in short, a very fine poet.

George Szirtes, "Winners and Losers," in The Times
Literary Supplement, No. 4150, October 15, 1982,
p. 1139.

ROGER LEWIS

The subject [of *Ring of Truth*] is the cruel world of professional
boxing. It might well be that a good writer is, among other
things, one who can interest us in an activity which would
otherwise remain unencountered. This is the case in this novel.
Dave, middle-weight champion of the world, is married to dull
Aileen, 'a sort of juvenile Baptist aunt'. But his mousy spouse
at least leaves him free to dedicate his energies to his sport.
Into his life comes temptation in the shape of shapely Judy,
'the popular Leeds soprano'. *Ring of Truth* charts Dave's dilemmas as he tries to cope with his mistress, 'a shop-cake,
thrilling, colourful, sweet . . . and bad for you', his silly scold
of a wife and an impending big fight in which his title has to
be defended.

Though the conversations and bad grammar of dialect pall, the
novel is dotted with excellent observations. (pp. 19-20)

Roger Lewis, "Enclosed Worlds," in New Statesman, Vol. 106, No. 2754, December 30, 1983, pp.
19-20.

D. A. N. JONES

Vernon Scannell is not the first British poet to have been keen
on boxing and, apparently, quite good at it: we may think of
Lord Byron and Robert Graves. But few others, surely, have
written and worried so concernedly about the ethics of this
sport, its moral justification. *Ring of Truth* . . . returns hungrily
to Scannell's old problem. Can deliberate wounding be good
sport? Scannell tells of dangerous, exciting weeks in the life
of Dave Ruddock, a boxer from Leeds, acknowledged as Mid-
dleweight Champion of the World. . . .

There are other challenges in *Ring of Truth*. David Ruddock's
wife, a pious Roman Catholic, feels challenged by the Pope's
visit to Britain and wonders if she ought to become a Bride of
Christ. Dave's young brother, a professional soldier, is called
to fight in the Falklands, meeting the reluctant challenge presented by the conscripts of the Argentine junta. The father of
the Ruddock brothers, once a physical-training instructor in
the British Army, is pretty well pleased with his sons' combative energies and skills: but even he has his pleasant confidence challenged by the reality of his sons' risks and wounds.
The Ruddocks' mother feels that men's fights are none of her
business: she is challenged rather by the split between Dave
and his wife, when Dave finds a more loving and lovable
girl. . . .

As Vernon Scannell grows older he becomes more expert or
plausible in his attempts to understand women's ideas and
imagine their conversations when no men are present. Is he a
'sexist'? He is certainly not the kind of man who finds women
boring. But he did once complain in a poem about poetry
readings: 'There are always more women than men.' (Does he
complain that there are always more men than women at box-
ing-matches?) The well-timed reissue of his autobiography of
1970, *The Tiger and the Rose*, gives us some excuse to consider
his life and character—helpful toward the appreciation of his
writing (as with Byron and Graves, again).

None of the women in *Ring of Truth* can appreciate boxing:
Scannell sets up women characters to argue against the sport.
Dave Ruddock's mate, Tom, persuades him to appear on Radio
Leeds, to be interviewed by Tom's girlfriend. She says re-
proachful things: 'You know quite well that the kind of blow
you've been trained to deliver could kill a man.' Dave pon-
derously replies:

> Women don't understand boxing . . . You'll hear a
> boxer say something like 'I knew I had hurt him so
> I went in for kill.' Now, he doesn't mean it, not like
> you mean 'hurt' or 'kill'. You never feel vicious . . .
> You've got to have a bit of danger, a bit of pain, or
> there wouldn't be no point, would there?

The interviewer does not understand. She goes home to Tom
and he tries to tell her boxing is remarkable for its 'purity'.
He claims that a boxing match is 'a moment of truth'—to be
distinguished from more rational expressions of courage, during wars, natural disasters, Acts of God. 'The soldier's being
used by politicians. The hero of the flood or fire's manipulated
by special circumstances. With the fighter it's an end in itself.'
Scannell has tried out similar arguments in his own nonfictional
voice, in *The Tiger and the Rose;* but he is evidently not quite
satisfied with them. . . .

Vernon Scannell's novel is largely didactic: though the conversations are sometimes 'true-to-life' (as if tape-recorded in
a pub snug), they are more often artificial and rhetorical, designed to instruct the audience and provoke thought. . . . An
editor could have pulled out half this talk and still left us with
the exciting story of Dave Ruddock's women and Dave Ruddock's big fight—very well described, blow by blow.

When I reached the page where Dave Ruddock boasts of having
defeated 'Johnny Bain', I put down the novel and picked up
the autobiography to check my memory. Yes, I was right,
'Johnny Bain' was the name Vernon Scannell used when he
was a professional boxer—and he also used it as a pseudonym
when entering literary competitions in the weeklies. It is worth
reading *The Tiger and the Rose* before *Ring of Truth*, so that
one may have Scannell's straightforward memories of Leeds
and London gyms, and the resemblances and differences he
sees between boxing, soldiering and the writing of poems, to
serve as a background to his imaginative use of the same material in the fiction of *Ring of Truth*.

His autobiography is like his novel, in that the grave arguments
are kept separate from the racing, punchy narrative. *The Tiger
and the Rose* has one chapter headed 'Then', describing an
army experience: this is followed by a chapter headed 'Now',
with an older Scannell gravely reflecting upon the incidents.
The alternating 'Then' and 'Now' chapters form a good pattern
for telling a life-story, worth copying by any novelist who
wants his story to look like a biography. (p. 17)

D. A. N. Jones, "Fighting Men," in London Review
of Books, Vol. 6, No. 2, February 2-15, 1984, pp.
17-18.

GERALD MANGAN

Although written in the form of a novel, *Argument of Kings*
is "a kind of confession", whose, first and most startling
revelation is that Scannell's final flight after VE-Day, when
he considered the war to be over, was in fact preceded by a
more serious desertion from the frontline in North Africa, which
ended in court-martial and a sentence of three years' penal

servitude. Cowardice seems not to have been his motive, in the usual sense, and he was released prematurely to take part in the invasion of France; but this episode evidently left a more enduring sense of shame, whose depth may be measured by the forty-odd years of concealment. Considering his careful suppression of it in *The Tiger and the Rose,* whose "factuality" he chose to emphasize in a preface to the 1983 edition, it does seem strange that his conscience should finally have been moved by so casual an occurrence as a radio interview, given some two years later; but this is the explanation he provides in his preface.

Reservations are swept aside, however, by the sheer pace and quality of this book, in which Scannell gives his third-person hero his own real name, "John Bain". *Argument of Kings* is remarkable not only for the disturbing immediacy of its realism, but for acute explorations of complex states of mind. Bain's unpremeditated retreat from a corpse-strewn desert hillside, in the still aftermath of a battle which had not even involved his own regiment, is propelled less by fear than by a combination of desert-hypnosis, dislocation of the will, and a vague disgust at the sight of his comrades looting the bodies of compatriots. This almost metaphysical revulsion remains frustratingly inarticulate throughout his trial and imprisonment—as it has, presumably, through much of the author's life. . . .

The long comic-romantic epilogue, in which he escapes from the tedium of hospital to conduct a touchingly awkward affair with an ATS girl, would make an ungainly and anti-climactic resolution to a novel, if it were to be judged as such; but the episode is compulsively readable, and its affectionate portrait of "Maxie", like those of his fellow swaddies, is well served by an unusually accurate ear for Scottish speech. Its atmosphere of absurdity is not at all incongruous, and it does serve to illuminate the confusion of grief, frustration and mental stagnancy which he brought back to civilian life. From this viewpoint, as from others, it may well speak for many of his generation.

The most resonant poem in his latest collection [*Funeral Games*], **"The Long Flight"** (a response to a recent news-item) sees a crashed Nazi bomber buried since the war under a ploughed field in Wales, "flying blind with shattered instruments for more / than forty years in fossil silence". If this could be an image for his own long-buried secret, the poem **"Sentences"** is further proof that he can now make comedy from the nightmare—translating the New Testament into a barrack-room ballad, that makes Christ and both crucified thieves "Soldiers Under Sentence" like his younger self: "Who fed the whole battalion / On one man's rations? Guess!"

This gently abrasive wit enlivens his portrait-miniatures, and a boozers' lament ("Drinking up time, as we have always done"); but the larger part of *Funeral Games* is in a pastoral-lyrical mode that suffers from his fidelity to early models. His rather tired iambics are still laced with sonorities of a 1940s vintage ("How long and lovely were the summers then / Each misted morning verdant milk . . ."); and his admiration for Yeats and Hardy has prepared him too well for the roles he has now adopted—in wistful memories of childhood and youth, and rueful acknowledgements of advancing years. **"Bona Dea"** is one of the few lyrics that suggest what he can do when he sharpens his ear, and resists the more seductive echoes.

Gerald Mangan, "A Long-Buried Secret," in The Times Literary Supplement, *No. 4411, October 16-22, 1987, p. 1132.*

Charles Simic

1938-

Yugoslavian-born American poet, translator, nonfiction writer, and editor.

Simic is credited with writing some of the most inventive verse in contemporary poetry. He often employs abstract terms to describe commonplace objects so that the reader, through a series of phenomenological reductions, may sense his underlying existentialist themes. In his poems "The Spoon," "Fork," and "Knife," for example, Simic scrutinizes dining utensils with such intensity that they become imbued with primordial significance. Peter Stitt commented: "The world of Simic's poems is frightening, mysterious, hostile, dangerous; by focusing on such unimportant, everyday objects, the poet is able to achieve, however briefly, some degree of order, comprehension, and control within this world." Because of its density and its various layers of meaning, Simic's verse is often compared to the work of Theodore Roethke. Similarly, the elements of Eastern European folklore and mysticism contained in many of Simic's pieces reflect the influence of Yugoslavian poet Vasko Popa. The contrasting bleak and playful tones in much of his work, underscored by his inclusion of violent and comic details from recent history, prompted Robert B. Shaw to note: "[Simic's] poems oscillate between two dominant moods—one of ritualistic dread evoked in austere, enigmatic scenes, and one of antic exuberance with touches of surrealism and black humor."

Simic grew up in Yugoslavia during the Nazi occupation of his homeland. Following World War II, his family emigrated to Paris and then to New York before settling in Chicago. His first volumes, *What the Grass Says* (1967) and *Somewhere among Us a Stone Is Taking Notes* (1969), were later collected in *Dismantling the Silence* (1971). Critics praised the poems in these books for Simic's thematic application of simple diction and sentence structures and for their Eastern European allusions. Richard Howard stated: "*Dismantling the Silence* reinstates an ancient wisdom, as well as an ancient fooling, which, by its presence, we suddenly realize has been absent from recent American verse—a gnomic utterance, convinced in accent, collective in reference, original in impulse."

While some critics consider the conversational style and use of foreboding images in Simic's subsequent collections to be overly stylized, most acknowledge that these books display considerable imagination. *Return to a Place Lit by a Glass of Milk* (1974), *Charon's Cosmology* (1977), *Classic Ballroom Dances* (1980), and *Austerities* (1982) evidence Simic's increasing reliance on ironic humor, details of urban life, his European heritage, and historical concerns. *Selected Poems, 1963-1983* (1985) includes "White," an extended piece written in two-line stanzas that was originally published in 1972 and revised in 1982. *Selected Poems* also contains works from *Weather Forecast for Utopia and Vicinity: Poems, 1967-1982* (1983), a volume of previously uncollected verse. In *Unending Blues* (1986), Simic continues to examine familiar themes while expanding his scope to accommodate a more personal tone and rural settings.

(See also *CLC*, Vols. 6, 9, 22; *Contemporary Authors*, Vols. 29-32, rev. ed.; *Contemporary Authors New Revision Series*,

University of New Hampshire Media Service. Courtesy of Charles Simic.

Vol. 12; and *Contemporary Authors Autobiography Series*, Vol. 4.)

ALAN WILLIAMSON

[Somehow the] European outlook has not been successfully imitated in American poetry, where the experiences that shaped it are obviously missing. Even Charles Simic, who spent his early childhood in wartime Yugoslavia, seems to turn it into something less serious, more like the "one-of-the-guys" tone Robert Pinsky detects in contemporary American "surrealism." In **"East European Cooking,"** one of the poems in *Austerities,* Mr. Simic looks back to the times when "the Turks / Were roasting my ancestors on a spit" and argues (not very forcefully, since no evidence of modern horrors is given) that "It wasn't half as bad then as it is today." A friend gets so incensed at this as to scream at him, "I make no distinctions between murderers." But the poem ends:

> Luckily, we had this Transylvanian waiter,
> This ex-police sergeant, ex-dancing school instructor
> Regarding whom we were in complete agreement
> Since he didn't forget the toothpicks with the bill.

There is the ghost of a wry moral here: A mild atavism saves the two friends from the greater atavism of fighting over an idea. But one mainly feels that Mr. Simic is rather enjoying subordinating ideas to the "reality" of earthy tastes and lowlife connections.

Such easy anti-intellectualism makes *Austerities* a slightly disappointing book, unlikely to dispel the impression that the poet has not quite fulfilled the promise of his brilliant early *Dismantling the Silence*. But in some of the more straightforward, reminiscent poems, there are still marvelous details—details that convey something significant and felt about poverty and suffering.... Occasionally Mr. Simic dwells on this remembered world long enough for a character to emerge, usually an Eastern European woman lost in America. Two of these poems, **"Spoons With Realistic Dead Flies on Them"** and **"Thus,"** seem to me incomparably the best and most touching poems in the book. (pp. 15, 34)

Alan Williamson, "Pasts That Stay Present," in The New York Times Book Review, *May 1, 1983, pp. 15, 34.*

EDWARD LARRISSY

The title poem of Charles Simic's *Austerities* serves as an introduction to his book.... This magnificent poem is admittedly simple in everything but its implications, which go beyond mere condemnation of the machine State to that of all loveless utilitarianism. The anger in the bitter reversal of the last stanza shows that it inhabits a different world from [Sean] O'Brien's. Is it a matter of taste to find it a nobler one?

The style of ["**Austerities**"] is characteristic of the book as a whole, which is austerely gnomic, bleak even. It is a recognisably East European manner (Simic was born in Yugoslavia, but moved to America and now lives in New York), but subject-matter also appears to be strongly influenced by East European experience. Occasionally, though, there is a recognisable hint of the 'New York school', as in **"Madonnas Touched Up with a Goatee"**, where metaphysics, 'decked up in imitation jewelry', goes for a stroll with the poet:

> It's still the 19th century, she whispered.
> We were in a knife-fighting neighbourhood . . .
> In the back of a certain candy store only she knew about,
> The customers were engrossed in the
> *Phenomenology of Spirit.*

But on the street corners are 'young hoods' with 'crosses and iron studs on their leather jackets' who look as if they've read Darwin and Pavlov. Whimsy? Yes; but amusing enough.

It has to be said, however, that Simic's gnomic style can degenerate very easily into mannerism. It depends for success on the interest of what is being said, and on a certain judgment about timing. The fact that Simic has a taste for compressed ironic narratives means that the overall impression is of a series of grim or black-humorous anecdotes. Sometimes the anecdotes, or the irony attached to them, can seem slight. (p. 65)

Edward Larrissy, "Home and Abroad," in Poetry Review, *Vol. 73, No. 2, June, 1983, pp. 64-6.*

PETER STITT

Curiously, it may be through one of his least strong, least characteristic poems that we can best define the métier of the Charles Simic of *Austerities*. In **"The Great Horned Owl,"** a

"Grand Seigneur" appears in the poet's backyard. Simic shows him "my belt, / How I had to / Tighten it lately / To the final hole." The owl is not impressed; he "Studies the empty woodshed, / The old red chevy on blocks. / Alas! He's got to be going." We can easily imagine what Robert Penn Warren, Donald Hall, Dave Smith, Mary Oliver, or a dozen others would do with this subject; it would be a visit from a god, a serious, symbolical moment. None of them would prance before the bird like a clown, however, showing it how thin they've become lately. Simic's interest is not out there, on the bird; it is with his own performance, the song and dance of his own internal Grand Seigneur, the imagination.

Much has been made by critics of the folk influence which was so pervasive in Simic's earlier work, his preoccupation with "pre-verbal, pre-conceptual consciousness," with "childhood, folklore, eroticism, foods, animals, and plants" (to quote an anonymous reviewer in *Virginia Quarterly Review*) [see *CLC*, Vol. 6]. All this seems well behind Simic now; the poems in *Austerities* are pre-eminently verbal performances, conceptual and sophisticated, allusive to a wide range of western thought and literature. There are overt references here to Kepler, Newton (twice), Parmenides, "Pharaonic avenues," Homer; the speaker's wife is said to be "Pascal's own / Prize abyssologist / In marriage"; he and she take a walk and see "young hoods on street corners" who "all looked like they'd read Darwin and that madman Pavlov, / And were about to ask us for a light"; and a dissertation on **"East European Cooking"** begins: "While Marquis De Sade had himself buggered, / O just around the time the Turks / Were roasting my ancestors on a spit, / Goethe wrote 'The Sorrows of Young Werther.'" Veiled allusions abound as well, as the reference to Frost in **"Crows"** ("The absolutely necessary / Way in which they shook snow . . ."), at least two to Whitman, another to Pound, demonstrate. In short, Simic is a post-modernist par excellence, heir to Eliot (in ironic literary allusiveness) and Stevens (in commitment to a world of imagination).

Austerities is a masterfully entertaining book, even at its most somber. Simic is famous for his handling of human cruelty, which he keeps at bitter and witty distance through the use of irony. **"Rough Outline"** is typical of his best. . . . [It] is both serious and not serious, which, of course, makes it all the more serious. It is a tone and situation we are familiar with, and the author indicates his own similar familiarity through the use of "etc.," as well as the generally sketchy form. This kind of thing shows best in such short poems, each a sort of jazzy intermezzo. Thus a book of such pieces never becomes a symphony, or even a "Rigoletto"; rather, a series of short concerti, or an album of popular songs. If the book is at all disappointing, it is as a whole; the parts which make it up are a complete, and rarely a shallow, delight. (pp. 46-8)

Peter Stitt, "Comment: Imagination in the Ascendant," in Poetry, *Vol. CXLII, No. 1, October, 1983, pp. 39-50.*

PUBLISHERS WEEKLY

[*Weather Forecast for Utopia and Vicinity: Poems, 1967-1982*] is even richer than most lengthier collections. In the best style of our time, Simic's poems are digressions almost without text, originating from a "compulsive ratiocination on the subject of the self"—though the self may be energetically disguised by an elliptical style that avoids statement. He often speaks through archetypes who reside on a plane where fantasy intersects pure imagery. Through these dreamy veils Simic describes those alien moments of pure, intense, almost mystical feeling often associated with John Keats—flashes so inimical to our sense of everyday reality that they leave us in a minute, unless we happen to be poets. . . . We come by way of Simic's accounts of the fantastic, the momentary and the unsayable to a genuine experience of the self. (pp. 67-8)

A review of "Weather Forecast for Utopia and Vicinity: Poems, 1967-1982," in Publishers Weekly, *Vol. 224, No. 18, October 28, 1983, pp. 67-8.*

PAUL BERMAN

[*Weather Forecast for Utopia & Vicinity: Poems, 1967-1982*] contains 35 previously uncollected poems about tenement life, morbid children, love, and intimations of another existence. The poems are short and perfectly shaped. They float past like feathers, turning one way, then another, and then they're gone. Occasionally Simic ends on too obvious a note, with a big thwack on his drum. Occasionally he's not obvious at all, and you wonder what he's talking about. More often he amazes you, for instance in **"Ariadne,"** where he writes about the keen desperation of love and manages to be witty, vulnerable, and grisly all at once. The poet looks at Ariadne's eyes and sees "two loopholes." No, "two sadistic schoolboys pulling off the legs of a fly." "To hell with her eyes!" He looks at her mouth, which is "the famous cottage where the wolf swallowed grandma." No, it's a "toy fire engine." "Ah, the hell with her mouth!" He looks at her breasts. These he can't describe. Mere thought of them makes him shiver. So he looks at her legs. . . .

Weather Forecast for Utopia & Vicinity is a little book, and in that book are little poems, and the little poems say: "Charles Simic is indeed very good."

Paul Berman, in a review of "Weather Forecast for Utopia & Vicinity: Poems, 1967-1982," in The Village Voice, *Vol. XXIX, No. 9, February 28, 1984, p. 46.*

RODNEY PYBUS

Born in Yugoslavia but brought up in the United States, Charles Simic reveals [in *Austerities*] his East European origins in verse at times reminiscent of Holub or Popa. None the worse for that: his spare, wry, linguistically uncomplicated approach has a black-edged wit which deepens and darkens many of these poems. . . . His themes are drawn mostly from the physical and spiritual poverty of urban life (the streets 'of compulsory misfortune'), and echoes of Eastern Europe, a world of crows, bridegrooms and burials. It's as if these poems were miniatures presided over by Chagall or Isaac Bashevis Singer, for, while there's nothing overtly Jewish in Simic's work, he has that same vision of the world where there is no obvious dividing line between ordinary and extraordinary, between mundane and magical. He avoids whimsy, mostly, by the acuity of his realisation of human relationships and of loneliness in 'these dark, hell-bent days'. His fables may be at times cryptic, but even the enigmas of **"Crows"** or **"Drawing the Triangle"** at least forcefully present the notion of the enigmatic. More often these poems release accessible images of a corrupted and corrupting world where temporary salvation is possible only through ironically self-aware optimism and various forms of loving. In **"Front Tooth Crowned with Gold"** the hooker in 'scarlet wig,

rabbit fur coat, / Hot pants, boots' edges forward, wide-eyed, to watch a demonstration 'Just for her' of 'the world's most amazing Potato-peeler' by a man who is

> Some Greek Arab Slav Scythian Longobard
> Gold tooth and no winter overcoat,
> Everybody's venerable and future partner.

A sense of exile and loss is partially compensated for by the precision evinced in Simic's presentation of the lonely or unsuccessful figures who people his poems. 'The one who lights the wood stove / Gets up in the dark', he begins **"February"**. The woman has to use wood that 'smells of rats and mice' rather than of woods, and the dark mood of this piece is only briefly lit by the stark closing image of Life and History:

> By its flare you'll see her squat;
> Gaunt, wide-eyed;
> Her lips saying the stark headlines
> Going up in flames.

(p. 59)

Rodney Pybus, "American and Australasian Poetry," in Stand Magazine, *Vol. 25, No. 3, Summer, 1984, pp. 56-62.*

ANTHONY LIBBY

Dave Smith commented in a 1982 interview, "that one is going to write a great poem about a knife and a fork." Well, reasonable readers must agree that Mr. Simic's poem **"Fork"** [in his *Selected Poems, 1963-1983*] is not exactly "great," but it has a loony rightness that is certainly something. "Good" seems wrong as well; in fact, what the poem does to our subsequent apprehension of utensils may be pretty horrible. Consider the impact of its opening: "This strange thing must have crept / Right out of hell." The blunt declaration seems precisely right, as do the grotesque twists of the rest of the poem's images.

In his plain-style Surrealist poetry, Mr. Simic's talent lies in imagining the true strangeness of such ordinary household objects; his curse is that he can't stop doing it, so that after a short while the strangeness feels imposed rather than discovered. After **"Fork,"** naturally we get **"Spoon,"** and, yes, **"Knife,"** which is perhaps inevitable. But then there are **"My Shoes"** and **"Brooms."** Of course, the brooms are also connected with hell, or at least the devil, and among other things they mutter "that most sacred of all names: / Hieronymous Bosch," as things begin to get corny. Breasts become household objects too—to irritate any passing feminists—just hanging around like jars "of forbidden jam" or "freshly poured beer mugs." This collection is arranged chronologically, but as the years pass, we come upon the same sort of things—**"A Wall"** and **"Eraser"** and **"Shirt,"** and, as Mr. Simic moves toward simple realism, a plain description of a black dress called, tritely, **"Piety."**

Many other subjects appear in *Selected Poems,* and at times, as in **"Empire of Dreams"** or **"Prodigy,"** Charles Simic takes us to his mysterious target, the other world concealed in this one. But more often the customary devices of Surrealism are used with more cleverness than vision. There is an echo, as if we have heard much of this before. In part Mr. Simic is the victim of history, of changes in taste bred by familiarity. A phrase like "This light is our sperm" may have been an eye-opener in 1971, but now it seems forced. And Mr. Simic's forays into straight description can sound more obviously flat, as when he notes the "Chill / of the late autumn in the air."

In a 1977 poem he invokes the image of snowflakes in the horse's mane, which already seemed perhaps too consciously Japanese when Robert Bly used it in a 1962 epiphany poem.

What distinguishes the deep poems in this collection from the many that leave little impression? Because Surrealism tends to resist the claims of logic, there are no clear rules. The images work better when they are not derivative or embedded in derivative verbal patterns, when Mr. Simic thinks more about the pleasures of language than his blunt lines usually allow. But there is something else: in the most striking poems there emerges, beneath the irrational associations, an underlying logic, often the ghost of a narrative to hold scattered perceptions together. A poem like **"Classic Ballroom Dances"** is not only striking but also conceptually coherent. Still, Mr. Simic is generally most memorable in bits and pieces; his best subject remains the trivial, which becomes profoundly trivial only in periodic flashes. Then it leaves its strange mark on our seeing.

Anthony Libby, "Gloomy Runes and Loony Spoons," in The New York Times Book Review, *January 12, 1986, p. 17.*

HARRY THOMAS

There ought to be a law against reviewing a book of selected poems in less than twenty pages. One feels this all the more strongly when the book is as lovely, humorous, unflappably desperate, and mysterious as Charles Simic's [*Selected Poems, 1963-1983*] sometimes is. Since the publication, in 1971, of *Dismantling the Silence,* Simic has been our best poet of parables, riddles, and parables composed of riddles. He is essentially a religious poet; his subject from the first, born "of a presentiment of a higher existence," has been if not God, then spiritual transcendence. But unlike Whitman, Eliot, Roethke, and Bly, the American poets whose projects his own most resembles, Simic undertakes his quest often with small hope of success. Unlike Whitman and Roethke, he is utterly impersonal and non-ecstatic; unlike Eliot, he embraces no creed, is non-devotional; unlike Bly, he possesses a good deal of talent.

As each of Simic's seven books came out one often had the impression of a crushing sameness of matter and manner. Even the really good poems—**"Stone," "What the White Had to Say,"** and **"Great Infirmities"**—differed so little from the rest they tended to get lost in the shuffle. For this reason one is happy to have the chosen highlights of a selected volume. The volume makes clear that Simic's career falls into two almost equal parts, with **"White,"** a poem in many sections that originally appeared as a chapbook, being the central and transitional piece. The first part records the poet's efforts to woo the soul from its invisible realm; the second presents the poet's renunciation of the quest. **"White"** reformulates the first and announces the second. Basically the progress is from aspiration to denial.

Simic's method is the familiar one of modern poetry, though it is indebted specifically to the work of medieval mystics and to the phenomenological poets of Eastern Europe, chiefly Popa and Herbert. Briefly the method is to attempt to ascend to spiritual oneness by penetrating an object or landscape chosen as a sign or correlative of the self. **"Stone"** is both an allegory of the experience and of the poet's method. . . . The stone is the just-right emblem for Simic, for he has the mystic's suspicion of movement and, more importantly, language. The suspicion explains in part Simic's obsession with whiteness,

the standard symbol of purity and oneness; the poet knows that the unmarked page can be the only true poem. "Nor can you call me saint," he writes in **"White."** "If I didn't err, there wouldn't be these smudges." So the suspicion also helps to explain Simic's eventual denial of his quest. Being a contradiction—summoning through words that which exists beyond words—his modus operandi dooms him from the start.

The poems written after **"White"** turn to consideration of things *of* (not just *in*) the world and of the poet's autobiography. Still, the tendency to treat everything in parable is pronounced. . . .

Even the best-intentioned and sympathetic reader will find it hard, however, to overlook the limitations of this poetry. Simic has virtually no interest in the movement of a poem across the page. Indeed, one is mildly shocked to realize that nowhere in this volume is there even a trace of the British-American tradition of formal verse. Wyatt to Wilbur, it's all gone. Unrelieved flatness takes its place. Second, Simic is, as I have said, utterly impersonal. Thus the lack of affect at times makes the relation between poem and resonant life hard to see or tenuous at best. And last, there is the built-in limitation of the parable as a form. As Jesus points out to the disciples in the first Gospel, it is a secondary mode of instruction, meant to serve only those who do not perceive the truth. Foregoing direct statement, Simic's poetry operates always at a second level of intensity.

Harry Thomas, in a review of "Selected Poems, 1963-1983," in Boston Review, *Vol. XI, No. 2, April, 1986, p. 28.*

PETER STITT

Charles Simic's *Selected Poems 1963-1983* is an unusual book in at least two important senses. For one thing, it is easily the best volume of poetry published in 1985, so good that it should have won all the prizes. For another thing, it is cumulatively superior to its parts; that is, by leaving out poems that critics of his earlier books felt were silly, reductive of the deep seriousness of his vision, Simic has forced his readers to concentrate upon his very best work. What was silly in the earlier books were the merely funny poems that some critics interpreted as surrealistic. Far from being a surrealist, however, Charles Simic is in fact one of the fiercest—though also one of the most indirect—realists writing today. (p. 564)

One thing that makes Simic unique among American poets is the fact that he was born in Yugoslavia in 1938 and only came to the United States at the age of eleven. He is not a directly personal poet, but he has included here one poem that gives some details of his own past. **"Prodigy"** is based upon the metaphor of chess as representative of life: "I grew up bent over / a chessboard. // I loved the word *endgame.*" Even the most innocent details in a Simic poem ("*endgame*") give off sinister implications. Later he tells us that he lived in "a small house / near a Roman graveyard. / Planes and tanks / shook its windowpanes." Of the ending of the War, he says: "I'm told but do not believe / that that summer I witnessed / men hung from telephone poles." It isn't that this did not happen or that Simic was not there to see it; rather, he says, his mother "had a way of tucking my head / suddenly under her overcoat." I am reminded of the story told by a Belgian man who was ten or eleven when the war ended. He remembered watching from the street as a Nazi collaborator was hounded to the roof of a five-story house, then hounded off the roof.

Given this background, it would seem that **"Empire of Dreams"** might stand as an ars poetica for the shadowy and disturbing content of Simic's poems. . . . The poem has a narrative structure, though the meaning of its action, like the meaning of its details, is more suggestive than exact. Thus the poem is vaguely allegorical and resembles a fable, all of which makes it both typical of and descriptive of Simic's generally allusive and indirect practice.

As for theme, Simic's most persistent concern is with the effect of cruel political structures upon ordinary human life. Thus the series of almost miniaturist poems he has written on such subjects as **"Fork," "Spoon," "Knife," "Ax,"** and **"Stone"** should be seen not as constituting his major achievement, as some critics insist, but as a momentary stay against confusion. The world of Simic's poems is frightening, mysterious, hostile, dangerous; by focusing on such unimportant, everyday objects, the poet is able to achieve, however briefly, some degree of order, comprehension, and control within this world. (pp. 564-65)

While the subject matter of Simic's poems is grim, their writing is not, and it is this that saves them from a hopeless and self-destructive nihilism; even the most somber poems here exhibit a liveliness of style and imagination that seems to re-create, before our eyes, the possibility of light upon the earth. Perhaps a better way of expressing this would be to say that Simic counters the darkness of political structures with the sanctifying light of art. (p. 566)

By now Charles Simic has become a thoroughly American poet. The fact that he spent his first eleven years surviving World War II as a resident of Eastern Europe makes him a going-away-from-home writer in an especially profound way. . . . He is one of the wisest poets of his generation, and one of the best. The publication of his *Selected Poems* was a major literary event in 1985, and the Pulitzer committee should hang their heads in shame. (p. 567)

> *Peter Stitt, "Staying at Home and Going Away," in* The Georgia Review, *Vol. XL, No. 2, Summer, 1986, pp. 557-71.*

LIAM RECTOR

With George Oppen gone, I look now to the work of Creeley, Strand, and Charles Simic to provide the weight of an absolute spareness. . . . Here not only is poetry "the best possible words in the best possible order," utterly shorn of anything which doesn't, as Pound demanded, "contribute directly to the presentation," but it has also the presence of what's absent, a sound of spareness that goes beyond mere economy and brevity and is always at the gates of the unsayable—as Beckett always is. Charles Simic's *Selected Poems* has recently appeared and triumphantly illustrates what such a book can offer the old admirer, the new fan. It includes selections from all the books published from 1967 to 1982, as well as a revised version of *White,* published in 1972, and *Weather Report for Utopia and Vicinity,* a collection of previously unpublished work published in 1983. (pp. 510-11)

Simic's poetry is a kind of philosophical insomnia, one wherein the present is noted and remembered but soon floats off into the formulas and imaginings of history and the unlikeliness of the future . . . The imagination in these poems, which I think takes as its source *innocence,* is continually taking its first look at a first world, reacting with both awe and horror, wisdom and austerity. This imagination has done a great deal to animate

the supposedly inanimate, in poems like **"Fork," "My Shoes," "Ax," "Brooms,"** and many others which now figure a kind of 'surrealism' for their time; but in addition, and this the *Selected* makes painfully obvious, Simic's work has about it a purity, an originality unmatched by many of his contemporaries.

"White," a book-length poem, is a welcome inclusion in its re-edited form. A helpful and hilarious discussion of that poem, with George Starbuck, is included in *The Uncertain Certainty,* a collection of interviews, essays, and notes on Simic's poetry, by Simic himself. . . . It's a useful companion volume to the *Selected,* and collects many of the few prose pieces Simic has written and published. One would hope there will be more of this from Simic. His essay, **"Negative Capability and Its Children,"** is an important *entrée* into his work and into the whole of contemporary poetry. (p. 512)

> *Liam Rector, "Poetry Chronicle," in* The Hudson Review, *Vol. XXXIX, No. 3, Autumn, 1986, pp. 501-15.*

MATTHEW FLAMM

Simic's humor runs through all his poetry, from his celebrated first poems to those in his new collection, *Unending Blues.* It's a fatalistic, Eastern European humor, and part of why I find it hard to believe that he is really, through and through, an American poet. The question of nationality, as it concerns Simic, may seem moot: Although he speaks with a distinctly Serbian twist and looks Slavic enough, with a bit of the bulkiness I associate with characters in early Milos Forman movies, he has always written in English—11 books, some essays, and translations. It's an imaginative, precise, essentially native's English. . . .

Some of Simic's "foreignness" has to do with trends in recent American poetry. In the late '60s and '70s, he was linked with the so-called neosurrealist school, whose poets, influenced by European and South American fabulists, were after a certain archetypal or mythic experience in their work. Simic's mysterious "utterances" about elemental things—a stone, a knife, "the invisible"—became some of the (over-used) models for this group. But he stood out, both for his inventiveness and for something distinctive and inimitable about his voice. There's that irony, inseparable from an Eastern European's sense of history: the joke's on us, whether it's the cosmos or a tyrant who's playing it. It's a curiously detached voice, removed from its author's self. Simic's "I" is always impersonal, collective—another difference from most other American poets.

I ask him about growing up (in Belgrade, then New York and Chicago) but Simic, who likes to talk, turns out to be only a little more open about his past in person than he is on the page. "It was your typical Eastern European war childhood" closes the subject. That he arrived here at 15 and was writing poems in English three years later he finds hardly worth noting. When I ask, finally, if he might be a Yugoslav poet in an American disguise, he answers simply, "I've been translated over there [in Yugoslavia]. They don't see me as one of them." These *are* old questions for Simic, but I am getting back more than just boredom. This is also his point of view, which regards the individual as anonymous, shaped by forces that couldn't care less about character. Which is the subject Simic keeps returning to: the ways we're affected all of the time by things we barely understand.

"One of the things in the poems," he says, "that for me personally has always been the issue, is that we live in a series of endless contradictions. Just take the view of the self, or the dozens of theories of the universe. We have dozens of theories about everything. And the poor individual, if you're not inclined to believe in something easily, if you're a skeptic, if you have a sense of humor—then you have to make sense of it all, by yourself. It's a very heroic and incredible situation to be in. Very different from the Greeks, or from Mr. Hamlet, who had only a few options before him."

Simic likes that confusion; he's at home in it. So are his poems, which are best read as a self-portrait in negative space: Simic tells us about his past all the time, by what he leaves out. It has to do with what he went through during his childhood, which included pilfering "war-junk" from dead German soldiers, and going hungry after the war. But what's important is not that he suffered (he's described the war as "fun") but that ordinary expectations were shattered. Therefore his "I" has to find its own way—"make sense of it all," by itself—despite the tricks constantly played on it. The anonymity of the poems, their puzzled nature, their amnesialike scattering of the few autobiographical details, all reflect this experience. He's writing about bewilderment, about being part of history's comedy act, in which he grew up half-abandoned in Belgrade and then became, with his Slavic accent, an American poet.

Simic's devotion to his themes has its drawbacks. He tends to write too many of the same kind of poem, to the point that his surreal asides and ironic send-ups seem merely glib. You have to pick and choose with Simic; fortunately, he has pretty much done the job for us in his *Selected Poems*, which fits 20 years of work into less than 200 pages, including poems (notably **"White"**) previously available only in small-press editions. Just as important, though, *Selected Poems* shows how over the years Simic has become a sharper, more economical writer, while moving on to new ways of thinking about his past.

Early Simic seems to have nothing to do with the poet's personal life. The concerns throughout the first half of *Selected Poems* are "ancestral and archetypal": experience that predates history, or carries on regardless of it. Or, as Simic describes it in one of his essays, "to lower oneself one notch below language . . . to recover our mute existence." In *Dismantling the Silence,* Simic's first major collection, that means trying to observe the act of thinking, or knowing, just as it takes place, prior to any conceptions. The results are oracular, unexplained, and loaded with menace, as if to say there's always been history, it's in our blood. But there's anger in the work that has to do with Simic's staking out his territory: with his background, he couldn't have written any of the more conventional types of autobiographical poem. He had to respond to history—posed as the conditions of consciousness and its attempts to keep him confused, fogbound. Simic's way to truth was through chance: He followed only the random—and therefore pure—associations his mind made at that deeper level ("below language"), encountering ordinary things as if for the first time. (p. 18)

"It was an attempt to go back to beginnings," Simic says, "to go to the things that one really loves—stones, household objects, objects of immense affection." Not surprisingly, in those days, he detested anything artificial ("'50s academic poetry, the school of Eliot and Lowell") or casual ("poems of the sophisticated, literate traveler—someone goes to Europe and writes about a painting"). Taking off from Roethke's *The Lost Son* (Simic credits Roethke and the Yugoslav Vasko Popa as

his main influences), he went primitive—no people, no places, no literary trappings—and bragged about it. "Go inside a stone / That would be my way. / Let somebody else become a dove," begins **"Stone,"** Simic's most famous poem of this period, and a kind of *ars poetica*. But he wouldn't stay this ornery for long. By the time of his second major collection, *Return to a Place Lit by a Glass of Milk*, he was writing love poems and at least mentioning, if not describing, people. There's also a playfulness in *Return,* a sense of delight in letting the mind make discoveries, as in . . . the lovely and ingenious **"Watch Repair."** . . . The poem's eerie power, entirely out of proportion to its size, derives from the sense it gives of being just the visible tip of another world, one that's the imaginative reverse of our own, metaphor its only fact.

Simic experiments with letting imagination guide him; the poems are exercises in exploration. But the desire to behold inspiration rather than its products, to visit metaphor at its source—as impossible as knowing what we think before we think it—reaches (mock) epic proportions in the minisaga **"White."** The poem, by Simic's standards, is immense. Some 250 lines long, it sits in the middle of the *Selected Poems,* the culmination of all his earlier phenomenological quests. Its theme is of a kind of marriage, "the White" being the muse, or bride, of Simic's poems. Her groom, though, can barely get a glimpse of her:

> Touch what I can
> Of the quick,
>
> Speak and then wait,
> As if this light
>
> Will continue to linger
> On the threshold

The series of short poems that follows tells the history of this romance while acting it out, the poor poet mixing riddles, ditties, incantations—anything to get a closer look. Not that his expectations are terribly high. Simic relishes a certain lowliness in himself, a peasant grunginess that's like a whoopie cushion to his metaphysics. He's just the opposite of White; little wonder she's always slipping away. . . . ["**What the White Had to Say"** is] an account of poetic inspiration, and not the sophisticated, literate kind. Inspiration is—metaphorically, which, with Simic, means literally—the source of life. It leads him out of darkness. That being the case, though, inspiration also owes darkness a debt. In Simic's world, neither desolation and joy nor violence and art are ever far apart. (pp. 18-19)

Beginning in the late '70s, the poems examine what actually happened. History enters the picture undisguised, along with people, places, and names, as in the title of Simic's 1977 collection, *Charon's Cosmology.* He keeps his mythic tone, applying it to events from daily life. The book was a breakthrough for Simic, though one he describes with his usual understatement: "The earlier poems are phenomenologies of perception, of consciousness," he says. "But at this point, I simply realized, yes, there was all this history I had lived. And I started writing poems which had that in mind. You get all the atrocities, all the craziness, all the killings—you know, all the things that happened in the 20th century." And nowhere more so than in **"The Lesson":** "It occurs to me now / that all these years / I have been / the idiot pupil / of a practical joker."

The poem chronicles the pupil's discovery of the dark bent of the universe, showing, as well, the temptation to believe in a benevolent order. He thinks, at first, he's part of a "picaresque novel," the conclusion of which will be "given over / entirely /

to lyrical evocations / of nature,'' but gradually, the things he finds to be real turn out to be the most mundane; in fact, he trusts these details either because they're too trivial to be part of the joker's pattern, or because they're painful and disturbing: ''The haircut of a solider who was urinating against our fence; . . . the day / My mother and I had nothing to eat.'' The irony is pure Simic—the poet's traditional awakening turned inside out, the source of lyricism become the apparently meaningless. And it's a real lyricism, not a parody. The poem is touching rather than cynical, the pupil almost fond of his illusions, which have lingered on like a phantom limb. After all, the lesson never ends; he can still be surprised. . . .

Initially, the books that follow—*Classic Ballroom Dances, Austerities*—seem to be more of the same. But the changes in the work are subtler now. Simic has begun to reflect, not just on his past, but on his peculiar relationship to it. He's a poet who's forgotten his biography, but rather than simply reacting to that condition, as he did earlier, he recognizes it as just another joke. **"Prodigy,"** in *Classic Ballroom Dances*, describes his predicament through a faintly comic reminiscence of learning chess in 1944. The poem gives a child's eye view of war: the planes and tanks shaking the windowpanes are just part of the landscape. But the child's clarity of vision—he remembers everything, down to the chipped paint on the black pieces—can be too much. Some things he has to forget. ''I'm told but do not believe / that that summer I witnessed / men hung from telephone poles. / I remember my mother / blindfolding me a lot.'' That amnesia will be his handicap, as well as a source of inspiration, of even greater vision, as long as he can learn to live with it. . . .

Unending Blues, Simic's first book since the *Selected Poems,* shows him turning toward a more personally accessible poem, one with a bit less irony between himself and his feelings. The lines are longer, the language more discursive, the settings more specific. They're also rural instead of urban, the result, Simic says, of living in New England for the last 13 years (he teaches at the University of New Hampshire). The book includes landscapes (**"Trees in the Open Country"**), some relatively straightforward, domestic love poems (**"Dear Helen"** and **"To Helen"**), and a long meditation addressed to Emily Dickinson (**"Birthday Star Atlas"**), which shows the intellectual side of Simic's contact with New England. History appears more as topic, less as disturbing force within the work, though Simic can still conjure up haunting scenes. **"Toward Nightfall"** moves from country road, to grocery store, to rooming house, brooding over tragedy and how it affects us in an age when ''in the proper Greek sense'' it supposedly doesn't exist. Overall, though (and in spite of the title), *Unending Blues* is Simic at his most cheerful. Against this homespun landscape, Europe, with all its insanity, stands out sharper than ever before as comic relief. In **"A Place in the Country,"** those old ideas are not only funny but positively soothing, having lost their power to mystify.

> And the fire is roaring in the stove,
>
> While up above in what are still called the heavens,
> There's our own chimney smoke
> Like an oldtime coachman's whip
> For both the good and the bad angels.
>
> (p. 19)

Matthew Flamm, ''Impersonal Best: Charles Simic Loses Himself,'' in VLS, No. 51, December, 1986, pp. 18-19.

ROBERT ATWAN

[Charles Simic] is one of the truly imaginative writers of our time.

Most anthologists, however, have concentrated on a handful of [Simic's] brief, brilliant poems about ordinary objects (**"Fork," "My Shoes,"** etc.), giving the impression that Simic is primarily a poet of deep vision and small range. But anthologies cannot adequately represent the overall richness of his figurative language. This richness shows up not in isolated poems but in the densely-woven texture of interlocking images that Simic creates from poem to poem.

A book like *Unending Blues* jolts us out of a ''set-piece'' mentality. It reminds us that a new book of poems can be a literary item in itself and not just a miniature anthology of a poet's latest efforts. So intertwined are all of the 44 poems in this book that each poem seems to reflect all of the others, an aesthetic accomplishment that becomes apparent only after several re-readings. The impression is of poems without clear verbal boundaries, poems that drift unendingly in and out of each other.

If American poets can be said to fall roughly into two schools—the vocal and the visual—then Simic is primarily a visual poet. In fact, Simic's own awareness of these two modes of imagination plays a dominant role in the book. It is especially apparent in the lovely interplay of visual and auditory imagery in the volume's final poem, **"Without a Sough of Wind."**

But despite the pun, the ''blues'' of the title seem more connected to color than song. Deliberately low-keyed in tone, Simic achieves astonishing effects through recurrent imagery. An image in one poem will turn up embedded in another, and yet again in another. The images, moreover, do not repeat themselves exactly. As in some highly inventive computer graphics programs, they keep recurring in new contexts and surprising configurations.

Take the book's brief opening poem. Considered by itself, **"December"** seems slight, somewhat journalistic. It consists of a single image: Even in the snow, two derelicts go ''carrying sandwich boards— / one proclaiming / the end of the world / the other / the rates of a local barbershop.'' The terms of this humorous juxtaposition, however, will branch out into the entire book: A winter chill, snow, street life and reduced circumstances dominate the volume's imagery. Nested in the image, too, is the interplay of global and local, the universal and the concrete.

But, more important, we see projected from this first poem the problem of signification. The sandwich boards are literally *signs;* in this instance, signs that point to both the eternal and the everyday. Such signs appear throughout the book, from the various emblems of prophecy to a madwoman on a sidewalk marking X's on the backs of lovers. There are signs in the clouds, in the stars, in the movement of insects, the call of birds, in ordinary objects.

Though Simic is always alert, as in **"First Frost,"** to ''sign and enigma in the humblest of things,'' just what the signs ultimately point to is another matter. Perhaps they merely point to each other in some Escher-like illusion; or possibly, as in **"Birthday Star Atlas,"** to an awesome infinite: ''The great nowhere, the everlasting nothing.'' Or perhaps they signify the poetic afterimages of a once clear religious vision. In any case, the recurring images of blindness, obscurity, darkness, labyrinths and loss give the volume an unmistakable religious dimension.

T. S. Eliot once noted that a poem might be religious not because of the "quality of its faith but because of the quality of its doubt." The poems in *Unending Blues* suggest a highly meditative frame of mind, an imagination groping for a coherent vision. Such contemplative activity might well be called devotional, even without a discernible theology.

> *Robert Atwan, in a review of "Unending Blues," in*
> Los Angeles Times Book Review, *December 7, 1986,*
> *p. 8.*

MICHAEL MILBURN

Charles Simic is a poet of original vision. There is nothing technically new in his [*Selected Poems*], no radical experiments with structure, syntax or rhythm, and certainly no exotic subjects. In fact, Simic practically taunts the reader with a familiarity bordering on cliché. He seems to challenge himself to write as plainly as possible, while still producing works of freshness and originality. Titles such as **"Fork," "Spoon," "Knife," "Stone," "History"** and **"Charles Simic,"** literally beckon us off the street and into a world that at first looks indistinguishable from our own. . . . But a brilliant method lies behind Simic's plainness. Three stanzas into his **"Butcher Shop"** the reader finds himself looking past

> knives that glitter like altars
> In a dark church
> Where they bring the cripple and the imbecile
> To be healed,

to

> a wooden block where bones are broken.

In these lines, casual, unobtrusive language expresses the most fantastic images. Two familiar phrases, "wooden block," and "broken bones," combine in the simplest of sentence structures—"There is a . . . where . . ."—to create a picture of archaic cruelty and dementia. . . . Again, in **"Butcher Shop,"** frequently misused words such as "cripple" and "imbecile," become properly heartbreaking. If, as Emerson said, language is fossil poetry, then Simic's poems are miniature archeological sites committed to its preservation.

Born in Yugoslavia in 1938, Simic has been a tireless translator of foreign poetry—echoes of some Eastern European poets can be heard in his stark, straightforward language and often violent imagery. This imagery, however, is less a form of graphic protest than a way of enhancing our powers of observation and imagination. Similarly, Simic's language, far from an inevitable compromise of translation, constantly repossesses and rejuvenates the most popular and occasionally the most neglected English idioms. (p. 7)

In all of his poems, Simic mines ingredients of language and experience that readers may take for granted, and fuses them in a singular music.

With one brilliant exception, the weak points in this book occur when Simic moves away from the brief, focused poem, which is his forte. Some of the relatively complex pieces state their multiplicity in their titles and are less interesting, though all include ingenious passages. . . .

At least one critic has wondered how long Simic can succeed in so brief and precise a form. Simic addresses this question

in the volume *White,* excerpted here. Originally published in 1970, and revised during the subsequent decade, *White* differs in both ambition and execution from anything else he has written. A long meditative sequence composed primarily in sections of two-line stanzas, *White* represents not only a departure from Simic's characteristic form, but an occasion for a more general and far-reaching imagery. . . .

In spite of its difference, *White* springs from the same source as Simic's shorter poems. In concept, it's a logical extension of his attempt to write as plainly and originally as possible. He shifts temporarily from quick and specific nine-line poems about forks to a sort of verse study of that ultimate surrealist joke—the simultaneously visible and invisible, present and absent, knowable and unknowable color that is white. In its very blankness, and clean, simple beauty, it's an ideal metaphor for Simic's work.

All of this may sound experimental and fragmentary and self-indulgent—another poet trying not to do what he's good at. But what is important about *White* is not so much Simic's decision to expand and experiment as the fact that he knows well enough to do so within the limits of his own voice. So many poets try to avoid repetition and self-imitation by abandoning their talents. *White* is both a confirmation and a prophecy of Simic's genius. . . .

It should be no slight upon Simic to say that his poems are not demanding, and that reading them is less a matter of self-discipline than of giving in to the temptation of beauty. There is no need to steer a reader through this selection of twenty years—any three or four poems will undoubtedly include at least one that gives great pleasure. With the exception of *White,* Simic writes individual gems rather than brilliant sequences or fragments. Similarly, in seeking patterns and developments over the course of the seven books excerpted here, one concludes that each poem's quality has little to do with when it was written or the company it keeps. In the end, the abundance of turned-down pages will be the most deserved critical statement about this book.

Simic has won numerous prizes and most of the prestigious grants. This fact, and his publication of a *Selected Poems* at the age of 47, would seem to confirm his acceptance by readers. One may be cynical to hope that his deceptively simple poems will be seen as the masterpieces that they are, and that he won't, like Robert Frost, be initially ignored by serious critics in favor of more allusive, prolific, analyzable and often boring poets. For Simic's poems are the kind one thinks of when asked to define poetry. Some critics, confronted with that question, will explain all night. No, a reader of this book wants to say, this is poetry—read it. (p. 10)

> *Michael Milburn, "Fresh Forks & Original Vision,"*
> *in* New Letters Review of Books, *Vol. 1, No. 1,*
> *Spring, 1987, pp. 7, 10.*

ROBERT B. SHAW

I have a longstanding liking for Charles Simic's poetry, to which I have testified several times in print. It troubles me to have to say that I felt somewhat let down by [*Unending Blues*]. In too many of these poems he seems to be going through accustomed motions with a minimum of conviction. He seems, in fact, to have slipped into the self-parody which is the primary threat to a voice as unique as his. It is hard to see how existentialist alienation could become a complacent attitude, but such is the impression this volume projects.

It is still worth reading, still recognizably Simic. The trouble is that it is often *too* recognizably Simic. As before, his poems oscillate between two dominant moods—one of ritualistic dread evoked in austere, enigmatic scenes, and one of antic exuberance with touches of surrealism and black humor. On this last method in particular Simic appears to have lost his grip. **"The Marvels of the City"** begins:

> I went down the tree-lined street of false gods
> The cobbled street of two wise monkeys
> The street of roasted nightingales
> The small twisted street of the insomniacs
> The street of those who feather their beds. . . .

Thinking of some of Simic's earlier catalogues, so much more animated and inventive, we can easily lose interest in this speaker's destination. And there are equally flat passages in some graver pieces, in which images meant to be ominous remain inert, unpersuasive props. (p. 228)

Unmoved by much of this, I was relieved to find some pieces which sound the note of foreboding which is uniquely Simic's—dark landscapes like **"Trees in Open Country"** and **"October Arriving"**—and also some of those disturbing fragments of parables which can't be pieced together in time to save us— **"At the Night Court," "The Implements of Augury,"** and . . . **"Early Evening Algebra."** . . . (pp. 228-29)

It may be that Simic himself is weary of what he calls in one poem "nostalgia for the theological vaudeville." If so, it might be better to put them aside altogether rather than to invoke them flippantly or absentmindedly. He has, after all, other themes and tones thus far less prominent in his work which could be developed further. I for one would be happy to see in future volumes more poems of the intimacy and quieter humor of **"Dear Helen."** . . . It is really a poem about the ungainly beauty of language, about stumbling upon a pair of words which even without being understood can serve as a love token. . . . This is not a momentous poem, but its sturdy delicacy is a quality Simic might bring into play more frequently while giving some of his broader effects the rest they seem to need. (pp. 229-30)

> *Robert B. Shaw, in a review of "Unending Blues,"*
> *in Poetry, Vol. CL, No. 4, July, 1987, pp. 228-30.*

STEPHEN DOBYNS

A sense of the world and a sense of history are rare among contemporary American poets, but they are qualities one always finds in the poems of Charles Simic. This is especially true in *Unending Blues,* his most recent book since the marvelous *Selected Poems* appeared in 1985. Mr. Simic was born and raised in Yugoslavia during World War II. His poems create a small bright space between darkness and mystery. He fills that space with men and women of the humblest sort— people looking for enough to eat, for a few moments of happiness, while around them the darkness hunkers and the mystery swells huge and incomprehensible.

He has often been called a surrealist but that seems a mistake. His poems are sometimes obscure and impossible to paraphrase, but they never try to portray the gratuitously odd or peculiar. When they work, and most do, one has a sense of the world made bigger and taken out of the hands of the bandits and the captains. A poem may create only a very small scene, but that scene continues to expand and ramify within the imagination. An example is **"Avenue of the Americas."** . . .

Highly detailed, yet sparse and almost minimalistic, [**"Avenue of the Americas"**] is typical of much of Mr. Simic's poetry. Such poems defy traditional analysis. The surface meaning and the occasion of the poem are perfectly clear, but they work together to create something considerably vaster and unexplainable.

Mr. Simic moves through his work as a kind of affable outlaw. He is not respectful of traditions and never decorative. His characters tend to be nonheroic pragmatists slogging their way through a hostile world. Even his sense of history is anti-heroic and revisionist. In **"Department of Public Monuments,"** he places history on a pedestal next to justice and liberty:

> It could be that fat woman
> In faded overalls
>
> Outside a house trailer
> On a muddy road to some place called Pittsfield or Babylon.
>
> She draws the magic circle
> So the chickens can't get out,
> Then she hobbles to the kitchen
> For the knife and pail.
>
> Today she's back carrying
> A sack of yellow corn.
> You can hear the hens cluck,
> The dogs rattle their chains.

The sound of dogs rattling their chains is in the background of many of Mr. Simic's poems. This menace is the darkness that people live pressed up against. In charting that space, Mr. Simic writes poems that help me live my life.

> *Stephen Dobyns, "Some Happy Moments, Some Very*
> *Tall Language," in The New York Times Book Re-*
> *view, October 18, 1987, p. 46.*

Wallace (Earle) Stegner

1909-

American novelist, nonfiction writer, short story writer, essayist, editor, and biographer.

Best known for his novels and histories set in the western United States, Stegner is primarily concerned with questions of personal identity and the problem of achieving stability amidst the impermanence and dislocation of the modern world. Writing in a traditional, realistic style, Stegner explores such themes as the effect of the past on the present, conflicts between generations, and the importance of place and history in defining cultural origins. James D. Houston noted: "Wallace Stegner is a regional writer in the richest sense of that word, one who manages to dig through surface and plumb a region's deepest implications, tapping into profound matters of how a place or a piece of territory can shape life, character, actions, dreams."

Stegner's literary sensibility derives from his childhood, when his family moved frequently to various regions of the western United States and Canada. Although his early novels, *Remembering Laughter* (1937), *The Potter's House* (1938), *On a Darkling Plain* (1940), and *Fire and Ice* (1941), lack the expansive focus, profundity, and richly developed characterizations of his later fiction, these works are respected for their insight into his mature style. Stegner's early books typically feature a young male protagonist who attempts to escape his past and test his personal convictions against the realities of human nature. *On a Darkling Plain,* for example, illustrates Stegner's suspicion of radical political, philosophical, or economic answers to human injustice in its story of a wounded World War I veteran who rejects modern civilization to live in isolation in the Canadian province of Saskatchewan. When an influenza epidemic compels the man to lend aid to his neighbors, he gradually realizes that life is meaningless without human contact.

Stegner achieved widespread popular and critical success with his next novel, *The Big Rock Candy Mountain* (1943), which most critics agree exhibits greater range and depth than his earlier works. A semiautobiographical chronicle of a nomadic family's travels through the western United States in pursuit of material rewards, this novel cautions against the overzealous exploitation of land by Western settlers and, by extension, modern developers. *Second Growth* (1947), about the invasion of a traditional New England community by urbanized vacationers, addresses the conflict between small-town puritanical values and modern morality. In *The Preacher and the Slave* (1950), Stegner combines history and fiction to relate the story of Joe Hill, a poet associated with the International Workers of the World who was convicted of murder and executed in 1915 on the basis of what many believed to be circumstantial evidence. *A Shooting Star* (1961) focuses on the wife of a wealthy doctor whose feelings of uselessness lead her to a guilt-provoking extramarital affair and, ultimately, to a search for a more meaningful life. Although several critics faulted this work for its melodramatic subject matter, others praised Stegner's sympathetic portrayal of his female protagonist. *All the Little Live Things* (1967) examines differences between generations through the memories and observations of Joe Allston, a retired literary agent. Allston moves with his wife from New

Photograph by Leo Holub. Courtesy of Wallace Stegner.

York to California following the sudden death of his rebellious son, whose suspected suicide, combined with the death of a young friend and the appearance of an antagonistic counter-culture youth, forces him to come to terms with his fears of parental inadequacy and betrayal.

Angle of Repose (1971), for which Stegner won a Pulitzer Prize in fiction, centers on Lyman Ward, a retired history professor confined to a wheelchair who relates a fictionalized biography of his Western pioneer grandparents. Through a combination of research, memory, and exaggeration, Ward also espouses ideas concerning the relationship between history and the present, the Eastern and Western United States, art and life, parents and children, and husbands and wives. William Abrahams lauded *Angle of Repose* as "a superb novel, with an amplitude of scale and richness of detail altogether uncommon in contemporary fiction." *The Spectator Bird* (1976), for which Stegner received a National Book Award, again depicts Joe Allston, protagonist of *All the Little Live Things.* This novel alternates Allston's sardonic ruminations on aging and the decadence of contemporary society with intimate confessions concerning his adulterous affair with a Danish heiress, which he reveals to his wife while reading from his private journal. P. L. Adams deemed *The Spectator Bird* "consistently elegant and entertaining reading, with every scene adroitly staged and each effect precisely accomplished.'' In *Recapitulation* (1979), Stegner resurrects Bruce Mason, a character from *The Big Rock Candy Mountain*. He relates Mason's return to Salt Lake City, Utah, after an absence of more than forty years to attend a relative's funeral, using flashbacks to reveal his protagonist's long-suppressed memories and to show him reassessing the course his life has taken. Stegner's recent novel, *Crossing to Safety* (1987), traces the turbulent friendship of two college professors and their wives over several years. This book examines many themes central to his work, including the importance of place, the value of family and friends, the conflicts of youth and age, and the impact of history on the present.

A professor of English and Humanities at various American universities since the late 1930s, Stegner is also an active conservationist, an editor of many books on topics related to writing, and an avid researcher of Western American history. He has written two books on Mormon culture, *Mormon Country* (1942) and *The Gathering of Zion: The Story of the Mormon Trail* (1964). In *Wolf Willow: A History, a Story, and a Memory of the Last Plains Frontier* (1962), Stegner delineates his personal and cultural roots and provides a history of Saskatchewan. In his essays collected in *The Sound of Mountain Water: The Changing American West* (1969) and *One Way to Spell Man* (1982), Stegner describes the history, geography, culture, and literary tradition of the Western United States. Stegner's short stories, for which he has received several O. Henry Awards, explore such characteristic themes as generational disputes and the search for identity; *The Women on the Wall* (1950) and *The City of the Living and Other Stories* (1956) collect much of his short fiction. Stegner has also published two biographies, *Beyond the Hundredth Meridian: John Wesley Powell and the Second Opening of the West* (1954) and *The Uneasy Chair: A Biography of Bernard DeVoto* (1974).

(See also *CLC*, Vol. 9; *Contemporary Authors*, Vols. 1-4, rev. ed.; *Contemporary Authors New Revision Series*, Vols. 1, 21; and *Dictionary of Literary Biography*, Vol. 9.)

V. S. PRITCHETT

[*Remembering Laughter* is] strange. This is a Maupassant story set in an Iowa farm, about a Scotch woman who virtually imprisons her husband and her sister in a lifetime's fear of impending accusation. The brevity and economy of the story heighten its dramatic effect and suggest an inevitability which, however, is not really there. The sister and the husband have, in Calvinist speech, ''sinned,'' but it is hard to believe that for a lifetime they would have submitted to the wife's refusal to have the matter out. Neither is timid or without will. A Maupassant would have made that menacing speechlessness convincing; with only a few more words he would have given the whole of the lives of these people, instead of the rigid façade. But Mr. Stegner, having pointed out that the wife has sublimated her jealousy until it is indistinguishable from Calvinist doctrine, leaves it at that. If there is to be any theory at the bottom of a story it should surely be deducible from the behaviour of the people—not the behaviour from the theory. Still there are good things in the book. The farmer husband with his tall talk and his drinks is a real person and the passages describing his behaviour immediately after his *affaire* has been discovered are brilliant. (pp. 448-49)

V. S. Pritchett, in a review of ''Remembering Laughter,'' in The New Statesman & Nation, *Vol. XIV, No. 344, September 25, 1937, pp. 448-49.*

WILLIAM SOSKIN

Like Mrs. Wharton's [*Ethan Frome*], this romantic tragedy [*Remembering Laughter*] concerns three people whose entire lives are locked in a cold prison of frustrated emotion as the result of an illicit love affair. Over this drama, as in the case of *Ethan Frome*, there hovers an unbearable, tight-lipped silence, as though its characters have withdrawn from humanity to live out their days in a vacuum.

Mr. Stegner's story is laid in the rich Iowa farm country, and its physical scenes are clean and washed—a landscape of white farm houses, flourishing elms and oaks, trim fences, intense green squares of meadow and pasture. All of it has the native design of a Grant Wood picture, the clear lighting and the physical excitement of one of Frank Capra's motion pictures of a rural scene.

The women of the triangle are sisters. The man, Alec, a healthy, good-humored, full-blooded and prosperous farmer, is the husband of the elder sister. We come upon the women in a prologue at Alec's funeral—years after the heat of their passionate drama has subsided. They are contained, stiffly starched women now, sitting in their dark parlor with only a suggestion of a sympathetic, affectionate light in their icy-blue eyes to indicate that they have emerged to some semblance of sisterly affection.

Years earlier, when Elspeth came from Scotland to live with her older sister, she brought a youthful eagerness and a quick vitality that were in striking contrast with Margaret's Calvinistic restraint. Elspeth's beauty and her spirits led almost inevitably to a surreptitious love affair with Alec, and inevitably to discovery by Margaret.

The author's greatest effectiveness lies, perhaps, in his restrained handling of this melodramatic situation. He can convey successfully both the immediate flare of emotion and the strength of character that finally subdues emotion. He develops the story of the years of barren restraint and furtive living which grow out of the situation, in a succession of quick scenes, most economically depicted. He lends true poignance, never thick, to the story of the life of the child who springs illicitly from this unfortunate affair. Finally he leads us to an epilogue which, while it mellows some of the drama in human tolerance, remains nevertheless an uncompromising conclusion.

William Soskin, ''Locked in a Cold Prison of Emotion,'' in New York Herald Tribune Books, *September 26, 1937, p. 6.*

EDITH H. WALTON

Some comparisons are so obvious that one hesitates to make them. *Remembering Laughter*, however, is filled with such irresistible echoes of *Ethan Frome* that one can hardly evade the parallel. Less stark and uncompromising, its pattern and plot remind one forcibly of Mrs. Wharton's without being unduly imitative. As in *Ethan Frome*, an impulse toward passionate escape results in tragedy and long retribution, binding together in cruel proximity a man and two women who harbor anguished memories. In *Remembering Laughter*, it is Scotch Calvinism, not New England austerity, which is the true villain of the piece, but its blighting influence is the same and has equally dire results. Mellower, lighter in tone than its memorable precursor, Mr.Stegner's novelette is cut from the same bolt of cloth.

Gracious, dignified, at bottom kind, Margaret Stuart is warped by a stiff, prim Puritanism. Much as she loves her husband, wealthy Iowa farmer, he is too lustily and exuberantly pagan for her Calvinist instincts to approve.... Sweet and fond as she is, Margaret cannot understand him. In her perpetual efforts to tame him, she wrongs him more than she knows. Unlike her young sister, Elspeth, who arrives from Scotland to live with them, Margaret is incapable of responding as Alec would have her respond.

Elspeth is a different kind of person. A gay, high-spirited, eager girl, she has something of Alec's own quality, kindles to him immediately and inevitably, shares his joy in the fertile, teeming land. Almost before they are conscious of it, the two are drawn together, and though Elspeth at first fights desire out of shame and affection for Margaret, in the end her passion is too tameless and too strong for her. Naturally, paganly, she and Alec become lovers, and for a brief, joyous, unabashed while savor in stolen moments the fullness of delight. Then Margaret discovers them together, and in a fury of bitterness and wounded pride delivers them over as victims to her stern Calvinist God. Neither her jealousy nor her religion will permit her to forgive them. She is ready to preserve appearances, but she will do nothing more.

During the dreary, sunless years which follow, Alec and Elspeth acquiesce in the punishment allotted them. For all their native joyousness, they, too, have Calvinist blood. When Elspeth's baby is born, she forfeits her natural claims to him, represses all evidences of affection, assents to the rumor of his parentage which Margaret spreads in order to avert suspicion of the truth. In a household where too much remains unspoken, from which all spontaneity has fled, these three drag out a long, obscene mockery of what their lives once were. With Alec's death, eighteen years later, the worst of their purgatory ends, but by that time it is too late for any but Elspeth's son. The sisters are gaunt old women, prematurely aged, who though they have lost their original bitterness have lost everything else besides. They are sentenced for life to a prison of their own making.

Told with a clean-cut crispness and simplicity, this story, oddly enough, is not as dour as it sounds. It is the early, sunlit scenes which leave the sharpest impression.... Regrettably perhaps—since his tale is ostensibly tragedy—Mr. Stegner is less convincing about the grim aftermath which follows. One never quite believes that two people so alive as Elspeth and Alec Stuart would have submitted so docilely to their ghastly expiation. Margaret one understands, complex and tortured as she is, but these two—granting their remorse—somewhat belie their natures.

For this, no doubt, the limitations of the novelette form are to some extent responsible. The brevity of *Remembering Laughter* scarcely permits leeway for a searching analysis of character. Inevitably, Mr. Stegner's three protagonists are sketched in rather lightly; the process of their dissolution is merely hinted at, not shown. *Remembering Laughter* has the quality of a rueful, ironic legend, is neither as powerful nor as realistic as the unforgettable *Ethan Frome*. Where Mrs. Wharton told one all that one needed to know, Mr. Stegner leaves one with a slightly unsatisfied feeling. If one is content, however, to accept its superficiality, *Remembering Laughter* has a great deal

in its favor. It is adroit and moving; it is notably well written; it is full of promise for what can be done in the field of the short novel. (pp. 6-7)

        *Edith H. Walton, " 'Remembering Laughter' and Other
        Recent Fiction," in* The New York Times Book Review, *September 26, 1937, pp. 6-7.*

MILTON G. LEHMAN

On a Darkling Plain is the story of Edwin Vickers, poet and philosopher, who leaves a world "where ignorant armies clash by night" to pacify his own turbulence, to build a hermit's hut on the somber plains of Saskatchewan, with only a few scattered farms around him. There he undertakes to measure his own mind. He had fought and had been wounded in the last great war; now he tries to escape from confusion into solitude.

"The only way to get at reality was to throw out everything that most people call reality," he decides. "In all the spectacle of people living in groups there was not a thing called by its real name, not a person who dared to take off the mask." What he does is attempt to throw out not only the labels, but the people as well. "This matter of curiosity in the pack, this ganging together to strip everyone not strictly what the pack thought he ought to be, angered him like a pebble in a shoe. So damned empty themselves they had to empty everyone else and paw among the entrails." But Vickers is drawn inexorably back to the group—by a dreamlike maiden and a nightmare epidemic of influenza. Smiling at his own heroics, he volunteers to help the hard-pressed country doctor. Returned to the world because his individualism is not quite invulnerable, he will escape to society now, rather than to solitude.

The passing generation of writers examined man with a minifying glass, made him smaller, baser, more miserable than life-size. Inevitably, the characters became too small to be seen; and new writers are returning to their only possible tool, the magnifying lens, and establishing man once more above the ground. In this tradition Mr. Stegner has written a rich and moving study. Perhaps it is in spite of himself that he is romantic, mystical, compassionate and warm. The interbellum generation had been taught by the war generation to distrust these qualities; but in Mr. Stegner—as in Steinbeck, Wolfe and Saroyan—they are what we value most.

        Milton G. Lehman, "New Generation," in The New
        Republic, *Vol. 102, No. 9, February 26, 1940, p.
        284.*

EARLE BIRNEY

[*On a Darkling Plain*] is set in southwest Saskatchewan during the last year of [World War I].... The author obviously chose the time and place not because he had any special knowledge of them but because they were the most plausible time and place he could safely use to illustrate his theme. This last is foreshadowed in the book's motto, quoted from MacLeish: "Men are brothers by life lived and are hurt for it."

A young Canadian invalided home in the spring of 1918 bears wounds of the flesh which have healed and wounds of the mind from which he can recover only by withdrawing himself from the human jungle. He leaves a too-loving mother in green Vancouver and (having cash enough to live without farming) hikes to an isolated pre-emption, digs out a sod-hut, and gives himself over to morose contemplation under the lone and quiet sun. It does not take him long to discover that he must be active, that "to live on the tangled froth of the mind's motion" is not enough. And, by summer's end, the demands of both flesh and spirit drive him willy-nilly into comradeship with his Danish neighbor and the latter's daughter.

When the influenza epidemic reaches even their remote plain, he is dragged back into the human world of suffering and sacrifice, and finds that his will to be "honestly himself, without the mask" cannot be satisfied by a Timon of Athens hermitage, but must be achieved in society. . . .

This is a timely as well as a timeless theme and one which the author develops with skill and sincerity. The central character comes easily to life, and the adolescent farm girl is sketched with delicacy. The other figures are few and shadowy, for the technique is still the novelette, with the focus almost continuously upon the hero. There is some monotony in this, but it is relieved by the author's close attention to the varied aspects of the prairie background. The style is clear and unaffected, seldom flat and occasionally vivid.

> Earle Birney, "Saskatchewan Hermitage," in The Canadian Forum, Vol. XX, No. 231, April, 1940, p. 28.

WILLIAM JAY GOLD

[*Fire and Ice*] clearly carries the hallmark of [Stegner's] individual style, but otherwise it falls sadly short of the standard set by either of his previous books [*Remembering Laughter* and *On a Darkling Plain*]. A very brief story, it is little more than a character study of Paul Condon, a student at what seems to be a large Midwestern university. He is a member of the Young Communist League, on fire with hatred of the capitalist system and all those who benefit from it. He is desperately poor, and has to work at all kinds of jobs, menial and dull, to keep himself in school. The dialectic forms all his thought, but passion urges all his actions. He waits impatiently for the day of the open revolution, and in the mean time he is unable to see a pretty girl without reflecting bitterly that her charms are at least partly the product of expensive clothes and beauty treatments.

The action of *Fire and Ice* takes place in less than a week. Condon gets out of favor with the party because of his characteristic impetuosity in distributing pamphlets against aid-for-Britain. At the same time he is provoked by a girl to whom he has taken a special dislike: a pretty girl, obviously rich, with a cool, impersonal facial expression which he believes to be assumed for her benefit. He encounters her wherever he goes, and she is finally the medium whereby he discovers the real meaning of his hatred and bitterness.

It is this girl who shows him that what he professes to hate he really desires; what he wishes to overthrow is that which he feels he cannot possess; no real revolutionary at heart, his attitudes are all personal, and his affiliation with the Communists is a result of his confusion about his own impulses.

Mr. Stegner's portrayal of Condon is convincing in itself, particularly as a picture of the really poor who "work their way through" many of our colleges and universities. Nevertheless, the book as a whole doesn't come off successfully. The machinery of the plot creaks badly in several places, which is astonishing in a writer who has heretofore exhibited such painstaking craftsmanship; for one thing, the girl pops up altogether too conveniently too many times, simply because it seems necessary to the movement of the book. Also, Condon's sudden

understanding of himself comes too abruptly to be easily accepted by the reader, the more so since it is the result of an unconvincing rape scene which is heavily charged with symbolism.

Candor requires the admission that *Fire and Ice* does not in any way represent an advance in Mr. Stegner's art, but it can be added with equal truthfulness that it ought not to diminish our interest in the work he has yet to produce. (p. 12)

> William Jay Gold, in a review of "Fire and Ice," in New York Herald Tribune Books, April 27, 1941, pp. 10, 12.

FRED T. MARSH

[Stegner's novels] are of the Flaubert school—emotions and passions running high within the story, the approach that of the detached observer, the temperate recorder, the whole kept strictly within the bounds of form. They are effective and very moving studies, losing nothing as dramatic stories from the atmosphere of detachment in which they are enveloped. His kind of story teller does not ask the reader to identify himself with the hero, even for the moment's sake, but to consider the hero and to understand and, understanding, warm to him. *Fire and Ice,* slighter than the others but most timely, has the same general qualities as its predecessors. It is a good story, thoughtfully wrought: and sympathetically, for Mr. Stegner is of the more humane, generous wing of his school.

It is a college story of our time. Young Paul Condon, a big clean husky lad, has emerged from the very poor to fight his way up as a young workingman during depression years until he has the necessary secondary education to enter the university. He is so ambitious out of his driving need to realize his possibilities that it is painful. A junior when the story opens, he has spent two and a half years in college without any social life—has been on no parties, gone to no games, raised no hell, dated no girl. He has not had time. . . . Thus far, Paul might be any one of thousands of American boys, and particularly over the last ten years (jobs used to be easier and pay better), working their way through college in a tradition, the value of which has been vastly overemphasized.

But Paul has had a bitterer youth than others, is a little older than most, has been a real workingman, is mature in that sense—as immature in others. He is immature, for instance, with respect to any understanding of middle-class mentality, particularly the young woman, one of the art students, a perfectly nice, ordinarily intelligent college girl of liberal sentiments, who becomes the focus of his thoughts—desperately attractive and repellent at one and the same time to him in his monastic self-torture. Just so, as a party member of communist youth (another drain on his time and energy) he is immature as a revolutionary. He has not had a chance to fight his way through and come out on the other side, whether as a revolutionary or in the tradition of the self-made man. But after the tragic scene of unreasoning violence which brings the story to its climax, Paul comes to himself, not without a few painful digs from a young girl in his own dedicated circle, in jail; comes to himself sufficiently to realize he will have to start all over again, humbly, on first principles in his thinking. What will come of it remains in doubt. Young Condon might become almost anything, and for better or for worse. There is stuff in him.

The story has its faults in structure—common faults but not as forgiveable in a careful craftsman and artist like Stegner as in cruder realists—faults which are the virtues of melodrama, suggesting contrivance rather than development. But the faults are only of framework. It is as sound a study and as moving a story of youth of today as you are likely to come across.

Fred T. Marsh, "Mr. Stegner's Tale of Groping Youth," in The New York Times Book Review, May 11, 1941, p. 7.

JOSEPH WARREN BEACH

Wallace Stegner's latest book [*The Big Rock Candy Mountain*] shows great advance in power and grasp over the shorter novels for which he is chiefly known, and is a much more satisfying example of regional fiction. Maturity of experience and human insight are brought to the treatment of a serious theme; characters unusually vivid and convincing are involved in a story of deep human interest. An exacting reader may note with surprise that, in spite of all this, he somewhat misses that peculiar pleasure that is to be derived from a work of literary art. He will ask himself how this is possible. And he will reluctantly conclude that Mr.Stegner has yet to find himself a thoroughly distinctive style, an esthetically significant point of view.

Mr. Stegner is exceptionally well equipped by personal experience to stake out his claim in that vast and glamorous country which has not yet found its Faulkner, Wolfe, Glasgow, Caldwell or Rawlings, though it has found its Vardis Fisher and H. L. Davis. Born on an Iowa farm, and living successively in Washington, Saskatchewan, Montana, Utah, Nevada and California, Stegner is prepared to give an inside view of the great Northwest as it was passing from the pioneer to the settled agricultural stage. . . .

With *The Big Rock Candy Mountain* the author takes real hold on his subject. He starts out with the heroine's background in a Minnesota village, takes her to a "populated locality" in North Dakota, where she marries Bo Mason, the keeper of a blind pig, and follows her through a heartbreaking series of moves across the American and Canadian Northwest as her husband tries, one after another, the possible ways of making easy money. . . .

Mr. Stegner has felt the spell of mountain and prairie, of drought, flood and blizzard; he can write of moving accidents and hair-breadth escapes which give us the feel of frontier life better than phrases about the stars and seasons. Perhaps the most intensely interesting passages are those which describe the rum-running drives of Bo Mason through treacherous back roads in peril from weather, law, and hijackers.

Of course the serious novelist will want to give us something more than exciting episodes and local color; and Mr. Stegner's narrative is held together by themes significant on several levels of interest. His title recalls that land of Cockaigne where plenty comes easy for the man who knows how to beat the game. Plenty comes less easy since the closing of the frontier, and Bo Mason leads his family a vagabond underground life in which the satisfactions of home and society are tragically missed.

That is the upper or cultural level of interest, typifying much in our rootless America. At the deeper, psychological level is the still more significant theme of personal relations in a family dominated by a strong-willed he-man, whose imagination is all used up on his buccaneering enterprises, leaving none to guide him in his private life.

Between husband and wife, the day is saved by the courage, loyalty and staying power of Elsa Mason. . . . The real character creations are Elsa and Bo. Bo is a fascinating figure, many-faceted and intensely human, interesting in himself, and doubly interesting as the typical man (or grown-up boy), a little more than life size. Elsa is also rather more than life size, and it is with her that the reader most often identifies himself. If she cloys a little in her sweet and brave long-suffering, blame it on the author's style rather than his substance.

And what of the distinctive pleasure which one takes in a work of art? There is little in the book which has not some pertinence to the theme; yet one might wish to see a more jealous selection of detail for more particular effect. The scrupulous author refrains from using the "distortions" of art, and he does not greatly command the finer tools of irony, suggestion, pathos, fancy, or intellectual abstraction, which variously serve in the masters to give esthetic point to a neutral subject.

The patient, realistic method is adequate to the plain truth of the situation, but the point of view is indeterminate. It is not sharply objective, as in pure naturalism; and at the same time the impressions of the several characters, through which the action is interpreted, are not nicely individualized in tone. They are all presented in a uniform soft middle style, a trifle hesitant and apologetic, and not remarkable for either beauty or precision. The book is full of languid echoes. Bruce, driving west through Dakota, is half-hearted Thomas Wolfe. What is here referred to is not something peculiar to Wallace Stegner. It is the average well-bred "sensitive" style of contemporary American "realism" where we do not have the intervention of an artistic individuality that speaks with authority.

Joseph Warren Beach, "Life-Size Stegner," in The New York Times Book Review, September 26, 1943, p. 4.

MILTON RUGOFF

Hamlin Garland once gave us a memorable picture of American pioneers as men made epic by discontent, pursuers of mirages, stems too overgrown for any roots. In writing about those restless men, Garland—and Rolvaag, too—inspired by their magnificent energy, wrote magnificently. So Wallace Stegner, tracing the destiny of a man of that same breed in modern America, fired by the spectacle of his wasted powers, his furious energy turned desperate and corrupt in a world rifled before he came, has told this man's tale with superlative vigor and skill. It is plain that Stegner's earlier novels, almost tentative in their brevity, were only preludes to the 250,000-word symphonic scale of *The Big Rock Candy Mountain*. This is his bid for a place among our major novelists.

Harry "Bo" Mason was born too late. He came of age at the turn of the century, when the Forty-niners were only a memory and the measure of the West had been taken. But his eyes were fixed on a "big rock candy mountain" beyond whose summit a man would make his pile overnight; and he was equipped, surely by a mocking fate, with an inexhaustible body, iron nerve, few scruples and the kind of temper that outdoes itself when challenged and boils over when thwarted. Bo is destined to be thwarted; it is proper that such blind and overweening ambition should be. But the record of his duel with that destiny provides a chronicle alive with action, rocked by alternations of exuberance and despair.

When we first meet Bo he is a brash, fiery young poolhall owner in a Minnesota town and he is laying siege to Elsa, sweet, even-tempered daughter of strait-laced Norwegians. He sweeps her off her feet and into a life which is for him one endless cycle of heaven-soaring hope, followed by slow disillusion, restlessness, and boundless hope all over again, and, for her, pleading, following by resignation, making the best of it. . . .

A master of those sensory details that evoke the whole feeling of day-to-day living, Stegner recreates, segment by segment, the homes and ways of life the Masons tried up and down the western land during the first three decades of the century. The result is a lavish variety of sequences and scene after scene that sticks in the memory. . . .

As the book progresses two new points of view are added—those of the sons, Chet and Bruce. Like his father, Chet is the flashy, aggressive extrovert, but, lacking that very excess of obstinacy which enabled his father to outface every disappointment, he disintegrates after his first major defeat—but that is a story in itself, a study in a heritage that went, so to speak, one generation too far. On the other hand, Bruce is slight and sensitive, on the surface his father's opposite yet fortified by a pride and will that somehow owe something to the very parent he hates. Together with Elsa he lends the book a vein of tenderness and compassion, and, as he grows older, of brooding thoughtfulness, of inquiry. It is he who, challenged by his parents' lives, ponders their characters, finding in them the contradictions of human nature and seeking in them the sources of his own mind and heart. It is he who sews a lining of significance into the fabric of the book's physical action, and it is he who comes to see Bo Mason whole.

Bo Mason's career is a fictional footnote to the era that saw the end of the American dream. It may be said that Mr. Stegner does not quite do justice to the larger social implications of Bo's failure to make his way or of his being forced into anti-social pursuits, or even that there is a little too much dramatizing of Bo's violence and ruthlessness. Yet who Bo Mason was and what he did and how he lived Wallace Stegner conveys to us with a vividness and a fullness hardly less than that with which we know our own fathers.

Milton Rugoff, "Born Too Late: Saga of an American Dreamer," in New York Herald Tribune Weekly Book Review, October 3, 1943, p. 3.

THE CHRISTIAN SCIENCE MONITOR

In his *Second Growth,* Wallace Stegner has written about a New Hampshire village that is part native, part vacation, land, with a handful of persons who belong wholly to neither group, but are caught midway in the clash of opinions and codes. Just as truly as there is lack of understanding between white and black, between Jew and Gentile, there is also lack of understanding between the old stock of a New Hampshire town and the more progressive, fluid summer people who have come to look upon the village as theirs because they love it and feel themselves better fitted to direct it. There can be as much conscious and unconscious cleavage between such social groups as between those divided by race.

There is also a touch of racial discrimination in the case of Ruth Liebowitz, who, through a misunderstanding, got in among the summer folk at the "restricted" little inn, and was equally a misfit among the village women when she married the local tailor.

Though Mr. Stegner's previous novels have made his readers associate him with the West, and though he does actually live on the West Coast, he is much at home in this New Hampshire village. . . . [He] knows and loves the natural setting; and, in not frequent but exquisite passages reveals, with the delicacy and precision of a poet, the summer skies and mountains of New Hampshire, especially the changing effects of light.

In the story itself, it seems for several chapters that nothing happens or is going to happen. Then, with a tightening of all the cords of action, the fortunes of those persons who were in the middle, those who did not quite belong with the villagers or the summer people, come to a climax. It is characteristic of Mr. Stegner, who is a true realist in that he sees bright as well as dark, that, in two scenes out of three, the climax has a hopeful direction. In all events, it is not the story, but the situation, that is important to the author. Just exactly why he felt it necessary to bring in Miss Flo Barnes and her abnormal affection for Helen Barlow is not easy to understand. It is true that Miss Barnes served to drive Helen to throw herself into the lake; but, if the author believes that Helen's lack of adjustment to her environment must inevitably have a tragic conclusion, a less unsavory means could surely have been devised to accomplish it, one that would have had some real significance in this story of the rift between groups.

W. K. R., "In a New Hampshire Village," in The Christian Science Monitor, July 26, 1947, p. 18.

RICHARD SULLIVAN

A special, localized, peculiarly American state of society is the real subject of Mr. Stegner's novel [*Second Growth*]. Three human beings, ingeniously studied in turn, with about equal emphasis, seem to make up the matter of the narrative; but dominant in the lives of all these characters, over-riding them in real importance, is the formidable life of the community. Ultimately, Westwick, New Hampshire—with its collective attitudes and responses, its admirable old virtues and simplicities, its mean, tight notions, its static severity, its rigor—becomes the great and common antagonist against which the assorted protagonists of the novel make their variously successful—and unsuccessful—struggles.

Westwick is a "dying village in a dying state." . . .

Against this place, this congealed, sometimes pleasant, often ominous social background, Mr. Stegner carefully locates the characters of his book. One of them is a "notional" local girl, timorous, repressed, dissatisfied in a deep but inarticulate way with her prospects as town schoolteacher. Another is a Jewish tailor, immigrant to the village, aware of its prejudice, yet proud of its general adoption of him. A third is a local boy, torn between his good and valid allegiances to the village and his sudden opportunity to go away to school.

The affairs of these characters occasionally intersect, but there is no single dramatic involvement taking in all three. Each proceeds in separate conflict with the community. It is simply this common struggle, unknowingly shared, which unites them—and the novel—not in a single sequence but in three parallel sequences which brilliantly illuminate both the individual persons and the even more impressive spirit of the place.

The local girl, after suffering a thoroughly unsavory relationship with a woman staying in the village for the summer, finds her way out in suicide. The immigrant tailor, having quickly married a guest who had been ostracized for racial reasons at the village inn, settles with his new wife, gratefully though with some preliminary difficulty, into the permanent life of Westwick. The young boy, at the very end of the book, is on his way, somewhat reluctantly, to a new life at boarding school. Thus in death, in arrival, and in departure he symbolized the "second growth" of a community which "History touched . . . once, in the Revolution," but which now is only a "confusion of two ways," a muddle of "summer folks" with "Village folks."

Because it is such a very easy-looking, fluid, apparently simple little book, *Second Growth* is likely to seem to some readers a piece of quick and casual work. Actually, it is a creation of remarkable penetration and skill. Its small, accurate touches build up to a full and firm whole. Its objectivity, its air of knowledge and judgment, are accompanied by an almost lyrical, delicately restrained tenderness. Its prose is disciplined, sensitive and luminous. As a novel, achieving effortlessly and exactly its subtle intentions, it deserves honest admiration.

> Richard Sullivan, "Life and Death in Westwick, N.H.," in The New York Times Book Review, *July 27, 1947, p. 4.*

HARRY SYLVESTER

Half a dozen solid books . . . testify that Wallace Stegner is a serious writer—serious in the good, straight, French sense of the term. Now these collected short stories [in *The Women on the Wall*], interesting and well written, add to that testimony. Moreover, these stories are indicative of how one writer responded to the influences of the time.

Mr. Stegner is a regional writer in the usual sense that a certain geographical area engages him. Three subjects particularly intrigue him: memories of a prairie boyhood; a sudden and often belated revelation to one character of the incubi that haunt another; and what might be called the He-man pastoral, a highly American form found at its purest in the work of Sherwood Anderson and in such stories as Hemingway's "Big Two-Hearted River," and Faulkner's "The Bear."

Mr. Stegner writes with clarity and power, enough of the latter to produce a cumulative annoyance in the reader that this author should be so often concerned with the trivial. All too often Mr. Stegner sets out after sentimentality with the same equipment that could and sometimes does permit him to achieve tragedy.

Stories such as **"Beyond the Glass Mountain"** and **"The Double Corner,"** with their sudden sharp moments of insight, find him at his most admirable, sure of his subject, free from sentimentality and with form and substance happily united. . . .

Other ambitious stories, such as [**"The Women on the Wall"**] and **"The View From the Balcony"** are less successful. In the former, women on a California sea wall are waiting for their men fighting in the Pacific. Variously pregnant, addicted to drugs or drink, they are observed daily at mail time by the aging Mr. Palmer, three parts bumbler and one part prurient. Compassion alone could have saved this story and Mr. Stegner does not quite achieve it.

"The View From the Balcony" finds an English bride realizing the same dark forces she endured at home during the war also pervade an American campus in forms subtle or diffuse. Yet I found it somewhat pat that the professor of psychology should be the one to go temporarily berserk and the professor of the social sciences the one to become concerned over his young wife's whereabouts after the student party.

But there is substance to these stories, and they reveal a genuine attempt to grapple with the life of our time.

> Harry Sylvester, "Regional Stories," in The New York Times Book Review, *January 1, 1950, p. 15.*

SAMUEL HOPKINS ADAMS

Stark, unrelieved violence is the beginning, substance and end of Mr. Stegner's biographical novel [*The Preacher and the Slave* (republished as *Joe Hill: A Biographical Novel*)]. If its swarming hoboes, bums and soapbox evangelists are not committing crimes in the name of the I.W.W. and the O.B.U. which so alarmed the nation in the early days of this century, they are glorying in past depredations or planning future outbreaks.

Notwithstanding the author's insistence that his book is "an act of the imagination," it has the impact of history. Its protagonist is the Industrial Workers of the World which, with its ideal of the One Big Union, for fifteen militant years fought the hated "System" with every resource of terrorization, and was itself the victim of methods hardly more defensible. Its hero is Joe Hill, poet laureate of the attempted revolution.

Born Hillstrom in a Swedish village, and brought to this country in boyhood, Hill is here pictured as a poet, musician and fanatic in the cause of labor. His creed is "one enemy, the System"; his guiding principle, "everything the boss makes is stolen from labor." In this simple faith he travels from railroad yard to itinerant fruit-camp to embattled dock-front to riotous city street, fomenting trouble, fighting police, finks and scabs, and composing his songs. Such is the body and spirit of the Odyssey of his sanguinary wanderings, his exchanges and plottings in missions, flophouses and wobbly meeting halls, with his fellow evangelists of the movement which was to unite all labor in a single and victorious front against the nefarious wage system.

So engrossed is Joe Hill in these activities that he has scant time left for romance, amusement, or gainful occupation. The one explicit love item in the novel is notable chiefly for its pace. It starts, flowers and culminates in approximately fifteen minutes, elapsed time. . . .

As regards Joe Hill's compositions, one may agree with the labor men who complained that the cause could not advance further to the strains of "Hallelujah, I'm a Bum," yet remain unimpressed by the Hill parody of "Casey Jones," the faintly Tennysonian echo of his farewell poem. . . .

It was not his poetry, however, that brought Joe Hill into the clutches of the law but a murder perpetrated in the course of a hold-up. Whether innocent or guilty (and the evidence points strongly to the latter), Hill stubbornly declined to present any defense other than an unsupported alibi based upon a chivalrous refusal to sully a woman's fair name.

"I want to die a martyr," he proclaimed. And again, "I have lived like an artist. I shall die like an artist."

After which brave words, he fought like a cornered rat against the sheriff, come to lead him out to execution. It is only fair to the author to say that he stacks no cards of sympathy to set a halo upon the final scene of his hero's martyrdom.

The story is enriched by vigorous dialogue, some shrewd character sketches, insight into the motivations of the fanatics, and at least one powerfully nauseating description of an itinerant labor camp. Herein lies its best quality. As fiction it lacks the power, the drama, the emotion which characterizes such a work as *Grapes of Wrath*.

> *Samuel Hopkins Adams, "A Novel about the Fanatics of the I.W.W.," in* New York Herald Tribune Book Review, *September 10, 1950, p. 4.*

RICHARD SULLIVAN

The real Joe Hill, of whose life, background and personality not much is known, was one of the several "martyrs" who rose out of the Industrial Workers of the World during the first quarter of this century. As Mr. Stegner . . . presents Joe Hill in *The Preacher and the Slave* the central figure is primarily "an act of the imagination."

In the early sections of his novel Mr. Stegner strays far from known biographical fact; and it is in these sections that the central character remains somewhat dim, never quite emerging from the dark reality which is so sensitively rendered as surrounding him. The Seattle and San Pedro of 1910 are made living cities; the bindle stiffs and Wobblies come through; the feeling for people and place and time is charged with conviction. Still, Joe Hill, to whom the narrative keeps returning, stays somehow outside the texture. It is not until the book is well along that he begins to participate in its movement.

Possibly this initial shadowiness of the main figure is an effect the author worked for; in some ways it is a fascinating introduction; and it may be that the second half of the novel is made more emphatic by the early tentativeness. Yet the question is whether the possible gain is worth the cost—whether the sturdy, solid writing of the second half is not partly the result of its being grounded more generally on fact than on invention.

Once Joe Hill is engaged in his passionate crusading for the One Big Union, he begins to stand out as the prickly, deadly, not quite humorless writer of I.W.W. songs, the militant partisan, the ruthless believer, hating the system and full of indignation on behalf of its "slaves." He emerges as the intellectually limited, genuinely artistic, somewhat pitiable exponent of a compulsive "fighting back" with no holds barred.

> *Richard Sullivan, "Worker of the World," in* The New York Times Book Review, *September 10, 1950, p. 4.*

ROBERT GORHAM DAVIS

[The tales collected in *The City of the Living and Other Stories*] are regional stories in the sense that they catch exactly and often brilliantly the manifest qualities of life in very different places and social circumstances—in Egypt and on the Riviera and through the American West. Mr. Stegner records physical details and human responses with a persuasively sure touch whether he sets his scene in a duck marsh or a grade school, a Mexican slum in Los Angeles, an isolated Northwestern farm in a blizzard, or a millionaire's home, with floodlighted swimming pool and a thirty-foot barbecue grill, on a hill overlooking San Francisco. . . .

In a profounder human and creative sense, the stories in *The City of the Living* are not regional. The central characters are not really at home in the regions where the events occur, and they are often not at home with themselves. . . .

In the last analysis, in fact, every story in *The City of the Living* is filial or parental, or deals with the distance between youth and middle-age. In **"The Volunteer,"** an eager, unhappy schoolboy struggles to make a clay model of a Roman military camp in a home his bootlegger father has turned into a house of assignation. Even when the ties are not of blood, as in the case of the arrogant, tormented young Jewish pianist, or of the Negro delinquent, or the farm boy discovered in the storm, the attitude of the story's central observer is still parental, as are his responsibilities.

The psychological or regional not-at-homeness of Stegner's main characters makes the stories dominantly reflective in tone. The changes are mostly inner. What begins as condemnation of others becomes self-criticism. A deepened sense of what others are and need results in a deepened and chastened sense of self. Such detachment and reflectiveness are not likely to go with passionate commitment, and the stories do not usually drive dramatically toward some final outer resolution. They are wise and humane as well as observant, however, and teach what must happen in ourselves before we can love and understand others, and by what steps we can move toward effective sympathy with those who, most needing love, are most unlovable.

> *Robert Gorham Davis, "Voices Speaking from the Lonely Crowd," in* The New York Times Book Review, *October 28, 1956, p.6.*

JOSEPH M. DUFFY, JR.

The City of the Living is a good example of Stegner's capability. The eight stories represented here have artistic integrity; they are varied, proficient, and interesting. They range in length from ten to eighty pages; they move in setting from Luxor to Salt Lake City; in technique they display Stegner's competence in managing different points of view, in handling physical detail effectively, and in employing unforced symbolic devices. Through all eight stories one thematic concern predominates: a concern with what Stegner in one story calls "the most chronic and incurable of ills, identity." Character after character is nagged by the lonely burden of his own identity and calls for recognition from another over a space planetarily vast and desolate—to the other side of a room. In the majority of the stories the conflict is provided by the alienation of parents from children—the pain of the desire for communication frustrated by the inability of one to act or the other to receive.

Several of the stories are very good, notably ["**The City of the Living,**"] **"Impasse,"** and **"The Traveler."** Two are weak, one of which is the longest story in the volume, **"Field Guide to the Western Birds."** Nearly all of them, however, are poignant in insight, skillful in construction, and impeccable in manner. Despite this praise their merit is limited and a single reading will catch most of it. In the best of them, even, one misses a significant thickening of import and notes a complacency of form. These stories are too unruffled, too imperturbably "right." They are admirably contrived academic pieces. And in them one looks in vain—perhaps precisely because they are academic—for the very quality of life itself captured and enriched by the artist, that moral reverberation sounding from all the world's discordant brass upward to the sure, silent harmony of art. (pp. 213-14)

Joseph M. Duffy, Jr., "Between Distinction and Popularity," in Commonweal, *Vol. LXV, No. 8, November 23, 1956, pp. 213-14.*

WINFIELD TOWNLEY SCOTT

Wallace Stegner is a reliable novelist, and the excellences of his writing are uncommonly high. Because his craftsmanship is informed with a fine intelligence and integrity, Stegner can be relied upon for the novelist's fundamental job of telling a significant story; for casting it with completely believable people who are conceived in the round; for re-creating a time and place and society with astonishingly acute observation.

The immense care which he brings to narrative leads him at times—as it does a similar novelist, James Gould Cozzens—to loquacity and a slow motion. [In *A Shooting Star,* Stegner's] young schoolteacher, Leonard MacDonald, will spin a fanciful tale for his little daughters, and it is a good tale for children, but we wonder if we needed every last syllable of it recorded. . . .

On the other hand, the novel begins with an immediate dramatic stroke: Sabrina's contrite confession of adultery to her husband, Dr. Burke Castro. And as for drama, few novelists could equal the great confrontation scene. It blazes with the momentary, indelible revelations of lightning-flash. If nowhere else the novel attains quite such realistic tensions, nonetheless a God's plenty take place and the reader is never in doubt as to their authenticity.

This strong sense of reality comes in part from Stegner's decor. He has a nose as quick as Sinclair Lewis' for the precise American detail. . . .

A Shooting Star is not primarily a novel about adultery. That is only the rawest of several situations which dramatize the struggle between the present and the past. The real drama is the drama of change. The past is summed up in Sabrina's mother, Mrs. Hutchens, old, ailing, rich, obsessed nearly to the point of being unbalanced with the history of her family; and this is made the more foolish since the family's history is that of nonentities—with wealth. However, Sabrina's brief, thoughtless, "modern" infidelity is less shocking than some of the marriage arrangements in that family's past.

Sabrina's brother Oliver most overtly sums up the present in his quarrel with his mother over her hundreds of acres of land.

The solutions to these and lesser struggles are compromises, and that's pretty real too.

Old Mrs. Hutchens is the novel's outstanding triumph. She is stubborn, set, and silly, but is also in many ways a very nice old lady, sweet and generous and tremulously unhappy. This is not duality, it is reality. And so with the others. If Sabrina is spoiled and willful, she is, too, attractive and is trying earnestly if helplessly not to be useless and meaningless. Her thin-lipped husband is cool, but he is also in his way a dedicated man. . . .

It is in these full-bodied, fully understood characterizations that *A Shooting Star* exhibits its greatest distinction. Whatever Wallace Stegner's other abilities as a story-teller, it is these which make this his maturest novel.

Winfield Townley Scott, "Mature Novel of Modern Americans," in New York Herald Tribune, *May 21, 1961, p. 27.*

MARTIN TUCKER

The pace of this long novel [*A Shooting Star*] dealing with one major character and the many people with whom she forces her way into contact is leisurely, even when the woman is frenetic. In some ways Stegner's book is reminiscent of Arnold Bennett, except that this novel is a young wife's tale of a sustained disintegration rather than a momentary misdemeanor. But the multiplicity of details, the reportorial distinctions, and the insights into character are all handled through the cool, feeling lens of the artist who places his material into order. The heroine Sabrina Castro is a combination of Madame Bovary and Mrs. Malicious Rich—a woman proud, complex, destructive and at war with everyone till she makes peace with herself.

The novel opens when, after a twelve years marriage of convenience and boredom, Sabrina has her first extramarital affair in Mexico while on vacation there alone. She returns to her husband, and in a moment of honesty (but she is not sure it is *only* honesty) blurts out the truth. When her husband neither forgives her nor slaps her, but turns coldly to his work—he is a physician, and his professional duties have in Sabrina's eyes been her chief rival—Sabrina begins to travel the road that takes her first to her mother's mammoth estate near San Francisco, later to a wild escapade in Nevada, and finally to a knowledge of her limitations.

Sabrina is a typical American heroine in her vague discontent with the well-heeled furniture of her life, but Stegner's compassion and clarity of style keep her from becoming a predictable cliché. She is a species of the energetic woman who, although she has travelled all the roads, cannot get anywhere because she has no destination in mind. Her outlets for expression have not so much been closed as never opened.

The novel's greatest shortcoming is that Sabrina has no issues in which she can become interested; she turns on people because she is more involved with her wounds than her experiences. A novelist's job is not to deal with ideas or issues *per se,* but to make people the issue. Stegner himself has said, "ideas are not the best *subject matter* for fiction. They do not dramatize well. They are rather a by-product. . . ." Yet the absence of social, political, even philosophic ideas in a specific context does weaken Stegner's story. . . .

In the past, such women as Sabrina have come from the Midwest, and there has been more than a hint that they deserved the blows they gave themselves so mercilessly. Stegner has shifted both the scene and the tone. In doing so, he has created a book that captures the daily quixoticism of life. At all times genuine, [*A Shooting Star*] brings the reader into a world in which money has impoverished many lives. At all times kind, it does not have a villain. . . .

The ever-radiant undercurrent of compassion, of the idea that everyone needs love-and-understanding, and that the only way to get it is to start giving it, streaks through the book and cannot fail to make it a moving experience. Yet Sabrina's neuroses, while they remain representative, finally become annoyingly familiar. Ultimately, incessant understanding of such a limited character as Sabrina carries with it the kiss of love—and monotony.

Martin Tucker, "The Sad Country of Love," in Commonweal, *Vol. LXXIV, No. 16, July 14, 1961, p. 406.*

JAMES F. LIGHT

A Shooting Star is painfully dull. Completely conventional in form, the novel tells the pitiful saga of a poor little rich girl named Sabrina Castro. As the narrative opens, Sabrina is telling her husband of an affair she has had. She has experienced "ecstasy" for the first time, but her Puritan conscience torments her. To her revelation, Sabrina's husband reacts coldly, and his lack of loving sympathy leads Sabrina to an emotional orgy. "Sick in the soul," she searches for a way "to matter to somebody, or to myself," and the quest leads her to an obsession with the useless lives of her wealthy ancestry, as well as to some melodramatic questions:

> What if all unexpectedly you found yourself vulgar, hysterical, spiteful, and uncontrolled? What if one hour you were frantic with lust for one man, and the next anguished with pity and duty for another, and the next wild with revenge against them both, and all the time full of desperate loathing for yourself?

By the end of the novel, Sabrina has learned something about the small tragedies of her mother's life, and she has gained a little pity for her forbears. That knowledge helps her toward the beginnings of selfless love. In a spirit of renunciation she sets out to try to control her wild and unattainable desires and to accept a life with her mother "of repetitive tears in gray or golden afternoon light." The fact that she is pregnant with an illegitimate child brings hope that she will be able to give and to receive the love she so much needs.

In contrast to the agony of Sabrina, Stegner tells of the contented lives of two of Sabrina's friends, Barbara and Leonard McDonald. Barbara is the selfless inspiration for Sabrina's desire "to learn how to love people, the way Bobbie does, just as the sun shines." Leonard is a man who has learned to retain his freedom even in suburbia and to control his ambitions by an act of willed temperance. . . . When one of his children is born with a club foot, Leonard takes the misfortune without whining. Full of homely wisdom, he lives by a simple code:

> I believe in human love and human kindness and human responsibility, and that's just about all I believe in. . . . The political revolutions will blow us all up at last, probably, but I'm not working for any. The only revolution that interests me is one that will give more people more comprehension of their human possibilities and their human obligations.

It is hard to object to the Jamesian renunciation of Sabrina and unmannerly to quarrel with Leonard's obeisance to virtue. What is unfortunate is that Sabrina's story is all surface, and her tiny tragedy seems so personal that it lacks real emotional power. Even worse, the materials of Sabrina's saga are those of soap opera, and they are dramatized with a puffed-up, repetitive agonizing of situation and language that is only slightly removed from the afternoon world of Proctor and Gamble. And as for Leonard? He is undoubtedly Stegner's idea of a decent man, without religious faith but nevertheless with a real moral sense, and certainly it is time that someone asserted that Updike's running Rabbits are not the only animals in the zoo. Unfortunately, Leonard is not recognizably human. He may not be too good to be true, but he is not made true by Stegner. The fact that Stegner puts abundant hair on Leonard's chest and calls him an ape does not make Leonard either virile or alive. (pp. 103-04)

James F. Light, "A Motley Sextet," in The Minnesota Review, *Vol. II, No. 1, October, 1961, pp. 103-10.*

JUDITH RASCOE

How can [*All the Little Live Things*] be a good book when it is not very satisfying as a novel?—when its story is slight, its characters not always substantial? It's good because Wallace Stegner has let anger and concern spill over the confines of his small story, which seems to have begun as a funny and meticulous sketch of a corner of California society and finished as a series of angry, unanswered questions—questions which put the reader in the center of more than one contemporary dilemma and force the act of moral choice upon him.

We are given Joe Allston, a retired literary agent, who has come with his wife to a cottage in the countryside a few hours from San Francisco—a harmless, Sunset magazine life of gardening and a few neighbors (but no close friends) that anesthetizes the pain of their son's death. California is full of nice people like the Allstons: decent and a little deadened, successful escapees from urban or emotional chaos.

Then, out of the blue come three people who jar them into full waking. First their son's spiritual buddy, a hippie on a Honda named Jim Peck, who squats on a neglected corner of their property; next Marian Catlin and her husband, who buy a house nearby and become the kind of close friends Joe and Ruth left behind in New York. One day they learn that Marian is fatally ill, and Joe Allston has to face simultaneously the process of her dying and the ghost of his son conjured up by Jim Peck.

Joe, the narrator, is an unobtrusive triumph: he is likable, funny, unsentimental, warm, a tough old man who tries hard to live up to a Roman ideal of ironic, even generous, and unillusioned stoicism. Those who know Wallace Stegner's work will know how very sympathetic the author feels towards his crotchety storyteller. . . . Stegner is among other things a fine amateur natural historian, who knows the trees and animals, the smell and weather of the West, and can, through Joe Allston, convey the sensuous experience of the California countryside better than any other writer today.

But if Stegner shares some of Joe's values, he is also using this novel to challenge them, and the reader is drawn into the heart of Joe's folly: Joe is, in many ways, the elder counterpart of his hippie squatter, for they have both tried to escape the price men pay for consciousness and love. Joe has fled into irony and occasional drinking at neighborhood barbecues, while Jim Peck prefers Zen, pot, and sex. It is the presence of Marian, not of Jim Peck, that makes Joe acknowledge the forces of good and evil in the paradise Joe and Jim share so uneasily.

Most of us have known someone like Marian, but it is no easier to believe she exists in this novel than it is to believe she exists in real life. Joe Allston stands right behind your shoulder, talking in your ear, and we only know about Marian what he chooses to tell us. He says he thought of her as the daughter he never had, that she loved him and Ruth and that they loved her—he says these things, and yet his deepest feelings about her seem shut away from the listener; for Marian seems more disturbing (*that* quality of hers Joe conveys wonderfully) than lovable. She sees not death but transformation, not evil but misunderstanding, and she trusts the pushing force of life.

Joe cannot see the world this way, and all around him he finds the tokens of mortality and wrong. In the world Joe calls reality, the cost of love is outrageous, and to accept every living thing, exploded cell or fellow human, with love means to accept dehumanizing pain, lost hopes. At the book's end he pays that price, in order to accept his memory of Marian and her affection for him and the grief he feels for his lost son. . . .

Whether he is Wallace Stegner or Joe Allston, the educated Westerner living in California is an exile in his own country— so this novel suggests—where developers' bulldozers and flower children and exhausted refugees grab, grab, with greed or despair for "the good life." Neither Stegner nor Joe Allston can resolve that "uneasy alliance." It is for the reader, really, not for Joe Allston, to decide.

Judith Rascoe, "No Choice but the Need to Choose,"
in The Christian Science Monitor, *November 16, 1967,*
p. 15.

WILLIAM ABRAHAMS

[*Angle of Repose*] is a long, intricate, deeply rewarding novel by Wallace Stegner. It has been written seriously and deserves to be read seriously, not dynamically or speedily, though whether or not there are enough such readers still around—a form of the real thing in themselves—to assure Mr. Stegner the large audience he ought to have is an open but lesser question. What is important is that he has written a superb novel, with an amplitude of scale and richness of detail altogether uncommon in contemporary fiction.

Mr. Stegner ranges widely: in his settings—California, New York, the Dakotas, Idaho, Mexico; in his time span—from 1870 to the present; and in the number and variety of his characters. Yet what he has written is neither the predictable historical-regional Western epic, nor the equally predictable four-decker family saga, the Forsytes in California, so to speak, from the first sturdy pioneers even unto the fourth and declining generation—though to the superficial eye it may appear that he has done both. For all the breadth and sweep of the novel, it achieves an effect of intimacy, hence of immediacy, and, though much of the material is "historical," an effect of discovery also, of experience newly minted rather than a pageantlike re-creation. Stegner's method is to keep us up very close to his principal characters, close enough to hear, to see, to recognize, to understand and sympathize, as they reveal themselves to each other and to themselves: notably, from the first generation, Susan Burling, in her time a famous writer-illustrator, "some sort of cross between a humming bird and an earth mover," who leaves her genteel artistic circle in New York to marry and go West with Oliver Ward, from one ditched hope to the next, as he, a mining engineer, seeks his fortune; to the third generation, their grandson Lyman Ward, a historian, who is narrator, commentator, and interpreter of the action at one level, and participant in it at another.

It is Lyman Ward's voice we hear first, for the strategy of the novel is to have us believe that we are reading what this middle-aged historian, the victim of a crippling bone disease that keeps him prisoner in a wheelchair, speaks to a tape recorder through the spring and summer of 1970 in the house Oliver and Susan Ward had built in Grass Valley, California, at the turn of the century. Deserted by his wife, patronized by his son, Rodman, a confident sociologist, he spends his time sorting out his dead grandparents' papers (and their lives), feeding them onto the tape—in effect, bringing them and himself back to life. . . .

All this is quite beyond sociology. Rodman disapproves: If the papers have any value, give them to the Historical Society and "get a fat tax deduction"; as for Pop, he should be sensible (that is, save Rodman tiresome anxiety) and let himself be "led away to the old folks' pasture down in Menlo Park where the care is good and there is so much to keep the inmates busy and happy." (p. 96)

Implacable and pessimistic, "Nemesis in a wheelchair," Lyman Ward begins his exploration of the past. But however bleak his expectation, he is historian enough to wait and see: he has no predetermined notion of what he will find—that life was different is not to say that it was automatically better—or indeed of what he will make of what he finds—a biography, a monograph, or mere historical doodling. Gradually other voices are heard on the tape: Susan's, in particular, in letters that are a triumph of verisimilitude, perfectly matched to Mr. Stegner's carefully rendered locales and social discriminations. As she and Oliver come into clearer focus—she perhaps the more vulnerable, but finally the more fascinating and memorable of the two—and as more and more of their extraordinary experience is brought into the foreground, the device of the recorder is discreetly modulated: for long stretches nothing is allowed to break the communication that has been established. What is communicated proves to be of a different order than might have been anticipated from Lyman Ward's first bleak estimate. For what we see, what the historian sees, is the essential changelessness of human behavior; the relationship of the Wards, the strains of their marriage, the conflict of their deeply contradictory natures, transcends time and place. "What interests me," their grandson observes,

> is not Susan Burling Ward the novelist and illustrator, and not Oliver Ward the engineer, and not the West they spend their lives in. What really interests me is how two such unlike particles clung together, and under what strains, rolling downhill into their future until they reached the angle of repose where I knew them. That's where the interest is. That's where the meaning will be if I find any.

And he does find a meaning—virtually on the final page— which joins, illuminates, and in a sense reverses the two parallel stories that have been deployed. But here let me abandon the conceit that the book of which I have been speaking is *by* Lyman Ward. For he, his grandparents, and all the other figures of the tale are created by Wallace Stegner; we are speaking of a novel, not history; and if Lyman Ward is moved by "a sense of history," his creator is moved by a sense of the past. (pp. 96-7)

"We have been cut off, the past has been ended . . ." So it would seem. But a novel like *Angle of Repose,* admitting the possibility of the past as still a part of fiction, suggests its possibility still as a continuing part of our lives. Between art and life, past and present, the moment and its aftermath, Mr. Stegner reminds us, there are still connections to be made, and we are the richer for them. His novel stands out already; it may prove a landmark. (p. 97)

William Abrahams, "The Real Thing," in The Atlantic Monthly, *Vol. 227, No. 4, April, 1971, pp.*
96-7.

WILLIAM DU BOIS

Well-made novels seldom turn up as news flashes in our Sunday supplements. A remarkable example of the genre is . . . *Angle of Repose,* a jumbo that illumines one man's Western heritage, a dynastic chronicle that contrasts the American past and present with dazzling expertise. . . .

Though it was evident that [Stegner's] theme would be the Timelessness of Time, I found [the book's] well-orchestrated melodic line both colorful and convincing; his counterpoint for the Then and the Now seemed entirely justified in its frame of reference.

Why, then, did I close this big but never boring novel with a sense of circular motion in a maze?

The answer is not far to seek. *Angle of Repose* is a well-made novel *in extenso*. . . . [It is] well made as Marquand used to make them. . . . Unfortunately, it's *too* well made. The paradox is defensible.

David Copperfield and *The Brothers Karamazov* (highly unfair comparisons, but it's the point at issue) hardly seem "made" at all. Dickens and Dostoevsky often wrote badly. Wallace Stegner almost never does. In both these multi-deckers, chapters are launched with jerry-built plotting that seems on the point of collapse. Mr. Stegner's plot is as sturdy as the best Meccano on the market.

Whole chunks of *Copperfield* and *Karamazov* recall Huck Finn's sermon: very good, but poison long and tiresome. Nonetheless, these books teem with characters who are both larger than life and completely real; they are people, not postures, who somehow become part of us forevermore. In addition (and this is another point at issue), D&D seldom overlooked Lewis Carroll's advice on how to hook an audience. They begin at the beginning, keep on till they get to the end, then stop.

Stegner and his mouthpiece (a curmudgeon history prof who once won the Bancroft Prize) disdain this elementary logic. What's more ominous, they ignore the ancient proverb that warns us never to mention a rope in the hangman's house. Not for a moment do they let us forget *they're* creating a novel, even when they're in the heat of gestation. *Angle of Repose* begins at the end. It returns with cadenza flourishes to the beginning—the first encounter of narrator Lyman Ward's grandparents, in the Brooklyn of the 1870's—then segues again to Ward and his tape-recorder. It continues this facile shuttle-service to the finale: never mind if the switcheroos leave the reader breathing hard, as he adjusts and readjusts to the changes in altitude.

Susan and Oliver marry and go West, where they fight bitter battles with the frontier, most of them predestined to be lost. In the process, Susan emerges as a sometimes appealing, sometimes bitchy, sometimes baffling archetype—the eternal blue-stocking with minor pen-and-brush talents who never reconciles her craving for Paris and conversation (even as Carol Kennicott) to the cabins of a still-perilous wilderness. Oliver is the taciturn pragmatist, the miner who always gets his ore wagons to the rail head, where he's generally bilked by the bad guys. Though he's worth two of her, he somehow remains his wife's inferior.

Other well-balanced unions of opposites carry over into later times. The shuttle never fails to deliver the requisite wars of wills—and, for the coda, the near and actual adulteries that link generations in matching skeins of tragedy. . . .

This author never loses control of his raw materials or his story-lines. Taken individually, those roller-coaster *recherches du temps perdu* are always apropos. And yet—the disappointment

is worth stressing—I reached page 569 convinced that an essential element was absent. . . .

Angle of Repose, let me add instantly, is anything but low-pulsed. It has, in fact, more than its quota of blood and guts and Rabelaisian laughter—its own built-in inducements to go on reading. It is head-and-shoulders above most of the navel-chewing that passes for fiction on our current lists. But it is the work of a forthright craftsman. A well-made novel, neither more nor less.

Oliver and Susan are antagonists to be respected. I, for one, sensed their heartaches without sharing them; I empathized with the collywobbles of the decent, irascible Bancroft Prize-winner who was researching them so diligently. I could never forget the time machine he was using, or close my ears to the busy hum of its bearings. I could never lose myself in Lyman Ward's artful re-creations. As I was once lost in Dmitri's madness, in Copperfield's passion for that little nitwit Dora Spenlow. . . .

As well-made novels go, *Angle of Repose* fills an aching void. . . .

The addict can be forgiven for wanting something even better.

William Du Bois, "The Last Word: The Well-Made Novel," *in* The New York Times Book Review, August 29, 1971, p. 31.

JANET BURROWAY

Peace-seeking in the poisoned American West is a recurrent theme of Wallace Stegner's novels. He seems now to have found its ideal image in *Angle of Repose,* the geological term for the slope at which rocks cease to roll. This is a novel-within-a-novel, narrated by a historian who, short half a leg and rigid up the spine, abandoned by his wife and edged towards an asylum by his son, sets out to chronicle his grandmother's adjustment to the West.

Most of the book's almost 600 pages are devoted to Susan Ward, and she is its great strength. Following Bancroft's advice to historians, 'Present your subject in his own terms, judge him in yours,' Lyman Ward presents his grandmother as a proud, gay, inquisitive and self-regarding Eastern illustrator who marries a man too rugged for her sensibilities; who puts her minor talent to good use precisely because of the exile she resentfully endures. The vitality and hypocrisy of her letters are superbly caught, as is the mulish integrity of her husband Oliver, and the relationship that emerges is one of complex unease between two people who both, like the Brownings, erroneously regard the woman as superior.

Stegner's hero fully understands that people like his grandfather were responsible for the current California mess:

> Afflicted . . . with the frontier faith that exploitation is development, and development is good, he was simply an honest man.

And to a large extent the book is a plea that the Victorian way of handling inadequacy and error was not a bad way. (p. 369)

In two ways the argument is weakened and the stature of the book slightly diminished. The first is that Stegner expends so much more compassion on the grandparents than on the contemporary young. . . . Secondly, if we are to be convinced that the rigid Victorian marriage was a better frame for dealing with the human predicament than current licence, then he must convince us that Susan Ward did find the 'angle of repose' in some more positive form than penance and duty. He suggests but does not show this, and the novel ends on a query some hundred pages too soon. This is, of course, for so long a book, a left-handed complaint. (pp. 369-70)

Janet Burroway, "Limping Westward," in New Statesman, Vol. 82, No. 2113, September 17, 1971, pp. 369-70.

TIME, NEW YORK

"How to live and grow old inside a head I'm contemptuous of, in a culture I despise." The voice belongs to Joe Allston, a retired talent agent who serves as protagonist of Wallace Stegner's latest novel [*The Spectator Bird*]. But the problem is one that seems to have much preoccupied Stegner himself.... [For] some time his narrators have been older people (70 and upward). They mount the crow's-nest of age to look back (and down) on current civilization. The resulting author's voice is full of a distinctive sardonic ruefulness that produces a style of its own.

Joe Allston, for example, describes himself as "a wisecracking fellow traveler in the lives of other people, and a tourist in his own." He is aching from rheumatoid arthritis but resents all treatment.... His wife Ruth worries about him, and keeps urging him to write "something, anything." So he begins "the way a kid lost in the mountains might holler at a cliff just to hear a voice."

What Allston writes is a recollection of a trip to Denmark made 20 years earlier. It is, as Stegner admits, a gothic tale complete with a brief interlude with Baroness Karen Blixen herself and a teasingly slow revelation of the sins of the Danish aristocracy. Allston, looking for his ancestral past, concludes that many things are rotten in the state of Denmark, and always have been, as they are in any place the human race inhabits.

For a man like Joe Allston, who lives off other men's talents and is a failed talent himself, the book becomes a study on how to survive in a world where "most things break, including hearts. The lessons of life amount not to wisdom, but to scar tissue and callus." The way of survival most celebrated here is the bittersweet process of an aging marriage.... Wallace Stegner's message seems to be that, as in the ark, mankind and other animals go more gently into that good night if they go two by two. (pp. 65-6)

A review of "The Spectator Bird," in Time, New York, Vol. 108, No. 2, July 12, 1976, pp. 65-6.

PETER WILD

The Spectator Bird provides intriguing opportunities for comparison and contrast with *Angle of Repose*, while at the same time showing [Stegner's] skill in taking risks with his craft. For one thing, it is a shorter work, less comprehensive in time and space, and in this sense less ambitious. The central figure is another aging, sickly male, a carry-over from the previous novel. But this time Stegner throws out much of the historical propping; instead he is interested in the psychic life of his character as influenced by events having little to do with panoramic history. The plot is simple, approaching cliché, and one holds his breath to see if the novelist can bring it off.

Joe Allston is a retired literary agent from New York, comfortably settled with his wife Ruth in the hills around Palo Alto, California. In his seventies, Joe struggles with the pains of aging, the occasional sore back, the twinges in his joints during rainy weather. Unlike his wife, he no longer wrestles with politics and social issues; he wants to be left alone to enjoy his less than original musings and the company of his dying friends. "I am just killing time till time gets around to killing me," he says. Nights he walks in his garden, meditating on the wisdom of Marcus Aurelius. Inside, Ruth worries that he'll catch cold, frets about his increasing spates of introspection. The beginning of the novel does not seem propitious.

The wily Stegner, of course, knows what he is doing. Trudging up the hill to his house from the mailbox, Joe notices among the standard pleas for help from Boys' Town, the NAACP, and the Association for the American Indian a post card from a countess on the financial skids, a friend he and Ruth made twenty years ago while vacationing in Denmark. The unexpected note sparks Joe to life again, and he rummages around until he finds his diary of the trip. Motherly Ruth catches him flicking through it; thereafter, [*The Spectator Bird*] saws back and forth between the couple's reliving of the past through nightly sessions with the diary and the resulting change in Joe's perspective. Along the way the reader beholds revelations of the unsuspected, the goings-on in a Gothic castle, suicide, experimentation with human genetics, Joe's one extramarital love affair, and incest. In a small but personal triumph Joe is rejuvenated by coming to terms with the past and achieves a new appreciation for the present. The delight lies in seeing Stegner succeed within the limitations of such a scheme, proof of a master hand at work. Wallace Stegner will be remembered for other canvases, works that impress with their large scope, but this one also is worthy, a miniature, almost perfect. (pp. 278-79)

Peter Wild, in a review of "The Spectator Bird," in Arizona Quarterly, Vol. 33, No. 3, Autumn, 1977, pp. 278-79.

BENJAMIN DeMOTT

Fare forward, says the poet, and most people do, including Bruce Mason, hero of Wallace Stegner's [*Recapitulation*].

Mason, a bachelor ex-diplomat in his mid-60's, is universally admired and trusted, edits a quality magazine, handles spot assignments for the State Department and usually is too busy for nostalgia. Even his areas of expertise—the Organization of Petroleum Exporting Countries, oil diplomacy—are tomorrow-oriented. The company of a sympathetic woman occasionally induces Mason to talk a little about his youth, but only a little. Like the rest of us, he's comfortable with the notion that growing up means forgetting, and he seldom looks back.

Everything changes, though, owing to an intrusion of family duty. Except for an aged aunt in a nursing home, Mason is the last of his clan. When the aunt dies, in Salt Lake City, scene of the hero's boyhood and adolescence (he hasn't returned in 45 years), he comes home to bury her and the return plunges him deep into his past.

It's a painful descent, as it happens, because the feelings familiar to this grown-up—confidence, self-esteem—are remote from those that dominated his youth. In chapters that interleave memory and confession, Wallace Stegner awakens his hero's sleeping past....

The emotional particulars of the story—dependence on a loving mother, unvarying touchiness before the father, ceaseless competitiveness and envy—are obviously not new to fiction. As in Mr. Stegner's other novels, ... the writing is more often workmanlike than striking. And because Bruce Mason's intention, as ultimately revealed, is to expunge the past absolutely from his memory, the author sometimes seems at pains to prevent the past from returning too vividly—too ineradicably. This holding back from complete imaginative engagement lessens the impact of several crises (among them, the end of a first love affair).

Yet, despite all this, *Recapitulation* is an easy book to respect. The author's often-praised gift for the re-creation of place is partly responsible. . . .

More important, *Recapitulation* is rich in the grittier American truths—the kind I associate with (and admire in) the works of Edward Dahlberg. Wallace Stegner knows that the problem for many of our kind isn't just that we can't bear connection but that we find continuity still more unendurable. And he's alert to many intricacies in our standard heroes of success—figures who, inhabiting the glowing skin of luxury, remain gaunt and wounded within. *Recapitulation* is unsurprising in design and slightly under-animated in execution, but it has a piece of our pathos at its core.

Benjamin DeMott, "Mixing Memory and Desire,"
in The New York Times Book Review, *February 25, 1979, p. 10.*

JONATHAN PENNER

Against the ways and means of movies, what chance has fiction? Not much, suggests this novel by Wallace Stegner. *Recapitulation* is a capitulation to cinema vision, cinema technique. It is a book whose dominating metaphor is the movie, and which pursues that metaphor so doggedly that its failure is a criticism of film itself.

Bruce Mason, 67, ex-ambassador and the State Department's leading Arabist, returns to Salt Lake City to bury his last surviving relative. But he hardly knew Aunt Margaret, and realizes that he wouldn't have come had he not a more pressing need.

A nearer person must be interred: his younger self, who—he now finds—has become a set of mental newsreels. . . .

The action is minimal. Mason arrives in town, consults with the funeral director, drives around to see how the place has changed, spends the night in a hotel, and attends Aunt Margaret's funeral the next morning. He does learn that someone has been trying to call him; there is a hint (which Mason strangely fails to catch) that his best friend and his best girl of those bygone days may now be married. But he never makes the return call that we're waiting for, and this thin current of plot sinks into the desert sand.

Such slight forward momentum can be overborne by the retrograde motion of flashback, and a series of flashbacks is what *Recapitulation* chiefly is. Indeed, the main time frame of the story—Mason's visit to Salt Lake City—turns out to be a slim excuse for a guided tour through the newsreel archives. This design flouts the conventional wisdom of the craft: let present action run until some background to it is necessary; defer flashback until the reader has been made hungry for its contents.

Here present action comes to nothing; all we have are shards of the past to assemble. Bruce, the ashamed son of a liquor smuggler. Bruce stealing a cabbage. Bruce feeling a girl in a crowd. The jagged pieces fall into place until we see young Bruce whole.

But he has been gone for half a century; and why—apart from a novelist's convenience—the Bruce of today should systematically remember all this is more than the reader can imagine. Just as puzzling as his prodigious remembering is the mechanical way his memory works. . . .

In movies—which usually lack narrators—memory must be made to serve: someone looks out a window and sees, on the lawn, himself as a child. But in fiction, flashback need not, often should not, work this way. A third-person novel, which this book is, can simply tell us what happened, never pretending that someone is reliving these events in his mind. This is truer to how we think than the remembered flashback that we agree to accept (granting the art its limits) in movies. . . .

Despite irruptions of pedantry, the language is often startlingly good: "His childhood had been a disease that had produced no antibodies. Forget for a moment to be humorous or ironic about it, and it could flare up like a chronic sinus." And many of the remembered vignettes are fine set pieces—for instance, a game of strip poker and its aftermath. A different, better novel could have been built by arranging these events chronologically—the story of Bruce Mason's youth—and leaving out the Bruce Mason of 50 years later.

That would free us from the camera and the computer, another term for memory in this novel—the goddess and god of our technology. The mind is no such simple machine as either of these.

Jonathan Penner, "Through the Camera's Eye," *in*
Book World—The Washington Post, *March 11, 1979,
p. F3.*

PETER LA SALLE

The protagonist [of *Recapitulation*] is Bruce Mason, and readers of Stegner's *The Big Rock Candy Mountain* will remember last seeing him as a young man in that novel. Now he is a respected State Department official on the brink of old age. He goes to Salt Lake City to oversee the burial of a maiden aunt. He grew up there and hasn't been back in 45 years. The visit is jarring, conjuring up memories from a more bitter than sweet youth populated by a seemingly heartless father, a seemingly mistreated mother and a seemingly special girl whom he intended to marry after finishing law school and whom he lost. The narrative thrust is Mason's probing those *seemingly's*—in a series of extended flashbacks, he examines the past with near-Proustian obsession to see if the years of success since have given him any more insight into what he has been trying to repress for so long.

The novel's strengths lie in those remembered sequences themselves. The best of them read like complete short stories. Stegner, through Mason, doesn't back away from the most painful scenes. . . .

He creates a solid feeling for time and place, detailing in rich language the beauty of simple things ranging from a scarlet-and-white University of Utah athletic sweater to a dazzling sunset seen from a restaurant. Also there is much graceful wisdom here, a commodity all too rare in fiction nowadays when so many writers appear to be delivering their raucous fare just to jolt a shock meter, rather than to appeal to human sensibility. For instance: "He told himself that it is easy enough to recover from a girl, who represents to some extent a choice. It is not so easy to recover from parents, who are fate."

The novel is lacking, however, in the framework encompassing the memories. The reader doesn't see enough of Mason in the present; the few scant details about his adult life as a diplomat in the Mideast seem forced, as if the author had to research the matter simply so Mason would have a profession. And though Stegner probably doesn't want Mason to reach any neat conclusions about his youth, Mason never seems to realize fully that maybe he can't come to any conclusions. In other words, the narrative never quite falls together, even in confirmation of the perplexing.

> *Peter La Salle, in a review of "Recapitulation," in America, Vol. 140, No. 18, May 12, 1979, p. 400.*

GILBERTO PEREZ

Recapitulation is a carefully crafted novel, smoothly shifting back and forth between the present and the pieces of the past that surface in Bruce Mason's mind. Almost anything he encounters in his old city can act to trigger his memories, the things that still remain as well as those he finds changed or gone. He recalls his unhappy boyhood with the family he felt ashamed of, the father who was a bootlegger, the suffering supportive mother; recalls the young man whose friendship helped Mason pull himself together in the years of his early manhood; recalls Nola, the love of his life, or so it had seemed back then, before their relationship ended in grief. The present time of Mason's visit is recounted in the past tense; the past of his memories and dreams is sometimes given in the present tense, to correspond to those moments when it becomes especially vivid in his mind. Everything, however, is recounted in the third person: Stegner follows the venerable Jamesian method of third-person narration limited to the consciousness of one person in the story. When, as here, that person is the protagonist, this method serves at once to encase us in his frame of reference—it's his story as it appears to him—and to keep us at a certain distance from him, since he's not the one telling the story.

For me this method, even in some of the master's own longer works, can often become irksome, generating neither sufficient subjectivity nor sufficient detachment. I found Stegner's novel intermittently absorbing but more frequently frustrating in its calculated withholding of information. I wanted to know more about the past than Mason remembers, or would like to remember: not until more than halfway into the book, for example, do we learn that a certain licentious fellow Mason has been recalling with distaste was the man Nola betrayed him with. Nor did I get a clear enough picture of Mason himself, of the satisfactions he must have obtained from his diplomatic career, of the reasons why even now, on this trip into the past, he won't quite come to terms with it. Thinking he ought to get in touch with his old best friend, he looks him up in the phone book and discovers that his number is the same one as that left by the woman who called the funeral parlor; but Mason can't bring himself to call that number back, though we're led to expect he will until the end, when he's relieved of doing so by an assignment from Washington which he gladly accepts. We are to understand that his rushed departure from Salt Lake City parallels his escape from it as a young man, when Nola perhaps had sought a reconciliation with him and he left without speaking to her—as now it was perhaps Nola who called him at the funeral parlor. Still, I wanted to find out who that woman was, and to know more about Nola, in the present and in the past, than the restrictive compass of Mason's repressive consciousness permits.

What had happened with Nola was bound up with another, still more important relationship in Mason's past. He had virtually invited her seduction by that distasteful fellow, whose vulgarity and coarse masculinity Mason seems to have associated with his own father. It transpires that the relative who, in his mind, Mason has really come back to bury is his hated bootlegger father, long in the grave yet the crucial unresolved figure in his past. But this takes an inordinate length of time in transpiring, and we never learn enough about that father, again because Mason is reluctant to summon him back. Stegner's novel is not a recapitulation but a thwarted attempt at one, thwarted because Bruce Mason would really rather not know; but that's not, in my opinion, a good enough reason why *we* shouldn't. (pp. 475-76)

> *Gilberto Perez, in a review of "Recapitulation," in The Hudson Review, Vol. XXXII, No. 3, Autumn, 1979, pp. 474-76.*

LARRY WOIWODE

[*One Way to Spell Man,* a collection of essays], is divided into two sections, the first concentrated on writing, on attitudes toward it, and on basic beliefs; "pitons," as Stegner puts it in his foreword, "driven into the cracked granite of uncertainty to establish a temporary foothold." "Belief and attitudes form the base from which one projects a life and the writing that is its by-product," he adds. A quote from Conrad, bearing on the same point (from a Conrad essay entitled "Books," which Stegner refers to more than once), seems the guiding light for his own book's entire composition: "A novelist who would think himself of a superior essence to other men would miss the first condition of his calling." Wonderful distillation, this.

The second half of the collection explores the area that shaped Stegner and has provided a good deal of his material, the West. In these essays, dealing with frontier attitudes and the vision of the West, and with the sensibilities of men identified with it, such as A. B. Guthrie, Walter Van Tilburg Clark, Ansel Adams, and John Muir, Stegner pins down, at least partially, particular objectifications of his beliefs. These are "not susceptible to the quantitative or mensurative or statistical methods of social science," because they deal with creativity and "art is all variables, all particulars—and yet at the moment of meeting, both work and reader must operate as wholes and must collaborate toward meaning." (p. 3)

[In his essay **"One Way to Spell Man"**], Stegner says, "What anyone who speaks for art must be prepared to assert is the validity of nonscientific experience and the seriousness of non-verifiable insight. The second is easier. For nearly a hundred years now, literature has assumed for some people the spiritual responsibilities traditionally belonging to religion." Undoubtedly this is true, and if this age wants its prophets and philosophers and talk-show shamans to be writers, then that's what it'll get. But what about zeal in this particular realm? In later essays, Stegner speaks of the excesses, of language and of sex, that he sees invading contemporary fiction, along with a deterioration of standards by those who ought to be arbiters of usage (he implies that Updike, "a lord of language," has trouble with lie/lay verbs, from the evidence of *The Coup*).

Which implies too that there is another side to what he is saying, one having to do with language and rhetoric. When you formulate beliefs without a cosmology of moral reference, or the theology that most established religions supply, those beliefs might seem commendable, if one has Stegner's articulate, reasoned overview. But then the next man will formulate his beliefs, and values that would otherwise be subjected to the systematic "spiritual responsibilities traditionally belonging to religion," become secularized and free-floating. As a result, you can have a Great Society, for instance, looking out from a New Frontier, which is able to perpetrate a war like the one in Vietnam. For whatever reasons.

It's this very lack of relative reference, it would seem, that causes the "go-for-broke" attitude that Stegner decries in much of modern writing. And causes, too, the depredations, mentioned in later essays, that are taking place in the parks and wildernesses of the West. This is a problem somewhat touched upon in **"The Writer and the Concept of Adulthood,"** when Stegner writes "if the present tendency toward accentuated ethnicity continues, there may never be a recognizably American adult, but instead the continuation and hardening of diverse and possibly hostile patterns within many subcultures." Yet isn't "ethnicity" less a central cause than basic standards, or a lack of them? And don't personalities, as easily as ethnic groups, harden in their own directions? What's the real source of divisiveness? Or of chaos? These are questions Stegner's essays provoke.

The best parts of *One Way to Spell Man* are those that deal with writing, and the specifics of it, as seen from the inside, after 50 years of practice and some 40 years of teaching. . . . [Surprisingly], considering how prolific he's been, the most telling of his insights are into the darker side of the business, relating to "blocks," or the problems of being "written out." Or to this: "The writing habit can be a carefully prepared schizophrenic closet into which one retires to make intolerable reality into something bearable."

These passages, and passages from the essays on the West as a purely physical phenomenon—where a "baptism in space and night and silence" on the plains brings Stegner to an understanding of his identity—make this a book that many literate and literary and space-bound travelers on this westward-tending continent will want to have handy as a point of particular reference in an age that is going. Or gone. (pp. 3, 13)

Larry Woiwode, "Wallace Stegner: On Literature and the Land," in Book World—The Washington Post, *May 2, 1982, pp. 3, 13.*

VANCE BOURJAILY

[*One Way to Spell Man*] is a collection of essays, written over 30 years, which express the attitudes and beliefs of a humane and civilized man who is both an artist and a Westerner.

The opening essay, **"This I Believe,"** sets the tone and, in a way nearly always perceptible, lays a foundation for the others:

> Passionate faith I am suspicious of. . . . I fear immoderate zeal. . . . The code of conduct to which I subscribe was preached more eloquently by Jesus Christ than by any other. About God I simply do not know. . . .

Though the two men are quite dissimilar, except that both write fine prose, it is still not altogether preposterous to suggest an image of E. M. Forster in a Stetson hat.

Mr. Stegner did not, as he tells us, possess "civilization from childhood." He recalls being taken by wagon, driven by his father across 50 miles of uninhabited Western prairie to the place on their homestead where the house was to be built.

"I . . . came hungrily . . . from the profound barbarism of the frontier, and was confronted with the fairly common task assigned American would-be writers: that of encompassing in one lifetime, from scratch, the total achievement of the race."

His mastery of this assignment is evident in Part I of the book, in which he writes of art and literature, science and language, work and pleasure, esthetics and ethics, expressing attitudes which, as he says, may not be "very bizarre or very new" but are nevertheless lucid, interesting and always consistent with his basic beliefs. That he is still a son of the region in which he grew up is equally evident in the second section of the book, where he writes of the land itself and of the work of some of its other artists—A. B. Guthrie, Walter van Tilburg Clark and Ansel Adams.

Vance Bourjaily, "An Artist and a Westerner," in The New York Times Book Review, *May 30, 1982, p. 19.*

KERRY AHEARN

More than anything else, we long mightily for something to believe in. Wallace Stegner's latest book of essays [*One Way to Spell Man*] speaks to the same need, though without the simplifications necessary to gain it top rating. The sixteen essays, in fact, give an overview of the author's concern over the past 35 years with belief, tradition, and principle. It is a catholic gathering. Seven of the essays (Part I) approach in various general ways the subject of belief and its relationship to literature, and the question of the writer's obligations. The rest of the volume deals with western themes, from A. B. Guthrie, Jr. to James Watt. . . . Truly there is the consistency we have come to expect of him: the earnest tone, the softening humor, the emphasis upon moderation and the writer's humility before his task. But there is also an encouraging impression of change (I hope I am not inventing): Stegner writes even more skillfully now than he did a quarter-century ago.

"One Way to Spell Man," by its defense of art ("the validity of nonscientific experience and the seriousness of nonverifiable insight"), sets the tone for Part I, and with **"Fiction: A Lens on Life"** constitutes Stegner's best theorizing on art in general. Every reader should know them. But even more interesting as investigations of ideas are two essays from the past five years, **"The Writer and the Concept of Adulthood,"** and **"Excellence and the Pleasure Principle."** They illustrate how much the early Stegner seems self-conscious dealing with "Ideas." By the 1970s, Stegner-the-Essayist is a more confident and comfortable persona who can use personal experience and even risk self-deprecation ("a bewildered pilgrim") in pacing an essay and in clarifying and dramatizing concepts.

The same can be said of the volume's western essays. **"That New Man, the American,"** **"The Provincial Consciousness,"** and **"The Gift of Wilderness,"** though they do not equal in substance the best work in *The Sound of Mountain Water,* show Stegner a master of communicating a hard message in a most affecting manner. (pp. 52-3)

The prophet is yet among us, not much honored, but we can enjoy these reminders of his presence. He makes a case for hope, but refuses to promise or pontificate: "Yes, this I believe, this I will stick with, or am stuck with." (p. 53)

Kerry Ahearn, in a review of "One Way to Spell Man," in Western American Literature, *Vol. XVIII, No. 1, May, 1983, pp. 52-3.*

ALAN CHEUSE

[*Crossing to Safety*] recalls to us the old grand highway of novels about youth and age, family and friends, work and poverty and success and failure, sickness and health, loving and cherishing, the value of place and how to live with *dis*-placement, art and life, yes, yes, yes, all these marvelous motifs growing out of the story of a life span of not always easy friendship between two couples who will, by the time you finish the book, become confused, probably, with your own special friends and acquaintances; that's how splendidly crafted this novel is.

Larry Morgan, the septuagenarian writer who tells the story, can take all the credit for that. From the beginning, his felicitous gift for making the ordinary into the beautiful catches our attention, from the odor of the air in the room in northern Vermont into which he wakes in the opening scene ("Standard summer-cottage taint of mice, plus a faint, not-unpleasant remembrance of skunks under the house, but around and through those a keenness as of 7,000 feet. . . .") on through the portraits of academic life in a Midwest college town in the '30s and an upper-middle-class summer retreat in the old woods of Vermont with its road that curves "out of wet ground thick with cedars, and up onto a plateau meadow where Jersey cows, beautiful as deer, watch . . . with Juno eyes. . . ."

That's a little how I felt, watching, bewitched, as the story of Larry and Sally Morgan and Charity and Sid Lang unfolded with such ease before me, their love for each other and for life, their defeats and victories in their attempts to make ordinary decent lives in a world born of economic depression and, later, global war. And I watched, read quickly, fascinated with the way in which the novelist's novelist, narrator Larry Morgan, makes the telling of his and his wife's and his friends' life stories the occasion for dealing with the larger issues that seem to have loomed behind most of Stegner's work.

"How do you make a book that anyone will read," Morgan poses the question at an appropriate moment toward the end of the novel,

> out of lives as quiet as these? Where are the things the novelists seize upon and readers expect? Where is the high life, the conspicuous waste, the violence, the kinky sex, the death wish? . . . Where are the hatreds, the political ambitions, the lust for power? Where are the speed, noise, ugliness, everything that makes us who we are and makes us recognize ourselves in fiction?

None of these things, the elements that make up the materials of novels written by just about everyone we read and praise, appears in Stegner's latest novel (though a touch here and there has shown up in some earlier books)—yet *Crossing to Safety* stands as a triumph because of these absences, not in spite of them. Stegner is a surpassing master at showing victory in the everyday activities of life, and though he admits to the darker places of the human heart, for who couldn't and still remain honest, he depicts a world in which, because of the angle of vision, we see more by sunlight than shadow.

Consider the way in which Larry Morgan describes the prospect before him as he surveys the scene in Vermont where he and his wife Sally have been visiting the Langs for nearly 40 years. "The view from Folsom Hill," he says,

> is not grand in the way of Western landscapes. What gives it its charm is the alternation of wild and cultivated rough woods ending with scribed edges against

smooth hayfields—this and the accent dots of white houses, red barns, and clustered cattle tiny as aphids on a leaf. Directly below them, across the shaggy top of a lesser hill, is the lake, heart shaped, with the village at its southern end. . . .

This is a literary landscape, with its "scribed" woods and houses like "accent dots," and a literary landscape of a particular sort. The epic master of *Big Rock Candy Mountain* and *Angle of Repose* ends here on a quiet, Eastern note, as the lyricist of the rational showing us his source, the New England lake, heart shaped. (pp. 3, 12)

Alan Cheuse, "*Making the Ordinary Beautiful,*" in Los Angeles Times Book Review, *September 6, 1987, pp. 3, 12.*

DORIS GRUMBACH

What I am extolling [in *Crossing to Safety*] is the appearance of a superb book at the other end of a consistently accomplished career, heartening proof that [Stegner] has continued to grow, is still maturing in his late maturity, has added to his accomplishments a sympathy for his contemporaries' condition: the miseries of old age, the resentment of physical decay and, most of all, the pleasures of enduring marital love.

Crossing to Safety moves back and forward in the middle of the 20th century, from 1937 to 1972, when the narrator, Larry Morgan, and his polio-crippled wife, Sally, return after many years to the Lang family compound in Vermont to attend a farewell picnic. Charity Lang and her husband, Sid, have been friends of the Morgans since both men were instructors in English in Madison, Wis.

The couples could not have been more different. The Morgans were young, struggling and happy. "In a way, it is beautiful to be young and hard up. . . . Deprivation becomes a game," says Larry. They are from the West; the Langs are Eastern and Harvard, Sid is Jewish, both are determinedly ambitious, and their families are wealthy. The Langs are attracted to the Morgans by Larry's literary talent: during his temporary appointment at the university he has already begun to publish short stories.

The novel's fulcrum is Charity, a strong woman whose sense of how things should be done extends to everyone around her. Her husband is weakened by her strength, her friends rebel against her need to control. Larry says of her, "And with Charity it was organization, order, action, assistance to the uncertain, and direction to the wavering." When she knows she is dying of cancer, she decides to control and direct the conditions of her death. . . .

There is some question about Charity's life, for her determination is not so easily dismissed as harmless. The bittersweet tone of Larry's reminiscences is echoed in his thoughts about Charity's family, the Ellises:

> How do you make a book that anyone will read out of lives as quiet as these? Where are the things that novelists seize upon and readers expect? Where is the high life, the conspicuous waste, the violence, the kinky sex, the death wish? . . . Where are speed, noise, ugliness, everything that makes us who we are and makes us recognize ourselves in fiction?

Mr. Stegner's success with this story lies precisely in the absence of all these currently popular subject matters and the presence of quiet re-examination of what, close to the end, seems to have made a life not only worth living but happy and almost fulfilled. Larry realizes that "Sid Lang best understands that my marriage is as surely built on addiction and dependence as his is." Sid needed Charity's domination even as it debilitated him. Larry is tied by the inexorable chains of love to Sally, whose polio is doomed to return at the end of her life. He doubts if he can survive her, just as the reader is left to wonder, until the last lines of the book, if Sid will survive Charity.

Mr. Stegner is a wise man as well as a skilled writer. His narrator, very close to him in biographical detail as well as quality of mind, recognizes the truth that the affliction of a loved one (Sally) can be "a rueful blessing. It has made her more than she was; it has let her give me more than she would ever have been able to give me healthy; it has taught me at least the alphabet of gratitude."

John Webster (in *Westward Hoe*) said that "old lovers are soundest." Mr. Stegner has built a convincing narrative around this truth, has made survival a grace rather than a grim necessity, and enduring, tried love the test and proof of a good life. Nothing in these lives is lost or wasted, suffering becomes an enriching benediction, and life itself a luminous experience.

Doris Grumbach, "The Grace of Old Lovers," in
The New York Times Book Review, *September 20,
1987, p. 14.*

BARBARA A. BANNON

[*Crossing to Safety*] is Wallace Stegner's first novel since *Recapitulation* in 1979 and it is one of his finest and most moving. What Stegner has dared to do is show us over the years how love grows and deepens between two husbands and wives from the Depression years of the 1930s to the early 1970s and how love grows and deepens, too, among the four of them as friends, with never a hint of either man lusting after the other's wife.

It is such an old-fashioned way of looking at things as to be downright iconoclastic. And it is going to find an awful lot of readers out there who will recognize joyously that there are other people besides themselves who value true friendship this deeply. . . .

Stegner writes of starry-eyed and pretty desperate young academics in the 1930s as if he had been one of them, and undoubtedly he was. Not the least of this novel's interest is not only the fictional story it has to tell us, but what it tells us about Stegner himself. No one could write a novel like this without drawing on deep personal experience.

Yet it would be a mistake to try to personalize *Crossing to Safety* too much. When Stegner . . . writes about earnest, anx-

ious, desperately caring, very young academics in the Depression years of the 1930s, he is obviously writing about something he experienced himself. All those pot luck suppers, the rallying around each other in childbirth, the growing fear as the time approached when contract renewals would or, more likely, would not be made, these must have been part of Stegner's own experience. Nor does he portray everything as wine and roses. Under pressures such as these, bitter rivalries and feuds flourished even more, if possible, than they do in today's academia, and Stegner can be pretty funny about these, ruefully so, when he wants to be.

But his major characters, Charity and Sid, Sally and Larry (who narrates the story), however fictional they may be, are achingly real and very believable. Meeting in Madison, Wisconsin in the thirties, where Sid and Larry are on their first teaching assignments, Charity and Sally both pregnant, they begin the start of a deep, lifelong, loving friendship.

On the surface they have little in common. Charity, as her name suggests, comes from an old, deeply intellectual, but thoroughly warm-hearted New England family. Sid's father despised anything but money-making but left him a fortune with which to achieve whatever he wanted. Sally is an orphan of Greek background. Larry, who comes from the Southwest, has no money at all, but he will make it first, selling a story to the *Atlantic* in his initial teaching year.

Where Stegner is so convincing right from the beginning, is in giving us each of these four as individuals yet making perfectly clear the attraction that draws them all closer and closer as loving friends. He knows how to let us see, little by little, however, as Sally and Larry perceive it, what the blight of Charity and Sid's marriage is, and what it will come to mean in time to all four of them.

The jacket of *Crossing to Safety* displays a glorious picture of golden autumn leaves and a winding road. That sense of place is essential every step of the way here in terms of what it has brought into the lives of Charity and Sid, Sally and Larry. And it is marvelously conveyed by Stegner. (p. 630)

However deep and enduring their loving friendship, Sally and Larry, Charity and Sid, are mortals. As their relationship deepens, so does Sally and Larry's perception of the very real problems the other pair faces. A lot of things will happen here, but the most important of all remains Stegner's ability to keep us, his readers, caring. (p. 631)

Barbara A. Bannon, "Old-Fashioned Ways of Knowing," in Commonweal, *Vol. CXIV, No. 19, November 6, 1987, pp. 630-31.*

James Still

1906-

American novelist, poet, short story writer, and author of children's books.

Still is highly regarded for his prose and verse in which he documents life in the Appalachian region of Kentucky. Like Jesse Stuart, to whom he is often compared, Still attempts to convey the humanity, dignity, and humor with which rural families confront economic and environmental hardships. His acclaimed novel, *River of Earth* (1940), and the short stories collected in *On Troublesome Creek* (1941), for example, rely on descriptions of everyday events rather than plot to convey the effects of the Great Depression on the family of Kentucky miner Brack Baldridge. These books, along with two other volumes of short stories, *Pattern of a Man* (1976) and *The Run for the Elbertas* (1980), as well as *Sporty Creek: A Novel about an Appalachian Boyhood* (1977), are praised for Still's disciplined use of language and natural rendering of the region's diverse dialects. Still's verse, collected in *Hounds on the Mountain* (1937) and *The Wolfpen Poems* (1986), is similarly praised for its restrained and evocative qualities.

(See also *Contemporary Authors*, Vols. 65-68; *Contemporary Authors New Revision Series*, Vol. 10; *Something about the Author*, Vol. 29; and *Dictionary of Literary Biography*, Vol. 9.)

R. P. HARRISS

The grain of James Still's poetry is the grain of his ancestry and of the Appalachian range, ''rock-ribbed and firm . . . from Maine to Alabama.'' He is of an old American segment; its memories stretch far back, and the Stills, though hill folk, date back three hundred and one years ago to Scots-Irish people who landed at Charleston, South Carolina. The poetry in *Hounds on the Mountain* reflects this. There is none of the Western sweep of a Robinson Jeffers, nor does it hold any of the distinctly Southern overtones of a Timrod or a Lanier. Rather it suggests Frost, the Frost who can describe unforgettably a frightened little Morgan colt alone in a stone-walled pasture during the first snowfall. It is not easy to align James Still with living Southern poets. DuBose Heyward has often summered in the Great Smokies and has told, in more than fair verse, of mountain lads and their guns and hounds—but his were the softer modes and notes of the sojourning lowlander. Perhaps the closest kinship is with John Crowe Ransom, a Southern poet whose diction is hard and cleanly shaped into sprung rhythms. . . .

What is apparent all through [Still's] verse is this: that memories of his up-country boyhood were continually stirring in his head. It would, indeed, have been impossible for him not to have absorbed, while a young journeyman horse doctor, much horse lore and hound lore. The unearthly cry of hounds is a haunting thing. His hounds on the mountain, then, are more than figurative hounds of spring upon winter's traces;

Photograph by Warren Brunner. Courtesy of James Still.

they are those lovable creatures, so unequivocally *right* in their proper setting—mellow-voiced coldnosers, fed on sow-belly and corn pone, who lie beneath the puncheon floor near the chimney's warmth until the thin-scraped cowhorn (or sheephorn) hunting bugle calls them out. . . .

[*Hounds on the Mountain*] is a young poet's first book. He began trying to write not long ago—it was an attempt, he says, ''to express my horror and disgust after seeing a young man shot to death while I stood helplessly watching.'' Much of it, and the best of it, harks back to those archaic mountain farms. More contemporary are his **''Court Day''** and realistic, unlovely pictures of coal towns and coal camps; and there is much that should appeal to Donald Culross Peattie and his readers notably the poem, bitter and thoughtful, on the slaughtered passenger pigeons. Mr. Still appears to write slowly, carefully, even with difficulty; he is articulate in a fine sense, not glib.

> R. P. Harriss, ''Granite Appalachian Poetry,'' in New York Herald Tribune Books, *July 4, 1937, p. 5.*

JOHN HOLMES

[In *Hounds on the Mountain*, James Still] does not waste words ever, and he concentrates into his lines all the mountain nouns possible, and there lies much of his strength. If it were not for the image-making, his lines would seem like prose lines (never prosy, however) but his images rise from deep in his mind, and mark him for a true poet. He sounds solemn, slow; now and then some passion quickens the words, but one feels that he is most like his mountain people in his quietness. One feels that he would not chatter, would keep his thoughts to himself unless he had the outlet of poetry. A reticent poet, but genuine. His love for his valleys and the names of their ridges and creeks is also very deep, and these names ring again and again in his lines and titles.

The fact that . . . ["**Heritage**"] rises to such a climax as the statement that he cannot leave his hills, cannot and will not, makes speculation interesting. Of course, he need not. But one who had no fear of staying, nor of what departure might do to him, would hardly be so vehement. It may be that the hills and the hounds, the fox hunts and the creeks and men and music, are his world and his poetry, and these alone. No poet need travel to improve his writing, if he makes journeys within. But in regional writers who insist that they are forever at home and happy in their chosen valley, there may be already some foreboding of limitations.

Reading James Still's poems several times over, one is increasingly impressed with the curious unmetrical run of the lines. "He is waiting under the shadow of these hills." "I have gone up to the graveyard on a laurel-thicket hill." "The traces and forks carved like wagon tracks on stone." Yet in each of these lines and in all the poems there is the emotion and the chosen word that keeps poetry. . . .

James Still is a poet aware of the language in which he writes; words mean much to him, and he treats them with scrupulous honor. He values those names of his country, Troublesome Creek, Carr, Buckalew Ridge, Sand Lick, Honey Gap; and the names for things familiar every day, piggings, dulcimer, sow-belly, catamount. Not that these are over-used, but they are there to flavor the lines. But this would be a small part, and it is the larger number of words common to everyone that he chooses from with such skill. He has this craftsman's taste for discrimination, rather than the wordy outrush of Jesse Stuart, or Thomas Wolfe.

Of the thirty-five poems in the book, I like "**Infare**," "**Journey Beyond the Hills**," "**Spring on Troublesome Creek**," "**Pattern for Death**," "**With Hands Like Leaves**," and "**Horseback in the Rain**." . . . Naming the poems above does not mean that I did not like many others as well, but I find myself inclined to like poems in which I can see the man most. James Still is a poet sure of himself as he writes, and has brought together a firm, quiet collection of real value. It is full of mountain weather and the feel of things against the body, rich with sounds and weight, deep in emotion and beyond question sincere. It is a fine book.

John Holmes, "A Poet from the Rugged Hills of the South," in Boston Evening Transcript, *Part 5, July 17, 1937, p. 2.*

JOHN GOULD FLETCHER

Mr. James Still, who is a young poet, has found his poetic background in the Cumberland region of Kentucky. [In *Hounds on the Mountain,* he] is aware of the beauty and interest of this region: the brawling mountain streams, the lonely cries of the birds, the remote coal camps, the deep brush of the woods, the pattern of piety and violence that flowers in the lives of the people. Yet the general effect of his poems, after two readings, is one of monotony. They lack variety and they lack life. Their author has carefully assimilated his detail, has studied his background, but has had little to add to it that may be called his own. Too frequently, he writes the kind of poem that depends for its total effect only on complete and exact precision of observation; he cannot strike a fire that burns on, line after line, whether the observation is precise or not. In other words, he is too much the photographic realist, plodding along where a rustic furrow leads him, rather than turning and running with the wind.

John Gould Fletcher, "Camera in a Furrow," in The New Republic, *Vol. LXXXXI, No. 1182, July 28, 1937, p. 343.*

ROSE FELD

When *Hounds on the Mountain* was published, its author, James Still, was at once acclaimed as a poet who sang his native song with stirring note. *River of Earth* sustains the lyric quality of his writing in a full-length novel. In it Still tells the simple story, no doubt autobiographical, of a boy growing up in the mountain country of Kentucky. That his tale will be compared with Marjorie Kinnan Rawlings's *The Yearling* is inevitable. To mention it seems trite; to ignore it stupid. The comparison does honor to both writers, to Mrs. Rawlings for creating an unforgettable boy; to Still for coming close to the same high standard of characterization if not of dramatic appeal.

The story is told through the eyes of the boy, one of Brack Baldridge's "chaps." It goes back to the time the lad is 6 and becomes aware of his surroundings. . . .

There is no formal story in this novel, no plot rising to a climax and falling in proper release. Its virtue lies in characterization and incident and the manner of their development and expression. When Uncle Jolly is jailed the boy is sent to stay with his Grandmother Middleton. At 78 she wants help and pity from no one, her "chaps" included. She has pride and she has courage and a bit of learning. "I larnt to figure," she tells the boy, "but I never larnt to read writing. My man could read before he died, and he done all the reading and I done the figuring. We allus worked our larning like a team of horses."

After a hard Winter the boy, grown homesick for his own people, feels the stirring of Spring. "One morning I saw a redbird sitting in a plum bush, its body dark as a wound," he says. "'Spring's a-winding,' I told Grandma, 'Comin' now for shore.'"

When he got home there was plenty and the boy's mother got the good of it by having a belated funeral service for the baby who had died months before. Brother Sim Mobberly officiated. "We have come together to ask the blessed Saviour one thing pint-blank," he intoned over the grave. "Can a leetle child enter the Kingdom of Heaven?" Relatives and friends came from miles around to hear him and to partake of the feast.

But when Grandmother Middleton died there was neither service nor feast. "Send nary word to my chaps," she had instructed Uncle Jolly. "They wouldn't come when I was low in health. No need they haste to see me dead."

This is the quality of the book, this is what gives it eminence. To call it homespun is not enough. Still's language and native idiom, joyfully wedded, give it special excellence as a regional document.

Rose Feld, "The Tale of a Kentucky Boyhood," in The New York Times Book Review, February 4, 1940, p. 6.

WILLIAM JAY GOLD

About *On Troublesome Creek* one may say with fairness that it is like a footnote to the author's only novel, *River of Earth.* The present book is made up of ten short stories in which James Still tells us more about his Kentucky mountain people. In most of the stories the family is obviously the same as that which figured in *River of Earth.* The locale is the same, there is evident the same feeling for effective and vivid detail, together with the sureness in handling dialect that help make the novel an outstanding contribution to our regional literature.

In the stories which make up the first half of the book, *Up-Creek,* the narrator is the young boy who told the story of *River of Earth.* . . . [These stories] are admirable for their craftsmanship. They exhibit economy of movement and material, deftness in character development, a good feeling for the dramatic, and skill in the manipulation of form. But they also betray a sameness in structure that leads one to believe that Mr. Still is perhaps willing to play again and again the same tune on an instrument that has become as comfortable to him as an old pair of shoes.

Two stories in the last half of the book, *Down-Creek,* do not follow the same pattern, however. Here there is the story of the old man, so old as to be "brother to Methusalem," who decides to take another wife after he has passed 100; and "**The Scrape**," a story of mountain courtship, fighting with knives and much drinking of corn "likker." Oddly enough, these stories are among the poorest in the book. They have a smooth finish and a glibness, even a conventionality, that is not at all like Mr. Still's writing. They resemble *River of Earth* much less than they remind us of Li'l Abner of the comic strips, and their humor is at about the same level. . . .

[In] seeking to determine why the book as a whole fails to register a strong and unified impression even though it deals with more or less the same characters throughout, one cannot help reflecting that these stories are skimmings—the best of them and their kind have already seen print in *River of Earth.* In fact, with some rearrangement in order and the omission of two stories, *On Troublesome Creek* could pass as a connected story, even as a novel which would be an anemic parallel to the earlier book, and the fund of moving and universally meaningful material out of which that book came is not, after all, inexhaustible.

At least two stories, nevertheless, should be singled out for praise: "**Snail Pie**," which tells how old Grandpa, vinegary and mischief-minded, is put in danger of being sent back to the county home through the innocent tattling of his greatest admirer, a young boy; and "**The Moving**," which feelingly portrays the departure of the family from the mining camp shut down by slack times.

William Jay Gold, in a review of "On Troublesome Creek," in New York Herald Tribune Books, *October 26, 1941, p. 16.*

THE CHRISTIAN SCIENCE MONITOR

James Still continues his genial portraits of Kentucky backwoods folk in his new volume of short stories [*On Troublesome Creek*]. As in his earlier book, *River of Earth,* the chief narrator is again a one-gallused barefoot boy whose powers of observation are agreeably enhanced by a gift of expression in the gentle, rippling speech and unique phrasing of the people who live deep in the hills which roll westward from the Alleghenies and the Great Smokies.

Few of the many authors who are attracted by this setting are successful in attempting to duplicate the vernacular in their stories, even when they limit such expression to the dialogue. It requires temerity indeed to clothe the entire narrative with it, and in such a case only a native like James Still or Jesse Stuart can be counted on to impart the authentic flavor. When this is successfully done, a notable contribution is added to our regional literature. *On Troublesome Creek* is therefore worth commendation, for its tang is as American as the candy jacks in a molasses kettle. . . .

In "**The Proud Walkers**" and in "**The Stir-Off**," gusts of laughter seem to breathe through the pages as the boy tells how he and his family enter into their new life. The other stories in this section supplement the family's adventures, ending at a point some years later, with "**Journey to the Forks**," in which the boy and his brother finally set out for school. . . .

Four brief sketches, unrelated to the first stories, but similar in background and style, are added, although they are inferior in quality to the others. The first group, however, make up the bulk of the book, and they could indeed serve as the framework for a novel of considerable stature, if Mr. Still were ever to feel inclined to expand his work beyond the excellent, but undeniably repetitive, tales which have occupied him hitherto.

M. W. S., "Tales from Kentucky Hills," in The Christian Science Monitor, *November 29, 1941, p. 13.*

DAYTON KOHLER

A curious parallel links the careers of Jesse Stuart and James Still. Products of the same general environment, graduates of the same small college on the Tennessee side of Cumberland Gap, they live less than one hundred miles from each other as the crow flies in the mountain section of eastern Kentucky. This is the region of ridge farms and lonesome hollows about which each has written, first in poetry and later in prose. In a way this similarity is misleading, for the effect of their writing is completely unlike. James Still is realistic where Stuart is melodramatic, poetic where Stuart is often sentimental. Between them, however, they have given shape and life to their green Appalachian hills.

The background of their work is familiar enough. At the end of the century Mary Noailles Murfree and John Fox reclaimed the Tennessee and Kentucky hill country as a segment of older America. But one can describe a region without participating in its life. Today this sense of participation is the very center of all regional matters. A generation of local-color writers from Miss Murfree to Maristan Chapman exploited only the picturesque and sentimental in the lives of mountain characters; their stories failed to reveal the essential humanity of the people themselves.

Jesse Stuart and James Still have an advantage over these earlier writers in having been born into the life they write about. They use the materials of the local colorists, but it is clear that much of their freshness and gusto derives from a sense of identity with a place and its people. We can mark a stage in the development of southern fiction if we put one of their books beside one by Miss Murfree, for example. The older writer demonstrates a landscape literature: bright scenes of local color enlivened by quaint dialect. Her stories are about a place rather than of it. No writer's notebook, filled with tourist observations of dress, weather, sayings, manners, crops, could give the casual yet familiar picture of a way of life which we find in Stuart's and Still's best work. Even their language has emotional roots in the common experience, for it takes its color and rhythm from the speech of people who have lived a long time in one place. This writing has value quite apart from its importance as regional documentation. (pp. 523-24)

If Jesse Stuart has escaped from strict localism by a renewal of frontier types and themes, James Still has gone beyond local emotions through the working of a poetic imagination which finds in regional experience the feelings common to very simple people everywhere. This was also the method of Elizabeth Madox Roberts, the one novelist to whom Still can best, although imperfectly, be compared. He is like her in his ability to join outward realism with intense inwardness of mood.

In Still we confront a serious writer. He has specifically those qualities that Stuart lacks: the precision and restraint which reflect a literary discipline of humility as well as sincerity in the handling of his material. Both men exhibit the same regional theme, the relationship between man and his natural world. In Stuart's fiction this kinship of man and nature leads him at times into vague landscape mysticism. Still has wisely given his sensibility a frame of reference and a point of view. His novel and short stories have been told by a boy whose recognition of objects in nature becomes a measure of his awareness of the world about him. This sensibility is effective because it sets a contrast between a boy's knowledge of the familiar natural world and the bewildering, mysterious world of human relationships.

The territory of Still's fiction is the region of hill farms and coal camps scattered along the branch waters of Little Carr and Troublesome creeks. For him this is adopted country. Born on Double Creek in the Alabama hills, he came into Kentucky by way of Tennessee. His boyhood ambition was to be a horse doctor like his father, and among his earliest recollections are nights he spent with his father while they nursed a sick animal on some neighbor's farm. At Lincoln Memorial University, where he worked in a rock quarry and in the school library to pay his way, he became interested in writing. After some postgraduate study at Vanderbilt he went to Hindman as librarian at the Hindman Settlement School. There one of his duties was to carry boxes of books over mountain trails to supply one-room schools that had no libraries of their own. He has tramped over every ridge and hollow mentioned in his books. At Hindman he wrote his first poems, published in 1937 as **Hounds on the Mountain.**

These poems are minor but authentic. Their subjects are those of much regional verse—people, a horse-swapping, a court day, the sights and sounds of nature—but the quiet tones of his lines surprise us with a sudden sharp image that reveals the true poet. His descriptions of the hill country are always warm and homely and clear. **"Earth-Bread"** tells of the miner's life: "This is the eight-hour death, the daily burial." **"Year of the Pigeons"** stirs ancestral memories. **"Heritage"** is his regional affirmation. . . . (pp. 528-30)

One way of becoming an artist is to accept those limitations of material imposed upon the individual by the nature of his social experience. This acceptance implies an act of discipline, the necessity of the writer to distinguish what is his own from what he admires in other men's books. It was this discipline which Thomas Wolfe, for example, could never learn, but which turned Willa Cather from the Jamesian manner of *Alexander's Bridge* to a use of native materials in *O Pioneers*. James Still has known this discipline from the first. All of his writing is of one piece, for it comes straight out of the region which has shaped his own life. Perhaps that is why he reverts to a boy's world in *River of Earth,* where the experiences of a growing boy make the regional pattern clear.

River of Earth covers two years in the life of a mountain family. The novel begins shortly before the boy who tells the story has his seventh birthday, and it ends two winters later, after he has learned something of a man's responsibilities. The boy is one of Brack Baldridge's young ones. Brack is a miner, moving his family about from one coal camp to another as he follows the precarious wages the big companies pay. Although he will take to farming when work in the mines grows slack, he has no desire for the homeplace his wife talks about. She wants a house with windows and a real puncheon floor, a garden patch, and some trees without smoke-grimed leaves. She is one of the mild Middletons, but she speaks her mind when Brack's worthless cousins and lazy old Uncle Samp come to live with them at the end of a hard winter. But Brack says, "As long as we've got a crust, it'll never be said I turned my folks from my door." Mother has another plan. She moves the furniture into the smokehouse and burns the cabin. It is a life of hardship and violence. School closes when the teacher is shot for whipping one of the pupils. After Uncle Jolly has been taken to jail, the boy goes to Lean Neck Creek to look after Grandma Middleton through a starvation winter. At seventy-eight Grandma is still spryly carrying on her secret feud with the man who killed her husband years ago. Next spring the baby dies. In September the Baldridges hold a funeralizing, with Preacher Sim Mobberly from Troublesome Creek to preach the text. "Oh, my brethren," he begins, stroking his white beard, "we was borned in sin and saved by grace." Lifting his hands toward the sky, he thunders, "We have come together to ask the blessed Saviour one thing pint-blank. Can a leetle child enter the Kingdom of Heaven?" In Blackjack they face another hungry winter after the mines close. Then Grandma Middleton dies. "Send nary word to my chaps," she says. "They wouldn't come when I was low in health. No need they haste to see me dead."

From incidents like these James Still has made a simple but moving regional novel. There is no dramatic structure to his book, for it is a boy's story that falls into a clear pattern of memory as he tells what he saw and did during those two full years. He has learned the feel of tools in his hands and back-breaking labor in the fields. Birth and death, men's anger and hate, women's tolerance for clumsy masculine ways, summer's plenty and winter's hungry pinch have become as much a part of his life as the sights and sounds of mining camp and farm, the smells of plowed ground, an empty house, cooking food.

River of Earth is regional, but it is first of all a novel about people, not more literary business about folkways in the manner of so much regional literature. People are never folk to any but outsiders, and Still happens to be writing about friends and neighbors into whose lives he has entered with the instinctive knowledge and feeling of true imagination. They belong to the life he himself shares. The signs are hopeful for his future. The writer who can reveal the life of his own region with perception and meaning usually ends up by writing about the world.

Beneath the regional feeling of the novel there is another meaning which is never put into words because it lies just outside the boy's understanding of his world. Brack's son can describe his mother's fears and his own hunger, but he can only listen to talk of puzzled resentment and bitterness when men are out of work. He knows Uncle Jolly's anger over good farmland ruined when the timber was cut off, leaving the plowed fields to wash away in gullies during the summer storms. But if he is too young to realize what is happening, the reader can understand the terrible importance of work and food to America's dispossessed. The Baldridges are not Joads or Lesters; nevertheless they speak to the social conscience of our time.

On Troublesome Creek is a collection of short stories in the same clear, luminous pattern of measured emotion and unstudied drama. At first glance it may seem that Still is trying to write a lesser *River of Earth* in these stories, for some use the same background and the same theme and all are loosely linked by the bright-eyed boy who tells them. Although the book as a whole is likely to give an impression of sameness because the point of view does not vary, most of the stories, taken singly, will stand on their own merits. In any collection like this each reader must find his own favorites. One of the best is **"I Love My Rooster,"** in which the boy's longing for a gamecock and a striped shirt becomes an expression of the desires of an inarticulate class in which the sense of possession is strong but seldom satisfied. **"Snail Pie"** is a pathetic picture of old age. **"Brother to Methusalem"** shows that Still can write fantasy and humor in the tall-story tradition. A boy's revenge on a miserly cattle-driver gives another kind of humor to **"On Quicksand Creek."** **"The Moving"** tells what happens to these people when the mines close, and several of the stories deal with the hardships of finding a new home in a new place.

James Still has been praised for his simplicity. Much of the effectiveness of his writing comes from a clear and often lovely style with the occasional incorrectness of folk speech in its idiom. This is the best kind of style that a regional writer can have, for it shows the habits of thought and language found in the sayings, stories, and proverbs that indicate the history and simple wisdom of a region. "Even come spring," says Grandma Middleton, "we've a passel of chills to endure: dogwood winter, redbud, service, foxgrape, blackberry. . . . There must be seven winters, by count. A chilly snap for every time of bloom." Still's style is flexible enough for more than one effect. It can bear a considerable burden of emotion that is within a boy's range of response, and it can record sensory impressions with poetic finality. . . . In Preacher Sim Mobberly's sermons this style broadens with homely metaphor into rude folk poetry. It can also weight a situation with a deeper meaning that adds to our understanding of life. In *River of Earth* there is a scene in which Brack, newly hired at the mines, brings home several sacks of food from the company commissary. The mother sits quietly touching the meat and flour and then suddenly throws her apron over her head as she bursts into tears. The words of that passage are not the language of realism, but something as flat and final as the realist can offer has been said about a way of life.

Perhaps one should not grow too critically solemn over the books Stuart and Still have written. Stuart has probably shown us the whole range of his talent. Still has the manner of a young writer feeling his way, and as yet he has not attempted a direct portrayal of the larger adult world. But as regionalists they have added another panel to the long record of American life, for in their books the southern mountaineer has found his own voice for the first time. This regionalism is as genuine and untainted as any we have in America today. (pp. 530-33)

> Dayton Kohler, "Jesse Stuart and James Still: Mountain Regionalists," in College English, Vol. 3, No. 6, March, 1942, pp. 523-33.

DEAN CADLE

The difficulties of writing about Still's prose are akin to those presented by the best stories of Chekhov, of Katherine Anne Porter, and of Bernard Malamud in that the reader is placed in the position of a listener enjoying classical music. The listener does not have to be able to relate an accompanying narrative or recognize the techniques employed in order to appreciate the music. It is true that if his listening apparatus is supplemented by a knowledge of such concrete and mechanical facts he might be able to discuss his appreciation more factually and more intelligently. But what is more important is that he and the music are conducting an exhilarating conversation in which any form of kibitzing would be deadening. Like music, Still's better stories (such as **"A Ride on the Short Dog,"** **"Mrs. Razor,"** **"The Run for the Elbertas"**) and *River of Earth* are more meaningful if they are "experienced" rather than read critically and analytically, if they are approached as incidents happening rather than as stories that are being read. Their effect is closer to that gained from hearing an oral tale or from watching a staged play.

The reader who approaches Still's writings equipped with the kit of critical tools now issued with most college diplomas is apt to dismiss them as exercises in regional naïveté or terminate his tinkering in bafflement because his custom-made tools do not fit the model. For there is little conscious use of symbols, no allusions to classical or other literatures, and no reference to anything outside the immediate situation in which the characters are involved.

However, the machinery is there, just as it is in all writing—or in any other artistic creation—the only difference being that the nuts and bolts and pistons are fewer and are more finely tooled than in most writing.

Qualities that a careful reader may find in Still's writing are his convincing characterizations, the exactness and colorfulness of his language, his emphasis on sense of place, his reliance on poetic interludes, his use of humor, and his themes. Perhaps less obvious, but equally as important, are his point of view and his use of foreshortening.

Because his methods of characterization are unobtrusive and because the characters do and say what seems appropriate, the reader's impression likely is that character delineation must be the easiest part of writing for Still. We do not learn the traits of the characters from either the author or his narrators. Rather, Still unfolds characterization by implication in much the same way a skillful dramatist presents it on stage; through dialogue, through gestures, and through remarks that characters make about each other. And it is to Still's credit that he succeeds without the dramatist's crutch of stage directions preceding the acts, in which we too often are told point-blank the nature of the individuals we are about to meet, or what changes have transpired in their attitudes since last we saw them.

A character is revealed gradually in response to the friction of the other characters and to the incidents he must contend with.

Presentation in this manner can be a series of surprises as the reader watches the character react as he thinks he should but is not always certain he will. It can also be a disastrous method in the hands of a writer not thoroughly familiar with his characters.

In **"The Run for the Elbertas"** we first see Riar Thomas as he glances at his watch then stops his truck to pick up two teen-age boys who are to make the trip with him to South Carolina. He pulls the cardboard out of the broken window and opens the door from the inside, because "it's cranky." "'Let's go,'" he commands the boys; "'a body can't fiddle in the peach business.'"

However, there is considerable "fiddling" as the boys prod, prick, cheat, and prank, and draw out the character of Riar. His character is implied in the short opening paragraph: He is punctual, thrifty, honest, determined, irritable, business-like, suspicious, and a bit impatient. But it is only after many miles of defensive argumentation and after numerous delays initiated by the boys that we realize that the entire story is a development of the implications of the opening paragraph.

What is perhaps most delightful in Still's writing is the colorfulness and exactness of his language. Whether the individual words are strange or familiar, it is the manner of expression that gives them conviction and demonstrates that the author is a creator, as well as a listener and lover, of language, and that he sees and hears with the senses of a poet. (pp. 239-41)

Still's language is so filled with the creations of a real people, with his own experiments, and with folklore and Elizabethan expressions and influences, that perhaps a linguist could not easily separate the borrowings from the creations. However, even a waving familiarity with Elizabethan literature can help us spot numerous words and expressions in Still's work that have passed out of common use in English but have remained lodged in the mountain language, some unchanged and others twisted to fit the tongue, as apt reminders of what the Elizabethan spoken language sounded like. Especially noticeable is that the people have retained one of the more marked and lively peculiarities of the Elizabethan language, that of using any word as almost any part of speech. (p. 242)

It may seem far-fetched but is entirely likely that the sententious, elegant deflection of the language that came to be known as Euphuism, primarily written rather than spoken, may be partially responsible for the brief, balanced, often witty, proverbial statements of the mountain people which Still enjoys hearing his characters speak. (p. 243)

Some of Still's best writing appears in rhythmic passages that may be called poetic interludes which he uses as transitional devices to bridge space between scenes or to indicate the lapse of time or change of locale. Usually they deal with the look of a place or the change of seasons, and they are always brief, sometimes no more than a sentence. (p. 245)

A discussion of humor can be as unreliable as the writing of it. Nothing can spoil so soon or stay fresh so long. There are few guides, no assurances. What seemed humorous yesterday may be embarrassing today. The printed page often becomes a paper coffin for what in real life is hilarious. And exactly because of its mercurial nature, from what was entombed in Egypt and Greece centuries ago there may yet sprout full-blown laughter in outer space.

Still knows this, and so what may be humorous in his stories is not often specifically intended as such. His use of humor is inescapably a part of characterization and of theme.

For instance, when Harl and Tibb Logan, the wild, undisciplined brothers in **River of Earth,** cut off the thirty-year-old, carefully-tended mustache of Uncle Samp, the incident may be humorous. But the real function of the fact is to characterize them, to show the reader that their lives are sustained by such practical jokes. And Godey and Mal in **"A Ride on the Short Dog"** and in **"The Run for the Elbertas"** turn to practical jokes and speak only in clever, cliché remarks not because they necessarily enjoy them or because they possess a sense of humor but as a means of relieving the tension, of reducing the monotony, of their static lives.

Such acts and such language are presented as inherent human reflexes that act as alternatives against loss of will, against defeat. They serve as pacifiers and preoccupiers, in somewhat the same way that counting the bricks of his cell guards the prisoner against insanity. And while they may be humorous today and even several generations from now, Still is too wise a writer to bet on humor: On Uncle Jolly, a humorous character he has written knowingly about, he has more than one relative pass judgment: "'There goes a born fool.'"

Just as one mentions point of view in discussing Laurence Sterne or William Faulkner because they made an art out of misusing and overusing it, so it is mentioned here because Still has rendered it as nonexistent as possible. The reader is so little aware of point of view in his stories that it is difficult to recall whether they are told through the third person or the first. Actually, most of them are related by a first-person narrator. But Still has skirted most of its traps and has evaded the violations which some writers read into their license to use the first person. He has veritably erased the author.

In **River of Earth** and **On Troublesome Creek** Still chooses the even more risky path of taking the reader into the immediate world of a seven-year-old boy. He uses the unnamed narrator as an eye or window to keep the reader's attention riveted at all times inside the story, and to keep the narrative "tight," never accepting the privilege granted the author to wander or to use the narrator as a chorus. And what remains to delight the reader even years after reading the stories is the seen, heard, and felt child-view of a small mountain world, with hardly a false note to betray its passage through the mind of the author.

When Still's themes are enumerated outside his writings they seem as blatant as trumpet blasts, but when their almost unobtrusive weavings are traced through his stories they are no louder than the simple, traditional affirmations that have always plagued and honored mankind: concern with love, loyalty, hunger, death, and with the reactions of the individual when he is cornered, when he reaches the breaking point, either by force or choice. Reworded, they mean the will to endure, self-preservation.

More than twenty years before the Appalachian region was labeled a poverty pocket and before the somewhat artificial reactions of experts and government officials to the problems of poverty, as though they had encountered some recent wonder, Still had presented in **River of Earth** the heartbreaking account of what it means for a human being to live out his life hungry and cold. His is not a socioeconomist's collection of figures, causes, and possible cures, but the dramatized plight of human beings accepting poverty without accusations or judgments and without rantings against ephemeral institutions.

Acceptance of life as it is and refusal to admit defeat aptly describes the philosophy of most of Still's characters. They are always on the move in search of better living conditions. Like migrating birds, they move with the seasons back and forth from coal camps to hillside farms, always confident that this is the last move, that a life of plenty is ahead.

The father in **"The Burning of the Waters"** sees Tight Hollow as a paradise in which "'We can sit on our hands and rear back on our thumbs.'" And with the coming of each fall Brack Baldridge in *River of Earth* announces: "'A long dry spell it's been, but they'll be working at Blackjack,'" or "'We'll feed right good down at Blackjack this winter. I hear tell the mines are to open the middle of October—this time for good.'"

And when the mines close and the crops fail, there is little complaining. They simply pack up and move again, accepting, hoping, laughing to make their misfortunes bearable. After the father has pitted himself against common sense, the advice of friends and family, a merciless winter, crop failure, and even the animals of Tight Hollow which betray him by taking food from his traps then escaping, he bends to his family's pleas. But he is undaunted, and even as they prepare to move, "A gale of laughter broke in father's throat."

When Riar Thomas is pushed to the edge of lunacy in **"The Run for the Elbertas"** by his teen-aged tormentors, he fends them off until they near the Kentucky line, putting up every reason at his command against their case for the joy to be found in revenge, then he strikes back in the only way he knows will be effective, in their own manner. For him it is a difficult choice, but he realizes it is necessary.

Family loyalty, independence and self-reliance, and a sense of honor are themes that are prevalent throughout Still's writing. Season after season Brack Baldridge boards his relatives when there isn't even enough food for his children. "'I can't turn my kin out,'" he argues with his wife. "'As long as we've got a crust, it'll never be said I turned my folks from my door.'"

When Grandma Middleton's husband is murdered, she calls her sons together and has them swear against their will to an oath: "'There's been blood shed a-plenty. Let Aus Coggins bide his time out on this earth. Fear will hant his nights. Hit'll be a thorn in his flesh. Let him live in fear. He'll never prosper nor do well. Let him live in sufferance.'"

And he does. We never see or hear Aus Coggins nor even know what he looks like. But we do know that here is a man who has lived in sufferance.

If social injustice is one of Still's themes, then it is present only by implication, for his people never begrudge the better fortune of others nor express a desire to move farther than the few miles that separate mining camps from hillside farms. "Being of these hills," Still seems to say in prose as well as in poetry, they not only "cannot" pass beyond them but have no desire to. They complain, of course, the men less out of a sense of social maltreatment than because they must work a garden patch instead of dig coal, the work they do best; and the women's complaints are softened into good-natured resignation: "'It takes a man-person to be a puore fool,'" or "'Oh, man-judgment's like the weather. Hit's onknowing.'"

Still's interest in endurance, self-preservation, and the reactions of people under stress are themes he likely finds akin to the motives that drive men to climb mountains. Not the Appalachians, but the big ones which are spoken of as being "scaled" and "conquered," the ones of which records are kept, those which men continue to challenge in the face of promised death: Everest, K2, Kangchenjunga, Nanga-Parbat. And from his interest in and knowledge of mountain climbing Still has derived the word "foreshortening," which he applies to his practice of giving early in a story a synopsis, or telescoped view, of the entire narrative, characterization, and theme.

It is a geometrical term applied primarily to the effect of visual perspective, meaning "to cause an object to be apparently shortened in the direction not lying in a plane perpendicular to the line of sight." In painting a mountain or other large object, for instance, a painter must shorten some lines and make some parts disproportionate in order to create an illusion of true perspective. Since he must crowd a tremendous bulk of earth, stone, foliage, snow, and shadow onto a small canvas, it is the illusion, not the true picture of the mountain, that the painter wishes to present. For when a viewer looks at a mountain from a distance he sees it all at once. But he does not realize its distance, size, details, nor complexity until he gets close to it.

Likewise, in the first paragraph or early in a story Still attempts to give a preliminary view of the entire narrative, a silhouette. And just as foreshortening in painting is a misrepresentation in order that the complete figure will have visual proportion, so Still's practice is a negative form of foreshadowing, for what transpires in the story is often the opposite of, and at the same time much larger than, what is implied. (pp. 245-50)

Unlike most writers, Still does not want to put into writing or have printed what he has learned about the theories or techniques of the craft of writing, perhaps feeling that putting it into print would be equivalent to establishing a system of rules, which, like a law that has been put on the books, would be most of all binding on the maker, as though he fears that any opinion in black and white might assume the authority of a dictum that would somehow permeate to the source of his creativity and do irreparable damage.

And even when he talks about writing it is often in a puzzled, questioning tone, as though he is not certain how it is done and would not object to finding an inclusive code that would not be dangerous, one that he would not have to claim if the time came when he found that it instead of his characters was dictating to him. (pp. 251-52)

Dean Cadle, "Man on Troublesome," in The Yale Review, *Vol. LVII, No. 2, December, 1967, pp. 236-55.*

DEAN CADLE

The sureness with which James Still weaves his patchwork of light, shadow, and colors into [*River of Earth*'s] drab, joyless landscape surely creates one of the presences of artistry that we can recognize and appreciate in all the arts but cannot isolate and define. Marjorie Kinnan Rawlings had this quality in mind when she referred to Still's work as "vital, beautiful, heartbreaking, and heart-warmingly funny," as did poet Delmore Schwartz who called *River of Earth* "a symphony," and the *Time* reviewer who considered it "a work of art."

Still's "secret" lies in his ability to use language so that it performs the functions of both music and painters' pigments. Whether the individual words are strange or familiar, it is the manner of expression that gives them conviction and demonstrates that Still is a creator as well as a listener, and that he sees and hears with the senses of a poet. (p. vi)

Published within a year of each other by the same publisher, *River of Earth* and *The Grapes of Wrath* are the only books chronicling the demoralizing Depression years that have continued to gain readers in more affluent ones. The major difference between them is that Steinbeck's story deals with a calamity that has struck America only once in its lifetime, while Still is writing of the struggles that have plagued the mountain people since the country was settled. (pp. vii-viii)

More than twenty years before the region has labeled a "poverty pocket" and prior to the surprised reactions of experts and government officials to the problems of destitution, as though they had encountered some recent wonder, James Still had presented the heartbreaking account of what it means for a human being to live out his life hungry and cold. His is not a socioeconomist's collection of figures, causes, and possible cures, but the dramatized plight of human beings accepting poverty without accusations or judgments or rantings against outside institutions.

That fiction for Still obviously is a scenic art is evident in the visual clarity with which he creates scenes and develops characters and in the deceptive ease with which he keeps the author out of the story. Most any section of the novel reads like a mini-play that could be transferred to the stage with a minimum of directives, for the narrative is continually pushed forward by credible action and by dialogue designed more for hearing than for silent reading. And though the reader may insistently remind himself that the story was set down on paper by James Still, he will have to search for overt signs of the author's presence. It would be ridiculous for a playwright to circulate on stage giving cues and interrupting the action to inform the audience of the thoughts of the actors, Still seems to be saying, so why should I muddy the story for the reader by intruding my directives, commentaries, and evaluations? Using the first person point of view of a young boy as his "center of consciousness," Still has achieved a fine balance between erasing the author and creating the impression that the story moves of its own volition. And however far in the background he may be, he is there in the form of a magician busy with one hand entertaining the audience with anecdotes, echoes of folklore, and mountain dialogue while with the other hand he is unobtrusively shaping incidents, bridging-in poetic interludes, and disguising signs that direct the story toward his intended climax. (pp. viii-ix)

With each "discovery" and each exploitation of Appalachia, *River of Earth* assumes new meaning and increasing significance both as a chronicle of change and as a work of art. Read today with the strip-mined region as a map—the scalped hills and gashed mountainsides, the ruined farmlands, the dead streams, the flash waters the earth can't contain—even the title assumes a prophecy of doom undreamed of by Brother Mobberly.

An emotional response is the one quality above all for which Still works. There are no games, no literary or historical allusions, no puns, no symbolism, sentimentality, didacticism, or redundancy. He gives no motives, airs no theories, states no beliefs. He simply sets down the experiences of a few human beings during a season of change in a certain place. And he does it in a manner that is simple and unposed and with the perception and restraint that denote an imagination as honest, as controlled, as the needle of a compass. And the emotion is present as certainly as the leaf is in the bud. In giving order to "a handful of chaos" Still has created a new and fresh view

of a range of mountains seventy million years old and of a people that promise to survive all industrial upheavals. (p. x)

Dean Cadle, in a foreword to River of Earth *by James Still, The University Press of Kentucky, 1978, pp. v-x.*

CLEANTH BROOKS

[*The Run for the Elbertas*] is doubly welcome. It makes generally available in book form pieces of highly interesting Americana and it also goes far toward insuring that an excellent contribution to our literature will not be lost to sight. When *On Troublesome Creek,* from which several of these stories are taken, appeared in 1941 it received the acclaim of the thoughtful and sensitive reader. So had Still's novel, *River of Earth,* published a year earlier. But Still's literary virtues are solid and quiet, not flashy and sensational. Still's work needs to be absorbed by the reader and by a considerable body of such readers before it can take its due place in the accepted canon of our literature. (p. ix)

Most readers will be startled by the revelation of such primitive life still surviving in the southern Appalachians at so late a time. Yet if present-day Americans are to understand themselves, they need occasionally to step out of what we like to think of as the rushing mainstream of American life. Life in a backwater community may provide an illuminating glimpse into the older America, the frontier America, which was a necessary preliminary stage of our present civilization.

The culture depicted in Still's [*The Run for the Elbertas*] though quite primitive, is not brutish; in such a culture men have to be ever mindful of the elemental facts on which their very existence depends but they do not allow those pressures to make them inhuman. In fact, the people who live along Still's mountain creeks are actually more warmly human than many of the men and women who live the more insulated life of our great cities. For they are to each other never mere cyphers— they are always fellow creatures, if sometimes all too human— even on occasion downright ornery.

The boy who narrates several of the stories is the perfect observer through whose eyes we are allowed to see this old-fashioned world. He has a boy's curiosity and freshness of vision. He is alert and properly inquisitive about the world in which he finds himself. He is an "innocent" in the pristine sense of that word, yet nevertheless a realist. The terms here are not contradictory: the boy has no illusions that the world is less than harsh or that life is easy. The people of the stories are never far away from real hunger. They live far below what we now know as the poverty line, but that circumstance has not destroyed their basic good humor or sense of hope. All of them seem to find life good and living a joy.

What one notices at once is the language used in these stories. It is idiomatic, highly concrete, richly metaphoric, and has the true lilt of oral speech. It is not precisely the dialect that Faulkner's novels have made familiar to so many twentieth-century readers, for it has its own peculiar characteristics. Yet there is a large overlap with Faulkner's and with the "Southern" dialect in general. (pp. ix-x)

Yet Still is sensible in not requiring that his readers struggle through a thicket of dialect spellings, with elisions and dropped letters marked by inverted commas. For instance, he does not even indicate the dropped *g*'s in such words as "going," "doing," and "living," though one may be sure that the dropped form is general among his speakers. (pp. x-xi)

To give the flavor of the dialect, Still is content to rely on the use of occasional dialect words such as "mort" or "bunty" or "roust," plus folk expressions such as "I'm a hicker-nut hard to crack," or "couldn't make a hum-bird a living," or "it would take Adam's grands and greats to rid that ground." One must not assume, however, that these Southern highlanders have either debased the English language or coined a new language all their own. (p. xi)

The ordinary reader, of course, will hardly be disposed to look up such words in the *OED* or in the special dialect dictionaries, nor need he do so in order to enjoy these stories. The context will usually indicate the basic meaning. Furthermore, the derivation of many of these expressions is transparent. Thus "whiter than a hen and biddy dish" obviously refers to a white china dish, the cover of which is shaped like a hen brooding her chicks, the "biddies," one or two of which are usually represented peeping out from under her feathered body. When Peep Eye asks "Air you have been dranking john corn?" she is referring to whiskey, which in Burns's Scotland was called "John Barley Corn." But barley was not the grain used in the Kentucky mountains. It was plain corn (maize); hence "barley" properly dropped out.

Why do I put such emphasis on Still's language? Because it is central to what his stories so powerfully render: the ways of a culture which sharply differs from that of twentieth-century urban America. Any culture is most deeply and sensitively reflected in its language. There we find the expression of its central concepts and its basic modes of feeling. If we are to be given an insider's view of that culture—that is, if we are to be made to experience it as the person within it does, we must enter it through his language.

I remember having witnessed in Chicago thirty-odd years ago a play about mountain folk of North Carolina. It may have been originally written from an insider's point of view, but once it was deemed to have possibilities for a Broadway production, the play doctors got to it and "improved" it for the benefit of the urban outsider. The play now stressed the quaintness, bawdy realism, and provincial depravity of its characters. The aim became titillation at the bizarre speech and sexual activities of a culture to be viewed as comically decadent.

There is no nonsense of this sort in *The Run for the Elbertas*. The people in these stories take their culture for granted, for they obviously know no other.

The real weakness of the old local color fiction of the 1880-1910 era derived from its condescending attitude toward the regional characteristics that the author undertook to exploit. The local colorist played up what would appear quaint or funny or at any rate outlandish. He was the spielman for a rubberneck bus taking tourists through the hinterland. His job was to amuse the sophisticated by exhibiting the antics of the natives. In short, he could not afford to take his characters seriously as human beings in their own right. James Still does not make this mistake. (pp. xi-xii)

The stories in [*The Run for the Elbertas*] are indeed stories, with simple but adequate plots, a due measure of suspense, and an interesting variety of characters. In those stories narrated by the boy, things, good and bad, happen to his family and happen to the boy as he grows toward an adult's possession of his world. These stories thus make up a modest *Bildungs-*

roman, a mode that has clearly provided some of the best fiction in the whole range of American literature. One thinks immediately of Twain's Huck Finn, or Hemingway's Nick Adams, or Faulkner's young Isaac McCaslin, or Sherwood Anderson's Kentucky boy who is the narrator of "I Want to Know Why." Still has made a worthy contribution to this genre.

It is sheer gain, then, to have the stories in *The Run for the Elbertas* now available in this one volume. They need not merely to be preserved as an item in our literary history, but made accessible to the reading public as a piece of living literature. (p. xiii)

Cleanth Brooks, in a foreword to The Run for the Elbertas *by James Still, The University Press of Kentucky, 1980, ix-xiii.*

JAMES DICKEY

The Wolfpen Poems seems to me to establish Still as the truest and most remarkable poet that the mountain culture has produced. He is a more permanently valuable writer, for instance, than his fellow Kentuckian, Jesse Stuart, who shared some of Still's background but was shamelessly exploitative of it, very nearly to the point of becoming a professional hillbilly. There is none of this attitude in Still's example. The poems are quiet, imaginative and sincere, and the poet's terrible grief over the loss of a way of life ("when the dulcimers are gone") registers with double effect because of the modesty of statement. Throughout everything, Still writes that there is a continual sense of both custom and uniqueness, of tradition and at the same time the strangeness of the tradition, of work and wonder, of the everyday things one does in order to survive, taking place in a kind of timelessness, a world of sacramental objects.

His people are equally archetypal, timeless, interpenetrative with the country they live in, so that the two resemble each other: The human being is himself land walking, weathered by seasons, loving, aging, dying and coming back in spring, and the land bears not only the spiritual but the physical imprint of the man who has lived his life on it, in it, and with it. In the life-landscape, even the wounds are duplicated; the land takes them on. (p. 1)

It is much to Still's credit that he does not bring dialect into his poems, and it is a considerable feat that he projects the sense of "countryness" without resorting to this most obvious of devices. He is sparing of metaphor, so that when he makes a comparison by means of his sharpness of eye and his remarkable aptness of selectivity, he is able to bring an extra dimension from the simplest physical details, such as the measurement made from one place to another. Seldom has the concrete highway, for example, appeared as so sinister and destructive an agency as in the few words where Still admonishes us not to go "upon these wayfares measured with a line/ Drawn hard and white from birth to death." Still believes that a sense of harmony is not so abrupt and final as the line by which the highway is laid down, but that "quiet and slow is peace, and curved with space."

His sense of home is strong but is in a marvelous way counterbalanced by his sense of wandering, of lying not in his "rope-strung bed" in the log cabin where he lives, but somewhere out on the hills, under the open fall of water. . . . To those who tend to think of mountain people in terms of "The Beverly Hillbillies," or country people in terms of "Hee-Haw," I suggest a thorough reading of these poems, or better still, a living with them and *in* them; the reader's vision is likely to change, in a quiet and profound way, in the company of a man who sees in the death of a fox he himself has run over the doom of a part of the Earth, and perhaps the promised end of us all. *The Wolfpen Poems* bring home, among many other good and painful things, the necessity of Appalachia and the things it stands for, even to those who have never seen it. From the curves of his land, Still has more than the right to ask for all of us, as the fox goes, and the dulcimer, as we destroy the natural world and its traditional cultures, "is there no pardon anywhere?" (pp. 1, 19)

James Dickey, in a review of "The Wolfpen Poems,"
in Los Angeles Times Book Review, *December 7,*
1986, pp. 1, 19.

Vladimir (Nikolaevich) Voinovich

1932-

(Also transliterated as Vojnovič) Russian novelist, short story writer, essayist, nonfiction writer, poet, dramatist, and script-writer.

An exile from his native country, Voinovich is credited with reviving satire as a mode of expression in Soviet literature. Widely praised in Europe and the United States for his sardonic treatment of Russian existence, Voinovich began his writing career in the early 1960s, a time when the Nikita Khrushchev regime tolerated a degree of freedom in the arts. Most writers of this period adhered to the tenets of socialist realism, a format stressing the didactic use of art, music, and literature to develop social awareness and Marxist beliefs. In response to conventional portrayals of Soviet protagonists who triumph against overwhelming odds, Voinovich redefined the Russian hero as an individual concerned with discovering and preserving personal integrity within a totalitarian society. In his works, Voinovich lampoons such Soviet institutions as the Red Army and the KGB as well as scientific research and agricultural collectives. His novels have been compared to those of nineteenth-century Russian satirist Nikolai Gogol for their accurate rendering of dialect and their critiques of social and political corruption.

Many of Voinovich's early short stories were first published in the Russian literary magazine *Novy Mir* and are reprinted with previously unpublished works in *Putem vzaimnoj perepiski* (1979; *In Plain Russian*). While most pieces in this collection express no direct criticism of the Soviet government, several provoked censure for their portrayal of young idealists who question the values of their society. In ''What I Might Have Been,'' for example, a construction engineer refuses to clear an unfinished apartment building for occupancy because he considers the dwelling unsafe. Although the man loses his job, he retains his ethics and personal dignity. ''By Way of Private Correspondence'' concerns a young soldier who is trapped into marriage by a female pen pal. Through his depiction of a man's manipulation by his wife and her family, Voinovich alludes to the lack of personal freedom in Soviet life as well as to the ways that individuals resign themselves to government control. Although Voinovich continued to publish fiction throughout the 1960s and early 1970s, his work met with increasing censorship. Critics generally agree that his harsh view of the Soviet political system and his open support of dissident writer Aleksandr Solzhenitsyn led to his expulsion from the Union of Soviet Writers in 1974.

Zhizn' i neobychainye prikliucheniia soldata Ivana Chonkina (1975; *The Life and Extraordinary Adventures of Private Ivan Chonkin*), Voinovich's best-known work in Europe and the United States, was originally published in Paris. Set during World War II, this novel revolves around Private Chonkin, an amiable bumbler who resists authority through his innocent pursuit of personal pleasure. After ordering him to guard a crashed airplane near a remote collective farm, the Soviet bureaucracy forgets him, and Chonkin becomes involved with a local postmistress. Following a series of comic mishaps, Chonkin is charged with treason after arresting a group of secret police he has mistaken for German soldiers. Theodore Solo-

taroff called Voinovich's choice of a satirical style ''inspired, for it unearthed a first-rate comic talent that had been lurking beneath the sober gritty surface of his early realism and a new and powerful gift for rendering the transactions between reality and fantasy, the ordinary life haunted by the phantoms and phantasmagoria of the police state.'' Several critics compared *The Life and Extraordinary Adventures of Private Ivan Chonkin* to such novels as Jaroslav Hašek's *Good Soldier Schweik* and Joseph Heller's *Catch-22* for its portrayal of an ordinary individual who perseveres against absurd bureaucratic obstacles.

Pretendent na prestol: Novye prikliucheniia soldata Ivana Chonkina (1979; *Pretender to the Throne: The Further Adventures of Private Ivan Chonkin*) begins where *The Life and Extraordinary Adventures of Private Ivan Chonkin* ended, with Chonkin awaiting trial in prison. A rumor circulates that Chonkin is Prince Golitsyn, the illegitimate son of a pre-Soviet ruler, and that he is in league with Adolf Hitler to replace Joseph Stalin's government with a czarist monarchy. Attempting to rescue the ''German spy,'' Hitler erroneously diverts his military forces to the village where Chonkin is held and is defeated by Stalin's Red Army. A ludicrous Soviet investigation into Chonkin's case culminates in orders to pardon Chonkin for his heroic role in Hitler's defeat and to issue a death warrant for Prince Golitsyn. Several critics contended that Voinovich's portrayal of the KGB and its inept but dangerous methods in *Pretender to the Throne* led to his exile from the Soviet Union in 1980. Following his expulsion, Voinovich emigrated to West Germany.

In *Ivan'kiada: Ili rasskaz o vselenii pisatelia Voinovicha v novuiu kvartiru* (1976; *The Ivankiad; or, The Tale of the Writer Voinovich's Installation in His New Apartment*), Voinovich presents a mock-epic account of one of his encounters with the Soviet government. Since Voinovich and his wife are expecting a child, they are thus entitled to a larger apartment, according to the Soviet maxim "To each according to his needs." A minor bureaucrat requests use of the apartment, however, to provide room for his new household appliances, and the committee appointed to oversee the matter vacillates in deciding whose claim to honor. By the novel's end, Voinovich's victory seems more the product of persistence than merit. According to Mary Ann Szporluk, *The Ivankiad* "satirizes the methods by which the bureaucracy rules and reveals the discrepancies between official values and laws and real values and practices."

Antisovetskii Sovetskii Soiuz (1985; *The Anti-Soviet Soviet Union*) collects Voinovich's essays and prose pieces on such topics as his expulsion from the Soviet Union and the ways in which ordinary citizens resist governmental control in contemporary Russia. Dragan Milivojević asserted that with this book "Voinovich reaffirms his position as the leading Russian satirist of our time." In his recent novel, *Moscow 2042* (1987), Voinovich employs science fiction and self-reflexive satire to relate the adventures of an exiled Russian writer who returns to the Soviet Union, now a single city called Moscowrep, in the twenty-first century. Ostensibly a communist utopia, Moscowrep is revealed to be tainted by the evils of previous regimes. Offering insight into the situations of Soviet exiles and the fundamentalist attitudes of Westerners, this novel was praised for its effective blend of humor and social criticism. Designating Voinovich "one of the greatest and most courageous of . . . modern satirists," Malcolm Bradbury called *Moscow 2042* "a work both of historical pain and massive comic ebullience."

(See also *CLC*, Vol. 10 and *Contemporary Authors*, Vols. 81-84.)

DRAGAN MILIVOJEVIĆ

The fate of most outstanding Russian writers both in Tsarist and Soviet Russia has been perilous when their artistic endeavors followed their social and philosophical commitments. Solzhenitsyn's strident clamor for freedom and his subsequent repression was followed by Voinovich's satirical portrayal of totalitarian society on behalf of sanity and common sense. Both writers suffered social ostracism, and both were exiled from their homeland. In a peculiar way, their fates were interwoven as Voinovich stood up to defend Solzhenitsyn's right to artistic freedom and thereby caused his own downfall and exile. (p. 55)

Voinovich's first prosaic literary works belonged to the so-called "new prose" of the sixties. Writers of that period, Gladilin, Aksyonov, Kazakov, to name just a few, were moving away from Socialist realism. The upbeat tone of official optimism is missing in Voinovich's early works. The grayness and dullness of everyday life surround his characters. The main

character of **"I Want To Be Honest"** oscillates between a meaningless job and a meaningless love affair. The short story ends on a flat note of resignation. In **"Two Friends"** adolescent friendship was portrayed along with corruption and betrayal. The theme has a universal meaning, and the moral is applicable to adults as well. It is very appropriate to totalitarian societies where people, for gain and advancement, denounce their friends who have committed a political indiscretion.

Nowhere else in the early works of Voinovich is the description of Soviet reality so downbeat and so starkly unvarnished as it is in his short, ironic story, **"By Way of Private Correspondence."** Ivan Altynnik, a soldier in the Soviet army, in his long leisure hours corresponded with unknown girls with the intention of getting acquainted. For Altynnik, women were objects of pleasure, and he hunted them for the sexual pleasures they could provide. In his quest he met a formidable opponent who was as singleminded in her desire to get married as Altynnik was in his fixation. Lyudmila was getting on in years, and she was at that point in her life where a marriage to anybody became imperative. Enticed by Lyudmila's snapshot taken many years ago, Altynnik stopped at Lyudmila's village with high hopes of having fun; but instead, became drunk and was led to the altar by the scheming bride and her brother. Later, after returning to his unit, he received a letter from Lyudmila in which she informed him that she had gotten a baby by him. Altynnik, the hunter, became the victim. He had to get married and return to the village henpecked and depressed, drowning his sorrow in vodka.

Altynnik is a victim of circumstances over which he has no control, quite unlike the positive hero of socialist realistic works who perseveres against all odds and handicaps. The society depicted here is corrupt in its entirety so that it is impossible to take a positive and optimistic view of its future. The realism here is in the tradition of Tolstoy and Chekhov; it is critical realism conveying a critical picture of the society as a whole.

For Voinovich, the writing of *Ivan'kiada*, or *A Story of Writer Voinovich Moving into the New Apartment* was a therapeutic exercise which prevented him from going insane or ending up with a heart attack. He succeeded in staying mentally and physically healthy by considering his own troubles with Soviet bureaucracy from a detached, third person viewpoint.

"To each according to his own needs and from each according to his own ability" was an early egalitarian slogan of the Soviet revolution. It was an ideal to be emulated and applied. Against the background of this ideal and other ideals of early revolutionary morality, such as the desire for common good and welfare and the disinterest in private gain, the author superimposed a microcosmic photographic reality of the mores of the seventies. The ideals have remained the same, and they are constantly repeated, but the abyss between ideals and practice, between sham and reality, between words and deeds, is enormous.

The writer's council has decided that the next free apartment should be given to the author Voinovich who lives in a one-room apartment and whose wife is expecting a baby. By standards of socialist morality, he is entitled to it. The only problem is that the same apartment is coveted by a man of power and influence, Ivan'ko, who needs additional living space to install his newly purchased American appliances. His is a matter not of need but of greed, and the issue from the moral point of view would be overwhelmingly in Voinovich's favor, if these matters were to be solved by moral criteria alone. They are not, and power and influence appear, initially, more important. The writer's community sways opportunistically between the justice of Voinovich's cause and the power and influence of Ivan'ko. The story ends on an optimistic note with the triumph of Voinovich's just cause. The reader is left with an impression that the victory of justice in this particular case was not in the order of things but that it was an exceptional case won by dint of sheer persistence.

Ivan'kiada is a sociological-literary documentary of the seventies in an urban intellectual environment. It is a unique literary genre in which the author succeeded in distilling his own private experience by endowing it with the presence and the mores of the whole period. (pp. 57-9)

Voinovich's most ambitious work is undoubtedly, *Zhizn' i neobychayniye prikl 'ucheniya soldata Ivana Chonkina (Life and Extraordinary Adventures of Private Ivan Chonkin)*. This novel is the chronicle of a Red Army misfit who is ordered on the eve of World War II to guard a plane that crash-landed on a remote collective farm in central Russia. Although he is promptly forgotten by his unit, he has vowed to quit his post only when properly relieved. Private Chonkin imprisons a detachment of secret policemen who attempt to arrest him for desertion. A whole army regiment is sent to capture him. At the end, Chonkin is led away, but his spirit remains high and undefeated.

Chonkin is an anti-ideological, satirical novel. One of the many definitions of satire concerns opposition between appearance and substance or between form and content, or between manner and matter. This aspect appears very appropriate to both the concept of the novel as such and to the portrayal of individual characters.

The concept of the novel is based on the contrast between truth vs. lie, humanity vs. inhumanity, common sense vs. irrationality, and the highest ranking contrast which includes all the previously mentioned is the opposition between the dead hand of the ideology and the creative force of life. The effectiveness of the satire centers around the juxtaposition and the collision of these principles. Each character in *Chonkin* is divided within himself between the ideological precepts of how life should be lived or what individual behavior should be under certain circumstances and what natural impulses or common sense prompts him to do.

It is generally assumed that life whose only purpose is vegetative existence is not worthy of being lived and that life should have a goal and a mission. Viewed from this angle, Chonkin's life is indeed worthless, since his only preoccupation is survival. His simplicity and lack of education as well as his low position in the military prevent him from having any high aspirations or ambitions. The very fact, however, that he did not have any notions of "saving mankind" or contributing to its welfare saved him from inflicting damage on the society and harm to his countrymen and prevented him from becoming enslaved to the ideology. Chonkin, along with his girlfriend Nyura, lives spontaneously from the center of his being, and out of this spontaneity come pity, compassion, and even sparks of wisdom. (pp. 59-60)

At the other end of the spectrum are individuals who have subordinated and suppressed their humanity to ideological exigencies so completely that only traces of their humanity are apparent, e.g., the chief of the secret police Milyaga and Aglaya, the wife of Revkin, the secretary of the district party committee.

Unlike Chonkin who did not believe that in the cosmic order of things his own life had any special importance, Captain Milyaga believed that his life had a purpose. The awareness of this purpose did not arise in Milyaga from the depth of his own being through reflection and cogitation. It came to him from outside through the propagandistic, instructional material which he had been receiving as a part of his ideological education. The most prominent influence on his view of the world and his mission in it was a big poster on the wall facing his desk with Stalin's words, "We should organize pitiless struggle with all kinds of disorganizers in the rear, scaremongers, rumormongers and we should destroy spies. . . .". Confronted by a newly apprehended, innocent-looking, old Jew, Milyaga decides right on the spot without any supportive evidence, that Stalin's words from the poster apply to the victim. Aglaya and her husband Andrey followed the new Communist morality according to which the allegiance to the party exceeds any other loyalty including family loyalties. Andrey has been behaving strangely lately, and his wife is suspecting him of ideological errors. Before bedtime an intimate conversation between husband and wife takes place in the following way:

> "Andrey," quietly and inexorably asked Aglaya, "If you feel unhealthy inclinations in yourself, you should disarm yourself before the party."
>
> "Yes, I should," agreed Andrey, "but what will happen to our son? He is only seven years old."
>
> "Don't worry. I will educate him as a real Bolshevik. He will even forget what your name was."

In both examples ideological purity runs counter to the common precepts of humanity and compassion. Because of such examples, it may appear that the prevailing mood of the novel is that of depression. That this is not so is due to the author's belief that human beings are basically good insofar as they exist close to the earth and live from the center of their beings untouched by ambitions, pretentions, and ideologies. Voinovich, also, does not believe in the totality and absoluteness of evil in human beings. Even the most depraved characters have retained deep down a spark of humanity. Even the chief of the secret police, Milyaga, through the windows of his prison is able to appreciate the beauty of the Russian landscape. The evil and the corruption come from outside, and they consist in abdicating individual morality to the collective ideological thinking. (pp. 60-1)

Voinovich in his lampooning of the ideology used the language of the ideology itself. This is the cliche-ridden language of "Pravda," official pronouncements, party meetings, and public speeches. Whatever emotional content this language possessed in the beginning of Soviet power subsequently disappeared, and words like worn out coins, have lost their freshness and originality. The Russian language appears to be divided into two variants: the one used in public and the other used in private. A party organizer has to tell a group of peasants that the war between the Soviet Union and Germany had broken out. He is visibly moved, choking with profound emotions and grasping for words. The only word he can utter is "comrades," and he keeps repeating this word several times. Finally, taking control of himself, he slips into fluent jargon of official announcements describing the German attack in official parlance as "Verolomny" (faithless). To the extent that the fluency of his delivery increased, his emotions diminished, until the speech lost any vestige of originality.

It has been frequently stated that the physical separation of a writer from his homeland and the language tends to affect his creativity negatively. Bunin continued writing during his stay abroad without any signs of decline, but other writers were not so fortunate. It is too early to say to which group Voinovich belongs. . . .

Voinovich's importance in contemporary Russian literature is that he opened up new possibilities of literary expression which have been in disuse since the twenties in the Soviet Union. Socialist realistic precepts were not suited to the emergence of satirical literature. Voinovich had to reach back to Zoshchenko and also to foreign writers like Heller in *Catch-22* and Hashek in *Good Soldier Schweik* to revive this tradition. It is unfortunate that his works cannot be enjoyed by his countrymen at the present time. (p. 62)

> Dragan Milivojević, "The Many Voices of Vladimir Voinovich," in Rocky Mountain Review of Language and Literature, *Vol. 33, No. 2, Spring, 1979, pp. 55-62.*

JOHN BAYLEY

Opening any issue of *Soviet Monthly* . . . , I am struck by the same revelation. In none of the well-tailored, adequately written stories, which range conscientiously over all the peoples and activities of the U.S.S.R., is there such a thing as an *I*, a real I. The main figure is usually a he or a she, a sound representative type whether old or young; but even if the tale should be in the first person the I might just as well be a *we*.

Modern Anglo-American literature makes one thoroughly sick and tired of *I*, just as readers of *Soviet Monthly* in the U.S.S.R. must be fed up with *we*. The trouble is that our I's are not really I's at all: they are really just the same as everybody else, though at least they do have the sense of themselves as individuals, writing their own thing. A real I in literature is very rare indeed; and in contemporary Soviet literature, practically unheard of.

Hence the remarkable importance and interest of Vladimir Voinovich's stories. Let me say at once that [the pieces collected in *In Plain Russian*] are the best stories I have read for a long time, in any language. Most of them are earlier than the two works that have made Voinovich famous in the West—and infamous to the Soviet literary establishment—*The Life and Extraordinary Adventures of Private Ivan Chonkin* and *The Ivankiad*. These elaborate, full-length, often very funny burlesques reveal an enormous, wholly individual talent; but as the titles suggest, they make extended use of the picaresque or mock-heroic form. The stories give the essence of Voinovich's unique talent in a purer, more naïve and subtler form.

Vladimir Voinovich was born in 1932, in Soviet Central Asia. His mother was Jewish, and his father was a Serb who worked as a journalist. Thus, in an important sense, the author is not really Russian at all. . . . But like all very gifted authors (and Pushkin is the greatest Russian example) Voinovich knows how to get the best of both worlds into his art; he knows how to be at once local and universal, national and cosmopolitan. His Russian has a classic succulence and flavor. . . .

Voinovich has many ancestors, some of them rather surprising; but their presence only strengthens our impression of a remarkable *I* who is giving us his own entirely uninfluenced and unadulterated view of the universe. The lead story, one of the earliest, written in 1962, draws the reader effortlessly into a world that is quite new to him and yet mysteriously familiar, from Anglo-American as well as Russian literature. Called

"What I Might Have Been," its narrator is a construction engineer working to finish a block of flats in a large Soviet city. This, of course, is a good old *Soviet Monthly* situation; and part of the esthetic interest of the work is the way in which the narrator—simply by being a real and totally individual *I* whom we at once accept as such—finds himself parodying the standard Soviet "construction site" story. (p. 9)

But there is more to it than that. The daily life of the narrator here—his flat, his workmates, the cafeterias he eats in, his elderly girlfriend—is put before us with vivid authority. The author knows this life through and through. But that in itself would be a minor accomplishment. Nor is the parodic "point" of the story—the narrator's refusal to hand over the buildings in an unfinished state under pressure from the local politicians—particularly compelling. It is the standard story ploy of an honest fellow in a locally corrupt situation. But what *is* compelling is the extraordinary originality the author has shown in emancipating hero and tale from these set-piece stereotypes.

This point was not lost on Khrushchev's adviser on cultural affairs, who first noted down a black mark against Voinovich that led to his expulsion from the Writers' Union 10 years later. The interesting thing is that stories about dishonest contractors and incorruptible foremen are two a penny in *Soviet Monthly*: it was not the theme that upset Khrushchev's man but what lay behind it—the fact that the narrator did what he did, not for the cause or on Communist principle, but because he was an *I*, an individual who had a mind of his own.

And, insofar as any stereotype is involved, it is an American and not a Russian one. Voinovich's narrator has something in common with those just men who go their way in O'Hara, Dos Passos, Raymond Chandler—and most of all, perhaps, the hero of Lionel Trilling's immensely distinguished novel *The Middle of the Journey*. Who knows how familiar Voinovich is with these types? What is certain is that he avoids any suspicion of the second-hand where either Russian or American themes are concerned. The plain Russian element in these stories is their complete spontaneity, humor, fantastic merriness of perception, apparent absence of art. (pp. 9, 32)

Voinovich points out that he has no wish to be a martyr, as so many remarkable recent Russians—from Solzhenitsyn on—have eagerly sought to be. He advocates no counterrevolution, as they implicitly do. He has said of himself: "My character is absolutely not that of a dissident. I am a completely apolitical person. I have never held literature to be a part of politics." This is disingenuous, of course, for Voinovich must know quite well that the "apolitical" person is precisely the one most disliked, even feared, by regimes like the Soviet. . . . [All] Soviet literature has political implications, and never more so than when a writer says exactly what he thinks.

Voinovich put this much more forcefully when summoned before the Writers' Union. "We have nothing to discuss and nothing to argue about, because I express my own opinions while you say what you are told to." And this was the young man who had composed the lyrics for the song **"Fourteen Minutes to Go,"** which became the unofficial anthem of the Soviet cosmonauts. . . . (p. 32)

A clue to this conflict is given by a section of the present book called "Autobiographical Stories," where the author is glimpsed doing his service in the air force and working on a construction site. It is a little like Kipling's *Stalky and Co.* but less heartless: most of the bosses and bullies show themselves to be afraid, and not so bad underneath it all. Indeed the analogy between the Soviet system and the worst sort of school (a comparison once made by Isaiah Berlin) hovers in the background of Voinovich's creative psychology. One of the liveliest sketches, called **"A Circle of Friends,"** is about a party in the Kremlin on the eve of Hitler's invasion. The author manages to convey the crudity and odiousness of the group in a manner much more devastating than his lighthearted treatment would suggest. (pp. 32-3)

[*In Plain Russian*] contains two examples of what the Russians call the *rasskaz* (a slight but effective tale) and two more serious *povesti*, or novellas. Both are stories about simple people, plain Russians, and like the best of Chekhov's have the gift of making one cry without being in the least sentimental. The funnier— a perfect masterpiece—is [**"By Way of Private Correspondence"**], about a young go-ahead air force sergeant who acquires a promising female pen pal in some god-forsaken hick town. Unexpectedly ordered to pick up equipment nearby, he takes the chance of going to see her and—to make a long story short—never gets away. The resonance of this story lies in the collision between the new technocratic Russia and the old unchanging one. The end is not unlike that of Waugh's *A Handful of Dust* but much more human and believable. Strange that the author himself, still holed up in Russia, still writing somehow, may well be leading a similar sort of life. And on the evidence of his work he will not be minding too much. (p. 33)

John Bayley, "A Soviet 'I'," in The New York Times Book Review, *October 7, 1979, pp. 9, 32-3.*

GEOFFREY HOSKING

Devotees of the unassuming Red Army soldier Ivan Chonkin, whom Vladimir Voinovich introduced to the world some years ago, may be faintly surprised to hear that the next volume of his adventures is entitled *Pretender to the Throne*. Judging by the first volume [*The Life and Extraordinary Adventures of Private Ivan Chonkin*], it would be difficult to imagine anyone less like a prince than red-eared, bow-legged Chonkin. In any case, one thought the monarchy had long been abolished in Russia.

Well, anything is possible in the Soviet Union—and also in a story of Voinovich, where, to misquote Hegel, "All that is fantastic is real, and all that is real is fantastic". The misquotation is not entirely frivolous: some crazy end-product of Hegel's dialectic really is at work here. George Orwell called it "doublethink", which one might think of as the mechanism by which man's imaginings confront him and enslave him. . . .

Of all the writers of recent years, there is none who exposes "doublethink" in all its varieties so skillfully as Voinovich. . . .

Voinovich's work is full of satirical revelations . . . , and this gradually unfolding novel, *Chonkin*, is especially remarkable: its humble, good-natured "hero" constantly and unwittingly unmasks the duplicity of others, and its conscientious, slightly obtuse narrator plods gamely along, always one step behind the reader in understanding the implications of his own story.

"Doublethink" cannot, however, be overcome just by revealing the discrepancy between reality and words. Human beings cannot live on reality alone. At the very least they need to bring to it their own preconceptions and predispositions. To cope with reality, in fact, people need some kind of fantasy. That is why "doublethink" is so tenacious, why human beings are always ready to half-believe any old mumbo-jumbo served

up at them consistently and repeatedly. Not only do we need to be rescued from sterile and noxious fantasies, we also need to be offered creative and humane alternatives.

This is where the humble figure of Private Ivan Chonkin comes in. He is not only an excellent satirical catalyst, his naivety inducing people to relax their guard and reveal their underlying motives. He is also, in his own incongruous way, a "positive hero". But not at all of the traditional Soviet type: he is not the least interested in tractors, ball-bearings or the output of pig-iron. He comes from an older and simpler world in which the stupid peasant lad, Ivan the Fool, could win the princess's hand because of his cheerful, open-hearted honesty and his magical capacity to communicate with plants and animals. Of course, nowadays something more than this is needed to enable him to aspire to the throne in a socialist republic.

But then he has a priceless asset on his side: the inexhaustible imagination of the NKVD and the Soviet propaganda machine. In [*Pretender to the Throne*] Chonkin does in fact more or less nothing: he is a helpless prisoner, being shunted from one investigator to another. But those investigators, true to their NKVD routine, build great edifices of fantasy on tiny scraps of evidence—for example, the rumour in Chonkin's home village that he is the illegitimate son of a prince. They provide the material which enables the state procurator at the trial to reach the dizzy heights of absurdity where he accuses Chonkin of being the leader of a massive White Guard movement acting in league with Hitler to restore the monarchy. Both Hitler and Stalin dream of Chonkin as a *bogatyr'*, the hero-knight of Russia's folk epics, leading his people to victory.

And perhaps, in a totally different sense, that is what he is. Viewed through the prism of popular rather than state-sponsored fantasy, through the traditional folk-tale, he is a kind of foolish-Ivan-cum-prince bringing his people salvation by freeing them from the grip of the paranoid make-believe in which they have been forced to dwell. His good-hearted simplicity, and that of his unregistered but very real wife, Nyura, re-establishes contact with ordinary, unschizophrenic humanity. . . .

[*In Plain Russian*] is a rewarding collection by any standards, and fascinating in its revelation of the elements out of which Voinovich's masterpiece, *Chonkin*, has been built up. From the ironically self-deprecating first-person narration of **"What I Might Have Been"** have developed the naive and earnest understatements of the narrator of *Chonkin*, leading the reader on to insights slightly beyond the mental capacities of that narrator himself. In the same story one sees Voinovich's gift for capturing the muddled, even perverse texture of everyday life and work, its irreducible distance from rule books and ideals. . . .

In **"From an Exchange of Letters"** a young man, newly out of the army and with the world before him, becomes trapped by a woman's desperate longing for a husband. His own epistolary flirtation, conducted as a form of compensation for the bleak and unfeminine surroundings of the barracks, forms the initial thread by which she entwines him, using an indomitable mixture of affectionate cajolery, low cunning and straightforward bullying. In its homely way, her method has something in common with the process by which the totalitarian state traps men in their own fantasies. . . .

In his autobiographical sketches of life in the air force Voinovich presents military routine as yet another system of tightly organized fantasy imposed on a cussed reality which keeps resisting it. The disciplinary code, which everyone has to take very seriously, even when they do not observe it, constantly reveals itself as ill-adapted to ragged, unpolished humanity. Some of Voinovich's most unforgettable characters are army officers whose natural gentleness occasionally breaks through the military mask. Such is Major Dogadkin, in the story named after him, or the officer in **"From an Exchange of Letters"**, who only really seems at ease with himself when he suddenly has to change the dirty nappies of a baby abandoned at the roadside.

Perhaps the most interesting of all these stories is the previously unpublished **"A Circle of Friends"**, which portrays Stalin's Politburo of 1941, thinly disguised, in a drunken summer midnight get-together. The fabric of propaganda and self-deception by which this boorish, undignified and servile bunch have been living is abruptly torn apart at dawn, when news reaches them of the German invasion. The final image is of Stalin, having torn off his paste-board moustache (strictly for the public), faced in the mirror with a truthful image of himself as an ugly and deluded old man. Horrified, he shoots at the apparition and shatters it; but, unable to rid himself of himself, he falls into a deep coma which lasts for ten days. Thus, in Voinovich, images of reality and illusion deftly change places, continually throwing light on one another.

Voinovich still lives in Moscow, but, since his expulsion from the Writers' Union in 1974, he has only been able to communicate with a foreign and émigré public. That makes the standard of translation all the more important. Richard Lourie . . . has done on the whole a good job. My only reservation is that I should have preferred to see Voinovich in English English (if I may call it that), since American colloquial diction tends to be a little too direct to do justice to the delicate circumlocutions and understatements which are such a distinctive feature of his style. All the same, *In Plain Russian* is a marvellous introduction to Voinovich for English-language readers.

> Geoffrey Hosking, *"The Bow-Legged Prince of Single-Think,"* in The Times Literary Supplement, *No. 4010, February 1, 1980, p. 109.*

R. C. PORTER

"The future of Russian literature, if it is destined to *have* a future, is being nourished by jokes, just as Pushkin grew up imbibing the tales his nanny told him. The joke is a pure demonstration of the miracle of art, which thrives on the savagery and rage of dictators. . .". Thus Sinyavsky in the first issue of *Kontinent*. The subtitle of "roman-anekdot" for Voinovich's novel *The Life and Extraordinary Adventures of Private Ivan Chonkin* in fact understates the powerful jolt that the work gives one even on a superficial reading, and demonstrates exactly Sinyavsky's contention. None of the reviewers of the book deny its humour, and the sad facts surrounding its publication are well known. . . . [The novel] was first published in Paris in 1975, and shortly after its appearance Voinovich had two interviews with KGB agents . . . ; after the second, during which he was threatened with sudden death, he was seriously ill for several days, and realised he had been given a poisoned cigarette. Clearly the book had aroused the "rage of dictators". At the time he wrote to the KGB: "Murder too is no mean estimate of a writer's work—I am not afraid of threats, Private Chonkin will avenge me."

At first sight Chonkin hardly seems to be the sort of character to avenge anyone. But his qualities have attracted Voinovich repeatedly and work as the most effective antidote to the evil he sees around him. These qualities, for the sake of convenience, may be called collectively "innocence", though they comprise elements of the Tolstoyan "simple man", the *Ivan-durachok* (Ivan the fool) of folk tales and an instinctive moral awareness, unashamedly devoid of intellectual basis. The possessor of "innocence" is usually a simpleton, by no means at odds with the system, but always a thorn in its side, because of his ostensible incompetence. It is not that he does not want to, he simply cannot. In this, he differs from the more notorious—underground—men of Soviet literature like Olesha's Kavalerov and Zamyatin's D-503, who consciously set themselves up in opposition to the establishment, and in this he would seem to be more a phenomenon of post-1945 Russian literature, rather than of Soviet literature as a whole. (pp. 97-8)

Perhaps the most eloquent expression of Voinovich's "assumed innocence" occurs in his latest book *Ivankiada,* where he stubbornly insists on what seems to become a fairly small principle, as the conflict it generates spins out in ever-increasing and heated circles. The story of Voinovich moving into a new flat which he badly needs and which he has been promised by the housing co-operative, becomes a sort of Soviet *Clochemerle,* except that it is pure documentary, not fiction. When the author takes possession of the flat he lies there "like Chonkin" expecting attack. The serious, even tragic, subtext of the comedy comes through at the end of the story when Voinovich recalls Victor Nekrasov's question as to why so many talented citizens have to leave the Soviet Union, and he replies, because of people like Ivanko, the self-seeking unprincipled bureaucrat. (p. 99)

In *Chonkin* there is the author's "assumed innocence", which operates through the mode of narration, and the natural innocence of most of the main characters, which manifests itself in their various reactions to events. The two kinds support each other, and clear the ground of established myths and stereotypes for authentic existence. In this way the novel is truly subversive to any society. If it were to be read simply as a biting satire on peasant backwardness, the shortcomings of collectivisation, and Russia's unpreparedness for war in 1941, it might just be accomodated. . . . (pp. 99-100)

The full title of the novel *The Life and Extraordinary Adventures of Private Ivan Chonkin* suggests an episodic, picaresque novel, and the book has been, justifiably, compared with Hašek's *Good Soldier Svejk.* A recent emigré critic, Yuriy Mal'tsev, feels that the comparison goes no further than the titles, and while one might disagree with such a bald dismissal, there are important differences. Unlike *Svejk,* *Chonkin* is not repetitive or episodic. It has a strong plot-line throughout; the initial event—the crash-landing of an aeroplane—animates all the characters right to the end (at least to the end of Part two); the relations between all the protagonists are explored and developed, with the exception of the old Jew, Moisey Solomonovich Stalin; despite the fine comedy he brings with him, he remains at this stage extraneous in terms of the plot. Likewise, the characters, particularly the hero, have a ring of authenticity about them, being self-sufficient and familiar. Chonkin himself, the military drop-out, has a long literary pedigree. Minor characters like Baba Dunya and Ninka are the stock-in-trade of village life. Golubyov, the harassed book-cooking chairman of the collective farm, is a type common enough to be known to everyone, and easily enough presented as an aberration rather than an everyday and inevitable phenomenon, to be ridiculed in the pages of *Krokodil*. On several occasions the novel is deliberately derivative. The first exchanges between the pilot of the plane and the collective farm chairman parallel closely the conversation between the mayor and Khlestakov in *The Government Inspector,* and when rumours start to circulate about Chonkin and his band the echoes of the rumours surrounding Chichikov and the legend of Captain Kopeikin can hardly be due to either accident or literary fecklessness.

What Voinovich is doing is to give his story an aura of respectability and authority the better to denigrate it through his own assumed innocence. He achieves this by constantly interrupting his strong plot-line with digressions and interjections, by appealing to the reader not to read on if he is irritated, by apologising for his characters when they refuse to submit to any external authority, even their creator's. (p. 100)

The author creates situations of which the characters fail to see the relevance or importance. The very first chapter is built on a series of digressions and misunderstandings. Being literate, Nyura knows that superstitions are just remnants of the dark past, therefore she tries not to believe in the "iron bird" that has just landed by her vegetable garden.... Nyura finds it difficult to take in this piece of modern technology, even when she does realise what it is—she uses the word *aeroplan* instead of the modern *samolyot.*

Moreover, understanding what it is in abstract terms, hardly helps the locals communicate with the pilot. Plechevoy "was not surprised, not afraid", and launches into a long diatribe on the history of the name of the village and its environs.... The pilot, by his status in Soviet society, should enlighten and direct the collective farmers, but he lapses into embarrassed speechlessness. The locals might all be dismissed as variously ignorant, superstitious, cowardly, impressionable, or pushy; but their common trait is spontaneity. Casting aside all preconceived notions, be they from the dark superstitious past or the new, scientific present, they confound the newcomer by their very naturalness. This first chapter then gives the first round to "the people" who, as Golubyov with fine unwitting irony and truth tells us, "sees everything and knows everything."

Chapter II simply reverses the situation. Chonkin, the peasant, is defeated by the unnatural life he is forced to lead in the army. Once he is slotted back into where he belongs, the illusions, the false fabric of social life, collapse and the *narod,* or common people, really come into their own. "With the sort of folk who live here—they don't even lock up their huts", Nyura tells him to his surprise, and in the village Chonkin is able to give full vent to his instinctive morality and his intuitive sense of duty, which depend on his day-to-day existence rather than on an artificially constructed hierarchy. Without any external stimuli he becomes an efficient farmer, a good husband, even something of a sensible businessman, and most astonishingly, a fine soldier. (pp. 101-02)

One of the most salient features of Chonkin's make-up, and something that gives the novel as a whole a wider perspective, is the occasional dream sequences. Their immediate functions would seem to be to summarise the plot so far, to define the tensions in the hero's psychology, and to indulge in blatant ridicule of Soviet sacred cows—Stalin appears as a transvestite, human beings are turned into animals. However, they go far beyond this. It is clear that most of the protagonists are constrained by officially sponsored illusions. Golubyov is trapped by an economic system that just does not seem to work, Milyaga is in pursuit of a band of cut-throats that does not exist, and more than all the others Gladyshev is shaped entirely by

a bogus scientific ambition; it is in the nature of things that he, misguided by a spurious example imposed from above, should eventually clash with Chonkin, who has managed to liberate himself and achieve total inner integrity and self-realisation. (p. 102)

Chonkin's dreams—he has two major ones and a number of short daydreams—stand in opposition to the illusions that already exist. They provide a counterweight to them and hint at a fundamental philosophical objection to them. In his waking moments they provide harmless escape from boredom (usually induced by political indoctrination classes); in his sleep, they annihilate all the laws of nature. Yet two positive things emerge in these series of mad, jumbled events. Firstly, the world of men and the world of animals become interchangeable; secondly, Chonkin is by no means master of the situation.

In the first dream a horse tows the aeroplane across the sky, and Yartsev, the political instructor, turns into a beetle and then back again. Trofimovich becomes a horse and paws the ground. Just before he wakes up, Chonkin is about to be shot for desertion, having spent most of the dream trying futilely to catch the aeroplane. In the second, Plechevoy takes Chonkin to Nyura's wedding, where everyone turns into pigs and the hero is forced to grunt like a pig, and even made to enjoy grunting like a pig. The guests are served human flesh (*chelovechina*)!... [Chonkin's] dreams proper may take on the semi-harrowing, semi-humorous world of Kafka, but they are kept firmly in their place and the hero always wakes up in time to be saved. Yet these innocent fantasies form a definite system of cross-references with the real world that Chonkin has entered on arriving in Krasnoye, and the two spheres tend to validate each other. In this way man gains at least as much as he loses by being repeatedly compared with animals.

In *Cancer Ward* Solzhenitsyn uses the world of animals in the zoo scene as an allegory of man's various qualities, life-styles and moral standing. Earlier in the novel, Shulubin has mentioned Kropotkin's *Mutual Aid,* a work designed to refute Darwin and to point out that man can learn from the example that higher animals give us in the way they offer each other mutual aid. In Voinovich's work there is not a trace of didacticism, but the same notion is nonetheless there. (p. 103)

The morality exuded by man in his natural state, when he is animal-like, stripped of abstract theories and superimposed moral norms (often depicted in [*The Life and Extraordinary Adventures of Private Ivan Chonkin*] as norms of etiquette rather than virtue), is at the centre of Chonkin's innocence. Any attempts to categorise, generalise, or attribute this quality are severely censured. When Golubyov and Chonkin get drunk on samogon they both end up crawling around on all fours. "Jean-Jacques Rousseau said that man should get down on all fours and go back to nature." "And who's this Jean-Jacques?" asked Chonkin, struggling over the peculiar name. "God only knows. Some Frenchman or other."

The attempt by Gladyshev to differentiate between man and beast not only fails, but works directly in favour of the innocent and to the detriment of the abstract thinker. Gladyshev tries to instil some crude Darwinism in Chonkin by explaining that toil turned the monkey into man. It takes Chonkin some time to voice his objection, but when he does Gladyshev is found to fall back on popular oaths rather than enlightened debate. Chonkin argues that the horse works more than the monkey and therefore he should be the true ancestor of man.

Gladyshev's rationalism fails to make headway with Chonkin; but Chonkin's wild, unbridled dreams infect the village scientist, and bridge the remaining gap between innocent, benign fantasy and the destructive illusions of rationalism. Gladyshev's horse visits him in a dream, having achieved human status through toil; he now has human ambitions of going to Moscow, yet retains his moral superiority—he cannot fight for either the Germans or the Russians since he still has hooves and cannot pull a trigger. This time the dream does not so much sum up the action, as presage what is to follow. Gladyshev finds the horse's shoe, the horse runs away and is killed, Lyosha's message is found by it. Thus the "real" world of Krasnoye with its man-made illusions and neurotic bigwigs is being ousted by the sweet, innocent dream-world of Chonkin, with its natural morality. It remains to be seen if this process will be continued in the subsequent parts.

Chonkin's triumph by proxy over Gladyshev still leaves a great many square pegs in round holes. There are a number of passages where a natural rhythm and order predominates, where characters are at one with their environment and situation, and any implicit violence in the air is as nothing compared to the uproarious scenes of psychological and physical conflict—one recalls the evening scene where war is announced on the radio while Chonkin's attention is turned more to the snatches of popular song, concertina-playing, and domestic altercation; all this occurs immediately after his row with Nyura. However, these scenes of serenity are rare. Voinovich's business is more with the nature of social conflict and its causes. There seems to be a contrast between the *authority* of spontaneous human response which persists in confounding the system, and the *naked power* of the system, which operates without any authority, through a rigid hierarchy and a gradation of threats and sanctions. . . . While military life is clearly the best example of this power devoid of authority, the same factors are present in all sections of society. The power of the MTS, with its political section, allowed for little rationalism in agricultural economics, and as an institution was widely resented. This, plus the party regional committee and the local KGB, would be enough to put the average collective farm chairman in a position not much different from an NCO. Moreover, the official language of the media throughout the thirties was militaristic in the extreme.

It is in language particularly that one sees the discrepancies between what is officially expected and what actually happens. If nothing else, *Chonkin* provides a first-rate glossary of terms not to be found in Smirnitsky's dictionary. Not just peasant dialect, but racy and obscene language too. One of the finest examples of the dichotomy between language as it is and language as the establishment would like it to be is the title of the hybrid plant Gladyshev is trying to perfect—"Put' k sotsializmu"—or *Puks*, for short, which is a children's word for "breaking wind". However, the argument goes beyond bawdy puns.

The whole area of official language—the radio, newspapers, lectures, and even literature—comes in for bitter indictment. One of the main reasons for the pre-requisite of "realism" in official Soviet literature has been to "get the message across", to make art comprehensible to the masses. Yet the over-simplified, high-sounding jargon of the news flashes and political lectures drives Chonkin and his kind to either boredom or total confusion. . . . The lack of communication brought about by the manipulation of the language is refined to its most comic state in the scene between Milyaga and his interrogator; perhaps

the upshot of this passage is not so much the inevitable incomprehensibility of official jargon as the inevitable limits that all language has when it comes to communication. Chonkin's animal-like seduction of Nyura, almost wordless, reflects far more mutual understanding than dialogue ever can.

The manipulation of language leads to greater problems than comic misunderstandings. Ultimately it leads to distorted conscience and morality. . . . In *Chonkin* language would seem either to strip the characters of all conscience and morality, or deform conscience to an absurd degree—one thinks of Revkin, the first secretary of the party regional committee, who, suffering from "unhealthy moods", turns himself in to the KGB, while his wife promises to bring up their son as a true bolshevik so that he'll forget even his father's name. Chonkin's conscience is certainly troubled from time to time, but it is always by domestic things—even the aeroplane, which gains a certain symbolic meaning as the novel progresses, has to be domesticated, i.e. dragged into Nyura's garden, before it presents an authentic moral issue. (Even then, at one point its wings are still described as "absurd".) Conscience only becomes valid when it springs from inner harmony and complete self-realisation. The fact that these two conditions are so rarely fulfilled gives Private Chonkin all the fire-power he needs. (pp. 105-07)

> *R. C. Porter, "Vladimir Voinovich and the Comedy of Innocence," in* Forum for Modern Language Studies, *Vol. XVI, No. 2, April, 1980, pp. 97-108.*

MORDECAI RICHLER

[In reading *Pretender to the Throne*], Vladimir Voinovich's rich, inventive satire about Russia, it is all too easy for the reader to sit back smugly and reflect what a fearful society the Communists have made, and how fortunate we are to be living in the freedom-loving West. Well, yes. *Yes, certainly*. For, after all, what distinguishes our society from theirs is that it is not rooted in fear of the informer or the midnight knock. But, beyond that, the most startling thing about Voinovich's entertaining novel is not the odious Russia it so convincingly describes, but that too many of his nicely calculated targets also flourish here. Corrupt, lying politicians. Sleazy officials on the take. Third-rate writers toadying for official favor. Demented Secret Servicemen. Everybody looking out for No. 1.

Pretender to the Throne is set in wartime Russia, Stalin's Russia, shortly after Hitler's attack, the Red Army poorly disposed because a comically inept general staff has paid no heed to warnings about the exact time and place of the attack, just as (come to think of it) Americans ignored clear signs about the time of the attack on Pearl Harbor, allowing their fleet to be trapped at anchor. At the very core of this satire is the tale of a cowardly little captain, acclaimed a hero for propaganda purposes and given a grand state funeral. The hero of *Pretender to the Throne* is an engaging, thickheaded peasant, Ivan Chonkin—short, puny and lop-eared—whose triumph is that somehow or other, possibly because he is informed by a fundamental decency, he endures Stalin's crazed Russia. Unjustifiably imprisoned, Private Chonkin, through a series of incredible misunderstandings, is mistaken for a certain Prince Golitsyn, who becomes crucial to the war plans of both Stalin and Hitler. How this comes about, and how he blunders through, is too joyously contrived a web to unravel here, but en route a gleeful Voinovich provides telling descriptions of prison life in Russia and the rules that operate on what is theoretically the outside. (p. 14)

The novel abounds in devastating portraits of officialdom, the absurd ideological hopes willingly negotiated if only to protect perks; and always there is the fear that permeates even deeper than the frost. Possibly the most brilliant of the set pieces is a meeting of the district committee in which everyone, protecting his flanks, outdoes everyone else in condemning an innocent comrade. And one of the most memorable characters in a veritable Communist rogues' gallery is the abject newspaper editor Ermolkin. (pp. 14, 28)

Finally, even as diluted ideologies muddy distinctions, there is another difference between American and Russian society. A literary one. To compose such a satire about American life could be to invite fame and fortune. But to write about Russia as Voinovich does with such assurance calls not only for talent but also for courage; last year Voinovich was forced to emigrate from the U.S.S.R.

Someday in the future it will be seen that in this time of obloquy Russian honor was redeemed by a fistful of writers and scientists, Vladimir Voinovich among them, who risked everything, to bear honest witness. (p. 28)

Mordecai Richler, "Say Stalin 12 Times," in The New York Times Book Review, September 20, 1981, pp. 14, 28.

JAMES CAMPBELL

[*Pretender to the Throne* takes] up the story of Private Ivan Chonkin from the end of *The Life and Extraordinary Adventures of Private Ivan Chonkin* at which point the hapless soldier had ended up in prison as a traitor; in fact, he had obstinately *obeyed* orders and stuck to his sentry post even as a garrison of Russian troops attempted to gain entry. Thereafter, word gets around among 'the Right People' that Chonkin, nicknamed 'the prince', is actually a member of the monarchy, Prince Golitsyn. This sets in motion a ludicrous chase, involving interrogations, enquiries and the uncovering of non-existent spies, with the aim of proving that the prince is in league with Hitler and plotting to restore the monarchy.

While the unsuspecting private languishes in his cell, plotting nothing but what he would do with his beloved Nyurka if only she was beside him in the prison bunk, the investigation into his alleged activities takes on an absurd life of its own, leading the reader into the homes and offices of numerous Soviet officials, some of whom are never sure whether they are at home or in the office. 'Most suspicious is he who is not seen doing anything suspicious', reads the directive of Major Figurin, otherwise known as Idiot Idiotovich. Together with Stalin's motto, 'One internal enemy is more dangerous than a hundred external enemies', it provides an excuse for investigating just about everybody.

That the trail of universal suspicion spreads furiously but altogether independently of Chonkin, so that he figures in the story less than some of the other characters, popping up now and again as if only to remind the reader of his unimportance, is a necessary formal characteristic of a narrative in which the terrifying absurdity of the endless pursuit is the whole point. . . .

Many readers will enjoy the farcical relating of, for example, how in the newspaper *Bolshevik Tempos* an editorial reading 'Comrade Stalin's instructions have become, for all soviet peoples, the gilding of wisdom', is misprinted as "gelding" of wisdom. . . . On the other hand, some may find the rambling maze of stories, anecdotes and authorial intrusions, with its

slapstick humour and two-dimensional characters, repetitive and ultimately boring.

Voinovich is an honest and brave man and the message at the heart of *Pretender to the Throne* is a true and important one. 'I fear no threats,' he has written elsewhere, 'Soldier Chonkin will avenge me . . . your security officers will not defeat him.' However, beneath the tangle of false leads which make up this novel, I would like to have discovered a character who resembled a real person; but Voinovich's comic style is of a sort which excludes any such realism. This is displayed everywhere in the book and nowhere more prominently than in the sex scenes; flat characters in a novel cannot have satisfactory sex. . . . Elsewhere, the possibly intentional facelessness of the many officials leads to confusion which a 'Cast' of the sort provided in other Russian novels would have pre-empted. Nonetheless, admirers of Chonkin will be pleased to have him back and will want to discover how, without knowing it, he becomes embroiled in the military strategies of both Russia and Germany.

James Campbell, "More Red Herrings," in New Statesman, Vol. 102, No. 2636, September 25, 1981, p. 25.

CARL J. PROFFER

This summer the Supreme Soviet announced that it had stripped Vladimir Voinovich of his citizenship for "slandering" the Soviet state. (p. 35)

Pretender to the Throne was published in Paris two years ago, so the Supreme Soviet's KGB informants knew what they were dealing with. The new book's main subject is the system itself, the secret police, and terror in Stalin's Russia. Loyal, simpleminded, perplexed Private Chonkin plays the role of catalyst; the main actors are party and police functionaries, prosecutors, judges, editors, and informers. As the novel opens, Chonkin, who cannot really understand the absurd things happening to him, is in jail, arrested on a false charge of desertion. The series of bureaucratic foul-ups which has led to this (in Volume I, *The Life and Extraordinary Adventures of Private Ivan Chonkin*) pales compared to what happens next.

A few simple misunderstandings, combined with universal incompetence, lead the sycophants and paranoids who run everything to the fantastic conclusion that Chonkin is not only an ace German spy, but a direct descendant of the Princes Golitsyn who has come to foment rebellion and restore the monarchy. A Soviet rule is that one hand never knows what the other is doing, and by the end things get so crazy that simultaneously Chonkin is 1) ordered shot, and 2) ordered brought to Moscow to get a medal from Stalin. The two telegrams are even signed by the same officer.

Voinovich's main characters represent the whole chain of command, from local lieutenants up to Beria. He shows the psychology of each type, using satirical hyperbole which Russians who lived through this period say is not hyperbole at all. . . . [Everybody] is afraid, no matter how much power they wield. Secret police chief Beria is terrified because he has to face Stalin directly. And in his own terror Stalin lives underground in a blocked-off subway station. Voinovich's sketch of Stalin has a worthy place in the growing anthology of the generalissimo's literary portraits (notably by Solzhenitsyn and Iskander). Indeed, Stalin occupies the imaginations of Russian fiction writers approximately as much as sex occupies the thoughts of American writers. . . . (p. 37)

Obviously there are national differences in what excites readers. A fairly common reaction of Americans reading novels by Russian dissidents is, "Yes, that's awful. But what's the fuss about?—we've known that for a long time." I'm not sure everyone really has known, but people living on one-sixth of the earth have not been able to say such things out loud, much less get them in print. In the USSR there is so little about which a writer can write honestly that every new kernel of truth has great weight.... So it is no wonder that Russians reading *Pretender to the Throne* are stunned. (I mean emigrés, or the few thousand in the USSR lucky enough to see it in *samizdat* or smuggled copies.)

Virtually nothing in *Pretender* would have the slightest chance of being printed in the USSR. It deals exclusively with banned subjects, and that automatically galvanizes Voinovich's natural audience. Moreover, Russians have the advantage of immediate comprehension of names, characters based on real-life Soviet celebrities, and literary and historical allusions which the American reader cannot possibly understand.... Thus Voinovich's wonderful parodies of bureaucratic documents, Soviet newspaper styles, or political jargon are either diluted or lost in English. Like most comic writers Voinovich is at a disadvantage in translation; the common experience and knowledge which satire presupposes is absent.

This is not to say that *Pretender* is closed territory for non-Russians. Voinovich creates a world which is sufficiently autonomous for anyone to understand the main lessons he is teaching, often in a direct Tolstoyan way.... Voinovich has a profound understanding of Soviet Marxist mentality. He is especially enlightening, and funny, when showing how perfectly decent fellows learned the doublethink which allows them to rationalize their destruction of innocent people, including their own best friends. As anyone who has spent time with Voinovich can attest, he has a natural storytelling gift, particularly for something like American tall tales, and along with *Chonkin, Pretender to the Throne* is his most sustained achievement. (pp. 37-8)

> Carl J. Proffer, *"Absurdity as a Way of Life,"* in The New Republic, *Vol. 185, No. 13, September 30, 1981, pp. 35, 37-8.*

D. M. THOMAS

Soviet dissident authors are no more immune than anyone else to the temptation to try to repeat an earlier success, and Vladimir Voinovich is no exception. Rarely are second parts as successful as the first; and I do not think these "Further Adventures of Private Ivan Chonkin" match the comic vitality of *The Life and Extraordinary Adventures of Private Ivan Chonkin* though they are always entertaining and at times brilliant.

Voinovich's reluctance to let Private Chonkin go is understandable. Ivan is a young and simple peasant, related to the archetypal "Ivan the Fool" of Russian folklore—whose naïveté, muddle-headedness, and common good nature are constantly getting him both into and out of trouble at the hands of corrupt officials.... The author, who was himself a manual worker, and who later got into deep trouble with the Soviet authorities because of the straightforward honesty of his stories, is obviously very much at home with Chonkin. The character is Russian but also universal....

In the first book, Chonkin had been sent by his unit to guard a plane that had come down in the middle of nowhere. The

army had forgotten his, and the plane's, existence, and he had doggedly gone on guarding it, consoled by the warm body of a postmistress, Nyura, who lived in a nearby house. At the end of the novel, however, he is arrested as a traitor. In [*Pretender to the Throne*], published since Voinovich's move to the West, we see Ivan languishing in prison (while Nyura vainly struggles to procure his freedom), convicted of being a White Guard agent attempting to restore the monarchy, and sentenced to death. The absurd accusation arises from the fact that an investigator, visiting Chonkin, hears a rumour that an "Ivan Chonkin" was the bastard son of Prince Golitsyn....

Both Hitler and Stalin become involved in the Golitsyn affair. The Führer orders Guderian to switch his tank attack from Moscow to the small town where Ivan is awaiting execution: hence the miraculous escape of Moscow. In the Soviet High Command, confusion is so rife that the local garrison commander receives simultaneously, from the same official, an order to shoot Golitsyn at once and to send Chonkin to Moscow to receive an award. The wilder Voinovich's imagination becomes, the funnier he is, and the better he writes. He follows Gogol in these passages, and is worthy of the master....

Where the novel seems to me less successful is in its more believable satire on pretension, bureaucratic muddle, and vice: on the venality of everyday Soviet life. With this—the greater part of the book—Voinovich seems largely to be repeating what he wrote in the first book. The satire is effective enough, but becomes so unremitting that its effect is weakened. There is a good deal of rather heavy-handed slapstick; one begins to suspect that Voinovich himself is growing weary of exposing the crimes and follies of Soviet man, and the cancer so all-pervasive that the satirist tires of exposing it to useless radiation. He is happier when, like a mad Gogolian surgeon, he slashes at the body.

Perhaps significantly, there are several passages in which he briefly deserts the satirical mode for one which, if comic at all, is comedy at its blackest: a conscience-stricken official tries to shoot himself, but only succeeds, by accident, at the moment when he changes his mind and decides to live; Chonkin, glancing high up on his cell wall sees, dumbfounded, that "a certain Kuzyakov or Puzyakov, not desiring to vanish without a trace, had scribbled his name in shit, which had petrified in time." At this instant, and in a few others, there is neither Gogolian extravagance nor Swiftian *saeva indignatio*: we are in the Inferno of Dante or Solzhenitsyn.

> D. M. Thomas, *"Slapstick and Body-Slashing,"* in The Times Literary Supplement, *No. 4097, October 9, 1981, p. 1153.*

DONALD M. FIENE

Pretender to the Throne begins where its predecessor (*Zizn'i neobycajnye priključenija soldata Ivana Čonkina,* 1975) leaves off—with good soldier Ivan jailed as a German spy by the NKVD. The earlier work, containing the first two parts of five projected, is almost good-humored in its satire as it focuses primarily on its hero in the village of Krasnoe, in the summer of 1941. The continuation, adding two more parts to this Ivan-kiad, is by contrast treasonous as it pitilessly, though with deadly wit, rakes Stalinist Russia from bottom to top. The difference in tone between the two books is accounted for by the author's having given up in the interim any hope of publishing his work in the Soviet Union. (pp. 439-40)

In *Pretender* Vojnovič abandons his hero to the NKVD jail for much of the novel, bringing him out only at the end to be publicly tried and convicted in the provincial center of Dolgov. The author gives most of his attention to Ivan's tormentors—all those inept investigators who must manufacture evidence for the rigged trial. . . . Vojnovič contrives to save his hero, however, by causing Hitler to divert an entire army division from Moscow to Dolgov to rescue the by now notorious "German spy." This action does in fact allow Ivan to stumble free of both his Russian and German enemies—while Moscow has been saved as well. We leave Ivan as he speeds away in a stolen German jeep—whither we know not. But we do know he will return, as the author has promised us five parts, while but four have been published.

Čonkin, as the type of the holy fool (*jurodivyj*) or the folklore figure Ivan Duraček, is certain to emerge whole, perhaps even victorious, in the end. Already in this second book Čonkin is seen to have such a powerful influence on his accusers (with his appearance of undoubted innocence), as to cause one of them, the *prokurator* at his trial, to commit suicide in remorse. In this there seems to be a slight departure from the satirical mode; nevertheless, Vojnovič's satire is at least as consistent as Gogol's, which it greatly resembles. In particular, the investiture of an absurdly wrong identity on Ivan, which becomes a central plot element for several hundred pages, seems an obvious borrowing from *The Inspector General*. In Gogolian satire, Vojnovič has no peers in all of Soviet literature.

Vojnovič's style is rich in puns, non sequiturs, dialect words and jokes, though in its basic organization and sentence structure it is not fancy—just good plain Russian. (p. 440)

> Donald M. Fiene, in a review of "Pretender to the Throne," in The Modern Language Journal, Vol. LXV, No. 4, Winter, 1981, pp. 439-440.

S. FREDERICK STARR

Mr. Voinovich's sardonic volume *The Anti-Soviet Soviet Union* opens fresh vistas to humor—and to social science as well—on the ways Soviet life confounds the Soviet system.

Mr. Voinovich, well known as the author of *The Life and Extraordinary Adventures of Private Ivan Chonkin,* focuses in his new book on his expulsion from the Union of Writers, the Gogolesque quarantine slapped on him by former colleagues and his final departure from the Soviet Union under the embarrassed gaze of Soviet customs inspectors whom he had mocked for rifling his meager luggage. He presents a grotesque funeral as seen through the eyes of the smiling corpse.

Mr. Voinovich has a keen sense of absurdity, and the loose form of these essays . . . permits him to indulge it. He speculates on what would happen if a Soviet official refused to patronize the special stores to which privilege entitles him or if an average citizen were to try passing out on the street copies of the proceedings of the 20th Party Congress, at which Stalin was denounced. He muses over the way Soviet officials endlessly invoke the word "sacred," as in "sacred names," "sacred flags," "sacred faces" and "sacred ideas." . . .

As in his earlier works, Mr. Voinovich's tone is wry and boisterous. He chuckles as he relates how the mathematician Yuri Gastev published a book in which he expressed his great debt to "Doctors Chain and Stocks" (actually John Cheyne and William Stokes) for their support of his career. These gentlemen, it turns out, gave their names to Cheyne-Stokes

breathing, the agonized gasping that occurs just before death; Stalin, it is known, experienced this phenomemon in his final moments. Similarly, Mr. Voinovich delights in recounting the heroic lives of writers like Mikhail Zoshchenko and Vasily Grossman, both of whom proved in their martyrdom that "true literature is beyond [politicians'] control; that anyone encroaching on its sovereignty will suffer inevitable defeat."

Maybe. But just how will the deadly dance of genius, repression and martyrdom ever be broken? For this to happen, Soviet society will probably have to produce a large number of citizens—not subjects—who have outgrown the smug comforts of true belief and blind loyalty and accepted the tenuousness and true diversity of view that is the hallmark of modern life. This may be happening. Youth culture in the Soviet Union today has more in common with that of Turin, Manchester or Minneapolis than with that of Stalin's Moscow. . . . At the Congress of Writers of the Union of Soviet Socialist Republics in June, there were hints that more pragmatic attitudes may be spreading among the intelligentsia.

Mr. Voinovich, however, remains deeply skeptical that the old dogmatism is on the wane. He tells of a Moscow friend who formerly would browbeat him with quotes from Lenin's holy writ. This friend then threw Lenin overboard and embraced, in turn, Bertolt Brecht, Ernest Hemingway, Che Guevara, Fidel Castro, Boris Pasternak, Aleksandr Solzhenitsyn and Pavel Florensky (a Russian Orthodox religious philosopher and linguistic theorist)—all with the same fanatic intolerance of other views. "My friend's pattern of development is typical of many people in my generation," Mr. Voinovich ruefully observes.

So long as this is so, the old cycle will continue, and there will be plenty of room for mordantly entertaining books from Mr. Voinovich and future satirists. It's a sad thought, even though the reading will be good.

> S. Frederick Starr, "Laughing All the Way to the Border," in The New York Times Book Review, August 31, 1986, p. 5.

DRAGAN MILIVOJEVIĆ

[*The Anti-Soviet Soviet Union*] does not belong to belletristic literature but rather to documentary material pertaining to life and literature in the Soviet Union in the sixties and seventies. Much of the writing in the book is autobiographical and based on eyewitness observation. Voinovich's fate as a writer and as a human being has been clearly involved with political and literary events and with the ebbs and flows of Soviet economic and political life.

The book is divided into three parts: "Life," "Literature," and "Politics," in descending order of size. As in his earlier works, Voinovich is a satirist here, seeing absurdity and nonsense in hallowed Soviet institutions: the Communist Party, the KGB, Soviet propaganda, an almost endless list. (p. 651)

In the section on literature a prominent place is allotted to the Union of Soviet Writers and its methods of operation. Prominence and reputation in this organization, according to Voinovich, are not based on literary skill or popularity among readers; he cites the case of Georgi Markov, who possesses a list of superlative accomplishments. . . . Markov has been widely published in the Soviet Union, and his books appear in thousands of copies. Voinovich conducted a private survey in which he asked anybody he met whether they had read anything by Markov; he could not find any who had done so. In "**Nostalgic**

Suffering'' Voinovich discusses the fate of Russian immigrants in the West, with particular reference to Svetlana Aliluyeva, Stalin's daughter. Svetlana, according to Voinovich, was a privileged person both in the Soviet Union and in the West. her dissatisfaction with the West was, in Voinovich's opinion, unjustified. His conclusion is that "she fled from herself, and as we know, one cannot flee very far from oneself." For Voinovich, the main advantage of living in the West is being free, being able to buy a ticket and travel wherever one wishes: Italy, America, Ireland.

With [*The Anti-Soviet Soviet Union*], Voinovich reaffirms his position as the leading Russian satirist of our time. Each one of the short entries has the potential of being developed into a longer satiric narrative. Voinovich is an iconoclast, a destroyer of false idols and false values, of sacred cows and sacrosanct institutions. He sees the hypocrisy behind the official act, the dark side of propaganda and the struggle for peace. He has identified the big lie which stands at the foundation of the system—the lie of universal brotherhood, equality, and happiness. (pp. 651-52)

> *Dragan Milivojević, in a review of "The Anti-Soviet Soviet Union," in* World Literature Today, *Vol. 60, No. 4, Autumn, 1986, pp. 651-52.*

GEORGE GIBIAN

This anti-Utopian novel [*Moscow 2042*] by Vladimir Voinovich is easily the most amusing and readable fantasy yet produced by the third wave of Soviet émigrés. Satire has of course been richly represented in the output of writers who have recently left the USSR. . . . None, however, has succeeded in treating with so light a touch the profusion of targets that Voinovich hits in *Moscow 2042*. (p. 30)

The protagonist and narrator of *Moscow 2042*, Vitaly Nikitich Kartsev, is himself an émigré writer living in West Germany. In 1982 he manages to secure passage on a marvelous new kind of airplane that will, in a matter of three hours, transport him to Moscow 60 years in the future. The first third of the story is a hilarious account of Kartsev's life in West Germany, his preparations for the upcoming journey, and the various approaches made to him prior to his departure.

Friends, acquaintances and strangers—ranging from Arab representatives and CIA agents to one Sim Simych Karnavalov, a writer exiled in Canada who bears many similarities to Solzhenitsyn—have somehow gotten wind of the hero's forthcoming trip. Most want to use Kartsev to gather future intelligence. Karnavalov-Solzhenitsyn, however, is eager to have the way readied for his return to 21st century Russia on a white horse, to take power as Emperor. Voinovich's digs at this character are masterful (whether or not you think the parody of Solzhenitsyn is justified), and the pictures of Germany and Canada are perfect takeoffs on Soviet émigrés' impressions of Western culture and life styles.

Initially, Kartsev is received in the Moscow of 2042 as if he were a visiting VIP, but the atmosphere gradually becomes frosty. The USSR, he finds, has shrunk to the point where it consists of the capital and its immediate environs, which are surrounded by a tall wall. . . .

The diminution in scope and stature of the once frightening Soviet empire evidently reflects Voinovich's belief that the USSR is on an inevitable course of decay and backwardness relative to the rest of the world. He makes broad fun of the Brezhnev-Andropov-Chernenko gerontocracy. Gorbachev, seen retrospectively, is an ephemeral bubble of trifling attempts at rejuvenation, quickly overwhelmed by stagnation and lethargy.

While the country's material and technological condition has dwindled into unrelieved shabbiness, the horrors of 20th-century Soviet Russia have survived quite nicely. Lawlessness, violence, oppression, and totalitarianism are the norm in the Moscow of 2042; pettiness, nastiness and spying—often double or triple—define the tenor of everyday life.

Voinovich's innumerable funny thrusts work well: We all get it when, as a quasi-religious gesture, the Muscovites "star" instead of cross themselves, and when a Ukrainian sings the same old pseudo-folk song she has sung under all the previous regimes. But some specific satirical references may elude the American reader. . . . Happily, the inside jokes are rare, and the book on the whole is universal in its appeal.

The zany atmosphere of *Moscow 2042* could only have been concocted by a literary exile who has been away long enough to see his country from a detached perspective, yet not so long that he has grown indifferent or out of touch. It is almost surrealistic in some places, a future world pervaded by vodka fumes. Other Soviet émigré authors may be long-winded, parochial, heavy-handed—not Voinovich. You can read his novel for its jokes, for its prophecies, for the points it makes about the Soviet Union (and the West) today. You can even pit your own crystal ball against his. Whatever your approach, you will admire his ingenuity and freewheeling wit. . . .

While this book is sometimes reminiscent of 1930s satirists like Ilya Ilf and Yevgeny Petrov, Voinovich's primary literary antecedents are George Orwell's *1984* and Yevgeny Zamyatin's *We* (in Russian, *My*). Where he goes beyond these two works is in leavening his vision of Soviet evil with comedy. His success in permitting lightheartedness to coexist with revulsion is high tribute to his skill. Orwell and Zamyatin . . . were trenchant and grim. Voinovich is trenchant and amusing. Perhaps Voltaire is the closest comparison. (p. 31)

> *George Gibian, "Dying of Terminal Absurdity," in* The New Leader, *Vol. LXX, No. 7, May 4-18, 1987, pp. 30-1.*

JOHN GROSS

Satirists have often set their fables in the future, and *Moscow 2042* falls squarely within an established literary tradition. It is as futuristic as its title proclaims, and as satirical as you would expect it to be, coming as it does from Vladimir Voinovich—author of *The Ivankiad,* creator of Private Chonkin, probably the most purely comic talent among leading Soviet dissidents.

In propelling us 60 years forward Mr. Voinovich doesn't waste many words over technological wonders. One day in 1982 a Russian writer called Vitaly Kartsev, who is living in exile in West Germany (like Mr. Voinovich himself), learns from a friend that there is a travel agency in Munich that can arrange journeys back and forth through time. He manages to get a booking for a three-hour trip scheduled to arrive in Moscow in 2042. . . .

When he gets to Moscow, Kartsev discovers that it has become a city state known as Moscowrep surrounded by three "Rings of Hostility": a ring of filial republics, a ring of fraternal socialist countries and ring of capitalist enemies. Within the city itself the regime claims to have achieved the world's first "classless and systemless communist society."...

Such, at least, is the official story. In reality, however, life in Moscowrep is characterized by shortages, shabbiness, blind uniformity and an unsurpassed proliferation of doubletalk....

Repugnant though he finds much of what he observes, Kartsev at least has the consolation of learning that his memory is still honored and his work still studied. He is even shown a copy of *Moscow 2042*, a book he can't recall having written, and which indeed he sees isn't due to be published until 1987.

The authorities have a pressing reason for showing it to him. They want him to remove all reference to Sim Simych Karnavalov ... who is the object of a widespread underground cult. Simych's followers, the "Simites," are convinced that one day he will return to Russia in triumph....

When the hour strikes, [Simych] is defrosted and comes riding back to Moscow to take over power. The exact details—how the Genialissimo is overthrown, who he really is, what his secret agenda has been all along—ought perhaps to be allowed to come as a surprise. But what can fairly be said, I think, is that the whole "Simite" sequence, like much else in the book, gives the effect of having been improvised: it is scrappy and rather spun out.

The true strength of *Moscow 2042* lies in its portrait of a bogus utopia. Here, too, the humor is occasionally labored; but there are some bitingly effective episodes—at their best, on the whole, when they contain an element of the squalid or the sinister as well as the outright absurd. Some genuinely eerie scenes are enacted in the Palace of Love and in the public bathhouse (or Hall of External Washing), and I don't think anyone who reads about it will readily forget the menu at the communal cafeteria, complete with something called "Progress" vegetarian pork.

Have we heard it all before? To some extent, yes; and if the policy of glasnost is what it says it is, Mr. Voinovich's prophecies may soon be of strictly historical interest. But if it isn't, they may turn out to be uncomfortably close to the mark in their portrayal of repression wearing a bland and smiling face.

> *John Gross, in a review of "Moscow 2042," in* The New York Times, *June 2, 1987, p. C17.*

MALCOLM BRADBURY

One of the greatest and most courageous of ... modern satirists is Vladimir Voinovich, an extraordinary and wonderful Russian writer now living in West Germany and the author of the brilliant *Moscow 2042*, his first novel from exile.

While he was still living in the Soviet Union, Mr. Voinovich, in his *Ivankiad* and various other books about his glorious hero Private Chonkin, chose to mock such sacred institutions as the Red Army, state bureaucracy and the spirit of political and artistic opportunism. He wrote his books with a heroic ebullience that insured they could appear only in the West....

In a 1981 *New York Times* essay, Mr. Voinovich did not care to call himself a dissident. He was, he said, just a writer, and a writer is a writer only when his view of the world is uncommon, unique. Mr. Voinovich viewed himself as dissident only in the sense of thinking differently; differently, that is, from the way official writers are supposed to think. Now he has applied this same satirical energy to his splendid *Moscow 2042*. Like many modern satires, it is a dystopian work, an antiportrait

of utopia, that plaything of fixed minds. A work both of historical pain and massive comic ebullience, it reads like a strange potpourri of Orwell's dark and visionary *Nineteen Eighty-Four*, Andrei Bely's fantastic view of modern Russia and Gogol's inventive extravagance. It finds a way of revisiting a Russia from which Mr. Voinovich is an exile and also of making many telling points about our own fundamentalist tastes in the West.

The hero of *Moscow 2042*, Vitaly Nikitich Kartsev, is an exiled Russian writer living in Munich ... who in 1982 suddenly receives an extraordinary opportunity to take a Lufthansa flight to Moscow 60 years into the future.... He lives in a world where no action goes unobserved and soon he is being enlisted by various agencies, including the K.G.B. and the West's dissident Soviet émigré community—not least among them Sim Simych Karnavalov, a charismatic Russian dissident suggestive of Aleksandr Solzhenitsyn. He lives modestly in the Canadian wilderness, with no more than a few armed guards, an enormous house, two cottages and his own church and lake, producing great slabs of dissident writing and cultivating czarist dreams. (p. 36)

But Kartsev himself is just a writer—one whose work, he explains, is always based on something, though sometimes nothing, which after all is a version of something. He is no guru, and no science-fiction fantasist either, which is why he drinks himself stupid on the three-hour flight to Moscow 2042. Moscow—now Moscowrep—is still Communist, indeed more so than before, though it has now incorporated Christianity, with the sole proviso that God is not mentioned. Past errors have been purged, especially the view that Marxism should dominate the world or indeed an entire country; it has been purified down to one city. Moscowrep's great leader is the Genialissimo, who has all the properties of a true leader, being Party General Secretary, Army Generalissimo and great literary and scientific genius. (pp. 36-7)

And here Kartsev finds himself given a hero's welcome. His works are "preliminary literature," much studied though not read, precursors to the achievements of the Great Leader. Kartsev's hundredth jubilee, just due, will be publicly celebrated by the people.... [For] a time at least Kartsev becomes one of [the] elite.

He is also—in a brilliant postmodern piece of fictional play—given the book of his adventures to read, even though he has not yet written it. Indeed he is pressed to correct it—since it contains some inadmissible and erroneous references, mostly to Sim Simych. Kartsev refuses, explaining that if he had been able to correct his novels that way he would have had no reason to come to Moscowrep.... But plots, he finds, are dangerous and do affect history. Sim Simych himself appears, there is a revolution, and Sim establishes a new czarist regime, little different from what went before.

Moscow 2042 is a comic delight, not least because it is a satire on satires, on itself. Books like his, Kartsev says, would be simply the products of an idle, inoffensive imagination, were it not that history made fictions true. "May the reality of the future not resemble the one I describe here," he says in conclusion....

And so, if Kartsev/Voinovich has presented a totally false vision of the future, he would not object at all, even if he were accused of writing a totally inoffensive book.

In the era of glasnost and possible new détente, we may well think, as we watch our difficult century turn, that Mr. Voinovich has got some of it wrong, and that his dystopia is a historical exaggeration. Alas, the world of the new millennium is already becoming an era of revived fundamentalism, of gurus bearded and beardless, of new doctrinal faiths burgeoning in the West as well as the East. For such a changing, late-20th-century world Mr. Voinovich's ebullient and zany satire offers two options. One is the despairing future of life according to ideology, even if it is an ideology in which no one believes. As the Genialissimo finally confesses, when he explains he had intended to take Communism to its absurd extreme so that people would become immune to it for generations, the problem is that masses are different from individuals: "The people are stupider than any one person. It's much more difficult to convince one individual of an idiotic idea than an entire people."

The other is the view of satire itself, a vision of comic and anarchic humanism, in which fictions serve not fixed ideologies but our own inventiveness. As a result, *Moscow 2042* captures a sense not only of historical anxiety but great comic freedom, and mixes social vision with a very modern view of the game of fiction. It is, quite simply, a wonderful book, written by a man who has been forged within our difficult modern history but who still manages to possess a profound sense of literary play. It shows Mr. Voinovich as the doyen of late 20th-century satirists, with targets on both sides of the wall, and a major international writer—a writer of the highest comic energy who makes us hope that, when the time comes to celebrate his jubilee, it will be a great and free one, quite different from that of his own fictional hero. (p. 37)

> *Malcolm Bradbury, "Cosmic Misunderstandings,"*
> *in* The New York Times Book Review, *June 7, 1987,*
> *pp. 1, 36-7.*

THOMAS D'EVELYN

It takes a special kind of satirist to reveal the reality of the Moscow seen today through the rose-colored glasses of *glasnost*. But that Moscow has found its satirist in Vladimir Voinovich. (p. 23)

Despite the shopworn elements of his description of the communist utopia—the vegetarian food, the calculated sex, the control of the weather, the dismissal of the old and feeble—*Moscow 2042* is consistently entertaining because of its style.

The style reflects the odd mixture of sad and funny things, of real and imaginary, that make up the human world. That mixed style, so true to life, is precisely what gets Kartsev in trouble: It deflates pomposity! For instance, the authorities gag on his description of the food in their utopia, especially since that description comes after a lyrical passage about "the sun shining all the time and the palm trees growing and the birds singing and the girls in their little tennis skirts . . ."

"There I was all excited," says the examiner, "and you hit me with that business about the vegetarian pork!"

Moscow 2042 unfolds in seven parts, and the parts unfold in brief, sometimes beautifully turned chapters. In the chapter called "A Secret Revealed," Kartsev is taken on a tour of a writing center in which authors are encouraged to compose on computers. These computers are linked to a mainframe that doesn't exist. ". . . There are people who just want to write," says his guide.

Clearly, Vladimir Voinovich does more than just write. And yet, ironically, compared to the ideologues and the millennialists, Voinovich is "just a writer"—and suspect because of it! *Glasnost* or no *glasnost*, *Moscow 2042* is superior entertainment. The only word that seems to describe it is one that current politics has almost ruined, the old word "gay."

Perhaps that's fitting. The gaiety of *Moscow 2042*—so piercing so elegant, so free—makes it a very special novel. It should make Voinovich, already popular at home, known everywhere. (pp. 23-5)

> *Thomas D'Evelyn, "Millennium in Moscow, 2042,"*
> *in* The Christian Science Monitor, *June 10, 1987,*
> *pp. 23, 25.*

Manly Wade Wellman

1903-1986

(Also wrote under pseudonyms of Levi Crow, Gans T. Field, and Hampton Wells) Portuguese West African-born American novelist, short story writer, nonfiction writer, critic, editor, poet, dramatist, scriptwriter, and author of children's books.

A prolific author in several genres who is frequently associated with the "Golden Age" of science fiction of the 1930s and 1940s, Wellman is perhaps best known for his fantasy fiction. His most popular stories and novels feature an occultist known variously as Silver John, John the Minstrel, John the Wanderer, or John the Balladeer, who roams the Appalachian mountains of North Carolina chancing upon malevolent supernatural forces. Frequently praised for the credibility of his fiction, Wellman infused his works with authentic dialogue, believable characters, and references to southern folklore, historical texts, and **published pieces on witchcraft and the occult. Nicholas De** Larber noted: "Wellman's North Carolina is convincing as a place where magic and fundamental religion co-exist. . . . Though the stories [about Silver John] are set in the present, there is a feeling that little has changed since earlier days and that little will change, thereby giving the series a timelessness that keeps it from becoming dated."

Born in what is presently Kamundongo, Angola, Wellman came to the United States with his father, a medical missionary, at the age of six and received a predominantly southern upbringing. After obtaining degrees from Wichita University in 1926 and Columbia University in 1927, Wellman began his literary career as a reporter, critic, and feature writer for various Kansas newspapers. In the late 1920s, he began selling horror stories and poetry to magazines under the pseudonyms Levi Crow and Gans T. Field, and in 1932, he published his first science fiction novel, *The Invading Asteroid*. Wellman wrote several sequences of fantasy and science fiction stories for pulp magazines beginning in the early 1930s. One of these, known as the "Hok" series, was originally published in *Amazing Stories*. This saga relates the heroic adventures of the title character against a backdrop of mythic earth civilizations. When popular demand for works in these genres declined following World War II, Wellman largely limited his output to adult mysteries, historical fiction, and nonfiction. He also wrote several science fiction and fantasy novels during this period, however, including *The Devil's Planet* (1951), a blend of science and detective fiction in which a human and an android investigate intrigue on Mars; *Twice in Time* (1957), about a time traveler who arrives in seventeenth-century Italy and discovers that he is Leonardo da Vinci; and *Giants from Eternity* (1959), in which the greatest intellects of history are resurrected to combat a plague brought to the earth by a meteorite.

Wellman's stories featuring Silver John first appeared in *The Magazine of Fantasy and Science Fiction* between 1951 and 1962 and were republished in one of his most famous short fiction collections, *Who Fears the Devil?* (1963). In these stories, Silver John manages through virtue, knowledge of the occult, and the talismanic power of his silver-stringed guitar to overcome such traditional monsters as witches, ogres, and giants, as well as creatures derived from Appalachian folklore and menaces of Wellman's own creation. Wellman continued

Photograph by Billy Barnes. Courtesy of Frances Wellman.

the adventures of Silver John in a series of highly popular novels. *The Old Gods Waken* (1979), which Richard E. Geis described as "disciplined, very enjoyable fantasy," chronicles Silver John's attempts to stop a cult of contemporary Druids from combining their supernatural powers with those of the Cherokee Indians of southern Appalachia. The next novel in the series, *After Dark* (1980), concerns the Shonokins, an ancient race of humanoid beings who claim to have inhabited North America before the Indians and who seek to regain the continent through legal and supernatural trickery. Tom Easton described *After Dark* as "classic ghost-story fantasy, told with a flavor that is half modern and half Appalachian hills." Other novels in the Silver John series include *The Lost and the Lurking* (1981), in which Silver John is forced to choose between joining an alliance of devil-worshipers and death; *The Hanging Stones* (1982), about a commercial project to construct a "new Stonehenge" in the Appalachian mountains that prompts an invasion of supernatural creatures; and *The Voice of the Mountain* (1984), in which an evil sorcerer attempts through deception and magic to entice Silver John to join forces with him.

Several of Wellman's stories related to the Silver John series, first published in such magazines as *Weird Tales* and *Strange Stories* during the late 1930s and early 1950s, feature John Thunstone, a paranormal detective who differs from Silver John in his active pursuit of malevolent supernatural forces. Many of these pieces are collected in *Lonely Vigils* (1981), a volume that also includes tales Wellman wrote under the pseudonym of Hampton Wells featuring independently wealthy occult investigators Judge Pursuivant and Professor Nathan Enderby. In addition, Wellman wrote two novels involving John Thunstone: *What Dreams May Come* (1983), in which Thunstone must prevent the resurrection of an ancient pagan god in a remote English village, and *The School of Darkness* (1985), which is set at a university founded by a coven of witches. According to Paul Granahan, *The School of Darkness* ''has a kind of nostalgic, comfortable charm to it, reminding us of a time when works of dark fantasy weren't quite so gruesome as today's best sellers.''

Wellman also earned critical acclaim for his adult mysteries, historical novels, and works of nonfiction. His first mainstream novel, *Find My Killer* (1947), is a mystery that features both male and female private investigators. Wellman's historical novels include *Candle of the Wicked* (1960), about an ex-Confederate cavalryman's return to Kentucky following the Civil War and his search for a missing pioneer, and *Not at These Hands* (1962), in which a man of principles is forced into conflict with the law by the corrupt head of a small southern town. Wellman also wrote over sixty books of historical and other fiction for boys. His most notable nonfiction works are often concerned with the Civil War and the history of North Carolina. These volumes include *Giant in Gray: A Biography of Wade Hampton of South Carolina* (1949), *Dead and Gone: Classic Crimes of North Carolina* (1954), for which Wellman received an Edgar Allan Poe Award from the Mystery Writers of America for best nonfiction study of crime, and *Rebel Boast: First at Bethel—Last at Appomattox* (1956).

Wellman's last novel, the posthumously published *Cahena: A Dream of the Past* (1986), is set in eighth-century Northern Africa and combines elements of fantasy and historical fiction to chronicle the downfall of a warrior queen who attempts to defend her civilization from Moslem encroachment. Michael M. Levy described *Cahena* as ''a satisfying novel and a fitting end to a fine literary career.''

(See also *Contemporary Authors*, Vols. 1-4, rev. ed., Vol. 118 [obituary]; *Contemporary Authors New Revision Series*, Vols. 6, 16; and *Something about the Author*, Vols. 6, 47.)

WILL CUPPY

In the earlier pages of [*Find My Killer*] you'll find a murdered man in a suicide set-up, a collection of guns, a young widow with green eyes and red hair, a male grinner, several starers of both sexes, Pettigrew the butler and other phenomena showing that we're deep in the heart of Mystery Land. Jackson Yates, fairly tough narrator, gets a job as assistant to J. D. Thatcher, private investigator, and who is this person but a pretty girl with one dark blue and one light blue eye—and very becoming it is, too.... She and Jackson make an amusing enough pair as they face guns, argue with Winkle the cop and trace a hideous slayer, meanwhile pepping themselves up with coffee for a change. This rather daring innovation, ruling out drunken deductions for a whole book, struck us as a good idea.

We cared more for Jackson and J. D. than the other pair of sweethearts, Diane of the green eyes and Jim, a lawyer who resembles Ernest Hemingway, as so many mystery characters do. We hated them most when they suspected each other of the crime and rang all the changes on that dead and gone motif. For the rest, Mr. Wellman . . . comes off nicely in his first full-length mystery. Since he has included so many gadgets from the mystery grab bag, we thought of giving him another prize for practically total recall in the whodunit field, but why pick on a likable new baffler?

> Will Cuppy, in a review of ''Find My Killer,'' in New York Herald Tribune Weekly Book Review, March 9, 1947, p. 21.

P. SCHUYLER MILLER

Back in the early 1940s the two Standard magazines, *Startling* and *Thrilling Wonder,* were trying out every possible variation on every conceivable SF theme, in the interests of pure entertainment. Maybe there were few memorable stories or superior writing, but you could count on fun and frolics. In this period, Manly Wade Wellman, a very skilled practitioner who has since become far more so, was perhaps the first to do the yarn about the man from our time who was really Leonardo da Vinci. . . .

[In *Twice in Time*], Leo Thrasher, nineteen-year-old physicist-cum-painter, builds a time reflector—a new gimmick, that has been freshly updated in the rewriting of the present version—that sends him back to the Italy of Lorenzo the Magnificent, Botticelli, Columbus, and of course Leonardo. He is cornered and hypnotized by a magician whose ''ward'' is Mona Lisa, and who milks young Leo's fuzzy memory of enough wonders to make them both prominent. And so it goes, with Leo blundering in and out of what is known of the real Leonardo's career.... (p. 143)

Far be it from me to cast aspersions on the author's Renaissance scholarship, but the fact is that it reads like a fast job of library work, much like one I once did for a similar story of time travel to Periclean Athens. Months went into it, but my story no more brought Athens to life than this does Italy. What makes the shortcoming so obvious is that Robin Carson's magnificent *Pawn of Time*, out just a little while before Wellman's book, brings the same scene, fifty years later, to stirring life and reality with every sound, smell and color pushing out of the paper at you. That took several years of writing and certainly more of study: nobody can put that kind of work into a novelette for *Thrilling Wonder*. (pp. 143-44)

> P. Schuyler Miller, in a review of ''Twice in Time,'' in Astounding Science Fiction, *Vol. LXI, No. 3, May, 1958, pp. 143-44.*

P. SCHUYLER MILLER

When you realize that [*Giants from Eternity*] originates in a one-shot novel in *Startling Stories* for July 1939 . . . you will also realize that Avalon has dug deep for this one. This, I'm afraid, was a pot-boiler for the author even in '39, for he was doing much better then, and had gone right on carving out a foothold for himself as a serious novelist and fantast. The ''essence of life,'' fallen from the stars, which converts a few grams of dust into fully clothed reconstructions of Pasteur, Darwin, Newton, Edison and Madame Curie, is presented with all the plausibility of a current monster movie, and the creeping red blight could be an ancestor of that raspberry-colored Glob that has been oozing across the drive-in screens.

Actually, the basic idea is a good one: which scientific "giants" of the past would you resurrect for help in combating an Earth-threatening menace? Might make a program for your SF club some night when you're desperate. But I'm not sure the answer isn't "None," and I'm very sure that Darwin and Edison were lousy choices. (pp. 147-48)

> *P. Schuyler Miller, in a review of "Giants from Eternity," in* Astounding Science Fiction, *Vol. LXIV, No. 4, December, 1959, pp. 147-48.*

WALTER HAVIGHURST

In [*Candle of the Wicked,* a] novel "Based upon several facts in the history of the Kansas frontier," Mr. Wellman traces the fortunes of an ex-Confederate cavalryman who had campaigned with Bedford Forrest. Like many Southern soldiers after 1863, Spanish McCready found no life left for him in the South. With his friend, Drury Randolph, he set his hopes on the beckoning and spacious land of Kansas. Randolph went ahead to buy a farm in the Osage lands recently surrendered by the Indians. A few weeks later McCready was to join him there.

This is the situation which *Candle of the Wicked* develops into melodrama. Toiling over the empty road under a blazing April sun leading a lame horse and wondering about his future, McCready makes two fateful encounters in the lonely country. At the farm of hulking Jake Ritter he is turned away as a Rebel. The war is not over for this somber German settler, though his pretty daughter has only kindness for the footsore traveler. A few miles farther McCready is taken in by another German family and again there is a handsome daughter to make him welcome. This girl, Kate Bender, "Professor Kate Bender" in her professional role, is a spiritualist, ready to give information about the departed, or the merely distant. During a seance she tells McCready that his missing partner has gone to Texas.

The puzzled McCready soon learns of other mysterious disappearances, and the novel becomes a search not for the missing Randolph so much as for an understanding of the actions of these strange German settlers.

Despite the sustained focus upon Spanish McCready, his hopes and fears, his memories of war's violence and his desire for a life of peace and simplicity, he never emerges as a really credible man. . . . The vanished Drury Randolph, footloose and laughing, is better realized than this blurred protagonist.

After two puzzling days in the uneasy prairie community, McCready begins to see the answer to his questions, but the answer requires resolute action. Blood flows thickly in the final episode, and only then can he see for himself and Emmy Riker a clear, clean future under the bright Kansas sky. *Candle of the Wicked* ends on a pretentious note which has been suggested by its murky foreword: "The behavior of these actual and fictitious persons, as here described, may recognize a certain necessary starkness which was an active principle of the American pioneer character." The novel is like that.

> *Walter Havighurst, "Kansas Melodrama," in* Lively Arts and Book Review, *January 29, 1961, p. 34.*

DONALD WETZEL

[*Not at These Hands*] concerns itself, as have most of Mr. Wellman's other books, both fiction and non-fiction, with the American South in its earlier days, in this instance, the com-paratively recent days of the first world war. The place is Portici, county seat of Lawson County.

The book's main characters are two: young George Cobbett, the gifted son of a tenant farmer who becomes editor of the Portici Weekly Globe, and Ira Drumm, the rich and powerful, high-handed ruler of Portici, who, for reasons both darkly secret and tragically in error, becomes first George Cobbett's benefactor and later his mortal enemy. . . .

The story follows the fortunes of George Cobbett from his arrival in Portici, a raw country youth indebted to Ira Drumm for this chance at a better life, through his rapid rise to prominence in the little town, his successful wooing of Ira Drumm's daughter, Til, to the ultimate clash between the two men and its dramatic outcome in which the story's elemental issue of right and wrong, of power versus principle, is finally joined and more or less happily resolved.

The author's sentiments are kind and liberal, and his style is straightforward; taken on its own terms, his story does pretty much what it set out to do, and does it quite well, with a courtroom scene near the book's close that is particularly effective, both as the story's logical denouement and a suspenseful bit of first-rate courtroom drama.

> *Donald Wetzel, "Small-Town Carolina," in* Books, *February 4, 1962, p. 11.*

JOSEPH BLOTNER

[*Not at These Hands*] is set in the South: specifically, in the towns of Portici and Myrtle, county of Lawson, state of North Carolina. Much of the story is bound up in the way Lawson became a county, so that though the action has a 1915-17 time span, its antecedents go back to coercion, blackmail and murder committed in 1880. These crimes had figured in the rise of Ira Drumm—planter, financier and political boss of Lawson County—who dominates this novel and whose protagonist he encourages, helps and nearly destroys.

Young George Cobbett is a promising country boy, son of one of Drumm's tenant farmers. After the father's death. Drumm secures for George a job on The Portici Globe which, like nearly everything else in Portici, he half-owns and dominates. The story quickly comes to focus upon the relationship between the two: the intelligent, honorable, romantic boy and the shrewd, unprincipled man. As the boy approaches the point of capitulation or rebellion, the author violently wrenches his story into a different concern and mode: defending himself, George kills Drumm, and the novel thereupon degenerates into a standard courtroom drama.

Drumm is an interesting character, a politician reminiscent of the New England mortgage-holding bosses in novels the American Winston Churchill wrote shortly after the turn of the century. George is not quite so solid or deep as Drumm, despite his being constantly in the forefront of the action. Lovely Tilford Drumm is one-dimensional, sharing with George the role of star-crossed lover. Many of the other characters are clichés. . . .

Technique in *Not at These Hands* is conventional and uninspired. The plot turns on Drumm's thinking that George is his illegitimate son and that his projected elopement with Tilford will be incest. In novels such as *The Holy Sinner* and *Absalom, Absalom!* the incest theme is used for exploration of human psychology. Here it is used for melodrama.

The author confines himself to straightforward, omniscient narration except for short italicized passages of interior monologue. Paragraphs of vital statistics are employed to create a sense of time and place while a steady stream of references keeps World War I muttering in the background until George is ready to join up. Mr. Wellman is more successful in creating his effects when he uses the old songs, stories, jokes and speech-patterns of the region. In its best passages the novel is convincing and interesting, but it never rises above this level.

> *Joseph Blotner, "The Boss and the Boy," in* The New York Times Book Review, *February 11, 1962, p. 35.*

DONALD M. WINKELMAN

Manly Wade Wellman's book *Who Fears the Devil?* is a collection of stories and sketches about John, a wayfaring citizen of the Southern Appalachians, and his guitar, strung old style with silver strings. Although they are reprinted from *The Magazine of Fantasy and Science Fiction,* it is difficult to classify these tales as purely in that genre. Rather, the extensive use of folklore makes me classify the book as a collection of tales which rely heavily upon traditional elements.

The book's main character, John, speaks in mountain style. When introduced, he "makes his manners"; if someone is a fool, he is "gone gump"; and if he is surprised he says "I declare to never!" John's travels bring him into contact with witches and warlocks, revenants, a Genesis Giant, and pacts with the devil. Especially interesting for the folklorist is Wellman's mastery of the folk idiom. He writes ballad texts surprisingly similar to those in oral tradition....

The folklorist will enjoy *Who Fears the Devil?* not only because of Wellman's use of a motif or ballad as the basis for his stories, but because this is enjoyable literature.

> *Donald M. Winkelman, in a review of "Who Fears the Devil?" in* Journal of American Folklore, *Vol. 78, No. 308, April-June, 1965, p. 181.*

J. B. POST

Among the stories [collected in *Worse Things Waiting*] there are a few clinkers..., but a Manly Wade Wellman clinker is still pretty good reading. The collection is definitely fantasy, often relating historical ghost stories. Wellman is at his best when dealing with the backwoods (OK, Appalachia), the Civil War (the U.S. one), and the Amerindian. He has a real feel for these subjects and his stories, however much fantasy they may be, reflect and convey this feeling. I find it hard to decide which is my favorite and equally hard to decide which I liked the least because even the poorer stories have redeeming features.

> *J. B. Post, in a review of "Worse Things Waiting," in* Luna Monthly, *No. 53, August, 1974, p. 29.*

PUBLISHERS WEEKLY

Wandering the Appalachian countryside singing venerable songs to the music of his silver-stringed guitar, John the Balladsinger has dealt with all forms of evil magic in many popular short stories by Wellman. [*The Old Gods Waken*], however, is the first novel about John's adventures, a tale about a supernatural threat so powerful that John must call on help from Chief Reuben Manco, a Cherokee medicine man and expert on the world's folkways and arcane practices. Together they overcome the sinister and mysterious Voth brothers (who prove to be modern-day Druids . . .) and save the lives of two friends. Readers may initially be uncomfortable with the backwoods dialect in the narration, but it soon becomes a natural and effective part of the scene-setting. Wellman's creation feels authentic in a way that goes beyond well-done research, and, although not truly novelistic, it is good old-fashioned story-telling.

> *A review of "The Old Gods Waken," in* Publishers Weekly, *Vol. 216, No. 19, November 5, 1979, p. 59.*

RICHARD E. GEIS

[In *The Old Gods Waken*], Silver John is a rootless man of goodwill and arcane knowledge who becomes involved in a supreme struggle against revived Druidism and the Old Ones' evil powers, in Southern Appalachia.

Set in now, told in the idiom of the region, it is a story of considerable power, realism and intensity. The last half of the book has mythic structure as John and an older Cherokee medicine man face seven magical tests in their struggle to save a young man and woman from death as sacrifices atop Wolter Mountain.

Wellman knows the ways and talk of the people. . . .

The turns of phrase and use of words is a delight.

This is the first of a series of Silver John novels. This is disciplined, very enjoyable fantasy.

> *Richard E. Geis, in a review of "The Old Gods Waken," in* Science Fiction Review, *Vol. 9, No. 2, May, 1980, p. 26.*

TOM EASTON

Wellman is well known as a producer of beautifully crafted tales of occult horror set in the Appalachians. . . . [*The Old Gods Waken*] is the story of what happens when two Englishmen take over an Appalachian mountaintop with an eye to reviving Druidism and are confronted by John, Wellman's minstrel hero, a woman anthropologist specializing in magic, and an Indian medicine man with a college education. The premises are occult, but the outcome depends strongly on Wellman's rational approach to his subject. To him, magic is a kind of science. . . .

> *Tom Easton, in a review of "The Old Gods Waken," in* Analog Science Fiction/Science Fact, *Vol. C, No. 6, June, 1980, p. 163.*

BILL CRIDER

Manly Wade Wellman's first book about John [the Balladeer], published a little more than fifteen years ago, was *Who Fears the Devil?* . . . In that volume, John encountered One Other beside the Bottomless Pool on Hark Mountain, killed the Ugly Bird, and even caught a glimpse of the Behinder. He has a knack for dealing with such outlandish creatures; and this knack stands him in good stead in *After Dark,* when he meets the Shonokins, an ancient humanoid race who claim to own the North American Continent. They have decided to press their claim. . . . Good wins out in the end, of course, but not before there is quite a battle of supernatural powers, with John pitting his knowledge of such forces against that of Brooke Altic [the Shonokin leader].

Wellman has the ability to conjure up what John might call "a jangly feeling" in the reader's blood. He also has a true storyteller's gift, and his rendering of Southern mountain speech is a pleasure to read. Those who have met John before are probably on the way to their bookstores now. Anyone else who likes a good fantasy or a well-written story is advised to join them.

> *Bill Crider, in a review of "After Dark," in* Best
> Sellers, *Vol. 40, No. 11, February, 1981, p. 393.*

TOM EASTON

Manly Wade Wellman's second Silver John novel is out now. It's *After Dark,* and it's the tale of what happens when John meets the Shonokin. . . .

Who are the Shonokin? They have no song, but they can be known. Non-human, here before the Indians, hidden among men for ages past, dwellers in gardinels. Encouraged by the results of Indian lawsuits, they plan to sue Washington to regain their ancestral lands—the works. To do this, they need money. To gain money, they hold a country concert and plan far, far darker deeds. However, the concert attracts John, and he meets a fan who takes him home to meet her Dad, who is threatened by the Shonokin's wish for his land. It seems they wish to extend a ley line across his place and thus gain the power to raise the dead. They want Dad's alexandrite, too, and Silver John holds the only hope.

[*After Dark* is] classic ghost-story fantasy, told with a flavor that is half modern and half Appalachian hills. It's strong stuff, delicious in a way that fantasy set in alien times and climes cannot be. It's home-grown, set in homey traditions, and its shivers are thereby the more heart-felt.

> *Tom Easton, in a review of "After Dark," in* Analog
> Science Fiction/Science Fact, *Vol. CI, No. 8, July
> 23, 1981, p. 164.*

JAMES J. J. WILSON

Manly Wade Wellman has been publishing since the early thirties and is one of the best known of the nontraditional SF/fantasy writers. One of the strangest series in the genre is Wellman's "John the Minstrel" or "Silver John" stories. . . . (p. 45)

These stories are written in an intriguing, back-woods dialect, appropriate to the setting. Silver John is a man whose only possessions are the clothes on his back and the silver-strung guitar he carries and plays to earn occasional friends.

In *After Dark* John comes across a settlement or a race of people known as "Shonokins". These people supposedly evolved from a different form of animal long before man but were driven from their land by the Indians. Now, they want to use legal and other means to get their country back. . . .

The story of the novel is how John and a local landowner defeat this particular group of Shonokins. The uniqueness is due to Wellman's back-woods dialect and the rustic charm of his characters. *After Dark* is a welcome addition to the "Silver

John" series and a perfect book to curl up with on a stormy night. (p. 46)

> *James J. J. Wilson, in a review of "After Dark," in*
> Science Fiction Review, *Vol. 10, No. 3, August,
> 1981, pp. 45-6.*

NICHOLAS DE LARBER

[*The Lost and the Lurking*] is the third novel in the series about John the Balladeer ("Silver John"), a modern minstrel who wanders through the North Carolina hills, armed only with his knowledge of the occult and his silver-stringed guitar as he encounters witches, giants and other supernatural phenomena. In this novel John, who usually travels of his own volition, has been asked by a government agent to investigate some strange happenings in the small Appalachian town of Wolver. But the townsfolk are suspicious of John until he bests the town's strongest man in a fair fight, despite the man's talisman. Figuring that he has some kind of power (and due to a few of the songs he sings), John is introduced to Tiphaine, a beautiful, yet malevolent witch. She offers John a choice: either join her cult of devil-worshipers or become its chief sacrifice. In short, *Lost* presents a conflict between a human good and a supernatural evil in a modern rural setting.

Of the characters, John is the most fully developed, despite the lack of a last name. John acts as the narrator of this and other novels/stories in the series, and he presents himself as a very human character who knows the folk music of the region and how to combat "haunts," but he is less than infallible, rather humble, and a good man (but no saint). As in the other novels of the series . . . , John has a group of supporting characters, less defined but visible. Here, they include Tiphaine, Ottum Orcutt, Quill Norbury, and Lute Baynor (cult members), and Simon Latchney (an ex-preacher who lives outside Wolver and is John's ally). One major difference between this novel and the others is that John primarily works alone for most of the book. But Wellman also allows John to reveal more of his background (his family, schooling, army hitch, and some indications of the extent of his occult learning) than in earlier works.

The North Carolina setting is also very important to the series. Wellman . . . knows the region and its people and he blends the knowledge into his works. Wellman's North Carolina is convincing as a place where magic and fundamental religion co-exist: a place where a man can wander anywhere and find food and shelter for the price of a few songs on a silver-stringed guitar or some chores; a place where spells and counter-charms are known by most. Though the stories are set in the present, there is a feeling that little has changed since earlier days and that little will change, thereby giving the series a timelessness that keeps it from becoming dated.

Also, some elements of realism take this series from the realm of other series about supernatural adventurers. . . . The lyrics to the folk songs and hymns John sings are legitimate; the historical references to witch hunters and witchcraft may be found in histories of the occult, and the spells and charms have their roots in folk custom. Even the dialect spoken by the characters seems very realistic as opposed to the "pseudo-southern" dialect used in other works or on television. . . .

The "Silver John" series contains some of Wellman's most popular work of his career which began with his first story for *Weird Tales* in 1927, and *The Lost and the Lurking* is one of the best of the series. With this novel, Wellman seems to have reached a proper pacing for a novel-length "Silver John" story.

> Nicholas De Larber, in a review of "The Lost and the Lurking," in Science Fiction & Fantasy Book Review, No. 3, April, 1982, p. 16.

TOM EASTON

Manly Wade Wellman's latest is *The Lost and the Lurking,* in which the government sends Silver John to investigate the hamlet of Wolver. Wolver turns out to be a hotbed of genuine witchcraft involved in an international conspiracy of evil, and John (of course) defeats its plans. Yet he does so only with the aid of a talisman which, though he has had it in past stories, here seems too contrived. It is a ragged little book, *The Long Lost Friend,* whose simple possession protects its bearer against all manner of magical evil. Yet John remembers this cardinal virtue only in the nick of time. Through most of the story, the book resides in his pack, stashed in the bushes.

I quibble, yes. One does not read Wellman for rigors of plot, but for flavor, for Appalachian color and the sound of old ballads, and *that* is all here. It's a treat.

> Tom Easton, in a review of "The Lost and the Lurking," in Analog Science Fiction/Science Fact, Vol. CII, No. 7, July, 1982, p. 166.

MARK WILLARD

[*The Lost and the Lurking*] is Wellman's third Silver John novel and the least noteworthy of a rather disappointing trio. Like the previous two, it seems like an inflated short story—Wellman even runs out of events and has John locked in a prison room where nothing too significant happens until it's time for the climax.

The title opens with wandering balladeer John, who's become known for his brushes with the supernatural in the rural South, being invited by the U.S. government to investigate an isolated Appalachian town with a sinister reputation. This executive commission seems unnecessary, in the light of John's wandering proclivities—why couldn't he just come across the town himself?—and his sentiments about the President of the United States make him sound like a simple-ass peon who's never heard of Watergate. The town turns out to be a whole community of devil-worshippers, and it's hinted that it's but one of many worldwide, but this is never followed up. The bunch abjectly abandon their faith when their leader dies at the end; John demonstrates no particular wit or initiative and foils a lot of the magic directed against him evidently just because he's so darn *good.*

The book does have some interesting characters, lots of background for its supernatural events and themes, and Wellman writes smoothly in a low key. . . . The best Silver John material is still the collection *Who Fears the Devil?,* which I highly recommend; [*The Lost and the Lurking*] comes nowhere near it in inventiveness and execution.

> Mark Willard, in a review of "The Lost and the Lurking," in Science Fiction Review, Vol. 11, No. 4, November, 1982, p. 32.

JEFFREY M. ELLIOT

[*In the essay from which this excerpt is taken, Elliot provides a biographical overview of Wellman's career and then interviews the author.*]

For as far back as he can recall, Wellman wanted to be a writer. As early as 1925, at the ripe young age of twenty-two, he found a market for his poetry, as well as short stories, all written while he was in prep school and college. Despite his success at writing, he received little encouragement from family or teachers, who tried to dissuade him from becoming a writer. One of his first stories, **"Back to the Beast,"** prompted a teacher to remark: "Your work is impossible!" That story later found a home in the pages of *Weird Tales* and was his first professional sale.

From 1927 to 1930, Wellman worked as a reporter in Wichita until a personal altercation with a "hungover editor," who made the mistake of cussing him out for something he hadn't done. Wellman promptly quit and turned to freelancing on a full-time basis. This was a particularly bold decision, as it was the height of the Depression and jobs of any kind were hard to come by. Wellman, however, persevered, wrote whatever he was asked, and made it by on a shoe-string budget. (p. 6)

It was in this period that Wellman made his first foray into the science-fiction field, with several sales to the poorly-paying Hugo Gernsback chain. Indeed, Gernsback bought a number of his early tales, including *The Invading Asteroid,* a space-opera thriller, and the first of many novels to come. . . . In 1934, hoping to improve his standing, [Wellman] moved to New York in order to be closer to the markets. Although times were rough, he made a number of quick sales to the Macfadden chain, and then, in 1935, sold **"Outlaws of Callisto"** to *Astounding* for $150, a story that would later become one of his classic tales. This sale proved to be a major turning point in his career.

Although Wellman wrote prolifically and well in several fields, he remained, for the most part, a writer of science fiction and fantasy, at least until the end of World War II, when the bottom dropped out of the market. However, it was in the fantasy field that Wellman did his best writing, owing perhaps to his lifelong interest in the genre. During these years, he forged a close working relationship with Farnsworth Wright, of *Weird Tales* fame, for whom he wrote dozens of stories, and proved to be one of *Weird Tales'* most popular writers.

It didn't take Wellman long to crack all of the field's major markets, as well as most of its minor ones, selling numerous stories to *Unknown* and *Strange Stories.* His most famous fantasy series, though, appeared in *Fantasy and Science Fiction,* which published his popular stories of John the Balladeer. . . . (pp. 6-7)

[Following World War II], most of the major markets for which [Wellman] wrote previously—pulps and comics—were on their last legs. Anticipating rough times ahead in the fantasy field, Wellman shifted his efforts to other areas of writing, chief of which were hardcover novels and nonfiction works.

In 1946, Wellman left New Jersey and moved to Pine Bluff, North Carolina, a move that satisfied his Southern instincts and upbringing. An ardent student of Civil War history, he saw the move as extremely promising in terms of future research. In 1947, Wellman published his first hardcover volume—*Find My Killer*—a highly popular mystery novel. He then turned his hand to writing juvenile books, a move which later resulted in several awards and citations. And then, in 1949, Wellman published **Giant in Gray,** his best-known biographical work. Based on his namesake, Confederate General Wade Hampton, the book served to win him a reputation as a first-rate Civil War historian.

Wellman moved to Chapel Hill, North Carolina in 1951, where he has continued to reside for the last thirty years. With that move, he extended his forays into mainstream and nonfiction writing.... (p. 7)

Despite his popular success in the science fiction-fantasy field, Wellman virtually stopped writing his popular yarns with the demise of *Weird Tales* in 1954. He turned his attention, instead, to hardcover writing—juvenile books, mainstream novels, Civil War history, and regional history. He also taught classes in creative writing at the University of North Carolina and at neighboring Elon College.

In 1974, Wellman retired from teaching. With more time to write, he decided to heed the mounting requests from editors who wanted new fantasy tales.... Wellman, who felt at home in his new mountain habitat, started writing stories about mountain people and their ways. Around this time, Carcosa Press published a collection of Wellman's best fantasy stories—**Worse Things Waiting**—which received high praise. (pp. 7-8)

•   •   •   •   •

[Elliot]: *You've written both science fiction and fantasy. Do you prefer the latter genre? If so, why?*

[Wellman]: Yes. I prefer fantasy to science fiction. I can't keep up with science as I should to write about it. A scientific mind is needed for it, anyway. I'm fascinated by how science fiction becomes science fact. As for fantasy, maybe I've been deeper into it, thought more about it. But both genres appeal to the human sense of wonder....

You've said that you owe your development as a writer to Weird Tales, *and its pioneering editor, Farnsworth Wright. What role did Wright play in your early career?*

Farnsworth Wright was tremendously patient with anyone he thought worth the effort. His criticism was painstaking and constructive. He had considerable education and appreciated nuances in writing. (p. 9)

Your most well-remembered fantasy series was Fantasy and Science Fiction's *"John the Balladeer." What explains the extraordinary appeal of these stories?* ...

The stories about John have succeeded most gratifyingly, have been praised and valued highly and embarrassingly. Perhaps that is because I did my best, and still do, to speak for the Southern mountains and their people, in their own language. Some have called these stories "poetic." If so, I'm not the poet. These natural men and women are the poets.

Would you agree that the John stories represent your best writing?

I don't know what my best writing is. I've done a lot of mainstream fiction and nonfiction, and critics have mostly been kind. Whatever I happen to be writing at the moment is what I try to write best. (p. 10)

Why did you virtually stop writing fantasy and science fiction after the death of Weird Tales?

I stopped writing fantasy and science fiction because I was busy writing Southern history and regional fiction, with good book contracts. I stuck with *Weird Tales* to the end because of affectionate memories. (p. 11)

Has your approach to writing fantasy changed significantly with the passage of years? Do you still experiment with new methods, new techniques?

By and large, I suppose I've always tried to tell simple stories, written as plainly as I can, in language I hope people can understand. If I've changed, it's by experience and by observation of life, literary and otherwise. I hope I've become better by diminishing old faults.... Some think of Poe's stories as quaint and somewhat old hat. But if Poe had kept on living and writing until now, he'd be writing to enchant the readers of today as he enchanted readers of the 1830s and 1840s.

Do you do a great deal of research in the course of laying out a story? How concerned are you that the story details conform to historical fact? Would you distort history in order to tell an engaging story?

I'm a good researcher, and I do lots of it. It's painful to read something that shows a lack of research. I don't plot out short things in writing, as we used to have to do for themes in school, but any book I write has a carefully written organization, plus stacks of notes and pictures and things. If I write something historical, I do my best to recognize what happened in history. Lots of historical fiction suffers from distortion, but if this is true, it's the writer's fault. It's his responsibility to make fiction conform with fact. Too many readers are looking down your throat to see if the truth is there. (pp. 11-12)

Are most of the names and places cited in your stories more the product of historical research or a fertile imagination?

I use real places in my stories, and, now and then, actual people. I've used, fictitiously, Charles II, John Smith, George Washington, Robert E. Lee and Ulysses S. Grant, among others, always trying to recognize the realities. I've based characters on real persons I've known, and sometimes, with permission, used real names. Imagination goes into this, of course. But, if you're trying to make a story real, where is the faint boundary between fact and fiction? Nowadays, a great deal of stuff that is offered as fact is fiction, anyway.

You're particularly adept at writing dialogue. How important is it to match a character with his dialect, especially in fantasy writing?

It's important in all writing. I keep a ready ear for how people talk, because the talk proclaims the person. I deplore stilted dialogue, written out by an author for a character to read out loud, so to speak. For God's sake, let the man say what he's got to say, in his own terms. Speech must be the greatest of all inventions mankind has achieved, and certainly what you say shows what you are. Perhaps one of the greatest modern masters of dialogue was John O'Hara. If any of his characters talked in a stilted fashion, the character himself was stilted. (p. 12)

Very often you employ a format where "innocents" wander into a bizarre happening and become actively involved. Is this an important element in the fantasy genre?

Yes. The encounter of an "innocent"—usually a child—with the supernatural situation is too manifestly dramatic to need much comment. Many fine writers have used this technique, notably M. R. James, John Collier, and H. G. Wells.

You are particularly deft when it comes to making frightening things one would consider powerless to frighten. For example, the imps in "For Fear of Little Men." What is the secret of this skill? . . .

[The] sudden frightening menace of small things is manifest. When I was in Africa, whole villages would get out of the way of a march of driver ants in their myriads; if you didn't get out of the way, they'd polish your bones. How about the Bishop of Bingen, devoured by mice? How about the excessive smallness of deadly germs? Small things can turn out horribly powerful. So much **"For Fear of Little Men,"** and again for **"Frogfather,"** where a cruel gigger of frogs suddenly comes face to face with a frog the size and power of an aquatic grizzly bear. I've always liked stories of the short-end coming out ahead in a fight. (p. 14)

From your vantage point, what makes for a successful fantasy story? What ingredients must it possess?

A fantasy tale should take the extraordinary situation, make it real, and make the reader believe it and accept it. Farnsworth Wright's favorite word was "convincing." I used to get tired of it, but I know how right he was to insist. (p. 15)

Do you view fantasy, especially as you write it, as "escapist" in nature? Is escapism a good thing?

Fantasy is "escapist" literature, which, by the way, is badly needed these sordid days. Escapist literature is somewhat akin to dreams. If you dream a dream with a happy ending, you wake up and are happy to have dreamed it. If it's a horrible dream, you wake up and are glad you're awake. Escapism is sometimes used as a derogatory term. But I feel it's like falling into a cesspool. You're supposed to stay in there and brilliantly adjust to your environment. But if you scramble out and have a bath, you're an escapist. (p. 16)

How do you view your own contribution to the fantasy field? How would you like to be remembered?

If I've made an appreciable contribution, I hope it was for honesty and for writing my best. I've been flattered by the expressed opinions of folklorists that I have some value as an interpreter of the natural American and things he may believe. And I've tried to write with decent restraint, too, tried to do it without capital letters and exclamation points. (p. 18)

> *Jeffrey M. Elliot, "Manly Wade Wellman: Better Things Waiting," in his* Fantasy Voices: Interviews with American Fantasy Writers, *The Borgo Press, 1982, pp. 5-18.*

WALTER E. MEYERS

[In] the last few years, Wellman has maintained a steady output of fine fantasy, rich in local detail and sensitive to the setting he now inhabits, and clearly loves.

These fantasies of the Carolina mountains began as a series of short stories all published in *Fantasy and Science Fiction* from 1951 through 1962. Their central character was a wandering singer, Silver John, named for the silver strings on his guitar, who moves through the lushly described Appalachians, encountering and overcoming various kinds of supernatural evil. The original stories were collected (with some additions linking them) as **Who Fears the Devil?** (pp. 50-1)

The strength of the [early] short stories lay in their use of the copious folklore of the Southern mountains. While Wellman

by no means exhausted that folklore, the Silver John novels have tended to move out of the region for their villains, though their settings all remain within a day or so's drive of Asheville, North Carolina. . . .

[Wellman's] most recent work, **The Hanging Stones,** returns to European sources for its fantasy themes: the establishment of a "New Stonehenge" as a tourist trap attracts John at the same time that it provokes an invasion of honest-to-goodness shape-changers. Although they provide the climax of the story, the werewolves are almost secondary in their villainy: they evoke as much pity from John as they do contempt. Continuing a theme found in several of these tales, John is more disgusted by the wealthy, especially by the nouveau riche who have no higher goal than the acquisition of more money. John disagrees with the choice of those who are attracted by the black arts but he can understand their motives; but those who use their wealth for power seem almost more alien to him.

The Hanging Stones gives the admirer of the series a chance to renew acquaintance with John's wife, Evadare, a character who could well have stepped out of a mountain ballad. The novel is a welcome addition to one of the outstanding fantasy series now in print. (p. 51)

> *Walter E. Meyers, in a review of "The Hanging Stones," in* Science Fiction & Fantasy Book Review, *No. 14, May, 1983, pp. 50-1.*

TOM EASTON

Manly Wade Wellman is back with **The Hanging Stones,** another Silver John novel. Here John climbs Teatray Mountain, on whose flat top a would-be millionaire is building a copy of Stonehenge, with tourists and dollars in mind. John soon discovers that there are degenerate locals who do not like interference with their own local sacred site. Too, they are werewolves.

In the end, the werewolves are defeated by a corps of the original Stonehenge's builders, brought into the present by a "white" magician. John is largely an onlooker, a vehicle for the rich local color and song we expect from Wellman. He brings us very little of the Appalachian arcana we have seen in past yarns, and we miss it.

Has Wellman run out of steam with Silver John? I'd hate to think so, for I like both character and style. Yet earlier stories seem more vigorous, fresher, at least in memory. Perhaps the next will suit me better.

> *Tom Easton, in a review of "The Hanging Stones," in* Analog Science Fiction/Science Fact, *Vol. CIII, No. 7, July, 1983, p. 103.*

MARK MANSELL

[**Lonely Vigils** is] a collection of Manly Wade Wellman's occult detective tales in *Weird Tales* and *Strange Stories* between 1938 and 1951. They deal with three dabblers in the occult—Judge Pursuivant, Professor Nathan Enderby and John Thunstone. Each of course, is well-educated in various and sundry aspects of the supernatural and each does his best to challenge and defeat the malevolent aspects of the occult. . . .

Although this volume shows Wellman's ever-present craftsmanship and storytelling ability, they don't reach the sheer heights of delightful fantasy as displayed in his other works, such as *Who Fears the Devil?* Of course, none of these tales were meant to be preserved for the ages, and the occult detective genre is a difficult one to pave new ground in. As these types of stories go, they are entertaining and there are some innovations like the depiction of ectoplasm as a kind of jelly exuded from a person's body and the characters of the Shonokins, who are humanlike beings predating the Amerinds in America and who appear in Wellman's more recent Silver John novel *After Dark* (which also features an offstage John Thunstone).

Like Seabury Quinn's Jules de Grandin stories, those in *Lonely Vigils* are best taken in small bites. Despite not reaching the quality of *Worse Things Waiting*, *Lonely Vigils* is still a worthwhile purchase. . . .

> *Mark Mansell, in a review of "Lonely Vigils," in* Science Fiction Review, *Vol. 12, No. 3, August, 1983, p. 35.*

GENE DeWEESE

[In *What Dreams May Come*, the] latest of John Thunstone's adventures, his "instinct" for the supernatural leads him to a small English village where preparations are being made to awaken something that has slept for ten-thousand years. This is not a book for anyone who wants only fast-paced action or edge-of-the-chair suspense or a lot of sex and gore, because *What Dreams May Come* has none of these. Instead it takes the reader on a pleasant amble through an everyday world where the supernatural is taken for granted, where everyone is polite and even courtly, and where even the final confrontation between Thunstone and the ancient, awakening evil is low key. This sort of thing wouldn't make a good steady diet, but it does make a nice, relaxing change of pace. (pp. 22-3)

> *Gene DeWeese, in a review of "What Dreams May Come," in* Science Fiction Review, *Vol. 13, No. 2, May, 1984, pp. 22-3.*

TOM EASTON

Here's Manly Wade Wellman, with *What Dreams May Come*, a tale of John Thunstone, friend of John the Balladeer, poking into a strange little English town where every July 4th they overturn the Dreamer Rock. The town is Claines. It is almost wholly owned by the strange Gram Ensley, who also owns the hillside which bears Old Thunder, a figure limned by turf cut away to reveal the chalk beneath. The Dreamer Rock is a supine megalith which, when John prods it with his silver sword-cane, delivers an alarming tingle.

John moves into a small boarding house run by a middle-aged woman with an eye for an unattached man. The help is a local girl who claims to be a white witch. At night, the walls fade away, and John finds himself sitting on a rock in a paleolithic countryside. He has the spells to escape, though, and he does, returning once with a flint-tipped spear and a second time with blood upon his sword.

There is clearly a mystery to Claines, centering on Old Thunder and Dreamer Rock and Gram Ensley. But what is it? John pokes and prods, and he discovers the truth. Almost, he comes to grief, and perhaps he saves the world. The story is very much in the Wellman style, folksily told, peopled with real-seeming characters, without wind and stodge, and with such

deftness that we barely miss the Appalachian ambiance we may be more accustomed to from him. I recommend it heartily.

> *Tom Easton, in a review of "What Dreams May Come," in* Analog Science Fiction/Science Fact, *Vol. CIV, No. 7, July, 1984, p. 167.*

NICHOLAS S. DE LARBER

What Dreams May Come is the first novel-length work to feature author John Thunstone, another of Wellman's occult investigators. In this tale, Thunstone's travels have led him to the quiet English village of Claines to study its two claims to fame: a huge, ancient chalk outline called "Old Thunder" on the cliffs outside town and the annual ritual of overturning a sandstone obelisk called the "Dream Rock" each July 4. But this July marks the ten thousandth anniversary of the rite, and this fact, plus strange visions experienced by Thunstone and others, indicate the impending return of a prehistoric, supernatural evil. The battle to prevent this, waged between Thunstone and his allies and Gram Ensley and the other human minions of the power, is the basis of this adventure.

After a lengthy absence, John Thunstone remains essentially the same character who appeared in the *Weird Tales* stories recently collected in *Lonely Vigils*. But Thunstone has aged slightly and he has become a bit more dependent upon his silver sword cane and upon allies like Constable Dymock, Mr. David Gates, the town minister, and Constance Bailey, a white magic witch. However, this has allowed more development of these other characters and made this a stronger story.

Like other Manly Wade Wellman novels, *What Dreams May Come* utilizes its setting to a large extent to help establish mood and plot development. In this case, the clash of the modern and the ancient and traditional in Claines parallels the struggle between Thunstone and Ensley. Further, the English locale, the home of much of our magical heritage and folklore, adds to the feeling of unfamiliarity and suspense.

Also, as in earlier works, Wellman has introduced references to other texts on occult events to add verisimilitude. . . . Wellman also continues to connect Thunstone with his other psychic detectives with references to Judge Pursuivant and Silver John (here described as a "witch master") and to Seabury Quinn's Jules de Grandin, thereby maintaining a consistent vision with this motif.

What Dreams May Come is a supernatural novel in the tradition of *Weird Tales* at its best, and it tells its narrative effectively and economically, with none of the blood and gore and little of the filler of many modern horror novels.

> *Nicholas S. De Larber, "Further Adventures of John Thunstone," in* Fantasy Review, *Vol. 7, No. 7, August, 1984, p. 31.*

LEN HATFIELD

That good ol' boy Silver John rambles through another of his amiable tall tales in [*The Voice of the Mountain*, the] fifth novel about his wanderings . . . based in the folklore of the southern Appalachians. John learns of Cry Mountain and sets out to discover the secret to its mournful call. Nearby, he meets the friendly hill folk of Larrowby who all warn him to stay away from the place; no one has ever returned from there, and spooky things have been happening thereabouts. Nevertheless, after some pleasant dalliance, off goes John to climb the mountain and learn the truth. Once at the summit of the old flat top, John encounters the sinister cause of the mountain's reputation, Ruel Harpe. A powerful black magician, Harpe tries to charm John into joining forces with him; but the minstrel resists, and eventually their struggle of wills turns into one with fists. The story has the strengths and weaknesses of many such folktales told in dialect: it's strong on the flavor of the hill life and lore, and offers warm pictures of the old ways still practiced in secret mountain valleys. But this novel also drags in spots, especially if you have a limited tolerance for pone and licks of Silver John's foot-stompin', heart-squeezin' music. Too, the dark magician and his creatures offer only slight menace, and the occasional moments of suspense are too short lived and predictable to raise much interest. This will feel comfortable enough to those with a taste for mountain lore and Silver John's exploits. To me it seemed more like an overlong short story: slow, episodic, not very gripping. . . .

> Len Hatfield, "A Tepid Mountain Folktale," in Fantasy Review, *Vol. 8, No. 4, April, 1985, p. 29.*

TOM EASTON

Manly Wade Wellman brings back Silver John the Balladeer one more time with ***The Voice of the Mountain.*** Once more we hear the Appalachian rhythms of a master storyteller, though he gives us less of the folklore. In ***Mountain,*** a wandering John finds the mountain called Cry, which periodically moans aloud. The locals avoid it, though some years before one boastful young man had gone off to climb it and never returned. John decides to follow his predecessor's path.

Naturally enough, John survives. Atop the mountain, he finds a stockade enclosing the home of wizard Ruel Harpe and his three female associates. There are also such legendary monsters as the flat, the bammat, and the hide-behind. And there is a dream of world destruction and restructuring to suit Harpe's wishes, a dream that hinges on finding the long-lost Book of Judas, and an invitation for John to join the effort.

Cry Mountain reeks of evil, and John has a keen nose. He resists, though he is tricked into helping gain the coveted Book. He balks, and he inevitably must fight a desperate battle. ***Mountain*** is an elemental story, perhaps the perfect distillation of Wellman's appeal: he writes drawn-out fairy tales, with all the drawing power of absolutes and high places. He writes the cautionary dreams of simpler peoples in simpler times, and they resonate with our modern discomforts.

Don't miss this one.

> Tom Easton, in a review of "The Voice of the Mountain," in Analog Science Fiction/Science Fact, *Vol. CV, No. 6, June, 1985, p. 167.*

ROBERT COULSON

Most but not all of Wellman's fantasies are of the sub-genre of horror fantasy. Unlike many of the younger writers in the field, he does not use the technique of a long, slow building of suspense, with many psychological details of his major characters (a technique called "building the mood" if one is in favor of it, and "padding" if one is not). Neither has he continued to use the old pulp formula of plunging immediately into the action, and bringing in background details only as needed, and never before the reader has theoretically been hooked. He prefers a straightforward story, with a short period

of scene-setting, whatever space is necessary to state the problem, and action scenes leading to a logical and preferably surprising climax.

His best stories incorporate elements of folklore; white, Indian, and very occasionally Negro. He's fond of including references to the book *Pow-Wows, or Long Lost Friend,* by John George Hohman. . . . Another item frequently mentioned in his stories is the "magic square":

S	A	T	O	R
A	R	E	P	O
T	E	N	E	T
O	P	E	R	A
R	O	T	A	S

Both this and the *Long Lost Friend* are invariably described as powerful charms against evil magic. In one of the best of his early stories, **"Fearful Rock,"** these both appear, plus such country lore as that a woman who looks into a mirror after reciting a particular incantation will see the face of her future husband, or her fate. This story also has the Civil War setting which is a common background in Wellman's stories.

The magic square and the *Long Lost Friend* also appear in his best, and best-known series; the stories of John the Balladeer. These stories are much involved with folkmusic as well as other folklore. John is a wandering singer with a silver-strung guitar who disposes of such evil as he meets in the Appalachian Mountains. Many of the songs mentioned in the stories are standards. . . . Some are written by Wellman specifically for the stories; they're a part of the plot. . . . The genuine songs used are always appropriate but not usually vital to the plot.

The use of silver as an antidote to evil is fairly common in folklore, and Wellman has used it in two other series; Judge Pursuivant and John Thunstone both carry sword-canes with silver blades. These are quite useful against sorcery, however much of a handicap they might be in a swordfight. The use of silver guitar strings against evil, however, seems unique to John.

The stories themselves are briskly told; the evil is shown, sometimes but not always identified, battled, and overthrown. The characters are all described well enough to become individuals, and they fit their mountain background. . . . The assorted menaces are generally tied in with mountain legends, though a few like Mr. Onselm and his ectoplasmic Ugly Bird [in **"O Ugly Bird!"**] are more general fantasy types. A few I had encountered before; I went to school with a boy from the Kentucky hills, and one afternoon he regaled me with stories of the "Behinder," the "Toller," the "Flat," the "Sammat" and others. But generally Wellman's menaces were new to me, and to most other readers, which increased the impact of the stories. There are certain rules and regulations concerning vampires, werewolves, and other popular creatures of evil; they've been arrived at either from legend or from the very quantity of stories about them. We know how they are supposed to act, and the suspense must lie entirely in the originality of the hero's attempts to outwit them. There is no such consensus of reader opinion concerning One Other, or the Ancients, or Kalu; part of the suspense lies in finding out just what they are. This originality is present in most of Wellman's fantasies, but is particularly well handled in the John stories.

The popularity of the stories is also enhanced by the fact that John, himself, is an interesting character, and since the reader usually finds out a bit more about him in each story, there is none of the overfamiliarity that one associates with other series characters such as Conan, Jules de Grandin, or the "Star Trek" crew.

While Wellman's straightforward writing and conciseness is refreshing in the horror field, it's occasionally overdone. In several of his very short stories and a few of the slightly longer ones, there is almost no suspense or horror at all. The sequence of scene-setting, problem, action and climax is shortened by leaving out most of the action. This is particularly evident in the short stories about John Thunstone, and, rather surprisingly, in many of his recent short stories. In **"Rouse Him Not,"** Thunstone investigates a mystery, probes the menace once, and then dispatches it. No worrying, no fumbling, no suspense. (pp. 100-03)

Very rarely does Wellman indulge in a variant of the *deus ex machina,* but the short story **"Willow He Walk"** provides one. The protagonist and the victim struggle through the story, achieve nothing, and in the last half-page are saved by the victim's girl-friend, who appears for the first time with a solution she's obtained offstage from Judge Pursuivant. Admittedly the story wasn't done for a major market, but it's an unusual failure for Wellman. (p. 103)

Most of Wellman's recent work has been in his novels. The first John the Balladeer novel, *The Old Gods Waken,* abandoned the folkmusic theme but provided an entertaining mixture of Cherokee and Druid wizardry. For once, John abandons his reliance on silver to fight sorcery with cold iron. The plot is closer to that of the "standard" horror novel, but characters and setting retain the individual Wellman touch.

After Dark returns to the folkmusic emphasis and pits John against the Shonokins, an Elder Race of humanoid sorcerers, whose only fear is of their own dead. The Shonokins have appeared in other Wellman stories, mostly in opposition to John Thunstone, and provide a fascinating menace; they're among the best of Wellman's creations.

In *The Lost and the Lurking,* John tangles with devil-worshippers and disciples of the Earth Mother. A fair number of our modern religious cults would surely resent this book, but Wellman's description of the Earth Mother rites are probably much closer to the original than are the modern imitations. The book has two flaws; the menace is less original than most, and the plot is advanced by having John captured by a gabby High Priestess, who helpfully explains things to him. This is the first of the stories of John which isn't entirely a success.

The Hanging Stones provides an assortment of oddities. Wellman is usually economical with his characters and plot elements; here he's used them liberally. . . . In a way, there are too many characters; some of them are not fully realized, and the actions of the spiritualists in particular seem a trifle arbitrary. A big plus is the first appearance of John's wife Evadare since the final story in *Who Fears The Devil?* She's more interesting than most of Wellman's female characters. Judge Pursuivant also turns up, to give John a hand in the final struggle.

The latest novel as of this writing is *What Dreams May Come.* For the first time in his novels, Wellman has dropped John and the Appalachian setting for John Thunstone and an English village. The sorcery here is connected to the English chalk carvings, the Old Religion, and an attempt to reawaken one of the old gods. The only flaw is that the reader knows what's coming before Thunstone does, which doesn't enhance Thun-

stone's status as an occult expert. This is a problem with most modern horror novels; if the protagonist knew as much about evil as the regular reader does, a good share of the action would be unnecessary. Wellman normally avoids the problem by having menaces that are unknown to the reader, but the habits of Druids and the "old religion" have been extensively chronicled recently. (pp. 103-04)

On the whole, Wellman has been both a good and a prolific writer of horror-fantasy for over fifty-five years. His flaws are an occasional story in which the suspense is too much curtailed, and a certain sameness to his female characters—though his women are better drawn than are those of most former pulp-magazine writers. His strengths are the authenticity and believability of his settings, particularly the southern mountain backgrounds, the originality of his menaces, and his use of folklore, which adds both authenticity and a touch of alienness for modern city-dwelling readers. His straightforward, concise writing style is also an asset when it's not overdone. His master work in fantasy to date is *Who Fears The Devil?,* but he's still writing, and may surpass that work at any time. (p. 104)

Robert Coulson, "The Recent Fantasies of Manly Wade Wellman," in Discovering Modern Horror Fiction, Vol. I, *edited by Darrell Schweitzer, Starmont House, 1985, pp. 99-105.*

LAUREL ANDERSON TRYFOROS

The School of Darkness is Manly Wade Wellman's latest novel about John Thunstone, psychic scholar and troubleshooter. The action takes place at an American folklore conference hosted by a university founded by a demonic pact. . . . Strange, eerie events follow; then Thunstone spots his old enemy Rowley Thorne, practitioner of black magic, formerly banished to another dimension—and the forces of good and evil begin to fight in earnest. Thunstone is aided by other psychic experts. . . . [One] familiar character is Sharon Hill, Countess of Monteseco, with whom Thunstone is in love. Together they use their individual expertise and Thunstone's knowledge of folk magic (the manual entitled *The Long Lost Friend*) to defeat the cult of diabolism on campus.

School of Darkness follows the formula of other Silver John novels, but here the formula works very well. The strengths (specific detail about occult practices and interesting asides about American folklore) overcome the weaknesses. In the last Silver John novels, the villains have been too easily disposed of; in *School of Darkness* the showdown is more prolonged, and there are more encounters with evil throughout. Also, charming as Silver John is, Thunstone's more sophisticated point of view is more consistently interesting. Wellman's women characters are still a little colorless, though Sharon is a nice enough heroine and Grizel Fian a sexy witch.

I have always felt that Wellman's novels do not match the quality of his shorter fiction, particularly the wonderful collections *Who Fears the Devil?* and *Worse Things Waiting.* But *School of Darkness* is, I think, a good sustained work. . . .

Laurel Anderson Tryforos, "Diabolism on Campus," in Fantasy Review, *Vol. 9, No. 2, February, 1986, p. 27.*

PAUL GRANAHAN

The School of Darkness continues a . . . Wellman sequence, the *John Thunstone* series about a psychic investigator which originally appeared in *Weird Tales* during the '40's and '50's. In this novel, Thunstone is invited to Buford State University to speak at a symposium on folklore and legend. Also participating are a Jesuit expert in the field of exorcism, a Cherokee Phi Beta Kappa graduate of Dartmouth who is a powerful medicine man of his people, and a Japanese scholar well-versed in the mythology and tradition of his people. All, however, is not as it seems, and Thunstone enlists the aid of these worthy companions when it becomes apparent that an evil miasma permeates the town of Buford, one which is entwined with the very founding of the university. For Buford is a hotbed of black witchcraft, home to a coven practicing a particularly diabolic aspect of the "old religion." Compounding the supernatural danger for Thunstone is the unexpected involvement of his old enemy, the corrupt sorcerer Rowley Thorne, back from whatever nameless dimension to which he was last banished while attempting to destroy Thunstone.

Taking into account Mr. Wellman's considerable reputation, I must assume that his earlier works surpass this novel. It is brief not only in number of pages, but in texture as well. Little is revealed to the uninitiated regarding Thunstone professionally or personally, or about any of the recurring cast. There is little true terror conveyed, and even the scarcity of real action would be more tolerable if the conversation had more substance. All that said, I must confess that I did enjoy the book. It has a kind of nostalgic, comfortable charm to it, reminding us of a time when works of dark fantasy weren't quite so gruesome as today's best sellers. I really would *like* to know more about Thunstone and company, and hope to see a future adventure of greater length and complexity from their creator. (pp. 446-47)

> *Paul Granahan, in a review of "The School of Darkness," in* Best Sellers, *Vol. 45, No. 12, March, 1986, pp. 446-47.*

TOM EASTON

[*The School of Darkness*] is not the best thing Wellman has ever done, but it is still a pleasure to read. Its hero is John Thunstone, poker into dark corners, invited for this occasion to participate in a symposium at Buford State University, a school founded in thanks for the healing efforts of a coven of witches. The witches remain, they have dark designs upon the future, and they have recently retrieved from Hell Thunstone's old foe, Rowley Thorne. . . .

Perhaps because of the setting—a prosaically contemporary campus—the atmosphere suffers. BSU is a stage for dramatic posturings, an impression strengthened when so much of the action occurs on a literal stage and before an array of groundlings. Too many people are mere background, without even spears to carry, and the tale might as well have happened in one of Silver John's Appalachian forests. But the tale nevertheless carries the Wellman flavor, and for that alone it is worth the price. (p. 183)

> *Tom Easton, in a review of "The School of Darkness," in* Analog Science Fiction/Science Fact, *Vol. CVI, No. 7, July, 1986, pp. 182-83.*

PUBLISHERS WEEKLY

[*Cahena: A Dream of the Past*] is a historical novel based on the life of the warrior queen known as the Cahena, who lived around the beginning of the eighth century in Northern Africa

and the Near East and led her people, the Moors, against the Moslems. The novel is told from the point of view of the Saxon career soldier named Wulf who comes to be the Cahena's right-hand man and eventually her lover. The story moves smoothly through its numerous military campaigns and romantic complications. Wellman has written a superior historical adventure (with a bit of fantasy—an encounter with a vampire) that, despite occasionally being too talky, always remains interesting.

> *A review of "Cahena," in* Publishers Weekly, *Vol. 230, No. 19, November 1, 1986, p. 56.*

MICHAEL M. LEVY

Cahena is quite different from the often horrific, sometimes lyrical fiction Wellman has recently published. In flat, understated prose he relates the story of the Imazighen of North Africa and their resistance to the first advance of Islam in the eighth century.

The book's narrator, Wulf, is a Saxon who has fought his way across Europe and North Africa; fleeing the destruction of Carthage, he is saved from the desert by Imazighen warriors. They take him to their charismatic ruler, the Cahena, who, impressed with Wulf's military prowess, makes him her counselor and, later, her lover. Things go well for the Imazighen at first; using Wulf's tactics they defeat a larger Moslem force in battle. Then the Cahena, who evidently has an eye for exotic younger men, takes Khalid, a Moslem prisoner, to her bed. Wulf, though deeply hurt, continues to serve her, but increasingly his advice is ignored and Khalid's accepted. This quickly leads to military ruin, the Cahena's death, and the collapse of Imazighen civilization.

Cahena reads like a straight historical novel and works as one. The Imazighen culture, a hodgepodge of Judeo-Christian and pagan concepts, is well if briefly sketched. The Cahena's prophetic powers have little impact on daily life. Only on the eve of battle does the supernatural come to the fore as Wulf spies Khro, the horned god of death, stalking the battlefield, contemplating those fated to die. Late in the novel, however, Wulf kills a lamia. The monster claims to be responsible for the Cahena's prophetic powers and, after the creature's death, all magic leaves the land of the Imazighen. It is this loss of her powers as much as her infatuation with Khalid which leads the Cahena to her downfall, but the situation is confusing. Is Wulf's killing of the lamia—seemingly a good deed—the cause of the disappearance of magic, or is the disappearance triggered by the Cahena's mistreatment of Wulf? We never know.

Despite this minor confusion, *Cahena* is a satisfying novel and a fitting end to a fine literary career.

> *Michael M. Levy, "Manly Wade Wellman's Last Novel," in* Fantasy Review, *Vol. 10, No. 2, March, 1987, p. 45.*

TOM EASTON

[*Cahena*] is not a tale of Silver John or any other of Wellman's patent, delightful folky heroes. Instead, it is the tale of an ancient North African warrior queen, the Cahena, whose Moorish troops fought off the Moslems until an invidious traitor induced the Cahena to order her land's life-support systems—orchards, fields, and towns—destroyed to deny the enemy his potential spoils. . . .

The tale is told by Wulf, a kind and gentle Saxon Conan who had advised the Cahena in war, fought for her, and loved her. The time is many years later, in the tent of Charles Martel, a Frankish general opposing a different Moslem horde. Wulf is instructing in tactics, proving how much he knows of Martel's foe, and striving for a place in the front lines where, if he is lucky, death will erase his painful memories. Yet the point is something more. *Cahena* is a historical novel, yes, and it has enough touches of fantasy to justify its coverage here. But it is also a cautionary morality tale, a message to rulers everywhere who ignore the elemental concerns of their peoples. It is, perhaps, addressed specifically to Washington, with its perennial short-sheeting of our environmental bed.

> *Tom Easton, in a review of "Cahena," in* Analog Science Fiction/Science Fact, *Vol. CVII, No. 7, July, 1987, p. 183.*

Terence de Vere White

1912-

Irish novelist, short story writer, biographer, nonfiction writer, memoirist, and editor.

White's novels combine mild social and political commentary with sophisticated humor to satirize the conventions of Irish gentility. His works have been characterized as comedies of manners that explore the decline of Ireland's Protestant aristocracy. White's fiction typically features droll, polished dialogue, detailed evocations of upper-class milieus, and stereotypical characters who reflect the attitudes of many high-society sophisticates. While often faulted by reviewers for trivial fictional concerns, White has been praised for his urbane wit and the craftsmanship of his prose.

A successful lawyer who also served as literary editor of the *Irish Times* from 1961 to 1977, White published several books of nonfiction before writing his first novel, *An Affair with the Moon* (1959), a stylish seriocomic story that derives from his experiences as a solicitor. In this and other early works, including *Prenez Garde* (1961), *The Remainderman* (1963), and *Lucifer Falling* (1966), White examines many of the concerns he has continued to investigate throughout his career, including the changes in Ireland's social structures due to the demise of British rule, relationships between young people and their elders, and snobbery and eccentricity among the Irish gentry. In *Tara* (1967) and *The Distance and the Dark* (1973), White expands his thematic scope by presenting the strife in Northern Ireland as a significant factor in the development of the personal, political, and social sensibilities of his characters. Among his subsequent books, *The Radish Memoirs* (1974) and *Johnnie Cross* (1983) satirize academia by exposing the churlishness that is often masked as intellectual pretension, while *Chat Show* (1987) investigates the British television industry and reveals the ephemeral nature of fame and wealth.

In addition to his many novels, White has published several collections of short stories, including *Big Fleas and Little Fleas* (1976), *Chimes at Midnight* (1977), and *Birds of Prey* (1980). He has also written biographies of several literary personalities as well as *A Fretful Midge* (1957), a volume of memoirs.

(See also *Contemporary Authors,* Vols. 49-52 and *Contemporary Authors New Revision Series,* Vol. 3.)

NYT Pictures

THE TIMES, LONDON

Mr. Terence de Vere White's Jane in *An Affair with the Moon* ("I had an affair with the moon," wrote Laurence Sterne, "in which there was neither sin nor shame") is, to put it vulgarly, a filly of a very different colour. Jane carries amorality to the point of genius, but there is no particular credit in the feat since she was born without any moral sense worth speaking about. She is, however, beautiful; she is generous; she is innocent of self-seeking and many other of the convenient social deceptions, and her mental age is that of a radiant twelve.

Her husband for the moment—the "I" of the narrative—a stolid Yorkshire solicitor is, in marrying her, as much out of his element as though he were in truth on the moon, but he is no fool and he is quick in perceiving that in meeting Jane, he has not "encountered Diana of the Crossways or Rhoda Fleming, the dialogue was much closer, perilously close to Anita Loos." The scene shifts to Eire and Mr. White, who has a shaky sense of construction, introduces, for no discernible purpose, a number of more or less comic Irish types and spends pages on a detailed account of a *farouche* day's hunting. The novel's description of itself as one of "rich comedy with a dying fall" will pass, but a little of Jane in real life would be quite enough and in fiction, as Mr. White would seem to feel, it is hard work making a book of her.

A review of "An Affair with the Moon," in The Times, *London, August 20, 1959, p. 11.*

THE TIMES LITERARY SUPPLEMENT

Mr. Terence de Vere White's *Prenez Garde* . . . has as its background a tableau of violence, excitement and collapsing British rule . . . in Ireland during the Troubles, 1920-21. But well in the foreground of the story is Brian, a nine-year-old boy imagining himself in love with a pretty governess, who eventually comes to terms with adult realities at a cruelly early age. The governess, living in the circle of a comfortably well-off West British family, is pursued by a decaying aristocrat and an English officer who carries, to the boy, all the sinister associations of the Black and Tans. Death claims one, the other just escapes it; the boy loses his innocence and suddenly grows up.

This aspect of the novel reminds one of Mr. L. P. Hartley's *The Go Between;* an adult complication seen through the eyes of a child at a crucial time. But often the book's style flags into whimsy and sentiment, coming alive only when it evokes the last dying moments of ascendancy Anglo-Irish life spluttering out to the accompaniment of battles between the I.R.A. and the Tans. *Prenez Garde* may well be remembered more for this nostalgic quality than for any attempt to create character and plot.

"Conflicts and Backgrounds," in The Times Literary Supplement, *No. 3085, April 14, 1961, p. 237.*

BERNARD BERGONZI

[*The Remainderman*] is a charming account, told in the first person, of a few packed months in the life of 17-year-old Michael Whaley, set in the Dublin of 1929. Michael's father is already dead; his mother dies suddenly, reading *Pride and Prejudice,* and the orphaned Michael is shabbily treated by the uncles who are supposed to look after him. He wants to be a writer—or, as he unwisely confesses at one point, a writer *and* an actor—but he has to go into a solicitor's office, articled to the bland and hypocritical Mr Daunt. He is a poetry addict and fancies he is in love with an off-hand girl called Sheila with whom he makes no progress at all. He then goes on to make rather too much progress with his Uncle Arthur's glamorous and faithless wife, Philippa. He gets out of this entanglement and is finally rescued from his dull life by the intervention of Daunt's daft old clerk.

Mr White has skilfully avoided the various sentimental pitfalls that await writers about Dublin and/or adolescence. His Michael is no stammering Salingeresque goof, but a witty young moralist, highly articulate even when he is most miserable.... The book reaches a level of subdued hilarity when Michael improbably attends a hunt ball given by the horsy Anglo-Irishry of Limerick. Mr White is an economic writer who doesn't waste his effects, and he carefully plays down the oddity of the various eccentrics who surround his hero. His drily told story is light without being superficial, and I recommend it. (pp. 175-76)

Bernard Bergonzi, "Two Adolescents," in New Statesman, *Vol. LXVI, No. 1691, August 9, 1963, pp. 175-76.*

JOCELYN BROOKE

I started *The Remainderman* on the wrong foot, and I rather suspect that its author did too. In my own case, I was misled by the blurb—and by 'quotes' about Mr White's previous book— into thinking that this was a comic novel; but though amusing in parts, it is in fact a rather sad little tale. As for Mr White, he seemed to me, for the first chapter or two, to be unsure of himself, and his writing struck me as dull and plodding; then, suddenly, his characters started to come to life, and I found the book engrossing. Michael Whaley is left an orphan at sixteen; his parents' money goes to his three uncles, all of them too stingy to contribute to the cost of his education, though one of them instals him as an articled clerk in the office of the

family solicitor. Poor Michael, who reads Joyce and Eliot and wants to write himself, is miserable; he falls in love, first with a dreary and witless girl of nineteen, then with a glamorous aunt-by-marriage, who flirts with him shamelessly and then bolts off to Kenya with an older lover. It is the lawyer's chief clerk, a Dickensian *deus ex machina,* who finally rescues Michael from his servitude by a gift of £400. Such unexpected happy endings are unfashionable, and usually seem contrived, but Mr White makes this one seem quite plausible. The scene is Dublin in the late 'twenties, and the story, told in the first person, has an air of being autobiographical. (Oliver Gogarty appears briefly as a minor character); yet apart from a few specific references to street-names and so on, the atmosphere of the book is singularly un-Irish.

Mr White's writing is so low-toned and unemphatic that the highlights of the novel shine the brighter by contrast: there is, for instance, a really brilliant description of a huntball in which Mr White evokes most amusingly—and rather movingly—the social agonies of a timid and gauche young man at his first grand party. There are a few anachronisms: I don't think one spoke of someone being a 'drip' in 1929, and surely the expression 'You've had it' hadn't come into use as early as that. And certainly no Anglo-Irish lady, then, or now, would say 'Fix yourself a drink', unless she had lived in America. This is an old-fashioned, not very exciting, yet oddly likable novel.

Jocelyn Brooke, in a review of "The Remainderman," in The Listener, *Vol. LXX, No. 1794, August 15, 1963, p. 249.*

DAVID LODGE

[*The Remainderman*] concerns an idealistic, innocent young man whose romantic illusions do not survive the experience of bourgeois professional and social life.... [The] setting is Ireland, and the mode is comedy. Michael Whaley is seventeen and has lost both his parents when the novel begins. Dependent on his relatives for support and guidance, he despises his crass Uncle Hilary, admires his sophisticated Uncle Arthur, and falls deeply in love with Arthur's entrancing wife Phillipa. Most of his judgments prove to be wrong, but the plot (heavy-handedly spelled out by the blurb) is not greatly important.

What one admires about the book is the fresh, gentle comedy, coloured by the pleasing innocence of the hero, which Mr. White manages to create out of very familiar routines: cutting oneself while shaving for an important social occasion, for instance, or taking a woman to an expensive restaurant for the first time. Like many Irish novels, *The Remainderman* is rich in eccentrics, and Mr. White has the literary tact to describe their antics with scarcely a flicker of surprise. This novel is a slight but graceful achievement.

David Lodge, "The Unities Mastered," in The Spectator, *Vol. 211, No. 7051, August 16, 1963, p. 210.*

MARTIN LEVIN

The law of the jungle as it operates in the Groves of Academe is the thematic basis of *Lucifer Falling* by Terence de Vere White. Specifically, Mr. White's sparkling satire deals with the efforts of Prof. Arnold Power, department head in a place that loosely resembles Dublin's Trinity College, to hang on to his prerogatives in the face of encroachments from the lower ranks.

"A wit among scholars and a scholar among wits," Power is an amiable faker who embarks on a pair of projects designed to bolster his self-esteem: the writing of a book and the engineering of an affair. The book, a biography of his Victorian predecessor, leads through the by-ways of *fin de siècle* literature into a half-buried scandal; the professor's girl, an American graduate student, leads to other surprises. Mr. White is a brilliant, witty and humane guide as he conducts his hero through successive varieties of self-defeat. The academic air, though its flavor is Irish, has a whiff of universality about it, as has the savage confrontation between young don and old.

> *Martin Levin, in a review of "Lucifer Falling," in* The New York Times Book Review, *May 14, 1967, p. 48.*

NICHOLAS J. LOPRETE, JR.

It is rare that a reviewer agrees with the incantatory prose of dust-jacket blurbs, but, in Mr. White's case, I am compelled to give my vigorous assent to what is described as "a witty and explosive journey into the world of the academe." True, Carlos Baker, Stringfellow Barr, Mary McCarthy, and C. P. Snow have produced academic novels, but *Lucifer Falling* is superior to the productions of those authors, if for no other reason than that Mr. White's people are human beings in a university setting.

For over twenty years, Professor Arnold Power has been chairman of the department of English literature in a university not unlike Dublin's Trinity College. In Power's case there was something like the religious "laying on of hands", for he was personally pushed to an early undeserved prominence by his predecessor, the great Victorian critic, Edward Jameson. And Power has lived with that burden consciously and conscientiously declaring, to the annoyance of friends, enemies, and family, that he owes all to Jameson. Jameson's objets d'art clutter Power's rooms, his bust glowers at all who visit Power.

It would be unfair to reveal Mr. White's plot. Suffice it to say that Arnold Power, after years of delay, determines to write his definitive study of Jameson. Complicating his decision, however, is an invitation to visit Harvard for a year, and the boorish, brutal nastiness of a young-academic-on-the-make who would like nothing better than to have Power's university position and the Harvard visit. Pressed on all sides, Power deliberately involves himself in an affair with a young American graduate student in whose inspiration he hopes to find encouragement during the waning of his middle-aged career. A trip to Brussels and the discovery of Jameson's scandalous scholarship lead to the tragic collapse of the man Jameson had once called, "Lucifer, son of the morning."

Mr. White is literary editor of *The Irish Times,* and a novelist, biographer and critic. *Lucifer Falling* is urbane and witty, sophisticated and tender. It is stylistically literate in the grand tradition. (pp. 126-27)

> *Nicholas J. Loprete, Jr., in a review of "Lucifer Falling," in* Best Sellers, *Vol. 27, No. 6, June 15, 1967, pp. 126-27.*

THE TIMES LITERARY SUPPLEMENT

Tara does not strike sparks, but it is vastly entertaining and beneath its urbane surface there is an awareness of darker forces. Nearly all of Mr. de Vere White's characters are fail-

ures: there is a failed Dublin poet, a failed Dublin rebel, now fat with complacency and affluence, a thwarted lesbian, a social climber with no head for heights and so on. Even the one happily resolved relationship seems doomed, for it is the elopement of a young Catholic Irish girl with a middle-aged Protestant English actor.

The plot, involving the missing manuscript of the poet's verse play and the infanticidal activities of the I.R.A., is deftly handled, and among many fine comic scenes there is a particularly funny one where the poet reads his dreadful play to the sponsors who had not suspected what they were letting themselves in for. *Tara* is a lightweight, but, as is often the case, offers much better value than many of the hopeful heavyweights.

> *"Missing," in* The Times Literary Supplement, *No. 3411, July 13, 1967, p. 613.*

FLORENCE O'DONOGHUE

Mr. de Vere White sets his scene [in *Tara*] in Ireland. An undeserving hero of the "Troubles" becomes vastly rich and his decent but silly wife aspires to a high social place, limping over solecisms. Their son, schooled at Ampleforth, broods on Ireland's historic grievances and takes part in IRA attacks on border barracks, and only the blowing-up of a child finally arrests the malaise and sends him confessing to the Southern police, with the father desperately hoping that influence with a powerful Minister may keep the boy out of prison. A failed poet shuffles his way through the setbacks of his kind. Mr. de Vere White writes, quite plainly, from an intimate knowledge of Ireland, and *Tara* is a most agreeably told story.

> *Florence O'Donoghue, "The Irish Spirit," in* The Tablet, *Vol. 221, No. 6643, September 16, 1967, p. 973.*

R.G.G. PRICE

The Lambert Mile half-reminded me of several authors, from Somerville and Ross to Jane Austen, though hardly ever of a recent writer. Setting a light novel in Ireland allows many freedoms, including freedom from literary conformism. Perhaps the term "light novel" makes the humour sound too sunny and ignores the sharp social observation. In the tiny, genteel community, where the gentry are absentees and calm is always threatened by incursions from the vulgar rich, things are always happening which are amusing, on the surface. Comic stereotypes are used—selfish, muddled parson, landed tomboy, elegant, horsy crook—but the parts they play gradually diverge from the expected. The writing is swift and very enjoyable. Mr. de Vere White is one of the few authors who has ever made me laugh aloud with a single adjective. Only jogtrot Irish fun, of course, only a grin at the follies of the natives—but behind the charm and the open smile is a deadly wit and something colder and older than English authors provide when they frolic.

> *R.G.G. Price, in a review of "The Lambert Mile," in* Punch, *Vol. 256, No. 6707, March 26, 1969, p. 474.*

THE TIMES LITERARY SUPPLEMENT

The Lambert Mile, focusing on the great mansion of Mount Lambert, is an estate of lodges in which live a tight, exclusive circle of genteel and well-to-do Irish families. The affairs of the estate are left in the hands of the bailiff and lawyer by its bored owner, Sir Julian Lambert; but his daughter Elizabeth, beautiful and unscrupulous and "taking a high moral tone about everything except morals", is both an attractive romantic proposition and an important social catch when she decides to visit the locality. Around the flutter caused by her return, Mr. de Vere White weaves an entertaining, if not particularly substantial, tale of social snobbery and personal eccentricity among the respectable rural Irish.

His concern to present a broad panorama of life on the Mile leads to the sketching of a very wide variety of local characters, so that the narrative runs the risk of getting lost in a maze of amusing minor episodes and personal quirks; but the novel shakes down finally into a unity which shows the contrivance of a skilful, if whimsical, plot. The satire is very mild and genial, with all the caricatures gentle: neither ruthlessness nor penetrating social observation are really the author's purpose. But the book is likeable in an unassuming way. The portrait of Major Christian Paul, variously nicknamed "The Count" and "Ritzy", a smiling local charlatan, is the most lively element in it: old-fashioned stuff, but pleasing for its humorous simplicity. Mr. de Vere White's prose is craftsmanlike and witty.

"Genteel Eccentrics," in The Times Literary Supplement, *No. 3505, May 1, 1969, p. 457.*

ANNE O'NEILL-BARNA

Both the connoisseur of comedies of manners and the armchair sociologist will recognize Terence de Vere White's novel [*The Lambert Revels*, published in Great Britain as *The Lambert Mile*] as vintage stuff.

The story unrolls with the mouth-watering quality of exclusive gossip, for it carries us into the Lambert Mile, an Irish village jealously guarded by its Anglo-Irish and Anglo inhabitants. The plot, if such it can be called, hangs on a bogus Count— who is neither Irish nor English—and his 11th-hour attempts to ward off creditors and buy Mount Lambert (the Big House) to use as a stud farm. The complication is the arrival from Majorca of 21-year-old Elizabeth Lambert, daughter of the absent owners of the House—who, like her mother, is a lover of the Count—and the arrival of the Coppingers (upstarts by the standards of the mile), who also want to buy Mount Lambert.

What fleshes out the story, just like life, are the dozen or so people who get involved in the bankruptcy, the purchase or the series of disastrous parties held in honor of Elizabeth. In these unfolding events the oneupmanship of the English character is shown and shown up; the only thing that keeps some of the author's characters from seeming as horrible as those English people in *A Passage to India* is, paradoxically, his deadly humor, truly all-embracing humor which includes in its scope such sacrosanct things as sex, money and the nonentity of most human beings, and which couldn't care less about nationality.

The characters are so familiar they must be types, but if so they are types with the idiosyncracies of individuals; a laconic exact phrase here, a perfect reproduction of speech there, produces them in the round because the reader already recognizes them. But what sparks our interest is what Mr. White so deliciously adds, not only the view from within this assorted group, but the view very much from without.

For instance, the Canon is a bore, never mind him, but from his (of course) long-suffering wife flash some memorable considerations, such as: "She had seen him in his shirt and even less. . . . She had been his partner in moments when his feelings got the better even of his syntax." When the bulky Mrs. Browne, who is a particularly active social climber, and Captain Loftus, who is the lowest in the Mile pecking order, somehow share champagne: "After the first bottle, the Captain realized what never struck him or anyone before, that Mrs. Browne was a desirable woman. . . . Lying back in the chair her thighs had a certain magnificence . . . like the entrance to the War Office."

Or we recognize Barbara Beddington as a type, but a type seldom described. Here, with an exquisite blend of admiration and amusement, she is delineated for all time: the correct, beautiful and beautifully preserved spinster who is witty, poised, perceptive, self-aware and eventually in love (with the Count). (pp. 4-5)

The Count himself is a rare achievement; not everyone can deal with a complex mesomorph whose phoniness is as convincing as his authority. Michael the gentle simpleton is deftly sketched as the only one in the story who sees clearly and acts rightly. But it is Elizabeth, a new-style young woman, who is as real as this minute and as appealing—generous, honest, unblinking, sexually free, wise beyond her years. Her authentic tone comes through in her conversation—perhaps most typically when the Count gives her an old pitch of his about comradeship. She says, "O cut it out, Ritzy. You know I can't live without you."

As you can see, a civilized pleasure lies ahead. (p. 5)

Anne O'Neill-Barna, "A Pleasure to Meet Some Horrible English People," in The New York Times Book Review, *January 18, 1970, pp. 4-5.*

CHARLES DOLLEN

Life in a modern Irish village can be viewed as a carry-over from the late nineteenth century where gentry and peasant preserve their once-charming relationships for lack of anything else to do. That, at least, is the scene that Mr. de Vere White would have his readers believe as he plunges [in *The Lambert Revels*] into the lives and eccentricities of a dozen assorted people who live on the Lambert Mile.

Since the Anglo-Irish gentry are the subjects of this witty novel, there just has to be a Canon, and there is. Like most fictional Canons of the Anglican Church, Canon Ormsby has nothing to do for the Church except preside in monsignorial fashion over carefully chosen events. For the rest of the time he spends his wife's money and putters about in other people's lives.

Then, there has to be the village spinster, genteel, prudish and quietly aging. That would be Miss Beddington. The villain is also predictable with the introduction of the mysterious Count Paul who throws lavish parties, runs up excessive debts, and employs Italian servants. The absentee landlords, Sir Julian Lambert, his wife and his beautiful daughter, along with the village dolt, the village constable and every other stock character from a vaudeville event are trotted out at predictable intervals to perform according to a rigid etiquette.

The effect is to produce a novel so "veddy, veddy British" that the reader is supposed to double up with laughter. Well, it does manage to muster up a few smiles here and there but the humor is either so wry or so common that it never really produces anything creative. The simple-minded Canon and the conniving Count have just been used too often in recent literature.

According to the publisher's blurb the novel, first published in England as **The Lambert Mile,** has enjoyed some critical success, even being praised by *Punch*'s reviewer [see excerpt above by R.G.G. Price]. Maybe that explains why there is an American edition; it doesn't excuse it.

> Charles Dollen, in a review of "The Lambert Revels," in Best Sellers, *Vol. 29, No. 21, February 1, 1970, p. 416.*

SARA BLACKBURN

There are at least a couple of very entertaining characters in [**The Lambert Revels**], Terence de Vere White's novel about what happens when the Anglo-Irish "aristocracy" of a small Irish village have their enormous pretensions toward wealth and status shaken and then shattered by a conspiracy among two of their own. The novel is a kind of comedy of manners which readers of another age might have referred to as "civilized"; it is occasionally very funny, because the author has an admirable skill for creating characters so absurdly pompous that they are richly deserving of the vicious delight with which he sets about deflating them. The cast includes a remarkably boring canon who is deeply respected by his fellow villagers for no detectable virtue; his vapid lawyer son; a Count who is not a count but quite a scoundrel; assorted retired army officer types; and a lively young girl whose return to her ancestral home provokes a competition of ghastly social events in her honor that culminates in the virtual death of the old order.

As the residents of The Lambert Mile have almost literally nothing to do but spy on and gossip about one another and go about the calls which pass as their social life, there is a great deal of speculation about intention, misinterpretation of actions, and blundering into unexpected events. The novel has one serious flaw which makes it impossible to recommend with real enthusiasm: Somewhere in his heart, de Vere White harbors an affection for his fading gentry, and, for all of his good-natured malice, he means them to be rather touching, and, for example, often attempts to indicate their real virtues by the degree of their kindness to the working class. Perhaps "civilized" reading was always meant specifically for those who were capable of mourning the passing of an aristocracy. Left-handed as it is, **The Lambert Revels** is a long tribute to a group that deserves a quick and unmourned demise. The result is worse than anachronism; it is superfluousness, and that is a shame.

> Sara Blackburn, "'Civilized' Values," in Book World—Chicago Tribune, *February 15, 1970, p. 10.*

CLAIRE TOMALIN

Terence de Vere White's **The March Hare** is . . . highly entertaining and told with the lightest touch: the snobberies of families watching one another's rise and fall in the social scale, the problems of Protestant boy and Catholic girl, the pretensions of a penniless sponging uncle, the bossiness of titled patronesses; clearly there is little he does not know about Dublin society circa 1905.

But he adds to this an insight into the minds of his women. In those days it was important to be a lady, and ladies had their delicacy carefully preserved by parents and husbands: but they must sometimes have wondered about the other, hidden side of those same fathers' and husbands' lives, spent with women who were not ladies. The consequences of this division were not always comic, and Mr. de Vere White allows accordingly a strain of realistic sadness to enter his otherwise cheerful book.

> Claire Tomalin, "Funny Serious," in The Observer, *September 20, 1970, p. 28.*

EDWIN MORGAN

The March Hare is a very readable comic novel set in Dublin at the beginning of the present century. The action, as the author cannot help inserting during a chaotic country-house weekend, is 'like an Irish comic novel', but some shrewd thrusts are made at Irish society, manners and politics. It is against the background of Home Rule and the decline of the Protestant Ascendancy that the class-conscious little dramas are played out: has impoverished-genteel Catholic Milly any chance with her Protestant boyfriend Alan who is under the thumb of his smooth Bishop uncle? The dénouement is a somewhat melodramatic accident which nevertheless coolly sorts things out: art in Paris for the scarred Milly, law in Burma for Alan, who was a poor fish anyhow.

> Edwin Morgan, "Private Flashpoints," in The Listener, *Vol. 84, No. 2165, September 24, 1970, p. 428.*

THE TIMES LITERARY SUPPLEMENT

"All they had"—Carrie Preston and her two daughters, Dolly and Milly—"was respectability". So Mr. de Vere White sums up [in **The March Hare**] his little nest of Edwardian gentlewomen living in Dublin "in reduced circumstances" as the phrase went in the early 1900s, the relics of Arthur Preston, a prosperous, spendthrift lawyer who dies untimely right at the story's beginning by falling off an outside car.

For Milly, the younger daughter, however, respectability is no precious jewel. Situated as they are, pressed for money, linked to the best society only through the less than good offices of the patronizing Lady Kelly, Milly looks on it as a jewel made of paste. She will make her own way, be a "new woman"; she can draw prettily and knows she has sufficient good looks to attract men; she has small patience with the droopy dependence of her mother and Dolly; she can shrug off the ton-weight of convention which middle-class women of about the year 1902 were required to stagger round with; she has her father's raffishness.

Mr. de Vere White develops his comedy with deft assurance and some accurate social observation. Inexperienced though she is, Milly sails briskly ahead through choppy waters with the other two clucking behind her. Her Uncle Joe, a con-man in a frock coat, doesn't make her progress any easier, but Alan, a very suitable young man, does fall in love with her. She is well on her way to fixing him when an accident, caused by Uncle Joe's happy-go-lucky handling of one of these dangerous new motor cars, sends her back to the starting-line. We leave her, with a nasty scar on the forehead and with all to do again.

A review of "The March Hare," in The Times Literary Supplement, *No. 3586, November 20, 1970, p. 1368.*

EDWIN MORGAN

Mr De Vere White's may not be a major talent, but his novels give a great deal of pleasure and have a flavour of their own—witty, worldly-wise, sly. He is also a good craftsman, and the well-engineered moves and turns of his narratives are part of the entertainment. *Mr Stephen* is surely one of his best stories. It sets down an apparently clear-cut moral dilemma in the confusing sphere where personal, professional and political areas of influence all overlap. Mr Stephen is a Dublin lawyer at the top of his profession who has been offered a job in the Government as Minister of Justice: a straight and honest man, well-liked and much respected. But a little wasp of quasi-blackmail begins to sting him when an ex-secretary of his, egged on by her penniless fiancé, accuses him of technically forging a will by forgetting to witness it at the time and signing later. The matter is of importance to her, since if the will can be invalidated, or if a cash settlement can be squeezed from him out of court, her fiancé's deceased aunt's fortune will no longer go to charity but to the hopeful if gormless couple. As a very wealthy man himself, he could settle for cash without missing it, but his pride refuses any such admission of guilt. If the case is taken to court, and by a rival firm of solicitors at that, what will happen to the new Minister of Justice?

This piquant situation is complicated by the tiresome fantasies of his fading mistress, Barbara, who sees herself becoming a great hostess though she knows he hates ostentation, and by the weird machinations of the odious but grinningly irrepressible property developer and tax-dodger Mr Woodhouse, a client of Stephen's who acts as a sort of Iago to his Othello. Woodhouse, who takes a 'macabre delight' in upsetting people and causing as much trouble as he can, is the most interesting character in the book, and the satirical comedy of his actions (not unlike that of the medieval demon attaching squibs to the robes of the mighty) is pointed as well as skulduggerous.

Edwin Morgan, "Dublin Pride," in The Listener, *Vol. 86, No. 2210, August 5, 1971, p. 185.*

THE TIMES LITERARY SUPPLEMENT

Terence de Vere White has contrived [in *Mr Stephen*] a tale about a Protestant Dublin lawyer, head of a well-established firm, and a will which was wrongly witnessed. A former solicitor himself, and now the distinguished literary editor of *The Irish Times*, he is comfortably at home in the lawyer's offices and the Stephen's Green Clubs, less so among what the reader uneasily feels to be the lower orders: "porter" is something that has not been manufactured, let alone drunk, for a good many years; and the almost illiterate but cunning property speculator who is opposed to the staid, able and on the whole attractive central figure suffers from a common fault in class-characterization—he is both a cliché and unreal at the same time. None of this would matter so much except that a primary theme seems to be the remnants of the old order intermingling with the new. *Mr Stephen* is mildly readable and exhibits some insight into men and their worldly affairs. To say it is no more is not to demean it: its author does not seem to have been any more ambitious.

"Unwilled," in The Times Literary Supplement, *No. 3630, September 24, 1971, p. 1138.*

THOMAS LASK

The Minister for Justice [published in Great Britain as *Mr Stephen*] is refined entertainment: civilized, clever, intricately but plausibly plotted, full of honest sentiment and a pleasure to read. Mr. White, an Irish novelist and biographer, is shameless in manipulating the feelings of his readers. He lines them on the side of virtue and they go through the book cheering for the right side to win. I am gratified to report, without the danger of diminishing anyone's enjoyment, that it does. Although the ins and outs of the plot resemble a path in an English ramble that time and again turns back on itself, Mr. White gives his audience the credit of being able to keep up with him. He does not explain; he lets the events as they unfold do it for him.

Stephen Foster, a lawyer honored by his colleagues, respected by his opponents and revered by his staff, receives a visit in his slightly rundown house in the outskirts of Dublin from a onetime secretary. She has an odd tale to tell. She remembers a will, drawn and witnessed by Foster, that had not been executed to the last letter of the law. It was a will that deprived a man of his aunt's inheritance. The aunt had cut him off, and all the money had gone to charity. The secretary went on to say that she was now being courted by the disinherited nephew, who had not a sixpence to his name. She had come to the lawyer to point out the error and to get back some of the charity money for her husband-to-be.

Her visit opens a big can of worms. She is saying in effect that this pillar of the Irish bar did something illegal and would want to cover it up. Mind you, neither the nephew nor his girl friend have moral scruples about the business. They only want money. They are willing to settle for half of the aunt's estate, which Stephen Foster can afford to pay. But such an action would be giving in to blackmail and Foster refuses. The onetime secretary involves others in her suit to try to make Foster see the light. The nephew falls into the hands of a sharp operator who offers to help him. A shoddy real estate scheme adds more complications; lawyers and clients play a game of musical chairs, well-meaning people rush in to help with disastrous results. Foster is not just encumbered with help; he is strangled by it. He has to fight off enemies and well wishers alike. For a while he is on the razor's edge, but he makes it.

He's a character who would confound most of the heroes in today's fiction. A modern Parson Adams. He believes in the good and does it. Villainy simply must not be allowed to conquer. Obviously this is not a fashionable view to hold today. Mr. White will almost persuade you that it should be.

Thomas Lask, "The Quick and the Dead," in The New York Times, *November 27, 1971, p. 29.*

R. J. THOMPSON

This new novel [*The Distance and the Dark*] by the most interesting of present-day Irish novelists of manners does not offer the same quicksilver and unequivocal delight that is to be found in his last two novels published in America, *The Lambert Revels* (1969) and *The Minister for Justice* (1971). Here, as in those books, the plot grows thin as soon as its main idea sinks in, but unlike those previous works *The Distance and the Dark* is not supported by a beautifully realized social background. White's forte is the development of an almost palpable upper-crust ambience that is civilized by a richly drawn, eccentric, and spirited field of folk—his novels are often called, as they are on the blurb here, "Trollopian." The present book is miserly in its presentation of White's special values.

The narrative concerns the murder of the son of an Anglo-Irish landowner, Everard Harvey, in County Meath by a branch of the I.R.A. A divided and permissive government is afraid to deal harshly with the crime; despite Harvey's family reputation and status, the government wants to play all sides of the political game for selfish reasons. So far, so good: White is marvelously competent in delineating both the timidity of the government . . . and the reckless contempt heaped upon some of the Protestant gentry by bully-boys who plunder and kill by night in the name of freedom. To confuse Harvey's quest for justice all the more, his wife runs off with an English jockey and horse-owner, and Harvey himself lapses into a dependent flirtation with the wife of his best friend. If things sound bad, they are about to worsen, right through to the end where Harvey loses everything, including his life.

White's problem lies in the blandness with which he handles the "big" culminating scenes toward which his narrative builds, e.g., his hero's confrontation of the terrorist thug Gallagher in which the reader expects a one-on-one shoot-out or at least a psychological resolution between their warring minds, or the potentially exciting Sligo Plate horse race. Instead, the story swerves away from its expected high moments in favor of Victorian chat ("You have brought me peace," says the best friend's wife to Harvey, who replies, "I went in search of it.") Only at the very end does White gird himself to deliver sterner stuff: Harvey's wife importunes him to allow her to return, the best friend waxes furious, the paternity of Harvey's murdered son is put in doubt, and the wretched Gallagher, or his coevals, turns up yet again. But even these whiz-bang elements are not enough to galvanize the book into final life, which is a pity—White is so good that one expects him to be great.

> *R. J. Thompson, in a review of "The Distance and the Dark," in* Best Sellers, *Vol. 33, No. 1, April 1, 1973, p. 8.*

FRANCIS GRIFFITH

You don't have to be Irish to like *The Distance and the Dark*—but it would help.

The current strife in Northern Ireland provides this novel's background, but the events themselves occur just beyond the Ulster border. Everard Harvey, a well-to-do Anglo-Irish landowner, holds views about the Catholic minority's struggle for civil rights which do not sit well with the other members of his social class, who regard him as a traitor to their traditions. They share his abhorrence of terrorist tactics but not his sympathy with minority aspirations.

When Everard tries to bring a gunman to justice, he becomes the target of an illegal military organization which, in an attempt to kill him, accidentally kills his infant son.

Sally, Everard's British wife, leaves him, ostensibly because she believes his political activity occasioned their child's death but actually because she is infatuated with a bachelor sportsman, Percy Dalrymple.

Everard, who knows the murderers of his son, relentlessly attempts to bring them to justice but is confronted by formidable legal and social obstacles. Lonely and unsupported by the local farmers and gentry, he falls in love with Aileen Greville, the wife of his neighbor. Aileen at first reciprocates his affection but later refuses to abandon her husband and children.

Sally, disillusioned with Percy, begs to return and Everard generously assents, but the terrorists strike before she can reach him. Again they escape punishment.

The Distance and the Dark is the tragedy of a well-intentioned man who finds himself trapped by malevolent forces which, no matter how he opposes them, overcome and destroy him. Although it is a bit protracted, it is a sophisticated, deftly crafted and satisfying novel. It is an engrossing exploration of characters and loyalties under the stress of extraordinary events. The chilling dramatic moments never spill over into melodrama and are effective because they are handled with subtlety.

> *Francis Griffith, in a review of "The Distance and the Dark," in* America, *Vol. 128, No. 14, April 14, 1973, p. 340.*

DOUGLAS DUNN

Terence de Vere White has already written many novels on Anglo-Irish themes, and a non-fictional study of the Anglo-Irish. *The Distance and the Dark* is more turbulent than any of these. Mr White dramatises the fate of an Anglo-Irish landowner singled out for attention by the IRA, or rather an affiliated violent group known as the Gallowglass. Ironically, he is the only one among his neighbours of the same social position who 'feels' Irish. There are bombings, shootings, and intimidations, and Mr White comes down severely on an ineffectual Irish government, on tight-lipped, puritanical or conniving villagers, on the IRA, and the inability of the Anglo-Irish to put some service in. Harvey's failed marriage to an English bitch parallels the public disasters but the novel is overly tragic, and although Mr White is a skilful judger of pace, he is, at times, a bit repetitive. Many characters are stereotypes, and, in the Irish context, that is its own comment. The pity of recent Irish history is that it is populated with blandness in high places, men who yield too easily to what was thought before, the sentiment of the streets. It was too early in the day to write this book—it bears the marks of haste and formula, and although its implied judgments contain much genuine pathos, they are unsettled, and this may well lead readers into believing them biased. (p. 774)

> *Douglas Dunn, "Black Destinies," in* New Statesman, *Vol. 85, No. 2201, May 25, 1973, pp. 773-75.*

HAYDEN MURPHY

Mr. de Vere White's characters in [*The Distance and the Dark*] are, despite the social class he may try to portray, all doggedly paper thin, pennant bearing, middle class dullards.

The plot is of tabloid depth and seems to be a mish-mash of various incidents that have occurred in this island over the last few years. Protestant landowner Everard Harvey with his silly second wife called Sally and a catatonic coterie of friends becomes involved in an I.R.A. plot. It is not really the I.R.A. but rather one of their tail wings colourfully called 'The Gallowglass'. His informant, a loyal serf straight out of Canon Sheehan, his son and a nurse are blown up by a car bomb set for him. Revenge and a sub plot involving renegade wife and loathesome cad, set-piece racing scene, compulsive homosexual, and a 'character' carrying a gossip dimension of bosom bring the book to its sober end.

And a sobering book it is. Why a mind as eruditely closed, a wit as clear and a writer as experienced as Mr. de Vere White ever allowed his theme to escape from a conservative after dinner conversation is perplexing. These are not simple days where all the 'baddies' are on one side. Despite, or maybe because, of the liberal meanderings of Harvey this becomes a dangerous book in the hands of either an ill informed Irishman or an outsider curious about our 'problem'. Its simplistic re-hash of history just will not do particularly from a man of Mr. de Vere White's prestige. Those who read his *Sunday Tele-graph* column will realise that 'men of violence' could not expect any support from him, but to deliberately introduce this theme and then to scurry behind insipid pastiche is cowardly.

Unlike a number of people, mainly people who neither read him or have his dedication to writing, I have found Mr. de Vere White in the past an entertaining novelist. However after this slight piece of myopic mischief I doubt if I will go to the trouble in future. (p. 114)

> Hayden Murphy, "Nice Cautery," in The Dublin Magazine, Vol. 10, No. 2, Summer, 1973, pp. 113-14.

THE TIMES LITERARY SUPPLEMENT

Cheerfully tooling—and on occasion, it must be conceded, even toiling—its way round the nooks and corners of the Lon-don-Dublin literary scene, *The Radish Memoirs* busies itself inspecting some of the dirty-pranks departments of the letters business, anxious to prevent at least some literary venials and violents from lurking unseen. The novel delightedly charts the series of flutterings in the cultural dovecotes caused by news of the impending publication of the memoirs of Sir Romney Radish, radical man of letters, energetic hobnobber with the famous and notorious, and egregiously lustful midget (his friends know him as Runty; others recall Pope).

Eleanor Hartley and her husband Leonard are in quite a tizzy since she has been generously free, not only with the week-ending hospitality that has made her much mentioned in the literary memoirs of the 1930s, but also with her own person. Always sharply tuned in to signals of budding reputations, she also worked on the liberal principle of repairing—again and again—the human loss of Fanny Brawne's refusal to give her-self to Keats. Her house, Bloomdale, is of course now no longer what once it was when it was serving as "epicentre of the creative volcano", and Eleanor has very little going for her now except memories of what Lawrence did and what Huxley said to the gardener. But, anxious though she is to feature in memoirs, Romney's might hurt her pride—after all they quar-relled over his new false teeth. And there's also the consid-erable threat to her mulish and aging offspring's belated mar-riage to his colonel's daughter: the Chetwynd-Skopwiths, "third-best family in the border counties", aren't amused by "third-rate literary gossip".

Eleanor's bright emptiness and knowing prattle are never less than exactly and devotedly observed (her plight brings to her mind "dear Tom: 'And I Tiresias have fore-suffered all'"), and equally aptly placed is Leonard's numbly accommodating acquiescence in her outside interests: he grins and forces him-self to bear it to the tune of her smugly squawking assurances about the perfect understanding and rare maturity of their re-lationship.

Much more turbulently possessive about his woman, however, is Angus MacDonnell, a disgruntled scribbler, "born in bloody Australia and thrown into Fleet Street at twenty years of age", and now lightening the tax burden in Ireland. He once enjoyed a certain success with *In the Spring a Young Man's Fancy*, but perhaps because, as he plaintively insists, "to be an artist and to come from Australia is like being a pock-marked beauty queen", he is increasingly unremembered in the offices of publishers and literary editors. Natively aggressive, he refuses to take lying down his wife's embroidered tales of rape by Romney on a scratchy Madagascan beach. Not for him Lionel's gentlemanly legal menacing of Haymaker's, Radish's fast-buck publishers—the one owned by the fish-and-chip-shop million-aire. MacDonnell goes in rather for the more fruitless accost direct, incited by visions of Radish tearing off his wife's blouse behind a tropical plant at a nuclear disarmament conference.

No less briskly, Terence de Vere White goes in for jeering at the peccadilloes and vanities of what is presented as a too seamless package of tenth-rate creators, tawdry journalists and chummily collusive hacks. Though he aims publicly to outdo Don Juan in life and letters, Radish privately confides that his secret pride is his parabolical, scrubbed-down tales, "little ivory figures" as C. P. Snow has called them. Radish has also been dubbed the "Aesop of the atomic age" by another per-ceptive reviewer. And the Sunday newspaper which is seri-alizing his memoirs is arranging for a puffing reviewer to com-pare him, "to his advantage, with Plato, Darwin, George Eliot and Max Beerbohm". To be sure, this kind of attack on the grubbier denizens of New Grub Street is available enough for instant mounting—this is the kind of *roman à clef* with several possible keys to every lock—but Mr White does contrive a fairly consistent and pleasing comic level in what could easily have turned into a tedious polemic.

He gets some nice comic yardage out of his appropriate im-patience with the uniform liberal trendiness that makes Radish the world's most dependable signer, protester, demonstrator and advocate of advanced opinions. For example, the moment is neatly chosen when, at a Trafalgar Square demo against the British presence in Ulster, MacDonnell gets duffed up by in-censed building workers for shouting "Rapist" (naturally misheard as "Papist") at Radish in full spout on the plinth. But the novel's warmth towards the only major alternative it offers to all that Radish represents—the bone-headed Che-twynd-Skopwiths—is a bit surprising.

Still, perhaps one must not come down too heavily on a con-servatism that rarely manages to present either side of its case in other than fairly stereotyped terms.

> "The Dirt on Grub Street," in The Times Literary Supplement, No. 3771, June 14, 1974, p. 679.

PETER ACKROYD

[Our] product this week comes in an attractive red, yellow and white package. Its brand-name is *The Radish Memoirs* and it is from the fine old family firm of Terence de Vere White. There is a list of ingredients on the outside, but I am afraid that there is a great deal of colouring ("the ending is delight-fully ironical") and more than a touch of artificial preservative ("wickedly funny . . . vividly malicious"). It can be taken with tea or after any main meal, but I would not suggest that you try it more than three times a day, unless you care to suffer undue discomfort. There is such a thing as an excess of laxity.

The Radish Memoirs offers a smoked mirror-image within a beautiful surround, and our common aspiration should be to become what we read. The novel is a palliative as well as a laxative, exciting a gentle and safe emotion at the same time as it lifts us back into our accustomed niche. Mr de Vere White's world is that of drawing-room farce, a world in which age is calculated on the number of parties held, and death is announced by a sudden auction. Randy Radish is writing his memoirs, as small bores will do, and there are some members of society who pretend to be outraged when they are mentioned and others who are genuinely outraged when they are not. Among the former is Eleanor Hartley, a lady who has sacrificed intensity to variety and is lying to this effect somewhere in the book, and among the latter a second rate Australian novelist known as the Laird of Smogg who should be the proud possessor of something known as the *Cliché at Bay*. Randy knocks them all with a straight bat, treating everyone with the self-righteousness which is natural to a writer of memoirs and behaving as if he were already stuffed above the ancestral fireplace. (pp. 742-43)

Mr de Vere White does wield a style but it is one only by default, and his realism is of the valedictory sort. There are moments of irony and pawky humour, and the protagonists have a chirpy way with language which is familiar in the brightly lit world of middle-class fiction, but no one quite rises to the occasion and the whole novel finishes as an exercise in *nature morte*. (p. 743)

> Peter Ackroyd, *"Consumer Durables," in* The Spectator, *Vol. 232, No. 7616, June 15, 1974, pp. 742-43.*

VALENTINE CUNNINGHAM

Apparently *Big Fleas and Little Fleas* is only [White's] first collection of short stories, but the tinier tactical space suits him as well as the novel's ampler zones have previously done. Admittedly, what his characters have to learn—all they have time to learn—is necessarily not much. But the glimmerings and gleanings of self-knowledge are always scrupulously marshalled. The settings are mainly Irish, but there's little that's ethnically unique about the tales: their coolly contoured integrities, their morally concerned nibblings, could spring, in fact, from almost anywhere in the English-speaking West. To be sure, success in short stories appears to come less elusively than success in novels, but with this volume Mr de Vere White praiseworthily joins the ranks of, to say no more, the very good short-fictionalists.

> Valentine Cunningham, *"Godabout," in* New Statesman, *Vol. 91, No. 2342, February 6, 1976, p. 165.*

ANNE DUCHÊNE

In so far as short stories must contain some element of discovery, the surprise in [*Big Fleas and Little Fleas*] lies chiefly in the satisfaction of finding "life's little ironies" so neatly upheld: the lovers deceived by the husband for whom they have taken such generous thought, the meek unrewarded, mistakes and misunderstandings carefully perpetuated from one generation to another. Set mostly in a politely undifferentiated, unassertive Ireland, the span of the stories is either very short—a lunch-time reunion of erstwhile schoolgirls in a "vogueish" restaurant, the narrator's recollection of his first encounter with white port—or else rather long, embracing a number of years.

In the latter case, one must, necessarily, take a good deal for granted—the writer has to concentrate on the articulation of his story, rather than on its flesh—and so forfeit Terence de Vere White's strongest, rather malicious gift, his alertness to the unexpressed interaction between people. This is best demonstrated in close focus, as in ["**Big Fleas and Little Fleas**"]. Nothing "happens", except that resentment and small revenges ricochet successively off one character on to another. The autocratic millionaire needles his art consultant; the art consultant, who is a bit of a fraud, and vexed about missing his golf, upsets the typist; the typist offends the simpleminded manservant; the simpleminded manservant kicks his cat. It is not a new situation but there are some mordant sideswipes along the way. . . .

Mr White himself is rather wayward: sometimes at pains to load a sentence well, sometimes letting one run to ruin. In sum, though, his stories indicate a respect for the fiction writer's craft, a kind of seriousness and innocence—quite refreshing, jaded palates may find it, in a time of experiment and exhaustion—seldom experienced since the days when, say, *The Summing Up* of Somerset Maugham was seriously annotated by aspiring adolescent Tolstoys.

> Anne Duchêne, *"The Meek Unrewarded," in* The Times Literary Supplement, *No. 3856, February 6, 1976, p. 131.*

DUNCAN FALLOWELL

Terence de Vere White is [rounded and civilised] . . . as a writer, and gives the impression that Dublin is where Nero's court went when Rome snuffed it and where they fiddle still. His prose is what is known as considered. Assembled on the principles of carpentry it is calculating all its effects with the self-conscious irritation of those Irish who have fallen victim to the fantasy that no one can speak English like they do. South of Ulster Mr Wilde remains the preponderant influence in the culinary selection of an epithet and the moulding of a bar-stool anecdote into sonata form. Everywhere else in the Western world the coming of the cocktail lounge killed off the perambulatory raconteur, fortunately. In the speakeasys there simply wasn't time. One had to sharpen up. But in Ireland, disfigured by a grudge against humanity, they continue to provoke indulgent applause and override any chance of clever conversation by their insistence upon taking the floor. In his twentieth book, and first of short stories [*Big Fleas and Little Fleas*], Mr de Vere White circumscribes the deluded vanity of these rancid hams.

It cannot of course add up to very much. That is in the nature of the subject. There can be no creative tension between personalities who in every case regard friends and acquaintances as a tied audience. It is a very Irish trait, this equation between personal confidence and ability to disregard the feelings of one's associates, that truth must always be at the expense of other people. Such tiresome poppycock originates in a genetic inferiority complex of national proportions, and as a result it is possible to see this collection as so much writing on the wall. The social consequences of such an attitude are extremely boring and cleverly set out in ["**Big Fleas and Little Fleas**"] which leads from the lofty and immensely considerable obliviousness of a millionaire down to the orphaned dogsbody who can only take it out on the cat.

All the stories, from the opening fantasy "**Journey By Air**" onwards, are concerned with the callousness of cheap pride, how one slight begets another and the helpless cruelty which builds up as a result. Like egotistical children everyone "fails to realise" and would no doubt apologise profusely "had they known". But in this society of charlatans and flotsam—writers, painters, drunks, whores, lords, *femmes fatales*—the penny never drops. Such theatrical concern for self and the impression it makes is certainly an excellent compost for the raising of eccentrics, the "characters" about which we hear so much. But the luxuriance is superficial. De Vere White's writing for all its arch elegance is perforce a symptom of the sterility which lies beneath. Nor does this seem his proper medium. There is the sensation of loud satin being stuffed into cracked egg cups. And it may come as a revelation to him but the short story is not obliged by an act of God to end with a twist. Despite many a dainty sentence his sense of form is appalling. In an autobiography, he christened himself "the fretful midge". One need not quarrel with his entomology. (pp. 22-3)

> *Duncan Fallowell, "Real Tears," in* The Spectator, *Vol. 236, No. 7703, February 14, 1976, pp. 22-3.*

A. N. WILSON

"This all happened", we are told in one of the short stories in *Chimes at Midnight*, "when the moral climate in Ireland . . . was still such as Jane Austen would have recognized". It is a climate in which the fundamental things in life—money, success, death and love—are far too important to be taken seriously.

Terence de Vere White is a delicate and witty writer who achieves moments almost worthy of Jane Austen herself. . . . "**At Mrs Preston's**", in many ways the best of this collection, is a wonderfully tender account of a shabby-genteel woman who takes in guests, seen through the eyes of one of her lodgers forty years on.

It is said that novelists should not write stories. And, in at least one of the tales here "**Very Like a Whale**", the theme is too diffuse and complicated, and the timespan too leisurely, to make a perfect short story. It concerns the obsessive way in which a woman attempts to woo a homosexual away from a *ménage à trois*, the "whale" of the title (actually a rock) being made to do rather heavy duty as a symbol of the woman's failure to perceive her man's proclivities, as well as being the cause of her rival's death. For all that, there are some marvellous sentences. "In the 'thirties in Dublin a girl like Charlotte didn't know much about queers" would throw light on Captain Grimes's assertion that, however hard he tries, a man can never get into the soup in Ireland.

The range of the collection is admirably broad, and every story has some magnificently rounded characters: Michael, the incorrigible gambler, who fails to redeem his fortunes on Kildonan's Hope; the best-selling author Howard Harper whom the protagonist of "**Caesar's Platter**" "classed in his mind with detergent powders"; Mirabelle, the central figure in "**The Widows**", who, "left to herself would have dug a hole in the garden and put [her late husband] comfortably in, as she put the dogs and cats that she had loved through the years when they died"; Mr Seaver, the publisher in "**Fair Exchange**", who wants one of his authors to rewrite the New Testament after the plan of Durrell's *Alexandria Quartet* ("So much was missing from the gospels").

Perhaps the most technically achieved of the stories is "**The Open Mind**". It describes how a committee, choosing between two candidates for a job, persuades itself to appoint a woman whom almost none of them want, and who is plainly less suitable than her rival. What leads them astray is partly a desire not to appear disapproving of the second-rate candidate's divorce. Wretches hang, or anyway get jobs, that jurymen may dine.

> *A. N. Wilson, "Making Up the Numbers," in* The Times Literary Supplement, *No. 3928, June 24, 1977, p. 751.*

LORNA SAGE

Chimes at Midnight by Terence de Vere White brings together 12 neat, knowing and slightly overripe comedies. He gets most fun out of the spectacle of people's perverse self-defeats. A committee managing by mutual distrust to give a job to the applicant none of them wants, or a punter contriving to lose while betting on the winner, are the sorts of happenings he savours. Sometimes the pattern is over-obvious . . . , but he makes up for that with minor triumphs of tone. . . .

In this atmosphere of amused tolerance he is thoroughly at home, and can afford (as he does from time to time) to doze off.

> *Lorna Sage, "Jigs for Geriatrics," in* The Observer, *August 7, 1977, p. 29.*

JOHN MELLORS

In *Chimes at Midnight*, Terence de Vere White turns his dry, laconic wit on to ill-assorted couples and misunderstandings between lovers, spouses, and parents and children. Mirabelle and Ernest in "**The Widows**" have not had a conversation for over 20 years. One night, Ernest stands by her bed saying he has a pain. She rings the doctor, who says he will come in the morning. 'I'll be dead,' Ernest says. And he is. 'Your father never liked a fuss,' Mirabelle tells her daughter.

White, like Ernest, doesn't fuss. He writes with quiet elegance, suffusing his comedies with sympathy for his cast of misfits. A marriage is doomed because Peter had married Daphne only 'to silence wagging tongues and secure domestic comfort'; while she sunbathes and craves for sex, he sits in his study, 'a man wrapped up like a brown-paper parcel'—but what he is studying is porn, and he finds that more exciting than his wife's 'large soft breasts' and 'electric razor' kisses.

> *John Mellors, "Brown-Paper Man," in* The Listener, *Vol. 98, No. 2525, September 8, 1977, p. 318.*

PAUL TAYLOR

The stories in [*Birds of Prey*] are nasty, brutish and short—as, indeed, is the life they convey. Most of them pivot on the theme of snobbery, distantly recalling the Angus Wilson of *A Bit Off the Map*, though this comparison does not work to their advantage. What is piercing and exact in Wilson's venomous vignettes comes across, in de Vere White, as pinched and crabbed.

In ["**Birds of Prey**"], Cyril and Emma Wolfe condescendingly establish themselves in a terrace which they feel, having once lived in Mecklenburgh Square, several degrees too smart for. A power struggle ensues for the control of the lane that runs from their house to the manor opposite. They aren't very close to each other as a couple, but have a wily tactical partnership that comes from their paranoid attempt to keep up with and get back at others. . . .

But snobbery, in these stories, has the tendency to backfire on its unfortunate practitioners. Cyril and Emma are eventually isolated by their absurd calculations. In like vein, **"Portrait of a Lady"** sourly shows how the divided Miss Mulligan, ashamed of being a Liverpool Catholic, too embarrassed to tell how she has sacrificed her career to looking after a mentally handicapped sister, unwittingly destroys her chances of a job with the Homeworkers' Association by charmlessly harping on her connections with colonels and Conservative Clubs. At the end, still jobless, she merely feels she should have used this ploy more insistently.

De Vere White falls between two stools. The writer on snobbery can either take an exultant delight in the baroque extravagance of his material or thoughtfully explore snobbery's destructive workings. These stories lack both the sheer operatic vivacity of E. F. Benson's wonderfully waspish *Lucia* stories and the sensitivity to another's social sensitiveness of, say, Dickens in *Great Expectations*. De Vere White seems glumly trapped in the spite he is attempting to outface.

Two of the tales deal with homosexuals, but one must search hard in **"Talking in the Train"** or **"Carnal Knowledge"** for the "understanding" and "wide-ranging sympathies" that so impressed the blurb-writer. The former, by nudgingly overdoing understatement, ruins a good idea. The narrator, an Irishman, has sold his small business and moved to England. On a train journey, he falls into conversation with an Englishman, Charles. Being gay and bereaved (a paradoxical set-up), he is quick to misinterpret Charles's friendliness and imagines the latter is attracted to him, an error compounded when Charles helps him to buy a house near his own. Their relationship slides downhill rapidly, reaching rock bottom when, on the day of an outbreak of anti-British violence, the narrator accidentally sends Charles a postcard depicting an idyllically Irish rural scene. Think what Kingsley Amis (who in "All the Blood Within Me" has written one of the great short stories on unstated love) might have done with both the pathos and the absurdity of this situation. De Vere White tricks it out with unnecessary twists and turns. We only realize at the end that the Irishman is telling the story to yet another victim on a train. "I see from your luggage that you live in Bournemouth; it's a place I've always meant to visit." Far from opening up horrifying vistas, this "clever" ending emasculates the impact of what has gone before: the pay-off in these stories hardly ever pays off.

The portrayal of relations between the sexes is dourly stereotyped: the women are manipulative and whining, the men obstinate and oppressed; and there is no Thurberesque humanity to leaven the cliché. In a rather good story, **"Lily Coe"**, the husband returns from a conference with mother to find that his wife has poured herself a drink. This unspeakable outrage has "the effect of a blow. It was almost as if he had found her with another man". This is going it a bit even for Ireland and 1945.

> *Paul Taylor, "Struggling with Snobbery," in* The Times Literary Supplement, *No. 4053, December 5, 1980, p. 1378.*

PETER ACKROYD

John Walter Cross married George Eliot just eight months before her death; in his *Life of George Eliot as related in her Letters and Journals* he does not linger on the nature of this apparently doomed marriage. The title of the book is almost his longest original contribution. In the brief space he allows himself between George Eliot's massive jottings, he simply recounts how he was enlisted and had no choice but to serve. The assaults and skirmishes are not mentioned. If it was a happy marriage, it would seem that happiness did not suit his wife. On her return to England after their honeymoon in Venice, she returned also to her usual state of sickness and so died.

Mr de Vere White, with his own particular conflation of research and intuition, proves once again [in *Johnnie Cross*] that fiction can be a more than adequate substitute for biography. Cross himself is the central figure in this novel, and is presented here as an elderly 'club-man' now in his eighties (the setting is 1924) who is quite happy to be known as a famous 'widow'. He approaches a vapid young journalist, Colin Cathcart, and invites him to become George Eliot's next biographer. Since he had found it difficult to confront the truth about himself, let alone about his wife, his own attempt had been necessarily selective. *Johnnie Cross* gradually reveals the true nature of the brief marriage, and specifically of the honeymoon during which George Eliot's exaltation exhausted her much younger husband: 'She knew nothing of the jog trot pace at which most mankind was satisfied to live'. *Middlemarch* must have been an aberration.

The main trouble seems to have been sex. George Eliot not only expected it but also craved for it—she was too eager for the passion of which in the last years of her 'marriage' to Lewes she had been denied. It is the classic story of the elephant and the mouse: and Cross is trampled upon. He had thought of himself as a dear companion, almost a son; and it came as something of a shock when mother decided that she wanted something more than baby kisses at bedtime. In his desperation Cross plunges into a convenient canal; for once, the gondoliers do the noble thing and he is rescued. Mrs Cross, cursed by that pre-marital sensitivity which she had tried so hard to abandon, understands everything and every second thought is her grave.

The sexual explanation is plausible enough, but Mr de Vere White is actually more convincing in his presentation of George Eliot herself. (His only mistake is to capitalise the pronoun and call her She throughout. It breaks the rhythm of the sentence, and brings back unfortunate memories of Rider Haggard.) Here is an extraordinary woman who combines enormous intellectual and creative powers but who suffers from a kind of nervous hysteria. She is haunted by her plainness, and has developed a capacity for becoming infatuated with any man who cares to look upon her with anything approaching approval. It is a familiar account, but Mr de Vere White has rendered it convincing. The novel offers a substantial portrait of a woman who even *in extremis* remained bewilderingly self-absorbed, able to impose her own interpretations of the world upon those less skilled in the art of disavowal which is fiction's real name: 'Once a fact passed through that great mind and massive imagination,' Cross remembers, 'it became so convoluted in the process that I couldn't recognise it as the simple thing I saw before it went in.'

As his own hesitations and perplexities gather, John Cross himself emerges as a recognisable figure, but only faintly: like a watermark, he can only be seen when the shape of George Eliot is held up to the light. He is an innocent, virginal although in his forties, ready to serve the great woman in any position except the recumbent one; despite the hours of Dante under his wife's tutelage, he remains resolutely and reassuringly dim. It is a situation which George Eliot could not help but dominate and although Mr de Vere White has presented a difficult woman he has not created an unsympathetic one. Her behaviour would only shock those romantics who expect the writer to be as magisterial and as moralistic as the writing.

Although *Johnnie Cross* follows a pattern familiar from more popular genres—that of using real people in a fictional guise (imaginary toads in a real garden)—this is very much a 'literary' novel. That is not only because of its theme, but also because it relies upon a certain converse with the 19th century among its readers. It is elegantly as well as ably done—but fortunately not without that acid humour which Mr de Vere White has put to good use elsewhere—and suggests that what was once easily dismissed as the 'historical novel' has become transformed into something much more elaborate and interesting. (pp. 24-5)

Peter Ackroyd, "Mrs Cross," in The Spectator, *Vol. 251, No. 8097, September 17, 1983, pp. 24-5.*

BARBARA HARDY

In its compressed and foreshortened use of biographical materials, and its avoidance of tempting anachronisms of scholarship, [*Johnnie Cross*] is adroit. It is also occasionally amusing, as in the scene where Cross tactlessly quotes Browning in a gondola, but not funny enough to justify its sour depreciations. The language is not brilliant Victorian pastiche, though tolerable enough as coming from Cross's mouth or mind. This is George Eliot: "I love you when you put on that disapproving voice. We cannot be such hypocrites as to say we derive great advantages from reading the classics and then pretend to be shocked when we see their themes enacted in real life." I thought it might be a novel about two unreliable narrators, but no such luck. Cross is scarcely a dignified figure, but his masculinity, whatever its frailty, is thoroughly endorsed. . . .

George Eliot is presented by the husband who is supposed to be devoted to her as aggressive, demanding, nagging, insensitive, highly-sexed, and a terrible bore about Venice. A note of inconsistency: Cross is snubbed and fatigued by her erudition, though he also says he would be having a wonderful time in Venice with her if it weren't that she unreasonably and unexpectedly wants the marriage to be consummated. The real George Eliot wrote the real Cross a love-letter in which she teasingly forgives his lack of learning and lovingly praises his lovingness. Read in cold blood it is ludicrous and embarrassing, but it wasn't intended to be read in cold blood. Sorting out letters at the age of sixty-one, she hated "the thought that what we have looked at with eyes full of loving memory should be . . . read with hard curiosity." She was merely anticipating scholarship. This book satisfies hard curiosity by fiction's permitted slanders.

The terrified bridegroom glimpses his wife sadly inspecting the charmlessness of her "flaccid stomach", breasts "like dry wrinkled figs", "sad grey mat and legs as thin as arms". But there's no pleasing Johnnie. He also runs away from the whore, whose shapelessness is fat, whose huge nipples are "like prunes", whose wiry black hair sprouts "in all directions". The real George Eliot may have been plain, the real Mrs Cross was twenty years older than her husband, but the image of woman in this novel is a compound of qualities invented to scare the sensitive and demanding man. She is that unforgivable combination, an ugly woman of strong passions. Her unconven-

tional adventures with Brabant, Chapman, Spencer and Lewes are also quoted in evidence against her. (The sad Spencer letters can't be drawn on because they weren't to be published for over fifty years.) For a finishing touch the novel says that Cross never proposed to her. She made the running.

This is not unpleasant because of its curiosity. We are interested in the secret lives of the great dead, and their stillness seems to license our scholarly gossip. Everyone has a go at guessing the Venetian secret. Terence de Vere White's solution may not be far from the truth, though he deals with masculine virginity more crudely and less soundly than Eliot did. Her novels have an uncanny way of forecasting events in her life. The reunion of Tom and Maggie looks ahead to the reconciliation of Mary Ann and Isaac. The inequality of the Casaubon marriage anticipates, in reverse, that of George Eliot herself. The omniscient narrator observes that no one would ever know what Dorothea thought "of a wedding journey to Rome". In guessing what George Eliot thought of a wedding journey to Venice, we may remember her ironic suggestiveness as she refused to tell us clearly what is wrong with Casaubon, whose thoughts were "entangled in metaphors" as he assumed that his long-preserved virginity had stored up potent passion, like compound interest. The doctor in the novel, Sir James Paget, is an innocent by comparison, as he heartily assures the virginal Johnnie Cross that gentle marital intercourse, in moderation, would be good for George Eliot's art and health.

Of course you have to be made of stone or straw never to laugh at George Eliot's solemnities and intensities, but her overstrained highmindedness is the defect of power. In this book some of her flaws, like priggishness or pedantry, are deliberately associated with others for which she cannot be held responsible, like age and a lack of beauty, and mocked, along with qualities which are not defects at all, like affectionateness and sexual vitality. Fiction can always seize the chance to be parasitic upon scholarship. The result in this instance is dexterous in its craft, conventionally unpleasant in its sexism.

Barbara Hardy, "The Venetian Secret," in The Times Literary Supplement, *No. 4201, October 7, 1983, p. 1095.*

LINDSAY DUGUID

Terence de Vere White's last novel *Johnnie Cross* (1983) concocted a persuasive and intriguing scenario for George Eliot's marriage, in her late sixties, to a man thirty years younger, a scenario which took in the man and the world he inhabited. His new book [*Chat Show*] tackles a social rather than a literary mystery, and attempts to show what lies behind the apparent vacuity of the small screen by filling in the details of the life of Miles O'Malley, television presenter and professional Irishman, and providing authentic glimpses of his London life. From the less salubrious reaches of the Parnell Hotel, Lindsay Road, NW6 (which Miles owns), via the plusher purlieus of the New King's Road and Bohemian Clapham, to a final fatal encounter in Fleet Street, the background is as plausible as Miles's charm.

What led Miles to cross the water and become "the Brian Boru of the medium" is briefly recounted: the Roman Catholic childhood with superior friends at the Deanery; the father who held the saloon bar spellbound and advised "Keep away from the women"; the successful business (Shannonwear) in a 1960s Ireland of RTE and Dublin boutiques. Miles's "discovery" ("He was someone special. He knew it always, but television had to tell him where he could demonstrate his quality'') has brought him to William Trevor-land.

Against this background we see Miles pitifully exposed. He has a grudge against the BBC. He looks into mirrors and does not like what he sees, has a rather florid taste in clothes, a hair-piece he hasn't the courage to wear, a weakness for betting, whisky and flash hotels; his sexual fantasies are absurdly lubricious evocations of *houris*. Abandoned by his muse, he feels life slipping away fast. "After I found my vocation", he recalls, "ordinary life became terribly dull." Television has been the ruin of Miles. Not only did it provide him with money, it had the power to give life meaning: "To be on television was to them the closest to God mere mortals were permitted to attain." In a precarious state since his forced retirement, he continually anticipates a relief from present dullness and a return to the public eye. An invitation to address the Alma-Tadema Society, written on lavender writing paper and signed "Lalage Dubonnet", seems to offer the chance to reminisce, settle old scores and gain publicity.

For the most part life keeps pace, just about, with Miles's fantasies, but now a new kind of reality—generally of a grim nature—breaks in. The junketings at the Alma-Tadema dinner are interrupted by the news that the Parnell Hotel has been set on fire and that hunchbacked Willie, his greatest fan and willing messenger, has been brutally murdered at Camden Town Underground station. The pleasures of getting to know his new friends in a lunatic household of Pre-Raphaelite relicts do not prepare Miles for finding the mutilated body of Lalage Dubonnet. The IRA, drugs, arson and murder entail visits to solicitors, and, worse, visits to the police. Life takes over from fantasy for a brief period before Miles is run down by two sinister men in a van.

Despite these Dick Francis-ish elements, **Chat Show** is on the whole an old-fashioned entertainment. Miles and his milieu are undeniably engaging and, like a good chat-show guest, de Vere White slips in a smattering of good jokes, dropping bizarre names and quoting a full-blown *Evening Standard* paragraph.... Those who complain that the novel lacks decorum or a higher purpose, like those who complain that television is worthless, are condemned to dullness and will miss a lot.

Lindsay Duguid, "Abandoned by the Muse," in The Times Literary Supplement, *No. 4374, January 30, 1987, p. 109.*

WALTER NASH

Chance brings [Miles O'Malley, hero of **Chat Show**], into chat-showmanship at the age of 42—and Miles is indeed a chancer, a shamelessly obsessive promoter of himself, accurately described by one of his few friends as 'deeply frivolous'. His chance to shine lures him away from his sound business and his devoted Irish wife, into an English marriage, a contract with the BBC, and two decades of the fame for which he insatiably hungers, as a folk-hero who puts down the mighty and is adoringly recognised in the street. When his English wife dies, she provides him with the security of a seedy hotel and entrusts him to the conniving care of a dubiously-connected pair of Hibernian hustlers who rackrent most of the hotel's rooms to the temporarily homeless. His fortunes, too, turn seedy; the BBC refuses to renew his contract, and soon he is ready to try any expedient that might help him recover his lost public face.

He angles unsuccessfully for the opportunity to officiate at the funeral of a colleague.... Then he accepts an invitation to speak at the annual dinner of the Alma Tadema Society, founded to boost the decaying fortunes of an aged RA, and used by some of its exotic backers as a cover for less laudable projects, including a traffic in drugs that involves the use of a certain conveniently-located hotel. Here the fable begins to drift from satirical fancy into grand Guignol melodrama. Several people are grotesquely murdered, and Miles, implicated, is able to clear himself only with the help of his friend Gideon Russell, an ex-bank official and compulsive gambler, and Gideon's friend and omnicompetent lawyer Moriarty, BA, TCD, an Irishman of a very different pinstripe. At length, when it seems that the chancer's luck has once more taken an upward turn, that he will sell his story to a national daily, find a new mistress, perhaps be reunited with his first wife, he goes for an enthusiastic trot down Fleet Street and runs into the path of a speeding van.

The plot is intricate, perhaps a little overburdened, as comic plots tend to be, and wrought into a continuous narrative with no chapter divisions to mark the story's progression as Miles, self-absorbed and lethally gullible, wanders through blending worlds of fact and fancy. There is a darkness in the tale, but the telling is always elegantly witty. (I shall treasure Mr White's lapidary dismissal of bedroom business: 'It was not what she wanted at the moment, but it gave him a good opinion of himself.') The ironic vivacity of the style, and the author's capacity for macabre invention, make for what is known in blurbspeak as a 'wonderfully zany' tale. But the zany is fitfully shadowed by a serio-comic moral theme. Miles readily confounds the actual and the fanciful; he is too well rehearsed in his televisionary trade to distinguish clearly between image and substance, reportable fact and adjustable fiction. This becomes a playful thesis to which Mr White's book is committed. Throughout the story, and indeed into its very last paragraph, he plays a game of false cognisances and dubious identities, until we are left with the feeling that in his mingling of real and fictional persons, of accurate and misleading perceptions, of realism and melodrama, of the resolved motive and the unresolved mystery, he has brilliantly scripted a chat show that will allow neither the principal performer nor the reader-onlooker to know the true facts of the fiction. (p. 22)

Walter Nash, "Father Bosco to Africa," in London Review of Books, *Vol. 9, No. 3, February 5, 1987, pp. 22-3.*

ROSALIND WADE

Through his ageing, ailing Miles O'Malley, Terence de Vere White presents [in **Chat Show**] the ultimate of human disintegration. Those who depend for a living on mammoth corporations such as the British Broadcasting Corporation will appreciate the difficulty, even the impossibility, of recovering a foothold once lost. Miles O'Malley goes to almost any lengths to ingratiate himself with his faceless bosses of yesteryear, yet to no avail. Added to which, he is beleaguered on the domestic front. His late second wife, Rowena, the one who set him up in the London scene, has bequeathed to him a sleazy bed and breakfast hotel which was intended to provide him with a permanent home. Instead, the place has virtually been taken over by an unscrupulous couple of domestics so that he is little more than a prisoner in his own property. The situation blows to a crisis with the incursion of 'squatters' and IRA agents, and Miles himself falsely accused of murder. A pity, for the lurch towards a farcical element, reminiscent of an 'Ealing' comedy, detracts from the subtle investigation of Miles' character. As a result, some interesting side-issues are insufficiently explored, as for instance his relationship with his first wife, Jean, and her wish to return to him when things turn ugly for her still-loved former spouse.

What becomes of the once lively Irishman and the devoted Jean must not be revealed in the interests of narrative suspense. Sufficient to say that the finale is unconvincing, relying as it does too heavily on coincidence, always unsatisfactory as a fictional device, however frequently it may occur in real life. (pp. 213-14)

Rosalind Wade, in a review of "Chat Show," in Contemporary Review, *Vol. 250, No. 1455, April, 1987, pp. 213-14.*

William S(mith) Wilson

1932-

American short story writer and novelist.

An author of experimental fiction, Wilson attracted significant critical attention with his first work, *Why I Don't Write Like Franz Kafka* (1977). In the short stories in this collection, Wilson employs scientific and philosophical terminology and methodology to explore such topics as human relationships, epistemology, and the nature of fiction. The stories "Love" and "Fatherhood" are characterized by Wilson's analytical tone, satirical humor, and lucid examination of ideas. Kenneth Baker commented: "The intellectual texture of Wilson's work is finer than that of most current fiction. . . . For reader and writer alike, these fictions are ways of considering ideas and feelings that are normally unthinkable."

Wilson's first novel, *Birthplace: Moving into Nearness* (1982), is set in the future on a Caribbean island called Primavera. Taking the form of a long letter written by an old man to his grandson, *Birthplace* also features a series of letters composed by the grandfather's descendants that reveal the island's unusual history. This correspondence allows the old man to discourse on such concerns as death and rebirth and the relationship of language to memory while he attempts to restore order and meaning to his life in preparation for death. Jonathan Baumbach observed: "What moves us in this work are the esthetic qualities and not tragic events, not what happens to the characters but the language and form in which events are revealed. *Birthplace* is a long philosophical poem in the guise of utopian fiction."

(See also *Contemporary Authors*, Vols. 81-84.)

Photograph by Toby Spiselman

JOSEPH McELROY

[*In the essay excerpted below, McElroy analyzes stories written by Wilson for various magazines prior to their republication in book form as* Why I Don't Write Like Franz Kafka.]

> If you mean that you don't love me, say so.
> Remember, we were going to say what we feel.

These words from William S. Wilson's story **"love"** point to the fundamental effort he writes about. But they do not begin to suggest the strange, rigorous, and original methods which reveal and are that effort. To say what you feel, you may have to know what you feel. I think one reason Wilson calls his stories "science fiction" is that the root sense of *science* is *knowing*.

"If you are going to know my books, you need to know what I know," says the main character in another of Wilson's stories. But Wilson's method is in one respect unlike the spirit of that remark, for all the thinking in any one of his stories is, as he has said, "retrievable" from the story itself. If this at first seems obvious, it may seem less so as we become caught in the sequences of these beautifully clear fictions and are tempted to forget one ground of Wilson's search for truth: "Thinking is a social act."

Wilson is true to this proposition and to his reader. His stories are demanding and at times obsessive. But they are enthralling and then liberating by virtue of their passion to find and follow and make observable a feeling, a thought, a thought about a feeling.

What happens in these stories?

Two of them define operations. **"marriage"** maps the narrator's pain after surgery that has grafted onto him a woman—so that "through the extension of my veins and intestines, joined to hers by a hinge of flesh, she shares my life." **"men: the man who ends his story"** looks forward to and moves into an operation that is to be a sequence of amputations designed by the patient so that he may witness the process of his dying.

If the first story is a combining, and the second a separation, the two stories are also alike. In each, the writer's attention to phenomena is so free of irony, so plain in its detailed exactness as to approach an instrumental lyricism like what Gaston Bachelard calls "informed dreaming." And in each, the operation of the mind upon its body matters as much as the opening of concrete surface and function, the "heartbeat visible," the torso unlimbed.

413

I say "as much as," because the mind's experience of alien, identifiable fingers moving over the nose and lips is not only a traced form with grades of mutual meaning; it is also a touch on skin. Conversely, if the sole anesthetic against the pain of being cut bit by bit from life is to be the patient's own focused attention, that attention may enable the patient to receive the information and discover the "principle" of his own dying. . . . Wilson's sentences are contemplative X-rays. The attention in his story **"men . . ."** will focus "on death as it enters a plane among other observables."

The point in **"marriage"** and in **"men . . ."** is that no plane disappears into any other. Degrees of abstraction hold like electron orbits promising and recollecting the cadence of flesh. The palpable logic of deathbed dreaming earns the fiat of resolved continuity: "Everything that happens after I die continues the story of my life." The Siamese hinge of **"marriage"** and the process endured in **"men . . ."** are passages among modes; they are transits—they are simultaneities—through the tissue of whole consciousness where concrete never abandons abstract nor is abandoned by it.

Now since these bonds are kinetic, the distances they claim may be notably active and emphatic. Distance may make for strangeness, and a strange distance may yield unexpected freshness. This is what happens in Wilson's story **"love,"** a dialogue between two lovers. The issue between them is their love and the concept of love, the truth about their feelings toward each other, and the language for these feelings. We seem to have not the lovers but their words; and yet throughout the relentless argument (which brings to mind voices as different as Plato and Doris Lessing), we are pressed and gripped by two distinct personalities so that the differences are intimate and the presences seem physical. This is not mainly in spite of but, astonishingly, because of the distance Wilson seems to put between his drama and his method. Astonishing because the central event of **"love"** is a dialectical demonstration that turns upon the use of mathematical logic.

What logic? A three-stage quest which concludes that (1) love is an open system that cannot be made consistent, (2) there is a positive value in the proof of these inconsistencies, and (3) if you can't prove an axiom, you go ahead anyway and improvise—you construct a decision yourself. (pp. 7-8)

Wilson takes us away in order to take us closer. In the grim operation of **"men . . ."** we may recall the physicians of Donne's "Hymn to God, my God in my Sickness" who "by their love [i.e., attention] are grown / Cosmographers" examining the body of the dying man. But even if we substitute Wilson's "continuity" or "the principle of my death" for the New World of heaven which Donne's straits of death lead to, Wilson's prime focus (unlike Kafka's in "In the Penal Colony") . . . is on the process of dying.

In **"marriage,"** the operation—or post-operative condition—is so closely examined that its function as a metaphorical illumination of marriage shifts, and the two parts of the equation become convertible. In **"love,"** thinking approaches, touches, and becomes laminally congruent with its object. Thinking redefines, and is marvelously redefined as, demonstrativeness.

Yes: "thinking is a social act," and (as the main character in **"métier: why I don't write like Franz Kafka"** is quoted by his harrassed interviewer as having written) "philosophy and friendship are convertible."

So are love and thought. Or so I warily conclude from Wilson's story.

His stories are haunted essays which seem to say a story should be as well-written as an essay, thought through as thoroughly as it is thought up. If these are haunted stories, they are haunted by their own clarity and by the colleague-reader's own sense of the rarity of what Wilson is attempting to do.

But his stories are more than attempts. They answer questions. For instance, "Why is my writing not like Franz Kafka's?"

Wilson is content to surprise us here, but not with caprice. "Questions and Answers" is a pivotal chapter in one of his favorite books, R. G. Collingwood's *Autobiography;* Wilson shows that the question about Kafka is the right question. In **"métier: why I don't write like Franz Kafka"** he proceeds to answer it.

That is, Wilson's writer answers it in the taped interview which is the story. But the substance of the interview is not only the question and its answers; it is the writer, his interests, his principles, his view of the interviewer's view or non-view of the process of interviewing. And as the interview is self-referring in that the writer is faithful to his interviewer in telling her all he can, so is the story self-referring in that it displays the writer's faithfulness to his own experience, a faith which includes the formulation and adoption of an explicit purpose for and in his own writing: to teach himself to hold his own beliefs.

This purpose is shown in a lesson from his life. The lesson is itself a story, an intriguing dossier of psycho-cultural archaeology. Joyce, Freud, Kafka, and others join the ever-present source, Michelangelo's *Moses,* and we (like the interviewer who may play back the tape just as we may read Wilson attentively) are led to a climax of detection expressed in the form of a stunning equation that is one of the three answers Wilson and Wilson's writer provide to the original question **"why I don't write like Franz Kafka."**

For Wilson and his story insist upon what can be shown; they celebrate "moments when appearances and experience successfully survive the interpretations that would annihilate them." (pp. 9-10)

One meaning of Wilson's stories is definition—the setting of (lower-case) limits in the compilation of some dictionary of experience. But a more important meaning is the wholeness and fullness possible within a given self. If **"marriage"** and, then, in its widening range, **"men . . ."** seek wholeness in a collaborative interpenetration of meaning and being, of abstract and concrete modes whose operative distinctness is not sacrificed, **"love"** and **"métier . . ."** think more comprehensively about the self—about its dialectical existence with the other, and with others, with phenomena, and with itself.

Does Wilson agree with the writer in **"métier . . ."** that wholeness, unity, totality are no longer possible for consciousness? There remains an old faith that intellect and feeling are opposed categories. With this notion there goes—even further back than the "absolute truth" Chekhov said he aimed at—the idea that in fiction the authentic resistance of life can be recreated only in some absence of overt abstraction. Abstract is bad; concrete is good. And insofar as we admit some explicit superintendence or immanence or laminate congruence of shape or equation or abstract pattern into the experience of a story, that force or presence must be assimilated to the point of dissolution.

Wilson opposes that faith. His stories may be humble in their clear desire to serve certain principles, but they are also didactic and discomfiting and passionately convincing.

Yet in the midst of their moral rigor I now and then hear myself asking a question. I'm uneasy about it because somehow I feel it represents in me some moral relapse, as if I've forgotten for the moment the lessons this writer has been teaching me. I find myself asking how much observed life there is in the action of these stories. From what density of experience do these stories emerge?

One answer is on view in this preface, and it is the power and rightness of Wilson's thought; and the question that goes with this answer is: What good is your "concrete" experience if you haven't made anything of it? Yet reading **"marriage"** and **"men . . ."** I sometimes wonder what has happened to the body, and I wonder if behind the analysis of pain there lies any acquaintance with pleasure. And in **"love"** I sometimes wish for some sensual vacancy to invade all this clear talk. There are moments in his stories when Wilson seems to me to have "made" so much of his experience that we may be too much less aware of a weight of accrued, particular knowledge of the world than we are of the thinking subject's conscious operations. These operations, for all their generous refusal to be secret, tricky, or condescending to the reader, are sometimes so near to domineering that the reader may feel that some thinness or curtailment is being disguised. (pp. 11-12)

But these stories are processes I cannot step away from. To follow and be part of them is to find new energy both given and gained. . . .

When I think of much of our contemporary American literature, when I think of the masses of literal or poetic naturalism, the commerce in nostalgic rearmament, and all those adventures in parodic or apocalyptic defense, Wilson's stories seem new—perhaps a new form which might be called abstract naturalism. But whatever we call them, his stories are so firm, so precise, so explicit, and so dialectically rich that they call into question the standards by which most fiction is written. (p. 12)

Joseph McElroy, "Wilson's Métier," in Antaeus, *Vol. 19, Autumn, 1975, pp. 7-12.*

KIRKUS REVIEWS

"You seem to have more of the spirit of a scientist than a writer of fiction." So says the unctuous interviewer to the sneering eminence in the title story of this first collection [*Why I Don't Write Like Franz Kafka*] from a distinctive, often disarming, occasionally difficult talent. And indeed the spirit and vocabulary of modern science—medical science, social science, logic, evolution, Lévi-Strauss, Freud—pervade these thirteen sharp or stringy arrangements of near-non-sequitur dialogue, almost-rambling memoir, and parodied professionalese. The emotional ramifications and psychic symbolism of wonder surgery: a lonely man seeks out the woman who received his mother's transplanted heart; an "alien Caucasian male aged thirty-eight" chooses "Elective Surgery"—suicide by rampant amputation; sniffy doctors defend their revolutionary operations—using aborted fetus cells for ultimate cosmetic repair, penis transplant (father to son) and regeneration. . . . If Wilson's social satire doesn't always score and if his obsession with logic and numbers renders a few pieces inaccessible, he seems far more concerned with communication than other *Antaeus* headliners—and endowed with far more humor. Two

stories especially make direct emotional assaults: a Scotsman reacts to the death of his newborn child by planning the reforestation of Scotland; a student-writer widow sends Bill Wilson a devastating letter. And throughout—an ear for the frightening or ironic music in words . . . that should soon have the likes of Donald Barthelme looking to their laurels. (pp. 1011-12)

A review of "Why I Don't Write Like Franz Kafka," in Kirkus Reviews, *Vol. XLV, No. 18, September 15, 1977, pp. 1011-12.*

ANATOLE BROYARD

"The meaning of the story is in learning how to read it," says a writer who is being interviewed in one of William S. Wilson's stories. "I taught myself to write," he adds, "in order to find the boundaries of my belief—to learn how to read existence."

This is an apt description not only of Mr. Wilson's approach to writing, but also of a whole genre of experimental stories as well. In *Why I Don't Write Like Franz Kafka,* the author free-associates to being, toys with perspective, with the harmonics of life. Sometimes the results are brilliant and sometimes—as with all adventures—they are less so. Mr. Wilson almost always begins well in these 13 pieces, but, as in modern-jazz solos, the further he gets from his initial inspiration, the more likely he is to lose himself in improvisation.

I would prefer not to hold up this last observation as a verdict. Whether his stories—they are not "stories," but this, too, is a profitless quibble—"succeed" or "do not succeed" is irrelevant in a sense because they are provocative and they take you to unfamiliar places, and that should be enough to forestall verdicts. I think one should criticize such pieces in the spirit in which they are written, "in order to find the boundaries of beliefs—to learn how to read existence."

I am especially taken by **"Love,"** which is a formal, philosophical attempt by two people to ascertain whether or not they are indeed in that condition, "I believe that I love you, and you can't deny that you've been investigating the possibility that you love me, and the effect of your investigation of feelings, at least for me, has been to bring the feelings into existence." The other person replies: "Listen, we're two different people."

"Whatever we have," the first continues, "we have constructed by probing. I'm questioning whether we've constructed anything objective." "You must love me to go to this trouble," the other says.

"I'm as tired of being overestimated by you as I am of being underestimated by other people," one observes, adding, "Stop seeing how beautifully you see me." "I love you, you love me," the other says. "Don't you feel the tautology? There's no friction."

And so it goes, a lesson to each of us in learning how not to read love, how to let it alone instead of nagging it into "meaning." The mood of the piece is rather like Paul Valery's "Mr. Head," who says, "I know my heart by heart." . . .

I won't go through all 13 of Mr. Wilson's pieces, one by one, because this smacks of the compulsive, the plodding inquisitor, the heavy-footed literalist. Let's just talk of pleasure. At this moment, for whatever reason, it seems to be the sensible thing to do. **"Fatherhood,"** for example, gives pleasure by introducing a psychological premise that offers a long view, like the view of certain historical towns as seen from the top of neighboring mountains, the kind of view that includes elements of history, morality, ontology and teleology.

"Fatherhood" concerns itself with all the male infants who are born without, or lose through an accident, their sexual organs. The narrator has developed an operation in which, if the father gives his organ to his son for a transplant, he will afterwards regenerate his own. The opportunities for speculation that this piece arouses should be apparent to everyone. Unfortunately, no father so far has volunteered for the operation, and the narrator wistfully concludes: Think of the pathos of the fact that we shall never know what could be felt by a son who had been made such a gift or by the father who then regenerated himself.

"Desire" revolves around the thought of people eating light, of comprehending themselves as "thickenings of light." **"Metier"** invites us to consider Freud and Kafka worrying the question of whether the "Moses" of Michelangelo is just sitting down or about to spring up, together with the attendant implications. **"Metier"** also contains this line: "Each failure of irony is the proof of an appearance." I realized as soon as I read this that I had been wondering for some time what to make of all the failed ironies I am obliged to read. I am grateful to Mr. Wilson for this and for other things. I think you should read *Why I Don't Write Like Franz Kafka*. But read it as if you were going to your doctor for a checkup.

> Anatole Broyard, in a review of "Why I Don't Write Like Franz Kafka," in The New York Times, December 7, 1977, p. C27.

KENNETH BAKER

Several of these extraordinary stories [in *Why I Don't Write Like Franz Kafka*] by William S. Wilson, describing "operations," satirize the rhetoric and emotional tone of scientific writing. Wilson evidently has grasped the modern sciences as ways of using language and metaphor, not just as canon of thought. "Every problem of medicine is a problem of language," says the inventor of the operation **"Fatherhood,"** "and this operation was malapropism." . . .

Wilson's writing probes repressed feelings and images inscribed in the content and practice of science. When one voice in his dialogue **"Love"** says "I don't want to think about it," the other responds, "We are thinking about it whether we know it or not. I want to know it." In **"Men: The Man Who Ends His Story,"** a man's design of an operation by which he is dissected alive is a metaphor for ambition, and for the abstract toughness men demand of each other and of themselves. "You will be tempted to spare me pain," says the man to his surgeons, "but pain will be my information as to what you are doing to me. . . . My only anesthetic will be my attention focusing on death as it enters a plane among other observables. As I die, I will feel the principles of my dying that will not themselves ever die." Another story, **"Interim,"** evokes more compassionately a madness peculiar to rationalism. **"Interim"** vividly envisions the future depopulation and "reforestation" of Scotland proceeding from one man's conviction that nature, to be itself, must be rid of mankind.

Wilson writes about ideas with a directness most fiction writers don't even risk, constructing, in his story **"Love,"** a demonstration of love in dialogue on principles found in a mathematical theory (Gödel's) and devising, in another story, **"Anthropology: What Is Lost in Rotation,"** a mystery whose solution

lies in the formality of Lévi-Strauss's thought. Wilson's writing is so brilliantly precise that you need not have encountered his sources previously to appreciate his stories. His use of numbers as a narrative device in **"History: A Story Has Only a Few Good Years"** is unforgettable.

The intellectual texture of Wilson's work is finer than that of most current fiction. Reading his stories you feel the intensity of his attention to whatever he writes. For reader and writer alike, these fictions are ways of considering ideas and feelings that are normally unthinkable. *Why I Don't Write Like Franz Kafka* is the most powerful new American fiction I have encountered in years. A demanding, exhilarating work.

> Kenneth Baker, "Fancy Fiction," in The New York Times Book Review, January 1, 1978, p. 6.

JONATHAN BAUMBACH

This eccentric, often brilliant first novel [*Birthplace: Moving into Nearness*] . . . is difficult to describe without seeming to fall into parody. Set in the near future on an Edenic island called Primavera, *Birthplace* is a novel in the form of an extended letter from an old man to his long-absent grandson, Octavio. There are recognizable human transactions in William S. Wilson's literary tour de force—births and deaths, adoptions and marriages—but the novel is mainly about its own engendering. Its true subject is the relationship of language to the workings of the imagination.

"I have been the librarian of time, able to see and to feel with my hands the shape of things to come ever being reshaped," the maker of this book of letters, Salathiel, says of himself. His is the role of the artist giving coherence and form to fragments of memory. In writing to his grandson, the septuagenarian Salathiel is also seeking to make sense of his own life as he readies himself for death. Letters are included within the larger letter, communications from other members of the family—notably, the boy's parents, Orlando and Olivia, and his aunt and uncle, Aurelia and Oliver. Although playful and at times parodic, *Birthplace* is essentially a meditative work, an implicit wisdom text (advice from experience to innocence) dealing with death and renewal. It is related both in theme and imagery to Shakespeare's *A Winter's Tale* and *The Tempest*. In their sharing of knowledge and experience, the letters occasion themselves as gifts, the written word as gesture of love.

Although composed solely of letters, *Birthplace* has almost nothing in common with conventional epistolary novels, such as Samuel Richardson's *Pamela* or *Clarissa*. Mr. Wilson has only passing interest in the psychology of character. The figures in his cast at times seem interchangeable, defined only by their occupations. Aurelia is a doctor (a scientist in her predilections), Olivia a film maker ("Content is merely the accident of the era," she says), Oliver a poet and Orlando (a once backward child) a father and failed novelist. The Mayan Indian, Delenda Kinh, a godlike figure who comes to rule Primavera, is inchoate and wise. Salathiel, as artist, includes the qualities of the others as he includes their letters in his book. At the end, Salathiel marries a young woman named Yolanda and fathers a child. The title of the book, like a prophecy, achieves literal fulfillment.

A narrative of sorts—the oblique exposition of an embryonic story—evolves through the letters that Salathiel shapes for his grandson. We learn of the overthrow of the tyrannical ruler, Kwant—a figure representing the inhumanity of the past—by the enlightened Delenda Kinh.... Under Delenda's benign authority, money is replaced by writing paper as a mode of transaction. After 14 years of wise rule, Delenda is killed by his beloved Aurelia in a self-devised ritual: He is cut open and a calcified fetus sewn up inside him. His death is intended as a sacrifice, the taking on of the "infections" of his people. We learn eventually of the deaths of Orlando, Oliver and Olivia, though their letters, at times delivered posthumously, live after them. Renewal is the book's central issue. Salathiel gives up the notion of dying, becomes a father and completes the letter to his grandson. The rest is implication.

Not all of this self-conscious novel is as good as when it is at its best. On occasion, obsession extends itself into tedious repetition. The notion that life on Primavera is a "party" palls after excessive reiteration. Still, this odd species of experimental fiction sustains itself at an impressively high level much of the time. What moves us in this work are the esthetic qualities and not tragic events, not what happens to the characters but the language and form in which events are revealed. *Birthplace* is a long philosophical poem in the guise of utopian fiction....

Instead of being a memorial to the past, this book-length letter becomes an invitation to the present. Salathiel finds his absent grandson in himself and so renews his own life as he completes the letter. It is art that Mr. Wilson cares most about, that frozen moment when the imagined world—the world itself—achieves an illusory completion. *Birthplace* as it ends offers us that triumphant illusion.

Jonathan Baumbach, "Life in Primavera," in The New York Times Book Review, *August 8, 1982, p. 12.*

CARYN JAMES

Plato banned poets from his Republic and Shakespeare wrote, "Let's kill all the lawyers." William Wilson's Kwant has a better idea: "I will have no semioticians on this island," announces the owner of Primavera, site of a 21st century Caribbean community. Unfortunately, Kwant is the novel's villain, and *Birthplace* itself is a semiotician's puzzle. A series of letters within one long letter explaining the history of Kwant's descendants, it is full of signs which can be neatly cross-referenced and interpreted. Promising depth and intellectual rigor, the book delivers cultural and literary commonplaces. Using modernist theories of time and language, Wilson attacks capitalists and literary dilettantes, pleads for simple, direct responses to life.

Kwant loses his power during an unspecified disaster and Primavera reverts to a preindustrial society. The island becomes a kind of modernist paradise with language as its controlling force: every person must compose a letter a day to be delivered years later. People create experiences in order to write about them; anticipating the future to which they are dictating the present and the past, they become aware of time as a continuum.

Salathiel (Kwant's son) writes to his grandson, Octavio, passing on in random order letters from Octavio's parents, his aunt and their cousin. As readers, we are in Octavio's position, piecing together the life stories of the previous generation from the letters Orlando, Olivia, Aurelia, and Oliver address to each other and to him.

The youthful idealism of these four in their idyllic setting (as well as their names) echoes *As You Like It* and *Twelfth Night*. Their self-conscious description and creation of each other's identities recall *The Waves*. But while Wilson never relates his work to these literary predecessors directly, neither does he quite let them disappear. *Birthplace* is frustrating because it is full of such faint echoes. (pp. 4-5)

With great fluidity and an effective, ironic eye, Wilson controls each character's distinct style.... Aurelia, a scientist, dissects every experience, while Oliver, a poet manqué, measures life against literary quotations. Orlando, the community's scribe, compiles layered references which are often unintentionally bad puns....

Wilson is most convincing when he allows these characters to push against their limits. At odd moments Aurelia indulges in romance, saying "What was I learning to believe before I loved that man, my believable Delenda, my beloved?"... More often, however, Wilson's stylistic consistency limits each character's development to a predictable nervous tic.

Recalling his youth, Orlando diagnoses a problem which Wilson himself fails to solve. "We did not know how to be simple," he says, "We were unwitting prisoners of our own overwrought style which conveyed our overelaborated meanings." Although the last section of the novel is headed "Coherence," in fact it offers easy simplifications. In his seventies, Salathiel remarries and fathers a child. "I named our daughter Renata, my attempt to govern the meanings," he explains. But the overwrought past gives way to this obvious renewal of life and language too readily, making Primavera seem more primitive than springlike.

Wilson tries hard to make us care about these people, but for all its ambitious linguistic devices, *Birthplace* is really someone else's family album, and a little of that goes a long way. (p. 5)

Caryn James, in a review of "Birthplace: Moving into Nearness," in VLS, *No. 13, December, 1982, pp. 4-5.*

JAY McINERNEY

[*Birthplace: Moving into Nearness*] mixes social critique and self critique. It is on the one hand, a Utopian fantasy in the tradition of William Morris's *News from Nowhere*, that nineteenth century vision of arts-and-craft Socialism. It is also meta-fictional in the manner of the epistemological adventures of John Barth and Gilbert Sorrentino. These two sets of concerns are never fully integrated, and *Birthplace* is unsatisfying on both levels.

The place in *Birthplace* is Primavera, an island-state somewhere in the Caribbean. Time is methodically problematical, but basically we are in the early twenty-first century. The Primaverans have started a new calendar, the year One marking the arrival, by flower-laden canoe, of a Mayan mystic who deposes the European Kwant, neocolonial ruler of the island's Indian-Creole population. Delenda, the Mayan, defrocks Kwant in the public square, revealing a large colostomy bag strapped to the old despot's leg—a symbol, we can be sure, of the anal retentiveness of European culture. Delenda's first decree—not exactly a decree since this gentle ruler abjures coercion—is that all inhabitants of the island write a letter each day, dated for delivery some years in the future. Letters replace sugar as the island's main product, and stationery becomes the national currency. Letters wait at various points in the future to explain the past.

Delenda is welcomed not only be the dark-skinned islanders, who are as quaint and voiceless as the "natives" in Tarzan movies, but also by Kwant's four white grandchildren—Oliver, Olivia, Orlando and Aurelia. The four have been raised and educated together on Primavera, which may explain why they sound, like their names, so much alike. (p. 12)

The bulk of the novel is composed of the letters these four write to each other. Their voices are almost indistinguishable. Although Aurelia occasionally strikes the note of cheerful scientific positivism, the overwhelming tone is that of the self-absorbed artist manque.... Though they are all usually in immediate physical proximity, the dearth of physical and social detail leaves the impression of four hermits in four caves.... Qualities are ascribed but never demonstrated. There are vague references to deaths, fights, meals and marriages. (pp. 12-13)

The arrival of Delenda is styled a revolution by the four correspondents, but its consequences, except for increased letter production and some chanting of Mayan syllables, do not seem extraordinary. Delenda himself is a drugstore Indian via Castaneda. He appoints Orlando, the novelist, to the post of scribe for the island's illiterate Indian population, who must also compose letters. Oliver learns to make paper from the local flora. After many years as the official amanuensis Orlando comes to the realization that he has composed a novel, the fragmentary history of the island in letters, while at the same time serving a useful social role. The point seems to be that Delenda has led his disciples to the Old Eldorado where social

and aesthetic goals merge. It is difficult to know how seriously we are to take this Utopian vision, since it floats in a near vacuum of physical, social and economic detail.

Wilson's apparent desire to advance a social vision seems to be at odds with his post-modernist sense that a novel should be a self-referential object, an artifact which is about nothing, finally, but itself. Describing an open-ended party which is in progress when the novel closes, one of the correspondents writes: "The party veered, for a few days, into a celebration of our wedding, an escapade of social sympathies, but now I think we celebrate the party, itself a rather complicated self-activating old object...." For "party" read "novel." In this and in other passages, Wilson makes it clear that he is not throwing the kind of party Fielding and Dickens hosted. Form is subject. What is finally most disappointing about *Birthplace* is a lack of ingenuity in developing the promise of its self-critical structure. The scrambled epistolary style raises interesting and important questions about chronology and causality: letters posted into the future, a past waiting to be explained. However, the letters seldom qualify or subvert each other. The method seems finally gratuitous. The story which eventually emerges is thin and fragmentary, but the persevering reader will eventually discover that the pieces fit in a way which does not significantly challenge his expectations, that past, present and future interpenetrate more or less as they do in more traditional novels. Only less so. (p. 13)

Jay McInerney, in a review of "Birthplace: Moving into Nearness," in The American Book Review, *Vol. 5, No. 2, January-February, 1983, pp. 12-13.*

George C. Wolfe

1954-

American dramatist and librettist.

Wolfe received considerable attention for his play *The Colored Museum* (1986). Comprised of eleven playlets, or "exhibits," that satirize and lampoon various elements of black American culture, *The Colored Museum,* according to Frank Rich, addresses the theme of how black Americans can "at once honor and escape the legacy of suffering that is the baggage of their past." The scenes center upon characters attempting to establish their identities, some of whom repress past hardships by embracing glamorous lifestyles or by affecting gentility. In "The Last Mama-on-the-Couch Play," generally considered the most effective of the exhibits, Wolfe parodies the social realism of Lorraine Hansberry's play *A Raisin in the Sun* and sentimentalism in popular black musicals to explore the intentions and expectations of artists and audiences. While several critics considered *The Colored Museum* uneven, most applauded Wolfe's examination of racism and self-perpetuated stereotypes of black culture. Jack Kroll commented: "[Wolfe] is as angry at racism as Richard Wright or James Baldwin. But he's just as angry at the worn-out cultural and psychological patterns that in his view prevent blacks from achieving and celebrating their own identities. *The Colored Museum* is true satire, fiercely funny writing that wraps Wolfe's anger and compassion in an effective theatrical structure." Previous to *The Colored Museum,* Wolfe wrote the musical *Paradise* (1985) and composed the libretto for the posthumous production of Duke Ellington's musical fantasy *Queenie Pie.*

FRANK RICH

There comes a time when a satirical writer, if he's really out for blood, must stop clowning around and move in for the kill. That unmistakable moment of truth arrives about halfway through *The Colored Museum*. . . . In a sketch titled "The Last Mama-on-the-Couch Play," the author, George C. Wolfe, says the unthinkable, says it with uncompromising wit and leaves the audience, as well as a sacred target, in ruins. The devastated audience, one should note, includes both blacks and whites. Mr. Wolfe is the kind of satirist, almost unheard of in today's timid theater, who takes no prisoners.

The target in this particular sketch, the longest of the 90-minute entertainment's 11 playlets, is nothing less than *A Raisin in the Sun,* Lorraine Hansberry's breakthrough play of 1959 and a model for much black American drama that came later. Mr. Wolfe's new version of it is introduced by an elegant "Masterpiece Theater" type announcer in black tie, who promises us "a searing, domestic drama that tears at the very fabric of racist America." The principal inhabitants of the tenement setting are a "well-worn mama," forever sitting with her Bible on her "well-worn couch," and her son Walter-Lee-Beau-Willy, whose "brow is heavy with 300 years of oppression." . . .

[If] Mr. Wolfe is merciless in mocking the well-made plays, "shattering" acting and generational conflicts of a 1950's black American drama preoccupied with "middle-class aspirations," he doesn't stop there. "The Last Mama-on-the-Couch Play" eventually satirizes a more pretentious, latter-day form of black theater (blamed on Juilliard in this case)—and finally turns into an all-black Broadway musical that spirals into a nightmarish indictment of the white audience's eternal relationship to black performers. By then, Mr. Wolfe, too, has torn "at the very fabric of racist America"—but not before he has revealed the cultural blind spots of blacks and whites alike. Although the letter of Miss Hansberry's work has been demolished, the spirit of its political punch is upheld.

Not all of *The Colored Museum* is as funny as "The Last Mama-on-the-Couch Play," but even the lesser bits are written at the same high level of sophistication. The evening as a whole amounts to more than its uneven, revue-like parts. . . . The issue raised by [Mr. Wolfe's] Hansberry parody percolates in every sketch: How do American black men and women at once honor and escape the legacy of suffering that is the baggage of their past? . . .

The opening sketch sharpens Mr. Wolfe's conflict. . . . [A stewardess wearing a hot-pink outfit] and a hideously perky grin welcomes us to a "celebrity slaveship" whose Savannah-

419

bound passengers are forced to obey a "Fasten Shackles" sign and are warned that they will have to "suffer for a few hundred years" in exchange for receiving a "complex culture" that will ultimately embrace the Watusi, "Miss Diahann Carroll in 'Julia'," and such white hangers-on as Gershwin and Faulkner.

The other "exhibits" in Mr. Wolfe's museum are contemporary blacks torn between the cultural legacy of oppression and revolt and the exigencies of living in the present. Perhaps the prototypical Wolfe character is a pin-stripe-suited businessman who tries to throw away his past ("Free Huey" buttons, Sly Stone records, his first dashiki) only to discover that his rebellious younger self refuses to be trashed without a fight. . . .

Mr. Wolfe's characters "can't live inside yesterday's pain," and yet they can't bury it, either. When two *Ebony* magazine fashion models try to retreat from their past into a world of narcissistic glamour, they find only "the kind of pain that comes from feeling no pain at all." Another would-be escapee, a campy homosexual nightclub denizen known as Miss ROJ, looks beneath the surface of his glittery nocturnal existence to find maggot-laced visions of "a whole race trashed and debased."

While *The Colored Museum* may sound depressing, it's not. Mr. Wolfe is always lobbing in wisecracks about Michael Jackson's nose or *The Color Purple*. . . .

[It's] clear that the baggage of slavery cannot really be banished from *The Colored Museum*. But the shackles of the past have at the very least been defied by Mr. Wolfe's fearless humor, and it's a most liberating revolt.

Frank Rich, "'Colored Museum': Satire by George C. Wolfe," in The New York Times, *November 3, 1986, p. C17.*

THULANI DAVIS

Near the beginning of *The Colored Museum*, as an Aunt Jemima clone appears stirring a cauldron and singing "First ya add a pinch of style / and then a dash of flair / now ya stir in some preoccupation / with the texture of your hair," you know not to be surprised that she's cooking "a batch of Negroes." When she ends by saying "but don't as' [sic] me what to do with 'em now that you got 'em 'cause child that is your problem," you have to wonder if the playwright knew what to do with them. I'm not sure he did.

George Wolfe's comedy is a smart collection of vignettes, some of them quite funny, displaying a mixed batch of black media stereotypes, many of whom were created by black folks themselves. They are a very entertaining lot, the kind of plastic black folks we've all gotten too used to hearing from over the years. They know they're soulless, lost, and getting over, and so what about it? They parade through, doing monologues mostly, singing occasionally, and cracking jokes about what it takes to get by. The serious is trivialized as the trivial is enlarged, and the causes of their ugly transformations get lost right along with the victims.

I was told by someone I respect that *The Colored Museum* was a coon show, a nasty parody of black theater. I even expected to be offended. I also expected it to be well done and written with some facility—which it is—because I'd heard basically good things about Wolfe's work on the book of Duke Ellington's *Queenie Pie*. But the show is too slick to be really of-

fensive. It's more like a satirical glimpse through Donald Bogle's film history *Toms, Coons, Mulattoes, Mammies, and Bucks*, with some other folks thrown in. Performed in a broad, vaudevillian style, the writing is smooth, effortlessly humorous, and wickedly stylized when Wolfe parodies other writers. At the end we are told that these stereotyped folks are "celebrating in their cultural madness." Perhaps this too is satire, but it seems to be soft-pedaling, calculated to keep anybody from getting mad. . . .

The most interesting moments here are visual: the stewardess fastening shackles on herself; the passengers in rags, looking every bit like slaves on an auction block, but crouched among the American Tourister luggage rolling by for collection. Miss Pat's description of the time passing is most alarming: "Oh look, now we're passing over the '60s. . . . 'Julia' with Miss Diahann Carroll—and five little girls in Sunday school—Martin Luther King—Oh no! The Supremes just broke up!" Here's where the trivial starts to get mixed up with the significant. . . .

Most of the characters in *The Colored Museum* are women—Sapphires to be exact—who, like Topsy Washington, are not fretting over the painful past, but have "everything I need to get over in this world." In a send-up of Lorraine Hansberry's *Raisin in the Sun*, we have several of these bloodless survivors: Mama, a Claudia McNeil parody; the Lady in Plaid, an Ntozake Shange cutout; and Medea Jones, who seems to be part Beneatha Younger (the daughter in *Raisin*), part Diana Sands, and who knows who else. The announcer passes each of these characters an award for her performance. . . .

I found myself laughing as these familiar sisters strode onstage. But I left feeling they were more the center of the author's intentions than he wants to let on. While the poor males are tormented, driven, sweating, and serving duty, the Lalas are all self-satisfied, reveling in their own glory, rewriting their bios, hiding mothers, abandoning daughters, tying up the rich white lover. Amos and Andy must have been out for lunch while these women were carrying on.

If Wolfe really wants to complain about the divas or Sapphires, he should just do so. The African slave trade resulted in more than minstrelsy, jheri curls, rap music, and naturalism in black theater, if these are his complaints. The process of transformation, the willful desire to shed the culture in order to "get over," seems to be his subject—*how* we have come to be pinups of decadence, if that is what we have become. Every time I think about Miss Roj, the disco habitué, crying out to her listeners, "Come on everybody and dance. A whole race of people gets trashed and debased. Snap those fingers and dance," I think somebody ought to bring Little Richard by so he can sit that child down and tell him a few things—Sapphire style.

Thulani Davis "Sapphire Attire," in The Village Voice, *Vol. XXXI, No. 45, November 11, 1986, p. 91.*

JACK KROLL

Playwright George C. Wolfe's savagely hilarious parody of the slave ships that brought blacks to America is the first "exhibit" in his *The Colored Museum*, a work that brings forward a bold new voice that is bound to shake up blacks and whites with separate-but-equal impartiality.

Wolfe is one black writer who's less concerned with castigating Whitey than with directing his razor-sharp shafts against the stereotypes and sacred cows of the black culture. Not that Wolfe is a New Conservative, the Thomas Sowell of the theater. He is as angry at racism as Richard Wright or James Baldwin. But he's just as angry at the worn-out cultural and psychological patterns that in his view prevent blacks from achieving and celebrating their own identities. *The Colored Museum* is true satire, fiercely funny writing that wraps Wolfe's anger and compassion in an effective theatrical structure.

That structure encompasses 11 sketches, the exhibits in Wolfe's museum of antic anthropology. Not all of these mini-plays are equally successful, but . . . they fuse into an organic whole. . . . (p. 84)

In an insanely funny section, [two] hairpieces (one Afro, one straight and flowing) . . . engage in a fiery debate over which one will adorn the head of their mistress . . . , who has gone bald through years of torturing her hair. The miracle is how Wolfe can be both merciless and loving while skewering his characters, as in one sketch [which concerns] . . . LaLa, a Mississippi girl who's had to go to Europe and french-fry herself to become a star, just like "the Paul La Robesons, the James La Baldwins, the Josephine La Bakers" before her.

This loving mercilessness reaches a peak in the *Museum*'s central exhibit, an all-out assault on "The last mama-on-the-couch play," which of course is *A Raisin in the Sun*, Lorraine Hansberry's breakthrough play that brought black revolt into the middle-class living room and created a genre that's still going strong. It's all here—the worn-out but indomitably religious mama; her son Walter-Lee-Beau-Willie, eternally imprecating against "the Man, Mr. Charlie, Mr. Bossman"; his wife, who sees herself as a degraded African princess; his sister, who talks in nonblack classical verse she's learned at Juilliard. (pp. 84-5)

"Black American culture is a very fragmented thing," says Wolfe. "We're all trying to come up with some definition of what we are. My absolute definition of me *is* the schizophrenia, the contradiction." At the end of the play . . . [the character] Topsy Washington describes the ultimate party where all the contradictions meet—Bert Williams and Malcolm X, Angela Davis and Aunt Jemima. "I can't live inside yesterday's pain," says Topsy, "but I can't live without it." (p. 85)

                    Jack Kroll, "Zapping Black Stereotypes," in News-
                    week, *Vol. CVIII, No. 20, November 17, 1986, pp.
                    84-5.*

JOHN SIMON

The Colored Museum is a near-musical revue that is young in spirit, gifted in most aspects, and black. Written by George C. Wolfe, . . . this is a sophisticated, satirical, seriously funny show that spoofs white and black America alike. It is remarkably unafraid of lampooning black foibles, which is a sign of artistic maturity. We come of age —all of us, black or white— when we can laugh at ourselves.

Not all the numbers are equally funny and mordant, but the best ones are mightily both. We start with a bang: In "Git on Board," the smarmy stewardess on a Celebrity Airlines flight to Savannah takes the passengers through three centuries of black-American history, from slavery to the ambiguous present. . . .

Though "The Photo Session" and "Soldier With a Secret" are less fully realized, they do make pointed comments. "The

Gospel According to Miss Roj" presents, performing in a nightclub, a glitzy black transvestite whose monologue blending past and present as well as two put-upon minorities is witty and feral, pathetic as well as frightening. Like the Socratic aporias, it forces us to reconsider our preconceptions. . . .

Even funnier and more ferocious is "The Last Mama-on-the-Couch Play," which starts as a deadly satire on *Raisin in the Sun* and proceeds to make mincemeat of every type of black theater and its white audience. . . . ["Symbiosis" concerns] an assimilated young black careerist in the process of discarding the treasures of his youth over the protests of . . . his former self. Everything must go into an elegant trash can, from *Soul on Ice* to an early Michael Jackson album that "proves he had a black nose." But can one eradicate one's origins?

The same question surfaces in "LaLa's Opening," where . . . a Frenchified, Josephine Bakerish songstress [tries] to *Franglais* away her poor-black beginnings. She'll say things like "I told him my name, whatever my name was back then," but she cannot lose the little-girl-lost she once was, who comes back to haunt her. That little girl blends into a somewhat older girl who, in "Permutations," gives illegitimate birth in a literal and figurative closet. This number, championing the proliferation of all-but-doomed babies, strikes me as unsound as well as maudlin. . . .

Aside from a slight structural flaw—two contradictory framing devices, a plane flight and a museum (the skits arch their way in on a turntable, like art exhibits)—it all works well. . . . (p. 119)

                    John Simon, "Wolfe at the Door," in New York
                    Magazine, *Vol. 19, No. 45, November 17, 1986, pp.
                    119-20.*

MICHAEL FEINGOLD

[In the article excerpted below, Feingold responds to a review by Thulani Davis of The Colored Museum *(see her excerpt above). Excerpts of Davis's reply to Feingold follow this excerpt.]*

It's ironic that such a feeble piece [as *The War Party,* by Leslie Lee], by a black theater with considerable glory in its past [the Negro Ensemble Company], should have opened the week after George Wolfe's *The Colored Museum* . . .—ironic because Wolfe's acerb statement about the forms of black American culture is in effect both an indictment of the NEC's artistic policy and—in a backhanded way—the greatest tribute the company could have. Since Thulani Davis's review in last week's *Village Voice* seemed to misunderstand Wolfe's intent almost willfully, I think the subject is worth discussing again.

The Colored Museum is a satirical revue on the subject of black American cultural identity—on the dilemma of assimilation that comes to every ethnic group in this nation of immigrants sooner or later, and that has taken its time hitting home with blacks because their immigration was not voluntary (to put it mildly!) and was not followed by anything remotely resembling equal opportunity. One pole of the debate has naturally been the need to take on the forms of white culture and white behavior, as a demonstration that black people are equal: In theatrical terms this was the significance of *A Raisin in the Sun;* Lorraine Hansberry demonstrated that a black woman could write a quintessentially Broadway play—on a subject pertinent to blacks—as easily as any white man or woman, and that a black director and actors could put it on for the approval of a largely white audience. At the opposite pole was the contrary need to be as nonwhite as possible, to refuse on principle to look for any kind of approval from the white majority, on the very good historical ground that black people had come here under white duress, and after 200 years of systematic victimization had no obligation whatever to the larger society. (pp. 95, 98)

The Colored Museum does indeed, as Davis complained, display a range of black stereotypes from both sides of this cultural debate. But what Wolfe does is hoist the stereotype high to show its cardboard underside, to assert that neither version of black life is complete without the other. Far from denying black history, he reaffirms its completeness: Yes, black people can fly first class and own chic luggage, but they can't pretend that slavery is not part of their history. It's altogether peculiar of Davis to assert that Wolfe's female characters are not "fretting over the painful past." Lala, the glamorous diva who has changed her name and escaped to Europe to become a star, spends her entire time onstage doing exactly that—rewriting her history in compulsive desperation over her need not to be an ordinary black American, to invent a different version of her life. Far from "strutting and carrying on," she's reduced at the end to tears and suicidal nightmares.

If women are, as Davis asserts, the locus of Wolfe's examination, there's a reason: From domestics to divas, women have been the black world's principal points of communication with the white; their opportunities for crossing over have been numberlessly greater, because white society has found the image of black men, from Nat Turner to Superfly, so much more threatening. The black businessman trying to shed his rebellious street-smart past in "Symbiosis," Wolfe's most mordant sketch, declares, "Being black is too emotionally taxing; therefore I will be black only on weekends and holidays." But murdering his past and tossing it into a dumpster isn't enough—at the end of the sketch, his street-kid self has come back to life and is clutching him by the throat, a stage image that says more about poverty and crime in the black community than all the ponderousness of *War Party*. It can do so because of Wolfe's predecessors, because of the entire history of black suffering and black artistic expression in this country—which means, in the theater, because of the NEC. As Wolfe would surely be the first to admit, even while in the process of slugging down his forebears with comedy. (p. 98)

Michael Feingold, "Push Comes to Schlock," in The Village Voice, *Vol. XXXI, No. 46, November 18, 1986, pp. 95, 98.*

THULANI DAVIS

Its opening vignettes set *The Colored Museum* apart from any other satire of assimilation I can imagine. A "spoof" of the horrors of Middle Passage is followed by the glamourous posing of an *Ebony* couple—rather like a campy send-up of the Holocaust followed by an arch parody of Jewish immigrants changing their names. There's something wrong. It's disturbing that Frank Rich, Clive Barnes, Allan Wallach, and Michael Feingold were able to laugh at the Celebrity Slaveship. That playwright Wolfe is laughing is devastating, a sign of how very deep self-hatred has run in the black psyche.

It is also no small slight that the person who gives "I-Will-Not-Rebel" training is a black woman rather than the slaver. *The Colored Museum* is a misogynist work, and anyone who apologizes for it must use, as Feingold does, a misogynist's argument. "If women are . . . the locus of Wolfe's examination, there's a reason. . . ." If he's pointing the finger at them they must deserve it. When Feingold claims that black women have been "the black world's principal points of communication with the white," or that our opportunities have been "numberlessly greater," he stoops to a galling fabrication. Feingold is fully aware that like white women we were restricted from the stage in the early days—a woman minstrel, technically speaking, is a contradiction in terms. I'm sure he knows about our general absence from the ranks of produced playwrights until very recently, and he should be equally familiar with our long tenure in the maid's position in Hollywood. As for the histrionic Lala and her suicidal desperation, she is the prime example of Wolfe's drag-queen-deep understanding of black women.

Black women writers have come under attack in recent years, but their most glaring sin seems to have been a modicum of success. Hansberry proved, Feingold says, that a black woman "could write a . . . Broadway play . . . and that a black director and actors could put it on for the approval of a largely white audience." It's a racist view of significance to hold that such things need to be proved. Hansberry's importance to blacks, then and now, is that she succeeded in expressing something felt deeply and widely among black people. (p. 98)

Thulani Davis, in an extract from "Push Comes to Schlock," in The Village Voice, *Vol. XXXI, No. 46, November 18, 1986, pp. 95, 98.*

SYLVIANE GOLD

The author of *The Colored Museum,* George C. Wolfe, hasn't even tried to write a play. He's strung together a series of bitter, strident sketches about black life in America, and his characters range from talking hairpieces to walking magazine ads, from dead soldiers to flaming transvestites. With that kind of range, it should be no surprise that this piece is erratic at best. . . .

If "Please fasten your shackles" is your idea of incisive humor, it's an auspicious start to the evening. If, on the other hand, you choose to make a distinction between satire and sarcasm, you're amply warned right at the start that this will be, for the most part, an evening of the latter.

There is one genuine, if too-easy, satire in "The Last Mama-on-the-Couch Play," in which Mr. Wolfe rings some changes on *Raisin in the Sun*. And there is genuine feeling in a sequence in which a businessman in conservative suit and horn-rimmed glasses is accosted by his bejeaned, besneakered former self as he's about to throw out his Afro comb, his hightops, and sacrilege of sacrilege, his favorite Temptations record. The tone here is rueful rather than angry, and that's why it's the best thing in the museum.

Sylviane Gold, in a review of "The Colored Museum," in The Wall Street Journal, *December 10, 1986, p. 32.*

ROBERT BRUSTEIN

[*In his review of* The Colored Museum *excerpted below, Brustein discusses assertions made by Thulani Davis in her two reviews excerpted above.*]

Two recent New York productions begin with overtures from Bach but couldn't be more different in tone or purpose. Simon Gray's *The Common Pursuit* . . . is about a quintet of Cambridge-educated whites completely at home with the tradition of European classical music. George C. Wolfe's *The Colored Museum* . . . features a gallery of American blacks seeking to establish their own identity among the oppressive artifacts of Western culture. The first piece, a drama, tends to shallowness, possibly out of overcomplacency. The second, a satire, tends to overstatement, perhaps out of a sense of cultural displacement. Both have charms; neither fulfills its implied intentions. (p. 24)

[*The Colored Museum*] is lively and loud and full of fiery jive. The Brandenburg Concerto that opens the evening is soon undercut by reggae, New Orleans jazz, gospel, and snatches of Ellington, Satchmo, Miles Davis, Billie Holiday, Bessie Smith, and the Supremes. Apparently, *The Colored Museum* is going to have something cogent to say about the clash of cultures, and about the awkwardness of black assimilation, voluntary or involuntary, into the white world. Some of this is provocative: the opening sequence aboard a "Celebrity Slave Ship" flying at high altitudes where "shackles must be worn at all times" and earphones can be purchased for "the price of your first-born male," and a skit involving a prosperous member of the black bourgeoisie who carries a Saks Fifth Avenue shopping bag and plops everything connected to his past (his first pair of Converse All-Stars, his autographed photo of Stokely Carmichael) into a dumpster, finally adding to the pile a contemptuous street kid who represents his repressed rage ("Being black is too emotionally taxing; therefore I will be black only on weekends and holidays"). Other sketches are thinner, less coherent, overextended. . . . (pp. 24-5)

"The Last Mama-on-the-Couch Play"—perhaps the most celebrated "exhibit" in Wolfe's "museum"—displays both the felicities and the weaknesses of the piece as a whole. (p. 25)

Bravely pinpointing the creaky conventions and clichéd themes of Broadway-bound black realism, the sketch doesn't always rise above the level of a drama school takeoff. And this is generally true of the entire show, which is uneven, both in writing and performance. On the other hand, *The Colored Museum* is significant less as an artistic achievement than as a signal advance beyond the imperatives of black pride. It is easy enough to satirize white attitudes toward racial issues (a staple of black drama since the war). What is considerably rarer—and more difficult—is to satirize black attitudes as well. Richard Pryor has done this, albeit with more wit and intensity, and so, with more energy, has Eddie Murphy. But *The Colored Museum* is still a work of considerable courage for which the author is bound to pay a price.

Indeed, he is paying it already. The play has been savagely reviewed in the *Village Voice* by a black woman, Thulani Davis [see excerpt above dated November 11, 1986]. Charging that Wolfe's satire is primarily aimed at successful black woman entertainers, Davis has indicted him for misogyny, hauling him before a feminist court in a display of the kind of resentment that black women are increasingly expressing toward black men. Returning to the fray one issue later [see excerpt above dated November 18, 1986], in response to a positive review

by a white critic [Michael Feingold (see excerpt above)], Davis asserts that the opening sequence is "rather like a campy send-up of the Holocaust followed by an arch parody of Jewish immigrants changing their names," adding: "It's disturbing that Frank Rich, Clive Barnes, Allan Wallach, and Michael Feingold were able to laugh at the Celebrity Slaveship. That playwright Wolfe is laughing is devastating, a sign of how very deep self-hatred has run in the black psyche." If Davis is insinuating that these (mostly Jewish) critics are praising Wolfe for satirizing certain subjects in a way that Jews would never tolerate in their own case, then I urge her to revisit the movies of Woody Allen and Mel Brooks (whose *The Producers* actually *does* feature "a campy send-up of the Holocaust"). There she might see that self-satire is not necessarily equivalent to self-hatred; indeed, it signifies a capacity to transcend one's preoccupation with oppression. As for Wolfe's "devastating" laughter, I believe it more accurate to call it "liberating," since it is a sign of genuine racial confidence.

I regret putting myself in the crossfire between black men and black women, or black artists and Jewish critics, or engaging myself in the internecine battles of the *Village Voice*. But *The Colored Museum*, like most suppressed things finally exposed to the air, is bound to inspire considerable rancor and misunderstanding. It's too bad the ideological climate is still so choked that it won't permit such works to be evaluated on their own terms, free of external imperatives or intimidated criticism. It's that kind of well-tempered world that produced Bach, as it also produced Miles Davis and Duke Ellington. (pp. 25-6)

> Robert Brustein, "*Bach Goes to Town*," *in* The New Republic, *Vol. 195, No. 24, December 15, 1986, pp. 24-6.*

JIM HILEY

Even after its official close, the London International Festival of Theatre continues to bear fruit in bitter-sweet profusion. . . . Now a fast, ferociously witty, all-black American revue pounds politically delicate territory where home-grown groups seldom tread. *The Colored Museum* . . . satirises every black cultural cliché you've ever known, and—for British audiences—several you haven't.

In a domestic melodrama called 'The Last Mama-On-The-Couch Play', one of the show's best sketches, each fervently stricken character recalls a stereotype of stage or soap. They include the eponymous matriarch, a mountainous figure, clutching an almost equally vast Bible, and her son, Willy, who curses the iniquities of 'The Man' with rampantly gesticulated despair. When the boy is shot for over-acting, Mama bemoans his not having been born into an all-black musical. 'No one dies in an all-black musical,' she announces, as the cast swing into a song-and-dance parody of wicked exactness.

But author George C. Wolfe goes further. Willy's sister, a posturing actress, commends the training which has made her 'classical, and therefore universal'. I don't think the idea here is to chastise blacks participating in classical theatre. Their presence may, Wolfe suggests instead, be so exploited as to generalise suffering, and to sidestep the realities of black life. As elsewhere in *The Colored Museum*, a subtle point is made in raucous cartoon style, through a barrage of digs at black snobberies and talismans. Again and again, though, the show affirms idiosyncracy, not as entertainment for whites, but to defend black identity in a yuppified, post-positive-discrimination, yet Reaganite world.

Black British companies don't often embrace such complexities, because they are still (necessarily) establishing the fact of racism, which *The Colored Museum* assumes. And it's interesting to compare this show with the local, white-produced *The Emperor*, which will shortly transfer to the same stage . . . , its smug ambiguities no doubt intact. *The Colored Museum* spotlights contradictions, but its message is proud and clear. (p. 31)

Jim Hiley, "Cliché Crunching," in The Listener, *Vol. 118, No. 3024, August 13, 1987, pp. 31-2.*

Charles (Stevenson) Wright

1932-

American novelist, essayist, and journalist.

Wright's fiction focuses upon the difficulties black men encounter in their quest for the "American dream." Unlike many other black writers who have dealt with similar themes, however, Wright employs humor, sarcasm, and surrealism to depict his protagonists' struggles to rise above the limited roles that he believes society has forced upon them. Jerome Klinkowitz remarked: "Wright's 'blackness' is closer to the hue of Nathaniel Hawthorne, Franz Kafka, and the other great artists who looked past the reality of our lives toward what was really going on. His novels and essays try all aspects of that reality, from the Great Society ambitions to the dead end of the last, drug-spent frontier."

Wright's first novel, *The Messenger* (1963), is loosely based on his personal experiences. Charles Stevenson, the title character and narrator, views New York City both as a land of boundless opportunity and as a sordid underworld replete with drugs, violence, and sexual aberration. Charles is equally fascinated and repulsed by both aspects of New York yet is unable to find a place in either existence. William Barrett commented: "As a novel, [*The Messenger*] is very slight, but manages nevertheless to carve out a pretty large slice of New York life; and it is all done with an economy of means that would be admirable in an older writer but is little short of amazing in a first novel."

Wright turned to satire in his second novel, *The Wig: A Mirror Image* (1966), which several critics interpreted as a denunciation of racial self-hatred. In this work, Wright recounts Lester Jefferson's chaotic attempts to assimilate into mainstream society. Taking the advice of a disreputable Harlem pharmacist, Lester, a fair-skinned black man, chemically straightens and bleaches his hair blond in order to become more socially acceptable. Naively confident with his new hairstyle, or "wig," he embarks on a picaresque journey through Manhattan in search of wealth and power. During his adventures, Lester's faith in his wig subsides and his fortunes turn sour, resulting in disillusionment and, ultimately, physical mutilation. While Conrad Knickerbocker hailed *The Wig* as "a brutal, exciting, and necessary book," most reviewers found its satire unconvincing. Since the novel's recent critical reevaluation, however, Wright has been acknowledged as one of the first contemporary black writers to employ humor and farce to delineate racial injustice.

Wright is also the author of *Absolutely Nothing to Get Alarmed About* (1973), a collection of columns and autobiographical essays first published in the *Village Voice*. These pieces offer an eclectic depiction of life on the fringes of New York society.

(See also *Contemporary Authors*, Vols. 9-12, rev. ed. and *Dictionary of Literary Biography*, Vol. 33.)

ROBERT KIELY

The Messenger by Charles Wright is . . . a first novel with a cast of characters who cannot or will not fit into the structure of respectable society. . . . Charles Wright presents a series of vignettes—some only two or three pages long—that distill the frustrating and anchorless life of a young messenger in New York City. Mr. Wright's brevity demonstrates, at its best, a stylistic control and a consistently implied moral attitude. . . . But even more important, Mr. Wright's narrator sounds like a human being rather than a committee of recent graduates of the introductory course in abnormal psychology at New York University night school. The messenger talks about himself and his world without affecting the theoretical gibberish of an amateur sociologist. At a dinner party of well-to-do homosexuals he reacts with characteristic candor: "If they're so unreal in real life, how is it possible for their sex lives to have any meaning? And the answer is: perhaps it doesn't."

Mr. Wright's hero is a Negro, and one of the reasons he lives on the fringe of the "normal" world is that he is forced to do so. . . . The narrator's account of his relationship with his pious grandmother, the humiliations suffered at the hands of Southern police and Army superiors, his pathetic attempts to join the middle class, give point and poignancy to his later dissipations. There are repeated flashes of humor and compassion in his narration which convince us that he has remained human in the face of great odds. And that is something worth writing about. (p. 550)

Robert Kiely, "Exercises in Extremity," in The Nation, *New York, Vol. 196, No. 25, June 29, 1963, pp. 549-50.*

NAT HENTOFF

Following the decline of Jack Kerouac and his genre of misty disaffiliation, there has been less talk recently about the Beats. Still among us, however, are those who reject the "square" world. They prefer to subsist on the periphery of society rather than commit themselves to full-time upward mobility, with—by their criteria—its debatable rewards and chronic compromises.

In his first novel, [*The Messenger*], Charles Wright speaks for one such outsider. His protagonist, Charles Stevenson, is apparently not greatly different in background and attitude from the author himself. Stevenson is a messenger only in order to eat and pay his rent. For the rest of the time, he wanders—more as an observer than as a participant—through intersecting demi-mondes. Most of his acquaintances are homosexuals, prostitutes, and con men. The messenger has writing aspirations; but in his twenty-ninth year, he is a transient in New York with no specific goal except to move on somewhere else. He stands, as he puts it, "at a distance from life."

Unlike Kerouac and his boyish emulators, Wright views the microcosms of the disaffiliated with a total lack of sentimentality. The fact that the messenger and his associates scorn middle-class values has brought them few positive satisfactions. The messenger himself is acutely lonely. . . .

Hardly anyone he knows, in bleak fact, is really honest, and that realization is the cold core of *The Messenger*. He admits this condition, common to both squares and hipsters, without self-pity or self-righteousness. His defensive stance is ironic, but he can be surprised into acknowledging his own vulnerability. There is, for example, a spare, painfully direct description of a Puerto Rican woman whose drunken husband has smashed their month-old son against the wall. The messenger cannot help but respond with compassion, but then he walks away; there is nothing he can do for her.

The messenger is a Negro; and inevitably he has to confront dimensions of hypocrisy and guilt that white drifters are spared. Yet the messenger's color is only part of the reason for his detachment. Looking at a crowd of office workers, he sees "my people too, like dark dots in a white field"; and he recognizes that "I could become one of the horde, despite the fact that I am Negro." But his conception of meaningful living calls for more than getting "a soft, white-collar job, save the coins, marry, and all in the name of middle-class sanctity."

The messenger does not yet know, however, what it is he *does* want. He tries to force himself into a posture of not allowing himself to care what becomes of him. . . . Nonetheless, there is enough hope in Stevenson-Wright to have produced a book and to drive the messenger at its end to get a bus ticket to Mexico.

Charles Wright may not yet have "found" himself, but he has an advantage over the more self-adulatory Beats in that he knows who he is not. As a writer, he has developed a deceptively simple style that is clearly the result of honest distillation of experience and hard-won craftsmanship. And in this discipline itself there is a kind of commitment.

Nat Hentoff, "Neo-Beat," in The Reporter, *Vol. 29, No. 1, July, 1963, p. 40.*

VICTOR S. NAVASKY

In critical discussions of Claude Brown's moving autobiography, *Manchild in the Promised Land* one happy discovery recurs with the frequency of rats in a tenement—that Brown managed to emerge "without bitterness." The realization that an ignorant, delinquent Negro can survive the degradations of Harlem life and go on to good citizenship and bookwriting, (not to mention law school and the intention to defeat Adam Clayton Powell for Congress) is apparently an occasion for celebration. After all, the implicit logic goes, if Brown can triumph over his oppressive environment then so can others. The unstated premise is, of course, that the others aren't trying hard enough and that's where the *real* blame lies, not with white hypocrisy, exploitation, prejudice, apathy.

The Wig, Charles Wright's ugly second short novel, is a book about the others. Like its predecessor, *The Messenger*, it is peopled with a procession of transvestites, junkies, schizophrenics, ladies of the night, twilight and daylight, and just plain thieves, all inhabiting the surreal subworld of the young Negro narrator. If *Manchild* is a story of hope told without rancor, *The Wig* is a tale of bitterness told with malice, alleviated only by satiric relief. Mr. Wright has lots of talent but little compassion. White folks won't find much to celebrate in *The Wig*.

Narrator Lester Jefferson's aim in life is to join the Great Society, i.e., the great white world. At the beginning of the novel he employs Silky Smooth Hair Relaxer to convert his kinky head of hair to burnished silken curls. His "wig" (slang for hair) is to be his badge of entry to this other world. Lamenting only that "If my parents had been farsighted I would have gone to bed with a clothespin on my nose" he sets out on his episodic, morbid, occasionally hilarious journey. (p. 4)

The cast of characters Lester encounters have vast comic potential. They include Miss Sandra Hanover, nee Alvin Brown, whose black stubble is visible under two layers of hormone powder; Little Jimmy Wishbone, who Tommed his way to movie stardom signing checks with X's (for public relations purposes), and now wants to appeal his downfall to the Supreme Court. ("I worked for the government, man. I kept one hundred million colored people contented for years"); Nonnie Swift, the Negro who claims she is a Creole but is living in Harlem so that her baby (she doesn't really have one) can see how the underprivileged live; Duke, a *National Review*-reading pusher with a collection of "antiques" which include such items as an expensive, brassy hose nozzle dented by human skulls, and a hunk of hair from a Georgia policeman's dog; and an omnipotent undertaker named Mr. Fishback, who dispenses fake credit cards.

The trouble is that with the exception of Little Jimmy Wishbone, a truly inspired creation, these characters don't transcend the ideas behind them. They seem to pass by, like the Negroes in blackface at the Mardi Gras Zulu Parade, without really engaging the reader or each other. Each has his own *shtick*, but that is about all. Nevertheless, the author has done more than portray a moral slum. On a conceptual level, in a way reminiscent of Ralph Ellison's *Invisible Man*, the varying guises adopted by his people suggest the ambiguous relationship man's social masks bear to his true identity. And in a masochistic, searing climax, he seems to argue, with James Baldwin, that the Negro may be damaged beyond repair, that only through continued pain and self-inflicted suffering can he make contact with reality.

The Wig is a disturbing book by a man with a vicious, significant talent. One assumes that despite the ambitions of his protagonist, the author has only contempt for white kudos—and would rather be Wright than a member of the Great Society. It is therefore ironic that, with the publication of *The Wig,* he becomes the first certified Negro black humorist. (pp. 4-5)

> Victor S. Navasky, "With Malice toward All," in The New York Times Book Review, *February 27, 1966, pp. 4-5.*

CONRAD KNICKERBOCKER

Charles Wright's Negro world explodes with the crazy laughter of a man past caring. In *The Wig,* he strops his razor on white men's intentions and then lunges for the jugular vein, but one cannot be sure it is our neck he is after, or his own. He joins James Baldwin to testify that the worst burden the Negro must bear is not racial discrimination, but self-loathing.

The Wig saves its deepest contempt for the Negroes who accept at face value the roles the white world imposes on them. Malevolent, bitter, glittering, the book calls a plague on both houses and thumbs its nose at everything in between.

Like *The Messenger,* Mr. Wright's excellent first novel, *The Wig* is a comic portrait of the loser as a young man. Its narrator, Lester Jefferson, hungry as a Greek mountain dog, sequestered in the racial outhouse, wants his share of the Great Society—pretty girls, credit cards, and fine shoes. He has already tried being a Negro, which means masquerading as an Arab waiter in a Greenwich Village coffee house and tap dancing in front of the Empire State Building for $1.27 a week. Nor can he make it as a Spaniard, American Indian, or Jew. His social security card is silent on the point of whether or not he is human. It is time for a miracle. . . .

Silky Smooth turns Lester's wig into a rich reddish-golden cascade. He sets forth to make his fortune, filled with dreams of being able to leap from the ocean and shake the water triumphantly from his hair like any white boy. At last, he has "a dog's sense of security."

But Silky Smooth is not divine grace, and Lester's sub-basement world contains no doors leading upward. His new wig, like every other gimmick foisted off the Negro, merely gives him false hope. In the weird carnival of people Lester encounters, Mr. Wright categorizes the disguises the Negro assumes in order to survive. Most of these roles are escapist in nature; some are fraudulent; a few are evil. And all, according to him, are as funny, quite literally, as hell.

Mr. Wright's Harlem is almost as nightmarish as the real thing. Human hair rugs, clipped from "live Negro traitors," are on sale in a department store. A shop window advertises coats of arms done on "rat proof antique paper." The police wear Brooks Brothers shirts, and their night sticks are trimmed with lilies of the valley. A group of Black Muslims sells chances on a special armored tank guaranteed to go from New York to Georgia and back on a gallon of gas. . . .

Mr. Wright's style, as mean and vicious a weapon as a rusty hacksaw, is the perfect vehicle for his zany pessimism. On Lester's visit to Fifth Avenue, "gouty, snobbish mongrel dogs howled discontentedly. Infected infants sat in Rolls-Royce baby carriages guarded by guant nursemaids. Good Humor men equipped with transistor laughing machines hawked extrasensory and paranoiac ice-cream bars. The unemployed formed a sad sea in front of the apartment buildings . . . while merry apartment wives peered from plate-glass windows, hiding smiles behind Fascisti silk fans."

In Mr. Wright's view, the whole gamut of Negro behavior—even drugs and sex—involves one form or another of "Tomming it:" being like Uncle Tom. Like all good satirists, he sees no hope. His jibes confirm the wounds no Great Society will ever salve, and his laughter has no healing powers. *The Wig* is a brutal, exciting, and necessary book.

> Conrad Knickerbocker, "Laughing on the Outside," in The New York Times Book Review, *March 5, 1966, p. 25.*

WILLIAM JAMES SMITH

The Negro novelist today is faced with a peculiar dilemma. On the one hand his work is sought eagerly by publishers and readers, and on the other hand the nature of his work is circumscribed by a number of preconceptions. He has to talk about "race." The white novelist may talk about race if he wishes to, but the Negro is obliged to, whatever his predilections.

That the injustices of their situation is a burning matter to most Negro writers is certainly to be expected, but that they should all be exclusively preoccupied with it is hardly realistic. "Bitter social protest" is a phrase that the Negro novelist knows will automatically be used to describe his book, no matter what he says in it. It was used, for example, to describe Mr. Wright's first novel, *The Messenger,* and it will inevitably be used for his second, *The Wig.* But both books are social protest only in the sense that any work which attempts to tell the unsparing truth about life is a social protest. The white masochist who wants to scourge himself once more for what he is doing to the Negro will find few kicks in Mr. Wright's books. Mr. Wright's eye is jaundiced indeed but he tends to see black and white alike in a similar unflattering light.

Mr. Wright's predicament as a novelist is complicated by the fact that he is basically a humorist—"black humorist" he calls himself. This is overt in *The Wig* but it was apparent even in the more conventionally serious first novel. *The Wig,* in fact, very nearly goes overboard with its humor. In it Mr. Wright joins the Pop Art School, which is in great danger of becoming a cliché before it fairly gets started. Lester Jefferson, his hero from Harlem, experiments with a bottle of hair-straightener and the life it promises to open out for him. His new hair, "the wig," promises a great deal but produces nothing except the same old frustrations.

The novel is short, episodic, bizarre. It succeeds best when it tries most casually, as with Lester's "Creole" neighbor Nonnie Swift, a widow of fancied elegance and a continual imaginary pregnancy—and least when it tries hardest, as when Lester and Little Jimmie Wishbone, the ancient movie star, try to break into the pop music field. But there are a number of successfully funny incidents, such as Lester's job as publicity agent for The King of Southern-Fried Chicken. . . . (p. 182)

Unfortunately the novel is not successful as a whole. I attribute this not so much to any lack of talent on Mr. Wright's part as to a misplaced faith in the whole notion that the Pop Art silliness can sustain attention even for the length of a quite short novel. It is a recalcitrant aspect of literary humor that you have to believe in the characters in a novel before you can regard their doings as more than flickeringly funny—or, for that matter, before you can take much interest in the characters whatsoever. It is the shortcoming of the Pop Art approach that the characters tend to be unbelievable even in the most elementary sense in which Popeye, say, is believable, or Jack Benny is believable.

Lester Jefferson is not so much a real person as a rack on which to hang a wig or a comic costume. And he is unreal for the oddest of reasons—he is too complicated for the comic strip-atmosphere in which he moves. If he were simpler, "less real," he would be more real. Mr. Wright has attempted to weld two irreconcilable elements. Lester with one or two simple traits (Popeye's spinach or Jack Benny's avariciousness) might have worked. The alternative was a much more ambitious novel which could have fleshed out Lester to full size. This latter was obviously not what Mr. Wright intended.

All of which strictures do not take away Mr. Wright's real accomplishments—a dose of dark laughter and the pleasure of watching an artist who is being venturesome in dangerous directions. He has that quality which is most admirable and most promising—the refusal to deliver *quite* what is expected. Mr. Wright may make a "bitter social protest" but he will do it in his own sweet way. (pp. 182-83)

> *William James Smith, in a review of "The Wig," in*
> Commonweal, *Vol. LXXXIV, No. 6, April 29, 1966,*
> *pp. 182-83.*

FRANCES S. FOSTER

When the Black protagonist of *The Wig,* Lester Jefferson, discovered his hair had turned "a burnished red gold," he said, "At least I was the first. . . . a minority within a minority." These words could have been spoken just as well by Charles Stevenson Wright when certain white critics began to agree with Victor Navasky's judgment that Wright as author of *The Wig* is "the first certified Negro black humorist" [see excerpt above]. Disregarding the ideas of whether he actually is the first and of what *certified* actually implies, the fact that he is so proclaimed places him as a "minority within a minority." Like any other Black Humorist, he is isolated from the American literary mainstream by his constant concern with a realization of new perspectives on all aspects of reality: one which includes a search for new artistic means of presenting contemporary experience as well as a question of the established ideas concerning the reality of this experience. However, like any other Black author, he is because of his race generally isolated from even the Black Humor tributary of American literature. Yet being a Black Humorist, he represents a deviation from what is considered the usual course of the Black writer. Nevertheless, Charles Stevenson Wright does fit the criteria of Black Humor. He shares the same slightly-raised-eyebrow attitude about the same concerns as the other authors included in that casually coined term of Black Humor. (p. 44)

In general Black Humorists are among those who have concluded that traditional Western literature ultimately fails in its primary aim: that of exploring and explaining the meaning and relationship of man to himself, his society, and the universe, or, in other words, to life. They are concerned that traditional

Western literature has through its usual means of selecting and ordering somehow missed the essence of the reality of (at least) contemporary existence. Rather than considering life as literature usually shows it as an orderly progression of events, they have discovered that life is simultaneously comic, tragic, humane, inhumane, unpredictable and seemingly illogical. In short, it is absurd. Unlike most existentialists who in traditionally structured and polished literary works argue the absurdity of life, the Black Humorists maintain that a literature which arbitrarily selects its topics, incidents and events and which adheres to an equally arbitrary literary structure is not only misleading, it is fraudulent. Thus they seek alternatives to Aristotle and Henry James. They seek to discuss what has heretofore been ignored and they seek new forms which can be integrated with these new subjects in an effort to present alternative concepts of reality. In short, they are characterized by dispassionate attempts to exhaust the varieties of possible experience in an effort to challenge the traditional concepts of temporal, spatial, and causal order while searching for the Reality(ies) of existence. . . . Charles Wright like other Black Humorists does not theorize, he presents his novel and through its form and content we see his suggested reality.

One way in which he differs from tradition is through his development of plot. (pp. 44-5)

In *The Wig* there is a plot or sequence of events that make up a story. Lester Jefferson is attempting to join The Great Society. He says, "Everyone seemed to jet toward the goal of The Great Society, while I remained in the outhouse, penniless, without 'connections'. . . . I had to make it." Therefore, he Silky Smooths his hair, attempts to attain the dream of overnight success and then to succeed in the Horatio Alger tradition. He ends up as a chicken man wearing a suit of electrified feathers and crawling on his hands and knees ten hours a day, five and a half days a week for ninety dollars a week. He also masquerades as a Swede, uses credit cards, and collects rat pelts in an effort to win his "All-American Girl," The Deb. All efforts fail. Deciding that his "impersonation had caused the death of a bright dream," he visits Madame X, but rejects her offer of ritual, marijuana, and money as the realities with which to replace the American Dream. Then he discovers his wig has turned red-gold. He is picked up by a mysterious woman who offers him money to become her lover. He finally runs into Mr. Fishback who, following another concept of reality, shaves his head and renders him impotent.

The book, however, contains many episodes which have little or nothing to do with this plot. The false labor of Nonnie's false pregnancy is one example of the extraneous incidents. There is also an extended description of a walk through Harlem where "Everything's still the same . . . But it's different now." There is the meeting with the mother who kills her son because he doesn't want to attend a segregated school. There is the appearance and disappearance of Little Jimmie Wishbone which does not form a sub-plot or double plot but which simply enters Lester's life, parallels the action for a while then exits. There is the episode of the rat fight. Finally, the marijuana session with The Duke is still another of the numerous examples of incidents unrelated to the main action.

Not only is much of the action unrelated, but it is also unmotivated. There is no foreshadowing nor reason given for Nonnie's imaginary pregnancy, for Miss Sandra Hanover's decision to go to Europe, for Mrs. Tucker's death, or even for Lester's decision to leave the mysterious woman and to acquiesce to Mr. Fishback's solution.

Although Mr. Fishback seems to have connections with several of the characters, the exact relationship to these persons and the degree of his responsibility for any one incident is always obscure. Thus coincidence or chance appears to bring about most of the climactic incidents. Lester accidently meets The Deb. His hair accidentally turns red. He accidentally meets the mysterious lady in Central Park. He also just happens to meet Mr. Fishback who tells him The Deb is dead and who provides a solution to his dilemma.

Unmotivated action, chance, and coincidence are vital to the novel. This is contrary to the tradition that novels must make order from chaos and that fiction must be less strange than fact. Instead, their emphasis supports an idea of irrationality in life. This is not the same as merely copying chaos, nor is it simply a rebellious "anti-novel" technique. It is an attempt to examine, in other ways, other views of life. It is an exploration of reality by adapting, improvising, or in some cases, abandoning techniques in a studied attempt to discover what life is, not by picking examples to illustrate an ideal, but by observing experiences to form conclusions. By ignoring the usual constraints concerning plot, Wright presents an alternative and possibly more realistic method of giving artistic expression to the twentieth century experience.

His use of character is another example of a varied literary technique. M. H. Abrams says, "Whether he remains stable or changes, we require 'consistency' in a character—he should not suddenly break off and act in a way not plausibly grounded in his temperament as we already have come to know it."

Charles Wright disregards these requirements. His characters' motivations are vague. Their actions seem arbitrary. They are neither convincing nor lifelike, rather they are grotesque. They have no specific past nor future but exist only in their particular episodes, then disappear. Their purpose is not so much to advance the plot or to 'show human nature in all its complexity and multiplicity" in order to know or understand people as [Laurence] Perrine demands, but to suggest alternative views of human nature. By choosing a protagonist whose real self is unknown to him, his society, and ultimately to the reader, and by refusing to present any character who is clearly motivated, consistent, and plausible, Wright raises questions concerning the possibility of any reality other than the assumed masks of his characters and thereby questions the idea that man is a complex but rational being and not simply at any given moment a variation of one (or all) of the types presented here. In *The Wig,* a wide variety of characters exist only to support the statement of "Miss Sandra Hanover, ex-Miss Rosie Lamont, ex-Mrs. Roger Wilson, nee Alvin Brown" that "Everybody's got something working for them." Miss Hanover is a black man who believes he is a white Southern lady, "does" people, and plays the roles of leading ladies in old movies. Miss Nonnie Swift maintains she is a "Creole from New Orleans" who lives in Harlem so that her unborn child of a two-year pregnancy will know all the good and bad things in the world. Mr. Sunflower Ashley-Smith appears to be "a thoroughbred American Negro" whose life is devoted to plotting the future of his "golden-voiced colored brethren." Tom Lacy portrays an Uncle Tom who beneath a placid mask has the face of a natural killer and who spends his time counting the deaths of whites. Even the central character, Lester Jefferson, is known only by the roles he plays. . . . Not one character stands out as having a sure grasp of reality. The author presents his characters as harmless humorous examples of modern man's loss of individuality in an attempt to fit into life as they have been conditioned to see it. Each of the characters is trying to maintain a masquerade, to acquire a gimmick in order to fit a pre-established and thus more desirable mode. Not one is trying to comprehend or to assert his own individuality. Max Schultz in "Pop, Op, and Black Humor" describes this kind of activity as a character's search "to realize the authenticity of his self through his identity with its commonplaces" and warns that this leads not only to submission to "a code of behavior more determinedly abstract than that of the Waverly hero," but that this also results in an inability to relate to any other person "because of the reduction of his being to a contrived ratio which renders the extremes of personality nonexistent." This behavior is seen in *The Wig* in so far as the characters are not only anxious, frustrated, and imitative social misfits but also are preoccupied with appearances.

The first indication of this interest is the novel's subtitle, *A Mirror Image*. It is with this clue that The Wig emerges as a multi-dimensional symbol. The author explains in a prefatory note that *wig* is a slang word for hair. The idea that changing one's hair, or one's appearance in general, makes one a new person connotes an identity which is based entirely upon appearance. It brings to mind the mentality of a nation that seriously considers, if not believes, the version of reality symbolized by the question, "Is it true that blondes have more fun?" An example of this is when The Deb says, "When I get my hair fixed tomorrow I will be like you. Almost, anyway. And pretty soon us colored people will be as white as Americans." *Wig* also carries the connotation of masquerade. Clarence Major sheds more light upon the possibilities of this term in his *Dictionary of Afro-American Slang* when he reveals that *wig* means "a man's or woman's natural hair that has been processed or straightened; one's mentality, brain, skull, thoughts." Thus, the word *wig* becomes a symbol for the idea of reality and illusion on several levels.

Exploration of the idea of illusion and reality begins on page one. The narrator, "a desperate man," is finding it "hard to maintain a smile." He is desperate because everyone but he "seemed" to be part of the Great Society. The illusion motif is strengthened by the purchase of Silky Smooth, a hair relaxer, with its Faustian promise, "With this you may become whatever you desire." Les' adaption of The Wig represents a new attempt to achieve what he considers Reality, for we are told that before this, he had "masqueraded as a silent Arab waiter in an authentic North African coffeehouse in Greenwich Village" where he'd been successful in "tempting dreamers of Gide, Ivy League derelicts, and hungry pseudo-virgins" until "unmasked by two old-maid sisters." He now says, "I realize people have to have a little make believe. . . . Sooner or later though, you have to step into the spotlight of reality. You've got to do your bit for yourself and society. I was trying to do something real, concrete, with my Wig." Like the other characters in the book, he recognizes the illusory worlds of others. Furthermore, he seems to be able to recognize specific instances when he has been mistaken, but in seeking to replace an illusion with reality, he inevitably chooses another illusion.

The point of view used in *The Wig* is primarily first person narration, a method which usually increases a reader's sense of immediacy and reality. Wright uses it for a slightly different purpose. Because the narrator has revealed himself as shallow, gullible, vacillating, and often intoxicated, the reality of the view presented is always questionable. Thus Wright can present incidents which pass from realistic to plausible to fantastic with no clue as to how or when the boundaries were crossed. An example of this is Les' tale that the fifth floor of The Duke's mansion had fallen into the street killing three ricket-ridden children, raising the ire of the Sanitation Department, and causing a joyous Welfare Department to send The Duke a twenty-five-year-old quart of Scotch and to officially ax the children from their list. . . . Wright's use of a narrator who blurs reality and fantasy presents the idea that reality being a mental construct exists on multiple levels anyhow. This preoccupation with reality and illusion is Wright's most outstanding Black Humor characteristic and constitutes the central concern of the novel.

Though the characters are Black and the setting is Harlem, *The Wig* is not a story of Black people only. Charles Wright seems to agree with Richard Wright's idea that "The Negro is America's metaphor," for his characters are actually reflections of American society. Les' values are those of the American Dream. He completely accepts the Horatio Alger legend. He believes he has no limitations and needs only an "acquisitional gimic," i.e. education, connections, or The Wig, to succeed. His resolve is fortified by a slogan he'd heard, "You are not defeated, until you are defeated," and he exhibits the famed optimism of the American people. At one point he says, "No, I like drama. I had to be someone else. I had such a celestial picture of being someone else, and a part of that picture was that my luck would change. But had he?. . . Oh, well, tomorrow's Monday." The closest he comes to recognizing his illusions is when he says, ". . . I had progressed to the front door of hell when all I had actually been striving for was a quiet purgatory," but then he sees a girl. Unsure whether she was "a trick of nature or a goddam trick of my eyes" he follows her anyway. Even when The Wig is clipped and that dream has ended, he says, "I smiled at my bald-headed reflection. 'It's over, I can always do it again'." Les is an incurable role player, a nutty-putty creation who can assume as many identities as desired and who may be easily flattened, but destroyed only with difficulty. The conclusion of the novel is not the end. Lester is still determined to make it. Furthermore, there is no proof that this incident is not another of a series for Black Humor is less concerned with the fate of a protagonist than with the multiplicity of experience possible. The story of Lester Jefferson's struggle to enter the Great Society is, then, exemplary. It is a catalogue of some forms of illusion and reality accepted by contemporary man. When viewed from this perspective, the previously discussed extraneous incidents become an integral part of the novel because they represent alternative visions of reality. Like Bruce Jay Friedman, Thomas Berger, and other Black Humorists, Wright peoples his books with anonymous, undistinguished persons. His protagonist is the reluctant hero—the convention any / everyman trying to make it in contemporary society. (pp. 46-52)

Frances S. Foster, "Charles Wright: Black Black Humorist," in CLA Journal, *Vol. XV, No. 1, September, 1971, pp. 44-53.*

DAVID FREEMAN

Ten years ago, in a widely praised novel, Charles Wright described the first stops on his journey toward self-understanding. The trip then was through the semisecret world of junkies and homosexuals. But the demimonde has come up town, and what was once subterranean is now public information, the stuff of that endless talk show called television. To continue the journal of his life, Wright has had to find newer, more private lower depths to chronicle. He remains in the streets, but the drama is more internal now, a private battle waged in the mind. Street life is still Wright's turf, but the young hustler of *The Messenger* has grown up. He no longer carries packages to strange offices and neighborhoods, little bundles of someone else's success. Now he cleans their floors and their silver.

Absolutely Nothing to Get Alarmed About is the story of Wright's life as dishwasher and porter, drunk and lover, in and out of back rooms and Bowery hotels. As in *The Messenger* Wright continues to see his life as a novel, and one of the pleasures of this book, which is rich in pleasures, is that one is never certain what is fact and what is fiction. There is a slide show of vignettes, characters quickly etched, observations on the washing of other people's dirt and on the nature of welfare. This material in lesser hands and lesser minds would come out new journalism. Charles Wright brings it closer to old truth.

Today, as he pushes into his forties, Wright is looser than the young messenger he once was; the tension has slipped from the surface and burrowed deeper toward the bone. The writer has exploded and now floats above the Bowery and the Lower East Side like a Chagall fiddler in the air, landing long enough to wash a dish, capture a moment, skewer a soul and then rise again on wine or Nembutal. . . .

He's an over-wined and over-pilled poet whose truest commitment is to eavesdropping on the world and bearing witness. Cool and isolated, his love for language is finally greater than his love for himself. Wright has rejected the fellowship America offers its outsiders and has chosen to remain a dishwasher. One wonders if he's made that choice out of self-destructiveness, or out of a creative need to maintain the habit of the fictional persona he has created. Art and life sit down to dinner, and Charles Wright is the waiter.

This journal-novel, an act of self-definition, appears at first to be more an act of the will than of the imagination. But at its best, the two worlds—private imagination and harsh reality—merge and hover between gentle evocations of the sad eccentricity of street life and canny social and political views. Wright calls that being "stoned in [my] hall of mirrors.". . .

Tired of the youth culture, the woman's movement and the black middle class, Wright's passion ebbs and he slips closer to numbness. . . . The sad and inescapable conclusion is that this book, about a lost passion, and a weariness that envelops Wright in ennui as much as any wine, feels like the rough draft of a suicide note. I hope not, and I suppose if one confronted Charles Wright with that thought, he'd just say it's *Absolutely Nothing to Get Alarmed About,* and have another drink.

David Freeman, in a review of "Absolutely Nothing to Get Alarmed About," in The New York Times Book Review, *March 11, 1973, p. 34.*

ANATOLE BROYARD

Somewhere under all these affectations there's a promising black author named Charles Wright. He says he's about 40, which means he's pretty old to be promising. You would think with two highly praised books already to his credit, he would be further along in the evolution of his style. He should have outgrown for example lines like "pierced with cut crystal sensitivity"; "the uric sperm of those years has flooded my mind"; "hoarded prejudices beget slaves who impale their masters on the arrow of time"; "mankind prepares not to scale the summit but to take the downward path into the great valley of the void''; "life's eyedropper is being sterilized with ant [urine].''. . .

When is the last time anybody speaking his own language ever talked about scaling summits? Has any black man outside of politics or the church used the word scale in that sense in the last 50 years? What is life's eyedropper, anyway, and why is it being sterilized with ant urine?. . .

Sonny Liston had better lines, on the average, than you'll find in *Absolutely Nothing to Get Alarmed About.* As an uneducated prize fighter like Liston proved, there *is* a rich black idiom, but so few black writers use it. Here and there, Mr. Wright shows that he has a good ear for genuine speech rhythms, but he keeps falling instead into a forced, amphetamine splutter or a drone of Cadillac oratory. In the middle of a nice blues-like scene with an ironic obbligato, he'll remember that he has read Faulkner—but it will probably be Faulkner crossed with a Lower East Side social worker.

When he's relaxed and moving naturally, Mr. Wright can bring life—sad, bleak, painful, embarrassing or funny life—to the drug, wino, East Village and Bowery scenes that are his territory. (Much of this book appeared as separate essays in *The Village Voice.*) Sometimes he's so good-humored in these unpropitious environments that he makes it sound as if being black was a form of entertainment. And perhaps it is, under certain circumstances. Perhaps the human comedy is even funnier when your laughter has a touch of hysteria in it. At other times, though, Mr. Wright sounds all smug and buttoned up. Although he rarely *is* alone, he's always telling us how much he *wants* to be alone, how sufficient unto himself he is, how far beyond the blandishments of poor, deluded humanity. He pontificates as if meditation was his thing, yet he's always popping dexies or drinking enough for half a dozen Madison Avenue executives.

As you read on in *Absolutely Nothing to Get Alarmed About,* a question is likely to arise in your mind. Why do many black writers deal only in extreme experiences? It's too easy: the drama is already there, and all too often it is the *same* drama. Don't any blacks lead bourgeois, or even ordinary working-class lives? Mr. Wright's cards are so stacked that, even when we know the elements of the scene are real, we feel that the characters are self-consciously posing too. The first to protest against stereotyping, many black writers seem determined to create one of their own.

The day has come, also, to reconsider one of their fundamental propositions: that ''whitey'' will never let you forget you're black. In Mr. Wright's case, the patent leather shoe is on the other foot. A further assumption that needs re-examination is the notion that a life thrown away constitutes a tragedy, a ''horror,'' as the author would say. If a man shoots heroin into his arm, or a woman takes up prostitution, it is still possible that he or she, individually, is responsible and not ''society.'' They are not always ''forced'' into it. If we take that line, who shall we blame for forcing the forcers into *their* special brands of unhappiness? Are we seriously to suppose that all American society is a hierarchy of imposed unhappiness with President Nixon at the top, a primum mobile?

Mr. Wright is at his best in his throw-away lines, like the time he described two junkies trying to sell him a pair of ice-skates. When he sums up a particular kind of white girl as having ''a ban-the-bomb-air,'' we feel that, yes, we've met her. We're even willing to forgive him his dangling clauses when he goes down to the Chelsea health center to show up a busy surrealist

day at the V.D. clinic. We want to like him—he's appealing in his cranky way—but he keeps fading out of focus on us. He insists on blowing both hot and cool, and the two don't jive.

At one point in his hot phase, he says that blacks have nothing to lose but their lives—and it ain't necessarily so. Mr. Wright, for example, can lose his audience, his talent, his dignity, his sense of humor—oh, any number of things.

Anatole Broyard, ''It Ain't Necessarily So,'' in The New York Times, *April 9, 1973, p. 35.*

EBERHARD KREUTZER

Although Charles Wright is a writer with only a modest output of prose, his work justifies our interest because it brings together some of the most prominent literary tendencies of the sixties within a black context. Thematically as well as technically it reflects a period stirring with the revived awareness of the social environment and set on new approaches in dealing with it. His first novel, *The Messenger* (1963), presents a neo-realistic slice-of-life by focusing on a shabby New York segment and giving glimpses of the city's other milieus through the eyes of a young black drifter from the South. *Absolutely Nothing to Get Alarmed About* (1973) collects Wright's *Village Voice* chronicle of the sub-cultures from the East Village to Harlem in a black version of the New Journalism, which evokes the fantasy element in the contemporary scene. Between these two, not only chronologically, comes *The Wig* (1966), a farcical novel blending reality and fantasy in the story of a young Harlemite's vain attempt at economic and personal self-realization during the Johnson era. It is mainly for this novel that Wright has caught the critics' attention as one of the first black writers to turn to black humor. His frontline position of the ''black black humorist'' implies a dissatisfaction with the realistic tradition of the black protest novel. Rather than confronting the reader with a fictional picture, however stylized, of authentic reality, he decides to counter reality with the fantastic distortions of satire. More directly, the book dramatizes the disillusionment with the Great Society, which confirmed the suspicions of those blacks who criticized it as yet another mirage of liberal rhetoric. The black community's thwarted hopes for a substantial improvement in their situation, most manifest wherever this belated version of the American Dream would be put to the test, makes up the theme of the novel. *The Wig* exemplifies this theme in the episodic plot of the hero's quest and its interwoven parallels drawn from America's archetypal ''dark ghetto.'' (pp. 145-46)

[Lester Jefferson's] quest for his admission into the Great Society is from the start beset with the psychodynamics of despair and delusion, pursued with the doggedness of one who will not admit the contradictions of his behavior, and finally given up in utter resignation to the dehumanizing forces around him. When he expects from his changed Wig the subsequent miracle of a ''new life,'' he is led by the forced optimism of a destitute man who seeks refuge from past failures in attacking his future. At first, glances at himself in the mirror and reactions of the people he meets seem to confirm that he is ''reborn,'' a different person altogether. But the most flattering compliments about his appearance ironically come from those who share his identity problem in one way or another: his neighbor Sandra Hanover, a queen in high drag, and The Deb, a girl extremely self-conscious about her kinky hair. He gets the impression that he literally blinds people in the street and with the additional help of a British accent, an elegant suit, a forged credit card and similar aids from the conman's bag of tricks, he brings off an even more elaborate façade. But he cannot deceive anyone for long and, more poignantly, as a fraud he alienates most strongly those who are his closest friends. (p. 148)

But most of all he deceives and alienates himself. If he intends to develop his personality and, more basically, ensure his humanity his efforts are misguided and they push him into the worst of black stereotypes and conformist attitudes—a living parody of the invisible man made visible. Wright uses his eager, yet ludicrous hero-narrator as a *persona* to play the fool in a racist, capitalist society and to demonstrate the catch that only the economically successful may "become human," yet to be eligible for such an advancement they have to have learned the "art of being human," that is "the art of being white." The psychological and social terms of this absurd notion inevitably lead the black man into self-destruction, especially since they are constantly reinforced by the media: Lester's mind is flooded by their delusory images of a consumer's good life and disturbed by the message in their weird job descriptions. Like everybody else he does try to "make it," dreaming of fame and fortune or, more plainly, money and girls. Not surprisingly, however, even the modest successes within his reach abound with ironies. When he eventually becomes a minor TV celebrity it is as the Chicken Man cackling and crawling through the streets, the anonymous innards of an artificial animal. When he first meets The Deb he draws on his appeal as a "foreigner" wittily pleading for free love, only to be rebuffed by this cash-and-carry girl's trade union slogan "No finance, no romance." When he later takes his revenge it is in a typical shift of roles: as soon as he has proved himself to her as a sexual performer he acts the mean *macho*.

The lesson he is supposed to draw from one encounter after another is spelled out in an oracular manner by his two magician-guides, Madam X and Mr. Fishback. Madam X gives him to understand that as long as his people do not enjoy a naturalized status their only worthwhile passion will be hard cash—as opposed to love—and she interprets the Wig as a sign of his fearful, self-destructive vanity, a flaw in his "portrait" he will be lucky to get rid of. This forebodes the final scene as much as Mr. Fishback's obscurer and earlier piece of advice: "you're almost a man. It's time you learned something. That Harlem skyline is the outline of your life. There is very little to discover by looking at the pavement." By way of explaining this unenlightening eye-opener he tells Lester that he is "on his own for now" and that his guide's *"presence won't be required until . . ."* It is not until the final scene with its perverse rite of passage, performed in the acts of unmasking and castration, that the ominous meaning of the image becomes clear. Only superficially could it have been taken as an encouragement to widen one's horizon and look up to a dynamic life; rather, it must be understood as a warning not to transcend the enclosed world of the ghetto, whether in the capacity of the charming foreigner or the talked-about Chicken Man. Fishback himself symbolizes the ambivalent relation of the white downtown world toward the uptown ghetto. Indeed, early on it is implied that Lester may leave Harlem only with Fishback's permission. And although he has received from him the gift of a credit card—apparently forged and thus a limited open-sesame anyway—he knows perfectly well that some day he will have to pay for such favors. When this day comes it will come with a vengeance: the price he has to pay is the humiliating acquiescence in the brutal fact of his "nigger" status.

Rather than continue to strive for his naturalization as an American he yields to the release from his neutralization as a lover.

The immediate context of the climactic scene stresses the exemplary character of Lester's development and reveals the author's apocalyptic undertone. Shortly before the final encounter Lester receives a telepathic message from Fishback: "when love waxes cold, said Paul in 'The Third Coming . . .'" On the face of it a corny joke about the weakening of sexual prowess, this travesty alludes to Christ's prophecy of his Second Coming at a time when "iniquity shall abound" and hence "the love of many shall wax cold." The context of the source, applied to the black man's situation, suggests a dystopian significance. Lester, of course, does not see more in it than a foreboding of his aggravated misery when he hears from Fishback about The Deb's death in a traffic accident. Ironically, The Deb provides the most obvious mirror image of his own life, thus reinforcing the representative quality of his case: in a way, she is more successful when she becomes café society's darling—her greatest asset being precisely her "natural" hair according to a new vogue—but she is also more completely undone; and at least in her death both Madam X and Mr. Fishback once more seem to have conspired. When Lester first experiences the separation from The Deb as "the death of a bright dream" and puts the blame on his wretched impersonation, he speaks only half the truth because he has known for some time that Fishback is the "prime mover of people" always hovering over him and that he alone would have the authority to decide whether his pursuit of happiness is an unalienable right or a crime and a sin. In the final scene Fishback clearly assumes the role of a *deus-ex-machina* in an upside-down world where the guide gives misleading counsel, the sponsor takes more than he gives, the doctor mutilates the healthy. Above all, both Mr. Fishback and Madam X allegorize the death-and-money principle. They make an odd pair of unholy "saints" obstructing natural instincts and creative purpose. . . . The sorceress specializes in deadening love as a painful habit, the undertaker in loving the dead in their irresponsive availability, and both of them teach the capitalist gospel while combining business with pleasure. More specifically, they play mother and father to Lester's inverted initiation, turning him back into the bare existence of the black boy.

This ironically brings him full circle since his strongest motivation for self-improvement derives from an unhappy childhood. While watching his new self in the mirror, he dreams the old dream of succeeding where his parents have miserably failed. He also remembers how as a child, sniffing someone's opium, he had sensed for the first time what it must mean to fly and be free, and he now seems on the brink of following countless Americans who with confidence and diverse strategies have liberated and fulfilled themselves: "American until the last breath, a true believer in The Great Society, I'd turn the other cheek, cheat, steal, take the fifth amendment, walk bareassed up Mr. Jones's ladder, and state firmly that I was too human." Meek religion, criminal competition, legal insistence, unashamed social climbing make an odd mixture to ensure success but, again, the "land of hope" is out of reach for blacks anyway despite the ever renewed promise of endless opportunities. (pp. 148-51)

When Wright sends his hero "studying the map of the Great Society" after the maxim "One is not defeated until one is defeated" he makes him the quixotic dupe of precisely the delusion in the Dream rhetoric, the tragicomic victim acting out the brutal consequences of the accomodationist's incentives. By ridiculing the fallacy of such ready belief and un-broken optimism it does not, however, advocate black mili-tancy: a side glance at Black Muslims in front of the Theresa Hotel hawking chances on an armored tank which is supposed to make a round trip to Georgia on a gallon of gas satirizes what [sociologist Kenneth B. Clark] calls the fantasy of mil-itancy. In contrast to Clark and other social critics Wright does not provide an alternative: his perspective remains that of the debunking satirist as he explodes the myth of the Great Society and deflates the delusions of the black man in a mirror image of distorted realities without allowing for much insight or future policy on the part of the hero or any other character. Rather, the novel's dystopian illustrations function as a future warning for America and its farcical treatment of contemporary ghetto life is all fixed upon destroying the various fantasies. Given this intention and accepting it as a feasible objective of fiction, the impact of the book depends to a considerable degree on the author's satirical imagination and stylistic execution. It is here, unfortunately, that Wright largely fails: some of his tar-gets are too worn-out to yield more than hackneyed reflections or they are simply shortlived (the concept of physical beauty would soon change and give rise to black pride). Too often his use of ironic contrasts seems predictable, whereas his efforts to impress us with the extraordinary usually results in either strained or crude effects. Not that one expects much character development, a subtle point-of-view or a complex structure from a book that uses for its main device the caricature of a quester who gets involved in a series of episodes and encounters with other characters as typified as himself (see the name sym-bolism). And the piecemeal experiences of the hero delivered in a fast nervous style may be seen to convey his disorientation among the flood of images in the hectic urban environment. But the intended tragi-comedy cannot convince us because the comedy boils down to cheap jokes and the tragedy never makes itself felt for the sheer inadequacy of expression. (pp. 159-60)

The third part of the novel is set on April Fool's Day and indeed the whole book has something of a series of practical jokes with everybody trying to fool everybody else. It contains a lot of slapstick situation comedy in a structure resembling that of vaudeville acts. It also employs the more strictly literary methods of satirical inversion, exaggerating or diminishing dis-tortion, ironical juxtaposition and word-play. Since the hero is essentially a satirical *persona*—gullible, contradictory, and vacillating—who attempts to fool his way into the Great So-ciety in one impersonation after another and rebounds from each rebuff the episodic structure lends itself to a pattern of parallelisms. Keywords and catchphrases recur and bring their connotations into play, especially the main theme of the "Wig" in its manifold contexts and the associated leitmotif of "making it," or they assume an ambiguous undertone as in the use of "slave" and "progress:" Lester, originally willing to "work like a slave" in order to overcome the obstacles on "the road to progress," maneuvres himself in his repeated autosuggestion into his final enslavement and regress. There are also the com-plementary motifs of (re)birth and death, crucial in Lester's hope for a new lease on life that is thwarted by the various forms of death toward the end of the book, and the concomitant rise-and-fall pattern, which is demonstrated with some consis-tency and a diversity ranging from slapstick instances to a macabre symbolism: Nonnie collapses in the hall, queen Sandra topples from the sofa, the civil servant drops dead in the street, Jimmy Wishbone is a fallen star; and Lester himself, getting high on pot and playing haughty roles, proves himself a flop (Paradise Records), is knocked down (Tom), turned down (The Deb), and finally, as it were, cut down to size (Fishback).

Since the book is conceived as a "mirror image" one can see in these motif patterns a method of narrative and linguistic reflection, yet again, the parallels are often obtrusive and the overall structure is largely repetitive.

Wright's division of the book into three parts seems equally superficial although it gains some importance from the mottos attached. Part I is prefixed by a quotation from *Ulysses:* "Every phenomenon has its natural cause," a statement significantly picked out of the phantasmagoric Circe episode and implying the context of Bloom's first encounter with the 'madam' of nighttown whose fan ensures his subservience while he attri-butes his present predicament to the fact that he parted with his talisman. The motto, thus, introduces the novel's cause-and-effect pattern and the trauma of slavery. More immedi-ately, it signals Lester's departure as he resorts to the magic hood of his Wig and tries to free himself from racial history's nightmare conjured up in a cluster of memories toward the end of the first part. . . . Part III has an equally ironic motto quoting a phrase from the ambivalent ending of *The Great Gatsby* where Nick Carraway's outlook suggests a pursuit of one's dream against the currents carrying one back in the vague expectation: "And one fine morning—." This hope against hope, which makes the pursuer run faster and faster, is a recurring reference in Wright's books and receives in the ending of *The Wig* its most pessimistic interpretation. Another quotation of similar significance from another of Wright's favorite authors occurs toward the end of the central, ninth chapter. When Lester is startled by the runaway slave and tries to make his escape, he suddenly finds himself in front of a plaque commemorating Nathaniel West with a quotation from *Miss Lonelyhearts:* "Life is worthwhile for it is full of dreams and peace, gentleness and ecstasy, and faith that burns like a clear white flame on a grim dark altar." It is a consoling wisdom belied by the development of both West's hero and Wright's, two unmasked impersonat-ors. A closer parallel even suggests itself between Lester and Lemuel Pitkin in *A Cool Million* as both heroes are naive young men who try to make it in the surreal metropolis and suffer a brutal dismantlement. The integration of these references seems to set Wright firmly in the modern tradition but the models referred to also reveal the wide gap in artistic achievement.

He may be on safer ground with the oral tradition of black America. The largest section of the book, Part II, takes as its motto a line from "How Long Blues," a classic in its own genre: "If I could holler like a mountain jack. . . ." For one thing, the implied context of the song, expressing the lament for lost love in the code of black folklore, sets the tone for the increasingly blue mood in this section which leads up to the visit with Madam X. . . . If one can generalize from here, Wright's style seems most promising where he tries to combine the traditions of black folklore and literature within the modes of fantasy and comedy. There is a considerable thematic and technical range reflecting such a background. In particular, he draws on the rich resources of indigenous humor: the street culture ingenuity of the shoeshine boys' tricks of the trade; the rapping rituals of swaggering and insult; the ridiculed stereo-type of food tastes in Lester's sudden dislike for watermelon and his later change into a walking reminder of the inordinate love for chicken; the standard joke about the black passenger and the white taxi driver; and, above all, the many varieties of disguise and roleplaying in Tomming it, including the re-course to cosmetic and magical panaceas. The remarkable ca-pability of black America to create laughter out of a depressing situation goes back to the early days of slavery and has proved psychologically the most effective mechanism by exposing the paradoxes of a racist society and releasing the pent-up aggression toward it. The humor of absurdity undermining racism by playing up to it usually involves some form of inversion and often employs the rhetoric of exaggeration. Wright obviously stands in this tradition and may even remind one of the once popular form of the animal trickster tale since the Chicken Man episode has something of the fable about the trickster getting himself entrapped.

In the more literary tradition of the black novel Wright takes up where the Harlem Renaissance satirists left off with such assimilationist fantasies as George Schuyler's *Black No More* (1931). The difference lies, among other things, in the fact that Wright's fantasy develops out of a realism pushed to its limits and tipping over into hallucination and farce, a process which can be traced back to the atmospheric touches in *The Messenger,* an otherwise blatantly realistic—and largely autobiographical—novel in the tradition of Richard Wright. It is directly related to the fantasy element in the all too real city which constantly catches up with one's wildest imagination. *The Wig* takes its essential material from the physical, psychological and social realities of the dark ghetto and, in a way, blows them up into grotesque fantasy. Perhaps the most interesting example in this respect is the episode of the rat fight recalling the opening scene of *Native Son* (1940), a *locus classicus* of black realism turned into a mock-heroic feat: it keeps in view the ghetto reality and ironizes the scope it allows for black heroism. The episode also clearly indicates Wright's departure from the traditional protest literature, his revival of the black folklore tradition and his alignment with the parodist-fantasists among such modern classics as Joyce and West. Whether the rat episode deserves a whole chapter is another question and shows once more a lack of artistic economy.

The novel sets off with some of the stock features of environmental realism, such as the tenement microcosm, and displays a considerable variety of fantasy elements—day-dreaming, roleplaying, drug hallucination, nightmarish allegory. It ridicules the latest version of the old American Dream bringing in some of the oldest stereotypes of American literature, the conman and Uncle Tom, presenting, as it were, a black Horatio Alger in whiteface. If this seems to be a new attempt to make black laughter serve its old regulative purpose, it is undercut by the author's scathing pessimism which aims at a more radical response in the reader. The accomplishment of his purpose is, however, limited by the inadequacy of the style. As an author who made his name in a transitional period of postwar (black) American literature [Wright] is symptomatic in the recapitulating and anticipating aspects of his work, but never comes near a major achievement. His fantasy will appear rather coarse compared with Ellison's subtle symbolism and rather uninventive compared with Ishmael Reed's verbal dexterity. He wrote, of course, at a time when many writers felt that writing in balanced fictional structures had become obsolete and when . . . the various American movements were still in their experimental stage. Asked about his literary approach, he has pointed to the interpenetration, and even interchangeability, of realism and fantasy and the thin line between fiction and journalism. This associates him with the contemporary neo-realism and New Journalism as well as the emerging fantasists. Such an open approach must have proved too much for his limited capabilities. He may also have been constrained by the fact that the public was not quite ready yet for the special blend of "black black humor." (pp. 160-65)

Eberhard Kreutzer, "Dark Ghetto Fantasy and the Great Society: Charles Wright's 'The Wig' (1966)," in The Afro-American Novel Since 1960, *edited by Peter Bruck and Wolfgang Karrer, B. R. Grüner Publishing Co., 1982, pp. 145-66.*

Appendix

The following is a listing of all sources used in Volume 49 of *Contemporary Literary Criticism*. Included in this list are all copyright and reprint rights and acknowledgments for those essays for which permission was obtained. Every effort has been made to trace copyright, but if omissions have been made, please let us know.

THE EXCERPTS IN CLC, VOLUME 49, WERE REPRINTED FROM THE FOLLOWING PERIODICALS:

America, v. 140, May 12, 1979 for a review of "Recapitulation" by Peter LaSalle; v. 150, February 11, 1984 for a review of "Waltz in Marathon" by David Castronovo. © 1979, 1984. All rights reserved. Both reprinted with permission of the respective authors./ v. 128, April 14, 1973. © 1973. All rights reserved. Reprinted with permission of America Press, Inc., 106 West 56th Street, New York NY 10019.

The American Book Review, v. 3, May-June, 1981; v. 5, January-February, 1983; v. 7, July-August, 1985; v. 8, May-June, 1986; v. 8, November-December, 1986. © 1981, 1983, 1985, 1986 by *The American Book Review*. All reprinted by permission of the publisher.

American Mercury, v. V, August, 1925 for a review of "God's Stepchildren" by H. L. Mencken. Copyright 1925, renewed 1953 by American Magazine, Inc. Reprinted by permission of the Literary Estate of H. L. Mencken.

The American Poetry Review, v. 9, March-April, 1980 for "One Man's Music: Some Recent American Poetry" by Dave Smith; v. 15, May-June, 1986 of "Kenneth Rexroth's 'Selected Poems'" by Sam Hamill. Copyright © 1980, 1986 by World Poetry, Inc. Both reprinted by permission of the respective authors.

Analog Science Fiction/Science Fact, v. C, June, 1980 for a review of "The Old Gods Waken" by Tom Easton. Copyright © 1980 by the Condé Nast Publications, Inc. Reprinted by permission of the author./ v. CI, July 23, 1981 for a review of "After Dark" by Tom Easton; v. CII, July, 1982 for a review of "The Lost and the Lurking" by Tom Easton; v. CIII, July, 1983 for a review of "The Hanging Stones" by Tom Easton; v. CIV, July, 1984 for a review of "What Dreams May Come" by Tom Easton; v. CVI, July, 1986 for a review of "The School of Darkness" by Tom Easton; v. CVII, July, 1987 for a review of "Cahena" by Tom Easton. © 1981, 1982, 1983, 1984, 1985, 1986, 1987 by Davis Publications, Inc. All reprinted by permission of the author.

Antaeus, v. 19, Autumn, 1975 for "Wilson's Metier" by Joseph McElroy. Copyright © 1975 by the author. Reprinted by permission of the author.

Arizona Quarterly, v. 33, Autumn, 1977 for a review of "The Spectator Bird" by Peter Wild. Copyright © 1977 by *Arizona Quarterly*. Reprinted by permission of the publisher and the author.

Art in America, v. 72, February, 1984 for a review of "Marbot: A Biography" by Douglas Blau. Copyright © 1984 by Art in America, Inc. and the author. Reprinted by permission of the publisher and the author.

Artforum, v. XXII, November, 1983. © 1983 Artforum International Magazine, Inc. Reprinted by permission of the publisher.

Astounding Science Fiction, v. LXI, May, 1958 for a review of "Twice in Time" and v. LXIV, December, 1959 for a review of "Giants from Eternity" by P. Schuyler Miller. © 1958, 1959 by Street & Smith Publications, Inc. Renewed 1986, 1987 by Davis Publications, Inc. All rights reserved. Both reprinted by permission of the Literary Estate of P. Schuyler Miller.

Bailin, George. From "A Shining in the Dark: May Sarton's Accomplishment," in *May Sarton: Woman and Poet.* Edited by Constance Hunting. National Poetry Foundation, 1982. Copyright 1982 © by The National Poetry Foundation. Reprinted by permission of the publisher.

Benedikt, Michael. From an introduction to "Suicide Prohibited in Springtime," in *Modern Spanish Theatre: An Anthology of Plays.* Edited by Michael Benedikt and George E. Wellwarth. Dutton, 1968. Copyright © 1968 by Michael Benedikt and George E. Wellwarth. All rights reserved. Reprinted by permission of Georges Borchardt, Inc. for the author.

Brooks, Cleanth. From a foreword to *The Run for the Elbertas.* By James Still. University Press of Kentucky, 1980. Copyright © by The University Press of Kentucky. Reprinted by permission of the publisher.

Bryant, Paul T. From *H. L. Davis.* Twayne, 1978. Copyright 1978 by Twayne Publishers. All rights reserved. Reprinted with the permission of Twayne Publishers, a division of G. K. Hall & Co., Boston.

Bush, Douglas. From *Mythology and the Romantic Tradition in English Poetry.* Cambridge, Mass.: Harvard University Press, 1937. Copyright 1937 by the President and Fellows of Harvard College. Renewed © 1964 by Douglas Bush. Excerpted by permission of the publishers.

Cadle, Dean. From a foreword to *River of Earth.* By James Still. University Press of Kentucky, 1978. Copyright © 1978 by The University Press of Kentucky. Reprinted by permission of the publisher.

Calvino, Italo. From an introduction to *Words in Commotion and Other Stories.* By Tommaso Landolfi, edited and translated by Kathrine Jason. Viking Penguin, 1986. Translation copyright © 1986 Viking Penguin Inc. All rights reserved. Reprinted by permission of the publisher.

Clark, Norris B. From "Gwendolyn Brooks and a Black Aesthetic," in *A Life Distilled: Gwendolyn Brooks, Her Poetry and Fiction.* Edited by Maria K. Mootry and Gary Smith. University of Illinois Press, 1987. © 1987 by the Board of Trustees of the University of Illinois. Reprinted by permission of the publisher and the author.

Coffman, Stanley K., Jr. From *Imagism: A Chapter for the History of Modern Poetry.* University of Oklahoma Press, 1951. Copyright 1951 by the University of Oklahoma Press. Renewed 1979 by Stanley K. Coffman, Jr. Reprinted by permission of the publisher.

Coulson, Robert. From "The Recent Fantasies of Manly Wade Wellman," in *Discovering Modern Horror Fiction, Vol. I.* Edited by Darrell Schweitzer. Starmont House, 1985. Copyright © 1985 by Starmont House, Inc. All rights reserved. Reprinted by permission of the publisher.

Elliot, Jeffrey M. From *Fantasy Voices: Interviews with American Fantasy Writers.* The Borgo Press, 1982. Copyright © 1982 by Jeffrey M. Elliot. Reprinted by permission of the publisher.

Esslin, Martin. From *The Theatre of the Absurd.* Anchor Books, 1961. Copyright © 1961, 1968, 1969 by Martin Esslin. All rights reserved. Reprinted by permission of Doubleday, a division of Bantam, Doubleday, Dell Publishing Group, Inc.

Ferguson, Suzanne. From "To Benton, with Love and Judgment: Jarrell's 'Pictures from an Institution'," in *Critical Essays on Randall Jarrell.* Edited by Suzanne Ferguson. Hall, 1983. Copyright 1983 by G. K. Hall & Co. All rights reserved. Reprinted with the permission of the publisher.

Finney, Kathe Davis. From "The Poet, Truth, and Other Fictions: Randall Jarrell as Storyteller," in *Critical Essays on Randall Jarrell.* Edited by Suzanne Ferguson. Hall, 1983. Copyright 1983 by G. K. Hall & Co. All rights reserved. Reprinted with the permission of the publisher.

Fowler, Douglas. From *S. J. Perelman.* Twayne, 1983. Copyright 1983 by Twayne Publishers. All rights reserved. Reprinted with the permission of Twayne Publishers, a division of G. K. Hall & Co., Boston.

Gale, Steven H. From *S. J. Perelman: A Critical Study.* Greenwood Press, 1987. Copyright © 1987 by Steven H. Gale. All rights reserved. Reprinted by permission of Greenwood Press, Inc., Westport, CT.

Gates, Norman T. From *The Poetry of Richard Aldington: A Critical Evaluation and an Anthology of Uncollected Poems.* Pennsylvania State University Press, 1975. Copyright © 1974 the Pennsylvania State University Press, University Park, PA. All rights reserved. Reprinted by permission of the publisher.

Hughes, Glenn. From *Imagism & the Imagists: A Study in Modern Poetry.* Stanford University Press, 1931.

Kent, George. From "Gwendolyn Brooks' Poetic Realism: A Developmental Survey," in *Black Women Writers (1950-1980): A Critical Evaluation.* Edited by Mari Evans. Anchor Books, 1984. Copyright © 1983 by Mari Evans. All rights reserved. Reprinted by permission of Doubleday, a division of Bantam, Doubleday, Dell Publishing Group, Inc.

Kreutzer, Eberhard. From "Dark Ghetto Fantasy and the Great Society: Charles Wright's 'The Wig' (1966)," in *The Afro-American Novel Since 1960.* Edited by Peter Bruck and Wolfgang Karrer. Grüner, 1982. © 1982, B. R. Grüner Publishing Co. Reprinted by permission of the publisher.

☐ Contemporary Literary Criticism

Indexes

Literary Criticism Series
  Cumulative Author Index
Cumulative Nationality Index
Title Index, Volume 49

This Index Includes References to Entries in These Gale Series

Contemporary Literary Criticism

Presents excerpts of criticism on the works of novelists, poets, dramatists, short story writers, scriptwriters, and other creative writers who are now living or who have died since 1960. Cumulative indexes to authors and nationalities are included, as well as an index to titles discussed in the individual volume. Volumes 1-49 are in print.

Twentieth-Century Literary Criticism

Contains critical excerpts by the most significant commentators on poets, novelists, short story writers, dramatists, and philosophers who died between 1900 and 1960. Cumulative indexes to authors, nationalities, and titles discussed are included in each new volume. Volumes 1-29 are in print.

Nineteenth-Century Literature Criticism

Offers significant passages from criticism on authors who died between 1800 and 1899. Cumulative indexes to authors, nationalities, and titles discussed are included in each new volume. Volumes 1-18 are in print.

Literature Criticism from 1400 to 1800

Compiles significant passages from the most noteworthy criticism on authors of the fifteenth through eighteenth centuries. Cumulative indexes to authors, nationalities, and titles discussed are included in each new volume. Volumes 1-8 are in print.

Classical and Medieval Literature Criticism

Offers excerpts of criticism on the works of world authors from classical antiquity through the fourteenth century. Cumulative indexes to authors, titles, and critics are included in each volume. Volumes 1-2 are in print .

Short Story Criticism

Compiles excerpts of criticism on short fiction by writers of all eras and nationalities. Cumulative indexes to authors, nationalities, and titles discussed are included in each new volume. Volume 1 is in print.

Children's Literature Review

Includes excerpts from reviews, criticism, and commentary on works of authors and illustrators who create books for children. Cumulative indexes to authors, nationalities, and titles discussed are included in each new volume. Volumes 1-15 are in print.

Contemporary Authors Series

Encompasses five related series. *Contemporary Authors* provides biographical and bibliographical information on more than 90,000 writers of fiction, nonfiction, poetry, journalism, drama, motion pictures, and other fields. Each new volume contains sketches on authors not previously covered in the series. Volumes 1-124 are in print. *Contemporary Authors New Revision Series* provides completely updated information on active authors covered in previously published volumes of *CA*. Only entries requiring significant change are revised for *CA New Revision Series*. Volumes 1-23 are in print. *Contemporary Authors Permanent Series* consists of updated listings for deceased and inactive authors removed from the original volumes 9-36 when these volumes were revised. Volumes 1-2 are in print. *Contemporary Authors Autobiography Series* presents specially commissioned autobiographies by leading contemporary writers. Volumes 1-6 are in print. *Contemporary Authors Bibliographical Series* contains primary and secondary bibliographies as well as analytical bibliographical essays by authorities on major modern authors. Volumes 1-2 are in print.

Dictionary of Literary Biography

Encompasses three related series. *Dictionary of Literary Biography* furnishes illustrated overviews of authors' lives and works and places them in the larger perspective of literary history. Volumes 1-68 are in print. *Dictionary of Literary Biography Documentary Series* illuminates the careers of major figures through a selection of literary documents, including letters, notebook and diary entries, interviews, book reviews, and photographs. Volumes 1-5 are in print. *Dictionary of Literary Biography Yearbook* summarizes the past year's literary activity with articles on genres, major prizes, conferences, and other timely subjects and includes updated and new entries on individual authors. Yearbooks for 1980-1987 are in print. A cumulative index to authors and articles is included in each new volume.

Concise Dictionary of American Literary Biography

A six-volume series that collects revised and updated sketches on major American authors that were originally presented in *Dictionary of Literary Biography*. Volumes 1-2 are in print.

Something about the Author Series

Encompasses two related series. *Something about the Author* contains heavily illustrated biographical sketches on juvenile and young adult authors and illustrators from all eras. Volumes 1-51 are in print. *Something about the Author Autobiography Series* presents specially commissioned autobiographies by prominent authors and illustrators of books for children and young adults. Volumes 1-5 are in print.

Yesterday's Authors of Books for Children

Contains heavily illustrated entries on children's writers who died before 1961. Complete in two volumes. Volumes 1-2 are in print.

Literary Criticism Series
Cumulative Author Index

This index lists all author entries in the Gale Literary Criticism Series and includes cross-references to other Gale sources. For the convenience of the reader, references to the *Yearbook* in the *Contemporary Literary Criticism* series include the page number (in parentheses) after the volume number. References in the index are identified as follows:

AITN:	*Authors in the News,* Volumes 1-2
CAAS:	*Contemporary Authors Autobiography Series,* Volumes 1-6
CA:	*Contemporary Authors* (original series), Volumes 1-124
CABS:	*Contemporary Authors Bibliographical Series,* Volumes 1-2
CANR:	*Contemporary Authors New Revision Series,* Volumes 1-23
CAP:	*Contemporary Authors Permanent Series,* Volumes 1-2
CA-R:	*Contemporary Authors* (revised editions), Volumes 1-44
CDALB:	*Concise Dictionary of American Literary Biography*
CLC:	*Contemporary Literary Criticism,* Volumes 1-49
CLR:	*Children's Literature Review,* Volumes 1-14
CMLC:	*Classical and Medieval Literature Criticism,* Volumes 1-2
DLB:	*Dictionary of Literary Biography,* Volumes 1-68
DLB-DS:	*Dictionary of Literary Biography Documentary Series,* Volumes 1-5
DLB-Y:	*Dictionary of Literary Biography Yearbook,* Volumes 1980-1987
LC:	*Literature Criticism from 1400 to 1800,* Volumes 1-8
NCLC:	*Nineteenth-Century Literature Criticism,* Volumes 1-18
SAAS:	*Something about the Author Autobiography Series,* Volumes 1-5
SATA:	*Something about the Author,* Volumes 1-51
SSC:	*Short Story Criticism,* Volume 1
TCLC:	*Twentieth-Century Literary Criticism,* Volumes 1-29
YABC:	*Yesterday's Authors of Books for Children,* Volumes 1-2

Author Index

Author Index

Author Index

Author Index

Author Index

Author Index

Author Index

Author Index

Author Index

Author Index

Author Index

Author Index

Author Index

CLC Cumulative Nationality Index

Nationality Index

Nationality Index

CLC-49 Title Index

Title Index